D1614047

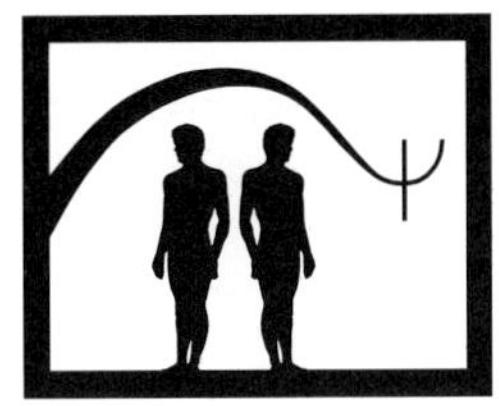

Encyclopedia of PSYCHOTHERAPY

VOLUME 2
I–Z

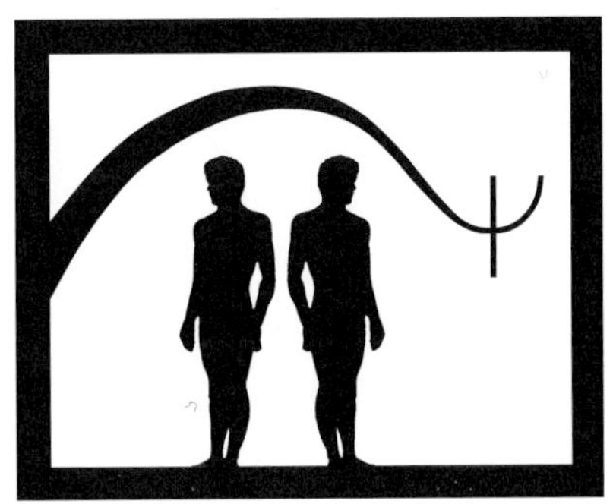

Encyclopedia of PSYCHOTHERAPY

Editors-in-Chief

MICHEL HERSEN
Pacific University
Forest Grove, Oregon

WILLIAM SLEDGE
Yale University
New Haven, Connecticut

VOLUME 2
I–Z

ACADEMIC PRESS
An imprint of Elsevier Science

Amsterdam Boston London New York Oxford Paris
San Diego San Francisco Singapore Sydney Tokyo

The acquisition editors for this encyclopedia were Nikki Levy and George Zimmer, the editorial assistant was Anya Kozorez, the production manager was Jocelyn Lofstrom, and the marketing manager was Trevor Daul. The cover was designed by G. B. D. Smith. Composition was done by Hermitage Publishing Services, Ossining, New York, and the encyclopedia was printed and bound by the Maple-Vail Book Manufacturing Group, York, Pennsylvania.

This book is printed on acid-free paper. ♾

Academic Press
An imprint of Elsevier Science
525 B Street, Suite 1900, San Diego, California 92101-4495, USA
http://www.academicpress.com

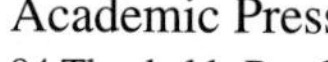

Academic Press
84 Theobalds Road, London WC1X 8RR, UK
http://www.academicpress.com

Library of Congress Catalog Card Number: 2001099034

International Standard Book Number: 0-12-343010-0 (set)
International Standard Book Number: 0-12-343011-9 (Volume 1)
International Standard Book Number: 0-12-343012-7 (Volume 2)

PRINTED IN THE UNITED STATES OF AMERICA
02 03 04 05 06 07 MM 9 8 7 6 5 4 3 2 1

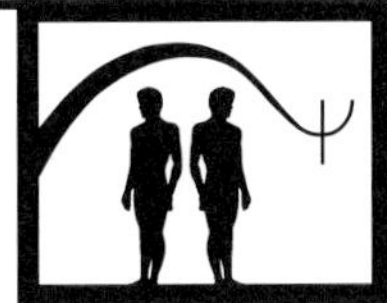

Contents

Contents of Volume 2

I

J

L

M

N

O

P

T

U

Contents of Volume 1

C

F

G

H

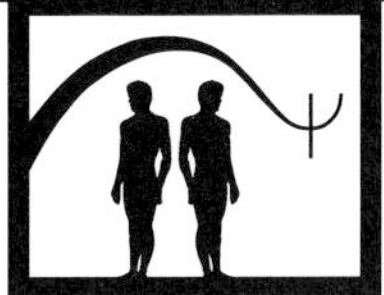

Preface

When we began this project, it would have been beyond our most radical beliefs to think that we would be seeing a nation fraught with intense worry, anxiety, acute stress disorder, post-traumatic stress disorder, grief, and depression less than three years later. So now, as we put our finishing touches on this work, and following the terrorist incursions, we regrettably have been forced to see the graphic proof of the inherent value of psychotherapy. The critical contributions and the value of the psychotherapeutic arts have never been clearer to us than in the aftermath of the terrorist strikes. We say this with much humility, in that we would have preferred to continue to talk about the sometimes small theoretical differences in various psychotherapeutic applications, in what now seem to be needless polemics between such psychotherapeutic camps. Nonetheless, the original intent (which continues today in spite of world events) was to present a compilation of both the science and art of psychotherapy.

Psychotherapy has been a vital treatment in health care since development of the great innovative and technical approaches embodied by psychoanalysis and behaviorism at the beginning of the 20th century. In the course of its development, many questions have been raised about this treatment: What is psychotherapy? How does it work? Which forms are cost effective? Who can do it? How does it fit into a comprehensive approach to health care? What is its scientific basis? How does theory drive treatment? What is the role of complementary treatments such as pharmacotherapy in combination with psychotherapy?

The *Encyclopedia of Psychotherapy* strives to answer the aforementioned questions. It is a comprehensive reference to extant knowledge in the field and written in clear expository language so that it will be of value to professional and lay persons alike. Within its pages, this encyclopedia addresses over 200 topics by experts in psychotherapy. Topics were selected in order to give broad coverage of the field (albeit not exhaustive) so as to encompass the most contemporary schools and approaches that have clearly defined techniques, some form of systematic study, and measurement of outcomes. Eclectic and integrative approaches have also been considered. Additional topics that transcend all schools, such as the impact of culture and the importance of the therapeutic relationship, have also been included as well as discussion of the treatment for some specific disorders.

Psychotherapy is an extremely complicated process that is difficult to fully capture even in a work of large scope, such as this encyclopedia. The interplay between scientific confirmation of particular strategies and the actual implementation of a given therapeutic technique is not always isomorphic. Also, how theory drives practice and ultimately the empirical confirmation of such practice, is not always clear cut. Moreover, how cultural, financial, legislative, and forsensic issues act in confluence further complicate the intricacies of what we refer to as psychotherapy. However, it is these very intricacies and complexities which make psychotherapy such an interesting field to examine. In many ways, this work may raise more questions than it does provide answers, and that, perhaps, is the way it should be.

The *Encyclopedia of Psychotherapy* is designed to serve the needs of a multi-faceted audience. As a reference work, we see it being used by students and professionals from counseling and clinical psychology, psychiatry, psychiatric nursing, and social work. Certainly, other disciplines will make reference to it as well. But the encyclopedia will also be of use to interested lay individuals seeking information about this burgeoning field. Topics are arranged alphabetically. As appropriate, a good many of the entries have case descriptions to illustrate the specifics of theory and technique. The topics addressed span clinical, theoretical, cultural, historical, and administrative and policy issues, as well as the matters of schools and specific patient conditions. Most importantly, a comprehensive user friendly Index is provided.

Early on it was apparent that a project of this magnitude would require associate editors and an advisory board to ensure broad coverage of issues and topics. The inclusion of these colleagues has added immeasurably to the fruition of this work. The associate editors (Alan M. Gross, Ph.D, Jerald Kay, M.D., Bruce J. Rounsaville, M.D., Warren W. Tryon, Ph.D.) were chosen in order to represent the cross-fertilization between the medical and the psychological, adult and child, theoretical and pragmatic, research and practice, and behavioral and non-behavioral. Similarly, the 18 advisory board members (both M.D.s and Ph.D.s) were selected because of their broad range of interests and expertise in all aspects of the psychotherapeutic endeavor.

The iterative process began with a large list of topics selected by the two editors-in-chief, which was then refined by the associate editors and the advisory board members. Excellent suggestions for authors were made and the solicitation process began. When received by Academic Press, each entry was evaluated by an appropriate associate editor, revised to the editor's specifications, and then sent on to one of the two editors-in-chief for approval and/or further modification. All entries were reviewed on the basis of accuracy, completeness, clarity, brevity, and the absence of polemics. The resulting *Encyclopedia of Psychotherapy* is a product of complete collaboration between the two editors-in-chief, and hence the order of editorship is alphabetical.

We are grateful to the many individuals who helped make the *Encyclopedia of Psychotherapy* possible. Thank you to the four associate editors who performed in an exemplary fashion. Thank you also to our 18 members of the advisory board for their wise counsel and excellent suggestions. Thanks also to our contributors who took time out from their busy schedules to become part of our project, sharing their expertise as well as articulating their views on where this field stands. We thank Alex Duncan, Angelina Marchand, and Angelina Basile for their research efforts. We appreciate Carole Londeree's technical assistance. We thank all at Academic Press who were involved in the production effort, especially the acquisitions editor, George Zimmar, and the coordinator of the *Encyclopedia*, Anya Kozorez, for helping us to conceptualize this work and overcome obstacles to see it through to publication.

We dedicate this work to our colleagues who work on a daily basis to relieve the suffering of their clients.

Michel Hersen
William Sledge

How to Use the Encyclopedia

The *Encyclopedia of Psychotherapy* is intended for use by students, research professionals, and practicing clinicians. Articles have been chosen to reflect major disciplines in common topics of research by professionals in this domain, and areas of public interest and concern. Each article serves as a comprehensive overview of a given area, providing both breadth of coverage for students, and depth of coverage for research and clinical professionals. We have designed the encyclopedia with the following features for maximum accessibility for all readers.

Articles in the encyclopedia are arranged alphabetically and are addressed at three levels of detail depending on the broadness of the topic itself. A good many of the entries have case descriptions to illustrate the specifics of a given technique. A comprehensive user-friendly index is provided to make this work amenable to all level of readers. A particular topic which may appear not to have coverage may be subsumed under a broader entry. The index, rather than the table of contents, should be used as the primary road to accessing information.

Articles in the title list vary in length, as a reflection of each article's importance to the field. Most articles follow a similar format, including:

1. description of treatment (an overview of the treatment process),
2. theoretical basis (conceptual underpinnings of the treatment),
3. applications and exclusions (patient populations, diversity issues, etc.),
4. empirical studies (review of treatment efficacy),
5. case illustration (showing main features of the treatment), and
6. summary (an abstract of the treatment).

Entries dealing with theoretical, empirical, and sociocultural aspects of treatment have a suitably modified format. For ease of reading no references have been included in the body of the text.

Each article contains an outline, a glossary, cross references, and a list of further readings. The outline allows a quick scan of the major areas discussed within each article. The glossary contains terms that may be unfamiliar to the reader, with each term defined *in the context of its use in that article*. Thus, a term may appear in the glossary for another article defined in a slightly different manner or with a subtle nuance specific to that article. For clarity, we have allowed these differences in definition to remain so that the terms are defined relative to the context of the particular article.

The articles have been cross-referenced to other related articles in the encyclopedia. Cross-references will always appear at the end of an article. The cross-references are listed in alphabetical order by title. We encourage readers to use the cross-references to locate other encyclopedia articles that will provide more detailed information about a subject.

The suggested readings at the close of each article list recent secondary sources to aid the reader in locating more detailed or technical information. Review articles and research articles that are considered of primary importance to the understanding of a given subject area are also listed. This section is not intended to provide a full reference listing of all material covered in the context of a given article, but is provided as a guide to further reading.

Implosive Therapy

Donald J. Levis

Binghamton University, New York

GLOSSARY

implosive therapy A technique that involves use of an *in vivo* or imagery presentation procedure designed to extinguish via repetition those aversive conditioned cues responsible for eliciting and maintaining symptom execution.

neurotic paradox Why neurotic behavior is at one and the same time self-defeating and self-perpetrating.

imagery exposure Imaginal exposure of the feared or anxiety-evoking stimulus, using flooding in implosive therapy.

Implosive (flooding) therapy is a learning-based exposure technique of psychotherapy designed to treat a wide variety of maladaptive behaviors in a relatively short time period. The underlying theoretical model for this behavioral cognitive treatment approach to therapy is based on an extension of two-factor avoidance learning theory.

I. DESCRIPTON OF TREATMENT

A. Introduction

Imagine the suffering of a woman who becomes so panic stricken by the obsession she has cancer that psychiatric hospitalization is required. No matter how much medical assurance she is given that she is in excellent physical health, the nagging doubt somehow persists that she is not. Or consider a man who is forced to relinquish his professional career because he is afraid to leave his home out of fear that dog feces may be in his yard. His day becomes dominated with disturbing thoughts that find relief only in repetitious washing of his hands, clothes, and body. Perhaps it is hard to comprehend how one could become so frightened of bath water that a life preserver must be worn, or that a sound of a locomotive whistle in the distance evokes such terror in an individual that he runs around in a circle screaming at the top of his voice. The range of human fears may be extended almost indefinitely. Some individuals break out in a cold sweat at the sight of a car, an airplane, or a tall building. Others become so afraid of their own sexual feelings that they avoid the opposite sex, having become convinced they will be sent to hell for such feelings. Still others fear failure, loss of control, taking responsibility, being angry, or giving love and expressing compassion.

Committed to the goal of seeking methods to ameliorate such psychological suffering, the mental health worker is confronted with the difficult task of selecting from hundreds of different treatment techniques. The rather chaotic state of the field today suggests the need to isolate and maximize the central procedural variables that appear to be reliably correlated with behavior change. One factor common to most treatment techniques stems from the observation that behavior change appears to occur following the elicitation from the patient of a strong emotional response to material presented during the therapeutic interaction. Implosive therapy is a treatment technique that is designed to maximize in a systematic manner the last-noted common denominator of therapeutic interaction, that of emotional responding and its resulting effects. Disillusioned with the insight-oriented emphasis of the time period, Thomas G. Stampfl in the late 1950s developed the technique of implosive therapy which some authors today call flooding therapy or response prevention therapy. Each of these terms is frequently used interchangeably in the literature since the goal of therapists is to maximize emotional responding by getting patients to confront their fears directly. Stampfl was the first investigator to extend systematically his learning-based exposure treatment approach to the treatment of a wide variety of clinical nosologies. Borrowing a term from physics he labeled his newly developed cognitive-behavioral approach implosion, to reflect the inwardly bursting (dynamic) energy process inherent in the release of affectively loaded environmental and memorial stimuli encoded in the brain.

Stampfl was initially influenced by the extensive clinical experience he gained from conducting "nondirective" play therapy with emotionally disturbed children. He concluded from this experience that exposure to the emotional stimulus features of the play material could account for virtually all the positive effects of therapy. Consistent with his clinical observations was the insistence by Abraham Maslow and Bela Mittleman in their 1951 abnormal text that the neurotic's symptoms, defense mechanisms, and general maladaptive behavior resulted from a state of anticipation or expectation of an impending catastrophic event, which, in turn, provided the motivating force for symptom development. These authors concluded that, although the catastrophic even usually remained unspecifiable by the patient, it generally involved fears associated with anticipation of abandonment, injury, annihilation, condemnation and disapproval, humiliation, enslavement, loss of love, and utter deprivation. Stampfl reasoned that if therapy was to succeed, these anticipatory fears, as was the case for the children he treated, needed to be confronted directly in order for the unlearning of the emotional response attached to these fears.

B. *In Vivo* Exposure Approach

Stampfl at first adopted an *in vivo* exposure approach in which he instructed patients to confront directly in real life their feared stimulus situation. For example, one of his patients, a college student, reported a compulsive behavior he had engaged in for years. Upon retiring at night, this patient reported an urge to check to see if he had left the radio on. Every night (without exception) he checked the radio up to 50 times. He reported that any time he failed to engage in radio checking he developed much apprehension and anxiety and the feeling that something "terrible" or "catastrophic" might happen. He would fear, for example, that perhaps a short circuit would occur and a fire would result. Stampfl then instructed the patient to confront his fears directly by forcing himself not to check the radio and imagine that his worst fears would happen. He was asked to let himself tolerate as much anxiety as possible. The patient was able to follow the therapist's instruction; he reported seeing the radio burst into flames and hearing his father's voice telling him to "turn off the radio." Following additional repetitions of the therapist's instructions, the patient recalled a number of traumatic memories involving his father. Once the affect associated with these memories was eliminated, his compulsive symptoms disappeared.

C. Imagery Exposure Approach

Thomas Stampfl recognized that although this patient followed his *in vivo* instructions to confront directly the anxiety he experienced, most patients avoid engaging in an *in vivo* task because of the strength of the fear response associated with the task. He also recognized that many of the fears motivating the patient's symptoms did not lend themselves readily to an *in vivo* approach. He then developed his implosive imagery procedure, which was capable of being presented within the context of a therapy session. In an attempt to illustrate the above point, consider the case of an airplane phobic. Although most phobic behavior is clearly amenable to an *in vivo* exposure approach, the use of this procedure with an airplane phobic would entail the therapist's accompanying the patient on repeated airplane trips. Stampfl recognized that his imagery exposure procedure had the advantage of presenting the feared cues in the therapist's office. Furthermore, and most importantly, the imagery technique has the additional advantage of introducing the more salient and emotionally intense fear cues associated with the phobic reaction that do not lend themselves to direct *in vivo* presentation. Examples of such fear cues include the fear of the plane crashing, the fear of dying, and the fear of being punished for guilt-producing behavior in the after-life. Imagery scenes involving the incorporation of these non *in vivo* presented fears have been clinically shown to produce a powerful emotional reactivity and subsequently a lasting therapeutic effect.

In summary, the fundamental task of the implosive therapist is to repeatedly re-present, reinstate, or symbolically reproduce those stimulus situations to which the anxiety response has been learned or conditioned. By exposing the patient to the stimulus complex of fear cues that are being avoided, the patient will be confronted with the full emotional impact of these cues. As a function of repetition, this emotional exposure weakens and eventually eliminates the connection between the eliciting stimulus and the resulting emotional response. For example, imagine a patient who is terrified of viewing horror films and takes a job as a movie projectionist which requires him to show such a movie. Although terrified during the first showing, by the tenth time he is exposed to watching the film little emotional reactivity is left.

It may at first seem that the goal of specifying the aversive learned events in the patient's life history represents a difficult, if not impossible, task. Stampfl noted that it is feasible for a trained clinician to locate "key" stimuli associated with the patient's problem area following in-depth diagnostic clinical interviews. This information allows a trained clinician to formulate hypotheses as to the type of traumatic events that may have contributed to the client's problems. Of course, these initial hypotheses must be conceived as only first approximations in the quest to determine the aversive cues controlling the patient's maladaptive behavior. As therapy progresses, it is usually possible to obtain additional information as to the validity of these cues and to generate new hypotheses. The elicitation of these hypothesized cues in imagery frequently results in the reactivation of the patient's memory regarding the initial historical events associated with development of the patient's conflict and fears. However, it is not essential to present imagery scenes that are completely accurate since some effects of emotional unlearning or extinction effects will occur through the established learning principle of generalization of extinction. Naturally, the more accurate the hypothesized cues are and the more realistically they are presented by the therapist, the greater will be the emotional arousal obtained and subsequently the greater the emotional unlearning to the cues presented. This process is continued until the patient's symptoms are reducd or eliminated.

D. Procedural Instructions

Following the completion of two to three interview sessions, a treatment plan is developed. Patients are provided the rationale and theory behind the technique. A commonly used approach is to ask patients the following question: if they were learning to ride a horse and fell off the horse, what would the instructor have them do? (The usual answer is to get back on the horse.) The therapist might then comment that failure to get back on the horse might result in an increase in fear and possibly the generalization of that fear to events surrounding riding horses. The point is to illustrate that fears can be overcome by directly confronting them. Patients are told that the procedure being used involves an imagery techneque and they will be asked to imagine various scenes directed by the therapist. Patients are instructed to close their eyes and play the part of themselves. They are asked, much as an actor or actress would be, to portray certain feelings and emotions that represent important parts of the process. They are told that belief or acceptance, in a cognitive sense, of the themes introduced by the therapist is not requested, and little or no attempt is made to secure any admission from patients that the cues or hypotheses actually apply to them. Following the administration of neutral imagery practice sessions, the therapist is ready to start. Once the implosive procedure is started, every effort is made to encourage patients to "lose themselves" in the part that they are playing and "live" or reenact the scenes with genuine emotion and affect. Compliance with the technique is readily obtained and rarely do patients terminate therapy prematurely.

Thomas Stampfl's procedure encompasses an operational feedback approach that is self-correcting. If the hypothesized cues introduced into a given scene presentation elicit emotional affect, support for their continued use is obtained. The greater the emotional arousal elicited by these cues, the greater the support for their use. Cues that do not elicit emotional arousal are abandoned and replaced by new hypothesized cues. This process is continued until the desired emotional affect is obtained and unlearned. Therapy continues until symptom reduction occurs. Significant levels of symptom reduction usually occur within 1 to 15 hours of treatment.

E. Stimulus Cue Categories

As a guide in using the therapy, Thomas Stampfl has outlined the use of four cue categories that can be conceptualized in terms of progression along a continuum that ranges from extremely concrete to hypothetical. These four cue categories, in order of their presentation, are as follows: (1) Symptom-contingent cues, those cues correlated with the onset of the patient's symptoms; (2) reportable internally elicited cues, those verbally reported thoughts, feelings, and physical sensations elicited by presentation of the symptom correlated cues; (3) unreported cues hypothesized by the therapist to be related to the second cue category; and (4) hypothesized dynamic cues, those fear cues suspected to be associated with an unresolved conflict situation being avoided by the patient.

As an illustration of the application of these cue categories, consider the case of a woman who had to wear a life preserver while taking a bath. The symptom-contingent cues would encompass the presentation in imagery of all those cues surrounding her taking a bath without wearing a life preserver. Upon presentation of these cues, she reported the feeling that the bathtub consisted of a "bottomless pit of water," the second category. This in turn led to the therapist's hypothesis that she was afraid of drowning (third category). Because the patient manifested considerable feelings of guilt, the therapist hypothesized that the patient's fear of drowning related to her fear of being punished in hell (the fourth cue category). The systematic presentation and repetition of all these fear cues led to the elimination of the patient's phobic response and to the recovery of a memory in which she almost drowned in a bath tub when she was a child. Since repetition of the feared stimuli is considered an essential requirement in producing symptom reduction and elimination, patients are expected to conduct homework that involves 20 minutes daily of repeatedly imagining the scenes assigned to them by the therapist.

II. THEORETICAL BASES

Implosive theory is unique in its ability to integrate areas of psychology, in its resolution of the neurotic paradox, and in its ability to define complex behavior according to basic principles of experimental psychology. To explain theoretically the development, maintenance, and unlearning (extinction) of psychopathology, Stampfl adopted and extended O. Hobart Mowrer's 1947 version of two-factor avoidance learning. Mowrer was influenced by Sigmund Freud's conclusion in 1936 that human symptoms reflecting psychopathology resulted from patients' attempts to escape and avoid the anxiety elicited by stimuli ("danger signals") associated with past exposure to traumatic experiences. Mowrer then concluded that the development and maintenance of human and animal avoidance (symptom) behavior involved the learning of two response classes.

A. Emotional Learning

The first response learned is how one becomes afraid of a previously nonaversive stimulus situation. To explain how fear is learned, Mowrer relied on the well-established laws of classical conditioning. Fear and other emotional conditioning result from the simple contiguity of pairing this nonemotional stimulation, in space and time, with an inherent primary (unlearned) aversive event resulting in the production of pain, fear, frustration, or severe deprivation. This biologically reactive, pain-producing stimulus is referred to as the unconditioned stimulus (UCS). Following sufficient repetition of the neutral stimulus with the UCS, the neutral stimulus becomes capable of eliciting the emotional response with which it was paired. Once the process is learned, the neutral stimulus is referred to as a conditioned stimulus (CS) and its elicitation of the emotional response (e.g., fear) as the conditioned response (CR). Stampfl believes the conditioning events of humans to be multiple, involving a complex set of stimuli comprising both external and internal CS patterns. Such conditioning events are believed to be encoded in long-term memory and capable of being reactivated at a later point in time.

B. Avoidance (Symptom) Learning

Mowrer viewed the resulting conditioned emotional response as a secondary or learned source of drive, possessing motivational or energizing properties, as well as reinforcing properties. These motivational properties of the conditioned emotional response set the stage for the learning of the second class of responses, referred to as avoidance or escape behavior. Avoidance or symptom behavior is believed to be governed by the established laws of instrumental learning. Avoidance behavior is learned because the response results in the termination or reduction of the emotional state elicited by the CS. It is this reduction in aversiveness that serves as the reinforcing mechanism for the learning of the avoidance behavior.

C. Emotional-Avoidance Unlearning

Finally, Mowrer's two-factor theory argues that both emotional responding and subsequent avoidance behavior can be readily unlearned via the well-established principle of Pavlovian extinction. This principle states that the repeated presentation of the classically conditioned CS will weaken and cease to elicit emotional responding via the principle of nonreinforced CS exposure. The extinction of the CS results in the extinction of its drive properties. Without any motivating state to elicit and reinforce the avoidance behavior, it also will undergo an extinction effect. This is the therapeutic premise on which implosive therapy is based.

D. The Neurotic Paradox and Symptom Maintenance

Implosive theory has been instrumental in resolving Freud's expressed concern and puzzlement as to why patient's symptomatology may persist over the course of a lifetime. Mowrer labeled this concern the "neurotic paradox." In Mowrer's words it is a question as to why neurotic behavior is at one and the same time self-defeating and self-perpetuating. In other words, why does the neurotic's neurosis persist to the point of seriously incapacitating the individual when the behavior has long outlived any real justification?

To resolve theoretically the issue of sustained symptom maintenance, Thomas Stampfl developed his serial CS hypothesis. He observed that, although some clinical symptoms do appear to last for lengthy periods, the CSs initially eliciting the symptom frequently undergo a change over time, with the cues originally triggering the symptom failing to serve as an eliciting stimulus to repeated CS exposure. However, as they weaken, these cues are replaced from memory by a new set of previously unexposed fear cues that upon exposure recondition secondarily the first set of cues. When the new set of released cues also undergo an extinction effect from nonreinforced CS exposure, the stage is set for yet another set of new cues to be released. This process continues until all the encoded fear complex of cues undergo an extinction effect. In other words, implosive theory maintains that there is a network of cues representing past conditioning events involving pain which are stored in memory and which, upon reactivation, are capable of motivating a symptom over time. Thomas Stampfl believes these conditioned cues are stored in memory in a serial arrangement along a dimension of stimulus intensity, with the more aversive cues being least accessible to memory reactivation. Repeated symptom execution prevents further CS exposure to these cues and to the elicitation of those cues stored in memory. As a result, the anxiety and fear level attached to these unexposed CSs are conserved or maintained until they are exposed by being released from memory. The presence of these unexposed cues stored in memory, along with the intense emotional reactions conditioned to them, can be observed by preventing symptom occurrence.

III. EMPIRICAL STUDIES

Over the last 50 years, O. Hobart Mowrer's two-factor avoidance theory and related fear theories have generated an abundance of experimental support at both the human and animal level of analysis. It still remains the dominant avoidance theory within the field. Stampfl's extension of the theory to the area of psychopathology has also received strong empirical support at the human, animal, and clinical levels of analysis. This includes his serial CS hypothesis and his extension of the conservation of anxiety hypothesis to explain symptom maintenance and the neurotic paradox. Stampfl's techniques of *in vivo* and imagery implosive therapy and related CS-exposure techniques of treatment have been experimentally supported by a host of controlled clinical outcome studies, including studies involving the treatment of phobias, anxiety reactions, obsessive compulsive behavior, trauma victims, depression, and psychotic behavior. The procedure has also been shown to be nonharmful. Today, CS exposure techniques of treatment are regularly recommended as the treatment of choice for a number of clinical nosologies.

IV. SUMMARY

Implosive (flooding therapy) therapy is a cognitive behavioral treatment approach to psychopathology. It was first developed by Thomas G. Stampfl and extended to encompass the treatment of a wide variety of clinical nosologies. Treatment effects are regularly reported to occur within 1 to 15 treatment sessions. The technique involves the use of an *in vivo* or imagery presentation procedure designed to extinguish, via repetition, those aversive conditioned cues responsible for eliciting and maintaining symptom execution. The therapist's task is to help the patient confront these cues directly within and outside the therapist's office. The underlying theoretical framework behind this technique is based on two-factor avoidance theory which Stampfl has extended to account for symptom maintenance and symptom extinction. Both the theory and treatment technique has been supported by considerable experimental research over the last 40 years at the human, patient, and animal level of analysis.

See Also the Following Articles

Avoidance Training ■ Classical Conditioning ■ Coverant Control ■ Emotive Imagery ■ Exposure *in Vivo* Therapy

Further Reading

Boudewyns, P. A., & Shipley, R. H. *Flooding and implosive therapy: Direct therapeutic exposure in clinical practice.* New York: Plenum Press.

Levis, D. J. (1985). Implosive theory: A comprehensive extension of conditioning theory of fear/anxiety to psychopathology. In S. Reiss, & R. R. Bootzin (Eds.), *Theoretical issues in behavior therapy* (pp. 49–82). New York: Academic Press.

Levis, D. J. (1989). The case for a return to a two-factor theory of avoidance: The failure of non-fear interpretations. In S. B. Klein, & R. R. Mowrer (Eds.), *Contemporary learning theories pavlovian conditioning and the status of traditional learning theory* (pp. 227–277). Hillsdale, NJ: Erlbaum Associates.

Levis, D. J. (1995). Decoding traumatic memory: implosive theory of psychopathology. In W. O. Donohue, & L. Krasner, (Eds.), *Theories of behavior therapy* (pp. 173–207). American Psychological Press, Washington, DC.

Levis, D. J., & Boyd, T. L. (1985). The CS exposure approach of implosive therapy: In R. Turner, & S. L. M. Ascher (Eds.), *Evaluation of behavior therapy outcome* (pp. 59–94). New York: Springer.

Levis, D. J., & Brewer, K. E. (2000). The neurotic paradox. In R. R. Mowrer, & C. B. Klein (Eds.), *Handbook of ccontemporary learning theories* (pp. 561–597). Hillsdale, NJ: Erlbaum Associates.

Stampfl, T. G. (1970). Implosive therapy: An emphasis on covert stimulation. In D. J. Levis (Ed.), *Learning approaches to therapeutic behavior change* (pp. 182–204). Chicago: Aldine.

Stampfl, T. G. (1991). Analysis of aversive events in human psychopathology, fear and avoidance. In M. R. Denny (Ed.), *Fear, avoidance and phobias: A fundamental analysis* (pp. 363–393). Hillsdale, NJ: Erlbaum Associates.

Stampfl, T. G., & Levis, D. J. (1973). Implosive therapy. In R. M. Jurjevich (Ed.), *The international handbook of direct psychotherapy Vol. 1: Twenty-eight american originals* (pp. 83–105). Coral Gables, FL: University of Miami Press.

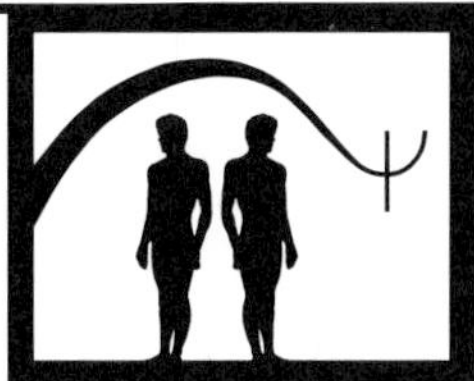

Individual Psychotherapy

Larry E. Beutler and T. Mark Harwood
University of California, Santa Barbara

GLOSSARY

behavior therapy A theory of psychotherapy in which problems are assumed to have been learned because the consequences of problematic behavior and feelings are rewarding. These treatments attempt to directly alter behavior and feelings by changing the pattern of consequences. The development of these models of treatment is most closely associated with Joseph Wolpe and B. Fred Skinner.

cognitive therapy/cognitive-behavior therapy Models of psychotherapy that attribute problematic feelings and behaviors to one's inappropriate or dysfunctional ways of thinking. The most recognized of these approaches was developed by Aaron T. Beck.

effectiveness studies Research designs that employ representative clinical populations of patients, as well as samples of therapists and psychotherapy. This type of research typically sacrifices some degree of experimental control for procedures that are closer approximations of actual clinical settings, procedures, and populations.

efficacy studies Research designs that employ randomized assignment, closely controlled and monitored treatments, and carefully selected and homogeneous samples of patients. This type of research typically sacrifices some degree of generalizability for experimental control.

experiential therapy Approaches to psychotherapy that emphasize the positive role of feelings and current experience. These approaches assume that efforts to stifle or avoid certain feeling states are at the basis of most human problems. They emphasize the role of the present, of feeling recognition, and of the innate human drive to grow (self-actualization) as processes that produce beneficial change.

exposure therapy Approaches to treatment that emphasize the importance of systematic exposure to situations and objects that evoke avoidance. This is a form of behavior therapy but has been incorporated into many models and approaches to cognitive and cognitive-behavior therapy as well.

integrative/eclectic psychotherapy Methods of intervention that draw from multiple theories. These approaches emphasize that the effectiveness of the procedure rather than its theoretical framework should be the guide to its application. These approaches range from those that blend different theoretical constructs to those that develop a case mix of specific techniques. Newer models are based on the development of cross-cutting principles of change rather than amalgamations of either specific techniques or general theories.

psychoanalysis The method of uncovering unconscious impulses and wishes that was developed by Sigmund Freud.

psychodynamic therapy Approaches to psychotherapy that generally assume that behavior is caused by inner conflict and by disturbed psychic processes. These models of individual psychotherapy are generally short-term or less intensive variations of psychoanalytic therapies. Some of these variations include those built on object relations theory, ego psychology, and self-psychology.

Individual psychotherapy is the most typical form of psychotherapeutic treatment. It consists of one patient and one therapist. The psychotherapist, assuming the role of healer, authority, facilitator, or guide, employs a variety of theories and procedures to assist the patient or client to modify behaviors and feelings, gain understanding of self and others, change perceptions and beliefs, and reduce fears and anxieties. This entry will describe some of the more dominant methods of psychotherapy and the current status of research on its effects.

I. DEVELOPMENT OF INDIVIDUAL PSYCHOTHERAPY

The field of modern psychotherapy is over 100 years old. Freud is typically credited as the individual most responsible for introducing contemporary psychotherapy, in the form of psychoanalysis, to the Western world at the end of the nineteenth century. Almost from its inception, the developmental history of modern psychotherapy has been one of conflict, controversy, and change. Freud's early views were under attack nearly from the beginning, both from his students and from the established medical system. Conflict continues with the trend of growth and the emergent influence of various groups who present views that contrast with established schools of thought. In this environment, we have seen the emergence of literally hundreds of different theories and approaches to psychotherapy. Presently, psychotherapies differ in their theoretical constructs, their mode of delivery, their techniques, and the processes to which they attribute the patient's problems.

Those who are endowed by society with conducting and overseeing the field are also diverse, ranging from those with medical and psychological degrees to those with degrees in sociology, human development, social work, anthropology, group process, biology, and the like. Opinions about the nature of desirable credentials, advantageous types of experience and training, and the nature of psychotherapy itself are far from uniform. Yet, the prototype of "Individual Psychotherapy," a process that occurs between an individual person who has a problem and an individual practitioner who offers assistance, as originally set by Freud, continues to be the dominant model. Although there has been a good deal of research and writing on group therapy and to a lesser extent on marital and couples therapy, it is individual psychotherapy that has stimulated the most research and to which most conclusions are addressed.

Psychotherapy has increasingly come to be defined as a health-related activity and has thereby come under the purview of third-party payers and political bodies. Cost containment concerns have placed increasing pressures on practitioners to justify their procedures and to demonstrate that they are effective. This, in turn, has led to increasing emphasis being placed on those who conduct psychotherapy research to demonstrate the value of these procedures in ways that have scientific credibility.

II. Theoretical Models of Individual Psychotherapy

It has been estimated that there are over 400 different theories of individual psychotherapy. However, most of these fall within five general classes.

Cognitive psychotherapy models of intervention focus on identifying specific problems and changing the processes and mechanisms by which patients evaluate themselves, others, and their environments. A central assumption of this model is that beliefs rather than facts determine how one will evaluate one's own behavior, remember the past, and anticipate the future. If one's beliefs are distorted and inaccurate, then one's evaluations and memories will be distorted as well. Moreover, one may develop behavioral or emotional disturbances in which the behavior and feelings, too, are inappropriate to one's present situations. Distortions and misperceptions of events are assumed to be at the root of or associated with many problems that impair daily functioning. Cognitive psychotherapy applies methods that encourage re-inspection of these assumptions and the application of rational analysis to correct distortions and cognitive errors. This type of treatment focuses on directly altering one's symptoms through a process that involves the rational and realistic appraisal of situations and the application of thoughtful and systematic problem solving strategies.

Behavior therapy models of individual treatment focus on immediate events and consequences. Symptoms are thought simply to reflect patterns of learning that are cued by the presence of evoking environmental stimuli. That is, behavioral models eschew the use of mental or biological events as explanations for behavior. They look for both causes and consequences within the person's immediate environment or in the concomitant occurrences of sequential cues that progress to more remote consequences. The focus of such treatments is on the development of new skills and on repeated exposure to aversive stimuli leading to extinction of behaviors that are excessive and repetitive. In this model, the therapist is a guide and instructor rather than a philosopher and healer. Indeed, postulations of illnesses are thought to obfuscate the factors that support and reinforce dysfunctional and disturbed behaviors.

Interpersonal psychotherapy models emphasize that all behavior, whether problematic or adaptive, occurs within a social context. That is, they focus on social and intimate crises such as loss and expected loss, transitions to new social environments, skills to navigate social expectancies and demands, and mediating the competing expectancies and desires that emerge when one enters into relationships with other people. This form of treatment assumes that there are a finite number and type of interpersonal problems that relate to such conditions as anxiety and depression. Interpersonal treatment involves identifying the problematic interpersonal patterns, creating understanding of the interpersonal nature of one's problems, learning to anticipate when problems will emerge, gaining a meaningful understanding of one's own behavior, and developing skills of communication and assertion that can be applied in competitive environments. The therapist assumes an authoritative role in directing the patient through a process of identifying and exploring the nature and causes of one's problems and directs the patient in a process of selecting and using effective procedures for ameliorating these problems and developing improved interactions with others.

Psychodynamic/psychoanalytic psychotherapy models are widely varied but are bound by a common emphasis on the indirect relationship between behavior and environment. That is, disturbed behavior and feelings are thought to reflect internal conflicts rather than current events. The conflicts are symbolized by symptoms and are thought to derive largely from primitive experiences that predispose patients to continue to reenact certain dysfunctional patterns of behavior in a vain effort to obtain a resolution in the present for a conflict whose nature is out of awareness and whose genesis is in the past. Thus, in contrast to other models, neither immediate situations nor dysfunctional thoughts cause disturbance. Indeed, these situations and thoughts are thought to more likely be the consequences of the individual's effort to resolve conflict rather than the causal agents of psychopathology. That is, current behaviors and situations may reflect the disturbance that is caused by the turmoil of inner struggles between contrasting impulses and wishes. Usually, the nucleus of these inner conflicts is kept unconscious by innate efforts to protect one's self from painful awareness. Thus, the patient does not acknowledge, understand, or know the motivation behind behavior. Improvement is thought to relate to the development of insight and awareness, uncovering these unconscious processes, and becoming aware of how past experiences and filial needs, rather than current demands and exigencies, are determining one's current behavior.

Experiential psychotherapy models focus on problems that are associated with the failure to integrate emotional experience with either thoughts or behaviors. They adopt the viewpoint that from traumatic experience and interpersonal crises early in life, individuals learn ways to protect themselves from experiencing strong emotions. These defensive patterns typically involve separating one's self from one's emotional state and learning to be oblivious to personal emotional cues. Overreliance on rationality, on action and "doing," rather than on feeling and awareness is thought to arise when social forces encourage one to lose sight of inner experiences or to distort and suppress emotional drives and experiences. Experiential treatment is based in the here and now of immediate experience. It endeavors to identify current feelings and to bring these into high relief, often magnifying and enhancing these experiences in order to encourage emotional processing. In this process, the therapist attempts to foster the integration of emotional, behavioral, and cognitive life.

Experiential treatments strive to keep patients in the emotional present rather than retreating to thoughts of the past or future. They encourage patients to learn to tolerate strong feelings without withdrawal, attempting to help them remove their internalized, socially imposed sanctions against such feelings.

III. THE EFFECTS OF INDIVIDUAL PSYCHOTHERAPY

A. Models and Theories

Scientific research over the past 40 years confirms that individual psychotherapy is an effective method for initiating personal change and reducing feelings of unhappiness, stress, and conflict. Its effects are substantial and compare well to alternative treatments for emotional problems, such as psychoactive medication. In recent years, considerable attention has turned to efforts to identify which of the many available models and theories of treatment yield positive effects among different patient groups. Research on these various models or types of psychotherapy indicates that substantial improvements are associated with their use—relief can be reliably achieved in various kinds of symptoms and problems.

Among the most widely accepted methods and models, those based on cognitive-behavioral, behavioral (e.g., exposure therapy), and interpersonal therapy principles have been most consistently identified as being effective. Models that have received some, but less, support from research, include those that are constructed around psychodynamic principles and emotional awareness or emotion-enhancing therapy (e.g., experiential therapy). Cognitive therapies have been identified as especially effective for treating depression, anxiety, general distress, chemical abuse, and specific anxiety disorders (e.g., obsessive-compulsive disorder, agoraphobia, panic disorder). Behavior therapies are identified as effective for treating depression, psychophysiological disorders (e.g., headache, rheumatic disease), and habit control problems (e.g., smoking, drug/alcohol abuse, enuresis, etc.). Experiential therapies are identified as effective for depression and relationship problems. Interpersonal therapy is identified as being effective for treating depression and eating disorders. Psychodynamic therapies are considered useful for depression, chemical abuse, and social distress.

B. Specific versus Common Contributors to Change

In his classic treatise on *Persuasion and Healing*, Jerome Frank defined psychotherapy as a form of interpersonal influence that involves (1) a healing agent in the person of the therapist, (2) a patient who seeks relief of his or her suffering from the healer or healing agent, and (3) a healing relationship comprised of a circumscribed, more or less structured series of contacts between the healer and the sufferer in which the healer attempts to bring about relief.

By restricting his definition of psychotherapy to these three elements and excluding specific mention of any of the myriad procedures and therapeutic models used by therapists to effect recovery or improvement, Frank underscored what has become a major point of controversy in the field. Namely, does the use of particular psychotherapeutic models and procedures add benefit to that which is obtained from a supportive and caring psychotherapeutic relationship alone? The essential controversy embodied in this question can be distilled to a conflict between those who attribute healing to the use of specific techniques and procedures (i.e., specific "antipathogenic" psychotherapeutic interventions) and those who attribute psychotherapeutic healing to the effects of a supportive, caring, and evocative therapeutic relationship in its own right—a medical versus a humanistic view of change.

Adherence to a medical analogy has resulted in the admonition that practice be restricted to the use of interventions that have been supported by scientific research. Scientists who look for the differences among psychotherapeutic treatments have advanced and published lists of effective treatment brands and have identified various diagnostic conditions for which each brand of treatment is considered to be effective. However, this line of investigation may oversimplify the difficulty of garnering evidence of efficacy on the 400+ different models of psychotherapy that are currently practiced in contemporary Western society. Restricting practice even to the 150 or so treatments that have been scientifically supported would mean that much of the service that is currently provided in hospitals and clinics throughout the world would have to be discontinued. Furthermore, even if society were to embrace this view and undertake a systematic study of these various treatments, the results may tell us very little about some of the more important and powerful contributors to treatment gain. Research strictly based on fitting brands of treatment to diagnoses of patients will tell us very little about the various modes and formats through which psychotherapy is applied and virtually nothing about the contributions of important nondiagnostic patient qualities and individual therapist variations.

To those who emphasize the similarities among treatments, rather than the differences, such lists of brand-name models inappropriately imply that there are more differences among the various models than have been consistently demonstrated. The qualities that contribute to the development of a healing relationship and those that dictate the specific use of different treatments may have little to do with the patient's diagnosis or the brand name of the treatment provided. By extension, many authors suggest that focusing on differences among brands and models of psychotherapy discourages research on ways both to enhance the presence of therapeutic relationships and to blend interventions across therapeutic models.

Many of these same authors suggest that the effort to identify certain brands of treatment that fit with patients who are identified only by diagnosis would both require that therapists learn many different and frequently contradictory treatment models and that clinicians could only treat a limited and perhaps insignificant number of patients—those who comply with certain inclusion and exclusion criteria.

The use of a medical analogy and the corollary assertion that practice should be restricted to empirically supported treatments applied within the confines of patient samples on which they have been systematically tested is one way to increase the credibility of mental health treatment in a political world. It reflects an effort to place psychotherapy on a parallel with medical treatments for diseases—effective treatment depends on accurate diagnosis, and once diagnosis is established, one should select and apply a treatment that has been scientifically demonstrated to be safe, practical, and effective in the treatment of that condition. From this perspective, the field would do well to consolidate around a uniform effort to find or develop specific procedures that work with particular kinds of problems and conditions.

Working from this viewpoint, clinicians and researchers alike are continuing to develop new theoretical models and technical methods of intervention, with the implicit assertion that these specific techniques and procedures are responsible for the effects of treatment, either positive or negative. This point of view has generated hundreds of theoretical constructs and causal inferences that describe the nature of effective psychotherapy. Each of the resulting theories and procedures vies for the status of being "most effective."

Controversies between those who attribute change to the elements that are common to all treatments and those who attribute change to specific and unique treatments that derive from certain brands of treatment are not unique to psychotherapy. The past decade has seen the emergence of similar conflicts in the general area of health and medicine as well. Placebo effects, expectancy, hope, and other constructs are implicated in the treatment of a wide array of medical and health conditions and compete for effectiveness with active drugs, surgery, and other interventions that are based on contemporary notions of illness. Clearly, whatever else is working, both physical health and emotional/behavioral well-being rely more than most would acknowledge on the forces of interpersonal persuasion, expectation, faith, and relationship, and less than some would wish on the specifics of pathology-based treatments.

In contrast to the specific treatments approach, the common factors viewpoint focuses on the interpersonal qualities that are correlated with change rather than with the technical ones. Scientists from this camp point out that virtually no direct comparison of one legitimate treatment against another yields any meaningful differences between them. Most who review this latter body of literature conclude that "all have won and all must have prizes." From the bulk of existing data, it is not scientifically sound to conclude that there are any treatments that are uniquely effective. To many of these scholars, it is the ubiquitous qualities of support and caring within the patient–therapist relationship that are seen as signals in evoking change in all of these treatments. Proponents of the common factors model consider these relationship qualities to be relatively independent of the specific procedures and techniques used—they are based largely on the nature of the relationship or the bond that develops between patient and therapist. That is, common factors proponents conceptualize a healing relationship as one that instills hope, facilitates communication, conveys safety, and is imbued with the patient's respect for, and trust of, the therapist.

These two viewpoints color how one perceives the extant research literature. For example, investigators who seek to identify specific treatments that work best with patients who carry different diagnostic labels are gratified by evidence that some treatments may produce substantially better effects among patients with different disorders than various comparison treatments or control groups. However, these same investigators tend to ignore the abundance of evidence indicating that all treatment studies produce essentially equivalent results. At the same time, researchers who believe that all treatments owe their effects to common interpersonal processes find their viewpoint reinforced by evidence that relationships and alliances are consistently related to outcomes but ignore the absence of direct evidence of a causal (rather than simply a correlational) relationship between alliance and outcomes. These investigators see the similarity of outcomes among different psychotherapy models as evidence for the causal nature of common factors, but no studies have been published that clearly demonstrate such a causal chain. For example, alliance may simply be a consequence of change rather than a cause of change.

It is certainly persuasive to look at the consistent correlation that exists between treatment qualities and outcomes, and to conclude that the many diverse therapeutic procedures that are effective all exercise their effects through the medium of improving the patient's sense of safety, comfort, and support. Thus, it is popular to conclude that therapists who provide safety, while being collaborative and supportive, are likely to produce good effects regardless of the specific procedures or theories used. Such a conclusion lacks the necessary scientific support to conclude that the observed correlation is the result of a causal chain of events. It is equally plausible that change itself may cement and foster warm and caring relationships, for example. It is also scientifically unjustified at present to conclude that some treatments are better than others.

Out of this awareness has emerged a third group of individuals within the individual psychotherapy movement who have attempted to integrate the opposing views of therapeutic specificity and therapeutic commonality. Members of this third group hold that the principal reason treatments don't show significant differences is that they have been tested on groups that are too homogeneous. They observe that within any treatment, there are some patients who get better, some who get worse, and some who fail to change. This pervasive pattern constitutes strong evidence that undisclosed patient factors are interacting with treatments. These scientists also hold that most research fails by attending only to therapy or relationship factors, and they assert that patient qualities themselves as well as the fit between patient qualities, and the procedures used also contribute to outcome. Indeed, they assert that patient qualities, therapy procedures, treatment relationship, and the fit or match between patient and treatment qualities are likely to make independent contributions to treatment benefit and that if relevant patient and matching qualities could be identified, the accuracy of predictions and the power of treatments could be substantially improved.

Contemporary research provides some evidence that while no specific procedure holds a mean or average advantage over others, there are some patient characteristics that mediate or moderate the effects of treatment, moreover, while the therapeutic relationship is very important, it may be more or less important depending on a variety of patient proclivities and the psychotherapeutic techniques utilized. Integrative and eclectic psychotherapy models accept the assumption that at least some interventions from widely different models are equally appropriate for some symptoms, some people, or some occasions. These models also assume that all treatment models are inappropriate for some people and that different people may benefit from different treatments. Some of these models simply blend two or more theories to make one new theory that is compatible with the techniques from more than one theoretical position. Other models attempt to directly identify patient markers that will indicate when to use different procedures and techniques of treatment, each representing different broad-band models.

Relatively new approaches within integrative and eclectic field have directed attention away from deriving finite lists of either theories or techniques, asserting that integration is best achieved by identifying cross-cutting principles that govern behavioral change in any of several different individual therapy formats. These latter approaches attempt to develop prescriptive treatment programs based on trait and statelike characteristics that the patient brings into the treatment relationship. Research is accumulating to support this point of view and to suggest that cross-cutting principles and discriminative use of different treatment procedures tend to enhance treatment outcomes. At present, these three points of view are yet to be reconciled. Moreover, the diversity of viewpoint and of research interpretation embodied in these views underlie the presence of other cardinal issues in the field of individual psychotherapy.

C. Lesser Issues in Individual Psychotherapy

As individual psychotherapy begins its second century as an accepted treatment for emotional, behavioral, and mental disorders, it is faced with a variety of complex and difficult problems. These problems are largely occasioned by threats to the credibility of this form of treatment.

1. The Proliferation of Psychotherapy Models

In the past three decades, the sheer number of available and practiced psychotherapies has grown exponentially, now reaching several hundred. All or at least most of these theories purport to offer both an explanatory model of psychopathology and a model of treatment change. In almost all theories, the model of psychopathology, incorporates an explanation of normal behavior by invoking developmental and situational factors, as well as an explanation of deviance by invoking pathogens and insidious precipitators of disorder and disease. The explanations extend to all disorders and identified conditions, and, if they exclude a causal explanation of any type of psychopathology at all, it is an explanation of those disorders that are judged to be outside the influence of interpersonal persuasion methods. Thus, all theories undertake to explain virtually all behaviors and to develop concepts that can fit all persons. Although psychotherapists may be comfortable with this breadth, it does not instill great faith in the idea that psychotherapists really know what produces change and what is healing in the patient–therapist exchange. Those within the managed health care environment who are in charge of assigning treatments to patients are likely to find the process of distilling the truly effective treatment from among 400 or so theoretical descriptions rather daunting they may conclude that a theory that explains everything really explains nothing.

Even among clinicians, the proliferation of theories and models may be taken as an indication that none of the models really works well. Clinicians are likely to develop new models when old ones don't work. Certainly, the fact that the highest percentage of clinicians identify themselves as being "eclectic" supports the view that no one theory is satisfactory. It is no wonder that psychotherapy has lost credibility both among patients and among managed health care providers, both of whom seem to believe that the various models and methods are interchangeable—there is no real or meaningful difference among them. Thus, a patient is recommended for or seeks psychotherapy for a condition or symptoms like depression; patients rarely seek a specific type of psychotherapy. In the rare instances in which a patient does seek a particular kind of therapy, typically one in which he or she has become familiar through friends or through reading, these treatments are likely to be rather exotic or unusual therapies. Predominantly, patients seem to view the particular therapist as being more important than the theoretical model from which he or she practices.

2. *Criteria of Effectiveness*

One of the major controversies in the field is how treatment effectiveness should be judged. Many psychologists believe that the best test of the worth of a psychotherapeutic treatment is in the observations of the clinician who exercises judgement and forms an opinion based on his or her theories of psychological disturbance and the elements that facilitate change. Such opinions, however, are by their nature very subjective; they cannot be reliably replicated, and their validity is highly suspect.

The usual criteria by which a treatment is judged to be effective is based on how persuasive, sincere, and articulate a clinician may be. These factors determine how effective a therapist is in persuading fellow clinicians to adopt his or her philosophy and perspective about psychotherapy. Political and legal criteria of a treatment's value are equally subjective and rarely focus on what the actual impact of the treatment is at the level of the patient's problems. Factors such as treatment cost, number of people accessed, popularity, and acceptance among peers are all considered in these criteria and frequently take precedence over actual effectiveness at altering symptoms and resolving problems.

In North America, as health care companies continue to struggle with the cost containment of mental health services, managed health care has increasingly turned to more objective methods of assessing whether a treatment is appropriate. Some professional groups have emphasized the need for a scientific standard by which to judge a treatments worth and have suggested certain research-informed standards by which to assess effectiveness.

By far the biggest obstacle to developing a uniform, research-based standard of care is that most contemporary approaches to treatment have not been subjected to empirical test. Nonetheless, a number of well-developed efforts have been made to translate the available research into standards of care or guidelines to direct practitioners. These guidelines typically specify the priority of various models and identify which ones among them have achieved empirical support through scientific research. A continuing obstacle to the implementation of these guidelines involves the sheer number of treatment models available.

Recognizing that it is difficult for clinicians to learn several different theoretical models and that often these guidelines are overly rigid, some authors have argued for a set of standards that emphasize empirically derived principles of psychotherapeutic change rather than either techniques or whole theories. This approach identifies various principles of selecting and applying treatments that are sensitive to ways in which patients differ from one another in their receptivity to different techniques, models, or therapeutic styles. It also emphasizes the need to customize the treatment to each patient, usually by mixing and fitting specific interventions or general styles to defined patient characteristics.

3. *Integration of the Science and Practice of Psychotherapy*

In these several ways, research findings are becoming more central to clinical practice, though this merger is frequently mandated by law and policy rather than being the result of a voluntary effort. Moreover, without a clear standard for assessing the scientific standing of various models of intervention, whatever merging or integration does occur is difficult to evaluate.

One of the most enduring and complex problems facing the practice of individual psychotherapy is the way in which scientific and clinical observers come to integrate their findings. This problem is complicated both because clinicians who practice psychotherapy and scientists who evaluate it have very different belief systems and perspectives. These differences underlie many of the disputes over the criteria by which to evaluate effectiveness and undermine the credibility of the treatment itself. Some of the differences that exist between scientists and practitioners are embodied in what kind of research methodologies are most valued. Scientists have tended to value studies of efficacy, whereas practitioners tend to value studies of effectiveness.

Efficacy studies are typically characterized by the use of a highly defined sample of patients, a well-trained cadre of clinicians, random assignment to well-structured and specific treatments, and systematic measurement of outcomes. They contrast with effectiveness studies, which are often less controlled, with more typical samples of therapists and patients, clinical assignment procedures, and less systematic treatments and measures. Although these labels represent the end points of control and generalizability in psychotherapy research, there is ample reason to believe that the distinction between them is more arbitrary than real. Efficacy studies frequently use complex, clinically representative samples, real therapists, and clinically meaningful measurements, whereas effectiveness studies often include random assignment and controlled treatments. In the final analysis, the critical question is the clinical utility of research, by whatever method it is conducted.

Perhaps a more important factor in keeping scientists and practitioners apart is that within both the camp of practitioners and the camp of scientists, there are many factions. In this chapter, we have already pointed to the many different clinical theories that guide treatment, but equally problematic is the fact that scientists themselves have disparate interpretations about what contemporary research tells us.

At the present time, there is no well-accepted way to translate research findings directly into practice or for researchers to be very responsive to clinician opinions and needs. Some argue that a new model of research is needed that adequately addresses the problems of practice. This model would systematically include clinical as well as research perspectives in treatment.

IV. SUMMARY

Over the 100 plus years since it emerged as a formal professional activity, psychotherapy has proven itself to be both popular and effective. Individual psychotherapy is by far the most widely researched and practiced, and it sets the general standard of efficacy and effectiveness by which other approaches can be assessed.

With the popularity of individual psychotherapy has come a burgeoning number of practitioners representing various professional backgrounds and types of training. Moreover, there has been an exponential growth in the number of theories used to describe the psychotherapeutic process and to guide one's work. Research has demonstrated that some of these approaches are effective, but most psychotherapeutic practices do not rely on scientific research for justification. Clinician experience and impressions are the most frequently used yardsticks by which to judge when treatment is effective and is working. However, this situation seems to be changing, and contemporary political movements and health care programs are recognizing the need to identify which treatments are effective and which ones are not. This movement has introduced a number of changes in the field of psychology. It has brought increasing pressure on clinicians to justify their practices in terms of research findings, and this development has placed more emphasis on making research that is clinically applicable.

As a result of changes in the health care environment, the disparities within the field of psychotherapy research as well as those between science and practice are becoming more apparent. New models are needed and are developing, both for making research more applicable and for applying research findings to the task of directing the course of treatment.

See Also the Following Articles

Behavior Therapy: Historical Perspective and Overview ■ Cognitive Behavior Therapy ■ Effectiveness of Psychotherapy ■ Efficacy ■ Exposure ■ Group Psychotherapy ■ Integrative Approaches to Psychotherapy ■ Interpersonal Psychotherapy ■ Neuropsychological Assessment ■ Objective Assessment ■ Research in Psychotherapy ■ Single Case Methods and Evaluation

Further Reading

Bergin, A. E., & Garfield, S. L. (Eds.). (1994). *Handbook of psychotherapy and behavior change*, 4th ed. New York: John Wiley & Sons.

Beutler, L. E. (2000). David and Goliath: When empirical and clinical standards of practice meet. *American Psychologist 55*, 997–1007.

Corsini, R. J. (1981). *Handbook of innovative psychotherapies.* New York: John Wiley & Sons.

Frank, J. D. (1973). *Persuasion and healing.* Baltimore, MD: Johns Hopkins University Press.

Freedheim, D. K. (Ed.). (1992). *History of psychotherapy: A century of change.* Washington, DC: American Psychological Press.

Nathan, P. E., & Gorman, J. M. (Eds.). (1998). *A guide to treatments that work.* New York: Oxford University Press.

Norcross, J. C., & Goldfried, M. R. (Eds.). (1992). *Handbook of psychotherapy integration*. New York: Basic Books.

Roth, A., & Fonagy, P. (Eds.). (1996). *What works for whom? A critical review of psychotherapy research*. New York: Guilford Press.

Wampold, B. E., Mondin, G. W., Moody, M., Stich, F., Benson, K., & Ahn, H. (1997). A meta-analysis of outcome studies comparing bona fide psychotherapies: Empirically, "All must have prizes." *Psychological Bulletin, 122,* 203–215.

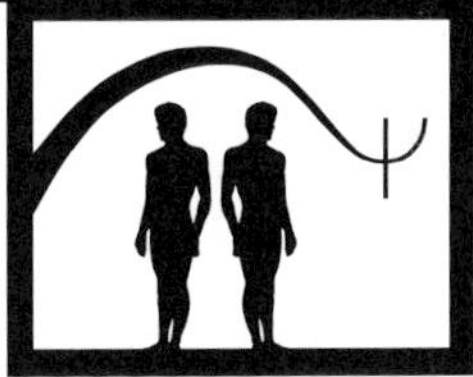

Informed Consent

Catherine Miller
Pacific University

GLOSSARY

confidentiality The ethical (and often legal) requirement to restrict disclosure of client information outside the therapy sessions.

mandated reporting of child abuse The legal requirement in all 50 states that psychologists report to authorities reasonable suspicion of physical, sexual, and/or emotional abuse of a child under the age of 18.

reasonable patient standard The prevailing standard employed when determining the amount of information to provide to clients in order to obtain consent for treatment. Although it is not clearly defined, this standard requires clinicians to provide as much information as a reasonable patient would desire.

Clinicians have an ethical and often legal obligation to obtain consent from clients prior to treating them. In order to obtain valid consent, clients must be fully informed regarding the nature of psychotherapy, including, for example, the potential benefits and risks of treatment, alternative treatments available, and limits of confidentiality. This article provides a description of the components of informed consent and methods of obtaining valid consent. Next, the article discusses the legal and ethical bases of the concept. Finally, a review of the available research on ways of obtaining informed consent and the impact that written forms have on the therapy process is provided.

I. DESCRIPTION OF INFORMED CONSENT

Initially, informed consent was a medical concept applying only to physicians and surgeons. The concept was circumscribed, requiring only that doctors tell patients the type of treatment recommended. Within the medical community, the concept eventually was expanded in scope, requiring physicians to give patients enough information about different available treatments so that patients could make educated decisions as to whether to accept a particular form of treatment. More recently, the concept has been incorporated into other disciplines, such as psychology.

As it applies to psychotherapy, the current doctrine of informed consent requires a client to be informed of the potential benefits and risks of the contemplated treatments, the expected prognosis with and without treatment, and any possible alternative treatments. Barring exceptions such as emergency treatment, a person cannot be given therapy without his or her informed consent to such procedures. Underlying the concept of informed consent is the principle that allowing a client to make an informed decision respects that person's autonomy and self-determination.

Valid consent implies that the client agrees to treatment intelligently, knowingly, and voluntarily. Intelligence, sometimes referred to as competency, is defined as a client's capacity to comprehend and evaluate the specific information that is offered, whereas knowledge is defined as a client's ability to appreciate how the given treatment information applies to him or her specifically. Finally, the voluntary element suggests that a client's consent may not be coerced or enticed by the treating agent. All three elements must be present in order to consider consent truly informed and valid.

The first element of competency or intelligence is a difficult concept for two reasons. First, there has been considerable debate over how much information should be given to a client to allow him or her to make an informed decision. Second, the concept is often difficult to assess with child clients.

Regarding the debate over the extent of information provided, historically there have been two standards employed to determine whether the client has received adequate information. The first is a professional standard, which requires that the amount of information provided to a client be what other professionals in the community typically provide. The professional standard has been criticized for being somewhat paternalistic, in that clinicians determine the extent of the information that is provided to clients. The second standard is the reasonable patient standard, which requires the professional to give as much information as a reasonable patient would desire to make treatment decisions. The major problem with this standard is the difficulty in quantifying the exact amount of information a reasonable patient would desire. This standard does, in addition, put the onus squarely on clinicians to provide information, even when not requested by a particular client. In recent years, the reasonable patient standard has been the prevailing model.

Regarding child clients, it should be noted that the right to give consent is a legal one that is based on a client's presumed ability to understand the information given. In general, only adults are considered able to understand treatment information and to be legally competent to give consent. In many states, minors are not legally competent to give consent; instead, consent for treatment must be obtained from a legal guardian or parent. However, some state statutes give minors limited rights to consent to treatment. For example, in Oregon, state law allows children 14 years of age and older to give valid consent for outpatient mental health treatment without the consent of parents. Other states' statutes recognize the mature minor exception, granting minors near the age of majority or mature enough to understand and weigh treatment options the right to consent to treatment. Regardless of state law, it is important to involve even young children in the process of obtaining consent. Despite the fact that state laws often do not recognize their capacities, research has found that even young children may be capable of understanding and weighing treatment options. Given these findings, clinicians should endeavor to obtain assent to treatment from children ages 7 and older. The term assent does not imply legal consent; however, it suggests that young children should be given relevant treatment information and asked whether or not they wish to participate in treatment. If a child does not want to participate in treatment, despite parental consent, ethical principles dictate that the clinician should consider the best interests of the child. Such a dilemma would involve considering and respecting the child's autonomy while recognizing the legal authority of the child's parents.

Although providing information about treatment is necessary to ensure a person's consent is done intelligently, it is not sufficient to obtain informed consent from a client. In addition, a client's knowledge or ability to appreciate that the material is relevant to him or her specifically must be assessed. In order to ensure that a client fully appreciates the information provided, a clinician must regularly question the client's comprehension of the material. One way of assessing comprehension is to ask a client to repeat, in his or her own words, treatment information that was presented previously. Only with a reasonable appreciation of the information will consent to treatment be considered valid. By the reasonable patient standard, clinicians bear the responsibility of ensuring that clients understand and appreciate the treatment information given.

Finally, in order to satisfy the requirement that consent be given voluntarily, no undue pressure may be placed on the client by the treating agent. For example, clinicians should avoid promising miraculous and timely cures; they should also avoid offering financial incentives for participating in treatment. To ensure the voluntary element necessary to valid consent, clients must be told that they can withdraw from treatment at any time.

The limits of informed consent should be noted by clinicians. Obtaining informed consent does not provide permission to clinicians to perform illegal or unethical acts. For example, a therapist cannot justify sexual acts with a client by claiming that informed consent for these acts as part of treatment was obtained from the client. In other words, there clearly are limits on those things to which a client can validly consent.

Given the three elements of valid consent, it should be clear that obtaining informed consent is not a one-time incident but instead is an ongoing process throughout treatment. Several authors have suggested that clinicians adopt a process model rather than an event model of informed consent. Ongoing discussions with clients throughout the treatment process may be necessary to ensure that they have sufficient opportunities to ask questions and have information clarified. At a minimum, there are two discrete times during the therapy process when informed consent should be obtained: at the initiation of therapy and when particular treatments are proposed.

At the initiation of therapy, clinicians should provide general information on the nature and process of therapy to potential clients. Informed consent for treatment generally should be obtained at the beginning of the very first session, prior to obtaining potentially sensitive information, conducting assessments, or implementing any treatment techniques. The following information should be given at the initial session to assure informed consent. First, clients should be told the qualifications of the therapist and any supervision that is required. Second, clients should be told the limits of confidentiality (e.g., mandated reporting of child abuse) and general client rights (e.g., the right to withdraw from therapy at any time). Finally, clients should be told logistical information, such as scheduling practices and fee structures.

In addition to general information on the nature of therapy, the informed consent process should continue when specific treatments are proposed. At this time in the therapy process, clinicians should provide information on the purpose of the proposed treatment, any possible discomforts or harms, and any potential positive benefits. In addition, clients must be told about alternative treatments available and the possible risks and benefits of these treatments. Finally, clients must be told that no treatment is an option and must be informed of the possible consequences of opting out of treatment.

It is imperative that clinicians document this ongoing process of obtaining informed consent. The first major point of documentation is at the first session. At that time, clinicians are advised to employ a written information sheet that is read and signed by the client. Although there are many variations of this form, it should be written in plain language free of jargon or legalistic phrases and should contain the information necessary for the client to make an informed choice regarding whether or not to participate in therapy. However, it should be noted that a signed informed consent form is not enough to demonstrate knowledge, one of the three elements of informed consent. To document client knowledge, clinicians should include in a progress note any client questions or statements that indicate that the client has a full appreciation of the information given. The second major point of documentation is when specific treatment techniques are proposed. At that time, clinicians should carefully document in progress notes the treatment options presented to the client and any questions asked by the client. Standard of care issues now dictate that clinicians should determine which treatment to employ by reading available literature and using empirically supported treatments. If a clinician decides to employ an unusual or experimental treatment, he or she should thoroughly document that the client has been fully informed about the nature of the experimental treatment and the possible risks and benefits. In addition, the clinician should document that the client was given information about standard treatments.

The documentation requirements ensuring valid consent may become more time-consuming when clinicians conduct family or couples sessions. In those instances, informed consent should be obtained from all participating members at the initiation of therapy and throughout the treatment process. In addition, progress notes should document that discussions have been held regarding any issues that are unique to family or couples sessions. For example, clinicians should discuss with all family members how to handle difficult confidentiality issues faced when more than one client is in the room and should document these discussions in the progress notes.

II. LEGAL AND ETHICAL BASES OF INFORMED CONSENT

Several legal cases illustrate the importance of obtaining informed consent. The first major legal statement of the need for consent occurred in the 1905 case of Mohr versus Williams. In this case, the plaintiff used a physician for performing an unauthorized surgical operation. While the plaintiff did consent to an operation on her right ear, the physician instead performed an operation on her left ear, as he had found the left ear to be more in need of treatment once the surgical procedures had commenced. Following the operation, the plaintiff claimed that she had not previously experienced any difficulty with her left ear but that she currently was having trouble hearing out of that ear. The court found in favor of the plaintiff and stated that a surgical operation by a physician upon the body of his patient is unlawful when performed without either the express or implied consent of the patient.

In 1914, the case of Schloendorff versus the Society of New York Hospital expanded on the requirements for informed consent. The court stated that a patient must be apprised of the potential benefits and major risks of any proposed treatment, as well as the available alternative treatments. However, the court did not give specific guidance on how much information is sufficient. A later case, Canterbury versus Spence (1972), appeared to support the reasonable patient rather than the professional standard of information provision. The court in this case stated that physicians have "a duty to impart information which the patient has every right to expect." Since this 1972 case, physicians have been considered to have an affirmative duty to impart as much information as a reasonable patient would require, regardless of whether a particular patient asks for such information.

It is clear from the above brief review that case law has supported obtaining informed consent for medical procedures. However, courts have not directly addressed whether or not informed consent is applicable to typical psychological or counseling services. Likewise, state statutes that address the concept of informed consent have typically addressed only physician obligations to obtain consent. Currently, all states have statutes mandating some type of informed consent procedures for physicians and psychiatrists. Not every state, however, clearly specifies that psychologists or other mental health providers must obtain informed consent for psychological treatments. For example, Oregon law on informed consent states only that physicians and surgeons must obtain informed consent for treatment, with no mention of any such obligation on the part of psychologists. On the other hand, Colorado and Indiana statutes mandate that psychotherapists obtain informed consent. Other state legislatures currently are considering bills requiring psychologists to obtain informed consent prior to treatment. It appears that the recent increase in legislative activity stems from controversy surrounding therapy techniques designed to activate repressed memories. These techniques supposedly help adults recover or unlock previously repressed or forgotten memories of childhood sexual abuse. Critics claim that these techniques result in false memories rather than true memories of abuse and that the techniques lack a scientific basis. Critics have introduced legislation requiring psychologists to inform clients of the scientific basis of all treatment techniques, as part of their efforts to reduce the use of repressed memory techniques. Clearly, clinicians should be aware of the statutes in the states in which they practice, as laws regarding informed consent for therapy vary across state lines.

Regardless of whether state statutes or case law mandate that clinicians obtain informed consent prior to mental health treatment, ethical codes of conduct typically dictate that clinicians apply the concept of informed consent with all clients. For example, the ethical codes developed by the American Psychological Association (APA) and the American Counseling Association (ACA) contain sections dealing with informed consent. In the APA code, Principle 4.02 states that psychologists must obtain informed consent by using "language that is reasonably understood by participants." If a client is a child or otherwise unable to give consent, psychologists must obtain consent from the legal guardian. In addition, psychologists must provide information to a child or other legally incompetent person and obtain assent from that person. The overarching principle espoused in ethical principles is that clinicians must consider the client's best interests, autonomy, and self-determination.

Clinicians should be aware that not obtaining valid consent prior to treatment places them in a precarious position. Due to ethical principles requiring informed consent, a client may file an ethical complaint with the state licensing board for a clinician's failure to obtain valid consent. Complaints regarding lack of informed consent may be based on the three areas discussed previously: lack of competence to consent to treatment, lack of voluntary consent, or lack of sufficient information. To be found in violation of the ethical code, a psychologist must only be found to have neglected standard and reasonable informed consent procedures. It is not necessary for the client to have been harmed due to the psychologist's negligence for a clinician to be found in violation of the ethics code. In egregious cases, the result may be suspension or loss of the license to practice psychology in that state.

In addition to an ethical complaint, clinicians who neglect to obtain valid consent from clients may find themselves facing a civil lawsuit. Despite a lack of case law directly addressing the concept of informed consent for psychological services, it is only a matter of time until such a suit is filed. In contrast to an ethical complaint, the client in a civil suit must show, among other things, that the client was harmed by the clinician. To win a suit based on a failure to obtain informed consent, the client must prove all of the following five things: (1) that the risks involved with a therapy should have been disclosed; (2) that the risks were not disclosed; (3) that the risks materialized; (4) that the materialized risks resulted in injury; and (5) that the client would not have accepted the therapy if he or she knew of the risks involved. It is true that such lawsuits are uncommon and difficult to prove currently. However, the rise of empirically supported treatments may increase the frequency of complaints made by clients who did not receive information and full disclosure regarding such treatment options. Injury or harm may be demonstrated by a client who incurred expenses while participating in an ineffectual therapy for a long period of time, when a more time-efficient and empirically supported therapy was available but was not disclosed to the client. In our increasingly litigious society, clinicians should be aware of the growing possibility of legal liability for failure to obtain fully informed consent.

III. RESEARCH ON INFORMED CONSENT PROCEDURES

There has been little research conducted on the process or effects of obtaining informed consent. The limited research that is available has addressed three main areas: prevalence of informed consent procedures, optimal methods of obtaining informed consent, and effects of informed consent procedures on client disclosure or attendance.

First, research has not supported the idea that all clinicians employ some form of consent procedure. As stated previously, consent procedures include utilizing a written informational form and documenting ongoing discussions with the client. As recently as 1993, Daniel Somberg, Gerald Stone, and Charles Claiborn found that only 60% of psychologists reported utilizing any type of consent procedure with all clients. Thirty-seven percent of the remaining psychologists stated that they did not employ informed consent procedures with all clients due to believing that such procedures were irrelevant, while 16% stated that they often simply forgot to obtain informed consent.

As should be clear from previous sections, the use of both written forms and ongoing discussions with clients is encouraged. Research has found that the sole use of written forms to convey information on the therapy process and treatments has increased over the past two decades. However, research does not support the exclusive use of a written informational form as a method of obtaining valid consent. There are two major problems with sole reliance on such forms. First, researchers have found that the average length of consent forms doubled from 1975 to 1982, in order to include more information about client rights and confidentiality. Second, the written forms typically employed generally require that the reader have at least a college education. One study found that the average readability of consent forms was grade 15.7 (third year college level), while some reached grade 17+ (postgraduate level).

Given the increasing length and complexity in such forms, it is important to ask whether the typical client can comprehend such information. It is possible that longer and more detailed forms, while covering all of the required consent elements, are primarily utilized to protect clinicians against ethical complaints or lawsuits rather than as a way to educate and inform clients. Clearly, understanding is an important element in giving informed consent; without it, a signature on an informational form is not valid. Although not directly addressing clinical or treatment forms, a 1994 study by Traci Mann on the understanding of research informed consent forms is relevant. Overall, Mann found that longer consent forms inhibited the amount of information retained by participants. Mann concluded that research participants often agree to engage in studies that they do not understand, which belies the whole idea of informed consent. His findings imply that long, complex consent forms should not be employed with clinical clients.

An alternative to employing detailed informed consent forms is a procedure suggested by Mitchell Handelsman and Michael Galvin in 1988. These authors developed a question sheet that includes a list of commonly asked questions. This sheet also instructs potential clients that they have a right to ask any or all of these questions to their therapist. Handelsman and Galvin directed that some of the questions must be answered by the therapist even if not asked by the client; examples of such questions that therapists are ethically obligated to discuss with clients would be those dealing with confidentiality and the general nature of treatment. However, the remaining questions are left to the discretion of the client, respecting the right of clients to not be given information that is not wanted. It may also encourage the use of a process format of obtaining informed consent, rather than a single event model. To date, no studies have been done investigating the level of client retention of information presented in such a format.

Several studies have examined the effects of informed consent procedures on the therapy process, with most of the research examining the effects of written informational forms. Clearly, some clinicians have been reluctant to employ informed consent procedures, particularly written forms, on a regular basis. The primary concern may be that the use of legalistic forms and terms is detrimental to the establishment of a therapeutic relationship. In other words, informed consent procedures, particularly written forms, may create a negative impression of therapy in general and the therapist specifically. It is also possible that clinicians are concerned that too much information on the limits of confidentiality may deter clients from revealing important but sensitive information. However, in general, the literature does not support these negative effects of informed consent procedures; instead, research has found primarily positive results from the process of obtaining informed consent.

In regard to the therapeutic relationship, in 1990 Mitchell Handelsman surveyed 129 undergraduate students regarding their impressions of a hypothetical therapist. Holding level of experience of the therapist constant across conditions, Handelsman varied the amount of written information provided to survey participants. In all conditions, participants were provided minimal written information about the therapist, including his educational background and years of experience. In the first condition, participants also were provided the question sheet. In the second condition, participants were given a legal disclosure form, outlining client rights, limits to confidentiality, and other information often considered part of informed consent procedures. Finally, in the third condition, participants were given a brochure that provided general information to commonly asked questions (e.g., What is the difference between a psychologist and a psychiatrist?). Based on the information provided, participants were asked to complete a questionnaire regarding their impressions of the hypothetical psychologist. Overall, Handelsman found that the use of more written information increased participants' positive judgments of therapists' experience, likeability, and trustworthiness, in addition to their likelihood of referring the therapist to others. This study suggested that written information, whether disclosed in a more legalistic document or through a question sheet, may improve therapist ratings. The study was not able to conclude that the question sheet was more beneficial than the legal disclosure form.

In a separate study in 1990, Mitchell Handelsman surveyed 137 undergraduate students to assess whether varying level of therapist experience would affect the previously established positive impact of legal disclosure forms. For this study, half the participants received the legal disclosure form; the other half received both the legal disclosure form and the question sheet. In addition, therapist level of experience varied. In the first condition (the low-experience condition) participants were told that the hypothetical therapist was recently licensed within the past year. In the second condition (the moderate-experience condition), participants were told that the therapist had been practicing for at least 9 years. Finally, in the third condition (the high-experience condition), participants were told that the therapist had been in practice for 19 years. Overall, Handelsman found that participants rated experience highly. However, with more information provided, the less experienced therapist was rated more highly. Handelsman's findings suggest that adding more written information in the informed consent process improves client ratings, particularly with less experienced therapists.

In 1993, Therese Sullivan, William Martin, and Mitchell Handelsman conducted a survey of 124 undergraduate psychology students to further investigate the impact of information on ratings of clinicians. Participants were assigned to one of two conditions. In both conditions, participants were given a hypothetical transcript of a first therapy session. In the first condition (informed consent transcript condition), the transcript was accompanied by a written consent form and included discussion of confidentiality, alternative treatments, and risks and benefits of therapy. In the second condition (control transcript condition), no written form accompanied the transcript and no discussion on informed consent issues was included. Following presentation of materials, all participants were asked to complete a questionnaire regarding impressions of the therapist. The authors found that the combined presentation of oral and written information positively impacted therapist ratings.

To date, only one study has found any negative effects of written forms on client impressions of therapists. In 1992, Mitchell Handelsman and William Martin found that male adult clients reported lower ratings for therapists who provided written informed consent forms than no information at all. However, the forms employed in this study were difficult to read, as they required at least a 10th-grade reading level, had complex sentences, and were single-spaced. As previously reported, less readable forms are likely to be misunderstood by clients. It appears from this study that therapist ratings also suffer from complex information forms.

As the above brief review demonstrates, the limited research that has been done appears to support the idea that informed consent procedures improve client ratings of therapists. Further research has examined whether informed consent procedures affect client behaviors in therapy, such as termination rates and the frequency of disclosures of sensitive information.

Termination and no-show rates of clients at a counseling center of a state university were examined in 1995 by Patricia Dauser, Suzanne Hedstrom, and James Croteau. In the partial disclosure condition, participants received only the counseling center's standard written information, including the services provided at the clinic, limits of confidentiality, length and frequency of sessions, and the client's right to terminate treatment. In the full disclosure condition, participants received the standard written form as well as written materials containing more detailed information. Specifically, participants were told the name of the assigned therapist, the therapist's experience and typical treatment procedures, anticipated positive results of therapy, possible risks, potential alternatives to therapy, fee structure, the name of the therapist's supervisor (if applicable), and the name and number of the state licensing board. Overall, the authors found no differences between the two conditions in no-show or termination rates during the course of therapy, suggesting that more information does not negatively affect client attendance.

The results of research on the impact of informed consent procedures on client disclosures have been mixed. In recent years, legislation in most states has mandated that certain information revealed by clients (e.g., child abuse, imminent harm to others) be disclosed to authorities. This legislation is based on the idea that society has more of an interest in preventing harm than in protecting client confidentiality. Informing clients of the limits of confidentiality is a standard part of most informed consent procedures. Some studies have found that warning clients of the limits of confidentiality reduces client disclosures, whereas other studies have found that it has no impact. As an example, Daniel Taube and Amiram Elwork examined rates of disclosure of sensitive information in 1990. These authors assessed 42 adult outpatient clients regarding level of self-disclosure following either minimal information on confidentiality limits or full information regarding this topic. The authors found that information on confidentiality limits does reduce self-disclosure for some patients in some circumstances. In particular, more informed clients did not admit to as many child punishment and neglect behaviors, nor did they admit to as many socially unacceptable thoughts and behaviors as the minimally informed group. The authors suggested that legislation on mandated reporting of certain client information may not achieve its intended aim of protecting society and may also hinder the therapy process. Due to conflicting findings in the literature, further research is needed to clarify the impact of informed consent procedures on client disclosures.

IV. SUMMARY

Obtaining informed consent of all clients is an ethical requirement for psychologists. In addition, it is likely that psychologists will increasingly be legally required to obtain informed consent prior to treatment. Informed consent is valid only if given intelligently, knowingly, and voluntarily. The reasonable patient model is now the standard of care, suggesting that clinicians must take the responsibility for initiating dialogues with clients regarding consent issues. An ongoing, process model is advisable, rather than a single event model that relies exclusively on a written informational form. Both written forms and continual discussions are helpful, as long as the client understands these basic areas: nature of therapy in general, limits to confidentiality, treatment techniques available, and the risks and benefits of potential techniques (including the option of no treatment).

Research has found that not all therapists currently utilize informed consent procedures, believing it may be irrelevant or even harmful to the therapeutic relationship. In general, research has supported the positive effects of providing more information to the client prior to treatment. For example, research has found that increased information appears to improve client ratings of clinicians. Although not directly studied, it is possible that providing more information to clients reduces the risk of exploitation of clients by informing them of rights and expectations. In addition, it is possible that utilizing informed consent procedures may align client and clinician expectations of therapy, resulting in a better therapy outcome, as well as fewer lawsuits or ethical complaints for clinicians. Clearly, further research should be conducted on these hypotheses.

It should be noted, however, that research has not been uniformly positive as to the effects of informed consent procedures. When long or complex written materials are utilized, client comprehension suffers. Also, research is mixed on the effects of informed consent procedures on client disclosure of sensitive information. At least one study has found that disclosure of sensitive material may be inhibited when more information on the limits of confidentiality is provided to clients. Further research on this issue is needed to clarify the extent of client censoring of sensitive materials.

See Also the Following Articles

Bioethics ■ Cancer Patients: Psychotherapy ■ Economic and Policy Issues ■ Flooding ■ Legal Dimensions of Psychiatry ■ Medically Ill Patient: Psychotherapy ■ Supervision in Psychotherapy

Further Reading

American Psychological Association. (1992). Ethical principles of psychologists and code of conduct. *American Psychologist, 42,* 1597–1611.

Appelbaum, P. S. (1997). Informed consent to psychotherapy: Recent developments. *Psychiatric Services, 48,* 445–446.

Crowhurst, B., & Dobson, K. S. (1980). Informed consent: Legal issues and applications to clinical practice. *Canadian Psychology, 34,* 329–343.

Gustofson, K. E., & McNamara, J. R. (1987). Confidentiality with minor clients: Issues and guidelines for therapists. *Professional Psychology: Research and Practice, 18,* 503–508.

Koocher, G. P., & Keith-Spiegel, P. (1998). *Ethics in psychology: Professional standards and cases* (2nd ed.). New York: Oxford University Press.

Marczyk, G. R., & Wertheimer, E. (2001). The bitter pill of empiricism: Health maintenance organizations, informed consent, and the reasonable psychotherapist standard of care. *Villanova Law Review, 46,* 33–93.

Zuckerman, E. L. (1997). *The paper office* (2nd ed.). New York: Guilford Press.

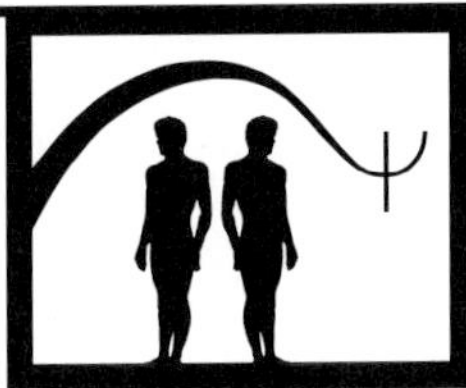

Integrative Approaches to Psychotherapy

Jerry Gold
Long Island University

GLOSSARY

assimilative integration A system of psychotherapy integration that depends largely on one approach but that incorporates concepts and methods as dictated by clinical necessity. These new elements are transformed to fit into the primary approach.

common factors That group of variables that have been found to be the effective ingredients of most psychotherapies.

common factors integration The combination of therapeutic approaches based on the ability of particular methods to deliver the desired common factor of change.

psychodynamic A synonym for psychoanalytic, it refers to unconscious motivations, perceptions, emotions, and conflicts that determine behavior, and to forms of psychotherapy that emphasize these factors.

psychotherapy integration The combination of techniques and/or concepts from two or more psychotherapeutic approaches into a single method of psychotherapy.

technical eclecticism The most pragmatic and common form of psychotherapy integration, in which interventions are matched to patient characteristics, symptoms, and problems on the basis of research findings and clinical knowledge.

theoretical integration The most conceptually complex form of psychotherapy integration, in which the underlying theories of personality and psychopathology are synthesized and are the foundation of a new therapeutic approach.

This article will introduce the reader to progress in the area of psychotherapy integration. This is a new and exciting subdiscipline in the field of psychotherapy. It is concerned with using and combining the most effective elements of psychotherapy theory and practice in ways that accentuate the power of integrated psychotherapies to help a wider range of patients, with a broader spectrum of problems, to change.

I. DESCRIPTION OF TREATMENT: A HISTORICAL AND CONCEPTUAL OVERVIEW OF PSYCHOTHERAPY INTEGRATION

From the earliest foundations of modern approaches to psychotherapy, practitioners and students of psychotherapy have been extraordinarily unwilling to learn from systems of psychotherapy other than their own. Each school of psychotherapy has developed in a state of isolation from the other schools. This state of segregation within the field of psychotherapy has had dramatic and important effects. It has led to unwanted hostility between adherents of the various psychotherapeutic schools, and to efforts to dismiss out of hand the ideas and methods of competing approaches without systematic study or intellectual consideration. This self-imposed therapeutic "apartheid" also has prevented psychotherapists and patients from benefiting from clinical and theoretical innovations introduced by colleagues who are loyal to other psychotherapeutic approaches. Michael Mahoney argued in 1985 that these schisms in the field were political in nature and did not reflect clinical reality, which indicated that none of the therapeutic schools could claim to be vastly superior to any other.

This stubborn isolationism in the field of psychotherapy stands in contrast to the fact that psychotherapists have always been interested in, and long have attempted to use, new developments in the natural and social sciences, philosophy, theology, the arts, and literature. A small group of scholars and clinicians have been able to cross sectarian lines and have countered the segregation of the various schools of psychotherapy. These integrationists have aimed at establishing a useful dialogue among members of the various sectarian schools of psychotherapy. Their goal has been the development of the most effective forms of psychotherapy possible. The integration of therapies involves the synthesis of the "best and brightest" concepts and methods into new theories and practical systems of treatment.

Integrative forms of psychotherapy vary greatly depending on the particular version that is being considered, yet all share one common goal and purpose. Integrative psychotherapies are the result of the synthesis of theoretical concepts and clinical techniques from two or more traditional schools of psychotherapy (such as psychoanalysis and behavior therapy) into one therapeutic approach. It is hoped and assumed that this therapeutic synthesis will be more powerful and will be applicable to a wider range of clinical populations and problems than were the individual models of psychotherapy that formed the basis of the integrated model.

Histories of early efforts at integrating compiled by Marvin Goldfried and Cory Newman in 1992, and by Jerold Gold in 1993, identified scattered but important contributions as early as 1933, when Thomas French argued that concepts from Pavlovian models of learning should be integrated with then current psychoanalytic insights. In 1944 Robert Sears offered a synthesis of learning theory and psychoanalysis, as did John Dollard and Neal Miller in 1950, whose translation of psychoanalytic concepts and methods into the language and framework of laboratory-derived learning principles was a watershed event.

Early clinical efforts at integrating behavioral and psychoanalytic interventions in a single case were introduced by Bernard Weitzman in 1967, in 1971 by Judd Marmor, and by Benjamin Feather and John Rhodes in 1973. These clinical efforts demonstrated that unconscious factors in a patient's psychopathology could be ameliorated through the use of behavioral methods, along with traditional psychodynamic exploration and interpretation.

In the past two decades a number of important integrative approaches to psychotherapy have been developed. In 1977 Paul Wachtel published a groundbreaking book that advocated an integration of psychoanalytic theory with social learning theory, and in which he demonstrated ways in which clinicians could effectively use behavioral and psychoanalytic interventions with one patient. This integrative approach received enormous attention within the behavior therapy and psychoanalytic communities, and was followed by other efforts at promoting a dialogue between clinicians of various orientations, as well as a relative torrent of articles and books that focused on integrative topics. In 1984 Hal Arkowitz and Stanley Messer published an edited volume in which prominent behavior therapists and psychoanalytic therapists discussed and debated the possibilities of extensive integration of the two systems.

In 1992 John Norcross and Marvin Goldfried published a handbook that presented a variety of fully developed integrative systems of psychotherapy. This effort was followed in 1993 by a volume edited by George Stricker and Jerold Gold in which an even greater number of integrative models was presented, and the clinical utility of psychotherapy integration was explored with regard to a variety of clinical problems and populations. These volumes illustrated that integrative models were no longer focused exclusively on the synthesis of psychoanalytic and behavioral systems. Newer integrative efforts have combined humanistic, cognitive, experiential, and family systems models with each other and with psychoanalytic and behavioral components in ever more sophisticated combinations and permutations. Process-experiential psychotherapy, an innovation introduced by Leslie Greenberg, Laura Rice, and Robert Elliot in 1993, and acceptance and commitment therapy (ACT), described by Steven Hayes, Kirk Strosahl, and Kelly Wilson in 1999, are important examples of integrative approaches that rely heavily on the integration of humanistic and experiential approaches with cognitive-behavioral therapies. Similarly, an integrative model that blended existential, humanistic, and narrative therapies was described in 1999 by Alphons Richert.

These psychotherapeutic systems have received increasing attention on the part of clinicians and researchers alike, and have become established and viable alternatives to traditional schools of psychotherapy.

In 1992 John Norcross and Cory Newman identified eight variables that have encouraged this rapid proliferation of integrative psychotherapies after decades during which these efforts were scanty. These included (1) The ever-increasing number of schools of psychotherapy; (2) a lack of clear-cut empirical support for superior efficacy of any school of therapy; (3) the failure of any single theory to adequately explain and predict pathology, or personality and behavioral change; (4) the growth in number and importance of shorter term, focused psychotherapies; (5) greater communication between clinicians and scholars that has resulted in increased willingness to, and opportunity for, experimentation; (6) the intrusion into the consulting room of the realities of limited socioeconomic support by third parties for long-term psychotherapies; (7) the identification of common factors in all psychotherapies that are related to outcome; and (8) the development of professional organizations, conferences, and journals that are dedicated to the discussion and study of psychotherapy integration.

II. THEORETICAL BASES OF PSYCHOTHERAPY INTEGRATION

A. Modes of Psychotherapy Integration

The three most commonly discussed forms of integration are technical eclecticism, the common factors approach, and theoretical integration.

1. Technical Eclecticism

This is the most clinical and technically oriented form of psychotherapy integration. Techniques and interventions drawn from two or more psychotherapeutic systems are applied systematically and sequentially. The series of linked interventions usually follows a comprehensive assessment of the patient. This assessment allows target problems to be identified and identifies the relationships between different problems, strengths, and the cognitive, affective, and interpersonal characteristics of the patient. Techniques are chosen on the basis of the best clinical match to the needs of the patient, as guided by clinical knowledge and by research findings.

a. Multimodal Therapy The most influential and important integrative approach that is representative of technical eclecticism is multimodal therapy, described by Arnold Lazarus in 1992 and studied extensively by him and many others since that time. Multimodal therapy was derived from Lazarus's experiences as a behavior therapist, and particularly from his follow-up studies of patients who relapsed after seemingly successful behavioral treatment. His research and clinical experience indicated that most behavioral problems had more extensive psychological and social causes and correlates than then current behavior therapy had addressed. Seeking to expand the range of his ability to work in a more "broad spectrum" way, Lazarus arrived at a multimodal, or broad-based, eclectic therapy.

Multimodal therapy is organized around an extensive assessment of the patient's strengths, excesses, liabilities, and problem behaviors. Upon completion of this assessment, that patient's clinically significant issues are organized within a framework that follows the acronym of the *BASIC ID:* Behavior, Affect, Sensation, Imagery, Cognition, Interpersonal relations, and Drugs (or biology). As the firing order or causal sequence of variables in the BASIC ID is identified, interventions are selected and are implemented. More microscopic BASIC ID profiles of discrete or difficult problems and of components of a firing order can be attempted once the initial, global assessment and interventions are completed.

Lazarus states that he prefers to use methods that have been demonstrated through empirical tests to be effective with specific problems and skills, and his theory and technical strategies are more heavily aligned with social learning theory and with cognitive-behavior therapy than with any other therapeutic school. However, in his broad-spectrum approach, he often includes imagery work, techniques drawn from couples and family therapy, gestalt exercises and some affective and insight oriented interventions.

b. Systematic Eclectic Psychotherapy This system of psychotherapy integration was described by Larry Beutler and Amy Hodgson in 1993. This is an empirically informed system in which a thorough assessment of the patient is followed by the prescription of techniques, if available, that have received the most research validation for efficacy with that specific clinical profile. When such research-based matching is not possible, techniques are selected according to accumulated clinical findings drawn from the literature and from the experience of the individual therapist. Beutler and Hodgson choose therapeutic interventions by considering the interaction of three variables: the stage of involvement in psychotherapy that the patient has reached; the necessary change experiences for which the patient is prepared; and the dominant aspects of the patient's immediate clinical status. Clinical techniques can be matched with four psychological spheres that are assessed on an ongoing basis: overt dysfunctional behavior, faulty thinking, inhibitions of affective and sensory experience, and repressed unconscious conflict. Therapists who work in this framework are free to draw on interventions from any existing system of psychotherapy ranging from psychoanalytically oriented interpretations, to experiential, emotional work, to efforts at modifying thoughts and overt behaviors.

2. Common Factors Approaches to Integration

Common factors integration starts from the identification of specific effective ingredients of any group of therapies. This way of thinking has its origins in the 1936 paper by Saul Rosenzweig, who argued that all therapies shared certain effective ingredients of change, despite their overt ideologies and technical procedures. Also critically important in this area is the work of Jerome Frank, who in 1961 suggested that all systems of psychological healing share certain common, effective ingredients, such as socially sanctioned rituals, the provision of hope, and the shaping of an outlook on life that offers encouragement to the patient. Integrative therapists who rely on common factors concern themselves with the task of identifying which of the several known common factors will be most important in the treatment of each individual. Once the most salient common factors are selected, the therapist reviews the array of interventions and psychotherapeutic interactions to find those that have been found to promote and contain those ingredients. The integrative therapies that result from this process are structured around the goal of maximizing the patient's exposure to the unique combination of therapeutic factors that will best ameliorate his or her problems.

a. Transtheoretical Psychotherapy The most important and widely accepted integrative psychotherapy that exemplifies the common factors mode is transtheoretical psychotherapy, described by James Prochaska and Carlos DiClemente in 1992. In this system, the therapist selects intervention techniques after three patient characteristics are assessed. These are the change mechanisms or common therapeutic factors that are required, the stage of change at which the patient seeks help, and the level of change that is necessary. Prochaska and DiClemente identified 10 possible change factors that operate in the entire range of the psychotherapies, including consciousness raising, self-liberation, social liberation, counterconditioning, stimulus control, self-reevaluation, environmental reevaluation, contingency management, dramatic relief, and helping relationships. Each of these factors is linked to particular therapeutic interventions, although most therapies contain only 2 or 3 of the 10. The concept stage of change refers to the patient's readiness and motivation to change. Five stages have been identified, including precontemplation (the patient is not actively considering change), contemplation (consideration of change without current readiness), preparation, action, and maintenance. Depth of change refers to the sphere of psychological life in which the targeted problem is located, including situational problems, maladaptive thinking, interpersonal conflicts, family conflicts, and intrapersonal conflicts. The transtheoretical therapist selects interventions that will have maximal impact at the desired level of change, will be consistent with the patient's readiness for change, and will convey the highest level of exposure to the most powerful change factors.

b. Common Factors Eclectic Psychotherapy Sol Garfield described in 2000 another influential integrative model that is grounded in common factors research. Garfield integrates interventions from a variety of psychotherapies, with the aim of providing the patient with a number of positive experiences and skills. The common factors that guide Garfield's selection of therapeutic techniques include an empathic, hope-promoting therapeutic relationship; emotional release or catharsis; explanation and interpretation; desensitization; reinforcement; confrontation of problems; provision of new information and skills; and time as a healing factor.

3. Theoretical Integration

Theoretical integration refers to the most complex and sophisticated mode of psychotherapy integration. Psychotherapies that are theoretically integrated rely on the synthesis of concepts of personality functioning, psychopathology, and psychological change from two or more traditional systems. These integrative theories explain behavior and internal experience in cyclical, interactional terms, by looking for the ways in which environmental, motivational, cognitive, and affective variables influence and are influenced by each other. Perhaps the best known version of theoretical integration is a form of psychotherapy that is so well established that it is recognized only rarely as integrative:

cognitive-behavior therapy. As described by Marvin Goldfried in 1995 in an important work on psychotherapy integration, cognitive-behavior therapy is based on a theory of psychopathology and of personality change that is greater than the sum of its behavioral and cognitive parts. This expanded, integrated theory guides the therapist in the selection and use of interventions that are drawn from each school of therapy.

The systems of psychotherapy that are based on theoretical integration use interventions from each of the component theories, and lead to original techniques that may be added to the technical repertoire of the originating therapeutic schools. At times, the clinical efforts suggested within a theoretically integrated system substantially may resemble the choice of techniques of a technically eclectic model. The essential differences may lie in the belief systems and conceptual explanations that precede the clinical strategies selected by the respective therapists. Theoretical integration goes beyond technical eclecticism in clinical practice by expanding the range of covert and overt factors that can be addressed therapeutically. Subtle interactions between behavioral and interpersonal experiences and internal states and processes can be assessed and targeted for intervention from a number of complementary perspectives. Expected effects of any form of intervention in one or more problem areas can be predicted, tested, and refined as necessary. This conceptual expansion offers a framework in which problems at one level or in one sphere of psychological life can be addressed in formerly incompatible ways. That is, the therapist might target a problem in cognition not only to help the patient to think more adaptively, but to promote change in interpersonal behavior, or to rid the patient of a way of thinking that maintained powerful unconscious feelings.

a. Cyclical Psychodynamics Paul Wachtel introduced the most important and influential integrative approach that exemplifies theoretical integration in 1977. This system is known as cyclical psychodynamics and was the first psychotherapeutic model in which psychodynamic theory and therapy were integrated completely with other systems, including especially behavioral theory and behavior therapy techniques. The integration of psychoanalytic and behavioral theories led to the integrative theory that posited that human beings are influenced by unconscious factors that reflect their ongoing perceptions of significant interpersonal relationships. Further, these unconscious issues were seen as maintained and reinforced by the responses of the persons with whom the patient was interacting.

With this cyclical theory as a foundation, Wachtel pioneered the viewpoint that those clinical issues that were the typical concern of psychodynamic therapists could be addressed in therapy through the use of behavioral techniques such as desensitization and assertiveness training. Wachtel argued convincingly that these active behavioral interventions could reach and change unconscious conflicts, fantasies, and depictions of the self and of other people, and as such were useful within a psychodynamically informed psychotherapy. In an updated work on cyclical psychodynamics that was published in 1997, Wachtel expanded his integrative approach to include concepts and methods that were drawn from family systems therapy and gestalt therapy.

b. Cognitive-Analytic Therapy Cognitive-analytic therapy was developed by Anthony Ryle in his role as a consulting psychiatrist in the British National Health System, and has been described in two books that were published in 1990 and 1997. Cognitive-analytic therapy is a theoretical and technical integration of psychoanalytic object relations theory with schema-based cognitive theory and therapy. Ryle found that it was possible to reconceptualize psychoanalytic concepts as the unconscious images of self and of others in explicit, cognitive terms. This theoretical integration allows the cognitive-analytic therapist to introduce and to emphasize the use of cognitive techniques for the purpose of actively modifying these depictions of the self and of other people that exist outside of the patient's awareness but that exert powerfully negative influence on the patient's behavior, symptoms, and relationships.

c. Assimilative Integration A particular subset of theoretical integration that has been the focus of much recent interest is assimilative integration. This way of thinking about psychotherapy integration was introduced into the literature in 1992 by Stanley Messer. Messer suggested that many integrative approaches could best be termed assimilative due to the impact that new techniques have on the existing conceptual foundation of the therapy. As therapeutic interventions are used in a context other than that in which they originated, the meaning, impact, and utility of those techniques are changed in powerful ways. Essentially, these interventions (such as psychodynamic interpretation used by a behavior therapist) are assimilated into a different model and thus are changed in meaning and in impact. In his discussion of assimilative integration of psychotherapies, Messer pointed out that all actions are defined and contained by the interpersonal, historical, and physical context in which those acts occur. As any therapeutic intervention is an interpersonal action (and a highly complex one at that) those interventions are defined, and perhaps even re-created, by the larger context of the therapy. Therefore, a behavioral method such as systematic desensitization will mean something entirely different to a patient whose ongoing therapeutic experience has been largely defined by psychodynamically oriented exploration, than that intervention would mean to a patient in traditional behavior therapy.

George Stricker and Jerold Gold introduced an influential version of assimilative integrative psychotherapy into the literature in 1996. This integrative approach is one in which the basis for the therapy is traditional psychodynamic exploration. Most of the therapeutic work is carried out through the usual psychoanalytically oriented techniques of clarification, confrontation of defenses and resistances, and interpretation of unconscious conflict and of transference phenomena. However, there are frequent occasions during which an intervention that originated in cognitive, behavioral, or experiential therapy will be introduced into the treatment. Even though these interventions may seem identical to those used by therapists from those other schools, the assimilative nature of this therapy means that the intention, meaning, and potential impact of these interventions will differ, reflecting the basic psychodynamic foundation of the therapy. As an example, when a common behavioral intervention such as assertiveness training is assimilated, it is chosen as much for its ability to bring unconscious conflicts about anger into awareness for the patient as it is for its behavior benefits. Similarly, the use of a cognitive restructuring technique may help a patient to lessen his or her resistances to therapy by reducing anxiety, as well as helping that person to learn a more adaptive way of thinking.

III. RESEARCH ON INTEGRATIVE APPROACHES TO PSYCHOTHERAPY

Research on systematic eclectic psychotherapy as described by Beutler and Hodgson has yielded promising empirical support for the effectiveness of matching patient characteristics and specific therapeutic interventions. Larry Beutler, Paulo Machado, David Engle, and David Mohr conducted an important study of this approach to integrative psychotherapy in 1993. These authors reported that when depressed patients were assigned randomly to three different forms of psychotherapy, two patient characteristics were crucial in predicting the effectiveness of the different therapies. As predicted, cognitive therapy was most effective for those patients who externalized responsibility for their depressions, while those patients with an internal locus of control showed the greatest improvement in the insight-oriented, focused expressive psychotherapy. Patients with higher levels of defensiveness and with greater resistance to authority were helped most by a self-directed therapy.

In 1999 James Prochaska and John Norcross summarized the research literature concerned with the effectiveness of technically eclectic psychotherapies. Although they were appropriately concerned with the limitations of the methodologies used in many of these studies, Prochaska and Norcross concluded that this approach had, on average, a moderate to large effect size and performed better than control therapies in about 70% of the studies that were located.

The transtheoretical model of psychotherapy and its basis in the stages of change in psychotherapy as described by James Prochaska and Carlos DiClemente in 1992, has been studied extensively. These studies, summarized by Carol Glass, Diane Arnkoff, and Benjamin Rodriguez in 1998, have demonstrated the maximized effectiveness of psychotherapies that include interventions that are drawn from several different dimensions of psychological life, as does our model. These studies impressively support the idea that technique serves the patient best when interventions are matched to the patient's immediate clinical need and psychological state.

Clinical trials of integrative psychotherapies that synthesize psychodynamic formulations and exploration with active interventions have yielded preliminary but positive results. For instance, the integrative, interpersonal psychotherapy for depression developed by Gerald Klerman, Myrna Weissman, Bruce Rounsaville, and Eve Chevron in 1984 has outperformed medication and other psychological interventions in a number of studies. Haim Omer, writing in 1992, offered empirical support for integrative interventions that heighten the patient's awareness of his or her participation in psychotherapy, thus improving the impact of the basic exploratory stance of the psychotherapist. Carol Glass, Brian Victor, and Diane Arnkoff pointed out in a 1993 publication that several systems of integrative psychotherapy, such as the "FIAT" model (Flexible, Interpersonal orientation, Active, and Teleological understanding) have been demonstrated, albeit in limited numbers of studies, to outperform either strictly psychodynamic or cognitive-behavioral interventions.

Anthony Ryle reported in 1995 that short-term and long-term versions of cognitive analytic therapy (CAT) have been found to be more effective than purely psychodynamic or behaviorally oriented approaches. Perhaps the most impressive and important collection of studies of integrative psychotherapy that compare the synthesis of two or more approaches with traditional therapies have been carried out by David Shapiro and his colleagues at the Sheffield Psychotherapy Project. Shapiro and Jenny Firth-Cozens reported on this work in an important paper published in 1990. These workers studied the impact of two sequences of combined psychodynamic and cognitive-behavioral therapy: dynamic work followed by active intervention or vice versa. They found that the greatest gains were made, and the smoothest experiences of treatment were reported, by those in the dynamic-behavioral sequence. Patients in the behavioral-dynamic sequence more frequently deteriorated in the second part of the therapy, and did not maintain their gains over time as often as did patients in the other group.

An integrative approach to treating agoraphobia that combines behavioral, systemic, and psychodynamic theories and techniques was evaluated by Diane Chambless, Alan Goldstein, Richard Gallagher, and Priscilla Bright in 1986. These authors found that their integrated model led to marked or great improvement for almost 605 of the patients. Specific treatment effects included lessened avoidance, depression, social phobia, and agoraphobic symptoms, and enhanced assertiveness for their subjects. When this treatment was compared to standard drug therapy and to behavior therapy, the patients treated with the integrated therapy had a much lower dropout rate then either of the other therapies.

Another theoretically integrated approach that has been tested empirically is process-experiential therapy, an integration of principles and methods derived from client-centered, gestalt, and cognitive therapies that was described in 1993 by Leslie Greenberg, Laura Rice, and Robert Elliot. This therapy has been found to be more efficacious than control therapies such as standard behavior therapy. The effectiveness of this integrative model has been demonstrated with individuals on a short-term basis for problems such as anxiety and depression. Glass, Arnkoff, and Rodriguez pointed out in 1998 that a version of this approach that had been adapted for use with couples also has been demonstrated to be more effective than standard control measures.

Dialectical behavior therapy (DBT) is an integrative psychotherapy aimed at alleviating borderline personality disorder. Marsha Linehan described this approach to this disorder in 1987. DBT integrates skills training, cognitive restructuring, and collaborative problem-solving from cognitive-behavior therapy, with relationship elements (such as warmth, empathy, and unconditional positive regard) from client-centered therapy, and with aspects of psychoanalytic works as well. Borderline personality disorder is recognized by most clinicians as among the most difficult forms of psychopathology to treat, yet DBT has gained wide acceptance among clinicians in recent years, due in great part to the research support for its effectiveness. Glass, Arnkoff, and Rodriguez reported that patients who received DBT demonstrated better treatment retention, had fewer suicide attempts and episodes of self-injury, fewer hospitalizations, decreased anger, greater social adjustment, and more improved general adjustment when compared with those who received standard therapies. These results were maintained over a 1-year follow-up period, and were replicated in a second study.

The first psychotherapeutic approach that has been demonstrated empirically to be effective for treating chronic depression (dysthymic disorder) is an integrative model developed by James McCullough in 2000. This psychotherapy is known as CBASP, for the systems that it synthesizes: Cognitive, Behavioral, Analytic, and Systems psychotherapies. CBASP has been found to be as or more effective as antidepressant medication and traditional forms of psychotherapy in alleviating the symptoms and interpersonal problems involved in chronic depression. As importantly, its results are more enduring and more resistant to relapse than are other treatments.

IV. RANGE OF PATIENT POPULATIONS AND ISSUE OF DIVERSITY

Marvin Goldfried, an early, influential advocate of psychotherapy integration, summed the dilemma of the psychotherapy patient in a cartoon that he included with an article published in 1999. Goldfried's cartoon shows a therapist and patient shaking hands, with two thought bubbles above the head of each person. The therapist is seen to be thinking, "I hope he has what I treat!" while the patient silently worries, "I wonder if he can treat what I have?"

Integrative approaches to psychotherapy would seem, at least in theory, to be uniquely suited to the needs of patients with diverse backgrounds and problems. The problem highlighted by Goldfried may best be avoided by employing an integrative outlook. The hallmark of effective integration is the flexibility of the therapist and the therapeutic approach, and the overriding concern for the individuality of the patient. Unlike many traditional psychotherapeutic systems and schools, wherein the patient is made to fit into, or to conform with, the therapist's preconceived notion of what works for whom, the integrative therapist tries to tailor the therapy to meet the needs and characteristics of the patient.

Similarly, it would be difficult to think of a specific psychological disorder or patient population for which integrative approaches could not be considered. Since the cornerstone of psychotherapy integration is using the best of what works, any therapeutic approach to any problem may, at least in theory, be improved by the addition of active ingredients from other models.

Presently there exist a number of important contributions to the literature on psychotherapy that are concerned with improving the lot of patients from diverse backgrounds. Sheila Coonerty demonstrated in 1993 that an integrative model of psychotherapy that combines behavioral and psychodynamic elements could be used successfully in the treatment of school-aged children. Mary Fitzpatrick published in 1993 the application of a similar integrative model to the problems of adolescents. Iris Fodor introduced into the literature in 1993 an integrative therapy that was designed particularly for the needs of female patients. Fodor's model integrated concepts and methods from gestalt therapy and cognitive-behavior therapy with feminist theory and therapy. Many integrative therapists have focused on improving the effectiveness of family therapies by adding elements from other schools of psychotherapy. Among the more influential approaches of this type are William Pinsof's integrative family therapy, published in 1995, which assimilated behavior, cognitive, and psychoanalytic methods into family therapy, and Mary Joan Gerson's 1996 integration of psychoanalytic and family systems therapies.

In 1993 Anderson Franklin, Robert Carter, and Cynthia Grace described an integrative approach to psychotherapy with Black African Americans in which issues of race and culture were synthesized with clinical concepts and methods. These authors illustrated how an understanding of the adverse social and cultural factors in American life that shape African American identity development and family structure can be integrated with a variety of therapeutic approaches within a systems framework. Nicholas Papouchis and Vicky Passman, also writing in 1993, described an integrative model of psychotherapy specifically designed to meet the needs of geriatric patients. These authors described how the cognitive deficits, personal losses, and physical illnesses that often afflict the elderly make the traditional psychodynamic therapist less accessible to many older people. However, Papouchis and Passman pointed out that the judicious integration of structured cognitive-behavioral techniques into a psychodynamically oriented psychotherapy may be used effectively by this population, allowing these patients to benefit from the curative factors contained in both approaches.

A number of integrative psychotherapists have explored the ways in which an integrative perspective can be helpful in extending the reach of Western psychotherapies to other sectors of the world. These contributions collectively demonstrate the cultural sensitivity and respect for indigenous traditions, meanings, and ways of life that must be part and parcel of any effective psychotherapy. Articles by Sylvester Madu and Karl Pelzer, both of which appeared in 1991, described integrative therapeutic systems that synthesized several Western therapies with traditional African modes of healing. Both of these writers noted that the openness and flexibility of integrative therapies made these approaches more likely to be able to accommodate the cultural necessities of African life than were standard forms of treatment. Willi Butollo published in 2000 a report of an integrative therapy that he had developed while working in refugee camps in Bosnia during and after the civil war and ethnically motivated atrocities that occurred in the Balkans. Butollo's approach synthesized elements from humanistic, interpersonal, psychodynamic, and cognitive-behavior therapies, and was found clinically to be extremely effective in helping trauma survivors to recover from posttraumatic syndromes.

Integrative therapists have been concerned with expanding the effectiveness of psychotherapy to include politically and economically disenfranchised individuals. In 1989 Paul Wachtel expanded his pioneering integration of psychoanalysis and behavior therapy by focusing on the economic, political, and societal factors that lead to psychopathology. Wachtel then expanded his clinical methodology to include intervention in these areas.

In 1990 Jerold Gold described an integrative therapy that was aimed at helping institutionalized inner-city children and adolescents recover from the mixed impact of individual psychopathology, family dysfunction, and social problems such as divorce, poverty, drug abuse, malnutrition, and substandard housing. Gold's synthesis of psychodynamic, family systems, and behavioral methods also included a strong emphasis on understanding and utilizing the cultural framework within which each patient lived, and posited for the therapist the role of social and political advocate when appropriate.

Integrative psychotherapies have been applied successfully to a wide range of clinical syndromes and patient populations. Anxiety disorders and related conditions such as panic disorders and phobias are the focus of at least three integrative models. As noted above, Diane Chambless and her colleagues demonstrated in 1986 that an integrative treatment model for agoraphobia was highly successful in alleviating that difficult condition. Barry Wolfe described an integrative approach to anxiety disorders that has been highly influential since it appeared in print in 1992. Wolfe proposed a developmental model for anxiety disorders in which unconsciously processed experiences of self-endangerment are established and maintained during traumatic interpersonal experiences. Wolfe demonstrated how an integration of imagery, behavioral, experiential, and interpersonal techniques could be used to treat this disorder. Another integrative therapy for anxiety disorders was published in 1993 by Jerold Gold, who based his integrative model on a synthesis of concepts and methods from attachment theory, behavior therapy, and humanistic therapy. Obsessive-compulsive disorder was targeted for treatment by R. Harris McCarter in 1997. This author based his approach on a combination of behaviorally oriented exposure techniques with psychoanalytic interventions that were aimed at enhancing the patient's ability to regulate his or her internal emotional experience.

Depression, in its acute and chronic manifestations, has been the focus of much effort on the part of integrationists. We have already encountered the integrative, interpersonal psychotherapy for depression developed by Gerald Klerman, Myrna Weissman, Bruce Rounsaville, and Eve Chevron in 1984. In 1992 Hal Arkowitz presented an integrative approach to depression that exemplified a common factors model. In 1993 Adele Hayes and Cory Newman wrote about an integrative model for depression that allowed the therapist to intervene with techniques drawn from behavior therapy, cognitive therapy, experiential therapy, interpersonal therapy, psychodynamic therapy, and biological psychiatry. As discussed earlier, the most effective therapy for chronic depression that has been introduced to date is the integrative CBASP model that was described by James McCullough in 2000.

Other integrationists have turned their attention to more severe disorders that often are impervious to the effects of traditional psychotherapies. One of the most important examples of this work was discussed earlier in this article, that being Marsha Linehan's dialectical behavior therapy for borderline personality disorder. Anthony Ryle wrote in 1997 of his successful attempt to treat borderline and narcissistic disorders with cognitive analytic therapy. Other important integrative models that have been applied to severe psychopathology include Mitchell Becker's treatment for organic disorders that he wrote about in 1993; the integrative therapy for bulimia proposed by David Tobin in 1995; Nicholas Cummings' integrative psychotherapy for substances abusers, reported on in 1993; and integrative therapies for schizophrenia discussed by David Hellcamp in 1993 and by Giovanni Zapparoli and Maria Gislon in 1999. Finally, integrative models have made inroads into areas such as health psychology, as discussed by Robert Dworkin and Roy Grzesiak in 1993. These authors described an integrative psychotherapeutic approach to the treatment of chronic pain that combined the behaviorally oriented procedures of biofeedback, hypnosis, and relaxation with psychodynamic exploration and medical interventions.

V. CASE EXAMPLE

This brief case report is drawn from the author's practice and exemplifies aspects of theoretical, assimilative integration and an instance of technical eclecticism. It overlaps to a large degree with other integrative approaches but cannot be assumed to illustrate exactly the many approaches that have been discussed in this article.

Mr. X was a 35-year-old single man who had entered psychotherapy suffering from dysthymic disorder of several years' duration. He was seen in weekly psychodynamic psychotherapy sessions. As the therapy unfolded the unconscious determinants of Mr. X's depression were explored and were interpreted to him. It became clear that Mr. X had never gotten over the dissolution of his relationships with his parents, which had occurred when the patient was in his late twenties. At that time he had abandoned a lucrative career in the financial industry to become a high school teacher. This decision was highly satisfying to him on an emotional and interpersonal level, but was experienced by his parents as a major disappointment and betrayal. After trying to "mend fences" and receiving only continued anger and criticism from his parents, Mr. X had stopped seeing and speaking to them.

As far as the patient was aware, he had gotten over his hurt, anger, and longing for contact with and approval from, his family. However, as his dreams, free associations, and reactions to the therapist were explored, it became apparent that he was stuck in a process of interrupted mourning for his parents. In this state he was beset by helpless rage at his mother and father, guilt and shame at having hurt them, and an unrealistic hope that they would one day come to love and accept him for his choice. All of these emotions were kept outside of his awareness through active defensive processes, among which was the unwitting decision to turn his anger against himself. The outcome of these unconscious attacks on himself was to feel sad, listless, and depleted, and to be constantly plagued by self-critical thoughts and images.

Interpretation of these unconscious processes and emotions helped to gain some distance and relief from his self-critical, attacking stance, but he was still unable to feel the anger and longing that he agreed intellectually seemed to be at the core of his depression. At this point, a period of cognitive restructuring was begun, with two goals: first, to further alleviate the patient's suffering, and second, because it was assumed that the presence of these thoughts continued to turn Mr. X's anger at his parents back toward himself to externalize his anger. The use of the cognitive intervention to test this was typical of assimilative integration, as it involved using a technique from cognitive therapy in order to promote change at a psychodynamic level.

As Mr. X became increasingly successful at countering his self-critical thinking, his depressive symptoms improved significantly. He began to have longer periods during which his self-esteem was maintained. As importantly, he began to recognize that the internal stimuli for his self-criticism often were dimly perceived reminders of his parents, and he began to fully feel the anger that their rejection still evoked in him. It seemed that the integration of cognitive restructuring had in fact accomplished its assimilative goal of reaching and making more accessible to the patient previously disavowed, unconscious emotional conflicts.

As Mr. X gained more access to his anger and feelings of rejection, his guilt and sense of failure diminished greatly. However, he also experienced a powerful upsurge of longing for his parents and for their love and approval. These feelings led him to contact them, but he was rebuffed in a cold and cruel way when he refused to give into their demands to return to his old job. This experience was, of course, entirely disheartening to the patient, but did help him to recover a series of memories from his childhood, all of which were concerned with his inability to satisfy his parents' demands for academic, social, and athletic success on his part. These memories echoed his present-day experience in their emotional tome of longing for love, and of feeling essentially unlovable because of his inability to attain it from his parents.

Mr. X explored these memories, emotions, and the connected image of himself as unlovable, for a number of weeks without much progress. Remembering the success he had had with the introduction into the therapy of cognitive techniques, Mr. X asked the therapist if there might be another way to approach these issues. The therapist suggested that Mr. X might try using the empty chair technique. This method originated in gestalt therapy and involves speaking to an imaginary person whom the patient imagines is sitting in a chair in the therapist's office. This technique has been found empirically to be highly effective in helping people with "unfinished business" in this case, with Mr. X's incomplete mourning and with his longing for parental approval and love that did not seem possible to obtain. This prescriptive matching of an effective technique with a specified problem is typical of technical eclecticism, but in this case it also has an assimilative purpose. The therapist hoped that any unconscious factors that were maintaining the patient's longing could become more accessible by having Mr. X interact with the images of his parents in the sessions. As Mr. X spoke with the imaginary figures in the empty chair he was able to experience his need for love and approval in an expanded way, and found that this catharsis left him sad but comforted at the same time, with a lessened sense of need. He also became aware that he had always blamed himself for his parents' coldness and criticism. His dialogue with them helped him to become more aware of their intrinsic emotional limitations, and to separate his sense of worth and of being lovable from their inability to love. Again, the integrative technique had been successful at two levels, in this case at the experiential level for which the method had been designed, and at the psychodynamic level for which it had been integrated in an assimilative mode.

After about 11 months of therapy, Mr. X had freed himself of his dysphoric mood, but had begun to experience frequent bouts of anxiety that bordered on panic. It became clear that he also suffered from significant social anxiety that had been disguised and warded off by his depression.

Attempts to explore Mr. X's anxiety symptoms, and to identify the situational precipitants or the psychodynamic meanings of these symptoms, were fruitless and frustrating. Mr. X felt helpless and incompetent during these discussions, and the therapist eventually began to consider these interactions as constituting a transferential repetition of some past relationship in which Mr. X's distress had been responded to with a lack of concern or competence on the part of a significant other. The therapist then suggested a change of tactics: the introduction of cognitive-behavioral techniques that were aimed at relaxation, anxiety management, and self-soothing.

These techniques were employed for a number of simultaneous purposes. The first purpose was to address the clinical situation and to enable Mr. X to master his anxiety and to gain a new level of comfort when faced with anxiety. Second, these active interventions were a way to move the therapy past this stalemate, and thus to resolve the resistances involved in the patient's anxiety symptoms without addressing those resistances directly. Attempts to explore and interpret the unconsciously motivated, resistive nature of the patient's anxiety had led only to Mr. X feeling criticized, ineffective, and "stupid," and to a perception of the therapist as hostile and demeaning. Finally, the therapist hoped that by actively helping Mr. X to lessen his anxiety, the patient would have an immediate (corrective emotional) experience of being valued and cared for that would illuminate and correct the negative enactment in which patient and therapist were caught.

As Mr. X became more capable of managing his anxiety he also became more aware of the interpersonal precipitants of these symptoms, and was better able to explore the warded-off meanings as well. Most important, patient and therapist were able to reestablish a positive working alliance and to explore fruitfully the past relationships, particularly with Mr. X's father, in which Mr. X's pain and fear had been met by indifference and ridicule. As he stated, "By showing that you cared how I felt and that you were willing to help in an accepting way, you proved how different you are from my father. That allowed me to see and feel how hurt and angry I am at him for how he made fun of me when I was scared, and how I expect that, and get it from others now."

This case example demonstrates the ways in which interventions from another therapeutic system can be assimilated into psychodynamic therapy, changing the meaning and impact of that intervention, and eventuating in psychodynamic and interpersonal changes that would not be anticipated in the original (here, cognitive-behavioral and experiential) systems. The active interventions led to the reduction of painful symptoms and the acquisition of new skills, but also to a radical shift in the patient's defenses, transference situation, and his understanding of his psychodynamics. Most important, the active provision of help led to the establishment of new and benign ways of perceiving himself and important people in his life, which became the bases for hopefulness, a sense of self-worth, and a newly independent, grief-free, way of life.

VI. SUMMARY

Integrative approaches to psychotherapy blend together techniques and ideas that are drawn from the widest possible ranges of schools of psychotherapy. The goal inherent in these approaches is maximizing the patient's exposure to those factors that induce change. As such, integrative approaches represent an attempt to develop and apply, custom-fitted, broad-spectrum psychotherapies that will meet the needs of the majority of patients.

Among the many useful integrative approaches there are a number that synthesize psychoanalytic, cognitive, and behavioral features. Others emphasize the integration of humanistic and experiential therapies with more active approaches, while still a third group has focused on the combination of family systems and integrative models. Some integrative therapies are empirically tested and are guided by data, while others reflect clinical wisdom and experience.

See Also the Following Articles

Alternatives to Psychotherapy ■ Existential Psychotherapy ■ History of Psychotherapy ■ Humanistic Psychotherapy ■ Individual Psychotherapy ■ Interpersonal Psychotherapy ■ Multimodal Behavior Therapy ■ Research in Psychotherapy

Further Reading

Beier, E. G. (1966). *The silent language of psychotherapy.* Chicago: Aldine.

Bohart, A. C., & Tallman, K. (1999). *How clients make therapy work.* Washington, DC: American Psychological Association.

Cummings, N., & Cummings, J. (2000). *The essence of psychotherapy.* New York: Academic Press.

Gold, J. R. (1996). *Key concepts in psychotherapy integration.* New York: Plenum.

Hubble, M., Duncan, B., & Miller, S. (1998). *The heart and soul of change.* Washington, DC: American Psychological Association.

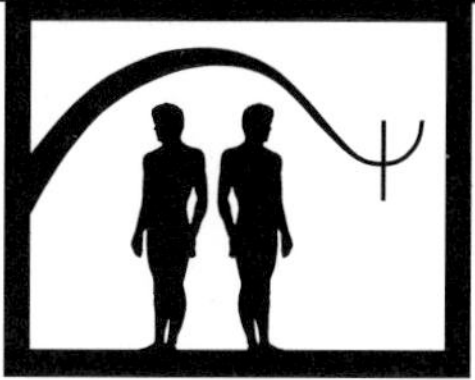

Interpersonal Psychotherapy

Scott Stuart
University of Iowa and Iowa Depression and Clinical Research Center

Michael Robertson
Mayo-Wesley Centre for Mental Health

GLOSSARY

cognitive behavior therapy (CBT) A treatment which focuses on the patient's internally based cognitions in an effort to relieve symptoms, change behavior, and ease suffering.

content affect Refers to the dominant feeling experienced at the time of a significant event.

defense mechanisms Psychological structures that assist in the modulation of internal conflicts in order to achieve harmony, both internally with demands and prohibitions, and externally with social reality and individual desires, needs, and wishes.

ego strength A term broadly referring to the ability to modulate and balance internal needs and wishes with external reality. Sometimes the term is simply used to refer to the ability to withstand threats form the external world and to modify the external world.

here and now A term that refers to present, ongoing active events in interpersonal relationships, in contrast to fantasized future or past presentations.

interpersonal incidents Descriptions by the patient of specific interactions with a significant other.

interpersonal inventory A brief description of important people in a person's life, which include the amount and quality of contact, problems in the relationship, and expectations about the relationship.

interpersonal psychotherapy (IPT) A time-limited treatment that focuses on interpersonal relationships as a means of bringing about symptom relief and improvement in interpersonal functioning.

maintenance treatment The explicit agreement to continue treatment and contact at a "lower dose" than the agreed upon for active treatment.

process affect Refers to the emotion experienced by the patient as he or she is describing to the therapist events surrounding the cause of the affect.

transference The feelings and attitudes brought about towards a person in the present that stem from unconscious feelings and attitudes derived from a relationship with a person in the past.

treatment contract The conscious and explicit understanding between the therapist and the patient, which includes the number, frequency, and duration of sessions, the clinical foci of treatment, the roles of the patient and therapist, and the planning for contingencies such as illness, lateness, missed sessions, and acceptable and unacceptable contact for out of session and off hour emergencies and behavioral expectations, such as substance abuse.

Interpersonal psychotherapy (IPT) is a time-limited treatment that focuses on interpersonal relationships as a means of bringing about symptom relief and improvement in interpersonal functioning. This article will describe the fundamental characteristics of IPT, the theoretical basis of the treatment, and will detail several of the therapeutic interventions used in IPT.

I. TREATMENT DESCRIPTION

A. Introduction

IPT is a time-limited, dynamically informed psychotherapy that aims to alleviate patients' suffering and improve their interpersonal functioning. IPT focuses specifically on interpersonal relationships as a means of bringing about change, with the goal of helping patients to either improve their interpersonal relationships or change their expectations about them. In addition, IPT also aims to assist patients to improve their social support network so that they can better manage their current interpersonal distress.

IPT was originally developed in a research context as a treatment for major depression, and was codified in a manual developed by Klerman and colleagues in 1984. Since that time, a great deal of empirical evidence supporting its use has accumulated. As clinical experience with IPT has increased, its use has broadened to include both a number of well-specified *Diagnostic and Statistical Manual of Mental Disorders, 4th edition* (DSM-IV) diagnoses and the treatment of patients presenting with a variety of interpersonal problems.

IPT is based on both empirical research and clinical experience. Rather than being a static and codified treatment, IPT is designed to incorporate changes that improve the treatment, as additional data and clinical experience accumulate. Instead of being applied in a strict "manualized" form in which the clinician is required to follow precisely a treatment protocol, clinicians using IPT are encouraged to use their clinical judgment to modify the treatment when necessary in order to provide maximum benefit for their patients. The practice of IPT should be based on equal measures of empirical research, clinical experience, and clinical judgment.

B. Characteristics of IPT

IPT is characterized by three primary elements: (1) IPT focuses specifically on interpersonal relationships; (2) IPT is time limited as an acute treatment; and (3) the interventions used in IPT do not directly address the transference relationship.

1. Interpersonal Relationships

Interpersonal psychotherapy is based on the concept that interpersonal distress is linked with psychological symptoms. Thus the foci of treatment are twofold. One focus is the difficulties and changes in relationships that patients are experiencing, with the aim of helping patients to either improve communication within those relationships, or to change their expectations about those relationships. The second focus is helping patients to better utilize their social support network so that they are better able to deal with the crises that precipitated their distress.

Interpersonal psychotherapy therefore stands in contrast to treatments such as cognitive-behavior therapy (CBT) and psychoanalytically oriented psychotherapy. In contrast to CBT, in which the focus of treatment is the patient's internally based cognitions, IPT focuses on the patient's interpersonal communications. In contrast to analytically oriented treatments, in which the focus of treatment is on understanding the contribution of early life experiences to psychological functioning, IPT focuses on helping the patient to improve communication and social support in the present. Past experiences, although clearly influencing current functioning, are not a major focus of intervention.

Interpersonal psychotherapy seeks to resolve psychiatric symptoms rather than to change underlying dynamic structures. Although ego strength, defense mechanisms, and personality characteristics are all important in assessing suitability for treatment, change in these constructs are not presumed to occur in IPT. The question that should drive the therapist's interventions is, "Given this particular patient's personality style, ego strength, defense mechanisms, and early life experiences, how can he or she be helped to improve here-and-now interpersonal relationships and build a more effective social support network?"

2. Time Limit

The acute phase of IPT is time-limited. In general, a course of 12 to 20 sessions is used for the acute treatment of depression and other major psychiatric illnesses, and a contract should be established with the patient to end acute treatment after a specified number of sessions. Clinical experience has shown that having a definitive endpoint for therapy often "pushes" patients to make changes in their relationships more quickly. The time limit also influences both patient and therapist to focus on improving the patient's interpersonal functioning in current relationships.

Although empirical research is limited to controlled treatment studies in which weekly treatment is provided and then abruptly stopped, clinical experience has clearly demonstrated that tapering treatment over time is more effective. In other words, weekly sessions may be used for

6 to 10 weeks, followed by a gradual increase in the time between sessions as the patient improves, such that weekly sessions may be followed by biweekly and monthly meetings. Although acute treatment should be time-limited, both empirical research and clinical experience have clearly demonstrated that maintenance treatment with IPT, particularly for recurrent disorders such as depression, should be provided to reduce relapse risk. Maintenance IPT must be distinguished from the acute phase of treatment in IPT, and a specific contract must be negotiated with the patient for the maintenance phase.

3. The Interventions Used in IPT Do Not Directly Address the Transference Relationship

The third characteristic of IPT is the absence of interventions that address the transference aspects of the therapeutic relationship. It is readily acknowledged in IPT that transference occurs; it is a universal phenomenon in all psychotherapy. However, although in IPT the therapist's experience of transference is used to provide information about the patient and his or her interpersonal relationships, the transference relationship is not addressed directly. To do so detracts from the focus on symptom reduction and rapid improvement in interpersonal functioning that is the aim of IPT, and also typically leads to a longer course of treatment than is required for IPT. The goal in IPT is to work with the patient quickly to solve his or her interpersonal problems before problematic transference develops and becomes the focus of treatment.

Although the transference is not directly addressed, the use of transference in IPT to assess the patient's attachment style and to understand the patient's interpersonal functioning is crucial. The use of transference to formulate questions about the patient's interpersonal relationships outside of therapy is also important. The transferential experience should be used by the therapist to formulate hypotheses about the patient's interpersonal difficulties, and to ask questions about how the patient asks others for help, ends relationships, and reacts when others are not responsive to his or her needs. These questions are directed outside of the therapy relationship, however, to current interpersonal relationships.

As an illustration, consider a patient who forms a dependent relationship with the therapist. The patient may manifest this dependency as difficulty in ending sessions, calls to the therapist between sessions, or in more subtle pleas to the therapist for help or reassurance. This transferential relationship should inform the therapist about several aspects of the patient's functioning: (1) The patient is likely to have similar problems in relating to others; (2) the patient is likely to have difficulty in ending relationships; and (3) the patient has likely exhausted others with the persistent dependency. A hypochondriacal patient would be an excellent example of this kind of behavior, manifested in the ways described.

Further, the transferential experience should be used by the therapist to predict potential problems in treatment, and to modify the therapy accordingly. For instance, the therapist might hypothesize that the patient's dependency may be a problem when concluding treatment, and may begin discussing the ending of therapy much sooner than with less dependent patients. The therapist should also strongly encourage a dependent patient to build a more effective social support network, so that the patient's needs are more fully met outside of therapy rather than fostering a dependent or regressive relationship in the therapy itself. Appropriate modifications would also be made with patients who are avoidant or who manifest other personality characteristics.

C. Treatment Process

IPT can be divided into assessment (described later), initial sessions, intermediate sessions, treatment conclusion, and maintenance treatment phases. During each, the clinician has a well-defined set of tasks to accomplish. Undergirding these therapeutic tasks and techniques is the stance taken by the therapist. Clinicians should be active and maintain the focus of therapy. The therapist should also be supportive, empathic, and strongly encouraging, and should make every effort to convey a sense of hope to the patient and to reinforce his or her gains.

1. Initial Sessions

During the initial sessions of IPT (usually the first one or two meetings following the general assessment) the therapist has three specific tasks. These are (1) to conduct an interpersonal inventory; (2) to work collaboratively with the patient to determine which problem areas will be the focus of treatment; and (3) to develop a treatment contract with the patient.

The interpersonal inventory is a brief description of the important people in the patient's life, and for each includes the amount and quality of contact, problems in the relationship, and the expectations about the relationship. These descriptions need not be exhaustive; those that become treatment foci will be revisited in detail later. The purpose of the inventory is to determine which relationships to work on, and to gather further information regarding the patient's attachment and communication patterns.

Once the inventory is complete, the patient and clinician should mutually identify one or two problem relationships on which to focus. The therapist should frame the patient's problem as interpersonal, and should give specific examples of the way in which the problem fits into one of the four problem areas: grief and loss, interpersonal disputes, role transitions, or interpersonal sensitivity.

Establishing a treatment contract is an essential part of IPT. In general, the contract should specifically address (1) the number, frequency and duration of sessions, which in general will be about 12 to 20; (2) the clinical foci of treatment; (3) the roles of the patient and therapist, particularly the need for the patient to take responsibility for working on his or her communication between sessions; (4) contingency planning: issues such as missed sessions, lateness or illness; and (5) acceptable conduct: contact out of hours, emergencies, and behavioral expectations such as substance use.

Because of the injunction in IPT to limit discussing the transferential relationship directly, the contract must serve as a rock solid point of reference for both patient and therapist. Thus when contract violations occur, the therapist can remind the patient that both had initially agreed on certain guidelines for therapy, and that the patient, by failing to meet his or her responsibility, is in essence minimizing the benefit of the treatment. The therapist would then proceed to ask questions about similar behavior outside of the therapeutic relationship.

2. *Intermediate Sessions*

During the intermediate sessions of IPT, the patient and therapist work together to address the interpersonal problems identified during the assessment. In general, work on these issues proceeds in the following order: (1) identification of a specific interpersonal problem; (2) a detailed exploration of the patient's perception of the problem, including communication patterns and expectations about the relationship; (3) collaborative brainstorming to identify possible solutions to the problem; (4) implementation of the proposed solution; and (5) reviewing the patient's attempted solution, with positive reinforcement of the changes made and discussion of refinements to be carried out.

The tasks of the therapist in the intermediate sessions of IPT are to assist the patient in discussing his or her problematic interpersonal relationships, and to attend to the therapeutic relationship. In addition, the therapist must actively work to maintain the focus of therapy, rather than encouraging or allowing the patient to talk about peripheral issues.

Once a specific issue is identified, the therapist should encourage the patient to describe his or her perceptions and expectations about the relationship problem. Whether it is a problem in communication or a matter of unrealistic expectations, the patient and therapist work collaboratively to brainstorm and identify possible solutions. The patient is responsible for attempting to implement the agreed upon solution, and to provide feedback regarding the attempted solution and its results at the next session. The therapist and patient then review these results and make modifications as needed.

A number of solutions can be considered in IPT. For instance, a change in communication to a style that is more direct may be of help with a dispute. A change in circumstances, such as a change in location or in employment, may be of benefit during a role transition. Changes in expectations, with a movement toward other social support, are also viable options. In IPT, however, the endpoint of therapy is not simply insight; it is change in communication, behavior, and social support that leads to symptom resolution.

3. *Completing Acute Treatment*

Acute treatment with IPT comes to an end as specified by the therapeutic contract. There are both theoretical and practical reasons for keeping acute treatment with IPT time-limited. The time limit is very effective in generating change, as it often compels patients to work more rapidly on improving communication skills and building more effective social networks. In addition, the time limit influences both patient and therapist to focus on acute symptoms rather than on personality change. Moreover, to extend IPT beyond the acute time frame may lead to the development of problematic transference, as the relationship between patient and therapist assumes greater importance.

On the other hand, the success of therapy is also dependent on the patient's belief that the therapist is committed to helping the patient, and that the patient's needs supercede other considerations. The IPT therapist should prioritize helping the patient ahead of satisfying the dictates of a manualized protocol. Consequently, if extending the therapy beyond the number of sessions initially agreed upon is clearly in the patient's best interest, then it should be extended. The apparent conflict between maintaining the therapeutic contract and extending sessions when needed can be resolved by renegotiating a new treatment contract with the patient. Clinical judgment should be used to make such a decision.

Clinical experience with IPT strongly suggests that the best clinical practice is usually to extend the interval between sessions once the patient is in the recovery stage of acute treatment. Rather than continuing to meet weekly, the patient and therapist may choose to meet biweekly or even monthly toward the end of treatment. This gives the patient further opportunities to practice communication skills, to reinforce the changes that have been made, and to develop more self-confidence while remaining in a supportive relationship, all of which facilitate better and more stable functioning.

As the primary goals of IPT are symptom relief and improvement in interpersonal functioning, the specific aims of treatment conclusion are to foster the patient's independent functioning and to enhance his or her sense of competence. The therapist is still available should a future emergency arise, but the expectation is that the patient will quite capably function independently.

4. *Maintenance Treatment*

Rather than using the traditional psychoanalytic model in which "termination" is a complete severing of the therapeutic relationship, concluding acute treatment with IPT does not signify the end of the therapeutic relationship. In fact, in IPT it is usually agreed that there will be therapeutic contacts in the future, and provision is specifically made for these. Clinical experience, theory, and empirical evidence all make clear that IPT should be conceptualized as a two-phase treatment, in which a more intense acute phase of treatment focuses on resolution of immediate symptoms, and a subsequent maintenance phase follows with the intent of preventing relapse and maintaining productive interpersonal functioning. Therefore, the therapist should specifically discuss future treatment with the patient prior to concluding therapy. A specific contract should be established with the patient for the specific alternative for the provision of maintenance treatment that is chosen. Options include specifically scheduling maintenance sessions at monthly or greater intervals; concluding acute treatment with the understanding that the patient will contact the therapist should problems recur; or planning to have the patient contact another provider in the future. Decisions about how to structure future treatment should rely on clinical judgment.

In essence, IPT follows a "family practice" or "general practitioner" model, in which short-term treatment for an acute problem or stressor is provided until the problem is resolved. Once resolved, however, the therapeutic relationship is not terminated; as with a general practitioner, the therapist makes himself or herself available to the patient should another crisis occur, when another time-limited course of treatment can be undertaken. In the interim, the therapist may choose, like a general practitioner, to provide "health maintenance" sessions periodically. There is no compelling clinical or theoretical reason to come to a complete termination with most patients in IPT, while the data clearly support the benefit of maintenance treatment.

D. Techniques and Therapeutic Process

It is the focus on extra-therapeutic interpersonal relationships rather than any particular intervention which characterizes IPT. Not surprisingly, given its psychodynamic roots, IPT incorporates a number of "traditional" psychotherapeutic methods, such as exploration, clarification, and even some directive techniques. While there are no techniques which are actually forbidden in IPT, all should be used in the service of helping the patient to modify interpersonal relationships.

More important that any techniques, however, is the establishment of a productive therapeutic alliance. Warmth, empathy, genuineness, and conveying unconditional positive regard, though not sufficient for change, are all necessary for change in IPT. Without a productive alliance, the patient will flee therapy, an obstacle which no amount of technical expertise can overcome.

A primary goal of the IPT therapist should be to understand the patient. If the patient does not perceive that the therapist is truly committed to doing this, the patient will not readily disclose information, will not feel valued as an individual, and will not develop a meaningful relationship with the therapist. Working to understand the patient should always take precedence over any technical interventions. Further, all IPT interventions should be therapeutic; the ultimate value of an intervention is the degree to which it helps the patient. Techniques should not be used simply because they are included in a manualized protocol; the benefit to the patient should guide the interventions used in treatment.

1. *Nonspecific Techniques*

Nonspecific techniques are generally understood as those that are held in common across most psychotherapies. Examples would be the use of open-ended questions, clarifications, and the expression of empathy by the therapist. These techniques play a crucial role in IPT, as they serve to help the therapist understand the patient's experience, convey that understanding to the patient, and to provide information regarding the genesis of the patient's problems and potential solutions to them. Techniques such as problem solving with the patient, giving directives, and assigning homework can also be used judiciously in the service of facilitating interpersonal change.

2. Communication Analysis and Interpersonal Incidents

The analysis of the patient's communication patterns is one of the primary techniques used in IPT. The therapist's task is to assist the patient to communicate more clearly what he or she wants from significant others. Communication analysis requires that the therapist elicit information from the patient about important interpersonal incidents. Interpersonal incidents are descriptions by the patient of specific interactions with a significant other. If the identified dispute results in a pattern of fighting between spouses, the therapist might ask the patient to "describe the last time you and your spouse got into a fight," or to "describe one of the more recent big fights you had with your spouse." The therapist should direct the patient to describe the communication that occurred in detail, re-creating the dialogue as accurately as possible. The patient should describe his or her affective reactions as well as both verbal and nonverbal responses, and describe observations of his or her spouse's nonverbal behavior.

The purpose of discussing an interpersonal incident is twofold: (1) to provide information regarding the miscommunication that is occurring between the parties; and (2) to provide insight to the patient about the unrealistic view that the problem is intractable. The goal in working through an interpersonal incident is to examine the patient's communication so that maladaptive patterns of communication can be identified. The patient can then begin to modify his or her communication so that his or her attachment needs are better met.

3. Use of Affect

The more the patient is affectively involved in the issues being discussed, the greater the motivation to change behavior or communication style. Consequently, one of the most important tasks for the IPT therapist is to attend to the patient's affective state. Of particular importance are those moments in therapy in which the patient's observed affective state, and his or her subjectively reported affect, are incongruent. Examining this inconsistency in affect can often lead to breakthroughs in therapy.

Affect can be divided into that experienced during therapy (process affect) and that reported by the patient to have occurred in the past (content affect). Content affect refers to the predominant affect experienced at the time of a significant event. For instance, a patient might describe feeling "numb" at the time of the death and funeral of a significant other. Process affect, on the other hand, refers to the affect experienced by the patient as he or she is describing to the therapist the events surrounding the loss. The same patient, for example, might describe a "numb" feeling at the time of the funeral, but when describing the event to the therapist might be in tears, and feeling sadness, or perhaps anger. When met with this incongruence in affect, the therapist can focus directly on the discrepancy between content and process affect. In other words, when the report the patient gives about how he or she felt during an interpersonal event is different from the affect he or she is exhibiting during the session, it should be noted by the therapist and explored further.

4. Use of Transference

Transference is a universal occurrence in all psychotherapies, and plays an extremely important part in IPT. However, in contrast to longer-term psychodynamic therapies, information gleaned from the transference that develops during IPT, although an important source of data, is not typically a point of intervention.

By observing the developing transference, the IPT therapist can begin to draw hypotheses about the way that the patient interacts with others outside of the therapeutic relationship. Sullivan coined the term "parataxic distortion" to describe this phenomena: The way in which a patient relates to the therapist in session is a reflection of the way in which he or she relates to others as well. Attachment theory also supports the idea that individuals tend to relate to others in a manner that is consistent both across relationships and within relationships. Thus the transference or parataxic distortion recognized by the clinician provides a means of understanding all of the other relationships in the patient's interpersonal sphere.

Using these data, the therapist can then begin to draw conclusions about the patient's attachment style and problems in communicating to others. The therapist should ask questions to confirm or disprove these hypotheses. For instance, if the therapist notes that the patient tends to be deferential in therapy, hypothesizing that the patient tends to be the same way in other relationships is reasonable. The therapist may want to ask about the experiences (or difficulties) that the patient has had in confronting others, or in dealing with rejection. Similarly, if the patient behaves in a dependent manner during therapy, the therapist may ask about how the patient maintains relationships, or about experiences the patient has had in ending relationships.

The key difference between IPT and transference-based therapies is that the IPT therapist should avoid making transference comments, and particularly interpretations, about the therapeutic relationship. As long as a reasonably positive transference is maintained, therapy can proceed without the need to focus on it. The therapist should focus instead on the here-and-now problems in the patient's extratherapy interpersonal relationships. With well-selected patients, keeping the therapy short-term allows the therapist to assist the patient to solve his or her interpersonal problems before the transference becomes intense, and as a result, becomes the new focus of therapy.

E. Interpersonal Model

1. Problem Areas

IPT focuses on four specific interpersonal problem areas: grief and loss, interpersonal disputes, role transitions, and interpersonal sensitivity. Psychosocial stressors from any of the problem areas, when combined with an attachment disruption in the context of poor social support, can lead to interpersonal problems or psychiatric syndromes. Although these categories are useful in focusing the patient on specific interpersonal problems, it is important to be flexible when using them. Rather than "diagnosing" a specific category, the problem areas should be used primarily to maintain focus on one or two interpersonal problems, particularly as the time available in IPT is limited. Because the interpersonal problems experienced by patients are all derived from the combination of an acute interpersonal stressor combined with a social support system that does not sufficiently sustain the patient, effort should always be directed toward improving the patient's social supports as well as addressing the specific problem.

a. Grief and Loss. Grief in IPT can best be conceptualized as a loss experienced by the patient. In addition to the death of a significant other, a loss such as divorce may be seen by the patient as a grief issue. Loss of physical functioning, such as that following a heart attack or traumatic injury, may also appropriately be considered in the grief problem area.

The therapist's tasks are to facilitate the patient's mourning process, and to assist the patient to develop new interpersonal relationships, or to modify existing relationships to increase social support. Although new or existing relationships cannot "replace" the lost relationship, the patient can reallocate his or her energies and interpersonal resources over time.

Several strategies are useful in dealing with grief issues. Primary among these is the elicitation of feelings from the patient, which may be facilitated by discussing the loss and the circumstances surrounding it. The use of process and content affect may be quite useful. Often the patient will initially describe the lost person as "all good" or "all bad," and be unaware that this idealization (or devaluation) covers other contradictory feelings. Grief issues commonly involve layers of conflicted feelings surrounding the lost person, and assisting the patient to develop a "three-dimensional" picture of the lost person, including a realistic assessment of the person's good and bad characteristics, is a helpful process in the resolution of the grief.

This same process can be used for other losses as well, such as the loss of a job, a divorce, or loss of physical functioning. In such instances the patient will also need to grieve the loss, and to move toward establishing new social supports. Encouraging patients to develop a more realistic view of their loss is helpful as well.

b. Interpersonal Disputes. The first step in dealing with interpersonal disputes is to identify the stage of the conflict, and to determine whether both parties are either actively working to solve the problem, have reached an impasse, or have reached a point at which dissolution is inevitable. Successful treatment does not necessarily require that the relationship be repaired. Resolutions to the conflict may be to modify the relationship, to modify expectations about the relationship, or to exit the relationship. The important point is that the patient makes an active and informed decision about the relationship.

A primary goal of treatment is to assist patients with interpersonal disputes to modify their patterns of communication. Patients may become locked in patterns of communication with others that result in misunderstanding, or in cycles of escalating affect. The therapist can assist the patient to communicate his or her needs more clearly and productively, rather than provoking hostile responses. The therapist should model direct communication to the patient, and may engage the patient in role playing to reinforce the new communication. Although IPT is generally an individual therapy, inviting a significant other to therapy for several conjoint sessions can be an invaluable way to observe the communication *in vivo,* and to begin to help the couple to make changes in their interactions.

C. Role Transitions. Role transitions encompass a huge number of possible life changes. Included are life cycle changes such as adolescence, childbirth, and decline in physical functioning, and social transitions such as marriage, divorce, changes in job status, and retirement. Typical problems include sadness at the loss of a familiar role, as well as poor adaptation or rejection of the new role. Role transitions often result in the loss of important social supports and attachments, and may require new social skills.

The therapist should assist the patient in moving from his or her old role, which includes assisting the patient to experience grief over the loss, often using some of the techniques described for dealing with grief issues. It is crucial to help the patient to develop a realistic and "balanced" view of the old role, including both positive and negative aspects. Assisting the patient to develop new social supports is also essential.

d. Interpersonal Sensitivity. There are some patients who either because of personality traits, avoidant attachment styles, or other factors, may have problems with poor interpersonal functioning. "Interpersonal sensitivity" refers specifically to a patient's difficulty in establishing and maintaining interpersonal relationships. Patients with interpersonal sensitivities often require a different approach than is utilized with patients who have better social skills.

Patients with interpersonal sensitivities may have few, if any, interpersonal relationships to discuss in therapy. Relationships with family members, although they may be quite disrupted, may be some of the only relationships the patient has. The therapeutic relationship may also take on greater importance, as it too may be one of the patient's only relationships. The therapist should be prepared to give feedback to the patient regarding the way he or she communicates in therapy, and may utilize role-playing to practice skills with the patient. In addition, the therapist should assist the patient to get involved in appropriate social groups or activities in the community. Above all, the therapist and patient must keep in mind that the therapy is not designed to "correct" the social difficulties, but rather to teach the patient some skills to build new relationships, and to relieve his or her acute distress.

II. THEORETICAL BASIS

IPT is grounded in attachment theory, which as described by Bowlby among others, rests on the premise that people have an instinctual and biological drive to attach to one another. When crises occur, individuals seek reassurance and care from those important to them. Interpersonal communication is intrinsic to this process, and individuals who cannot effectively ask for care, and consequently cannot obtain the physical and psychological care they need, will suffer as a result. When interpersonal support is insufficient or lacking during times of stress, individuals are less able to deal with crises and are more prone to develop psychiatric symptoms.

Bowlby described three different types of attachment styles that drive interpersonal behavior. Secure attachment describes individuals who are able to both give and receive care, and are relatively secure that care will be provided when it is needed. Because securely attached individuals are able to communicate their needs effectively, and because they are able to provide care for others, they typically have good social support networks. Thus they are relatively protected from developing problems when faced with stressors.

Anxious ambivalent attachment, in contrast, is a style in which individuals behave as if they are never sure that their attachment needs will be met. Because of this, such individuals believe that care must be sought constantly. Such individuals often lack the capacity to care for others, since their concern about getting their own attachment needs met outweighs all other concerns. Consequently, they have a relatively poor social support network, which in combination with their difficulties in enlisting help, leave them quite vulnerable to interpersonal stressors.

Individuals with anxious avoidant attachment typically behave as if care will not be provided by others in any circumstances. As a result, they avoid becoming close to others. The paucity of their social connections, along with their tendency to avoid asking for help during times of crises, leaves these individuals quite prone to difficulties.

In essence, attachment theory states that those individuals with less secure attachments are more likely to develop psychiatric symptoms and interpersonal problems during times of stress. A persistent belief that care must be constantly demanded from others, or that care will not be provided by others, typically leads insecurely attached individuals to have more difficulty in asking for and maintaining social support during times of crisis. Severe disruptions of important attachment relationships, such as the death of a significant other, also lead to an increased vulnerability to psychiatric symptoms.

Interpersonal psychotherapy also follows the biopsychosocial model of psychiatric illness, resting on the premise that psychiatric and interpersonal difficulties result from a combination of interpersonal and biological factors. Individuals with a genetic predisposition are more likely to become ill when stressed interpersonally. On this foundation rests the individual's temperament, personality traits, and early life experiences, which in turn are reflected in a particular attachment style. The attachment style may be more or less adaptive, and has effects on the person's current social support network and his or her ability to enlist the support of significant others. Interpersonal functioning is determined by the severity of current stressors in the context of this social support.

Interpersonal psychotherapy is therefore designed to treat psychiatric symptoms by focusing specifically on patients' primary interpersonal relationships, particularly in the problem areas of grief, interpersonal disputes, role transitions, and interpersonal sensitivity. This is done by helping the individual to recognize and modify his or her communication patterns, which has a threefold effect. First, it leads to more effective problem solving, as conflicts can be more directly addressed. Second, it improves the patient's social support; communicating in a way to which others can more readily respond will more effectively meet the patient's attachment needs. Third, these improvements in communication and in conflictual relationships, and improved social support, help resolve the interpersonal crisis and result in symptom resolution.

III. APPLICATIONS AND EXCLUSIONS

The purpose of conducting an assessment is to determine when IPT should be used, and to whom it should be applied. The assessment may take several sessions to complete. It is only after the assessment, and the determination that the patient is suitable, that IPT should formally begin.

During the assessment, the therapist should evaluate the patient's attachment style, communication patterns, motivation, and insight. Assessment of DSM-IV diagnoses should also occur. IPT should not, however, be restricted only to patients with DSM Axis I diagnoses; it is quite suitable for patients with a variety of interpersonal problems such as work conflicts or marital issues. In fact, because patients without major psychiatric illness often have more secure attachments and better social support networks, they are usually able to utilize IPT very effectively.

Special attention should be paid to patients diagnosed with personality disorders. Those with cluster A disorders including paranoid, schizoid, and schizotypal personality disorders may be unable to form effective alliances with their therapists in short-term therapy, whereas those with severe cluster B disorders such as narcissistic, histrionic, borderline, and antisocial personality disorders may require more intensive therapy than can be provided in an IPT format. However, many patients with depression or anxiety superimposed on a personality disorder may benefit a great deal from short-term therapy with IPT if the focus is on the treatment of the depression or anxiety rather than on personality change.

The assessment should include an evaluation of the patient's attachment style. This should consist of information about the patient's perception of his or her patterns of relating to others, and an evaluation of the patient's past and current relationships. Questions regarding what the patient does when stressed, ill, or otherwise in need of care are particularly helpful. The patient should also be queried about his or her typical responses when asked to assist others.

The patient's attachment style has direct implications regarding his or her ability to develop a therapeutic alliance with the therapist and the likelihood that treatment will be beneficial. Those patients with more secure attachment styles are usually able to form a more productive relationship with the therapist, and because of their relatively healthy relationships outside of therapy, are also more likely to be able to use their social support system effectively. Individuals with more anxious ambivalent attachments can usually quickly form relationships with their clinicians, but often have difficulty with the conclusion of treatment. Those with anxious avoidant attachments may have difficulty trusting the therapist. Consequently, when working with anxious avoidant patients, the therapist may need to spend the initial sessions working on developing a productive therapeutic alliance, waiting until a good alliance is established before moving into more formal IPT work.

The therapist should also use the assessment to forecast and plan for problems that may arise during therapy. For example, because patients with anxious ambivalent attachment styles often have difficulty in ending relationships, the therapist may modify his or her approach by emphasizing the time-limited nature of the treatment, and by discussing the conclusion process earlier. Significant others may also be included in sessions more frequently to ensure that therapeutic dependency does not become a problem. When working with avoidant patients, the therapist should plan to spend several sessions completing an assessment, taking great care to convey a sense of understanding and empathy to the patient.

The therapist should conduct an assessment of the patient's communication style. The way in which the patient communicates his or her needs to others has profound implications for the therapeutic process, as well as for the likelihood that the patient will improve with therapy. The therapist should directly ask the patient for examples or vignettes in which a conflict with a significant other occurred. Patients who are able to relate a coherent and detailed story are likely to be able to provide the narrative information necessary to work productively in IPT. Insight can also be judged by noting the way in which the patient describes an interaction, and the degree to which the other person's point of view is accurately represented.

In general, patients who have characteristics that render them good candidates for all of the time-limited therapies will be good candidates for IPT. These include motivation, good insight, average or better intelligence, and sufficient ego functioning. Other characteristics specific to IPT include (1) a specific interpersonal focus of distress, such as a loss or interpersonal conflict; (2) a relatively secure attachment style; (3) the ability to relate a coherent narrative; and (4) a good social support system.

IV. EMPIRICAL STUDIES

Interpersonal psychotherapy has been demonstrated to be efficacious in a number of research studies; at present, with the exception of cognitive therapy, IPT enjoys more empirical support than any other form of psychotherapy. Since the initial studies of IPT in 1979 by Klerman, Weissman, and colleagues, IPT has been demonstrated to be efficacious with a number of depressed populations, including depressed geriatric patients, depressed adolescents, depressed patients who are HIV-positive, and patients with dysthymic disorder. IPT has also been used for both postpartum and antenatal depression. In addition, it has been tested with patients in the depressed phase of bipolar disorder and with eating disorders.

Largely because of the success of the early efficacy studies, IPT, along with CBT, was chosen as a comparative psychotherapeutic treatment in the National Institute of Mental Health Treatment of Depression Collaborative Research Program (NIMH-TDCRP). Both were compared to treatment with imipramine and with placebo over 16 weeks. IPT was found to be superior to placebo, and was equal to imipramine and CBT for mild to moderate depression. Neither psychosocial treatment was as effective as imipramine for severe depression. The consensus from the NIMH-TDCRP study is that IPT and CBT are effective for mild to moderate depression, but that antidepressant medication should remain the gold standard treatment for severe depression.

Another major study evaluating IPT involved maintenance treatment of patients with recurrent depression. Acutely depressed patients who had suffered at least three prior episodes were treated with a combination of imipramine and IPT over 16 weeks. Patients who recovered were then assigned to one of five maintenance treatments: (1) imipramine alone; (2) imipramine plus monthly IPT; (3) monthly IPT alone; (4) monthly IPT plus placebo; and (5) placebo alone. The patients were then followed for 3 years.

Mean depression-free survival time was significantly longer for those patients who received imipramine alone or imipramine plus IPT. Over 3 years, the mean time before relapse of depression was about 120 to 130 weeks for patients who received imipramine with or without IPT as an adjunct. The patients who received IPT alone or IPT plus placebo had a mean survival time of about 75 to 80 weeks. Although significantly better than the mean survival of patients who received only placebo (roughly 40 weeks), treatment with IPT alone was not as beneficial as treatment with maintenance antidepressant medication. The current consensus is that recurrent depression should be treated with maintenance antidepressant medication, with IPT a viable alternative for patients who do not want or who cannot tolerate medication.

Currently IPT is being investigated for use with social phobia and somatization disorder. The use of IPT has also been described with groups, couples, and in a family practice setting. Excellent reviews of this research can be found elsewhere.

The research on IPT clearly demonstrates its efficacy as a time-limited treatment for acute depression, and as an effective alternative to medication for patients with recurrent depression. Further, there are numerous studies that suggest that IPT may be efficacious for patients with a variety of DSM-IV Axis I disorders.

V. SUMMARY

Interpersonal psychotherapy is characterized by three essential elements: a focus on interpersonal relationships, a contract that specifies a time limit for therapy, and the use of interventions that focus on relationships outside of therapy rather than on the transference relationship. Attachment theory undergirds the approach used in IPT, and the attachment style of the patient should instruct the therapist about the patient's suitability for treatment, prognosis, and the potential problems that may arise in therapy. Further, the patient's attachment style should inform the therapist about the ways in which the therapy can be modified.

Interpersonal problems and psychiatric symptoms are conceptualized within a biopsychosocial framework. An acute interpersonal crisis, such as a loss, interpersonal dispute, or a difficult life transition, creates problems for patients for two reasons: (1) Their interpersonal communication skills within their significant relationships are not adaptive; and (2) their social support network is not sufficient to sustain them through the interpersonal crisis. IPT proceeds by helping patients to communicate their attachment needs more effectively, to realistically assess their expectations of others, and to improve their social support. This should help resolve interpersonal problems and relieve psychiatric symptoms.

The conduct of IPT is based on a three-point foundation. First, the practice of IPT rests on empirical research. Second, the practice of IPT reflects clinical experience. Finally, and most important, the practice of IPT includes the use of clinical judgment: The therapist must recognize the unique nature of the relationship with the unique individual with whom he or she works, and must always place the needs of the patient above a strict adherence to a manual. Given these foundational supports, IPT is an efficacious, effective, and extremely useful clinical approach to interpersonal problems.

See Also the Following Articles

Grief Therapy ■ Structural Analysis of Social Behavior ■ Sullivan's Interpersonal Psychotherapy ■ Time-Limited Dynamic Psychotherapy

Further Reading

Bowlby, J. (1988). Developmental psychiatry comes of age. *American Journal of Psychiatry, 145,* 1–10.

Klerman, G. L., Weissman, M. M., Rounsaville, B. J., & Chevron, E. S. (1984). *Interpersonal psychotherapy of depression.* New York: Basic Books.

Stuart, S., & Robertson, M. (2002). *Interpersonal psychotherapy: A clinician's guide.* London: Edward Arnold Ltd.

Weissman, M. M., Markowitz, J. W., & Klerman, G. L. (2000). *Comprehensive guide to interpersonal psychotherapy.* New York: Basic Books.

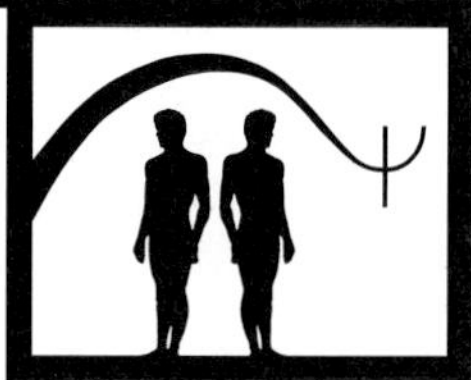

Interpretation

T. Wayne Downey
Western New England Institute for Psychoanalysis and Yale University

GLOSSARY

genetic History of the individual encompassing both biological influences, the temperamental givens in birth and development, and the prior influences of environmental nurture and stressors.

internalization Process by which the new knowledge conveyed by the interpretation becomes syncretic with the person's expanded sense of self.

interpretation Technique for reformulating the many competing and conflicting modes of thought from the multiple developmental epochs of the mind.

I. INTERPRETATION: A DEFINITION

Interpretation is a basic process in psychoanalysis and psychotherapy by which old information of the patient is translated into a new syntax of self-understanding by a therapist. It is a fundamental element of the process of psychological healing. The act of interpretation simultaneously promotes psychological repair and is the mode for bringing about psychological change in the individual. It is a technique by which one individual, the psychotherapist or analyst, plumbs the unconscious mind of the analysand or patient with the purpose of bringing to light new cognitive connections, new feeling states, and new perspectives on human relationships. Interpretation involves a reformulation of the affected mind to address the defensive intellectualizations, rationalizations, and denials of fact and outer reality that have been erected by individuals to salvage and preserve their limited and compromised sense of identity and being, such as it is. Interpretation connects the latent and manifest meanings that reside in a person's psyche as they emerge in the context of a special therapeutic relationship. This relationship consists of transference of past history on the part of the patient onto his or her image of the therapist and countertransferential empathic referencing of this transference on the part of the therapist. Interpretation provides a medium and context for further objectification of the individual's subjective experience, leading to an increase in capacities for insight, self-analysis, and self-interpretation. On another level these shifts in reflection are accompanied by new senses of self and identity in relation to others. When it works well interpretation brings about incrementally and occasionally dramatically a new language of self in a new key.

II. WHY INTERPRETATION?

To understand interpretation and its fundamental role in the therapeutic action in dynamic treatments, psychotherapy, and psychoanalysis it is first necessary to review some central concepts about the growth and functioning of the mind. The brain provides the biological engine of the mind. Dysfunctions of the brain can readily translate into disorders of the mind. The mind is also capable of its own disorders apart from neurophysiology that are related to its often imperfect attempts to synthesize the conflicting types of information that it is presented with and the divergent modes by which it processes that information. For instance, one of the great paradoxes of human existence involves the presence of a sense of both mindedness and mindlessness in our psychology. The evolution of mankind's capacities for consciousness, self-awareness, and self-reflection are central aspects of what separates homosapiens from other organisms. The human capacity for thought that extends beyond the immediate neural responses to stimuli for the purposes of obtaining pleasure, release, or avoiding unpleasure is present and developed in humans as in no other species. The capacity for mental activity that goes beyond the immediate and relatively fixed response to signal forms of activity adds variety to human behavior and to the possibility of thinking about things.

We have a potential and actual psychology that we share, communicate, and talk about in myriad ways. Many organisms may use signs and signals to communicate. These occur without a sense of memory and foreknowledge and the mutually reinforcing transfer of information and intellect that we both observe and infer in humans. In the realm of feelings and affective life, while flight and/or fight provides a foundation of basic organismic and affective responses, the dimension of time adds complexity, depth, and layers of feelings and shared understanding. The apprehension of a dangerous or painful future becomes the foundation for a complex of anxieties and is something that humans share. The memory of a noxious past in the form of depressive dread is part and parcel of human existence in a world of psychological infinitude that continues through and beyond time. We possess minds that meet, diverge, that are lost and found but that are nonetheless capable of thinking about a self or other selves through a unique medium that we call psychological mindedness.

The other part of the paradox of mindedness that I referred to earlier is mindlessness. Mindlessness in psychoanalytic terms represents preconscious and unconscious realms and aspects of our minds that are typically "lost" or unknown. We conceptualize the disavowed "mindless" unconscious as originating in our psychological prehistory. It emerges as part of the earliest psychological stirrings and questings of the infant-organism. As such it contains all the contradictions and conflicts of the organism's attempt to derive a structure and function of thought from rudimentary physical and psychological experience. In Freud's original terms we come to conceptualize this first infant area of psychological strata as primary process thought. Primary process thought is an "unminded" mode of thinking about perceptions that we think are experienced by the infant and are reported by the adult as occurring in a relatively monadic context. There are few social referents in this realm. It is a way of perceiving that will eventually give way through experience, learning, socialization, and neuropsychological maturation to the dyadic mindedness and organized cognition of secondary process thought.

The toll on the developing brain of managing these divergences of mind and consciousness is that certain modes of thought and experience are relegated to unconscious mental functioning. This is the price to be extracted for resolving conflicts between one part of the mind and another. We describe this as intrapsychic conflict resolution. This mode may also be active in resolving conflict between the psyche and forces or beings in the outer world, what we refer to as interpsychic conflict resolution. Both forms may be, and often are, sequestered in the "mindless," disavowed regions of unconscious thought although each area of conflict may also have its derivatives in consciousness.

The result of such syntheses is that we split our consciousness in our waking state and to some lesser extent in our sleeping state. We must think and act as though we know what we are doing and responding to in its entirety even when, in fact, we know only a portion, sometimes only a small portion, of the picture of perception and response. If our responses become stereotypic with fixed outcomes that seem not to benefit from experience and learning, we categorize such responses as "neurotic." Neurosis is a quality of experience that is driven more by the need to appease the internal psychic economy of the individual than it is geared to benefiting from novel experiences and attaining a newer and better adaptation of inner and outer worlds. What in the optimum sense should be a part of mindedness becomes instead coopted by conflict resolution that leads to repetitive behaviors and circular modes of thought. Thus the child who has been severely abused and neglected by a parent may continue to encounter such a parent in his many relationships throughout life as though to work out through repetition the trauma of the early parental catastrophe. Such neurotic modes affirm a mindless frozen psychological state in which what is unconscious dictates mental outcome rather than facilitating new levels of mentation and psychological organization. In the example just given that would mean having the psychological flexibility to move on to appreciate and appropriate the new opportunities for nurturing and nontraumatic mothering in later life figures or thought.

The therapist is the agent necessary to make interpretations and shed new light on dim repetitions. Such interpretations are delivered in a value-neutral manner except insofar as they carry with them an investment in the patient acquiring increasing self-perspective and making a psychological recovery. To cite another example, the power of an individual's anger may be blocked from perception and expression, or, conversely, it may be expressed in overly strong and inappropriate ways. In either case the person is unable to face the threat that anger poses. They may feel either paralyzed in the first instance or defeated by their own rage in the second. They require interpretation of what they are unaware of through the medium of a significant and trusted other to be able to link up all levels of the neurotic feeling state that has brought with it either such an overabundance or a paucity of action.

We equate "healthy" psychological development with a wholeness of consciousness; one that admits to opposites, similarities, ambiguities, and divergent lines of thought. We look for flexibility, adaptability, and the capacity to ride through life's inevitable conflicts so as to arrive at some sort of stability and interpenetration of conscious thought with unconscious fantasy that enlarges and deepens the individual's engagement with inner and outer worlds. The need for interpretation is always there, but healthy individuals are less blocked and more able to provide meaningful reformulations of everyday events. They are able to learn from their experience and the experience of others without the aid of special pleadings of special agents.

To approach the matter of interpretation from a somewhat different direction, in the ideal, because we are capable of empathy, putting oneself in the mind of another, there exists the possibility of psychological healing. The prototype for this experience is the mother's psychological work in intuiting and inferring the affective and cognitive state of her nonverbal infant and then taking the necessary steps physically or psychologically to remedy its distress. If the child was cold and wet, warmth and dryness would be the soothing response. This response would permit the infant to identify such a state, not from the affective perspective of anxiety and helplessness, but with the anticipation and optimism that the ministrations of another are correct, timely, and will bring relief. Ultimately this would allow for the development of the capacity for self-soothing through the process of internalization. If the infant is fearful of separation from the mother or the presence of strangers, the mother's adoption of a calm stance through verbal tone, words, and actions will eventually increase the child's sense of security in the mother's availability and protectiveness. Such interpretive understanding translates into the child's taking in the mother's loving presence. If things go wrong in such situations the child will end up afraid of anxiety and distrustful of the adult's abilities to understand and remedy their fear of the strange. Over time the infant becomes more able to take in, to internalize, the mother's empathic actions. This eventuates in the ability to consciously and unconsciously soothe and care for themselves in situations of potential estrangement or physical discomfort.

This empathic paradigm is the cornerstone of psychological healing. By means of it, one participant, the therapist, listens and observes another person, the patient, in distress and infers and interprets the hidden and unconscious elements that have led them to repeatedly hit the same mental block as in their love and work lives.

In 1901 Freud originally introduced the technical lynchpin of interpretation in his classic work *The Interpretation of Dreams*. In its initial guise in his attempts to treat hysteria, interpretation involved a "Rumpelstiltskin" sort of technique in which deep understanding by the therapist was converted into memory of genetic events that were expected to magically change the patient's symptomatology. In most versions of the fairy tale "Rumpelstiltskin" if the princess whom Rumpelstiltskin has given a baby can guess his name she may keep the baby and he will vanish. In his treatment of hysterics Freud had started from the notion that as a group hysterics suffer from their reminiscences. His remedy was to go to the heart of their problems and with his profound powers of intuition wrench into consciousness the unconscious amnesic event that was causing the hysteric's symptoms. This would lead to their cure. In this early theory, by finding the "gnome" of their neurosis and labeling it would cause it to vanish.

By 1901 Freud had progressed to the point past labeling the trauma to using the interpretation of dreams as the agent of therapeutic action by which what was unconscious in the manner of unacceptable wishes and impulses was made conscious. Thus he articulated the unconsciously dominated nature of dreams and the light that their interpretation could shed on the neuroses of everyday life and what had amounted to, heretofore, the individual's mindless domination by their unconscious. The interpretation of a person's dreams was conducted mainly in the context of their own personal meanings and metaphors. The previous historical emphasis had been on dreambook and cookbook kinds of understanding of generic dream symbolism. Inherent in such an approach was a grammar of dream symbolism that attributed meanings to symbols on an abstract basis that was divorced from the possibility that the dreamer might have developed idiosyncratic meanings of their own for the objects and dynamics encountered in their dream life. The analysis of a dream is an example par excellence of the proposition regarding healing that resides in the phenomenon of interpretation. It is the rare individual, and Freud was certainly one, who can interpret the multilayered meaning of one's own dream. To arrive at such meanings usually requires two minds and the convergence of the unconscious "mindlessness" of both parties. The exercise involved in this meeting with another mind may allow the dreamer to eventually carry on the work of dream interpretation independently, just as the exercise of analysis may set the stage for future self-analysis.

In the early era of id psychology, interpretation enjoyed a decade's reign during which it was considered "the royal road to the unconscious" and thus the avenue of therapeutic cure. As the subsequent development of analysis has borne out, innovations expand the range of treatment but they also reveal the shortcomings of the current dominant technique and point toward areas in need of further theoretical clarification. This heyday established the subsequent niche of dream interpretation in analytic technique but it also uncovered its shortcomings. Practitioners began to realize that id psychology with its emphasis on the understanding of forbidden wishes and desires located in the deep unconscious could only bring the treatment dyad so far. There were obvious limitations to its general treatment effectiveness. Other factors of therapeutic significance emerged that came to be categorized in terms of self and object relations. In order to promote the further understanding of symptom and character it became necessary to subject the person's internalized images of others as well as their actual social relations to interpretive attention. Although the initial premise still holds that the work of interpretation is to uncover hidden meanings and occult connections, the potential residence of such meanings took on more global consideration in personality functioning. Areas may be encountered in object relations, ego psychology, and in relation to the defensive activities of the ego, not to mention in relation to the meanings that reside in the unconscious conscience, that are subject to first the therapist's and then the therapist and patient's interpretive scrutiny.

III. WHAT GETS INTERPRETED?

There are now considered to be many dimensions to interpretation. It can be seen as a process that may extend through many aspects of space and time. Freud initially emphasized the temporal and historical aspects of interpretation. The earliest form of interpretation tended to have a genetic emphasis. That is, the ideal interpretation attempted to link up the individual's current difficulties functioning and the many "mindless" factors throughout life that had contributed to the difficulties and were being actively expressed through them. This approach aimed at positing as the nidus for a symptom an event that was either unconscious or not clearly conscious in its recall. "Your arm became paralyzed because you were in conflict about using it to strike your father" would be one such example. If presented in the proper emotional setting, this would expose the noxious forbidden element of trauma. It is brought into consciousness in a more fully and clearly focused manner that allows the individual a better view of the regressed elements of his or her history that his or her mind had hitherto deemed too painful or too awful to acknowledge. This is a technical point that has been emphasized many times by Loewald in his modern reformulation of psychoanalysis.

In an overall sense psychoanalysis is an ally of memory. This is the case to the extent that one of the goals of psychic exploration is to provide the individual with a fuller sense of the historical truth of his or her life as it courses back and forth through memory and time. Ernst Kris conceptualized the therapeutic process as an activity in which the personal myth of the individual is gradually replaced with a sense of conviction about the affective and experiential elements of a life that is both more compelling and more coherent than the one that had been woven into the fabric of their neurosis. Paradoxically adolescence, a period that often holds vivid memories, is also one in which the pressure of interpretation will yield a significantly altered story line through the reconstructions that inevitably accompany a dynamically founded treatment. A not uncommon statement might be "we can now understand your sense of dominance and distance with females during your teenage years as an outgrowth of several early stinging rejections by girls that became coupled with your own deep anxieties about sexual and emotional intimacy. This seems quite consonant with the manner in which you have kept me (your therapist) at a distance. It has also manifested itself in the conflicts of intimacy that you have attempted to defend yourself against by seeing me as sexually threatening and at the same time emotionally withdrawn." The interpretation presented here *en bloc* would in all likelihood be parceled out over time, eventuating in this summary interpretation. Such ideas when introduced in a timely fashion with a tactful tone of voice should lead over time to a gradual acceptance, acknowledgment, and further elaboration of the interpretive premise. This may lead over time to an equanimity that comes from possessing a sense of an apt and resonant relation to both inner and outer realities. It may be even more enhancing in introducing a larger acceptance of the objective and subjective mix of fantasy and fact that constitutes such "realities." Human experience being what it is, a state of relative equanimity is just that, and although neurotic difficulties may have been fixed, the mind is never fixated in any healthy state. We will always struggle to process our experience in a manner that updates our realities at the expense of our personal myths.

The upshot of any interpretation may be quite varied. The patient may respond with immediate recognition, what Ralph Greenson termed the "aha" phenomenon. Alternatively the reaction may be vague resistance, either in response to the sense of criticism that every interpretation inevitably conveys, or as a function of the partial nature of the interpretation. On the therapist's side of the treatment process or the couch, the reaction may be "oi vay!" The therapist, with or without reaction from his patient, immediately registers the vast error in his interpretation. When errors of interpretation occur, necessarily unavoidable but hopefully rarely, they require acknowledgment on the part of the analyst. Perhaps this would mean an apology, depending on the circumstances and the content of the errant ideas. Following this there should be a moving on to more fully understand how the patient interpreted the misunderstanding on the part of the therapist. For some patients it is the therapist's grace in responding to an incorrect interpretation rather than his or her acumen that saves the day. In addition there is currently developing an added appreciation that such spontaneous moments may reference memory and events that are beyond the usual realm of interpretation in declarative memory. They may bring in elements from the "noninterpretive" realm of nondeclarative memory for attention and objectification.

In addition to the dimension of time there is a metaphorical dimension by which interpretations extend through the layers of mind and consciousness, from surface to depth. In addition to placing the spotlight of interpretation on elements involving group and interpsychic dynamics of social relations and control, the operations of the ego per se need at times to be an object of attention. It is not only the conflicts that the ego works to control but also the workings of the ego as an organ of synthesis and adaptation and as a partner or hostage of conscience that needs to be taken into consideration.

In a stepwise fashion a series of interpretations may lead to a complex revision of the patient's sense of world and self. New and novel choices begin to appear in the mind's eye. Fresh ideas presented in the proper sequence can lead to paranoia evaporating over time, to be replaced by a less anxious, more confident, and less reactive sense of self. "Originally your independence in childhood served you well, given the discontinuities in care that you experienced with your mother and your need to put some space between the two of you. You sensed at several levels of awareness that she could not accept you for who you were. This left you with confusions about dependency and now in your work and in your love life this cloak of alienated independence that you cover yourself with serves to keep you apart from others and unfulfilled in terms of your self-esteem. You end up not safe, as you intended, but anxious and never fully relaxed or satisfied. Yes, your escape is swallowed up by anyone and anything but also you are never able to fully be yourself with another." Such a revisionist approach spans areas of history, defense, self-configuration, and neurotic adaptation while pointing the way toward a potentially less defended and restricted person with a more fulsome nature. Such interpretive syntheses may only be possible toward the end of an analysis when there is a fairly firm sense that all the facts are in and available for tally.

As the previous examples have indicated most interpretations follow from the content of the patient's thoughts, the subject matter of their consciousness. There are exceptions in which the process of associating becomes coopted by predominantly defensive dynamics. We are then confronted with the paradoxical situation that speaking one's mind serves mainly to cloud and obscure one's more cogent thoughts and feelings. This defensive maneuver was initially identified in relation to dreams where the telling of the dream became so elaborated and extended that there was no time or opportunity for its deeper examination and interpretation. The supposedly cooperative and compliant dreamer produced too much of a good thing and in the process defeated the central purpose of dream analysis. This profusion of information without the opportunity for comment or interpretive scrutiny may occur in the course of any string of associations. At those instances the content of the patient's communication becomes less interesting than the quality and the process of the associations as they exhibit more of the quality of an action. When a torrent of words drowns out the facts contained in the stream of associations, a comment acknowledging the diversion of words from meaning is indicated. "The pressure and volume of your words and speech, while seeming to communicate a great deal, actually confuses me and makes it more difficult to understand what is going on in you. I wonder if there is some anxiety behind your words that we need to examine?" This might be one among many possible comments that the therapist could make in such a situation.

A current associational emphasis that is popular among some therapists is that of "close process monitoring." This technique expands the usual emphasis in any treatment, the ebb and flow of verbal material toward or away from areas of conflict and concern. The defensive nature, particularly with regard to matters of aggression, is given a predominant focus. Comments and questions leading up to interpretive statements are restricted to here and now observations that call patients' attention to shifts in their train of thought away from more affectively loaded material. This often involves bringing to light hostile and aggressive thoughts and feelings about the analyst that the patient is consciously suppressing and unconsciously censoring.

IV. TIMING AND SCOPE OF INTERPRETATIONS

The timing and scope of an interpretation has everything to do with how successful or effective an interpretation is. It is also critical if the therapist's activity at a particular point is gauged toward building to a broader interpretation. Some treatments may hinge upon the proper and timely application of a very limited number of interpretive comments. Selecting the right moment when idea, emotion, and resistance is at a proper pitch is key. The therapist's ease in understanding and delivering a properly timed formulation is also a significant factor in its successful reception by the patient. Much of an interpretation's effectiveness is contingent on how much data, both affective and cognitive, the therapist has at his or her disposal. This may be a factor in setting apart analysis from most psychotherapies. In an analysis, with its greater frequency and often intensity of meetings, we anticipate that there will be less use of guesswork and intuition and a more refined processing of the unconscious into conscious thought. Therapists of different professional persuasions and different temperaments will vary widely in how much they rely on empathy and intuition in their interpretive activity. In Kleinian analyses and in briefer forms of psychotherapy the therapist may rely more heavily on "deep" intuition-rich verbal interventions to shortcut the defensive activities of the ego and get right to the heart of the matter. This is more in accordance with the technique of the early days of id analysis as opposed to current fashion that draws more on a constant assessment of object relations and the quality of the ego's defensive activity to determine how to proceed in a stepwise manner toward id interpretation.

Some versions of interpretation are met with immediate approval or disapproval. Depending on the quality of the therapeutic alliance, positive or negative, collaborative or combative, the degree to which an interpretation will be accepted for further internalization may be immediately apparent. At other times the impact of an interpretation is apparent only over time in the context of the further elaboration and working through of associations and defenses. This may be particularly the case when working with children, whose response to interpretations may appear minutes, hours, or days later. Children's responses may also show up in their play in apparent wide displacement from the therapist's words.

Central to determining what is healthy collaboration and what is neurotic compliance is the degree to which interpretations open up new avenues of information for inquiry and exploration. A premature interpretation may be greeted by a range of responses: incredulity at the therapist's cognitive lapse, confusion and self-blame, or the therapist may find himself the target of a withering attack of invectives and humiliation. Of course, it is impossible to assess the impact on the patient of tactfully delivered words until they are spoken. If the patient's reaction needs to be redressed with regard to the transference or countertransference elements elicited by an interpretive comment, that will require time and an open mind by both parties. Some patients are well-versed in contemporary or past therapeutic techniques and apply them easily and at will. They are also often too smart by half, bending their energies to making interpretive points before the therapist does. The quantity of clarifying comments is also important. Too many interpretations may cause them to fall on deaf ears. At other points such comments will only be received according to the criticism that is inherent in them. If that is the case the interpretive activity either has no effect or it has a negative countertherapeutic impact. Traumatically sensitized patients are more prone to experience the therapist's words almost literally as being struck by a cudgel or raped. These concrete, physically referenced reactions can be taken up as defensive reactions of one sort or another.

A tilted relationship is one aspect of any therapy in which a psychological "expert" is helping a psychologically in need "patient." There is always the risk and danger that the interpretations will be perceived as a manifestation of the analyst's legitimate or illegitimate authority. Likewise they may be taken as evidence by the patient of the therapist's investment in the power politics of the situation. If that happens, boredom and impatience on the part of either member of the therapeutic dyad may come to supplant the fervor of self–other exploration. If the patient is mainly reacting to suggestion and is in the process of succumbing to the analyst's need to be the authority, the treatment process will come to feel more and more predictable, stereotyped, and static. If there are narcissistic issues on the part of the analyst or analysand that are not accessible to insight and clarification then stalemate, breakdown, or a compromised therapeutic process is inevitable. In these occasional situations unanalyzed rage in the patient or therapist may lead to stultification or truncation of the treatment.

The scope of interpretations has become much more varied and vast as the varied and vast capacities of the human mind have become more accessible to understanding. It ranges from interpretations of content, process, and defense to the sorts of overarching historical and genetic interpretations on which this aspect of technique was founded. In the case of defense analysis, attention is drawn to largely unconscious mechanisms that restrain the patient in speaking his or her mind. These may be in place to avoid coming across to the therapist as too active, too passive, too involved or needy, or too affect ridden, to mention a few of the conditions of defense. Interpretation of the mythic history of the individual may possess a particular power if used sparingly and precisely, identifying and appreciating the compulsive and repetitive aspects of historical experience without taking up camp in the past at the expense of existential frame in the here and now. Care should be taken not to develop a historical mantra that becomes yet another version of the personal myth or that distracts or displaces in an exaggerated and unwarranted fashion from pressing dynamic issues in current-day experience.

There is as yet no agreed on objective standard for interpretation in the field. We are left with an activity that is still more art than science. The crucial element in interpreting is that it should always contain a question mark and rarely an exclamation point. It should indicate both what the analyst knows or thinks he or she may know as well as extending an invitation to the patient to provide further data from all levels of the mind to extend the interpretive moment to a clearer conclusion. As is continually emphasized, the overall treatment alliance is an essential part of therapeutic efficacy. In some instances the process of collaboration is as much or more important than the self-knowledge that emerges from it. At times it is not what is said that is most pertinent. At its core, self knowledge, including the growing ability to auto-interpret, should cause the distinction between what the therapist perceives and anticipates of the patient and what the patient's understanding of themself is, to be subject to more and more overlap. The other's understanding of one's self should become ever more one's self-awareness and self-acceptance.

At the point in a treatment where there are no new issues left to interpret and explore there should be an emerging sense of completion and wholeness to complement the feeling that what has been available for resolution and reformulation has, by and large, been apprehended. To put it another way, in the ideal therapy, a time of mourning, celebration, and parting emerges that signifies that a maximum (for the moment) of self-understanding and self-acceptance has been achieved. It is not the completion of a life's story but rather the end of a chapter in the life of an individual when the need for another to understand one's self has reached a developmental conclusion. This is much as the need for a child to have understanding and defining parents wanes with the ending of adolescence. The self-understanding that comes from interpretation has been internalized and "knowing thyself" in the universal (and idealized) dimensions of love and work has been optimized. For many this will include knowing that at some future time they may come again to be beyond their psychological depth. In addition to having a better sense of when they have reached the limits of self-help, they will be able to interpret their own need to once again rely on the help and interpretive powers of a therapist. Ultimately an open mind with better access to, and reciprocity with, conscious and unconscious mindedness should be the endpoint of interpretation.

See Also the Following Articles

Applied Behavior Analysis ■ Behavioral Assessment ■ Behavioral Case Formulation ■ Countertransference ■ Functional Analysis of Behavior ■ Psychoanalysis and Psychoanalytic Psychotherapy: Technique ■ Transference

Further Reading

Busch, F. (2000). What is a deep interpretation? *Journal of the American Psychoanalytical Association, 48,* 237–254.

Davis, J. (2001). Revising psychoanalytic interpretations of the past: An examination of declarative and non-declarative memory processes. *International Journal of Psychoanalysis, 82,* 449–462.

Freud, S. (1901). *The interpretation of dreams,* Standard Edition, V. IV. London: The Hogarth Press.

Greenson, R. (1967). *The technique and practice of psychoanalysis.* New York: International Universities Press.

Kris, E. (1975). *Selected papers.* New Haven, CT: Yale University Press.

Loewald, H. (2000). *The essential Loewald.* Hagerstown, MD: University Publishing Group.

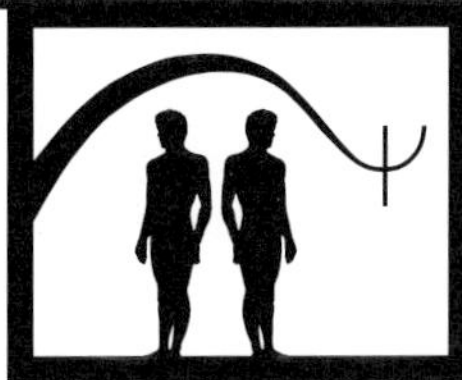

Intrapsychic Conflict

Alan Sugarman

San Diego Psychoanalytic Society and Institute and University of California, San Diego

GLOSSARY

abreaction A cathartic release of pent-up affect usually associated with trauma.

censor Synonymous with the term of repressive barrier anthropomorphosized in order to dramatically make the point of the fact of repression.

compromise formation The synthesis created by conflicting mental components.

defense The counterforce opposing the expression and emergence into consciousness of socially unacceptable or otherwise problematic biological and somatic urges.

instinctual drives Mental/somatic entities which are the mental representation of somatic stimuli.

intrapsychic conflict The basic psychoanalytic idea that almost all mental phenomenon and psychologically mediated behavior are the product of opposing mental forces or structures.

latent content An aspect of the dream that deals with underlying or repressed thoughts stimulated by the day's activity and seeking expression.

libidinal drive The tendency of the psychological structure seeking the satiation of biological needs, as well as psychological needs, for affiliation and merger.

manifest content Refers to the aspect of dreams that are expressed clearly and directly within the dream.

multiple functions The almost universal tendency of certain defenses to serve multiple functions at the time of their use.

primary process A mode of thinking in which logical and formal relations between mental contents are absent and there is a press for immediate gratification of pleasurable needs. Contraindications exist without difficulty. Temporal considerations are irrelevant.

psychic energy An imprecise term referring to the economic work or resource required on the part of the individual to accomplish a certain act or invest a psychological structure with capacity.

reality principle The tendency for an organism to orient itself to practical social dictates and requirements.

repression A form of defense in which unacceptable urges and materials are kept outside the realm of consciousness.

repression barrier The psychological structure that separates the contents of the system unconscious from the preconscious system by a defense and the function of the censor.

resistance A form of defense specifically oriented towards keeping certain thoughts and ideas out of the talk between analysis and anlysand.

secondary process functioning Refers to a mode of functioning in which logic, temporal relationships, and social and physical reality predominate as principles.

sexual drives Refers to drives emanating from specific bodily areas and following a development timetable, which have a pressure, an aim, an object, and a source.

structural model The psychoanalytic model developed by Freud that hypothesized the existence of three basic psychological structures that embody and mediate between the demands of external social reality and internal, biologically based, instinctual needs.

structures Psychological constructs of drive, representation, motivation, and function that exist to carry out psychological work and integrate various domains of mental functioning.

superego The agency within the structure model that is responsible for determining ideal social reality and measuring various aspects of the individual's function in relationship to this reality.

system conscious (CS) A set of structures oriented towards conscious and explicit experience.

system preconscious (PCS) Refers to the existence of psychological material that can be made conscious and has not attracted enough repression to render it incapable of being known consciously.

system unconscious (UCS) Refers to the psychological and biological structures that press for expression and satiation and are not capable of consciousness.

topographical model The model of the mind developed by Freud that postulates the existence of conscious and unconscious mental processes separated by repressive barrier.

transference The tendency for all people to "transfer" feelings, attitudes, and relationships more appropriate to a specific person in the past of the individual to some other analogous, present, and active social relationship.

The concept of intrapsychic conflict, also called internal conflict, psychic conflict, or neurotic conflict, is central both to the psychoanalytic theory of mind and the application of that theory to differential treatment strategies. This concept refers to the basic psychoanalytic thesis that almost all mental phenomena and psychologically mediated behavior are the result of opposing mental forces or structures. Thus, symptoms, personality structure, fantasies, emotions, and so on reflect the synthesis of more basic mental components. This synthesis of these conflicting mental components is referred to as a compromise formation. Psychoanalysts assume that virtually all complex mental acts are compromise formations designed to allow the maximum possible gratification of the conflicting components with the least possible mental pain. Intrapsychic conflict and its subsequent compromise formations are ubiquitous and not inherently pathological. Rather they are understood as essential aspects of the human condition. Thus, psychoanalysis has traditionally been viewed as a psychology of intrapsychic conflict. Conflict and compromise formations are pathological only when they lead to excessive inhibition of key human urges, when they give rise to excessive anxiety and/or depression, when they cause excessive inhibition of important psychological functions, when they lead to excessive self-destructiveness, or when they bring the individual into excessive conflict with his or her environment. Mental health occurs along a continuum in terms of intrapsychic conflict. Conflict and compromise formation move from the healthy to the unhealthy parts of the continuum as they interfere in one's life in the previously listed ways.

I. AFFECT—TRAUMA MODEL

Psychoanalysis' theory of mental functioning, and the technical implications drawn from it, has evolved over the past 100 years. Each phase in that evolution has defined the conflicting elements of the mind differently and derived different technical precepts from those definitions. Freud's first stage of thinking occurred between the mid-1880s and 1897. The psychological model that he developed during those years is commonly referred to as the affect-trauma model. While trying to understand the etiology and treatment of neurotic symptoms, Freud emphasized the role of environmental trauma and subsequently pent-up charges of affect. Essentially Freud said that neurotic symptoms derived from internal conflict between the individual's conscious moral standards and distressing affects or ideas that were incompatible with these percepts. In general, trauma, usually of a sexual nature, was understood to overstimulate the individual to a degree that an intense charge of affective energy developed. This affective charge was defended from consciousness to avoid the unpleasant feelings generated by it running counter to conscious moral standards. Damming up of affect occurred and became expressed in disguised ways through neurotic symptoms. Oftentimes symptoms would develop years later when a current event stimulated memory traces of early events that had not been experienced consciously as fully traumatic at the time they occurred. In these situations a conflict was postulated to arise between what was repressed as a child and the adult's current moral standards. During this earliest stage of psychoanalytic theorizing, the strategy of treatment revolved around helping the patient to remember the traumatic event and to cathartically release the pent-up affect associated with it. Freud called this cathartic release abreaction. In this way the pathological impact of intrapsychic conflict was thought to be overcome.

II. TOPOGRAPHIC STAGE

By 1897, however, Freud was finding this understanding of psychic conflict unsatisfactory and the treatment results from it disappointing. Thus, his topographic stage of theorizing was developed over the next 26 years as his understanding of intrapsychic conflict underwent radical revision. Perhaps most importantly, several events, including Freud's own self-analysis, led him to shift his focus away from memories of actual childhood sexual traumas and their related affects as a significant component of intrapsychic conflict. Instead Freud came to the conclusion that most of his patients' memories of childhood sexual seductions were, in fact, disguised unconscious wishes. These wishes had to be disavowed because they conflicted with other components of the mind, resulting in a false belief that an actual sexual trauma had occurred during childhood. The recent furor over the false-memory syndrome speaks to how slow nonanalysts have been to realize the intensity and ubiquitousness of childhood sexual wishes and the defenses against them.

During this second phase in the development of his thinking, Freud defined and elaborated his concept of libidinal drive as a key component of intrapsychic conflict. He introduced the concept of instinctual drive as a mental–somatic construct, defining it as a mental representation of somatic stimuli. The sexual drives had a pressure, an aim, an object, and a source. The source referred to a part of the body imbued with sexual energy, following a developmental timetable. These sources became synonymous with the stage of development at which they were primary—hence, the oral, anal, phallic, and genital stages of development. Inherent in this idea of a sexual drive following a developmental timetable was Freud's notion of libido or psychic energy. That is, this energy was postulated to arise in the somatic sources of the sexual drive and to provide the impetus for the mind to work. Freud maintained his belief in the importance of the sexual drive and its underlying energy, even when he ultimately rejected the topographic model in 1923.

Freud's topographic stage of thinking involved far more than the realization that childhood sexual wishes and fantasies exerted a profound impact on mental functioning into and through adulthood, however. That is, he had to explain the reason that patients experienced and reported such wishes as memories of actual occurrences. Furthermore, he needed to explain why such memories (in reality, fantasies) emerged only during treatment. These issues required the introduction of a counter force to becoming aware of such wishes or fantasies—that is, defense. During this stage in his model building, Freud used the term "repression" synonymously with defense. Repression did not refer to any particular type of defense mechanism but to the gamut of ways in which the mind could render a wish, thought, fantasy, or memory unconscious. It represented the work of the ego or self-preservative instincts that had as their aim the preservation of the individual.

Freud's topographic model did far more than redefine the conflicting elements of the mind. It also attempted to chart out the organization of the mind and to map the main components through which internal conflict was actualized. Thus, three systems or layers of the mind were described: (1) the system Unconscious (UCS); (2) the system Preconscious (PCS); and (3) the system Conscious (CS). These three systems were structures, each with its own type of mental contents, and each characterized by qualitatively different modes of functioning. Essentially these structures or stratas of the mind were viewed as the mind's attempt to harness the instinctual drives so that the individual could adapt to reality. Were the instinctual drives and wishes to succeed in their push for conscious awareness and discharge, the individual would experience unpleasant feelings as well as potential danger. During this era of Freud's thinking all sorts of mental phenomena including jokes, slips of the tongue, dreams, as well as neurotic symptoms were understood to involve a conflict between instinctual wishes and the mind's counter forces occurring within and between these mental strata.

The UCS was viewed as the deepest strata of the mind and the repository of instinctual drives and wishes, always pushing for conscious expression. This system is characterized by a very primitive mode of functioning or thinking that Freud called the primary process. In this mode of functioning, logical and formal relations between mental contents are absent. Contradictions exist without difficulty, temporal considerations are irrelevant, and so on. What Freud called the pleasure principle dominates. Drives and wishes push for discharge, gratification, and relief of tension without consideration for anything but pleasure. It is important to distinguish this system UCS from the descriptive term unconscious. Contents of the system UCS are kept unconscious through a repression barrier; that is, active amounts of psychic energy are used to keep the contents dynamically unconscious. In contrast, descriptively unconscious mental contents might be outside of conscious awareness only because attention is not directed at them. Were attention to be focused on them, they would become conscious. No defensive force is exerted against this possible occurrence.

This distinction becomes relevant when defining the system PCS. The contents of this system are also unconscious but only descriptively so. They are capable of becoming conscious once attention is focused on them.

Thus, Freud initially located the active censor or repressive barrier that kept dynamically unconscious content out of consciousness at the boundary between the system UCS and PCS. Intrapsychic conflict occurred first at this juncture. This barrier allowed the system PCS to function according to what he called the secondary process in which logical reason and moral concerns characterize the relationship between its mental contents. The reality principle predominates so that any discharge of instinctual drives or wishes has to be filtered, altered, and/or disguised to make it compatible to reality logic and the individual's moral standards. Freud eventually explained that the system PCS modified drive impulses at all levels on their way through the system to the system CS. Thus, repression or defense no longer became conceptualized as a static barrier occurring between the systems UCS and PCS. Instead unconscious wishes are continually transformed during their traversal of the system PCS and had to pass by a second censor at the boundary between the systems PCS and CS. Intrapsychic conflict could occur at any step along the way. To pass muster and get past the censor unconscious drive laden wishes have to be disguised—what psychoanalysts labeled drive derivatives. Only such derivatives can be allowed into the system CS to be discharged.

The system CS was described by Freud as on the mind's surface. All its mental contents are conscious, although only a limited range of contents can be attended to at any moment. Perception occurs in this system as does attention. Thus, the system CS receives input from both the deeper recesses of the mind as well as from the external environment. To become aware either of mental contents from inside or perceptual stimuli from without, the system CS has to invest what was called attention cathexis, that is, to invest content or stimuli with psychic energy that has become neutralized of its sexual and/or aggressive drive qualities. As with the system PCS, the contents of the system CS follow the reality principle and are characterized by secondary process functioning.

This stage of Freud's thinking in which internal conflict was viewed as occurring between the instinctual drives of the system UCS and the censorship and defenses of the system PCS continues to be important because all of Freud's papers on clinical technique were written during this era. For example, he formulated the important clinical concept of transference during this era and emphasized the importance of analyzing dreams. Dream analysis became synonymous with psychoanalytic technique during this stage as Freud described dreams to be the royal road to the Unconscious. Vestiges of this theoretical understanding of internal conflict continue to appear in modern day clinical literature because Freud never reformulated his theory of technique when he gave up this model in 1923. This failure to recast his theory of technique has impeded the development of modern-day thinking about technical matters as many analysts and nonanalysts alike seem to operate therapeutically out of an outdated understanding of mental functioning and conflict.

For example, the clinical dictum that psychoanalytic technique should aim to raise unconscious mental content to consciousness is still regarded by many as the means by which psychoanalysis cures despite it being overly simplistic and at odds with how most contemporary psychoanalysts understand the mind to work. But during the topographic era, Freud believed that one only had to make the patient aware of his or her unconscious sexual and, later, aggressive wishes derived from childhood in order to overcome the symptoms and/or character traits for which treatment was being sought. Resistance to analytic treatment at this stage was thought to reflect solely the operation of the defense mechanisms in the clinical encounter. That is, resistance was the patient's defensive attempt to protect against the analyst's attempts to make the analysand aware of unconscious wishes. Resistance analysis meant that one had to overcome the resistance so as to allow the patient to gain access to the recesses of the Unconscious. This formulation led to didactic if not coercive practices such as telling the patient that he or she was in a state of resistance with the implicit, if not explicit, idea that he or she should stop doing so. Such an approach has led many nonanalysts as well as analysts of more modern schools to criticize classical analysis as coercive and controlling.

III. TRANSFERENCE

In this theoretical vein, Freud introduced the concept of transference as a clinical phenomenon arising within the analytic situation. Originally Freud viewed transference as the displacement of unconscious wishes and fantasies about past individuals in the patient's life onto the person of the analyst. He first viewed such transference as an obstacle to making the unconscious conscious, but later came to view it as an ally in the work. That is, transference allowed the analyst to see the unconscious wishes, feelings, thoughts, and so on, and to bring them to the patient's conscious awareness.

But during this stage of thinking, too often, the emphasis was placed on demonstrating to the patient the unconscious wishes or fantasies about historical objects rather than on understanding the reasons that such contents had to be disguised or on the analyst's actual contributions to the patient's transference perceptions.

IV. DREAM ANALYSIS

Dream analysis also took priority during this era of psychoanalytic theorizing. Given the dream's latent content about unconscious wishes, the analysis of dreams took high priority in guiding the analyst's decisions about where to intervene. The prevailing theory of analytic cure, making what was unconscious conscious, led the analyst to interpret the unconscious or latent content of the dream to the patient. In particular, this approach to dream analysis focused on remembering or reconstructing the experiences and fantasies of childhood. At the same time, the defensive use of dreams to avoid other less comfortable mental contents received short shrift. So did the attempt to understand why a childhood drive-laden experience or fantasy had to be expressed through dreaming rather than remembered and experienced more directly. Such distinctions about whether to give dream analysis particular priority in determining analytic interventions or whether to regard the dream as just one of many types of mental content that can serve multiple purposes continues to be debated in the literature and serves, in part, to distinguish those analysts who continue to practice from a primarily topographic perspective from those who have integrated Freud's structural model and more recent advances in psychoanalytic thinking into their theory of technique.

V. STRUCTURAL THEORY

By 1923, Freud felt obliged to change his model again, first through his important book, *The Ego and the Id,* and then with *Inhibitions, Symptoms, and Anxiety,* published in 1926. These two volumes are considered to define the structural theory of psychoanalysis, a model which once again shifted the conceptualization of intrapsychic conflict. Essentially, theoretical inconsistencies in the topographic model along with the problem of how to formulate the newfound clinical phenomenon of unconscious guilt led Freud to revise his understanding about what sort of conflicts gave rise to mental phenomena. The terms conscious, preconscious, and unconscious remained in psychoanalytic theory but only as adjectives describing the nature of mental contents or processes. They no longer referred to strata or organizations of the mind.

Instead an explicitly tripartite model with the mind composed of three separate structures—id, ego, and superego—was described. The use of the term structure is a metaphor that refers to enduring patterns and configurations of mental processes that show a slow rate of change. That is, they are theoretical abstractions that have proven valuable clinically and can be inferred from behavior or mental content. The id is the structure that most closely approximates Freud's early concept of the system Unconscious. It involves mental representations of the twin instinctual drives of libido and aggression, operates according to the pleasure principle, and is organized according to the rules of the primary process. Freud conceived of the ego as developing out of and retaining roots in the id while the later ego psychologists such as Heinz Hartmann described the id and ego as differentiating out of an originally undifferentiated matrix. Regardless of its origins the ego is described as the mental structure that balances and mediates the pressure of the id drives and superego and integrates them with the need to adapt to the demands or pressures of the external world. As such it operates toward the goal of preservation of the individual. Thus, it involves multiple functions, the most important of which, in regard to intrapsychic conflict, is defensive functioning. At times it helps the id to gratify its drive impulses and, at other times, it exerts defense against them in order to adapt to the external world. Intrapsychic conflict occurs at such times. Because successful defenses must always allow some drive discharge, the ego facilitates the development of compromise formations.

The third structure, the superego, was added by Freud to help explain unconscious guilt. It is the internalized representation of parental values and prohibitions—in essence a conscience as well as an ego ideal. Conflict among these structures—structural conflict—was seen by Freud as the genesis of all subsequent mental phenomena. In this model, still used by many if not most American psychoanalysts, the genesis of symptoms or character traits is as follows. An id wish or impulse runs into conflict with an internal or external prohibition, which threatens the ego with a variety of unpleasurable situations causing signal anxiety or depression. This signal affect stimulates defensive functioning, which leads the ego to find a compromise formation that allows for some id gratification while also preventing the impulse from becoming manifestly conscious; the compromise formation also assuages the prohibitions of the superego. Symptoms and character traits are examples of such compromise formations as are other mental phenomena. Besides the intersystemic conflicts that can develop between these structures, intrasystemic conflicts also occur. These conflicts involve clashes between mental contents of the same structure, for example, between incompatible ideals in the superego or between opposing drive wishes in the id.

VI. TECHNICAL IMPLICATIONS

Only in the past 20 years have psychoanalysts begun to systematically revise their theory of technique to implement the implications of this new understanding of mental functioning and intrapsychic conflict. Expanding the ego's unconscious awareness of intrapsychic conflict has become the focus of clinical technique based on the assumption that such ego expansion will bring mastery. No longer are resistances viewed as obstacles to making the unconscious conscious. Instead the importance of understanding the reasons for resistance is emphasized as is an awareness that the occurrence of resistance can be used as an opportunity to teach the patient how to observe the manifestations of unconscious conflict as they occur in his or her free associations.

Increasingly the importance of addressing the conscious ego and intervening at the surface in a way that the patient's ego can grasp and observe is seen as more important than deep interpretations of id content. Psychoanalysts now assume that unconscious id content will emerge into consciousness under its own impetus as the anxieties and threats that motivate the ego to defend against them are understood. Self-analysis—the ability to continue to observe and analyze such resistances to full consciousness—is now a goal of technique and a definition of a successful analysis, as we accept that intrapsychic conflict never disappears. Instead psychoanalysis aims to increase ego mastery over such conflicts with the assumption that conscious awareness and understanding of such conflicts will lead to compromise formations that are more adaptive and less restrictive. Thus, contemporary structural theory promulgates an approach to analytic technique that studies all facets of intrapsychic conflict rather than giving therapeutic priority to one of them. As such it can be viewed as a comprehensive approach to analysis.

See Also the Following Articles

Oedipus Complex ■ Resistance ■ Structural Theory ■ Topographic Theory ■ Transference Neurosis ■ Unconscious, The

Further Reading

Brenner, C. (1982). *The mind in conflict.* New York: International Universities Press.

Dowling, S. (1991). *Conflict and compromise: Therapeutic implications.* Madison, CT: International Universities Press.

Nagera, H. (1966). *Early childhood disturbances, the infantile neurosis and the adult disturbances.* New York: International Universities Press.

Sandler, J., Holder, A., Dare, C., & Dreher, A. U. (1997). *Freud's models of the mind. An introduction.* Madison, CT: International Universities Press.

Sugarman, A. (1995). Psychoanalysis: Treatment of conflict or deficit. *Psychoanalytic Psychology, 12,* 55–70.

Job Club Method

Nathan H. Azrin
Nova Southeastern University

GLOSSARY

job-finding Viewed as a chain of responses from the initial step of identifying a job lead, each of the steps being taught and supervised in the Job Club session, rehearsed, and actually put into practice under the supervision of the Job Club instructor.

I. THEORETICAL BASIS

The Job Club method is based on established principles of learning similar to those used in behavior therapy and by applied behavior analysis for treating psychological problems. The process of job-finding is viewed as a chain of responses from the initial step of identifying a possible job lead, each of the steps being taught and supervised in the Job Club session, rehearsed, and actually put into practice under the supervision of the Job Club instructor. Also included are modeling (imitation), self-recording of each of the job-seeking behaviors, progress charting, and "homework" assignments for out-of-session behaviors. The same rationale governs the conduct of the Job Club instructor analogous to that of the therapist in behavior therapy; specifically, the Job Club instructor constantly reinforces the job seeker using descriptive praise that designates the specific behavior being praised. The instructor is always positive, praises any action in the direction of the final goal of obtaining a job, never criticizes, and directs attention to future constructive actions rather than past difficulties.

The program takes place in a group for reasons of cost/benefit but also to obtain group support including finding job leads for each other, transportation assistance (car pools), and assigning each job seeker a partner such that they work in pairs with the partner providing a role model, reminders, and assistance, thereby having each person receiving continuous individual assistance while still functioning in a group.

Also similar to behavior therapy, the Job Club program is highly structured with standardized forms and scripts that are individualized for each person.

II. EMPIRICAL STUDIES

Prior to 1975, many types of job-finding programs were being promoted and used, such as those relying on "Job Development," or subsidized priming (such as the G.I. bills), or motivational seminars, interview rehearsal, and public employment agency listings of openings by employers. Controlled evaluation of all of these programs using the accepted scientific requirement of a randomly assigned control group was absent, similar to the situation that had existed previously in medicine and clinical psychology.

In 1975 my colleagues and I, as part of an Illinois research group (see Further Reading) conducted the first controlled evaluation using the Job Club method to help normal job seekers to obtain jobs. The result was that in 3 months 92% of the Job Club members had obtained jobs compared with 60% of those in the comparable wait-listed control group.

In 1979, the Job Club program was evaluated with job seekers who had severe job-finding handicaps: former mental patients, retardation, prison records, physically handicapped, and other such difficulties. As compared to a control group of similar job seekers who were given a motivational and information counseling program, 95% of the Job Club members obtained jobs versus 28% of the information counseling members. In 1980, the Job Club method was evaluated in a controlled study with chronic welfare recipients by the U.S. Department of Labor. The results were that twice as many job seekers enrolled in the Job Club obtained jobs than did those counseled by the agency's existing program.

Since that time the Job Club has been evaluated by many different controlled studies, all of which have found the method to be more effective than any of the alternatives with which it has been compared. More specifically, the Job Club has been found effective in different studies with high school students, the elderly, the visually impaired, the intellectually handicapped, the chronically mentally ill, unemployed professionals, deaf people, workforce programs, physically handicapped, state hospital patients, halfway house and outpatient mental patients, alcoholics, drug addicts, those with psychiatric disorders, criminal offenders, and in several foreign countries.

The Job Club method also has been found empirically to decrease depression and to increase feelings of self-efficacy, indicating its value in improving one's psychological state as well as in obtaining employment.

III. DESCRIPTION

A. Setting

The job seekers meet as a group—preferably 8 to 12 persons in a room equipped with a large table for ease of writing. These should be several telephone lines and a extension phone for each primary phone such that the assigned "buddy" and instructor can listen to all calls made. The facility also provides a copy machine for résumé copies, secretarial assistance for typing résumés, daily copies of the help wanted advertisements in the local newspapers, and several copies of the Yellow Pages telephone directory. The room also contains a file of job openings uncovered by previous and current club members. A bulletin board displays for each member a visually conspicuous record in histogram form of the (1) number of telephone calls, (2) number of letters written, and (3) number of interviews obtained; these serve as a progress chart.

B. Schedule

The members attend each day for 2 weeks, arranging interviews during half of each day and attending the interviews during the other half of the day. The second half of the day after the first 2 weeks is attended by all those members who have not yet obtained a job during the first 2 weeks. The local telephone calls, photocopying, postage, stationery, and secretarial assistance are provided without cost to the job seekers. A new group can start every 2 weeks.

C. Initial Session

During the initial session, the members briefly introduce themselves to the group and identify what type of work they have had and hope to obtain. A written form is circulated on which members list their telephone number, address, and any transportation needs. This list is photocopied and distributed to all and arrangements are made to assist those with transportation needs. Each person is paired off with a "buddy" to work together. An explanation of the program and its record of successes is provided. The members are instructed to attend any interviews arranged in the sessions that day and all future days.

D. Specific Procedures

1. Job finding is treated as a full-time job; as stated, half of each day is spent in the Job Club office, and the remainder of the day is spent attending interviews.

2. Personal sources of job leads. Because surveys have consistently shown that the initial job leads for two-thirds of jobs obtained were first identified by a friend, relative, or acquaintance, the Job Club makes a systematic effort to contact those persons and not to rely primarily on published job listings.

3. Supplies and services. As noted above, the program provides all supplies and services necessary for the job seeker without cost. The actual cost to the agency has been found to be very slight relative to the usual cost of a job-finding person.

4. Group support. Members are instructed and prompted to assist each other with transportation, obtaining job leads for others and providing mutual encouragement and advice.

5. Buddy. Each member is paired with a "buddy" to provide each other with assistance. The buddy is given a checklist to record the other buddy's phone contacts with potential employers; they review the checklist recordings together.

6. Positive personal and social attributes. In addition to work skills, the Job Club approach stresses the communication of positive personal and social attributes. The job seeker is shown how to identify these attributes and how to stress these attributes during an interview, in the job resume, and when first contacting a potential employer to arrange an interview.

7. Open letters of recommendation. The job seekers are taught to obtain open letters of recommendation that can be given to interviewers and possible employers at the time of initial contact to maximize the initial positive impression.

8. Interview rehearsal. The program has each job-seeker rehearse being interviewed using common questions asked by job interviewers and is given written material describing how such questions might best be answered for maximum benefit.

9. Interview behavior reminder checklist. The program provides instruction and a checklist of behaviors to be considered in interviews, such as proper posture, eye contact, arranging a call-back date, handshake at start and end, describing positive personal attributes, and so on. The completed checklist is reviewed the next day with the Job Club instructor.

10. Assistance by family. The program sends a letter to the family (spouse, parent, or significant other) providing suggestions as to how they can assist the job seeker, such as by actively seeking job leads, providing needed transportation, relieving the job seeker of household activities that would interfere with Job Club attendance, providing encouragement, assistance in typing or letter writing, and so on. Surveys have shown that family members are typically a source of productive job leads.

11. Counselor individual attention. In order to provide the job seeker with continuing feedback, advice, and support in spite of the group setting, the counselor follows a "continuous rotation" rule in which the counselor observes each club member in systematic rotation, spending no more than about 1 minute per club member. The counselor examines the forms being filled out, listens briefly if needed on the extension phone to job seeker calls, praises for efforts made (e.g., number of leads collected), and gives brief instruction as to what to do until the next counselor contact. This procedure plus the "Buddy" procedure described earlier provides continuous feedback and support.

12. Telephone book. The "Yellow Pages" of the local telephone book is used as a major source of job leads in the session. Because companies are conveniently listed by the type of business, the job seeker contacting those businesses will know if they are likely to utilize the job seeker's skills. As noted above, surveys have consistently shown that jobs were obtained from contact with nonpublicized sources.

13. Current job leads leading to new leads. Because personal contacts have been found to be the most frequent source of productive job leads, job seekers are taught (and supervised in session) to request additional leads from any contact person who has no positions immediately available; this situation occurs often in the telephone book contact, with friends, or at the termination of unsuccessful interviews.

14. Auto transportation is often a problem for job seekers possibly because of insufficient funds, or relative lack of public transportation in rural areas. As noted in "Group support" earlier, the club members are encouraged to assist these members with this need. Also as noted previously in "Assistance by family," family members are sent a letter urging them to supply auto transport to interviews and indeed to the Job Club location as well as to the job site when a job is obtained.

15. Telephone as initial contact. Rather than using actual "drop-ins" as a method of contacting potential employers, which usually allows 2 to 4 contacts per day, the Job Club arranges for the telephone to be used as the initial contact to arrange an interview. The telephone contacts can be made under supervision in the Job Club session and in great number.

16. Number of sessions. The goal of the Job Club is to obtain employment for all (100%) of the job seekers. If a fixed number of sessions are allowed, the most needy or job handicapped are likely to remain unemployed. Therefore, the Job Club program allows and encourages continued attendance until a job is obtained. Even after a job is obtained, the members are encouraged to return if they again become unemployed. This continual access

is logistically made possible by having the continued access members meet in the afternoon each day, while new members meet in the morning hours, with a new group starting in the morning every 2 weeks. After the 2 weeks, the members attend in the afternoon. In practice, past club members attend only occasionally, usually to use the copy machine, or telephone, or to obtain postage or typing assistance, but this continued availability appears very important in assuring the most difficult-to-place persons that they will not be abandoned.

17. Multiple sources of job leads. Surveys reveal that productive job leads result from many sources, primarily from personal contacts, but also about a third from various public announcements. The Job Club accordingly emphasizes primarily the personal sources (see "Personal Sources of Job Leads" earlier), but also common public announcements that are obtained by visits to a local public service employment agency, and announcements in newspapers' help wanted advertisements and professional and trade newsletters.

18. Personal orientation of résumé. In recognition of the great role played by personal attributes, the résumé does not only chronicle the Job Club members' job-relevant experience but also positive personal attributes of the job seeker, such as being "a team player," a "leader," "dedication to one's employer," "motivates the employees reporting to him," "needs no supervision," "well-liked by customers and fellow employees," and so on, whichever attributes honestly apply to the specific job seekers. These personal attributes are noted and emphasized in the interview as well.

19. Type of job applied for. In recognition of the diversity of skills of a given job seeker, they are encouraged to apply for more than one type of position (grant writer as well as English teacher, for example) and also to list the diversity of their experiences that may not be evident from the listing of their work history, such as being multilingual, computer proficient, organizing groups for community service, or club projects leader.

20. Structured job-seeking schedule. The job seeker is given preprinted forms and taught by the counselor to use them to arrange each day's activities with regard to interviews (date, time, name of interviewer, address, telephone number, etc.), call-backs after an initial inquiry or after each interview, persons to contact for possible leads, and so on. By structuring each day's activities the job-seeker's job search is focused, organized, and full-time.

21. Job Seeker Progress Feedback. A major problem in the job search is the discouragement and loss of motivation that results when no job placement has resulted from one's initial efforts. To help overcome this problem, the program provides feedback to the job seeker via a visual display on the wall of the room depicting separately how many interviews, telephone calls, and letters were completed by the job seeker since the start of the research. Also on the wall is a chart showing how the probability of success increases as the number of interviews increases, as determined by the results of all previous Job Club members. A job seeker's attention is directed to this chart as feedback on how his or her efforts are increasing the probability of success even though no placement has yet been obtained.

22. Counselor's style. The counselor's style is consistently positive, never criticizing or pointing out shortcomings or errors in carrying out the specific steps of the search. Rather, the counselor praises all progress and all efforts, even the fact of attendance. To address any omissions or errors, the counselor follows a "future-oriented" style, describing to the client what changes or additions might be made in future efforts to improve the chances of success.

IV. SUMMARY

The Job Club method is a program for assisting job seekers to obtain employment that has been found effective in several controlled outcome studies. It requires an experienced counselor as the leader and functions in a group format. The members do not passively listen to suggestions, but rather are actively engaged and supervised in the job search during each session by obtaining job leads and arranging interviews. The sessions continue for each job seeker until he or she obtains a job or discontinues attendance. The results of this intensive program has been that more than 90% of the attendees obtain employment. The program is based on the principles of learning and motivation embodied in the psychological body of knowledge known as behavioral psychology, which emphasizes rehearsal and functional improvement.

See Also the Following Articles

Behavioral Contracting ■ Contingency Management ■ Good Behavior Game ■ Homework ■ Token Economy ■ Vocational Rehabilitation

Further Reading

Amvine, C., & Bullis, M. (1985). The Job-Club approach to job placement: A valuable tool. *Journal of Rehabilitation of the Deaf, 19,* 18–23.

Azrin, N. H., & Besalel, V. A. (1980). *A Job Club counselor's manual: A behavioral approach to vocational counseling.* Austin, TX: Pro-Ed Publisher.

Azrin, N. H., Flores, T., & Kaplan, S. J. (1975). Job-Finding Club: A group assisted program for obtaining employment. *Behavior Research and Therapy, 13,* 17–27.

Azrin, N. H., & Philip, R. A. (1979). The Job-Club method for the job-handicapped: A comparative outcome study. *Rehabilitation Counselors Bulletin, 25,* 144–155.

Azrin, N. H., Philips, R. A., Thienes-Hontos, P., & Besalel, V. A. (1980). A comparative evaluation of the Job Club program with welfare recipients. *Journal of Vocational Behavior, 16,* 133–145.

Elksnin, L. K., & Elksnin, N. (1991). The school counselor as job search facilitator: Increasing employment of handicapped students through job clubs. *School Counselor, 38,* 215–220.

Jacobs, E. (1984). A skills oriented model facilitating employment among psychiatrically disabled persons. *Rehabilitation Counseling Bulletin, 28,* 87–96.

McGurvin, M. C. (1994). An overview of the effectiveness of traditional vocational rehabilitation services in the treatment of long-term mental illness. *Psychosocial Rehabilitation Journal, 17,* 37–54.

Murphy, G. C., & Athanson, J. A. (1987). School to work transition: Behavioral counseling approaches to the problems of finding jobs for unemployed adolescents. *Behavior Change, 4,* 41–44.

Stilham, H. H., & Remley, T. P. (1992). The Job Club methodology applied in a workforce setting. *Journal of Employment Counseling, 29,* 69–76.

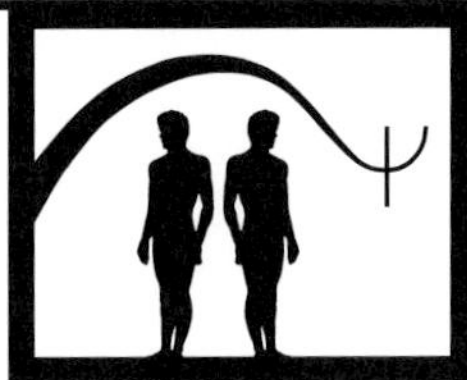

Jungian Psychotherapy

Jeffrey Satinover
Yale University

GLOSSARY

(Archetypes are preceded by asterisks. Some are also correlated [*in brackets*] to characters in the popular film series "Star Wars," as these were deliberately designed by George Lucas to represent Jungian archetypes.)

active imagination A practice whereby imagery is deliberately engaged as though one were participating in one's dreams while awake. [*As when Luke "feels the Force."*]

amplification Used chiefly as a method of dream interpretation, whereby the therapist explicates a patient's dream by relating those myths, legends, fairy tales or otherwise archived symbol, images, and stories that seem most pertinent to the dream.

analysis (Jungian) The formal designation given Jungian psychotherapy within the Jungian world, reflecting Jung's early role in the development of (Freudian) psychoanalysis. However, the practice of Jungian therapy is very unlike that of classical psychoanalysis.

* ***anima*** A personified representation (imago) of the undeveloped feminine potential in a man. [*Princess Leia*]

* ***animus*** A personified representation (imago) of the undeveloped masculine potential in a woman. [*Han Solo*]

archetypal (Jungian school) Followers of James Hillman. Hillman considers there to be no "Self"—and no "self" either. His school focuses on literary elaborations of archetypal motifs rather in the spirit of Lacan and of deconstructionist literary criticism. He terms his approach "archetypal psychology." While much admired throughout the Jungian world, it has no formal structure (e.g., training methods, programs, or institutes). It may be thought of as being focused on the technique of amplification, narrowly and for its own sake.

archetype An innate, latent nucleus of personality predispositions conforming to a consistent set of attitudes, ideas, emotions, and behaviors. Symbolically represented as the stereotyped characters of myth, fable, and literature.

classical (Jungian school) Followers of Jung's original formulations. The classical school is emphasized in this article and relates Jungian analysis as less a form of therapy than a modernized Gnostic spiritual discipline: a sacred journey or quest to achieve full realization of the Self. [*Luke Skywalker is the hero of the quest*]

* ***collective unconscious*** The various archetypes; the innate preformed structure of the psyche.

developmental (Jungian school) Followers of Jung whose primary interest is in practical therapeutics. Formerly termed the "clinical" school, which is more accurate. However, it is also true that this school assumes that adult personality develops largely on the basis of childhood developmental process. The classical school is more interested in adult developmental changes while the archetypal school considers development a "fantasy."

extraversion One of two fundamental orientations of a person. The extravert directs interest and adaptive effort chiefly toward the outer world and other people.

Gnosticism A perennial religious philosophy that identifies God (or a god) with an interior state of "illumination" available only to initiates. Gnostic strains accompany the mystical practices of most religions. Gnostic variants of Christianity have always been the chief source of heresy in the Church's view. [*The Jedi Knights*]

* ***Great Mother*** A personified representation (imago) of on the one hand the experience of being comforted and nurtured, and on the other, of being terrifyingly vulnerable to the withdrawal of same.

individuation process The process of achieving "wholeness," wherein all competing aspects of the personality are accepted, integrated and harmonized. Marked by the appearance of the Self, and by subjective states of a religious or spiritual character.

inflation Hypomania.

introversion One of two fundamental orientations of a person. The introvert directs his interest and adaptive efforts chiefly toward the inner world and himself.

mandala A term from Buddhist iconography, these are complex images whose basic structure consists of a circle subdivided into four major quadrants, and further subdivided or inscribed with complex, highly symmetrical, often recursive designs. Mandala-like imagery represents the Self and is expected to emerge spontaneously in dreams and visions as the sign of a successful individuation process.

personal unconscious Jung's term for what Freud called the unconscious (i.e., repressed material) in contrast to archetypes, that are presumed never previously to have been conscious.

psychoid A necessarily ill-defined term that refers to the puzzling mind-brain interface.

* ***Self*** The entirety of the personality encompassing both consciousness and the unconscious; an experienced unity of all archetypes; the endpoint of the individuation process. Often felt subjectively as the presence of God and so symbolized in dreams, visions, and in cultural products. [**The Force*]

* ***shadow*** A personified representation (imago) of the personal unconscious. [*Darth Vader*. But the "dark *father*" is not typical.]

synchronicity The relatedness of two events solely on the basis of their meaning to an individual, in the absence of any possible direct or indirect causal relation. This relatedness was held by Jung to be in some sense objective, however, and not merely in the mind of the individual(s) perceiving the meaning. Pathologically: ideas of reference.

* ***trickster*** A personified representation (imago) of a capacity for paradox, and concealed wisdom, messenger to the gods. [*C3PO and R2D2*]

types A set of innate personality predispositions on three orthogonal axes.

* ***wise old man*** A personified representation (imago) of a capacity for spiritual insight and experience. Leads to the Self [*apart from their ears, Joda looks exactly like Jung.*]

I. INTRODUCTION

Jungian therapy ("J_analysis") is a face-to-face psychoanalytic psychotherapy based on psychodynamic principles elaborated by the Swiss psychiatrist Carl Gustav Jung (b. July 26, 1875, Kesswil, Switzerland; d. June 6, 1961, Küsnacht) after his break with Freud and classical psychoanalysis around 1912. In sharp contrast to the early psychoanalytic model of the mind restricted to instinct, drive, and defense, Jung postulated an innate, irreducible, and thus additional psychic need to apprehend meaning and to express it symbolically. This need most commonly generates a religious impulse that cannot in every case be derived from (nor need always be a defense against conflict with) the biological drives. When ignored or blocked, this need can produce not only unhappiness, but psychological distress and eventually overt symptoms. Jung considered the now-widespread dismissal of religion as driven less by rational disillusionment than by hubris.

Classical Jungian therapy therefore aims at promoting an "individuation process," marked by an individually determined interior experience of a markedly mystical character. Jungian scholarship incorporates and interprets a vast, world-spanning body of mythological, religious, mystical, and occult references. Jungian ideas are widely embraced within artistic, literary, religious, and pastoral circles, but remain largely peripheral to academic psychology and psychiatry.

Jung anticipated many later trends: "ego-psychology," which defines, and focuses treatment toward expanding a defense-free domain of the ego; the ideas of Otto Rank, who similarly focused on free will; Heinz Kohut with his emphasis on a "self" developed out of "normal narcissism"; Hans Loewald's re-evaluation of regression as not merely restorative but creative; and Abraham Maslow's notion of "self-realization." Todays easy blending of "new age" psychotherapy and spirituality likewise parallels Jung's approach—and was in large part fostered by it.

II. DESCRIPTION OF TREATMENT(S)

A. Historical Backdrop

It took about 1000 years for European culture to consolidate around a relatively uniform body of Christian, creedal beliefs. That this would happen was by no means a foregone conclusion. The main competitors to early and medieval Christianity formed a group of philosophies and theologies loosely called "Gnostic." They shared with each other, and with many Eastern religions, the view that the goal of spirituality was a form of personal "illumination," a specific state of mind, if you will.

Jung considered his "analytic psychology" to be a modern reformulation of these same ancient Gnostic principles. The mass return to these ancient mysticisms that marked the 1960s was therefore unsurprisingly characterized as well by a sudden upsurge of interest in Jung. (Timothy Leary applied to the C. G. Jung Institute of Zürich in 1971 but was rejected.)

Jungian psychology arose within an unusually gifted, accomplished, and eclectic circle of continental scientists, artists, poets, writers, and theologians who gathered around the person of Jung (see, for example, the proceedings of the Eranos Conferences of the 1930s and 1940s). Most shared with Jung a deep hunger for the mysterious and a visceral dislike of the rationalism and materialism that they considered Freudian psychoanalysis to embody—indeed, modernism altogether. But they were also too sophisticated for the fading religiosity of pre–World War I Europe.

They were seekers, an intellectual elite that heralded the new-age spirituality that would explode in populist form worldwide two decades later. As Jung conceived it, "analysis" should stimulate the "Self" to emerge, heralded by imagery associated with God (dreams; induced visions called "active imaginations") and accompanied by the unique emotions attending divine revelation. This "individuation process," hence classical Jungian therapy itself, therefore has a markedly spiritual—specifically Gnostic—cast.

Nonetheless, Jung had a strikingly open mind toward what we now call "biological psychiatry." In the mid-1950s he chaired the First International Congress on Chemical Concepts of Psychosis, having formulated a prescient biochemical theory of schizophrenia—in the same book in which he first outlined his *religiously* based objections to Freudian psychoanalysis. Freud had specifically appointed Jung his "prince and heir," and as Jung was a rising young psychiatrist assigned him the task of "conquering for psychoanalysis the psychoses," as Freud himself had the neuroses, by showing that psychotic imagery, like dreams, consisted of the same infantile conflicts, in disguised form, as in neurotic fantasy. But Jung concluded otherwise: Psychotic imagery was a rigidified self-portrait of innate, biologically foundational brain processes. They were on this genetic basis universal, and did not arise from the idiosyncratic conflicts of an individual mind. Such imagery was accessible in normal states as well, mystical and creative ones in particular; their emergence and fixedness in psychosis was due neither to spiritual development nor creative genius but rather, he guessed, to a destructive toxin. To treat all such imagery as born of neurotic conflict at once grossly underestimated both art and religion and grossly overestimated both the neurological integrity of a brain affected by psychosis and the power of psychoanalysis as a treatment method. Empirically, if not strictly speaking scientifically, Jung was well ahead of his time on both points.

Jungians after Jung have been keen students of other schools of psychotherapy—object relations theory, the ideas of Heinz Kohut, Gestalt therapy, for example, even classical psychoanalysis—as much as they have been keen students of religion, both new and old. However, those Jungians most interested in other schools of therapy tend not to be the ones most interested in religion. This difference in "culture," as it were, underlies the major divisions in the Jungian world, markedly enough so that conferences in the 1970s and 1980s explicitly addressed the conflict between a second-generation "clinical" camp and Jung's first generation of followers. The clinical practices of the former are scarcely distinguishable from the clinical practices of any well-trained, psychodynamic psychotherapist, even if the language they use is different.

By the 1980s, yet a third strand in Jungian thought and therapy had developed, largely under the influence of James Hillman, whose talents and approach to treatment are chiefly literary, with a strong "deconstructionist" cast. Whereas Jung and his early followers sought a form of enlightenment as symbolized by the emergence of a unitary "Self," Hillman and his followers pursue rather a never-ending process of poetic interpretation and story-telling whereby any (and every) firm belief save one can ultimately be "seen through," as they put it: deconstructed not into a set of socially inculcated self-serving biases, but into a set of transcendental self-serving illusions ("gods"). Whereas Jung made an explicit analogy between the "Self" and God (or to a Gnostic Christ), Hillman makes an explicit analogy between his "archetypal psychology," and the god Hermes, messenger among all the gods—and trickster to their self-importance.

The sole firm belief opaque to Hillman's archetypal psychology is, of course, the firm belief that any and every firm belief can ultimately be "seen through," the belief on which depends the trickster's own self-importance.

These three Jungian camps have now acquired more or less formal names: the "classical," "developmental," and "archetypal" schools, respectively. (No school wants not to be called "clinical.") A brief analysis of the same case as approached by representatives of each of the schools may be found in *The Cambridge Companion to Jung*, and an excerpted web version at http://www.iaap.org/articles/ccj3approaches.html. What follows is a synopsis of classical, hence distinctively Jungian, psychotherapy.

B. Classical Jungian Therapy

1. Format

Jungian therapy ("Jungian analysis") is conducted face-to-face. Jung believed that the "neutrality" of the classical psychoanalyst was undesirable—because largely illusory. He was the first to argue for a more "personal" form of psychotherapy in which the mixing of the patient's problems and biases with those of the therapist would be accepted as a virtue. Treatment sessions last about an hour and take place no more than three times weekly, more typically once or twice.

2. Process

Classical Jungian therapy has two chief components: dream interpretation and "active imagination." Dream interpretation begins immediately; active imagination is a method usually employed later.

a. Dream Interpretation The Jungian approach to dream interpretation uses two main techniques: association and amplification. To associate to his dream, the patient freely expresses, without censorship, any thoughts that the imagery brings to mind. In contrast to classical psychoanalytic technique, however, Jungian-style association is interrupted, not free. It is akin to the limited association Jung asked of his subjects in his early word-association studies: Once a link is established by the patient between an element of the dream and some aspect of the patient's life —past or present— the therapist encourages him or her to set that element aside and associate to other aspects of the dream. Jung insisted that while associations eventually lead toward a patient's familiar conflicts (which he called "complexes") they wandered away from the specific meaning of the dream to which they were tethered. Inevitably, the lack of new information will lead both therapist and patient to devalue dream interpretation. Over the years, this is exactly what has happened in most schools of psychoanalytic psychotherapy. On the other hand, those classically trained Freudians in whose hands dream-interpretation remains a vital art (and those patients who have likewise learned its vitality) invariably interrupt free associations in precisely the way Jung argued they should—a matter more of common sense than of deep theoretical distinction. Jung's rather overly sharp argument with free association also reflects the relatively limited role played by conflict, repression, and compromise in the (early) Jungian psychodynamic theory of symbol and symptom formation, hence in the classical Jungian approach.

For both practical and theoretical reasons, in the early stages of a classical Jungian treatment, dream interpretation consists in teaching the patient (by commentary, not directive) how to make plausible links between the elements of the dreams and their personal concerns. Early on, the dreams are expected to be of the kind familiar to most psychotherapists: fleeting, fragmentary, often confusing.

Patients are encouraged to keep careful records of their dreams, and to note their responses both to the dream imagery itself and to any of the personal material evoked by the dreams. They are likewise encouraged to express both the dreams and their responses in plastic form: drawing, painting, poetry, story-telling, music, even dance, as the patient is inclined. For perhaps two years, a classical Jungian analysis may consist of little else but attention to dreams.

Over time, it is anticipated that the character of the dreams will subtly change. From reflecting a more or less self-evident preponderance of personal problems and concerns expressed in idiosyncratic images composed largely of memory traces, the dreams will begin to become more mysterious—harder to link to personal experiences—and will take on a more general character. More fable-like, such "big dreams" employ the universal characters of myth and legend: heroes, villains, monsters, kings, queens, princes and princesses, fantastic landscapes. They are also more likely to unfold as full-scale dramas, with a coherent structure. This kind of imagery is termed "archetypal," by which Jung meant to indicate at once their common and their fundamental nature. He considered these figures, and the dramas they engaged in, to be the intrapsychic representation of the innate structure and dynamic of the human psyche, the "images of the instincts." Out of the inherent repertoire of such dramas (aspects of brain function that presumably evolved as discrete patterns of adaptive response to being a human being in a typical human setting), the ones that are individually emphasized in each person reflect the psyche's deepest response to particular challenges constructed from the common, evolved responses of the human species to like challenges. Variations in this response unique to each individual's specific genetic background may be evident as well, especially if these reflect relatively long-term adaptational pressures that affected many ancestral generations.

Once criticized as dangerously racialist, such notions tend nowadays to be taken for granted in evolutionary medicine—as for example in the strong genetic pigment correlations and statistically near-perfect north–south geographic gradient in the distribution of seasonal affective disorder. Group differences in innate brain-based response patterns attenuate, naturally, as the human gene pool becomes increasingly mobile and admixed. It should be said, however, that the classical Jungian therapist attributes to these patterns a transcendent meaning that goes beyond purely biological explanations.

b. Active Imagination Once a patient has begun to experience "big dreams," they are encouraged to take their expressive engagement with the material a step further. The patient will be guided to converse with the dream figures in imagination. The goal is to achieve a state of mind akin to certain forms of meditation that utilize explicit visualization. These meditative practices can be found worldwide and are detailed, for instance, in Jewish Kabbalistic, medieval Christian-contemplative, Tibetan Buddhist, and Chinese Taoist texts, inter alia. When successful, the visualized dream characters are experienced as holding up their end of the conversation, as it were, on their own, not as being invented by the patient in the way that an author invents dialogue.

On the other hand, it is not uncommon for authors (indeed, anyone experiencing creative inspiration) to feel that certain ideas appear spontaneously. But the purpose of "active imagination" is not artistic but rather to learn from whatever the "characters" themselves have to say. "Active imagination" is a state of dissociation, cultivated for constructive purposes rather than for defense. Arguably, it has much in common with classical free association. The major difference between active imagination and free association—and between individuals drawn to the one and those drawn to the other—may precisely be the well-known individual differences in dissociability. The temperament of Jungians, both patients and professionals, may therefore tend on average to be more expressive, sentimental, and "hysteroid"; of Freudians, more restrained, intellectual, and "obsessive." An older parallel distinction is that between the romantic and the classical types. In sum: That which Freudians dichotomize by the abstractions "hysteria" and "obsessionality," Jungians poeticize as the enmity of Apollo and Dionysus.

3. Individuation

In any event, not everyone has a knack for active imagination. Those who do are considered to have the essential skill for the "individuation process." Utilizing active imagination as its chief vehicle, the Jungian analysand may now undergo a lengthy series of imaginative encounters with the major "archetypes." These appear as larger-than-life beings of mythic proportion and (in the meditative state) so real as to engender intense emotional response. The therapist's role at this stage is two-fold: First, to ensure that the emergence of this archetypal material is paced so as to minimize the risk of "inflation" (hypomania); and second, to guide the analysand toward literature that "amplifies" the meaning of the emerging themes.

Jung's own autobiography remains the best example in the literature of such a state, and of the difficulty of discriminating among deliberate active imagination, psychotic hallucination, and extreme dissociation. There are some individuals who are able to engage in active imagination but who should not, because of its potentially destabilizing effects.

In a successful individuation process, the encounter with the archetypes greatly expands the individual's sense of meaning and purpose in life, and their flexibility in adaptation. Potentials previously unrecognized and untapped may be awakened, and aspects of the personality that had lain fallow may now be cultivated and incorporated, yielding greater "wholeness."

Jung believed that such an expansion of the personality was marked in dreams and active imagination by the spontaneous appearance of symbols of the "Self." These are images whose basic geometric format is the quartered circle ("mandala"). They are strikingly similar to symbols utilized worldwide to represent God; in polytheistic cultures, the highest god; in Gnostic religions, the union of all gods.

The symbol system Jung considered closest to that which emerges in modern patients was that of the alchemists. Their journey to all the planets, their "sublimation" of lead through various metals to gold, their quest to unite ever higher-level opposite elements to form the Philosopher's Stone: All symbolized the transformation of personality by the progressive encounter with and integration of the "lesser" gods within to form the "Self"—hence the capitalization.

The ideal classical Jungian individuation process is expected to traverse the following stages: (1) Integration of the "personal unconscious," or "shadow," loosely equated with the unconscious as defined in psychoanalysis; this prepares the individual for integration of the "collective unconscious," that is, the archetypes; to wit (2) the "anima"—unrealized feminine aspects of a man, or "animus"—unrealized masculine aspects of a woman; (3) the "Great Mother," the embodiment of everything maternal, both nurturing and engulfing, as nature herself can be; (4) the "Wise Old Man," the embodiment of "spirit"; (5) the "Self," an overarching union of all of these, that is at once the superordinate representation of God and the foundation of individual identity (as in the equation of Atman and Brahman in Hindu mysticism; or of Christ and the person in orthodox Christian theology).

Individuation itself is a never-ending process. Jung considered the ignition of the process in therapy, and at least some substantial experience of the "Self," to be the goal of therapy. With the acquisition of a sense of meaning and higher purpose in life, symptoms may be expected either to disappear or, if not, to have taken on the kind of meaning that allows them to be accepted as a gift rather than a hindrance.

III. THEORETICAL BASES

In classical Jungian therapy, practice and theory are intimately intertwined. A common criticism of Jungian therapy is that it amounts to the indoctrination of the patient in a specific quasimystical worldview. The classical Jungian would sharply deny that this is criticism; Jung and many of his followers explicitly consider the individuation process to be a modern equivalent to antique rites of initiation into the cult and doctrine of certain gods and/or goddesses. But he would balk at "indoctrination." A central tenet of Jungian theory is that the "initiatory" sequence of archetypes emerges spontaneously from within the patient, rather than being overtly or covertly taught. Similarities to any external sequences arise because of innate predispositions that underlie the symbol-making potential of the human brain.

Evolution suggests that the brain should develop predispositions to apperceive experience according to common if flexible categories and patterns (like the newborn whose mouth conforms, without instruction, to the negative space of a human nipple). Fully formed "images" per se need not be embedded innately for common forms to emerge widely. Nor can simple commonality of experience account for all the overlap in imagery: Even motherless infants hunger for her expected presence. (This particular line of reasoning led to a rapprochement in the United Kingdom between followers of Jung and of Melanie Klein.)

A. Biology versus Spirit in Jungian Therapy

Against this one may argue that Jung developed Jungian therapy not empirically but much as did Freud: out of a lengthy attempt to define himself, free from serious outside accountability, with patients turning into followers, and with data from all. The importance and plausibility of the archetypal hypothesis notwithstanding, the vast body of Jungian writing detailing "archetypal imagery" in case studies can provide no compelling supportive evidence for it. Today's Jungian therapists are therefore far less likely to assume that something is archetypal just because it looks like it.

What exactly is an innate structure of the psyche? Jung's revolt against Freudian reductionism led to Jung's claim that there is a "level" of the psyche deemed "psychoid," that is at once both instinctive and transcendent. Critics argue that this is a mere assertion and that the concept "psychoid" is ill-defined. In effect, Freud argued that society strikes a never-wholly successful compromise between animal desires and a wholly pragmatic civility, religion of any kind serving to enforce the precarious dominance of the latter. Jung argued that society need strike no such balance, since in the form of spirituality he advocates desire and civility become one; only organized religion is a problem in stifling both spirituality and instinctive gratification.

The religious instinct, Jung thus argues, is real, not a defensive pose taken up by one of the animal instincts to help us avert our gaze from its true intent. Like any instinct, it has an underlying nervous system physiology that is relatively invariant among all human beings. Hence, its patterns of expression, and the sequence of maturational steps it follows, are similarly invariant. It may be ignored, as may any other instinctive drive, but only at significant cost: a sense that life is ultimately meaningless. On the other hand, Jung argued, spirituality that defines itself as unconnected to instinct tends to become sterile and unfulfilling, a criticism he leveled without cease at Christianity.

A dominant Eastern model for the individuation process in early Jungian circles (in the 1930s) was therefore Kundalini Yoga, a form of mystical practice in whose original (Tantric) form enlightenment could be achieved via the sacred sexual union of the male and female practitioners. The corresponding Western model was, again, alchemy, the symbolic content of which was explicitly sacred-sexual, the "union of opposites" depicted as the explicit sexual conjugation of a naked king and queen; and the practice of which involved a male alchemist and his "mystical sister" *(soror mystica)* working together in sacred precincts of the "laboratory."

In the classical Jungian model of therapy as individuation, an intense mutual emotional entanglement of analyst and analysand was anticipated and cultivated. As in psychoanalysis, these emotions are termed "transference" and "countertransference," but they are not interpreted as the emergence of long-repressed infantile longings whose original objects are found in the family. Rather, they are understood as the awakening of never-before experienced longings whose proper objects are divine.

To penetrate into the depths of the psyche in a classical Jungian analysis is therefore meant to be a profoundly spiritual journey whereby the tension between material drives and spiritual longings are resolved by their union. Such a journey has importance beyond the resolution of an individual's personal conflicts: To achieve in any significant measure a "union of matter and spirit" is to contribute to the building of a new explicitly post-Christian spiritual epoch. In light of modern culture-wide sentiments it is remarkable that Jung and his followers elaborated all these ideas well before World War II.

B. The Structure of the Psyche

1. *Conscious versus Unconscious*

For Freud the unconscious is primarily a set of primitive, unacknowledged desires that to remain out of sight require an ever-expanding construction of mutually reinforcing false ideas, self-serving attitudes, and conveniently filtered, distorted and, as needed, invented, memories. But such freedom from self-knowledge demands an exhausting vigilance. Psychoanalytic treatment therefore consists largely of a tactful undermining of this vast defensive fortress. Treatment releases the energy invested in defense for other "constructive" purposes.

To that aspect of the unconscious that is more than what has been repressed psychoanalytic theory did once accord a place—Freud recognized that some dream images, for example, represented "vestiges" of an early stage in the (biological) evolution of brain function. But as the term "vestige" suggests, he considered this material of little practical significance. It is rarely even mentioned anymore.

Jung's dislike of psychoanalytic theory, and of Freud's worldview, follows rather directly. Freud's insistence that all human activities are but distorted variations of material, instinctive drives—that "higher meaning" is therefore nothing but cheesecloth veiling the bleak truth of reality—seemed to Jung much like what the alchemists called "the universal solvent." In its attack, it excepts nothing: not even the beaker supposed to contain the solvent; not even, therefore, psychoanalysis itself. In such a bleak view, there are no "constructive" purposes in whose service all that freed energy can be placed without some new illusion to sustain it. "Sublimation" therefore is not sublime, it is merely the "highest' form of defense against reality.

For Jung, by contrast, the structure created by repression is the trivial and uninteresting aspect of the unconscious (the "personal unconscious"). What Freud considered a mere vestige, Jungians view as the essential, inherited anatomy of the psyche, and by virtue of its link to spirit, the pathway toward higher meaning. Jungians argue that meaninglessness is a priori pathogenic, and to train people to accept it is to induce, not alleviate, both psychological and societal disorder. The Nazis succeeded, Jung argued, because they offered Germans meaning, whereas Weimar deprived them of it. The power of his simple insight—that no one accepts meaninglessness—was severely compromised by Jung's own early flirtation with Nazi ideology.

The repressed material of the personal unconscious may need to be dealt with first, but the individuation process proper will only begin when material from the deeper levels of the collective unconscious begins to emerge. This deeper material is not considered to be a disguise for otherwise unacceptable but perfectly expressible thoughts and feelings. The mythic imagery is treated rather as genuine metaphor—that is, the best possible representation of profound states of mind otherwise inexpressible. The repressed material of the personal unconscious and the innate archetypes of the collective unconscious are related in that personal conflict, hence repression, develops only around matters that are of inherently profound import.

2. *Archetypes*

The infant is born hard-wired to form an attachment to a specific kind of external object. Later, to this latent expectation there becomes associated a specific set of sensory impressions. But the innate representation can never adequately be embodied by any real experience or memory. Instead, the mind, when released from the criticisms of rationality, will creatively weave together—from memory and from imagination—whatever fragments it needs to paint a portrait of the hidden, never before "seen," yet more "real," more deeply longed-for and feared "Great Mother," the "archetype" against which all human mothers—indeed, all women—are subtly going to be judged; and against which they subtly judge themselves.

Religion and therapy come together in this model when the compulsive philanderer, say, realizes that not only is he pursuing his mother in the guise of other women (the personal unconscious at work), but that his disappointment in his mother arises less from her flaws as a person than from his previously unacknowledged longing for a Mother of the sort not ever available in earthly form (an element of the collective unconscious). The latent, preformed imago of "mother" Jung called the "Great Mother" archetype. A family of archetypes constitutes the basic structure of the human psyche. Such a viewpoint has much in common with later "object relations" psychoanalytic theory except that for Jungians, "introjects" do not come from the outside—they begin within, are projected outward onto more or less suitable objects, and only then reintrojected.

Many Jungian archetypes have obvious parallels in typical human experience and so lend themselves to a more standard psychoanalytic or object-relations reinterpretation: Perhaps images of the "Great Mother" are energized not by innate, universally human expectations but by experiences that are universal, or nearly so, subjectively processed. (The Jungian model is closest to an interactionist model.) But other archetypes are not so easy to reinterpret this way. For example, the so-called trickster figure, common to many folk religions, and especially to shamanism, was the veritable patron god of alchemy in the form of Hermes (Mercurius). Why jokes, trickery, adolescent mischief-making, chicanery, and even outright duplicity should have so honored a place in certain forms of spirituality is hardly self-evident—unless one starts with the assumption that all such "higher" pursuits are cons.

3. The "Self"

The hermetic mysticisms of antiquity guided the seeker along a more-or-less well-known path toward a distinct state of illumination. The state is represented by a plethora of metaphors; the path likewise. But a common feature of most metaphors for the path is that of a synthesis of some sort: Initiation consists of the controlled identification with, incorporation of, and disidentification from a sequence of gods ("metabolized introjects"). The journey to each of the planets (named after the gods) is one such metaphor; the progressive transformation of base metals (lead) to noble ones (gold) is another (with each metal associated with a planet and a god). Hermes guides the soul on its planetary peregrination; Mercurius guides the alchemist in the progressive "sublimation" of the metals. As each "god" is encountered, identified with, and disidentified from, it is integrated to form a larger nucleus of personality that Jung called the "Self." Although experienced within, it is experienced as larger and other than one's personal identity.

4. Personality Types

Jung also authored the widely accepted distinction between "introversion" and "extraversion." He considered these traits as defining an important and universal dimension of human personality—an axis along which everyone tends toward a characteristic position that forms their most comfortable way of relating to the world. Jung extracted two other independent such axes as well: one defined by a polar contrast between "thinking" and "feeling"; the other by a polar contrast between "sensation" and "intuition." The eight types thus defined seem at first glance to have a rather forced symmetry. But of all of Jung's theoretical constructs, his typology has earned the most research-based confirmation.

A careful study of Jung's ideas about the archetypes and the collective unconscious on the one hand, and of his typology on the other, reveals very little compelling connection between them—they could easily be developed as two entirely different models of the psyche.

There is one critical point of contact, however, with respect to the concept of introversion. When he at first accepted Freud's plan that he should conquer the psychoses for psychoanalysis, Jung spoke of the essential problem in psychosis as being that of "narcissism"—the turning away from relationships to a solipsistic world of inner gratification. Freud's understanding was that this turning away was regressive and defensive—that the healthy capacity to spurn narcissism had been acquired by the psychotic and then split off (a defensive "vertical split in the psyche," as Freud would later characterize it when indirectly responding to Jung's abandonment of psychoanalytic theory), a variant of repression.

But eventually, Jung came to two very different conclusions: First, as noted before, that however it may first have been initiated, the profound entrenchment of psychosis was due not to psychological defense and resistance, but by a serious biochemical defect. The second conclusion was that narcissism per se was more than an early stage in psychic development and more than a defensive regression to that stage: It was a normal, natural, and absolutely critical component of the psyche at all stages of life, and perhaps especially necessary in later maturity in particular. That is why when he broke from Freud over just this issue, Jung ceased using the word narcissism and replaced it with "introversion."

When Jung rejected/was ejected from the psychoanalytic movement, a nascent psychodynamic understanding of healthy narcissism was ejected as well. The mutual bitterness of this parting ensured that it would take Jung's followers a good 50 years to accept the importance of the "personal unconscious," and that it would take Freud's followers the same 50 years to produce and accept the ideas of a Heinz Kohut and of related forms of self psychology.

C. Science or Religion?

Most people are unaware of this, but many major mainstream American churches have tacitly but extensively made of Jungian theory a new theological foundation. (This is especially true, for example, of the Episcopal church in general and of the female religious orders of the American Catholic church.) In many cases the incorporation of Gnostic and pagan themes is remarkably explicit given the flat contradiction between the Hebrew and Christian scriptures, on the one hand, and the Gnostic heretics to whom Jung explicitly relates his own ideas. To the extent that religions have felt that they need to justify themselves on psychological grounds—theology proper apparently being passé—they have frequently therefore become agents for the widespread social acceptance of Jungian psychotheological ideas, although these are rarely recognized for what they are. Jungian theory and therapy thus exerts an extraordinary cultural influence both via formal religion and informal post-sixties' spirituality.

Yet Jung also exerted an important influence—one that continues to grow—on arguably the most fundamental of the hard sciences, namely physics. Mathematical physicists with a keen interest in quantum mechanics cite certain Jungian ideas regularly in their writings. A few of the more prominent names include Christopher Isham, professor of theoretical physics at Imperial College, London, and Henry Stapp of the Theoretical Physics Group at Berkeley, Harald Atmanspacher of the Max Planck Institut and Kalervo Laurikainen at CERN. On the brief back flap biography of his *Lectures on Quantum Theory: Mathematical and Structural Foundations* Isham specifically mentions his interest in "the work of C. G. Jung," and on the cover, the letter "o" in "theory" is replaced by a snake biting its tail—the "ouroborous"—a favorite symbol of Jung's that he often interpreted as referring to a mysterious wholeness of everything that evades causality. This is no accident.

In the late 1920s and early 1930s Jung developed a theory of "synchronicity," the idea that events unrelated by any causal chain were nonetheless related via meaning, not merely as an invention of imagination, but objectively. Astrology, for example, claims that stellar arrangements as happen to be seen on earth, and perceived as forming images drawn from earthly experience (e.g., Scorpio the scorpion), influence both behavioral tendencies and chance events in the life of selected individuals, and that this influence is uniquely symbolized by the constellation's image.

The kernel of astrology is not the idea that stars influence people—one could contrive some chain of physical events, however farfetched, that might effect such an influence; perhaps some as-yet-to-be-discovered radiation, for example. What is nutty is rather the claim that the nature of the effect is reliably characterized by the earthly image to which in two dimensions an impossibly widely separated three-dimensional array of stars happen to conform—only for the moment!—and merely in someone's imagination.

Ideas of this sort strike most scientists as absurd beyond mention, but they have formed an important part of classical Jungian practice: Jung's daughter provided astrological charts for many new students at the C. G. Jung Institute in Zürich—not officially, to be sure, but wholly accepted; lectures on tarot and palm reading are unexceptional; divination via the I Ching has long held an especially esteemed place in classical Jungian practice. In his autobiography, Jung provides a number of examples where he would interpret an incidental event that occurred during a treatment session just as he would a dream reported by the patient—as when once a bird flew into the room. Synchronicity, in short, has never been a mere cognitive foible of classical Jungian therapy; it has been central to it.

But physicists (a minority, to be sure) of varying rank, from modest to the very best, find in "synchronicity" a rather startling analogy to certain bizarre features of quantum mechanics (e.g., "entanglement"), wherein two particles appear to function as though they were one, with an instantaneous orchestration of behavior between them, no matter how widely separated, and even backward in time: Neither causality nor physical interaction (e.g., forces) is involved. Out of early quantum hypotheses Einstein brilliantly drew such behavior as an inevitable consequence, hoping thereby to demonstrate their absurdity. But all subsequent experiments, over 80 years, have instead validated their reality. Physical reality as understood by the very foundations of physical science is exactly as Einstein said quantum mechanics describes it, a description he considered so absurd as to be its own self-evident impossibility proof. Yet so it is.

Marcus Fierz, an eminent Swiss physicist whose brother became a Jungian analyst and founder of the Jungian inpatient psychiatric facility Klinik am Zürichberg, assisted Jung with later corrections to the statistics in Jung's astrology paper. The corrections erased any statistical significance in the supposed correlations between constellations and psychology. Between hard modern science that does indeed unveil a mysterious universal correlation among subatomic particles everywhere, and Jung's unsuccessful attempt to statistically correlate astronomical orbits with human fantasy, there is a huge gulf—which Jung dismissed.

Having found that a better statistical analysis nullified his hypothesis, he changed his hypothesis. Synchronistic relations occur within statistical fluctuations, he then claimed, not in excess of them as do causal associations. By contrast, the physical relations created by entanglement are detected precisely in their violation of classically expected statistical results. It may be plausibly argued, therefore, that however poetic the analogy between modern physics and a Jungian model of psyche, there is no real connection whatsoever. How is it then that so many eminently qualified scientists have taken Jung's ideas, amateur statistics and all, so seriously? Is there something about the Jungian theory of synchronicity that should perhaps not be dismissed out of hand?

The answer is a qualified "yes," and arises out of an aspect of Jungian theory and history that is often alluded to but has yet to be fully clarified: The personal relationship and collegial interchange between Jung and one of the very greatest of the founders of quantum mechanics—Wolfgang Pauli. Within their relationship Jungian theory, practice, and history unite.

In 1904, Einstein had been Jung's dinner guest: "These were very early days when Einstein was developing his first [i.e., special] theory of relativity...," Jung recalled. "I pumped him about his relativity theory. I am not gifted in mathematics. I went fourteen feet deep into the floor and felt quite small." Nonetheless, says Jung, "...it was he who first started me off thinking about a possible relativity of time as well as space, and their psychic conditionality."[1]

Fifteen years later, in the early 1920s, Wolfgang Pauli was at work on the mathematics of "spin," a quantum phenomenon whose utter mysteriousness even today remains to be fully fathomed. Among other things, spin ensures that two identical particles with the same (half-integer) spin will tend to avoid each other—not via any force propagating at the speed of light, but by fiat, instantaneously, everywhere in the universe and probabilistically, as though orchestrated by some gentle omnipotent conductor who merely urges—and who leaves no physical trace of his existence.

For electrons—the foundational instance of such a spin-bearing particle—these probabilities conform to the mathematical relations of three intersecting rings, rotating about three perpendicular axes with a common center, but with some twists: Each ring may rotate simultaneously in both possible (opposite) directions. By the laws of classical physics (including those in which Einstein firmly believed) such "superpositions" are completely impossible—like one object being in two places at the same time; and to return to its original position, a ring must complete two identical rotations (a fact that is beyond human visualization). But superpositions do, in fact, exist. Recently, objects large enough to be seen by the naked eye have been made to exist simultaneously in two places at once. And on the fact that two-rotations-equals-one depends every diagnostic MRI scan ever taken. Furthermore, the speed of rotation for each ring, in either direction, was quantized—it could assume only discrete values, like pulses or rhythms, giving spin values what we might call "clock-speeds," that in multielectron systems are determined by certain special powers and inverse powers of 2.

Pauli's initial success in 1924 delineating these relations would win him standing as one of the very greatest of the founders of quantum mechanics, the 1945 Nobel prize, and on that occasion an unsurpassed accolade by Einstein, who designated Pauli his "spiritual son" and successor as director of the Institute for Advanced Studies at Princeton.[2] The strange relations of spin—now termed the Pauli Exclusion Principle—are directly responsible for the current explosion of quantum technology, including such astounding feats as quantum teleportation, quantum computation, and the emerging field of "spintronics."

But even this understates the matter: "There is no one fact in the physical world which has a greater impact on the way things *are* than the Pauli Exclusion Principle. To this great Principle we credit the very existence of the hierarchy of matter ... which makes possible all of nuclear and atomic physics, chemistry, biology and the macroscopic world that we see" (theoretical particle physicists Ian Duck and E.C.G. Sudarshan).

[1] Jung, C. G.: *Letters,* Vol. 2. p. 108.

[2] Before their estrangement, Freud had publicly deemed Jung his "spiritual son *and heir.*" The infinitely nuanced, unfailingly courteous Einstein, friend to Freud, and knowing of the true relationship between Pauli and Jung, gave Pauli his love with no strings attached. Quantum theory was Einstein's permanent *bête noir.*

But Pauli had also been wrestling with a profound twofold despair. In 1927 his mother poisoned herself after discovering that Pauli's father's was having an affair with a much younger sculptress whom he later married; and his scientific genius had early on led him to a deep estrangement from Catholicism. "I am baptized 'antimetaphysical,'" he wrote, "instead of Catholic." (To safeguard his rise in the professoriate at the University of Vienna in the 1890s, Pauli's Jewish father converted to Catholicism—much as today a conversion to leftism is *de rigeur;* near the end of his life Pauli seems to have made something of a return to his father's abandoned faith.) In May 1929 Pauli formally left the Catholic church and in December 1929 a beautiful and seductive cabaret performer married the lovesick physicist, even though he was her second choice. In 1930 she abruptly abandoned him and quickly married her first choice.

Pauli had by no means been happy with his 1924 formulation of spin, whatever his colleagues thought. "My nonsense is conjugate to the nonsense which has been customary so far," he wrote. Yet in 1927, the year that his mother killed herself, he fully satisfied himself with respect to spin, inventing the three famous "Pauli matrices," mathematical representations of the doubly valued quantum spin, one for each spatial axis. In anguish, regardless, Pauli drank heavily and provoked humiliating public quarrels until, at his father's urging, he consulted Jung.

Jung repeatedly claimed that he never "formally analyzed" Pauli because he found Pauli's natural psychological capacity so great ("He even invented active imagination for himself...") and because Jung was intent on studying and presenting Pauli's dreams as objective evidence for his theory of the collective unconscious, archetypes, individuation, the Self and the relationship of these to alchemy: "Now I am going to make an interesting experiment to get that material absolutely pure, without any influence from myself, and therefore I won't touch it," Jung stated. Instead, "[a]t the end of the year I am going to publish a selection from his first four hundred dreams, where I show the development of one motif only." Pauli was officially treated by Dr. Erna Rosenbaum who, since she was "a beginner," Jung "was absolutely sure she would not tamper."

Nonetheless, Jung supervised Rosenbaum's work and met weekly at noon with Pauli to discuss and interpret Pauli's dreams: "[H]e was doing the work all by himself," for 3 months, Jung says, but "for about 2 months, he had a number of interviews with me. ... I did not have to explain much."

In 1935, Jung discussed 400 of these dreams as the 1937 Terry Lectures in Psychology and Religion at Yale. They form the evidentiary backbone for all his volumes on alchemy. At Yale, Jung asserted that "the dreams I am going to relate ... represent an entirely uninfluenced natural sequence of events" and that in these dreams, his "well-educated intellectual" (and at the time anonymous) subject "worked out (among other matters) the problem of perpetual motion, not in a crazy way but in a symbolic way. He worked on all the problems which medieval philosophy was so keen on."

The climax of the series was not a dream, however, but a "visual impression" that "sums up all the allusions in the previous dreams." Jung called it "a turning point in the patient's psychological development ... in the language of religion—a conversion." The visual impression was (in Pauli's words, as quoted by Jung):

> There is a vertical and a horizontal circle having a common center. This is the world clock. It is supported by the black bird. The vertical circle is a blue disc with a white border divided into 4 × 8 = 32 partitions. A pointer rotates upon it. The horizontal circle consists of 4 colors. On it stand 4 little men with pendulums, and round about it is laid the ring that was once dark and is now golden formerly carried by 40 children. The world clock has three rhythms or pulses. (1) The small pulse—the pointer on the blue vertical disc advances by 1/32. (2) The middle pulse—one complete rotation of the pointer. At the same time the horizontal circle advances by 1/32. (3) The great pulse—32 middle pulses are equal to one complete rotation of the golden ring.

Jung refers to this vision as the "perpetuum mobile," and provides 64 pages of world religious commentary on it, representing it as the spontaneous emergence of the Self. Thereafter, Jung says, Pauli "became a perfectly normal and reasonable person. He did not drink any more, he became completely adapted and in every respect normal. ... He had a new center of interest." In 1934, Pauli discontinued his sessions with Rosenbaum and married that same year, for life.

Never in his many discussions of this prototypical vision does Jung mention Pauli's successful matrix model of three quantized spin axes, which this visual impression obviously reproduces; nor the admix of feelings over his personal losses (the black ring turning golden once again; the blue and white motif that Jung related to Mary, the Mother of God in Catholicism, but not to Pauli's own lost mother). Indeed, the particular problem that the Pauli Exclusion Principle solved was how and why the first four "magic" numbers of the periodic table arise: 2, 8, 18, and 32. Pauli was widely known to have continued his problematic drinking long after.

However weakened Jungian theory may be by the lack of evidence from one of its chief sources, and in spite of the fact that throughout their ensuing friendship Pauli made his own doubts clear about many of Jung's scientific claims, Pauli made no bones about his personal debt to Jung. He had wanted Jung to test "synchronicity" against the rigors of statistical evidence; Jung refused. When urged by colleagues not to damage his reputation by later copublishing a book with Jung, Pauli nonetheless insisted: "For there comes the time when I must give documentary evidence of what I owe this man."

IV. EMPIRICAL STUDIES

Only very recently has any attempt been made to assess the value of Jungian treatment with due consideration to the fundaments of experimental design. Numerous presentations on outcome have been delivered at Jungian conferences by Dr. Seth Rubin of the Society for Psychotherapy Research, and the first peer-reviewed article was published in 2002 in the *Journal of Analytical Psychology.*

However, a German Jungian society has published on the web and in print an extensive, lengthy, and independently funded study with attempt at controls and a clear delineation of its own limitations and weaknesses. This study found that "Even after 5 years, ... improvement in the patients' state of health and attitude ... resulted in a measurable reduction of health insurance claims (work days lost due to sickness, hospitalisation days, doctor's visits and psychotropic drug intake) in a significant number of the patients treated ... [with] long-lasting effects on the patients' psychological well-being. [However], there are numerous major methodological problems with these data including the lack of comparison sample, the non-representativeness of the sample, the unreliability of pre-treatment data, the high rate of attrition, the need for multi-variate statistics, and uncertainty about the actual treatments offered."

V. SUMMARY

C. G. Jung has exerted an enormous and steadily growing influence on modern culture, especially as the "search for meaning" has taken on special urgency in light of the triumphs of scientific materialism. Transplanted via analogy from physics to psychology, the seminal ideas of the theoretical physicist Wolfgang Pauli profoundly influenced Jung's theory of the psyche. Although greatly helped by Jung the person, and deeply grateful to him, Pauli predicted what has in fact happened: That for an era bereft by science of religion, Jungian theory would ultimately prove more worthy as a philosophy than as a strictly scientific model of psychology.

Jungian therapy is therefore most distinct when aiming its therapeutics primarily at the development of a spiritual life. Its practitioners root themselves theoretically in a model they find personally congenial and that provides for them, as it were, a larger myth within which to lead a meaning-infused life. In practice, the evidence for and against the comparative efficacy of a specifically Jungian treatment method is no better than for any other method—or worse. Given the many different approaches that have arisen among the various Jungian schools—and within them—a good argument can be made that the parameters defining Jungian therapy will surely evade adequate denotation, but that individuals who identify themselves as Jungian therapists do as good a job on the whole as do those who do not. There is no doubt that many individuals deliberately seek Jungian therapy for what the term "Jungian" connotes and that Jungian therapists favor a style of communication that is comfortable for such individuals.

See Also the Following Articles

Adlerian Psychotherapy ■ Beck Therapy Approach ■ Behavior Therapy: Historical Perspective ■ Dreams, Use in Psychotherapy ■ Existential Psychotherapy ■ History of Psychotherapy ■ Gestalt Psychotherapy ■ Oedipus Complex ■ Psychoanalysis and Psychoanalytic Psychotherapy: Technique ■ Self-Psychology ■ Sullivan's Interpersonal Psychotherapy ■ Unconscious, The

Further Reading

Archive for Research in Archetypal Symbolism. (1991). *An encyclopedia of archetypal symbolism.* Boston: Shambhala.

Cook, D. A. G. (1987). Jung, Carl Gustav. In *The Oxford companion to the mind* pp. 403–405. Oxford: Oxford University Press.

Edinger, E. F. (1973). *Ego and archetype; individuation and the religious function of the psyche.* Baltimore, MD: Penguin Books.

Jacobi, J. S. (1984). *The psychology of C. G. Jung: An introduction with Jungian analysis.* Edited by M. Stein (Eds.); Introduction by J. Singer. Boulder, CL: Shambhala.

Jung, C. G. (1989). *Memories, dreams, reflections.* Recorded and edited by A. Jaffé; translated from the German by R. and C. Winston. New York: Vintage Books.

Jung, C. G. (1970). *Collected works. 1953–1961.* Princeton, NJ: Princeton University Press.

Jung, C. G. (1973). *Letters.* (Selected and edited by G. Adler, in collaboration with A. Jaffe. Translations from the German by R. F. C. Hull.) Princeton, NJ: Princeton University Press.

Jung, C. G. (1984). *Dream analysis: Notes of the seminar given in 1928–1930.* Princeton, NJ: Princeton University Press.

Jung, C. G. (1996). *The psychology of Kundalini yoga: Notes of the seminar given in 1932 by C. G. Jung* Edited by S. Shamdasani. (Bollingen series; 99) Princeton, NJ: Princeton University Press.

Meier, C. A. (1959). *Jung and analytical psychology.* Newton Centre, MA: Dept. of Psychology, Andover Newton Theological School.

Meier, C. A. (1987). *The meaning and significance of dreams.* Boston: Sigo Press.

Meier, C. A. (Carl Alfred). (1989). *Consciousness.* Boston: Sigo Press.

Nagy, M. (1991). *Philosophical issues in the psychology of C. G. Jung.* Albany, NY: State University of New York Press.

Neumann, E. (1972). *The great mother; an analysis of the archetype.* Translated from the German by R. Manheim. Princeton, NJ: Princeton University Press.

Satinover, J. (1980). *Puer aeternus:* The narcissistic relation to the self. *Quadrant 13,* 2.

Satinover, J. (1984). Jungian Psychotherapy. In M. Sacks, P. Rubinton, & W. Sledge (Eds.), *Core readings in psychiatry: An annotated guide to the literature* pp. 306–308. New York: Praeger.

Satinover, J. (1986). Jung's lost contribution to the dilemma of narcissism. *Journal of the American Psychoanalytic Association, 34,* 401–438.

Satinover, J. (1995). Psychopharmacology and Jungian analysis. In M. Stein (ed.), *Jungian analysis* (2nd ed.). Chicago: Open Court Press.

Shelburne, W. A. (1988). *Mythos and logos in the thought of Carl Jung: The theory of the collective unconscious in scientific perspective.* Albany, NY: State University of New York Press.

Smith, R. C. (1996). *The wounded Jung: Effects of Jung's relationships on his life and work.* Evanston, IL: Northwestern University Press.

Steele, R. S. (1982). *Freud and Jung, conflicts of interpretation.* London; Boston: Routledge & K. Paul.

Storr, A. (1981). Jung, Carl Gustav 1875–1961. In J. Wintle (Ed), *Makers of modern culture* pp. 258–260. New York: Facts on File.

Ulanov, A. B. (1971). *The feminine in Jungian psychology and in Christian theology.* Evanston, IL: Northwestern University Press.

Vincie, J. F. (1977). *C. G. Jung and analytical psychology: A comprehensive bibliography.* New York: Garland.

The wisdom of the dream [videorecording]: Carl Gustav Jung [Wilmette, IL]: Public Media Video, c1989. v. 1. A Life of dreams (53 min.); v. 2. Inheritance of dreams (53 min.); v. 3. A world of dreams (53 min.)

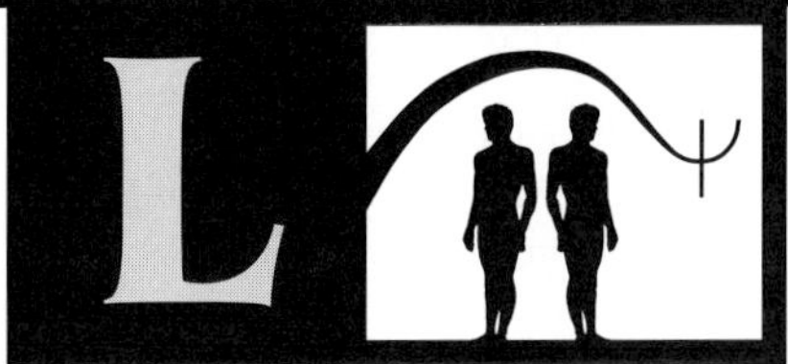

Language in Psychotherapy

W. Rand Walker
University of Idaho, Moscow

GLOSSARY

bridging Language that associates current thoughts and feelings with historical events or previous experiences. For example, "Is this a familiar feeling?" and "You said when she yelled at you the thought 'I am such a loser' popped into your head. Is that a new thought or is it a familiar one?"

clarification Clarifications are questions (or statements with the inflection of a question) that serve to confirm the perspective of the client. During instances when the client is vague, clarifications are used to encourage more description or explanation in order to bring clarity to the session. Importantly, a clarification can also be a way to convey an understanding of the client's situation or perspective.

confrontation Noticing, and bringing the client's attention to, events, behaviors, or content that are inconsistent with the goal of progress or change. Mixed messages, aloof behavior, and inconsistent remarks are examples of content that are typically confronted.

counterassumptive A counterassumptive statement is used to manage the working distance between the client and therapist. It targets the assumption of the client and counters it without arguing with the client. For example, when the client says "tell me what I should do" the therapist can respond with a counterassumptive instead of arguing or refusing the client's request ("It isn't obvious to me either ... I wish I knew").

description There is an important distinction between inference and description. Describing behavior is generally less threatening than inferring something from the client's behavior. "It doesn't look like you like your kids" is an inference and "when you talk about your kids your face becomes more constricted and strained" is a description.

dichotomous questions Presenting a choice between two statements is a dichotomous question. "What feels more true to you ... that you are angry or that you are afraid?"

edification Educating the client is an essential variable in the change process. Explanations regarding the etiology and causes of various problems, imparting treatment options, developing new skills, and Socratic discussions, are all examples of edification in counseling.

exclamations Exclamations are used to convey an active empathic stance. "Wow!," "How awful!," and "Outstanding!" are expressions that either convey an understanding regarding the intensity of a given situation, or welcome clients to experience something they are currently holding at an emotional distance.

extensions When clients constrict content and have difficulty acknowledging what might be obvious emotional dimensions of their life experience, the therapist can take an active empathic stance and state it for the client. This very delicate and advanced skill is used as an invitation to delve further into emotional content. For example, the client says "I am lonely" and when there is a reasonable amount of certainty, the therapist can use an extension "and it has been this way for a long time."

horizontal questions Horizontal questions are used when the therapist wants the focus to stay on the emotional and relational aspects of a client's experience. When the client makes a sensitive and personal self-disclosure, the therapist can respond either vertically (which focuses on the informational level of content) or can respond horizontally. "Now that you have told me this, what are you thinking?" or "What was happening right before you told me this?" are examples of horizontal questions.

imperatives A statement that elicits a specified action. "Tell me what you're thinking" or "Say the first thing that comes to mind when I say 'airplane'."

interpretations An interpretation is a well-timed and carefully constructed explanation of the client's experience, disorder, or interpersonal context. In most instances, this is where the theory of the therapist emerges. The primary difference between an interpretation and a clarification is that the interpretation introduces a new perspective to the client (it is the therapist's perspective).

minimal encourager These are sounds and statements that encourage the client to continue in a monologue. "Mmm," "uh huh," and "oooh" are examples of minimal encouragers designed to keep the process going without undue interference.

open-ended question A question that cannot be answered with a "yes or no" or single word response. "What did you do on your vacation?" as opposed to "Did you have a nice vacation?"

paraphrasing Putting the client's description into different words as a means of conveying an understanding of the client's thoughts and experiences.

performatives Statements that are also actions. "I do" in a wedding binds the individual in a commitment, a compliment like "That looks nice" has the effect of making the recipient feel good, or the therapist saying "I have confidence in your ability to handle this" is intended to instill a sense of self-efficacy.

probes These are statements and questions designed to elicit more information regarding a specific area of content. "I'm thinking you must have had a good reason to start drinking again after all the things you have been through" is a probing statement and "Why did you start drinking again?" is a probing question.

reflection Rephrasing or restating the emotional or affective part of the client's statement. Many therapists rely on reflections as a way of expressing empathy and acceptance of the client.

reflexive questions Posing questions that put the client in a position to consider new perspectives or alternatives. Reflexive questions start off with statements like "What would happen if..." and "Let's say you were assertive with your boss, what would you expect to happen?"

strategic questions Tactful use of strategic questions is an option when the therapist observes the need for more direct challenges. Strategic questions are often corrective and imply a desired outcome. "What keeps you from doing your own grocery shopping at this point?" and "Something stops you from speaking out about this to your boss (with the inflection of a question)" are examples of strategic questions.

summarizing Rephrasing the client's utterance as a means of clarifying and conveying an understanding of the client's disclosure.

verdictives These are performative statements that serve as verdict or implicit declaration. "I think you can handle this" or "It is necessary to deal with this" are verdictives.

vertical questions Interviewing often requires a number of questions regarding the client's history, family structure, educational background, and other facets of the individual's personal life. Vertical questions are designed to elicit information and logical details. When a client discloses something very personal, the therapist can either address the informational aspects of the disclosure (via vertical questions like "How long?" and "When?") or can focus on the emotional and personal aspects of the revelation (see horizontal questions).

I. INTRODUCTION

Throughout this encyclopedia, there are descriptions of specific psychological theories and novel techniques of therapy that set various orientations apart. In spite of numerous differences expressed by the respective denominations in psychotherapy, there is one common element that very few would dispute; the essential use of language as a mechanism of change. In the short time psychotherapy has existed, the field has evolved into a craft with its own language, conversational rules, and social structure. Although the process of therapy is more than word selection and phrasing, there is a growing accumulation of verbal strategies designed to assist the therapist through a number of situations and contexts. This article is a review of the actual verbal "tools of the trade" that serve as the staple of most therapeutic approaches.

II. EVOLUTION OF THERAPEUTIC LANGUAGE

The systematic use of conversation for therapeutic purposes is not a new concept. As far back as Hellenic Greece, rhetoricians were employed to challenge the logical errors of melancholic "patients" in order to effect a more positive outlook on life and to find solutions to problems. The Greek formulation of mental processes paved the way for the use of persuasion, motivational conversations, and encouragement, as a healing form.

In spite of the historical dominance of mystical and spiritual formulations of human suffering, it is clear that very few "lost faith" in the use of a confidential and abiding relationship to produce behavioral changes or to render assistance to those who needed it. Even the priests of the middle ages were purveyors of a healing conversation in the form of confession. This sacramental ritual included many facets of modern psychotherapy. A confidential setting, self-disclosure, focus on behavior change, and a redemptive relationship are all elements in common with the secular practice of psychotherapy. It was not until the "age of enlightenment" that the intellectual formulations of mental illness and human suffering returned to mainstream Western thought. As the ideas and attitudes shifted away from the more mystical views of mental disturbance, the medical field advanced concepts that served as the precursors to psychotherapy as we know it today. Importantly, the more humane and optimistic views posited by Tuke, in Great Britain, and Rush, in the United States, encouraged treatments based on rational and scientific formulations of mental illness and set the tone for the next century.

A culmination of theoretical contributions led to the ultimate invention of psychotherapy; however, psychoanalysis was the first type of therapeutic conversation to emerge as a discipline. By the time of Freud's death in 1939, psychoanalysis had developed an assortment of well-defined pragmatic verbal strategies. The verbal activity of the contemporary analyst is largely centered around the sequence of free associating, confronting, clarifying, interpreting, and "working through" material as it emerges in the session. In essence, the psychoanalyst's artful use of language creates a process of unencumbered exploration while striking a delicate balance between defensive self-preservation and a desire to access the troubling source of the individual's problem or neurosis. With a strict sense of restraint and economy, the analyst uses a series of prompts and other linguistic devices of language to accumulate enough data or material to form an interpretation. In many ways, it is initially a process of collecting pieces to a puzzle and then it proceeds to an interpretation, at which point the therapist actually attempts to put the pieces together. The interpretation brings to light connections that were, at one time, outside of the individual's awareness. With each insight, the individual is equipped to reallocate psychological resources previously dedicated to the unresolved intrapsychic conflict. Freud described the process as two travelers on a train with one looking out the window and describing what is on the landscape and providing details about the scenery. The other traveler is blindfolded, but is able to explain details and impart meaningful information regarding the countryside as they pass through. This one-sided and slow deliberation was unprecedented in terms of a social structure and seminal with regard to the development of therapeutic language.

The psychoanalytic approach to treating psychological and emotional problems was a dramatic departure from the "bootstrapping" and "advice giving" mores of the time. Society began to accept the notion that emotional suffering and mental illness was often too complex to resolve with simplistic solutions. Along with the changes in attitude came a rapid succession of new therapies, as well as more lively debates about what "active ingredients" of therapy make it effective.

Although psychoanalysis solidified the presence of the "talking cure" in the twentieth century, a proliferation of therapeutic approaches would lead to an expansion of ideas regarding therapeutic language. There was a notable transition from the "free floating" and noninstrusive stance of the psychoanalyst to a more active and broadly applied use of the therapeutic relationship. A new taxonomy of language developed around a number of core concepts in psychotherapy that included a collection of therapist behaviors and types of utterances. Therapeutic orientations began to offer ideas regarding language usage and presented techniques that were based on their respective theories of change. Whether it be insight, a corrective emotional experience, or an in-depth exploration of an important aspect of the client's life experience, clinicians and theorists were discovering how to make these types of conversations occur.

The new faces of therapy expanded well beyond the original constraints imposed by "psychodynamic" theory. Albert Ellis broke through the vales of neutral distance with his often blunt and usually directive approach to dialogue in his rational emotive therapy (now rational emotive behavior therapy). Conversely, Carl Rogers placed considerable importance on a nonjudgmental and supportive collaboration in his person-centered therapy. Mirroring techniques, passive empathic statements, and an emphasis on genuine dialogue, are all activities advanced by Rogers as "facilitative" therapist behaviors. Fritz Perls demonstrated a number of creative strategies that intensified the emotional experience in therapy, including cathartic techniques such as the "empty chair" where the client engages in a role-played conversation with an imagined person. Aaron T. Beck and his colleagues established a method of "collaborative empiricism" in his cognitive therapy approach. His method included the use of the Socratic method, engaging the client in a scientific inquiry using questions, and persuasive challenges to problematic thought processes and perceptions. The interpersonal theorist Harry Stack Sullivan attended scrupulously to the impact of his wording and phrasing on his patients and lectured extensively on the importance of deliberate syntax. His well-regarded work on interviewing and therapeutic processes articulated minute differences between well-constructed therapist statements and poorly constructed ones. Milton Erickson was widely known for his creative use of language and his effective use of metaphors. The full spectrum of contributions to therapeutic language is a vast and voluminous subject; however, it is clear that developments in therapeutic language have come from a multitude of sources. Close examination of the various techniques and approaches reveal a field that is willing to integrate new ideas and to learn from one another. The rapid growth of "integrative" and "eclectic" therapeutic movements is testimony to the widespread recognition of the need for the creative application of a variety of tools, rather than strict adherence to a narrow and dogmatic view of change.

III. THERAPEUTIC COMMUNICATION

The cornerstone of most therapeutic approaches centers on the mutual participation in a special type of conversation, a conversation that is implicitly different from everyday discourse and that is unique in terms of structure and content. The "way" the therapist phrases something, the timing of a given response, even the selection of words, have become a recognizable form of social interaction. The cliché "How does that make you feel?" may be the best known of the therapist's staples; however, the skilled therapist is capable of applying many more proprietary tools of the trade to help the client. Historically, it is clear that the development of therapeutic approaches was largely dependent on recognizing what worked in different situations. The remainder of this article focuses on the actual verbal behavior of the therapist, how language changes within different contexts of the process, and what the therapist hopes to achieve with different types of verbal responses.

Much of what we know about language in psychotherapy comes from the field of "process research." Studies of the actual behavior as well as *in vivo* observations of different forms of therapeutic communication have resulted in a reliable taxonomy of words and behavior that are unique to psychotherapy relative to everyday conversation. The seminal research of Clara Hill, William Stiles, Sol Garfield, Kenneth Howard, Carl Rogers, Larry Beutler, Leslie Greenberg, Michael Patton, Robert Russell, Hans Strupp, David Orlinsky, and numerous others, elevated the level of description from vague and theoretically laden inferences, to measurable entities. The content and scope of process research attends to complex variables within the session such as therapist intentions, types of utterances or "verbal response modes," probabilities of therapist responses within different contexts, conversation analysis, semantics, "good moments," and other interpersonal variables related to positive outcomes. The collective findings of this type of research have had a direct influence on the therapeutic terminology, the validity of outcome studies that use process measures to assess treatment integrity, and training. The glossary provides an overview of therapist statements, as well as the typical contexts in which they are used. Ultimately, these tools make it possible to engage the client in a conversation that is markedly different from other forms of social support, help, or advisement.

The fields of anthropology and "conversation analysis" observe that in most interpersonal contexts and cultures, verbal interactions fall into fixed patterns that are predictable and orderly. When people abide by these social tenets, it contributes to a sense of cooperation, safety, and compatibility. Even minor infractions of these rules can lead to anxiety, perceived disturbance, interpersonal distance, conflict, or the interpretation of rudeness. For example, a self-disclosure of emotional pain or suffering will typically lead to consolation, commiseration, or supportive comments. Beyond that point, however, intuitive signals cause one or both speakers to change the topic away from the delicate subject matter and on to a subject that is not so sensitive. Subsequently, a concern about intrusiveness or a fear of intensifying the person's emotional pain can effectively thwart a therapeutic conversation. Conversely, it is understood, even expected, that the collaborative relationship between the client and the therapist is in effect to talk about things that are difficult to share and to address issues beyond the normal scope of everyday conversation. Therapists develop the ability to depart from the social restrictions that limit the course and depth of everyday conversation with implicit permission to abandon conventional patterns of conversation in order to engage the client in a unique and constructive process. Probing questions, long silences, interpretations, *in vivo* descriptions of behavior, and clarifications, are but a few verbal events that are rarely observed in most other interpersonal contexts. This relatively new type of dialogue employs a variety of illocutionary strategies in order to promote positive movement in the therapy process. Therapists-in-training learn to use a variety of verbal strategies that have known effects on the direction of the session and that are introduced as a means of meeting identified therapeutic goals. Specific roles are adopted (e.g., teacher, redemptive listener, a guide through the healing process, motivational speaker, and persuader) to engage the client in different types of therapeutic interactions. In whatever the context, the skilled therapist relies on the systematic use of language to ensure the best chance of a positive outcome.

The appropriateness and quality of any therapeutic response is dependent on the situation at hand. Although there are over 400 identified "orientations" of psychotherapy, the conversation of therapy is fairly uniform when considering context. There is an initial greeting, then a brief gathering of information, a subsequent exploration or delving into more detail, and then a "winding down" period. Each session follows a general trend and provides a "frame" that guides the therapist's responses. Take, for instance, the statement "I feel bad." Again, the type of therapist response will depend significantly on when or in what context the statement was made. If it occurs early in the session, the therapist may ask questions, or direct the client to elaborate, as a means of establishing a focus, or to determine the context of the client's reported experience (e.g., "Tell me what has been happening" or "What has happened since our last session?"). The same statement, "I feel bad", elicits a different set of therapeutic responses when it occurs further into the therapeutic hour. It is notable that most of the "treatment"-oriented techniques occur during this part of the therapy session. It is not unusual for the therapist to use techniques to intensify the client's emotional experience or engage the client into a deeper exploration of content. Therapist empathy becomes more finely tuned and is accompanied by a due amount of encouragement, even pressure, to work through difficult material. Clients are sometimes guided through a courageous process of facing dreaded material, conquering personal demons, and are systematically exposed to fears and stimuli that provoke escape and avoidance. When the client says, "I feel bad" toward the end of the session, the constraints of time affect the therapist's response. The same disclosure might require attention to coping strategies that the client can use between sessions (e.g., "What do you expect to happen to this feeling later today? or "Do you think it would be helpful to go over some of the coping strategies we have discussed previously to get us through the week?"). The therapist will also summarize the session with relevant information, new insights, or present an objective view of the possibilities in the future. It follows then, that the quality of any given response depends significantly on the context in which it occurs.

The therapist is also mindful of "timing" a statement or question appropriately and is poised to respond to opportunities for positive movement. When to exert pressure and when to back off, is an hourly challenge that is largely determined by the readiness and competence of the client. Premature exploration often leads to flight responses or other types of resistance such as restricting content, dominating the session, attempts to change the therapeutic arrangement, and emotional withdrawal. An absence of exertion or movement can lead to meandering and even apathy. In both cases, there is a risk of a negative effect. One poignant example of this comes from an intake conducted by a seasoned psychologist working with a woman struggling to bond with her adopted child. She reported feeling repulsed by her new son's attempts to be close to her. At one point during a description of her son, she displayed a look of disgust and made a gesture that signified "go away." After observing the intensity of her emotion, the psychologist asked, "Is this a familiar feeling?" It did not take long to realize that the question thrust her into a dissociative state. Her history of abuse had yet to be disclosed to anyone and they scrambled for 2 hours using standard grounding techniques to get back to the "here and now." Although this kind of "bridging" question was not a bad one, the timing was clearly premature. If the same question occurred several sessions later, it may have resulted in a more fruitful outcome. Thus, it is not simply what the therapist says that makes a difference, it is also what the therapist chooses not to say. At any given moment, the therapist is considering options, restraining his or her own impulses, and choosing one response over another, based on what has the best chance of leading the conversation in a direction that will help the client.

For better or worse, each utterance has the potential of affecting the course and experience of the conversation. The study of pragmatics examines the interpersonal effect of phrasing and syntax. Each statement has a probability of influencing the direction and nature of the subsequent utterance. When the therapist makes a statement or asks a question, it is often "goal-directed" and made with specific intentions. For instance, if therapists believe that creating a "here-and-now" experience is important to therapeutic success, then they will ask questions differently than if they are interested in gathering basic information. Instead of the therapist asking "So what was it like in your house growing up?" the therapist might set up the question with a present tense like "It is 6 o'clock in the evening at your house when you were growing up ... what is happening around you?" This type of phrasing is more likely to be "experienced" than the past tense questioning.

Depending on the goal of a given session, the therapist will pose questions and initiate dialogue with a fair amount of attention to probability. Starting the session with "O.K., where is a good place to start today?" produces a different direction or set of responses than "So tell me about your week." An even more predictable outcome can be generated with a statement like "Last time we were talking about your relationship with your brother and how he was the prized son." In each case, the therapist uses language to shape the course and emotional depth of the session.

Mindful of the multiple layers of therapeutic communication and the known effects of certain types of statements, the therapist mentally juggles a variety of options and then selects a response according to the immediate goals of the session. An example of how the therapist considers the probable effect of one type of utterance versus another is observable in instances when the client discloses a closely guarded secret. After the disclosure, the therapist can ask "vertical" questions designed to generate information about the historical and factual aspects of the secret. "How long ago did this happen?" or "What makes you think that?" are examples of vertical questions. However, the skilled therapist might decide to prioritize strengthening the therapeutic relationship over gathering information. In this event, the therapist could ask a "horizontal" question such as "What was it like to say that?" or "Tell me what you were thinking before you told me this." Horizontal dialogue changes the focus from the content of the disclosure to the client's experience of therapeutic relationship. When a delusional patient discloses a fear of an "FBI plot" to assassinate him, the therapist can respond with at least two routes of exploration. It is tempting to assess and treat the delusion or psychosis; however, the seasoned therapist recognizes the tenuous nature of the therapeutic relationship with this type of problem. Subsequently, since the notion of an FBI plot is frightening to the patient, empathic language and supportive comments are appropriate responses. "Approximating" statements make it possible to express an understanding of the fear without endorsing the belief. "If I were convinced the FBI intended to kill me it would be very frightening and I wouldn't know who to trust" is different than "If I were in your shoes I would be very frightened." The therapist will attempt to side with the fear and express an understanding of the experience before attempting to confront the delusion. When it is time to confront the delusion directly, it is prudent to phrase the probe in a manner that elicits a description, rather than a belief. "What are you seeing that convinces you that this is happening?" leads to a description of external events and "Why do you think this is happening" generates a response depicting thought processes and theories. Therefore, the therapist can minimize problematic exchanges and lower the chances of exacerbating the patient's delusion with carefully crafted phrasing.

Countless situations are navigated and managed with the deliberate use of language. Although there is not a "right way" to respond to every situation, there are responses that have better probabilities of success than others.

IV. LANGUAGE AND THE THERAPEUTIC RELATIONSHIP

The therapist is also monitoring the quality and strength of the therapeutic relationship. Freud was the first to recognize the intense bond that forms when two individuals embark on the therapeutic journey and others have concluded that this is one of the most critical dimensions to successful therapy. It is necessary to establish intimacy and trust before the therapist employs any deep probes or challenges. In order to keep the focus on the client it is necessary to discard the most common means of achieving interpersonal intimacy, namely two-sided self-disclosure. When people pursue personal relationships, they willingly collaborate in a "do as I do" process that is proportional and rhythmic. When we meet someone for the first time, we often attempt to achieve a level of intimacy and comfort by beginning a search for things in common. "Where are you from?" "Where did you attend college?" and "What do you do for fun?" are questions that lead to a point of excitement when people find a mutual domain of experience or interest (i.e., "Me too!" or "Oh really, I have a friend at that university. Perhaps you know her...").

With emotionally and deeply personal information the implications of disclosure are more threatening. As the layers of self-protection peel away, there is a lingering state of vulnerability until the other responds with either an affirmation or a similar unveiling of personal content. Intimacy in psychotherapy is different. Client disclosures are met with expressions of understanding, empathy, and prompts to continue rather than reciprocal self-disclosures. Empathic sounds (e.g., "uh huh," "hmmm," and "oh") and positive nonverbal gestures serve to encourage, even invite the client to discuss sensitive material if it is needed.

The seminal work of Carl Rogers emphasized the importance of creating a strong alliance between the therapist and client. To be in "sync" with clients and to reflect an understanding of their experience is a necessary condition of therapy. Conveying a genuine interest in the individual, as well as making an effort to understand the client's emotional experience, or empathy, is the cornerstone of a functional therapeutic relationship. Upon disclosing the horror of a traumatic event, the client sees and hears indications of empathy and a human response. A grimace or the sound of a quiet gasp serves to encourage, even prompt the client into further exploration. Rogers emphasized the nonintrusive and tentative stance of "passive empathy" as a means of establishing a safe and "facilitative" environment. Although the therapist is encouraged to monitor (and even express) his or her own personal reactions within the therapeutic process, there is a clear separation between the therapist's experience and the client's reported experience. Instead of "me too" statements, the therapist attempts to acknowledge and validate the client's view of the world. Once the therapist is confident about the level of "intersubjectivity" or degree of shared knowledge, the therapist can tread carefully into the client's space. Sometimes it is a matter of expressing or conveying an "experience of the client's experience," but also verbalizing thoughts and feelings that the client is reluctant to admit. Therapy is brimming with opportunities for this type of connection. For example, as an exhausted and anxious single mother describes all of the activities and obligations that she encounters on a daily basis, the therapist can use a passive empathic statement such as, "That must be overwhelming" or he or she can choose an active empathic statement such as, "Wow, when I think of doing all of that I feel overwhelmed." In either case, the therapist uses empathy to fortify the therapeutic alliance and create a safe place for therapy to occur.

The therapeutic relationship is also subject to periods when it shifts into altered states. During the course of therapy, Freud noted that patients would develop a distorted view of the patient–analyst relationship. Frequently, the patient would transfer thoughts and feelings associated with parental figures to the analyst. It became evident to Freud that this phenomenon, which he labeled "transference," was an opportunity to work through unresolved conflicts of the patient's childhood. Harry Stack Sullivan expanded on the notion of transference with his concept of "parataxis," which included feelings about people in general rather than just parental figures. Nonetheless, when these feelings emerge in the therapy session it presents some opportunities for positive movement. The therapeutic dyad can serve as a microcosm of other relationships and facilitate an opportunity to work through pervasive issues that exist in the individual's social milieu.

Hostility, seductiveness, submissiveness, and dominance are all examples of behavior addressed in the safety of the therapeutic environment. In these cases, the therapist must establish and manage a "working distance." In his book *Making Contact,* Harvard psychiatrist Lesten Havens describes working distance as "being alone together" in a state of "noninvasive closeness." The instincts of the client might compel him or her to submit too readily to the will of the therapist, rebel against the therapeutic process, or to take over the process with his or her own preferred form of dominance. Language moderates imbalances created by these polar movements and prevents the therapist from colluding with the client's attempt to derail threatening but constructive movement. The seductive client may attempt to draw the therapist out of a neutral stance by appealing to the personal needs of the therapist. After disclosing in provocative detail, a sexual dream about the therapist and then conveying current sexual feelings, the therapist is saddled with the task of redirecting the focus without rejecting the client. When the client moves toward the therapist in this way, the use of horizontal questions such as "What is it like to tell me about these feelings?" can create an objective moment. A statement such as "It says a lot about the trust we have established that you are able to talk about this with me. You can speak openly about these feelings and know, with confidence that I will not betray you by changing our relationship in that way" is a "performative" (see glossary) statement that declares the status of the relationship. If the client exhibits embarrassment or regret, a counterassumptive statement such as "One thing I will ask is that the next time you have a dream like that about me could you give me a full head of hair and rippling stomach muscles?" This statement counters the assumption that the client did something wrong by disclosing the dream, but also reaffirms the safety of the therapeutic setting.

Managing the working distance involves keeping a perspective and thinking of these events in terms of data instead of personal dilemmas. Harry Stack Sullivan referred to a state of mind called "participant observer." Like the ethnographic researcher, the therapist is both experiencing and studying the situation. Instead of treating challenging situations as a problem, the therapist observes the behavior and assesses the degree to which the behavior is likely to be a problem in the individual's daily life. Using the example of the seductive client, rather than thinking about how appealing the therapist must be to elicit such feelings, the therapist considers the possibility that this behavior is a maladaptive response to psychological intimacy. The socially anxious client sometimes projects hostility or aloofness as a way of creating a safe distance from people whom they perceive as a threat. The therapist subdues the initial experience of rejection and, again observes the behavior as important data. By use of description, as well as carefully constructed questions, it is possible to capitalize on the emergence of the behavior and offer an opportunity that literally does not exist in any other setting. The therapist can offer "objective" feedback about potentially problematic behavior without an obligation to apologize or repair the relationship.

In addition to dealing with the challenges of direct "focal messages" or the literal content of any given utterance, there are "metamessages" that are equally important. Metamessages are the implicit messages that are not typically acknowledged as a message, but have a profound impact on the conversation nonetheless. If, for instance, a client pleas to the therapist "Just tell me what to do" the therapist has a few options. One common response to this type of plea is to refuse the request with an explanation. "It wouldn't be appropriate for me to tell you what to do in this case" or "This is your life and I think you are in the best position to make a decision of this importance." The focal messages in this case are "no" and "It isn't a good idea to tell you what to do." However, one of the metamessages might be perceived as "I am withholding my advice" and "I probably do have the answers but it is against the rules to tell you." In spite of the reasonable focal content, these metamessages could result in resistance, problems in the therapeutic alliance, and unnecessary arguments. One way to counter this metamessage would be to use a statement such as "I wish I knew what the right way to handle this would be ... it is not obvious to me either" (which is a "counterassumptive" statement). This response counters the assumption that the therapist knows what is best for the client and, for whatever reason, chooses to keep from the client, and sends another message acknowledging the complexity and difficulty of the client's situation.

V. SUMMARY

Psychotherapy resides in our culture as a widely accepted and specialized form of communication. The psychotherapist shapes the process by using a unique combination of verbal tools and well-placed responses to the client. Importantly, statements are selected on the basis of the known effects of specific devices or techniques, and are utilized as a means of meeting an identified therapeutic goal. The therapist adopts specific roles such as teacher, redemptive listener, a guide through the healing process, motivational speaker, and persuader, and engages the client in different types of therapeutic interactions. In whatever the context, the skilled therapist relies on a deliberate use of language to ensure the best chance of a positive outcome.

See Also the Following Articles

Acceptance and Commitment Therapy ■ Communication Skills Training ■ Confrontation ■ Functional Communication Training ■ History of Psychotherapy ■ Interpersonal Psychotherapy ■ Rational Emotive Behavior Therapy ■ Sullivan's Interpersonal Psychotherapy ■ Working Alliance

Further Reading

Havens, L. (1986). *Making contact: Uses of language in psychotherapy.* Cambridge, MA: Harvard University Press.

Nofsinger, R. E. (1991). *Everyday conversation.* Newbury Park, CA: Sage.

Schegloff, E. A. (1984). On some questions and ambiguities in conversation. In J. M. Atkinson & J. Heritage (Eds.), *Structure of social action: Studies in conversation analysis* (pp. 28–52). Cambridge, MA: Cambridge University Press.

Stiles, W. B. (1992). *Describing talk.* Newbury Park, CA: Sage.

Wachtel, P. L. (1993). *Therapeutic communication: Principles and effective practice.* New York: Guilford Press.

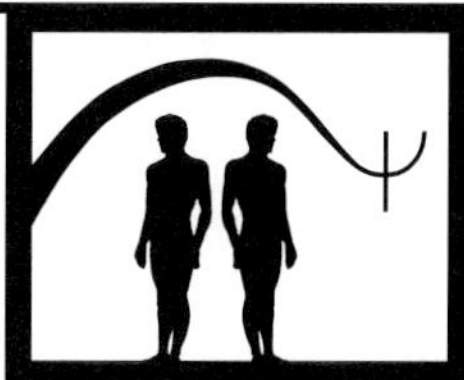

Legal Dimensions of Psychotherapy

Howard Zonana
Yale University and Connecticut Mental Health Center

GLOSSARY

adjudicate Refers to the process whereby differences and conflicts within the justice system are heard and settled.

confidentiality The right of a patient to have any information or communications made during the course of treatment and evaluation to be held in strict confidence unless authorized to be divulged.

due process The process whereby the rights of parties in a conflict are assiduously protected in the settlement of that conflict. Due process generally entails the opportunity to know and examine one's accusers and the chance to present one's own case in defense of an accusation.

HIPAA Health Insurance Portability and Accountability Act of 1996, which is federal law intended to rectify a variety of conflicting state laws concerning health related issues. It has stringent confidentiality protections.

privilege Refers to disclosures made in court or for legal reasons and is an exception to the general rule of evidence of the justice system, in which every member or party to a conflict has a right to every other person's evidence.

There are both ethical and legal underpinnings to the confidential relationship between a psychotherapist and a patient. Confidentiality here refers to the right of a patient to have communications, made during the course of evaluation or treatment, held confidential absent express or implied authorization. Although confidentiality is not absolute, and may vary with the professional qualifications of the therapist, it remains a core value for mental health professionals and patients.

A variety of professionals may fulfill the role of psychotherapist. Physicians specializing in psychiatry and psychoanalysis have the ability to prescribe medication for their patients in addition to performing psychotherapy in its varied forms. Clinical psychologists with master's or doctorate degrees have special training in administering and interpreting psychological testing as well as clinical training in psychotherapy. Other licensed professionals who conduct psychotherapy are social workers and nurses with master's or doctorate degrees. In addition there are marital and family counselors and the clergy.

Psychotherapy involves disclosures of the most personal nature, including wishes, fears, dreams, fantasies as well as detailed disclosures regarding one's personal, educational, legal, employment, social, sexual, and family history. This information is important, not just for the isolated facts and psychological symptoms, but also to learn how the person deals with stress and conducts personal and intimate relationships. This data is needed for accurate assessment and diagnosis, as well as treatment. The style and process by which the information is disclosed by the patient/client is also revealing of personality traits and cognitive styles of dealing with the inevitable stresses of daily life. It is not uncommon for a psychotherapist to be the recipient of information that has never been shared by the patient with anyone else. Unless there is some assurance of confidentiality, it is unlikely that individuals would be as open or free about making disclosures, especially as there remains a significant stigma associated with mental disorders and their treatment.

I. CONFIDENTIALITY AND PRIVILEGE

Confidentiality protections are derived from a variety of sources. The oldest derives from professional and ethical codes. Since the fourth century BCE, the Hippocratic Oath has required that physicians respect the confidentiality of patient communications:

> And whatsoever I shall see or hear in the course of my profession, as well as outside my profession, in my intercourse with men, if it be what should not be published abroad, I will never divulge, holding such things to be holy secret.

Professional organizations, such as the American Medical Association (AMA), since early in its history, have been concerned with the importance of confidentiality. The current code of medical ethics has a section on confidentiality:

> The information disclosed to a physician during the course of the relationship between physician and patient is confidential to the greatest possible degree. The patient should feel free to make a full disclosure of information to the physician in order that the physician may most effectively provide needed services. The patient should be able to make this disclosure with the knowledge that the physician will respect the confidential nature of that communication. The physician should not reveal confidential communications or information without the express consent of the patient unless required to do so by law.

The American Psychiatric Association (APA) publishes for its members *The Principles of Medical Ethics* with special "Annotations Especially Applicable to Psychiatry." Members are required to follow the basic AMA principles as well as the APA Annotations. The APA principles state that psychiatrists must "respect the rights of patients, colleagues, and other health professionals, and that they must safeguard patient confidences within the constraints of the law." The guidelines on confidentiality also tell psychiatrists that they "may release confidential information only with the authorization of the patient or under proper legal compulsion. The continuing duty of the psychiatrist to protect the patient includes fully apprising him/her of the connotations of waiving the privilege of privacy." Other therapists are also bound by ethical codes to keep information within the therapeutic relationship confidential. The American Psychological Association, in its *Ethical Principles of Psychologists and Code of Conduct,* informs therapists that "safeguarding information about an individual that has been obtained by the psychologists in the course of his teaching, practice, or investigation is a primary obligation of the psychologist." The National Association of Social Workers (NASW) also has a code of ethics with an elaborate confidentiality section. Section 1.07c states in part

> Social workers should protect the confidentiality of all information obtained in the course of professional service, except for compelling professional reasons. The general expectation that social workers will keep information confidential does not apply when disclosure is necessary to prevent serious, foreseeable, and imminent harm to a client or other identifiable person.

All clients must be informed by the social worker of the limits of confidentiality in a given situation. The American Counseling Association requires its members to adhere to a code of ethics that has a full section on confidentiality. Counselors must respect their clients right to privacy and avoid illegal and unwarranted disclosures of confidential information.

The concepts of confidentiality and privilege are related but separate. Privilege laws, strictly speaking, only relate to disclosures made in court whereas confidentiality statutes govern therapist's obligations outside the courtroom. Privilege is an exception to the general rule that the justice system has a right to every person's evidence. Confidentiality is both an ethical and legal duty that protects a patient from unauthorized disclosures of protected information. At this point all states and the federal courts recognize important confidentiality and privilege protections in the psychotherapist–patient relationship. At the same time statutes and courts have created numerous exceptions to the confidentiality/privilege rights.

By far the most influential rationale for recent privilege law is the traditional justification enunciated by Dean Wigmore. Essentially utilitarian in nature, this justification asserts that communications should be privileged only if the benefit derived from protecting the relationship is important enough to society that it outweighs the detrimental effect on the search for truth. In particular, Wigmore set out four conditions for the establishment of a privilege:

1. The communications must originate in a confidence that they will not be disclosed.
2. This element of confidentiality must be essential to the full and satisfactory maintenance of the relation between the parties.
3. The relation must be one which in the opinion of the community ought to the sedulously fostered.
4. The injury that would inure to the relation by the disclosure of the communications must be greater than the benefit thereby gained for the correct disposal of litigation.

The evolution of the privilege concept in law is helpful in understanding its current role for psychotherapists. The rule that an advocate could not be called as a witness against his client existed in Roman times. It is unclear whether the Roman tradition influenced the Anglo-Saxon attorney–client privilege, but English recognition of the privilege goes back at least to the reign of Elizabeth I. The purpose of the privilege was to prevent the attorney from being required to take an oath and testify against his client. Later, it was also considered that such testimony against one to whom loyalty was owed would violate the attorney's honor as a gentleman. Thus, the original justification for the privilege was nonutilitarian. Accordingly, the attorney, rather than the client, held and asserted the privilege. Today the privilege is the prerogative of the client. The client, not the lawyer, holds the privilege. The client has the ultimate authority to raise or to waive the privilege. In addition to the attorney–client privilege under English common law there was also a spousal privilege and, until the Reformation, a clergy–communicant privilege.

The physician–patient privilege did not exist under the English common law, and physicians were expected to testify as any other witnesses in court proceedings. In the United States, a New York court first recognized the clergy–communicant privilege in 1813. In 1828, New York also became the first state to grant a testimonial privilege to communications between a doctor and patient. This permitted a patient to prevent a physician from testifying about information relevant to the patient's treatment that was divulged to the physician in his professional capacity. The psychological counseling privilege has gained recognition since the 1950s, and more recently the privilege has been extended to cover other therapists and sexual assault counselors. Around 1970 there were some efforts by psychiatrists to assert the privilege in their own right. Psychiatrists argued that the patient could not fully understand what they were agreeing to when they signed a release of information. Only the analyst could understand the full implications of the disclosures made in therapy. Courts were by and large not sympathetic with this argument and have clearly held that it is the patient's privilege and is not the prerogative of the therapist.

By 1996 all 50 states and the District of Columbia had enacted some form of psychotherapist privilege. Federal courts, however, did not accept the privilege. In 1972 the Chief Justice of the Supreme Court transmitted to the Congress proposed rules of evidence for the federal courts that had been formulated by the Judicial Conference Advisory Committee and approved by the Judicial Conference of the United States. The proposed rules defined nine specific testimonial privileges, including a psychotherapist–patient privilege. Congress rejected this recommendation in favor of Rule 501, which was more general and authorized federal courts to define new privileges by interpreting "common law principles ... in the light of reason and experience."

Until 1996 only a few federal jurisdictions adopted a limited form of a psychotherapist privilege. Others rejected it entirely. Because of these conflicts in the federal courts the U.S. Supreme Court agreed to hear the case of *Jaffee v. Redmond.* Mary Lu Redmond was the first police officer to respond to a "fight in progress" call at an apartment complex in Illinois. As she arrived two women ran toward the squad car saying there had been a stabbing in one of the apartments. Officer Redmond relayed the information and requested an ambulance. As she was walking to the entrance of the building several men ran out, one waving a pipe. Two other men then burst out of the building, one chasing the other and brandishing a butcher knife. He disregarded her repeated commands to drop the weapon, and Redmond shot him when she believed he was about to stab the man. He died at the scene, and people came pouring out of the building, and a threatening confrontation followed before other officers arrived. A suit was filed against the officer claiming excessive force. There was conflicting testimony from the victim's relatives claiming that he was unarmed and that she drew her gun immediately on exiting the squad car. After the shooting Redmond saw a clinical social worker for 50 sessions. The plaintiff sought access to the therapy notes concerning the sessions in their cross-examination of Officer Redmond. The district judge rejected Redmond's assertion that the contents of the therapy notes were protected under the psychotherapist–patient privilege. Neither the therapist nor Redmond complied with the order to release the notes. The judge instructed the jury that they could presume the notes would have been unfavorable to Redmond, and the jury awarded approximately $550,000 in state and federal claims.

The U.S. Supreme Court majority opinion concerning this case held that confidential communications between a licensed psychotherapist and her patients in the course of diagnosis and treatment are protected from compelled disclosure under Rule 501 of the Federal Rules of Evidence. They explicitly recognized and extended the privilege for psychiatrists and psychologists to licensed social workers. They noted that there would be situations in which the privilege must give way, for example, if a serious threat of harm to the patient or to others could be averted only by means of the disclosure by the therapist.

In spite of the importance of the recognition of a psychotherapist–patient privilege, it is important to be aware that the patient's privilege is not absolute. There are several exceptions to both the psychotherapist–patient privilege and confidentiality statutes. The patient waives the right to confidentiality when he or she places his or her mental condition into issue in civil litigation, the so-called patient-litigant exception. This is permitted to allow the defendants to explore a patient's prior history to confirm that the current mental condition was related to the claimed injury and had not been present before. Since *Jaffee,* courts continue to differ about the breadth of this exception. The most frequent examples are plaintiff's claims in civil cases for emotional distress damages or in suits under the Americans with Disabilities Act in which a party's mental condition may be part of the case. Some courts have held that where a patient merely alleges "garden variety" emotional distress following an injury and not a specific psychiatric disability or unusually severe distress, this has not been deemed sufficient to waive the psychotherapist–patient privilege. However, there is wide variation in individual rulings. A waiver is frequently deemed to apply when parents cannot agree in custody disputes regarding who is best able to care for the child. In many jurisdictions, statutes also exclude the use of the privilege in involuntary civil commitment proceedings.

The dangerous patient exception to the privilege was explored in a case where a man was indicted for threatening to kill the president. The defendant moved to exclude from evidence his prior statement to a psychiatrist that he "wanted to shoot Bill Clinton." The government argued that under the *Jaffee* exception the privilege was not available, and the trial court agreed. On appeal the Tenth Circuit rejected the broad claim that the privilege does not apply in the criminal setting but remanded the case for an evidentiary hearing "to determine whether ... the threat was serious when it was uttered and whether its disclosure was the only means of averting harm to the president when the disclosure was made." If serious and the only means for averting harm then the privilege would not be available. On remand, the District Court heard from the psychiatrist that the man had been discharged to his father's care after his hallucinations of killing the president had stopped and he was stabilized on antipsychotic medication. Three days later the psychiatrist learned that the man had left the father's home, and his whereabouts were unknown. Concerned that he would again stop his medication without supervision, the psychiatrist now concluded that he posed a "serious threat" but commitment was not an option because he had disappeared. The Secret Service was concerned that he had money to travel and had once before been investigated for similar threats. Based on this evidence the court denied the defendant's motion to exclude the disclosure to his psychiatrist. Neither the trial court nor the appellate court considered whether the disclosure, designed to prevent a future harm, should be admissible in a subsequent criminal prosecution.

California has an evidentiary rule permitting this type of disclosure, which has led to psychiatrists and psychologists being called to give evidence of aggravation in capital sentencing hearings after making a *Tarasoff* warning that ultimately failed to protect a victim. The prosecutor was interested in showing long-standing hostility and premeditation by use of this testimony. Other state courts, without this rule of evidence, have refused to let such testimony into evidence.

Other exceptions to confidentiality include reporting laws, such as those relating to communicable diseases; child abuse and neglect; chronic health problems affecting safety to drive; disabled physicians; elderly abuse; and mentally retarded abuse. Most states also permit disclosures, without patient consent, when therapists wish to consult with other professionals for the purpose of diagnosis and treatment, when decisions need to be made regarding hospitalization of the patient, or when the patient poses a risk of harm to self or others.

There are also special rules that come into effect when the work setting or facility has developed specific guidelines. For example, correctional institutions, employee assistance programs, and the military all have additional exceptions to confidentiality. Prison wardens generally require, as a work rule, that any information regarding escapes or escape plans are not confidential and require disclosure to security staff. In employee assistance programs, some information concerning work performance issues may be available to the employer. Commanding officers in the military frequently must be told certain information that would be confidential in other settings. Such special settings frequently require a therapist to learn about and then inform the patient of any limitations on confidentiality that may be applicable.

There have not been many cases brought against psychotherapists for inappropriate breaches of confidentiality reaching appellate levels of review. Many explanations have been offered to account for this small number. The standard of care is not as clearly defined as in other areas of medicine, and causation and damages are hard to prove. There is rarely a physical injury, and courts have been reluctant to make awards for purely emotional damages. Patients may also be reluctant to file cases and expose their mental history in public. It is also possible that many cases settle before reaching open court. Nonetheless a small number of cases have reached public attention, and some are instructive.

In 1986 Diane Wood Middlebrook was writing an authorized biography of Anne Sexton, an American poet. Although Sexton had left detailed instructions regarding most of her papers including some therapy notebooks and a few tapes, her psychiatrist, Dr. Martin Orne, released 300 tapes after obtaining the permission of Sexton's daughter and literary executor, Linda Gray Sexton, to allow the biographer to review the tapes. The release of the tapes evoked great consternation from both literary and psychiatric circles. One professional called his actions a "betrayal of his patient and profession." Others felt the family's wishes did not matter and that confidentiality should survive a patient's death. Dr. Orne believed that the patient would have been eager to have the material reviewed. Eventually charges of an ethics violation were brought against Dr. Orne and adjudicated by the American Psychiatric Association. Ultimately a decision was reached that no ethical violation occurred. Although no lawsuit was filed, the situation illustrates the high sensitivity to these issues as well as the vulnerability of psychotherapists to ethical complaints.

Some liability for disclosures has been founded upon "breach of contract." In *Doe v. Roe* a psychiatrist and her psychologist husband wrote and published a book about a wife and her late husband eight years after the couple terminated psychotherapeutic treatment with the psychiatrist. The book reported extensive details of their lives with verbatim quotations on the feelings, fantasies, and thoughts of both husband and wife concerning the marriage that was breaking up. The therapist claimed that she had obtained verbal consent during the course of therapy. The suit was brought for breach of contract and in tort, for a violation of the confidentiality statute between physician and patient and for invasion of privacy. The court held that the defendant psychiatrist had entered into an agreement with her patients to provide medical care, and although not an express contract, the court stated that the physician impliedly covenants to keep in confidence all disclosures made by the patient concerning the patient's physical and mental condition "as well as all matters discovered by the physician in the course of examination or treatment." The court noted that patients would bring out "all manner of socially unacceptable instincts and urges, immature wishes, perverse sexual thoughts—in short the unspeakable, the unthinkable, the repressed." The psychologist husband who was a co-author was not in a contractual or physician–patient relationship with the plaintiff but the court held him equally liable as a co-violator.

The courts have used a similar means to hold nonphysician therapists to a standard of care encompassing confidentiality. In *Mississippi State Board of Psychological Examiners vs. Hosford*, a psychologist was suspended from practice by the state board for revealing confidential information about his patient. The patient and her husband had sought a treatment for marital difficulties. The psychologist voluntarily and unilaterally revealed information about the wife in a subsequent divorce and custody action to the husband's attorney and signed an affidavit attesting that the wife was not a competent parent. This disclosure was made without a court order requiring disclosure. The Mississippi Supreme Court reviewed the American Psychological Association's Ethical Principles, the psychologist patient privilege, and a "public imperative that the psychology profession as a whole enjoy a impeccable reputation for respecting patient confidences" when the psychologist appealed the decision of the licensure board. The suspension was upheld.

The complexity of the psychotherapist–patient privilege and the Fifth Amendment were illustrated in a case that arose on an Indian reservation and thus was heard in federal court. D. F. was a troubled 13-year-old adolescent who was admitted to a residential treatment program at a county mental health center. Over the course of 6 months she received very conflicting messages about the confidentiality of her statements made to center staff. She was suspected of harming two infant cousins who had died within a short time of each other. While at the center she was repeatedly encouraged by staff to write and discuss her abuse of young children to gain better ward privileges. At the same time some of the staff were in close communication with Protective Services and the FBI. The staff could never reach consensus about their role and responsibilities. Finally, after more than 6 months on the unit, she confessed. She was arrested and charged with second-degree murder. When the government attempted to introduce her confession, the defense argued that it was not voluntary. The admission into evidence of a confession that was not voluntary, within the legal meaning of the word, violates due process. The court found that the therapists were acting more like "state actors" (police) than they were therapists as they were directly communicating with law enforcement, and thus the confession was determined to be coerced and inadmissible. The staff never clearly defined their role as caregivers with a duty to look after the patient's best interests. Had they done so they would have thought of suggesting that she have a lawyer appointed to attend to her legal problems as well as obtaining legal guidance for the staff.

II. ACCESS TO ONE'S OWN MEDICAL RECORDS

Traditionally, medical records were considered the property of the physician or therapist and thus were under his or her full control. As recently as 1975 a woman, who had signed a contract to write a book about her own experiences as a patient, wished to read her psychiatric records. The New York court, at that time, had no difficulty in upholding the hospital's right to refuse such access. This rule has been altered as the vast majority of states have passed right-of-access laws permitting patient access to their own medical records. Generally, however, these laws allow therapists a limited ability to restrict access where there are reasonable grounds for a judgment that access would be harmful to the patient.

III. "DUTIES TO THIRD PARTIES" OR WHEN CAN VICTIMS OF A PATIENT'S VIOLENT BEHAVIOR HOLD THE PSYCHOTHERAPIST ACCOUNTABLE?

Prior to the mid-1970s psychotherapists had little exposure to lawsuits from individuals who were injured by their patients. This generally was limited to cases of (a) harm by a patient to other patients on an inpatient unit, or (b) negligent discharge from inpatient facilities that resulted in harm to families or strangers within a short period of time from the discharge. This was based on a common-law principal that imposed a duty on the person having custody of another to control the conduct of that person. This common law principle is stated in Restatement of the Law, Second, Torts § 320

> one who is required by law to take or who voluntarily takes the custody of another under circumstances such as to deprive the other of his normal power of self-protection or is subject him to association with persons likely to harm him, is under a duty to exercise reasonable care so to control the conduct of third persons as to prevent them from intentionally harming the other or so conducting themselves as to create an unreasonable risk of harm to him, if the actor

1. Knows or has reason to know that he has the ability to control the conduct of the third persons, and
2. Knows or should know of the necessity and opportunity for exercising such control.

As written this would not seem to apply to outpatients in psychotherapy.

A. The Tarasoff Case

In 1969 a case arose in California that substantially expanded the duty of care for psychotherapists. The facts are interesting, and although a jury (because of a settlement prior to trial) never heard the case, it has become a landmark case for psychotherapists. Prosenit Poddar was a 25-year-old Bengalese Indian student at the University of California in Berkeley when he murdered another student, 19-year-old Tatiana Tarasoff. Why he killed this young woman he "loved," but barely knew, gradually emerged. Poddar had risen with amazing success through the Indian educational system. In the 1960s he was one of a small number of

Indian students chosen because of his intellectual abilities to pursue graduate-level study in United States in the field of electronics and naval architecture. He grew up in a tiny village in a remote area of India. His upbrining was so the distant from that of Western society that when he first attended the University in India, his friend Farrokgh Mistree had to teach him how to eat with a knife, fork, and spoon and had to explain plates to him. He was a member of the lowest caste in India, the so-called untouchables. During his first year in the United States he did quite well academically. His friend Mistree then joined him in the states but was able to adapt much more quickly to U.S. culture. In the fall of 1968, during his second year, Poddar met Tatiana Tarasoff at an International Students' Organization folk dance. She talked, danced, and flirted with him. She told him of her background, being born in Shanghai of Russian parents, moving to Brazil and then the United States. She was studying languages at a local college and liked to practice at the International House where Poddar was living. She was outgoing and friendly with many of the foreign students but gradually Poddar's interest in her increased, and he told his friend Mistree of his powerful attraction. He did not understand how her behavior, that seemed more than friendly to him, was compatible with spending time with other male students. His friend explained that he thought her interest was genuine but probably only casual.

At a New Years Eve party, he was alone with her in an elevator. It was a festive occasion, and people had been drinking. Impulsively she kissed him for the New Year. He was stunned, as he had never had physical contact with a woman other than his relatives. He almost immediately fled to tell his friend of the new development. In the months that followed he became increasingly upset by her inconsistent behavior. He installed microphones in his room to record their conversations both on the phone and in person. His friend suggested that he end the relationship because it was interfering with his work. He did so, but a month later she called and said she missed him. Within a month he was again uncertain, and in an effort to clarify the situation, he proposed marriage. She did not accept but also did not clearly refuse. Shortly afterward he again confided to his friend that Tatiana's friends were now laughing at him. "Even you, Mistree," he said, "laugh at my state. But I am like an animal, I could do anything, I could kill her. If I killed her, what would you do?" He began to stay in his room for days. He told fellow students that he would like to blow up the house where she lived with her brother and parents. They persuaded him that it was not possible but did not say anything to warn anyone or call the police.

In June, Tatiana returned to Brazil for the summer, but nothing changed for Poddar. His friend suggested that he see a doctor, set up the appointment, and accompanied him. After the initial interview the psychiatrist placed him on antipsychotic medication and set up weekly appointments with a psychologist. During the summer months Poddar became friendly with Tatiana's brother, Alex, spent time with him, and planned to share an apartment with him in the fall. He began to fantasize about rescuing Tatiana from a contrived situation so she would understand the depth of his affection for her. When he told his friend Mistree that he planned to buy a gun to effect this plan, Mistree called the therapist and told him that Poddar planned to stop therapy and buy a gun. The psychologist consulted with the psychiatrist, and they decided that Poddar needed to be hospitalized. Because of peculiarities in California commitment law the psychologist wrote a letter to the University police requesting their assistance in hospitalizing Poddar. Shortly thereafter the Berkeley campus police found Poddar in his new apartment with Alex and interviewed him there. Poddar denied he had a weapon and denied any specific threats although he acknowledged that there had been a difficult relationship between him and the young woman. The police warned him to stay away from her and left without taking any other action. Tatiana's brother Alex was present during interview and knew that the threats were related to his sister but he did not take them seriously and did not report them to his family. When the head of the clinic reviewed the case, he ordered the therapist to destroy the letter to the campus police requesting hospitalization.

Tatiana returned in September, and Poddar overheard her recounting a summer affair to her friends. He began to follow her around. He then purchased a gun, perhaps to carry out his plan of rescuing her from a disaster situation. He consulted with Alex about what would be the best way to approach his sister but Alex recommended that he stay away from her and that it was all over and best forgotten. Poddar insisted that he must talk with her, but Alex told him not to go over to his parent's house, as his father was quite hot tempered. Poddar then made several efforts to see Tatiana at the house. After her mother turned him away, he returned in midafternoon before anyone else came home. As he left his apartment, he slipped a kitchen knife as well as the gun into his pocket as protection against her angry father. When she answered the door he tried to explain his need to talk with her and forced his way past the closing door. Tatiana screamed, pushed him away, and started to run away. He fired at her scream and followed her. He took the knife from his pocket as they plunged together through the kitchen door. Within minutes he dialed the phone number of the Berkeley City Police stating that he thought he had killed someone. Poddar was charged with first-degree murder. He pled insanity and diminished capacity. Although all experts agreed with the diagnosis of paranoid schizophrenia, the jury found Poddar guilty of second-degree murder. He was sent to California state prison. Five years after he had begun serving a sentence, the California Supreme Court issued its decision; overturning the jury verdict on the grounds the trial judge had given inadequate instructions on diminished capacity to the jury. Rather than retry him, a deal was struck. Because he had already served 5 years, if the state would agree to release Poddar from prison; his attorney personally guaranteed that Poddar would return immediately to India and would never come back to the United States.

Alongside the criminal case, *Tarasoff v. Regents of the University of California* also ended with a settlement. Tatiana's parents sued the University of California and the therapists for the wrongful death of Tatiana. They included a complaint that the psychiatrist's failure to warn them or Tatiana of the danger that Poddar posed to the family was a legal cause of action. Because the trial court dismissed the causes of action as groundless it was appealed to the California Supreme Court on their legal adequacy. After the Court rendered its first decision holding that psychotherapists had a duty to warn potential victims of their patient's threats and that the campus police could be found liable for a failure to warn Tanya, a rehearing was requested although such requests are almost never granted, it was in this case. The second decision reaffirmed but modified the original decision. It required therapists to "protect" intended victims, rather than just "warn" them and absolved the police from any liability. Although the Court expressed concern about the confidentially issues raised by psychiatrists and other mental health professionals, they concluded in both decisions "The protective privilege ends when the public peril begins." The major holding of the case was that the therapists could not escape liability on the grounds that Tatiana was not their patient. The Court held:

> When a therapist determines, or pursuant to the standards of his profession should determine, that his patient presents a serious danger of violence to another, he incurs an obligation to use reasonable care to protect the intended victim against such danger. The discharge of this duty may require the therapist to take one or more of various steps, depending upon the nature of the case. Thus it may call for him to warn the intended victim or others likely to apprise the victim of the danger, to notify the police, or to take whatever other steps are reasonably necessary under the circumstances.

Justice Mosk, in a concurring opinion (meaning that he agreed with the holding but not the legal reasoning), agreed that under the limited circumstances of this particular case, Poddar's therapists had a duty to warn Tatiana. Although Mosk believed the therapists' duty had been satisfied by warning the campus police, he considered this a factual matter to be raised by the defense on remand and did not dissent on this basis. He dissented from the majority's use of the term "standards of the profession." What standards? Psychiatric opinions of future violence were inherently unreliable. "The majority's expansion of that rule will take us from the world of reality into the wonderland of clairvoyance."

Justice Clark, in dissent, was concerned about the pressure on psychiatrists to protect themselves.

> Now, confronted by the majority's new duty, the psychiatrist must instantaneously calculate potential violence from each patient on each visit. The difficulties researchers have encountered in accurately predicting violence will be heightened for the practicing psychiatrist dealing for brief periods in his office with heretofore nonviolent patients. And, given the decision not to warn or commit must always be made at the psychiatrist's civil peril, one can expect most doubts will be resolved in favor of the psychiatrist protecting himself."

Because the case settled prior to trial, there was no discussion or expert opinion of what warnings or protective action were possible or appropriate in the above circumstances.

Although California went on to clarify the meaning of the principle in later decisions to cover only identifiable victims, other jurisdictions disagreed and expanded the scope of the decision. The broadest interpretation occurred in 1980 in the case of *Lipari v. Sears Roebuck & Co.* There, a patient fired a shotgun in a crowded nightclub, blinding a woman and killing her husband. There were no advance warnings to his therapists, and he never threatened any specific person. He did make clear that he was unhappy with his treatment. While still in treatment at the V.A. day care center he purchased a shotgun at Sears, but told no one on his treatment team. He terminated treatment 3 weeks later. One month after the termination he entered the nightclub. The Nebraska District Court allowed the plaintiffs to proceed in their lawsuit against the hospital. The court held it was for the jury to decide whether the therapist knew or should have known of the patient's dangerous propensity. It did not matter that the victims were not identifiable. The Court rejected the limitation to identifiable victims and focused on the foreseeability of the act.

A Vermont case extended the liability to situations where only damage to property was involved. In that case a patient informed his master's-level counselor that he intended to burn down another person's barn.

The duty has also expanded in some jurisdictions to the area of a patient's erratic driving. In one case a man diagnosed with paranoid schizophrenia, and with an extensive history of depression, self-mutilation, and noncompliance with neuroleptic regimens, was confined following his excision of his left testicle. One day prior to the expiration of his commitment he was observed driving dangerously on the hospital grounds. His commitment was not renewed, and he was released to outpatient follow-up. He promptly threw away his medication and resumed use of street drugs. Five days later he ran a red light at excessive speed and hit a vehicle, injuring the driver. She filed a suit, charging the state with negligent treatment by failing to recommit him or releasing information, regarding his violation of probation conditions. The court adopted the foreseeability standard from *Lipari* to hold that a psychiatrist has a duty to take reasonable precautions to protect anyone who might foreseeably be injured by the patient's drug-related problems. This line of cases requires therapists to protect victims from their patients' negligent behavior rather than just intentional harmful acts.

An interesting variant occurred in another California case where the question arose as to whether a therapist has to make a warning if the potential victim is already aware of the danger. In *Jablonski v. U.S.* the victim was the defendant's common-law wife, Melissa Kimball. Ms. Kimball was fully aware of her husband's violent tendencies in view of his prior beatings of her and his attempted rape of her mother. His more recent behavior included threatening the mother-in-law again. His psychiatrist recommended a voluntary hospitalization, which he refused. Prior psychiatric records from the V.A. were not obtained that would have revealed homicidal ideations toward his former wife. His wife brought him back for a second visit but the physicians felt that although he was potentially dangerous due to his antisocial personality he was not presently committable. Two days later he attacked and murdered his common-law wife. The victim's daughter claimed the psychiatrists were negligent by failing to warn her mother of her husband's foreseeable danger. The court agreed. "Warning Kimball would have posed no difficulty for the doctors, especially since she twice expressed her fear of Jablonski directly to them. Neither can it be said ... that direct and precise warnings would have had little effect." The reasoning of the Court seemed to be that, even though others had suggested she stay away from him, a warning from a doctor carries greater weight and might have influenced the victim.

Almost all jurisdictions have adopted some form of the *Tarasoff* duty, either through case law or by statute. Some courts have reasoned that this duty to protect third parties should be imposed because of the therapist's control over the patient, while others have taken a modified approach by broadening the therapist's duty to warn all foreseeable victims. Some have limited liability to specific identifiable victims or to a class of identifiable victims (e.g., children). A minority of jurisdictions has declined to recognize the obligation altogether, especially for outpatient therapists (Florida, Virginia, and Texas). The American Psychiatric Association has proposed model legislation to better define the nature of the liability as well as what actions are sufficient to fulfill the duty. They suggest language to include "actual" or "real" threats as well as identifiable victims. They also suggest that hospitalizing the patient or making reasonable attempts to notify the victim and calling the police is sufficient to satisfy the duty. This model statute was adopted in some 22 states with variations in wording.

There were many concerns that this decision would have dire effects on the psychotherapeutic relationship. Some felt that psychotherapists would be deterred from treating potentially violent patients or that patients would be deterred from seeking therapy. Others thought that patients would be less likely to share violent fantasies or that once a warning was issued the therapy would end as in the *Tarasoff* case. Subsequent studies and experience, however, have failed to confirm these fears. Psychotherapists have and should increase their use of consultation in potential *Tarasoff* cases, which is a useful step in planning carefully as well as averting liability.

Tarasoff and subsequent cases have defined and expanded the psychotherapist's obligations to victims of their patient's actions if they are deemed foreseeable. The challenge is how to maintain trust with patients while carefully assessing and evaluating risk of violence to third parties. Therapists must then consider how best to protect potential victims as well as their patients by considering increased contact, medication, hospitalization, warnings, or other protective actions. Problems have arisen when past medical records have not been reviewed or past therapists have not been contacted.

By contrast when patients reveal information about past crimes most confidentiality statutes (except for child abuse reporting) do not permit disclosure by the therapist. Yet therapists, unlike attorneys who hear such information are generally more uncomfortable keeping such information confidential, especially if the crime is serious, and often wish to call law enforcement authorities. They are concerned that patients are using psychotherapy to "get away with a crime." But for an expectation of confidentiality, patients would not disclose such information to therapists. In such circumstances a consultation with an attorney or knowledgeable colleague may be useful in reviewing duties and obligations.

IV. FEDERAL LAW AND REGULATIONS REGARDING CONFIDENTIALITY

Aside from comprehensive regulations regarding treatment of substance abusers in facilities receiving federal funding, the federal government has generally left confidentiality protections of medical information to the states. In 1996, however, Congress passed the Health Insurance Portability and Accountability Act (HIPAA). Concerns about the fact that more and more health care providers and plans are using electronic means of storing and transmitting health information caused Congress to attempt to develop privacy rules and to ask the Department of Health and Human Services (HHS) to provide regulations if there was no congressional action by August 1999. Congress did not act, and regulations were developed by HHS and went into effect in April 2001. Compliance is required by 2003. This Act covers all health care providers who have engaged in at least one standard electronic transaction or providers that use billing services that utilize electronic transactions as well as health plans. The Act distinguishes between consent and authorization. Consent must be obtained to release information for "treatment, payment, and health care operations" (TPO). Consent, in this context, is a general document that gives health care providers, who have a direct treatment relationship with a patient, permission to use and disclose all health information for TPO. Authorization is required for more specific releases of information. An authorization is a more customized document that gives providers permission to use specified protected health information (PHI) for specified purposes, which are generally other than TPO, or to disclose PHI to a third party specified by the individual. Psychotherapy notes have received some special protections if they are kept separate from the rest of the medical record and are for the use of the therapist only. In general, disclosures of information will be limited to the "minimum necessary" for the purpose of the disclosure. This provision does not apply to the disclosure of medical records for treatment purposes because physicians, specialists, and other providers need access to the full record to provide quality care.

States that have more stringent confidentiality protections under local state laws (like those covering mental health, HIV infection, and AIDS information) are not preempted by HIPAA. These confidentiality protections are seen as setting a national "floor" of privacy standards. This law was not designed to resolve disputes between insurers and providers nor prevent subpoenas of records for court-related issues. HHS is beginning to issue "guidances" so that practitioners will be able to understand the regulations and their requirements.

V. BOUNDARY VIOLATIONS: PSYCHOTHERAPIST–PATIENT SEXUAL CONTACT

The boundaries of any relationship define how the parties ought to behave toward each other in their respective roles. In the psychotherapist–patient relationship, these boundaries are derived from professional ethical guidelines, cultural morality, and jurisprudence. Generally, boundaries include agreements relating to scheduled sessions; fee agreements; establishing "treatment goals" that are modified through negotiation; therapy sessions focused entirely on the client; an understanding regarding confidentiality and any limitations; and finally, no sexual contact or even social contact with patients, except when "overlapping [social] circles" render such contact unavoidable. The purpose of these limits is to create an atmosphere of safety and predictability within which the treatment can proceed. These guidelines have evolved from the psychoanalytic method of treatment. They have not been codified or updated to include current modes of treatment especially involving treatment of the seriously and chronically mentally ill in the public sector. This work does involve professionals in their clients' lives especially when they live in supervised housing or are being delivered and administered medications in their homes or apartments.

Many of these patients or clients are also supervised and at times accompanied by staff to aid in shopping for food or clothes as well as helping with money management programs. Many of these behaviors have been deemed unethical when they have occurred in psychoanalytic-type treatment settings. Even within psychotherapeutic approaches, it has not been possible to articulate definitive guidelines, as most clinicians would agree that guidelines should be tailored to the particular requirements of the individual patient.

The fiduciary nature of the physician–patient relationship is fundamental to boundary setting and creates a covenant that controls the imbalance of power to ensure a safe and trusting relationship based on the patient's needs. In essence, the physician guarantees that, within the therapeutic relationship, the patient can feel comfortable revealing intimate personal information without fear of exploitation.

Not all boundary crossings are equivalent to malpractice or substandard care. Many do not harm the patient or threaten the treatment. Helping a patient who has fallen or consoling a patient who has just been informed that a close relative has died are humane responses that should not be discouraged. There are situations where some behaviors may be inappropriate in some contexts but not in others, for example some touching of terminally ill, geriatric patients or HIV-infected patients. Both culture and context are important factors to consider in reviewing behavior.

Any sexual contact, however, has been increasingly viewed as an egregious violation of patient trust. Here, psychotherapists are seen as allowing personal interests to supercede those of the patient in a manner that may cause significant harm.

In cases involving breaches of confidentiality courts have been more willing to look at physicians' ethical guidelines and fiduciary duties, than they have in cases involving physician–patient sexual contact. The courts' inconsistency in applying the ethical standards and fiduciary aspects of the psychotherapist–patient relationship to sexual conduct remains unclear. Judicial unfamiliarity with the medical professions standards may reflect the inconsistent statements made by different professional organizations and the relatively late response of the American Medical Association to develop specific standards.

Like confidentiality standards, the ethical proscriptions against sexual contact between physicians and patients are long standing and were emphasized in the Hippocratic Oath that was codified around 460 BCE: "In every house where I come I will enter only for the good of my patients, keeping myself far from all intentional ill-doing and all seduction, and especially from the pleasures of love with women or with men."

Prior to 1990, the AMA recognized the potential for power abuse in the physician–patient relationships and declared "sexual misconduct" in the practice of medicine to be unethical. However, the code did not define "misconduct" and thus did not clarify what type of sexual conduct was proscribed. Today the code expressly provides that sexual contact that occurs concurrently with the physician–patient relationship constitutes sexual misconduct. Sexual relationships that predate the physician–patient relationship, such as sexual contact with a spouse, are an exception to this general rule. In most other cases the AMA has explained that sexual contact between a physician and patient is almost always detrimental to the patient and is unethical because the physician's self-interest inappropriately becomes part of the professional relationship. Because a fiduciary relationship exists between a patient and a physician, physicians have obligations to act solely for the welfare of patients and refrain from engaging in sexual activity.

The American Psychiatric Association, in its annotations to the AMA Code for psychiatrists much earlier specified the possibility for exploitation of patients (1973–first edition of the Principles of Medical Ethics with "Annotations Especially Applicable to Psychiatry"): "The necessary intensity of the therapeutic relationship may tend to activate sexual and other needs and fantasies on the part of both patient and psychiatrist, while weakening the objectivity necessary for control. Sexual activity with a patient is unethical." This policy was promulgated in the 1970s along with the suggestion that if therapy was ended but the subsequent relationship was exploiting the patient it too was unethical.

Other psychotherapeutic disciplines have similar codes. The ethical code for psychologists states that "Sexual intimacies with clients are unethical." Likewise for social workers, "The social worker should under no circumstances engage in sexual activities with clients." Similarly the ethical code for marriage and family therapists maintains, "Sexual intimacy with clients is prohibited."

In one survey of psychiatrists in the 1980s, 7.1% of male and 3.1% of female psychiatrists admitted sexual contact with patients. In three surveys of psychologists, between 1977 and 1986, 12.1% of male psychologists and 2.6% of female psychologists reported sexual contact with patients. There are several indications that the incidence of sexual contact may be higher than admitted by therapists. For example, there were low return rates in some of the surveys, and some states have felony criminal penalties for such behavior. In one study, 63% of psychiatrists surveyed reported treating at least one patient who had experienced sexual contact with another physician. In another study, 50% of psychologists reported treating at least one patient who had been sexually involved with a previous therapist.

Indeed, between 1976 and 1986, sexual misconduct was the most frequent cause of lawsuits against psychologists insured under American Psychological Association policies, accounting for 44.8% of all moneys ($7,019,165.00) paid in claims. There is nothing to suggest that the incidence among the different mental health professionals differs greatly. In response to similar concerns, the American Psychiatric Association extended the prohibition from current patients to both current and former patients in 1993.

Problems abound in the implementation of remedies for victims of such misconduct and unethical behavior. There are now generally four avenues of redress and complaints can be filed simultaneously:

1. Traditional malpractice claim
2. Complaint to the state medical or professional licensing board
3. Criminal complaint
4. Ethical complaint to the professional association

A. Traditional Malpractice Claim

Health care professionals—including dentists, gynecologists, physicians, psychiatrists, psychologists, therapists, and medical technicians—spend millions of dollars purchasing medical-malpractice insurance from state, regional, and national liability insurers. For example, the St. Paul Fire & Marine Insurance Company, the largest medical-liability company in the nation, sells and renews thousands of medical-malpractice policies each year. The language appearing in St. Paul's medical-liability contracts is very similar to that appearing in legal-malpractice policies. Typically, the coverage provision states: "This agreement provides protection against professional liability claims which might be brought against you in your practice as a physician or surgeon. ... Your professional liability protection covers you for damages resulting from ... your providing or withholding of professional services."

For at least 30 years, St. Paul—as well as those professionals who were insured—has asked state and federal courts to decide whether St. Paul must defend professionals who allegedly seduced, battered, sexually assaulted, or molested their patients. As expected, St. Paul's defense has been consistent: These intentional injuries do not "arise out of" or "result from rendering professional services." The medical-liability carrier, however, has not prevailed in every case, even though the third-party patients' allegations involved allegedly intentional acts excluded by St. Paul's insurance contracts. State courts have either refused, or failed to employ, various legal doctrines to help determine whether "deviant" physicians and medical technicians are "rendering professional services." Instead, these tribunals have permitted some generalized notion of public policy to influence whether some insurers must defend their insureds in cases involving sexual assault.

In one early case in 1977, *Hartogs v. Employer Mutual Liability Insurance Company*, Dr. Hartogs was a practicing psychiatrist. Under the guise of medical treatment, Dr. Hartogs administered "fornication therapy" to cure his patient's lesbianism. The patient received judgment for $15,000.00 and Dr. Hartogs's insurer refused to pay the judgment on the grounds that the treatment did not constitute medical malpractice. They argued that sexual relations could not be considered a medical treatment. Dr. Hartogs brought an action against the insurer to recover his costs and expenses in defending the action, as well as the expenses incurred by him when he filed for bankruptcy to protect his property. As part of his argument for compensation, Dr. Hartogs noted that the jury had specifically found medical malpractice.

The court ruled that the insurer was not obligated to indemnify Dr. Hartogs for two reasons. First, the court held that a distinction should be drawn between medical malpractice in the mind of the patient, and medical malpractice in the mind of the doctor. The patient believed at the time that appropriate medical therapy was being administered. On the other hand, the doctor administering this treatment knew at all times that what he was doing was in no way pursuant to the doctor–patient relationship. As such, as between Dr. Hartogs and his insurer, his actions could not constitute medical malpractice.

Second, as a matter of public policy, the court would not allow itself to be used to enforce illicit or immoral or unconscionable purposes. The court held that to allow judgment in this type of case would be to indemnify immorality and pay the expenses of prurience. The Court did not deal with the question of how the plaintiff would collect judgment given that Dr. Hartogs had filed for bankruptcy.

On the other side of the same question, the issue of protecting the victim was focused on by the 1982 Michigan decision, *Vigilant Insurance Company v. Kambly*. In that case, Vigilant Insurance Company filed an action for relief, absolving it from liability under a professional insurance policy issued to a psychiatrist. The court's decision denied relief. In that case, Dr. Kambly had induced his patient to engage in sexual intercourse under the guise of treatment. In its judgment, the court stated that there was no reason for distinguishing between this type of malpractice and others. The court noted that in each situation, the essence of the claim is the doctor's departure from proper standards of medical practice. In addition, the court found that allowing insurance coverage would benefit the patient, not the physician. Therefore, Dr. Kambly would not unjustly benefit from the determination that coverage existed.

The court further held that it was unlikely that the insured was induced to engage in unlawful conduct by relying on the insurability of any claims. Therefore, allowing insurance coverage would not induce future similar unlawful conduct by practitioners. In addition, the policy was not obtained in contemplation of a violation of the law. Finally, the court noted that there was a great public interest in protecting the interests of the injured party.

A number of insurers in the United States provide funding for a defense in sexual abuse cases but do not pay a judgment on a finding of liability. There is a problem throughout the lawsuit, however, that any settlement negotiations are complicated and restricted by the fact that the organization providing the defense is not ultimately responsible for paying the judgment. Many policies now either exclude or place liability limits (e.g., $25,000) on policies for behavior or malpractice that stems from sexual interest or contacts.

The ethical guidelines in this area have also become the legal standard of care. Nonetheless, posttermination contacts continue to evoke much discussion in the clinical literature. Many allegations of abuse are based on allegations that transference continues after therapy ends. Transference, however, remains a complicated construct with multiple definitions. Freud initially used the concept to explain some of the irrational behavior of patients in treatment by the idea that feelings and other aspects of earlier relationships were "transferred" to the analyst who came to represent, often unconsciously, figures from the patient's past. Some therapists and treatment modalities do not accept or use the concept, while others believe that it exists in all therapies. Some psychoanalysts believe transference never ends and therefore taints any consent for posttermination relationships. This has led to conclusions that both former patients and patients are not capable of providing legally informed consent, even in the absence of a specific evaluation. A popular view of transference is that it refers to all feelings that arise between a patient and therapist. Others extend the concept to include all relationships, for example, a young woman falling in love with an older man. Given this uncertainty, it is not surprising that courts have frequently misunderstood the concept. Even for those adopting a transference paradigm, there is a need to assess what role it may be playing. Patients continue to make many decisions while in treatment and posttreatment, and there is no literature to support global incapacity to do so just as a result of being in treatment.

B. Complaint to State Licensing Board

Another option available to victims is to file a complaint with the state licensing board regulating the offending therapist. Virtually all jurisdictions have licensure laws and codes of ethics that prohibit therapist–patient sexual contact and specify that such contact is grounds for discipline. The primary purpose of licensure laws is to protect the public from incompetent and unscrupulous therapists. As a general rule, state licensing boards are responsible for establishing and enforcing codes of ethics for the professions they regulate. In addition, most licensing statutes give the boards authority to refuse to grant a license to a therapist who has committed sexual misconduct or been found guilty of a felony involving moral turpitude. Furthermore, licensing boards also have authority to investigate ethical complaints and impose disciplinary sanctions.

Therapists accused of sexual misconduct are entitled to a hearing before disciplinary action is taken. Most complaints, however, are resolved without hearings through the use of negotiated settlements. If the complaint is not settled informally, and an administrative hearing becomes necessary, the burden of proof is low, a preponderance of the evidence (the standard of proof required in civil cases), and the rules of evidence are relaxed. In addition, although licensing board hearings are not as private and confidential as those of professional associations, they do provide less public exposure than civil trials.

From the victim's perspective, licensing board regulation has several positive aspects. First, most licensing boards do not impose a statute of limitations on the filing of complaints. In many cases, the statute of limitations is 2 to 3 years for a civil malpractice action. Therefore, disciplinary action by the licensing board may be the victim's only available remedy. Second, state licensing boards have a range of sanctions available to them. Most boards are authorized to discipline by warning, reprimand, censure, or probation. They may also suspend or revoke a license to practice.

C. Criminal Complaints

Several factors have led to the enactment of specific statutes criminalizing psychotherapist sexual misconduct. First, although some mental health professionals feel that the intensity of the therapist–patient relationship impairs the patient's ability to consent to a sexual relationship with the therapist, courts have been reluctant to recognize this in criminal cases making it impossible to prosecute offending therapists under traditional sexual assault statutes. The second and more significant factor has been the public outcry and demand for specific legislation. In 1984, Wisconsin became the first state to enact a specific statute criminalizing psychotherapist sexual misconduct. At least 15 states have enacted some form of criminal penalty for psychotherapist or physician sexual misconduct, and most of these statutes have withstood constitutional challenges. The majority of these statutes impose criminal sanctions on therapists engaging in sexual contact while performing psychotherapy, defining those terms broadly enough to bring physicians within the scope of the statutes. Ten of the 15 statutes cover sexual contact both within and outside actual treatment sessions during an ongoing professional relationship. Two statutes apply to sexual contact outside the treatment setting only if the patient is emotionally dependent on the therapist, and two apply only to contact during therapy sessions or medical treatment or examination. All but one of the statutes applies a strict liability standard, expressly excluding consent as an affirmative defense.

Some private interest groups have argued that consent should not be eliminated as a defense in such cases because to do so "treats any person who consults a mental health professional as a child." Eliminating consent as a defense, however, does not treat the patient as a child but merely recognizes that "competent individuals may be unduly influenced in special relationships." Furthermore, as one commentator indicates, "patient consent to sex ... is not the issue." Rather, "it is the breach of fiduciary trust by the therapist who engages the patient in sex that is the appropriate focus of wrongdoing."

Proponents of criminalization point to its deterrent and retributive value, its function as an alternative form of redress for patients inadequately served by civil or disciplinary avenues, and its potential for raising money via fines for both victim treatment and prevention programs. In reality, however, very few people file charges under these criminal statutes, suggesting that the disadvantages of criminal controls far outweigh the advantages.

Furthermore, prosecution is completely dependent on the victim's willingness to come forward, and victims of physician sexual misconduct will be hesitant given the fact that a criminal conviction generally yields no monetary award, and the prosecutor, rather than the victim's own legal advocate, maintains control over the case. In addition, the threat of criminal sanctions may have a chilling effect on both colleague reports and patient complaints, masking the significance of the problem and limiting the effectiveness of other controls. Moreover most malpractice insurance coverage excludes coverage for criminal acts, eliminating access to civil damages to cover the costs of necessary subsequent treatment.

Criminalization may, indeed, make it more difficult for the victim to prevail or negotiate settlements in civil suits, in that admissions will be less likely, and therapist assertions of Fifth Amendment rights may delay discovery in civil and administrative actions, pending completion of the criminal trial. In addition, criminal conviction offers little or no opportunity for rehabilitation. Finally, prosecutors face the higher reasonable doubt burden of proof and the limitations of strict rules of evidence. Given these barriers to prosecution, it is clear that criminal statutes, like civil actions, are inadequate in and of themselves to deal effectively with the problem of physician sexual misconduct.

D. Ethics Complaints to the Professional Association

Although many professional groups use professional licensing boards to adjudicate ethical violations, some professional organizations like the American Psychiatric Association (and the American Psychological Association and National Association of Social Workers) have procedures to adjudicate ethical complaints directly. If a complaint of unethical conduct against a member is sustained, that person can receive sanctions ranging from reprimand to expulsion from the association. A formal complaint has to be made in writing, and the ethics committee of the local district branch has the ability to appoint an ad hoc investigating committee to conduct an investigation and to render a decision. Due process requires that the accused member will be notified of a hearing by certified mail at least 30 days in advance. The notice includes the day, time, and place of the hearing. In addition, it includes a list of witnesses expected to testify, notification of the member's right to representation by legal counsel (or another individual of the member's choice), as well as notification of the member's right to appeal any adverse decision to the ABA Ethics Appeals Board. In addition to sanctions the district branch may also, but is not required to, impose certain conditions such as educational or supervisory requirements on a suspended member.

Patients are sometimes reluctant to file complaints, because they do not want any publicity of the details of their lives to become fodder for the press. But after years of what was termed a "conspiracy of silence," several factors have changed the dynamics of reporting. First, as a result of both patient and women's rights movements, patients feel less protective of and less intimidated by physicians and other professionals and are more willing to speak out. Increased awareness of sexual abuse, child abuse, date rape, clergy abuse, and therapist–patient exploitation has resulted in an increased focus on the healing professions. Professional organizations have also spoken out against these transgressions, developed training programs, and treatment programs for impaired professionals.

This section highlights a few of the major themes that have come under scrutiny over the past few decades. The factors that influence the practice of mental health professionals are an algorithm of a professional's ethical, moral, and legal duties to provide competent care to patients. These duties are modified over time to reflect changing science, practice, and legal regulations as promulgated by courts, legislatures, professional organizations, and agencies that regulate professional practice. The mental health professional must learn to analyze clinical situations so as to know how to balance sometimes conflicting values and rules so that proper care can be rendered to a patient.

See Also the Following Articles

Bioethics ■ Confidentiality ■ Documentation ■ Economic and Policy Issues ■ Education: Curriculum for Psychotherapy ■ History of Psychotherapy ■ Informed Consent ■ Multicultural Therapy ■ Supervision in Psychotherapy ■ Working Alliance

Further Reading

Developments in the law – Privileged Communications. (1985). *Harvard Law Review, 98,* 1450–1454.

45 CFR Parts 160 and 164, Federal Register: December 28, 2000, volume 65, Number 250, pp. 82461–82829, RIN: 0991-AB08.

Jaffee v. Redmond, 518 U.S. 1, 135 L. Ed. 2d 337, 116 S. Ct. 1923 (1996).

Gutheil, T. G. & Gabbard, G. O. (1993). The concept of boundaries in clinical practice: Theoretical and risk-management dimensions. *American Journal of Psychiatry, 150,* 188.

Jorgenson, L., Randles, R., & Strasberger, L. (1991). The furor over psychotherapist-patient sexual contact: New solutions to an old problem. *William & Mary Law Review, 32,* 645.

Tarasoff v. Regents of the University of California, 17 Cal. 3d 425, 442, 131 Cal. Rptr. 14, 551 P.2d 334 (1976).

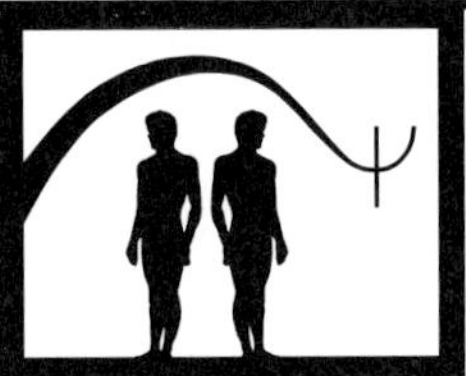

Logotherapy

Paul T. P. Wong

Trinity Western University, British Columbia, Canada

GLOSSARY

dereflection A logotherapeutic technique to redirect clients' attention away from their problems to more positive aspects of their lives. It is built on the human capacity for self-distancing and self-transcendence.

existential analysis Developed by Viktor Frankl, it refers to therapeutic techniques that bring the hidden meaning of existence into consciousness.

logotherapy Developed by Viktor Frankl, it refers to a spiritually, existentially oriented therapy that seeks to achieve healing and health through meaning.

meaning-centered counseling and therapy Developed by Paul T. P. Wong, it focuses on the transformation of cognitive meanings as well as life's purposes. It integrates both cognitive-behavioral and narrative processes.

paradoxical intention A logotherapeutic technique to encourage the patient to do or wish to happen what the patient fears. It is built on the human capacity for self-detachment.

I. INTRODUCTION

This article will present an overview of Viktor Frankl's (1905–1997) logotherapy and existential analysis. Known as the "Third Viennese School of Psychotherapy," logotherapy was developed in the 1930s because of Frankl's dissatisfaction with both Freud and Adler.

Frankl accepts Sigmund Freud's concept of unconsciousness but considers the will to meaning as more fundamental than the will to pleasure. Existential analysis is designed to bring to consciousness the "hidden" meaning or spiritual dimension of the client.

Frankl received training in individual psychology from Adler. He differs from Adler because he focuses on the will to meaning, while Adler emphasizes social interest and the will to power. However, some of the basic concepts of logotherapy, such as freedom and responsibility, bear the imprint of Adler's influence.

A major difference between logotherapy and psychoanalysis is that both Freud and Adler focus on the past, while logotherapy focuses rather on the future—on the meanings to be fulfilled.

Although logotherapy and existential analysis tend to be used interchangeably or together as a single label, it may be helpful to recognize the following difference between these two terms:

Logotherapy means therapy through meaning, and it refers to Frankl's spiritually oriented approach to psychotherapy. *Existential analysis*, on the other hand, refers to the analytical therapeutic process involved in addressing the patient's spiritual, existential needs. To the extent that logotherapy makes the patient aware of the hidden meaning of existence, it is an analytical process.

Logotherapy is a distinct branch of existential–humanistic school psychotherapy, because of its focus on the human spirit and "the meaning of human existence as well as on man's search for such a meaning." What sets Frankl apart from North America's existential psychotherapy is his unconditional affirmation of life's meaning. The main objective of logotherapy was to facilitate clients' quest for meaning and empower them to live meaningfully, responsibly, regardless of their life circumstances.

Logotherapy was put to severe test in a very personal way between 1942 and 1945, when Frankl was committed to Nazi concentration camps. His experience in these camps was recorded in his best-selling book *Man's Search for Meaning*. His personal triumph over unimaginable trauma has been the most compelling testimony to logotherapy. There are no other psychotherapists whose life and work are as inseperable as Frankl's. He is logotherapy, and vice versa.

II. THE SPIRITUAL DIMENSION

It is not possible to practice logotherapy without understanding the human spirit or the spiritual dimension of human existence. According to Frankl's dimensional ontology, human beings exist in three dimensions—somatic, mental, and spiritual. Spirituality is the uniquely human dimension. However, these different dimensions must be understood in their totality because a person is a unity in complexity.

A. The Defiant Power of the Human Spirit

One of the prepositions of logotherapy is that the human spirit is our healthy core. The human spirit may be blocked by biological or psychological sickness, but it will remain intact. The human spirit does not get sick, even when the psychobiological organism is injured.

According to Frankl, part of the human spirit is unconscious. When the human spirit is blocked or repressed, one experiences existential vacuum or neurosis. Existential analysis seeks to remove the block and brings to consciousness the will to meaning.

According to Joseph Fabry, the noetic dimension of the human spirit is the "medicine chest" of logotherapy; it contains love, the will to meaning, purpose, creativity, conscience, the capacity for choice, responsibility, sense of humor, and so forth.

The defiant power of the human spirit refers to people's capacity to tap into the spiritual part of the self and rise about the negative effects of situations, illness or the past. Paul T. P. Wong proposes that it may be more helpful for scientific and therapeutic purposes to conceptualize the human spirit as inner resources, which can come to one's aid in coping with life stress.

B. Logotherapy and Religion

Frankl differentiates between spirit, spirituality, and religion. Spirit refers to one of the dimensions of humanity. Spirituality is manifest in a person's quest for meaning. Religion encompasses the ultimate meaning, super meaning, as well as God. He clearly recognizes the importance of religion but is reluctant to be considered religious. He equates authentic religion with deep spirituality.

In an interview with Matthew Scully in 1995, when Frankl was already 90, he seemed to be more explicit about the important role of religion and faith in logotherapy. Frankl said:

> I have come to define religion as an expression, a manifestation, of not only man's will to meaning, but of man's longing for ultimate meaning, that is to say a meaning that is so comprehensive that it is no longer comprehensible ... But it becomes a matter of believing rather than thinking, of faith rather than intellect. The positing of a super-meaning that evades mere rational grasp is one of the main tenets of logotherapy, after all. And a religious person may identify Supermeaning as something paralleling a Superbeing, and this Superbeing we would call God.

III. THE MEANING OF MEANING

The Greek word *logos* represents the word, the will of God, the controlling principles of the universe, or meaning. Dr. Frankl translates logos as meaning. Therefore, logotherapy means healing and health through meaning. But what is meaning?

A. Specific versus Ultimate Meaning

According to Frankl, there are two levels of meaning: (a) the present meaning, or meaning of the moment, and (b) the ultimate meaning or super-meaning. Dr. Frankl believes that it is more productive to address specific meaning of the moment, of the situation, rather than talking about meaning of life in general, because ultimate meanings exist in the supra-human dimension, which is "hidden" from us. He cautions against addressing ultimate meanings in therapy, unless the client is openly religious.

Each individual must discover the specific meanings of the moment. Only the individual knows the right meaning specific to the moment. The therapist can also facilitate the quest and guide the client to those areas in which meanings can be found.

B. Meaning versus Value

In his earlier writings, Frankl often used meaning and value interchangeable. Fabry has clarified the difference between meaning and value:

> We create unique relationships and accept unique tasks, face unique sufferings, experience unique guilt feelings and die a unique death. The search for meaning is highly personal and distinct. But millions of people have gone through situations that were similar enough so they could react in a similar way. They found what was meaningful in standard situations. They found universal meanings, which is the way Frankl defines values: "meaning universals."

Therefore, values are abstract meanings based on the meaning experiences of many, many individuals. Frankl believes that these values can guide our search for meaning and simplify decision making. For example, life can be made meaningful if we realize three categories of values—experiential, creative and attitudinal.

Traditional values are the examples of the accumulation of meaning experiences of many individuals over a long period of time. However, these values are threatened by modernization. Frankl believes that "Even if all universal values disappeared, life would remain meaningful, since the unique meanings remain untouched by the loss of traditions."

Implicit in all his writings, Frankl gives the impression that values, like Kant's categorical imperatives, are somehow universal, from which specific meanings flow. Thus, every experience of meaning involves the realization of some values. But these values may lie latent and need to be awakened or cultivated through existential analysis. This kind of reasoning may explain why Frankl insists: "The meaning of our existence is not invented by ourselves, but rather detected."

IV. BASIC TENETS

The logotherapeutic credo consists of freedom of will, will to meaning, and the meaning of life. These are the cornerstones of logotherapy and existential analysis.

A. Freedom of Will

Frankl realizes that "Human freedom is finite freedom. Man is not free from conditions. But he is free to take a stand in regard to them. The conditions do not completely condition him." Although our existence is influenced by instincts, inherited disposition, and environment, an area of freedom is always available to us. "Everything can be taken from a man, but ... the last of the human freedoms—to choose one's attitude in any a given set of circumstances, to choose one's own way." Therefore, we always have the freedom to take a stand toward the restrictive conditions and transcend our fate.

Freedom of will is possible because of the human capacity for self-distancing or self-detachment: "By virtue of this capacity man is capable of detaching himself not only from a situation, but also from himself. He is capable of choosing his attitude toward himself."

B. Responsibility and Responsibleness

With freedom comes responsibility. Joseph Fabry once said responsibility without freedom is tyranny, and freedom without responsibility leads to anarchy, which can lead to "boredom, anxiety, and neurosis." Frankl points out that we are responsible not only to something but also to Someone, not only to the task, but to the Taskmaster.

Frankl differentiatess between responsibility and responsibleness. The former comes from possessing the freedom of will. The later refers to exercising our freedom to make the right decisions in meeting the demands of each situation. "Existential analysis aims at nothing more and nothing less than leading men to consciousness of their responsibility."

C. Will to Meaning

Frankl considers the will to meaning as "the basic striving of man to find and meaning and purpose." The will to meaning is possible because of the human capacity to transcend immediate circumstances. "Being human is being always directed, and pointing to, something or someone other than oneself: to a meaning to fulfil or another human being to encounter, a cause to serve or a person to love."

Self-transcendence often makes use of the power of imagination and optimism. Self-transcendence is essential for finding happiness, which is not the end, but the by-product of trying to forget oneself. "Only to the extent to which man fulfils a meaning out there in the world, does he fulfil himself."

D. Meaning of Life

Every meaning is unique to each person, and each one has to individually discover the meaning of each particular situation. The therapist can only challenge and guide the patient to potential areas of meaning: creative, experiential, and attitudinal values.

According to logotherapy, we can discover this meaning in life in three different ways: (1) by creating a work or doing a deed; (2) by experiencing something or encountering someone; and (3) by the attitude we take toward unavoidable suffering.

Attitudinal values are especially important in situations of unavoidable suffering. Frankl claims: "This is why life never ceases to hold meaning, for even a person who is deprived of both creative and experiential values is still challenged by a meaning to fulfil, that is, by the meaning inherent in the right, in an upright way of suffering."

V. EXISTENTIAL FRUSTRATION AND NOOGENIC NEUROSIS

Existential frustration is a universal human experience because the will to meaning can be blocked by external circumstances and internal hindrances. Existential frustration leads to noogenic neurosis or existential vacuum. According to Frankl, "Noogenic neuroses have their origin not in the psychological but rather in the 'noological' (from the Greek noos meaning mind) dimension of human existence." Therefore, logotherapy is uniquely appropriate in dealing with existential neuroses.

Existential vacuum refers to general sense of meaninglessness or emptiness, as evidenced by a state of boredom. It is a widespread phenomenon of the twentieth century, as a result of industrialization, the loss of traditional values, and dehumanization of individuals. People may experience existential vacuum without developing existential neurosis. Many feel that life has no purpose, no challenge, no obligation, and they try to fill their existential vacuum with materials things, pleasure, sex, or power, busy work, but they are misguided. Frankl believes that "The feeling of meaninglessness not only underlies the mass neurotic triad of today, i.e., depression-addiction-aggression, but also may eventuate in what we logotherapists call a 'noogenic neurosis.'"

Suffering is not a necessary condition for meaning, but it tends to trigger the quest for meaning. Frankl has observed that people are willing to endure any suffering, if they are convinced that this suffering has meaning. However, suffering without meaning leads to despair.

Logotherapists do not ask for the reason for suffering, but guide their clients toward the realization of concrete meanings, and choose the right attitudes. Often, logotherapists appeal to their clients to take a heroic stand toward suffering, by suggesting that unavoidable suffering gives them the opportunity to bear witness to the human potential and dignity.

Search for meaning is more likely to be occasioned by three negative facets of human existence: pain, guilt, and death. Pain refers to human suffering, guilt to the awareness of our fallibility, and death to our awareness of the transitoriness of life. These negative experiences make us more aware of our needs for meaning and spiritual aspiration. Neuroses are more likely to originate from our attempt to obscure the reality of pain, guilt, and death as existential facts. Logotherapy provides an answer to the tragic triad through attitudinal values and tragic optimism.

VI. LOGOTHERAPEUTIC TECHNIQUES AND APPLICATIONS

Frankl considers noogenic neurosis as the collective neurosis of contemporary Western society. The goal of logotherapy is to enable patients to discover their unique meanings and consider their own areas of freedom. In cases of psychogenic or individual neurosis, which may be treated by traditional psychotherapy or medication, logotherapy serves as a supplement and helps break the vicious cycles of neurosis.

According to E. Lukas, the four main logotherapeutic techniques are paradoxical intention, dereflection, modification of attitudes, and appealing techniques.

A. Paradoxical Intention

Frankl defines paradoxical intention as follows: "The patient is encouraged to do, or to wish to happen, the very things he fears (the former applying to the phobic patient, the latter to the obsessive-compulsive)."

This technique builds on the human capacity for self-detachment to break the vicious cycle, which traps people in psychogenic neuroses, such as phobia, anxiety, and obsessive—compulsive behaviour. Self-attachment enables to patient to adopt a new attitude, to stand back or laugh at the situation or self. In applying paradoxical intention, the therapist tries "to mobilize and utilize exclusive human capacity for humor."

For the phobic patient, he has a "fearful expectation" that a particular symptom might occur, and his fear creates "anticipatory anxiety, which in turn brings about what the patient fears to happen. Thus "fear of fear" creates a "vicious cycle." The most common reaction to "fear of fear" is "flight from fear," and the phobic pattern is maintained by excessive avoidance. This vicious cycle is broken when "the pathogenic fear is replaced by a paradoxical wish." As a result, the patient no longer avoids situations that create anxiety.

With phobic patient, paradoxical intention typically begins with self-detachment (often after invitation and persuasion). The second step is to ask the patient to develop a new attitude of not fearing but welcoming the symptoms. This typically results in a reduction of symptom, which allows therapist to work toward enhancing meaningful living.

In the case of obsessive–compulsive disorder, the patient fights against the obsessions or compulsions. However, the more he fights against these symptoms, the stronger they become. Again, a vicious cycle is created. To break this vicious cycle, the patient with compulsive hand washing because of fear of infection would be told to tell himself "I can't get enough bacteria, I want to become as dirty as possible."

According to D. Guttmann, paradoxical intention has been used with increasing frequency with good results especially in treating clients who suffer from phobias and obsessive–compulsive disorder.

B. Dereflection

Frankl developed dereflection to counteract hyperintention (trying too hard) and hyperreflection (thinking too hard). Examples of hyperintention include trying very hard to fall asleep, excessively pursuing pleasure, happiness, or power. Addiction is a form of hyperintention.

Hyperreflection involves excessively monitoring one's performance, and becoming very anxious about failure. Hyperreflection may turn everyday minor problem into catastrophes, and small obstacles into insurmountable hurdles.

This technique is built on the human capacity of self-distancing and self-transcendence. The clients are asked to redirect their attention away from their problems to more positive aspects of their lives. For example, instead of worrying about not being able to fall asleep, the client is asked to use the time to read a book or watch TV. Typically, the first step is to help clients to put some distance between themselves and their symptoms. Then, they are invited to use their defiant power of the human spirit to transcend their present conditions and move toward positive activities. This will result in a reduction of symptom.

Joseph Fabry points out that by immersing ourselves in work or by choosing the right attitude, we can transcend not only external conditions but also ourselves. The goal of dereflection is to help clients transcend themselves and move toward creative and experiential values.

C. Modification of Attitudes

It is used for noogenic neuroses, depression, and addiction by promoting the will to meaning. It can also be used in coping with suffering related to circumstances, fate or illness. Generally, the emphasis is on reframing attitudes from negative to positive. For example, the client may be asked: "Is there anything positive about the situation?" or "What freedom is still available to you in this situation?"

D. The Appealing Technique

These three logotherapeutic techniques are more likely to be effective, when the therapist appeals to the client's defiant power of the human spirit. The therapist makes use of the power of suggestion and directly appeals to the client to change for the better, regardless of the client's current circumstances, and physical–emotional condition. The therapist expresses trust in the client's dignity, freedom, responsibility, meaning orientation, and potential for positive change.

Frankl claims that "Logotherapy is neither teaching nor preaching. It is far removed from logical reasoning as it is from moral exhortation." However, appealing often involves exhortation on the value of taking a heroic stand against suffering. For example, a nurse suffered from an inoperable tumor and experienced despair because of her incapacity to work. Frankl tried to appeal to her sense of pride and moral obligation to her patients:

> I tried to explain to her that to work eight or ten hours per day is no great thing—many people can do that But to be as eager to work as, and so incapable of work, and yet not be despair—that would be as achievement few could attain. And then I asked her: "Are you not being unfair to all those sick people to whom you have dedicated your life; are you not being unfair to act now as if the life of an invalid were without meaning? If you behave as if the meaning of our life consisted in being able to work so many hours a day, you take away from all sick people the right to live and the justification for their existence.

E. The Socratic Dialogue

In Socratic dialogue, the therapist facilitates the client's discovery of meaning, freedom, and responsibility by challenging and questioning. The dialogue may begin with a struggle between client and therapist but should never become negative.

According to Paul Welter: "Socratic questions need to be asked that stretch the thinking of the client. This requires careful listening to find the circumference of the client's thought." Another consideration is that counsellors need to know the moment when silence is more curative. Often silence occurs when the clients reflect on the deeper meanings of words from the counsellors.

F. Family Logotherapy

J. Lantz has applied logotherapy to help the client family discover the meaning of opportunities within the family through social skills training, Socratic questioning, and existential reflection. According to E. Lukas, meaning-centered family therapy helps the family focus on meaningful goals rather than the obstacles; consequently, family members learn to overcome the obstacles to pursue meaningful goals.

G. The Therapist–Client Relationship in Logotherapy

Frankl tends to emphasize partnership between therapist and client in the quest for meaning. According to Lantz, logotherapeutic practice is based on the following assumptions: (a) commitment to authentic communication by the therapist, (b) the therapists' communication of essential humanness, and c) the therapist's ultimate concern being similar to that of the clients.

VII. RECENT DEVELOPMENTS

In the past 15 years, Dr. Frankl's classic logotherapy has been elaborated and extended by Alfried Langle and the International Association of Logotherapy and Existential Analysis *(Gesellschaft fur Logotherapie und Existenzanalyse)*. This Viennese society (GLE-Wien) is parallel to Viktor-Frankl-Institut–Scientific Society for Logothrapy and Existential Analysis *(Wissenschaftliche fur Logotherapie und Existenzanalyse)*, also in Vienna.

According to A. Langle, existential analysis is now a full-fledged psychotherapeutic method, of which Dr. Frankl's logotherapy is considered its subsidiary branch. Langle has applied existential analysis to cases of psychosocial, psychosomatic, and psychogenic disturbances.

Langle recognizes four fundamental preconditions for meaningful existence: (a) accept the situation, (b) find some positive value in the situation, (c) respond according to one's own conscience, and (d) recognize the specific demands of the situation.

He also postulates four types of fundamental human motivations:

1. The question of existence: I am, but can I become a "whole" person? Do I have the necessary space, support, and protection?
2. The question of life: I am alive, but do I enjoy it? Do I find it fulfilling? Do I experience a sense of abundance, love, and realization of values?
3. The question of the person: I am myself, but am I free to be myself? Do I experience validation, respect, and recognization of my own worth?
4. The question of existential meaning: I am here, but for what purpose, for what good?

Langle has developed additional methods, such as the biographical method of using phenomenological analysis to overcome unresolved past issues and the project analysis to elucidate areas that have proved to be a hindrance to one's life.

Joseph Fabry was largely responsible for introducing logotherapy to North America. Under his guidance and encouragement, Paul T. P. Wong has developed the integrative meaning-centred conselling and therapy (MCCT). It focuses on both the transformation of cognitive meanings as well as the discovery of new purposes in life. As an integrative existential therapy, it incorporates cognitive-behavioral interventions and narrative therapy with logotherapy.

See Also the Following Articles

Alderian Psychotherapy ■ Biblical Behavior Modification ■ Existential Psychotherapy ■ Humanistic Psychotherapy ■ Paradoxical Intention

Further Reading

Fabry, J. (1994). *The pursuit of meaning* (new rev. ed.). Abilene, TX: Institute of Logotherapy Press.

Frankl, V. E. (1984). *Man's search for meaning* (rev. and updated). New York: Washington Square Press/Pocket Books.

Frankl, V. E. (1986). *The doctor and the soul: From psychotherapy to logotherapy* (Rev. and expanded). New York: Vintage Books.

Guttmann, D. (1996). *Logotherapy for the helping professional: Meaningful social work*. New York: Springer.

Langle, A. (2000). Existential analysis. Ubersetzung von 1999 Fundamenta Psychiatrica: EA – die Zustimmung zum Leben finden.

Lantz, J. (1996). Stages and treatment activities in family logotherapy. *The International Forum for Logotherapy, 19*, 20–22.

Lukas, E. (1984). *Meaningful living*. New York: Grove Press.

Lukas, E. (1991). Meaning-centered family therapy. *The International Forum for Logotherapy, 14*, 67–74.

Welter, P. (1987). *Counseling and the search for meaning*. Waco, TX: Word Books.

Wong, P. T. P. (1999). Towards an integrative model of meaning-centered counselling and therapy. *The International Forum for Logotherapy, 22*, 47–55.

Manualized Behavior Therapy

Michael J. Zvolensky
University of Vermont

Georg H. Eifert
University of Hawaii

GLOSSARY

behavior therapy Application of interventions based on an understanding of learning principles.

effectiveness The degree to which a treatment produces positive outcomes in the context in which treatment most often is sought (i.e., "real world").

efficacy Demonstrations that an intervention improves psychological status in well-controlled, experimental studies.

functional analysis of behavior Isolation of proximate, contextual causes of problematic behavior and the tailoring of therapy protocols to reverse these causes once identified.

multicomponent treatment strategies Therapies that contain treatment elements that are based on behavioral and cognitive-affective processes.

treatment integrity Degree to which the implementation of a specific treatment matches the way it was conceptualized and intended to be employed.

treatment manuals Written materials that identify key concepts, procedures, and tactics for the delivery of a clinical intervention.

I. DESCRIPTION OF MANUALIZED BEHAVIOR THERAPY

A. Treatment Manual Description

In general, treatment manuals for psychological disorders are written materials that identify key concepts, procedures, and tactics for the delivery of a clinical intervention. Accordingly, treatment manuals are designed to help modify the variables and processes believed to produce, maintain, or increase the magnitude or frequency of problematic behavior. As is typical of treatment methods in general, there is considerable diversity in regard to the level of specification in a particular manualized therapy, which is contingent, at least in part, on the treatment strategy being employed. Despite this diversity, all manualized therapies provide rules and statements pertaining to how therapists are to prepare for treatment, describe what they should do during the session itself, and characterize how the process of therapy is to proceed over time. In the case of behavior therapy, which reflects the application of interventions largely based on an understanding of psychological learning principles, manuals serve to characterize the treatment process for persons with an identified psychological disorder.

At least initially, the primary aim of developing and implementing manualized behavior therapies was to improve the evaluation of particular treatment strategies and entire treatment programs. Within this context, manuals served to specify (in abbreviated form) the nature of the treatment, and articulate (in detail) how it was to be delivered. In this way, researchers would have available a precise and standardized clinical methodology that could easily be used in the evaluation of a particular treatment's efficacy. In addition, manuals provided researchers with the opportunity to standardize training in a specific treatment to increase the chance that the therapy would be delivered in the manner designated by and consistent with the theoretical underpinnings of the approach. Today, the development and utilization of manualized behavior therapies reflect an important breakthrough in the larger history of developing and evaluating psychosocial treatments for behavior disorders.

B. Reasons for Treatment Manuals in Mental Health Work

With the advantage of hindsight, it is quite easy to identify a number of key reasons why manualized therapies originally emerged in the mid to late 1970s. Prior to having standardized treatment methods and procedures, researchers often were left "in the dark" in regard to how a particular treatment was delivered. In the best-case scenario, questions about the effects of a clinical trial could be directed at how well a particular treatment was delivered. In the worst-case scenario, it was possible to question whether a particular treatment was really delivered at all, or at least whether the key components of that therapy were implemented. Other types of common concerns were aimed at such issues as whether the therapy under investigation was delivered in a consistent fashion across study participants. Still other concerns were aimed at how well the results could be replicated across independent research sites. All the questions, and others similar to them, essentially reflect questions of treatment integrity. A prerequisite for adequately addressing questions of treatment integrity from a scientific standpoint is to have a methodology that identifies the treatment of interest, and guides one in a step-by-step manner in regard to how it should be delivered.

In more recent years, the development and utilization of manualized behavior therapies have exceeded the boundaries of research circles. Indeed, the use of manuals in clinical contexts with no clear research objectives has been spurred on by health care policy changes demanding that psychological services follow guidelines for relatively brief treatments that have an empirical basis for outcome. Thus, despite the fact that manuals have helped to improve the quality of large-scale clinical trials in accordance with their original intended purpose, it is perhaps not surprising that they increasingly have been the subject of controversy and intense debate. In fact, the use of treatment manuals has called attention to clinical issues that strike at the very heart of what treatment should be considered clinically useful and in what contexts it should be implemented (e.g., controlled or real world settings).

II. THEORETICAL BASES OF MANUALIZED BEHAVIOR THERAPY

A. General History

At the time of inception of behavior therapy, the prevailing paradigm in clinical psychology was psychodynamic. Since that time there has arguably been a major paradigmatic shift from psychoanalytic approaches to behavioral approaches. This transition was based, at least in part, on the observation that psychoanalytic methods for treating behavioral disorders have not been consistently demonstrated to be superior to no treatment, placebo, or other treatment conditions. In contrast, investigations of behavior therapy have emphasized empirical scrutiny and quantifiable behavior change. As a consequence, behavior therapy applications have been widely recognized as being very successful for treating a wide variety of behavioral problems, ranging from anxiety disorders to developmental disabilities.

B. Function Oriented

Behavior therapy differs from other forms of psychological therapies in regard to its commitment to basic research and link with behavior theory. Specifically, behavior therapy is aimed at determining environment–behavior relations that either can explain the cause or maintenance of maladaptive behaviors individuals typically seek treatment for in clinical settings. Elucidation of these environment–behavior relations has emerged from behavioral research, most notably operant and classical conditioning. Congruent with the laboratory research on which it is based, behavior therapy focuses on the function rather than the structure of behavior. In the most general sense, structural analyses focus on how people behave (e.g., form of a particular response), whereas functional analyses focus on why people behave (e.g., purpose of a particular response).

In a functional approach, behavior therapists attempt to explicate the relation between observable behavior and the contextual variables of the environment, particularly focusing on observable antecedents and consequences of behavioral responses. For example, if a child's recurrent tantruming in a school classroom is routinely followed by attention from the teacher, a behavior therapist might encourage the teacher to praise the child when the child is not tantruming and ignore the child when a tantrum occurs. Thus, tantruming behavior aimed at receiving attention is not reinforced, thereby changing the function of such responding. This process of assessment, called a functional analysis of behavior, is the core of behavior therapy approaches.

C. Idiographic Oriented

The other major theoretical component of behavior therapies is that they have historically been idiographic (i.e., individual) rather than nomothetic (i.e., group) approaches to assessing and changing behavior. Nomothetic approaches, by definition, focus on the identification of the commonalities and differences among traits and dispositions that occur within and between groups of people. Idiographic approaches, on the other hand, focus on variability in the behavior of a person over time and across situations. As such, a second aim of the functional analysis is to identify consistent sources of variance for a particular person presenting to the clinic with a specific behavioral problem.

Despite the uniformity among behavior therapists commonly perceived by the public, it is important to note that not all behavior therapists are alike. Indeed, there are different behavioral approaches, differing in specific aspects of their clinical approach and the focus of treatment. This diversity is reflected in the numerous terms that have been employed to describe this general therapeutic approach (e.g., applied behavior analysis, behavior modification, cognitive-behavior therapy). Although these various terminologies capture relative differences in one's specific approach, behaviorally oriented therapists are all committed to changing maladaptive behavior through a functional, idiographic-based assessment of specified target behaviors. Thus, even in the case of standardized treatment manuals that identify the major processes functionally related to a particular disorder, treatments are tailored to the individual—at least at the level of practical implementation. Through this identification of the controlling variables, it has been possible to develop standardized treatment strategies that are based on behavior principles to alter problematic behavior. To achieve these goals, behavior therapists attempt to provide their patients with a new set of learning experiences that are in accord with positive behavior change within the patients' value system.

III. APPLICATIONS AND EXCLUSIONS

A. Empirically Supported Therapies and the Use of Treatment Manuals

There have a number of important developments within the behavioral health care that have come to shape the application of manualized behavior therapies. Perhaps most influential has been the push to establish empirically supported therapies for a variety of recognized psychological disorders. This movement has been at least partially in response to cost-containment efforts in the health care system in general and funding-related restrictions for behavioral health services specifically. For example, health care policy changes have strongly recommended, and in certain cases demanded, that psychological services follow guidelines for relatively brief treatments that have an empirical basis for positive outcome.

The movement to develop lists of empirically supported therapies for target populations defined by diagnostic categories has been pioneered by the Division 12 Task Force on Promotion and Dissemination of Psychological Procedures. The function of the task force has been to critically review the existing empirical psychological treatment literature in an effort to identify those psychosocial interventions that have shown promise in alleviating specific types of psychological distress. Once potential treatments are identified and agreed on, the task force communicates this information to the behavioral health community. The task of charting efficacious treatments is an ongoing process, as researchers are continuously examining therapies, refining their components, and assessing their utility across different populations, sites, and time periods (see Section IV). In all cases, the therapies that are evaluated by the task force have been manualized to facilitate the understanding and evaluation of the treatment's key concepts, procedures, and delivery tactics.

B. Behavior Therapy's Contributions to Standardization of Psychosocial Treatments

As behavior therapy always has been committed to empirical evaluation and time-efficient strategies, it is not surprising behavior therapists have been at the forefront of the major developments in the movement toward empirically supported treatments. In fact, behavioral and cognitive-behavioral therapies overwhelmingly top the list of empirically supported therapeutic interventions for a wide variety of disorders. In an illustrative example, the majority of empirically supported treatments can be considered behavioral in their theoretical foundations, content, and implementation procedures. For example, of the "well-established treatments," 93% are considered "behavioral" in content and procedures.

Whereas behavioral interventions were largely based on operant and classical conditioning principles through the late 1970s, cognitive treatment strategies have been increasingly added to these therapies from the 1970s through the 1990s. This evolution of behavior therapy reflects the growing recognition that internal processes such as thoughts and language characterize many important aspects of psychological dysfunctions. As an extension, many clinicians believe that by directly targeting cognitive-affective processes, they can facilitate positive behavior change along a greater number of different response domains. Thus, it is not surprising contemporary behavioral interventions can be best described as multicomponent strategies that contain treatment elements that are based on both basic learning principles and more recent developments in experimental cognitive psychology (e.g., research on memory biases). Hence, most behavior therapies are now described as cognitive-behavioral treatments and compiled in multiple component treatment manuals. Although it is not entirely clear at this juncture to what extent specific therapy components contribute to treatment outcome and maintenance, available evidence suggests that both cognitive and behavioral components contribute to the overall positive outcome achieved by cognitive-behavioral treatment protocols.

C. Contemporary Issues Related to the Potential Limitations of Manuals

There have been a number of controversies surrounding the use of manualized treatments (e.g., flexibility of therapist in treatment delivery, creativity of therapist, reification of treatment to a fixed manner). All these intensely debated topics differ in content but essentially rest on questions concerning the relative utility of manualized treatments as applied to "real-world" behavior problems. For the purposes of this article, only two of the most common concerns will be described.

1. Manuals as Standardized Treatment Strategies

Some scholars have suggested that manualized behavior therapy undermines and restricts clinical judgment of individual therapists in the practice setting. Manualizing treatments could be problematic because most clinicians are highly sensitive to the individual needs and characteristics of their patients. Furthermore, greater degrees of flexibility often are need to deliver treatment in the "real world" relative to when the treatments are developed and initially tested in clinical trials conducted in research settings.

Yet, these concerns must be weighed against the background of a large body of evidence that suggests personal biases typically are worse or at the very least not better than statistical prediction based on scientific analyses of persons with the same or similar type of problem. Thus, manualized treatments, which generally are based on scientific testing of groups of people, guide therapists in implementing what research rather than clinical judgment suggests is the most clinically appropriate thing to do. It is becoming increasingly evident that the "truth" lies somewhere between a strict individually tailored relative to a strict manualized approach. Indeed, insofar as a clinician can modify a manualized treatment to help identify and target aspects of an individual's behavior that might interfere with the successful implementation of a proven manual, success rates should continue to improve.

2. Manuals as Treatment Strategies for Comorbidity

Another concern raised about manualized therapies is that they often are developed from studies involving patients with a homogenous diagnostic profile yet are implemented clinically on patients with multiple behavior problems (i.e., diagnostic heterogeneity). Recent research in such areas as the anxiety disorders has seriously challenged this concern, as in the vast majority of clinical trials using manuals, patients have high rates of psychiatric comorbidity. In addition, many of these patients have not responded to alternative treatment strategies in the past, and in this respect, can be considered "treatment refractory" or at least "treatment resistant." Of further interest has been the finding that some manualized behavior therapies have been found to produce clinical improvement in other not specifically targeted behavior problems.

Taken together, then, it may be more appropriate to suggest that the clinical effectiveness of manualized treatment will be partially a function of presenting problem, nature of comorbidity, and the specific treatment being employed. With the recognition that this is a complex problem in need of further systematic study, it will be critically important for future research to address the generalizability of manualized behavior therapies across different clinical populations and settings. Along these lines, increased attention to questions of effectiveness will assume an increasingly critical role in determining the relative clinical utility and generalizability of particular psychosocial treatments.

IV. EMPIRICAL STUDIES

A. General Treatment Development and Evaluation Model

Psychosocial treatment development and dissemination is based on the stage model used by the Food and Drug Administration for the approval of drugs. Briefly, there are three primary units, each reflecting different stages in treatment development. Stage 1 reflects technological refinement and pilot research aimed at developing theoretically based treatment strategies that can usefully be applied to a specific type of psychopathology. Stage 2 is concerned with demonstrating that a particular treatment can produce positive behavior change in a controlled evaluation. In addition, in Stage 2, research can be aimed at ascertaining the mechanisms of action for a particular treatment (i.e., how it works). Stage 3 is field research involving larger samples of patients for the evaluation of treatments that already have shown initial success in Stage 2.

B. Empirically Supported Treatment Manuals

The empirically supported treatment task force evaluates all manualized therapies according to their efficacy; that is, demonstrations that an intervention improves psychological status in well-controlled, experimental studies. This research differs slightly from questions of effectiveness, defined as the relative degree of utility of a treatment to produce positive outcomes in the context in which treatment most often is sought. Typically, large-scale clinical trials are used to evaluate and demonstrate the efficacy of psychological interventions. Such evaluations are outcome oriented, that is, they typically are an evaluation of a particular type of therapy compared to some type of control group (e.g., placebo, other form of therapy), although a variety of different evaluation formats exist (e.g., series of single case studies).

The criteria for demonstrating efficacy are categorized as either "well-established treatments" or "probably efficacious treatments." Although it is not possible to review the criteria for each of these domains in their entirety, well-established therapies generally have demonstrated superior outcome compared to a control condition (e.g., placebo) or another treatment on two separate occasions by independent investigators. In contrast, probably efficacious treatments generally indicate that a treatment is superior to persons who desire psychological treatment but are on a waiting list for such treatment.

In all cases, the evaluation process involves persons with a particular type of psychological disorder being randomly assigned to a specified treatment condition. For example, patients with panic disorder may either be randomly assigned to receive an "active" psychological treatment or separate treatments such as a medical drug or a placebo pill. In these trials, patients are then evaluated in a standardized manner over the same amount of time using the same types of clinically relevant outcome measures. Overall, these efforts allow one to determine whether a therapy can reduce psychological distress in both a statistically and clinically useful way.

V. CASE ILLUSTRATION

For purposes of this article, a clinical case presentation of an individual with panic disorder may help illustrate the use of a multicomponent treatment manual that is prototypical for other treatment manuals used for the majority of psychological dysfunctions.

A. Case Description

Sam is a 33-year-old married white male with a 10-month history of recurrent panic attacks. His panic attacks occur in an unpredictable and uncontrollable manner and last for approximately 2 to 15 min. Sam indicated that his panic attacks occur at least once every other day and involve chest pain, difficulty breathing, racing and pounding heart, increased sweating, and lightheadedness. As a result of these symptoms, Sam believed he had cardiac disease. Due to the worry about the panic attacks, Sam had begun to avoid socializing with friends and family and declined professional opportunities to travel for his job as a computer programmer. After a thorough medical exam that found no indication of cardiac or other medical problems, Sam was referred to an anxiety disorders treatment center at a university hospital. After a psychiatric interview and testing, it was determined Sam suffers from panic disorder.

B. Manualized Therapy for Panic Disorder

We now discuss how Sam might be treated with a current well-established therapy for panic disorder and agoragaphoba termed panic control therapy (PCT). This multicomponent cognitive-behavioral intervention is guided by the use of a treatment manual entitled *Mastery of Your Anxiety and Panic–II (MAP–II)* that articulates the procedures for PCT in a step-by-step fashion. Manual-based therapies like the *MAP–II* also include self-report and behavioral assessment tracking instruments that can be readily employed to evaluate treatment progress of individual patients across different time frames.

MAP–II contains a number of key components, including exposure to bodily and environmental situations associated with fear and panic, relaxation, and breathing retraining, as well as cognitive interventions. Briefly, exposure to interoceptive bodily events is achieved through exercises that produce somatic sensations that are similar to panic (e.g., head spinning, breathing through a straw). Situational exposure involves contacting feared environmental stimuli without escaping from them if panic symptoms occur. For instance, a person with panic disorder with agoraphobia who fears crowds might be asked to go to a shopping center and stay there for a specified period of time or until potentially high levels of anxiety have subsided. Relaxation training refers to exercises that serve to decrease base levels of autonomic arousal, as this decreases the likelihood of future panic attacks. Breathing retraining refers to having patients breathe diaphragmatically at a normal rate in an effort to optimize the balance between oxygen and carbon dioxide in the patient's blood. Cognitive strategies typically are aimed at (a) correcting misappraisals of bodily sensations as threatening, (b) helping patients to predict more accurately the future likelihood of panic attacks, and (c) helping patients to predict more accurately and rationally the likely consequences of panic attacks.

C. Treatment Process with Manual

Sam's treatment would most likely be conducted in an individual setting over a period of about 2 months. As is the case for most psychosocial interventions, the *MAP–II* first provides Sam with educational information about the nature, origin, and course of panic disorder prior to the application of specific intervention strategies. This information helps patients realize that they are "not alone" and communicates that professionals understand their specific type of problem. The second and ongoing step in Sam's *MAP–II* treatment would be to have him monitor both negative emotional experiences and stressful life events to facilitate the recognition and identification of environmental events that contribute to the occurrence of recurrent panic attacks. Identifying such negative life events makes the potential occurrence of panic attacks more predictable and perhaps controllable, thereby lessening their aversiveness.

Third, the therapist would train Sam in relaxation and breathing exercises and have him practice these exercises until he has acquired the skill of reducing and controlling bodily arousal. Throughout *MAP–II* therapy, the therapist is instructed to guide Sam in correcting maladaptive cognitive errors related to worry about the negative consequences of panic attacks. For example, during cognitive restructuring, Sam would be taught to reconceptualize his panic attacks as harmless events that occur in response to "natural" stressors. Finally, Sam would participate in repeated trials of interoceptive exposure, and if necessary, exteroceptive exposure exercises in both the clinical setting and his natural environment. Such exercises would be continued until such stimuli no longer elicit significant levels of anxiety. Therapy would be discontinued when Sam's condition improved to a level that he can adequately perform his life tasks and his psychological status has returned to a healthy level.

VI. SUMMARY

In summary, treatment manuals are written materials that identify key concepts, procedures, and tactics for the delivery of a clinical intervention. In this manner, treatment manuals are designed to help modify clinically relevant variables and processes involved with problematic behavior. Although manuals can be quite diverse, all provide rules and statements pertaining to how the therapist is to prepare for treatment, describe what they should do during the session itself, and characterize how the process of therapy is to proceed over time. Manuals have greatly helped in efforts to improve the evaluation of particular treatment strategies by specifying the nature of the treatment and articulate how it is to be delivered. More recent, manualized behavior therapies have become apparent in clinical service contexts, calling attention to clinical issues that strike at the very heart of what treatment should be considered "clinically useful" and in what contexts it should be implemented (e.g., controlled or real-world settings).

An extension of the treatment utility issue has been the development of empirically supported therapies for target populations pioneered by the Division 12 Task Force on Promotion and Dissemination of Psychological Procedures. Testifying to the established place of manuals in contemporary clinical care, all therapies that are evaluated by the task force have been manualized so as to facilitate the understanding and evaluation of the treatment's key concepts, procedures, and delivery tactics. Perhaps because behavior therapy has always been committed to empirical evaluation and time-efficient strategies, it is not surprising the majority of empirically supported treatments can be considered behavioral in their theoretical foundations, content, and implementation procedures. Although the use of manuals has been controversial in a number of respects, few would challenge the contention that they likely will retain in an important and influential role in continued evolution of psychological treatment in upcoming years.

See Also the Following Articles

Behavioral Consultation and Therapy ■ Behavior Therapy: Theoretical Bases ■ Cognitive Behavior Therapy ■ Collaborative Care ■ Comorbidity ■ Effectiveness ■ Integrative Approaches to Psychotherapy ■ Multimodal Behavior Therapy ■ Panic Disorder and Agoraphobia ■ Research in Psychotherapy

Further Reading

Chambless, D. L., Sanderson, W. C., Shoham, V., Bennett-Johnson, S., Pope, K. S., Crits-Chiristoph, P., Baker, M., Johnson, B., Woody, S. R., Sue, S., Beutler, L., Williams, D. A., & McCurry, S. (1996). An update on empirically validated therapies. *The Clinical Psychologist, 49,* 5–18.

Eifert, G. H., Schulte, D., Zvolensky, M. J., Lejuez, C. W., & Lau, A. W. (1998). Manualized behavior therapy: Merits and challenges. *Behavior Therapy, 28,* 499–509.

Garfield, S. L. (1996). Some problems associated with "validated" forms of psychotherapy. *Clinical Psychology: Science and Practice, 3,* 218–229.

Heimberg, R. C. (1998). Manual-based treatment: An essential ingredient of clinical practice in the 21st century. *Clinical Psychology: Science and Practice, 5,* 387–390.

Persons, J. B. (1991). Psychotherapy outcome studies do not accurately represent current models of psychopathology. *American Psychologist, 46,* 99–106.

Society for Science of Clinical Psychology. http://pantheon.yale.edu/~tat22/

Task Force on Promotion and Dissemination of Psychological Procedures. (1995). Training in and dissemination of empirically validated psychological treatments: Report and recommendations. *The Clinical Psychologist, 48,* 3–23.

Wade, W., Treat, T. A., & Stuart, G. L. (1998). Transporting an empirically supported treatment for panic disorder to a service setting: A benchmarking strategy. *Journal of Consulting and Clinical Psychology, 66,* 231–239.

Wilson, G. T. (1996). Manual-based treatments: The clinical application of research findings. *Behaviour Research and Therapy, 34,* 295–315.

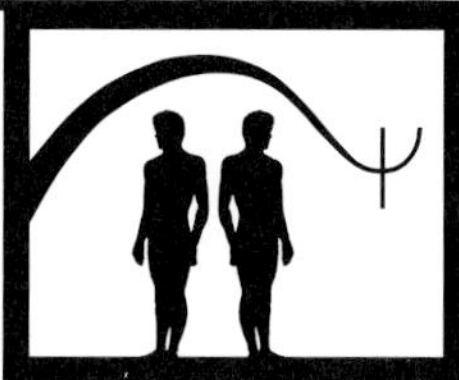

Matching Patients to Alcoholism Treatment

Margaret E. Mattson
National Institute on Alcohol Abuse and Alcoholism

GLOSSARY

alcoholism Alcoholism (also referred to as alcohol dependency) is an addictive disorder diagnosed by a series of specific DSM defined criteria such as, progressive loss of control over drinking, tolerance, withdrawal symptoms, continued drinking despite adverse consequences, narrowing of usual activities in favor of alcohol seeking.

clinical trial A clinical trial is a prospective experiment in which therapeutic interventions are evaluated. Desirable features which increase the rigor of the experiment include random assignment to treatment group, masking of clinician, research assessor and patient with respect to treatment assignment, and in the case of pharmacologic studies, use of matched placebo.

matching factors Matching factors are patient characteristics that affect outcomes differentially when two or more treatments are compared.

outcome predictors Outcome predictors are characteristics that influence the outcome of treatment across the board but do not have differential effects depending upon the type of treatment.

Patient-treatment matching is the concept that particular treatments may work better for some patients than others and that, in clinical practice, treatment outcomes can be improved by matching subgroups of patients with the therapy most suited to their particular needs using matching rules derived from previous experience.

I. DESCRIPTION OF TREATMENT

Patient-treatment matching occurs when treatment is prescribed based on the needs of the individual patient, as contrasted with providing the same therapy to all patients with the same diagnosis. It has been suggested that triaging clients to treatments based on their particular needs and characteristics might significantly improve outcome. The potential of the matching hypothesis has been of particular interest in the treatment of alcohol use disorders, prompting researchers and clinicians to search for assignment rules to individualize selection of psychosocial treatments. The literature in this area spans several decades and includes small-scale studies, reports from a large multisite clinical trial, and examinations of underlying theory and clinical practice implications. It provides a useful example to illustrate the rationale and implementation of the matching hypothesis and is used as the model here. Although the focus here is alcohol dependency as the target for patient treatment matching interventions, the concept is relevant to other disorders and has been used to varying extents in numerous medical, psychiatric, and educational contexts.

In its most basic form, matching is done informally by providers when, based on their clinical judgment, they provide treatment "tailored" to specific features of the patient and the patient's disorder. Patients may also practice "self-matching" when they contribute to varying degrees to treatment decisions based on, for example, their beliefs about various treatments and what will benefit them, or other influences, such as availability of resources, advice from others, and so on.

However, the formal practice of matching in clinical and research settings is based on validated rules that link particular patient characteristics with certain treatments. Typical steps in the matching process are: (a) systematic assessment of patient characteristics and needs, (b) availability of specific matching rules, and (c) consistent assignment of patients to well-defined treatment in accordance with the specified matching rules. Ideally, the guidelines should be based on validated research, and patient outcomes should be monitored to determine the extent of improvement and if modifications are necessary.

In addition to matching patients with treatments, matching of patients to therapists has also been of interest and is reviewed by the Project MATCH Research Group in 1998 who concluded that therapist effects on treatment outcome may contribute more toward explaining the variance in outcomes than either specific treatments employed or baseline patient characteristics. Reporting on a study of therapist influence on treatment outcome conducted as a part of the multisite Project MATCH, they found that therapist effects did indeed exert an effect on treatment outcome as well as patient satisfaction with treatment. Interestingly though, most of the observed effects were due to "outlier" therapists whose clients tended to show poorer outcomes. They advise that future studies take into account the potential effect of "outlier" therapists.

Until relatively recently, matching to treatments for alcohol dependence has involved interventions of a verbal nature, such as behavioral therapies, counseling, and psychotherapy. Beginning in the 1990s, the development of medications that target neurochemical systems implicated in the addictive process have brought a new and promising approach to treatment of alcoholism. In addition to clinical trials evaluating the efficacy of these drugs, (both alone and in combination with verbal therapies) matching hypotheses have also been tested. As knowledge emerges on the neurochemical and neurogenetic determinants of alcohol addiction, the rationale is strengthened for hypothesizing that outcome may be improved when particular neuroactive medications are linked to certain patient characteristics of known biological basis.

II. THEORETICAL BASES

Interactions differ from predictors in that predictors affect the outcome of treatments in a similar way (Figure 1A). In contrast, interactions arise when the patient characteristic of interest has a differential effect on the treatments being compared (Figure 1B and 1C). Thus, the main effects of different treatments may suggest that they have similar benefits, however, analyses that examine the interactions between certain patient and treatment types may make differential benefits evident.

The idea of matching is not new, having first been proposed in the alcohol treatment area in 1941 by K. Bowman and E. Jellinek and is common to other fields such as psychiatry, medicine, and education. R. E. Snow in 1991 discussed aptitude-treatment interactions as derived from the educational psychology literature as a framework for research on individual differences in psychotherapy.

Matching came to be of interest to alcoholism treatment researchers when despite decades of outcome research no clearly and generally superior treatment(s) that could be considered the "magic bullet" of alcoholism treatment emerged. In parallel, thinking concerning the nature of alcoholism diversified and a view of the disorder as the end result of a complex interaction of factors—environmental, personal, interpersonal, and biological—competed with the predominant medical model of alcoholism as a unidimensional disease. It was suggested that perhaps the "one-size-fits-all" approach was inappropriate for alcoholism treatment. The notion that perhaps the missing ingredient in the treatment selection process was the matching of patient to treatment began to evolve.

The hypothesis was that perhaps the addition of matching could enhance outcomes above and beyond what could be accomplished by simply choosing generally effective treatments and paying attention to generic curative elements such as support, rapport, and communication from the therapist. This concept was fostered by about 40 studies published in from the 1970s through the 1990s suggesting that a variety of patient features—demographic, drinking relating factors, intrapersonal characteristics, and interpersonal factors—appeared to "match" with particular treatments.

III. EMPIRICAL STUDIES

A. Early Studies

Development of the experimental database pertaining to the patient-treatment matching hypothesis may

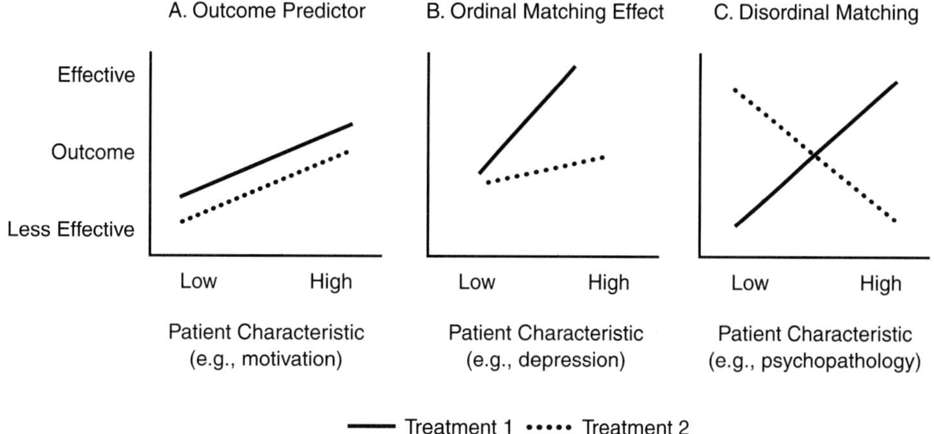

FIGURE 1 Three hypothetical examples of the relation of patient characteristics to treatment success are presented. The X axis (horizontal line) of each graph reflects the degree to which a patient has a certain characteristic. It may be a continuous variable (i.e., a patient may lie anywhere along a spectrum of characteristic levels varying from low to high), such as the degree of a patient's motivation, or a dichotomous variable, such as the presence or absence of a family history of alcoholism (not shown). The Y axis (vertical line) is a measure of treatment outcome (e.g., the percentage of days in a given period that the patient consumed alcohol). The relationship between the two lines that represent the two treatments being compared reveals information about the effects of varying levels of patient characteristics on outcome. (A) The relationship between an outcome predictor and two treatment types is shown. For example, how does a client's motivation affect the outcome of two different treatments? The outcome of treatment with both therapies is related to the patient's characteristic (i.e., the higher the motivation, the better the outcome for both treatments, although Treatment 1 appears a bit more beneficial than Treatment 2). The fact that the lines are parallel indicates that the effect of the patient's motivation is similar for both treatments. Therefore, the characteristic factor is an outcome predictor that does not affect the treatments differentially. (B) An ordinal matching effect is shown. Patients with low levels of the characteristic of interest, such as depression, appear to have about the same success regardless of the treatment they receive. For patients with higher levels of depression, the results diverge, and there is a definite advantage in choosing Treatment 1. (C) Disordinal matching is shown. Patients with low levels of a characteristic, such as psychopathology, have better success when receiving Treatment 2 than Treatment 1. For patients with high levels of psychopathology, the opposite occurs: Treatment 1 is more effective than Treatment 2.

be roughly divided into two eras. The first era consists of about 40 studies from the 1970s through the early to mid-1990s. These were mostly smaller scale, single-site studies. Some of the studies from the earlier portion of this period had methodological shortcomings, such as lack of a priori hypotheses; differing, less well documented therapies, and varying outcome measures that detracted from the studies and made comparisons across studies difficult. Nevertheless, the accumulating body of knowledge was viewed as promising not only for improving patient outcomes but also for making more effective use of ever-decreasing resources as reimbursement polices and other economic forces began to change the face of additions treatment in this country.

During the 1980s and early 1990s, methodologic advances occurred in addictions clinical research and numerous more sophisticated matching studies were reported, further strengthening the hope for matching as a clinical tool. An important catalyst were two reports from the Institute of Medicine in 1989 and 1990 calling for additional definitive and systematic research on this question. The matching hypothesis had become part of the national research agenda.

B. Project MATCH

The second era of matching studies was marked by the 1989 launch of a multisite clinical trial, Project MATCH, by the National Institute of Alcohol Abuse and Alcoholism (NIAAA) the principal sponsor of research on alcohol disorders in the United States. It was conceived of as the largest, most statistically powerful and most methodologically rigorous psychotherapy trial ever undertaken. The stated objective was to subject the matching hypothesis to its most rigorous test to date. Its research questions were based largely on the previous body of published studies and the latest knowledge of treatments believed to be generally effective and suitable for delivery both in a multisite clinical trial and in actual clinical practice.

1. Project MATCH Design

The details of the rationale and design of Project MATCH are described in a publication of the Project MATCH Research Group in 1993 and by D. Donovan and M. E. Mattson in a 1994 monograph. The study tested promising patient-treatment combinations involving 21 patient characteristics and three treatments: twelve-step facilitation (TSF), motivational enhancement therapy (MET), and cognitive-behavioral therapy (CBT). After determination of eligibility and an extensive baseline assessment, 1,726 patients were randomly assigned to one of the three treatments. The treatments were administered during a 12-week period by trained therapists following standardized manuals. Therapist supervision continued during the trial to ensure fidelity to the treatment protocol across all sites. The treatments are described in three therapists manuals written by their developers and published by the National Institute of Alcohol Abuse and Alcoholism as part of the eight-volume Project MATCH Monograph Series.

Drinking outcomes and other indicators of function were assessed at the end of treatment (3 months) and thereafter at 6, 9, 12, and 15 months. A subset (outpatients only) were recontracted 39 months after treatment. The two primary drinking outcome measures were percentage days abstinent and drinks per drinking day.

2. Project MATCH Sample

Patients were treated at nine locations in the United States. Five sites functioned as outpatient clinics, and five sites delivered Project MATCH treatments as aftercare following an episode of inpatient treatment or intensive day hospital. (One site had both an outpatient and aftercare capacity.) Treatment-seeking clients at the 9 locations were recruited from a total of 27 treatment facilities. Individuals with concurrent drug dependence diagnoses (other than marijuana) were excluded from the trial. The participants were almost exclusively alcohol dependent (as opposed to alcohol abuse only) and had an average of six (out of a possible nine) *DSM-III–R* dependence symptoms, and drank on average 25 days per month, with an average of 15 drinks per drinking day. Over one half had a history of prior treatment for alcoholism, approximately 75% were male, and almost all showed chronic effects of alcohol consumption on various areas of life functioning.

3. Project MATCH Hypotheses

Based upon previous research, a series of client characteristics were identified and tested as potential treatment-matching variables. The matching variables and the measures used to operationalize them are described in several publications authored by the Project MATCH Research Group. The patient-matching characteristics were alcohol involvement (i.e., severity of alcohol problems), cognitive impairment, conceptual level (a measure of abstraction ability), gender, meaning seeking (i.e., desire to find greater purpose in life), motivation (i.e., readiness to change), psychiatric severity, sociopathy, social support for drinking, alcoholic subtype, severity of alcohol dependence, psychiatric diagnosis (Axis I disorder), antisocial personality, anger, self-efficacy, social functioning, prior engagement in Alcoholics Anonymous, religiosity, treatment readiness, autonomy, and problem recognition. Hypothesized interactions between each of these client characteristics and the Project MATCH treatments were specified at the beginning of the trial. The matching hypotheses were a priori, that is specified in advance, and were not revealed during the trial to therapists and research assistants to maintain objectivity in treatment and assessment.

4. Project MATCH Results

In the following section, we consider how results of Project MATCH answered two questions: (a) How did patients fare in the different treatment conditions? and (b) Were any treatments particularly effective in subgroups of patients defined by the characteristics listed above?

a. Results: Main Effects. Patients in all three treatment conditions demonstrated major improvements in drinking, as well as other areas of functioning such as depression, use of illicit drugs, and liver enzyme status. Overall, MATCH clients were abstaining over 85% of the days throughout the year following treatment, and alcohol consumption decreased fivefold. Even those not successful in maintaining abstinence who continued to drink experienced a substantial reduction in alcohol consumption. In general, effects for the three treatments were similar, with the exception that 10% more of the outpatients receiving TSF attained complete abstinence over the 1-year follow-up period compared to the other two treatments. In addition, more aftercare patients were able to sustain complete abstinence throughout the year after treatment than the outpatients, despite the fact that the aftercare patients entered the study with more alcohol dependence symptoms.

b. Results: Matching Interactions. The findings of Project MATCH surprised many and challenged the belief that patient-treatment matching was critical in the treatment of alcoholism. Contrary to the expectations generated by the supporting literature, large and uniform effects for matches between single-patient characteristics did not emerge. Many hypothesized matches were not supported, and those found were, for the most part, of rather modest magnitude and often varied over time, between arms of the trial, and for the two primary outcome measures.

Of the 21 patient variables studied, the four with matching effects deemed more plausible were those involving, in the outpatient arm: psychiatric severity, client anger, and social network support for drinking, and, in the aftercare arm, alcohol dependence. These are briefly described.

Patients in the outpatient arm with low psychiatric severity treated with TSF had more abstinent days as compared to those treated with CBT, a differential as high as 10% for several months during the follow-up period. The largest difference occurred 6 months after the end of treatment, when clients without concomitant psychopathology had 87% days abstinent in TSF versus 73% in CBT.

Motivational enhancement therapy was postulated to be more effective for clients with higher anger scores presumably because of its non-confrontive nature. MET clients in the outpatient study who were high in anger were abstinent more often than clients receiving the other treatments (a differential of 9%, i.e., 85% vs. 76%) and drank less intensely when they did drink. Clients with low anger fared better in CBT and in TSF as compared to MET. The effect persisted throughout the 1 year after treatment and was also present at the 39 months follow-up. This finding was the most consistent matching result across time.

As predicted, clients having a social network supportive of drinking did better in TSF than in MET. This difference was not apparent in the first year after treatment, emerging among the outpatients at the 3-year follow-up. TSF patients reported abstinence on 83% of days versus 66% for the MET patients. This difference of 17 percentage points was largest size effect observed in Project MATCH. The effects appear due to a steady decline among clients with high drinking support in the MET group after the end of treatment, whereas the TSF group maintained their gains. An influential factor may be differences in levels of AA attendance, with attendance levels higher in the TSF group than in the MET group.

It had been hypothesized that clients high in alcohol dependence would do better in TSF whereas those lower in that trait would benefit more from CBT. Because TSF is a treatment that puts greater emphasis on total abstinence, it was postulated to be more effective with highly dependent clients than either CBT (which taught skills to deal with "slips") or MET (which focused on clients' own decision making to motivate them to become abstinent). Aftercare clients low in alcohol dependence had better outcomes when treated with CBT than TSF, (i.e., abstinence on 96% of posttreatment days vs. 89%). However, at higher levels of dependence, the better treatment choice was TSF, (i.e., 94 vs. 84% days abstinent). The effect was consistent for the posttreatment period of 15 months.

c. Results: Clinical Implications. The clinical implications of Project MATCH were described by the investigators in a 1998 publication as follows:

> In summary, the results of testing the *a priori* matching hypotheses showed several matches of modest-to-moderate magnitude, often with variability over time, outcome measures and arm of the study. These results suggest that matching clients on several of the attributes tested in Project MATCH to one of the three treatments appears to enhance outcomes to a modest degree, with the most robust of the confirmed effects constituting a moderate difference of 17 percentage points in abstinent days.

The Project MATCH Research group concluded that viewpoints differ on how clinically important these single characteristic effects are, although, overall, the findings do not suggest that major changes in triaging procedures are warranted. R. Longabaugh and P. Wirtz have extensively analyzed the mechanisms and "active ingredients" involved in the matching hypotheses and have discussed possible reasons for the failure to find a greater number of matches.

C. Medications as Matching Targets

The literature on pharmacological agents in the treatment of alcoholism have been reviewed extensively and point to the increasing potential of pharmacologic agents as aids in treatment of alcoholism.

In the early 1990s interest in the opiate antagonist naltrexone as an adjunct in the treatment of alcohol dependence was illustrated by key studies from two groups in 1992, that of O'Malley and colleagues and Volpicelli and colleagues. Previously used as a treatment for opiate dependence, naltrexone was approved for treatment of alcoholism by the FDA in 1994. Previously, the only approved drug for this purpose was disulfiram (Antabuse). Disulfiram functions as a deterrent to drinking by producing an aversive effect if alcohol is consumed through inhibition of aldehyde dehydrogenase, an enzyme involved in the metabolism of alcohol.

Data from studies of the efficacy of naltrexone were subjected to subsequent post hoc analyses by A. J. Jaffe and associates in 1996. These results illustrate the possibility of matching subgroups of patients to drug/psychosocial combinations. The question examined was "Do patients with certain baseline characteristics respond more positively to the drug/psychosocial combinations than those without these characteristics?" The authors concluded that naltrexone appears more beneficial for alcoholics with high craving and poorer cognitive functioning.

Research by Mason and colleagues in 1996 suggested that the use of the antidepressant desipramine may reduce the risk of relapse in depressed alcoholics, but not in the nondepressed. In 1994, H. R. Kranzler and others found that buspirone appeared more helpful to anxious alcoholics although the same had not been observed in a previous 1992 study by Malcom and colleagues. In 2000, two studies on the agent ondansetron, a 5-HT_3 antagonist, suggested it differentially affected drinking in early versus later-onset alcoholics. Early-onset alcoholics were defined as those who showed drinking problems earlier in life, had antisocial characteristics, and a family history of the disorder in first-degree relatives. They found that ondansetron reduced drinking preferentially in the early-onset group. In a small pilot study also in 2000 the same investigators combined ondansetron with naltrexone and found that the combination reduced alcohol consumption in the early-onset group to a larger degree than either of the two medications alone.

Based on preliminary studies such as these, it is tempting to speculate that perhaps new and better matching algorithms may be found when matches are based on pairing of pharmacologic treatments with biologically based patient characteristics. Much additional research remains to determine if intriguing, but preliminary, results can be replicated and extended. Needed are future studies with larger samples in multiple sites and settings, and greater understanding of the neurochemical mechanisms underlying clinical observations. The future of matching patients to pharmacologic treatments remains open pending further investigation.

IV. SUMMARY

Although many alcoholics indeed benefit from treatment, no single treatment has been shown to be effective for all those diagnosed with the disorder. For many decades it was suggested that assigning alcoholic patients to treatments based on their particular needs and characteristics might improve treatment outcomes. Interest in matching accelerated during the 1970s and 1980s as supporting evidence accumulated in the literature. However, these studies were small scale, and replication was required before specific recommendations for clinical practice could be advanced. In late 1989 NIAAA launched a multisite clinical trial, Project MATCH, with the goal of learning whether different alcoholics respond selectively to particular treatments. The study tested a promising set of patient-treatment combinations in 1,726 patients randomly assigned to three well-defined psychosocial treatments.

Patients in all three treatment conditions demonstrated major improvements in drinking, as well as other areas of functioning such as depression, use of illicit drugs, and liver enzyme status. However, in terms of matching the findings of Project MATCH challenged the popular belief that matching patients to treatment was needed to significantly improve outcome. Of the 21 patient characteristics evaluated, only four statistically significant matches with potential clinical implications were identified. These matches involved psychiatric severity, anger, social support for drinking, and alcohol dependence.

Viewpoints differ on how clinically significant these single characteristic matches are, given their overall variability over time and the rather modest size of most of the effects. The Project MATCH investigators in 1998 concluded that

> matching clients to particular treatment, at least based on the attributes and treatment studied in Project MATCH, is not the compelling requirement for treatment success as previously believed. The matches found, however, are reasonable considerations for clinicians to use as starting points in the treatment planning process.

It may be that other patient characteristics, or other treatments, or settings not studied in this large project may have matching potential. For example, continued future work involving matches of patient characteristics with pharmacological treatments that target the neurochemical pathways involved in addiction will assess the robustness of preliminary findings on this variant on the matching theme. Until such validation is forthcoming, no clinical guidelines can be made with reasonable certainty.

See Also the Following Articles

Addictions in Special Populations: Treatment ■ Controlled Drinking ■ Self-Help Groups ■ Substance Dependence: Psychotherapy

Further Reading

Donovan, D., & Mattson, M. E. (Eds.). (1994). Alcoholism treatment matching research: Methodologic and clinical approaches. *Journal of Studies on Alcohol, Supplement No. 12,* 1–171.

Friedman, L. M., Furberg, C., & DeMets, D. (1985). *Fundamentals of clinical trials.* Littleton, MA: PSG Publishing.

Hester, R. K., & Miller, W. R. (1995). *Handbook of alcoholism treatment approaches: Effective alternatives* (2nd ed.). Needham Heights, MA: Allyn and Bacon.

Project MATCH Research Group. (1998). Clinical implications of Project MATCH. *Journal of Mental Health, 7*(6), 589–602.

Project MATCH Research Group. (1993). Project MATCH: Rationale and methods for a multisite clinical trial matching patients to alcoholism treatment. *Alcoholism: Clinical and Experimental Research, 17*(6), 1130–1145.

U. S. Department of Health and Human Services, Public Health Service, National Institutes of Health, National Institute on Alcohol Abuse and Alcoholism. (2000, June). *10th Special Report to the US Congress on Alcohol and Health.* Washington, DC.

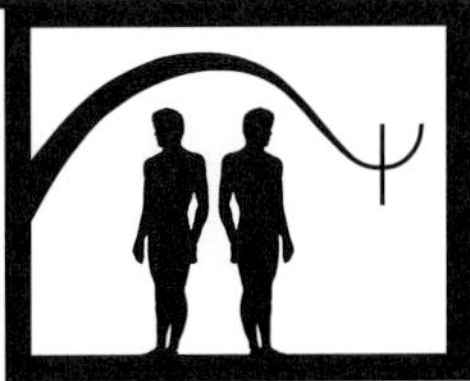

Medically Ill Patient: Psychotherapy

Randy A. Sansone
Wright State University School of Medicine

Lori A. Sansone
Alliance Physicians, Kettering Medical Center

GLOSSARY

countertransference The therapist's partly unconscious or conscious emotional reactions to the patient.

psychodynamics The systematized knowledge and theory of human behavior and its motivation, the study of which depends largely on the functional significance of emotion. Psychodynamics recognizes the role of unconscious motivation in human behavior. The science of psychodynamics assumes that one's behavior is determined by past experience, genetic endowment, and current reality.

psychoeducation Information in which the content is psychological or psychiatric in nature.

somatization The unconscious manifestation of psychological conflicts, either fully or in part, as somatic or body symptoms.

transference The unconscious assignment to others of feelings and attitudes that were originally associated with important figures in one's early life.

In this article, we highlight the complex relationship between medical illness and emotional or psychological distress and present options for psychotherapy treatment. This task is complex because of the variety of medical illnesses that individuals experience (e.g., from seasonal allergies to life-threatening forms of cancer), the unique psychological composition and reaction of each individual, and the many available treatment options that have been determined as efficacious.

Is there an association between medical illness and emotional distress? Among many patients, there appears to be. For example, 10 to 15% of individuals with medical illnesses suffer from depression, and among those with chronic illness, the prevalence of mood disorders increases up to 25 to 50%. It has been estimated that up to 25% of cancer patients suffer from depression, and that cancer treatment, itself, results in emotional distress for 40 to 60% of patients. Among patients with active medical illness, depression is one of the most common psychiatric complications in medical treatment and outcome. Surprisingly, not all patients with medical illness suffer from emotional distress, but no one knows exactly why this is.

Does emotional distress truly influence medical treatment and outcome? Among patients with similar types and severity of illness, those with depression remained in hospital for longer periods of time (up to 10 days). Depression among diabetic patients is associated with poor treatment compliance and an increased risk for vascular complications. Among cardiac rehabilitation patients, those who received treatment for depression had lower rehospitalization rates. Finally, following the hospitalization of one family member, studies indicate that there is an increase in the health care utilization of the remaining family members during the subsequent 3 years. These examples underscore that psychological factors appear to have an effect on one's response to medical illness and treatment.

In examining that effect, it is clear that medical illness is associated with some form of loss. Whether the loss is functional (e.g., use of one's legs), economic (e.g., inability to sustain employment), relational (e.g., loss of significant other, friends, or family), and/or self-esteem, a variety of factors affect how illness will be experienced. For example, there may be factors that predate the medical illness, such as early developmental psychodynamics, major psychiatric disorders, and/or personality traits or disorders, that affect the subsequent experience of illness. In addition, the arrival of medical illness may precipitate major psychiatric disorders as well as psychodynamic issues related to the illness experience.

I. DESCRIPTION OF THE TREATMENT

A. Assessment

1. Patient Reactions to Psychological Referral

Patients may be self-referred or referred by the treating clinician or family for psychological treatment. The patient's perception of the referral for psychological intervention may affect the entry into the treatment process. For example, negative reactions may result in failed appointments and, thus, prolonged psychological distress.

Referrals for psychological assessment and treatment may precipitate a variety of patient concerns. These may include social stigmatization (e.g., "Others will think I'm crazy!") as well as damage to self-esteem (i.e., "I can't do this on my own?"). Psychological referrals may be confusing to the patient who does not understand the relationship between emotions and medical illness. In addition, the patient may resist psychological referral if the recommendation is misinterpreted as an abandonment by the physician.

2. Selection Criteria for Psychotherapy Treatment

The selection criteria for entry into psychotherapy treatment vary from therapist to therapist. In general, the patient must be sufficiently intact on a cognitive level to enable participation in treatment. Among patients with medical illness, common concerns are the cognitive effects of drug treatment as well as delirium. Patients must be able to verbally interact (e.g., exclusions include aphasic patients) and reasonably able to relate to others (e.g., exclusions include severe personality disorders such as schizoid or antisocial personalities).

The ideal patient has a healthy and mature relational capacity. H. Levenson and R. E. Hales note the importance of the patient's ability to view issues in psychological terms, respond to a therapeutic experience in a positive manner, and make adaptations through personal strengths. These authors indicate that psychological pain may actually function as a potent motivation for treatment and emotional growth.

3. Contributory Factors to Psychological Distress among the Medically Ill

In the psychological assessment of the patient with medical illness, the psychotherapist must consider various contributory factors that might account for emotional distress. These factors, which become focal points in the subsequent development of a treatment plan, are described later and noted in Figure 1.

a. Early Developmental Issues Early developmental issues can temper the present-day experience of medical illness. Areas that might be explored with the patient include: (1) the relationship with parents, particularly parental effectiveness as caretakers (i.e., based on past experience, can the patient reasonably trust others to take care of him/her?); (2) the family philosophy of and approach to illness (e.g., acceptability, response patterns

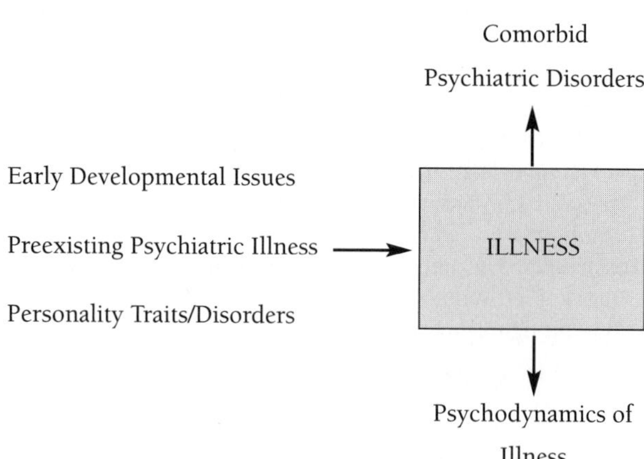

FIGURE 1 Contributory factors to emotional distress in patients with medical illness

to ill members, support and involvement; did parents effectively address, discredit, or dramatize illness in family members?); (3) prior personal experience with illness including illness among family members and friends; and (4) personal tolerability of dependency. It is also important to explore any cultural context or meaning of illness (e.g., the interpretation of hallucinations during delirium as a spiritual visitation from ancestors), and the expected response to illness within a specific culture, if applicable.

b. Preexisting Psychiatric Disorders Some of the current emotional distress may have actually predated the medical illness (i.e., the patient may have a preexisting psychiatric disorder). This possibility is based on the expected prevalence rates of major psychiatric disorders in the general population. For example, according to the National Comorbidity Survey, the lifetime prevalence of any depressive disorder is nearly 20%, anxiety disorder 25%, and substance abuse 27%. Therefore, it is worthwhile to explore for preexisting psychiatric disorders, particularly acute depression (major depression), chronic depression (dysthymic disorder), and substance abuse. These disorders may presently be comorbid, or co-exist, with the medical illness.

In addition to preexisting major psychiatric disorders, some adult patients also suffer from personality disorders. With their onsets in childhood, personality disorders result in long-standing and consistent deviations in cognition, behavior, and interpersonal relationships—all of which may influence the course and management of medical illness (e.g., medication compliance, appointment attendance, cooperation with treatment and medical personnel, reaction to illness, ability to elicit support from others). As an example of personality disturbance affecting illness, we have empirically determined that at least 7% of patients actively sabotage their medical care and that medically self-sabotaging behavior is typically associated with personality pathology, specifically borderline personality disorder.

Personality disorders can be difficult to diagnose during an initial evaluation, particularly if the patient is relatively high functioning and well educated. Oftentimes, diagnosis evolves with continuing or ongoing contact with the patient. However, health care personnel and family members may provide important historical information that suggests personality pathology, which is usually manifest in interpersonal functioning.

c. New-Onset Psychiatric Disorders After the onset of illness, patients may experience new-onset, or secondary, psychiatric disorders, most frequently either depression and/or anxiety. It appears that depression is particularly frequent among sufferers of neurological or cardiovascular disease. According to D. Spiegel and C. Classen, up to 50% of cancer patients experience clinical depression or anxiety, and the rate of depression in oncology patients is four times the prevalence found in the general population. Spiegel and Classen report that nearly 90% of these clinical syndromes are either manifestations of or reactions to illness or its treatment (i.e., secondary).

In addition to other factors, secondary mood disorders may be caused by a variety of medications administered to patients with medical illness. S. M. Valente and colleagues outline an extensive list of these medications (see "Further Reading") that include specific anti-inflammatory drugs and analgesics (e.g., ibuprofen, baclofen, opiates), anticonvulsants, antihistamines, particular anticancer drugs, caffeine, and propranolol. As with preexisting psychiatric disorders, these secondary mood disorders have the same potential to interfere with treatment by reducing compliance, optimism, and cooperation.

d. Medical Illness Psychodynamics There are well-known psychodynamics that are outgrowths of medical illness (see Table 1). Many of these psychodynamics center on the patient's experience of loss.

In addition to the themes relating to loss, D. Spiegel and C. Classen emphasize the importance of the patient's reaction to the disease, itself. For example, with

TABLE I
Psychodynamics That May Be Associated with Medical Illness

- Greater helplessness and increased dependency on others
- Need for social support
- Loss and mourning (e.g., disability, disfigurement, employability)
- Significant changes in usual activities, routines, life patterns
- Increased responsibility for own care (e.g., medication regimens, follow-up visits)
- Need to reexamine life priorities
- Feelings of alienation from others
- Threat of premature death
- Unpredictable course of illness
- Symptom control
- Secondary gain (e.g., nurturance needs, deserved punishment)

regard to cancer, some patients attempt to overly control their feelings in an effort to literally control the cancer. Some patients believe that maintaining a positive attitude, even at the cost of dealing with and sorting through by-product issues, is a means of curing cancer. These beliefs may result in the patient's unrealistic needs to remain strong and in control. Patients may also struggle to maintain a self-perception of being "normal" which can cause unrealistic overextensions of self.

Following diagnosis, the psychological demands on patients continue. For example, D. Spiegel and C. Classen describe cancer as a series of stressors, from beginning treatment protocols to the changes in the social and physical environment to fears of death. The complex demands of illness, as well as the stigma of illness, may result in social isolation and breaches in social support. In our experience, it appears that genuine support can be maintained in most families for about a year, but gradually, family members may lose their stamina and resilience.

4. Use of Psychological Measures in Medically Ill Patients

a. Mood Assessment Mood and anxiety disorders, the most common psychiatric disorders among the medically ill, may be assessed in a variety of ways. However, sometimes the direct approach is the best approach. In support of this, a group of investigators reported that, among a group of patients with terminal illness, asking the direct question, "Are you depressed?" was more valid than three sophisticated psychological assessments for depression.

b. Psychological Measures of Illness Experience Psychological measures specific to the illness experience have not been broadly utilized in clinical settings. However, examples of general measures include the Millon Behavioral Health Inventory; the Psychological Adjustment to Illness scale; and the Illness Behavior Questionnaire. The latter measure contains seven scales including general hypochondriasis, disease conviction, psychological versus somatic concern, affective inhibition, affective disturbance or dysphoria, denial, and irritability. Examples of illness-specific psychological measures, which are uncommon, include the Mental Adjustment to Cancer scale.

c. Psychological Measures of Health-Related Quality of Life Of the measures available, the Medical Outcomes Study 36-Item Short Form, or SF-36, is probably the most commonly used measure of health-related quality of life. This 36-item questionnaire, with known reliability and validity, contains eight subscales and measures health status, general functioning, and well-being. It has been used among broad samples of patients as a measure of outcome.

B. Treatment

Following assessment, the psychotherapist will hopefully have sufficient information to determine the initial foci of therapeutic work. These foci function as the basis for developing an eclectic and individualized treatment approach. Given the possible short duration of anticipated treatment, the therapist must, according to H. Levenson and R. E. Hales, select the symptoms, behaviors, or conflicts most amenable to treatment.

1. Timing of Psychotherapy Treatment

An important consideration for the therapist and patient is the timing of psychotherapy treatment. Coping strategies are ideally taught to the patient and family when motivation and physical stamina are relatively high (i.e., the early phases of illness), whereas treatment in the later phases of medical illness may limit efficacy.

2. Establishing the Therapeutic Relationship

a. The Paradox of Empathy Although most therapists have an understanding of what it feels like to be depressed or anxious, to suffer the loss of a relationship, or to mourn a death, far fewer have experienced the unique types of compromises precipitated by medical illness. This potential difference poses unique constraints with empathy in the therapeutic relationship because most of us do not understand what it is like to be burned beyond recognition or to deal with a disfiguring surgery. In this regard, we believe that it is important, when applicable, for therapists to actively acknowledge their lack of personal experience with a particular medical process, and the feelings associated with it, in an effort to promote a candid and sincere need to understand the patient. Likewise, therapists can explain their familiarity with a specific disease process and/or the illness experience from work with other patients.

b. Engagement with Emotional Boundaries Because of the potential devastation of medical illness and the resulting biological and psychological regression that occurs, the therapist needs to be sensitive to the extensive support needs of these patients. Spontaneity, genuineness, warmth, and the candid expression of support are important qualities in the building of rapport. At the same time, realistic internal emotional boundaries need to be established within the therapist to avoid emotional overinvolvement.

c. Transference As the treatment relationship unfolds, various types of transferences may evolve. A transference is the patient's unconscious assignment to others of thoughts and feelings that were originally associated with important figures in one's early life (American Psychiatric Association's *Psychiatric Glossary*). As an example, the patient may have been abandoned by parents as a child and now unconsciously expects that the treatment team will also abandon him or her. Examples of more subtle transferences might be the patient's unconscious resentment about the health and well-being of the therapist. Differences in age, gender, professional backgrounds, and level of education may cause breaches in the therapeutic relationship based on early issues. Finally, the early relationship with caretakers may affect the patient's reaction to being helped and supported by the treatment team as well as accepting the natural and expected dependency that occurs in a treatment relationship.

d. Countertransference Countertransferences may also develop. Countertransference is the therapist's partly unconscious or conscious emotional reactions to the patient (American Psychiatric Association's *Psychiatric Glossary*). As examples, the therapist may not feel comfortable working with patients who are going to die, due to earlier unresolved experiences with death as well as our cultural discomfort with death. The therapist may also be concerned about the patient's medical illness prohibiting an orderly exploration of issues. Likewise, the therapist's own prior experience of illness may affect his or her perception of the patient. As a final example, the therapist may feel uncomfortable with the medical overlay associated with the care of the patient (e.g., hospital setting, liaison with medical personnel, medical communication or jargon, uncertainty about the treatment process or outcome), which may be a reflection of an early sense of helplessness in undefined or overwhelming situations.

Beyond transference and countertransference issues, other relationship dynamics may emerge. For example, as therapy progresses, a mutual denial regarding the severity of illness may develop between the patient and the therapist. This dynamic may function to protect the continuity of the therapeutic relationship.

e. The Therapist with Medical Illness One final issue involving the therapeutic relationship needs to be considered—that of the therapist who suffers from medical illness. In these circumstances, the therapist may experience prominent defenses against his or her own illness including denial, omnipotence, and reaction formation (i.e., the latter being an unconscious defense mechanism in which the individual adopts thoughts and behaviors that are the opposite of what he or she is really experiencing). Reaction formation may be in response to dependency and debilitation. Medical illness may also result in empathic failure in the treatment relationship because of the therapist's emotional preoccupation and subsequent withdrawal from the patient. For therapists with medical illness, there is also the delicate issue of disclosure to patients about the illness, particularly its course and prognosis.

3. Psychotherapy Treatment Components

In the remainder of this section, we discuss psychotherapy treatment from a general perspective in an effort to accommodate the most generic patient with medical illness. We wish to emphasize that most effective therapies with patients with medical illness incorporate an eclectic and individualized approach. Several common components will be discussed (i.e., psychoeducation, acute problem solving, cognitive-behavioral techniques, psychodynamic psychotherapy, family intervention). The resulting treatment structure, including the various treatment components, is not limited to an individual-therapy format but may be incorporated into a group format as well. In addition, different treatment providers may captain the individual components.

a. Psychoeducation Psychoeducation is typically an ongoing process during treatment. Psychoeducation may occur while describing the process of psychotherapy, when inviting the mutual sharing of medical information (e.g., disease effects, prognosis, necessary medical intervention), and while validating key psychodynamic issues such as loss. In this regard, therapists who treat patients with medical illness need to understand the natural course and treatment of the illness, if such information is available.

b. Acute Problem Solving A variety of practical life issues may need to be addressed with the patient. These may include inexpensive resources for medical supplies, financial aid, child care, transportation, sexual functioning, and cosmetic concerns (e.g., hair loss with chemotherapy). The therapist plays an active role in triaging problems to appropriate adjunctive health care personnel (e.g., social work) and community resources (e.g., wig salons) as well as addressing issues relevant to psychotherapy treatment (e.g., telling a spouse the prognosis).

Acute problem solving may also be addressed in brief psychotherapy treatment models. H. Levenson and R. E. Hales describe two examples of specific models of brief, dynamic psychotherapy for medically ill patients. One model is Time-Limited Dynamic Therapy that is an interpersonal therapy approach based on the premise that present relational difficulties were learned in childhood. The preceding investigators report that this model is particularly applicable to patients with medical illness because chronic illness may initiate a pattern of disturbed interpersonal relationships. A second example of a brief psychotherapy model is Short-Term Dynamic Therapy of Stress Response Syndromes, a 12-session treatment developed by M. Horowitz in 1976. This model focuses on the alleviation of an immediate stressor and is intrapsychic, rather than interpersonal, in format.

c. Cognitive-Behavioral Techniques Cognitive-behavioral interventions can be very helpful for patients with medical illness by modifying thoughts, emotions, and behaviors. Cognitive-behavioral treatment focuses on the elicitation and "correction" of unintentional thinking errors or cognitive distortions that precede the exacerbation of emotional discomfort. Illogical thoughts (e.g., "I'll never feel better") are systematically elicited and processed to determine their nature (are they, for example, a result of magnifying or minimizing situations?). These thoughts, which are actively linked with emotional discomfort (i.e., "notice that when you think this, you feel like this"), are ultimately reformed, relabeled, or replaced ("you don't feel good now; you will feel better, later").

d. Psychodynamic Psychotherapy Although not applicable to all patients, many have early developmental issues, particularly parents' responses to caretaking and illness as well as the patient's experience of dependency, which relate to and affect the current medical illness. In working with the patient, the therapist needs to maintain an active mental checklist of prominent current issues with the intent of threading these back into the developmental history to explore for any former issues that might be affecting the current medical experience. We are fairly candid with patients about the purpose of this historical information (e.g., "I need to understand your childhood background to determine its possible influences on your illness."). When present, an understanding of the association between past and present relationships may help resolve excessive fears and address defenses such as denial.

Psychodynamic psychotherapy can assist patients by alleviating the complex issues related to loss and changing social and family roles. As an example, the therapist needs to explore and clarify the meaning of illness to the patient in terms of possible role reversal (i.e., being cared for by one's children). Other common psychodynamic themes are listed in Table 1.

Terminal illness is a particular challenge in the treatment process, in part because of the therapist's task of ascertaining the meaning and value of defense mechanisms such as avoidance and denial. For example, dying patients may avoid the disclosure of the extent of their disease to loved ones. Patients may even avoid asking the treatment team about the prognosis so as not to confirm a negative one. Denial may limit the patient's reality of being finite as well as sabotage personal closure needs. On the other hand, some of these defenses may be the psychological substance of immediate survival. Therefore, the therapist must delicately explore the function of these dynamics and determine their adaptability. Again, these defenses are not always pathological or problematic.

Another challenging issue in the treatment of patients with medical illness is the patient's personal determinism with regard to his or her own death. Although beyond the scope of this article, the patient's desire to end pain, suffering, family stress, and financial exhaustion may precipitate the contemplation of suicide. Unquestionably, there are a variety of complex social, spiritual, religious, moral, and legal dilemmas entailed in this issue. However, the immediate clinical dilemma is the intended meaning of the patient's disclosure of suicidal thinking. Is the disclosure a "cry for help" or is it the need to explore a difficult decision with another human being? Is the therapist's contemplation of intervention an overt need to rescue the patient or avoid legal prosecution for inaction, or the therapist's intolerance of the patient's decision? What are the legal risks of not intervening with such a disclosure, particularly if the family supports the patient's decision to suicide? Finally, is the decision to suicide a rational one or a decision driven by fear or untreated depression, and does it matter? As a general guideline for therapists, at this juncture, it is particularly important to reassess and treat (or alter treatment of) mood disorders as such intervention may result in the resolution of suicidal ideation.

e. Family Intervention Although most therapists do not undertake intensive family therapy work in the treatment of patients with medical illness, it is usually helpful to meet with the family. The family may provide additional background information, require individual professional support (e.g., the spouse who is depressed and needs antidepressant medication), and/or require a liaison between the patient and/or hospital personnel. In addition, families may require education about specific psychological issues (e.g., the role of depression, emergence of delirium secondary to the treatment) as well as some reframing about their loved one's behavior (e.g., the patient's low frustration tolerance, fear, confusion, inability to make decisions).

f. Group Therapy As noted previously, all the preceding treatment components may be undertaken in group format. The psychological advantages of group treatment of patients with medical illness include the ability to emphasize the universality of experiences, deal with disability on a mutual level, engage in emotional sharing, sort out relationships with family, and acknowledge and attempt to resolve grief and loss.

In working with cancer patients, D. Spiegel and C. Classen describe the goals of group therapy, many of which apply to all group treatments. These investigators emphasize the goals of building social bonds, using the group experience as a working lab to practice and express emotions, processing feelings about death and dying, redefining life goals, increasing social support, comparing health information, improving one's relationship with the health care team, and improving coping skills. With regard to the latter, a group experience is an excellent way to discover how others have dealt with and resolved specific issues or problems (e.g., having sexual relations while wearing a colostomy bag).

Group treatment is determined by the patient's individual needs (e.g., social comfort with groups, level of debilitation, type of medical illness), the available resources, and the availability of sufficient fellow patients (usually 7–10) who meet the group's criteria for entry (e.g., HIV infection). Some groups are very structured including an explicit number of sessions, while others are open-ended and continue as long as the need persists. In addition to patient groups, some therapists provide group intervention to families.

Group treatment is potentially more cost effective than individual treatment. However, potential difficulties in initiating group treatment include establishing the proper working group size, defining entry criteria (e.g., type of illness, stage of illness, age, sex), solicitation of members (e.g., bulletin board advertisements, physician referral only), duration of the group both per session and total duration, and whether the group is open to new members or not. Other potential problems include reimbursement, establishing and maintaining confidentiality, and leadership. Unlike typical psychotherapy groups, members may have to be prepared for the inevitable death of some participants, depending on the composition of the group.

4. Treatment Strategies for Major Psychiatric Disorders

a. Preexisting and Current Mood Disorders As noted previously, patients commonly develop depression and anxiety disorders, either prior to the onset of illness or during it. Mood and anxiety disorders are usually treated in a traditional fashion with antidepressant or antianxiety medications as well as the consideration of psychotherapy. Certain types of antidepressants, the selective serotonin reuptake inhibitors (SSRIs), are favored because of their ability to treat both depression and anxiety, and their minimal side effects, particularly the lack of cognitive and cardiovascular effects. With one exception (citalopram), these drugs tend to be very safe in single-drug overdoses.

b. Somatoform Disorders Somatoform disorders consist of a collection of psychiatric disorders that include somatization disorder (i.e., the presence of multiple physical complaints involving multiple body areas or body systems); conversion disorder (the presence of a symptom complex that is under unintentional but voluntary control and whose onset relates temporally to stress or conflict); pain disorder (pain symptoms in which psychological factors contribute in an unintentional way); and hypochondriasis (nondelusional, but persistent preoccupation with one's body or symptoms with regard to disease). These disorders may be associated with other types of psychiatric disorders, particularly mood and anxiety disorders. Because of the patient's focus on physical symptoms and the oftentimes unintentional generation of symptoms, there may be little interest in mental health support. However, symptoms may be reduced in some patients with supportive psychotherapy geared to stressors and interpersonal conflicts, frequent appointments with the primary care physician, conservative medical intervention, and the treatment of comorbid conditions such as mood and anxiety disorders with antidepressants. With regard to the latter, those antidepressants which exert an antiobsessive effect (e.g., SSRIs) may be particularly helpful in some patients. Among this group of patients, there is a great deal of heterogeneity and in some cases, more sophisticated types of psychotherapy may be utilized in particular patients as well as more complicated combinations of psychotropic medications. Some of these patients may even benefit from hypnosis (e.g., conversion disorder).

5. *Treatment Strategies for Patients with Personality Disorders*

We believe that the presence of a personality disorder is one of the most difficult issues in the treatment of patients with medical illness. Because of their longstanding nature, personality disorders tend to be tenacious and difficult to change. Most theorists believe that long-term treatment is required and the outcome or prognosis may be limited. In addition, there are few studies that clarify the efficacy of treatment for personality disorders. Indeed, some disorders, such as antisocial personality disorder, have questionable responses to treatment. The interplay of medical illness and personality disorder can be exasperating for the clinician as well as the family and health care team. For example, the management of diabetes may be extremely difficult among patients who sabotage their administration of insulin, resulting in repeated hospitalizations and medical complications.

It is important to emphasize that the presence of personality disorder is not always a meaningful issue in treatment. For example, in cancer victims with poor prognoses, personality disorder treatment is neither realistic nor appropriate. In these latter cases, the therapist may limit treatment to minimizing the impact and effects of the personality-disordered behavior on family, medical staff, and other patients.

II. THEORETICAL BASES

It is difficult, at times, to accurately measure and describe the psychotherapy process and why it works. Perhaps it is the psychological intimacy that provides immeasurable support. Perhaps it is the revelation of fear, anger, disappointment, and shame—all the feelings that incarcerate the spirit. It may also be establishing new conceptual paradigms to replace the previous ones that no longer work. Whatever the growth-promoting elements of psychotherapy treatment are, they certainly apply to the treatment of those with medical illness. The modifications in psychotherapy treatment of this population primarily center on the additional knowledge base required in working with a medical illness, the biological stress of the illness, and the ever-prominent issue of death. Although suicide is always a concern in working with patients with nonmedical illness, it remains an issue with the patient with medical illness as well, in addition to the threat of death from illness.

III. EMPIRICAL STUDIES

In a 1994 review of the literature, H. R. Conte reported that there were few controlled empirical studies, and only occasional case reports, exploring the efficacy of supportive psychotherapy for patients with medical illness. Results indicated beneficial effects, in general. Although it is impossible to compare outcome studies because of differing patient populations, therapeutic interventions, treatment settings, and types of medical illness, we present some highlights from the literature.

A. Psychoeducation

Among patients with chronical illness, researchers found that classroom as well as home psychoeducation (e.g., instruction on mind–body relationships, relaxation training, and communication skills) resulted in improvements with pain, sleep disturbance, mood, and anxiety. Formalized psychoeducation has also been undertaken with cancer patients and found to enhance both cognitive and behavioral coping skills.

B. General Psychological Intervention

In a group of patients with atopic dermatitis, those who entered into a psychological treatment demonstrated a greater improvement in their skin condition than did those patients in standard medical treatment. In a review of outcomes among those with chronic heart failure, it has been reported that psychological and behavioral interventions have the potential to substantially enhance treatment outcomes. Among patients undergoing coronary artery bypass surgery, those who participated in daily supportive psychotherapy had fewer medical complications and shorter lengths of hospitalization, compared with controls. Through meta-analysis, the efficacy of psychological interventions among both children and adolescents with chronic medical illness has been explored; despite a host of limitations, results support the overall efficacy of psychological intervention.

C. Cognitive-Behavioral Interventions

Cognitive-behavioral intervention has been found to improve depression among patients with chronic illness. Multicomponent behavioral therapy among patients with irritable bowel syndrome resulted in greater symptom reduction compared with controls.

D. Group Therapy

In examining the sense of well-being as an outcome measure for patients with serious medical illness in time-limited (12 sessions) group therapy, researchers found that although somatic concern remained sustained, all patients noted an improvement in their sense of well-being. Likewise, among cancer patients receiving radiation therapy, there were significant decreases in both physical and emotional symptoms for those who participated in 10 group therapy sessions of 90 min each. Through multicenter evaluation, group therapy with breast cancer patients has been empirically assessed and resulted in improved mood, fewer maladaptive coping responses, and improved support. Finally, group therapy (six sessions) among patients with malignant melanoma resulted in decreased stress, greater use of coping skills, and effective changes in the lymphoid cell system.

E. Cost Effectiveness of Psychotherapy

Researchers have found that psychotherapy can be cost effective among certain medical patients with concomitant psychiatric illness. In addition, there is evidence that psychiatric consultation-liaison services for medical patients reduces the overall cost of care. Studies indicate that psychiatric illness, notably depression, usually prolongs hospital stays for medical patients and intervention reduces cost. In summary, it appears that reducing psychiatric morbidity among medical patients also has the potential to reduce their overall cost of medical care.

F. Caveats

Although many studies clearly support the efficacy of psychological intervention in patients with medical illness, there are studies that do not. For example, the provision of group therapy for the relatives of patients with chronic aphasia was appreciated but did not lead to measurable improvements in participants' perceptions of personal, social, or family burdens. Among patients with testicular cancer, psychotherapy did not affect outcome when compared with controls. In examining the impact of treating depression among hospitalized veterans and the effect on participants' preferences for life-sustaining therapy, surprisingly, these preferences did not change, regardless of the improvement in depression.

IV. SUMMARY

The psychotherapy of patients with medical illness must be individualized to the needs of each patient. Treatment components may include psychoeducation, acute problem solving, cognitive-behavioral techniques, psychodynamic psychotherapy, family intervention, and group therapy. The unique aspects of medical illness temper the psychodynamics of the issues in the treatment process. The therapist must integrate both the knowledge of psychology and biological disease to effect an outcome. Although most studies underscore the effectiveness of psychological interventions in the medical patient, the documented limitations of psychological intervention in some populations underscores the importance of further investigation.

See Also the Following Articles

Bioethics ■ Cancer Patients: Psychotherapy ■ Collaborative Care ■ Comorbidity ■ Countertransference ■ Informed Consent ■ Integrative Approaches to Psychotherapy ■ Neurobiology ■ Transference

Further Reading

Levenson, H., & Hales, R. E. (1993). Brief psychodynamically informed therapy for medically ill patients. In A. Stoudemire, & B. S. Fogel (Eds.), *Medical-psychiatric practice* (Vol. 2, pp. 3–37). Washington, DC: American Psychiatric Press.

Spiegel, D. (1999). Psychotherapeutic intervention with the medically ill. In D. S. Janowsky (Ed.), *Psychotherapy indications and outcomes* (pp. 277–300). Washington, DC: American Psychiatric Press.

Spiegel, D., & Classen, C. (Eds.) (2000). *Group therapy for cancer patients: A research-based handbook for psychosocial care.* New York: Basic Books.

Spira, J. L. (Ed.), (1997). *Group therapy for medically ill patients.* New York: Guilford Press.

Stoudemire, A., & Fogel, B. S. (Eds.), (1993). *Medical-psychiatric practice.* Washington, DC: American Psychiatric Press.

Stoudemire, A., Fogel, B. S., & Greenberg, D. B. (Eds.), (2000). *Psychiatric care of the medical patient.* New York: Oxford University Press.

Valente, S. M., Saunders, J. M., & Cohen, M. Z. (1994). Evaluating depression among patients with cancer. *Cancer Practice, 2,* 65–71.

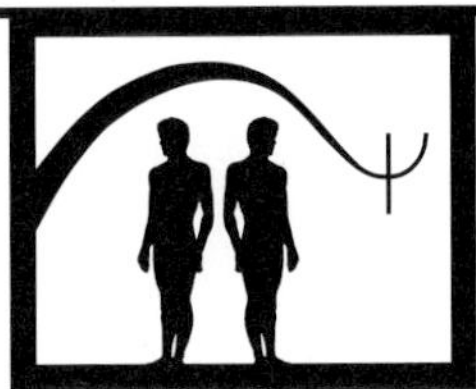

Minimal Therapist Contact Treatments

Anderson B. Rowan and Julie M. Storey

*Malcolm Grow Medical Center, Andrews Air Force Base, Maryland**

GLOSSARY

minimal therapist contact treatments (MCT) Rely heavily on out-of-clinic interventions. Often it is referred to as a "home-based" treatment.

cost-effectiveness Percentage improvement per minute of clinician contact.

Minimal therapist contact is a term used to describe psychological interventions that utilize alternative forms of instruction and treatment administration (e.g., written materials, computer programs, videotapes, audiotapes, and portable biofeedback equipment) to reduce professional contact time without compromising treatment intensity. Because minimal therapist contact treatment (MCT) relies heavily on out-of-clinic interventions, it is often referred to as a "home-based" treatment.

I. TREATMENT DESCRIPTION

For the purposes of definition, it is important to distinguish between other forms of intervention that utilize alternative delivery methods and MCT treatments. These other forms of intervention, including certain types of bibliotherapy and many self-help interventions, effectively reduce the amount of contact time, but they accomplish this by decreasing the intensity of the intervention. For example, efficiency may be improved solely by decreasing the number of sessions in the intervention, limiting the patient–therapist interaction to a one-time, informational exchange, or eliminating the patient–therapist relationship altogether (e.g., pure self-help). MCTs on the other hand, seek to deliver an intervention of equal intensity and duration to standard clinic-based treatments (SCT) while maintaining ongoing (although less frequent) patient–therapist contact.

MCTs offer many potential advantages over SCTs. First, at-home skill acquisition and practice eliminates the need for frequent, lengthy clinic visits, improving access to care for many patients. Specifically for patients living in rural areas who must travel significant distances for care, a decrease in clinic visits makes obtaining treatment more feasible due to a reduction in transportation costs and lost work time. A reduction in clinic visits, however, will likely improve access to care for all patients, not just those living in rural areas. For example, recent treatment utilization data suggest that 80% of patients attend fewer than six treatment sessions, suggesting the length of standard interventions may be a barrier to patient care in general.

* The views expressed in this article are those of the authors and do not reflect the official policy or position of the United States Air Force, Department of Defense, or the United States Government.

Second, MCTs reduce the total amount of therapist contact time that results in decreased provider cost per patient treated. Cost-effectiveness, defined as percentage improvement per minute of clinician contact, has been shown to be as high as five times greater in MCTs as compared to SCTs. This characteristic of MCTs fits in well with the prevailing method of health care funding and delivery: managed care. Health maintenance organizations (HMOs) are concerned with treatment cost, treatment quality, and patient access to care. As a method of cost containment, many HMOs limit the number of preapproved clinic visits. MCTs respond to this need to balance cost containment and patient care by decreasing cost without sacrificing treatment efficacy.

Compared to efficiency-enhancing methods that rely solely on reducing or eliminating therapist contact time, MCTs offer the potential benefit of greater patient involvement and skill acquisition without the loss of intervention and monitoring by a trained therapist. In addition, this utilization of alternative mediums of instruction and delivery allows the therapist to focus on tailoring interventions to specific patients and to respond to factors and circumstances that arise during treatment. MCTs are also flexible and can often incorporate the beneficial aspects of other efficiency-enhancing formats. For example, the first author has designed a group administered MCT protocol for the treatment of chronic headaches (HA). Finally, MCT's use of extensive at-home skill acquisition and practice theoretically may facilitate skill generalization and internal attributions for change. However, no studies have examined differences in generalization.

Some potential disadvantages may also exist for MCTs. The first author's experience with MCTs suggests they may require a higher level of motivation or cognitive ability than SCTs, although no studies have investigated such a requirement. In addition, the increased reliance on patient self-administration presents the potential for reduced adherence, although poor adherence has not been reported in the existing literature.

II. THEORETICAL BASES

The term "minimal contact" implies a form of treatment administration and delivery that is not limited to a particular theory. This represents a significant advantage for MCTs because they can potentially be applied to any type of intervention that is translatable into a standard protocol, regardless of clinical orientation. However, the MCTs described in the literature have, almost entirely, been developed from treatments based in cognitive-behavioral theory. This trend is not a random occurrence but is due primarily to the nature and developmental stage of cognitive-behavioral interventions that make them especially suitable for MCT methods.

First, cognitive-behavioral interventions rely heavily on education and exposure to new experiences for treatment efficacy. Both of these treatment components lend themselves to home-based interventions that utilize alternative mediums to communicate information. Second, treatment efficacies of many cognitive-behavioral interventions for a variety of disorders have received significant empirical support. Once an intervention has been established and its efficacy empirically supported, the amount of additional clinical improvement gained by modifying the content of the intervention will eventually plateau. Cognitive-behavioral interventions for chronic headaches reached such a plateau, leading researchers to look toward enhancements in treatment delivery for further improvement of the interventions. MCT methods provide one means by which the efficiency of established interventions can be enhanced while the treatment content, intensity and efficacy remain intact.

III. LITERATURE REVIEW

Research exists to support various forms of MCT for adult patients with both physical and psychological disorders, including migraine and tension HA, hypertension, and panic disorder. In addition, research supports the use of MCT for HA and enuresis in children.

The literature on MCT of HAs in adults consistently finds MCT to be equally as effective as the more intensive SCTs. Results of a recent meta-analysis of 20 controlled clinical outcome trials suggest MCTs, on average, are more cost-effective and require substantially less professional contact time, as well as, fewer clinic visits. In addition, MCTs produced similar or significantly better outcomes than SCTs requiring more professional contact.

More specifically, a 1996 review article including eight studies of MCTs for tension-type HA found MCTs to be equally as effective as SCTs for the reduction of HA activity. MCT for tension-type HA has also been compared to prophylactic, pharmacological intervention (Amitriptyline HCL). The results suggest MCTs are similarly efficacious in terms of decreasing HA frequency and intensity. However, compared to the medication group, additional benefits were realized in the MCT group, such as more internalized locus of control, fewer general somatic complaints, and fewer side effects. Although long-term follow-up studies of these interventions have been somewhat lacking, existing data have consistently shown good maintenance of effects throughout follow-up periods ranging from 3 months to 2 years.

Similar results have been reported for migraine HA. Three investigations comparing the efficacy of MCT and SCT relaxation/thermal biofeedback interventions suggest MCT is equally as effective as SCT for the reduction of migraine HA. One study to date has investigated the efficacy of MCTs as compared to abortive medication (ergotamine tartrate) for the reduction of migraine HA. The results found MCT to be equally as effective as this abortive intervention, although patients treated with medication experienced improvements more rapidly than those treated with MCT.

No research to date has been conducted comparing MCT to treatment with prophylactic medication. However, one study compared MCT alone to MCT plus propranolol (the most commonly used prophylactic agent for migraine HA). The results indicate that, although both interventions were effective, the addition of the prophylactic agent yielded significant enhancements in HA reduction.

MCT methods have also been used in the treatment of essential hypertension with equivocal results. One study investigated the efficacy of a 5-session, thermal biofeedback MCT for adults with essential hypertension who required at least two drugs for hemodynamic control. This intervention was compared to a standard, 16-session, thermal biofeedback SCT. The results suggest that patients in the MCT did significantly poorer controlling their blood pressures without medication than those in the SCT. However, a previous investigation comparing a 9-session thermal biofeedback MCT to a 20-session SCT found equivalent reductions in blood pressure and antihypertensive medication use. Methodological limitations, such as small sample size, suggest that more research is needed in the area of MCTs for hypertension.

A recent study also supports the efficacy of MCT methods in the administration of cognitive-behavioral treatment of panic disorder. When compared to a standard, 10-session cognitive-behavioral intervention for panic disorder, a minimal contact approach involving 5 sessions and supported by self-help materials yielded similar improvements both immediately posttreatment and at 12-month follow-up. In addition to applying minimal contact methods, this particular intervention also reduced the total length of therapy while maintaining the efficacy of the longer, clinic-based intervention.

Data have also been reported that support MCTs in pediatric populations. A review article including three school-based and four home-based MCT interventions concludes that MCT for pediatric and adolescent migraine, regardless of setting, is equally as effective as SCTs. The existing research on pediatric tension HA for both SCTs and MCTs are more modest, however, with the percentage of participants experiencing clinically significant improvement (defined as > 50% reduction in overall HA activity) being low, but similar, for both types of intervention. In terms of mixed-type HA, a recent treatment study of a home-based MCT for children (ages 10–12) found the MCT to be as efficacious as the SCT and over twice as cost-effective.

Similarly, data supporting the efficacy of MCTs for the treatment of nocturnal enuresis in children have also been reported. This treatment relied on the children's parents for the administration of the treatment. Although some limitations may exist for the application of MCTs with children, such as inability to read and the need for significant parental involvement in treatment, more research is needed on MCT in this population.

In general, research has fairly consistently shown MCTs to be as effective as more costly SCT for the treatment of a variety of disorders in both adult and child populations. The extensive body of research demonstrating the efficacy of MCTs for chronic HA suggest MCTs for HA are ready for widespread clinical application. However, additional research is needed to verify MCTs for the treatment of other disorders and to investigate the potential advantages and disadvantages of minimal contact methods beyond increased cost-effectiveness.

IV. TREATMENT ABSTRACT

Although MCT methodologies could result in many different therapy formats, a prototype based on a typical intervention is presented here as an example.

A prototypical MCT might take an 8-session, 8-week SCT and administer it utilizing three in-clinic sessions, two telephone contacts, and a series of audiotapes and manuals across the same 8 weeks. Table 1 compares a typical minimal therapist contact treatment (MCT) to a standard clinic-based treatment (SCT).

The first week of intervention looks almost identical in the two forms of treatment except for the use of training materials. During Week 2, the SCT therapist meets the patient for another 60-min session, while the MCT therapist speaks with the patient briefly on the telephone. During this telephone conversation, the MCT therapist will ask general questions regarding treatment progress, relaxation practice, and any behavior monitoring/recording that was assigned during Week 1. The

TABLE I
Example Minimal Therapist Contact Treatment versus Standard Clinic-Based Treatment Protocols

Week	Session content	Type of contact		Time (min)		Training material
		MCT[a]	SCT[b]	MCT	SCT	MCT
1	Education, treatment rationale, relaxation demonstration	Clinic	Clinic	60	60	Manual, audiotape
2	Progressive muscle relaxation (PMR) exercises; discrimination training (16 muscle groups)	Phone	Clinic	10	60	Manual, audiotape
3	PMR exercises (8 muscle groups)	None	Clinic	0	60	Manual, audiotape
4	PMR exercises (4 muscle groups)	None	Clinic	0	60	Manual, audiotape
5	PMR exercises (4 muscle groups); relaxation by recall, autogenic phrases, positive imagery, problem solving	Clinic	Clinic	60	60	Manual, audiotape
6	Same as Week 5	Phone	Clinic	10	60	Manual
7	Same as Week 5	None	Clinic	0	60	Manual
8	Review all components	Clinic	Clinic	40	60	Manual
Total		**3 visits 2 phone calls**	**8 visits**	**180**	**480**	

[a] MCT = Minimal Therapist Contact Treatment.
[b] SCT = Standard Clinic-Based Treatment.

MCT therapist will also briefly discuss the treatment activities for the upcoming weeks and remind the patient of the date and time of the second treatment session that will take place during Week 5.

During Weeks 3 and 4, the MCT patients do not have any contact with the therapist. They follow the readings and instructions regarding further development of relaxation and stress management skills that are contained in the manual and use the audiotapes to guide their skill acquisition and practice.

Week 5 for the MCT patients involves a 60-min clinic visit during which the therapist reviews the materials and the homework assigned during Weeks 3 and 4. The therapist also discusses problem solving, previews the information for Week 6, and schedules the final clinic visit for Week 8.

At the end of Week 6, a 10-min telephone contact is conducted. During this contact, the MCT therapist will ask questions regarding treatment progress, skills practice, and problem-solving exercises, discuss briefly the material for Week 7, reinforce the patient's effort and progress, and confirm the appointment for Week 8.

No contact is made with the patients in MCT during Week 7, and the patient meets with the therapist for a final 40-min session at the end of Week 8. During this visit, the materials and practice of skills from Weeks 5 through 8 are reviewed, posttreatment plans and goals are developed, and feedback is acquired regarding the treatment process.

Throughout the same 8-week period, SCT patients are exposed to the same information and skills, but they are delivered in weekly, 60-min, in-clinic sessions, with or without supplemental written and audiotape materials. It is important to recognize that many SCTs utilize supplemental materials such as manuals and audiotapes; however, in SCTs the intention of these materials is to review and reinforce the information and techniques presented by the therapist during in-clinic sessions. On the other hand, training materials used in MCTs are intended to be the primary delivery medium for the majority of the instruction.

See Also the Following Articles

Art Therapy ■ Bibliotherapy ■ Brief Therapy ■ Home-Based Reinforcement ■ Self-Help Groups ■ Self-Help Treatment for Insomnia ■ Single-Session Therapy

Further Reading

Blanchard, E. B., McCoy, G. C., McCaffrey, R. J., Berger, M., Musso, A. J., Wittrock, D. A., Gerardi, M. A., Halpern, M., & Pangburn, L. (1987). Evaluation of a minimal-therapist-contact thermal biofeedback treatment program for essential hypertension. *Biofeedback and Self-Regulation, 12*(2), 93–104.

Bollard, R. J., & Woodroffe, P. (1977). The effect of parent-administered dry-bed training on nocturnal enuresis in children. *Behaviour Research and Therapy, 15,* 159–165.

Botella, C., & Garcia-Palacios, A. (1999). The possibility of reducing therapist contact and total length of therapy in the treatment of panic disorder. *Behavioural and Cognitive Psychotherapy, 27,* 231–247.

Cote, G., Gauthier, J., Laberge, B., Cormier, H., & Plamondon, J. (1994). Reduced therapist contact in the cognitive behavioral treatment of panic disorder. *Behavior Therapy, 25*(1), 123–145.

Griffiths, J. D., & Martin, P. R. (1996). Clinical-versus home-based treatment formats for children with chronic headache. *British Journal of Health Psychology, 1,* 151–166.

Haddock, C. K., Rowan, A. B., Andrasik, F., Wilson, P. G., Talcott, G. W., & Stein, R. J. (1997). Home-based behavioral treatments for chronic benign headache: A meta-analysis of controlled trials. *Cephalalgia, 17,* 113–118.

Richardson, G. M., & McGrath, P. J. (1989). Cognitive-behavioral therapy for migraine head-aches: A minimal-therapist-contact approach versus a clinic-based approach. *Headache, 20,* 137–142.

Rowan, A., & Andrasik, F. (1996). Efficacy and cost-effectiveness of minimal therapist contact treatments of chronic headaches: A review. *Behavior Therapy, 27,* 207–234.

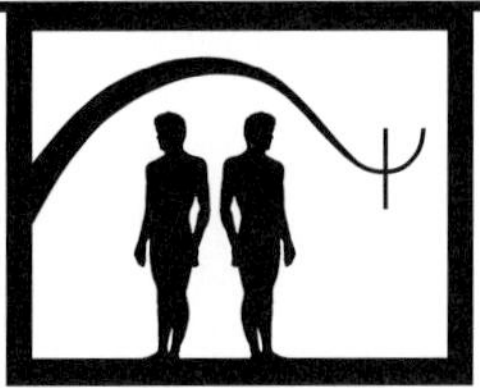

Modeling

Kurt A. Freeman
Pacific University

GLOSSARY

imitation Re-creation of an observed response.

vicarious learning Change in the likelihood that a person will demonstrate an observed behavior based on whether the observed model experiences reward or punish for engaging in the behavior.

Modeling is a psychotherapy technique utilized to produce changes in a client's behavioral repertoire by providing a demonstration of the desired behavior patterns and then affording opportunities for imitation. In this article, the basic components of the modeling procedure are discussed. Then, the theoretical bases on which the techniques are founded is explored. A review of the applicability of the technique follows, after which a synthesis of relevant research assessing the effectiveness of the approach is provided. Finally, a case example is given as an illustration of the process of using modeling as an intervention.

I. COMPONENTS OF MODELING INTERVENTION

As an intervention technique, modeling is relatively simple and is designed to assist clients in learning new behavior patterns. The procedure involves two primary components. First, the client is provided with an opportunity to observe the correct or desired form of behavior. Thus, theoretically any behavior that can be replicated in a form that is observable to the client may be taught through modeling. Second, the client imitates the observed behavior, demonstrating learning. For modeling to be effective as an intervention, the client must be able to demonstrate an imitative response. In other words, the client must be able to observe (i.e., pay attention to) the model (i.e., the person demonstrating the desired response) and then implement the skill that was just demonstrated. Clients who have particular characteristics that may interfere with attending to the model (e.g., blindness) or demonstrating the imitative response (e.g., physical disability) may not be good candidates for the use of this intervention.

Modeling is said to produce observational learning on the part of the client. Observational learning can be further divided into two forms of learning: imitation and vicarious learning. Imitation involves simply matching the topography of the observed behavior. For example, if a client observes a therapist demonstrate how to effectively introduce oneself to individuals unknown to the client (a skill that may be lacking in the client's behavioral repertoire), imitation involves the client simply repeating or matching the demonstrated introduction responses. Vicarious learning, on the other hand, involves a change in the likelihood of the targeted response being imitated as a function of observing the model being rewarded or punished for engaging in the targeted behavior. Using the earlier example, vicarious learning may result in the client being more likely to demonstrate the effective greeting response if the modeling situation involves the model being rewarded for implementing the skill (e.g., through a warm reception by "unknown" individuals).

Observational learning as a result of witnessing a model can produce three different effects. First, observing a model can result in the acquisition of previously unlearned behaviors. Thus, modeling can be used to increase a person's behavioral repertoire. In addition to establishing completely novel behavior patterns, modeling can facilitate chaining—the process of sequentially exhibiting various behaviors so that they form a complex pattern.

Second, modeling can result in a strengthening or weakening of inhibitory responses, referred to as inhibitory or disinhibitory effects, respectively. Regarding the former, modeling can strengthen inhibition to engage in a particular response via exposure to a model who is punished for engaging in the targeted behavior. Take, for example, a young child who tantrums. Assume that her parents are using time out as a punishment technique to decrease tantrums. If the time-out procedure is effective, it will inhibit the likelihood that the young girl will tantrum. Furthermore, if she observed (perhaps at school) another child being placed in time out after engaging in a tantrum, this could further decrease the likelihood that the she will tantrum. Through observing the model (in this case, the other child) being punished for the target behavior, she is now even less likely to engage in the tantrum, above and beyond the decrease produced by experiencing the time out directly. Alternatively, modeling can weaken previous learning that has inhibited responding. As an illustration, consider a student who was previously punished for participating in class (e.g., other students laughing at his incorrect answers, the teacher sternly correcting the student when he is wrong). If this student observes a model experience rewarding consequences as a result of participating in class, this may weaken the previous inhibitory learning, thus increasing the likelihood that the student will participate.

Finally, modeling may evoke previously learned behavior patterns, referred to as the response facilitation effect. Although seemingly similar to the disinhibitory effect, the response facilitation effect differs because of the previous learning that was involved. The disinhibitory effect occurs when behavior was previously punished. However, the response facilitation effect produces an increase in the likelihood of the occurrence of a response pattern that was not previously punished. In essence, then, the modeled behavior in this case simply serves as a cue to engage in behavior that has already been learned.

In 1977, Albert Bandura described the factors that influence the effectiveness of modeling as a behavior change technique. First, if modeling is being used to facilitate the demonstration of a particular behavior pattern by the observer, then the modeled behavior should result in successful (i.e., reinforcing) consequences for the model. Second, modeling is more likely to produce the desired impact if the model is similar to the observer(s), or has a high status. For example, if one is working with an adult African American client, modeling may be more effective if the model is also an adult African American individual. Thus, attention to factors such as age, gender, and ethnicity are important when selecting a model. Third, the complexity of the behavior modeled should be appropriate based on the abilities and developmental level of the observer. Fourth, the observer has to attend to the model for the exposure to have an effect. Fifth, the modeled behavior should occur within the proper context. For example, if a therapist is trying to teach the social skills necessary for successfully greeting a new person, the therapist should arrange a situation in which the client can observe one person demonstrate the necessary skills while interacting with a second person, perhaps in the waiting room or other similar situation. Sixth, the modeled behavior should be repeated as frequently as necessary for the learner to demonstrate correct imitation. To facilitate generalized learning, the desired behavior should be modeled in various situations and context. Finally, the observer should be given opportunities to imitate the modeled behavior as soon as possible after modeling has occurred, with corrective and positive feedback provided.

There are several variations in the format of presenting the modeling procedure to the client. The traditional form involves a live model demonstrating the desired responses. The client watches the model and then is provided with the opportunity to demonstrate the imitative response. Live, or *in vivo*, modeling is advantageous because of the ability to adapt and modify the model selected and the demonstration of the desired response to best meet the needs of a particular client. For example, specific appropriate models can be selected to match the characteristics of the client. Furthermore, particular behaviors of concern that are idiosyncratic to the client can be selected and demonstrated. However, the advantages of *in vivo* modeling can also be disadvantages in that it may be difficult to select ideal models or create the necessary conditions for the demonstration of various forms of behavior.

To provide for frequent exposure to the model, symbolic modeling may be used. Symbolic modeling can be achieved via the use of several different modeling formats, such as use of video, film, slide presentation, and so on. With symbolic modeling, the model is somehow recorded while demonstrating the desired responses. Then, the client is exposed to the recorded version of the modeling demonstration. Although the initial investment may be larger in terms of equipment and time needs, symbolic modeling can result in more efficient demonstration of the desired responses because once the model is recorded, it can be used repeatedly with the same client, or with multiple clients. In fact, there are commercially available resources to teach a variety of skills via symbolic modeling.

Finally, covert modeling has been described in the literature. Covert modeling involves carrying out the intervention via the use of imagery. With this variation, the client is instructed to imagine the model demonstrating the desired response, rather than actually witnessing the scenario *in vivo*. For a person to participate in covert modeling, she or he must be able to create detailed cognitive/mental images. Thus, careful assessment of a client's abilities to create detailed images is necessary prior to using covert modeling. Like live modeling, covert modeling has as an advantage flexibility in that a client can image models and scenarios that are particularly relevant. Furthermore, like video or film modeling, covert modeling has as an advantage ease of implementation in that a client can be repeatedly and frequently exposed to the model with minimal effort.

In addition to the general formats of modeling, the variants of this procedure can be further defined by whether they involve simple modeling or participant modeling. The former involves exposure to the model presented in any of the formats described earlier, followed by the opportunity for imitative responding. Participant modeling, on the other hand, also involves some form of guide practice either during or just after exposure to the model. With this form of modeling, the clinician physically guides the client to engage in the desired response, thus ensuring correct or successful performance.

Regardless of the form of modeling used, there are several components to the use of the intervention that should be considered, as described by Sherry Cormier and Bill Cormier in their 2000 text. First, the client should be provided with a rationale for the use of the modeling procedure. Essentially, the therapist should explain that by observing effective demonstration of skills/behaviors, the client should be better able to learn those desired responses. Second, Cormier and Cormier recommend addressing five components of the actual modeling scenario: (a) specifying and dividing desired goals into identifiable behavioral responses, (b) arranging the actual behaviors into a logical order of presentation, (c) selecting the appropriate model, (d) providing verbal instructions to the client prior to modeling, and (e) demonstrating the targeted behaviors repeatedly. Third, the client needs to be provided with an opportunity to demonstrate the modeled responses. At this stage of the intervention, the therapist should observe the client imitate the response, provide induction aids (e.g., verbal or gestural prompts), and offer positive and corrective feedback. Feedback and induction aids can be reduced and eliminated as the client demonstrates mastery of the responses. Finally, critical to the success of any modeling situation, the therapist should ensure that the imitated behavior produces desired, positive outcomes.

II. THEORETICAL BASES

Several authors have hypothesized about the theoretical reasons for why modeling produces observational learning. Those explanations have ranged from being firmly grounded within behavior analytic theory to being linked to cognitive and social learning theories. The cognitive-behavioral account provided by Albert Bandura, the researcher perhaps most strongly associated with modeling and observational learning due to his prolific research and writings about the topic, has received the greatest acceptance within the field of psychology.

Bandura proposed the contiguity theory (which eventually became part of his more expanded theory of social learning) as a means for understanding the impact of modeling. According to this theory, an observer acquires (i.e., learns) the modeled response through continuous associations between the observed behavior and sensory events, mental representations, and so on, that occur during the exposure to the model. These "cognitive" events then serve as cues for the occurrence of the behavior that was originally modeled.

According to Bandura, there are four main processes that influence the observational learning that occurs as a result of modeling. First, attentional processes are important in that they affect how much of an impact the modeled event will have on the observer. Attentional processes are affected by variables related to both the modeling stimulus (e.g., salience, distinctiveness, complexity, prevalence) and the observer (e.g., sensory capabilities, emotional arousal, past reinforcement history). Second, retention processes are involved, including such factors as symbolic coding of the modeled behavior, cognitive organization of the observed information, and symbolic and motoric rehearsal (i.e., imitation). Third, motor production processes are important influences in observational learning. Physical capabilities of the observer/learner, previous learning of similar responses, self-observation of imitation, and feedback regarding the accuracy of the imitative response are all variables that affect whether observing a model will result in imitative responding. Finally, motivational processes such as external reinforcement, vicarious reward and punishment, and self-reward or -punishment all are relevant to determining whether observing a model will produce imitation.

III. APPLICATIONS AND EXCLUSIONS

Unlike some psychotherapeutic techniques that are applicable for use with a limited number of clinical problems, evidence suggests that modeling strategies are effective with a wide variety of psychological, behavioral, emotional, and social problems. In fact, research evaluating the applicability of this intervention is so large that a thorough discussion is beyond the scope of this article. Instead, a brief discussion is provided to familiarize the reader with relevant issues.

As mentioned earlier, for modeling to be effective as a psychotherapeutic intervention, it is necessary for the person to be able to both attend to the model and engage in the imitative response. Thus, as the research supports, use of this intervention is possible with clients who meet these prerequisite skills. The clinician needs to determine whether the modeling procedure is the technique most likely to produce the desired effect. Thus, the clinician should consider various factors when determining whether to use this intervention, such as the clinical issue at hand, the complexity of the desired outcome, the ability to create the appropriate modeling conditions, and client interest and motivation.

Extending the applicability of the intervention even further, evidence suggests that modeling actually can be used with people who do not already demonstrate imitative responses. Through the use of prompting, shaping, and differential reinforcement, the generalized imitative response can be taught to clients who do not already exhibit such behavior. As a result, modeling may be used with people with severe or profound retardation, autism spectrum disorders, and clients with psychoses who do not already demonstrate the imitative response. In such situations, if use of modeling is desired, clinicians must first teach the imitative response to the clients. Once imitation is established, continued use of reinforcement for said responses will ensure that such clients will be able to benefit from modeling.

When considering the use of modeling strategies, one should also consider that particular formats of modeling have been shown to be more beneficial for use with certain clinical issues. For establishing new behavioral repertoires, evidence suggests that modeling (*in vivo* or symbolic) with guided performance may be effective. With this variant of modeling the client is first exposed to the model (with steps taken to ensure that the client is attending). Then, the client is guided to perform the desired behavior, after which reinforcement is provided for demonstrating the behavior. Use of the physical guidance is gradually decreased as the client demonstrates the imitative response with increasing independence.

Presentation of coping versus mastery models should also be considered. Coping models are those models who initially exhibit flawed or fearful performances, but then become increasingly competent in the desired behavior. This transition may occur during one or repeated modeling implementations. Mastery models, on the other hand, demonstrate the desired behavior perfectly from the beginning. Evidence suggests that coping models may produce more beneficial outcomes for clients, particularly when targeting fears, phobias, or other avoidance-based clinical problems. The opportunity to observe someone experience similar fear reactions, and then learn to overcome them, appears central to this finding.

Finally, evidence suggests that modeling techniques are useful with clients from diverse ethnic and cultural backgrounds. Studies have evaluated various modeling interventions with African Americans, Asian Americans, Hispanic Americans, gays, and lesbians. The use of ethnic and/or culturally similar models increases the salience and relevance of the model, thereby increasing the likelihood that clients will attend to the models. Although the general intervention format will not vary greatly across ethnic groups, Sherry Cormier and Bill

Cormier suggest in their 2000 text that clinicians consider three issues to ensure cultural sensitivity: (a) ensure that the live or symbolic model is culturally similar to the client, (b) ensure that the content to be demonstrated in the modeling scenario is culturally sensitive, and (c) be familiar with and account for differences in how people attend to, learn from, and use modeled information.

IV. EMPIRICAL STUDIES

Although the phenomena of learning via observing a model has been recognized for many years, methodologically sound research on the influence of models on observer's behaviors dates back to the 1950s and early 1960s. During this early research, experimenters designed investigations that documented the occurrence of observational learning. For example, researchers demonstrated that participants would engage in imitative responses of observed behaviors in the presence of the model who had demonstrated the behavior. This early research was important in that it demonstrated the phenomena of interest could be investigated under controlled, replicable conditions.

In 1961, Albert Bandura, Dorothea Ross, and Sheila A. Ross expanded on earlier non-clinical research by investigating whether the imitative response would occur in the absence of the model. To do so, they had 36 boys and 36 girls with a mean age of 59 months observe adult models engage in either aggressive or non-aggressive behavior with inanimate objects (i.e., toys). Following the observation period, the children were allowed to interact with the toys in the absence of the models while experimenters documented the presence or absence of aggressive imitative responses. Those children who observed the aggressive models were more likely to be aggressive with the toys than those children who had watched non-aggressive models. More important, Bandura, Ross, and Ross demonstrated that the influence of the model persisted in the absence of the actual model. Over the next 10 to 15 years, Bandura and his colleagues conducted numerous studies evaluating the effectiveness of modeling, the conditions necessary to produce observational learning, and the extent of learning produced via the process of modeling.

Applied research also has emerged and strengthened the position that modeling is an effective therapeutic tool. Since the initiation of this research, investigations have demonstrated the effectiveness of modeling with children, adolescents, and adults, and for various clinical problems (e.g., aggression, poor social skills). Furthermore, the intervention has proven effective with clients from various ethnic and cultural backgrounds. What follows is a sample of research on modeling in these different areas.

A significant amount of research has demonstrated the usefulness of various forms of modeling with children and adolescents. For example, in 1942 Gertrude Chittenden utilized symbolic modeling to alter aggressive responses by children. In this investigation, the participants were exposed to several "plays" in which an adult and a child used dolls to enact non-aggressive alternative responses in reaction to a situation in which both dolls wanted to play with the same toy, a scenario shown to produce aggressive responses in the participants. Furthermore, the plays involved the dolls receiving positive rewards for demonstrating the prosocial alternative responses. During observations conducted after watching the models, Chittenden found that there was a significant decrease in displays of aggressive responses and increase in modeled prosocial behavior.

In 1986, Eva Feindler, Randolf Ecton, Deborah Kingsley, and Dennis Dubey utilized modeling as one of several interventions to address anger management problems displayed by adolescent males residing in a psychiatric hospital. These experimenters used a between-groups wait-list control design to evaluate the impact of an 8-week group therapy program targeting anger control. The intervention group was taught various anger control strategies via the use of symbolic and participant modeling, which also included opportunities for role playing and behavioral rehearsal. Results indicated that the experimental group displayed significantly lower rates of anger problems posttreatment as compared to the members of the wait-list control group.

Research on the use of modeling to treat anger control problems and aggression is not limited to children and adolescents. In 1990 Frank Vaccaro assessed the impact of instructions, *in vivo* modeling, role playing, and feedback on verbal aggression displayed by 6 institutionalized older adults. Using an ABAB single-subject design, Vaccaro found that the intervention resulted in decreased instances of verbal aggression for all 6 participants. Further, improved behavior generalized from the experimental situation (i.e., the group therapy sessions) to the milieu setting.

A significant amount of research has been conducted assessing the utility of different modeling approaches to treating fears and phobias exhibited by both children and adults. In 1996, Rutger W. Trijsburg, Marko Jelicic, Walter W. van den Broek, and Annelies E. M. Plekker utilized participant modeling to treat phobic reactions to injections experienced by a 26-year-old female. According to the authors, this client demonstrated a "resistant-type" phobia in that she displayed strong, sometimes violent resistance to receiving a shot. Utilizing both scores on the State-Trait Anxiety Inventory and heart rate monitoring, the researchers found that the client's phobic reactions decreased as a result of exposure to a model receiving shots.

Matthew R. Sanders and Lyndall Jones provided a demonstration of the effectiveness of participant modeling with an adolescent female in 1990. In this investigation, the participant was a 13-year-old female with multiple medical and dental phobias, with comorbid oppositional defiant disorder. At the time of the investigation, she was scheduled for major surgery in 6 months. The investigators utilized coping skills training, systematic desensitization, and *in vivo* desensitization with participant modeling to help her overcome her fears.

As a final example of research demonstrating the utility of modeling to treat fears and phobias, consider a study conducted by K. Gunnar Goetestam and Dagfinn Berntzen in 1997. In this investigation, three pairs of adults with animal phobias participated. One person in each pair had stated that he or she was unable to participate in exposure therapy. Therefore, this person observed the other participant in the pair receiving direct exposure of the feared animal, thus creating a scenario involving *in vivo* modeling. Results showed that after observing the first person participating in direct exposure, the second person's phobic reactions reduced significantly. Furthermore, following modeling, the second person engaged in direct exposure to further reduce phobic responding. Results showed that treatment goals were achieved within 15 min for participants who had experienced modeling before desired outcome goals were met, as compared to within 1.5 to 2 h for the participants who experienced direct exposure only.

In addition to research demonstrating the usefulness of modeling to treat aggression and phobias, a significant amount of research has show that these procedures can be used effectively with individuals with developmental disabilities and/or mental retardation. Research with this population has utilized participant modeling, as well as various forms of symbolic modeling.

The use of modeling procedures with children and adults with autism has received particular attention. In 1986, Adeline S. Tryon and Susan Phillips Keane utilized participant modeling to target imitative play in 3 boys with autistic-like features. In this investigation, participants were exposed to a peer demonstrating appropriate play. Peers were selected for their similarity in age and gender to the participants and for their ability to engage in appropriate play with toys. Results showed that exposure to peer models resulted in increased appropriate play across a variety of toys, as well as a decrease in self-stimulatory behavior.

Researchers have also evaluated the effectiveness of video (symbolic) modeling with individuals with autism. Thomas G. Haring, Craig H. Kennedy, Mary J. Adams, and Valerie Pitts-Conway effectively used video modeling to teach 3 adults with autism skills used to purchase items from grocery and other stores in their research study published in 1987. Furthermore, Marjorie H. Charlop and Janice P. Milstein's 1989 research article describes the use of video modeling to teach 3 autistic children conversational speech. Finally, Marjorie H. Charlop-Christy, Loc Le, and Kurt A. Freeman demonstrated in their study published in 2000 that video modeling was more effective than *in vivo* modeling in teaching a variety of skills to 5 autistic children.

In addition to the research just mentioned, others have demonstrated the usefulness of modeling specifically with individuals with developmental disabilities to address developmental problems such as delayed social skills, deficits in expressive language, underdeveloped discrimination abilities (e.g., colors, shapes, on/under), and poor walking performance. Furthermore, researchers have demonstrated the utility of various modeling strategies with individuals with mental retardation who are experienced other clinical problems such as substance abuse problems, phobias and fears, selective mutism, and so on.

As should be evident from the brief review provided, modeling procedures are widely applicable and effective. The research described earlier only provides an introduction to the use of modeling, however. Evidence suggests that modeling procedures can be effectively incorporated into treatments for many different psychological, social, and emotional problems. Other clinical and social issues that have been shown to response positively to modeling include smokeless tobacco use, parenting, child safety, breast self-examination, self-defense skills, altruistic behavior, and gender stereotyping modification, to name just a few more. Thus, the research supports the general applicability and versatility of modeling interventions with a variety of psychological, social, and health-related issues.

V. CASE ILLUSTRATION

Consider Jeremy, a 13-year-old Caucasian male receiving services in a large-scale residential facility. In addition to full participation in the milieu therapy provided to all residents, Jeremy was also referred for individual psychological services due to social skills problems, oppositionality, and ongoing severe conduct problems. His behavior problems significantly affected his social functioning in that he was severely rejected by his peers. Teacher, peer, and other staff report all indicated that Jeremy was actively avoided, taunted, and made fun of by the majority of his peers. For example, it was not uncommon for Jeremy's peers to say something such as "Don't talk to me!" in response to his attempts to initiate interactions.

Further assessment on initiation of psychological services revealed the presence of significant social skills deficits that likely contributed to his social rejection. First, he was awkward in his attempts to initiate or maintain conversations. Specifically, he would attempt to start conversations by yelling hello to peers or adults from across the room and generally speak with a voice that was louder than conversational level. Second, Jeremy would attempt to procure interactions with popular peers by using age-appropriate phrases or wearing "trendy" clothes. Rather than elevating his social status, these attempts appeared to further alienate him from his peers, as evidenced by laughter and jeers directed toward him. Third, Jeremy tended to use mannerisms and gestures that were exaggerated and excessive. Fourth, Jeremy demonstrated poor table manners, as evidenced by him talking with food in his mouth, eating rapidly and/or with his finger, and eating in a messy manner (resulting in food being on his face and/or clothes). This particular behavior pattern often set the stage for ridicule and rejection during the lunch recess hour. Finally, Jeremy typically presented with a facial expression characterized by a clownlike vacant grin.

Modeling procedures were used during individual therapy sessions to target his social skills deficits directly. First, *in vivo* modeling was used to target his poor table manners. To accomplish this, the therapist conducted 3 one-half-hour sessions weekly while he and Jeremy sat together at a dining table in the lunchroom at Jeremy's junior high school. Sessions occurred during Jeremy's regular lunch period while he and his peers ate lunch. After establishing the need to target table manners, and describing the rationale for participant modeling, the therapist described verbally and demonstrated physically proper table manners (e.g., use of a napkin, appropriate rate of eating, chewing with one's mouth closed). Then, collaboratively the therapist and Jeremy selected a specific skill for focus, rather than attempting to intervene with all relevant behaviors at once.

Once the target skill was selected, the therapist initiated each session by verbally and physically reviewing the proper target behavior and then drawing Jeremy's attention to peers who were demonstrating that behavior while they ate lunch. During the observation, the therapist would verbally describe the behavior being modeled by the peer, as well as point out the positive social benefits of engaging in such behavior. After a brief period of observation, Jeremy was then instructed to eat his lunch while attempting to demonstrate the appropriate response. Positive and corrective feedback was provided during this time. Periodic prompts to observe his peers were also provided until Jeremy demonstrated the skill successfully.

In conjunction with *in vivo* modeling to target table manners, symbolic modeling was used to address various other social skills problems (e.g., facial expressions, voice volume). Sessions involving symbolic modeling typically occurred every other week in a therapy session room. Again, the deficit skills were identified and reviewed prior to implementing the intervention. Furthermore, appropriate skills were also discussed and modeled by the therapist. Examples of targets identified included taking turns appropriately, offering praise to his peer, and displaying facial expressions appropriate to the context. After establishing the target behaviors, symbolic modeling was implemented. Symbolic modeling in this case took the form of videotaped interactions between Jeremy, the therapist, and another similar-aged male peer. The peer was selected because care providers had identified him as being quite socially skilled. Interactions occurred in the context of involvement in some sort of board game. Following 10–15 min of playing the game while being videotaped, Jeremy and the therapist would review the videotape so that Jeremy could observe the peer implement appropriate social skills. Further, Jeremy's behaviors were evaluated, and positive and corrective feedback was provided. Then, Jeremy was provided with another opportunity to interact with the peer and the therapist while playing a game, thus allowing for imitation of the desired responses.

Modeling procedures were effective in altering some of Jeremy's serious social skills deficits in the therapeutic contexts. He learned how to eat in a more socially acceptable manner while the therapist was present, how to talk in a more normal tone of voice while playing a game with a peer, and how to change his facial expressions to more closely match the situation (e.g., smile when there was a joke told, scowl when losing the game). The level of prompting that was needed to ensure the use of these skills decreased during the therapy situation. Unfortunately, however, Jeremy was discharged from the residential program before specific measures could be taken to prompt generalization and maintenance of treatment gains, as these did not appear to be occurring naturally.

VI. SUMMARY

Modeling is a psychotherapy technique that is designed to create opportunities for the client to learn new behavior patterns or alter existing ones. Implementation of the intervention involves several relatively simple steps. First, the client is exposed to a model who demonstrates the desired response. The model can be presented live, symbolically, or cognitively. Second, the client is provided with an opportunity to imitate the desired response. Finally, corrective and positive feedback is provided to the client.

Modeling can produce two different forms of learning, imitation and vicarious learning. Imitation simply involves the observer matching the topography of the model's behavior. Vicarious learning, on the other hand, involves either an increase or decrease in the likelihood that the client will demonstrate the modeled behavior as a result of the model being rewarded or punished, respectively. As a result, the modeling situation should be created in a manner that capitalizes on the desired outcome. For example, if modeling is being used to decrease problem behavior, then the intervention should associate negative consequences with engaging in the behavior.

Research has demonstrated that modeling is an effective psychotherapeutic technique. Evidence suggests its utility with clients from diverse backgrounds, as well as those with diverse intellectual or developmental functioning. Furthermore, the intervention has been shown to affect a variety of clinical and social problems—such as smoking, phobias and fears, deficits in parenting skills—as well as important health-related behaviors (e.g., self breast examination). Finally, evidence suggests that the intervention may be most effective as a component of a larger set of strategies to address clinical or social issues.

See Also the Following Articles

Behavior Rehearsal ■ Cultural Issues ■ Heterosocial Skills Training ■ Race and Human Diversity ■ Retention Control Training ■ Role-Playing ■ Symbolic Modeling

Further Reading

Bandura, A. (1977). *Social learning theory,* New York: Prentice Hall.

Charlop-Christy, M. H., Le, L., & Freeman, K. A. (2000). A comparison of video modeling with in vivo modeling for teaching children with autism. *Journal of Autism & Developmental Disorders, 30,* 537–552.

Cormier, S., & Cormier, B. (2000). *Interviewing strategies for helpers: Fundamental skills and cognitive behavioral interventions.* Pacific Grove, CA: Brooks/Cole.

Dowrick, P. W. (1999). A review of self modeling and related interventions. *Applied & Preventive Psychology, 8,* 23–39.

Masia, C., & Chase, P. (1997). Vicarious learning revisited: A contemporary behavior analytic interpretation. *Journal of Behavior Therapy and Experimental Psychiatry, 28,* 41–51.

Masters, J. C., Burish, T. G., Hollon, S. D., & Rimm, D. C. (1987). *Behavior therapy: Techniques and empirical findings* (3rd ed.). New York: Harcourt Brace Jovanovich.

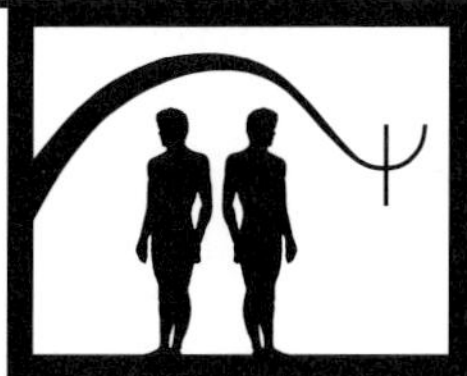

Mood Disorders

Michael Robertson
Mayo-Wesley Centre for Mental Health

Scott Stuart
University of Iowa and Iowa Depression and Clinical Research Center

GLOSSARY

depression An abnormal psychological state that is characterized by reduction of mood, interest, and vitality. It can be considered as the opposite state of mania. Depression differs from normal sadness in the severity of the symptoms and the lack of reactivity to otherwise pleasurable activities.

dysphoria An unpleasant emotional state that may be a mixture of sadness, low-grade anxiety, and negativity. Dysphoria is most likely a nonpathological alteration of mood state that represents a part of the normal spectrum of human experience.

dysthymia A chronic, persistent disturbance of mood that has some low-grade features of depression persisting over prolonged periods.

hypomanic episodes These share many features of manic episodes although they are considered to be not as severe as mania, or to cause as significant an amount of disruption to a sufferer's social or work abilities.

mania An abnormal psychological state that is characterized by overexcitement and elevation of mood. A "manic episode" is considered to be present if the symptoms create marked impairment for a person in his or her working and social interpersonal lives.

mixed mood states Characterized by the simultaneous presence of manic symptoms and depressive symptoms. Some clinicians refer to this condition as "dysphoric mania," which is characterized by the presence of irritability or an unpleasant sense of agitation or sadness rather than classically elevated mood.

I. INTRODUCTION

Disorders of mood or affect are among the most commonly recognized psychological disorders in both clinical and community settings. Individuals can develop a mood disorder at any time in their lives, although the nature, clinical presentation, and course of mood disorders vary greatly from individual to individual. This article will describe the features of mood disorders, their etiology, and their treatment.

The terms "mood" and "affect" are often used interchangeably; however, they refer to two different concepts. Mood is best defined as, "the prevalent emotional state described by an individual, consistently present over a prolonged period of day to weeks," as opposed to affect, which is best defined as, "the observable emotional state of an individual at a specific point in time, that may be changeable from moment to moment." Metaphorically speaking, mood refers to a person's climate whereas affect refers to the day's weather conditions.

The disorders of mood clinically recognized currently in the *Diagnostic and Statistical Manual of Mental Disorder, 4th edition* (DSM-IV) are:

1. Depression
2. Mania or hypomania
3. Dysthymia

4. Mixed mood states
5. Dysphoria

II. DEPRESSION

A. History of Depression

Depression is a heterogeneous condition that encompasses different types of illness. In ancient Greece the term "melancholia" (referring to "black bile") described a temperament characterized by lethargy, sullenness, and brooding. The concept infiltrated Western and non-Western cultures over time and numerous philosophers and physicians have written of its effects on the human psyche.

Sigmund Freud in his 1963 text *Mourning and Melancholia* conceptualized depression as a process of "internalizing" lost loved ones and "turning anger inwards" so that negativity directed at the loss would dominate the psyche. In the latter half of the twentieth century, psychological and psychiatric disorders were seen in more complex biological, psychological, and social terms, leading to a broader conceptualization of depressive disorders as having primarily psychological or biological origins. Currently, depression that is of clinical significance is referred to as a "major depressive disorder" by the American Psychiatric Association. This is the core concept around which our current classification of mood disorders revolves.

B. Phenomenology of Depression

The features of a major depressive disorder are shown in Table I. More severe forms of depression can occasionally have a number of unusual psychotic features such as delusions (false unshakeable beliefs) or hallucinations (disturbances of perception without a stimulus, e.g., hearing voices).

There is considerable variation in the experience and presentation of depression across the life span. In children and adolescents, depression may manifest in nonemotional ways such as behavioral deterioration, withdrawal, irritability, weight loss, school refusal, or self-injury. In the elderly, depression may manifest as preoccupation with health, paranoia, memory loss, cognitive impairment, or irritability. There is also a significant overlap between depression and responses to grief.

TABLE I
Features of Major Depression

1. Significantly depressed mood that is in excess of normal sadness
2. A loss of interest in an individual's usual activities
3. Marked loss of self-esteem, or self-reproach
4. Impaired sleep
5. Psychomotor agitation or retardation (a subjective sense of either psychological and physical perturbation or slowing)
6. Reduced or increased appetite with weight loss or weight gain
7. Feelings of hopelessness about the future
8. Suicidal thinking
9. Significant anxiety such as panic attacks or generalized worry or obsessional thinking

C. Epidemiology of Depression

Estimates of the prevalence of major depressive disorder by age and gender have been derived from the The Epidemiological Catchment Area (ECA) study of 18,000 community and institutionalized subjects over 18 years of age at five sites throughout the United States, according to Weissman and colleagues in 1991. The ECA found that the overall lifetime prevalence of mood disorders is 6%. This differs slightly from the 1994 DSM-IV data that suggest a lifetime prevalence of 10 to 25% risk of depression in women as opposed to a 5 to 12% lifetime risk for men. The ECA data indicate a much higher prevalence of all the mood disorders among persons under the age of 45. The ECA also reported a relatively higher prevalence of major depressive disorder in women than in men, which, although consistent across the ages, was more evident among the younger adult group than in the elderly or in childhood. The study also found alcohol abuse and dependence was more prevalent in men than in women, leading some to argue that depressive disorders and alcohol abuse and dependence may be different manifestations of the same biopsychosocial vulnerability.

Sex differences in depression begin in early adolescence and persist at least until midlife. However, women with a previous history of a depressive episode are no more likely to experience a new episode than men with a previous history of a depressive episode. This suggests that the higher risk in women results from women having a higher risk of experiencing major depressive disorder for the first time.

A number of studies performed prior to the ECA study suggested that the prevalence rates of depressive disorders may be changing. The findings seemed to indicate a progressively lowering of the age of onset of depressive disorders and a possible increase in childhood mood disorders as well as an observed reduction in suicide in the elderly.

D. Etiology of Depression

As with most psychological disorders, the causes of depression are multiple and overlapping. It is customary to divide etiological theories of depression into biological, psychological, and social factors.

1. Biological Factors

a. Biogenic Amines The human brain communicates with itself biochemically. The biological chemicals that are involved in this process are referred to as neurotransmitters. There are likely to be numerous neurotransmitters involved in the complex processes of the human brain; however two chemicals from the amine family have been implicated in the disordered functioning of the brain in depression, according to Nemeroff in 1998. The first, serotonin or 5-hydroxy–tryptophan (5-HT), is the most active biological amine in the human brain. A second biogenic amine, noradrenaline (NA), has also been implicated. The biogenic amine theory of depression postulates that levels of 5-HT and NA are present in subnormal levels in the parts of the human brain that regulate mood. The mechanism of action of virtually all antidepressant compounds is to effectively increase the level of activity of these compounds.

b. Neuroendocrine Factors Research by Nemeroff in 1998 indicated that the state of depression is associated with alterations in the level and activity of various endocrine glands, particularly the adrenal gland and the thyroid gland. This research demonstrated that higher levels of corticosteroids such as cortisol are associated with depression, as are alterations in responsiveness of the adrenal gland to the suppressive effects of artificial corticosteroids such as dexamethasone. Other hormonal disturbances include alterations in thyroid gland function.

c. Genetic Factors There have been numerous family and molecular studies of depression; however, progress has been limited by the fundamental problem of phenotypic identification. The controversy regarding the precise definition of depression has limited the study of depression to specific groups of individuals with "undisputed" depression. These patients tend to have more severe depression and are more similar in presentation than many patients treated in clinical settings. This has likely distorted the findings regarding depression to some degree, as most of the patients studied have had this more severe and uniform type of illness.

In general, most family studies highlight that depression and manic depression tends to cluster in families, according to Tsuang in 1990. The risk of developing depression in an individual with a first-degree relative with either depression or manic depression varies from 7 to 15% for depression and manic depression. Moreover, studies of identical (monozygotic) and nonidentical (dizygotic) twins indicate that the concordance for depression is approximately 60% for monozygotic twins and 30% for dizygotic twins, as discussed by Taylor in 1993.

Studies examining linkage of depression to other genes and molecular markers have been promising but inconclusive. In essence, the balance of opinion regarding the genetic etiologic factors in depression is that they are polygenic and multifactorial.

2. Psychological Factors

a. Attachment Style In the 1950s, John Bowlby evolved the concept of "attachment," which referred to the complex process by which animals and humans seek proximity to and interact with caregivers. Bowlby postulated that there was a biological and psychological drive to seek proximity to caregivers. Later studies, such as Ainsworth and colleagues' 1985 observations of infants' responses to separation from their caregivers, created the notion that human attachment could be either "secure" and flexible, or "insecure." The notion that attachment styles remained fixed throughout the life span suggested that adults could also be securely or insecurely attached. It is common to observe patterns of disturbed attachment in individuals who develop depressive disorders; however, insecure attachment in itself does not condemn an individual to depression. It is likely that a "poorness of fit" between a person with an insecure attachment style and his or her social environment will predispose an individual to depression.

b. Cognitive Style In the late 1960s, Aaron Beck formulated the idea that certain styles of viewing the world could predispose an individual to depression. Beck saw that individuals evolved a pattern of perceiving and interpreting events described as a "schema." A cognitive schema that was "depressogenic" was characterized by a triad of a negative view of self, present circumstance, and future circumstances. Further, depressed individuals have been found to have depressive attributional styles that are more global and stable than nondepressed individuals. Beck's clinical approach thus advocates identifying and altering factors in these types of schema.

c. Personality and Temperament Personality refers to the relatively enduring and stable patterns of thinking, behaving, and acting that are present consistently over time. The various recent psychiatric classification systems such as the American Psychiatric Association's 1994 *Diagnostic and Statistical Manual of Psychiatric Disorders 4th Edition (DSM-IV)* and the World Health Organization's *International Classification of Disease (ICD-10)* have highlighted the concept of "personality disorder" as a substantive clinical entity. This construct emphasizes the presence of persisting maladaptive patterns of interaction that produce clinically significant impairment in social, occupational, and interpersonal functioning. Certain types of personality, such as those with unstable emotions or relationships (borderline personality disorder) or excess perfectionism (obsessional personality disorder) may be at higher risk for depression.

Temperament refers to those biologically based dispositions that color personality. It was of interest in antiquity and has more recently enjoyed increased attention in a research and clinical context. Temperament is evident across the life span and relatively stable over time. Authors such as C. Robert Cloninger in 1987 have described temperament-based personality variables such as "novelty seeking," "harm avoidance," and "reward dependence" that may have their origin in neurophysiological states. These temperamental characteristics may have significance in the genesis of depression.

3. Social Factors

a. Early Environment Loss of a parent in early childhood has been long considered a risk factor for the later development of depression. More recently, loss of a parent either through death or family disintegration and the associated ecological disruptions have been associated with depression as well. Early childhood difficulties such as childhood anxiety disorders, behavioral problems, or illness may predispose an individual to later adult psychopathology.

b. Gender There has been an apparent higher incidence of depression in women as opposed to men. This has been debated, however, as some experts, including Jorm in 1987, have argued that the prevalence of mood disorders is roughly equal between the sexes, but that women are more likely to present for treatment or divulge depressive symptomatology.

c. Interpersonal Factors Specific studies including Brown's 1978 research, have isolated independent risk factors for depression in women including the lack of a confiding relationship and having more than three children. Similarly, the lack of a social support network seems to be a risk factor for depression in both sexes. Unemployment and other social adversity as well as abrupt loss of status are also associated with depression.

E. Treatment of Depression

As depression is invariably the product of a complex interaction of biological, psychological, and social factors, interventions in the treatment of depression are also grounded in these three areas.

1. Biological Treatments for Depression

a. Antidepressant Medication The current understanding of the biochemical origins of depression has led to several generations of medications that putatively correct the underlying "biochemical imbalance." At present these agents all have the effect of altering the activity of biogenic amines in the human brain. The classes of agent and their putative mechanisms of action are listed in Table II and depicted in Figure 1.

Duration of drug treatment. The duration of treatment with antidepressant agents has been an area of recent controversy. Studies have indicated that in many cases depression is a relapsing and remitting condition that requires long-term treatment, according to the American Psychiatric Association in 1993. Several useful terms describing the stages of treatment of depression include:

TABLE II
Classes of Antidepressants and Their Putative Mechanisms of Action

Selective serotonin reuptake inhibitors (SSRI)—Inhibit serotonin reuptake pump
Serotonin-noradrenaline reuptake inhibitors (SNRI)—Inhibit serotonin and noradrenaline reuptake pumps
Monoamine oxidase inhibitors (MAOI)—Inhibit the enzyme that catabolizes biogenic amines
Tricyclic agents—Inhibit serotonin and noradrenaline reuptake and alter postsynaptic receptor activity
Tetracyclic agents—Block alpha-2 noradrenaline receptor (stimulation of this inhibits release of biogenic amines)
Other agents—Varied degree of activity
- mirtazapine—blocks alpha-2 noradrenergic receptors and type 2 and 3 serotonin receptors
- nefazodone—inhibits serotonin transporter and type 2 serotonin receptors

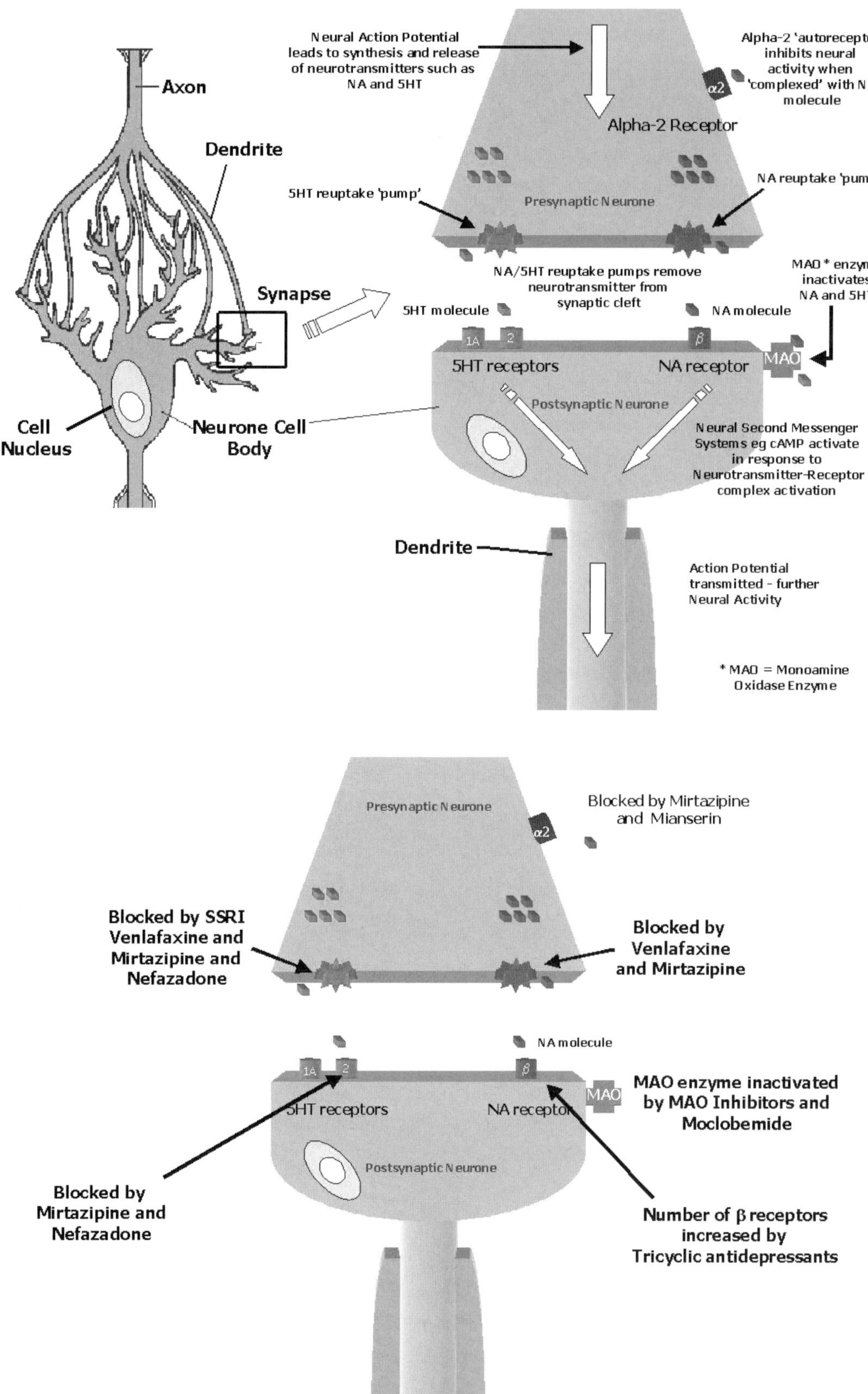

FIGURE 1 Putative mechanisms of action of antidepressant agents.

1. **Response**: the point at which depressive symptoms alter following treatment initiation. A 50% reduction in the level of symptoms is typically considered a response to treatment.
2. **Remission**: the point at which the diagnostic criteria for depression are no longer met. There may be residual symptoms at this point.
3. **Recovery**: the point of resolution of the depressive syndrome. This period requires 3 months of remission prior to being defined as remission.
4. **Relapse**: the reemergence of the depressive syndrome within the 3-month recovery phase.
5. **Recurrence**: the reemergence of symptoms during the remission phase.

The natural history of depressive disorders is for a 50% rate of recurrence after one episode of major depression and an 80 to 90% rate of recurrence after two episodes, according to the American Psychiatric Association in 1993. It states, therefore, that long-term treatment with antidepressant medication is necessary in cases where individuals are at high risk of recurrent depression.

b. Electroconvulsive Treatment Electroconvulsive treatment (ECT) is perhaps the most controversial area of psychiatric practice. In the late 1930s an Italian psychiatrist Ugo Cerletti experimented with convulsive treatments using electrical stimulation, as described by Abrams in 1988. This was based on observations that people suffering comorbid epilepsy and depression experienced improvements in their mood after seizures. According to Abrams, as technology and neuroscience have advanced, ECT has become a safe and effective treatment for severe biological depression.

It is thought that the therapeutic effects of ECT result from changes in the brain's biochemistry. Over a course of treatment, ECT has anticonvulsant effects that raise seizure threshold and decrease seizure duration. The so-called seizure threshold at which seizures will occur increases during ECT and it is thought that this may be a part of its mechanism of action. Periods of increased electrical activity in the brain, including seizures, promote the release of the compound adenosine, which in turn acts on several neuroreceptors to produce alteration of their chemical activity. Additionally, ECT increases norepinephrine turnover and α_1-adrenergic receptor sensitivity and decreases presynaptic α_2-adrenergic receptors. ECT also appears to enhance the effects of the serotonergic system but differs from antidepressant medication treatment in producing increases in serotonin (5-HT_2) receptor binding in the cerebral cortex. These findings suggest that ECT may have important actions on monoaminergic transmission that contribute to its therapeutic effects.

c. Rapid Transcranial Magnetic Stimulation Rapid transcranial magnetic stimulation (rTMS) uses an exter-

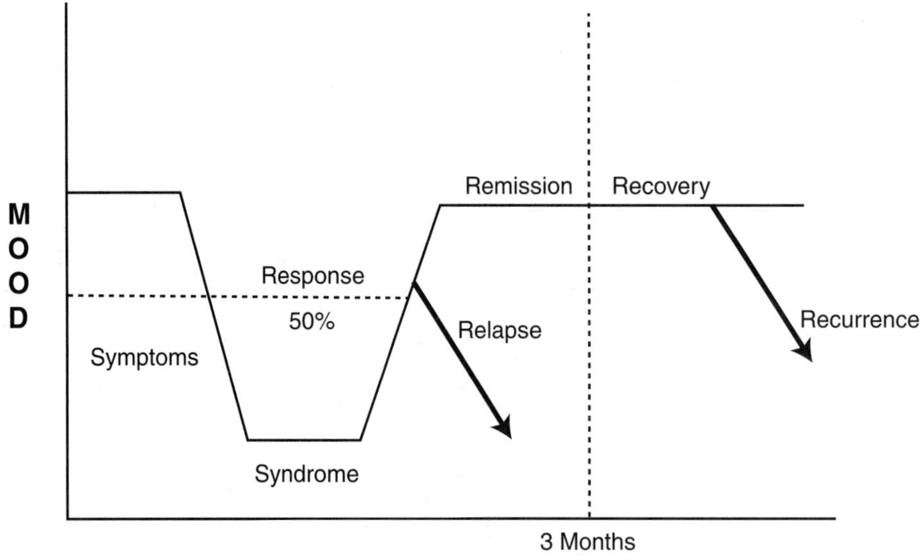

FIGURE 2 The stages of depression treatment.

nal magnetic field passed through a small coil applied to the scalp to allow focused electrical stimulation, which generates a focused magnetic field of 1.5 to 2 teslas. The magnetic field in turn depolarizes brain cells to a depth of 2 cm from the coil. Some evidence suggests that major depression may be characterized by hypoactive cortical areas. It was postulated by Post and colleagues in 1997 that rTMS stimulation of these frontal areas may help relieve symptoms.

Currently, the use of rTMS for the treatment of neurological and psychiatric disorders is still under investigation. Several open-label and controlled studies have suggested that rTMS may be at least temporarily effective in both animal models of depression and patients with major depression, according to Post and colleagues in 1997. A number of small, open-label studies have suggested that rTMS may be effective in some patients with treatment-resistant major depressive disorder as well as in those with milder major depressive disorder.

*d. **Phototherapy*** Phototherapy (light therapy) was first introduced in 1984 as a treatment for seasonal affective disorder (SAD; depression with seasonal pattern). In this disorder, according to Wehr and Rosenthal in 1989, patients typically experience depression as the sunlight period of the day decreases with advancing winter. Women represent at least 75% of all patients with seasonal depression, and the mean age of presentation is 40, as discussed by Blehar in 1989.

Phototherapy typically involves exposing the afflicted patient to bright light in the range of 1,500 to 10,000 lux or more with a light box that sits at face level for approximately 1 to 2 hours before dawn each day, according to Lam in 1994. As circadian rhythms are frequently disrupted in major depression, this is thought to be the basis of SAD and some of the features of depression. Exposure to light results in a phase advance that shifts the phase response curve earlier in the day. In addition, light suppresses the production of melatonin from the pineal gland at night. A number of controlled studies by Blehar in 1997 suggests that phototherapy is effective as monotherapy and as an adjunctive agent in the treatment of seasonal depressions.

2. *Psychological Treatments for Depression*

The specific details of this area are discussed elsewhere in this text. In brief, a number of studies have confirmed that the focal structured psychotherapies such as Beck's cognitive behavior therapy (CBT) and Klerman's interpersonal psychotherapy (IPT) are equivalent in antidepressant efficacy for depression of mild to moderate severity, according to Elkin in 1989. There is also evidence that the combination of antidepressant medication and psychotherapy has greater efficacy than either alone. Evidence suggests that a short-term psychotherapy, while efficacious in acute depression, confers little protection against further episodes. There is now a shift to studying and providing psychological treatments in maintenance fashion as well as acute treatment for depression.

III. MANIA AND BIPOLAR DISORDER

A. History of Bipolar Disorder

Aretaeus of Cappadocia (ca. 150 AD) is likely to have initially nominated that mania and melancholy were associated entities stating, "It appears to me that melancholy is the commencement and a part of mania" (see Goodwin and Jamison's 1990 work). In the 19th century, French psychiatrists offered the description "folie à double forme." Later that century, the German psychiatrist Emile Kraepelin elaborated the ideas that the core of depression was lowered mood and slowed mentation, wheras mania was characterized by elation and accelerated mental activity. Unlike depression, which may have significant "neurotic" contributions, Kraepelin saw manic states as being hereditary and biologically determined.

B. Phenomenology of Bipolar Disorder

Bipolar disorder is diagnosed when a person suffers a manic episode at some point in his or her lifetime. People who suffer from bipolar disorder are prone to develop episodes of hypomania, mania, and depression. The features of a manic episode are listed in Table III.

A "manic episode" is considered to be present if the symptoms create marked impairment for a person in his or her work or social and interpersonal functioning. "Hypomanic" episodes share many features of manic episodes although they are considered to be not as severe or to cause as significant amount of disruption to a sufferer's social or work functioning.

Current classification systems describe a number of different types of bipolar disorder:

1. **Type I bipolar disorder:** Diagnosed if an individual suffers an episode of mania. Depressive episodes may or may not be present as well.

TABLE III
Features of a Manic Episode

1. Distinct periods of abnormal or persistently elevated or irritable moods
2. Inflated self-esteem or grandiose behavior
3. A decreased need for sleep
4. Overtalkativeness
5. Racing thoughts
6. Being easily distracted
7. Overactivity including increased productivity, increased sexual drive, or purposeless agitation
8. Overspending
9. Disinhibition in social activities
10. Possible recklessness in behavior including gambling, sexual indiscretions, or exercising poor judgment
11. Psychosis including hallucinations (abnormal sensory experiences), severe disorder of thinking, or delusions (fixed unshakeable ideas that are often false).

2. **Type II bipolar disorder:** Diagnosed if an individual suffers episodes of both depression and hypomania.
3. **Mixed mood states:** Characterized by the simultaneous presence of manic symptoms and depressive symptoms. Some clinicians often refer to a condition known as "dysphoric mania," which is characterized by the presence of irritability or an unpleasant sense of agitation or sadness rather than classically elevated mood.

C. Epidemiology of Bipolar Disorder

The ECA data suggest that the lifetime risk for bipolar disorder is approximately 1.2% in the general population. It commonly affects young adults from 20 to 40 years of age. It tends to affect both men and women equally, and also appears to have a similar rate of occurrence across a variety of cultural and racial groups, according to Weissman and colleagues in 1991.

D. Etiology of Bipolar Disorder

1. Biological Factors

Unlike depression, mania is now regarded as primarily a biologically determined process. The general consensus is that during a manic episode the brain is usually overactive in terms of chemical activity, electrical activity, and generalized neurological processes. Most studies, according to Post in 1997, have consistently indicated that there may be imbalances or overactivity of a number of neurotransmitters including serotonin, noradrenaline, dopamine, glutamate, and other excitatory compounds during acute mania as well as possible disturbances in thyroid hormone or cortisol and newly described neurochemicals such as neuropeptides.

More recently, researchers have uncovered some possible disturbances in complex chemical processes occurring within the neurons including alterations in the activity of so-called second messenger systems involving compounds such as cyclic adenosine monophosphate (cAMP) and phosphatidylcholine, as described by Post in 1997.

There has been some additional interest in a process referred to as "kindling" (in which a number of neurons are chronically hyperactive and have a tendency to summate with produced marked neural overactivity, rather like kindling in a fire combining to produce a large flame) in the temporal lobe of the cerebral cortex and more specifically the deep nuclei that comprise the limbic system including the hippocampus and amygdyla, according to Post in 1997.

2. Genetic Factors

A first-degree relative (such as child or sibling) of someone suffering from bipolar disorder has approximately a 6% risk of developing bipolar disorder but a 15% risk of developing either depression or bipolar disorder, according to Tsuang in 1990. Tsuang notes that children of people suffering from bipolar disorder have approximately a 25% risk of developing a mood disorder if either parent suffers from bipolar disorder and a 75% risk of developing a mood disorder if both parents suffer bipolar disorder.

E. The Treatment of Bipolar Disorder

1. Medication

The treatment of mania and hypomania has two phases: an acute phase, in which the acute syndrome is quelled and social and occupational impairment is improved; and a maintenance phase, in which medications are administered long term to prevent the recurrences of the condition.

a. Mood Stabilizers

Lithium. In the 1940s Australian psychiatrist John Cade discovered the tranquilizing properties of lithium (see work by Goodwin and Jamison in 1990). Since that time lithium has been the primary treatment for acute and prophylactic treatment of mania. In comparative studies with antipsychotic agents, it yields better overall improvement in most aspects of manic symptomatology, including psychomotor activity, grandiosity, manic thought disorder, insomnia, and irritability, according to Post in 2000. The type of patient most likely to respond to lithium carbonate is someone with a classic presentation and euphoric mania (rather than dysphoric mania) and a pattern of mania followed by a depression and then a well interval. The number of patients with this "classic" presentation is relatively small, hence lithium's status as the "gold standard" treatment is under threat.

Valproic Acid. Studies by Bowden and colleagues in 1994 demonstrated that anticonvulsant medications such as valproic acid are efficacious in acute and maintenance treatment of bipolar disorder. This is possibly due to the effects on temporal lobe kindling and also its effects in acting on so-called inhibitory neurotransmitter systems that reduce neural activity. This research indicates that valproic acid seems to be the treatment of choice for dysphoric mania or mixed states as well as those patients with rapid-cycling types of bipolar disorder. Valproic acid also has the potential benefit of rapid oral loading in acute mania, which is usually well tolerated and associated with a rapid onset of response, according to Post in 2000.

Carbamazepine. Carbamazepine appears to have similar benefits as valproic acid, as described by Denikoff and colleagues in 1997; however, its side effect profile and potential for drug interactions tend to lessen its use.

Lamotrigine. Lamotrigine is a newly approved anticonvulsant for add-on therapy that has antidepressant and possibly mood-stabilizing properties, according to Calabrese and colleagues in 1999. Its place in the management of bipolar disorder is still being investigated; however, a significant risk of severe rash may limit its use.

Gabapentin. Gabapentin is a newly approved anticonvulsant for adjunctive therapy that may also have some mood-stabilizing effects in bipolar patients. The drug appears to have positive effects on sleep and anxiety.

Topiramate. Topiramate is a recently approved add-on agent for treatment of refractory epilepsy. Preliminary experience suggests that it may have mood-stabilizing properties in rapid-cycling patients, with better antimanic than antidepressant effects, according to Post in 2000.

b. AntiPsychotic Agents The use of major tranquilizers has historically been confined to the acute treatment of mania, particularly if there are psychotic features present. In recent years, a new class of major tranquilizers that lack the troublesome side effects of older antipsychotic agents has helped to improve the acute management of mania. These agents include risperidone and olanzapine (both serotonin-dopamine antagonists), which are frequently coadministered with mood stabilizers to control acute mania. In some cases, these agents need to be used for maintenance treatment as well.

2. Psychological Management

Psychosocial factors may contribute 25 to 30% to the outcome variance of bipolar disorder and despite optimal pharmacotherapy, up to 50% of sufferers may encounter further episodes, according to Joyce in 1992. It is important to note, however, that all of the studies of psychological interventions in the treatment of bipolar disorder have been used during the recovery phase of treatment, and have been used only to prevent relapse—there is no evidence that any psychological intervention is of benefit in the acute treatment of mania.

a. Family Therapies Several studies support the efficacy of brief family-focused interventions in both inpatient and outpatient settings, with an emphasis on education, problem solving, and reduction of ambient stress within the family, as discussed by Miklowitz and colleagues in 1996.

b. Group Psychotherapies Several studies suggest the benefits of group therapies, although no actual controlled studies exist. There is limited evidence of benefits in the areas of compliance with medication, problem solving, and interpersonal functioning, according to Scott in 1995.

c. Cognitive Behavior Therapy Cognitive behavior therapy for bipolar disorder has focused on improving compliance and in recognition of early symptoms of relapse. The results of some trials suggest that this reduces relapse rates, and there are some observations of improvement in social functioning and employment stability, as discussed by Robertson in 2000.

See Also the Following Articles

Cognitive Behavior Therapy ■ Pain Disorders ■ Psychopharmacology: Combined Treatment

Further Reading

Akiskal, H. S. (1995). Toward a temperament-based approach to depression: Implications for neurobiologic research. *Advances in Biochemical Psychopharmacology, 49,* 99–112.

American Psychiatric Association. (1994). *Diagnostic and statistical manual of mental disorders, 4th Edition.* Washington, DC: American Psychiatric Press.

Bowden, C. L., Brugger, A. M., Swann, A. C., Calabrese, J. R., Janicak, P. G., Petty, F., et al. (1994). Efficacy of divalproex vs lithium and placebo in the treatment of mania. *Journal of the American Medical Association, 271,* 918–924.

Calabrese, J. R., Bowden, C. L., Sachs, G. S., Ascher, J. A., Monaghan, E., & Rudd, G. D. (1999). A double-blind placebo-controlled study of lamotrigine monotherapy in outpatients with bipolar I depression. Lamictal 602 Study Group. *Journal of Clinical Psychiatry, 60,* 79–88.

Cytryn, L., & McKnew, D. (1996). *Growing up sad: Childhood depression and its treatment.* New York: Norton.

Denicoff, K. D., Smith-Jackson, E. E., Disney, E. R., Ali, S. O., Leverich, G. S., & Post, R. M. (1997). Comparative prophylactic efficacy of lithium, carbamazepine, and the combination in the treatment of bipolar disorder. *Journal of Clinical Psychiatry, 58,* 470–478.

Gabbard, G. O. (1994). *Psychodynamic psychiatry in clinical practice: The DSM-IV edition.* Washington, DC: American Psychiatric Press.

Kessler, R. C. (1997). The effects of stressful life events on depression. In *Annual review of psychology.* Palo Alto, CA: Annual Reviews.

Kessler, R. C., Davis, C. G., & Kendler, K. S. (1997). Childhood adversity and adult psychiatric disorder in the U.S. National Comorbidity Survey. *Psychological Medicine, 27,* 1101–1119.

Lam, R. W. (1994). Morning light therapy for winter depression: Predictors of response. *Acta Psychiatrica Scandinavica, 89,* 97–101.

Miklowitz, D. J., Frank, E., & George, E. L. (1996). New psychosocial treatments for outpatient management of bipolar disorder. *Psychopharmacology Bulletin, 32,* 613–621.

Nemeroff, C. B. (1998). The neurobiology of depression. *Scientific American, 278,* 42–49.

Post, R. M., Ketter, T. A., Denicoff, K., Pazzaglia, P. J., Leverich, G. S., Marangell, L. B., et al. (1996). The place of anticonvulsant therapy in bipolar illness. *Psychopharmacology, 128,* 115–129.

Post, R. M., Leverich, G. S., Denicoff, K. D., Frye, M. A., Kimbrell, T. A., & Dunn, T. M. S. (1997). Alternative approaches to refractory depression in bipolar illness. *Depression and Anxiety, 5,* 175–189.

Post, R. M., & Weiss, S. R. B. (1997). Kindling and stress sensitization. In R. T. Joffe & L. T. Young (Eds.), *Bipolar disorder: Biological models and their clinical application.* New York: Marcel Dekker.

Robertson, M. D. (1999). Interpersonal psychotherapy for patients recovering from bipolar disorder. *Australasian Psychiatry, 71,* 329–331.

Shea, M. T., Pilkonis, P. A., Beckham, E., Collins, J. F., Elkin, I., Sotsky, S. M., Docherty J. P. (1990). Personality disorders and treatment outcome in the NIMH Treatment of Depression Collaborative Research Program. *Am J Psychiatry, 147,* 711–718.

Suomi S. J. (1991). Early stress and adult emotional reactivity in rhesus monkeys. In *Childhood Environment and Adult Disease: Symposium No. 156,* Ciba Foundation Symposium Staff, editors. Wiley, Chichester, England.

Swann, A. C., Bowden, C. L., Morris, D., Calabrese, J. R., Petty, F., Small, J., et al. (1997). Depression during mania: Treatment response to lithium or divalproex. *Archives of General Psychiatry, 54,* 37–42.

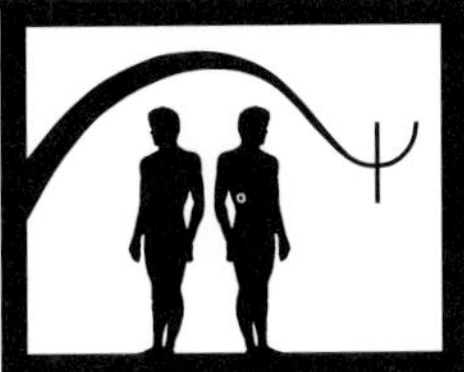

Multicultural Therapy

David Sue
Western Washington University

GLOSSARY

acculturation conflict Conflict between traditional ethnic values and the adoption of values of the host culture.

barriers to cross-cultural psychotherapy Values, expectations, and behavioral differences between the therapist and client that impede the therapeutic process.

cultural encapsulation Ethnocentric perspective that does not acknowledge cultural differences.

culture-specific (emic) therapy Therapies developed from the study of the helping processes found in specific cultural groups.

co-construction A process in which therapists work with and learn from clients in jointly developing appropriate intervention strategies.

ethnic identity models Models that indicate the "stages" that members of ethnic groups go through in attaining identity.

generic characteristics of counseling Traditional Euro-centered therapy that is based on the importance of openness of expression, individualism, action orientation, and a clear distinction between physical and emotional realms.

universal (etic) multicultural therapy Therapies based on hypothesized factors that transcend cultural differences and involve shared human experiences but holding that culture is universal.

worldview Frame of reference based on a particular set of values and beliefs.

I. THEORETICAL BASIS

Multicultural therapy (MCT) developed out of the recognition that current forms of psychotherapy were inadequate to meet the needs of ethnic minorities. In fact, some have suggested that ethnic minority clients have been harmed by psychotherapy as currently formulated and practiced. Barriers to effective cross-cultural counseling included the generic aspects of Eurocentric counseling: verbal and emotional expressiveness, individual centered, self-disclosure and intimacy, nuclear family orientation, and egalitarian relationships. These elements of counseling and therapy are often in opposition to the beliefs or values of ethnic minorities. Many ethnic groups value the family rather than the individual, have hierarchical family patterns, demonstrate different communication patterns and styles, and are more hesitant about revealing information of a personal nature. In addition, there has been little attention paid by humanistic, psychodynamic, and cognitive-behavior therapies to issues of racism, oppression, and acculturation conflicts. Because of the inadequacies of current counseling theories and techniques, there was a need to develop a multicultural therapy.

MCT has developed into two somewhat divergent camps, although both have stressed the importance of considering culture in counseling. Total immersion into the cultural group under study is a part of the emic approach (culture-specific model). It attempts to generate new theories of psychopathology and therapy from the study of different cultural groups. Current systems of the classification and treatment of mental disorders are considered to be "culturally encapsulated." As Uchenna Nwachuku and Allen Ivey in 1991 pointed out, "In contrast with the conventional approach of adapting existing counseling theory to 'fit' a new culture, the culture-specific method seeks to generate a new theory and technologies of helping." Only by adopting such a methodology can one prevent the imposition of an existing framework on other ethnic groups. New theories originating from the culture under study can be developed using anthropological methods and observations. Natural helping styles and means of problem solving for each cultural group are then identified. A culture-specific psychotherapy training model involving the African-Igbo, a tribe in Nigeria, was described by Nwachuku and Ivey. The steps involved:

1. Generating a culture-specific theory. Questions such as, "How do people in this culture view the helping relationship?" "What methods are used in solving problems?" "How similar or different are they from EuroAmerican approaches" were used to determine problem-solving approaches from the African-Igbo perspective. Study of the culture revealed a group, extended family, and community orientation. Childrearing was shared by the family and the entire community. The locus of decision making centered in the extended family and community, and problem solving involved participation by these units.
2. Generating training material based on the analysis of the culture. It was determined that effective helping approaches involved a multiperspective rather than individual frame of reference. The family and community values in decision making were stressed as well the need for harmony for cultural tradition. A more directive style was more in line with cultural expectations.

The emic or culture-specific orientation avoids the "imposed etic" or the presumed universality of theories developed in one culture and applied to another. Many EuroAmerican therapists apply psychodynamic, humanistic, or cognitive-behavioral techniques to members of different ethnic groups without questioning the validity of this practice. Donald Cheek was one of the first to point out the ethnocentric basis of traditional counseling approaches. He stated,

> I am advocating treating one segment of our population quite differently from another. This is implicit in my statement that Blacks do not benefit from many therapeutic approaches to which Whites respond. And I have referred to some of these approaches of counselors and therapists as "White techniques."

Many of the recommendations regarding therapy with ethnic minorities contain aspects of the culture-specific approach. With American Indians, there has been suggestions to incorporate cultural healing elements such as the talking circle, sweat lodge, and community interventions such as network therapy. African American therapists often indicate the importance of the Afrocentric worldview. This perspective has its roots in both the African heritage and experiences from slavery. As opposed to the Eurocentric view, there is greater emphasis on interdependence, extended family orientation, spirituality, and holism. Treatment modalities are expected to include Afrocentric elements.

In 1993, Paul Pedersen and Allen Ivey developed a description of four synthetic cultures that are actually based on the extreme grouping of the values of different cultural groups found in the world: (a) The Alpha culture is described as high in power distance. Inequalities as accepted and expected. Children are taught to obey and authority is respected; (b) The Beta culture is characterized as strong uncertainty avoidance. To deal with uncertainly, rigid rules have developed, and deviant or different ideas are suppressed. Citizen protest is repressed and conservatism and emphasis on the law is popular; (c) The Gamma culture is associated with high individualism. Emphasis is on the individual or the nuclear family. People have the right to express their own opinion and freedom of the press is supported. Education is the process of learning how to learn and evaluate; (d) The Delta culture is highly masculine. Money and possessions are dominant values. Men are expected to be assertive and tough while women should be nurturing and tender. Performance, strength and accomplishments are admired. Culture-centered therapy skills involve identifying culturally learned values and expectations and developing techniques and goals that are consistent with the specific groups.

In general, the culture-specific models have identified the differences in values, orientation, and philosophy that need to be addressed in counseling and the new therapy skills that need to be learned in working with culturally different populations. However, not all multicultural clinicians share the culture-specific perspective in multicultural therapy. Suzette Speight, Linda Myers, Chikako Cox, and Pamela Highlen argued in 1991 that the culture-specific approach makes multicultural psychotherapy an "extra skill area" that is somehow different from "regular counseling." They contend that culture-specific methodology could have negative consequences, particularly if a "cookbook" method of therapy is employed with a checklist of the values of each cultural group and directions on how counseling should proceed. Such a approach would overemphasize cultural differences, ignore individual variations, and lead to possible stereotyping ethnically different clients.

The second trend in multicultural therapy involves an etic or modified universal perspective. Under this framework, all counseling is considered to involve cultural factors (defined broadly to include differences between the therapist and client in terms of diversity issues such as age, gender, social class, religious background, and ethnicity). A proponent of the universal perspective to multicultural therapy is Mary Fukuyama who argued that cultural factors are present in all psychotherapy and must be addressed. In working with all clients it is important to consider the context and social environment when conceptualizing the presenting problem. Such a focus would enable the therapist to gain an understanding of the worldview of the client. The modified universal approach would also reduce the danger of stereotyping, encourage the assessment and consideration of cultural values and beliefs, and understand how societal norms and values can affect processes such as acculturation. Criticisms of the universal multicultural perspective include the continued reliance on therapy approaches based on individualistic and Eurocentric models with culturally different groups. Others are concerned that defining culture to include sexual orientation, age, religiosity, and other diversity issues will dilute the emphasis on the plight of ethnic minorities.

Although the culture-specific and universal forms of multicultural therapy have been espoused, neither has not been fully developed as a theory. Not until 1996 was a multicultural therapy theory presented in a complete form. In a book titled, *A Theory of Multicultural Counseling and Therapy* by Derald Sue, Allen Ivey, and Paul Pedersen, multicultural counseling and psychotherapy (MCT) is described as a "metatheory" of counseling or a "theory or theories." MCT incorporates elements of both the universal and cultural-specific perspectives. As currently constructed, the theory of multicultural counseling and psychotherapy is composed of six propositions:

1. MCT is considered a metatheory of counseling and psychotherapy that includes a culture-centered organizational framework in which to view different theories of counseling. All theories of psychotherapy are identified as stemming from a particular cultural context. Mental health professionals need to identify the values, assumptions, and philosophical bases in their work. Not recognizing these can result in the imposition of their worldview onto their clients. MCT accepts aspects of the psychodynamic, humanistic, behavioral, and biogenic approaches as they relate to the worldview of the client. MCT co-constructs definitions of the problem and solutions with the client that reduces the chances of oppression. The approach attempts to help individuals, families, and organizations develop new ways of thinking, feeling, and acting both within and between differing worldviews. Failure in therapy can result from an overemphasis on either cultural differences or similarities. Successful therapy involves utilizing a combined perspective.

2. Multiple levels of experiences (individual, group, and universal) and contexts (individual, family, and cultural) affect both the counselor and the client. Although the salience and strength of these identities vary from individual to individual and over time, they must be considered part of the focus of treatment. Elements of the similarities and differences between the therapist and client can either assist or obstruct development of a working alliance. It is important for the therapist to identify and strategize in dealing with these factors. The person–environment interaction is central to MCT. Both the therapist and client are affected on multiple levels through these identities, and this interaction can influence the conduct and success of therapy.

3. Cultural identity of both the client and the therapist can affect problem definition and the identification of appropriate goals and treatment. These dynamics are also influenced by the dominant–subordinate relationship among different cultural groups in the United States. Most theories of helping have ignored issues of dominance and power. The stage of ethnic identity for both White and ethnically different clients can affect the relationship. For many ethnic minorities, the cultural identity can go through stages such as unawareness or unacceptance of the self as a cultural being, recognizing the impact of cultural variables, redefining the self as a cultural being, and the development of a multicultural perspective. Therapists who are not members of ethnic minorities are also hypothesized to go through a parallel process.

4. When the processes of helping and goals are consonant with the experiences and cultural values of the client, the outcome is likely to be enhanced. This can be accomplished by matching the counselor and client on relevant variables or to have the counselor develop a

larger repertoire of multicultural skills. MCT recognizes the two aspects of culturally-sensitive therapy, that of the cultural specific and the universal. The cultural-specific approach can help generate new helping skills and theories whereas the universal can help identify therapy processes transcending culture. Co-construction with the client can facilitate these processes.

5. MCT stresses the importance of developing additional helper roles such as that of an advisor, consultant, advocate, systems interventionist, and prevention specialist. Traditional psychotherapy has emphasized one-to-one interactions. The new roles help focus attention on the family, community, and government policies that may also affect the mental health of a particular client.

6. Instead of self-actualization, insight, or behavior change, the basic goal of MCT is the "liberation of consciousness." It involves the expansion of consciousness as it applies to the individual, family, group, and context for behavior. The underlying cultural dimensions of specific problems are identified with the specific client. MCT therapists are able to draw on both Eurocentric and other cultural forms of helping. The psychoeducational component of MCT is emphasized in helping the client gain awareness of the cultural aspects related to the presenting problem.

II. DESCRIPTION OF TREATMENT

Cross-cultural psychotherapy is still in the evolving phase and has not developed a specific course of treatment. Instead it advocates incorporating a "culture-centered" perspective when employing the different therapeutic approaches and techniques. As mentioned earlier, there are two major models for MCT, the culture specific and the universal. Although the techniques for each are discussed separately, many are shared between the two approaches.

A. Culture-Specific Treatments

1. Assess and explore the indigenous cultural belief systems of the culturally different client. Study and understand culture-bound syndromes and the explanatory basis of disorders. For example, "sustos" is the folk belief among some Latinos and people from Mexico and other Latin American countries, that the soul has left the body because of a frightening event resulting in illness. Healing results in the return of the soul to the body. In "rootwork," a belief found in certain African- and EuroAmerican populations, generalized anxiety and somatic problems are thought to be the result of witchcraft or sorcery. Cure is effected by utilizing a "root" healer who can remove the spell. *DSM-IV* lists a number of culture-bound syndromes that reveal the belief system underlying the cause and treatment for disorders found in different cultural groups.

2. Become knowledgeable about indigenous healing practices. As opposed to Western beliefs and practices, indigenous practices often involve the support of the disturbed individual though the use of communal and family networks, efforts to problem solve or develop treatment through a group context, reliance on spiritual healing, and the use of shamans or a respected elder from the community. Although we may not subscribe to these particular beliefs or practices, the psychotherapist can assist as a facilitator of indigenous support.

3. Consult with and seek the services of traditional healers within a specific culture. A liasion with indigenous healers can help deliver treatment more effectively. When the problem is clearly defined as primarily rooted in cultural traditions, referral to traditional healers becomes necessary. Advice regarding specific intervention strategies and how they can be reinterpreted to fit the specific culture can lead to more effective outcome.

4. Developing indigenous helping skills entails working in the community, making home visits, and expanding roles to include activism, prevention, outreach and social change. The culture-specific approach can be helpful to therapists in exposing them to multiple cultural perspectives, becoming aware of different philosophical and spiritual realities, and developing a more holistic outlook on treatment.

Techniques based on the universal perspective on psychotherapy are discussed in the context of the multicultural counseling and therapy theory. MCT provides a culture-centered element in traditional forms of intervention. Indeed, the different Eurocentric approaches to psychotherapy can be effectively employed when modified to be appropriate with multicultural populations. Following are some suggested steps in multicultural psychoterapy:

1. Role preparation and establishing rapport. To establish a working alliance, a therapist must be able to establish rapport with a client. The client must feel understood and respected. Some ethnic group members are responsive to emotional aspects of the interview process; for others "credibility" can be demonstrated through the identification of appropriate issues. For many ethnic minorities, therapy is a foreign process. To

enhance the working relationship, it is helpful to explain what happens in therapy, the roles of the both the client and the therapist, and confidentiality. Determining the expectations of the clients, their understanding of the treatment process, their degree of psychological mindedness and difficulties they might have with the therapy is an important aspect of role preparation. The concept of "co-construction"—that solutions will be developed only with the input and help of the client is introduced. Explain that problems are often complex and can be influenced by family, social, and cultural factors, and that you work together to determine if these are areas that need to be addressed.

2. Assessment—incorporating contextual and environmental factors. A culture-centered assessment would begin with an exploration of issues that may be faced by members of ethnic minorities such as immigration or refugee experiences, difficulties at work or in school, language and housing problem, possible issues with discrimination or prejudice, and acculturation conflicts (Recent immigrants or even individuals from first and second generations often show a pattern in which the children acculturate more quickly than the parents, and this difference often leads to conflict within the family). Social and community supports should also be identified. The assessment allows one to determine the possible impact of environmental, cultural, and social issues on the presenting problem. If the therapist determines the problem is external in nature, the therapist must help the client not to internalize the problem. Instead, the therapist might assist the client with developing strategies to cope with the external issues.

a. Ethnic or cultural identity. The cultural identify of both the therapist and client can affect both the problem definition and goals. Different identity development models have been developed for specific ethnic groups, but they all describe the process in which an individual moves from the host culture frame of reference to an acceptance of one's own cultural group. Determining the degree of ethnic identity of a particular client can help prevent stereotyping. Some clients will show little adherence to ethnicity and consider it unimportant whereas others may have a very strong ethnic identity that may influence how they perceive the presenting problem. Intervention strategies will depend on the stage of ethnic identity of the client. Those with a strong desire for assimilation into White society may reject attempts to explore ethnic variables. If the clinician determines that the presenting problem does not involve a rejection of the client's own ethnic identity, then mainstream psychotherapy approaches can be useful. At another stage of ethnic identity, the individual may become angry over issues of racism and oppression and respond with suspicion to the therapist. They may feel that therapy attempts to have them adjust to a "sick" society. Ethnic identity issues have to be identified to determine if this should be a focus of therapy.

b. Although controversial, a number of ethnic researchers and clinicians posited models of White Racial Identity Development that apply to EuroAmerican therapists. Hypothesized stages are: (a) conformity or the obliviousness and lack of awareness of racism. Success in life is seen to be dependent on effort and not race. Ethnic minorities are evaluated according to EuroAmerican standards. The therapist professes to be "color blind" and does not question the relevance of applying therapy approaches to ethnic groups; (b) disintegration or the conflict produced by the beginning recognition of discrimination and prejudice against ethnic minorities. An individual at this stage may avoid contact with people of color; (c) Reintegration that involves resolving conflict by returning to beliefs of minority inferiority; (d) Pseudoindependence or the acknowledgement of societal biases and the recognition of White privilege. However, the individual may perpetuate racism by attempting to have minorities adjust to White standards; (e) immersion/emersion that is marked by a personal focus on one's own biases and to directly combat racism and oppression; and (f) autonomy in which the individual accepts one's whiteness and is comfortable acknowledging and accepting ethnic differences.

(1) Intake forms. Background information, history, description of the problem, mental status exam, and other means of gathering data should include a section determining whether the characteristics or behaviors are considered normative for the particular cultural group. If the clinician determines the problem may have cultural aspects, a determination has to be made if it applies to a particular individual. This would reduce the chances of stereotyping. When using *DSM-IV–TR*, it is especially important to do a thorough assessment of Axis IV (psychosocial and environmental problems) to eliminate the possibility that the presenting problems may actually be "other conditions that may be a focus of clinical attention" rather than a mental disorder. It is essential that the therapist remain aware of validity issues with different types of assessment and clinical judgments involving specific ethnic minorities. *DSM-IV–TR* warns that there may be a tendency to

overdiagnose schizophrenia in certain ethnic groups. Behaviors considered normative in a specific ethnic group may be seen as pathological from another group's perspective. Asian Americans tend to score low on assertiveness and high on social anxiety. Rather than being considered negative attributes, these may represent the Asian values of modesty and group orientation. African Americans may show a "healthy paranoia" or suspiciousness resulting from experiences associated with oppression and racism.

(2) Problem definition. Consider the clients' perspective on problems. How did they arise and how are they affecting functioning? Are specific cultural factors involved? In interviewing an individual make certain information about family, friends, and possible cultural/environmental factors is also obtained. When working with a family, these areas are also explored along with the possibility of acculturation conflicts between the parents and children.

(3) Goal definition. First, identify the different theoretical therapeutic techniques or processes used to attain goals. What assumptions underlie the techniques, and are they acceptable to members of other cultural groups? What kinds of modifications may have to be made or new techniques adopted? Second, the therapist should acquire knowledge of the experiences of ethnic minorities in the United States and issues involving oppression and discrimination. Many are still affected by their minority status and face conflicts over acculturation issues. There must be a willingness to acknowledge and address cultural and value differences with clients. Third, therapists should seek continuing education and consultation when working with ethnic minority populations and be willing to take on different roles such as advisor, advocate, and consultant.

B. Culture-Centered Interventions

Although psychoanalytic, humanistic, and behavioral models have differences in theory and techniques, they still share similarities in their "generic" approaches to psychotherapy and the conceptualization of the "healthy" client. There has been some movement in each of these approaches to make them more compatible for the different cultural groups. One such suggestion involves coconstruction. In *DSM-IV–TR*, it is noted that is important to identify possible "cultural explanations of the individual's illness." These explanations are how the particular individual views the problem and are part of the co-construction process.

In general, the research on therapy for ethnic minorities has revealed that they prefer techniques that are directive, action oriented, and concrete. Some have suggested that cognitive-behavioral approaches show promise. However, as with all therapies, the cultural elements have to be identified. For example, what constitutes an "irrational belief" for particular cultural groups would have to be determined. Also, as with all Eurocentric psychotherapies, the focus has to change from the individual to include family, community, and societal factors. An individual's current mental complaints might stem from oppression and discrimination.

Currently, there are no specific guidelines in modifying traditional forms of psychotherapy to make them more appropriate for the problems of ethnic minorities. Regardless of psychotherapeutic orientation, the suggestions for multicultural assessment and co-construction can be helpful. All Eurocentric schools of psychotherapy face similar problems. They tend to have an individual focus and only work with the client rather than to attempt to address social and cultural concerns. Psychodynamic approaches could perhaps include exploration of a family or cultural unconscious to determine how these influenced individual development. Questions related to how these affected the identity of the individual could be explored. Humanistic therapists might use Abraham Maslow's hierarchy of needs to help identify the satisfaction of needs and the consideration of environmental concerns. Again, there could be a developed focus on cultural and family dimensions.

Empathy and other helping skills could not only be directed to the individual but to interpersonal relationships, the family, and the environment. The notion of co-construction fits well in the humanistic framework. With both the psychodynamic and the humanistic therapies, action and concrete suggestions need to be included as part of the therapy. Cognitive-behavior therapies are direct and action oriented and fit well into the expectations of many ethnic minority clients. However, they are also focused on the individual and need to be modified in use with other cultural groups. Cognitions considered to be "irrational" may not be perceived that way be ethnic minorities. The challenge is to understand what thoughts might be considered irrational by members of different cultural groups. In addition, the "unit" of treatment may not be the individual but the family, community, or even society. Group therapy with ethnic minorities also has to involve alterations. Techniques such as "ice breakers" are often used to facilitate interaction among the participants. Again, many of the activities reflect a cultural basis, and as therapists, we must analyze it as such. Some members of ethnic minorities may be uncomfortable participating because of the seeming lack of structure and ambiguity of these activities. Pairing individuals up with other group members or providing structured tasks may generate more responsiveness. The focus of groups often is in personal development, and being a member of a family or particular ethnic groups is ignored. It may be valuable to focus on social identity and the increased understanding and responses to differences between groups.

Family therapy is also based on Eurocentric models and should not be imposed on families from different cultural groups. The family structure needs to be identified and relationships assessed. Therapy should be co-constructed with the help of family members. Systems theories should be expanded to included societal issues such as discrimination, poverty, and conflicting value systems. Reframe the concept of the "identified patient" as conflicts between different value systems. Again, the emphasis is to help the family develop better ways of handling problems within and between cultural constraints. It will be a challenge for individuals with training in Eurocentric therapies to develop more culture-centered treatment strategies.

III. EMPIRICAL STUDIES

There has been a number of studies examining some of the factors that affect cross-cultural therapy. However, most of these are not theoretically based, and few have addressed either the culture-specific or modified universal multicultural therapy models. For the culture-specific approach presented earlier by Uchenna Nwachuku and Allen Ivey on the African-Igbo culture, U.S. graduate students in a counseling program responded to problems presented by videotaped African-Igbo clients. The counselors displayed listening skills, allowed the client to determine direction, and focused clearly on the individual. The counselors were then trained in a workshop with information gained from the analysis of African-Igbo culture and were again rated on their performance with videotapes of African-Igbo clients. Improvement was noted in the use of more culturally aware responses but difficulty was still displayed in focusing on family and community values rather than the individual and the use of use of influencing skills such as giving advice. The study indicated that culture-specific information and training can improve sensitivity to different cultural styles, but that aspects of Eurocentric therapy remain difficult to alter.

There has been no direct research on either the modified universal model or the six propositions of multicultural counseling and psychotherapy. Indeed it can be argued that past research on culturally different populations is culture bound and difficult to interpret from a culture-centered perspective. However, although the theories have not been directly examined, some of the research can apply to the propositions in multicultural counseling and psychotherapy. It must be noted that many of the cross-cultural studies involve college populations, and the findings may not be valid with ethnic clients living in the community. The following are hypotheses and research support in the area of multicultural counseling and psychotherapy that could be predicted from MCT. These are from the chapter "Research and Research Hypotheses in Intercultural Counseling" by David Sue and Norman Sundberg.

1. Conceptualization of mental disorders and psychotherapy will influence access. In general, Southeast Asians are less likely to enter psychotherapy because they associate mental illness with stigma and shame and are not acquainted with the notion of psychotherapy. Asian American groups tend to believe that mental illness is due to a lack of willpower and believe that they should deal with the problem themselves. Hispanic American families are more likely to utilize family, relatives, or community resources for emotional problems. Both groups underutilize mental health resources. African American and American Indians may show cultural mistrust of psychotherapy feeling that the therapy symbolizes oppression. African Americans tend to overutilize mental health services but also tend to terminate more quickly and show little positive gain. There is also some evidence that they use the therapy session to deal with external problems such as problems with agencies and the law rather than personal issues.

2. The degree of similarity in the expectation between client and therapist toward the process and goals of counseling affects effectiveness. In a number of research studies, ethnic minorities are more likely to be responsive to approaches that are more directive and action oriented and rate therapists using these approaches as more "credible." Pretherapy explanations of the process of therapy and the responsibilities of the client and therapy lead to greater satisfaction of services.

3. Ethnic similarity between client and therapist will enhance the probability of a positive therapeutic outcome. Reviews of ethnic matching have produced mixed results. Some support has been found in some studies and not in others. There is some support that African Americans prefer an ethnically similar therapist and that stage of racial identity development is related to this preference. Among Hispanic Americans, a slight preference for an ethnically similar therapist was found, especially among those low in acculturation. In one study of clients in the Los Angeles area, ethnic

matching was a significant predictor of outcome for Hispanic Americans and approached significance for Asian Americans, especially among recent immigrants. For all groups, including EuroAmericans, ethnic match was related to length of treatment except for African Americans. In many of the studies, other similarities between the therapist and client involving attitudes, values, or style was as, if not more, important than ethnic matching.

4. Among ethnic minorities, degree of acculturation or stage of ethnic identity affects receptivity to counseling. In general, low-acculturated ethnic minority individuals appear to prefer an ethnically similar therapist. This has been found with Asian American, Hispanic American, and American Indian participants. For African American clients, there is some support for the view that those with a cultural distrust were more likely to terminate earlier with a White than a African American therapist. There is limited support for the view that the stage of ethnic identity is related to the types of problems presented and reaction to the counselor.

5. Exploring cultural and environmental variables can increase the "credibility" of the therapist. Cultural sensitivity as defined by the acknowledgment of culture, acculturation conflicts, and other issues faced by ethnic minorities demonstrated by therapists increased their ratings of credibility. The acknowledgement of ethnic differences between the client and therapist has also found to be related to positive outcome. Demonstrating a culturally sensitive approach by exploring cultural issues increased the therapeutic alliance, regardless of ethnic differences between the client and therapist. Cultural sensitivity displayed by the therapist has been found to be related to greater client self-disclosure and satisfaction.

6. The stage of identity for a EuroAmerican therapists can affect their reaction to ethnic minority clients. The concept of "White identity" is controversial in that EuroAmericans also go through a stage of racial identity. Certainly it would seem that if therapists denied the possibility of prejudice and discrimination faced by ethnic minority group members, they would not be able to understand the worldview of many culturally different clients and not be able to provide appropriate interventions. There has been limited support for the impact of the specific stage of White identity development and self-reported multicultural competencies.

7. Ethnic minorities prefer directive, concrete, and action-oriented psychotherapy techniques. Most of the studies indicate that ethnic minorities show a preference for a directive when compared to a client-centered approach. This appears to be more true for recent immigrants or those with low acculturation. Ethnic minority females show somewhat greater acceptance of a client-centered approach than males. However, what ethnic clients may want is more structure and guidance in therapy and advice or suggestions for different courses of action.

Thus, it would seem that some of the predictions made by multicultural therapy has received some support. However, what is needed are more explicit testable hypotheses to measure outcome in a varied of ways (symptom reduction, termination, and satisfaction) and to involve the use of actual patient populations.

IV. SUMMARY

Consideration of cultural factors in psychotherapy is being addressed by the different mental health organizations. It is receiving greater recognition in *DSM-IV–TR* where it is discussed both in the Appendix and as a subheading under the different disorders. The mental health field has responded primarily by drawing attention to possible cultural factors but not questioning the universality of psychotherapies developed according to Eurocentric models. Multicultural therapy approaches attempt to have practitioners understand the culture-specific nature of Western therapies and to identify assumptions and values under their system of psychotherapy. All therapies develop under some type of cultural framework. To deal with the inadequacies of current counseling theories and techniques in working with different ethnic groups, there is an increased attention to the impact of cultural factors.

Multicultural therapy has developed into somewhat different theoretical models. The culture-specific model or emic approach attempts to determine how a cultural group defines problem behaviors and problem-solving techniques. Anthropological observations and interviews are used to gather information. The concept of "healer" within the culture is identified to understand the philosophical nature of "therapy." From this, new theories of psychopathology and psychotherapy may develop. Criticism of the culture-specific model includes the possibility of overemphasizing culture, ignoring individual differences, and the necessity of developing a different approach for the cultural groups.

The modified version of multicultural therapy attempts to identify universals and considers all therapy to have cultural components that need to be identified. Some criticize the universal approach as just adding culture to Eurocentric psychotherapies. A multicultural therapy that lies in between the culture-specific and universal perspectives was recently developed. It emphasizes the cultural aspects of all forms of counseling, emphasizing that practitioners need to identify the value system underlying their therapeutic approaches, and the importance of considering behaviors in context and multiple levels of experience (individual, group, universal). This theory is considered to be a theory of theories and has formulated a number of testable propositions and corollaries.

Intervention strategies based on culture-specific models are developed specifically for the population under study. With the African-Igbo, U.S. counseling students learned the methods of therapy derived through interviews with indigenous "experts" and observation and workshop material. The universal and multicultural therapy models develop intervention based on a culture-centered approach. Cultural factors are identified and assessments modified. The culture-specific nature of psychodynamic, humanistic, and cognitive-behavioral theories are identified and modified to incorporate family, groups, and environmental considerations. To reduce stereotyping, the ethnic identity of the client is assessed along with the identity of the therapist. Co-construction or the understanding of the problem, solutions, and appropriate interventions are made with the help of the client. Individual, family, and group therapies need to go through the process of identifying the assumptions underlying the models and altering the techniques to fit the worldview and expectation of ethnic minorities.

Research on cultural factors in psychotherapy has been relatively limited and without a theoretical basis. Most studies involve college populations and deal with specific aspects of cross-cultural counseling such as the rating of credibility, preference, and expertise. Although the findings are mixed, there is some support for ethnic matching of the therapist and client, especially for African Americans and less acculturated Hispanic and Asian Americans. It also appears that ethnic minorities feel more comfortable with action-oriented and concrete approaches of helping. Therapists are also rated higher when they demonstrate cultural sensitivity when dealing with an ethnic minority client. These findings are only tentative and need to include more actual clients and therapists.

See Also the Following Articles

Bioethics ■ Cultural Issues ■ Race and Human Diversity ■ Transcultural Psychotherapy

Further Reading

American Psychological Association. (1993). Guidelines for providers of psychological services to ethnic, linguistic, and culturally diverse populations. *American Psychologist, 48,* 45–48.

Cheek, D. (1976). *Assertive Black ... puzzled White.* San Luis Obispo, CA: Impact.

Fukuyama, M. (1990). Taking a universal approach to multicultural counseling. *Counselor Education and Supervision, 30,* 6–17.

Pedersen, P. (1988). *A handbook for developing multicultural awareness.* VA: Alexandria, VA: American Association for Counseling and Development.

Pedersen, P. B., & Ivey, A. (1993). *Culture-centered counseling and interviewing skills: A practical guide.* Westport, CT: Praeger.

Ponterotto, J. G., Casas, J. M., Suzuki, L. A., & Alexander, C. M. (1995). *Handbook of multicultural counseling.* Thousand Oaks, CA: Sage.

Speight, S. L., Myers, L. J., Cox, C. I., & Highlen, P. S. (1991). A redefinition of multicultural counseling. *Journal of Counseling and Development, 70,* 29–36.

Sue, D. W., Ivey, A. E., & Pedersen, P. B. (1996). *A theory of multicultural counseling and therapy.* Pacific Grove, CA: Brooks/Cole.

Sue, D. W., & Sue, D. (1999). *Counseling the culturally different (3d ed.).* New York: John Wiley & Sons.

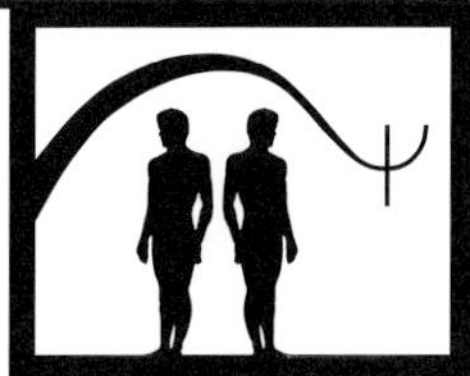

Multimodal Behavior Therapy

Arnold A. Lazarus
Rutgers University and Center for Multimodal Psychological Services

GLOSSARY

BASIC I.D. An acronym of Behavior, Affect, Sensation, Imagery, Cognition, Interpersonal relationships, and Drugs/Biological processes.

bridging A procedure in which the therapist deliberately tunes into issues that the client wants to discuss, then gently guides the discussion into more productive areas.

second-order BASIC I.D Focusing on a specific problem in the BASIC I.D. to flesh out more information; useful for breaking impasses in therapy.

social learning theory A system that combines classical and operant conditioning with cognitive mediational factors (e.g., observational learning and symbolic activity) to explain the development, maintenance, and modification of behavior.

structural profile inventory A 35-item questionnaire that assesses the extent to which one is apt to be active or inactive; emotional or impassive; aware of or indifferent to sensory stimuli; reliant on mental imagery; inclined to think, plan, and cogitate; gravitate toward people and social events or avoid them; and engage in healthful habits and activities.

technical eclecticism The use of techniques drawn from diverse sources without also adhering to the disciplines or theories that spawned them.

tracking the firing order A careful scrutiny of the firing order of the BASIC I.D. modalities to facilitate more effective sequencing of treatment procedures.

I. DESCRIPTION OF TREATMENT

Multimodal behavior therapy (also called Multimodal therapy) rests on the observation that at base, we are biological organisms (neurophysiological/biochemical entities) who *behave* (act and react), *emote* (experience affective responses), *sense* (respond to tactile, olfactory, gustatory, visual, and auditory stimuli), *imagine* (conjure up sights, sounds, and other events in our mind's eye), *think* (entertain beliefs, opinions, values, and attitudes), and *interact* with one another (enjoy, tolerate, or suffer various interpersonal relationships). By referring to these seven discrete but interactive dimensions or modalities as Behavior, Affect, Sensation, Imagery, Cognition, Interpersonal, Drugs/Biologicals, the convenient acronym BASIC I.D. emerges from the first letter of each one.

Many psychotherapeutic approaches are trimodal, addressing affect, behavior, and cognition—ABC. The outcomes of several follow-up inquiries pointed to the importance of *breadth* if treatment gains were to be maintained. The multimodal approach provides clinicians with a comprehensive template. By separating sensations from emotions, distinguishing between images and cognitions, emphasizing both intraindividual and interpersonal behaviors, and underscoring the biological substrate, the multimodal orientation is most far-reaching. By assessing a client's BASIC I.D. one endeavors to "leave no stone unturned."

The elements of a thorough assessment involve the following range of questions:

B: What is this individual doing that is getting in the way of his or her happiness or personal fulfillment (self-defeating actions, maladaptive behaviors)? What does the client need to increase and decrease? What should he or she stop doing and start doing?

A: What emotions (affective reactions) are predominant? Are we dealing with anger, anxiety, depression, or combinations thereof, and to what extent (e.g., irritation versus rage; sadness versus profound melancholy)? What appears to generate these negative affects—certain cognitions, images, interpersonal conflicts? And how does the person respond (behave) when feeling a certain way? It is important to look for interactive processes—what impact do various behaviors have on the person's affect and vice versa? How does this influence each of the other modalities?

S: Are there specific sensory complaints (e.g., tension, chronic pain, tremors)? What feelings, thoughts, and behaviors are connected to these negative sensations? What positive sensations (e.g., visual, auditory, tactile, olfactory, and gustatory delights) does the person report? This includes the individual as a sensual and sexual being. When called for, the enhancement or cultivation of erotic pleasure is a viable therapeutic goal.

I: What fantasies and images are predominant? What is the person's "self-image?" Are there specific success or failure images? Are there negative or intrusive images (e.g., flashbacks to unhappy or traumatic experiences)? And how are these images connected to ongoing cognitions, behaviors, affective reactions, and so forth?

C: Can we determine the individual's main attitudes, values, beliefs, and opinions? What are this person's predominant shoulds, oughts, and musts? Are there any definite dysfunctional beliefs or irrational ideas? Can we detect any untoward automatic thoughts that undermine his or her functioning?

I: Interpersonally, who are the significant others in this individual's life? What does he or she want, desire, expect, and receive from them, and what does he or she, in turn, give to and do for them? What relationships give him or her particular pleasures and pains?

D: Is this person biologically healthy and health conscious? Does he or she have any medical complaints or concerns? What relevant details pertain to diet, weight, sleep, exercise, and alcohol and drug use?

The foregoing dimensions or modalities are some of the main issues that multimodal clinicians traverse while assessing the client's BASIC I.D. A more comprehensive problem identification sequence is derived from asking most clients to complete the Multimodal Life History Inventory. This 15-page questionnaire facilitates treatment when conscientiously filled in by clients as a homework assignment, usually after the initial session. Seriously disturbed (e.g., deluded, deeply depressed, highly agitated) clients will not be expected to comply, but most psychiatric outpatients who are reasonably literate will find the exercise useful for speeding up routine history taking and readily provide the therapist with a BASIC I.D. analysis.

A. Placing the BASIC I.D. in Perspective

The treatment process in multimodal behavior therapy rests on the BASIC I.D., which serves as a template to remind us to examine each of the seven modalities and their interactive effects. It implies that we are social beings that move, feel, sense, imagine, and think, and that at base we are biochemical–neurophysiological entities. Students and colleagues frequently inquire whether any particular areas are more significant, more heavily weighted, than the others are. For thoroughness, all seven require careful attention, but perhaps the biological and interpersonal modalities are especially significant.

The biological modality wields a profound influence on all the other modalities. Unpleasant sensory reactions can signal a host of medical illnesses; excessive emotional reactions (anxiety, depression, and rage) may all have biological determinants; faulty thinking, and images of gloom, doom, and terror may derive entirely from chemical imbalances; and untoward personal and interpersonal behaviors may stem from many somatic reactions ranging from toxins (e.g., drugs or alcohol) to intracranial lesions. Hence, when any doubts arise about the probable involvement of biological factors, it is imperative to have them fully investigated. A person who has no untoward medical/physical problems and enjoys warm, meaningful, and loving relationships, is apt to find life personally and interpersonally fulfilling. Hence the biological modality serves as the base and the interpersonal modality is perhaps the apex. The seven modalities are by no means static or linear but exist in a state of reciprocal transaction.

A patient requesting therapy may point to any of the seven modalities as his or her entry point. *Affect:* "I suffer from anxiety and depression." *Behavior:*. "It's my compulsive habits that are getting to me." *Interpersonal:* "My wife and are not getting along." *Sensory:* "I have these tension headaches and pains in my jaw." *Imagery:* "I can't get the picture of my grandmother's funeral out of my mind, and I often have disturbing dreams." *Cognitive:* "I know I set unrealistic goals for myself and expect too much from others, but I can't seem to help it." *Biological:* "I'm fine as long as I take lithium, but I need someone to monitor my blood levels."

It is more usual, however, for people to enter therapy with explicit problems in two or more modalities—"I have all sorts of aches and pains that my doctor tells me are due to tension. I also worry too much, and I feel frustrated a lot of the time. And I'm very angry with my father." Initially, it is usually advisable to engage the patient by focusing on the issues, modalities, or areas of concern that he or she presents. To deflect the emphasis too soon onto other matters that may seem more important is only likely to make the patient feel discounted. Once rapport has been established, however, it is usually easy to shift to more significant problems.

Any good clinician will first address and investigate the presenting issues. "Please tell me more about the aches and pains you are experiencing." "Do you feel tense in any specific areas of your body?" "You mentioned worries and feelings of frustration. Can you please elaborate on them for me?" "What are some of the specific clash points between you and your father?" The therapist will then flesh out the details. However, a multimodal therapist goes farther. She or he will carefully note the specific modalities across the BASIC I.D. that are being discussed, and which ones are omitted or glossed over. The latter (i.e., the areas that are overlooked or neglected) often yield important clinical information.

In this description of the overview of treatment processes, it is important to explain several procedures that are employed by multimodal behavior therapists.

1. Second-Order BASIC I.D. Assessments

The initial Modality Profile (BASIC I.D. Chart) translates vague, general, or diffuse problems (e.g., depression, and unhappiness, and anxiety) into specific, discrete, and interactive difficulties. Techniques—preferably those with empirical backing—are selected to counter the various problems. Nevertheless, treatment impasses arise, and when this occurs, a more detailed inquiry into associated behaviors, affective responses, sensory reactions, images, cognitions, interpersonal factors, and possible biological considerations may shed light on the situation. This recursive application of the BASIC I.D. to itself adds depth and detail to the macroscopic overview afforded by the initial Modality Profile. Thus, a second-order assessment with a client who was not responding to antidepressants and a combination of cognitive–behavioral procedures revealed a central cognitive schema—"I am not entitled to be happy"—that had eluded all other avenues of inquiry. Therapy was then aimed directly at addressing this maladaptive cognition.

2. Bridging

A strategy that is probably employed by most effective therapists can readily be taught to novices via the BASIC I.D. format. We refer to it as bridging. Suppose a therapist is interested in a client's emotional responses to an event. "How did you feel when your father yelled at you in front of your friends?" Instead of discussing his feelings, the client responds with defensive and irrelevant intellectualizations. "My dad had strange priorities and even as a kid I used to question his judgment." Additional probes into his feelings only yield similar abstractions. It is often counterproductive to confront the client and point out that he is evading the question and seems reluctant to face his true feelings. In situations of this kind, bridging is usually effective. First, the therapist deliberately tunes into the client's preferred modality—in this case, the cognitive domain. Thus, the therapist explores the cognitive content. "So you see it as a consequence involving judgments and priorities. Please tell me more." In this way, after perhaps a 5 to 10 minute discourse, the therapist endeavors to branch off into other directions that seem more productive. "Tell me, while we have been discussing these matters, have you noticed any sensations anywhere in your body?" This sudden switch from cognition to sensation may begin to elicit more pertinent information (given the assumption that in this instance, sensory inputs are probably less threatening than affective material). The client may refer to some sensations of tension or bodily discomfort at which point the therapist may ask him to focus on them, often with a hypnotic overlay. "Will you please close your eyes, and now feel that neck tension. (Pause). Now relax deeply for a few moments, breathe easily and gently, in and out, in and out, just letting yourself feel calm and peaceful." The feelings of tension, and their associated images and cognitions may then be examined. One may then venture to bridge into affect. "Beneath the sensations, can you find any strong feelings or emotions?Perhaps they are lurking in the background." At this juncture it is not unusual for clients to give voice to their feelings. "I am in touch with anger and with sadness." By starting where the client is and then bridging into a different modality, most clients then seem willing to traverse the more emotionally charged areas they had been avoiding.

3. *Tracking the Firing Order*

A fairly reliable pattern may be discerned of the way that many people generate negative affect. Some dwell first on unpleasant sensations (palpitations, shortness of breath, tremors), followed by aversive images (pictures of disastrous events), to which they attach negative cognitions (ideas about catastrophic illness), leading to maladaptive behavior (withdrawal and avoidance). This S-I-C-B firing order (sensation, imagery, cognition, behavior) may require a different treatment strategy from that employed with a C-I-S-B sequence, a I-C-B-S, or yet a different firing order. Clinical findings suggest that it is often best to apply treatment techniques in accordance with a client's specific chain reaction. A rapid way of determining someone's firing order is to have him or her in an altered state of consciousness—deeply relaxed with eyes closed—contemplating untoward events and then describing his or her reactions.

One of my clients was perplexed at the fact that she frequently felt extremely anxious "out of the blue." Here is part of an actual clinical dialogue:

> Therapist: Now please think back to those feelings of anxiety that took you by surprise. Take your time, and tell me what you remember.
>
> Client: We had just finished having dinner and I was clearing the table. (Pause) I remember now. I had some indigestion.
>
> Therapist: Can you describe the sensations?
>
> Client: Sort of like heartburn and a kind of a cramp over here (points to upper abdomen).
>
> Therapist: Can you focus on the memory of those sensations?
>
> Client: Yes. I remember them well. (Pause) Then I started remembering things.
>
> Therapist: Such as?
>
> Client: Such as the time I had dinner at Tom's and had such a migraine that I threw up.
>
> Therapist: Let me see if I am following you. You started having some digestive discomfort and then you had an image, a picture of the time you were at Tom's and got sick.
>
> Client: Yeah. That's when I stopped what I was doing and went to lie down.

This brief excerpt reveals a sensation-imagery-behavioral sequence. In the actual case, a most significant treatment goal was to show the client that she attached extremely negative attributions to negative sensations, which then served as a trigger for anxiety-generating images. Consequently, she was asked to draw up a list of unpleasant sensations, to dwell on them one by one, and to prevent the eruption of catastrophic images with a mantra—"this too shall pass."

II. THEORETICAL BASES

Multimodal behavior therapy is behavioral in that is based on the principles and procedures of experimental psychology, especially social learning theory. According to this theory, all behaviors—normal and abnormal—are maintained and modified by environmental events. The initial behavioral theories rested on animal analogues and were decidedly mechanistic. They put forth rather simplistic analyses of stimulus-response contingencies. The advent of what is now termed cognitive-behavior therapy rests on a much more sophisticated foundation. Emphasis is now placed on the finding that cognitive processes, which in turn are affected by the social and environmental consequences of behavior, determine the influence of external events. The main focus is on the constant reciprocity between personal actions and environmental consequences.

Social learning theory recognizes that association plays a key role in all learning processes. Events that occur simultaneously or in quick succession are likely to be connected. An association may be said to exist when responses evoked by one set of stimuli are similar to those elicited by other stimuli. The basic social learning triad is made up of classical (respondent) conditioning, operant (instrumental) conditioning, and modeling and vicarious processes. Added to the foregoing is the personalistic use of language, expectancies, selective attention, goals, and performance standards, as well as the impact of numerous values, attitudes, and beliefs. A person's thoughts will determine which stimuli are noticed, how much they are valued, and how long they are remembered. In the brief space allocated, it is not possible to do justice to the nuances of social learning theory, but I hope that its level of sophistication and experimentally based outlook can be appreciated.

A pivotal concept in multimodal behavior therapy is that of technical eclecticism. As more therapists have become aware that no one school can possibly provide all the answers, a willingness to incorporate different methods into their own purview and to combine different procedures has become fairly prominent. There are several different ways in which methods may be combined. The first is to utilize several techniques within a given approach (e.g., exposure, response prevention, and participant modeling from a behavioral perspective). One may also combine techniques from different disciplines, especially when confronted by a seemingly intractable patient or problem. Yet another way of combining treatments is to use medication in conjunction with psychosocial therapies. In addition, one may treat certain clients with a combination of individual, family, and group therapy, or look to other disciplines (e.g., social work in the case of vocational rehabilitation).

There are three principal routes to rapprochement or integration: technical eclecticism, theoretical integration, and common factors. Those who attempt to meld different or even disparate theories (theoretical integrationists), differ significantly from those who remain theoretically consistent but use diverse techniques (technical eclectics). And those who dwell on the common ingredients shared by different therapies (e.g., self-efficacy, enhanced morale, or corrective emotional experiences), are apt to ignore crucial differences while emphasizing essential similarities. Unfortunately, there are still many school adherents who refuse to look beyond the boundaries of their own theories for ideas and methods that may enhance their clinical acumen.

In essence, there appear to be no data to support the notion that a blend of different theories has resulted in a more robust therapeutic technique or has led to synergistic practice effects. It cannot be overstated that the effectiveness of specific techniques may have no bearing on the theories that spawned them. Techniques may, in fact, prove effective for reasons that do not remotely relate to the theoretical ideas that gave birth to them. This is not meant to imply that techniques operate or function in a vacuum. The therapeutic relationship is the soil that enables techniques to take root. Theories are needed to explain or account for various phenomena and to try to make objective sense out of bewildering observations and assertions. And it is precisely because social learning and cognitive theories are experimentally grounded that multimodal behavior therapy embraces them rather than any of the other theories in the marketplace. It makes sense to select seemingly effective techniques from any discipline without necessarily subscribing to the theories that begot them.

In multimodal behavior therapy, the selection and development of specific techniques are not at all capricious. The basic position can be summarized as follows: Eclecticism is warranted only when well-documented treatments of choice do not exist for a particular disorder, or when well-established methods are not achieving the desired results. Nevertheless, when these procedures, despite proper implementation, fail to prove helpful, one may resort to less authenticated procedures or endeavor to develop new strategies. Clinical effectiveness is probably in direct proportion to the range of effective tactics, strategies, and methods that a practitioner has at his or her disposal. Nevertheless, the rag-tag importation of techniques from anywhere or everywhere without a sound rationale can only result in syncretistic confusion. A systematic, prescriptive, technically eclectic orientation is the opposite of a smorgasbord conception of eclecticism in which one selects procedures according to unstated and unreplicable processes. It needs to be emphasized again that arbitrary blends of different techniques are to be decried.

The cognitive–behavioral literature has documented various treatments of choice for a wide range of afflictions including maladaptive habits, fears and phobias, stress-related difficulties, sexual dysfunctions, depression, eating disorders, obsessive–compulsive disorders, and posttraumatic stress disorders. We can also include dementia, psychoactive substance abuse, somatization disorder, multiple personality disorder and various other personality disorders, psychophysiologic disorders, pain management, and diverse forms of violence. There are relatively few empirically validated treatments outside the area of cognitive–behavior therapy.

III. APPLICATIONS AND EXCLUSIONS

Multimodal behavior therapy is not a unitary or closed system. It is basically a clinical approach that rests on a social and cognitive learning theory, and uses technically eclectic and empirically supported procedures in an individualistic manner. The overriding question is mainly "Who and what is best for this client?" Obviously no one therapist can be well versed in the entire gamut of methods and procedures that exist. Some clinicians are excellent with children whereas others have a talent for working with geriatric populations. Some practitioners have specialized in specific disorders (e.g., eating disorders, sexual dysfunctions, PTSD, panic, depression, substance abuse, or schizophrenia). Those who employ multimodal behavior therapy will bring their talents to bear on their areas of special proficiency and employ the BASIC I.D.

as per the foregoing discussions, and, by so doing, possibly enhance their clinical impact. If a problem or a specific client falls outside their sphere of expertise, they will endeavor to effect a referral to an appropriate resource. For example, if a client who speaks only Spanish is to be treated by multimodal behavior therapy, obviously a therapist who is fluent in Spanish will be chosen. Thus, there are no problems or populations per se that are excluded. The only exclusionary criteria are those that pertain to the limitations of individual therapists.

IV. EMPIRICAL STUDIES

A crucial question is whether or not there is evidence that a multimodal approach is superior to more narrow or targeted treatments. During the 1970s and 1980s issues pertaining to focused versus combined treatment modalities were addressed in several quarters. Interestingly, for some disorders, specialized or highly focused interventions appeared superior to broad-spectrum approaches. For example, in weight-loss programs a specialized stimulus-control procedure was often favored over multidimensional treatments. Similarly, several other problem areas may respond better to specialized procedures: some phobias, compulsive disorders, sexual problems, eating disorders, some cases of insomnia, tension headaches, and the management of oppositional children.

On the other hand, a strong argument for combined treatments can be made for the treatment of alcoholism. Studies have shown that those treated only by aversion therapy were more likely to relapse than their counterparts who had also received relaxation training. And more recently, several studies have indicated that a combination of imipramine and exposure is more effective in treating panic disorder with agoraphobia than either exposure treatment or drug treatment alone.

In a carefully controlled outcome study conducted by Tom Williams in Scotland, multimodal assessment and treatment were compared with less integrative approaches in helping children with learning disabilities. Clear data emerged in support of the multimodal procedures. In Holland, M.G.T. Kwee and his associates conducted a multimodal treatment outcome study on 84 hospitalized patients suffering from obsessive–compulsive disorders or phobias, 90% of whom had received prior treatment without success, and 70% of whom had suffered from their disorders for more than 4 years. Implementing multimodal treatment regimens resulted in substantial recoveries and durable 9-month follow-ups.

The main criticism of multimodal behavior therapy is that it is so broad-based, so flexible, so personalistic and adaptable that tightly controlled outcome research is virtually impossible. Thus, it depends too much on the artistry of the individual therapist. This reproach is only partly true. Multimodal behavior therapy endeavors first and foremost to apply empirically validated methods whenever fessible. Beyond the cognitive–behavioral parameters, there is suggestive evidence, rather than hard data, to confirm the clinical impression that covering the BASIC I.D. enhances outcomes and follow-ups. Similarly, although there is considerable clinical evidence that the multimodal approach keeps treatment on target and often brings to light issues that remain hidden from therapists of other orientations, there are no hard data to confirm these impressions.

Aside from outcome measures, there is research bearing out certain multimodal tenets and procedures. For example, multimodal clinicians often use a 35-item Structural Profile Inventory (SPI) that provides a quantitative rating of the extent to which clients favor specific BASIC I.D. areas. Factor analytic studies gave rise to several versions of the SPI until one with good factorial stability was obtained. The instrument measures the extent to which people are action-oriented (behavior), their degree of emotionality (affect), the value they attach to various sensory experiences (sensation), how much time they occupy with fantasy and day dreaming and "thinking in pictures" (imagery), how analytical they tend to be (cognition), how important other people are to them (interpersonal) and the extent to which they are healthy and health-conscious (drugs/biology). The reliability and validity of this instrument has been borne out by research conducted by Steven Herman. One of the most important findings is that when clients and therapists have wide differences on the SPI, therapeutic outcomes tend to be adversely affected.

V. CASE ILLUSTRATION

A case illustration should amplify and clarify all of the foregoing elements and details.

Ken, a 46-year-old accountant employed by a large corporation, suffered from bouts of depression, had problems maintaining an intimate relationship (he was twice divorced), expressed concerns about his relationship with his son and daughter from his first marriage, and was unhappy at work. Previously, he had been in couples therapy, had seen various individual counselors and clinicians from time to time, but felt that he had derived minimal benefits from counseling and psychotherapy.

During the initial interview it was soon apparent that Ken tended to denigrate himself and seemed to have unrealistically high expectations for himself. These issues were broached and Ken agreed to read selected chapters of two books I handed him, one by Albert Ellis and the other coauthored by my son and myself. At the end of the initial interview, as is customary with literate clients who are not excessively depressed or otherwise too disturbed or distracted to focus on filling out questionnaires, Ken was handed the Multimodal Life History Inventory (LHI). This is a 15-page survey that covers the BASIC I.D. He was requested to complete it in his own time, but not to attempt to finish it in one sitting, and asked to bring the completed inventory with him to the next meeting. A depression inventory had also been administered and revealed that Ken's degree of melancholia fell within normal limits.

The therapist usually studies the LHI after session number 2, so by the time the client returns for the third session, the impressions gleaned from the inventory are discussed and treatment priorities are established. However, before perusing the entire document, it is my custom to turn to the bottom of page 4, which inquires about the client's "Expectations Regarding Therapy." Ken had written: "I want my therapist to remember the things I discuss with him. I also appreciate someone who will disclose pertinent things about himself. I am looking for someone to advise me, and point me in the right direction." Contrast this with another client's expectancies. She had written: "A good therapist is an active listener who says little but hears all." It would be naive to assume that clients always know what they want and what is best for them. But without slavishly following their clients' scripts, if therapists had more respect for the notion that their clients often sense how they can best be served, fewer blunders might result.

In Ken's case, the therapeutic trajectory was clearly enhanced by my willingness to self-disclose. (I revealed strategies that I found helpful in my own marriage and with my own children, and I discussed problems that I had encountered in various work situations and tactics that had proved useful for me.) He took very kindly to the fact that I transcended the usual clinical boundaries by meeting him for lunch on a couple of occasions. He also appreciated the fact that I was quite forthright in offering advice ("I don't see a down side to your asking for two things. (1) More challenging work. And (2) a raise.")

Several interconnected problems were brought to light. His behaviors were characterized by too much passivity; affectively, he was apt to depress himself needlessly; at the sensory level, generalized muscular tensions seemed widespread; his mental imagery was replete with pictures of his past failures; his cognitions were fraught with statements of self-denigration, perfectionism, and categorical imperatives; and his interpersonal relationships were characterized by unassertive and avoidant patterns.

Initially standard cognitive–behavior therapy strategies were employed: relaxation training, positive imagery exercises, cognitive restructuring (especially antiperfectionistic teachings), and assertiveness training. Ken made good progress across several dimensions but there seemed to be three sticking points: (1) Tensions between Ken and his woman friend were escalating; (2) he was feeling more resentful at work because his boss was so remote and unsympathetic; (3) his unsatisfactory relationship with his children remained a source of pain.

A Second-Order BASIC I.D. assessment was attempted by asking Ken to picture himself attaining some of his immediate goals—achieving harmony at home with his woman friend, coming to terms with his boss, mending fences with his son and daughter. These situations were addressed one at a time, and Ken was asked to discuss the repercussions in each modality.

It became clear that a few sessions with Ken and his significant other might prove beneficial and he agreed to ask Norma, his lady friend, to accompany him to our next session. Subsequently, during three meetings with Ken and Norma they were each able to express their specific complaints and learned how to derive more satisfaction from their relationship by avoiding traps into which they tended to fall. For example, Norma was inclined to dredge up negative events from the past, Ken was apt to say "No" too often even to simple requests, and they both rarely complimented one another. More intensive role-playing procedures were used to enable Ken to take the risk of approaching his boss and expressing his dissatisfactions. At his own initiative, Ken started actively pursuing a new job search.

With regard to his children, given they both lived too far for them to consider some family therapy sessions, Ken agreed to call them, express his love for them and his desire for a better relationship, and to continue a dialogue via letters and e-mail. These active methods primed Ken to approach all problems now and in the future by deliberately cultivating a forthright, assertive, outgoing, and nonavoidant modus vivendi.

A. Outcome

Multimodal behavior therapists have no ironclad adherence to weekly sessions, especially when clients need time to practice homework assignments. Thus, Ken had 16 sessions over a period of 8 months. His gains were clearly evident. He no longer described himself as depressed, and as the result of his newfound nonavoidant behaviors he reported having greater levels of interpersonal satisfaction and closeness. At a follow-up interview 6 months later he mentioned that he had obtained a new job at a higher salary.

It is noteworthy that although Ken was not a resistant, or especially difficult, combative, or seriously disturbed individual, he could easily have continued to suffer needlessly for the rest of his life. Many strategies and tactics were covered in the 16 sessions (e.g., relaxation training, mental imagery methods, cognitive disputation, and assertiveness training), but significant psychosocial gains accrued only after he started taking interpersonal risks. Because the therapist–client relationship is the soil that enables the techniques to take root, it must be remembered that the therapeutic alliance was deliberately tailor-made to fit Ken's needs and expectancies.

VI. SUMMARY

Multimodal behavior therapy draws on the same principles of experimental and social psychology, as do other cognitive–behavioral therapies. It emphasizes that for therapy to be comprehensive and thorough it must encompass even discrete but interactive modalities—behavior, affect, sensation, imagery, cognition, interpersonal relationships, and drugs/biological considerations. The first letters of the foregoing dimensions yield the convenient acronym BASIC I.D. This results in broad-based assessment and treatment foci.

Whenever feasible, multimodal behavior therapy practitioners use empirically supported treatment methods. The therapeutic relationship is pivotal. Rapport and compatibility between client and therapist is the soil that enables the techniques to take root. It is also considered essential to fit the requisite treatment to the specific client.

Multimodal behavior therapy is technically but not theoretically eclectic. As has been emphasized by Lazarus and Beutler, one need not draw on any theoretical underpinnings that gave rise to a specific technique when borrowing that procedure and applying it in a different context. The multimodal approach makes effective use of methods from diverse sources without relinquishing its social learning and cognitive theoretical underpinnings.

See Also the Following Articles

Biofeedback ■ Integrative Approaches to Psychotherapy ■ Neuropsychological Assessment

Further Reading

Keat, D. B. (1996). Multimodal therapy with children: Anxious Ashley. *Psychotherapy Private Practice, 15,* 63.

Keat, D. B. (1999). Counseling anxious male youths. In A. M. Horne, & M. S. Kilelica (Eds.), *Counseling boys and adolescent males.* Thousand Oaks, CA: Sage.

Lazarus, A. A. (1992). Multimodal therapy: Technical eclecticism with minimal integration. In J. C. Norcross, & M. R. Goldfried (Eds.), *Handbook of psychotherapy integration.* New York: Basic Books.

Lazarus, A. A. (1997). *Brief but comprehensive psychotherapy: The multimodal way.* New York: Springer.

Lazarus, A. A. (2000). Multimodal therapy. In R. J. Corsini, & D. Wedding (Eds.), *Current psychotherapies.* Itasca, IL: Peacock.

Lazarus, A. A., & Beutler, L. E. (1993). On technical eclecticism. *Journal of Counseling & Development, 71,* 381.

Negative Practice

Theodosia R. Paclawskyj
The Johns Hopkins University School of Medicine and The Kennedy Krieger Institute

Johnny L. Matson
Louisiana State University

GLOSSARY

affective variable A feeling or emotional response that follows a behavior or event.

habit Any learned way of living or fixed way of responding.

ideational variable Thought or belief regarding a behavior or event.

negative practice A technique in which a problem behavior is deliberately repeated or practiced by a patient to decrease the response in the long term.

paradoxical intention Therapeutic technique in which a patient suffering from a certain problem is encouraged to focus upon it and try to induce it rather than ignore it or avoid it.

reactive inhibition Principle which states that after any behavior there is an immediate increase in motivation not to perform the behavior.

I. DESCRIPTION OF TREATMENT

Negative practice is a technique in which a problem behavior is deliberately repeated, or practiced, by a patient to decrease the response in the long term. Negative practice has been used as a response reduction procedure primarily for habits, such as tics or nail biting; or in the treatment of specific types of anxiety. To treat nail biting, for example, clinicians prescribe scheduled practice sessions in which patients deliberately bite their nails until they learn to control the habit. Less often, negative practice has been used as a response reduction procedure for the modification of maladaptive behavior in persons with developmental disabilities.

II. THEORETICAL BASES

The origin of negative practice is associated with the work of Knight Dunlap, Ph.D. (1875–1949), Professor of Experimental Psychology at Johns Hopkins University. Dunlap published several critiques of imagery, consciousness, and instinct; however, his interests in neuropsychology and the impact of cognition on learning were closer to what is currently labeled as cognitive-behaviorism.

In 1928, Dunlap published a brief paper in Science in which he hypothesized that errors could best be corrected by repeatedly practicing those errors while acknowledging their incorrectness. He applied this technique to the correction of common typing errors (e.g., "hte" instead of "the") and found that negative practice remediated the error more rapidly than positive practice. Dunlap then wrote a monograph entitled *Habits, Their Making and Unmaking* in 1932 that outlined both his views on the formation of habits and his method to decrease these behaviors. He defined a "habit" as any learned way of living or fixed way of responding. His innovative suggestion for treatment was to repeat deliberately the response to unlearn it, that is, to implement negative practice.

Dunlap discussed several classes of habits, including stuttering (inadequate speech habit) and tics (obsessive motor habits). Although previous methods prescribed simply stopping the habit, for Dunlap this was the end goal, not the means to an end. In Dunlap's conceptualization of negative practice, the patient must understand the inappropriateness of the habit and the benefits of breaking the habit, have the desire to break the habit, and commit to the effort required to break it. In short, both motivation and effort are essential treatment components. Although contemporary psychologists may see this approach as similar to the cognitive-behavioral orientation, at the time Dunlap labeled his methods atheoretical.

In his monograph, Dunlap further explained his methodology using the example of stuttering. He took what a person who stuttered could consistently do (stutter) and used it as the basis of the treatment by which the behavior could be modified. Dunlap felt that if the patient could voluntarily practice stuttering under the conditions of wanting to eliminate the habit, then the habit could be modified. Voluntarily stuttering was the initial part of the process of eliminating the habit. However, Dunlap said that it was the desire to eliminate the habit that was the foundation of the curative process. The patient was not to avoid stuttering but should voluntarily practice stuttering for at least 30 minutes daily. After three or four weeks of practice, most people could then attempt to practice normal speech. If stuttering resumed, negative practice should be reinitiated. Dunlap noted that after three months of treatment, many adolescents responded with no trace of stuttering.

Dunlap wrote that treatment of tics generally paralleled the treatment of stuttering. The treatment of tics may be more rapid, but relapses are more likely. After approximately a dozen deliberate movements, the tic itself may disappear for an hour or two. Sometimes a tic may be completely eliminated, but another may take its place (this should be treated concurrently). Initially, daily practice should be performed with a subsequent schedule to be determined by the psychologist. Dunlap also successfully treated other habits similar to tics, namely, thumbsucking in children and nail biting in college students. Dunlap proposed extending negative practice to a range of personal habits, such as eating noisily or laughing while telling a story. He believed that the key to negative practice was not to yield to the impulse but to initiate the practice voluntarily in the absence of the impulse. Negative practice was the beginning of the learning process of not performing the habit.

Knight Dunlap's use of negative practice was intended to bring an involuntary behavior under voluntary control. In his perspective, this shift occurred due to both affective and ideational variables. When patients practice the behavior, they do so with a different purpose (ideational variable) and experience the behavior with a different feeling (affective variable). Dunlap believed these variables were essential in achieving voluntary control over the behavior. In fact, the subjective state of the patient was seen as more important than the behavior of the clinician.

Negative practice has been compared to other techniques such as paradoxical intention and therapeutic paradox, both of which have their origins in analytic psychotherapy. Although the techniques vary by theoretical orientation, in each case patients are encouraged to continue their problematic behavior on a schedule established by the clinician. A major distinction between negative practice and these methods involves the role of the clinician: for paradoxical intention and therapeutic paradox, the patient–clinician relationship is seen as paramount; in negative practice, patient variables are considered essential to therapeutic success.

Whereas Knight Dunlap considered negative practice devoid of a theoretical basis, in 1959, Aubrey Yates suggested a formulation of negative practice based on Hullian learning principles of reactive inhibition. According to the principle of reactive inhibition, after any response there is an immediate increase in motivation not to perform the response. The repeated rehearsal of the target response would lead to reactive inhibition. The reduction of the aversive state of reactive inhibition achieved by not performing the tic would lead to conditioned inhibition of the tic.

In 1982, Richard Foxx offered a more parsimonious explanation of negative practice. Based on an applied behavior analytic perspective, he suggested that the high response effort of repeating the behavior served as a punisher for the behavior.

III. EMPIRICAL STUDIES

Although Knight Dunlap provided extensive descriptions of his procedure in his 1932 monograph, the first empirical evidence to support the effectiveness of negative practice did not come until 1935. Winthrop Kellogg and colleagues compared the rate of maze learning across three conditions: in the first, participants were given no instructions regarding errors; in the second, participants repeated their errors (negative practice); and in the third, participants retraced a distance along the correct pathway that corresponded to the length of their error (positive practice). The negative practice group made significantly fewer errors than the original group and had a slight advantage over the positive practice group.

Since this time, negative practice has been researched periodically. Although initial studies showed successful results for repetitive behaviors and habits, positive outcomes tended to wane following the introduction of newer treatment approaches. This trend can be seen across research for the following behaviors.

A. Tics

Negative practice has been researched as a treatment for tics, although most studies used only one to two subjects. These studies were at least moderately successful in reducing tics such as eyebrow raising, eye blinking, mouth grimacing, head jerking, and multiple tics.

Frank Nicassio, Robert Liberman, Roger Patterson, and Eleanor Ramirez in 1972 used negative practice to treat successfully a single tic in one participant but had no success with a second participant who displayed multiple tics. In the case of the single tic, it subsided after 33 days of negative practice (approximately 16 hours total) and remained absent at 18-month followup. The second participant had multiple vocal and motor tics; three were targeted for intervention in a multiple baseline design. No reduction was observed in any of the tics, and rates remained at high at three-month followup. The authors suspected that this failure resulted from a lack of understanding of the complete behavioral complex (functions) of the multiple tics.

In 1974, Kenneth Knepler and Susan Sewall demonstrated rapid (80-minute) reduction of an eye-blink tic that maintained over a six-month period when smelling salts were paired with negative practice. The authors hypothesized that the use of smelling salts would accelerate the development of an aversive internal state. Negative practice was done as described by Aubrey Yates in 1958: five one-minute trials of practice interspersed with one-minute rest periods during clinic sessions.

Nathan Azrin, R. Gregory Nunn, and S. E. Frantz in 1980 compared negative practice to a newer procedure known as habit reversal. They found that habit reversal reduced tics by 92% by the fourth week, whereas negative practice only reduced tics by about one-third. Negative practice consisted of 30 seconds of practice every hour. With habit reversal, participants were taught to engage in a motor response incompatible with the tic.

Nathan Azrin and Alan Peterson (1988) reviewed the research to that date that had occurred with negative practice in the treatment of Tourette's Syndrome. Negative practice had a therapeutic effect in 10 out of 18 studies. For five studies with available data to analyze, there was an average of a 58% decrease in tics. Other studies showed an increase or recurrence in tics following treatment, and followup data indicated that the effect may not persist over time.

B. Nail Biting

Negative practice was used as an early treatment for nail biting by M. Smith, who eliminated the habit or markedly reduced it in about half of his sample of college students in 1957. During a two-hour session, the participants simulated nail biting in front of each other while telling themselves how ridiculous they looked. They were supervised by a therapist who explained the rationale, answered questions, and monitored practice. The participants were given instruction to practice nail biting for 30 seconds every hour until nail biting had been eliminated for four consecutive days. At that point, participants were to fade their practice schedule over a two-week period.

In 1976, however, John Vargas and Vincent Adesso found equal effectiveness between negative practice, self-imposed shock, and use of bitter taste. The effects for each of the three treatments were greater than those seen for self-monitoring (e.g., increased attention to the behavior) alone.

Nathan Azrin, R. Gregory Nunn, and S. Frantz in 1980 again compared habit reversal with negative practice in a study of treatments for nail biting. They found that habit reversal reduced nail biting by about 99%, whereas negative practice reduced it by only 60%, although both treatments had components of awareness, motivation to change, and repeated practice of a response. Negative practice within this study consisted of the identical method used by M. Smith in 1957. Azrin and colleagues then continued to pursue research on habit reversal, and subsequent studies of negative practice diminished in the research of treatments for this behavior.

C. Smoking

Negative practice has been used as a form of in vivo aversive conditioning to treat smoking. This procedure was used by J. H. Resnick in 1968 and again by James Delahunt and James Curran in 1976. However, Delahunt and Curran compared four groups: (1) negative practice alone, (2) self-control alone, (3) a combined treatment package, and (4) a control group of nonspecific therapy. They found that each component separately did not differ from the control group, while the combined group had a significant reduction of 70% from baseline rates. The authors hypothesized that this effect was due to a combination of operant and respondent factors that were in effect in the combined treatments group; both factors appeared necessary to reduce smoking according to the body of research on the reduction of this behavior. The specific method of negative practice in Delahunt and Curran's study involved having subjects smoke 1.5 times more than their usual average for one day, a day of abstinence, smoking 2 times their baseline rate for one day, and then quitting.

Although early studies reported the success of negative practice in the modification of smoking behavior, subsequent studies demonstrated that the effect did not last in followup data and that this therapeutic technique led to relapse, as did most treatments for smoking at the time. In 1968, Edward Lichtenstein and Carolyn Keutzer conducted a followup study of 148 participants who were involved in a treatment study that compared breath holding, negative practice, and coverant control (use of high-probability behaviors to reinforce covert thoughts). Although initial treatment gains were seen across all treatment groups at the end of treatment, by a six-month followup, the differences between treated and untreated groups were barely distinguishable. Richard O'Brien and Alyce Dickinson in 1977 compared negative practice, satiation, and control groups following one week of treatment. Initially, each treatment group had a significant decline in daily cigarette consumption. However, this effect was lost at three-month followup. This effect occurred despite manipulation of variables such as cigarette consumption within the negative practice and the baseline frequency of cigarette smoking.

D. Anxiety

In 1976, Richard M. O'Brien demonstrated that negative practice in the form of repeated exaggerations of anxious behaviors could decrease test anxiety and improve course grades in college students. A comparison group of students treated with group desensitization (graduated exposure to test-related stimuli paired with relaxation training) reduced their anxiety but did not improve their grades. The students practiced for 10 minutes each hour on the first day, 10 minutes each 2 hours the next day, and 10 minutes three times per day for the remainder of a week. However, when Richard Levine and Richard O'Brien attempted to replicate these results with a control group and another test group of systematic desensitization in 1980, they saw no significant treatment effects for any condition. They hypothesized that since this group of participants had lower scores on a test anxiety measure, the negative practice schedule was not intense enough to produce the desired treatment effect.

Richard Wolff in 1977 employed negative practice to treat the compulsive checking rituals of a woman who feared the possibility of intruders in her home after enduring a rape attempt. The participant was a 20-year-old woman who had a 13-step checking ritual that she performed following each return to her apartment. The woman was instructed to repeat the ritual five times contingent on each incident of checking for two weeks. The ritual was eliminated and remained absent at 6- and 12-month followup.

E. Bruxism and Oral Habits

The use of negative practice to treat bruxism (teeth grinding) was first reported by William Ayer, who did his research in 1969, 1973, and 1976. In the 1976 study, he reported successfully treating a group of adults with bruxism by having them schedule negative practice sessions six times a day for a total of 30 to 45 minutes of practice during a two-week period. All participants reported a decrease in bruxism, and 75% remained free of the behavior at one-year followup.

Although Ayer reported successful treatment in the above studies, these data were limited to patient or spousal report of occurrence. In 1988 Ross Vasa and Holly Wortman conducted a single-case study with a 22-year-old woman in which they restricted the massed practice time intervals to the period before bed time. Practice sessions were faded to alternating nights once a treatment effect was observed. A 90% reduction was observed in 10 weeks' time.

Nathan Azrin, R. Gregory Nunn, and S. E. Frantz-Renshaw extended their previous work with negative practice and habit reversal to oral habits such as biting, chewing, licking, or pushing of cheeks, lips, teeth, or palate in 1982. Again, a single-session treatment with followup across 22 months resulted in significantly greater reduction in the group treated by habit reversal (99%) as compared to that treated by negative practice (65%). The treatment method was identical to that used in their earlier studies treating tics. That is, a two-hour practice period was followed by 30 seconds of practice every hour until the behavior was eliminated. As previously mentioned, Azrin and colleagues proceeded to investigate habit reveral further and discontinued their work in nagative practice.

F. Applications for Individuals with Mental Retardation

In all reported applications, negative practice has been used as a contingent procedure for persons with mental retardation. That is, following an occurrence of an inappropriate behavior, the procedure is implemented with the anticipation that it will serve as a punisher and thereby decrease the chance of recurrence. For example, following an instance of clothes ripping, an individual may be guided to repeatedly tear a rag for a specified period of time. When used in this context, negative practice typically is considered a moderately aversive procedure.

Richard Foxx described the use of negative practice with persons with mental retardation and autism. He cautioned that the applicability of this procedure with this population was limited for several reason. First, negative practice as described in the general research literature requires a certain degree of motivation by the patient to eliminate a problem behavior, something that may not be present to the same level in persons with mental retardation. As a result, the use of negative practice would require physical guidance by a caregiver, which may lead to the patient becoming combative. Next, the treatment acceptability of this procedure may be low among caregivers. Both research and clinical observations have long held that if staff do not find a treatment acceptable, the will be less likely to implement it resulting in less behavior change in the client. Finally, this procedure is limited to a subgroup of the wide range of problem behaviors that are typically exhibited by the this population. It would not be appropriate, for example, to implement negative practice with aggressive behavior, self-injury, or destructive behavior that significantly disrupts a person's environment. The majority of these studies have shown effectiveness, especially when the problem behavior appeared not to be maintained by environmental consequences.

Lombana Durana and Anthony Cuvo in 1980 used negative practice in conjunction with differential reinforcement of other behavior (DRO) and restitution to eliminate public disrobing in a woman with profound mental retardation. This treatment proved effective even though DRO plus restitution plus positive practice (repeatedly putting on clothes) failed to significantly reduce the behavior.

Pieter Duker and Monique Nielen in 1993 decided to use a response-contingent negative practice procedure to reduce the pica (ingestion of inedible items) of a 33-year-old woman with mental retardation. Pica is a behavior that is often resistant to intervention and is therefore rarely researched. Negative practice in this case consisted of a caregiver approaching the participant when she engaged in pica attempts and pressing the object she was attempting to chew to her lips for a two-minute period. Pica was significantly reduced, and the authors concluded that the contingent negative practice served as a punisher for pica behavior. The authors hypothesized that the continuous repetition of the behavior may have become aversive to the participant.

G. Unique Applications

Several isolated studies exist that describe the application of negative practice to unique topographies of behaviors. For example, in 1974, Howard Wooden described the case of a 26-year-old married man who reportedly displayed nocturnal headbanging for 25 years. After four nights of negative practice (carried out before bed until the patient subjectively experienced physical fatigue), the behavior dissipated and recurred only twice in six months on followup data.

The effectiveness of negative practice for improving spelling ability has been researched with mixed results. Constance Meyn and others in 1963 compared negative practice and positive practice as correction techniques when fourth grade students misspelled words in a research study. There was no difference in outcome between positive and negative practice techniques. Other studies reported both increased errors and improvement in correct spelling with negative practice.

Negative practice has been used in conjunction with other elements of a treatment package treatment of fire-setting. Typically, the practice component would involve having the child set a fire (or as many fires as possible within a time period) while supervised by an adult who verbally reviewed fire safety procedures. The child would set the fire in a designated area and then be responsible for cleanup. The outcome of this study is difficult to discern because treatment was evaluated as a package and not by the individual components.

In summary, negative practice initially seemed promising as a treatment for many repetitive behaviors. As research progressed, however, most findings tended to show a lack of sustained effect in followup data or more beneficial effects from newer treatment approaches.

IV. SUMMARY

Negative practice is a therapeutic technique in which the patient deliberately repeats a problem behavior until the behavior is reduced or eliminated. Originally, it was hypothesized that negative practice functioned through the principle of reciprocal inhibition, a concept in Hullian learning theory. Due to a lack of supporting data, more recent hypotheses suggest that guided repetition of a behavior may lead to fatigue or another aversive state, thereby defining the technique as a punisher. Negative practice has been used to treat a limited number of symptoms with some success, although many of these symptoms (e.g., tics, smoking, anxiety) can be successfully treated with newer and more comprehensive approaches. In some cases, it can be successfully applied to certain problem behaviors exhibited by persons with mental retardation.

See Also the Following Articles

Avoidance Training ■ Habit Reversal ■ Negative Punishment ■ Negative Reinforcement

Further Reading

Azrin, N. H, & Peterson, A. L. (1988). Behavior therapy for Tourette's Syndrome and tic disorders. In D. J. Cohen, R. D. Bruun, & J. F. Leckman (Eds.), *Tourette's Syndrome and tic disorders: Clinical understanding and treatment.* New York: John Wiley & Sons.

Dunlap, K. (1932). *Habits, their making and unmaking.* New York: Liveright.

Foxx, R. M. (1982). *Decreasing behaviors of persons with severe retardation and autism.* Champaign, IL: Research Press.

Lehner, G. (1954). Negative practice as a psychotherapeutic technique. *Journal of General Psychology, 51,* 69–82.

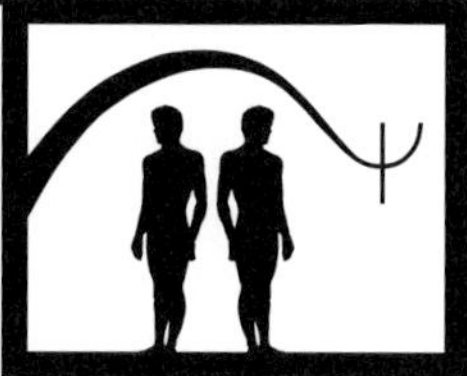

Negative Punishment

Alan Poling, John Austin, Susan Snycerski, and Sean Laraway
Western Michigan University

GLOSSARY

aversive A nontechnical term often used to refer to punishment and negative reinforcement procedures.

behavior Any action of a living creature. Behavior can be overt or covert.

consequence An event that follows and is produced by a behavior.

environment The natural world in its entirety, including all events that occur inside and outside living creatures.

functional assessment Procedures that are used to identify the variables responsible for a problem behavior.

negative punishers Punishers that involve removing or preventing the delivery of a stimulus.

negative punishment A procedure (or process) in which the removal or prevention of the delivery of a stimulus as a consequence of behavior weakens (e.g., reduces the likelihood of) that behavior in the future.

operant conditioning A form of learning in which behavior is controlled primarily by its consequences.

positive punishers Punishers that involve adding something to an individual's environment.

positive punishment A procedure (or process) in which the presentation of a stimulus after a behavior weakens that behavior in the future.

punishers Consequences that weaken behavior.

response cost A negative punishment procedure that involves removing something of value from an individual after an inappropriate behavior occurs.

rules Overt or covert statements of relations among stimuli and responses. Rules describing the consequences of behavior can evoke behavior similar to that associated with direct exposure to those consequences.

stimulus A physical event.

time out A negative punishment procedure that involves the temporary removal of an individual from an environment in which positive reinforcers are available.

token economy A therapeutic system based on providing appropriate consequences for important behaviors.

Most human behaviors considered by psychologists as important are operant behaviors. That is, these behaviors operate on the environment to produce particular changes, called consequences. Consequences are reinforcers if they strengthen the behavior that produced them and punishers if they weaken it. Punishment occurs when a behavior is weakened by its consequences. In 1953, B.F. Skinner noted that punishment was the most common form of behavior control. He strongly opposed its use in clinical applications and in society in general, and many other prominent people have done likewise. Nonetheless, punishment continues to be ubiquitous in everyday life. It is also used systematically to improve behavior in therapeutic applications, although ethical, practical, and legal considerations limit where, how, and with whom punishment can be utilized.

I. DESCRIPTION OF TREATMENT

Psychologists commonly distinguish between negative and positive punishment. Positive punishment occurs when the presentation of a stimulus, termed a positive punisher, weakens the behavior that caused this consequence to occur. In contrast, negative punishment occurs when the removal or prevention of delivery of a stimulus, termed a negative punisher, weakens the behavior that produced this consequence. As an everyday example of negative punishment, envision two friends who are sitting together having a friendly conversation when one makes a highly critical comment about a presidential candidate. The other person likes the candidate and is angered by the comment and abruptly gets up and walks away upon hearing it. If this results in fewer negative comments about the politician in the future, then negative punishment has occurred. In this hypothetical example, and in most cases, the response-weakening effect of punishment involves a decrease in the frequency of responding, although other changes in behavior (e.g., increased latency to respond or decreased intensity of responding) may be indicative of a punishment effect.

For negative punishment to be effective, the stimulus that is removed or avoided must have positive hedonic value. In general, such stimuli serve as positive reinforcers, which are stimuli that strengthen behaviors that produce them. Many writers describe negative punishment as a procedure that weakens a particular kind of behavior because that behavior removes a currently available positive reinforcer or prevents the delivery of an otherwise forthcoming positive reinforcer. Although this conception of negative reinforcement makes intuitive sense, stimuli that serve as negative punishers for a particular individual's behavior may never have served as positive reinforcers for that individual's behavior. For instance, a child who has been given CDs by family members may value them, and taking them away following an undesired behavior, perhaps cursing, might function as negative punishment. Thus, the CDs are negative punishers. But they were given to the child independent of her behavior, and no behavior was strengthened by their delivery. Thus, they have not functioned as positive reinforcers for any behavior of the individual in question. Whether they have the capacity to serve this function is not a fixed characteristic of the CDs but depends on the context in which their presentation follows behavior.

Basic and applied studies demonstrate conclusively that the behavioral function of a given stimulus is not fixed but rather depends on historical and current circumstances. Although stimuli that serve as negative punishers often also serve as positive reinforcers, this is not always, nor necessarily, the case. Moreover, thinking of the stimuli that are removed or avoided as positive reinforcers may cause confusion about the behavioral effects of negative punishment. Reinforcement always strengthens behavior, and punishment always weakens it; this principle holds regardless of whether either procedure is "positive" or "negative." In addition, these terms refer only to whether the procedure involves adding something to an individual's environment or taking something away. They do not refer to the kinds of behavior that are affected or to the "goodness" of the consequences that are arranged.

Although the behavioral functions of stimuli are not fixed, they are not capricious, and it is usually possible for psychologists and others to predict with some accuracy whether an event will function as a negative punisher in a given context. Personal experience, scientific reports, and theoretical deductions are all useful in predicting that a specific event will punish behavior, although the ultimate test is to arrange the event as a consequence for the behavior that is to be reduced. Operations that fail to weaken behavior do not constitute punishment, even if the persons who designed and implemented them intended them to reduce responding.

When used therapeutically, negative punishment is used to weaken inappropriate target behaviors. The two most commonly used procedures that involve negative punishment are time out (also spelled timeout or time-out) and response cost. As discussed later, these procedures have been effective in reducing a variety of target behaviors in various settings with diverse client populations.

Time out generally involves temporarily removing an individual from an environment in which positive reinforcers are available whenever the behavior that is to be reduced occurs. That is, when the client performs the undesired behavior, she or he loses the opportunity to earn positive reinforcers. The two broad classes of time out are exclusionary and nonexclusionary. In exclusionary time out, the client is moved from a setting that provides many positive reinforcers to a setting that provides few, if any, positive reinforcers. For example, a child who misbehaves in a classroom may be moved from the classroom to an empty room for a two-minute period as a form of exclusionary time out. If successful, this procedure would reduce the subsequent rate of occurrence of the undesired behavior.

Time out has been used most extensively in educational settings. In such settings (and some others as well), exclusionary time out commonly is implemented in one of three ways. In one, the client is required to spend the duration of the time out in a secluded time-out room whenever the behavior targeted for reduction (e.g., swearing) occurs. Time-out rooms should be well ventilated, well lit, and reasonably comfortable but should not contain obvious sources of positive reinforcement (e.g., toys, chairs that rock). If necessary, such rooms should be padded to protect clients from injuring themselves. Provision should be made for observing clients during time outs (e.g., through one-way mirrors) and intervening rapidly to terminate dangerous activities. Clients should not spend more than a few minutes in the time-out room. Long periods of time out do not necessarily reduce behavior more effectively than do short periods, and the former may be abusive to the client.

A second exclusionary time-out method uses a partitioning wall that separates the time-out area from the normal setting (e.g., a classroom). This method is similar to the use of a time-out room in that it involves a move from a more to a less reinforcing environment, but the client is moved to a place behind the partition instead of being moved to a separate room. One problem associated with the partition method is that disruptive clients can continue to disrupt normal activities from behind the partition. Furthermore, other individuals can still reinforce problem behaviors by laughing, making comments, or otherwise responding to the misbehavior.

A third, and perhaps the most popular, method of arranging exclusionary time out, involves taking the client to the hallway outside of the room where the problem behavior occurred. Although this method may be the only practical option for some situations, hallway time outs should generally be avoided because hallways typically contain many sources of positive reinforcement, such as other students, drinking fountains, windows into other rooms, bulletin boards, and posters.

To ensure the safety of students and to prevent them from running away, arrangements must be made for monitoring students placed behind partitions or in hallways during time out. These forms of time out, like all others, should be as brief as possible.

Exclusionary time out is likely to be effective in reducing behavior if four criteria are met. First, the time out must involve a move from an environment that provides a relatively high frequency of positive reinforcers to an environment that provides a relatively low frequency of positive reinforcers. If the frequency and quality of reinforcers in the time-out environment are equal to or greater than those in the regular environment, then time-outs will not punish, and may even reinforce, the undesired behavior.

Second, time outs must occur immediately after the problem behavior occurs. Delays in implementing time outs are apt to reduce their effectiveness substantially. Third, time outs should be ended only when the individual is engaging in appropriate behaviors. If time outs end while the individual is behaving unacceptably, or immediately thereafter, termination of the time out and return to the normal environment could reinforce the undesired behavior.

Finally, time-out procedures should be clearly explained to the client. This allows for rules about the consequences of behavior, as well as direct exposure to those consequences, to affect the target response. Rules specify relations among stimuli and responses and can engender behaviors similar to those produced by actual exposure to those relations. Helping clients to formulate and follow appropriate rules is apt to increase the effectiveness of any intervention and should be part of almost all treatments. This includes response-cost procedures.

Sometimes it is not possible or desirable to remove a misbehaving client from the situation in which the misbehavior occurs. In such cases, nonexclusionary time out is often used. In nonexclusionary time out, the individual remains in the setting where the problem behavior occurred but loses the opportunity to earn positive reinforcers. For example, a teacher may briefly ignore a student who behaves inappropriately. Ignoring, in this case, prevents the student from earning social reinforcers from the teacher.

Psychologists have developed four general methods of nonexclusionary time out: time-out ribbon, planned ignoring, contingent observation, and prevention of preferred activities. The time-out ribbon provides an excellent example of nonexclusionary time out. This method requires that all clients receive a ribbon when they enter the treatment setting. Possession of the ribbon indicates that the individual is allowed to participate in the reinforcement system (usually a token economy, which will be described later). Whenever a client performs a behavior targeted for reduction, the ribbon is taken from the client, indicating that the client can no longer obtain reinforcers from staff for some predetermined time. Unfortunately, this intervention is unsuited for reducing behaviors not maintained by staff-delivered reinforcers, or behaviors (e.g., self-injurious responding) maintained by staff attention that cannot be withheld for ethical or practical reasons.

As the name implies, planned ignoring involves having caregivers ignore predetermined problem behaviors. For example, in a therapy group designed to reduce interpersonal aggressive behaviors, the therapist (and others) may briefly ignore a client every time the client makes an aggressive remark (e.g., "I'm gonna kill you"). Planned ignoring tends to be most effective when the individual's social environment is highly reinforcing and when the therapist consistently implements the intervention. One problem with this intervention is that some behaviors are difficult or dangerous to ignore. Using the therapy group example, if a client actually engaged in an aggressive act against another person, it would be unethical simply to ignore this behavior. Another problem with planned ignoring is that this intervention is effective only if the client's behavior is maintained by social reinforcers that caregivers control.

Contingent observation is usually implemented in a group setting, such as a classroom. In contingent observation, a misbehaving client is asked to sit outside of a group of individuals and observe the group for a brief period of time (e.g., two minutes). During this time, the client cannot participate in group activities and, hence, cannot receive social reinforcers. In addition, the client observes others behaving appropriately and receiving reinforcers. Thus, this intervention uses negative punishment and modeling to achieve its effects. As with other time-out procedures, contingent observation requires that reinforcers are not available for the misbehaving client during observation periods and that the intervention be applied consistently and immediately after the problem behavior occurs.

A final nonexclusionary time-out procedure consists of preventing the client from engaging in a preferred activity, such as playing cards, whenever the target behavior occurs. For example, one study demonstrated that children's thumbsucking could be reduced by turning off the television the children were watching immediately following each incident of thumbsucking. In some cases, it may be appropriate and possible to reduce problem behaviors without clients' knowledge using this time-out technique. This may be important in situations where other behavior-weakening techniques have produced disruptive or aggressive behavior in clients.

There are obvious benefits and drawbacks to both exclusionary and nonexclusionary time out. Nonexclusionary time out is thought to be more beneficial to the client because he or she is allowed to remain in the educational (or therapeutic) environment. In addition, if the client does not have to be removed from the environment, there is less chance that he or she will become aggressive or hostile. As previously mentioned, however, nonexclusionary time out allows highly disruptive individuals to remain in the setting, providing them with the opportunity to disrupt further the ongoing activities. Exclusionary time out, on the other hand, has the virtue of removing disruptive individuals from the setting, allowing other clients to benefit from ongoing activities. Unfortunately, exclusionary time out removes from the instructional situation the very individuals who may need instruction the most. There is no obvious solution to these problems, and therapists must find a way to weaken inappropriate behavior while ensuring that clients receive the educational opportunities they require.

Whereas time out involves removing the opportunity for an individual to gain access to positive reinforcers, response cost involves taking valued stimuli away from an individual when misbehavior occurs. That is, response-cost interventions make problem behaviors "costly" in that the individual who emits these behaviors loses something of value. Put simply, the client has to pay for engaging in inappropriate behavior. Examples of response-cost procedures often appear in our daily lives in the form of fines and points lost in classroom settings. Implementing a response-cost procedure in no way guarantees that negative punishment will occur. In order for response cost to weaken behavior, the individual must lose something of greater value than whatever the individual gains by misbehaving.

Response-cost procedures are commonly implemented in four ways. First, response cost can be combined in a package intervention with procedures, such as differential-reinforcement-of-incompatible-behavior (DRI) schedules, that increase appropriate behaviors. Here, reinforcers earned under the DRI schedule for appropriate behavior would be lost if the undesired behavior occurred.

Second, response cost involving fines of specific amounts through loss of points, money, tokens, or quantifiable amounts of other valued stimuli already in the individual's possession can be used alone. Third, "bonus" or "free" reinforcers can be delivered at the start of the response-cost period and then removed if inappropriate behaviors occur. Finally, response cost can be implemented for a group of clients such that inappropriate behavior on the part of one group member will result in the loss of valued items for the entire group. In this case, the response-cost procedure results in group members exerting "peer pressure" on other members to remain well behaved. Although such peer pressure can maintain appropriate behavior, it may be too stressful for some clients. Thus, group procedures should be monitored carefully.

Psychologists often implement time out and response-cost procedures in settings where token economies operate. Token economies are behavior management systems that provide tokens, such as poker chips or points, for appropriate behaviors. The tokens can then be traded for a variety of backup reinforcers, such as tangible items like candy, soda, and toys, or for privileges like going to the park or checking out a book at the library. As a result of being exchanged for a variety of backup reinforcers, the tokens eventually come to function as generalized conditioned reinforcers and effectively maintain appropriate behaviors. In this way, tokens allow the psychologist to deliver consequences immediately following the performance of target behaviors, thereby maximizing the likelihood of the desired behavioral effect.

In the context of a token economy, time out involves the restriction of a client's ability to participate in the token system for a short period of time (e.g., two minutes) whenever the individual engages in an inappropriate behavior. Response cost in a token economy is relatively straightforward and involves the removal of a specified number of tokens whenever an individual engages in inappropriate behavior.

The implementation of a token economy requires: (a) specification of observable, easily measured behaviors to be reinforced or punished; (b) delivery or removal of tokens when the behaviors specified in (a) occur; (c) identification of effective backup reinforcers for which tokens can be exchanged; and (d) specification of rules by which the economy runs, including rules concerning exchange rates, magnitude of reinforcers and punishers, schedule of consequence delivery, and frequency of exchanges. In theory, token economies can be of any size if sufficient resources to manage the system are available.

Token economies must be flexible enough to support each client's personalized treatment goals and to provide consequences that may differ widely across individuals. As systems become more individualized, however, they become more complex, which can result in staff performance problems. No token system will function perfectly all of the time, so they should include mechanisms that allow treatment providers to monitor how well the system is performing and to correct any problems that arise. One way to increase the possibility that the token system will function smoothly is to obtain client's cooperation and input when designing the system. Including clients in the system development process increases their involvement in the system and gives them a greater degree of control over their lives.

Regardless of whether or not response cost is implemented as part of a token economy, the procedure is not likely to be successful unless the undesired behavior leads rapidly and consistently to the loss of enough of a valued item to be of significance to the client. A potential problem with the procedure is that, if response cost is implemented repeatedly, there may be no more of the specified valued item to take away. This difficulty sometimes can be averted by arranging a number of "different costs" for a target behavior. For example, tokens might be taken away until none are left; then loss of a specified series of privileges could occur.

What might be termed intermittent response cost is regularly used in educational settings. Here, something of value is lost after the target behavior occurs a specified number of times. For example, a teacher might make a check mark on the board each time a student talks out in class. When the third check mark appears, the child loses access to the playground during the next recess period. Although this procedure is often effective, some students might "figure out the system" and misbehave twice before behaving appropriately. This outcome might or might not be acceptable to the teacher, depending on the nature of the undesired behavior.

The procedure described in the preceding example was presented as a response-cost manipulation; this is legitimate because the student lost something of value—access to recess—because of misbehaving. But the procedure could also be construed as time out because the child lost access to reinforcers associated with the playground dependent on misbehaving. Although it is of heuristic value to distinguish between time out and response cost, the distinction often blurs in everyday applications.

II. THEORETICAL BASES

Punishment has generated a great deal of theoretical interest, although positive and negative punishments characteristically are not distinguished in these discussions. From the earliest days of psychology as a formal discipline, it has been widely acknowledged that consequences can weaken as well as strengthen behavior. For instance, Edward Thorndike pointed this out early in the 1900s in his famous Law of Effect. The version that appeared in his 1905 book, *The Elements of Psychology*, reads:

> Any act which in a given situation produces satisfaction becomes associated with that situation, so that when the situation recurs the act is more likely than before to recur also [this is reinforcement]. Conversely, any act which in a given situation produces discomfort becomes disassociated from the situation, so that when the situation recurs the act is less likely than before to recur [this is punishment].

Over time, however, Thorndike became convinced that punishment did not produce enduring effects. This view was based on limited studies of positive punishment that he conducted. The preeminent behavioral psychologist B. F. Skinner supported this view in his 1953 book, *Science and Human Behavior*, and elsewhere. Skinner contended that not only does punishment typically fail to produce lasting response suppression, but it also characteristically engenders negative reactions, including aggression, escape, and attempts at countercontrol. Consequently, punishment (and negative reinforcement, claimed to have similar adverse effects) should be avoided in clinical applications and in society at large. Skinner described a society without aversive control in his utopian novel, *Walden Two*, published in 1948.

Despite arguing forcefully against the use of punishment, Skinner recognized that operant behavior was sensitive to both negative and positive punishment. In fact, throughout Skinner's long life, both were included as principles of behavior in his analysis of operant conditioning. Skinner did not argue that behavior could not be reduced by negative punishment. Rather, he argued on practical and ethical grounds that behavior should not be reduced in this way because there are better alternatives (e.g., positive reinforcement).

Arguments against the use of punishment similar to those first advanced by Skinner half a century ago have been repeated and extended in the ensuing years. Over this same period, laboratory studies with nonhumans and humans and clinical studies with various client populations have provided clear evidence that both negative and positive punishment can produce strong and enduring reductions in operant behavior. Insofar as theory in psychology should be based on data, there is substantial theoretical support for the effectiveness of procedures based on negative punishment.

Whether such procedures are appropriate for therapeutic use in general, or in specific cases, is another issue altogether. Some theoreticians argue for and against therapeutic techniques based on the principles of behavior that underlie their effects. They claim, for instance, that positive reinforcement is good and negative punishment (along with positive punishment and negative reinforcement) is bad. But in the everyday world of the clinic and classroom, and in courts of law, the acceptability of procedures is usually based on their details (who does what to whom, for what reason, and with what real or anticipated result?), not on their mechanism of action. In the following section, we discuss general restrictions on the use of negative punishment and discuss appropriate safeguards for the use of procedures that involve negative punishment. Although such procedures should always be used with care, mild and generally accepted interventions (e.g., teachers' use of nonexclusionary time out for classroom management) typically are not subjected to the same scrutiny as more unusual and potentially intrusive interventions (e.g., time out in a secluded room to reduce severe self-injury in a person with severe mental retardation).

III. APPLICATIONS AND EXCLUSIONS

Even though negative and positive punishment can be distinguished procedurally and arguments against punishment have focused on the latter, procedures involving both forms of punishment (and negative reinforcement) are commonly considered as "aversive" and relatively restrictive (harmful) interventions. Therefore, the use of negative punishment is limited by both ethical and legal considerations, although the extent of these restrictions depends on the specific procedure, client, problem behavior, and setting under consideration. Like all "aversive" interventions, procedures involving negative punishment may generate negative affective behavior (e.g., crying), aggression, and escape responding. Moreover, negative punishment procedures are easily misused by ill-informed or ill-intentioned caregivers, as when clients are placed in a time-out room for long periods for staff convenience.

In view of the foregoing considerations, negative punishment should not be used until less restrictive interventions have proven ineffective. As with positive punishment, a clear decision-making process regarding the use of negative punishment should be in place. Specific guidelines must be established regarding the exact nature of the proposed punishment procedure, including who is to implement it and the specific standards of accountability. Unambiguous rules regarding the behavioral data that will support continuation, modification, and termination of punishment must be established and followed by a vigilant, expert, and caring treatment team before punishment is implemented. Input from clients, client's advocates, behavior-change experts, and the individuals responsible for implementing procedures is invaluable in formulating guidelines for the use of negative punishment in schools and other settings.

Before a negative punishment procedure is implemented, the treatment team, as Ray Miltenberger suggests in his excellent 1997 text *Behavior Modification*, should

1. Conduct a functional analysis to ascertain the consequences and other variables that are maintaining the problem behavior. This information is invaluable for planning effective interventions.
2. Determine whether the proposed intervention (e.g., time out or response cost) is practical in the present situation.
3. Determine whether the proposed intervention is safe.
4. Determine whether the client can readily escape from or avoid the proposed intervention.
5. Determine whether the intervention can be implemented consistently.
6. Determine whether all parties with a legitimate interest in the intervention find it acceptable.

Adhering to these guidelines often requires substantial time and effort. But doing so is essential to ensuring the well-being of clients.

In general, with the proviso that clients with special needs require special protections, issues of client diversity do not strongly enter into whether or not procedures based on negative punishment are appropriate. Interestingly, such procedures are frequently used with children and with adults with mental illness or mental retardation, and these are the very people most in need of special protections.

IV. EMPIRICAL STUDIES

The clinical literature relevant to negative punishment is sizable; numerous studies have shown that time out and response cost, if properly arranged, can effectively reduce a wide range of target behaviors in numerous settings with a variety of client populations. Time out is the negative punishment procedure most often examined in published studies, and it has a long history of success in the treatment literature. Published studies have demonstrated time out to be effective in reducing cursing, off-task behaviors, stereotypic behaviors, thumbsucking, pica, self-injury, disruptive meal-time behaviors, tantrums, self-stimulation, perseverative speech, noncompliant behaviors, physical aggression, verbal abuse, hoarding, and rule violations. Settings in which time-out procedures have been successfully implemented include psychiatric hospitals, elementary and high schools, juvenile facilities, and day-treatment schools. Among the clients with whom time-out procedures have been effective are children with autism, people with mental retardation and other developmental disabilities, people with mental illness, and children, adolescents, and adults without disabilites.

Response-cost interventions have been shown to be effective in decreasing smoking, cocaine use, opiate use, rule violation, off-task behavior, hyperactivity, aggressiveness, psychotic speech, stuttering, overeating, tardiness, perseverative speech, anxious and depressive behavior, and self-injurious behavior. Furthermore, response-cost interventions have been effective in improving academic performance and vocational training activities.

The effectiveness of response-cost procedures has been demonstrated in a wide range of settings. The literature shows these procedures to be effective in settings such as preschools, middle schools, high schools, and vocational education schools, as well as in prisons, psychiatric hospitals, day-treatment facilities, and home settings. This intervention has been used successfully with many client populations, including children with autism, people with mental retardation and other developmental disabilities, people with mental illness, prison inmates, predelinquent boys, and people without diagnostic labels. Furthermore, therapists often use behavioral contracts with response-cost components to benefit married couples, families, teachers, and individual clients. Behavioral contracts are agreements among committed parties regarding the consequences of specified behaviors.

V. CASE ILLUSTRATION

The director of a residential treatment facility wished to reduce the relative frequency of episodes of nonsensical speech in Ronald, a 15-year-old male diagnosed with schizophrenia. Ronald had engaged in nonsensical speech frequently over the past two years, and his statements usually centered around conversations with Ashtar, described by Ronald as the captain of an omnipotent space fleet. Because of his frequent episodes of nonsensical speech, other residents avoided Ronald. Indeed, nonsensical speech prevented Ronald from engaging in conversations with most people. In addition, the director realized that Ronald's bizarre speech interfered with the staff's ability to gather useful information about Ronald's needs. For example, when Ronald became ill, a reasonable description of symptoms might well facilitate his treatment, whereas statements concerning spacecraft and the beings who pilot them would be of no benefit whatsoever.

The director observed Ronald for five minutes at 30-minute intervals over a five-day period. During these baseline observations, the director recorded the percentage of intervals in which nonsensical speech occurred. In the process of collecting baseline observations, the director noticed that a few of the staff members spent time talking with Ronald about his conversations with Ashtar. From this, the director hypothesized that social reinforcers might help maintain Ronald's nonsensical speech.

The data indicated that Ronald engaged in nonsensical speech in 91% of the intervals. After collecting these data, the director met with Ronald's treatment team to discuss the results of the baseline observation. It was decided that a treatment package in which sensible speech was strengthened through positive reinforcement and nonsensical speech was weakened through a negative punishment component would be implemented. The positive reinforcement component consisted of a DRI schedule. The incompatible behavior that was reinforced was sensible speech (i.e., speech that did not contain references to Ashtar or the space fleet). Specifically, if Ronald spoke sensibly when a staff member came to observe him, then the staff member spent two minutes in conversation with Ronald and provided social reinforcers, such as smiles, eye contact, and questions about Ronald's interests. The negative punishment component consisted of a planned ignoring procedure in which the staff member turned and walked away when Ronald made a nonsensical remark.

After 10 weeks of treatment, the percentage of intervals in which Ronald made a nonsensical remark decreased from the baseline level of 91% to less than 25%. Unfortunately, in the eleventh week of treatment, volunteers from the local university visited the facility and spent much time speaking with the residents. After the volunteers' visit, the relative frequency of Ronald's nonsensical speech increased to nearly 50% and remained at that level for three weeks but declined to around 20% after another month.

At this point, a decision was made to add token reinforcers to Ronald's treatment package. These tokens (poker chips) were delivered when Ronald spoke sensibly. When he spoke nonsensically, one token was taken away. Social reinforcers continued to be provided when Ronald spoke meaningfully, and staff interacted only minimally when taking the tokens, then walked away. This altered intervention reduced intervals with nonsensical speech to approximately 5%. At that point, the frequency of reinforcement was gradually reduced, although the response-cost component stayed in effect. Ronald continued to talk appropriately most of the time, and there was general agreement that the problem was solved.

VI. SUMMARY

Negative punishment refers to a procedure (or process) in which the removal or avoidance of a stimulus as a consequence of behavior weakens such behavior. Response cost and time out are two common clinical interventions based on negative punishment. Published studies have shown these interventions to be effective in reducing a wide variety of inappropriate behaviors in several client populations in a variety of settings. Nonetheless, procedures based on negative punishment are widely construed as aversive and restrictive, and both ethical and legal considerations limit their range of utility.

See Also the Following Articles

Aversion Relief ■ Conditioned Reinforcement ■ Functional Analysis of Behavior ■ Negative Practice ■ Negative Reinforcement ■ Positive Punishment ■ Positive Reinforcement ■ Self-Punishment ■ Time-Out ■ Token Economy

Further Reading

Alberto, P. A., & Troutman, A. C. (1990). *Applied behavior analysis for teachers.* New York: Macmillan.

Coóper, J. O., Heron, T. E., & Heward, W. L. (1987). *Applied behavior analysis.* Columbus, OH: Merrill.

Kazdin, A. E. (1972). Response cost: The removal of conditioned reinforcers for therapeutic change. *Behavior Therapy, 5,* 533–546.

Klein, S. B. (1991). *Learning: Principles and applications,* 2nd ed. New York: McGraw-Hill.

Mazur, J. E. (1998). *Learning and behavior,* 4th ed. Upper Saddle River, NJ: Prentice Hall.

Miltenberger, R. (1997). *Behavior modification: Principles and procedures.* Pacific Grove, CA: Brooks/Cole.

Sidman, M. (1989). *Coercion and its fallout.* Boston, MA: Authors cooperative.

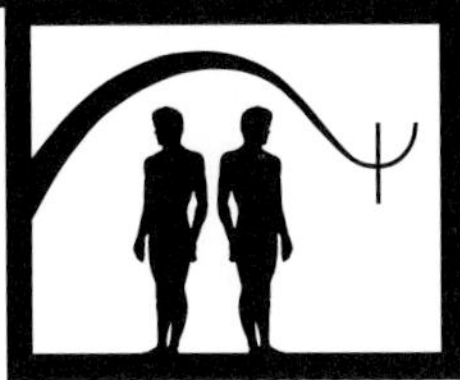

Negative Reinforcement

Alan Poling, Linda A. LeBlanc, and Lynne E. Turner
Western Michigan University

GLOSSARY

aversive A nontechnical term often used to refer to punishment and negative reinforcement procedures.

avoidance conditioning A procedure in which behavior postpones or prevents the delivery of an otherwise forthcoming negative reinforcer and is therefore strengthened.

behavior Any action of a living creature. Behavior can be overt or covert.

conditioned negative reinforcer An event that acquires its capacity to serve as a reinforcer through learning.

consequence An event that follows and is produced by a behavior.

environment The natural world in its entirety, including all events that occur inside and outside living creatures.

establishing operation An event that alters the reinforcing or punishing value of a consequence.

escape conditioning A procedure in which behavior terminates or reduces the intensity of an ongoing stimulus and is therefore strengthened.

extinction A procedure (or process) that reduces behavior by failing to reinforce a previously reinforced response.

functional assessment Procedures that are used to identify the variables that maintain a problem behavior.

negative reinforcement A procedure (or process) in which the removal or postponement of a stimulus after a behavior strengthens (e.g., increases the likelihood of) that behavior in the future.

operant A behavior that "operates" on the environment and is controlled by its consequences.

reinforcer A consequence that strengthens operant behavior.

respondent conditioning A procedure in which a previously neutral stimulus comes to control behavior by virtue of reliably preceding a stimulus that controls behavior at the onset of and throughout stimulus–stimulus pairings.

response A defined unit of behavior.

rules Overt or covert verbal descriptions of relations among stimuli and responses. Rules describing consequences can engender behavior similar to that produced by actual exposure to the consequences.

stimulus A physical event.

unconditioned negative reinforcer An event that does not require learning to serve as a reinforcer.

The term negative reinforcement refers to one of the basic principles of operant conditioning rather than to a specific therapeutic technique. Operant conditioning is a form of learning in which behavior is controlled primarily by its consequences, that is, by changes in an individual's environment that are produced by the behavior. When the consequences of behavior increase the future probability of that kind of responding occurring under similar circumstances, or otherwise strengthen behavior, the consequences are termed reinforcers and the process (and procedure) through which responding is strengthened is called reinforcement. Although a number of prominent psychologists have argued against the practice, theoreticians and practitioners commonly distinguish between positive and negative reinforcement. The definitions and examples provided here illustrate the similarities and differences between them.

I. DESCRIPTION OF TREATMENT

When a stimulus (physical event) strengthens behavior by virtue of being presented (or increased in intensity) following the occurrence of such behavior, the stimulus is called a positive reinforcer and the procedure is termed positive reinforcement. For example, the behavior "bringing home flowers" is strengthened when a pleasantly surprised spouse says, "Thank you, sweetheart. You are really thoughtful." The positive reinforcer is the appreciative statement, and bringing home flowers is strengthened because the behavior resulted in its occurrence.

When behavior is strengthened because it terminates (or reduces the intensity of) a stimulus, or prevents or postpones the delivery of an otherwise forthcoming stimulus, the procedure is termed negative reinforcement and the stimulus is called a negative reinforcer. For example, a teenager who picks up his room thereby prevents or postpones his mother's angry lecture about responsibility and cleanliness. Picking up the room is strengthened because it results in a negative reinforcer. The negative reinforcer (i.e., the angry lecture) is also commonly called an aversive stimulus.

The designation aversive stimulus is also applied to stimuli that serve as positive punishers. Perhaps for this reason, many people confuse negative reinforcement with positive punishment. The two procedures can be distinguished on one primary basis. While negative reinforcers strengthen behavior, positive punishers weaken (decrease the rate or intensity) behavior when delivered as consequences. For example, a child reaches toward a sharp knife (behavior) and a watchful parent exclaims sharply, "no" (positive punisher). The surprised child draws the hand back and does not reach for sharp knives again (weakened behavior). Stimuli that function as a negative reinforcer in one context frequently serve as a positive punisher in similar contexts. Nonetheless, negative reinforcement and positive punishment are independent processes that produce opposite effects on behavior, and the terms should never be used interchangeably.

Two variants of negative reinforcement can be distinguished: escape conditioning and avoidance conditioning. When behavior terminates or reduces the intensity of an ongoing stimulus and is therefore strengthened, the procedure is called escape conditioning and the behavior is termed an escape response. The reader should note that with escape conditioning the aversive stimulus is ongoing and thus is always present when the escape response occurs. For example, a person who is listening to the radio when a program that she dislikes comes on may turn a knob on the radio labeled "OFF–ON" to the left, terminating the aversive sound. If turning the knob to the left terminates the sound and knob-turning is strengthened, escape conditioning is evident. Here, the response-strengthening effects of negative reinforcement would most likely be evident not as a progressive increase in the rate of turning off the radio over time, but rather as reliably doing so each time a disliked program was aired. Reinforcement increases the rate of responding initially and subsequently maintains established rates and patterns of behavior.

When behavior postpones or prevents the delivery of an otherwise forthcoming aversive stimulus and is therefore strengthened, the procedure is called avoidance conditioning and the behavior is termed an avoidance response. Because the avoidance response prevents or postpones the occurrence of the aversive stimulus, the aversive stimulus is not present when the avoidance response occurs. A child who regularly says "please" when making requests because failing to do so historically has led to parental reprimands provides a good example of avoidance conditioning. Here, if "please" is not included as part of a request, then a reprimand is forthcoming. If, however, the child says "please," there is no reprimand. These consequences cause the child to say "please" consistently, as an avoidance response when no aversive stimulus is present.

Some stimuli, termed unconditioned (or primary) negative reinforcers, "automatically" strengthen behavior as consequences. That is, no conditioning history is required for them to serve this behavioral function. High-intensity sensory stimulation in any modality (e.g., loud sounds, bright lights, forceful pressure on the skin, extreme heat or cold) characteristically serves as a primary negative reinforcer.

As their name implies, conditioned (or secondary) negative reinforcers require a particular conditioning (learning) history to strengthen behavior as consequences. Respondent conditioning, in which a previously neutral stimulus reliably and immediately precedes presentations of an unconditioned negative reinforcer, can serve to establish the neutral stimulus as a conditioned negative reinforcer. So, too, can verbal mediation, as when a friend tells a person holding illegal drugs "that the guy in the brown sweater is a cop," and the drug-holder subsequently avoids the officer.

II. THEORETICAL BASES

A large number of studies have examined escape and avoidance conditioning in laboratory animals and in humans under laboratory settings. These studies provide clear evidence of the effectiveness of negative reinforcement in initially increasing the rate of, and then maintaining, operant behavior. They also have revealed much about the variables that influence the effectiveness of negative reinforcement in strengthening behavior, and therapeutic applications of negative reinforcement are built on a solid experimental foundation.

Since B. F. Skinner's early writings, most behavioral psychologists have favored explanations of operant behavior based on its more-or-less immediate consequences. Such explanations, which are termed molecular, work well with respect to escape conditioning. The usual theoretical explanation of escape conditioning is that responses immediately terminate an aversive stimulus, and this change in the environment is responsible for the strengthening of behavior. This analysis is straightforward and poses no conceptual difficulties. Explanations of avoidance conditioning are conceptually more difficult and have occasioned some debate.

Two variants of avoidance conditioning, signaled and unsignaled, are commonly distinguished. In signaled (or discriminated) avoidance, presentations of a forthcoming aversive stimulus are preceded (signaled) by a warning stimulus. A response during the warning stimulus terminates the warning and prevents the occurrence of the aversive stimulus. In unsignaled (also termed free-operant or nondiscriminated) avoidance, no specific stimulus precedes delivery of the aversive stimulus.

Signaled avoidance is easy to explain theoretically in terms of a two-factor theory initially proposed by Mowrer in the late 1940s. The essence of this widely accepted account is that the warning stimulus, which is highly predictive of the aversive event, comes through respondent conditioning to elicit what is commonly termed "fear." Fear is unpleasant. It ends when the warning stimulus ends, and this happens as soon as the avoidance response occurs. Therefore, the avoidance response does have an immediate consequence—it terminates the aversive warning stimulus and the accompanying "fear."

This account must be substantially modified to explain unsignaled avoidance, where there is no apparent warning stimulus. The general approach taken by molecular theorists is to posit that the passage of time since the last occurrence of the aversive stimulus, or of the avoidance response, serves as a warning stimulus that elicits fear. Occurrence of the avoidance response, which is never immediately followed by the aversive stimulus, terminates the fear, and it is this immediate outcome that strengthens responding. Although the results of some studies support this view, the results of others do not. Particularly troublesome for two-factor theories of avoidance are that (1) studies often fail to find unequivocal evidence of "fear" in subjects responding under avoidance procedures, and (2) studies regularly find that avoidance responding persists for long periods even though subjects never contact the aversive stimulus. This latter effect is evident when, for example, extinction is arranged for avoidance responding.

Unsignaled avoidance responding is notoriously slow to extinguish, in part because an individual who is efficient at avoidance responding never contacts the aversive stimulus either prior to or during extinction. Therefore, it is impossible to discriminate between the negative reinforcement and extinction conditions. This difficulty can be overcome by presenting the aversive stimulus regardless of whether or not the behavior that previously was an effective avoidance response occurs.

Because of the difficulties that molecular explanations of avoidance conditioning pose, molar, or one-factor, alternatives have been offered. The essence of these theories is that behaviors need not have immediate consequences to be strengthened by negative reinforcement, but need only produce a detectable reduction in the overall frequency of exposure to the aversive stimulus. Therefore, hypothesized fear produced through respondent conditioning is not necessary for unsignaled avoidance conditioning to occur.

Although the relative merits of various one- and two-factor explanations of avoidance responding have been debated for decades, and alternatives to both approaches have been offered, there is no general agreement as to which theory of avoidance conditioning is best. With respect to clinical applications, the matter is not of crucial importance, and the primary virtue of the debate has been in fostering a wealth of laboratory studies of avoidance conditioning.

III. APPLICATIONS AND EXCLUSIONS

Negative reinforcement is important clinically in two regards. First, procedures that involve negative reinforcement may be systematically arranged to strengthen desired behaviors of clients. Second, negative reinforcement may play a role in the genesis and maintenance of undesired behaviors. Therapeutic procedures that involve the direct (contrived) arrangement of negative reinforcement have not been used as often as procedures involving positive reinforcement because of the ethical considerations involved in presenting unpleasant stimuli to clients, just so those clients can learn appropriate behaviors that allow them to escape or avoid these stimuli.

More often than they arrange contrived negative reinforcement, therapists help clients to understand the role of negative reinforcement in controlling their own troublesome actions in naturally occurring aversive situations and assist such clients in developing appropriate escape and avoidance responses. For instance, many teenagers engage in risky behaviors (e.g., drinking and driving) in part to avoid criticism and ridicule from peers. A therapist may help the teenager by pointing out less dangerous response options (e.g., staying away from situations where risky behavior is encouraged and peers who encourage it) that also are effective avoidance responses.

Interestingly, as Brain Iwata points out in an excellent 1987 review, negative reinforcement appears to play a generally unrecognized role in a number of procedures generally construed as "positive." For example, an educator may arrange consequences such that (a) a student's incorrect responses to problems result in statements of disapproval or remedial trials and (b) correct responses lead to praise. The educator assumes that improvements in the student's performance occur because praise is a positive reinforcer. Although positive reinforcement may contribute to the improvements, correct responses may also be strengthened because they allow the student to avoid aversive statements (of disapproval) and repetitions of an unpleasant task. That is, negative reinforcement may play an important but unrecognized role in producing the treatment gains.

Similarly, a therapist may think that positive reinforcement stemming from social interaction is responsible for a married couple's self-reported completion of an instruction to spend a half-hour of quiet time alone each evening. Instead, negative reinforcement in the form of avoiding the therapist's disapproval may be responsible for the couple's inaccurate report that they spent time together. In truth, unintended negative reinforcement is very common in therapeutic settings, as in everyday life.

Even though negative reinforcement is common, clinicians should be cautious about its use because of the potential for engendering negative emotional responding, aggressive behavior, and escape from or avoidance of the situation in which negative reinforcement occurs. In these regards, negative reinforcement is similar to punishment, and the two often are considered together as aversive and relatively restrictive (harmful) strategies for changing behavior. For example, throughout his long life the eminent behavioral psychologist B. F. Skinner argued against the use of both punishment and negative reinforcement in clinical settings and in general society, although he recognized their ubiquity. Similarly, Murray Sidman (1999) considers procedures based on negative reinforcement as well as punishment "coercive" and advocates nonaversive alternatives to them wherever possible. These views are shared by many therapists as well as theoreticians.

Issues of client diversity bear on the use of negative reinforcement primarily when clients who are unable to make informed choices regarding their own treatment are concerned. For example, children and people with substantial intellectual impairment require special protections with respect to aversive interventions, including punishment and contrived negative reinforcement. In brief, a clear decision-making process regarding the use of negative reinforcement should be in place. This process should recognize that negative reinforcement is a restrictive (harmful) intervention and adhere to the doctrine of the least restrictive alternative intervention, which states that other, less restrictive interventions must be evaluated and found ineffective before negative reinforcement is considered.

Clear guidelines must be established regarding the exact nature of the negative reinforcement procedure, including who is to implement it and the specific standards of accountability. Input from clients and client's advocates, as well as behavior-change experts, should play a crucial role in determining treatment details, including who is to arrange negative reinforcement and how its effects are to be monitored. Unambiguous rules regarding the behavioral data that will support continuation, modification, and termination of the negative reinforcement procedure must be established by a vigilant, expert, and caring treatment team before treatment is implemented. These rules must be followed unless the good of the client dictates otherwise in the opinion of the team. When possible, negative reinforcement should be avoided entirely.

IV. EMPIRICAL STUDIES

Relatively few clinical studies have evaluated interventions that involved intentionally arranging aversive stimuli that clients could escape or avoid by emitting appropriate behaviors. Most of the studies that have appeared involve clients with mental retardation, although other client populations (e.g., people with schizophrenia, children and adults with no diagnostic label) have been studied. Several different target behaviors (e.g., slouching, naming pictures, recognizing objects, approaching adults, speaking appropriately, solving math problems, stretching burned joints, sitting quietly during dental procedures) have been increased through escape and/or avoidance conditioning. A variety of aversive stimuli have been used, including electric shock, unpleasant noises, dental procedures, and required work or exercise. Clearly, procedures that involve systematically arranging aversive stimuli that clients can escape or avoid can be effective in generating appropriate behavior. Unless, however, those stimuli are only mildly aversive and generally accepted as part of the client's everyday world (e.g., requiring a student to work on math during a study session, unless the assignment was completed during math class), the use of such procedures is widely restricted. Moreover, too little work has been done with specific procedures to allow for general statements regarding the costs and benefits of specific interventions based on negative reinforcement relative to alternative interventions.

In recent years, behavioral psychologists have emphasized that an important early step in the treatment of many troublesome operant behaviors is isolating the reinforcers that maintain those behaviors, as well as any events that reliably precede them. The term functional assessment refers to a variety of procedures used to identify important environmental variables that maintain behavior. Functional assessment provides a basis for developing rational interventions that directly address the causes of the troublesome behavior. As noted previously, naturally occurring negative reinforcement can be responsible for a variety of behavioral problems. Once this is recognized, it may be possible to plan effective interventions. Many different interventions have been used to treat troublesome behaviors maintained by negative reinforcement; we will make no attempt to review this extensive literature. Instead, we will describe a single intervention strategy for dealing with inappropriate escape/avoidance responses.

This strategy involves teaching clients an appropriate alternative to inappropriate behaviors. It is exemplified by functional communication training, an intervention developed by Edward Carr and Mark Durand. This procedure has proven effective in reducing a variety of inappropriate behaviors acquired because they historically produced reinforcement. As a case in point: a student with a developmental disability may have learned to scream and strike out during demanding academic tasks because doing so terminated the tasks. Functional communication training involves arranging conditions so that the inappropriate behavior no longer produces reinforcement (i.e., extinction is arranged) and teaching the person an appropriate communication response that allows the individual to escape the aversive situation. For instance, the student in our example might be taught to raise a hand to "request help" with aversive schoolwork rather than to engage in disruptive behavior. The value of functional communication training and similar interventions has been demonstrated in a number of published studies.

Strategies that involve reducing the aversiveness of the situation that a client historically has escaped or avoided by emitting an undesired response also can be effective in reducing troublesome behavior. For example, a 1999 study by Jennifer Asmus and her colleagues determined through functional assessment the variables that influenced the problem behavior of children during academic tasks. The results were idiosyncratic for each child, but relevant variables included the novelty of the task, the person administering the task, and the setting in which the task was conducted. In a similar vein, Richard Smith and his colleagues reported in 1999 that task variables such as rate of presentation of demands, task novelty, and duration of task affected the rate of problem behavior. Any of these task variables could be altered to decrease the aversiveness of the instructional situation without diminishing educational opportunities. Typical interventions might involve interspersing easier tasks with more difficult tasks, altering the task to match the student's current performance level, decreasing initial task requirements, and allowing additional time to complete difficult tasks. Such interventions should serve as establishing operations, reducing the effectiveness of escape or avoidance of academic tasks as a negative reinforcer and reducing the probability of occurrence of responses that historically have produced this outcome.

The clinical literature regarding negative reinforcement is neither extensive nor focused. Brian Iwata contends that further research in the area is warranted, and he suggests three interesting directions for it to take:

> First, negative reinforcement may provide an alternative means for establishing behavior when attempts to use positive reinforcement fail... If so, we will want to know the behaviors for which specific contingencies are useful and the conditions under which they should be applied. Second, it appears that the acquisition of adaptive behavior in our training programs is at least partially a function of negative reinforcement. Further research must evaluate the roles of escape and avoidance within the training context so that (a) we will have a proper estimate of the effectiveness of commonly used positive reinforcers (the results of this estimate may indicate that more potent reinforcers are needed), (b) we can determine whether procedures such as remedial trials, physical assistance, and so on, serve any useful function and if that function is one of negative reinforcement, and (c) we can base future training successes on the planned rather than the accidental use of negative reinforcement. A third promising application involves further elaboration of behavioral replacement strategies. If we are willing to entertain the assumption that it is impossible to eliminate all sources of aversive stimulation, the use of such stimulation to alter the topography of escape and avoidance behavior, from an undesirable one to a tolerabe one, makes eminent sense from a clinical standpoint.... As with punishment, we should conduct research on negative reinforcement with great care and under the appropriate conditions to determine how it might be used effectively and humanely, its limitations, and its proper role within the larger realm of currently available treatment. (1987, p. 78)

Negative reinforcement may well be coercive and unappealing, but it is also ubiquitous. Better understanding of its role in the genesis and maintenance of behavior disorders, and of its current and ideal role in treating those disorders, can only benefit psychologists and their clients.

V. CASE ILLUSTRATION

A study published by Nathan Azrin and his colleagues in 1968 provides a clear example of the logic of negative reinforcement. They treated postural slouching in 25 adults through the use of an automated device that detected slouching and, when it occurred, produced an audible click followed three seconds later by a loud tone. The click and tone could be avoided by standing upright (not slouching), and escape from the tone could be effected by standing upright after the tone had started. This procedure reduced slouching in all clients exposed to it. The aversive stimulation that they received was mild, and they agreed to its appropriateness. These factors helped to make negative reinforcement an acceptable intervention.

A study published in 1986 by Hegel, Ayllon, Vanderplate, and Spiro-Hawkins provides an excellent example of the therapeutic use of negative reinforcement in another kind of situation, one in which a necessary medical procedure caused pain. The clients treated were three men who were recuperating from extensive burn wounds in a hospital. As part of their rehabilitation, they were required to stretch burned joints to increase and maintain flexibility. The stretching, which was initially arranged as part of mandatory staff-directed physical therapy sessions held each day, was quite painful. None of the patients showed increased range of motion in the burned joint during the period of staff-directed physical therapy. Range of motion increased substantially in all of them in a subsequent condition, where staff-directed physical therapy sessions could be avoided by engaging in sufficient self-directed exercise to meet daily goals. If the client failed to meet a daily goal, he was required to participate in staff-directed exercise. Thus, self-directed exercise was maintained by negative reinforcement in the form of avoidance of staff-directed physical therapy. Although the exercise undoubtedly was painful, no alternative would produce the same long-term benefits for the client. Unfortunately, aversive situations and activities are sometimes an intrinsic part of the human situation.

VI. SUMMARY

Negative reinforcement, one of the basic principles of operant conditioning, is evident when behavior is strengthened because its occurrence results in the termination or avoidance of aversive stimuli. The technique is important clinically in two general ways. First, negative reinforcement can be responsible for the development and maintenance of both healthy and pathological behaviors. Knowing this can help therapists understand and, more importantly, develop effective interventions for their client's troublesome behaviors. Second, procedures that involve negative reinforcement can be systematically implemented to strengthen the desired behaviors of clients. Ethical and practical considerations place substantial limits on the range of situations where it is appropriate to use negative reinforcement as part of therapy, and whenever it is used due caution and appropriate safeguards are necessary.

See Also the Following Articles

Conditioned Reinforcement ■ Covert Positive Reinforcement ■ Differential Reinforcement of Other Behavior ■ Functional Analysis of Behavior ■ Negative Practice ■ Negative Punishment ■ Operant Conditioning ■ Positive Punishment ■ Positive Reinforcement ■ Reinforcer Sampling

Further Reading

Catania, A. C. (1998). *Learning*. Upper Saddle River, NJ: Prentice-Hall.

Crosbie, J. (1998). Negative reinforcement and punishment. In K. A. Lattal & M. Perone (Eds.). *Handbook of research methods in human operant behavior* (pp. 163–189). New York: Plenum Press.

Iwata, B.A. (1987). Negative reinforcement in applied behavior analysis: An emerging technology. *Journal of Applied Behavior Analysis, 20*, 361-378.

Michael, J. (1993). *Concepts and principles of behavior analysis*. Kalamazoo, MI: Association for Behavior Analysis.

Sidman, M. (1999). Coercion in educational settings. *Behavior Change, 16*, 79–88.

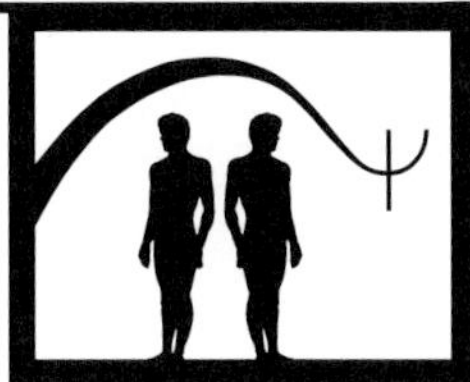

Neurobiology

Douglas S. Lehrer and Jerald Kay
Wright State University School of Medicine

GLOSSARY

amygdala A limbic system structure adjacent to the hippocampus that is responsible in part for regulation and valence of emotions (especially fear) and their related somatic expression.

brain-derived neurotrophic factor (BDNF) A molecule that is released by the targets of neurons and that promotes chemical alterations in the neuron responsible for its growth and maintenance.

explicit (or declarative) memory Learned factual knowledge and autobiographical information that requires conscious awareness and intact hippocampus.

glutamate An important excitatory neurotransmitter.

hippocampus The limbic system structure (extremely sensitive to high levels of stress hormones) responsible for significant aspects of both learning and memory.

hypothalamic-pituitary-adrenal (HPA)axis A feedback circuit between the hypothalamus, pituitary, and adrenal gland that regulates the release of glucocorticoids or stress hormones such as cortisol.

implicit (or nondeclarative) memory Nonconscious simple learning that although out of a patient's awareness, often has significant impact on behavior and perception.

neuronal plasticity The capacity of the central nervous system to strengthen and create neural connections (neurogenesis).

positron emission tomography (PET) A functional neuroimaging technique employing radioactive tracers that can demonstrate activation of brain regions through measurement of blood flow.

selective serotonin reuptake inhibitor (SSRI) A group of antidepressants that increase levels of the neurotransmitter serotonin in the synaptic cleft by impeding its degradation.

working memory A type of short-term memory, often referred to as the "blackboard of the mind," most often anatomically associated with the prefrontal cortex, that facilitates moment to moment perception, information processing, and explicit memory retrieval.

I. INTRODUCTION

Mental disorders and their treatments have long been viewed within a flawed intellectual framework, namely, that mental diseases are either biologically or psychologically based, and that treatment is best conducted with biological or psychotherapeutic tools, respectively. Many mental health professionals have adopted this view, as has an insurance industry that has often enforced criteria whereby treatment for "biological" illnesses (such as schizophrenia or bipolar disorder) is reimbursed while the treatment of "psychological" maladies (dysthymia or personality disorders, for instance) are less well supported. The very nature of professional practice has been affected, with a dramatic reduction in the number of hours that psychiatrists or hospital-based (and sometimes community-based) nonpsychiatric clinicians spend in the performance of psychotherapy. Combined treatment with psychotherapy and medication, although a common practice, founders within this theoretical quagmire, often leaving practitioners without a logically consistent theoretical framework in which to skillfully and rationally deliver treatment.

This conceptual dichotomy is indeed ironic and unfortunate, for a careful review of the remarkable contributions from the neurosciences and cognitive psychology describe a very different intellectual framework, one in which psychology and biology are indistinguishable, and in which mental disturbances may be understood simultaneously on both levels in a heuristically harmonious manner. As Nobel laureate Eric Kandel asserted, "all mental processes, even the most complex psychological processes, derive from operations of the brain." However, elucidating the neurobiological correlates of mental processes should not preclude the patient's need for the psychotherapist to appreciate their unique meaning.

In this article, we will attempt to explain the relation of biology to psychotherapy. Current knowledge about certain critical brain functions, particularly learning and memory, which form the basis for our understanding of the biology and cognitive psychology of all psychotherapies, will be reviewed. We will discuss the remarkable capacity of the brain to adapt to environmental changes, expressed in the construct of neural plasticity and findings related to new cell growth in the adult brain, followed by a brief review of the effects of stress on the brain. Finally, we will conclude by offering evidence that psychotherapy does indeed exert measurable biological effects in the brain, findings that may ultimately guide therapeutic decision making.

II. LEARNING, MEMORY, AND NEURAL PLASTICITY

A. Phenomenology of Memory

Memory is not a unitary function of the brain. Indeed, memory can be categorized into at least two major functional and neurobiological categories, namely, explicit (or declarative) memory and implicit (or nondeclarative) memory. Explicit memory refers to factual knowledge such as place, people, things, and autobiographical information. Working memory is one variety of explicit memory that is distinct from long-term explicit memory. Working memory refers to the short-term memory that facilitates active, conscious perceptual attention and initial processing of information, and later permits the purposeful retrieval of stored explicit memories. Implicit memory refers to the nonconscious effects of past behavior, and involves a heterogeneous set of abilities and knowledge, such as (1) associative learning (classical and operant conditioning); (2) procedural memory (learned skills and habits); (3) sensitization and habituation (exaggeration or attenuation, respectively, of behavioral responses to specific environmental stimuli); and (4) priming (enhanced recall aided by prior exposure to related stimuli, such as words or objects). In other words, and perhaps more germane to our understanding of psychotherapy, implicit memory refers to those past experiences that influence our current behavior even though we do not consciously remember them. Implicit memories form the rules that govern the interpretation of later life experiences. Because implicit knowledge is not readily available for conscious reflection, these rules self-perpetuate, even in the face of new life experiences that might demand a different (and more adaptive) perceptual bias.

As we might expect, there is an interaction between explicit and implicit memories that is utilized in psychotherapy. Implicit biases are examined and made explicit, creating an opportunity for conscious processing, reflection, and new experiences, hopefully leading to an adaptive change in the implicit memory system. To be more specific, the phenomenon of transference is understandable, for example, in light of the repetition of specific behaviors and beliefs that are governed by early experiences encoded in both implicit and explicit memories. In psychoanalytic psychotherapy, distortions that characterize transference within the doctor–patient dyad as well as throughout all sectors of a patient's interpersonal world can be examined and interpreted within a safe, nonjudgmental, and empathic new relationship.

It is worth pointing out that this discussion of memory, particularly as it applies to our understanding of psychotherapy, is by necessity simplistic. Most notably it neglects the phenomenon of consciousness, the neurobiology of which would justify an entire article. (For such a treatise, please see the reference to Regina Pally's work in the Further Reading section.) Consciousness, most often defined simply as awareness, probably represents a complex interaction between multiple brain functions and regions in the cortex and brain stem (at a minimum). Although a full elaboration of these systems and relationships is beyond the scope of this article, several points of relevance to psychotherapy are worth mentioning. If conscious perception is the product of the shaping influences of our conscious belief systems on environmental reality, then we may resist not only unconscious material, but the conscious as well if it conflicts with our belief systems. Yet the essential function of consciousness is, according to Pally, to "provide ... a means by which we notice changes and can flexibly choose the most adaptive response to that change." This is true of changes in the environment, as well as changes in our responses to those environmental events. Therefore, we simply cannot appreciate the processes of learning, growth, and therapeutic change without accounting for the role of conscious self-reflection.

Similarly, this article cannot address the broad field of human development as it relates to learning and memory. Questions about the relative stability versus alteration in these mechanisms at different stages in the individual's life cycle clearly have implications for clinical intervention as well as general understanding of learning and memory. This is a critically important area for further study.

B. Functional Neuroanatomy of Memory

An abundance of experimental data (human and animal, lesion and brain imaging studies) indicate that explicit and implicit memory depends on different brain structures and systems. Explicit memory relies on intact medial (i.e., inner surface) temporal structures, including the hippocampus, parahippocampal gyrus, and the entorhinal and perirhinal cortices, as well as association areas in the neocortex. New facts and event information are first processed in the association areas of the frontal, temporal, parietal, and occipital lobes. Working memory in particular relies on regions of left frontal lobes such as the prefrontal cortex. From the association cortices, information is conveyed to the parahippocampal and perirhinal cortices, and then to the entorhinal cortex, hippocampus, and adjacent structures (Fig. 1). Taken together, these steps represent the encoding and consolidation steps of memory formation. The specific functional tasks of each area remain unclear, and current investigations are under way to clarify the distinct roles. For example, the parahippocampal gyrus may support the encoding of information about the occurrence of an item, whereas the hippocampus may support the encoding of relationships between the item and its context.

The newly formed explicit memories return through the aforementioned systems back to the association cortices where long-term storage occurs. The fact that storage occurs in the association cortices explains why people and experimental animals that have bilateral lesions of the medial temporal lobes that damage the hippocampus are relatively unable to form new explicit memories but can recall previously stored (prelesion) knowledge. There is no single cortical storage area. Knowledge is distributed throughout the necortex and is "reconstructed" into a single data set during the retrieval process.

The functional neuroanatomy of implicit memory, taken as a whole, is somewhat less well defined than that for explicit memory, in part because of the heterogeneity of cognitive phenomena collectively grouped as implicit memory, but also due to methodological problems involved in the study of implicit memory (preventing the "contamination" of implicit memory processing with conscious or explicit memory activation). However, it is fairly clear that the striatum, a component of the basal ganglia (a system of several nuclei, or functionally related collections of neurons, located deep within the cerebral hemispheres) is involved. The striatum actually includes several discrete nuclei: the caudate, putamen, and ventral striatum. The striatum plays a role in a variety of brain functions, including cognitive functioning, mood regulation, and motor and nonmotor behaviors. As with explicit memory, various areas of the neocortex are also involved with implicit memory.

Another brain structure of paramount importance to memory function, especially as it relates to our understanding of trauma and psychotherapy, is the amygdala. The amygdala sits in the anterior temporal lobe, just in front of the hippocampus. It plays a central role in the regulation of emotions, including the mediation of conscious emotional feelings (such as fear) with related somatic expressions (autonomic and motoric expressions). Electrical stimulation of the amygdala in humans results in feelings of fear and apprehension. Rare bilateral lesions of the amygdala disrupt the ability of the individual to apprehend fearful facial expressions and discern other fear cues in the environment.

The amygdala is involved in the encoding and consolidation of emotion-laden explicit and implicit memories. Emotional arousal activates the amygdala, resulting in the modulation of other memory regions influenced by the amygdala, thus regulating the strength and persistence of affectively charged memories. Larry Cahill, James McGaugh, and colleagues at the University of California, Irvine, have performed a

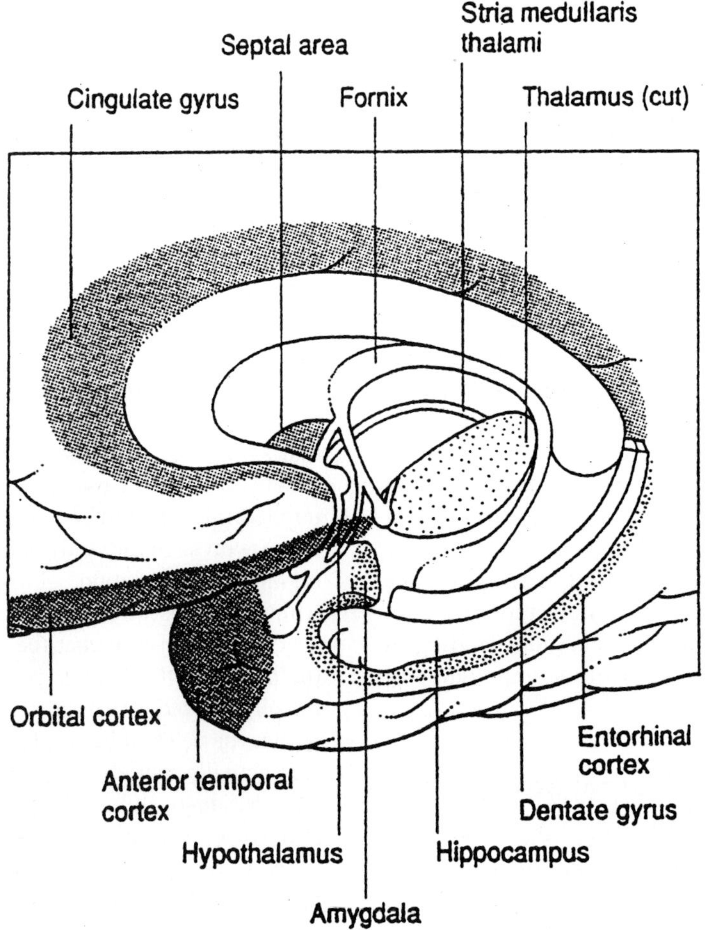

FIGURE 1 Medial view of cortical and subcortical limbic areas. From Fitzgerald (1992). "Neuroanatomy: Basic and Clinical," 2nd ed., W.B. Saunders Co.

number of experiments that demonstrate this phenomenon. For example, they showed emotionally neutral and emotionally arousing film clips to healthy volunteers who then underwent a functional brain imaging study (fluorodeoxyglucose positron emission tomography, or FDG PET) designed to demonstrate relative activation of various brain regions. The amygdala activated during viewing of the arousing films, but not the emotionally neutral clips. Later, the subjects were better able to recall the arousing clips, with the degree of amygdala activation correlating with the degree of recall.

The amygdala's memory role is therefore a selective one, with little involvement in the absence of emotional arousal. Furthermore, the amygdala is involved only in memory encoding and consolidation (prestorage activities), not retrieval.

C. Cellular Mechanisms of Learning and Memory: Neural Plasticity

We have reviewed known elements of how the brain, as a collection of macroscopic brain regions, obtains and retains new knowledge. But how do the actual individual functional units of the brain, that is, the nerve cells (or neurons), facilitate these changes?

Neurons communicate with one another through a process of chemical signaling known as neurotransmission. An impulse (action potential) traveling down the outbound fiber (axon) of a neuron reaches its terminus at the juncture between the signaling neuron and another nerve cell. This juncture is known as the synapse. The synapse may impinge on the body of the target neuron, or on one of its projections (an axon, or an inbound fiber, or dendrite). At the synapse, the "upstream," or presynaptic neuron releases chemicals (neurotransmitters) into the synaptic space. The neurotransmitter diffuses across the space and comes into contact with special proteins (receptors) imbedded in the outer membrane of the "down-stream" (postsynaptic) neuron. When the neurotransmitter interacts with the receptor in a chemical "lock-and-key" fashion, an excitatory or inhibitory effect is exerted on the postsynaptic neuron. The intended action of the signaling neuron is thus accomplished.

We now know that the brain possesses a remarkable capacity for structural change throughout the life cycle. This idea was first articulated in 1911 by the neuroanatomist Santiago Ramon Y Cajal, who postulated that repeated behavior must cause the neuron's dendrites and axons to undergo structural changes, revising the preexisting pattern of neuronal interconnections. In other words, learning is the product of new or enhanced connections between nerve cells. The neurophysiologist Donald Hebb experimentally demonstrated this phenomenon in 1949, resulting in what has become known as "Hebb's Rule." Hebb wrote: "When an axon of cell A ... excites cell B and repeatedly or persistently takes part in firing it, some growth process or metabolic change takes place in one or both cells so that A's efficiency as one of the cells firing B is increased." Hebb asserted that this change is the result of a strengthening of the connections between neurons. This phenomenon is known as neural (or neuronal) plasticity, and represents the process whereby learning experiences are physically encoded.

Eric Kandel was awarded the 2000 Nobel Prize in Physiology or Medicine for demonstrating the molecular mechanisms of this process in the marine sea slug *(Aplysia californica),* an invertebrate with a relatively simple nervous system consisting of about 20,000 nerve cells. The structural simplicity of *Aplysia*'s nervous system facilitated Kandel's demonstration of the mechanisms of implicit learning. A mild touch of the animal's siphon (a structure used to expel waste and seawater) normally elicits a reflexive withdrawal of its gill and siphon. This reflex is known as the gill-withdrawal reflex. Repeated stimulation of the reflex leads to habituation, or attenuation, of the reflex. On the other hand, the administration of a noxious stimulus to its tail produces a sensitization, or exaggeration, of the reflex. Briefly repeated trials of either kind of stimulus lead to a change in the reflex that is relatively short-lived (i.e., lasting minutes). However, the administration of four or five series of stimulations administered periodically over hours results in a change that lasts from days to weeks. Therefore, habituation and sensitization have short- and long-term forms. Kandel discovered that short-term habituation and sensitization result from a decrease or increase, respectively, in the amount of neurotransmitter released into the synapse (in the case of *Aplysia,* the connection between the sensory neuron bringing information about the stimulus and the motor neuron that mediates the withdrawal reflex). Importantly, although the exact mechanism of this alteration is unclear, changes in protein synthesis do not appear to be necessary.

Long-term alterations in the reflex were observed after repeated stimulus applications. It is noteworthy, although of little surprise to many behavioral scientists, that spaced training (small amounts of training spaced over many minutes or hours) produced substantially greater behavioral alterations than did massed training (a lot of training all at once). Long-term alterations were facilitated by changes in gene expression and the protein-manufacturing apparatus of the cell. This cascade of molecular events described by Kandel and subsequent investigators can be simplified as follows.

During repeated stimulation, a neurotransmitter known as glutamate accumulates in synapse. Activation of a subtype of the glutamate receptor, the so-called NMDA (*N*-methyl-D-aspartate) receptor, opens membrane channels that permit the entry of calcium into the neuron. In the interior of the cell, calcium triggers a series of enzymes (adenylate cyclase and protein kinases) to initiate gene expression in the nucleus of the cell. The activated genes encode proteins important for the regulation, growth, or elimination (pruning) of synaptic connections. When the cell's protein synthesis apparatus is turned on, and regulatory or structural proteins are manufactured, new receptors or synaptic sites are created, or existing ones functionally or physically eliminated. The ultimate result is a long-term change in synaptic excitability, effectively altering the way in which the brain's circuitry responds to later stimulation.

Evidence for anatomical changes in the brains of stimulated individuals is found in the work of Anita Sirevaag and William Greenough, who during the 1980s showed that different rearing conditions affect brain structure. Rats raised in a complex toy-rich environment showed indications of enhanced brain development compared to rats raised in isolated, uninteresting conditions. Specifically, the stimulated rats' brains had a greater density of synaptic nerve endings (boutons), higher volume of dendrites per neuron (more complex branching, implying more neuron-to-neuron communication), and more support structures, indicating more active neuronal activity (more blood vessels, for instance).

The individual genetic traits of an individual modulate the robustness of the plastic cellular adaptations. For instance, Joe Tsien and colleagues at Princeton University bred a genetic strain of mouse (dubbed "doogie the supermouse") in which the postsynaptic NMDA receptor density was intentionally increased (overexpressed). Compared to unaltered control mice, the mutant mice showed superior abilities in learning and memory in various behavioral tasks, as would be predicted by the neural plasticity model.

D. Neurogenesis

In addition to the above scenario, another mechanism may explain the remodeling of the nervous system in response to life experiences. Until the 1960s, neuroscientists had long believed that the adult brain was incapable of generating new neurons. In 1965, Joseph Altman at MIT described the production of new neurons in the brains of adult rats. Inexplicably, little work was done to further the study of the remarkable phenomenon of neurogenesis until the past decade or so, when several investigators resumed work on this critically important area of neuroscientific study. Elizabeth Gould of Princeton University has studied factors that appear to regulate neurogenesis in various animals, including primates. One of the most important findings was that neurogenesis is stimulated by environmental complexity and learning. Experimental training activities resulted in increased formation of adult-generated nerve cells (granule cells) in the black-capped chickadee. Training conditions also enhanced the survival of those cells. Conversely, conditions of deprivation reduced the generation and survival of new cells. Another important finding was that adrenal hormones, normally released in greater quantity during times of stress, suppresses the formation of precursor cells. We will discuss other effects of stress on the brain later in this article.

Even after neurogenesis was demonstrated in a wide variety of animals, the scientific community was resistant to accept that neurogenesis occurs in humans. That changed when Fred Gage and his colleagues at the Salk Institute for Biological Studies in La Jolla, California, studied the postmortem brains of cancer victims who had received a dosage of a diagnostic drug called bromodeoxyuridine (BrdU) before they died. BrdU is incorporated into the DNA of dividing cells and can be used as a marker for dividing and newly formed cells in the body. Gage found BrdU-containing cells in the studied brains, conclusively establishing that adult humans grow new neurons. Of great significance to our topic, the new cells were found in the hippocampus, already shown to be essential to learning and memory.

Last, although the exact mechanisms that regulate neurogenesis are still undetermined, existing work gives us every reason to believe that neurogenesis, like neural plasticity, results from interactions between experience and genes. Indeed studies by Liu and colleagues support that early life experiences can profoundly determine both brain structure and function. For example, high levels of maternal rat behavior promote hippocampal synaptogenesis, enhance memory and learning in adult offspring, and increase both NMDA receptors as well as brain neurotrophic factors that play a central role in the growth and maintenance of neurons. Conversely, rats experiencing maternal separation early in their postnatal development have decreased brain neurotrophic factors (BDNF) and in the presence of elevated levels of stress hormones that accompany acute stress, are unable to modulate BDNF as are sibs who are not separated from their mothers.

E. Implications

The implications of these findings about the biology of learning and memory are indeed broad. We now have an elegant scientific framework with which to understand the interaction between genes and environment. These models give us an idea why different individuals, with diverse genetic "blueprints," may respond to nearly identical environmental circumstances in strikingly different ways, including why some trauma victims may develop posttraumatic stress disorder (PTSD) whereas others survive with little detriment to their mental health. It also helps us to understand why identical (monozygotic) twins (with identical genetic content, but different life experiences) may have such divergent personal features. For example, we know that a monozygotic twin of an individual with schizophrenia—a mental disorder considered to be highly "genetic"—has no more than a 50% chance of developing the disease. Life experiences, through the previously described (and related) mechanisms, determine whether genetic predispositions and vulnerabilities are realized, or whether they remain latent throughout our lives.

In the case of depression, Kenneth Kendler studied more than 2100 female twins over 17 months. The probability for those twins at lowest risk for major depression increased from 0.5% to 6.2% and those at highest risk from 1.1% to 14.6% if a twin had experienced stressors such as a recent death, assault, marital problems, and divorce or separation. David Reiss' work with more than 700 multiconfigured families has demonstrated that when a parent differentially and persistently relates to one adolescent in a conflictual or negative manner, nearly two thirds of the variance in the teenager's antisocial behavior and one third in his depressive symptomatology can be accounted for by the conflicted parent–child relationship. Life experiences through the previously described (and related) mechanisms determine whether genetic predisposition and vulnerabilities are realized, or whether they remain latent throughout our lives. Moreover, recent research appears to support the possibility that psychotherapy and medication may share salutary effects through moderating the genetic effects of those with vulnerable phenotypes.

III. THE BIOLOGICAL EFFECTS OF STRESS

Most people who seek psychotherapy, or any mental health treatment for that matter, do so during times of increased subjective life stress or following a highly stressful, even traumatic, life experience. Psychosocial stress has long been recognized as a major contributor to the onset of mental disorders and to the recurrences or exacerbations of those maladies. For that reason, any attempt to understand the neurobiology of psychotherapy requires some understanding of the biological effects of stress.

Biologists have long been fascinated by the natural phenomenon of animal population crashes. Typically, environmental conditions favoring the exponential growth of a particular species' population results in intra- and interspecies competition for food and mates, and territory. When the population exceeds the carrying capacity of the environmental niche, vast numbers of the affected community die, sometimes losing 90% or more of its members within a very short period of time. Examinations of population crash victims typically reveal multiple organ abnormalities, including enlarged adrenal glands—the small hormone-producing organs that sit on top of each kidney and secrete adrenalin (also known as epinephrine) and corticosteroids. These substances are known collectively as the body's stress hormones.

Using less dramatic experimental and naturalistic research designs, many investigators have explored the consequences of stress in animal and human nervous systems. These investigations demonstrate that stress is associated with disruption or alteration of various mechanisms involved in learning and memory, and presumably, adaptation. We will illustrate this point with a description of selected findings.

A. Studies of Care-Related Stress

Stephen Suomi performed a series of experiments with rhesus monkeys that shed light on the interaction between genetic vulnerability, stress, and potentially corrective experiences. He first observed that infant monkeys separated from their mothers developed social anxiety–like behavioral responses. They were later reared by peers raised by the subject monkey's own mothers. The peer interaction resulted in some amelioration of the behavioral disturbance, but the subject monkeys remained prone to a return of the behavioral disturbance when placed in novel or stressful circumstances, accompanied by high levels of stress hormones (see later discussion). Suomi then observed that a minority of monkeys that were raised by their own mothers showed exaggerated separation disturbances that were similar to those shown by the original subject monkeys. This latter group of disturbed monkeys was placed in the care of highly nurturant foster monkeys. The change in rearing resulted in the relief of behavioral problems. But more surprisingly, the offspring that were "adopted" by the "supermothers" went on to rise to the top of the colony hierarchy, implying that the constitutional sensitivity of these monkeys was preserved in a way that conferred an attunement to the needs and cues of the colony, allowing them to respond in a socially adaptive and successfully manner.

A more dramatic example of the deleterious effects of separation (without subsequent surrogate caregiver nurturance) can be found in René Spitz's historic study of infants of unwed mothers placed in foundling homes in the 1940s. In order to reduce infection risk to the infants, handling was kept to a minimum, and the infant's view of caregivers' faces was blocked by masks and sheets. Despite receiving sufficient nutrition and an attractive physical environment, almost all of the infants died or developed mental retardation within 1 to 2 years. Spitz contrasted this to the healthy, normal outcomes of children raised by their mothers in a squalid prison environment. He concluded that nurturant human contact was as essential for growth and survival as was food and sanitary conditions.

Rosenblum and Andrews studied infant monkeys raised by either normal mothers or by mothers made anxious by an unpredictable feeding schedule. The monkeys with anxious mothers demonstrated social impairment and biochemical abnormalities (serotonin and norepinephrine abnormalities). Interestingly, the changes did not appear until adolescence, lending credence to clinical observations that early environmental disturbances may have long-ranging effects that do not manifest until later in life.

B. Role of Stress Hormones

The stress hormones have been an important focus of stress response studies. For the purposes of this discussion we will focus on the most important of the stress hormones—the category of corticosteroids known as the glucocorticoids—exemplified by cortisol. The glucocorticoids are involved in immune function and a number of other physiological processes as well as the stress response. Glucocorticoid release is regulated by a homeostatic feedback mechanism involving the hypothalamus, pituitary gland, and the adrenal glands (the hypothalamic-pituitary-adrenal, or HPA, axis). Many studies have examined the role of the HPA axis during stress, showing that glucocorticoid concentrations (and the levels of other brain chemicals that stimulate glucocorticoid production and release, such as adrenal corticotropic hormone [ACTH] and corticotropin releasing hormone [CRH]) go up during times of brief or prolonged stress. Elevated glucocorticoid levels are found in laboratory animals separated from their mothers or social groups, or otherwise placed in stressful conditions. Stress-related human cortisol elevations were demonstrated as long ago as the Korean War, when urinary cortisol levels of soldiers under random artillery bombardment were higher than during periods away from the battle zone.

The hippocampus, equipped with a high density of glucocorticoid receptors, is the principal target location in the brain for the glucocorticoids. The hippocampus is also an important inhibitory regulator of the HPA. Under conditions of modest stress, a resultant facilitation of hippocampal plasticity appears to enhance cognition. This is consistent with the observation that people tend to perform better when mildly or moderately challenged. However, major or prolonged stress produces sustained high levels of glucocorticoids that seem to have deleterious effects in the brain, including cell loss. The mechanisms of glucocorticoid-mediated harmful effects are unclear, but may involve inhibition of the chemicals inside the neuron that turn on gene transcription and protein synthesis. The consequences may include inhibition of neural plasticity (with reduced dendritic branching and alterations in synaptic structure) and/or neurogenesis, a decreased rate of new neuronal survival, and actual neurotoxicity with permanent cell loss (i.e., a direct lethal effect on hippocampal neurons, possibly through mechanisms involving the neurotransmitter glutamate, resulting in activation of programmed cell death processes known as apotosis). Animal studies and human brain imaging studies have demonstrated atrophy (shrinkage) of the hippocampus (and to a lesser extent, other brain regions) during prolonged periods of stress. As well, enduring hormonal changes throughout the life of an animal subjected to early maternal separation have been demonstrated. More will be said about the role of the HPA axis in depression and PTSD later in this article.

IV. EVIDENCE FOR THE BIOLOGY OF PSYCHOTHERAPY

In this section we will review present evidence that psychotherapy is a powerful tool that exerts its effects by changing the structure and function of the brain. Before presenting that evidence we will briefly describe background material regarding brain imaging methods, findings related to the biology of human emotions, and comments regarding the biology of personality.

A. Brain Imaging

It is beyond the scope of this chapter to attempt even a modest brain imaging primer. However, these tools have permitted the study of cognition and emotion, in normal and pathological states, to an extent that was previously impossible. A very brief description of imaging methods may therefore assist the reader as we subsequently present imaging data that inform the primary subject at hand.

Neuroimaging methods may be separated into structural and functional imaging techniques. Structural imaging methods provide information about the anatomy of the brain but say nothing about its present physiology. Many readers will be quite familiar with the two major structural imaging methods: computed tomography

(CT) and magnetic resonance imaging (MRI). Although CT has many valuable clinical applications, its resolution is inadequate to quantify the structural changes reflective of the processes described in this article. Therefore, research questions about brain structure are generally answered using MRI.

Functional imaging methods are less familiar to most clinicians as they have only recently found a limited role in clinical medicine. For now, their major role is still limited to research. These methods share a common theme: They provide information about the present physiology of the brain. Depending on the method chosen information about the metabolism or blood flow in a specific brain region (reflective of regional brain activity), and receptor and/or neurotransmitter levels, can be acquired. Brain activation studies may be performed under a variety of conditions, including a resting state, or when the subject is engaged in a specific sensory, cognitive, or emotional task. The most common functional imaging tools used to study emotional and cognitive function are positron emission tomography (PET), single photon emission computed tomography (SPECT), both of which involve introduction of a radioactive tracer into the subject's body, and functional magnetic resonance imaging (fMRI).

B. Functional Neuroanatomy of Human Emotions

Functional imaging tools can show us "real-time" information about brain activation during various emotional states and tasks. Eric Reiman performed a series of experiments with normal subjects and sufferers of panic or phobic disorders to characterize the biology emotions using functional brain imaging methods (PET), each constructed around a distinct mental task. His findings indicate that human emotional functioning is highly complex, involving multiple brain regions. To illustrate this point, we will present a selection of his findings.

A group of normal subjects underwent PET imaging while watching a series of silent film clips, some that were emotionally neutral and others that were emotionally arousing. He later performed a similar study using cognitive rather than visual stimuli. Subjects were instructed to recall (rather than view) happy and grievous events. A wide variety of regions again activated during the performance of both emotional tasks. However, when comparing the results of the studies, Reiman was able to make the following generalizations. Limbic areas (the hippocampal formation and amygdala) and paralimbic areas (anterior temporal cortex and parahippocampal gyrus) long thought to participate in emotion, while activated in both sets of subjects, were preferentially involved in the response to externally presented (film clips) emotional stimuli. In contrast, a region in the vicinity of the anterior insular cortex was preferentially involved in the response to distressing cognitive stimuli (recalled experiences).

Reiman concluded that the anterior insular region might serve as an internal alarm system, investing potentially distressing thoughts and bodily sensations with negative emotional significance. On the other hand, the anterior temporal region might serve as an external alarm system. Several structures activated in a way that indicated that they serve a general role in emotional response, irrespective of the quality or valence of the emotion. These areas included the thalamus and medial prefrontal cortex, the latter seeming to facilitate conscious experience of emotion, inhibition of excessive emotion, and monitoring of one's emotions in order to make personally relevant decisions.

Louis Gottschalk and Monte Buchsbaum also used PET to study the emotional phenomena of hope and hopelessness. Twelve healthy male volunteers were imaged during a state of silent, wakeful mentation. The thoughts that they experienced during the study were later rated using the "Gottschalk Hope Scale." As with Reiman's subjects, many regions activated during the mental task. The interesting conclusion made by the authors was that the metabolic changes associated with hope and hopelessness had some different regional locations and characteristics, indicating that from a neurobiological standpoint, hope and hopelessness are not simply opposite manifestations of a single emotional phenomenon.

It is too early to attempt a broad neurobiologically based explanation for mood and mood regulation. As can be surmised from the above discussion as well as earlier sections of this article (such as the role of the amygdala), the answer is likely to involve a complex interplay between numerous brain areas. In addition to those already mentioned, the anterior cingulate almost certainly plays a key role. John Allman at the California Institute of Technology has asserted that the anterior cingulate appears to be an area in which functions central to intelligent behavior, such as emotional self-control, focused problem solving, error recognition, and adaptive response to changing conditions, are juxtaposed with the emotions.

Whether mood disorders reflect a primary disturbance of the brain systems that control emotion, or involve dysregulation in other brain systems with secondary "downstream" disruption of mood regulation, remains to be seen. For additional reading beyond this discussion or that found in Section D later, see the reference to Dennis Charney's text in the Further Reading section.

C. Personality

If implicit learning is the result of experiential and genetic interactions, we are left to wonder about the biology of personality development. To what extent is personality already genetically directed at birth, versus a series of implicitly learned rules, perceptions, and emotional and behavioral responses? Anyone who has spent much time with infants has certainly observed the striking differences in behavioral responsiveness from one infant to another, yet we still traditionally think of personality as an acquired constellation of personal characteristics.

Robert Cloninger of Washington University has attempted to explain this conundrum with a psychobiological model of personality development. He suggests that personality consists of two independent multidimensional domains that he terms "temperament" and "character." Temperament consists of four independent dimensions, including novelty seeking, harm avoidance, reward dependence, and persistence. Temperament involves automatic, preconceptual, or unconscious responses to perceptual stimuli, reflective of biases in information processing by perceptual memory systems. Temperamental factors are independently heritable, manifest early in life, and are highly stable over time. The factors may be observed in childhood and predict adolescent and adult behavior.

The dimensions of character are self-directedness, cooperativeness, and self-transcendence, or, respectively, identification as an autonomous individual, integral part of human society, and integral part of the universe. In contrast to temperamental factors, character factors are concept-based and less stable (i.e., more malleable) over time, although genetics may still play a role in character development. Someone low in the first two character traits is, according to the author, likely to suffer a personality disorder. Although the importance of self-transcendence is of questionable value to the person early in life, it takes on great importance during times of death, illness, and misfortune.

This model has implications for the treatment of personality disorders. For instance, it is possible that temperamental factors may be attenuated using certain medications (some of which have already found an effective adjunctive role in the treatment of certain personality disorder traits). On the other hand, the factors of character may be more productive targets for psychotherapeutic interventions. Clearly more work must be done to test the validity of this construct, particularly as it translates to clinical settings with disturbed individuals.

D. Depression

1. Psychotherapy versus Antidepressant Medication: Imaging Findings

Psychotherapy of depression in its various forms is among the most well-validated of all psychological treatments. Yet fundamental questions about which form of psychotherapy to apply, when, to which patient, and whether a depressed person should receive psychotherapy, medication, or both, remain largely unanswered. Information from the neurosciences may soon inform these issues, and is already offering exciting clues.

Two investigators performed functional neuroimaging with depressed people treated with psychotherapy or antidepressant medicine. In the first study, Arthur Brody and Lewis Baxter used pre- and posttreatment PET imaging to examine regional brain metabolism changes in 24 people suffering from major depression treated with 12 weeks of either paroxetine or interpersonal therapy (IPT). The posttreatment changes in brain activation were very similar, with both groups showing a normalization of excessive pretreatment activation in a variety of brain regions (the right dorsolateral prefrontal cortex, left ventrolateral prefrontal cortex, right dorsal caudate, and bilateral thalamus). Only the medicated group showed a significant reduction in the right ventrolateral prefrontal cortex, possibly reflecting the fact that the medicated subjects were less symptomatic pretreatment and experienced a proportionately more robust response to treatment.

In a study performed in the United Kingdom, Stephen Martin used SPECT to measure changes in regional cerebral blood flow (rCBF) in 28 depressed people who were treated for 6 weeks with either venlafaxine or IPT. The two groups had a similar degree of pretreatment symptoms, and again, the drug group showed a more robust improvement, although 6 weeks of treatment is minimally adequate for an antidepressant trial, but probably not for IPT. The imaging studies showed that both groups showed increased rCBF in the right basal ganglia. Only the IPT group showed increased rCBF in the right posterior cingulate, an ambiguous finding due to potential confounding effects.

A preliminary study by Viinamaki and colleagues in Scandanavia suggests that psychodynamic psychotherapy, as is the case with CBT and IPT, may change brain function. A patient with both depression and borderline personality disorder was treated for 1 year with psychoanalytic psychotherapy and compared to another patient with the same conditions who received no treatment, as well as with 10 normal controls. Pre- and posttreatment SPECT scans demonstrated normalization of serotonin uptake in the prefrontal cortex and thalamus of the treated patient but not in the untreated subject.

Although not an imaging study, it is worth mentioning work done by Russell Joffe in which he treated 30 mildly depressed people with 20 weeks of cognitive therapy (CT), 17 of whom responded to treatment. Blood was drawn from the subjects before and after treatment, and assayed for concentrations of thyroid hormone. Prior studies have shown that thyroid hormone, a general regulator of the body's metabolic activity, is elevated in many people with depression, and tends to normalize after effective treatment with antidepressant medicines. Joffe found that thyroid hormone levels came down in CT treatment responders, but not in nonresponders. Although the implications of abnormal thyroid function is unclear as it relates to depression and its treatment, this study provides another piece of evidence that psychotherapy resembles medication treatment in terms of biological changes that follow effective treatment.

From these very preliminary studies we may conclude that there is little neurobiological evidence of differential antidepressant medicine–psychotherapy treatment effects, suggesting that a unitary pathway for relieving depressive symptoms might exist, shared by antidepressant medicines and psychotherapy. Yet even if there is, on some level, a common biological antidepressant mechanism, that possibility does not help us to decide which treatment might best help a given patient. Biological markers that predict response to one treatment or another could help the patient and clinician rationally choose the most promising treatment. Better understanding of the involved pathways may also provide a biological basis for synergistic antidepressant–psychotherapy combinations, analogous to the strategy commonly used in anticancer chemotherapy in which drugs are combined that attack a common biochemical pathway at different steps in the sequence.

2. Sleep Studies

Sleep studies have been used to identify just such a marker. Michael Thase and others at the University of Pittsburgh performed three studies of almost 300 depressed people treated with either antidepressant medication or psychotherapy (CBT in the first study; IPT in the subsequent studies). Prior to treatment, subjects underwent a sleep electroencephalogram (sleep EEG, or polysomnography). This test uses measurements of the brain's electrical activity to characterize a subject's sleep, in terms of the amount of actual sleep and the relative normalcy of the pattern of sleep stages. The investigators found that people with abnormal sleep profiles responded less well to CBT, and had a higher recurrence rate. Interestingly, the sleep EEG did not predict response to medication.

3. A Cellular Mechanism of Antidepressant Treatment

Hypotheses concerning the cellular mechanisms of effective psychotherapy are entirely conjectural at this time. However, the mechanisms of antidepressant medication action are being elucidated, and may offer us testable hypotheses about the mechanisms of action for psychotherapy.

Ronald Duman and colleagues at Yale University have studied the biology of mood disorders as well as possible cellular mechanisms of antidepressant treatments. Chronic administration of four different classes of antidepressant drugs and electroconvulsive shock increased levels of brain-derived neurotrophic factor (BDNF)—a chemical inside of the nerve cell that indirectly turns on gene transcription, and inhibits cell death pathways—in the hippocampus of unstressed rats. Furthermore, the antidepressant treatment blocked the expected downregulation of that chemical in response to stress. They concluded that antidepressant treatments might work by enhancing neural plasticity and supporting neogenesis and neuronal survival. Although this offers a hypothetical cellular mechanism of action for antidepressant treatments, it also raises the intriguing prospect, albeit conjectural at this time, that psychotherapy may act in a similar fashion. Duman hypothesized that depression (and possibly other psychiatric conditions) may result from a failure of neural plasticity in various brain regions, particularly the hippocampus and prefrontal cortex. Might effective antidepressant therapies, somatic or psychotherapeutic, act by restoring normal neural plasticity?

E. Posttraumatic Stress Disorder

Human history quickly dispels any notion that tragedy and trauma can ever become infrequent occurrences. Despite the best of societal intentions, wars rage, terror menaces, and trusted caregivers violate. Trauma survivors persevere in states ranging from health to mental debilitation. PTSD is a potential consequence of trauma that renders its victim chronically anxious and phobic, prone to awful reexperiencing episodes, avoidance behavior, and a range of behavioral, cognitive, and affective symptoms.

Our earlier discussion of the biology of stress is highly relevant to the study of PTSD. Douglas Bremner at Yale University has studied the biology of PTSD in combat veterans and victims of domestic violence. He and others have concluded that PTSD is associated with hippocampal defects that may result from the deleterious effects of stress-induced glucocorticoid exposure. Bremner showed that combat veterans had hippocampal volumes 8% smaller than control subjects. He also found that memory deficits correlated with hippocampal volume reduction. Later studies with abuse victims showed hippocampal volume reductions of 12 to 16% in people with abuse-related PTSD compared to abuse victims who did not develop PTSD. The age of traumatization (stage of development) may influence the nature of the memory deficits and hippocampal atrophy. For example, imaging studies of children who were maltreated demonstrate smaller hippocampal volumes than children who were not abused. Because of its central involvement in multiple memory- and stress-related functions, the hippocampus may also provide an anatomical explanation for the fragmented or delayed recall of highly stressful or traumatic memories.

Lisa Shin and Scott Rauch at Harvard University examined 14 Vietnam combat veterans, 7 with PTSD and 7 without, using PET. The subjects viewed pictures with various themes (emotionally neutral Vietnam-unrelated themes; emotionally negative Vietnam-unrelated themes; and emotionally negative Vietnam-combat-related themes). The PTSD subjects showed increased blood flow in the anterior cingulate gyrus and right amygdala when they were exposed to combat-related stimuli. They also had decreased blood flow in an important language area of the brain (Broca's area), which the authors conjectured "may be consistent with diminished linguistic processing while subjects with PTSD viewed and evaluated combat pictures." The subjects without PTSD did not show these changes.

Chris Brewin at the University College London has posited a novel "dual representation" theory of memory that he extends to understand PTSD and its behavioral treatment. He postulates the presence of two memory systems, which he terms verbally accessible memory (VAM) and strategically accessible memory (SAM). VAM relates to ordinary autobiographical information. Memories stored in the VAM system can interact with the rest of autobiographical memory base, and deliberate retrieval is straightforward. On the other hand, SAM is characterized by the processing of information from "lower level perceptual processing of the traumatic scene and of bodily response to it." Perceptions stored as SAM memory undergo less initial conscious processing, and such memories (that may take the form of "flashbacks") are more detailed and affect-laden.

Brewin extends this construct to psychotherapy, asserting that "therapy assists in the construction over time of detailed, consciously accessible memories in the VAM system which are then able to exert inhibitory control over amygdala activation." The therapy process creates new representations of critical retrieval cues stored in the VAM system. The new, verbally processed, trauma-related cues are identified as belonging to a specific past event that does not now constitute an ongoing threat ("that was then, this is now"). Initially, memories in the SAM and VAM systems compete when the patient is confronted with trauma reminder. VAM may be given a retrieval advantage if treatment strategies are used to "make the new representation highly distinctive," which may lead to encoding effects that improve memory retrieval. Brewin hypothesizes that EMDR may do just that: the EMDR cue (therapist's finger, for instance) encodes a very distinctive attribute to the new VAM representation. "Imaginal reconstructions" (i.e., deliberate fantasies about acting differently in the trauma) may also lend a distinctive cue to the new representations. His hypothesis, while intriguing, awaits experimental validation.

F. Obsessive–Compulsive Disorder

Perhaps no mental disorder has so represented each of the conceptual poles of the psychological–biological dichotomy as obsessive–compulsive disorder (OCD). Only a few years ago OCD was considered the classic psychological disorder, requiring the rigorous application of psychoanalytic psychotherapy. In recent years it has been conceptually transformed into the prototype of a "biological" malady that can only be truly relieved with serotonin-elevating drugs, with or without the aid of adjunctive behavioral or cognitive psychotherapy. However, as we learn more about OCD, and pay heed to the robust therapeutic potency of psychotherapy or pharmacotherapy monotherapy (as well as combinations), both models are revealed to be simplistic distortions of a complex environment–genetic interactive phenomenon (as we believe to be the case with the great majority of mental disturbances). Much research has been accomplished regarding the biology of OCD. We will concentrate on evidence for biologic change in response to psychotherapy.

Lewis Baxter and Jeffrey Schwartz at UCLA have published results from several experiments involving PET imaging of people treated for OCD. In their first study, they treated nine OCD sufferers with behavior therapy (BT) and nine with an SSRI antidepressant, fluoxetine (Prozac^{R}). Similar proportions from each group responded to treatment (6 of 9 BT, 7 of 9 fluoxetine). The responders' pre- and posttreatment PET images showed the same change, specifically a reduction in the metabolic activity of a part of the striatum called the caudate nucleus. They later treated nine more OCD patients with structured exposure and response-prevention behavioral and cognitive treatment. Again, PET scans showed a reduction in the metabolic activity in the caudate of responders, but not nonresponders. The shared ability of BT and SSRIs to reduce OCD symptoms may be partially explained by studies on classical conditioning in dogs. Injecting serotonin into the anterior limbic cortex of low-serotonin dogs decreases the effects of classical conditioning. Furthermore, high levels of conditioned and unconditioned reflexes in dogs are accompanied by low levels of serotonin in the blood. During exposure treatment, one tries to extinguish pathological, classically conditioned responses.

Baxter, Schwartz, and Arthur Brody conducted another study to attempt to identify a PET marker that might differentially predict response to BT or fluoxetine. They treated 27 OCD sufferers, 18 with BT and 9 with fluoxetine. Remarkably, the degree of pretreatment activity in a part of the left frontal lobe called the orbitofrontal cortex (LOFC) appeared to differentially predict response to the two treatments. Higher pretreatment activity in the LOFC was associated with a better response to BT, whereas lower LOFC activity was associated with response to fluoxetine. The investigators postulated that this effect can be explained by considering two of the (many) functions of LOFC. Specifically, the LOCF appears to (1) mediate behavioral responses to situations in which the affective value of a stimulus changes, and (2) mediate extinction. The authors pointed out that successful behavior therapy leads to a change in the affective value assigned to stimuli that had previously brought on compulsions. Subjects with higher pretreatment LOCF activity may possess a greater capacity to "change the assignment of affective value to stimuli and be better able to extinguish habitual, compulsive responses. These abilities may lead to a better response to BT." This represented the first study in which a single biological marker provided an explicit guide to differntial treatment planning.

G. Psychotherapy and Cancer

The study of the biology (and effectiveness) of psychotherapy need not be limited to psychiatric diseases. Fawzy I. Fawzy examined the outcomes of 80 people with malignant melanoma, an aggressive skin cancer with high mortality rate, who were treated at the John Wayne Cancer Clinic at UCLA. Some of the patients were enrolled in a 6-week supportive therapy group that provided education, stress management, enhancement of coping skills, and psychological support from group members and staff. The investigators compared the 6-year survival of the group-treated subjects and subjects who did not participate in the group. A significantly greater proportion of the group-treated patients were alive after 5 years than those who did not receive group therapy. Group-treated subjects also showed a trend toward lower recurrence rates.

David Spiegel studied 86 women with metastatic breast cancer. Fifty of the women participated in 1 year of weekly supportive group therapy, while 36 women did not. Because of the advanced stages of breast cancer in all subjects, most women (83 of 86) died within 10 years of participation. However, the mean survival time in the women who had group therapy was 36.6 months, whereas the control group lived for an average of 18.9 months.

Clearly, psychosocial factors influence the outcome of many (if not all) general medical illnesses. The mechanisms of this interaction deserve the attention of neuroscientists and psychotherapists alike.

V. CONCLUSIONS

We have sufficient evidence, some of which has been presented in this article, to reach certain neurobiological conclusions related to psychotherapy:

1. Psychotherapy is a powerful tool that produces functional and/or structural changes in our patients' brains.
2. These changes tend to reflect a relative normalization of the biological anomalies characteristically associated with the underlying illness.
3. Psychotherapy-induced changes occur in a variety of brain regions, including those involved in learning and memory.

4. Psychotherapy may exert its effects through the cellular mechanisms related to learning and memory, namely neural plasticity and possibly neurogenesis.
5. Psychotherapy may promote neural plasticity by inhibiting the cellular effects of stress.
6. Genetic diversity among individuals almost certainly contributes to the remarkable range of individual responses to stress, traumatic and nontraumatic life events, and to treatment.

Present knowledge and research tools (most notably brain imaging techniques) enable us to propose myriad testable hypotheses pertaining to psychotherapy and related topics. For instance, how is the interaction between implicit and explicit memory processes influenced or utilized by psychotherapy? Details about this interaction might guide the design of specific psychotherapeutic interventions.

Studies of stress and trauma raise many critically important issues. It is quite foreseeable that psychotherapy might be used to protect the brain from the deleterious effects of stress. Identification of the environmental conditions that are most likely to produce "toxic stress" (traumatic and subtraumatic) can facilitate that eventuality. As we clarify the interactions between genes and the environment, we may be able to identify genetically at-risk individuals to whom we could target our preventive approaches. Used in that manner, psychotherapy might reduce the likelihood of symptomatic mental illness (new onset or recurrence) during or following times of stress. It is worth noting that recent evidence indicates that critical incident stress debriefing (CISD) may not be as effective as we had thought in reducing the incidence of posttraumatic psychopathology in people who have recently experienced traumatic events. Thus, effective prophylactic psychotherapies must be as carefully tailored, delivered, and validated as therapies for existing mental disturbances.

Another important consideration involves the refinement of psychotherapies to best address specific mental diagnoses or symptoms. The scientific basis for selecting one psychotherapy over another is still weak, relying, at best, on empirical evidence that a particular type of therapy did or did not work in a particular sample population. A time may come when we will be able to rationally design optimal psychotherapy based on the neurobiology of the mental disease and the proposed treatment. On a related note, we hope that Cloninger's theories of personality development (or similar work) will be refined in a way that might also guide specific psychotherapeutic strategies.

Research described earlier in this article involving sleep EEG (in depression) and PET (in OCD) provides a tantalizing glimpse at the potential of diagnostic tools to identify predictors of treatment response. Brain imaging methods, HPA axis parameters, and other biological markers may someday offer accurate and practical ways to monitor progress in psychotherapy.

Substantial advancement in the effectiveness of combined psychotherapy and pharmacotherapy will certainly require additional research. Important questions concerning strategies for optimizing combined treatment abound. Ideally, combined therapies would offer synergistic, rather than redundant or even antagonistic mechanisms of action.

Do different psychotherapies act on different parts of the brain? Some have suggested that psychoanalytically oriented psychotherapy may have greater influence on the lateral hemispheres since this type of treatment focuses on internal representation and expectations of others. In contrast, behavioral therapy often focuses on simpler forms of learning and memory that may involve more directly the amygdala, hippocampus, and basal ganglia.

The healing professions have long paid insincere homage to the biopsychosocial model of human cognition, emotion, health, illness, and behavior. A true integration of biology and psychology into a coherent conceptual framework, subscribed to by medical and nonmedical clinicians and researchers, is essential if we hope to take full advantage of the remarkable healing power of psychotherapy and move from a reductionistic mind–brain dichotomy in understanding our patients in health and illness.

See Also the Following Articles

Biofeedback ■ Collaborative Care ■ Comorbidity ■ Neuropsychological Assessment ■ Organic Brain Syndrome ■ Psychopharmacology: Combined Treatment

Further Reading

Charney, D. S., Nestler, E. J., & Bunney, B. S. (1999). *Neurobiology of mental illness.* New York: Oxford University Press. For information about the biology of mood disorders, see in particular chapters 23 and 31.

Cloninger, C. R. (1993). A psychobiological model of temperament and character. *Archives of General Psychiatry, 50,* 975–990.

Gabbard, G. O. (2000). A neurobiologically informed perspective on psychotherapy. *British Journal of Psychiatry, 177,* 117–122.

Kandel, E. R., Schwartz, J. H., & Jessell, T. M. (Eds.). (2000). *Principles of neural science* (4th ed.). New York: McGraw-Hill.

LeDoux, J. (1996). *The emotional brain: The mysterious underpinnings of emotional life.* New York: Simon & Schuster.

Liggan, D. Y., & Kay, J. (1999). Some neurobiological aspects of psychotherapy. A review. *Journal of Psychotherapy Practice and Research, 8,* 103–114.

Pally, R. (1997). Consciousness: A neuroscience perspective. *International Journal of Psycho-Analysis, 79,* 971–989.

Reiman, E. M. (1997). The application of positron emission tomography to the study of normal and pathologic emotions. *Journal of Clinical Psychiatry, 58*(Suppl. 16), 4–12.

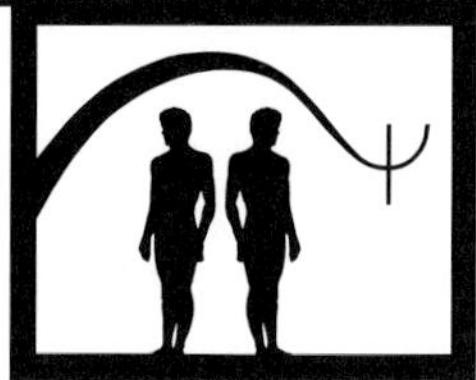

Neuropsychological Assessment

Linda Laatsch
University of Illinois College of Medicine at Chicago

GLOSSARY

dominant hemisphere The hemisphere of the brain dominant for language functioning.

frontal/prefrontal lobe The area of the brain anterior (in front of) the precentral gyrus.

intelligence Measures of overall capacity to process external and internal stimuli.

neuroimaging tools Nuclear medicine tools used to picture the functional and structural components of the brain in a systematic manner.

neuropsychological assessment (NPA) Systematic evaluation of the brain-behavior relationships in an individual.

neuropsychologist Clinician with specialized training in neuropsychology and involved in neuropsychological assessment.

normative sample Sample from population of interest with no known neurological impairments.

pathognomonic approach Use of a variety of measures that are designed to identify symptoms associated with characteristics of a particular disease.

premorbid ability Abilities prior to the neurologic event resulting in brain injury.

referral question The question for which the client was referred for the evaluation.

I. DESCRIPTION OF ASSESSMENT

Neuropsychological assessment (NPA) is the systematic evaluation of the brain–behavior relationships in an individual. The purpose of an NPA is to define the client's specific cognitive strengths and weaknesses and to identify the relationships between the neuropsychological findings and the client's medical and psychiatric condition. Tools used to complete the NPA are measures of cognition and intelligence that have been standardized on a neurologically normal sample. By administering the measures in the identical, systematic manner, as described in the instruction manual for the testing instrument, the evaluator can compare the individual's performance on the measure to the performance of a normative sample. It is optimal if the normative sample is subdivided by gender, age, and years of education. In that way a very specific comparison can be made. Neuropsychological test performance has been generally shown to vary according to gender, age, and years of education in control samples.

Localization of brain injury was the intent of neuropsychological testing in the 1970s but with current functional and structural neuroimaging tools, there is a reduction in the need to "localize" the brain injury. The purpose of neuropsychological evaluation is currently multifaceted and often is dependent on the referral question. A complete NPA helps the client, clinician, and referral source gain an understanding of the client's cognitive processes such as memory, language, and perception. In addition it can assist in diagnosis and identification of difficulties in cognition that might be related to psychiatric conditions and motivation. Finally, a thorough NPA can help to determine rehabilitation potential by identifying pathways for compensation and extent of cognitive involvement.

II. CASE ILLUSTRATION

The NPA report and raw data shown below provide an example of a case referred by a neurologist. This 55-year-old man was referred because, during a standard mental status evaluation, visual perceptual problems were observed.

A. Neuropsychological Testing Report

1. Relevant Past History

Dr. C is a right-handed, 55-year-old, Caucasian male, previously employed as an optometrist. Dr. C reported that he first noticed changes in his cognition while on an out-of-town visit. He became disoriented and he reported that he got lost for many hours while driving to a known location. He reported that he is happily married and has two children who have been very successful in their own vocations. Both his mother and father are deceased. His father died recently from a series of illnesses, including a bowel obstruction and pneumonia. His mother died in 1985 of Alzheimer's disease. Dr. C reported a recent fall from a horse while on a vacation, but he denied receiving a head injury from it, only reporting minor bruises. He also reported that last summer he was camping and his dog was exposed to ticks. He is concerned that the current problems that he is having may be related to Lyme disease. Dr. C denied other significant stressors in his life and continues to remain active, playing tennis regularly. He is on no medications.

2. Behavior During Evaluation

Dr. C arrived late for the interview because he was unable to find the location of the room. He was very guarded during the initial interview and overtly frustrated during some of the more difficult portions of the evaluation. Mood was observed to be slightly depressed but toward the end the session Dr. C was able to talk more freely and seemed to become more relaxed. His attention and effort were adequate and the current evaluation is thought to be an accurate measure of his current abilities.

3. Tests Administered

Tests administered included the Wechsler Adult Intelligence Test-R, Wechsler Memory Scale-R, Wide Range Achievement Test (Reading subtest), Stroop, Trails A & B, and the Adaptive Category Test.

4. Results of the Evaluation

Dr. C's full-scale intelligence was estimated to be within the very high average range but a significant discrepancy was noted between his verbal abilities and his visual–perceptual skills (Full-Scale IQ 124, Verbal IQ 130, Performance IQ 110). Dr. C demonstrated an exceptional vocabulary and understanding of the world around him. His speech was fluent and detailed, and no signs of expressive speech limitations were observed. When presented with visual stimuli Dr.C had difficulty identifying missing essential details within a visual percept. Dr. C also had great difficulty reproducing visual spatial designs. He was unable to segment accurately the design and work on parts to complete the whole design. Graphic motor speed was high average and he was able to copy simple figures accurately and rapidly. It is expected that, given his educational background and his vocation's emphasis on visual perception, his current visual perceptual skills represent a significant decline for him.

Speed of processing was found to be average and high average given simple material. Verbal short-term attention was average for his age. Dr. C was able to maintain seven digits in his head and present them forward. When asked to recall the numbers in reverse order, he was only able to recall four digits. Simple reading speed was average. In addition, Dr. C was able to keep a strategy in mind while he quickly read given words. When asked to scan for specific numbers and letters Dr. C demonstrated greater difficulty and he was unable to accurately alternate between number and letters. His performance on a difficult task requiring sustained attention and visual scanning with interference was significantly impaired.

Memory abilities were also variable and his pattern of performance is reflective of his memory complaints. Verbal memory skills are within the high average to superior range given his age. He was able to recall lengthy stories (98th percentile and 92nd percentile) immediately after presentation and again report the stories 20 minutes later accurately. He was also able to rapidly learn pairs of words. Dr. C had more difficulty recalling visual material presented. He was unable to encode essential details of the visual stimuli and his recall of the given visual designs was between the 25th percentile and 33rd percentile. Once he had learned the material, Dr. C was able to accurately reproduce the visual information even given a significant delay. His visual memory impairments are most likely related to his recent difficulty getting lost when not using a map. In addition, his memory is hampered by his difficulty identifying essential details and visual–spatial relationships in abstract visual percepts.

The complex visual problem-solving task administered on the computer was also difficult for Dr. C. He was inefficient in his ability to develop effective problem-solving strategies to apply to the sets of figures presented. He demonstrated difficulty planning and tended to act impulsively in response to the presented stimuli. This task was frustrating for him and his performance was severely impaired. Dr. C demonstrated excellent verbal abstraction abilities when he was given uncommon proverbs as part of the intelligence test.

Dr. C was administered the Symptom Checklist 90-R and denied all types of psychiatric symptoms. On this survey form, he did not acknowledge difficulty in thinking or a change in his appetite even though he had recently gained 65 pounds. His response pattern on the checklist and during the interview indicates that Dr. C is unable to fully acknowledge the significance of his cognitive changes. When his difficulties were pointed out, Dr. C had a tendency to use his excellent verbal skills to externalize the existing problem.

5. *Summary*

Dr. C has experienced significant neuropsychological changes that involve moderate visual–perceptual and visual–spatial impairments, moderate visual memory limitations, and moderate impairments in problem solving. In contrast, Dr. C continued to demonstrate exceptional verbal skills and verbal memory. Dr. C denied problems with mood or the recent occurrence of psychiatric symptoms.

Because of the importance of memory and visual-perceptual abilities in his work, it is not recommended that Dr. C return to his current job. It is recommended that Dr. C consider cognitive rehabilitation therapy to help him learn to compensate for his current limitations. In rehabilitation there will be an attempt to help him learn to use his verbal skills to compensate for his visual memory limitations. Because Dr. C displayed limited insight regarding his difficulties, his family will need to be involved in helping him learn to use compensation strategies. Supportive psychotherapy for himself and family members is also recommended.

Dr. C meets the criteria of dementia because of a decline in visual memory and problem solving. It is suspected that Dr. C is experiencing degeneration in both the right temporal and frontal lobes. This may be associated with frontal-temporal dementia. Repeated testing in 6 months will determine if the condition is progressive.

TABLE I
Neuropsychological Testing Scores

Wechsler Adult Intelligence Test-R

Verbal Tests		Performance Tests	
Information	15	Picture Completion	8
Digit Span	10	Picture Arrangement	9
Vocabulary	16	Block Design	7
Arithmetic	14	Object Assembly	9
Comprehension	15	Digit Symbol	13
Similarities	14		

Verbal IQ = 130 Performance IQ = 110 Full-Scale IQ = 124

Trail Making A: T = 38 *Trail Making B:* T = 36

Stroop Word T = 57, Color T = 55,
Color Word Interference T = 57

Wechsler Memory Scale-R

Logical Memory I	98th percentile
Logical Memory II	92nd percentile
Visual Reproduction I	25%
Visual Reproduction II	33%

Symptom Checklist 90-R
All 90 questions responded with "0" score.

Adaptive Category Test
Total Adaptive Error Score = 122

III. THEORETICAL BASES

Russia was one of the first countries in the world to begin NPA. In the early 1900s, A.R. Luria used a flexible, clinical evaluation approach in his work with patients who had brain injury. His model of brain functioning, published in English in 1970, outlined "three principal functional units of the brain ... a unit for regulating tone or waking, a unit for obtaining, processing and storing information ..., a unit for programming, regulating and verifying mental activity." Luria defines the purpose of NPA as being twofold: "to pinpoint brain lesions responsible for specific behavior disorders ... provide us with a factor analysis that will lead to better understanding of components of complex psychological functions" (p. 66).

In the United States in 1986 Donald T. Stuss and Frank Benson provided a behavioral anatomical theory of brain functioning to guide NPA. They stressed the global influence of the frontal/prefrontal lobe on mental activity. In their theory, executive functioning attributed to the frontal/prefrontal lobes of the brain provides conscious direction and efficient processing of internal and external stimuli. The second unit of the brain is associated with the posterior region of the brain and involves attention, visual–spatial processing, language, sensory perception, memory, motor, and emotional status. In their theory they create a hierarchy of brain functioning and they identify *self-awareness* as the highest cognitive attribute of the frontal lobes. Although many individual mental functions, assessed by neuropsychological tests, can be maintained without prefrontal and frontal participation, the responses are automatic and insight and planning are lacking. Adequate frontal/prefrontal functioning is essential for control of intelligence, consciousness of self, and independent thinking.

It has not been possible for neuropsychologists to develop specific measures that are 100% diagnostic of any type of brain injury. Instead most neuropsychologists now use a pathognomonic approach. This approach involves the use of a variety of measures that are designed to identify symptoms associated with characteristics of a particular disease. In the United States most neuropsychologists use a flexible battery approach. Instead of using standardized test battery in its entirety, a selection of tests from a variety of batteries and separate, individual tests are utilized. Standardized batteries that have been developed over the years are the Luria-Nebraska Neuropsychological Battery and the Halstead-Reitan Neuropsychological Battery. A flexible battery approach allows the clinician to match the referral question and the examinee's pattern of abilities to the test battery. It is the aim of the neuropsychologist to understand the reason for the evaluation, the questions being presented by the individual being evaluated, and the functional implications of the symptoms in making decisions concerning the assessment tools to be used in the evaluation. Although NPA batteries may differ, generally, a core set of assessment tools are used in each case. This core is included because the psychologist is most familiar with these assessment tools, understands the cognitive component skills that are part of the measure, and has appropriate normative data available. Flexibility in the NPA derives from the needs of the individual being evaluated. Clinical neuropsychologists regularly address a large range of referral questions, clinical behaviors, and patients with very disparate capacities. So although there is an overall structure to the NPA, there is significant diversity in the details of each NPA.

Generally a measure of intelligence is administered as part of the NPA battery. By administering a measure of overall general abilities such as an intelligence test, the clinician can compare overall level of functioning to specific cognitive skills such as memory, attention, and problem solving. Examination of the subtests may also provide clues to premorbid functioning. Most NPA batteries also include measures of expressive and receptive language, visual perception, visual scanning, and visual–spatial processing. A variety of measures of attention and memory are commonly included. Finally tests of executive processing such as problem solving are administered. Also included in an NPA will be at least a basic measure of emotional or psychiatric status. Because depression and anxiety can influence cognitive abilities, a measure of psychiatric symptoms needs to be administered to determine if there is an emotional component to the client's current cognitive status.

The battery of tests will generally be preceded by a clinical interview. Background information concerning the client's social history, present life circumstances, medical history and current medical complaints, and reasons for referral are obtained.

Information regarding social and medical history, psychiatric history, drug and alcohol abuse history, neurotoxin exposure, history of head injury, a list of current medications, family psychiatric and dementia history, and client's social, employment, and educational history should be obtained because these factors can influence test interpretation. The NPA will include an observation of the client's general appearance, ambulation, sensory limitations, and behavior. In an NPA the examiner needs to observe attention, distractibility, and motivation on all tests administered.

The entire test battery may require anywhere from a few hours to a day or two to complete, depending on the client's attention and stamina.

IV. APPLICATIONS AND EXCLUSIONS

NPA is most often not attempted in children younger than the age of 4 years. Normative data are available for the geriatric population on a select number of neuropsychological tests. Therefore, NPA is possible in individuals between the ages of 5 to 95 years.

Currently relatively few NPA tools used in the United States have been translated to languages other than English. The Wechsler Intelligence tests for children and adults are available in Spanish. Since the intelligence tests are some of few tests translated and normed for Spanish-speaking individuals, full NPA often takes place using informally translated NPA tools. It is very important to consider ethnic variations in administering NPA tools to individuals outside the normative sample on which standardization took place. Fortunately, many countries have developed NPA tools within their own culture.

NPAs vary extensively in length. Length of the testing will vary depending on the referral question, finances of the individual being evaluated, and complexity of the presenting symptoms or neurological condition. Therefore, testing is limited to individuals able to tolerate the interpersonal and lengthy testing situation. NPA is managed by a clinical psychologist trained in NPA but in many environments a student in clinical psychology or a testing technician may give some of the assessment tools. Because the assessment tools used in NPA are standardized in their administration, students and technicians can be trained to administer many of the tests. Close supervision is essential because the clinical neuropsychologist needs to be available if problems arise and to ensure that the tests are administered in the standardized manner.

As can be surmised, a psychologist involved in NPA needs to have extensive expertise. Generally specific neuroscience training while in a school of clinical psychology is required. Classes concerning normal child and adult brain functioning and neuropathology (neuroanatomy and neurophysiology principles) should be part of the student's experience. The clinician completing the NPA needs to have a broad understanding of brain function and its neuroanatomical correlates. Clinical experience in assessment of both neurologically normal and impaired individuals needs to be extensive. Given the complexity of each examinee's cognition and emotional status at the time of the evaluation, every NPA completed offers new learning experiences to the student in training. Currently graduating clinical psychologists are asked to continue their supervised experience for 2 years after completing an internship specializing in neuropsychology. This further training is called postdoctoral training in neuropsychology. The division of neuropsychology within the American Psychological Association offers these specialized training opportunities.

V. EMPIRICAL STUDIES

In 1981 Heaton and Pendleton completed one of the earliest studies of the predictive abilities of neuropsychological testing on everyday function. They reviewed the relationship between neuropsychological testing results and various aspects of everyday life: self-care, independent living skills, and academic and vocational achievement. They found that intelligence tests scores relate to the clients' ability to care for themselves and their understanding of everyday routine situations. The Category Test from the Halstead-Reitan battery was related to judgment and decision making in routine daily activities. Memory measures were related to learning capacity and forgetfulness in everyday functioning.

There is a continuing need for neuropsychologists to effectively address functional questions after the neurologic diagnosis has been established. Central to the success of NPA is its ability to present useful and valid information regarding issues for everyday living. Neuropsychologists, using the NPA, need to be able to identify the client's individual cognitive strengths and deficits. It is especially important for the NPA to identify residual strengths that can be used to improve everyday functioning within work and home situations. NPA should address the client's ability to function safely and efficently within an existing or new work environment, assess ability to perform adequately in school, and determine whether the client is able to remain at home without supervision. These are just a few of the many question needing to be addressed in a thorough NPA.

VI. SUMMARY

NPA is an applied science involving systematic measurement of brain–behavior relationships. It involves the complete and detailed assessment of behavioral expression of brain dysfunction. It is generally a lengthy process involving a clinical interview, a flexible battery of standardized cognitive measures, and measures of psychological functioning. The time and effort required of the client is compensated by the clinical neuropsychologist's careful consideration of questions concerning cognitive strengths and weaknesses, rehabilitation strategies, work and educational potential, and safety within home and outside environment.

See Also the Following Articles

Behavioral Assessment ■ Collaborative Care ■ Comorbidity ■ Formulation ■ Medically Ill Patient: Psychotherapy ■ Neurobiology ■ Projective Testing in Psychotherapy ■ Trauma Management Therapy

Further Reading

Heaton, R. K., & Pendleton, M. G. (1981). Use of neuropsychological tests to predict adult patients' everyday functioning. *Journal of Consulting Clinical Psychology, 49,* 807.

Lezak, M. D. (1995). *Neuropsychological assessment,* 3rd ed. New York: Oxford University Press.

Luria, A. R. (1983). *The working brain.* New York: Penguin Books.

Stuss, D. T., & Benson, D. F. (1986). *The frontal lobes.* New York: Raven Press.

Walsh, K., & Darby, D. (1999). *Neuropsychology: A clinical approach.* Edinburgh: Churchill Livingston.

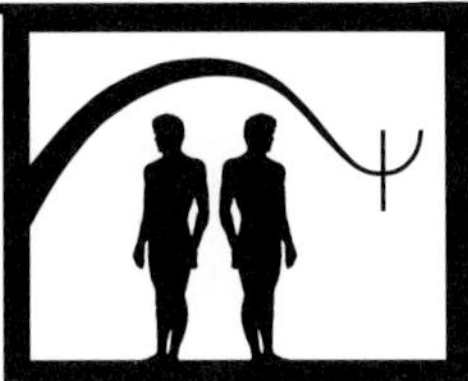

Nocturnal Enuresis: Treatment

Henry S. Roane, Cathleen C. Piazza, and Mary A. Mich

The Marcus and Kennedy Krieger Institutes and the Johns Hopkins University School of Medicine

GLOSSARY

classical conditioning Learning that occurs when a response is elicited by a particular stimulus. This process occurs when a previously neutral stimulus (e.g., a tone) occurs in conjunction with another (unconditioned) stimulus (e.g., food presentation) that results in a unconditioned response (e.g., salivation). Over repeated pairings, the neutral stimulus obtains the properties of the unconditioned stimulus and elicits the same response. The neutral stimulus is then referred to as the conditioned stimulus and the response is referred to as the conditioned response. Also known as Pavlovian conditioning.

dry bed training An intensive treatment for nocturnal enuresis that involves a combination of procedures, including urine alarm, retention training, and practice of correct toilet skills.

negative reinforcement Form of operant conditioning that occurs when a behavior is immediately followed by the removal of a stimulus that results in an increase in the future likelihood of the behavior.

nocturnal enuresis Repeated voiding of urine in one's bed or clothing at night that is inappropriate at a given age (5 years). Can be classified as primary (child has never been continent) or secondary (child previously has been continent). Also referred to as bedwetting.

operant conditioning Learning that occurs based on the consequences that follow a response. This process occurs when a behavior is emitted and the resulting consequences either increases or decreases the likelihood of the behavior occurring in the future.

positive reinforcement Form of operant conditioning that occurs when a behavior is immediately followed by the presentation of a stimulus that results in an increase in the future likelihood of the behavior.

punishment Form of operant conditioning that occurs when a behavior is immediately followed by a consequence such that there is a decrease in the future likelihood of the behavior.

retention training Treatment involving a gradual increase in bladder capacity by delaying urination for successively longer periods of time.

urine alarm Common treatment for nocturnal enuresis involving a pad placed on the child's bed and an alarm that is activated when the child urinates. Also known as the "bell-and-pad" treatment.

I. INTRODUCTION

Enuresis, the repeated voiding of urine into one's bed or clothing, is a fairly common childhood behavior problem. Based on the criteria described in the *Diagnostic and Statistical Manual, Fourth Edition*, a diagnosis of enuresis is appropriate if incontinent voiding has occurred for a minimum period of 3 months, and the child must be at an age where appropriate continence is expected (i.e., 5 years). The diagnosis of enuresis is divided into three types: diurnal, nocturnal, and combined, with the most frequently diagnosed type being nocturnal enuresis. Because of the frequency of the diagnosis, the majority of this article focuses on nocturnal enuresis.

As implied by the name, nocturnal enuresis refers to incontinent urination at nighttime. More commonly, the behavior is referred to as "bedwetting." Nocturnal enuresis can be classified as either primary or secondary, depending on the child's history of continence. If the child has never been continent, primary enuresis is diagnosed; conversely, secondary enuresis is diagnosed if the child previously has experienced a period of continence.

Nocturnal enuresis is a relatively common childhood problem. Prevalence estimates for the disorder vary widely; however, the occurrence of the behavior tends to decrease with age such that approximately 20% of 5-year-olds display the behavior compared to 10% of 10 year-olds. In addition to the variation with age, the prevalence of nocturnal enuresis varies with gender with an approximate 3:2 male to female ratio. Enuretic children often have an immediate family member who also displayed bedwetting. As noted by Shaffer this relationship is poorly understood. That is, it is unknown if this relationship is genetic in origin or if the families of enuretic children are more permissive in their views of the behavior (i.e., parents who displayed enuresis are more accepting of its occurrence).

Several hypotheses have been reviewed regarding the development of enuresis. A psychodynamic hypothesis posits that enuresis is related to the presence of an unresolved internal conflict. Psychological stressors (e.g., parental separation, poor academic performance) might also be related to the occurrence of enuresis. Some researchers have hypothesized that enuretic children have smaller bladder capacities than their nonenuretic peers. Finally, in some cases, it appears that enuretic children simply have not learned correct bladder control. The latter opinion is perhaps the most tenable hypothesis given that the teaching of correct skills has been shown to lead to a decrease in enuresis and other toileting accidents.

II. DESCRIPTION OF TREATMENT

As with all childhood behavior problems, the treatment of enuresis should begin with a comprehensive medical and psychological examination. Friman and Jones described several factors to consider in the assessment of enuresis. Examples of these factors include parental beliefs about the severity of the problem, parent and child motivation to implement treatment, and the child's concerns over the bedwetting. Knowledge of these factors may predict treatment efficacy in some cases. For example, Butler, Brewin, and Forsythe found that children who are not concerned with their enuresis are more likely to demonstrate treatment relapse than children who are concerned. Finally, it is recommended that the assessment of nocturnal enuresis include data collection prior to the onset of treatment. Such baseline data will assist in identifying the frequency of the behavior as well as other dimensions of the behavior (e.g., the time at which wetting occurs). In some cases, additional assessment procedures such as direct observation may be used to develop treatment alternatives.

Following assessment, treatment development should occur in accordance with the desires and needs of the child and the caregivers. That is, treatments of enuresis may vary in terms of caregiver vigilance in implementation or the occurrence of behavioral side effects. In addition, caregivers may find certain therapies unacceptable and may be less likely to implement the procedures. Regardless of the type of intervention employed, treatment application and its effectiveness should be monitored by either the prescribing physician or psychologist.

In general, treatment of nocturnal enuresis consists of medication or behavioral intervention. Among medications, the most frequently prescribed for the treatment of enuresis are the antidepressants, particularly imiprimine. Imiprimine has been shown to produce an immediate reduction in enuresis in many cases; however, withdrawal of the medication may produce a relapse in treatment in over 60% of cases as well as behavioral side effects (e.g., nausea, drowsiness). In addition, the use of imiprimine and other medications does not teach the child appropriate toileting skills.

Behavioral interventions have been the focus of many empirical investigations and have been demonstrated to be effective in reducing nocturnal enuresis. Thus, the remainder of this article summarizes the procedures and empirical support for the use of behavioral interventions in the treatment of nocturnal enuresis.

III. THEORETICAL BASES

Some research suggests that the occurrence of enuresis may be due to the improper learning of bladder retention and toileting skills. Thus, interventions that teach new skills (i.e., behavioral interventions) generally are more effective than pharmacological interventions. Various behavioral interventions have been described in the extant literature, with the most commonly employed procedures consisting of the urine alarm, bladder retention training, and dry bed training.

In general, the effectiveness of the various behavioral interventions has been attributed to both classical and operant conditioning. For example, it was initially hypothesized that classical conditioning was responsible for behavior change when using a urine alarm. That is, the alarm was conceptualized as the unconditioned stimulus, passing of urine was the condition stimulus, and waking was the conditioned response. More recently, an operant hypothesis has been used to interpret the learning mechanism that occurs with the urine alarm. Specifically, the alarm is an aversive stimulus and a full bladder or urine release is a stimulus associated with the activation of the alarm. The child awakens when the bladder is full and urinates in the toilet to avoid the activation of the alarm. Successful avoidance of the alarm increases the future likelihood that the child will urinate when internal cues (i.e., a full bladder) are present.

Successful retention training and dry bed training have been attributed to a combination of operant mechanisms. For example, the use of extrinsic reinforcers (contingent on bladder control) functions as positive reinforcement for bladder retention in both retention training and dry bed training. Waking and urinating in the toilet at night may function as negative reinforcement through the elimination of a full bladder and the avoidance of wet clothing and bedding. Finally, repeated practice of correct toilet skills and the changing of clothing and bed linens as a component of dry bed training may alter behavior through punishment.

IV. EMPIRICAL STUDIES

A. Urine Alarm

The urine alarm, also known as the bell-and-pad procedure, is one of the most well known and commonly used treatments for enuresis. Although there are variations of the treatment, the basic procedure is similar to that originally described by Mowrer and Mowrer. The child sleeps on a specially constructed pad covered by two foil outer shells. The top layer of the pad has holes, which are separated by an absorbent paper connected to a buzzer. The presence of urine on the absorbent paper activates an electric circuit that produces an alarm (e.g., a buzzer). Presumably, the alarm quickly awakens the child and teaches the child to associate a full bladder with awakening. The alarm may also inhibit additional urination as the bladder contracts. The child then progresses to the toilet and finishes urinating.

To produce maximum treatment effects, several manipulations should occur prior to the child's going to bed and following activation of the alarm. Before going to bed, the child should drink extra amounts of fluid. The buildup of fluid in the child's bladder throughout the night increases the probability that he or she will contact the "wetness equals alarm" contingency during the initial stages of treatment. In addition, the child should be put to bed with minimal clothing to ensure that only a small amount of urine is necessary to activate the alarm. That is, as less urine activates the alarm, the child awakens with more fluid in the bladder thus enhancing the training by teaching the child to associate a relatively full bladder with awakening. Other training procedures should be implemented following activation of the alarm. For example, if a child is clothed, he or she may be required to clean the soiled clothing or change into clean clothing. In addition, the child should be required to change the bed linens and wash the pad before going back to sleep. Finally, in an attempt to decrease the probability of relapse, an intermittent schedule of alarm activation has been effective in some cases (e.g., alarm activation on 50% of trials).

It is essential that parents become actively involved in the implementation of the treatment. For example, parents should be responsible for collecting data following each accident. Data may be collected on the frequency of accidents per night or week, the time of the accident, or the diameter of the wet spot. Such data are useful in determining minute treatment gains following repeated exposure to the alarm. In addition to data collection, parents should be responsible for reinforcing the absence of bedwetting and the occurrence of correct elimination in the toilet. For example, in our clinical practice, we often suggest that parents provide access to a highly preferred item or activity following no incontinence for a period of time (e.g., one or two nights, or one week). Toward this end, it is recommended that the supervising therapist conduct an assessment with the child and parents to identify potential reinforcing stimuli.

Training with a urine alarm is relatively brief and the results are relatively durable. In addition, the procedures implemented in urine alarm training are also easily modified for training skills in other settings. For example, one common modification involves the attachment of an alarm to a child's underwear. The alarm is connected to a pad that, when wet, sounds the alarm. Using a similar method, Edgar, Kohler, and Hardman successfully reduced the occurrence of urinary incontinence in 8 of 10 participants with profound mental retardation. More recently, Friman and Vollmer used a modified urine alarm to treat one girl's diurnal enuresis. Results showed that the use of the alarm produced an immediate reduction in enuresis; however, Friman and Vollmer noted that the participant experienced some social embarrassment on activation of the alarm.

B. Retention Control Training

It has been hypothesized that enuretic children have a smaller bladder capacity than nonenuretic children. Retention control training involves gradually increasing the bladder capacity of the child. As reviewed by Friman and Siegel and Smith, retention training involves a child drinking an amount of fluid (e.g., 8 oz.) and delaying urination for a set amount of time (e.g., 3 min) or for as long as possible after the initial urge to void. On subsequent days, the child is encouraged to refrain from urination for a longer period of time (e.g., progressing from 3 to 5 min). Successful bladder control should be reinforced through the use of extrinsic reinforcers. During the training, parents should collect data on the latency to urination after drinking and on the amount of urine emitted. Across successive days, the child holds the urine for longer periods of time, thereby increasing bladder capacity. Increasing bladder capacity within the course of a day indirectly may reduce the enuresis at night.

Retention control training does not yield as high of a success rate as does the urine alarm. However, this procedure may be preferred to the urine alarm because it does not require nighttime awakenings, and new bladder control skills are mastered.

C. Dry Bed Training

Dry bed training consists of a combination of the urine alarm and retention control training procedures. Due to the combination of these two practices, in addition to the incorporation of several other procedures, dry bed training is the most labor-intensive treatment for nocturnal enuresis. Dry bed training consists of a therapist coming into the child's home during at least the first night of treatment. In addition to the basic retention training and urine alarm procedures, Azrin and colleagues also suggested presleep practice of correct toileting skills, practice of changing clothes, and practice of changing the bed linens. That is, prior to going to bed, the child is exposed to the events that will take place should he or she wet the bed. Scheduled nighttime awakenings (e.g., once each hour) combined with prompts to go to the bathroom, checks for wetness, and additional fluids are incorporated into the treatment as well. At each waking, the child is reminded what will occur if the bed is wet. If the child appropriately urinates in the toilet when awakened, parents provide effusive praise. By contrast, if the bed is wet, the child is responsible for repeatedly practicing appropriate urination and is made responsible for cleaning all bedding and clothing. For each night without an accident, a reinforcement-based component is included such that the child receives access to a highly preferred reinforcer and praise contingent on appropriate bladder control. Using these procedures, Azrin and colleagues reported a 100% success rate in training 24 children within 7 days. It should be noted that almost 30% of the children relapsed following treatment; however, once the treatment was reimplemented, accidents decreased again. Finally, Azrin and colleagues found that the multicomponent dry bed procedure was more effective than the more commonly used urine alarm.

V. SUMMARY

In this article, several potential treatments for nocturnal enuresis were reviewed. One consistent finding in the literature is that behavioral treatments (i.e., urine alarm, retention control training, dry bed training) are generally as effective as pharmacological treatments. For these reasons, behavioral treatments represent the best practice for the treatment of nocturnal enuresis.

Initial implementation of behavioral treatments varies across children, with most children requiring several weeks of exposure before significant treatment gains are noted. Thus, the length of treatment exposure, combined with the treatment procedures that must be implemented by the parent and child, make behavioral interventions relatively labor intensive relative to medication. However, the relapse rate of children treated with behavioral interventions generally has been lower than relapse associated with medication. Finally, the focus of a medication-based treatment is the amelioration of enuresis, whereas the focus of behavioral treatment is the amelioration of enuresis plus the acquisition of appropriate replacement skills

Follow-up data suggest that behavioral treatments produce very durable effects. For example, Gustafson exposed 50 children to urine alarm treatment as described by Mowrer and Mowrer. All children were referred for the treatment of primary nocturnal enuresis, and each participant had displayed the behavior for at least 6 years. Results showed that 90% of the participants were trained successfully following one to three exposures to the treatment procedures. Furthermore, only five of the trained participants (11%) were reported to show relapse (defined as one or two wet nights) in the year following treatment. These results suggest that the use of the urine alarm is an effective and long-lasting method for treating nocturnal enuresis.

Regardless of the type of intervention used, practitioners should be aware of their patients' goals and their willingness to engage in various treatments. If caregivers find it unacceptable to awaken multiple times per night, or if they feel that certain procedures are unfair to the child, treatment with medication may be indicated. By contrast, if the child and caregivers are interested in teaching new skills with the lower probability of relapse, behavioral treatments should be prescribed.

One final consideration in treatment development should be the willingness of the caregivers or child to collect objective data on the occurrence of enuresis. Observational data can be graphed to yield a pattern of behavior that can be visually reviewed to determine the child's progress toward continence. In addition, data collection may facilitate child and caregiver implementation of a rather strenuous treatment (e.g., dry bed training) such that a visual representation of improvement may directly reinforce these behaviors.

See Also the Following Articles

Arousal Training ■ Bell-and-Pad Conditioning ■ Primary-Care Behavioral Pediatrics ■ Retention Control Training

Further Reading

American Psychiatric Association. (1994). *Diagnostic and statistical manual of mental disorders* (4th ed.). Washington, DC: Author.

Azrin, N. H., & Foxx, R. M. (1971). A rapid method for toilet training the institutionalized retarded. *Journal of Applied Behavior Analysis, 4,* 89–99.

Azrin, N. H., Sneed, T. J., & Foxx, R. M. (1974). Dry-bed: Rapid elimination of childhood enuresis. *Behavior Research and Therapy, 12,* 147–156.

Butler, R., Brewin, C., & Forsythe, I. (1990). Relapse in children treated for nocturnal enuresis: Prediction of response using pre-treatment variables. *Behavioral Psychotherapy, 18,* 65–72.

Edgar, C. L., Kohler, H. F., & Hardman, S. (1975). A new method for toilet training developmentally disabled children. *Perceptual and Motor Skills, 41,* 63–69.

Finley, W. W., Wansley, R. A., & Blenkarn, M. M. (1977). Conditioning treatment of enuresis using a 70% intermittent reinforcement schedule. *Behavior Research and Therapy, 15,* 419–427.

Fisher, W. W., Piazza, C. C., Bowman, L. G., & Amari, A. (1996). Integrating caregiver report with a systematic choice assessment to enhance reinforcer identification. *American Journal on Mental Retardation, 101,* 15–25.

Friman, P. C. (1995). Nocturnal enuresis in the child. In R. Ferber & M. H. Kryger (Eds.), *Principles and practice of sleep medicine in the child* (pp. 107–114). Philadelphia: Saunders.

Friman, P. C., & Jones, K. M. (1998). Elimination disorders in children. In S. Watson & F. Gresham (Eds.), *Handbook of child behavior therapy* (pp. 239–260). New York: Plenum.

Friman, P. C., & Vollmer, D. (1995). Successful use of the nocturnal urine alarm for diurnal enuresis. *Journal of Applied Behavior Analysis, 28,* 89–90.

Gadow, K. D., & Poling, A. G. (1988). *Pharmacotherapy and mental retardation.* Boston: College-Hill Press.

Gustafson, R. (1993). Conditioning treatment of children's bedwetting: A follow-up and predictive study. *Psychological Reports, 72,* 923–930.

Hagopian, L. P., Fisher, W. W., Piazza, C. C., & Wierzbicki, J. J. (1993). A water-prompting procedure for the treatment of urinary incontinence. *Journal of Applied Behavior Analysis, 26,* 473–474.

Luiselli, J. K. (1997). Teaching toilet skills in a public school setting to a child with pervasive developmental disorder. *Journal of Behavior Therapy and Experimental Psychiatry, 28,* 163–168.

Mark, S. D., & Frank, J. D. (1995). Nocturnal enuresis. *British Journal of Urology, 75,* 427–434.

Mowrer, O. H., & Mowrer, W. M. (1938). Enuresis: A method for its study and treatment. *American Journal of Orthopsychiatry, 8,* 436–459.

Rushton, H. G. (1993). Older pharmacologic therapy for nocturnal enuresis. *Clinical Pediatrics, 31,* 10–13.

Shaffer, D. (1985). Enuresis. In M. Rutter & L. Hersov (Eds.), *Child and adolescent psychiatry: Modern approaches* (pp. 465–481). Oxford: Blackwell.

Siegel, L. J., & Smith, K. E. (1991). Somatic disorders. In T. R. Kratochwill & R. J. Morris (Eds.), *The practice of child therapy* (pp. 222–256). Boston: Allyn and Bacon.

Starfield, B. (1967). Functional bladder capacity in enuretic and non-enuretic children. *Journal of Pediatrics, 70,* 777–782.

Object-Relations Psychotherapy

Frank Summers
Northwestern University

GLOSSARY

borderline syndrome A severe form of character pathology characterized by a high degree of instability, low frustration tolerance, impulsivity, demandingness, and little regard for others.

ego The part of the psyche charged with the responsibility of mastering competing pressures while maintaining the functional capacity of the organism.

narcissism An early state of infancy, often carried into adulthood in pathological states, in which the child is organized around the self and self-pleasures with little awareness of the desires of others.

object relation A relationship to an other seen from the viewpoint of the experiencing participant; includes both the way of relating to the other and the experience of the other in fantasy.

psychoanalytic therapy Any of a variety of psychotherapeutic approaches that seeks to uncover unconscious material and, thereby, achieve a depth understanding of the psyche.

resistance The tendency of psychotherapy patients to defend against the therapeutic process to protect against the uncovering of painful, unconscious material.

transference The unconscious tendency of psychotherapy patients to perceive the therapist in ways similar to important figures of the past, such as parents.

Object-relations psychotherapy is a growing and commonly used branch of psychoanalytic therapy. Beginning with the roots of this form of psychoanalytic therapy and its deviation from the classical model, this article shows the fundamental developmental principles on which this form of therapy is based and then demonstrates the basic concepts that define this therapeutic approach. Finally, the contributions of object-relations therapy to psychoanalytic treatment will be reviewed.

I. THE ORIGINS OF OBJECT-RELATIONS THEORY

When Sigmund Freud developed psychoanalytic theory and therapy, he did so on the basis of his view that repressed childhood memories were the source of neurotic symptoms, especially hysteria, the most prevalent form of psychopathology of his day. When he changed his view of pathogenesis from actual memories to fantasies, or wishes, he shifted psychoanalytic theory to a drive model. That is, Freud believed that the child's sexual wishes for the parent were the repressed material, rather than events. Freud's belief in the ubiquity of childhood sexual longings for the parent of the opposite sex led him to a drive-based view of human motivation. The eventual addition of the aggressive drive did not alter his view that our adult behavior manifests either repression or sublimation of our endogenous drives. These drives are biological in origin, seek satisfaction via tension relief, and have a fixed quantity of energy. The object of the drive is the means for its satisfaction. The child becomes attached to figures who provide this tension relief. Interpersonal relationships, for Freud, are motivated by tension relief. The child is born under the sway of the pleasure principle, the need for tension relief, and gradually, through the necessary frustrations of life, becomes adapted to the reality principle, the recognition that the world will not provide the gratification of drive pressures whenever and wherever the need is felt. Out of this frustration, the ego, the adaptive capacity of the organism, is born, and in the healthy personality, the ego is primarily in charge of the individual's relationship to both drives and the world.

W. D. R. Fairbairn was the first psychoanalyst to question the drive basis of human motivation and propose an alternative based on object relationships. Fairbairn contended that the baby is not pleasure seeking as Freud thought, but "object seeking." Fairbairn believed that Freud's theory ignored the role of the self's relationship to the object. That is, the ego can grow only through satisfactory object relationships. If the parental figures do not provide good care, the ego cannot develop, and pathology results. Consequently, according to Fairbairn, the child seeks relationships before pleasure. Indeed, he pointed out that one sees pure pleasure seeking only in states of severe pathology in which the ego is "fractionated." Fairbairn pointed out that children, and even adults, prefer painful relationships to none at all. This would not be the case were the child governed by the pleasure principle, as Freud thought. Part of Fairbairn's evidence was the behavior of abused children. According to the pleasure principle, children should not attach to their abusers. However, in fact, as Fairbairn and others have found in their work with such children, they actually attach more stubbornly to their abusers than other children do to their caretakers. Fairbairn took this as evidence of the primacy of object attachments over pleasure in human motivation. On this basis, Fairbairn developed a theory of the personality as formed from attachments to early figures. These object relationships, not reducible to drive gratification or any other motive, are, according to Fairbairn, taken in, or "internalized" in the form of objects. That is, the child makes a part of the psyche the images of the caretakers, and these images become the blueprint for all later relationships.

The idea of internalization was not new with Fairbairn or object-relations theory. Psychoanalytic theory since Freud had seen the ego as formed from the legacy of early relationships. The decisive difference between Freud and object-relations theory is that the latter does not see the motivation to internalize early relationships as reducible to any other motive, whereas for Freud the child internalized the image of the parent in an effort to master the frustration of childhood desires. That is, according to Freud, when the child finally realizes that longings will not be fulfilled, the child abandons the desire for the parent and internalizes the object to manage the loss. By contrast, object-relations theory sees internalization as motivated by the needs for self-development and a guide to navigate the interpersonal world.

II. DEVELOPMENTAL AND ETHOLOGICAL EVIDENCE

Fairbairn's intuitive insight that the infant seeks objects rather than tension reduction has now been substantiated by controlled empirical investigations. As early as 1960, Harry Harlow reported his famous experiment that baby monkeys attach to a cloth monkey that provides no nourishment rather than a wire monkey that gives them milk. At about that time John Bowlby began reporting ethological studies showing that subhuman primates will attach to whatever figure is available, even a different species, irrespective of whether the figure has a role in tension reduction. Bowlby also concluded that the available evidence indicated that human children also will attach to figures who have no role in the meeting of biological needs. Since this early pioneering work, a great deal of carefully controlled empirical investigations by a variety of researchers such as Daniel Stern and Beatrice Beebe has shown that the human child is "prewired" for a relationship with the caretaker. Distinguishing mother's voice and face from others in the early days of life, the child seeks interaction with others and shows pleasure when it is attained. This desire takes place irrespective of the meeting of drive reduction needs. The infant will learn tasks for the sole purpose of interacting with others. Furthermore, child and mother tend to form a relationship based on an interactional pattern from the inception of life. Independent of the meeting of tension reduction needs, the child not only seeks and helps to form and sustain this rule-based interactional system but also expects it. If the established patterns are not followed, the child becomes distressed. This evidence is but a small sampling of the data substantiating Fairbairn's claim that object relationships are autonomously motivated.

III. CLINICAL AND THEORETICAL BASIS

Since Fairbairn's pioneering work, a large group of psychoanalytic clinicians have adopted a clinical stance based on the primacy of object relationships. These psychotherapists follow a psychoanalytic model in that they believe in the importance of unconscious motivation, the patient's defenses against awareness of unconscious motivation, and the uncovering of underlying meaning. However, they are decisively different from classical psychoanalysts in that they do not adhere to the drive model. Rather, they see the human organism as autonomously motivated to form object relationships and personality formation as a product of the object relationships internalized in the developmental process. This theoretical shift, based on clinical findings and an abundance of experimental results, has led to the development of a variety of clinical approaches built on the importance of object relationships. Each theory within the object-relations model has a somewhat different emphasis, but each is built on the principle that object relationships are the primary building blocks of the psyche.

Object relationships are interpersonal relationships seen from the point of view of the experiencing participant. They differ from interpersonal relationships in that they are not the relationship viewed in terms of its external behavior as seen from the viewpoint of a third person. For example, a third party might describe two people as having a "good" or "friendly" relationship, or a "bad" or "hostile" relationship, but an object relationship is the experience of one party to the relationship. So, while an observer might say two people have a "bad" relationship, one person might experience the self as trying to please an implacable other whom this person regards as possessing exceptional qualities. That is the object relationship. As can be seen from this example, an object relationship always includes a self-state, an "object," who is the target of the experience, and an affective link between the two. The object relationship tends to be complex, including unconscious motives and affects and complex interplays between participant and object. As long as the relationship is viewed from the viewpoint of the experiencing participant, it is an object relationship.

Because of the overriding importance of the attachment to the caretaker, the child will do whatever is necessary to secure this attachment. If the relationship requires the suppression of aspects of the self, those potential components of the self are arrested, thus crippling self-development. For example, if the caretaker will not tolerate aggressive feelings and requires that the child avoid all angry or aggressive expression, the child will learn not to feel or act in an aggressive manner. The aggressive component of the personality will be arrested, thus crippling all areas that rely on aggression, such as self-assertion, ambition, and competitiveness. In this way, the object-relations viewpoint replaces the Freudian theory of symptom formation as rooted in internal defenses against drives with the conflict between the need for the object and the development of the self. What appears to be the repression of a drive is the child's burial of those potential aspects of experience that the child fears will be threatening to early caretakers. To some degree, such adaptations are an expectable part of life, as all caretakers require some adaptation from the child that does not allow for full self-development. However, when such accommodations interfere with the development of crucial components of the self, such as excitement, interest, enjoyment, aggression, and sexuality, the self will be fundamentally split in a way that arrests the development of essential components of the self. Winnicott called this division the split between the "true self" and the "false self." Those buried aspects of the self continue to seek expression and will gain it only through symptom formation. To continue with our example, the aggressive component of the self may seek veiled expression as a somatic pain or become part of a sadomasochistic sexual fantasy life.

From the object-relations viewpoint, all psychogenic pathology is a function of self-arrest induced by anxiety-driven object attachments. Pathological differences being due to the phase, degree, and type of arrestation, object-relations theory does not make decisive distinctions among causes and types of pathology. This view puts all psychopathology on a spectrum and makes distinctions among types of pathology a matter of degree.

All object-relations theories are built on the principle that development and psychopathology are a product of the object relationships internalized in the developmental process. However, theorists from various schools differ in emphasis and in details For example, followers of Melanie Klein, known as Kleinians, tend to see drives as important to the formation of object relationships even if they see object relationships as the building blocks of all development beginning in early life. Kleinians view problems with the aggressive drive as fundamental to pathological states, although they acknowledge that all drives are seen only within object relationships. Fairbairn, as mentioned earlier, sees no role for drives in development or pathology. In contrast to the Kleinians, Fairbairn saw the child's most fundamental motive to be the need to love and have that love accepted by the caretaker. Donald Winnicott, a primary English object-relations theorist, saw the child's dependence on the mother and the phases of its relinquishment to be the most important variable in development and psychopathology. According to Winnicott, each infant is born with potential that cannot be changed, but can be either facilitated or interfered with by caretakers. Impingement by the caretaker interferes with the maturational process, and this arrest in the development of the true self is the source of psychopathology, including the most severe forms. Many followers of Winnicott, such as Mhasud Khan, Margaret Little, and Andre Green, have used his work to apply object-relations concepts to the treatment of severe character and even psychotic disorders, thus broadening the scope of psychoanalytic therapy beyond the neurotic patients who tend to be the target of classical technique to the treatment of more severe emotional disorders.

Christopher Bollas, a contemporary Winnicottian, has shown how the mother's ministrations to the infant are taken in or "internalized" by the growing child. Bollas has pointed out that the original mother–child relationship becomes embedded in the psyche of the child in a way that results in a unique personal idiom the growing child and adult is unaware of, but always knows is there. Bollas calls this personal idiom the "unthought known."

Heinz Kohut developed a school of psychoanalysis that has come to be known as self psychology. In Kohut's view, the child is born with a nascent self that comes to fruition as a function of the interplay between the child's "nuclear program of the self" and the caretaker's ministrations. The child's experience of a caretaker is called a self-selfobject relationship. A selfobject is an other experienced as a provider of functions for the self. The degree to which the selfobject provides necessary functions abets the development of the nuclear program via a process of "transmuting internalization," a microscopic "taking in" of the selfobject until the internalizations replace the archaic forms of narcissism characteristic of infancy and early childhood. Disruptions in the self-selfobject relationship cause vulnerabilities in the emerging self and the need to protect this vulnerability by splitting off the original narcissistic state that, being unresolved, continues its influence on the personality. Although self psychologists prefer to regard their theory as wholly unique in psychoanalytic thought, the fact is that their view of self-development as a function of the relationship to early objects and the internalization process fits this school into the object-relations rubric. It is true that self psychology differs from other object-relations theories in its emphasis on the importance of self-esteem in normal development and vulnerabilities to self-esteem in psychopathology. However, this uniqueness exists within the object-relations paradigm that views self-development as a product of the relationship between self and object and the internalization of the latter by the former. Each form of object-relations theory has a unique emphasis; that is why there are different viewpoints within the object-relations model.

Whatever the particular differences in detail and emphasis, each object-relations theorist sees the child's absorption of the early relationships with caretakers to be fundamental to the growing personality of the adult. These internalizations are the legacy of the early object relationship and are often referred to as "internalized object relationships." From an object-relations viewpoint, who we are is fundamentally a product of our internalized object relationships. It is important, however, to emphasize that these internalizations are not regarded as copies, as though the mind is composed of the wholesale absorption of the childhood view of the early figures. What the child takes in from the parental figures is a complex creation based on the child's experience with the figures. If this were not the case, people would be photostatic copies of their caretakers. The child's internalized images of the parents are based on the child's experience with the caretaker, but the child creates meaning from this experience that cannot be reduced to the parental behavior. Again, this view of internalization is substantiated by developmental research. Virginia Demos, who researches affective development, has found that the child does not take in the parents' behavior, but makes meaning out of it, and this meaning is the legacy of the parent–child interaction. The lasting impact of the relationship on the child has been referred to by Christopher Bollas as "the shadow of the object." These "shadows" form the template of the child and growing adult's pattern of interpersonal behavior.

When the early caretakers do not meet the child's needs well, the child will experience the caretaking figure as traumatizing. To master the trauma while maintaining attachment to the traumatizing figure, the child will internalize the figure as a "bad object." These internalized bad objects become the source of psychic distress, self-abuse, and many forms of psychopathology. For example, the child may internalize the caretaker's attacks. Treating himself as he was treated, the child has an internalized bad object that may be relentless in flagellation of the self for every mistake or peccadillo. Such a patient will complain of being "hard on myself," or being a "perfectionist." Or, to take another example, the bad object may be projected onto others resulting in a paranoid stance to the world. These are just two of many possible outcomes. Whatever the result of the bad object experience, it will result in some form of pathological expression. All of this has far-reaching clinical implications.

IV. THE OBJECT-RELATIONS MODEL OF PSYCHOTHERAPY

This object-relations theory of development and pathology has direct implications for the conduct of psychoanalytic therapy. Due to its emphasis on the importance of attachments and the legacy of the child's interactions with caretakers, the focus of an object-relations clinical approach is the object-relations structure that gives rise to the symptoms or inhibitions. Consequently, the goal of any object-relations approach is to uncover the object relations internalized in childhood and early life and help the patient relinquish them and create a new object-relations structure that fosters self-development. Thus, in the object-relations model the traditional emphasis on discrete affects is replaced by a focus on the structure of the self.

Object-relations therapy looks at each symptom as an outgrowth of an anxiety-driven object relationship. For example, in the case discussed earlier of the patient who had to disavow any aggressive expression to secure the tie to the early caretaker, the emphasis in object-relations therapy would not be as much on "repressed aggression" as on the object relationships that required the disavowal of aggressive experience. In this case, the caretaker was threatened by aggressive expression, a threat that led to an internalized object relationship in which aggression threatens relationships. The developmental origins of the child's relationship with the caretaker who could not permit aggression would be a first critical step in the understanding of the patient's fear of her aggressive feelings. The internalized object relationship in which aggression is a threat to the object would then be the source of the aggressive inhibition. The consequence of this inhibition is an arrest of the patient's self-development that interferes with all aspects of life that require aggression, such as self-assertion, ambition, and competitiveness.

A. Resistance

One of the most vexing problems in any form of psychotherapy is the strength and resilience with which patients tend to cling to their painful and dysfunctional patterns. From the object-relations viewpoint, the patient's relational patterns reflect an underlying object-relational structure. Therefore, to relinquish the current patterns, no matter how painful or dysfunctional they may be, is tantamount to separating from the objects of the past. If the patient gives up the internalized bad mother, she has yielded the only tie to the mother of her childhood. This is an intense, painful loss for the patient. One might wonder why the loss is so painful and so strenuously avoided given that the object is "bad," painful. This is one of the great ironies of object relationships and the human condition: As mentioned in the first section of this article, the more painful the early relationships, the stronger is the clinging to the object. As Fairbairn pointed out a long time ago, the painful early relationships create anxiety and the need to attach ever stronger to the abusive object. The abused child is more attached to the abusive parent that is the healthy child to his parent. Similarly, the adult subjected to abuse and pain by an early caretaker holds on tenaciously to the internalized bad parent, whereas the child raised in a healthy environment tends to more easily separate from the internalized parental figures. Patients who suffered from abusive, painful parental relationships are filled with anxiety that leads them to cling desperately to bad internalized objects. This is why such patients are so difficult to treat.

Furthermore, this object-relations structure forms the fabric of the self. To give up the object is in a very real sense to give up the self. As Fairbairn pointed out many years ago, every internalized object is a piece of self-structure, so that to yield the object is to relinquish a part of the self, a loss that evokes annihilation anxiety, the dread of nonexistence. In this way, the object-relations approach makes a unique contribution to understanding the patient's attachment to painful and dysfunctional patterns.

It follows that a critical step in the resolution of pathological patterns lies in the understanding of the origin of the patient's unconscious object-relationship structure. The therapeutic task in each case is to identify and help the patient relinquish the object-relations structure that underlies the symptom or inhibition. For example, many depressed and masochistic patients will berate themselves mercilessly for seemingly trivial mistakes, and some will unconsciously seek out punishment for peccadilloes. They know that their behavior toward themselves creates pain, but they are unable to break free from their patterns. Even after the patient is well aware of the origins and meaning of her self-abuse, she is unable to control it. The object-relations model understands the patient's self-flagellation as an internalized bad object; the unconscious need to be punished is a product of a feeling of badness that originates in such an object. To change her self-abusive behavior is to separate from the abusive figure of the past. This example is prototypical of the object-relations interpretive emphasis on anxiety-driven early attachments and the resulting object-relations structure that strangulates self-development, in contrast to the classical emphasis on defenses against endogenous drives or discrete affects.

However, awareness of the object-relational structure in itself tends to have limited mutative effect. Here the object-relations model makes a contribution to the time-honored problem of "resistance." Clinicians from Freud to the present day have found that even after patients seem to have a good understanding of the underlying motivations and developmental origins of their problems, they tend to remain frozen in their patterns. They know what they are doing, but continue to do it anyway, and seem unable to control their repetitive patterns. Freud and generations of subsequent analysts have identified the problem of the persistence of pathological patterns despite insight, a problem classical analysts call "resistance." From this perspective, resistance is motivated by the patient's fear of knowing specific information regarding his wishes or past experiences. Here again the object-relations viewpoint has a unique contribution to make. The object-relations perspective sees the patient's attachment to these patterns as a reflection of an underlying object-relations structure woven into the fabric of the self. As we have seen, the patient is clinging to old objects and the sense of self. Awareness, no matter how meaningful, can have little mutative impact on the structure of the self. Therefore, from an object-relations viewpoint, the recalcitrance of patterns even after awareness is a product of a clinical strategy that: (a) focuses on understanding affects and "impulses" without appreciating the underlying self structure and (b) relies exclusively on interpretation. Because interpretation cannot alter the object-relations structure, pathological patterns will remain stubborn until the therapeutic relationship provides an alternative to the old, familiar patterns. The therapist is often opposed, or even disliked or hated, because she represents the effort to loosen the patient's bond to the object and thereby threaten the self. The patient's adherence to the bad object is not treated as resistance, but an anxiety-driven attachment that the therapist will understand and interpret. So, "resistance" from this viewpoint is not resistance at all, but clinging to a desperately needed object.

B. The Patient–Therapist Relationship

Although interpretation is important for making the patient aware of her object-relations structure, awareness by itself does not create new structure. Consequently, in most object-relations approaches to psychotherapy, making conscious the patient's early experience is considered necessary but not sufficient to effect lasting therapeutic change. It is here that the relationship between patient and therapist becomes crucial. The therapeutic relationship must create the conditions in which the patient can create new, more adaptive, authentic, and meaningful object relationships to form the basis for new psychic structure. Object-relations theorists vary in the emphasis they put on the therapeutic value of the patient–therapist relationship, but all, including Kleinians who have traditionally emphasized interpretation, see a critical role for the therapeutic relationship in the patient's ability to create a new object and healthier psychological structure.

Winnicott viewed the psychotherapeutic relationship as a "transitional space" akin to the child's use of a transitional object, such as a blanket or teddy bear. Winnicott pointed out these attachments are transitional between the world of omnipotent fantasy life of early infancy in which the child has the delusion that she meets her needs by their very existence and the later appreciation for the world of objective reality in which the child recognizes that people and material objects exist apart from her, outside of her control. There is a third world, according to Winnicott, between fantasy and objective reality, that must be traversed before the child can accept objective reality. In this transitional world, the child knows objects exist outside of her control but treats them as though they are part of her. Transitional experience is the basis for play, creativity, and aesthetic experience. To play one must know what objects are but treat them according to illusions of one's own creation. The clay is molded into a shape the child calls a "fish." The child knows the clay is not a fish but puts it in the water to swim. It is equally important that the child adapt to the materials at hand. The child must mold the clay for the play to work. The limitations of the materials differentiate play as a transitional experience from fantasy. If she tries to mold wood, or water, she will not see a "fish."

Winnicott viewed the psychotherapeutic relationship as a transitional space in which the therapist provides the conditions the patient can use to create new ways of being and relating. The patient has to operate within the objective constraints of the setting, analogous to play materials, but within that boundary creates the relationship she needs. What is created between therapist and patient is unique to the pair. The success of the therapeutic enterprise is a function of the degree to which the created relationship facilitates the development of the true self. Thus, it is not interpretation that is ultimately mutative for Winnicott, but what the patient creates in the transitional space of the therapeutic relationship. In object-relations therapy, the patient's use of the therapist is decisive for therapeutic outcome rather than the therapist's understanding. The therapist's role is not so much to offer information about the patient as to create the kind of relationship the patient can use to create something the patient has never had before. The therapist's role, then, is to adapt to the patient's needs, rather than find the correct understanding of the patient's unconscious. This adaptation is different for each patient, but it always includes the provision of a space that the patient can use to create something new. This conception of the therapeutic process is decisively different from the classical model in which the assumption is made that understanding is sufficient to produce the desired changes.

The therapeutic action, then, is the patient's use of the analytic space to create a new object relationship with the therapist that facilitates the articulation of arrested aspects of the self. Endemic to the therapeutic process is the creation of new ways of being and relating. This point requires emphasis because it is regarded by object-relations theorists as a major advantage over the classical psychoanalytic model in which the analyst is limited to interpreting the unconscious, and the patient's role is confined to receiving the analyst's understanding or "taking in" the analyst in the form of internalization. What the patient passively receives from the therapist may or may not be meaningful or authentic, but what the patient creates is the articulation of buried aspects of the self that are deeply authentic and meaningful because the patient created them.

In this model the concept of transference is broadened beyond the patient's projection of a past image onto the therapist. Just as in any other relationship, the patient forms the relationship she needs based on a variety of factors, one of which is past object relationships. Because this relationship is based on the patient's hopes and desires, adaptation to the current situation, defenses against the anxiety it causes, as well as the patient's history, this creation is rarely a simple copy of early relationships. This relationship will be a complex amalgam that shifts as the relationship evolves. Most object-relations theorists have a concept of transference broader than the traditional notion that includes the patient's creation of something new with the therapist, so that the transference is regarded as a complex blend of past images and present adaptations. That is to say, transference is not reduced to the repetition of past patterns; it includes the patient's contributions, often developed for the first time in the therapeutic process. For example, an inhibited patient may eventually explode with rage at the therapist, not because she is repeating an early relationship, but because she feels safe enough with the therapist to risk including an aggressive component in the relationship, an element that may be wholly new in the patient's experience. Or, sometimes the patient who feels cheated by having a weak father will idealize the therapist to create a relationship that he desires but never had. This type of object relationship has its own problems, but its very existence indicates that the transference is not the clear repetition depicted by classical psychoanalysis.

C. The Creation of a New Object Relationship

Like the classical psychoanalytic therapist, the object-relations therapist interprets the transference, but she is not prone to reduce every aspect of the therapeutic relationship to the patient's past experience. The object-relations therapist tends to search not only for the roots of the relationship in the patient's past, but also the adaptive function of the relationship in the present. Perhaps the patient idealizes the analyst because such an idealizing object relationship provides the protection lacking in the early caretaker relationship. The therapist interprets not only the lack of protection in the past, but also the safety afforded by the creation of an idealized therapeutic relationship. However, the object-relations therapist is never satisfied with interpretation alone. The therapist interprets the idealizing transference as a means toward helping the patient relinquish it so that a new type of object relationship may be formed. She then provides the opportunity for the patient to form a relationship that does not repeat the patterns of the past. In our example of the idealizing transference, the therapist attempts to facilitate the formation of a safe, protective relationship so that the patient may be able eventually to have this relationship without the unrealistic idealizing perception of the therapist. To use another example: The therapist helps the inhibited patient include aggression in his therapeutic relationship without feeling threatened that the aggressive expression will damage the relationship.

The therapist will include with interpretation the facilitation of a new relationship with the patient to replace the internalized bad object. Fairbairn referred to this new therapeutic relationship as the "beneficent parental figure." Some Winnicottians refer to the "good enough mother/therapist," and self-psychologists emphasize the provision of "selfobject functions."

Whichever nomenclature is used, all these terms signify the therapist as offering a new, different kind of relationship. The purpose of this relationship is to adapt to the patient so that the patient has the opportunity to create a more positive, benevolent object than the bad object it replaces. This active provision of a new, different relationship is one of the decisive differences between the object-relations model of psychotherapy and the classical psychoanalytic viewpoint. From the latter perspective, the therapist should never become a different object but rather interpret the patient's desire for her to become such an object. From this viewpoint, the object-relations strategy is a gratification of the patient's wishes and, therefore, is a technical error. By contrast, the object-relations model sees the fabric of the personality as consisting of internalized objects and the health or pathology of the individual as a direct product of the nature of these objects. Therefore, from this viewpoint, anything the therapist can do to facilitate the relinquishing of old, negative objects and their replacement with new, good objects is beneficial to the therapeutic process and the goals of the therapy. Having said that, it needs to be emphasized that the object-relations model does not believe that simply "being different" will effect the desired therapeutic effect. The old object-relations structure forms the very fabric of the self and will not be easily given up. This is why a new relationship in the patient's life will rarely affect lasting psychological change. In fact, often patients enter psychotherapy because they are in danger of damaging a potentially positive relationship by operating in accordance with their long-standing patterns. If psychotherapy is necessary, that is because a new relationship is insufficient to produce change and may even be threatened by the patient's old pathological patterns. As mentioned earlier, the object-relations structure formed in early childhood tends to be resilient because the patient is attached to not only her internalized objects but also her sense of self derived from them. The patient's object-relations patterns must be interpreted so that she can see their origins and damaging consequences before the therapist's influence as a new object can be experienced. The former allies the object-relations model with the classical psychoanalytic perspective, and the latter decisively separates it from the traditional viewpoint.

D. The Widening Scope of Psychoanalytic Therapy

A major advantage of this model is that is applies to a wide variety of patients, including many who were believed to be inaccessible to in-depth psychotherapy from the classical perspective. According to the latter viewpoint, the crux of psychoanalytic therapy is the resolution of intrapsychic conflicts caused by the repression of forbidden wishes. Consequently, patients for whom the very structure of the psyche is malformed were considered unsuitable for in-depth psychotherapy. The object-relations model blurs this either/or distinction between intrapsychic conflict and character pathology. If a conflict requires treatment, then the conflict has not been mastered by the structure, resulting in a symptomatic outbreak. Even the mildest case of neurosis must have some defect in the structure of the personality for the conflict to have erupted in a symptom. The distinction between intrapsychic conflict and character disorder is a matter of degree, as every patient has each to some extent. Consequently, the psychic structure must be addressed in every case. In terms of clinical strategy the implication is that both types of problem are resolved with a combination of interpretation and the provision of a new relationship. By including the importance of the therapeutic relationship in the therapeutic action, the object-relations model has found a way to address character issues, even primitive characterological expressions, with a psychoanalytic framework.

This widening scope of psychoanalytic therapy is one of the most profound implications of the object-relations approach to treatment. By addressing the object-relations structure of the personality via interpretation and the inclusion of the provision of a new relationship, psychoanalytic therapy becomes accessible to severe psychopathology. In the case of the most severe form of non-psychotic character pathology, the borderline syndrome, object-relations therapists have devised strategies designed to address the primitive needs and demands of those patients. Again, Winnicott was a primary leader in this movement. Following an object-relations model that sees the borderline patient as an arrest in the early development of the self, Winnicott responded to the expressed desires of such patients, rather than "setting limits" on them. His reasoning was that the patients' needs were not responded to in childhood, leading to a defensive protective response on the patient's part. This defensive shell buries the early needs and leads to the demandingness so typical of borderline patients. The hostility and oppositionalism of the borderline patient is seen as part of the protective posture. In fact, the patient defends against all needs and desires for others because the intensity of those needs is painful, frightening, and shameful. However, precisely because the needs are so intense, the patient is hungry and demanding. What makes these patients so difficult and perplexing to the clinician is the combination of the intensity of their longing and avoidance of all contact.

Winnicott's clinical strategy was to take seriously the patient's longings and respond to them any way he could. He regarded the therapist's responsiveness to the patient's needs to be far more important than interpretation in the treatment of such patients. He let the patient take the lead in where the treatment would go. If the patient needed to rage at him, he would allow that and "hold" the rage. If the patient needed to regress to infantile needs, he would allow the patient to curl up, hold a blanket, wander around the room, sleep, or do whatever the patient felt she needed. Any such patient behavior, if spontaneous and authentic, he regarded as an expression of a developmentally arrested state that must be met by the therapist's active responsiveness. He allowed the patient to determine what happened because in this way the development of the patient's arrested true self was facilitated. He conceptualized the therapist's role as the facilitation of the resumption of arrested growth. As can be seen, this is not a conflict model, but a model based on developmental arrest. Winnicott believed that such arrests required the meeting of the early needs in some way to stimulate arrested growth. Interpretation alone could never accomplish this type of renewal.

From this example of Winnicott's treatment of the borderline patient, one can see that the object-relations model is based on responsiveness to needs, rather than always interpreting them, a limitation of the classical viewpoint. According to object-relations theory, such gratification of the patient is not only called for but is a necessary ingredient of the treatment. Whereas for a neurotic patient, this meeting of "regressed needs" may be unnecessary or at most play only a small role in the process, with the borderline patient it is the essence of therapeutic action. Although this meeting of early needs can never replace what is missing from the past, it gains a responsiveness in the patient that allows for a new beginning, a beginning in which the patient can begin to live in accordance with her authentically experienced self. This meeting of regressive needs and the willingness of the therapist to allow the patient to stay in the regressed state as long as necessary is the crux of therapeutic action with severely disturbed patients, according to Winnicott. Harry Guntrip, a foremost object-relations therapist, called this process "meeting the needs of the regressed ego." Even contemporary Kleinians, such as Herbert Rosenfeld, see the relationship and the needs it meets for the patient as the most crucial factor in the therapeutic action with patients who are severely disturbed. The key for Winnicott as for most object-relations therapists is that the patient determines the depth and length of regression, and therapist's role is to be responsive to the patient. The elucidation of this treatment approach to character pathology, including substance abusers, food disorders, narcissistic personalities, and depression, among others is one of the seminal contributions of object-relations psychotherapy to psychoanalytic therapy and psychotherapy in general. There are many cases reported in the literature of successful psychotherapy conducted by object-relations therapists with borderline and other patients with character disorders.

SUMMARY

Object relations psychotherapy is built on the principle that the child's relationships with early figures are autonomously motivated. The child meets the parental ministrations with innate affective dispositions to form a unique personal idiom. This parental relationship is internalized by the child as internalized object relationships that form the character structure. The degree to which the child's innate direction is facilitated by the environment is the extent to which the personality becomes healthy. Impingements that interfere with the maturational process force the child's maturational process away from this inborn direction to a self protective stance that arrests the articulation of the personal idiom. If significant aspects of the self are blocked, this buried self will seek veiled expression as a symptom. Consequently, object relations therapy is directed both to understanding the defensive constellation and facilitating the articulation of buried affective dispositions that lie beneath it. Emphasis is placed on insight into the transference and the patient's creation of a new object relationship with the therapist. Thus, both interpretation and the therapeutic relationship are mutative factors in this type of psychotherapy. Insight helps to understand the patient's defenses and current character patterns, and the therapeutic relationship fosters the development of alternatives based on authentic affective experience. Consequently, the therapeutic relationship is given considerable weight in the therapeutic action of object relations psychotherapy. This model widens the scope of psychoanalytic treatment beyond neurotic conditions to characterological disturbances.

See Also the Following Articles

Character Pathology ■ Couples Therapy: Insight Oriented ■ Humanistic Psychotherapy ■ Oedipus Complex ■ Projective Testing in Psychotherapeutics ■ Rational Emotive Behavior Therapy ■ Sullivan's Interpersonal Psychotherapy ■ Working Alliance

Further Reading

Fairbairn, W. R. D. (1952). *Psychoanalytic studies of the personality.* London: Tavistock.

Greenberg, J., & Mitchell, S. (1983). *Object relations in psychoanalytic theory.* Cambridge, MA: Harvard University Press.

Guntrip, H. (1969). *Schizoid phenomena object relations and the self.* New York: International Universities Press.

Guntrip, H. (1971). *Psychoanalytic theory, therapy, and the self.* New York: Basic Books.

Kernberg, O. (1976). *Object relations theory and clinical psychoanalysis.* New York: Jason Aronson.

Modell, A. (1968). *Object love and reality.* New York: International Universities Press.

Summers, F. (1994). *Object relations theories and psychopathology.* Hillsdale, NJ: The Analytic Press.

Summers, F. (1999). *Transcending the self.* Hillsdale, NJ: The Analytic Press.

Winnicott, D. (1965). *Maturational processes and the facilitating environment.* New York: International Universities Press.

Winnicott, D. (1975). *Through paediatrics to psychoanalysis.* New York: Basic Books.

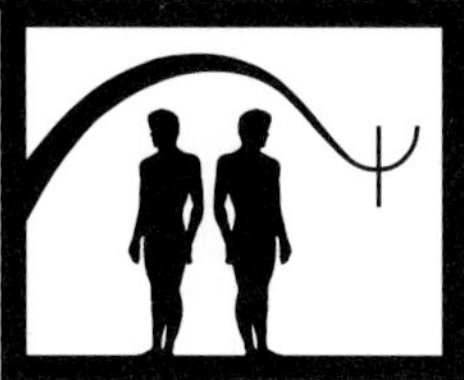

Objective Assessment

James N. Butcher
University of Minnesota

GLOSSARY

Butcher Treatment Planning Inventory (BTPI) An objectively derived, self-report, structured personality inventory that endeavors to obtain and organize relevant personality and symptomatic information into a cohesive picture to be used for treatment.

Minnesota Multiphasic Personality Inventory-2 (MMPI-2) A comprehensive, objective, self-report, personality inventory that provides the tester or practitioner with a general picture of the client's symptoms, beliefs, and attitudes.

multimodal therapy An approach to planning and delivering psychotherapy that takes into consideration a variety of different domains of functioning, including behavior, affective processes, sensation, images, cognitions, interpersonal relationships, and biological issues. These functions also relate to therapeutic techniques.

I. INTRODUCTION

Mental health professionals conducting psychotherapy are initially faced with the question of how to design a treatment regimen that suits the unique needs of the client. Clinicians must identify the patient's problem areas that need to be addressed and evaluate the client's personal qualities and strengths needed to solve the present problems. Regardless of the mode of psychological intervention, whether it is psychodynamically oriented psychotherapy or behavior therapy, the mental health practitioner must appraise the client's problems, motivations, strengths, and limitations if the intervention is to proceed toward a successful outcome. In an effort to understand these pertinent "patient variables" many therapists rely on personality and symptom information from psychological evaluations to accomplish this important task.

The assessment process typically involves using objective psychological tests that provide the practitioner with clues to the psychological and environmental characteristics involved in the problems and identify factors that might contribute to a positive outcome. Effective psychological assessment in pretreatment planning can add considerably to the likely success of psychotherapy by providing the therapist with an objective appraisal of the client's problems, psychological resources, and potential treatment failures due to resistance. Moreover, psychological test results can also be effectively incorporated into the treatment process as a medium for facilitating change in therapy.

There are several reasons why psychological assessment should be incorporated into the early stages of psychological treatment planning:

1. It is important in the early stages of therapy to assess the severity of the patient's mental disorder to ensure that the treatment focus is appropriate and effective for the client;

2. Obtaining an objective personality evaluation can also help the therapist uncover personality factors that could lead to treatment resistance. For example, some clients rely on psychological defense mechanisms such as projection and avoidance of blame to deal with conflict;

3. In the early stages of therapy it is also important to appraise the client's strengths that can be drawn on in crisis situations or circumstances that require change; and information on the client's personality characteristics in the early stages of therapy can be employed to facilitate the treatment process through providing personality feedback to the client.

II. TREATMENT PLANNING

Three assessment strategies used in pretreatment assessment are described briefly to illustrate the information that can be obtained in the assessment process. The assessment strategies described in this article are not tied to a particular treatment orientation or limited to a specific psychotherapeutic approach but address the important task of assessing the client's symptoms, motivations for treatment, and likely patterns of treatment resistance.

A. Multimodal Therapy

Although its initial focus and orientation was strictly behavioral in nature multimodal therapy has developed into a model in which all treatment orientations can be included. Lazarus noted in 1981 that its goal is not to fit clients to the "treatment," but rather to illustrate precisely how to fit the therapy to the requirements of the client. This approach by Lazarus employs a model of human personality that is composed of the following component behaviors, affective processes, sensations, images, cognitions, interpersonal relationships, and drugs (more accurately termed "biological functions"). Each of these areas of functioning must be understood before effective treatment can be initiated. The practitioner pays clear attention to excesses and deficits in each assessment area. The practitioner uses several approaches to assess these attributes, for example, interviews, observations, and questionnaires. Multimodal therapy begins with assessment, which traditionally has been considered to be the most important step in the process.

In terms of assessing behaviors in pretreatment planning, the therapist and client must consider what the client is doing or not doing that is interfering with his or her life. The therapist and client need to come to terms with what behaviors should be increased and decreased in frequency for therapy to be successful. For the assessment of the second area for multimodal therapy, affect, the therapist needs to determine what situations or events elicit different emotional responses in the client. What negative feelings, such as depression or anxiety, is the client experiencing. The third area to assess, sensation-related concerns, involve the clients' preferences for what they hear, see, smell, taste, and touch. Are they experiencing any particularly negative sensations, such as tension, dizziness, pain, or tremors? Next comes the assessment of images that require an evaluation of the effects particular images have on the clients' behaviors, affect, and sensations. The focus of the next assessment domain, cognitions, include opinions, values, beliefs, and attitudes. Do the patients hold any irrational beliefs or ideas that interfere with their functioning? An extremely important area to assess in pretreatment planning is the quality of the patient's interpersonal relationships. The final step in the assessment involves an assessment of the client's physical health including substance use or abuse. This task involves appraisal of the client's current use of alcohol, illicit drugs, and prescription medications.

Once the therapist has acquired the necessary relevant information, the next step in the process is to develop a modality profile, which provides a "blueprint" for establishing the goals of treatment and allowing both the patient and therapist input into what treatment will entail. In addition to being used to formulate treatment goals, the profile may also enable the client to aid the therapist in selecting the most appropriate psychotherapy strategies. Lazarus advocates the use of a wide variety of principal techniques representing a broad range of theoretical orientations, with particular emphasis given to behavioral therapy, rational-emotive therapy, and cognitive therapy.

B. Minnesota Multiphasic Personality Inventory (MMPI–2)

The most widely used personality measure used in pretreatment evaluation is the Minnesota Multiphasic Personality Inventory (MMPI). This inventory was developed in the 1940s as a means of evaluating mental health problems in psychiatric and medical settings. The original test developers considered it crucial in evaluating patients' problems to ask them about what they felt and thought. The MMPI is a self-report personality scale that includes a very broad range of problems and was developed according to rigorous empirical research methods. The MMPI was revised and updated in 1989 and provides a broader range of clinical information than the original test.

The MMPI–2 is a comprehensive objective self-report personality inventory that provides the practitioner with a general picture of the client's symptoms, beliefs, and attitudes. The MMPI–2 contains 567 true-false questions addressing mental health symptoms, beliefs, and attitudes that are grouped into scales (clusters of items) that address specific clinical problems such as depression or anxiety. An MMPI scale allows the clinician to compare the responses of the client with those of thousands of other people. To gain a perspective on what the patient's test results mean, the MMPI–2 scores are compared to the normative sample, a large representative sample of people from across the United States. This comparison allows the interpreter to determine if the person's responses are different from people who do not have mental health problems. If the patient obtains scores in the extreme ranges, for example on the Depression scale (compared with the normative sample) then they are likely to be experiencing problems comparable to the clinical samples of depressed clients that have been studied. The MMPI–2 results provide the practitioner with a clearer understanding of the patient's symptoms and personality features and help to identify possible areas to explore in therapy.

C. Butcher Treatment Planning Inventory (BTPI)

The BTPI was created for the purpose of incorporating objectively derived, self-report information into the treatment process when a tactical therapeutic approach is being formulated and time is crucial. The BTPI assists the therapist by obtaining and organizing relevant personality and symptomatic information into a cohesive picture early in the treatment process.

The BTPI is a structured personality inventory that takes about 30 min. to administer. It contains several empirically validated scales that were developed to provide treatment-relevant information about clients. Three types of scales are included: validity or response attitude measures, treatment-related attitudes, and major symptom areas. The first cluster of scales assesses the client's cooperativeness with the personality evaluation. Four scales address different test-taking strategies presenting an overly positive self-view, symptom exaggeration, inconsistent symptom presentation, and noncompliant treatment attitudes. The second BTPI cluster consists of five scales that assess specific treatment-related issues: problems in relationship formation, somatization of conflict, low expectation of benefit, self-oriented narcissism, and lack of perceived environmental support. The third symptom cluster addresses the following symptom areas: anxiety, depression, anger-in, anger-out, and psychotic thinking.

The practitioner obtains a summary of the client's likely cooperativeness in engaging into the therapy process, clues with respect to several areas of treatment resistance, and an indication of the extent to which anxiety, depression, anger, or unusual thought processes are likely to be encountered in the treatment process.

III. PROVIDING TEST FEEDBACK TO CLIENTS IN PSYCHOTHERAPY

Clients who are provided test results in the early stages of psychotherapy tend to improve as a result of the test feedback process. This strategy, referred to as "assessment therapy," is a procedure in which the therapist uses a feedback model to review psychological test information with the client and thereby promote the process of behavioral change. Several studies have shown that providing psychological test results to clients early in therapy can have powerful effects in terms of lowering symptomatic status and increasing self-esteem in patients. Research on assessment therapy has shown that providing psychological test feedback is an effective means of engaging the client in the treatment process early in the therapy and produces positive treatment effects by informing the client of likely problems, personality characteristics, and strengths.

In summary, psychological assessment in the early stages of psychotherapy can provide the clinician with a great deal of valuable, objective information concerning the clients problems and strengths. Moreover, the judicious incorporation of the test results into the therapy by using test feedback can facilitate the treatment by engaging the client in the process early in therapy.

See Also the Following Articles

Behavioral Assessment ■ Behavioral Case Formulation ■ Cultural Issues ■ Functional Analysis of Behavior ■ Individual Psychotherapy ■ Multimodal Behavior Therapy ■ Neuropsychological Assessment ■ Outcome Measures

Further Reading

Ben-Porath, Y. S. (1997). Use of personality assessment instruments in empirically guided treatment planning. *Psychological Assessment, 9*, 361–367.

Butcher, J. N. (1998). *The Butcher treatment planning inventory (BTPI): Test manual and interpretive guide.* San Antonio, TX: Psychological Corporation.

Finn, S. E., & Martin, H. (1997). Therapeutic assessment with the MMPI-2 in managed health care. In J. N. Butcher (Ed.), *Personality assessment in managed health care: Using the MMPI-2 in treatment planning* (pp. 131–152). New York: Oxford University Press.

Finn, S. E., & Tonsager, M. (1992). Therapeutic effects of providing MMPI-2 test feedback to college students awaiting therapy. *Psychological Assessment, 4*, 278–287.

Graham, J. R. (2000). *MMPI-2: Assessing personality and psychopathology* (3rd ed.). New York: Oxford University Press.

Lazarus, A. A. (1989). *The practice of multimodal therapy: Systematic comprehensive, and effective psychotherapy.* Baltimore: Johns Hopkins University Press.

Perry, J. N. (2002). Assessment of treatment resistance via questionnaires. In J. N. Butcher (Ed.), *Clinical personality assessment* (2nd ed,) (pp. 96–108). New York: Oxford University Press.

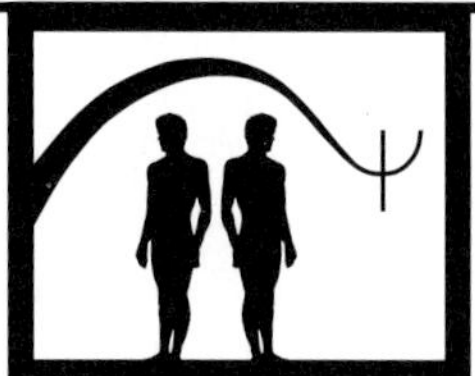

Oedipus Complex

Jodi H. Brown
The Institute of the Philadelphia Association for Psychoanalysis

Alan Sugarman
San Diego Psychoanalytic Society and Institute, and University of California San Diego

GLOSSARY

castration complex A universal unconscious fantasy that women are castrated and inferior because they do not possess a penis. Castration refers to real or fantasied loss or injury to the genitals of either gender in general psychoanalytic usage.

compromise formation Any mental phenomenon that is the product of internal conflict and that expresses all components of the conflict.

conflict Opposition between mental forces. These forces can be instinctual or Freud's structures of the mind (id, ego, superego).

defense The methods used by the ego to master and control id impulses or superego injunctions.

ego The hypothetical construct defined in Freud's structural model to enable the mind to organize its various components and to adapt to the external world.

ego ideal A set of functions within the superego. These include ideal representations of the self and idealized representations of the love object.

fixation Persistent, infantile modes of gratification, object relations, and defenses are thought to be fixed in the mind and available to be regressed to at later moments of stress.

identification The process by which a person borrows his or her identity from someone else through internalizing aspects of the other person into the self-representation. Identification is often seen as the most mature level of internalization by modern psychoanalysts.

infantile neurosis A confusing psychoanalytic concept that, at times, is used to refer to the childhood neurosis that is assumed to antedate all adult neuroses and, at other times, to the intrapsychic conflict that occurs during the Oedipus Complex.

libidinal wishes Wishes infused with affectionate or sexual urges thought to be ubiquitous in human functioning.

libido The hypothetical psychic energy attached to the sexual instincts.

narcissistic injury Experiences of having one's self-esteem lowered that are accompanied by painful affects of sadness, embarrassment, or humiliation.

neurosis Refers to psychological symptoms that develop from mental conflict that is primarily unconscious and derived from experiences in childhood.

object relations Refers to relationships to other people. In psychoanalysis, it is the internal representations of self and others that are important in motivating and mediating interpersonal interactions. A developmental distinction is often made between dyadic and triadic object relations. The former refers to relationships modeled on pre-Oedipal experiences where the major goals of the child revolve around need satisfaction by the mother. Triadic relations are seen as more mature, implying Oedipal engagement and the increasing mental complexity implicit in being aware of needs and wishes toward one parent vis-a-vis the other parent.

psychosexual Based on Freud's early finding that all aspects of mental functioning are affected by infantile sexual development and the wishes that derive from these experiences. The term is usually used as an adjective to imply that some mental or behavioral action is influenced by oral, anal, phallic, or genital urges.

regression A key psychoanalytic concept that thoughts, emotions, or behaviors can involve a return to developmentally immature levels. It also refers to a defense mechanism. Regression can occur along any developmental line.

signal anxiety Freud's second theory of anxiety stated that mental maturity brings with it the ego's ability to anticipate the danger of unconscious mental content becoming conscious so that appropriate defenses can be mobilized. Signal anxiety refers to the affective sense of danger that stimulates defense.

structural model Freud's final model of the mind introduced in 1923 in *The Ego and the Id.* The mind was conceived of having three structures (the id, ego, and superego). Interaction between these three structures is thought to account for all mentally mediated behavior.

sublimation This concept refers to mental contents or processes being separated from the drives that might have influenced their origins. As socially more acceptable motives affect these contents and processes, defenses are no longer needed against them.

superego The mental structure that creates and maintains ideals, values, prohibitions, and commands. It observes and evaluates the self's compliance with these ideals and generates affects to encourage compliance.

transference The process by which the patient displaces onto the therapist or analyst feelings, impulses, attitudes, or defenses derived from important interactions in the past.

"The Oedipus Complex" is a concept in which psychoanalytic history, theory, and clinical work converge. Freud described the Oedipus complex as a universal aspect of human psychological development. He found that in the life of every child, there comes a juncture at which the child strives for sexual union with the parent of the opposite sex, wishes for the death of the same-sex parent, and consequently fears retaliation. In short, Freud believed each of us has once been "a budding Oedipus" with fantasies of incest and murder. Since Freud, the Oedipus complex has been reexamined, reconceptualized, and integrated into different developmental theories of psychoanalysis. Though much of Freud's assertions have been reformulated, especially with respect to the development of the female, many psychoanalysts maintain that the Oedipus complex is a cornerstone in development, the "shibboleth" of psychoanalysis, the watershed of individuation, and one of the most influential and fundamental psychic organizers of mental life.

Currently, the Oedipus complex can be defined as a configuration in which the child's attachments to parents become infused with sexual feelings leading the child to compete with each parent for the attention of the other. With these emerging sexual strivings and their connection to the parents, fantasies form and shift, identifications deepen, interpersonal conflict becomes internalized, intrapsychic conflict results, and internal compromise formations become possible. This psychic organizer occurs between the 3rd and 6th years of life, at the height of "the infantile genital" or "phallic" phase: a phase that follows the oral and anal phases and that overlaps with the pre-Oedipal and Oedipal phases of development. Intense love and hate, envy and rivalry, fears of loss of love and bodily injury, a growing capacity to differentiate between fantasy and reality, and a new awareness of morality characterize a child in the midst of the Oedipus complex. Developmentally, the Oedipus complex is thought to signal a pivotal maturation, not only in the instinctual drives, but also in the ego and object relations. One cannot think about the Oedipus complex today without exploring the concepts of superego formulation, Oedipal and pre-Oedipal object relations, infantile neurosis, and differences in male and female development.

I. HISTORICAL CONTEXT

How Freud came to discover the Oedipus complex requires tracing his thoughts back before his conceptualizations of libido, dual-drives, and structural concepts to his famous 1887 note to Fliess. In that note Freud explained how his self-analysis led him to a radical revision of his seduction-trauma hypothesis. Exploring his own internal world brought the startling realization that the sexual experiences and seductions reported by some of his patients were really fantasies containing wishes, not actual memories. This turning point in his theory resulted from a discovery in himself of the fantasy he saw depicted in Sophocles' *Oedipus Rex.* In the play, the gods place a plague on Thebes for the murder of King Laius. "Oedipus" had been abandoned at birth by Laius and Jocasta for being defective. Oedipus means "clubbed foot." Now married to the widowed queen Jocasta after having solved the riddle of the Sphinx, Oedipus searches for the murderer only to find that he, himself, is not only the murderer but the murderer of his own father and the lover of his mother. In fact, in *The Interpretation of Dreams* (1900), in which Freud first published his formulation of what later he would call the Oedipus complex, he referred to the Greek myth of Oedipus as confirmation of the profound and universal power of the incest–parricide fantasy. Though it was not until his "Contribution to the Psychology of Love" in 1910 that Freud first used the term, "Oedipus complex," and not until a 1920 footnote added to *Three Essays on the Theory of Sexuality* in 1905 that he gave his first synopsis of the complex, from 1897 onward the discovered fantasy was already destined to be linked to the tragedy bearing the name of "Oedipus."

Though it percolated through his thoughts from 1887 onward, nowhere did Freud give a systematic account of the Oedipus complex. For Freud, the Oedipus complex was inseparable from sexuality, and, in his writings from 1905 to 1940, Freud integrated the Oedipal fantasy with his discovery of infantile sexuality and his understanding of psychosexuality. While Freud continued to develop, reassess, and revise his theories and models, the basis idea of the Oedipal fantasy remained a constant. However, the specifics of the Oedipus complex in relation to intrapsychic development were transformed as Freud's thinking and theories evolved. Prior to the formation of the structural model in 1923, Freud's understanding of development was influenced by his conviction that sexual and aggressive urges, otherwise referred to as "instinctual drives," provided most of the motivation for psychic function. These drives were mental representations or a "psychical representative of an endosomatic continuously flowing source of stimulation" and not simply somatic entities. In *Three Essays on the Theory of Sexuality,* Freud linked instinctual drives to erogenous body zones and proposed that a sequential progression occurred as the child matured. At birth the libidinal drives seek gratification through oral means. Later the anal arena becomes the focus of pleasurable sensations. Finally, in the infantile genital or phallic phase, the source of drives resides in the genitals, and, at this juncture, children show evidence of the Oedipus complex. While introducing a wealth of data on infantile sexuality that related to the Oedipus complex, Freud did not explain the complex as a whole until the addition of the earlier mentioned 1920 footnote that referred to the Oedipus complex as "the nuclear complex of the neurosis" representing "the peak of infantile sexuality" and the "shibboleth that distinguishes the adherents of psycho-analysis from its opponents."

Freud elaborated his understanding of infantile sexuality and development following his analysis of Little Hans in *On the Sexual Theories of Children* and *Analysis of a Phobia in a Five-year-old Boy.* He introduced the role of "castration threat" and "the castration complex" as well as fantasies of fertilization through the mouth, of birth through the anus, and of the woman having a penis in these writings. In *Totem and Taboo,* Freud linked the Oedipus complex to the cultural institution of totemism. He viewed the primitives' ban on killing the totem animal as an external representation of an intrapsychic prohibition against killing the father. In this way Freud elevated the Oedipus complex to a primary role in the origin and evolution of human psychic development. Freud further elaborated on the connection between castration and the Oedipus complex in his *Introductory Lectures.* Unfortunately these ideas were contaminated by his incorrect assumption that there was little difference in the early sexual development between boys and girls.

In *The Ego and the Id,* Freud broadened his theory by putting more emphasis on the environment and external experience as organizers of psychological development. Freud proposed that three hypothetical psychic structures—id, ego and superego—organized experience. The instinctual drives were subsumed into the metapsychological structure of the id. The ego was the psychological structure that synthesized and organized the personality by mediating between internal and external experience. The superego, referred to interchangeably in the 1923 paper as the ego ideal, was the structure that contained internalized real and fantasied approvals, criticism, threats, moral standards, and ideals of parents. Freud now expanded the idea of shifting developmental progression of erogenous zones to include the shifting progression of related wishes and fantasies with the structural model. And, perhaps most important, the structural model brought two new concepts to Freud's understanding of the mind: (a) the idea that these wishes and fantasies were connected not only to drives but also to objects and the child's shifting relationships to those objects, and (b) that these relational configurations were internalized. The Oedipus complex was further refined and highlighted in a new way within the structural model.

In 1923, Freud used the concept of identification in the context of the Oedipus complex to explain how the ego, like the rider on the horse, is able to rein in the drives of the id. First Freud wrote of the side-by-side existence of the "positive Oedipus complex" and the "inverted negative Oedipus complex." The former included the child's libidinal wishes for the opposite sex-parent and rivalrous feelings toward the same-sex parent. The latter referred to libidinal wishes towards the same-sex parent and rivalrous feelings toward the opposite-sex parent. Freud explained that the complete

Oedipus complex was "twofold, positive and negative ... due to the bisexuality originally present in children." He described a precipitate forming in the ego resulting in a special modification when mother and father identifications unite. This newly formed identification-based aspect of the ego was called the ego ideal or superego. Because this higher order structure was the means by which the child relinquished infantile sexual wishes, Freud declared the superego to be the "heir" to the Oedipus complex. Infantile sexuality would be left behind, and infantile omnipotence would now be dented by a new sense of reality that included inner reality and Oedipal identifications with the development of the new "heir." The Oedipus complex became a developmental landmark signaling a further and fundamental structuralization of the mind that resulted in the child's initiation into a moral order and an individuation founded on the basis of intrapsychic conflict.

Freud extended his theory on how the child resolved an Oedipal conflict 1 year later in *The Dissolution of the Oedipus Complex.* He emphasized the relinquishment of libidinal attachment to Oedipal objects and their substitution by identifications with parental authority. Freud spoke of the desexualization and sublimation of these Oedipal striving, and he stressed the importance of the ego's defense against castration anxiety. For the first time, Freud delineated different paths for the Oedipus complex in boys and girls. He emphasized that boys were driven to resolve their Oedipal longings after seeing the female genitals. With the sight of the female "castrated" genitals "the loss of his own penis became imaginable and the threat of castration takes its deferred effect." Fear of castration and guilt motivated the boy to identify with and internalize the father's moral rules and standards. In contrast, the girl's dissolution of the Oedipus complex requires the acceptance of her castrated state as an accomplished fact, something that occurred prior to the formation of the Oedipus complex. Freud had already elaborated on the weaker state of the female superego and, in 1924, he asserted that the dissolution of the Oedipus complex in the girl is never fully accomplished.

Freud's struggle to explain female development continued in *Some Psychical Consequences of the Anatomical Distinction Between the Sexes* in 1925 wherein he posited a developmental sequence for female Oedipal development. The core of this scheme centered on the vicissitudes of the questionable "penis-envy" phenomenon that Freud had first mentioned in *The Sexual Theories of Children* in 1908. The sequence was described as follows: (a) the girl discovered her lack of penis; (b) the discovery of her castrated state gave rise to feelings of inferiority, penis envy, and anger at her mother for not providing a penis; (c) consequently there is a loosening of the libidinal ties toward mother and a turning to father; and (d) the father is then looked to as a provider of a penis and a baby to compensate. Freud added a caveat at the end of the paper that his opinions could be wrong because they were based on a handful of cases, and that further observation was needed to validate his findings. Unfortunately, despite his own caveat and others' questions, these ideas became enshrined as the classical position on female sexuality for several decades.

Freud collaborated with Ruth Mack Brunswick prior to his death to write *The Preoedipal Phase of the Libido Development* that was published posthumously in 1940. In his final work, Freud wrestled with the importance and impact of pre-Oedipal attachment to the mother and clarified the fantasy of the "phallic mother." He had considered the girl's pre-Oedipal attachment to her mother earlier in *Female Sexuality* in 1931. In the 1940 paper, Freud rebutted those authors (Klein, Horney) who challenged his view of the female Oedipus complex. After discovering the Oedipus fantasy in himself, after dedicating years to understanding how the complex formed, how it evolved differently in boys and girls, how it may or may not resolve, and how it intensified to yield the superego, in the end Freud turned back developmentally. Although still holding to his shibboleth of psychoanalysis, Freud moved back toward that "dark continent" with which he was far less familiar to seek what nodal fantasies might be hidden beneath the Oedipal wish.

II. CURRENT CLINICAL RELEVANCE

Despite Freud holding his discovery of the Oedipus complex to be the "nucleus of neurosis", contemporary psychoanalysts continue to question its relevance to contemporary theory and practice. For a patient to have a successful analysis must today's analyst continue to whisper the Freudian shibboleth of "Oedipal fantasies" or "Oedipal conflicts?" Research on early childhood development in the decades following Freud has yielded findings that not only have resulted clearly in the redefinition of the Oedipus complex but have also led to a shift in the centrality of the Oedipus complex. Infant and child observational studies have provided new information about gender identity formation, female psychology, and sexuality. Freud's assumptions about the timing of several phenomena crucial to his theory that the Oedipus complex is the nucleus of psychical development have been challenged. For example, Freud was wrong when he stated that the discovery of the anatomical differences between the sexes occurred during the phallic phase. We now know that this discovery is made between 16 to 24 months, during the 2nd year of life. Freud was also inaccurate when he assumed that boys' and girls' development were the same up until the phallic years. We now know that gender identity (one's sense of whether one is a boy or a girl) is determined by the time the child reaches age 2 to 3. Such research has allowed analysts to rethink the concepts of penis envy, the negative Oedipal complex, and superego formation, and how they apply to both the boy's and the girl's psychological growth.

Penis envy was a concept which originated with Freud and became pivotal in his understanding of female psychology. This clinical concept of penis envy is manifested in an unpleasant feeling of inadequacy associated with and triggered by a covetous wish for the phallus. Freud asserted several ideas about penis envy: (a) the child discovered that the boy has a penis and the girl has no penis in the phallic phase; (b) the discovery led to castration anxiety and superego formation in the boy; and (c) in the girl, this discovery led to narcissistic injury with hostility toward the mother and subsequent turning to the father for a baby to replace the missing penis. The idea of penis envy in girls has been reconsidered and questioned as being a masculine or "phallocentric" perspective as psychoanalytic researchers have gained a greater understanding of female development. At the same time, clinicians have become more sophisticated in their attempts to understand clinical material about the penis and a wish for it in female patients. It is common these days for analysts to interpret such material as defensive against more pervasive feelings of inadequacy or as a desire for the penis to fulfill feminine needs (such as the wish to be penetrated). Rarely is penis envy interpreted as a primary issue. The concept of primary femininity was not available to Freud. Primary femininity implies an inborn sense of femaleness which predates penis envy, castration anxiety and the Oedipus complex. That is, femininity is innate and, at least in part, biological rather than simply a reaction to a disappointed inability to be masculine. Nonetheless, femininity is still subject to conscious and unconscious conflict and identifications with father as well as mother. Analytic observation of girls had led certain analysts to ask whether the phallic phase occurs at all in girls. If a phallic phase equivalent exists in girls, it is quite different from that of boys.

Penis envy is now recognized as occurring in both sexes. It means different things in boys and girls depending on a variety of factors including biology, environmental experiences with both parents, and fantasy formation. Boys have been observed to suffer from penis envy when they discover that an older male has a larger organ than they do. Some, but certainly not most, girls develop a fantasy that they have been castrated. Penis envy occurs in some girls but not in others. When it does occur it is dependent on the girls preexisting feminine identity and the experiences that formed it. Restitutive fantasies of a girl's illusory penis can occur in both sexes. Analysts have also wondered whether penis envy can cover a defensive devaluation of an all-powerful mother in both sexes. Penis envy in this context correlates with the feelings of smallness and helplessness with which every child must contend. The universal fantasy of the "phallic mother" can serve to deny castration or helpless vulnerability in a small child. Some analysts have suggested that shifts in fantasy content can be caused by cultural changes so that penis envy will decline and breast and womb envy will increase as gender roles continue to evolve in modern society. In summary, penis envy and narcissistic injury are no longer thought to be necessary factors initiating the girl's entry into the Oedipus complex. Neither is the female superego deemed to be "weak" or deficient. To date, however, penis envy remains part of the clinical vernacular of psychoanalysis though its meaning in girls and boys has been greatly amended and enlarged from Freud's original notions.

Penis envy is not the only aspect of Freud's concept of the Oedipus complex that has been reviewed and revised. New knowledge of gender identity and closer examination of the complexity of both male and female development has raised questions about the concept of the negative Oedipus complex. Freud had posited the negative Oedipus complex originally as a way to reconcile mixed identifications: The child, regardless of gender, identifies with both parents. Unlike penis envy, the negative Oedipus complex is not widely used in clinical contexts. Psychoanalytic writers have speculated that the diminished usage of the concept reflects the fact that it does not easily or even accurately fit observable clinical evidence. Some analysts have studied and questioned the negative Oedipus complex in girls, others in boys. Focusing on the girl, Edgecombe asked whether the negative Oedipus complex was a normal phase of Oedipal development if it existed at all. Others have reassessed negative Oedipal material and found it better explained in terms of a regression from an Oedipal to a pre-Oedipal level of object relations. What some label negative Oedipal material is seen by others as a wish to be nurtured, fed, and protected by mother: The girl relates on the basis of dyadic pre-Oedipal wishes rather than relating to the mother in an erotic way with rivalrous feelings toward the father. It remains an empirical question whether girls go through a normal negative Oedipal stage of development. Some analysts have reported finding such material only in women with histories of an absent father and a neglectful, depressed mother.

Blos is one of the few analysts who have examined the negative Oedipus complex in boys in his studies of the relationship of boys and their fathers. He prefers to use the terms "isogender dyadic and triadic complex" rather than "negative Oedipus complex." He prefers these terms because he challenges the idea that dyadic relationships are prerequisites for triadic ones. He views early male bonding as more complex than the boy's erotic love for the father as interpreted by concepts such as the Oedipal constellation. Blos emphasized that the boy's early relationship with the father not only consolidates gender identity but also provides a sense of security and safety. Furthermore, the boy's closeness with his father is not necessarily feminine or passive even if it has erotic components. For these reasons he views the term negative Oedipus complex as both misleading and pejorative. Another conceptual problem with the negative Oedipus concept involves whether to consider it as a defense against a positive Oedipus complex, a regression or fixation to a preoedipal level of development, or as pathological in its own right. Complicating the matter is the difficulty of differentiating clinically between oedipal and preoedipal. Furthermore, these two levels of object relatedness can co-exist in a superimposed, simultaneous manner. As a result the concept of the negative Oedipus complex does not appear often in psychoanalytic writings emanating from the United States.

Despite revisions in the way we understand the role of penis envy and negative Oedipus complex, the Oedipus complex remains alive and well in psychoanalytic theory and practice. Many psychoanalysts continue to conceptualize the Oedipus complex and the Oedipal phase as the developmental stage during which the mind either does or does not organize in a new and vital way: namely, a way that is defined as "neurotic." Neurotic mental organization refers to a special and unique structuralization that is thought to occur during the Oedipal phase. Such structuralization is a concept used to describe a reordering of mental functioning. This developmentally advanced mode of organization includes such new capacities as the integration of drives with triadic (rather than dyadic) objection relations, more selective identifications, and a more refined and differentiated sense of morality and authority. It is the most developmentally advanced level of organization available to the human mind. Psychoanalysts believe that the boundary between neurosis and normality is only quantitative, not qualitative. In "good-enough" circumstances, there is a nodal shift from the interpersonal to the intrapsychic that characterizes a neurotic organization. The danger of retaliation for wishes is no longer external but internal. The feared punishment is not in the form of the parent's action or attitude but involves guilt experienced as a failure to adhere to one's internalized ego ideal. This achievement of a capacity for guilt and intrapsychic danger reflects the maturation of the superego as a psychic structure that can regulate the individual's behavior. Most analysts believe that it is through the Oedipus complex, and during the Oedipal phase, that the superego, "heir to the Oedipus complex," is functionally consolidated. Many analysts correlate the formation of the superego with the Oedipus complex and, thus, couple the capacity for neurotic conflict with the Oedipus complex and Oedipal conflict. These analysts tend to view the Oedipus complex as what Spitz called the "fourth psychic organizer."

Spitz described three "critical periods" of psychic organization while applying embryological theory to ego development. These periods were defined by the emergence of new behaviors that Spitz took to indicate that different mental functions were brought into a new relation with one another. The result was new psychological growth manifested not only through a new behavior but also by a new affective expression. The three shifts that Spitz thought signaled a new level in psychic structuralization are: (a) the social smile, (b) stranger anxiety, and (c) the "no" gesture. Those who conceptualize the Oedipus complex as the fourth psychic organizer regard Oedipal conflict as evidence of a new level of organization; the ego now functions "neurotically," making internal compromises and becoming increasingly independent of the external environment. Many psychoanalysts equate Oedipal conflict with neurotic conflict and the infantile neurosis and, consequently, use Oedipal material in the patient's associations to assess whether psychic structure is neurotic or not. Thus, the presence of Oedipal conflicts in the patient's history takes on diagnostic significance. Oedipal content indicates neurotic symptoms or personality traits according to this equation. This diagnosis carries with it the treatment prescription that psychoanalysis is the treatment of choice. Likewise, patients whose conflicts are pre-Oedipal should be treated with psychotherapy according to adherents of this view.

However, child observation suggests that Freud was wrong in the timing of his central Oedipus complex. Not only do the discovery of anatomical differences and gender identity occur long before the emergence of the Oedipus complex, but, so too, does the formation of the superego. Precursors of superego development (along with the capacity for intrapsychic conflict) have been noted in the 2nd year of life, before the phallic and Oedipal phases. Ironically, they can occur during the critical period described by Spitz as the third organizer, "the no gesture." Occurring at the anal-rapprochement phase (a combination of Freud and Mahler's developmental theories), "the no gesture" initiates the child's struggle with compliance to mother's demands. Compliance indicates the beginnings of internal controls and internalized conflict. Margaret Mahler described the rapprochement subphase as the 3rd in the 4 stages of what she called the separation–individuation process. It is marked by notable ambivalence and the attainment of object constancy. Hence, the early superego arises in the context of ambivalence. When the child begins to say "no" to himself or herself the inchoate makings of the superego are unconsciously at work. If intrapsychic conflict and superego formation can begin in pre-Oedipal years, where does this leave the Oedipus complex? How can Oedipal conflict be a litmus test for presence of the capacity for intrapsychic conflict? Psychoanalysts have begun to wrestle with these questions.

If neurosis is thought to be an indication of superego modulation of intrapsychic conflict, our most recent knowledge of development indicates that neurotic internal structure begins before the appearance of the Oedipus complex. Thus, pre-Oedipal conflicts do not necessarily mean the mind is not organized neurotically. Similarly, the assumption that all Oedipal conflict is evidence of neurotic character structure is problematic. Psychoanalysts regularly bear witness to the fact that all that is Oedipal clinically—including manifestations of an Oedipus complex—is not necessarily indicative of neurosis. Symptomatology that could be viewed as a sign of neurosis (such as phobias or obsessional symptoms) may occur in individuals with borderline or narcissistic character structures. Moreover, Oedipal content can be observed regularly in the thoughts of patients organized at a borderline or psychotic level. It seems most reasonable to conclude, then, that psychoanalysis is indicated when the patient's symptoms or character traits are part of a personality structured at a neurotic level. Neurotic personality structure is characterized by internalized conflicts that arouse anxiety to which the ego responds with signal anxiety mobilizing appropriate defenses and/or compromise formations. The content of the wishes, fantasies, or conflicts that would lend themselves best to psychoanalytic treatment may be either Oedipal or pre-Oedipal, about either competing for the opposite-sex parent or seeking the security of mother. Likewise, a transference neurosis, often considered a *sine qua non* of psychoanalysis proper, does not absolutely require that its content be embedded in Oedipal themes. It is the mental structure and not the mental content that is most clinically significant.

In assessing whether to recommend psychoanalysis versus psychotherapy, the psychodynamically trained physician should assess the adaptability of the ego's functioning, not evidence of an Oedipus complex. One can be led to erroneous treatment recommendations if one looks for signs of Oedipal conflict, castration anxiety, penis envy, rivalrous wishes toward the same-sex parent object, and an eroticized transference. Though it provides one of the most complex conflicts to the developing mind, the Oedipus complex is not always proof of neurosis. Oedipal wishes can be organized in psychosis or borderline ways. The clinician should instead assess for autoplastic (rather than alloplastic) modes of conflict resolution. Autoplastic means that the individual's psychic structure allows for psychic shifts to be made so that conflicts are resolved "internally" rather than by attempting to make the world accommodate to the self (alloplastic). Furthermore, the capacity for affect regulation (specifically signal affects), a sense of self-responsibility, and a superego that controls impulses before they are expressed behaviorally should be looked for as core indicators of neurotic structure.

III. CONCLUSION

In conclusion, although the Oedipus complex and the Oedipal phase of development remain indelible in the history of psychoanalysis, vital to contemporary theory and practice of psychoanalysis, and nuclear to the formation and understanding of unconscious mental structure, the Oedipus complex and Oedipal conflict are no longer necessarily central to the diagnosis of neurosis. The clinician who blindly holds the Oedipus complex as the unshakeable shibboleth of psychoanalysis is in as precarious a position as was Oedipus on the road to Thebes.

See Also the Following Articles

Alderian Psychotherapy ■ History of Psychotherapy ■ Intrapsychic Conflict ■ Jungian Psychotherapy ■ Object-Relaitons Psychotherapy ■ Psychoanalysis and Psychoanalytic Psychotherapy: Technique ■ Structural

Theory ■ Topographic Theory ■ Transference Neurosis ■ Unconscious, The

Further Reading

Blanck, G. (1984). The complete Oedipus complex. *International Journal of Psycho-Analysis, 65,* 331–340.

Blos, P. (1987). Freud and the father complex. *Psychoanalytic Study of the Child, 42,* 425–442.

Calogeras, C., & Schupper, F. (1972). Origins and early formulations of the Oedipus complex. *Journal of the American Psychoanalytic Association, 20,* 751–775.

Edgecombe, R. (1976). Some comments on the concept of the negative Oedipal phase. *PSC, 31,* 35–61.

Moore & Fine. (1990). *Psychoanalytic terms and concepts.* New Haven, CT: Yale University Press.

Simon, R. (1991). Is the Oedipus complex still the cornerstone of psychoanalysis? *Journal of the American Psychoanalytic Association, 39,* 641–668.

Tyson, P. (1990). Neurosis in childhood and in psychoanalysis: A developmental reformulation. *Journal of the American Psychoanalytic Association, 44,* 143–165.

Tyson, P., & Tyson, R. L. (1990). *Psychoanalytic theories of development.* New Haven, CT: Yale University Press.

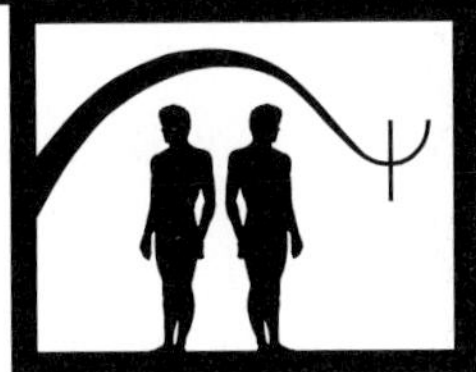

Omission Training

Ruth Anne Rehfeldt
Southern Illinois University

GLOSSARY

differential reinforcement of incompatible behaviors Reinforcement is provided contingent on an individual's engaging in behaviors that are incompatible with an undersirable target behavior.

differential reinforcement of other behaviors Reinforcement is provided contingent on an individual's engaging in behaviors other than an undesirable target behavior.

extinction Decrease in behavior following the removal of reinforcement.

overcorrection An intervention in which an individual is required to improve the setting beyond the way in which it appeared before a disruptive behavior was emitted, or to repeatedly practice behaviors that are alternative to the disruptive behavior.

punishment A contingent relationship between a behavior and a consequence such that the consequence causes the particular behavior to decrease in frequency.

reinforcement A contingent relationship between a behavior and a consequence such that the consequence causes the particular behavior to increase in frequency.

stimulus generalization The spread of the effects of reinforcement to settings different from that in which the original procedure was conducted.

time out An intervention in which an individual is removed from sources of positive reinforcement for a specified period of time.

I. DESCRIPTION OF TREATMENT

Omission training is a procedure that is used to reduce or eliminate behaviors that are deemed undesirable. Omission training is typically used to reduce behaviors that occur at a moderate-to-high rate. In general, the procedure requires that a time interval be established, and, if at the conclusion of that time interval, the target behavior has been "omitted," a reinforcer is delivered. Reinforcement is thus provided contingent upon the absence of the target behavior. The name omission training is for this reason often used synonymously with the term DRO schedule, or differential reinforcement of zero rates of the target behavior. As an example, consider an elementary school-aged child who gets up out of his or her seat at a high rate during the teacher's lessons. To implement an omission training procedure, the teacher might first determine the longest duration of time that the child can sit without getting up out of the seat during lesson time and establish this as the specified time interval. The teacher may then observe the child during that time interval, and if the child refrains from getting up out of the seat, the teacher may reinforce the child with a gold star, to be later exchanged for additional recess time. After a sufficient number of reinforcers are earned, the teacher may gradually and successively increase the length of time for which the child is required to refrain from getting up out of the seat to earn a gold star. This omission training procedure is likely to be effective in reducing the rate with which the child gets up out of the seat during lesson time.

There are a number of advantages associated with the use of omission training. First, because all that is required is that an interval of time be recorded, an observation be made as to whether or not the target behavior occurred, and, if it did not occur, a reinforcer is delivered, this procedure is fairly easy to implement. Teachers, parents, or human service agency staff who wish to reduce a behavior need only a rudimentary understanding of behavioral principles. In 1979, for example, Howard Hughes, Anita Hughes, and Hardy Dial reported the successful use of an omission training procedure by parents of a 4-year-old child who engaged in excessive thumb sucking. Likewise, in 1980 Edward Barton and Jennifer Madsen demonstrated that teachers' aides could effectively use omission training to reduce the extreme drooling exhibited by a child with severe mental retardation.

Second, ethical issues that are raised with other behavior reduction procedures are not of the same magnitude of concern here. Providing reinforcement contingent on the absence of a response is considerably less intrusive than other frequently utilized procedures, such as overcorrection and time out. A third and related advantage is that omission training does not produce the undesirable side effects (such as frustration, aggression, or other emotional behaviors) that are often observed with more intrusive behavior reduction procedures. Fourth, several studies have shown that the deceleration in the rate of the target behavior often occurs rapidly following the onset of an omission training procedure. This makes omission training a desirable procedure to use for reducing behaviors that are particularly disruptive. Fifth, the effects of omission training have been shown to be relatively long lasting, and to generalize to settings other than that in which the original treatment was implemented.

II. THEORETICAL BASES

Omission training as a treatment poses some theoretical difficulties. Specifically, the definition of reinforcement is an increase in the rate of a behavior when that behavior reliably produces some consequence; reinforcement hence describes the contingent relationship between a behavior and its consequence. One might ask, how can this same relationship hold with the absence of a particular behavior, as is the case in omission training? One way of reconciling this dilemma is by acknowledging that while the individual is refraining from engaging in the target behavior during the specified time interval, that individual is engaging in other behaviors. It is the other behaviors that are correlated with reinforcement, and hence, the other behaviors that increase in rate. For example, in our previous example, while the child is refraining from getting up from the seat, the child may be playing with a pencil, drawing on the desk, or listening attentively to the teacher. The gold star deliveries might serve to increase the rate of these other behaviors. Omission training, then, might conceivably be regarded as differential reinforcement of other, or alternative, behaviors.

Because behaviors occurring during the specified time interval may increase in rate due to their correlation with reinforcement, it is possible for other undesirable behaviors to increase in rate. For example, it would certainly not be beneficial if the omission procedure was successful in reducing the child's getting up out of the seat, but also in increasing the rate of the child's talking to a neighbor. For this reason, it is important to specify socially appropriate behaviors in which it is believed to be beneficial for the individual to engage. If behaviors that were deemed desirable for the individual to engage in during the specified time interval were determined and reinforcement was provided contingent on their emission, an increase in desirable behaviors would occur concomitant with the decrease in the undesirable behavior. This procedure could be conceptualized as a differential reinforcement of incompatible behavior, or a DRI, schedule. For example, if the child was provided with gold stars for listening attentively during specified time intervals, this behavior is incompatible with getting up out of the seat and would be expected to increase in rate. So, it may be useful to gradually fade a DRO schedule into a DRI schedule, so that desirable behaviors are specified and increased. It is also important that the individual's opportunities for reinforcement be maximized. The omission training procedure must begin with a specified time interval during which baseline levels of behavior suggest that the target behavior will not occur. When a certain number of reinforcers have been acquired, the time period can be gradually increased.

III. EMPIRICAL STUDIES

A. Use of DRO to Reduce Self-Injurious Behavior

In 1990, a dramatic demonstration of omission training was reported by Glynnis Cowdery, Brian Iwata, and

Gary Pace. The procedure was used to reduce the frequency of severe self-excoriation (scratching or rubbing) that was displayed by a boy who was not developmentally disabled. Functional analysis results revealed that the boy's self-injurious behavior was maintained by automatic reinforcement. A treatment plan was established in which pennies, tokens, or social praise were delivered following periods of time during which the boy refrained from scratching. Initially, the interval was set at 2 min, which was the longest amount of time the boy had been observed to refrain from scratching. As the boy met the criterion for reinforcement, the time interval was gradually increased to 18 min, and eventually expanded to where the boy was able to leave the facility in which he lived to visit his parents. Four months of treatment were required to reduce the boy's self-injurious behavior to less harmful levels; it was never completely eliminated.

B. Effects of Omission Training as Compared to Extinction

In some situations, caregivers may wish to determine what function a maladaptive behavior is serving, or what specific reinforcer is maintaining the behavior. When that has been identified, it seems reasonable to expect that withdrawing that reinforcer should extinguish the behavior, or cause it to decrease. For this reason, some investigators have compared the effectiveness of omission training to extinction. For example, in 1975, F. Dudley McGlynn, William B. Miller, and John Fancher established a key-pressing response by individuals with chronic schizophrenia. For one half of the participants, key pressing was then put on extinction, while the other one half of the participants received reinforcement contingent on not pressing during specified periods of time. Response rate was shown to decrease more rapidly for participants in the extinction condition; extinction was also shown to result in overall more response suppression than omission training. In 1976, Jeff Topping, Helen Thompson, and Billy Barrios reported slightly different results using a similar procedure with institutionalized individuals with Down's syndrome. Neither procedure was more effective in reducing response rate initially, but greater overall suppression resulted from omission training. The degree to which these results would also be obtained in clinical settings is not clear from either of these reports.

C. Durability and Generality

The effectiveness of an intervention can be evaluated on the basis of durability and generality. Durability refers to the degree to which the effects of the intervention persist over time after treatment has been terminated. For example, Brian Iwata and Andrew Lorentzson showed in 1976 that the effects of an omission training procedure in controlling seizure-like behavior persisted for 13 weeks following treatment withdrawal. Generality refers to the degree to which the effects of the treatment are shown to generalize to settings different from that in which the original procedure was implemented. In the study described previously by Cowdery, Iwata, and Pace, treatment was conducted in an institutional setting, but the effects were shown to generalize to the child's home when he visited his parents. As with most behavioral interventions, generalization of treatment effects is likely when the settings in which the intervention is performed in are varied, the frequency of reinforcement in the original training situation is reduced sufficiently so that the training situation more closely resembles the natural environment, and when common stimuli are programmed between settings.

D. Side Effects

As mentioned previously, omission training does not produce the worrisome side effects that other procedures might. However, emotional responses may still occur. Cowdery and his colleagues noted that emotional behavior (e.g., crying) did occur when the boy did not earn his scheduled reinforcers. Thus, an individual may experience frustration if scheduled reinforcers are not earned, but such effects would seem to be a by-product of any reinforcement-based intervention. Such effects are presumably of a lesser magnitude than those resulting from more intrusive procedures. It must be noted, however, that there may be clinical situations in which the target behavior poses such concern, either because it is harmful to others or harmful to oneself, such that caregivers do not have time to wait for omission training to take its effect. In fact, more harm may be caused if the behavior is allowed to continue to occur. In such situations, a more intrusive procedure may be warranted.

IV. SUMMARY

Omission training has been shown to be an effective procedure for reducing or eliminating undesirable behavior. It is not as intrusive as other behavior reduction procedures and produces few side effects. Its effects may be seen relatively soon after its onset and may be relatively durable over time. The reduction in the rate of the undesirable behavior can be expected to occur in settings different from that in which the original training was conducted. Omission training is an easy procedure to implement and will be most successful if opportunities for reinforcement are maximized, and if a DRI schedule is gradually implemented.

See Also the Following Articles

Chaining ■ Extinction ■ Differential Reinforcement of Other Behavior

Further Reading

Catania, A. C. (1997). *Learning.* Englewood Cliffs, NJ: Prentice Hall.

Cooper, J. O., Heron, T. E., & Heward, W. L. (1990). *Applied behavior analysis.* Upper Saddle River, NJ: Prentice Hall.

Homer, A. L., & Peterson, L. (1980). Differential reinforcement of other behavior: A preferred response elimination procedure. *Behavior Therapy, 11,* 449–471.

Kazdin, A. E. (2000). *Behavior modification in applied settings.* Belmont: CA: Wadsworth Publishing Co.

Martin, G., & Pear, J. (1999). *Behavior modification: What it is and how to do it* (6th ed.). Upper Saddle River, NJ: Prentice Hall.

Sulzer-Azaroff, B., & Mayer, G. R. (Eds.). (1991). *Behavior analysis for lasting change.* Orlando, FL: Holt, Rinehart, & Winston.

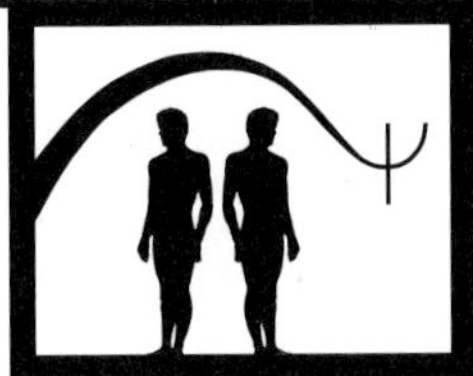

Online or E-Therapy

Zebulon Taintor

New York University School of Medicine

GLOSSARY

e-therapy Doing therapy by electronic communication.

online Generally is used to denote the subset of e-therapy done in real time, aiming for pauses between messages that are as brief as those between two people in the same room.

unmet e-therapy E-therapy where client and therapist have not met.

webcam A camera used in conjunction with a personal computer for video communication via the Internet.

E-therapy is doing therapy by electronic communication. At present this means exchanging text messages. Web sites offering e-therapy sometimes do not distinguish between therapy and counseling. E-therapy has evolved empirically because of the availability of technology, which includes both e-mail for communication, and the Internet, where therapists' web sites attract potential clients. There are no controlled studies of efficacy, although anecdotal testimonials abound. It is derived from older technologies (letters, telephone, facsimiles) that did not achieve the status of distinct therapies. E-therapy has emerged as yet another way the Internet may alter radically the way we do things. Although most professional associations agree e-therapy is not as effective or safe as when the therapist and patient are in the same room, proponents argue it is more convenient and can reach out and involve those who cannot or will not meet a therapist bodily. E-therapy is better than no contact for certain populations and may lend itself to frequent contacts in some forms of therapy. Potential disadvantages abound. Future use is likely as an adjunct to therapy that includes meeting in the same room, but unmet e-therapy depends on the ability to achieve adequate evaluations, and overcoming negative trends in liability, regulations, and reimbursement.

I. DESCRIPTION OF TREATMENT

The Internet, established in 1969 at the University of Southern California for national defense uses, has emerged as a major form of communication, with unanticipated qualities and effects. Electronic mail was used for years among users of terminals of main frame computers. Specialized offers to certain customers date to 1973 with Lexis legal information services available to clients of Mead Data Central. CompuServe began the first online access service for customers in 1979. E-mail has been increasingly accepted in general medicine, especially for anything a patient might have to write down if told on the telephone, such as test results, written instructions, directions, phone numbers, and so on. E-mail messages can be linked to web sites for patient education. Increasing use has been recommended by the Institute of Medicine's report, "Crossing the Quality Chasm."

E-mail can be contrasted to older technologies, long used in therapy.

A. Letters

An e-mail is basically a letter, the most ancient regular form of communication across distance. Even between people who know and see one another, letters can be used to develop and give a particular form to relationships. Many teenagers have pen pals, often in a distant country, that they do not meet for years. There are published exchanges of letters of people who have and have not met, in which the correspondence was more important than face-to-face encounters. For instance, Tchaikovsky and Najda von Meck corresponded for decades while living in the same city. They chose never to meet by plan, although reacting in their letters to their chance sightings of one another. Numerous examples show the process of therapy in traditional letter writing. Sigmund Freud developed several therapeutic correspondences. There is a rich literature of therapeutic exchanges, which typically took weeks. The big advantages of e-mail over letters are seen at every stage of the process: ease of composition by typing or dictating onto a screen, editing on screen, speed of delivery, ease of retrieval, legibility, ease of response, and storage. Retrieval can be so quick as to allow a conversation in real time, or at one's leisure, which means that the recipient is likely to be in a mindset favorable for communication. Cost per communication is insignificant in that monthly charges through Internet service providers usually provide unlimited e-mail for a monthly fee of $20 or less. These advantages are so self-evident and overwhelming that no studies have had to be done to quantify these advantages.

B. Telephone

Calls have been used to help people feel better since the invention of the telephone in 1885. They are immediate, and convey nonverbal data through pauses, tone of voice, inflections, and so on. Usually costs are charged by the amount of time taken, so telephone calls tend to be brief. However, therapists have routinely scheduled long sessions with patients when one or the other is traveling. Unless recorded, they are not retrievable, which may or may not be an advantage. If recorded, playback speedup is essential to achieve evaluation times that can match the ease with which written exchanges can be scanned. Telephone rings tend to be intrusive, and may not catch the recipient in a receptive mind set. Leaving messages on answering machines frustrates the very urgency that led to the call and is complained about as "telephone tag."

There is extensive experience with telephone therapy in the form of suicide prevention centers and other "hot lines." Answerers are always available. The caller and answerer have not met previously. Suicide prevention centers were once publicized extensively and were busy, answering many calls and serving many people in a crisis mode. Studies showed suicide prevention centers did not reduce suicide rates in the cities they served, a phenomenon attributed to the likelihood that more seriously suicidal patents did not call but killed themselves instead. Generally callers used hot lines once or twice. They got support and were urged to go to services where they could be seen and helped. Some of those served did so immediately, others used crisis hot lines and emergency rooms for months or years before getting involved in more regular treatment, and others did not progress beyond use of crisis hot lines. Crisis hot lines are widely used in emergencies and are accepted as one part of the range of services. Some proponents of e-therapy argue from the hot line experience that some people in need of therapy will get involved via the Internet because of its convenience and anonymity. However, web sites offering unmet e-therapy do not resemble crisis hotlines in avoiding diagnosis, treatment, and ongoing relationships.

C. Facsimile Transmission (Fax)

The fax offers a chance to preserve the handwritten, sometimes illustrated, letter format while using the electronic speed of immediate delivery. The novelist Isabel Allende described writing a letter to her mother daily for 30 years, in recent years by fax. She and her mother tie each year's faxes with a ribbon and store them in a closet. Although the writer knows of patients and therapists who communicate by fax, there are no scientific reports. Fax communication is closest to e-mail in that it can occur in real time, but uses the telephone system rather than the Internet and is stored as an image rather than retrievable text. Use of the computer as a facsimile machine may increase as therapists grapple with the regulatory issues described below.

Although the above forms of communication have been available for years, physicians in almost all training programs in all specialties receive no specific education in how to use them.

E-mail poses the following problems:

1. *Junk:* The problem of junk e-mail (spam) can be worse than junk mail, since there is no cost for paper, postage, or handling. For less than $20, a marketer can purchase a CD with millions of e-mail addresses. In April 2001 more than 10,000 "spam attacks" were launched daily. The estimated annual cost of spam is $8.5 billion, even though it can be sent without postage to a large number of addresses. Responding to spam, however negatively, actually provokes more, since it shows there is a live person behind the address.

2. *Volume:* Many therapists are on professional and other mailing lists, getting some of 6.1 billion e-mail messages sent daily.

3. *Loss of contact:* E-mail addresses and service providers, which may not reflect a person's name or location, are changed easily by people, often to avoid getting so much mail. Addresses may be upper or lower case sensitive, multiple (used for different purposes by one or more people), and can change without notice. That mail went undelivered is not always known by the sender; that mail was delivered to the wrong recipient is known by the sender only when the recipient takes the trouble to write back. Most e-mail users report having received someone else's mail.

These problems can be eased by getting an unpublished address only for e-therapy using a service provider easily accessed from any Internet browser. An ongoing relationship should include ways of contacting the client other than through e-mail.

4. Less easily resolved is *Disinhibition and projection:* The very ease with which e-mail can be sent quickly to anyone results in quick messages and responses before feelings have cooled. The improbability of any local, real-life repercussions in virtual communities on line is disinhibiting. Miscommunication, distortion, emotionality, and projection abound, thought to be a result of the lack of social cues and context. Angry messages constitute a greater percentage of e-mails than of regular letters. "Flaming" and other angry outbursts have led to the development of "netiquette," which may have its own class distinctions in various settings that provide a further complication. Proponents for e-therapy argue that spontaneity in online therapy is helpful. E-therapists practicing asynchronously garner praise for taking time to think about their responses. E-therapists will have to be able to write well, expect to be misunderstood, and deal with unexpected feelings stirred up by messages.

E-mail has evolved beyond simple transmission of text. It is possible to send images (e.g., remote art therapy) as an accompanying file, but this is rarely done. Voice dictation is used increasingly, but longer messages tend to slow interaction, and those using it find themselves employing longer words. Some proponents argue that the problem of the lack of physical cues can be overcome by using webcams, but video phones have been available for years without becoming popular. Use of webcams would change the modality to teleconferencing, which has emerged as a clearly defined therapy with limited reimbursement. At present e-mail belongs to the typists. For data gathering purposes this trades whatever can be gained from scrutinizing handwriting, itself the subject of a formidable literature, for legibility and retrievability.

II. GUIDELINES

E-therapy is a subset of patient–therapist electronic communication, so it must proceed within the general guidelines developed for such communication. These have been developed as follows.

The first comprehensive set of guidelines for physician–patient communication was developed by a committee within American Medical Informatics Association and adopted and published in 1998. The guidelines were passed on to the American Medical Association, which modified them slightly and adopted them in its assembly in June 2000. The American Psychiatric Association (APA) assembly adopted the guidelines in November 2000 and requested the APA Board of Trustees to accept the guidelines pending the adoption of APA guidelines. The APA Trustees did so in March 2001. Guidelines have been developed by the Psychiatric Society for Informatics (also highly derivative of the AMIA guidelines) and submitted to the APA. The guidelines adopted thus far are given here in their entirety.

The AMA Board of Trustees recommends:

1. That for those physicians who choose to utilize e-mail for selected patient and medical practice communications, the following guidelines be adopted.

Communications guidelines

A. Establish turnaround time for messages. Exercise caution when using e-mail for urgent matters.

B. Inform patients about privacy issues. Patients should know:
  Who besides addressee processes messages during addressee's usual business hours and during addressee's vacation or illness; and
  That the message may be included as part of the medical record, at the discretion of the physician. [The AMA subsequently stated this decision should be joint between patient and physician, while the Clinton administration privacy guidelines, barely modified (so far) by the Bush administration, offer no choice, stating such messages are to be part of the patient's record.]
C. Establish types of transactions (prescription refill, appointment scheduling, etc.) and sensitivity of subject matter (HIV, mental health, etc.) permitted over e-mail.
D. Instruct patients to put the category of transaction in the subject line of the message for filtering prescription: prescription, appointment, medical advice, billing question.
E. Request that patients put their name and patient identification number in the body of the message.
F. Configure automatic reply to acknowledge receipt of messages.
G. Send a new message to inform patient of completion of request.
H. Request that patients use autoreply feature to acknowledge reading clinician's message.
I. Develop archival and retrieval mechanisms.
J. Maintain a mailing list of patients, but do not send group mailings where recipients are visible to each other. Use blind copy feature in software.
K. Avoid anger, sarcasm, harsh criticism, and libelous references to third parties in messages.

Medicolegal and administrative guidelines

A. Develop a patient–clinician agreement for the informed consent for the use of e-mail. This should be discussed with the patient and documented in the medical record. Agreement should contain the following:

  Terms in communication guidelines (stated above).
  Provide instructions for when and how to covert to phone calls and office visits.
  Describe security mechanisms in place.
  Hold harmless the health care institution for information loss due to technical failures.
  Waive encryption requirement, if any, at patient's insistence.

B. Describe security in place, including:

  Using a password-protected screen saver for all desktop workstations in the office, hospital, and at home.
  Never forwarding patient-identifiable information to a third party without the patient's expressed permission.
  Never using patient's e-mail address in a marketing scheme.
  Not sharing professional e-mail accounts with family members.
  Not using unencrypted wireless communications with patient-identifiable information.
  Double checking all "To" fields prior to sending messages.

C. Perform at least weekly backups of e-mail onto long-term storage. Define long term as the term applicable to paper records.

D. Commit policy decisions to writing and electronic form.

2. That the policies and procedures for e-mail be communicated to patients who desire to communicate electronically.
3. That the policies and procedures for e-mail be applied to facsimile communications, where appropriate.
4. That the Board of Trustees [AMA, APA] revisit "Guidelines for Patient-Physician Electronic Mail" when the proposed HIPAA guidelines, encryption, and pertinent federal laws or regulations have been proposed or implemented.

The American Psychiatric Association has issued no statements on e-therapy, but has on telepsychiatry. These guidelines do not deal per se with special demands of the therapeutic process, but do show some of the regulatory burden involved in e-therapy. Subsequently the Health Insurance Portability and Accountability Act (HIPAA) regulations of 2000, themselves the subject of so much controversy as to have generated more comment than any other proposed regulation, have been adopted. They specifically provide for the protection of "notes recorded (in any medium) by a healthcare provider who is a mental health professional documenting or analyzing the contents of a conversation during a private counseling session or a group, joint, or family counseling session" as well as defining "covered professionals" as those who engage in electronic transactions. As of this writing, the requirement is that all e-mails must be included in the patient's record. The AMA and APA have asked that the physician and patient have the option of including e-mail or not. While protection for such notes is reckoned in advance, it may be difficult for an e-therapist to comply with all parts of the regulation at once.

Although the HIPAA regulations do not distinguish between counseling and psychotherapy notes and counseling in medicine may not be related to psychotherapy and still need to be confidential (e.g., genetic counseling might be of interest to insurers), the term "psychotherapy" has been avoided in statements issued by professional associations. The Ethics Committee of the American Psychological Association (www.apa.org/ethis/stmnt01.html) issued statements in 1995 and 1997 relating to its existing ethics code. While noting that there are no rules prohibiting electronically provided services as such, the statement refers to existing standards on practicing within one's boundary of competence, assessment, therapy, structuring the relationship, informed consent, doing no harm, and others. Most online therapists are marriage and family counselors and psychologists, with almost half possessing PhDs, so it is not surprising that other guidelines refer to counseling, particularly those adopted by the American Counseling Association in 1999 (www.counseling.org/gc/cybertx.htm) and the National Board of Certified Counselors in 2001 (www.nbcc.org/ethics/webethics.htm). "Suggested Principles for the Online Provision of Mental Health Services" were adopted in 2000 by the International Society for Mental Health Online, a self-constituted group of online therapists (mostly psychologists) founded in 1997 in conjunction with the Psychiatric Society for Informatics (mostly psychiatrists) (www.ismho.org/suggestions.html). Requirements include disclosure of credentials, performing an "adequate" evaluation, informed consent, performing within one's general competence (not dealing with any problem online one would not handle face-to-face), procedures to be followed in an emergency (the therapists should have the name of a local health care provider who can be contacted in an emergency), and so on.

The word "therapy" cannot be found in the suggestions or any other document cited earlier, since their framers see psychotherapy as requiring assessments and protections that are not possible without face-to-face meetings. Teleconferencing does not avoid such concerns, having been granted reimbursement mostly for consultations. A California law requires that whatever services are reimbursed when rendered in person be reimbursed as well when provided electronically, but third-party payers have indicated a willingness to deny claims for e-therapy on the grounds that it is not an equivalent service. Proponents of e-therapy urge reimbursement, but are accused of trying to have things both ways: avoiding liability by describing what they do as counseling, but wanting reimbursement for medically necessary psychotherapy. Persons needing psychotherapy must have some impairment to be reduced by treatment, yet patients with serious problems cannot be evaluated adequately on the basis of remote exchanges of text.

At least one professional organization unequivocally has opposed the practice of unmet e-therapy. The Clinical Social Work Federation voted to do so in its 2001 annual meeting, citing concerns about efficacy, liability, and jurisdiction. Its press release says, in part

> This area is totally unregulated and potentially very dangerous for clients and therapists alike. ... This new, very powerful medium blurs all the usual boundaries. Most organizations believe that it cannot or should not be evaluated by well-accepted professional standards. That just is not the case. The standards developed by the U.S. Department of Health and Human Services and Coordinated by the Office for the Advancement of Telehealth, are used by the federal government to assess federal policy on an ongoing basis. ... We have yet to see the first law suits in this area, but we know they're coming. Our concern with establishing a position on the delivery of online therapy services is in absolute alignment with the mission of state licensing boards ... the protection of the consumer. The standards used to analyze the growing area of text-based counseling include principles related to confidentiality, informed consent, quality of treatment, competence of the therapist, and basic ethical and professional requirements. These standards cannot be ensured when the client and therapist know each other only from a text on a screen. Assessment is the first phase of psychotherapy and frequently significant information about the client is based on nonverbal cues. Psychotherapy has at its heart a profoundly human connection, a connection that is, in itself, the major vehicle for change. Healing and restoration occur when the therapist and the client together find the bridge leading back, and forward at the same time, to the true self. Alienation from others and the self will not be healed through a virtual connection in cyberspace, a connection that is fraught with risks and hazards for both clients and clinicians.

Despite these cautions, it is clear that many online therapy practitioners are social workers not bound by the strictures above. This writer appeared on local television in tandem with a social worker treating a ballerina online for $80 per hour. They said they did not meet face-to-face because of the inconvenience, although separated only by a few blocks in midtown Manhattan. A marriage and family counselor confidently treated a patient he had never met, as they were separated by 2,100 miles. The press release correctly describes most other professional organizations as neutral about unmet e-therapy, but this does not reflect the intraorganizational debates, which turn on three variables: (1) "adequate evaluation", (2) data reduction, and (3) priorities for the underserved (those who cannot come for meetings in person. There is no controversy about the usefulness of e-therapy where therapist and client meet regularly.

III. DISADVANTAGES OF UNMET E-THERAPY

A. Deception

Michael Lewis has chronicled various deceivers, including teenagers who posed as a stockbroker and a lawyer. The first would pick any obscure stock that struck his fancy, promote it in chat rooms, and sell into the resulting victims's rally. The second passed online as a legal expert until he was exposed, after which demand for his advice continued. Lewis sees these young people as leaders in a populist electronic revolution, but they offer good examples of massive deception and an ongoing demand for advice in a climate that is not likely to be regulated soon. In New York State, as in most, anyone can call themself a psychotherapist, just as anyone can call himself or herself a fortune teller, astrologist, or palm reader. Periodically newspapers report crimes in which the victim was lured into a meeting after meeting the perpetrator on the Internet. Investigations of those offering online services found many did not give their professional credentials or offered incomplete ones (e.g., "M.S." in a context that implies it is in counseling when it may not be). Similarly, potential clients often give themselves fictional names. Not all deception is deliberate. Couples who met on the Internet have appeared to get married only to discover they mistook one another's sex. Tom Hanks, in the film "You've Got Mail," showed how a person's nature as expressed in e-mail can be very different from that expressed in the face-to-face workaday world. This problem is minimized when the patient and therapist have met enough in the same room for adequate evaluation and development of a therapeutic alliance.

B. Data Capture

Text-based messages leave out too much to be the sole basis of an evaluation for therapy. The data captured in e-mail are a complete set of a narrow band of communication. Although controlled studies show patients divulge facts more rapidly and completely to computers, most of the studies were done with substance abusers before the Internet and rise of confidentiality concerns. Computer-based assessments have not replaced live interviews because communication of facts still does not convey how a person thinks or feels about them.

C. Confidentiality

E-mails leave copies of themselves in almost all servers through which they pass. In this respect e-mail is less of a sealed letter than a postcard copied at each post office through which it passes. Although the regulations and guidelines included above require attention to confidentiality, they should be understood as raising the bar of difficulty of access to content. It is reasonable to assume that a highly motivated, intelligent person with enough time and other resources can eventually access all files. Thus confidentiality is likely to be sacrificed to the determined hacker.

D. Safety

Although the Internet seems well-enough dispersed to survive most catastrophes, both the Baltimore Tunnel fire and World Trade Center disaster either demolished cables or switching stations that help the Internet and e-mail to flow well. On the other hand, the World Trade Center disaster included such destruction that regular phone lines were out or overcrowded and cell phones highly variable, especially as cell towers atop the buildings were lost. E-mail was extremely effective in reassuring the worried, offering chances to send the same message to many people in one's address book. But systems crash, computers fail, and service can be interrupted by failure of any link in the chain. Other safety issues in e-therapy are, in some cases, a derivative of the deception issue in that text carries so little affect compared to a person's actual presence that most thoughtful therapists fear missing depression, especially suicidal intent. Safety concerns highlight the undesirability of doing e-therapy with a patient not evaluated face-to-face.

E. Liability

As of August 2001 only one lawsuit has been brought, but 31% of state regulatory agencies have had complaints about e-therapists. Not following the guidelines stated earlier would weaken a therapist's defense. Practicing across state lines to patients located where the therapist is not licensed is an added risk, especially as the local means for handling a crisis will also be remote. California legislation, likely to be replicated in other states, requires that anyone providing mental health services to its citizens be licensed in California. Liability is judged in art on the expectations created in plaintiffs, and web sites are careful to avoid statements that diagnosis and therapy are being offered, instead offering help with "problems, stress," and so on. More court tests are likely.

F. Lack of Definition, Standards, and Controlled Studies

This emerging field is not defined. Perhaps it is only a technology, perhaps a new technique, or some blend. It does not have standards per se; professional association standards are cautionary. The International Society for Mental Health Online maintains a web site of reported studies (94 as of September 17, 2001). Most reports are how-to-do-it anecdotes and testimonials to the promise of e-therapy. There are no controlled studies. Although some web sites have been set up by disappointed patients to describe negative experiences with e-therapy, such opinion tends to be reflected more in newspaper articles. In contrast, telemedicine, videoconferencing, telepsychiatry—anything in which video and spoken words are used—is being subjected to controlled studies with random assignment of subjects.

IV. ADVANTAGES OF E-THERAPY

E-therapy is best practiced when the patient and therapist feel comfortable in a progressing relationship that has clearly defined shared goals and objectives. Within this context, the disadvantages cited earlier can be minimized and the following advantages realized.

A. Distance

The Internet and e-mail know no distance, since they are available at any computer, any time, usually for the cost of a local telephone call.

B. Time

E-therapy can be done in real time or through a more leisurely back-and-forth exchange of messages. In real time there is an intensity and density of exchange very much like (although less expensive and slower than) a telephone call. One misses the affect a voice can convey. On the other hand, a record is produced (that must be encrypted for any hope of confidentiality) that can be useful for both patient and therapist later. A more leisurely exchange is more like an exchange of letters and can include elements of a journal kept by the patient with comments by the therapist. Cognitive therapy often proceeds well this way. Supportive therapy is enhanced by the therapist providing another means of access than the telephone, which is more intrusive than e-mail.

C. Convenience

E-therapy can be done without the trouble of travel, dealing with one's appearance, or taking other trouble.

D. Written Record

E-therapy can be used to generate a written record of exactly what texts were exchanged. Present regulations require this or inclusion of e-therapy exchanges in an electronic medical record or computerized patient record.

E. Stigma

There is a general impression that e-therapy carries less stigma because visits to a therapist's office are reduced, and one need not be identified. Because e-mail is fashionable, some of its cachet may spill over to e-therapy.

V. INDICATIONS FOR E-THERAPY

Proponents argue that e-therapy is particularly well-suited for the following:

1. Those who would not otherwise get involved. The Internet indeed attracts many people who are looking online for relationships. One indication is the number of people looking for mates, as evidenced by the membership numbers of the major services: Match.com (1 million), AmericanSingles.com (1.3

million), Matchmaker.com (40,000 new members each week), Jdate (150,000), Blacksingles.com (20,000). The impression that "the Net is packed with depressed people" is supported by at least one study showing an association with heavy Internet use and depression. There are many anecdotes of patients becoming involved in therapy as they developed relationships over the Internet, and outreach programs on the Internet may be useful.

2. Anyone who would benefit from having a written record of patient-therapist exchanges. This writer has routinely given copies of whatever he writes about patients to them. Patients report that it helps them remember what has happened and to see the process of treatment.

3. Those who live in remote places, are physically handicapped, suffer from severe agoraphobia, or communicate already by keyboard, the hearing impaired already communicating by text.

4. Cognitive-behavioral therapy. This form of therapy, which tends to emphasize intellect over affect, with its use of daily journals, labeling and categorizing thoughts, correcting cognitive distortions, and so on, is well-suited for a written record that can be parsed for insight and reinforcement.

5. Supportive therapy. The immediate availability and ease of communication via e-therapy allows ongoing contact as often as indicated and is reassuring.

VI. CONTRAINDICATIONS OF E-THERAPY

Contraindications of e-therapy include:

1. Patients who prefer to have no written record of treatment. Although such patients are rare and always pay themselves without making insurance claims, they have a variety of reasons for wanting no record. A therapist may merely make a note that it was agreed that no record would be kept. Because current regulations stipulate that electronic communication become part of a patient's record, maintaining no record would be a violation.

The following contraindications are "relative" in that they depend on the amount of electronic communication versus the amount of time meeting face-to-face. The crucial variable is maintenance of the therapeutic relationship.

2. Patients for whom nonverbal communication is important. This problem is related not only to patient expressive difficulties but also to what data a therapist would need to understand what a patient might be feeling. Here the problem is that "high tech" does not substitute for "high touch." Meeting face-to-face involves many nuances of body language, facial expression, eye movement, and so on. Therapists who can get a good idea of how patients are feeling when meeting with them in the same room often find that patients may not come across as clearly via e-mail, a communication problem resulting from insufficient data.

3. Patients requiring more than text can provide. Anecdotal evidence from therapists who have attempted to provide a presence through electronic communication indicates that it is insufficient for some patients who need to be in the same room as the therapist. This is a therapist problem of matching a high return for patients who need it.

4. Combined psychotherapy and psychopharmacology. Pharmacotherapy requires routine physical assessment of signs, which by definition may be different from the symptoms patients report. It is unethical to prescribe medication without baseline observations and periodic examinations.

5. Psychodynamic therapy. Psychodynamic therapy typically involves mobilization and communication of affect, which is difficult for most people when exchanging texts.

There are many forms of psychotherapy. Those previously mentioned because the special requirements of an approved residency in psychiatry that took effect January 1, 2001 stipulate that a graduate be assessed as competent in each before graduating. It will be interesting to see if the teaching of these forms evolves to include the use of electronic text communication. This may parallel development of the interpersonal and communication skills that are one of the six competencies required of all physicians.

Other forms of therapy available on the Internet include chat rooms, self help groups, and support groups moderated by mental health professionals. Family and group therapy have been reported.

VII. FUTURE OF E-THERAPY

In the late 1990s there were many rosy predictions for what seemed to be an unstoppable Internet revolution that would reach into all aspects of our lives. An example of hype: "the hottest and certainly the most controversial new trend in therapy" with only five therapists practicing on-line in 1996 (a 1997 study found

275) and more than 500 in 2001 (the American Psychological Association panel in August noted many had left the field). Advantages cited include: "It's tailor made for business travelers and employed parents who find it hard to carve out daytime hours or keep appointments in one city. It costs less. E-mails average $25 to $50 each. ... Even rates of $90 an hour fall below typical therapy charges of $125 to $165. It can work faster. There is evidence that people self-disclose more quickly to a computer than face-to-face. ... It may attract those too embarrassed to face a therapist: childhood sexual-abuse victims, the obese, those with physical deformities or painful secrets." But many changes predicted as a result of the Internet have not come to pass. Here are some that affect e-therapy.

A. Political Upheaval

Politics seemed changed in 1994 when Thomas Foley, Speaker of the United States House of Representatives with many years of incumbency, was upset by an unknown candidate waging his campaign through e-mail and the Internet. The Internet was touted as democratizing the political process, by offering direct democracy, more information available free to anyone interested, and a venue in which groups unable to afford conventional communication could be heard. However, politics has been documented as relatively unchanged after all, as established political forces have adapted to the new medium and incumbents have continued to be re-elected, often having more resources to devote to the Internet as well as other media. Therapy has its own political upheavals, and an e-therapy revolution connotes a therapeutic revolution, with all sorts of new types of therapy and therapists, a la the heady days of the community mental health center era. This seems no more likely than overall political change.

B. Dot Com Failures

It seemed that e-therapy might be part of the on-line shopping revolution, which fell short as the buying public has continued to want to experience potential purchases up close and making money on the Internet has proved to be difficult. In 1999 there were hundreds of sites offering e-therapy services to anyone who wanted to get involved. Many of these sites are no longer active, including here2listen, which had attracted large amounts of venture capital. Commercial failures in e-therapy have been attributed to unrealistic business plans, difficulty in sustaining growth, massive infrastructure costs, and difficulty in communicating benefits. However, although businesses have trouble making money on it, the Internet continues to grow and is expected to be a $20 trillion industry by the year 2020.

C. Paperless Offices and E-Books

Although the rise of the Internet, local area networks, and e-mail were expected to lead to a paperless office, use of paper has been expanding rapidly in the Internet's go-go years. Studies show e-mail, in particular messages over half a page in length, tends to be printed and that people retain roughly 30% more of what they read on paper than on computer screens. Paper documents are easier to annotate and compare. Ink on paper, for example from a laser jet printer at 600 dots per inch, has six times the resolution of computer screens. Hewlett Packard estimates laser jet printers spewed out 1.2 trillion sheets of paper in 2001, a 50% increase in 5 years. Canadian exports of printing and writing paper to the United States grew 14% in 2000.

Although e-books were expected to replace paper, and it was predicted that books published only on the Internet would account for 10% of all book sales by 2005, only one book has been commercially successful when published on the web, and sales of handheld devices for reading such books have been very disappointing. People prefer to be reading something they have in their hands. At least it is unlikely that e-therapy manuals and other materials will exist solely in electronic form and there may be resistance to much use of e-therapy. E-therapy notes will almost certainly be printed and stored as paper, especially with the current interpretation of the need to maintain documentation under HIPAA.

On the other hand, telemedical consultations have mushroomed in specialized sectors and now account for 30% of all consultations done in prisons, where security and incarceration make direct access laborious. Telemedicine is beyond the scope of this article, except to say that (1) the remoteness of the patient from the therapist often leads to e-mail contacts as additional input, and (2) telemedicine and telepsychiatry have gained some reimbursement through being evaluated in controlled studies that find it worthwhile, despite loss of some of the input gained in face-to-face meetings.

The future of e-therapy depends on regulation (too much regulation will put it beyond the reach of all but highly committed therapists willing to invest the resources required to meet the regulatory requirements), clarification (Is it a conversation continuing by other means or separable from other therapies?), and its eventual reimbursement (present pressures for nondiscrimination [parity] in health insurance may create an atmosphere of cost containment that would preclude reimbursement for e-therapy). Technical advances are likely to take it beyond its present definition.

See Also the Following Articles

Alternatives to Psychotherapy ■ Confidentiality ■ Engagement ■ Outcome Measures ■ Tele-Psychotherapy ■ Virtual Reality Therapy

Further Reading

Ainsworth, M. (2000). The ABC's of Internet counseling [Online] Available: http://www.metanoia.org/imhs

Bloom, J. R., & Walz, G. R. (Eds.). *Cybercounseling and cyberlearning: Strategies and resources for the millenium.* Alexandria, VA: American Counseling Association.

HIPAA (2000). 45 CFR Subtitle A, Subchapter C, 164.501, as reported in the *Federal Register,* Vol. 65, No. 250, Dec 28, 2000, at 82805.

Institute of Medicine. (2001). Crossing of the quality chasm: A new health system for the 21st century. Report issued March 21, 2001 <www.iom.edu>

International Society for Mental Health Online. (2000). Guidelines for therapists and consumers communicating online. <www.ismho.org>

International Society for Mental Health Online. (2001). Studies of e-therapy. <www.ismho.org>

Kahn, R. E. (1994). *Realizing the internet future: The internet and beyond* (pp. 20–30). Washington: National Academy Press.

Kane, B., & Sands, D. (1998). Guidelines for the clinical use of electronic mail with patients. *Journal of American Medical Informatics Association, 5,* 104–111. It can be accessed at <mail@mail.amia.org>

King, S. A., & Moreggi, D. (1998). Internet therapy and self help groups—the pros and cons. In J. Gackenbach (Ed.), *Psychology and the internet: Intrapersonal, interpersonal and transpersonal implications* (pp. 77–109). San Diego, CA: Academic Press.

Rothchild, E., McMahon, D., Taintor, Z., Alessi, N., Jones, B., & Hilty, D. APA resource document on telepsychiatry via videoconferencing (adopted by Board of Trustees 5/98) URL: www.psych.org/pract_of_psychiat/tele*psychiatry.*html

TelehealthNet. (2001). http://www.telehealth.net/articles/essays.html

Yellowlees, P. (2000). *Your guide to e-health.* Brisbane, Australia: University of Queensland Press. Available through http://www.ebooks.com

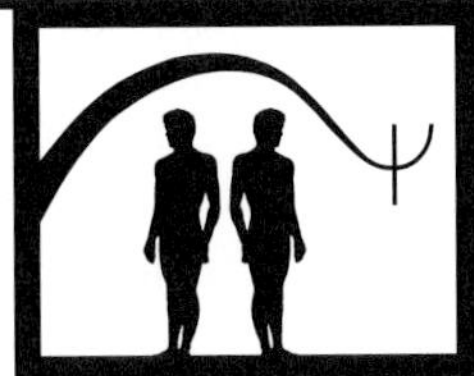

Operant Conditioning

Alan Poling, James E. Carr, and Linda A. LeBlanc
Western Michigan University

GLOSSARY

antecedent An event that precedes a behavior.

behavior Any action of a living creature. Behavior can be overt or covert.

consequence An event that follows and is produced by a behavior.

differential reinforcement A procedure used to establish stimulus control in which a particular behavior is reinforced in the presence, but not the absence, of a particular stimulus.

discriminative stimulus An antecedent stimulus that *(a)* given the momentary effectiveness of some form of reinforcement, *(b)* increases the frequency of occurrence of a particular behavior because, *(c)* historically, that kind of behavior was more successful in producing reinforcement in the presence of that stimulus than in its absence.

environment The natural world in its entirety, including all events that occur inside and outside living creatures.

establishing operation An event that alters the reinforcing or punishing value of a consequence.

extinction A procedure (or process) that reduces behavior by failing to reinforce a previously reinforced response.

fading An intervention that is used to transfer stimulus control from one discriminative stimulus to another.

functional assessment Procedures that are used to identify the reinforcer for a problem behavior.

negative punishment A procedure (or process) in which the removal of a stimulus after a behavior weakens (e.g., reduces the likelihood of) that behavior in the future.

negative reinforcement A procedure (or process) in which the removal or postponement of a stimulus after a behavior strengthens (e.g., increases the likelihood of) that behavior in the future.

operant A class of responses that "operate" on the environment to produce particular consequences. These consequences affect the future likelihood of occurrence of members of that response class.

positive punishment A procedure (or process) in which the presentation of a stimulus after a behavior weakens (e.g., decreases the likelihood of) that behavior in the future.

positive reinforcement A procedure (or process) in which the presentation of a stimulus after a behavior strengthens (e.g., increases the likelihood of) that behavior in the future.

response A defined unit of behavior.

rules Overt or covert verbal descriptions of relations among stimuli and responses.

stimulus A physical event.

stimulus control Control of behavior by an antecedent stimulus that is evident when some characteristic of a response (e.g., its rate, magnitude, or probability of occurrence) differs in the presence and absence of a particular stimulus.

stimulus equivalence A phenomenon in which stimuli that share no physical resemblance come to evoke the same behavior. If verbal humans are taught that A = B and B = C, the relationship A = C emerges without formal training.

stimulus generalization The spread of the effects of reinforcement (and other behavior-change operations) in the presence of one stimulus to other stimuli that differ from the original stimulus along one or more dimensions.

token economy A therapeutic consequence system, based on conditioned reinforcement, that is frequently used in hospitals.

verbal behavior A behavioral term for language and related phenomena. The defining feature of verbal behavior is that other people mediate its effects on the environment.

The term operant conditioning does not refer to a specific technique for dealing with behavioral problems. Instead, the term, which was coined and popularized by the late B. F. Skinner, refers to a form of learning, or conditioning, in which behavior is controlled primarily by its consequences. Skinner called the new learned responses *operants* to emphasize that they operate on the environment to change it in some way: that is, to produce consequences.

I. INTRODUCTION

Edward Thorndike's work with cats in puzzle boxes, performed in the closing years of the 19th century, is a good example of operant conditioning. In those experiments, Thorndike placed individual cats in large crates from which they could escape by either pulling a string that was tied to a latch on the crate's door, or by pushing down on a pedal that would likewise open the door. If either response was made, the cats, which were mildly deprived of food, could get out of the box and get food. Thorndike found that all cats eventually made the response that opened the door, and on successive trials, it took progressively less time for the response to occur. Eventually, escape from the box occurred very quickly.

After many experiments with different animals in puzzle boxes yielded similar findings, Thorndike formulated one of the first psychological laws, the law of effect. It stated: Of the many responses made to a situation, the ones that are closely followed by satisfaction will be strongly connected to the situation and will be more likely to recur in that situation, while those that are followed by discomfort will be less likely to recur. The law of effect emphasizes that the historical consequences of a particular behavior in a given context are the primary determinant of current behavior in that context. Cats that previously escaped from a puzzle box and secured food by pulling a string do so rapidly and reliably when placed in such an apparatus. In contrast, cats without that history do not reliably pull the string.

B. F. Skinner did not use puzzle boxes. Instead, he developed a device known as an operant conditioning chamber, or Skinner box. The first such device, used with food-deprived rats, was a small box that contained a metal lever and a small cup into which food pellets could be delivered. Depressions of the lever were counted as responses, and food was delivered as a consequence for such responses. In Skinner's experiments, a rat could press the lever at any time and at any rate, and Skinner manipulated observable variables (e.g., degree of food deprivation, frequency of food delivery) to determine how they affected the rate and pattern of responding. For example, he compared responding when food followed every response and every 20th response, and he observed what happened when food was no longer delivered.

By observing the effect of changes in events before and after specified responses on the rate and pattern of recurrence of such responses, Skinner demonstrated the fundamental orderliness of operant behavior and determined how many different variables affected such behavior. In *The Behavior of Organisms,* published in 1938, Skinner reported the results of his early experiments and described several behavioral processes including reinforcement, extinction, discrimination learning, and punishment. In that book, he also drew a clear distinction between operant and respondent (or classical) conditioning. The fundamental distinction is this: operant behaviors are controlled by their consequences whereas respondent behaviors are controlled by stimulus–stimulus pairings. This distinction may be clarified by contrasting the arrangements used by Skinner to study learning in rats with that used early in the 20th century by the famous Russian physiologist, Ivan Pavlov, to study learning in dogs.

Pavlov observed that food placed in the mouth of a food-deprived dog reflexively elicited salivation. When he arranged conditions so that the sound of a metronome immediately preceded food delivery, after several pairings the sound also elicited salivation, although it did not initially do so. Here, the capacity of the sound to control salivation depended on the pairing of two events, or stimuli: the sound of the metronome and the presentation of food.

Although he did not overlook the importance of respondent conditioning in his well-known book titled *Science and Human Behavior,* Skinner emphasized the importance of operant conditioning in the genesis and maintenance of inappropriate as well as appropriate human behaviors. He also argued that an understanding of operant conditioning provides an excellent basis for developing rational and effective treatments for a wide variety of behavioral problems. His argument has proven to be valid. From the 1950s to the present time, interventions based on principles of operant conditioning have been demonstrated in controlled studies to benefit people with many different clinical problems. For example, a task force commissioned by Division 12 (Clinical Psychology) of the American Psychological Association reviewed the entire psychological treatment outcome literature. Their findings, which were reported in 1995, indicated that the vast majority of successful interventions were either behavioral or cognitive-behavioral in orientation. Such interventions rely heavily on the principles of operant conditioning.

The fundamentals of operant conditioning are presented in the following sections. The key to understanding operant conditioning is the premise that operant behavior is determined in large part by its historical consequences under particular conditions. Therefore, the probability that such behavior will occur under current circumstances depends on *(a)* the nature of the historical consequences of the behavior, *(b)* the extent to which current conditions resemble the historical conditions under which particular consequences occurred, and *(c)* the current importance to the individual of the events that historically were consequences.

II. THEORETICAL BASES

B. F. Skinner repeatedly pointed out the similarity between operant conditioning and natural selection. In both cases, processes of variation, selection, and retention are apparent. Neither Darwin nor Skinner was able to specify the mechanisms underlying these processes. Skinner believed, however, that changes in physiology were responsible for the control of behavior by its consequences. In recent years, some progress has been made in understanding the physiological processes responsible for positive reinforcement and other principles of operant conditioning. For example, there is evidence that synaptic change is involved in learning via operant conditioning. Future work by neuroscientists may provide a detailed account of the proximal mechanisms that underlie operant conditioning, and in that sense, explain why environmental events affect behavior in particular ways. Some scholars hold the view that there can be no adequate "theory" of operant conditioning until this occurs.

Others, however, hold the view that operant conditioning is itself an adequate theory, insofar as the work of Skinner and others has led to a system of principles and assumptions that are useful for explaining and predicting behavioral observations. We hold this view. There are a great number of specific interventions based on operant conditioning, and those interventions usually are closely tied to its basic principles. For this reason, in this section procedures are introduced at the time that the behavioral principles that form their basis are explained.

A. Consequences of Behavior

Operant behavior is primarily controlled by its consequences, which are events (stimuli) that are produced by (and follow) such behavior. A behavior's consequence(s) can either increase or decrease the future likelihood of the behavior occurring under similar circumstances. The term reinforcement is used to refer to the former relation (i.e., increased likelihood), whereas punishment is used to describe the latter (i.e., decreased likelihood).

1. Reinforcement

Reinforcement is evident when a response is followed by a change in the environment (reinforcer) and is thereby strengthened. The response-strengthening effects of reinforcement typically involve an increase in the future rate of the response, although other changes in behavior (e.g., an increase in response intensity) may also be indicative of a reinforcement effect. It is important to recognize that, by definition, reinforcement always strengthens targeted behaviors. If a behavior is reliably followed by a consequence and its future likelihood is not increased, then the consequence was not a reinforcer.

Psychologists have traditionally classified reinforcers according to whether they are added to (e.g., presenting food) or subtracted from (e.g., turning off a loud noise) the environment. When a stimulus strengthens behavior by virtue of being presented as a consequence, the stimulus is termed a positive reinforcer, and the outcome is termed positive reinforcement. A spouse who responds with sympathetic statements to a mate's complaints about feeling "down and worthless" is positively reinforcing the occurrence of such statements, if such consequences increase the likelihood of such statements occurring in the future. In this case, the effects of the spouse's attention would be both unintentional and undesirable. Unintentional positive reinforcement frequently plays a role in the development and maintenance of psychopathological behaviors.

Clearly, the "positive" in "positive reinforcement" does not mean "good"; instead, it refers to a stimulus being "added" to the environment. For example, abused drugs (e.g., alcohol, heroin, the nicotine in tobacco) are positive reinforcers for the behavior of people who abuse them, but they cause untold suffering for those individuals and others.

Of course, in many cases, positive reinforcement is used intentionally and to good effect. Praising a young girl when she says "Da Da" when her father picks her up is an example of such positive reinforcement. Here, praise occurs dependent on the child's vocalization, and the relationship between the response and the outcome constitutes positive reinforcement if the behavior is strengthened as a result of that relationship. A response-strengthening effect probably would not be evident after praise followed "Da Da" on a single occasion, however. The effects of reinforcement are cumulative, and a reinforcer often must be delivered on multiple occasions before behavior changes noticeably. Moreover, once an operant behavior is well established, the effects of reinforcement are primarily to maintain, not to increase, responding. There are obvious limits on how reliably and how rapidly a child can say "Da Da" when picked up by dad and, for most children, those limits are reached fairly quickly.

Like positive reinforcement, negative reinforcement also strengthens behavior, but it does so because behavior *(a)* postpones or prevents the delivery of an otherwise forthcoming stimulus, or *(b)* terminates or reduces the intensity of a stimulus that is currently present. The former relation (a) is termed avoidance conditioning and the latter relation (b) is termed escape conditioning. A spouse who calls home to say "I'm sorry, but I'll be working late tonight" before going to a motel with a lover is emitting an avoidance response, if so doing prevents unpleasant interactions on returning home and is for that reason strengthened. A person who terminates aversive questions regarding fidelity by saying "Don't be silly, you're the only one I want and love; a bunch of us just stopped for beers after work" is emitting an escape response if the questions stop and such responding is therefore strengthened. Although both responses are incompatible with having an honest and healthy marriage, and may well be maladaptive in the end, their historical short-term consequences are sufficient to maintain them. This is often the case with respect to troublesome operant behaviors, regardless of whether they are maintained by positive or negative reinforcement. Neither positive nor negative reinforcement is intrinsically good or bad. Both processes can foster and maintain pathological as well as adaptive actions. Moreover, both processes can be used clinically to alter troublesome behaviors that do emerge.

An important early step in the treatment of many troublesome operant behaviors is isolating the reinforcers that maintain those behaviors, as well as any events that reliably precede them. This process, termed functional assessment, can be performed in a number of different ways and provides a basis for developing rational interventions. Consider a child diagnosed with mental retardation who sometimes loudly taps a pencil on a classroom desk. Observation suggests that teachers attend to the child each time this occurs. This relation suggests, but does not prove, that attention from teachers is a positive reinforcer that maintains the troublesome behavior. If this is the case, teaching staff not to attend to the child's pencil tapping, and to attend to some incompatible and appropriate activity, such as working on assigned materials, might well be an effective intervention.

Although the distinction between positive and negative reinforcement is simple logically (see Figure 1), in practice it can be hard to tell the two apart. For example, does a person adjust the tuning on a blurry television because doing so in the past has produced a clear image (positive reinforcement), or because doing so historically has removed a blurry image (negative reinforcement)? Because of such difficulties, and the possibility of confusing negative reinforcement with punishment, there is good justification for not differentiating positive and negative reinforcement, although the practice remains common.

A variety of environmental changes (i.e., stimuli) can serve as reinforcers. Unconditioned (or primary) reinforcers strengthen behavior in people without any particular history. Many primary reinforcers are of direct biological significance. Air, food, and water are examples of positive reinforcers that fit into this category. Primary negative reinforcers, which organisms will escape (respond to terminate) or avoid (respond to postpone), include high-intensity stimulation in most modalities (e.g., loud noises, extreme temperatures).

In contrast to primary reinforcers, conditioned (or secondary) reinforcers gain their ability to strengthen behavior through learning. Conditioned reinforcers can be established through respondent conditioning, that is, by being paired with (i.e., immediately preceding the delivery of) primary reinforcers or other established conditioned reinforcers. They also can be established through verbal mediation. Money is the prototypical example of a conditioned reinforcer.

	Consequence is presented	Consequence is removed
Behavior is Strengthened	Positive reinforcement	Negative reinforcement
Behavior is Weakened	Positive punishment	Negative punishment

FIGURE 1 Operant Conditioning.

The stimuli that serve as conditioned reinforcers vary substantially across people because of differences in their conditioning histories. For instance, certain kinds of painful stimulation (e.g., being struck with a leather belt) are in some situations positively reinforcing for people labeled as masochists, but not for other individuals. This is probably because such stimulation historically preceded a powerful positive reinforcer, most likely sexual stimulation, for some people, but not for others. Being struck with a belt initially was not positively reinforcing, but it eventually came to be so by virtue of reliably preceding sexual stimulation. Like other conditioned reinforcers, it will maintain its reinforcing ability only if it continues to be paired (actually or verbally), at least occasionally, with some other reinforcer. Once a conditioned reinforcer is no longer paired with another reinforcer, it loses the ability to strengthen behavior.

Although reinforcers typically are construed as stimuli, in some cases it is the opportunity to behave in certain ways that a stimulus affords, not the stimulus per se, that is important. For instance, access to food allows eating and access to a beverage allows drinking. During the 1950s, David Premack developed a response-based model of reinforcement that emphasizes that the opportunity to engage in a more preferred behavior will reinforce a less preferred behavior, a relationship known as the Premack principle. In this context, preference refers to the relative amount of time that an individual will engage in the behaviors if unconstrained. If, for example, an eighth-grade student is given a choice between playing basketball and doing math problems and spends more time playing basketball, then that behavior is the more preferred one. It this is so, then according to the Premack principle the opportunity to play basketball (the more preferred behavior) will be an effective reinforcer for solving math problems. Parents could use this relation to increase the time that their child spent working on math. That is, in order to play basketball for a given period, the child first must solve a specified number of math problems.

Environmental events may reinforce responses that precede them even if the response does not actually produce the reinforcer. For instance, a pool player shooting the nine ball may say "roll fast, sweetheart" as the nine ball slowly approaches a pocket. The player is apt to repeat the phrase under similar conditions in the future if the ball drops, winning the game, even though there is no plausible mechanism whereby the verbal response could influence the ball or table. This type of reinforcement, termed superstitious or adventitious, may control behaviors that appear counterintuitive. It should be noted, however, that explaining a behavior as being superstitiously reinforced begs the question of how the behavior is actually controlled, unless the nature of the superstitious reinforcement is apparent.

a. Variables That Influence the Effectiveness of Reinforcers Several factors affect the degree to which reinforcing consequences strengthen behavior. Four factors are especially important.

1. The quality and magnitude of the consequence. Stimuli differ in their effectiveness as reinforcers across people and within people across circumstances. Isolating effective reinforcers for clients often is an important part of therapy, and specific procedures have been developed for identifying reinforcing objects and activities. For example, objects that will positively reinforce behavior in a person with mental retardation can be isolated by presenting putative reinforcers (e.g., a car, a whistle, and a toy dog) and determining which, if any, object the person contacts. If, for instance, a child regularly selects and plays with the stuffed dog, it is reasonable to assume that the toy will serve as a positive reinforcer for that person's behavior. The car and whistle might do likewise, but they probably will be less effective as reinforcers. In general, reinforcer effectiveness tends to increase with the magnitude or intensity of a given stimulus. For example, $20 is a more effective reinforcer than $2 for most people's behavior. Ultimately, however, reinforcer effectiveness must be directly assessed, not simply inferred.

2. The level of motivation relevant to the consequence. The importance of this variable, which is discussed in detail later, is evident if one considers the reinforcing effectiveness of a given kind of food (e.g., a hamburger) as a function of how recently and how much one has eaten.

3. The delay between the response and its consequence. In the absence of verbal mediation, delaying consequences substantially reduces their effectiveness as reinforcers.

4. The schedule of delivery of the consequence. Many different relations, termed *schedules* (or, if behavior is strengthened, schedules of reinforcement), can be arranged between consequences and the events that produce them. For example, under a continuous reinforcement schedule every response produces the reinforcer. Behavioral interventions are typically implemented initially on continuous schedules and eventually the schedule is changed to some type of intermittent reinforcement schedule. The term intermittent reinforcement indicates that some instances of the behavior result in reinforcement whereas others do not. Most human interactions occur under intermittent schedules. For example, the gambling of individuals who play slot machines is maintained under an intermittent reinforcement schedule. Not every coin dropped into the slot results in a payoff. In fact, most do not; but eventually one of the coins is followed by a reinforcing payoff. Casino operators program this arrangement, which would be technically described as a variable-ratio schedule, because it generates a high rate of responding that persists for a relatively long time, even if no reinforcers are forthcoming.

The schedule of reinforcement that is arranged is one variable that determines response effort, which is the amount of force, exertion, or time required to execute a response, or to earn a reinforcer. Research has shown that *(a)* response rates generally decrease as response effort increases, *(b)* behavior weakens more rapidly during extinction as effort increases, *(c)* individuals will escape from situations that require particularly effortful responding, and *(d)* individuals prefer lower-effort responding to higher-effort responding. Knowing these effects of response effort can be of benefit in dealing with clients' troublesome behaviors.

As a case in point, broken health care appointments are a major problem in medicine. Something in the neighborhood of 10 to 30% of appointments are broken, and in such cases patients fail to receive needed services, and the schedules of service providers are disrupted. One strategy for reducing the number of appointments that patients miss is to reduce the effort required to keep an appointment. This tack was taken in the 1980s by Pat Friman and his associates, who mailed a parking pass and a reminder to patients who had scheduled appointments at pediatric clinic. Their notion was that the reminder made it easier to remember the appointment and the parking pass made it easier to park, therefore, the effort required to keep the appointment was reduced. This cheap and simple intervention was effective, insofar as it reduced missed appointments by approximately 20%.

As the preceding example illustrates, understanding of schedules can be used to good advantage in dealing with some clinical problems. Consider as a second example, a child diagnosed with autism who often flaps his hands in front of his face during school sessions. The behavior is considered undesirable because it interferes with educational activities. A possible strategy for reducing hand flapping to acceptable levels is to arrange conditions such that access to some reinforcing activity or object depends on the passage of a specified interval during which hand flapping does not occur. If the response occurs, the interval is reset. Initially, only a short time without hand flapping is sufficient to earn reinforcement. Over time, and only when hand flapping is adequately controlled, the interval without responding required for reinforcement is increased. Such procedures, which often are termed differential-reinforcement-of-other-behavior (DRO) schedules, have been used to good advantage in reducing various problem behaviors.

But how is it that behavior can be reduced by reinforcement, which by definition always strengthens behavior? The answer is that the unit of behavior that is reinforced under DRO schedules is an interval of not responding. For instance, if the child in our example were exposed to a DRO 5-min. schedule, 5 min. must elapse without hand flapping for the reinforcer (e.g., teacher attention) to be delivered. If the child is sensitive to this arrangement, 5-min. (or longer) intervals without hand flapping will increase in frequency. When this occurs, incidents of hand flapping will decrease. People can learn through reinforcement to omit as well as to emit particular responses.

2. *Punishment*

When laypeople think of learning-based procedures for reducing responding, they often think of punishment. Punishment occurs when behavior is weakened by its consequences, which are termed punishers. Many psychologists differentiate between positive and negative punishment, and the basis for the distinction is the same as that for distinguishing between positive and negative reinforcement (see Figure 1). If behavior is weakened because such responding adds something to an individual's environment, positive punishment is involved. If, however, behavior is weakened because such responding removes (or decreases the intensity of) some stimulus, the procedure is termed negative punishment.

Like reinforcers, punishers can be conditioned or unconditioned. The same processes that establish stimuli as conditioned reinforcers are also effective in establishing neutral stimuli as conditioned punishers. A common example of a conditioned punisher is the word "no." Without any prior training, a toddler will not have any specific reaction to "no." However, early in the life of most English-speaking people, the word is paired with unconditioned punishers and is thereby established as a conditioned punisher. For example, a young child may touch an electrical outlet in the presence of his parents. A quick, forceful grab of the child's arm (an unconditioned punisher), accompanied by a stern "no," will likely decrease the probability of the child touching outlets in the future. It will also be an initial step toward establishing "no" as an effective punisher. Of course, several pairings with another punisher may have to occur before the word alone has a response-reducing function. Once it does, the word can be used as a positive punisher to reduce various undesirable behaviors emitted by the child.

Relatively few people object to parents saying "no" to prevent their child from electrocution. But there has been considerable controversy about the use of punishment in therapeutic settings. Many therapists advocate the use of reinforcement-based procedures and consider punishment-based procedures unnecessarily intrusive. Others maintain that clients have a right to effective interventions and, if reinforcement-based procedures have failed, then other interventions that have been proven efficacious in similar cases, including punishment, should be used. A substantial literature documents the efficacy of punishment-based procedures when other interventions have failed, although applications have been largely limited to dangerous behaviors, such as self-injury, exhibited by people with developmental disabilities in controlled settings. When punishment is used, it typically is incorporated into an intervention package that also includes reinforcement procedures.

In general, negative punishment is better accepted than is positive punishment. When negative punishment is arranged, the consequence of an undesired behavior is that a person loses access to something of value. For example, exceeding the speed limit may result in a financial loss when the cost of a speeding ticket is paid. If the person is less likely to speed in the future as a result of receiving a ticket, negative punishment has occurred.

Two common procedures based on negative punishment are timeout and response cost. Timeout refers to the removal of access to positively reinforcing objects and activities for a preset time when a specified behavior occurs. For instance, when a child has broken a family rule (e.g., hit a sibling), the parents may arrange timeout by placing the child in a corner of the room with no access to interaction or toys for 3 min. If the behavior is weakened, negative punishment has occurred. Response cost typically involves removal of a specified amount of a reinforcer when an unwanted behavior occurs. Being fined for a traffic violation as described earlier is an example of response cost.

Overcorrection is another procedure based on punishment principles. It is based on the notion, originally advanced by David Premack and sometimes included as part of the Premack principle, that forcing an individual to engage in a less preferred behavior as a consequence of a more preferred behavior will punish the more preferred behavior. As an example of overcorrection, a child who has had a tantrum and thrown food on the dining room floor (a more preferred behavior) might be required to pick up the food and scrub the floor (a less preferred behavior). This procedure is apt to reduce the future likelihood of food being thrown and is appealing to many people because it is restitutional in nature—the child repairs the damages caused by inappropriate behavior. The primary problem with overcorrection is that it can be difficult to force people to engage in nonpreferred activities.

Critics sometimes argue that the effects of punishment are short lived. This may or may not be true and depends on specifically how punishment is arranged. Moreover, the effects of reinforcement also are short lived, in the sense that the changes in behavior produced by reinforcement eventually disappear when reinforcement no longer occurs. In general, operant conditioning procedures affect behavior only so long as they are in place, regardless of the specific nature of the procedures.

Other criticisms are that punishment produces undesirable emotional behavior, as well as escape from and avoidance of the individual who delivers the punisher. In addition, punishment may produce a generally passive and unresponsive individual. Although all of these adverse effects may occur, they are most probable with severe positive punishment. Mild punishment, both positive and negative, is a common and accepted part of human interactions that also occurs in many therapeutic contexts. For instance, a therapist treating a depressed client may say, "no, that's no really true – you're not that way at all" when the client describes him- or herself as helpless and unwanted. The intent is to reduce the future likelihood of the client making such statements. If the intent is realized, punishment has occurred, and the client has probably benefited.

In general, the same kinds of variables that influence the effectiveness of reinforcement also determine the effectiveness of punishment. Therefore, maximal response reduction is apt to occur when strong punishers are delivered after each occurrence of an undesired response. Making available an alternative and appropriate response that produces the same reinforcer that maintains the undesired response also increases the effectiveness of punishment. In practice, it often is difficult to arrange effective punishment for troublesome behaviors. For example, many people drive over the speed limit, although doing so may result in expensive tickets. They do so because the likelihood of receiving a ticket for a given instance of speeding is low, and the cost of the ticket is not great relative to most people's income. If every motorist received a ticket costing one month's pay each time they drove over the speed limit, and if this relation were assured, there would be few speeders.

3. Extinction

As long as a behavior produces an effective reinforcer, that behavior will recur. However, when responding no longer produces the reinforcer that once maintained it, the behavior eventually ceases. This process, and the procedure used to arrange it, is called extinction. The example described previously in which a child's striking of a desk with a pencil was eliminated by having teachers stop attending to the behavior is an example of extinction. Reducing abusers' intake of heroin by treating them with the drug naltrexone is another example of extinction. Here, naltrexone blocks the subjective and physiological effects of heroin, so that when a person takes the drug, there are no reinforcing consequences. Under these conditions, heroin self-administration eventually ceases. A serious problem, of course, is that individuals can stop taking naltrexone, ending the pharmacologically induced extinction.

Responses that have an extended history of reinforcement are likely to persist for a substantial period despite failing to produce a reinforcer. In fact, when extinction is first implemented, an individual may respond at higher rates or intensities than usual. This is known as extinction-induced bursting. Emotional responding and increases in the variability of behavior also commonly occur during extinction. As examples of these phenomena, consider what happens when a person puts a dollar in a vending machine, pushes a button in a manner that historically has produced a favored soda, and gets nothing. She or he is likely to curse, pound the machine, and push other buttons. The individual may even put more money in the machine. Eventually, however, machine-related behavior ceases.

The overall persistence of responding when reinforcement is no longer available is called resistance to extinction and is one measure of response strength. Even when responding falls to near-zero levels during extinction, the behavior remains in the organism's repertoire and may return quickly to previous levels if reinforcement once again becomes available. More interesting, when motivation relevant to a particular kind of reinforcer is high and responses that recently have produced that reinforcer are unavailable or ineffective, previously extinguished responses often occur. This phenomenon is termed resurgence.

Avoidance responses often persist for long periods, even indefinitely, in the face of extinction. In large part, this is because it is difficult for an individual to ascertain that conditions have changed. Successful avoidance responses prevent an event from occurring, and that event does not occur during extinction, unless extinction is arranged so that the event that served as a negative reinforcer is now presented repeatedly regardless of whether the historical avoidance response occurs or not. Under the latter condition, responding weakens relatively quickly.

4. Complex Consequence Systems: Token Economies

Both in everyday and therapeutic settings, consequences typically do not occur as single events in isolation. Instead, complex consequence systems may be implemented for several different behaviors simultaneously. One of the most common and effective therapeutic consequence systems is the token economy. Ted Ayllon and Nathan Azrin developed token economies in the mid-1960s as an intervention for chronic psychiatric patients. Since then, token economies have become widely accepted and are included as a standard part of many inpatient hospital treatment programs. A token economy typically allows a person to earn rewards and privileges (positive reinforcers) for emitting appropriate behaviors, such as attending therapy sessions and attending to personal hygiene. Typically, privileges are lost (i.e., negative punishment is arranged) when inappropriate behaviors, such as hoarding items or stealing, occur.

A token economy has three vital components: *(a)* tokens, *(b)* backup reinforcers that can be obtained with a certain number of tokens, and *(c)* schedules for reinforcement, punishment, and token exchange. The tokens function as conditioned reinforcers. Conditioned reinforcers have no intrinsic value, but they acquire the capacity to function as positive reinforcers because they can be exchanged for highly preferred items or for access to preferred activities. Generally, a person may earn tokens throughout a day or week and then trade them in for backup reinforcers at a preset exchange time and rate. Once appropriate behavior is established under stringent conditions, schedules can be altered to better approximate those that clients will encounter outside the inpatient setting.

B. Antecedent Influences on Behavior

The previous sections have considered how events that occur after operant behaviors (i.e., consequences) affect such responding. The following two sections discuss how operant behaviors are affected by prior, or antecedent, events.

1. Stimulus Control

As Thorndike suggested with the law of effect, the effects of reinforcers and punishers are relatively situation specific. That is, the behavioral effects of reinforcement (or punishment) that occurs in one context may not be evident in another context. Because of this, an individual's behavior often differs substantially across settings. Consider our previous example of a girl who has learned to say "Da Da" when picked up by her father. Initially, the same response might occur when another person, perhaps her mother, picked her up. However, before long mom would not evoke "Da Da," although dad would continue to do so. Another verbalization, probably "Ma Ma," might well occur when the mother picked up the daughter. In this situation, the person who holds her determines what the baby says and the child's verbal behavior is controlled by an antecedent stimulus, that is, by an event (i.e., the presence of the father or mother) that occurs before the behavior.

In general, stimulus control is evident when some characteristic of a response (e.g., its rate, magnitude, or probability of occurrence) differs in the presence and absence of a particular stimulus. Stimulus control can be excitatory or inhibitory. In the former case, the likelihood of the response occurring is higher in the presence of the stimulus than in its absence. In the latter, the likelihood of the response occurring is lower in the presence of the stimulus than in its absence.

Stimulus control is ever present in everyday life. It can be established through respondent conditioning, but most of the stimulus control that is evident in human behavior occurs as a result of operant conditioning, in which the consequences of behavior differ in the presence and absence of a stimulus. For example, in the example of the girl responding differently to her two parents, saying "Da Da" was reinforced (probably by attention, praise, and cuddles) in the presence of the father, but not the mother. Saying "Ma Ma," in contrast, was reinforced when mom, but not dad, picked up the child. As a result, the two people evoked different responses in their daughter.

In the context of operant conditioning, excitatory stimulus control typically occurs with discriminative stimuli. The term discriminative stimulus (S^D) is used to refer to a stimulus that *(a)* given the momentary effectiveness of some form or reinforcement, *(b)* increases the frequency of occurrence of a particular behavior because, *(c)* historically, that kind of behavior was more successful in producing reinforcement in the presence of that stimulus than in its absence. The mother and father are S^Ds in our example of the child learning to talk. Other examples of S^Ds controlling behavior include saying "4" when presented with "2 + 2 = __," beginning to play a musical instrument when a conductor's baton is raised, and taking food from an oven when the timer rings. In each case, doing so has "paid off" (i.e., been reinforced) in the past. A history of success in the presence of an S^D gives that stimulus the capacity to control behavior. Behaviors controlled by S^Ds continue to be so controlled only if reinforcement is at least occasionally arranged for those behaviors. If not, stimulus control eventually disappears.

If the historical consequences of behavior are punishing in the presence of a particular stimulus, then that stimulus is likely to acquire inhibitory control over such responding. Consider, for instance, two college students at a party who are talking about their favorite TV show. An influential professor, who in the past has criticized (punished) their comments about TV, approaches them, and they stop talking about TV. This is inhibitory stimulus control—if the professor were not around, comments about TV would occur more frequently. Stimuli present during extinction, as well as during punishment, also may acquire inhibitory control over behavior.

In clinical situations, it is often important to identify the S^Ds that operate in a client's environment and, if possible, to manipulate those stimuli to evoke appropriate behavior. Assume, for instance, that a functional assessment revealed that a child made rude noises in class primarily because the student sitting in the next seat laughed appreciatively when such sounds occurred. Given this, it is reasonable to assume that the laughter reinforces the noisemaking, and that the child who laughs is an S^D for the other child's disruptive behavior. If so, moving the noisemaker to a seat where the other child could not be readily seen would be a simple, and probably effective, intervention. It would be made even stronger if the noisemaker was seated beside another classmate who was an S^D for working quietly on tasks.

In some cases, establishing appropriate stimulus control is an important therapeutic goal. Consider, for example, the treatment of a convicted date rapist. It may be the case that such an individual has not learned to respond appropriately to social stimuli, such as a potential partner moving away, or saying "that's enough." Persisting in the face of such stimuli may have resulted in sexual gratification in the past. Establishing appropriate stimulus control of sexual behavior would be a necessary part of the treatment of the rapist. Practical and ethical considerations, however, probably would make this task relatively difficult to accomplish, and verbal mediation or contrived feedback in controlled settings, not direct exposure to consequences in a dating setting, would have to be used to establish stimulus control. A potential problem with such procedures is that the stimulus control established in the therapeutic setting might not generalize to actual dating situations.

In some cases, simply presenting a stimulus under conditions where responding is reinforced may be insufficient to establish stimulus control. Suppose you were trying to teach a child how to learn math facts with flashcards. Your instruction might include presenting a flashcard (e.g., 10 ÷ 2 = ___), requesting the answer, and providing error correction or praise, depending on the response. You would probably consider the child successful if the answer were correct following three consecutive presentations of the card. In addition, you would probably assume that the child "knew" the answer to "10 ÷ 2." Suppose, however, that the child merely guessed at the correct answer initially and subsequently provided it not in response to the actual numbers printed on the card, but instead in response to the size and color of the numerals. Therefore, the answer "5" would be given to any set of two black numbers printed in 12-point font, not just to "10 ÷ 2 = ___." This example illustrates the problem of "attention" in stimulus control. Individuals occasionally respond to unintended features of an antecedent stimulus, such that effective stimulus control is not developed. To counteract this effect, it is crucial to correlate differential consequences with the presence of the specific antecedent stimulus features that should control the behavior. In our example, the child would need to be exposed to other flashcards bearing problems different from "10 ÷ 2 = ___," but of the same size and color. The response "5" would be reinforced only when it was appropriate to the numbers presented, and in this way attention could be focused on that dimension of the flashcard, which is the sole relevant dimension in this example.

As this example illustrates, discrimination training can be used to establish behavior so that it only occurs in the presence of a specific S^D. In discrimination training, only instances of the target behavior that occur in the presence of the target S^D are reinforced. All other behaviors are placed on extinction in the presence of the S^D. In addition, the target behavior is placed on extinction in the presence of all antecedent stimuli except the S^D. The degree to which you reinforce only the target behavior determines how "tight" the stimulus control becomes (i.e., the degree of stimulus discrimination). For example, a classroom in which student questions are answered following both hand raising and calling out would most likely appear somewhat chaotic. If, however, the instructor only answered the questions of students whose hands were raised, and the answers were reinforcing, then the class would appear more orderly. In other words, tight stimulus control over the students' behavior would be achieved.

In some cases, consequences occur only when two or more stimuli, or stimulus dimensions, are present, and as a result a conditional discrimination is formed. For example, a child asking (behavior) his parents (antecedent) for money (consequence) only on or after payday (conditional antecedent) constitutes a conditional discrimination. The behavior occurs only when both antecedents (i.e., parents and payday) are present because, historically, that was the only time that the behavior was reinforced.

2. *Antecedent Stimulus Classes*

The stimulus control of human behavior is subtle and complex. In many cases, a number of different stimuli control equivalent behaviors in the same person. That is, they are members of the same stimulus class and are functionally equivalent.

One way in which different stimuli can acquire the same function is through stimulus generalization, which can be conceptualized as the counterpart to stimulus discrimination. Generalization occurs when antecedent stimuli that share a physical resemblance with an established S^D control the behavior evoked by that S^D. For example, suppose a child learns to say "dog" in the presence of a dog. The child might later say "dog" in the presence of a cat, not because this behavior was previously reinforced, but instead because dogs and cats share certain physical similarities (e.g., four legs, fur, tails).

A second way in which stimuli can come to control the same behavior is by being correlated with the same consequences for that behavior. For example, a stop sign, a red traffic light, and a traffic control officer with an outstretched palm may constitute a functionally equivalent class of S^Ds for stopping a car. These physically different antecedents acquired the same stimulus control properties because of a shared history of reinforcement for stopping.

A third way in which functionally equivalent stimuli can be established is through a phenomenon known as stimulus equivalence. Stimulus equivalence is thought to be a product of learning certain conditional discriminations. Specifically, individuals learn that A = B and B = C. As a result of such learning, the transitive relation "A = C" automatically emerges, although it is not specifically trained. After the relation emerges, the stimuli A and C are functionally equivalent. For example, a person may learn that Jessie is a Harvard graduate, which can be construed as learning A = B (Jessie = Harvard graduate). That same person may also learn that Harvard graduates are exceptionally intelligent people, which can be construed as B = C (Harvard graduate = very intelligent person). As a result of learning these two relationships, the person would "automatically" know that Jessie was a very intelligent person and would respond to her by emitting whatever behaviors that person historically had learned to emit in the presence of "very intelligent people." Similar behaviors would be occasioned by anyone described as a Harvard graduate and, depending on the history of the person responding to them, a wide range of behaviors may occur in their presence. Some people, for instance, learn to avoid highly intelligent people. Others ridicule them, whereas some seek them out as companions. Stimulus equivalence plays an extremely important role in determining how humans behave, and researchers have demonstrated the relevance of the concept to areas as broad as language development and adult psychopathology.

3. *Fading*

A common intervention that achieves its effects due to stimulus control is fading. The purpose of fading is to transfer stimulus control from an S^D that currently evokes the desired behavior to a new S^D that should evoke the behavior. In a fading procedure, the S^D for a particular behavior is gradually removed while the new S^D is gradually introduced. Thus, the target behavior occurs throughout the procedure, only the S^Ds are altered. This can be beneficial in that the individual frequently contacts reinforcement for the behavior. There are two general categories of fading.

Prompt fading occurs when a response prompt is physically removed from an individual's environment. For example, an individual in rehabilitation for a traumatic brain injury might initially require physical assistance to walk. In this case, the individual is walking, although dependently, at the onset of rehabilitation. As therapy progresses, the physical assistance is gradually removed so that the patient walks independently. In this example, stimulus control was transferred from the S^D of physical guidance to the S^D of physical independence through prompt fading.

Stimulus fading occurs when a stimulus prompt is physically removed from an individual's environment. For example, a teacher might use ruled (lined) paper when teaching a child how to write. The lines could eventually be lightened and/or spaced closer together such that the child learns to write smaller and straighter text. In this case, the child's writing is reinforced throughout the fading procedure. Stimulus control was transferred from the S^D of dark/wide lines to lighter/narrower lines through stimulus fading.

4. *Motivational Control*

One factor mentioned, but not discussed, in the section dealing with variables that influence the effectiveness of reinforcers, is the level of motivation relevant to the consequence. In operant conditioning, "motivation" is often explained in terms of a behavior's reinforcer. That is, if an individual is "motivated" to perform a behavior, then there is most likely a reinforcer available for that behavior. Although this approach has been useful, an adequate account of motivation must include antecedent influences on behavior. The previous section described how events that occur immediately before behavior can influence responding. However, some events that occur immediately or long before a response can also affect its occurrence, as well as the value of its consequences (i.e., motivation). Such events are the focus of the next section.

5. *Establishing Operations*

In general, an establishing operation (EO) is an antecedent event that produces two effects. One is a function-altering effect, which momentarily changes the value of a reinforcer or punisher. The other is an evocative effect, which momentarily alters the likelihood of occurrence of behaviors that have been previously reinforced or punished. As an example of a function-altering effect, a period without any interpersonal interactions might make a conversation more reinforcing. In other words, we might say that deprivation (i.e., lack) of social interaction establishes a conversation as a reinforcer. Social deprivation probably also would have an evocative effect: in addition to establishing conversation as a reinforcer, it also increases the probability of behaviors that have been previously reinforced with attention (e.g., making a telephone call to a friend). Thus, EOs alter the effectiveness of reinforcers (or punishers) and alter the likelihood of occurrence of behaviors that have produced those reinforcers in the past.

It is important to note that an EO can make an event either more or less reinforcing (or punishing). For example, food deprivation increases the reinforcing effectiveness of food, but free access to food reduces its reinforcing effectiveness. It is also important to note that an EO's effects usually are not permanent. EOs characteristically produce relatively short-lived effects; such is the nature of "motivation."

EOs can be either conditioned or unconditioned effects. Unconditioned establishing operations (UEOs) produce their effects in the absence of any particular learning history. A clinically relevant example of a UEO is the duress that a person who is physically dependent on heroin experiences during withdrawal from the drug. During the highly unpleasant withdrawal syndrome, the effectiveness of heroin as a positive reinforcer increases, as does the likelihood of occurrence of behaviors that have produced heroin in the past.

In contrast to UEOs, conditioned establishing operations (CEOs) are developed through several different associative processes. That is, they are learned. An example of a CEO is the host of a TV game show saying to the audience, "I'll give $1,000 for every broken pencil you can show me." Following that statement, but not prior to it, broken pencils would have substantial reinforcing value. Behaviors likely to produce broken pencils (e.g., rummaging through purses), therefore, would be far more likely to occur.

One example of a clinical intervention that most likely achieves its effects via EOs is noncontingent reinforcement (NCR). NCR has recently been used to treat the undesired behavior (e.g., self-injury) of individuals with developmental disabilities. Before NCR is implemented, the reinforcer responsible for maintaining the behavior is identified through functional assessment. This reinforcer is subsequently delivered to the individual on a time-based schedule regardless of whether or not the undesired behavior occurs. In other words, the individual receives "free" access to the reinforcer. Hence, the "motivation" to engage in the behavior is reduced. In this case, the free delivery of the reinforcer is an EO that results in a reduced probability of undesired behavior.

Methadone maintenance treatment of heroin abusers is another example of a treatment with an EO component. Methadone "substitutes" for heroin, reduces the likelihood of withdrawal occurring, and decreases the reinforcing value of heroin and the likelihood of occurrence of behaviors that in the past produced heroin. Because many of those behaviors are harmful to the heroin abuser, as well as to other members of society, this is a desirable effect. So, too, is reduced contact with heroin.

C. Verbal Behavior

Humans are like other animals in many regards, but verbal behavior makes humans unique. Verbal behavior is the term that B. F. Skinner used to refer to what many people call language. In his 1957 book, *Verbal Behavior*, and in other writings, Skinner emphasized that talking, writing, and signing is operant behavior that affects the world indirectly, through the mediation of someone else's behavior. In contrast, nonverbal operant behavior affects the world directly. For example, consider a thirsty 3-year-old girl who is sitting in the living room playing with her father. She can gain access to water by walking to the kitchen, getting a glass, and filling it with water from the tap. She can achieve the same outcome by saying, "Dad, please get me a glass of water." In the first case, the girl's actions directly produce water. Therefore, her behavior is nonverbal. In the second case, the girl's actions cause her father to behave in a way that produces water. Because of this mediation by another person, her behavior is verbal.

Verbal behavior is like nonverbal operant behavior in that it is acquired and maintained as a result of its effects on the environment. The specific environment that is affected by verbal behavior is a social one comprising other people. Verbal behavior is developed and maintained because it is reinforced by the actions of a social community that is taught, although not formally, to reinforce such behavior. Because different people reinforce different patterns of verbal responding, relatively strong audience control of verbal responding is common. As an example, consider how differently most people talk to friends, parents, lovers, employers, clergy, and police officers.

In general, verbal behavior allows speakers to ask for things (e.g., "Please get me a glass of water") and to describe the environment for others (e.g., "The tap in the kitchen isn't working"). Asking for things benefits the speaker, who often gets them, and may benefit the listener, insofar as they provide an indication of how the speaker is likely to behave. A speaker's description of relations observed in the environment, however, is apt to be especially useful for listeners. These descriptions may involve only stimuli ("When the stove is red, it's very hot"), antecedent stimuli and responses ("When the phone rings, answer it"), or antecedent stimuli, responses, and consequences ("When you hear a Beatles' song, be the first person to call in, and win $5,000"). Skinner called descriptions of relations among stimuli and responses rules.

Rules specify relations among stimuli and responses and usually change the behavioral function of those stimuli. For instance, after hearing a disc jockey say, "When you hear a Beatles' song, be the first person to call in, and win $5,000," a person who hears a Beatles' tune may well call the radio station. Absent the announcement, however, calling the station is highly unlikely. In this example, the announcement gives the Beatles song a capacity to control behavior similar to that of an S^D. The song is not an S^D, however, because the person has no previous history of calling in and winning. What she or he has, instead, is a history wherein following rules is generally productive. Whether or not a particular rule is followed by a given individual depends in large part on her or his prior experience with respect to the rule giver (and similar people) and the accuracy of similar rules provided in the past. We learn through operant conditioning to follow rules or to refrain from following them. For instance, a parent says to a child, "Don't touch the stove; it's hot and you'll get burned." Despite the rule, the child touches the stove and gets burned. As a result of the correspondence between real and described consequences, the future likelihood of rule following increases. If, however, the child touches the stove but is not burned, the future likelihood of rule following decreases.

The most important characteristic of rules is that listeners can learn from them. For example, a person can acquire new behavior, with very little effort, through rules such as "To get to the barbeque at my house, turn left on Main, turn left at the second light, and it's the fourth house on the right, 3117 Market Street." Without the rule, the listener would have to learn appropriate behavior through direct exposure to the environment. Imagine how difficult it would be to find 3117 Market Street in a large city with no map or directions. A rule makes doing so much easier. In fact, rules mimic the effects of classical and operant conditioning by allowing people to be affected by environmental relations that they have never directly experienced. Rule-governed behavior is of crucial importance to humans because it *(a)* provides for very rapid behavior change and *(b)* enables people to behave effectively without requiring direct exposure to environmental events that might prove harmful or ineffectual. Rules also can increase the effectiveness of delayed consequences. These are important, and often beneficial, effects.

Rules can interact with the consequences of behavior in three major ways. First, as noted earlier, rules can alter the behavioral function of consequences. A person who is exercising to improve health in the presence of a personal trainer may be told, "No gain without pain, make it hurt" while doing bench presses. This rule might alter the function of mild pain in the pectorals from punishing to positively reinforcing. In many cases, people who behave in the face of what appear to be unpleasant consequences are following rules that modify the behavioral function of those consequences.

Second, rules can alter the range of behaviors that are available to contact naturally occurring consequences. A depressed person who is repeatedly told to "Call your sister; she'll be glad to hear from you" probably is more likely to make the call, during which any of a variety of desirable verbal responses might be reinforced.

Third, rules can alter a person's sensitivity to consequences that are contacted. In general, if a rule accurately specifies the consequences of a particular kind of behavior, then sensitivity to those consequences increases. If, however, the rule is inaccurate with respect to actual consequences, then sensitivity to those consequences decreases. Rules can foster a kind of behavioral rigidity, wherein a person responds in a manner consistent with the rule, almost regardless of the consequences of so doing. Because of this, it is crucial that accurate descriptions of operant interventions be provided before those interventions are put in place. A token economy, for example, is apt to produce faster and greater improvements if the schedules it comprises are clearly stated to participants than if they are not.

Rules can be covert as well as overt; "talking to one's self' is behavior that is not fundamentally different from talking aloud. Rules also can be self-generated as well as provided by others. In either case, they sometimes provide inaccurate descriptions of relations among events in a person's environment. For instance, a person with anorexia may say, "When I weigh over 100 pounds, people think I'm fat and ugly." In fact, this is untrue. People think (i.e., say) that the client is seriously underweight at 100 pounds and that 130 would be a far better, and more attractive, weight. Were the higher weight to be attained, the actual consequences are very different from those described by the client. By following an erroneous rule, however, the client will never encounter those consequences. Moreover, even if they are encountered, other "bad" rules might change their function. If, for instance, the client got up to 125 pounds and several friends offered compliments, the client might well say "Everyone humors a fat person," or "That's what they say to my face; behind my back they're laughing." Either rule would prevent the compliments from functioning as a reward.

Most humans are verbal organisms, and most outpatient therapies are based heavily on verbal interactions between patients and therapists. In many cases, the aim of those interactions is to alter the client's rule-governed behavior, although they are not always conceptualized in this manner. In recent years, Steven Hayes and his colleagues have developed a comprehensive analysis of the role of verbal behavior, and of rules specifically, in human psychopathology. For example, Hayes and Ju offer the following explanation of suicide:

> The purposeful act of taking one's own life is an instance of rule-governed behavior based on derived relations involving time and the verbal construction of expected consequences of action ... For example, "death" can participate in if ... then verbal relations with many other events that have acquired desirable functions both directly and through the transformation of stimulus functions tied to direct events, such as, "If I am dead, I will no longer suffer, everyone will be happier, they will all be sorry for what they've done to me, I will finally be at peace," and so on ... [Death therefore] becomes a verbal consequence of importance ... Once death becomes a verbal consequence of importance, rules can be followed that give rise to it ... However, the impact of such rules as "If I die, then I will be at peace" depends upon the degree to which they conflict with other functional rules, such as "Suicide is an offense against God." If is for this reason that the psychotherapies and religious institutions around the world strive to create meaning, values, and purpose in the lives of individuals.

Hayes and his colleagues have developed a therapeutic technique, "acceptance and commitment therapy" (ACT), that is intended to overcome unhealthy forms of verbal control and to foster healthy forms. Although relatively new, ACT appears to hold promise for treating a variety of serious behavioral problems in clients for whom direct control of the environment is impossible.

Although altering the rules that an individual generates and follows can be a valuable therapeutic technique, it is important to realize that these activities are themselves influenced by their consequences. If there is nothing in a client's everyday social or nonsocial environment to support (i.e., reinforce) appropriate rule-governed behavior, then such behavior usually will not endure over long periods. In some cases, naturally occurring consequences in the client's everyday environment are sufficient to support appropriate behaviors that emerge. In other cases, however, contrived consequences may be needed. A significant problem in providing treatment for outpatients is arranging such consequences.

III. APPLICATIONS AND EXTENSIONS

The behavior of essentially all people is sensitive to operant conditioning, and procedures based on operant conditioning have proven useful in dealing with an enormous range of problems in clients with a wide variety of diagnostic labels. Many of the early therapeutic applications of conditioning principles involved children or people with developmental disabilities, and a few skeptics have argued that consequences do not affect the behavior of verbal adults. This contention is patently untrue. What is true, however, is that it often is difficult or impossible to arrange effective consequences for the behavior of adult humans unless they are in tightly controlled settings (e.g., inpatient treatment wards), which rarely occurs. Procedures based on operant conditioning obviously can be effective only when they can be consistently implemented, and they cannot be effectively implemented for some clients in some settings. When this occurs, therapists must attempt to alter rule-governed behavior and hope that naturally occurring consequences are sufficient to maintain any appropriate behaviors that are generated.

Moreover, in verbal individuals rules can diminish sensitivity to consequences. This may make it appear that these individuals are not affected by the consequence of their actions but, in fact, they are—the primary reason that they follow rules today is that behaving in similar fashion paid off in the past. Rule-governed behavior, which is indirectly controlled by consequences, is just as important as is behavior directly controlled by its consequences. Effective therapists work to change the two in parallel.

With certain clients, procedures based on operant conditioning may be more effective as adjuncts than as primary treatments. For example, antipsychotic drugs typically are first-choice treatments for schizophrenia and related conditions, even though operant interventions are useful in dealing with specific behavior problems in individuals with these conditions. Combined pharmacological and conditioning treatments also are useful in treating behavior problems in people with conditions other than schizophrenia, including depression and attention-deficit/hyperactivity disorder (ADHD).

Client diversity is not a consideration with respect to procedures based on operant conditioning in general, although appropriate sensitivity to this issue is required to evaluate the acceptability and probable effectiveness of specific interventions. Some clients object to interventions based on the manipulation of consequences as unnatural, controlling, or contrived, and such objections must be overcome if treatment is to have any hope of success.

IV. EMPIRICAL STUDIES

A great deal has been written about operant conditioning and clinical interventions based on it, and many research articles have been published. For example, a recent search of the psychological literature (using the PsycINFO database) with the keywords "operant conditioning" yielded 7,844 publications. It is very difficult to summarize this vast literature, save to point out that procedures based on operant conditioning are useful in treating a wide range of behavioral problems in many different kinds of clients in a variety of settings. As noted previously, results of a 1995 evaluation of the entire treatment outcome literature in clinical psychology indicated that the vast majority of successful interventions rely heavily on the principles of operant conditioning.

Such interventions have been used to good avail in dealing with behavioral problems in children and adults without diagnostic labels, in people with developmental disabilities, and in individuals with various mental disorders (e.g., ADHD, schizophrenia, depression, anxiety disorders, eating disorders). People with brain injuries and other medical problems (e.g. obesity, hypertension) also have responded favorably to operant interventions. Of course, not all clients respond favorably to a given intervention, and no client is helped by an ill-conceived treatment, regardless of its alleged theoretical basis. Over the years, poorly trained and misguided caregivers have placed children in closets for long periods as a kind of "timeout." Others, equally misguided, have deprived people with mental retardation of clothes and food, which they had to work to earn back, as a kind of "reinforcement." Such treatments cannot be justified and would not be recommended by any legitimate clinician.

V. CASE ILLUSTRATION

Jack is a 15-year-old male diagnosed with ADHD. He currently participates in outpatient therapy with his parents to address a variety of their concerns regarding his behavior. The presenting concerns include inappropriate behaviors at home (e.g., noncompliance, disrespectful language, breaking curfew) and at school (e.g., noncompliance, fighting, failure to complete homework). Most of these inappropriate behaviors have developed and worsened in the 2 years since Jack started high school.

The behavior therapist has decided to use a token economy to both increase appropriate behaviors (e.g., homework completion, compliance) and decrease inappropriate behaviors (e.g. fighting, breaking curfew). The token economy includes the following components: *(a)* tokens, *(b)* backup reinforcers, and *(c)* schedules for token delivery and removal and an exchange rate. In addition, the token economy provides consequences for clear, observable behaviors and provides unambiguous criteria for delivering those consequences. The token economy was developed through collaboration among the parents, therapist, and Jack. Jack's parents had final approval on the details of the treatment program.

The tokens used for Jack are points recorded in a check register by his parents. Only his parents can deliver or remove points, and they keep track of all delivery and exchange. Jack can earn a preset number of points each time he completes certain behaviors and he can lose a preset number each time he engages in other behaviors (see table 1). Points are exchanged on Saturday morning for a variety of activities and privileges (i.e. backup reinforcers) for Saturday and the next week. The list of these backup reinforcers was generated by having Jack provide a list of items and activities for which he would like to work, which ensured a variety of potentially effective reinforcers. His parents then either eliminated items (e.g. a new stereo) or approved items (e.g., watching movies) from Jack's list and established a point exchange rate for the Saturday exchange (see table 1). Each week in session the therapist reviewed the targeted behaviors and assessed Jack's progress and helped the family make changes in the token economy when necessary. Jack's progress was tracked by counting the number of points earned each week and counting the number of appropriate and inappropriate behaviors occurring each week.

The baseline condition indicates that Jack had high rates of problem behavior before the implementation of the token economy. The first week of the operant treatment resulted in a decrease in problem behavior and an increase in appropriate behaviors. Jack earned several points and was able to trade them in on the first Saturday for a delayed curfew (60 min.) on Saturday night and the opportunity and funds to see a movie. His progress continued in the next 3 weeks of treatment with even greater decreases in problem behaviors. The family continued to use a version of this token economy successfully and eventually Jack's behaviors remained at a satisfactory level as the treatment system was stopped.

Several principles of operant conditioning are evident in this case example. First, there is a schedule of reinforcement included in the token economy. Occurrences of an appropriate target behavior resulted in a positive reinforcer in the form of points delivered under a specified schedule. These points are conditioned reinforcers because they have no inherent reinforcing value but acquire such value because they can be exchanged for the backup reinforcers (i.e., items from the menu). A

TABLE 1
Token Economy Targets, Point Schedule, and Reinforcer Menu

Target behaviors

A. *Complete homework assignment:* An assignment is defined as all task materials due the next day in one particular class (e.g., algebra, biology). The assignment must be completed by 9:30 p.m.
B. *Meeting curfew:* Jack must be inside the house by 9 p.m. with no arguing, complaining, or prompting from his parents.
C. *Following instructions:* If Jack is instructed to do something (e.g., set the table, clean up your room, put away your shoes, lower the stereo), he will complete the task (e.g., turn down the stereo) or initiate completion of the task (e.g., cleaning room) within 5 min.
D. *Fighting:* Fighting is any activity that is called fighting by school personnel.
E. *Using respectful and disrespectful language:* Respectful language includes "please," "thank you," "yes/no maam/sir," and other phrases in an appropriate tone and volume of voice. Disrespectful language includes name calling and agreed-on statements (e.g., "shut-up," "leave me alone," "no way.")

Point schedule

Appropriate behavior	*Points earned*
Completion of each homework assignment	1
In house by 9 p.m. (curfew)	3
Following instructions within 5 min.	1
Respectful language	1
Inappropriate behavior	*Points lost*
Fighting	15
Disrespectful language	5

Back-up reinforcer menu

Item/activity	*Point cost*
Extended curfew (1 hour/1 day)	40
Movie (paid by parents)	25
Driving range with Dad on Sunday	25
$5 and trip to video arcade	25
Rent 2 movies	15
(This menu will be edited every 2 weeks)	

variety of reinforcers, selected by Jack, is available to ensure high quality reinforcers and to prevent satiation (i.e. maintain motivation). The number of points gained or lost for performing a behavior depends on the importance of that behavior. Because each occurrence of an inappropriate target behavior resulted in the immediate removal of points, a schedule of negative punishment is in effect. Finally, the relations between behavior and its consequences are explained carefully to Jack in the interest of generating appropriate rule-governed behavior and maximizing the sensitivity of his behavior to its consequences.

VI. SUMMARY

"Operant conditioning" does not refer to a single therapeutic technique. Instead, the term refers to an important form of learning, or conditioning, in which behavior is primarily controlled by its consequences. The consequences of a particular kind of behavior in one setting can either increase or decrease the probability of such behavior occurring in similar settings in the future. Descriptions of the consequences of behavior, called *rules*, can have similar effects. A great deal is known concerning how consequences affect behavior, and this knowledge has been put to good use in designing interventions shown to be effective across a wide range of client populations, behavior problems, and settings.

See Also the Following Articles

Classical Conditioning ■ Conditioned Reinforcement ■ Differential Reinforcement ■ Extinction ■ Fading ■ Functional Analysis of Behavior ■ Negative Punishment ■ Negative Reinforcement ■ Positive Punishment ■ Positive Reinforcement ■ Token Economy

Further Reading

Catania, A. C. (1998). *Learning* (4th ed.). Upper Saddle River, NJ: Prentice Hall.

Clayton, M. C., & Hayes, L. J. (1999). Conceptual differences in the analysis of stimulus equivalence. *Psychological Record, 49*, 145–161.

Cooper, J. O., Heron, T. E., & Heward, W. L. (1987). *Applied behavior analysis*. Columbus, OH: Merrill.

Hayes, S. C., & Ju, W. (1998). Rule-governed behavior. In W. T. O'Donohue (Ed.), *Learning and behavior therapy* (pp. 374–391). Boston: Allyn and Bacon.

Kazdin, A. E. (1982). The token economy: A decade later. *Journal of Applied Behavior Analysis, 15*, 431–445.

Michael, J. (1993). *Concepts and principles of behavior analysis*. Kalamazoo, MI: Association for Behavior Analysis.

Miltenberger, R. (1997). *Behavior modification: Principles and procedures*. Pacific Grove, CA: Brookes/Cole.

Sakai, K., & Miyashita, A. (1991). Neural organization for the long-term memory of paired associates. *Nature, 354*, 152–155.

Skinner, B. F. (1953). *Science and human behavior*. New York: Macmillan.

Skinner, B. F. (1957). *Verbal behavior*. New York: Appleton-Century-Crofts.

Skinner, B. F. (1984). Selection by consequences. *The Behavioral and Brain Sciences, 7*, 477–510.

Task Force on Promotion and Dissemination of Psychological Procedures. (1995). Training in and dissemination of empirically-validated psychological treatments: Report and recommendations. *The Clinical Psychologist, 48*, 3–23.

Tryon, W. W. (1995). Synthesizing animal and human research via neural network learning theory. *Journal of Behavior Therapy and Experimental Psychiatry, 26*, 303–312.

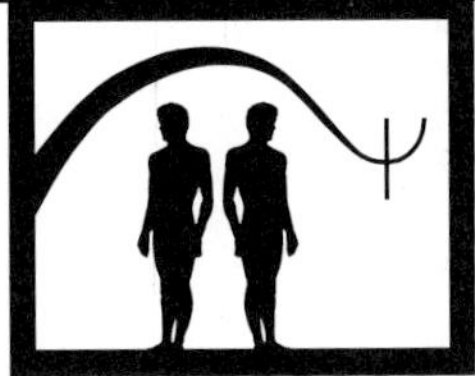

Organic Brain Syndrome: Psychotherapeutic and Rehabilitative Approaches

Avraham Schweiger
Academic College of Tel Aviv, Israel

Jason W. Brown
New York University Medical Center

GLOSSARY

cognitive therapy/remediation Refers to several forms of rehabilitation/treatment addressing the cognitive and behavioral consequences of brain damage. This treatment involves procedures that address impaired functions by using a variety of computer programs, as well as other exercises. In addition, cognitive therapy involves the teaching of a variety of compensatory strategies to increase functioning despite residual impairments. Cognitive therapy may include supervised practice of real-life situations outside the office. Cognitive therapy refers to treatment of individuals with brain damage and is distinguished from the psychotherapeutic technique by the same name.

organic brain syndromes (OBS) Refer to dysfunctions in the intellectual/cognitive, behavioral, social or emotional spheres, whose primary effective cause is brain pathology. These syndromes are defined in contrast to dysfunctions in the same spheres, whose etiology is believed to be primarily emotional or psychological.

traumatic brain injury (TBI) A category of OBS, used to describe the cognitive, emotional, and behavioral consequences of traumatic injuries to the brain (such as an injury sustained in a motor vehicle accident, or as a result of a gunshot wound). TBI is contrasted with other forms of brain pathologies, such as tumors, strokes, infections, and degenerative conditions, that do not result from a sudden, violent event, although the latter's consequences can be no less traumatic to the individual.

I. OVERVIEW OF ORGANIC BRAIN SYNDROMES

The term organic brain syndrome (OBS) refers in the literature to both organic mental disorder and organic brain disorder. This reflects the dualist mind–body distinction, which gave rise to it. That is, it implies a distinction between "physical" and "mental" causes of behavioral-emotional-cognitive dysfunction. The latter are also known by the general term psychopathology, but can there be an organic mental disorder, or even normal behavioral/cognitive functioning that is not related to brain function (try functioning without it)? And can there be a brain disorder that is not "organic," in the sense that it refers to something other than normal or impaired function of brain tissue? Current knowledge suggests a negative answer to both questions. There is a long tradition of dualism in psychiatry of "functional" and "organic" disorders (expressed in the diagnosis of OBS) that reflects the belief that some behavioral abnormalities originate in brain pathology, whereas others result from "psychological" or "functional" factors, such as maladjustment in the domains of emotional, social, and familial function.

Today it is recognized that a variety of medical conditions can cause the full range of psychiatric syndromes and symptoms. Therefore, many diagnostic categories of psychiatric symptoms resulting from specific medical conditions are recognized and are typically classified together with other clinical entities with similar clinical manifestations. When applied judiciously, OBS has important diagnostic, prognostic, and therapeutic implications: it implies that the appropriate strategy for dealing with the symptoms is to attend to the underlying brain pathology, whereas the behavioral-affective manifestations may be of secondary concern. To the extent that OBS is secondary to some underlying brain pathology, and to the extent that this pathology is treatable, the treatment of choice is medical intervention. However, for various forms of OBS (for example, degenerative disease), medical intervention may be limited to the pharmacological management of symptoms related to behavioral problems. For other subcategories of OBS, such as mild to moderate TBI or strokes, medicine offers little beyond symptomatic relief, and it is left for other professions to provide rehabilitation of impaired functions. It is therefore important that practicing clinicians consider the various forms of OBS in their differential diagnoses, because brain pathology can give a spectrum of psychiatric symptomatology, and because many of these disorders may be reversible with medical intervention. For similar reasons, the presence of documented brain pathology, in the context of psychiatric symptoms, may preclude common psychotherapeutic approaches. Thus, for example, insight-oriented psychotherapy for a patient whose insight is impaired by frontal lobe damage is quite ineffective.

As brain tissue does not regenerate to an appreciable extent, damage resulting in OBS, is in a sense "irreversible." Thus, many forms of OBS result in permanent dysfunction. In cases of degenerative conditions, the dysfunction gets worse. But in many other forms, such as in cases of TBI, various infections, and strokes, when occurring in the context of otherwise healthy individuals, where some form of new learning can still take place (which may be well into the 7th or 8th decades of life), functional improvement can take place. In such cases, motivation to exert the effort required, therapeutic intervention and environmental support are the main ingredients in turning the consequences of OBS around, and returning the individual back to his or her premorbid level of functioning, as quickly as possible. In this article, the focus is on the consequences and treatment of TBI, but it should be emphasized that these are appropriate for all other forms of OBS where there is a potential for recovery.

II. DESCRIPTION OF TRAUMATIC BRAIN INJURY

Traumatic brain injuries (TBI) do not form a well-defined category of symptoms, as injuries vary in their severity and location within the brain. This category of syndromes is the leading cause of OBS among young people and is the form of OBS most likely to come to the attention of psychotherapists. TBI include a large variety of syndromes, with varying degrees of disabling symptoms and pathologies. There is a considerable body of research on the topic, and space allows for only introductory discussion. TBI can result in a wide range of psychiatric and cognitive symptoms. No two traumatic injuries are alike, and the clinical picture following brain injury, as well as long-term adjustment, are always a combination of premorbid personality, psychological adjustment, intelligence, and the extent and location of the injury, together with the availability and quality of treatment and the patient's social support system. Thus, any prior history of drug or alcohol abuse, in itself a risk factor for TBI, may complicate both diagnosis and return to "normal" functioning. In part due to the age of the population with head injuries, there is typically significant recovery, albeit rarely back to the premorbid level of functioning.

Brain traumata are usually classified into cases of severe, moderate, or mild injuries, according to scores on the Glasgow Coma scale (GCS, a 15-point assessment tool, using measures of verbal, motor, and eye-opening responses), and on the length of time the individual has been unconscious. Roughly speaking, loss of consciousness for less than 20 min and a GCS of 13 to 15 are considered to reflect a "mild" injury. Any history of coma beyond 6 hr with a GCS of 3 to 8 is considered to indicate "severe" injury. However, there are substantial variations in the severity of symptoms and outcomes that do not respect the classification described earlier. Most often the injured person has amnesia for the injury, and depending on the severity of impact to the brain, there is often retrograde amnesia as well (amnesia extending from the onset of injury backward in time). The length of retrograde amnesia varies among injuries but does not correlate well with severity. There is often posttraumatic amnesia as well, referring to the period following onset of injury, during which the patient is alert but for which the patient later exhibits amnesia. Posttraumatic amnesia provides a measure of the severity of the impact to the brain and gives some indication of the prognosis (although variations are common). In addition, short-term memory deficits and impairment in new learning following brain injury are ubiquitous and are referred to as anterograde amnesia.

Traumatic brain injuries can result from a penetrating foreign body (as from a gunshot wound). They can result from acceleration–deceleration of the head, as in cases of motor vehicle accidents, falls, or from a blunt blow to the head, in which case they are referred to as closed head injuries. The mechanism of injury to brain tissue is different in each type, and from one situation to another. In some cases intracerebral bleeding occurs, and in some cases focal tissue damage can be seen on brain imaging. But almost always there is diffuse injury as well, involving disruption of cell membranes, especially in the brainstem and shearing of neuronal processes (axons). In addition to actual tissue damage, TBI may result in other pathological processes that may affect cognition, such as tissue swelling (edema). TBI can result in clinical pictures ranging from persistent vegetative state to a seeming absence of residual neurological symptoms. When the injury is severe, the individual usually does not return to premorbid functioning and may need lifelong assistance in all aspects of living, even after a long course of rehabilitation. In moderate and mild cases, a fast return to functioning is often possible, although residual deficits may, and often do, remain for the rest of the person's life, as damaged brain tissue does not regenerate.

Occasionally, the brain injury impairs the patient's insight (expressed as the inability to monitor and judge one's own behavior and/or thought process), so that the patient is not aware of the deficits and may even deny them altogether. This impairment makes intervention and rehabilitation much more difficult, as the patient sees no reason for the rehabilitation efforts, and cooperation may be limited. Nevertheless, intervention with the aim of improving overall functioning may still be necessary. Needless to say, when insight is impaired by TBI, or any other brain damage, any attempt to treat the disorder with insight-oriented therapy is doomed to failure (see later for more details on treatment).

Mild TBI can present a challenge to the clinician, because such injuries are often dismissed as representing either exaggeration of symptoms for secondary gains (especially when litigation is involved), or outright malingering. Such cases often received psychiatric diagnoses in the past, because the typical symptoms were headaches, concentration problems, memory loss, depression, mood lability, and even personality changes, among others. Nevertheless, research over the past 30 years indicates that between 5 to 10% of mild TBI, despite only brief loss of consciousness, or merely short alteration in consciousness, and without any symptoms of major impairment in thought processes, intellectual ability, or language skills, do not return to normal functioning. This symptomatology has been supported by techniques of functional imaging of the brain, such as positron emission tomography, and by research in patients who are not involved in litigation, where financial incentive may seem the basis for the complaints. Such disability was found to be due to residual symptoms of poor short-term memory, reduced attention/concentration (especially on tasks of divided attention), impaired organization, and reduced speed of cognitive processing, together interfering with cognitive performance. This clinical presentation is known as the postconcussion syndrome (PCS). This subtype of TBI can be seen in the absence of litigation, and there is evidence that microscopic changes do take place in the brains of these individuals, such as axonal shearing. The microscopic changes, however, are too subtle to be visualized by any imaging technique, and most often a general neurological evaluation produces no focal findings.

Deficits associated with the PCS can only be documented on comprehensive neuropsychological testing. In addition to the cognitive deficits mentioned earlier, patients with the PCS often suffer from headaches for many months, sleep disturbances, fatigue, and depression. Occasionally, a change in personality is noted, and symptoms of anxiety, irritability, dizziness, and apathy are present. Individuals who had been high functioning prior to the injury are particularly disturbed by PCS, even when their test performance is still in the normal range for the general population. That is due to their intact insight, so they are acutely aware of their deficits. Patients with the PCS frequently have the added burden of "convincing" their families that something is wrong with them; it is not obvious, given the relative minor nature of their injury, that they indeed sustained a lasting injury to their brain (see later for further discussion of treatment and diagnosis of PCS).

Recovery from any TBI is most rapid in the first 6 months following the injury, with continuing noticeable recovery up to about 1 year. Over the first year, the rate of recovery decreases gradually. Beyond 1 year, additional recovery may still take place, albeit at a frustratingly slow pace. Depending on the age at the time of the TBI, patients have shown recovery for several years postinjury, especially with regard to increased independent functioning. However, the latter depends to a significant extent on the social support system of the patient, availability of rehabilitation, and motivation.

One of the most significant, and almost universal, consequences of TBI and any other form of brain damage is affective disturbance. Most commonly, depression is seen, but other mood disorders can result as well. Thus mood swings, anxiety, phobias, hypomania and even posttraumatic stress disorder have been reported following TBI. Sometimes mood disorders reflect the effects of brain damage directly; in other cases, affective symptoms (mostly depression) are secondary and reactive to the cognitive deficits. A combination of both etiologies together is also possible. Mood disorders themselves in TBI can impair normal functioning, and therefore they require professional attention.

III. DIAGNOSTIC ISSUES

In cases of severe TBI, there is little question as to the presence of underlying brain damage. However, in cases of mild to moderate head injuries, especially where brain imaging reveals no positive findings of damage, and the neurological evaluation also produces no pathological findings, the diagnosis of TBI requires a different approach. Such diagnosis is crucial when litigation is involved, as motivation becomes part of the clinical question of diagnosing brain damage. It is also essential when the injury is mild, but the individual complains of persisting problems in function.

The most effective approach to identify the presence of cognitive deficits and determine their extent, to date, is the neuropsychological evaluation. The neuropsychological assessment, through the use of standardized tests, provides the most accurate, noninvasive, picture of the functional status of the individual, which in turn allows the inference of brain dysfunction, if present. Neuropsychological testing utilizes a comparison between the estimated premorbid, intact intellectual function of the individual, against his or her present performance on cognitive testing. This comparison is done under the assumption that the overall cognitive performance on different cognitive tasks of a given individual is fairly uniform within a certain range of variations. Therefore, an observed large deviation from the expected performance in a given skill, relative to the estimated intellectual functioning of the individual, raises the suspicion of impairment. If such a deviation is consistent with similar findings in other cognitive skills, the latter known from research to be readily affected even by mild brain damage, a diagnosis of TBI (or PCS) is made. Because TBI involves, by definition, pathology of brain tissue, it is likely that even if the presenting symptoms of TBI seem to be psychiatric (say, depression, mood swings, or poor concentration), some cognitive deficits will be present as well. These are most likely to be short-term memory and attentional deficits. In fact, despite the prevailing notion that depression results in cognitive deficits on testing, recent research on this topic has found little, if any, correlation between scores on neuropsychological tests and depression. Problems with daily and occupational functions, however, can be and often are seen with depression. As neuropsychological assessment identifies the presence or absence of brain pathology, positive findings on neuropsychological testing greatly increase the likelihood that the underlying cause of the patient's complaints is brain pathology. Neuropsychological testing is appropriate in mild to moderate cases of TBI, and where brain damage is known to be present (e.g., in cases of severe TBI with damage seen on brain imaging). The neuropsychological assessment should also be used to determine the extent of dysfunction and to aid in developing an optimal treatment plan.

IV. THEORETICAL BASIS OF TREATMENT

The World Health Organization formulated a part model to conceptualize deficits following TBI: impairment, disability, and handicap. Impairment refers to deficits in the actual underlying cognitive skills (such as memory, attention, fluency, inhibition of action). Impairments are detailed on the neuropsychological evaluation. Disability refers to deficits noted in the injured individual's function in everyday life (for example, memory impairments may cause problems in carrying out the task of shopping for food, keeping appointments, etc.). Handicap refers to difficulties imposed on the injured person by the demands of the outside world (e.g., a return to work may be impossible due to disability in dealing with more than one thing at a time). Within this framework, improvement in disabilities may not necessarily result from improvement in impairments: using a list for shopping can lead to improvement in performance of this task without any change in the underlying memory impairment. Nor is an improvement in a disability by itself a guarantee for progress of a handicap: the use of a list may not suffice to overcome the memory demand required by taking an oral examination at school. The goals of treatment in TBI are improvements in both disabilities and handicaps, although often impairments are targeted as well, especially within the initial phase of treatment.

Any therapeutic approach must be based on the presumption of a potential for recovery. Indeed, it is a common observation that people after TBI recover to some extent or other, often even spontaneously, in the absence of intervention. What does this recovery represent in terms of brain functions? TBI results in several pathophysiological (i.e., abnormal) processes in brain tissue that have been identified experimentally. Some of them (e.g., swelling, or edema) in and of themselves may cause disruption in normal functions beyond the effect of the brain damage itself. Thus, when swelling resolves, for example, it is accompanied by some recovery of TBI symptoms. As brain tissue does not regenerate, further functional recovery involves, most likely, (1) some measure of reorganization in tissue functions (perhaps the assumption of function by a healthy tissue heretofore not specialized for the impaired function), combined with (2) the residual function of damaged neuronal networks. But beyond the recovery of basic perceptual, conceptual, memory, attention, and motor skills, functional recovery observed can, and often does, reflect (3) the development of compensatory strategies. Various combinations of these three processes most likely form the basis for observed improvement following injury.

What we know from functional brain imaging about the neuroanatomical substrate of recovery is that reorganization takes place shortly after an injury to brain tissue. New neuronal networks seem to take over functions that premorbidly were subserved by the now-damaged tissue. But in addition, new learning can take place in neurologically intact individuals even into the seventh decade of life, albeit at a reduced rate and extent. Thus, there are good reasons to believe that as long as healthy, viable tissue remains after trauma, the individual may still be able to learn new tasks, or be capable of doing old tasks in new ways (i.e., compensation for deficits). Such new learning involves, quite likely, formation of new synapses (contacts among nerve cells), changes in membrane properties and firing characteristics of nerve cells, as is the case with learning in general. It is true, however, that even mild TBI is likely to reduce the overall capacity of the nervous system, so that any new learning requires more time and effort, depending on the extent of injury.

The general principles forming the basis for recovery outlined earlier cannot provide detailed guidelines for addressing a specific impairment or disability in a specific way. As individuals present with different injuries, different premorbid abilities, occupational background and adjustment, as well as varying psychosocial and familial contexts, treatment must be tailored to the individual needs of the patient. Individualizing treatment implies that long-term goals and specific treatment plans are synthesized from all the factors known to affect the outcome of treatment. Treatment approaches may include, in addition to individual therapy, group treatment when appropriate. Group therapy, whether as a form of cognitive treatment or psychotherapy, can have an important role in promoting recovery. Indeed, several rehabilitation programs around the world are based on group treatment approach (see later for details). Another implication of the knowledge we have on reorganization in the brain is that initiation of therapy should be as soon as the injured individual can participate in treatment. When treatment is initiated early, reorganization can incorporate easier new approaches to old tasks, and patients better adapt to new learning. During the first year following a TBI, the majority of recovery takes place. Beyond that, progress is far slower. Individuals with TBI who begin treatment a year following onset or later, may actually have to unlearn ineffective compensatory strategies they have acquired on their own during the initial phase following injury. This is an unnecessary burden.

V. COGNITIVE THERAPY AND PSYCHOTHERAPY IN ORGANIC BRAIN SYNDROMES

A. Cognitive Treatment

Cognitive treatment (CT) must address the complete range of skills involved in normal functioning, in the context of psychosocial, cognitive, occupational, and emotional readjustment. In reality, cognitive, occupational, physical, group, and psycho -therapies are intertwined in the process of assisting an injured individual to negotiate a return to normal functioning. Improvement in functioning can be observed even when test performance of basic skills does not change. This happens when treatment aims to improve the actual functioning in the context of real-life occupational and psychosocial settings.

In general, CT is said to be "restorative" when it addresses cognitive impairments directly by, say, rote repetitions of tasks involving impaired skills. Therapy is regarded as "compensatory" when new skills are taught to patients, such as procedures designed to reduce disabilities despite persistent cognitive impairments. Cognitive treatment follows the general knowledge acquired through more than half a century of research on principles of cognitive learning. Examples include strategies in improving memory functions (e.g., through the use of mnemonics), attention and visual scanning training, the utility of distributed versus concentrated practice, and so on. These principles are used but extended beyond the clinic in CT, through generalization into real life situations.

Any systematic activity that requires the purposeful use of the brain can be utilized as CT, as long as it is part of an effort to reduce impairment, disability, or handicap. Thus, anticipating and responding to a target on a computer screen, making a supervised trip from the home to the clinic using public transportation, interacting socially in a group moderated by a therapist, are all forms of cognitive treatment. Cognitive treatment might take the form of sensory stimulation for a partially comatose patient and ends with assisting an injured lawyer with strategies for reading and preparing legal briefs. A great deal of material exists commercially which can be used for CT: computer software, videos, tapes, workbooks, reading material, games, puzzles, and so on. Elaborate guidebooks and materials for addressing specific areas of problems can be purchased commercially (such as, for example, the Attention Process Training designed by McKay Moore Sohlberg & Catherine Mateer, 1989, and many other computer-based programs). But the resources are limitless, as many other, even daily encountered objects and situations can serve the same purpose of increasing functioning. Thus the home environment may be modified to provide an injured person with the structure necessary to stimulate recovery and reduce disability. Material from the patient's premorbid occupation may serve as context for developing specific compensatory strategies for skills needed for work; so can environmental objects serve the same therapeutic purpose for better functioning in daily life. For example, the pictures at a museum may serve to exercise both attentional and expressive purposes; searching topics on the Internet can provide exercises of attention, reading, visual-spatial and abstract skills, and so on. In short, the range of tools used in cognitive treatment is only limited by the therapist's imagination. In our center, for example, it is not unusual for patients to go shopping with a therapist, play a musical instrument, practice the use of public transportation, or attempt work at a local store, all as part of an individualized treatment plan. The only requirement is that any therapeutic activity is aimed at specific functional goals, appropriate for the individual's needs, and that it is executed with sights on actively challenging the patient.

Cognitive therapy must be performed at a specific level for the individual TBI patient: it cannot be too easy, as boredom will be quick to set in. Equally problematic is CT that aims too high for the patient: frustration and even a catastrophic reaction may ensue. Treatment must be just challenging enough for the individual, within a rather narrow window of difficulty, so that progress will take place without undue negative reactions. This requires constant, careful monitoring of both the mood and performance of the patient. For this reason, treatment plans for a CT session can never be rigidly adhered to. Fluid movement from one level of difficulty to another, or from one task to another may be required when unanticipated reaction from the patient renders the plan obsolete. It must be emphasized that individuals with brain damage may often exhibit not only shorter attention span than intact people, but also lower tolerance for frustration and a more rigid approach to problem solving. These abnormal reactions in themselves may become the focus of treatment.

Although the therapist–client relationship is somewhat different in the context of CT then it is in regular psychotherapy, rapport and trust are important elements of treatment. Eliciting cooperation requires, at times, a great deal of skill on the part of the therapist. For instance, clients may be profoundly depressed and feel hopeless, anxious, embarrassed or they may believe nothing is wrong with them. All these reactions to brain damage, and many more, may result in minimal motivation to cooperate in treatment. Cajoling a TBI patient to participate in therapy may call for the most elaborate inducements and reinforcements. Often it is necessary to recruit the assistance of family or significant others to promote participation. Group treatment can also be effective, provided the discrepancy in patients' abilities within the group is not too large. Thus, symptoms of impaired social functioning can be addressed in a group setting, where members' interactions provide both stimulus for and context of therapy. Other cognitive symptoms can be addressed well in a group settings, such as expression and comprehension skills, attentional deficits, sequencing, self-monitoring, and turn taking. Needless to say, psychosocial issues, such as acceptance of deficits, can be addressed well in group therapy (see later for more on this issue).

Survivors of brain damage present with an infinite variety of symptoms, and no two patients are quite alike. Premorbid adjustment and psychosocial factors influencing recovery are never at the control of the therapist. Therefore, understanding the totality of both symptomatology and psychosocial background must form part of the treatment plan. Whether a TBI patient lives alone, with parents or with spouse, will have bearing on the goals of treatment. Therefore it is always important to involve the family, or significant others, in the therapeutic process. At times, CT may take the form of educating the injured person's family regarding the altered cognitive status, the abilities and disabilities of their loved one. A family may hinder or facilitate the individual's recovery process, depending on their attitude toward the cognitive/behavioral changes they face.

B. Psychotherapy

Throughout human development, changes from infancy to childhood, into adulthood, and later maturation into old age are gradual. The process is slow, allowing ample opportunity for making such adjustments so as to preserve some sense of the individual's continuous identity. Thus, a person perceives himself or herself as possessing the same identity across significant changes in size and cognitive abilities. Brain damage, in contrast, is abrupt in TBI, and the demand for readjustment is both substantial and immediate, and always in the direction of reduced capacity (that is, it results typically in negative emotional response). Therefore, brain damage is a devastating event in all spheres of human experience, creating bewilderment and often a sense of loss. It may profoundly shake the person's sense of identity. Even in cases of mild impairments, awareness of reduced cognitive proficiency can injure the individual's sense of self. The experience, common after mild brain damage, of forgetful episodes, difficulties with handling more than one thing at a time, or reduced stamina, will require significant adjustment on the part of the patient. Typically, the more severe the damage, the more adjustment will be required; not only in terms of recovering of premorbid functions, but in the demand for emotional adjustment in the face of irreversible changes.

The most common presentation of psychological reaction to brain damage is problems of acceptance. These problems may appear as lack of awareness of deficits (especially with more severe injuries), over which the patient has no volitional control. In cases where awareness is intact, accepting the changes following brain damage presents a serious challenge, as it entails viewing oneself as less competent than before. High- and overachievers have particular difficulties with this kind of readjustment, which requires psychotherapeutic intervention. Reduced self-esteem and depression are very often the consequence of awareness of cognitive deficits. The role of psychotherapy is, then, to facilitate acceptance and the readjustment process, so that recovery and return to functioning are maximized. Without acceptance, people with brain damage can rarely negotiate the compensation needed for good adjustment. The process of acceptance includes grieving, as in a real sense individuals with brain damage must deal with the loss of part of their identity.

Psychotherapy should include educating patients concerning the effects of brain damage, so as to reassure them that their experience of changes is not unique. For example, mood swings, irritability, fatigue, bursts of uncontrolled anger (all common symptoms following TBI) in heretofore friendly and patient individuals can be very alarming, but understanding of such symptoms in and of itself can have a calming effect. Supportive psychotherapeutic techniques should be combined with more directive approaches to assist patients with the use of new strategies to deal with changes. For example, using a behavioral self-monitoring log to comprehend and control undesired anger outbursts can be taught to individuals exhibiting such symptoms. Families, when available, must be part of the adjustment process, as they, too, need education regarding the changes in their loved ones, support, and guidance in assisting the injured family member. Several approaches have been used with reported positive results, such as the cognitive therapy of Aaron Beck in addressing depression, cognitive-behavioral therapy, and even psychodynamically based intervention. Often psychotropic medications, such as antidepressants, are indicated and should be used as an adjunctive to psychotherapy.

In some cases of impaired insight, behavioral management techniques with the injured individual may be the only effective intervention. In such cases, substantially reduced abstract thinking ability and limited awareness render insight-oriented psychotherapy totally ineffective. As in dealing with individuals with dementia, in such cases it is the caregivers who are usually the focus of intervention, through counseling and teaching them behavioral management techniques to facilitate life at home.

Group therapy is quite effective in affecting what Irvin Yalom called "universality": the feeling that one is not unique in his or her experience of cognitive deficits. Group therapy is also useful in creating a context for social support from others who understand the changes following brain damage. It provides an opportunity to try new compensatory behaviors in a safe environment, with immediate supportive feedback. Patients who require relearning of social skills will do so better in a group setting.

Unlike traditional psychotherapy, the therapist working with individuals with brain damage must take a more directive role in the therapeutic process, as noted earlier. In addition to educating the client, the therapist may provide alternative approaches to a variety of problem-solving demands on the client, who may now be showing deficits of insight, initiative, and abstract abilities. Thus, not only is the patient devastated emotionally in the face of catastrophic changes, the patient now lacks efficient means of dealing with them. Merely supporting and facilitating grieving of loss, although important in the initial stages of recovery, may not be sufficient in the stages of returning to society at large.

Cognitive deficits do not have to prevent a survivor from returning to work. Thus, memory and attentional deficits can be circumvented using a variety of compensatory strategies. But, as noted earlier, to utilize these strategies, it is crucial for the individual to accept this new condition and recognize the necessity for compensation. For example, in our center we commonly recommend the use of organizers (electronic or not), as a compensatory strategy of dealing with memory deficits. But to make it useful, the individual must use the organizer. Again and again we observe patients who superficially accept the strategy but do not implement it in daily life. Using it presupposes accepting the need for it and, therefore, admitting to reduced cognitive ability.

It is very common to encounter individuals with mild brain damage who think "they are going insane" due to the perceived changes in function. This is especially common following TBI where patients are told they will get better in about 6 to 8 weeks, but no relief is experienced. In such cases, psychiatric referral may result, with the unfortunate implication that the patient has "neurotic" problems, or else, when litigation is involved, is greatly exaggerating the symptoms for financial gains. When the latter is not the case, such implications only serve to exacerbate emotional symptoms and hinder recovery.

Although the consequences of brain damage will be expressed in many forms, both cognitive deficits and emotional problems are often seen. Whereas mood disorders can result directly from impairment to the brain processes involved with affective responses, they can also be secondary to awareness of cognitive deficits. In turn, these psychological symptoms will intensify the symptoms of dysfunction that originally resulted from damage to brain tissue. Thus, it is necessary to treat both the cognitive and psychological symptoms observed in individuals with brain damage as they are inextricably entangled following injury. For this reason, overall improved functioning can be seen in survivors of brain damage when either cognitive or psychological symptoms improve.

VI. REVIEW OF TREATMENT EFFICACY

What is the role of cognitive therapy in promoting the rate of recovery and its final steady state? There are inherent methodological difficulties in assessing outcome of cognitive treatment. To mention a few, it was already noted that no two individuals with brain damage are alike, either in their life history, premorbid adjustment, support system, extent, and location of injury. In addition, defining and measuring outcome is very difficult, in a manner similar to that encountered in research on the effectiveness of psychotherapy. Recovery may be measured on a neuropsychological test battery, or in terms of returning to work and/or function in the family or the community. Each aspect of recovery has its place but may not correlate highly with each other, thus making the study of treatment outcome very complex. Despite the difficulties, the research evidence to date provides general support for the efficacy of cognitive treatment (CT). Thus large, multicenter studies indicate that rehabilitation in general will result in better functional recovery, higher rate of return to gainful employment, and better psychosocial adjustment, even when residual symptoms remain. In contrast, studies on the effect of CT that addresses just the basic cognitive processes, outside the context of functional utilization in the real world, are not as encouraging. The inference is that treatment should focus on disabilities in real life, that is, at work and in the psychosocial environment.

The efficacy of psychotherapy in the population with brain damage has not been well studied on a large scale, but many rehabilitation centers report positive effects of therapy in many, although not in all, individuals with brain injuries. This might be expected, given that patients with brain damage do not choose to receive psychotherapy, as do clients who turn to psychotherapy on their own. Such patients do not always recognize their own needs as a result of the injury, nor do they always have the cognitive wherewithal to form therapeutic alliance and benefit from the psychotherapeutic process. Often the effects of brain damage require pharmacological intervention before any adjuvant psychotherapy can have any effect. At other times, impaired memory, attention, and concentration do not permit good carryover from one session to the next, requiring a repetition of material dealt with before.

For these reasons, and due to the variability of the population with brain damage in general, no definitive information on efficacy is available. Yet any one who works in treatment with persons with brain injuries can attest to the dramatic positive responses, the improvement in psychosocial functions exhibited by some patients, with less remarkable effectiveness in others. Given the effects of brain damage on psychosocial functions, and the negative effects of the emotional consequences of brain damage on functioning, it would be unethical to await results of large-scale efficacy study of psychotherapy, and not provide intervention as needed.

VII. SUMMARY

Brain damage results in a wide variety of cognitive, affective, psychosocial, and occupational symptoms. Depending on the location and extent of damage, as well as on the developmental history, premorbid adjustment, overall intelligence, motivation, and available support system, the consequences can range from mild impairments with a full return to function, to total disability. Therapy for the symptoms must address the needs of the individual in all possible spheres, as they overlap and interact to produce a clinical picture of disability. Therefore, cognitive treatment, psychotherapy, psychosocial and vocational intervention all must form part of a comprehensive treatment plan if positive outcome is to be achieved. A return to normal function does not require a complete remission of deficits, something rarely achieved in this clinical population. Instead, it is contingent on acceptance of irreversible changes, emotional adjustment, and the integration of compensatory strategies that allows functioning despite residual impairments. For this purpose, the totality of the injured person's cognitive, social, physical, and emotional spheres (in short—the identity) must be readjusted in the process of treatment, to accommodate the new changes in the most adaptive fashion within the individual's life.

See Also the Following Articles

Collaborative Care ■ Comorbidity ■ Medically Ill Patient: Psychotherapy ■ Vocational Rehabilitation

Further Reading

Dixon, R. A., & Backman, L. (Eds.). (1995). *Compensating for psychological deficits and declines: Managing losses and promoting gains.* Mahwah, NJ: Lawrence Erlbaum.

Luria, A. R. (1963). *Recovery of function after brain injury.* New York; Macmillan.

Prigatano, G. P. (1991). Disordered mind wounded soul: The emerging role of psychotherapy in rehabilitation after brain injury. *Journal of Head Trauma Rehabilitation, 6*(4), 1–10.

Raskin, S. A., & Mateer, C. A. (Eds.). (2000). *Neuropsychological management of mild traumatic brain injury.* New York: Oxford University Press.

Uzzell, B. P., & Stonnington, H. H. (Eds.). (1996). *Recovery after traumatic brain injury.* Mahwah, NJ: Lawrence Erlbaum Associates.

Wilson, B. A. (2000). Compensating for Cognitive Deficits Following Brain Injury. *Neuropsychology Review, 10*(4), 233–243.

World Health Organization. (1980). *International classification of impairments, disabilities, and handicaps: A manual of classification relating to the consequences of disease.* Geneva.

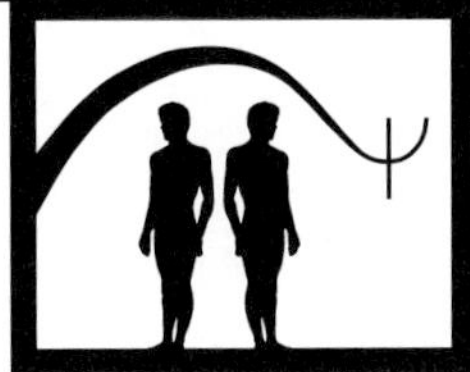

Orgasmic Reconditioning

Nathaniel McConaghy

University of New South Wales

GLOSSARY

expectancy effects Responses that follow a treatment but are not specific results of the treatment but are placebo responses due to the participant's expectancy of improvement. They can be difficult to exclude from specific effects in studies of psychological therapies that use placebo procedures as controls, because the treatment may appear to the participants to be more likely to be effective than the placebo.

multiple-baseline design Employed in single-case studies with the aim of demonstrating that the change following a treatment is a specific effect of the treatment. Frequency or intensity of a number of behaviors is assessed at baseline. Treatment aimed at changing only one of the behaviors is the introduced. If that behavior and none of the others change following treatment it is considered that the treatment has specifically produced the change. The procedure can be repeated with a treatment aimed at changing a second behavior and so on. The design will not control for expectancy effects if the treatment appears to the participant to be more likely to affect the behavior targeted than the other behaviors.

I. DESCRIPTION OF TREATMENT

Orgasmic reconditioning, also termed masturbatory reconditioning, was introduced for the treatment of participants seeking modification of their sexual preference. In early studies they were mainly homosexual men but in last two decades they have been mainly male sexual offenders. In their 1991 review, Laws and Marshall described four forms of orgasmic reconditioning that had been reported in the literature. Combinations of the four could be regarded as a fifth form.

A. Thematic Shift

In thematic shift the participant is instructed when he masturbates to use his habitual "inappropriate" or deviant fantasy to produce an erection and to maintain sexual arousal. At the point of ejaculatory inevitability he is instructed to switch his fantasy to one of an "appropriate" nature, thus pairing that fantasy with orgasm. Over time the participant is to introduce the nondeviant fantasy earlier and earlier during masturbation. If following the thematic shift he begins to lose arousal he is to shift back briefly to the deviant fantasy to regain high arousal and then shift again to the nondeviant fantasy. Ultimately he is expected to always masturbate using appropriate fantasies.

B. Fantasy Alternation

It was considered by some workers that as thematic shift was usually carried out by the participant without direct supervision he may not maintain the required temporal relationships between deviant and nondeviant fantasy. They changed the procedure to make it easier for the participant to follow. Rather than shift the thematic content in each session of masturbation, he was instructed to use alternate sessions, in one of which he used deviant fantasies exclusively and in the other, nondeviant fantasies exclusively.

C. Directed Masturbation

With this form of orgasmic reconditioning, the participant was instructed to masturbate exclusively to nondeviant fantasies and to totally avoid masturbating to deviant themes.

D. Satiation

In satiation as described by Marshall and Lippens in 1977 and subsequently termed verbal satiation by some authors, the participant under auditory supervision masturbated continuously beyond ejaculation for a prolonged period, usually about an hour, while fantasizing aloud every variant he could think of on his deviant activities.

Subsequently it was reported the procedure could also be carried out by the participant at home, where he recorded his verbalizations, for the therapist to check he was following the instructions.

E. Combined Directed Masturbation and Satiation

A subsequent development was for the participant to commence with directed masturbation until ejaculation and then employ satiation. This was further modified by the participant repeating directed masturbation until he was completely unresponsive to sexual stimuli and then commencing satiation while masturbating a flaccid penis. Laws and Marshall commented that duration of satiation with this procedure was brief, usually 20 min. Another variant was for the participant to initially masturbate to slides and audiotapes considered appropriate, then following ejaculation, to masturbate a second time while listening to a relaxation tape under instructions to avoid any sexual fantasy, then masturbate a third time when refractory, while exposed to deviant slides and audiotapes for 1 hr.

II. THEORETICAL BASES

Thorpe, Schmidt, and Castell in their 1963 report of the treatment of a homosexual man by showing him the picture of an attractive scantily dressed woman as he reached orgasm, described the procedure as a positive conditioning technique. Presumably it was expected that the sexual arousal associated with orgasm would by conditioning occur to women. Laws and Marshall in their 1991 review considered orgasmic reconditioning was based on the assumption inherent in conditioning accounts of sexual deviation that the content of masturbation fantasies guided the overt expression of sexual behavior. They stated that Marquis in 1970, though not the first to use the technique of thematic shift, provided the first theoretical rationale for its employment. The aim was to maintain the nondeviant fantasy as continuously as possible throughout the masturbatory sequence until ejaculation. The repeated pairing of sexual arousal and orgasm with appropriate fantasies was expected to initiate conditioning processes that would alter sexual desires in an appropriate direction. Thoughts of appropriate sexual acts with appropriate partners would become attractive. In addition, through the discontinuation of pairing deviant thoughts with masturbation, deviant acts would lose their attraction by simple extinction. Laws and Marshall commented of directed masturbation that it was not clear if it was expected to reciprocally reduce deviant arousal. However, as with the procedure, participants avoid masturbating to deviant themes, simple extinction should operate to reduce this arousal as with thematic shift.

Laws and Marshall stated that satiation was based on the concept that continuous unrewarded repetition of an undesired behavior will lead to its extinction. They cited the 1977 report of Marshall and Lippens that many of their clients had told them their masturbatory fantasies often became boring and they changed them to maintain arousal. Marshall and Lippens reasoned that the continued repetition of favored masturbatory themes during a period when the client was in a low state of sexual arousal should lead to a reduction in the arousing properties of those themes.

III. EMPIRICAL STUDIES

A. Penile Circumference Response Assessment of Outcome

Most of the empirical studies of orgasmic reconditioning report its use in one or a few patients with no or inadequate controls. They usually rely for assessing change in the individual participant's sexual preference by measuring his penile circumference responses (PCRs) to appropriate and deviant stimuli prior to and following the procedure. The validity of these responses as measures of sexual preference has been increasingly questioned. As early as 1971 Bancroft reported that though the mean PCRs of 30 homosexual men as a group were greater to pictures of nude men than nude women, in only 14 of the 30 as individuals were correlations between their "erection" and ratings of arousal statistically significant. In 1975 Mavissakalian, Blanchard, Abel, and Barlow found the mean PCRs to pictures of a nude young woman failed to discriminate as groups, six homosexual from six heterosexual men. In articles published by McConaghy in 1989 and 1991 and reviewed along with further evidence in 1998 the lack of consistent findings in studies attempting to discriminate groups of rapists or pedophiles from controls by their mean PCRs to deviant stimuli was pointed out. Evidence was also advanced of the ability of their penile volume responses unlike their PCRs to discriminate heterosexual and homosexual men as individuals rather than as groups.

To support the validity of PCR assessment Lalumiere and Quinsey in 1994 reported that meta-analysis of the findings of selected studies investigating the PCRs of rapists demonstrated that the assessment did discriminate rapists from nonrapists, as groups. Hence it was necessary to combine the responses of several groups of rapists and nonrapists by meta-analysis to obtain convincing statistical evidence that PCR assessment discriminated the two groups. This indicated it could weakly discriminate as groups men who differed in sexual preferences, but certainly not as of individuals.

Nevertheless the authors considered the result supported the use of the assessment in individual men. In 1996 Marshall commented that

> for a test to have merit, it must be shown that it is in a standardized form that is broadly acceptable, that it is reliable and valid, and that either it is resilient to faking or faking can be reliably discerned. Unfortunately, the available data on phallometric assessments (i.e. PCR assessment of sexual preference) do not meet any of these empirical and technical requirements ... the wisest course of action may be to withdraw its clinical use until more adequate data are available.

Subsequently in 1998 Lalumiere and Harris decided it was unclear whether changes in participants' PCRs following treatment should be thought of as changes in sexual preference or changes in men's ability to control arousal, a suggestion made previously by Quinsey and Earls in 1990.

In their 1991 review Laws and Marshall accepted that changes in PCRs of individual men to pictures of nude males and females were valid measures of change in their sexual preference that demonstrated the effectiveness of orgasmic reconditioning. Penile volume assessment though consistently demonstrated to validly assess the sexual preference of individual men has not been used to evaluate orgasmic reconditioning.

B. Thematic Shift

In their 1963 report of thematic shift orgasmic reconditioning of a homosexual man Thorpe and his colleagues stated that following the procedure his masturbatory fantasy remained entirely homosexual. The procedure was then alternated with electrical aversive therapy to pictures of nude males, after which he reported great reluctance to use homosexual fantasy with masturbation. Following treatment he had "occasional homosexual patterns" of behavior but continued the new pattern of masturbating to female pictures and fantasies. In a subsequent study Thorpe and colleagues used directed masturbation, instructing a homosexual man to masturbate as often as possible using heterosexual fantasies only. Initially he took a long time to reach orgasm, but later the time decreased, and he reported satisfying fantasy. He was then treated with aversion relief. The participant was said to have experienced heterosexual interest for the first time in his life during and following treatment.

In their 1991 review Laws and Marshall pointed out that unlike these and other early studies in which orgasmic reconditioning required some form of aversive therapy to dampen the attractiveness of the deviant stimuli, in his 1970 study Marquis reported its effective use alone. In the uncontrolled study 12 of 14 participants treated for a variety of sexual deviations reported that they were much improved or cured. Marshall relied on use of PCR assessment in a 1973 study that included thematic shift in 12 clients of mixed diagnoses but pointed out that as aversive therapy was used also causal inferences could not be made.

Ten years after introduction of orgasmic reconditioning Conrad and Winzce in 1976 pointed out the evidence of its efficacy had not gone beyond the case study level. They investigated use of thematic shift in three homosexual men who received this procedure alone and one in whom its use was followed by aversive therapy.

In evaluating their results they attached importance to failure of the participants' reported improvement, PCRs, and their written records of sexual feelings to change in relation to the periods of withdrawal and reintroduction of the treatments. As discussed by McConaghy in his 1977 review expectation that treatment effects would disappear when treatment was withdrawn was accepted at the time in applied behavior analysis theory. That this meant that treatment effects would be evanescent was overlooked. McConaghy concluded the study could be considered an uncontrolled report of a positive response to orgasmic conditioning in three patients, and a negative response in a fourth, who subsequently responded to aversive therapy. Conrad and Winzce accepted the validity of the individual participants' PCR assessments and considered they may have reported changes they did not feel and that both treatments were unsuccessful. Laws and Marshall in their 1991 review decided the study was the only well-controlled study of thematic shift and accepted the authors' interpretation that it failed to demonstrate any effects for the procedure.

C. Fantasy Alternation

Laws and Marshall reviewed the use of fantasy alternation in studies with one to four subjects that used self-report and PCR assessment as outcome measures. Some studies attempted to causally relate the treatment to outcome using a multiple-baseline design. This design relies on demonstrating that the introduction of the treatment targeting one behavior modifies only that behavior and not others that were not targeted. If this occurs it is accepted that the modification is a specific effect of the treatment. This methodology ignores the possibility that the targeting of one behavior has induced an expectancy effect in regard to that behavior and not the others not targeted. In any case in a study cited of a bisexual pedophile, though arousal to female children was targeted and declined, that to male children declined without having been targeted. Laws and Marshall attached significance to one study of four confused, apparently ego-distonic homosexuals, in two of whom the procedure produced increase rather than decrease in deviant arousal as assessed by their PCRs. They also pointed out that from the theoretical basis of orgasmic reconditioning use of masturbation to deviant fantasies as in fantasy alteration would increase rather than decrease the ability of such fantasies to excite sexual arousal. They concluded it was hard to see any justification for further investigation of the procedure.

D. Directed Masturbation

Laws and Marshall considered there was some evidence that directed masturbation might be effective. At the same time they raised the issue of whether it was appropriate to attempt to reduced men's sexual arousal to deviant fantasies by encouraging them to masturbate exclusively to nondeviant fantasies if they were already strongly sexually aroused by such fantasies. The evidence they cited supporting the procedure was again that of single-case uncontrolled studies using either self-report and/or PCR circumference assessments. It is difficult to see how this evidence was stronger than that supporting the efficacy of thematic shift, which they considered inadequate.

E. Satiation

Laws and Marshall cited single-case studies evaluating satiation, which were also uncontrolled and used participants' self-report and PCR changes as outcome measures. In one a multiple-baseline design was used in which PCR assessed reductions in sexual arousal occurred to stimulus categories targeted in sequence by the satiation procedure. Laws and Marshall did not discuss the possible confounding influence of expectancy effects and/or the ability of the participant to consciously or unconsciously modify his penile responses. Men's ability to modify their PCRs had been well documented by the time of their study. They considered satiation was clearly responsible for the reduction in inappropriate arousal that they considered had been demonstrated by the change in the participant's PCRs. The participant's assessed arousal to adult females showed only a modest increase. In another participant satiation produced marked decline in deviant arousal and a modest increase in arousal to adult women, as assessed by his PCRs. The participant had previously failed to respond to self-esteem enhancement and electrical aversive conditioning. Laws and Marshall criticized single-case studies evaluating combinations of directed masturbation and satiation as providing inadequate data concerning the outcome, or lacking appropriate control. Gray in 1995 reported a comparison study of verbal satiation alone and directed masturbation followed by ammonia aversive therapy in 28 participants, 14 nonrandomly allocated to one or other procedure. Outcome was assessed by participants' PCRs to audiotapes of sexual interactions with adults and children. Seven of those who received satiation and six of those who received the combined procedure showed reduction in assessed arousal to appropriate stimuli, a finding not discussed by the author. Significant reduction in assessed arousal to deviant stimuli followed the procedure incorporating aversive therapy but not satiation, and it was concluded the former was more effective.

F. Conditioning Theory Basis of Orgasmic Reconditioning Questioned

Accepting the theoretical basis of orgasmic reconditioning that pairing of sexual cues with orgasm would increase sexual arousal, Marshall and Eccles in 1993 concluded concerning pedophiles that

> Each time the offender has sex with a child, he obviously pairs heightened sexual arousal with vivid, realistic visions of children and the proprioceptive stimuli produced by his own actions. These contacts provide powerful conditioning trials, and if repeated often enough, should entrench a growing attraction to sex with children even in the absence of masturbating to children.

Evidence that would appear to question this belief was provided by McConaghy in a 1978 study that has been consistently ignored. Using the valid penile volume assessment of the sexual preference of individual men, the arousal to moving films of nude men as compared to that to films of nude women was determined in 181 men seeking treatment for compulsive homosexual feelings. Married men who had repeatedly experienced orgasm in the presence of female cues, namely their wives, but had not had intercourse with other women showed no evidence of increased penile volume arousal to films of women or decrease to films of men, compared to single men with no history of heterosexual intercourse. If all the married men utilized exclusive homosexual fantasies during their intercourse with their wives, it could be argued that these fantasies inhibited the effect of any physical cues from the bodies of the women with whom they were in intimate physical contact. However fewer than 20% of these men reported that they used homosexual fantasy during intercourse with their wives. All had sought treatment to cease homosexual activity and wished to continue the relationship with their wives with whom they frequently stated they were in love. Most said they were sexually aroused by thoughts of their wives, though they felt no sexual attraction to other women. It is possible that in men who report no sexual arousal to women generally, the repeated experience of heterosexual intercourse with one woman does condition sexual arousal to her, but it does not generalize to other women.

G. Need for Penile Volume Response Assessment of Effects of Orgasmic Reconditioning

The finding that the orgasmic reconditioning procedure experienced regularly by married homosexual men produced no change in their validly assessed sexual preference strongly indicates the need for valid empirical evidence of the ability of the procedure to modify the sexual preference of sex offenders, in whose treatment it remains widely used. The empirical research evaluating it in uncontrolled case studies using self-report and PCR assessment has been conducted in participants most of whom wish to experience or to report changes in their sexual orientation either for their own emotional comfort or to impress therapists who may be influential in regard to legal decisions concerning them. Given the superior validity of penile volume responses to films of nude males and females in assessing sexual preference, studies utilizing it to evaluate the various forms of orgasmic reconditioning used in current sex offender programs would seem urgently required. As stated earlier, Lalumiere and Harris suggested in 1998 that treatments which induce change in PCR assessments may do so not by changing men's sexual preference but by increasing their ability to control inappropriate arousal. If so, orgasmic reconditioning procedures that involve prolonged or repeated masturbation on instruction would seem to require comparison with more acceptable procedures that increase this ability. These include alternative behavior completion (imaginal desensitization), demonstrated in placebo-controlled studies to do so. The conclusion of Laws and Marshall that the combination of directed masturbation and satiation needs to be evaluated in a systematic study could stimulate a randomized controlled comparison of the combination with alternative behavior completion. Unfortunately this seems unlikely.

H. Incorporation of Orgasmic Reconditioning in Multimodal Approaches

As various forms of orgasmic reconditioning are now usually combined with a variety of treatments in multimodal approaches, research evaluating any forms alone is unlikely to be carried out. Quinsey in 1986 reported the response of self-referred sex offenders treated with covert sensitization and masturbatory satiation, cognitive restructuring, social and assertiveness skills and sex education; 89% of 44 contacted at 6 months and 79% of 19 contacted at 12 months under confidential conditions reported no recidivism. Travin, Bluestone, Coleman, Cullen, and Melella in 1985 reported a somewhat lower rate of recidivism over a shorter follow-up period with similar therapy in more highly selected sex offenders. These results were not superior to those reported by McConaghy and colleagues in 1985 and 1988 with therapy using alternative behavior completion combined with brief nonstructured counselling carried out during follow-up interviews. However comparisons of the results of these studies cannot be accepted to be meaningful in view of the lack of control of participant differences. McConaghy and colleagues treated all participant who sought treatment for deviant urges they could not control in a cost-free program tailored to allowed those employed to continue to work. The selection procedures and cost of the other programs was not specified, as is common. A further indication that research evaluating individual behavioral procedures is unlikely to be conducted is implicit in the comment of Quinsey and Earls in 1990. They considered that cognitive therapies for sex offenders may not require the addition of behavioral approaches, as the variety of behavioral treatments used to modify sexual arousal patterns all appeared to be at least somewhat effective, and hence all may act nonspecifically.

IV. APPLICATIONS AND EXCLUSIONS

Orgasmic conditioning procedures would appear to have been abandoned in the management of participants reporting problems in relation to homosexual feelings by some therapists because they consider that changing sexual preference by these and other methods is impossible, and others because they consider such attempts are unethical. The American Psychiatric Association in 1998 issued a statement opposing reparative therapy, that is, attempts to change homosexual preference. Currently orgasmic conditioning procedures are used in men with paraphilias, mainly sex offenders. Such men are under considerable social and often legal pressure to comply with treatment. The use of procedures that encourage them to masturbate particularly for long periods would seem likely to be experienced as demeaning by many such participants whose self-esteem is usually already low. In view of the lack of evidence of the effectiveness of the procedures in changing the sexual preference of men with paraphilias in an appropriate direction, they would seem unlikely to encourage them to form appropriate social relationships. It would seem acceptable to encourage men with paraphilias when they do masturbate to attempt not to use deviant fantasies. However to instruct them, particularly if they are under legal pressure to comply, to masturbate as a therapeutic procedure could be considered unethical when no acceptable evidence has been advanced of its value.

V. SUMMARY

Orgasmic reconditioning aims to change participants' sexual preference so they are more aroused by persons deemed appropriate in age, sex, and ability and willingness to consent, and less by those deemed inappropriate. The various forms that are or have been used are described, and their theoretical bases discussed. Associating pictures, verbal descriptions, or fantasies of appropriate persons with orgasm was considered to act by conditioning to increase arousal to the group to which such persons belonged. Associating similar representations of inappropriate persons with reduction of sexual arousal by repeated masturbation producing satiation was considered to inhibit arousal to the group to which such persons belong. Empirical research considered to support the value of the procedures lacked validity as it was based on self-report and/or change in treated participants' penile circumference responses to representations of appropriate or inappropriate subjects. Penile circumference responses unlike penile volume responses lack validity as measures of individual men's sexual preference. Using penile volume to assess their sexual preference, it was no different in married homosexual men who had repeatedly experienced orgasm with their wives compared to single homosexual men who have never had heterosexual intercourse. This finding casts considerable doubt on the theoretical basis of orgasmic reconditioning and indicates a need for valid research evaluating the procedures that remain in widespread use in the treatment of sex offenders. Until such evidence is produced as the procedures could be experienced by the subjects treated as demeaning, their use particularly by legal compulsion could be considered unethical.

See Also the Following Articles

Arousal Training ■ Bioethics ■ Electrical Aversion ■ Emotive Imagery ■ Multimodal Behavior Therapy ■ Sex Therapy ■ Thought Stopping

Further Reading

Lalumiere, M. L., & Harris, G. T. (1998). Common questions regarding the use of phallometric testing with sexual offenders. *Sexual Abuse: A Journal of Research and Treatment, 10,* 227–237.

Laws, D. R., & Marshall, W. L. (1991). Masturbatory reconditioning with sexual deviates: an evaluative review. *Advances in Behavior Research and Therapy, 13,* 13–25.

Marshall, W. L. (1996). Assessment, treatment, and theorizing about sex offenders. *Criminal Justice and Behavior, 23,* 162–199.

McConaghy, N. (1977). Behavioral treatment in homosexuality. In M. Hersen, R. M. Eisler, & P. M. Miller (Eds.), *Progress in behavior modification* (pp. 309–380). New York: Academic Press.

McConaghy, N. (1998). Assessment of sexual dysfunction and deviation. In A. S. Bellack & M. Hersen (Eds.), *Behavioral assessment: A practical handbook* (4th ed.) (pp. 315–341). Boston: Allyn and Bacon.

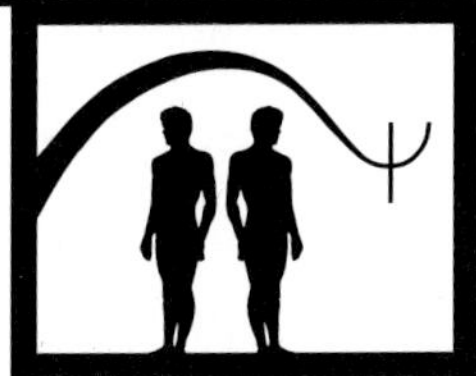

Outcome Measures

Michael J. Lambert and Dean E. Barley
Brigham Young University

GLOSSARY

clinical significance Refers to the relevance or meaning of change for the individual client. This is in contrast to statistical significance, which refers to the differences between group means on a measure.

efficacy research Designed to determine the success of specific treatment interventions for a particular disorder.

effectiveness research Intended to discover the overall success of interventions with typical clients in the usual clinic setting.

patient-focused research Centers on observing the individual client's progress throughout the course of therapy to determine how that particular client is responding.

reliable change index The least number of units a score can change on a measure to be certain that the change was not a chance fluctuation due to measurement error inherent from the reliability of the instrument.

Outcome measures are procedures used to document client functioning before, during, and after participating in psychotherapy. These can include self-report questionnaires, therapist and clinician rating scales, scales completed by the clients' relatives, or even records such as school, medical, insurance, or employment history.

I. THE PURPOSE OF OUTCOME MEASURES

The accurate measurement of clients' responses to psychotherapy is vital in order to (1) improve psychotherapy services both at the individual clinician level and at the level of establishing viable treatment protocols for specific disorders; and (2) demonstrate the effectiveness, including cost-effectiveness, of clinical interventions to interested parties (i.e., consumers, clinicians, researchers, third-party payers, administrators, and those who develop policy).

II. MULTIDIMENSIONAL NATURE OF CLIENT CHANGE

The accurate measurement of client response to psychotherapy is complex due to the multidimensional nature of change. For example, a group of clients who meet the diagnostic criteria for depression may experience to a different degree each of the clinical symptoms (i.e., sadness, suicidal ideation, and so forth). In addition to these distinctions, clients may also experience variations in other areas such as interpersonal difficulties, physical problems, financial concerns, work impairment, or substance abuse. These various difficulties are frequently the focus of therapeutic interventions, and proper assessment of a client's response to therapy requires that these areas also be evaluated. Hence, outcome measures by necessity must focus on many different areas of performance to give a complete picture of client functioning. Various researchers have proposed that outcome measures could conceivably evaluate aspects of client functioning such as (1) psychological symptoms, (2) interpersonal functioning in close relationships, (3) social role functioning in work or school, (4) physical health, (5) the cost of care and treatment utilization, (6) reduction in public health and safety threats, (7) client satisfaction, and (8) global well-being or quality of life.

III. EXPERIMENTAL DESIGN AND OUTCOME MEASURES

The purpose of an outcome study influences the type of outcome measures used. Efficacy research is designed to determine the relative success of specific treatment protocols for a particular disorder. This type of research uses experimentally controlled conditions with homogeneous populations. Different treatment interventions are given to the experimental and control groups. The responses of the experimental and control groups to the different interventions are measured with scales designed for that population and/or disorder. For example, a study exploring the response of clients to different interventions for depression might use the Beck Depression Inventory (BDI, a short self-report instrument that the client completes), the Hamilton Depression Rating Scale (HDRS, a rating scale completed by a clinician), a structured diagnostic interview, a client self-report scale to assess cognitive distortions, and so on. Differences between the experimental group and the control group on such scales are compared. Conclusions concerning the relative efficacy of interventions are based on tests of statistical difference between the means of the experimental and the control groups.

Effectiveness research measures the mean response of a more heterogeneous group of clients in naturalistic clinic settings. This type of research is designed to discover the overall success of interventions with typical clients in the usual clinical environment. Outcome measures in such studies often evaluate a wider range of difficulties because clients are not screened and come with more diverse problems. Examples could include instruments with a wider range of symptoms such as the Symptom Checklist 90-Revised (SCL-90-R, a 90-item self-report instrument completed by the client), program evaluation surveys, or client satisfaction questionnaires.

Patient-focused research centers on observing the individual client's response throughout the course of therapy and afterward. This approach determines how each particular client is responding in therapy. Outcome measures that sample a wide range of symptoms are also appropriate for this kind of study. Patient-focused research concentrates on the clinical significance of the individual client's responses to interventions rather than just the statistical significance of differences between group averages as is common in efficacy and effectiveness studies. Establishing the clinical significance of change reveals not just the magnitude of change but also the meaning of change for the individual client.

The most commonly accepted method of defining clinical significance has two components. First, a cutoff point that distinguishes between the "normal" and "dysfunctional" populations on the outcome measure is established. For example, the cutoff point could simply be defined as one standard deviation above the mean of the "normal" group on the measure (or below, depending on which way is more dysfunctional). The second step is to determine the reliable change index (RCI). The RCI is the minimal number of units the client's score must change between administrations to reliably say that the change is not due to chance fluctuation. The RCI is calculated by dividing the absolute change between two scores on the same instrument by the standard error of measurement for that instrument. For a clinically significant positive change to occur by this two-part definition, a client's change in score between the initial administration and subsequent administrations of the scale would have to (1) move from the "dysfunctional" side of the cutoff point into the "normal" range, and (2) move at least as many units as the RCI to ensure that the change was not due to measurement error. Cutoff points and RCIs have been established for many of the most commonly used outcome instruments. For example, on the BDI a client's total score after the initial administration would have to be under 14 (the cutoff score to be in the "normal" population), and would have to be at least 7 points lower than the initial administration in order to comply with this definition of a clinically significant change.

IV. BRIEF HISTORICAL REVIEW AND COMMON OUTCOME MEASURES

The theoretical orientation of researchers has historically influenced the type of instruments used to measure client change. For example, due to the influence of Freudian dynamic psychology, early measures such as the Thematic Apperception Test and the Rorschach Ink Blot Test attempted to measure changes in unconscious processes as a result of participation in psychotherapy. Later, measures such as the Q-Sort Technique were used because of their congruence with client-centered theory. Such procedures are no longer used due to poor psychometric qualities, dependence on inference, and the amount of time and cost required to administer and score them. Measures consistent with behavioral theory (behavioral monitoring) and cognitive theories (e.g., Irrational Beliefs Inventory) have also been used with interventions consistent with those theories.

Early efforts to document client outcome also relied heavily on unstandardized procedures and therapists' ratings of the clients' general improvement in one dimension. More recent efforts have focused instead on measuring outcome in many areas of functioning from a variety of viewpoints. This could include samples from the client, outside observers, relatives, physiological indices, and institutional information such as employment of school records. Current outcome measures have also improved in that they focus on specific symptoms without being theory-bound. Some measures can be used to examine patterns of change over time because they are brief and can be repeated many times through the course of therapy.

Several reviews have demonstrated which instruments have been most frequently used in outcome studies over the past three decades. The most frequently used standardized self-report measures include the State-Trait Anxiety Inventory (STAI), the Minnesota Multiphasic Personality Inventory (MMPI), the Rotter Internal-External Locus of Control, the S-R Inventory of Anxiousness, the BDI, and the SCL-90. A more recent measure, the Outcome Questionnaire-45,(OQ-45,a 45-item self-report questionnaire that measures the clients symptoms and self-distress, functioning in close interpersonal relationships, and social role functioning in society) has been used in a variety of studies to examine patterns of change in psychotherapy. The Hamilton Rating Scale for Depression (HRSD) is the most common scale used by therapists or expert raters, and the Locke-Wallace Marital Adjustment Inventory has been used most frequently with significant others to describe changes in relatives participating in therapy.

Unfortunately, researchers studying client outcome in psychotherapy have more frequently created their own unstandardized measurs to study client response to treatment. The use of unstandardized measures results in difficulty in communicating, interpreting, and integrating findings between treatment approaches and across studies. Many researchers have therefore proposed the notion of individualizing outcome measures. This usually entails creating specific treatment goals for clients and rating their progress on a graded series of possible outcomes from least to most desirable. The Target Complaints Measure and Goal Attainment Scaling are examples of this type of approach. These approaches have not yet produced valid, reliable, unbiased measures of outcome with findings that are easily integrated across studies.

V. CATEGORIZING OUTCOME MEASURES

As has been mentioned, client outcome to psychotherapy is complex due to (1) the different purposes of outcome research and the resulting variations in research design (efficacy, effectiveness, and patient-focused research; statistical vs. clinical significance); (2) the multidimensional nature of client change; (3) the diversity in psychological theories and approaches to treatment (4) the lack of consistent use of standardized instruments; and (5) the need to evaluate outcome from a variety of viewpoints (such as the trerapist, patient, and significant others). One way to bring order to this complexity is to categorize outcome measures on four dimensions: content, temporality, source, and technology. It is possible to categorize any outcome measure on each of these dimensions.

The content dimension refers to the aspect of functioning that is being sampled. This could include intrapersonal events (affect, cognitions, behaviors, symptoms), interpersonal events within close relationships, and the fulfillment of social roles through the client's interaction with society at large (i.e. work and/or school performance).

The temporality category refers to two aspects of a measure. First, it can reflect whether the instrument measures unstable state-like constructs that are expected to show change as a response to psychotherapy versus stable trait-like constructs that are more likely to remain consistent. Second, the temporality category also calls attention to the number of times the researcher uses the instrument during the course of the study. Some researchers administer an instrument both before and after therapy, whereas others utilize repeated administration throughout the course of therapy to establish a pattern of change both during and following treatment.

The source dimension refers to who completes the instrument: the client, the therapist, relevant others, trained observers, or a social where records are maintained. This dimension is a continuum moving from those most involved with therapy to those least involved. A robust finding is that studies using measures of outcome from different sources do not always yield consistent results. For example, treatment of a phobia may produce a reduction in behavioral avoidance as rated by observers, but it may not produce a decrease in levels of self-reported discomfort. This highlights the need for careful consideration of the source of outcome data in discerning the true impact of therapeutic intervention.

The technology dimension refers to the method or process of data collection. For example, this could include subjective global retrospective ratings of improvement at the end of therapy by the therapist or the client, more careful descriptive procedures that pinpoint specific symptoms at the time of the assessment, frequency counts of observed behaviors by trained observers, or measures of physiological status (e.g., electrodernal response, heart rate). The type of technology used influences the findings of outcome studies. For example, studies using measures that are more open to bias, such as posttherapy retrospective global ratings of change, will produce larger treatment effects than studies that use measures that are less susceptible to rater bias. Scales that are less susceptible to bias, such as those requiring descriptions of specific symptoms at the time of the administration of the instrument, lead to smaller estimates of treatment effect sizes. Thus researchers and consumers of outcome research need to consider carefully the type of technology used in the study when interpreting the findings.

The most common outcome instruments sample intrapersonal content (symptoms or distress) with descriptive technology (assessing current functioning at the time of administration) using self-report as the source. On the temporality dimension, the instruments are usually used as both pre- and posttherapy measures, and are intended to measure state-like client characteristics that hopefully change as a response to therapy. This means that the typical outcome instrument requires that the client rate his or her own behavior, feelings, and symptomatic distress on a paper-and-pencil measure. This would include instruments such as the BDI, the SCL-90-R, or the OQ-45.

VI. CHARACTERISTICS OF GOOD OUTCOME MEASURES

Researchers have often called for the creation of a "core battery" of outcome instruments to facilitate the comparison and integration of research findings. No such battery has materialized, but the following guidelines in outcome research and the use of instruments have evolved: (1) Specify clearly what is being measured to facilitate replication; (2) examine client functioning from diverse perspectives; (3) use a variety of type of scales and methods; (4) utilize symptom-based atheoretical instruments; (5) examine patterns of change over time with repeated administrations of the measure; (6) instruments should be inexpensive, and should be easy to score and administer; (7) scales should be appropriate for clients with a variety of diagnoses; (8) instruments must be psychometrically sound (standardized, reliable, and valid) and be sensitive to change; (9) instruments must be less susceptible to bias by focusing on the current functioning of the client; (10) they should have enough items in the "normal" and "dysfunctional" range to correct for possible floor and ceiling effects; and(11) they should sample a variety of content areas such as symptoms, interpersonal functioning, and performance in social roles.

VII. FUTURE RESEARCH POSSIBILITIES

With cutoff points and reliable change indexes available on many of the most commonly used instruments, clinicians can now use repeated administrations of brief symptom-oriented measures to see how well clients are progressing in therapy. Both clients and clinicians could be given feedback on how the client is responding, and studies could examine how such immediate feedback improves the outcome and process of therapy. In addition to this, normal patterns of change or "recovery curves" that typify the usual progress of clients during therapy could be formulated for specific outcome instruments. The progress of the individual client could then be compared with the usual progress of clients with the same initial level of disturbance. If patients are not progressing as well as their cohorts, therapists could use that information to reassess and restructure therapeutic interventions.

With sound outcome measures, therapeutic effectiveness could be established for specific disorders, interventions, programs, and even individual providers. Questions concerning "dosages of therapy" for different patient subtypes or disorders could be explored. Further work could be performed linking client outcome with the process of psychotherapy. It would be possible to correlate client progress with specific behaviors during therapy. It would also be possible to study the relationship between clients' pretherapy characteristics and their distinct responses to therapeutic interventions. This would help answer the question of which types of clients respond best to which kinds of interventions or processes.

With sound outcome measures, the target of defining cost-effective treatment becomes more attainable. This would entail identifying which interventions, therapists, and therapeutic processes result in the best outcomes for which kinds of clients suffering from which kinds of disorders for the least expenditure in time and money.

The wise use of solid outcome measures can give feedback to clinicians about how to help improve their own practice. Master clinicians who repeatedly produce better outcomes can be studied so that other practitioners can learn from their procedures.

VIII. SUMMARY

Outcome measures examine the client's response to psychotherapy. The use of such measures can improve psychotherapy services and can inform the decisions made by all parties involved in the process. Client change is multidimensional (i.e. personal distress, interpersonal functioning, social role fulfillment), and needs to be assessed from a variety of viewpoints (such as the therapist, the client, and significant others).

Different experimental designs (efficacy, effectiveness, patient-focused research) have different purposes and require different types of outcome measures. Patient-focused research centers on the clinical significance of a change for the individual client rather than on the statistical significance of a difference between group means on a scale score. One definition of clinical significance is that (1) the client move from the "dysfunctional" to the "functional" range on the measure; and (2) the client's change is greater than a chance fluctuation due to the measurement error of the instrument (is greater than the reliable change index).

Early outcome measures were linked more heavily to theoretical trends of the day, and may have relied more heavily on therapist global retrospective ratings of client improvement. More recent measures are atheoretical, pinpoint a wider variety of specific symptom complaints at the time of the administration, are brief, and can be administered repeatedly to examine patterns of change. The widespread use of unstandardized measures in the past has resulted in difficulty coordinating and integrating findings.

Outcome measures can be classified according to the dimensions of content (the aspect of client functioning sampled), temporality (the degree to which the measure focuses on state or trait characteristics, and the utility of the instrument in being administered repeatedly), source (who completes the instrument), and technology (the process by which the information is gathered). The type of instrument chosen influences the reported effect sizes of the interventions. Careful researchers need to pick the type of outcome measure that will best answer their research question, and that will most clearly add to the body of growing outcome literature. "Core batteries" of outcome measures have not been established, but the characteristics of a good outcome measure have been identified. As good measures are utilized, future research could more clearly examine what interventions work best with which types of clients and disorders. Cost-effectiveness of interventions can be more clearly investigated, client progress can be monitored during the course of therapy, and clinicians can more easily learn from each other.

See Also the Following Articles

Economic and Policy Issues ■ Effectiveness of Psychotherapy ■ Efficacy ■ Individual Psychotherapy ■ Objective Assessment ■ Research in Psychotherapy ■ Termination

Further Reading

Lambert. M. J., & Finch, A. E. (1999). The Outcome Questionnaire. In M. E. Maruish (Ed.). *The use of psychological testing for treatment planning and outcome assessment,* 2nd ed. Mahwah, NJ: Lawrence Erlbaum Associates.

Lambert, M. J., & Hill, C. E. (1994). Assessing psychotherapy outcomes and processes. In A. E. Bergin, & S. L. Garfield (Eds.). *Handbook of psychotherapy and behavior change,* 4th ed. New York: John Wiley & Sons.

Lambert, M .J., & Lambert, J. M. (1999). Use of psychological tests for assessing treatment outcome. In M. E. Maruish (Ed.). *The use of psychological testing for treatment planning and outcome assessment,* 2nd ed. Mahwah, NJ: Lawrence Erlbaum Associates.

Ogles, B. M., & Lunnen, K. M. (1996). Assessing outcome in practice. *Mental Health, 5,* 35.

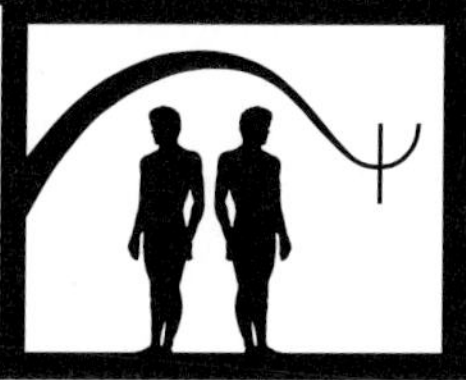

Overcorrection

Steven A. Hobbs, Benjamin A. Jones, and Julie Stollger Jones
Georgia School of Professional Psychology

GLOSSARY

graduated guidance Adjustment of the amount of force applied to the client's body to provide the minimum amount of physical assistance necessary for completion of required movements.

manual guidance Therapist placement of hands on the client's body to physically assist the client through required movements.

stereotyped behavior Repetitive acts that have no apparent functional effect on the environment.

Overcorrection is a diverse set of treatment techniques that involve contingent delivery of aversive consequences following undesirable behavior. The unique element of overcorrection is that the aversive consequences involve correct forms of behavior directly related to the undesirable act. This use of topographically similar responses is regarded as the critical feature that distinguishes overcorrection from other punishment techniques.

I. DESCRIPTION OF TREATMENT

Overcorrection procedures involve the contingent use of aversive consequences that are directly related in form (i.e., topographically similar) to the undesirable behavior they follow. In a 1982 review of overcorrection research, Richard M. Foxx and D. R. Bechtel identified several other important features of overcorrection.

1. The client is made to experience the effort that would be required of other individuals to correct the personal or environmental effects of the client's undesirable behavior.
2. The client also is required to rapidly perform overcorrection procedures, thereby increasing the effort involved.
3. Physical or manual guidance is employed to ensure client cooperation with, and completion of, the overcorrection procedures.
4. Manual guidance is graduated in that it is adjusted according to the degree to which the client voluntarily responds to directions to perform the required overcorrection acts.

The sequence of procedures used in overcorrection involves several important steps. Initially, the client is informed of his or her inappropriate action. Then the client receives brief verbal instruction regarding the overcorrection responses required. If the client does not immediately initiate the instructed responses, graduated guidance is provided. Finally, graduated guidance is terminated when the client complies with and/or completes the overcorrection procedure.

Originated in the early 1970s by Nathan H. Azrin and Richard M. Foxx, overcorrection procedures were classified by their developers as consisting of either restitutional or positive practice procedures. Restitutional overcorrection is employed in the treatment of maladaptive behaviors that result in disturbance to the environment (including harm to the client). Such procedures require an individual who demonstrates a maladaptive target behavior to restore the environment and him- or herself to a state that is vastly improved in comparison with conditions prior to the maladaptive behavior. The objective of overcorrecting environmental effects is achieved after first identifying the specific and general disturbances created by the misbehavior and identifying the behaviors needed to greatly improve the consequences of the disturbance. The individual then is required to perform corrective actions in the appropriate context whenever the undesirable behavior occurs. Useful examples of restitutional overcorrection procedures from Foxx and Azrin's initial studies include procedures referred to as oral hygiene training and household orderliness training. Oral hygiene training was employed as a consequence for repetitive mouthing, a behavior that may cause self-infection. The procedure involved verbal instruction and physical guidance directing the client to cleanse the teeth, gums, and lips with mouthwash for a period of 10 min. Household orderliness training was employed as a consequence for acts involving property damage. After throwing or overturning furniture, the client was required to spend 30 min or more wiping tables, emptying ashtrays, and rearranging magazines as well as returning the furniture to its original position.

Positive practice overcorrection is employed in the treatment of maladaptive behaviors that result in no apparent disturbance to the environment or harm to the client. Positive practice procedures require the individual who demonstrates a maladaptive target behavior to repeatedly practice appropriate responses that are relevant to the maladaptive behavior and the context in which it occurred. This objective, repeatedly practicing correct forms of relevant behavior, is achieved after first identifying appropriate behaviors that should be practiced. The client then is required to perform the correct behaviors after each occurrence of the target behavior. In Azrin and Foxx's initial applications, positive practice overcorrection procedures referred to as functional movement training were used to treat forms of self-stimulatory behaviors such as stereotyped head weaving and repetitive hand clapping. The procedures involved physically restraining either the client's head or hands and then verbally instructing and physically guiding the client through a series of head or hand movements for a period of 5 min.

Overcorrection procedures have been employed in the treatment of self-injurious behaviors, inappropriate toileting, and undesirable social and academic behaviors, as well as inappropriate oral behaviors, aggressive-disruptive behaviors, and self-stimulatory behaviors such as those cited in the preceding examples. Incorporating correct forms of behavior that are topographically similar to a wide range of target behaviors, numerous procedural variations of restitutional and positive practice overcorrection have been developed. In addition to oral hygiene training, household orderliness training, and functional movement training procedures, clinicians have developed overcorrection procedures labeled as medical assistance training, cleanliness training, quiet training, personal hygiene training, personal appearance training, social apology/reassurance training, required relaxation, hand control and awareness, autism reversal, and theft reversal.

Due to potential confusion that may arise from the various procedural labels used to characterize overcorrection treatments, Richard Foxx and D. R. Bechtel have recommended the elimination of all procedural terms and labels, including restitution and positive practice. These authors contended that overcorrection procedures consist of consequences that should be individually designed for each specific target behavior. Accordingly, overcorrection procedures should be described on a case-by-case basis, thus limiting the usefulness of procedural terms and labels.

Foxx and Bechtel noted that the use of the term positive practice has resulted in erroneous inferences regarding the inclusion of negative practice and positive reinforcement as components of overcorrection. It is important to recognize that overcorrection procedures do not include either of these elements. Overcorrection procedures are different from negative practice, a procedure whereby the client is asked to repeatedly practice the undesirable behavior. Moreover, the inclusion of positive reinforcement as a component in overcorrection procedures would alter the aversive nature of these procedures and possibly lead to increases in the target behavior. In those overcorrection studies in which positive reinforcement has been employed, such reinforcement was administered for appropriate behaviors that occurred during times when overcorrection was not delivered, rather than for correct forms of behavior that were required as part of the overcorrection sequence.

II. THEORETICAL BASES

As aversive stimuli that produce decrements in the behaviors they follow, overcorrection techniques clearly function as punishment procedures. When delivered immediately following undesirable behavior, overcorrection also includes timeout from positive reinforcement, as the client's ongoing behavior is interrupted and opportunities to obtain reinforcement from the environment are eliminated during overcorrection. Negative reinforcement, in the form of removal of manual guidance and termination of the overcorrection procedure, also occurs for the individual's compliance with and completion of the required overcorrection acts.

Overcorrection procedures have been regarded as unique compared with other punishment procedures because of their use of correct forms of behavior that are topographically similar to the maladaptive target response. Whether this element of topographical similarity results in behavioral outcomes that are different from outcomes of other punishment procedures is a question that has not been adequately addressed. Several studies have demonstrated that variations of overcorrection that employ topographically dissimilar forms of behavior can also produce suppression of target behaviors. Moreover, few studies have included data or anecdotal reports of increases in appropriate behavior associated with the use of topographically similar overcorrection procedures. Accordingly, Foxx and Bechtel have recommended the elimination of terms referring to the "educative" and "training" functions of overcorrection. Thus, researchers are left with the question of whether overcorrection entails anything more than an elaborate, albeit effective (as is discussed in the next section), set of punishment procedures.

III. EMPIRICAL STUDIES

Although overcorrection procedures have been utilized most commonly with persons with mental retardation in institutional settings, these procedures also have been employed in the treatment of autism, emotional disturbances, and behavior disorders in a variety of settings. Although many of the treatment studies have focused on children, significant numbers of studies have been conducted with adults as well. In their 1982 review of 97 overcorrection studies, Foxx and Bechtel classified the maladaptive behaviors treated with overcorrection techniques into categories of aggressive-disruptive behaviors, self-stimulatory behaviors, self-injurious behaviors, toileting behaviors, inappropriate oral behaviors, and educational-social development behaviors. Historically, the vast majority of applications of overcorrection have occurred with aggressive-disruptive, self-stimulatory, and toileting behaviors.

The initial application of overcorrection procedures occurred as a method of toilet training individuals with mental retardation in institutional settings. An extensive set of procedures known as dry-bed training was used following bowel and bladder accidents. The procedures usually consisted of mopping the floor, cleaning wet and soiled items, redressing oneself in clean clothing and replacing bed linens, and repeatedly walking to the toilet and performing a series of responses (pulling pants down, sitting, etc.) involved in appropriate toileting. These procedures later were modified for application to normal children with greater emphasis placed on the positive practice component (i.e., repeatedly walking to the toilet and rehearsing appropriate toileting behaviors). Similar procedures have been applied to children diagnosed with enuresis or encopresis. Despite some variation across studies and populations treated, the duration of overcorrection with toileting behaviors usually has been 30 min or greater, often ranging up to 45 min. Because overcorrection procedures usually have been combined with other effective procedures such as Mowrer and Mowrer's bell-and-pad training and reinforcement for appropriate voiding, it is not possible to determine the relative contribution of overcorrection to the successful outcomes reported in such multicomponent treatment programs. However, reductions of greater than 80% in wetting and/or soiling usually have been reported, with near 100% reductions often being achieved within 1 to 3 months and maintained at 2- to 18-month follow-up.

With aggressive-disruptive behaviors, overcorrection has been employed rather extensively in treating relatively mild problems, such as out-of-seat behavior or talking out, as well as in treating more extreme acts, such as hitting, biting, and assaultive sexual behavior. Typical overcorrection procedures for aggressive-disruptive behaviors include picking up thrown or ripped items, apologizing to the victim, and/or assisting in medical care of the victim. In a few studies, overcorrection has involved requiring the aggressor to lie down, to pat and stroke the victim, or to engage in a series of arm movements. The duration of these overcorrection procedures has ranged from less than 1 min to 2 hr, with the most frequent durations being 5 to 10 min. In relatively few of these studies has overcorrection been used as the only treatment procedure. Instead, many studies have combined overcorrection with procedures such as verbal warnings and positive reinforcement during periods when the client was not engaged in overcorrection acts. Using DRI (differential reinforcement of incompatible behaviors) or DRO (differential reinforcement of other behaviors) procedures, positive reinforcement has been made contingent either on responses that are incompatible with the target behaviors or on the absence of aggression or disruption for specified intervals. In investigations of overcorrection treatments, reductions of greater than 85% have been observed within 2 weeks to 2 months for most aggressive-disruptive behaviors, with a large number of researchers reporting reductions of near 100%. Maintenance of behavior change has been reported in most studies, with follow-up periods ranging from 5 weeks to 1 year.

In a large number of studies, overcorrection has been used to treat a variety of self-stimulatory behaviors including hand flapping and posturing, stereotyped vocalizations, rocking, hair pulling, and mouthing objects. Behaviors most frequently treated have been hand flapping, rocking, and mouthing. The most commonly used overcorrection procedures for these responses consist of required movement of the body parts involved in the self-stimulatory behaviors. Other common procedures have included enforced toy play and required toothbrushing. The duration of the overcorrection procedures for self-stimulatory behavior has ranged from 30 sec to 20 min, with a typical duration of 2 min. Relatively few treatments for self-stimulatory behaviors have employed overcorrection alone, as most combine overcorrection with other procedures. Additional treatment procedures have included verbal warnings, prevention of self-stimulatory behavior by physical restraint or other means, and/or positive reinforcement (i.e., DRI or DRO procedures). Nearly all investigators reported reductions in target behaviors of greater than 80%, with near 100% reductions observed in the majority of studies. However, follow-up data have been reported in very few studies, with maintenance of behavior reductions rarely reported for longer than 1 to 3 months.

Self-injurious behaviors, such as face slapping, head banging, hand biting, and eye poking and gouging also have been the focus of a relatively small number of overcorrection studies. The most frequently treated self-injurious behaviors have been head banging and biting. Overcorrection procedures for these behaviors usually have consisted of required movement of the body part involved in the self-injury, sometimes combined with required toothbrushing for self-biting, hair combing for head banging, required bed rest, and applying medication or cream to the affected area. The duration of these overcorrection procedures typically has ranged from 5 to 10 min. Overcorrection has been utilized as the only treatment procedure in most studies but has been combined with positive reinforcement of alternate behaviors in a few instances. Reductions in self-injurious behaviors of 95 to 100% have been reported in less than 1 week of treatment for most cases. The majority of studies have reported follow-up data, with maintenance of treatment effects being demonstrated for 4 to 33 months posttreatment.

A handful of investigations have addressed maladaptive oral behaviors in individuals with mental retardation. This category of behaviors includes drooling, vomiting, rumination (the repeated rechewing and swallowing of regurgitated food), pica (the ingestion of nonnutritive substances such as paper or cigarette butts), and coprophagia (the ingestion of fecal material). Overcorrection procedures have consisted of picking up trash, required practice in correct vomiting, cleaning of vomited matter from various surfaces including walls and floors, and required handwashing, toothbrushing, and mouth wiping. Durations for such procedures have varied considerably, often involving periods of less than 2 min for rumination, drooling, and pica as contrasted with 20 min to 2 hr for coprophagia and vomiting. Brief durations of overcorrection have been used most often combined with other procedures such as DRO and positive reinforcement for appropriate behaviors. Except for drooling, near 100% reduction in these maladaptive oral responses has been reported at posttreatment. The majority of studies conducted follow-up assessments and reported maintenance of these reductions at 3 to 12 months posttreatment.

A limited number of studies have addressed various responses identified by Foxx and Bechtel as educational-social development behaviors. Maladaptive responses in this broad category include errors on academic-related tasks (e.g., oral reading, spelling, writing proficiency, manual signing) and failure to comply with directions/demands to stay on-task, attend class, share with other children, make eye contact, vocalize, eat appropriately, and perform tasks with adequate speed. Overcorrection procedures for these behaviors typically have consisted of requiring clients to repeatedly correct academic errors, complete written academic tasks, comply with verbal instructions, and engage in required movements of specific body parts (e.g., hand movements with eating utensils or puzzle pieces, head movements in the direction of the therapist). Modeling and reinforcement procedures often have been included as treatment components in these studies. Combinations of these procedures usually have resulted in significant decrements in maladaptive responses, as well as significant improvements in compliance with instructions and accurate responding. However, relatively few studies examining the use of overcorrection procedures with social-academic behaviors have addressed issues of maintenance of behavior change.

As with other punishment procedures, the literature on overcorrection is replete with numerous reports (usually anecdotal in nature) of positive and negative side effects. The majority of studies that have provided data-based observations of side effects have examined stereotyped behaviors of a self-stimulatory or self-injurious nature. Associated with overcorrection have been reported increases in prosocial behaviors such as compliance, cooperation, and appropriate toy play, as well as increases in negative responses such as aggression, emotional outbursts, and nontargeted self-stimulatory behaviors.

IV. SUMMARY

In general, overcorrection represents a response-suppression method that has been demonstrated as highly effective in the treatment of a variety of maladaptive behaviors. Especially when combined with treatment procedures that promote appropriate behaviors, overcorrection has resulted in near elimination of aggressive and disruptive behaviors, self-injurious behaviors, inappropriate oral behaviors, and inappropriate toileting, as well as impressive decrements in self-stimulatory behaviors. Brief (i.e., 5 min or less), as well as extended, administrations of overcorrection have been demonstrated to suppress maladaptive behaviors with nearly equal effectiveness. As with most punishment procedures, many studies have reported positive and/or negative side effects with the use of overcorrection. Although a number of single case studies suggest the superiority of overcorrection when compared with other behavioral treatments, methodological problems inherent in these studies severely limit the conclusions that can be drawn from such comparisons. For this reason as well as ethical and practical considerations, inclusion of brief durations of overcorrection are recommended as a component of treatment protocols that provide positive reinforcement for incompatible responses and for alternate forms of appropriate behavior.

See Also the Following Articles

Aversion Relief ■ Positive Punishment ■ Positive Reinforcement ■ Retention Control Training ■ Self-Punishment

Further Reading

Axelrod, S., Brantner, J. P., & Meddock, T. D. (1978). Overcorrection: A review and critical analysis. *Journal of Special Education, 12,* 367–391.

Foxx, R. M., & Bechtel, D. R. (1982). Overcorrection. In M. Hersen, R. M. Eisler, & P. M. Miller (Eds.), *Progress in behavior modification* (Vol. 13, pp. 227–287).

Hobbs, S. A. (1976). Modifying stereotyped behaviors by overcorrection: A critical review. *Rehabilitation Psychology, 23,* 1–11.

MacKenzie-Keating, S. E., & McDonald, L. (1990). Overcorrection: Reviewed, revisited and revised. *The Behavior Analyst, 13,* 39–48.

Marholin, D. H., Luiselli, J. K., & Townsend, N. M. (1980). Overcorrection: An examination of its rationale and treatment effectiveness. In M. Hersen, R. M. Eisler, & P. M. Miller (Eds.), *Progress in behavior modification* (Vol. 9, pp. 49–80). New York: Academic Press.

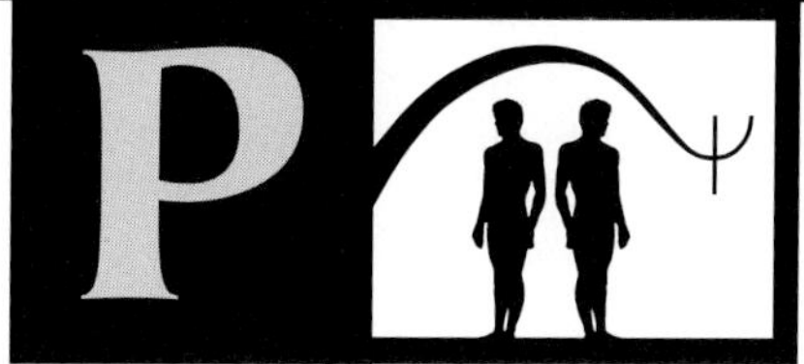

Pain Disorders

Douglas A. Songer
Wright State University

GLOSSARY

acute pain Pain from an obvious nociceptive source. It is generally self-limited and short-lived.

automatic thoughts Spontaneous and rapid, often inaccurate, interpretation of a situation.

biofeedback The technique of making unconscious, physiological processes perceptible to the senses through the use of a monitoring device in order to manipulate them by conscious mental control.

chronic pain Over 6 months, the original nociceptive cause can no longer explain the duration or severity of the pain.

continuous pain Long-standing pain from an obvious source (e.g., cancer pain).

hypnosis Induction of a state of selective attention, usually through a combination of imagery and relaxation techniques.

nociceptor A specialized peripheral nerve receptor the function of which is to receive pain stimuli.

The treatment of pain is a difficult challenge for all physicians. Recently, JCAHO has made adequate treatment of pain a priority for all hospitalized patients. Clinicians treating pain need to consider factors such as the duration and intensity of the pain, its psychosocial context, and its associated psychiatric comorbidity. This article will examine the treatment of pain in a biopsychosocial framework, concentrating on psychotherapy as a tool to help treat the pain patient.

I. TYPES OF PAIN

A. Overview

Pain was initially perceived as being purely a sensory event, resulting from tissue damage. The fact that patients respond to the same pain-generating stimulus in vastly different manners suggests that such an explanation is much too simplistic. Pain should more appropriately be viewed as a perceptual phenomenon rather than a sensory one. In a perceptual framework, both sensory and psychological factors are incorporated, and there is a much greater recognition of the importance of the attentional, cognitive, affective, and social components to the pain experience.

Physicians often question whether their patients are experiencing "real pain" or not. Such concern is generally useless, as it views pain solely as a sensory rather than a perceptual experience. Accepting patients' pain complaints as real is important; treatment can then be based on the sensory and psychological experience unique to that patient. Pain is often described as acute, continuous, or chronic in nature. Table I examines the differences between these types of pain.

B. Acute Pain

In most instances, the treatment of acute pain is uncomplicated. Adequate pharmacological analgesic relief is the first guiding principle. Physicians have often been leery of using narcotic medications even for severe pain because of a fear of the patient becoming addicted. This fear is grossly exaggerated, and narcotics can be used when clinically appropriate with minimal risk of addiction. Patients occasionally do not respond as well as expected to standard pharmacological analgesic treatment, and, in these instances, psychiatric consultation is sometimes requested. Psychosocial components to the pain should be explored in depth, and nonpharmacologic interventions can often be quite helpful. Many of these interventions will be described below.

C. Continuous Pain

Patients suffering from continuous pain pose very different challenges. For example, a patient with bone metastases may suffer some degree of pain no matter how aggressively he or she is treated with narcotic medications. The goal in managing pain in these patients is to help the patient learn to accommodate to the pain. A variety of psychotherapies can accomplish this task and may also permit the patient to decrease the dose of pain medication, minimizing the overall side effect burden. Biofeedback, cognitive-behavioral therapy, and hypnosis have all been demonstrated to be effective in such patients and will be described in further depth below.

D. Chronic Pain

Psychiatric consultation is most frequently requested for patients suffering from chronic pain. In these patients, the original nociceptive cause of the pain is no longer sufficient in explaining the current level of pain that the patient is experiencing. Pain behavior demonstrated in chronic pain patients often leads the physician to question the veracity of the pain complaints. The patient may complain of being in agonizing pain, but appear quite comfortable, or he may only cry out in pain only when the health care professional walks past his hospital room. Such behavior happens when the patient begins adapting to the pain. If the physician questions whether the pain is real because of this, then the patient may feel he needs to prove that his pain is real. Often, the disruption of the doctor–patient relationship that may ensue in such instances may further complicate the treatment. Patients need to be assured that their pain is real, and that the request for a psychiatric consult does not mean that the physician believes the pain is "all in their head." The consulting psychiatrist should emphasize that the goal of treatment is not cure of the pain, but instead to help the patient deal with it better. Aggressive treatment of underlying psychiatric conditions such as depression or anxiety that are often present in patients with chronic pain is necessary. Pharmacologic treatment must address both the pain and the underlying psychiatric issues to be successful. Psychotherapy interventions must do the same.

II. COGNITIVE-BEHAVIORAL THERAPY FOR PAIN DISORDERS

A. Overview

Cognitive-behavioral therapy has been shown to be effective in patients suffering from either continuous or chronic pain. Patients are taught skills such as distraction, imagery techniques, and calming self-talk, and learn to decrease negative, catastrophizing thoughts that are present in pain patients. Restructuring the patients'

TABLE I
Differences in Pain Types

Pain type	*Obvious nociceptive source*	*Response to narcotics*	*Time course of symptoms*	*Associated with psychological symptoms*
Acute	Yes	Good	Short, generally 1 month or less	No
Continuous	Yes	Good	Over 6 months	Sometimes
Chronic	No	Fair to poor	Over 6 months	Frequently

cognitive approach to pain is important. Beliefs about their condition, their expectations for the future, and cognitive distortions must all be examined. A catastrophic, overly negative view of the future has been found to be correlated to more intense pain reports. Helping the pain patient to have a more realistic assessment of the future may enable him or her to deal with the pain in the present.

B. Automatic Thoughts

Discovering the automatic thoughts that are present can enable them to be replaced with more realistic thoughts. For example, when the pain becomes worse, an automatic thought may be triggered such as "I'm never going to get better" or "I can't do anything." Such automatic thoughts often lead to more emotional distress, and increased physical and psychological dysfunction. Challenging the patients' inaccurate automatic thoughts can provide the patient with a more realistic and adaptive view of the problem. These same cognitive-behavioral techniques can also be used to treat the comorbid depression and anxiety that are often found in patients with pain.

C. Homework

Homework assignments are always an important part of cognitive-behavioral therapy. In patients with pain disorders, homework assignments may include asking patients to keep track of which specific thoughts, actions, and behaviors exacerbated or helped the pain. Homework can also be used to aid the patient in utilizing the coping strategies discussed in the therapy session. Homework should start easier and get progressively harder as the therapy continues. When easier tasks can be accomplished, the patient is more likely to be motivated to attempt to accomplish the more difficult tasks.

D. Relaxation Training and Imagery

Relaxation training and imagery are important components of cognitive-behavioral therapy for pain patients as well. Progressive muscle relaxation, stretch-based relaxation, and breathing relaxation are all techniques that have been shown to be beneficial. Progressive muscle relaxation involves tensing a muscle group for several seconds, passively focusing on how the tensed muscle feels. The tensed muscles are then released, with passive focus of attention on how the muscles feel as the relaxation takes place. This sequence is then applied to the major muscle groups of the body.

Stretch-based relaxation is utilized when tensing muscle groups exacerbates the pain. In stretch-based relaxation, series of muscles are very gently stretched without the tensing and relaxing techniques utilized in progressive muscle relaxation. For patients immobilized by their pain, stretch-based relaxation rather than progressive muscle relaxation is often utilized. Once patients become more mobile, progressive muscle relaxation techniques can begin to be used in combination with a stretch-based program.

Breathing relaxation focuses on slow, patterned abdominal breathing. Patients are instructed to inhale slowly and deeply through the nose, allowing the abdomen to expand. With inhalation, the abdomen rises, and the diaphragm moves downward. As the breath continues, the lower part of the chest expands and eventually the upper part of the chest does so as well. When the breath is completed, the patient is instructed to hold the breath for approximately 1 second, and then begin exhaling. The process is reversed with exhalation. The breath is slowly released as the abdomen is drawn back in and the diaphragm is lifted back up. The previously expanded chest now relaxes and exhalation is completed. The empty lungs are held this way for 1 second, and the cycle is again repeated. The entire process should take approximately 8 to 10 seconds, with inhalation and exhalation each lasting 3 to 4 seconds, and pauses following the completion of inhalation and exhalation lasting 1 second.

The use of imagery is often a part of cognitive-behavioral treatment as well. Patients can imagine returning to a calm, relaxing place. For pain patients, this allows their attention to be taken away from their pain. Imagery can also be more specific to the pain. The patient who suffers stabbing, intense trigeminal neuralgia pain, may imagine a knife stabbing into his cheek and can then be guided in therapy into imagining the knife becoming duller, and then ultimately becoming a blunt piece of wood. Other patients may be asked to focus intently on their pain, paying particular attention to its character. Pain does not remain at a constant level, but worsens significantly at times. When the patient becomes more aware of the pain and its inconstant nature, they can be more successful in utilizing imagery to help decrease the pain.

E. Coping Skills

Cognitive-behavioral therapy also involves the practical application of techniques enabling better coping with day-to-day pain. Diversional techniques such as reading or listening to music can be encouraged. Finding an appropriate pace for activities is equally important. Patients frequently alternate between doing too much, then being nearly immobilized from pain as a result. Encouraging activity, but in a restrained manner that is not likely to exacerbate the pain, is crucial for these patients. Other patients may be too inactive for fear of worsening their pain. Setting concrete, attainable goals may enable them to slowly become more active.

Cognitive-behavioral groups are utilized frequently in hospital-based pain programs. These groups often have a coping skills training component. Coping skills emphasized in such groups often emphasize assertiveness training, acknowledging and expressing feelings appropriately, and self-acceptance. When patients can hear from other fellow pain patients possible coping strategies, they are more likely to utilize them. Groups also offer the benefit of allowing patients to realize that they are not facing their problem alone.

F. Relapse Prevention

Relapse-prevention and maintenance of the learned skills in dealing with pain is an important part of cognitive-behavioral therapy as well. When patients have a flare-up of pain, especially when they have been relatively pain-free for a while, they will often become quite distressed, and feel that they need to "start all over" or that they will never get better. They frequently can forget the coping strategies and cognitive-behavioral techniques described above and can benefit from a short "refresher course." Emphasizing that one bad day does not undo all the good days that came before it is important as well. Patients can often benefit from a systematic approach to identifying the cause of the increased pain and discovering ways to prevent future flare-ups.

III. OTHER THERAPIES

A. Operant-Behavioral Therapy

In the operant-behavioral approach to the patient with pain, the goal is simply to change behavior by reinforcing well behavior and ignoring pain behavior. The operant model pays particular attention to the role that the patient's family may play in contributing inadvertently to pain behavior. Pain behavior may have been reinforced by providing attention, or permitting the patient to avoid undesirable activity. The family of the pain patient is told to ignore pain behaviors such as lying in bed moaning, while even small steps toward increased function are strongly reinforced. Homework assignments for both the patient and the family are often a part of the treatment. When both the family and the treating physician are involved, the benefits of this approach are magnified. An operant-behavioral approach to pain is often used in conjunction with a cognitive approach for additional therapeutic benefit.

B. Biofeedback

Biofeedback has often been used for a variety of pain complaints, including chronic tension headaches, low back pain, temperomandibular pain, fibromyalgia, and arthritis pain. Patients undergoing biofeedback become adept at monitoring physiological processes such as heart rate, muscle tension, and galvanic skin response. Patients learn to control these processes and thereby control overall physiological arousal. Biofeedback treatment often involves 10 to 20 sessions in which a physiological monitoring device is attached to the patient. The patient is then instructed to do whatever possible to alter the physiological parameter (e.g., skin temperature) in the specified direction. Biofeedback training typically includes training in specific relaxation strategies, such as progressive muscle relaxation or diaphragmatic breathing to aid patients to better control their physiological processes. The success of biofeedback is greatly dependent on the patient continuing to use the techniques learned in the biofeedback sessions at home.

C. Hypnosis

Hypnosis can also be a useful psychotherapeutic tool in the management of the pain patient. It has been shown to be effective in alleviating the chronic pain associated with cancer, irritable bowel syndrome, tension headaches, temperomandibular disorders, and a variety of other chronic pain disorders. Hypnosis is defined as the induction of a state of selective attention, typically through relaxation and imagery techniques. Hypnosis has both presuggestion and postsuggestion components. The presuggestion component involves attentional focusing through the use of imagery, distraction, or relaxation, and has features quite similar to relaxation techniques discussed earlier. During the suggestion component, the specific goal is introduced (e.g., a change in the nature of the pain from intolerable to mildly annoying). The postsuggestion phase involves continued use of the new behavior after hypnosis is terminated.

The hypnotherapist can, at times, teach patients to hypnotize themselves. Self-hypnosis has the potential to be an effective method for controlling both acute and chronic pain as well, especially for the motivated patient that will practice the technique at home. While not all patients can master this technique, benefits for those who can may include an increased sense of control over their illness and less dependency on the health care system. As with any pain treatment technique, hypnosis works best when it is employed early in the pain cycle, before the pain has become severe enough to impair concentration.

Meditation serves a similar function to hypnosis or self-hypnosis for patients but does not involve suggestion, autosuggestion, or the induction of a trance state. Mindfulness meditation focuses on development of an awareness of bodily sensations and mental activities in the present moment to allow the body to relax and the mind to calm. Chronic pain patients generally feel at the mercy of their illness and are quite frustrated by how much their pain controls their life. Offering tools such as meditation and self-hypnosis that patients may utilize on their own empowers them and allows patients to feel that they are once again in control of their life.

Biofeedback, hypnosis, and meditation are often used in conjunction with cognitive-behavioral therapy. As described earlier, the relaxation techniques utilized in cognitive-behavioral therapy are used in biofeedback to aid the patient in garnering more control over physiological processes, and used in the presuggestion phase of hypnosis. There is an underlying presumption in cognitive-behavioral therapy, biofeedback, and hypnosis that it is possible to attenuate the effects of pain through the use of the mind. Each of these therapies requires active intervention on the part of the patient, especially when self-hypnotic techniques are added to regular hypnotherapy. The patient must take not only an active part in his or her therapy, but must continue to do so once at home to ensure that gains made will be sustained. Table II describes the similarities and differences in cognitive-behavioral therapy, operant-behavioral therapy, biofeedback, and hypnosis.

IV. COMBINED TREATMENT OF PAIN AND PSYCHIATRIC DISORDERS

Patients with pain disorders often have comorbid psychiatric disorders. Patients who have either continuous or chronic pain are very likely to develop depression. Other psychiatric disorders, including anxiety and somatoform disorders, can frequently be found as well. The psychotherapist treating the patient who has a pain disorder must be alert to the likelihood of psychiatric disorders and ensure that they too are aggressively treated. A better treatment outcome is likely when both the comorbid psychiatric illness and the pain disorder are treated, rather than exclusively focusing on one or the other.

Many of the therapeutic methods utilized to treat the comorbid psychiatric illnesses can also be helpful in treating the pain disorder. Pharmacologic approaches such as antidepressants are often used as adjunctive agents in the treatment of pain disorders, as well as being a primary method in the treatment of depression. Anticonvulsant medications such as carbamazepine and gabapentin have often been used in a variety of pain disorders and are considered useful as augmenting agents in the treatment of anxiety or depression.

Cognitive-behavioral therapy techniques useful in the treatment of pain disorders are also helpful in the treatment of depression and anxiety. Relaxation therapy techniques utilized in the treatment of pain disorders are also frequently used in the treatment of anxiety disorders. Other cognitive-behavioral techniques, such

TABLE II
Therapies for Pain Disorders

Therapy	*Automatic thoughts*	*Relaxation techniques*	*Homework*	*Family involvement*	*Monitor physiological process*	*Induction of state of selective inattention*
Cognitive-behavioral	Yes	Yes	Yes	Yes	No	No
Operant-behavioral	No	No	Yes	Yes	No	No
Biofeedback	No	Yes	Yes	No	Yes	No
Hypnosis	No	Yes	No (except in self-hypnosis)	No	No	Yes

as cognitive restructuring and changing automatic thoughts, are common to the treatment of pain disorders, depression, and anxiety. The patient who has learned these techniques in one context should be able to more easily apply them when the other illness is being treated.

When treatment for the comorbid psychiatric illness is initiated, the therapist must be careful not to imply that this means that the therapist feels that the illness is "all in the patient's head." Most patients will readily accept the concept that psychiatric illness and pain disorders amplify each other's effects. For example, when a patient's pain becomes worse, this will often worsen a depression. A worsened depression makes it even harder to handle the pain, and this can lead to further pain, and even more depression. If the depression can be treated, then the patient's capacity to tolerate pain may increase as well.

In a similar vein, anxiety disorders must be appropriately treated as well. Patients with anxiety disorders frequently suffer from muscle tightness and have a constant low-grade muscle tenseness. For the chronic pain patient, this constant tension can be a source of additional discomfort. Treatment of anxiety with psychotropic medications or psychotherapy is necessary for complete treatment of the underlying pain.

V. SUMMARY

The treatment of the patient with a pain disorder poses a significant challenge for any clinician. Patients often resent being referred to a mental health professional, and are hesitant to accept that there may be an emotional overlay to their pain complaints. Clinicians need to take care not to suggest that the pain experienced is anything less than real, but also need to treat the comorbid psychiatric illnesses that are often present in the chronic pain patient population.

Psychotherapeutic approaches that have been shown to be effective in the treatment of patients with pain disorders include cognitive-behavioral therapy, operant-behavioral therapy, biofeedback, and hypnosis. Relaxation techniques such as progressive muscle relaxation are often used in cognitive-behavioral therapy, biofeedback, and hypnosis and are an important component of the treatment of pain disorders. Patients with psychiatric disorders such as anxiety or depression can often benefit from a psychotherapeutic approach that utilizes many of the features found in the treatment of pain disorders.

See Also the Following Articles

Biofeedback ■ Comorbidity ■ Medically Ill Patient: Psychotherapy ■ Somatoform Disorders ■ Stretch-Based Relaxation Training

Further Reading

Bone, R. C. (Ed.). (August 1996). Management of chronic pain part II. *Disease-a-Month, 42,* 459–506.

Brose, W. G., & Spiegel, D. (1992). Neuropsychiatric aspects of pain management. In S. C. Yudofsky & R. E. Hales (Eds.), *The American Psychiatric Press textbook of neuropsychiatry* (2nd ed., pp. 245–275). Washington, DC: American Psychiatric Press.

Eimer, B. N. (2000). Clinical applications of hypnosis for brief and efficient pain management psychotherapy. *American Journal of Clinical Hypnosis, 43,* 17–40.

Gaupp, L. A., Flinn, D. E., & Weddige, R. L. (1994). Adjunctive treatment techniques. In C. D. Tollinson, J. R. Satterthwaite, & J. W. Tollison (Eds.), *Handbook of pain management* (2nd ed., pp. 108–135). Baltimore: Williams & Wilkins.

National Institutes of Health. (1996). Technology Assessment Panel on Integration of Behavioral and Relaxation Approaches into the Treatment of Chronic Pain and Insomnia. *Journal of the American Medical Association, 276,* 313–318.

Turk, D. C., & Rudy, T. E. (1994). A cognitive-behavioral perspective on chronic pain: beyond the scalpel and syringe. In C. D. Tollison, J. R. Satterthwaite, & J. W. Tollison (Eds.). *Handbook of pain management* (2nd ed., pp. 136–151). Baltimore: Williams & Wilkins.

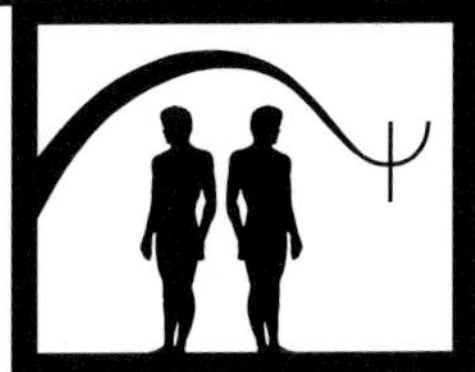

Panic Disorder and Agoraphobia

Stefan G. Hofmann
Boston University

GLOSSARY

agoraphobia Significant anxiety about places or situations from which escape might be difficult or in which help might not be easily available in the event of having a panic attack. Approximately one-third of patients with panic disorder meet this additional diagnosis.

panic disorder An anxiety disorder that is characterized by recurrent and unexpected panic attacks, which are discrete episodes of intense fear that are accompanied by a number of typical somatic and cognitive symptoms. Approximately 3% of the population is affected by this disorder over the course of a lifetime.

This article presents the therapeutic techniques, the theoretical basis, and the empirical evidence of cognitive-behavior therapy, an empirically supported intervention for the treatment of panic disorder and agoraphobia.

I. DESCRIPTION OF TREATMENT

The most effective psychological treatment for panic disorder with agoraphobia to date is cognitive-behavior therapy (CBT). This treatment is usually delivered in 12 weekly 60-min individual treatment sessions but can also be conducted in a small group format consisting of two therapists and between four and seven patients. Between each session, the patients are given clearly specified "homework" assignments to practice the newly acquired skills that are discussed in treatment. In addition, patients are expected to complete daily monitoring forms in order to identify specific panic attack triggers. These monitoring forms also serve the purpose of monitoring the patients' progress throughout treatment and of enhancing the patients' sense of predictability and controllability.

One of the best-studied CBT manuals for panic disorder is the Panic Control Treatment protocol (PCT) developed by David H. Barlow and his colleagues. The treatment consists of the following components: *(a)* education about the nature of anxiety and panic; *(b)* training in slow breathing; *(c)* cognitive restructuring; *(d)* interoceptive exposure exercises; and *(e) in vivo* situational exposure exercises for individuals with high levels of agoraphobia.

A. Education about the Nature of Anxiety and Panic

During the first two sessions, patients are taught about the nature and function of fear and its nervous system correlates. The fear response is presented as a normal and generally protective state that enhances the individual's ability to survive. Panic attacks are conceptualized as inappropriate fear reactions arising from spurious, but otherwise normal, activation of the body's fight-or-flight response system. Like other fear reactions, panic attacks are portrayed as alarms that stimulate the person to take immediate defensive action. Because the individual normally associates the fight-or-flight response with the presence of danger, panic attacks typically motivate a frantic search for the source of threat. When none is found, the treatment model assumes that the person looks inward and interprets certain bodily symptoms as signs of a physical or psychological catastrophe (e.g., "I'm dying of a heart attack," "I'm losing my mind").

In addition to normalizing and demystifying panic attacks, the educational component of PCT provides patients with a model of anxiety that emphasizes the interaction between the mind and body and provides a rationale and framework for the skills to be taught during treatment. A three-component model is utilized, in which the dimensions of anxiety are grouped into physical, cognitive, and behavioral categories. The physical component includes bodily changes (e.g., neurological, hormonal, cardiovascular) and their associated somatic sensations (e.g., shortness of breath, palpitations, lightheadedness). The cognitive component consists of thoughts, images, and impulses that accompany anxiety or fear (e.g., thoughts of dying, images of losing control, impulses to run). The behavioral component contains behaviors that are associated with anxiety (e.g., pacing, carrying a safety object, or simply avoiding or escaping the situation). These three components are described as interacting with each other, often with the result that anxiety is heightened. The therapist then explains that the goal of treatment is to learn skills for controlling each of the three components of anxiety. To manage some of the physical aspects of anxiety, such as sensations due to hyperventilation (e.g., lightheadedness and tingling sensations) or muscle tension (e.g., trembling and dyspnea), patients are taught slow, diaphragmatic breathing. To reduce anxiety-exacerbating thoughts and images, patients are further taught to critically examine, based on past experience and logical reasoning, their estimations of the likelihood that a feared event will occur, the probable consequences if it should occur, and their ability to cope with these consequences. In addition, they are assisted in designing and conducting behavioral experiments to test their predictions.

B. Breathing Retraining

Beginning with Session 3, patients are taught a breathing technique that encourages slow, diaphragmatic breathing over fast chest breathing. When introducing this treatment component, the patients are usually asked to first voluntarily hyperventilate by standing and breathing fast and deeply, as if blowing up a big balloon, for approximately 1 min. This exercise typically induces intense and unpleasant bodily sensations (e.g., racing heart, dizziness, tingling sensations in hands and feet), which often resemble some of the sensations that patients experience during a panic attack. Once the symptoms have abated, the therapist educates the patients about the physiological basis of hyperventilation and suggests that this may often be associated with panic attack episodes. It is then suggested that chronic hyperventilation, which may be caused by relatively fast and shallow chest breathing, might lower the threshold and therefore increase the risk for experiencing recurrent panic attacks.

In the next step, the therapist introduces a breathing control technique, which encourages patients to rely on the diaphragm rather than on chest muscles when breathing. In addition, patients are instructed to concentrate on their breathing by counting their inhalations and thinking the word "relax" on exhalations. The therapist models the suggested breathing patterns and then provides corrective feedback to patients while they practice this technique in the office setting. In Session 4, patients are further taught a technique to slow the rate of breathing with the goal of comfortably spanning a full inhalation and exhalation cycle over 6 sec. Again, the therapist models and then provides corrective feedback as practice is conducted during the session. As part of the homework assignment, patients are instructed to practice diaphragmatic breathing at least two times a day, for at least 10 min for each of the remaining sessions.

C. Cognitive Restructuring

The PCT manual introduces this treatment component in Session 4 by suggesting that thoughts are hypotheses or guesses rather than facts. The therapist explores the patients' thinking errors that are typically associated with panic attacks. Two main types of cognitive errors are described. The first error is probability overestimation, or jumping to negative conclusions and treating negative events as probable when in fact they are unlikely to occur. The second error is catastrophic thinking, or blowing things out of proportion.

The method for countering overestimation errors is to question the evidence for probability judgments. Typical probability overestimations are: "The feeling of dizziness are caused by a brain tumor," or "the feeling of breathlessness is a sign of a heart attack." Patients are encouraged to examine the evidence for these predictions, while considering alternative, more realistic hypotheses. This is best done in a Socratic style (i.e., leading questions) so that patients examine the content of their statements and reach alternative explanations.

Similarly, the method of countering catastrophic thinking is best be done by using Socratic questions. This type of error typically arises from viewing an event as "catastrophic" when, in actuality, it is not. Typical kinds of catastrophic thoughts are "If I faint people will think that I am weak and this would be unbearable," or "If people notice my anxiety, I will make a fool of myself and I could not deal with this." By challenging and modifying these catastrophic thoughts ("decatastrophizing") the patients begin to realize that the actual occurrences are not as "catastrophic" as originally assumed because there are ways to cope with these situations.

D. Interoceptive Exposure

To change maladaptive anxiety behaviors, patients learn to engage in graded therapeutic exposure to cues they associate with panic attacks. The exposure component (interoceptive exposure) focuses primarily on internal cues, specifically, frightening bodily sensations. The rationale for needing to perform interoceptive exposure exercises is very important for facilitating generalization from in-session practices to daily exposures. For this purpose, the therapist explores the way in which avoidance of feared sensations serves to maintain fearfulness. Activities that are avoided because of the associated physical sensations may not be immediately obvious to patients. They may include physical exercise, emotional discussions, suspenseful movies, steamy bathrooms, drinking coffee, and other arousing activities.

The purpose of these interoceptive exposure exercises is to repeatedly induce sensations that are feared and to weaken the fear response through habituating and learning that no actual danger results. In addition, the repeated inductions allow practice in applying the cognitive techniques and breathing strategies. As a result, fear of physical sensations that occur naturally is significantly reduced.

During exposure, patients deliberately provoke physical sensations like smothering, dizziness, or tachycardia by means of exercises such as breathing through a thin cocktail straw, hyperventilating, spinning, or strenuous physical exercise. These exercises are done initially during treatment sessions, with therapist modeling, and subsequently by patients at home. As patients become less afraid of the sensations, more naturalistic activities are assigned, such as drinking caffeinated beverages, watching suspenseful movies, or going to a sauna.

E. *In Vivo* Situational Exposure

An optional situational exposure component can be added for patients with significant agoraphobic avoidance. As currently administered, exposure therapy typically begins with the construction of a hierarchy of feared situations, which the patients are encouraged to enter repeatedly, starting with easier ones, and remain until anxiety diminishes. Sometimes the therapist accompanies the patients initially, but ultimately they are expected to do the task alone.

The most challenging aspect of this treatment component is to motivate the patients to engage in these exposure exercises without using any avoidance strategies. Before conducting the exercises, the therapist needs to thoroughly explore any forms of avoidance and anxiety-reducing strategies that patients typically use, some of which might be more obvious (e.g., carrying medication or a cell phone) than others (e.g., carrying quarters for a public phone, sunglasses, or chewing gum). Ideal situations at the beginning of the exposures are situations that are under the therapists' control and in which escape and avoidance strategies are difficult (e.g., leaving patients alone in a shopping mall). Once the patients have successfully mastered those situations, the therapist will then choose situations that are less controllable by the therapist (e.g., driving long distances in the car alone).

II. THEORETICAL BASES

A. History of Diagnosis and Treatment Models

Panic disorder was first officially recognized as a distinct diagnostic entity after a series of pharmacological experiments conducted by Donald Klein and his collaborators in the late 1950s and early 1960s. Klein and his colleagues observed that imipramine, an antidepressant, was effective against spontaneous panic attacks, but not against chronic and anticipatory anxiety. Klein concluded that panic and anticipatory anxiety reflect two qualitatively different underlying biological processes. By the 1980s, the efficacy of pharmacological treatment with imipramine in patients with panic disorder had been well established, and imipramine became the pharmacological criterion standard for the treatment of panic disorder for more than 20 years, until the emergence of the selective serotonin reuptake inhibitors.

Prior to including panic disorder as a distinct type of anxiety disorder in *DSM-III* in 1980, psychological therapies tended to focus primarily on the behavioral pattern of situational avoidance that frequently occurs in patients with panic attacks. During the 1960s and 1970s, systematic desensitization, consisting of imaginal exposure to feared situations paired with muscle relaxation, was the principal form of treatment. That approach was preferred to *in vivo* exposure, because it was thought the latter might engender too much anxiety for patients to manage. However, subsequent studies showed that *in vivo* exposure was superior to systematic desensitization for treating agoraphobia. During the 1980s, paralleling with the increasing recognition of the importance of fear of panic attacks as a factor in the development and progression of panic disorder, investigators began to experiment with treatments aimed more specifically at patients' experiences of anxiety related to panic and somatic sensations. These treatments are now called exposure therapy, behavior therapy, cognitive therapy or cognitive-behavioral therapy, depending on the theoretical orientation of the clinician or the emphasis placed on the treatment components, although in practice there is considerable overlap among them.

Researchers today generally agree that a combination of cognitive and behavioral strategies is the most effective psychological treatment for panic disorder and agoraphobia. Some researchers believe that exposure therapy primarily targets agoraphobic avoidance, whereas CBT either enhances the efficacy of exposure therapy or specifically addresses the panic attacks and associated features. Others assume that the treatment effects are primarily due to either exposure therapy or CBT.

B. Contemporary Psychological Models

The most popular psychological model of panic and agoraphobia today is the cognitive model. This model assumes that preexisting beliefs about the harmfulness of bodily sensations predispose people to regard them fearfully. Panic attacks are therefore viewed as resulting from the catastrophic misinterpretation of certain bodily sensations, such as palpitations, breathlessness, dizziness, and so on. An example of such a catastrophic misinterpretation would be a healthy individual perceiving palpitations as evidence of an impending heart attack. The vicious cycle of the cognitive model suggests that various external stimuli (i.e., the feeling of being trapped in a supermarket) or internal stimuli (i.e., body sensations, thoughts or images) trigger a state of anxious apprehension if these stimuli are perceived as threatening. It is assumed that this state is accompanied by fearful bodily sensations that, if interpreted in a catastrophic fashion, further increases the apprehension and the intensity of bodily sensations. Moreover, this model states that the attacks appear to come from "out of the blue" because patients fail to distinguish between the triggering body sensations of the subsequent panic attack and the general beliefs about the meaning of an attack.

Another popular psychological model is the anxiety sensitivity hypothesis by Steven Reiss and Richard J. McNally. Anxiety sensitivity denotes the tendency to respond fearfully to anxiety symptoms and is based on beliefs that these symptoms lead to harmful consequences. Similar to the cognitive model, the anxiety sensitivity hypothesis assumes that beliefs about the harmfulness of bodily sensations predispose people to respond fearfully. In contrast to the cognitive model, however, the anxiety sensitivity hypothesis does not require that patients misconstrue anxiety as something else (such as a heart attack). Instead, the model assumes that people with high anxiety sensitivity may be well aware of what causes the feared bodily sensations. Rather, patients believe that the high arousal itself might eventually lead to heart attacks, insanity, or other catastrophes.

C. Contemporary Biological Models

Biological models of panic assume that the disorder is associated with the dysregulation of a number of different biological systems. One of the most popular biological models today is the suffocation alarm hypothesis by Donald Klein. This model assumes that panic disorder is characterized by a pathologically low threshold for firing of an evolved "suffocation alarm," which can be activated by a number of biological (e.g., carbon dioxide inhalation) and psychological challenge procedure (e.g., feeling of being trapped) that signal impending loss of oxygen.

III. EMPIRICAL STUDIES

The efficacy of CBT has been demonstrated in numerous clinical studies. For example, it has been shown that PCT is superior to a relaxation condition or alprazolam, a frequently prescribed benzodiazepine to treat panic attacks. More recently, the PCT protocol was compared to imipramine, an antidepressant, which is often considered to be the gold standard pharmacological treatment for panic disorder. This study compared the efficacy of imipramine, a pill placebo, and combinations of PCT with imipramine or a pill placebo in a large, multicenter trial conducted by David H. Barlow and his colleagues. A total of 312 panic disorder patients with mild or moderate agoraphobia were randomly assigned to imipramine, PCT, PCT plus imipramine, PCT plus placebo, or placebo only. Participants were treated weekly for 3 months. In addition, responders were seen monthly for 6 months and then followed up for an additional 6 months after treatment discontinuation. The results of this study showed that combining imipramine and CBT had limited advantage acutely but more substantial advantage in the longer term: Both imipramine and PCT were superior to placebo on some measures for the acute treatment phase and even more pronounced after the 6 monthly maintenance sessions. Six months after treatment discontinuation, however, people were more likely to maintain their treatment gains if they received PCT, either alone or in combination with a pill placebo. Individuals who received imipramine were more likely to relapse than those who did not receive the antidepressant.

Similar results were also reported with a CBT protocol that focuses more on cognitive restructuring. For example, a study by David M. Clark and his colleagues compared cognitive therapy, applied relaxation, imipramine, and a wait-list control group. At posttreatment, 75% of the cognitive therapy patients were panic free, compared with 70% in the imipramine condition, 40% in the applied relaxation condition, and 7% in the wait-list control condition. Cognitive therapy was superior to the wait-list control group on all panic and anxiety measures, whereas imipramine and applied relaxation were better than the wait-list control group on approximately one-half of the measures. At 9-month follow-up, after imipramine had been discontinued, the panic-free rates were 85% for cognitive therapy, 60% for imipramine, and 47% for applied relaxation. These results are consistent with reviews and meta-analyses of treatment outcome studies utilizing *in vivo* situational exposure, suggesting that 60 to 75% of treatment completers experience clinical improvement with fairly stable treatment gains at treatment follow-ups.

It is not known at present which components of CBT are most important for treatment efficacy or whether they all contribute uniquely to efficacy. Panic patients with high levels of agoraphobia seem to respond best to *in vivo* situational exposure. Patients with moderate or mild agoraphobia seem to respond best to CBT protocols that combine cognitive restructuring, psychoeducation, interoceptive exposure exercises, and breathing retraining and relaxation exercises. Unfortunately, except for the use of a relaxation control condition in some studies, direct comparisons of the various components are lacking. However, there is some indication in the literature that repeated interoceptive exposure practices alone are effective in reducing panic attacks even without any explicit cognitive restructuring techniques. Similarly, *in vivo* situational exposure practices seem to be effective in treating panic disorder and agoraphobia without explicit cognitive interventions. Thus, although CBT for panic disorder and agoraphobia is clearly effective, little is known about the most important active ingredients in treatment and the mechanism of treatment action.

IV. SUMMARY

Panic disorder is a debilitating disorder that is characterized by recurrent and unexpected panic attacks. Approximately 3% of the population is affected over the course of a lifetime, and one-third of those individuals also develop agoraphobia, usually within 1 year of the initial occurrence of the panic attacks.

A number of biological and psychological models of the disorder have been proposed. A prominent biological model, the suffocation alarm hypothesis, assumes that panic disorder is the result of a pathologically low threshold for firing of a "suffocation alarm." The two most prominent psychological models are the cognitive model and the anxiety sensitivity model. The cognitive model assumes that panic attacks result from the catastrophic misinterpretation of certain bodily sensations. The anxiety sensitivity hypothesis does not assume that all panic attacks are caused by catastrophic beliefs. Instead, this hypothesis is based on the assumption that individuals with panic disorder have inherited a tendency to respond fearfully to anxiety symptoms.

CBT and *in vivo* exposure therapy are the most effective treatments for panic disorder with agoraphobia. A typical CBT protocol combines education about the nature of panic attacks, controlled breathing procedures, cognitive restructuring, interoceptive exposure exercises, and situational exposure practices. The treatment is usually delivered in 12 weekly 60-min individual sessions. The efficacy of this treatment protocol is well documented. Controlled studies show that this intervention is more effective than relaxation techniques and at least as effective as alprazolam or imipramine. Cognitive restructuring, interoceptive exposure practices, and *in vivo* situational exposure exercises all seem to be important components for the treatment of panic disorder and agoraphobia. However, it remains unclear which component is most effective for treating the disorder and what the mechanism of action of treatment is.

See Also the Following Articles

Anxiety Disorders ■ Applied Relaxation ■ Breathing Retraining ■ Complaints Management Training ■ Exposure *in Vivo* Therapy ■ Homework ■ Relaxation Training

Further Reading

Barlow, D. H. (2002). *Anxiety and its disorders* (2nd Ed.). New York: Guilford Press.

Barlow, D. H., Gorman, J. M., Shear, M. K., & Woods, S. W. (2000). Cognitive-behavioral therapy, imipramine, or their combination for panic disorder. *Journal of the American Medical Association, 283,* 2529–2536.

Clark, D. M. (1986). A cognitive approach to panic. *Behavior Research and Therapy, 24,* 461–470.

Hofmann, S. G., Bufka, L., & Barlow, D. H. (1999). Panic provocation procedures in the treatment of panic disorder: Early perspectives and case studies. *Behavior Therapy, 30,* 307–319.

Hofmann, S. G., & Spiegel, D. A. (1999). Panic Control Treatment and its applications. *Journal of Psychotherapy Practice and Research, 8,* 3–11.

Klein, D. F. (1964). Delineation of two drug-responsive anxiety syndromes. *Psychopharmacologia, 5,* 397–408.

McNally, R. J. (1994). *Panic disorder: A critical analysis.* New York: Guilford Press.

Reiss, S. (1991). Expectancy model of fear, anxiety and panic. *Clinical Psychology Review, 11,* 141–153.

Taylor, S. (1999). *Anxiety sensitivity: Theory, research, and treatment of the fear of anxiety.* Mahwah, NJ: Lawrence Erlbaum.

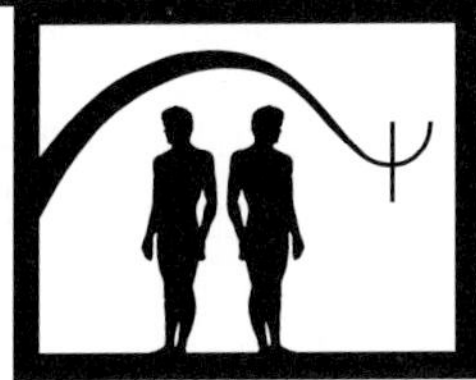

Paradoxical Intention

L. Michael Ascher
Philadelphia College of Osteopathic Medicine

GLOSSARY

fear-of-fear The concern that anxiety will result in the experience of negative physical consequences; these consequences can range from life threatening (e.g., cardiac arrest) to seemingly innocuous (e.g., perspiration).

logotherapy An existential approach to psychotherapy—developed by Viktor Frankl—that postulates meaning in one's life is a basic human need and that the failed search for such meaning underlies much neurotic distress.

recursive anxiety An extreme form of social phobia that is based on the concept of fear of fear and the additional suggestion that a self-maintaining process contributes to the experience of excessive anxiety.

reframe A common therapeutic procedure that involves changing the valence of a reported event from negative to positive without changing the facts.

Although paradoxical intention has been popularly identified with Frankl's logotherapy, and with family therapy, more recently the procedure has gained some favor with behavior therapists. As a behavioral strategy, it is typically presented as a directive by the therapist to an individual who is experiencing a problem associated with activity of the sympathetic nervous system—usually within a social context. For example, a person may complain about perspiring in public. In general, the behavioral difficulty is exacerbated by the anxiety about the effects of anxiety (i.e., fear of fear) and with the attempt to take voluntary control of this anxiety to avoid these unwanted effects. The paradoxical intention directive generally contains two elements common to most other paradoxical procedures: It is unexpected and counterintuitive (i.e., contrary to common sense) and it requires the individual to maintain the discomforting focal behavior as it is presently being experienced. Thus, an effected person might be told to seek as many opportunities as possible in which he or she might expect to perspire and, once in the situation, to try to become anxious and perspire.

I. DESCRIPTION OF TREATMENT

Paradoxical intention (PI) is one of a group of—not easily differentiated—techniques and strategies all of which are classified under the rubric of therapeutic paradox. It is an approach employed in a variety of schools of psychotherapy, especially family and Gestalt therapy—although its name was coined by Viktor Frankl whose use of the technique in logotherapy, an existential approach to psychotherapy, predates these. This article is confined to its use as a behavioral procedure.

Paradoxical intention is generally employed with responses that are impeded by recursive anxiety—a concept associated with fear of fear. A typical example would involve individuals complaining of anxiety when giving a public address. If a behavioral analysis suggested that discomfort were associated exclusively with factors external to the speaker (e.g., the size of the audience, aspects of the attendees, effect of the speaker on those assembled), then conventional behavioral procedures would be appropriate (e.g., systematic desensitization *in vivo*). In contrast, if discomfort were largely related to internal factors associated with anxiety, then paradoxical intention would be the treatment of choice. A characteristic complaint would be "I am afraid that when giving a public address, I will become very anxious and my heart rate will increase to the point that I will have a heart attack." The core instruction administered to such a client—provided within the context of a behavioral program, which would include procedures designed to support the paradoxical intervention—would be to make a presentation while focusing on, and attempting to augment, the most salient aspect of sympathetic activity—in this case, "try to increase your heart rate."

The role of PI is that of assisting individuals with recursive anxiety to enhance their desired performance by circumventing the goal of remaining calm. To do this, clients are directed to enter those situations in which they experience recursive anxiety, focus on the most salient aspect of sympathetic discomfort, and attempt to augment that process. Then they are instructed to remain in the situation until they have regained their composure. Thus a person who is afraid of blushing in front of others at work would be asked to participate in as many of these discomforting circumstances as possible and "really try to blush—turn as red as a traffic light—become so bright red that people will have to turn away to avoid being blinded by the light."

Naturally, a great deal of collateral work must be done to support these individuals in engaging in behavior that may at least be seen as dreadfully embarrassing and at most, life threatening. Frankl, and before him, Allport, discussed the role of humor in neutralizing anxiety. They believed that neurotic clients had taken a significant stride toward their therapeutic goals when they could laugh at their neurotic complaints. Frankl therefore considered humor to represent a important part of PI with respect to both its administration and its effectiveness. In fact, one of the components of PI that is a necessary part of humor is the opposition to expectation: the element of surprise. Practically speaking, before individuals consult a psychotherapist, they generally seek formal and informal guidance from a variety of acquaintances, both nonprofessional and those in relevant professions (e.g., a family physician). The longer the problem is extant, the more advice and counseling they accumulate. They combine all this information with their own preconceived notions and bring the result to the therapist. The therapist, applying PI gives them instructions that are counter to that which they expect, that is, in essence: Remain the way you are, stop trying to change.

Of course, as with most therapeutic procedures, considerable rapport must first develop. In addition, the manifestation by the therapist of great confidence in the procedure is necessary. These are the very minimal aspects required to form a supporting basis for the successful use of PI in the behavioral approach to recursive anxiety. Finally, paradoxical procedures have commonly been employed to enhance cooperation. In this context, clients are generally not provided with information about the techniques. In contrast, PI when utilized as the behavioral treatment of choice for problems associated with recursive anxiety requires, like any conventional behavioral technique, that the therapist provide the client with as many details as possible regarding the operation of the procedure (e.g., suitability of PI for the specific problem, available research, the experience of the therapist with the procedure, full instructions on intersession self-administration). The client and therapist are seen as equally important members of the team that must first formulate and then administer treatment to a successful conclusion. Therefore, the client must be as informed as is the therapist.

II. THEORETICAL CONSIDERATIONS

The myriad descriptions of the effective use of paradoxical interventions as a group, and especially PI, that are replete throughout the literature of psychotherapy are accompanied by an equal abundance of explanations for this efficacy. Because the scope of this article does not permit a survey of these hypotheses, discussion is confined to an explanation of the operation of PI from a behavioral perspective. Within that context, PI is presented as the treatment of choice for behavior that is impeded by recursive anxiety.

Fear of fear refers to concern about possible negative physical effects of anxiety on oneself. This phenomenon is typically associated not with all anxiety but with that experienced in specific locations or situations. Such an individual who is afraid of crowded places may notice an increase in cardiac rate at such times and can become afraid that the anxiety experienced under these circumstances will result in a rising cardiac rate that eventually reaches a level that produces a heart attack. So although most people with phobias attribute their anxiety to aspects of the external environment on which they remain focused, those with fear of fear shift their attention from external factors to internal stimuli and to the effects of anxiety on the functioning of certain physiological processes.

Recursive anxiety that is based on the concept of fear of fear adds two additional complications. The first concerns the sympathetic mechanism that maintains these individuals at a high level of anxiety. Suppose that circumstances require the person in the earlier example to participate in an event that involves a crowd. This individual will become apprehensive and will begin to focus on that aspect of the sympathetic syndrome that is of most concern. In the case of individuals who fear having a heart attack, that sympathetic component would be heart rate. As the time for the presentation draws near, anxiety will increase and the cardiac rate will be elevated. This in turn will be associated with a further increase in anxiety and a consequent additional elevation of the cardiac rate. The resulting pernicious circle is self-maintaining because it is based on this recursive process.

The second complication associated with recursive anxiety refers to observations of Michael Ascher, Tom Borkovec, Diane Chambless, and Alan Goldstein, among others, who have written about processes related to recursive anxiety. They have emphasized the significant role of social anxiety and have suggested that *in vivo* exposure to the social environment is of considerable importance. Ascher has further hypothesized that no matter what the person with recursive anxiety initially reports fearing—heart attack, passing out, losing bladder control, going crazy—the basic concern is loss of control. Such loss of control will result in emitting embarrassing behavior that will engender the negative evaluation of observers. The consequence will be a significant negative life change.

Individuals with recursive anxiety generally exhibit low-self esteem. They focus on what they believe to be substantial deficits in the qualities or skills necessary to maintain significant aspects of their lives. Because of their perceived inadequacies, people with recursive anxiety feel that they must depend on others for support and therefore place a great deal of importance on these interpersonal relationships.

At work, for example, affected people may attend to negative aspects of their skill, education, or performance profile, infusing these presumed inadequacies with disproportionate importance. They believe that by maintaining themselves in their positions they are perpetrating a fraud—no matter what evidence exists to the contrary. They, like Blanche DuBois, must rely on the kindness of strangers or, in this example, colleagues, both to assist them in the performance of their responsibilities and to maintain their—self-determined—fraudulent facade.

Thus, the person in our example who is anxious in crowds may be concerned that while participating in a business meeting at which the attendance of a large number of people is required, he or she will become very anxious and, fearing a heart attack, may run out of the room at an inopportune time. The horrible soap opera continues with all of those in attendance assuming that the departure had negative associations (e.g., "______ was obviously psychotic." or, "______ is certainly not "executive material" and should leave the firm"), and the CEO will demand resignation from their highly compensated position. In the final scene, the loss of this income and status results in the rapid deterioration of lifestyle, divorce, and finally descent into alcoholism and homelessness.

Because of their perceived dependency on these relationships, individuals with recursive anxiety will devote extraordinary effort to developing and nurturing associations with people deemed to have a significant role in their lives. They do this by advancing themselves as "nice" people and will do all that is necessary to support this perception. They believe that people who are "nice" are more likely to garner assistance when necessary and to have their shortcomings overlooked.

All individuals who perform goal-directed behavior have as their object the satisfactory achievement of the ostensible purpose of these actions. Those giving public addresses, for example, aim to educate or influence their audience in an entertaining manner. Or, supermarket shoppers wish to fill their grocery lists as efficiently as possible. Again, individuals driving across bridges simply want to get from one side to the other without encountering any difficulties or delays. Of course, those with recursive anxiety aim for the same goals as everyone else. However, they also have a second goal that is of more immediate concern: that of remaining calm while attempting to accomplish the ostensible goal.

They must remain calm to avoid the hypothesized disastrous consequence (e.g., heart attack, going crazy, looking foolish to others). This latter objective is difficult, if not impossible to accomplish. Moreover, in any case, attempts to remain calm subvert the professed aim of the performance by diverting the attention and effort necessary for accomplishing the ostensible goal.

Recursive anxiety represents a significant impediment over and above that resulting from simple phobias (i.e., those that are confined to aspects of the environment external to the individual). Thus people who exhibit simple public-speaking phobia are uncomfortable when giving a public lecture, but they remain largely concerned about the quality of their performance and direct their effort toward improving their presentation. Those with public-speaking phobia complicated by recursive anxiety initially attend to external aspects of their performance. But, at high levels of anxiety, they shift their focus to internal stimuli and begin to worry about the possibility of emitting some embarrassing behavior in front of an audience (e.g., freezing, vomiting, losing bladder control). They believe that this would be disastrous, and it therefore becomes vital that they remain free of anxiety to preclude this disaster. Remaining calm, then, becomes their primary commitment.

A number of hypotheses have been offered in an attempt to explain the efficacy of this procedure with recursive anxiety. Most recently, Ascher has advanced a proposal that combines his position on recursive anxiety with some of the formulations of Daniel Wegner. To understand Ascher's suggested explanation, it is first necessary to briefly describe Wegner's view of cognitive control.

Wegner describes the process of cognitive control by postulating a bimodal system. When individuals wish to exercise cognitive control (e.g., when there is a wish to inhibit specific classes of disconcerting, distracting thoughts in order to fall asleep or study or work on last year's taxes), activity on the part of the "operating" system (OS)—the active, effortful cognitive regulator—is initiated to ensure this control. A complementary "monitoring" system (MS) is an effortless component that is constantly searching for cognitions in opposition to the desired state of control. When the MS detects an errant thought it acts to bring this thought into the focus of attention of the OS and initiates the OS to control the incompatible cognition. In the normal individual, under ordinary circumstances, cognitive control by the OS generally occurs smoothly and effectively.

In contrast, when the person is under cognitive stress, the OS can become overloaded and increasingly less effective. In addition, if sufficiently bereft of resources, the OS will be able to do nothing with the incompatible thought that has now been released into the individual's focus of attention. In this way, a thought that is in opposition to the specific goal of cognitive control is very likely to be expressed.

Ascher hypothesizes that the difference between individuals who experience phobias with and without a recursive anxiety component is that the former attempt to control their cognitive state, whereas the latter are more concerned with the characteristics of the external situation. In addition, when recursive anxiety is associated with the phobic system, the result is the development of a "fundamental" fear of a significant negative life change. This would seem to add a considerable degree of stress and, therefore, cognitive load, relative to those exhibiting a simple or "common" phobia.

Thus, individuals with a simple public-speaking phobia, for example, would be absorbed in monitoring and enhancing their performance while observing audience response to measure their success. In contrast, those with recursive anxiety complicating their public-speaking phobia would be engaged in controlling their cognitive environment. They would attempt this by monitoring their thoughts and related emotional experiences in an effort to minimize stimuli incompatible with their objective of remaining calm. The more significant they deemed this goal of calmness to be—this depends on the details of the hypothesized disastrous consequence—the more cognitive load is generated, and the weaker becomes the OS. The result would be an increasing frequency of incompatible thoughts brought by the MS to the attention of the powerless OS that would be permitted to remain unmodified. This bimodal explanation of cognitive control is also compatible with the self-maintaining recursive component of the fear-of-fear process. That is, awareness of incompatible, anxiety-provoking thoughts increases cognitive load and decreases the ability of the OS to control them, thus permitting further discomforting thoughts, additional cognitive load, and continuing deterioration of the OS.

Combining the bimodal explanation with PI suggests the utility of the procedure with recursive anxiety. Paradoxical intention is based on instructions—to relinquish control and to accept whatever cognitive and physical experiences are present, but primarily—to try to protract the duration and the degree of discomfort of the most unpleasant of these symptoms. In such cases, the MS would be engaged in seeking thoughts that are incompatible with the goal of attempting to generate more profound discomforting symptoms—that is, thoughts of calmness and control, and also neutral, distracting thoughts. These cognitions enter the OS and become the focus of attention because these individuals begin their presentations with an already weakened OS. The thoughts that are incongruous with the PI are compatible with diminished stress and reduced cognitive load in situations that are uncomfortable for the individual with a public-speaking phobia and recursive anxiety. The result is a more positive experience for these affected individuals.

III. APPLICATIONS AND EXCLUSIONS

As a conventional behavioral procedure, PI for disorders associated with recursive anxiety and similar processes is appropriate for most groups of individuals. However, because of its counterintuitive nature, it may not be practical for those with cognitive developmental disabilities. At the very least, considerable repetition of instructions will be necessary. In addition, supervision of the *in vivo* practice conducted by family members, or others, can be a valuable adjunct to therapy and increase the probability of success with this population.

Although a careful behavioral analysis is the necessary preparation for the administration of any behavioral program, when the therapeutic program includes PI as its central focus, the behavioral analysis takes on an even more crucial role. As Ascher has written on several occasions, and demonstrated in his recent study with public-speaking phobia (described in the next section), it is important to differentiate between those experiencing simple phobias and those whose phobias are complicated by recursive anxiety. Simple phobias are adequately addressed by systematic desensitization, and covert conditioning, among a host of conventional behavioral strategies. But, the use of PI with simple phobias has been shown not only to be less useful than the established treatments of choice, but actually to impede the course of therapy and thereby protract its length in many cases.

In contrast, when the phobia is complicated by recursive anxiety, then PI becomes the treatment of choice, behavioral procedures devoid of the *in vivo* exposure to the interpersonal milieu tend to provide less satisfactory results.

Finally, it seems almost unnecessary to caution against the use of paradoxical procedures with individuals who are severely depressed or suicidal or with those attempting to control maladaptive approach responses (e.g., sexually offensive behavior, difficulties with alcohol, drugs, or tobacco).

IV. EMPIRICAL STUDIES

Since Viktor Frankl began writing about PI in the 1920s, many case studies have been published demonstrating its effectiveness with a wide variety of behavioral problems. Of course, uncontrolled case studies are of very limited value, at best.

In 1978, Michael Ascher and Jay Efran published the first controlled investigation of the procedure. They used a multiple-case study design with clients whose latency to sleep onset did not diminish as the result of a standard 10-week behavior therapy program appropriate for this problem. Subsequent to this 10-week segment, these clients were exposed to PI instructions. By the end of the next 2-week period, all clients reported that their sleep onset latency had reached a satisfactory level.

Rather than presenting an exhaustive review of the numerous experiments that followed the work of Ascher and Efran, many based on designs incorporating sophisticated controls, this section is intended to present a survey of studies that exemplify the research associated with paradoxical intention.

The first study to utilize the random assignment of subjects to groups in testing the efficacy of paradoxical intention was conducted in 1979 by Ralph Turner and Michael Ascher. In this study, PI was compared to two treatments of choice for reducing clinically significant levels of latency to sleep onset (relaxation, stimulus control). Two control groups were also included (attention-placebo and waiting-list). Analysis of the results failed to find any significant differences among the three treatment groups, each of which was significantly superior to the control groups. No differences were found between the two control groups. In a partial replication of their study, Ascher and Turner in 1979 confirmed the efficacy of PI with sleep onset insomnia.

When administered like any conventional behavioral technique, all aspects of the procedure and its goals are fully disclosed to the client. However, when used in other contexts (e.g., family therapy) this is not always the case. Then, PI, used to reduce resistance, is presented in a more obscured manner. In 1980, Ascher and Turner investigated the relationship of these two methods for administrating PI. They randomly assigned volunteers who complained of clinically significant levels of sleep onset insomnia to all groups. These conditions included two treatment groups (PI with veridical or obfuscated instructions) and two control groups (attention-placebo and waiting-list). Clients receiving the veridical instructions showed significantly greater treatment effects than did the group from whom the purpose of the procedure was obscured.

Ascher went on to conduct controlled multiple-case study investigations of PI with the travel restriction associated with agoraphobia and with psychogenic urinary retention. The results of these studies supported the hypothesis that PI, when administered as a conventional behavioral procedure, could be an effective component of a treatment program.

Subsequent to Ascher's study, Matig Mavissakalian, Larry Michelson, and a number of co-workers conducted a series of large-sample randomized groups experiments. Their target behavior was agoraphobia, and one of the treatment strategies in which they were interested was PI. This research extended from 1983 through 1986 and produced variable results with all treatment groups. One conclusion that might have been drawn from their final study was that although randomized assignment of clients to groups was a powerful method of control, it might have distorted the actual relationship of the treatment with the specific clinical profile of the client. That is, were a clinician to assign individuals with agoraphobia to treatment groups following a behavioral analysis, the results might have been more consistent, and of more benefit to the individual. Such clinically focused assignment might also reduce the variability of the resulting treatment data.

In 1999, Ascher tested this hypothesis with groups that had public-speaking phobias. Using a 2×2 design, he randomly assigned individuals with a simple phobia or with a phobia complicated by recursive anxiety to one of two treatment groups. One treatment condition involved a standard behavioral approach to public-speaking phobia, the other, added PI to the standard behavioral program. The results supported the idea that a better outcome was possible when clients are paired with treatment on the basis of clinical criteria as opposed to random assignment. Those with simple public-speaking phobia showed significantly greater improvement when the standard behavioral treatment program did not include PI. When this technique was added, the course of therapy was greatly protracted. The reverse was the case with clients exhibiting recursive anxiety. When their treatment included PI, their performance improved significantly relative to those who did not receive PI instructions. Of course, this selective assignment is fraught with design problems that can only be adequately addressed with sophisticated controls. However, a more valid picture of clinical operations may possibly be the outcome.

The body of research investigating the efficacy of PI from Ascher and Efran's study in 1978 through the mid-1980s grew in frequency and in sophistication of design. It generally suggested that PI was an effective procedure with a variety of behavioral complaints. The results were not uniform, nor were they based on designs that were above criticism. The data do support the impression that in the hands of an experienced clinician, PI viewed as a conventional behavioral procedure can be a useful and effective addition to the behavior therapist's repertoire.

V. CASE ILLUSTRATION

A 30-year-old, married, white male complained of becoming anxious and experiencing tremors at inopportune times. He was a psychologist who worked in the student health center of a private university. Each morning all members of the counseling section were required to participate in a meeting whose general focus was case presentation and case management. During the course of these meetings, coffee and cake were available; the coffee was served in ceramic cups on sauces (it was a well-endowed university). It was under these daily circumstances that the client experienced the most disconcerting occurrence of the problem.

He was afraid that if he were experiencing tremors when he removed his cup from the saucer, the resulting tapping would be noticed by others. On the basis of this behavior, the other members of the counseling team would conclude that the client had a serious mental health problem that would preclude him from continuing to work in the center. This information would become available to those in the mental health field at large, and he would be permanently denied employment in his profession.

He had been at the student health center for more than one year. He enjoyed his work and seemed to be doing well. He was popular with his student clients, had been commended by his supervisor on several occasions, and appeared to have the respect of his colleagues. Yet he felt that he could not quite meet the standard that was expected by these colleagues. As he explained it, this deficit was because all the professionals in the center had degrees in clinical psychology whereas his was in counseling psychology—which he deemed to be inferior.

Each workday he would be awakened early by what he described as an anxiety attack. He would monitor himself for tremors, squeezing his hands tightly into fists or around objects in an effort to moderate these attacks. His anxiety would remain fairly high until he entered the conference room for the morning meeting, whereupon his anxiety would increase markedly. Along with the anxiety would appear sporadic, mild intention tremors. His thoughts would shift from strategies for dealing with these tremors to their catastrophic consequences. He attended most meetings and did not generally leave before their conclusion. However, each meeting was an ordeal that never seemed to diminish.

Because the social phobic component of these complaints was immediately manifest and clear to the client, a good deal of the preparation generally necessary with cases involving recursive anxiety was precluded. The PI instructions are greeted by most people as counterintuitive and anxiety provoking. They are not only told to do something that may be in opposition to what they thought would be useful but are directed to do exactly what they fear. Here again, the client's professional training proved to be helpful. He was able to grasp the reason for the paradoxical suggestion and, rather than viewing it as counterintuitive, could understand its underlying logical structure.

With the assistance of the client, the therapist composed a hierarchy of anxiety-provoking, social situations. Emphasis was placed on those circumstances in which the client had experienced tremors or feared that he might have such an experience. Of course, the top of the hierarchy was occupied by the daily clinic meetings. The client was then encouraged to enter a situation that was of a lower degree of discomfort and to "try to become anxious. Practice exhibiting your tremors." He was not to exaggerate them, but to attempt to display them as realistically as possible. He first practiced them in the office but had a great deal of trouble making the tremors look realistic. They were jerky and spastic, and he devoted considerable effort to producing authentic tremors that, in so doing, served to create a good deal of attendant entertainment for both the client and the therapist. The client left the office in apparent good spirits and with a professed sense of confidence based on his new perspective.

On returning the following week, the client reported that he had practiced the procedure in a social situation, midway on the hierarchy, and he indicated his pleasure with his performance. He went with the expectation of acting as though he had tremors, he felt quite calm, and found it difficult to produce them in a realistic fashion.

It is important when using PI with recursive anxiety that the therapist not reinforce clients for success, because an effusive response on the part of the therapist will generally serve to impede progress. The reasons for this vary with the client. One common possibility is that it places additional pressure on acquiescent clients to meet what they consider to be the expectations of their therapists. The safest thing for the therapist to do is to reflect clients' positive emotion associated with their demonstration of efficacy. In this way, the therapist can remain relatively neutral and thereby reduce his or her role in client's *in vivo* activities. In the present case, the therapist encouraged the client to discuss his uncharacteristic comfort in the party that he had attended, and how it contributed to his enjoyment of the evening. In another effort not to bring the client's expectations to an unrealistic level, the therapist cautiously introduced the point that the client still had a good deal of work to do in this area, and that although it was pleasant that he was able to begin with a successful experience, impediments and setbacks were certain to appear sporadically. The instructions were repeated, and the client selected his next target.

During the next three sessions, the client continued to report improvement, but on the fourth session, he described an encounter that resulted in considerable anxiety and what the client described as a failure. The therapist reframed the event to support a more positive view and suggested that perhaps the client went into the situation with too much confidence. Possibly he was not prepared to allow his anxiety-free reign and to display his tremors. Maybe he thought that he was "cured" and was no longer in need of such preparation. The therapist reaffirmed the idea that the client should assume that he would be employing the paradoxical strategy in social situations for a considerable length of time. This seemed to have the desired effect, because the client's progress in dealing with his social anxiety resumed its positive trend in subsequent weeks.

With regard to his comfort during the morning meetings at the student counseling center, the client began to feel more comfortable after his first reported success in another social context. For some time, however, he was unwilling to take the chance of "trying to become anxious" in that most difficult setting. Finally, after some weeks, having gained some confidence in the PI procedure, and experiencing somewhat less anxiety at these morning meetings, he began to apply the procedure in the counseling center and found it to be quite helpful.

The focus of this case description was intended to rest on the administration of PI with recursive anxiety. Naturally, substantial ancillary activity was necessary to support the paradoxical intervention. In addition, other significant aspects of the client's life were addressed. Very often in the past, case studies illustrating the efficacy of PI emphasized this procedure to the point that its role in the therapeutic process was unrealistically exaggerated. PI as a conventional behavioral treatment of choice for recursive anxiety is, like other behavioral procedures, administered in an appropriate behavioral context.

VI. SUMMARY

Paradoxical intention as described in this article is a conventional behavioral treatment of choice for recursive anxiety—a phenomenon associated with fear of fear that reflects extreme social anxiety. Individuals who complain of anxiety about exhibiting the secondary aspects of anxiety in public (e.g., flushing, perspiration, tremors, urinary frequency or retention) represent good examples of this behavior. The paradoxical instruction, administered within the context of a standard behavioral program, requires clients to increase the frequency of that which they would prefer to inhibit, or to inhibit that which they would prefer to increase. Thus, a woman who has been avoiding public places for fear of being embarrassed by blushing would be advised to seek as many opportunities as possible to blush in front of others. Such suggestions often have the effect of reducing some of the anxiety that the person associates with interpersonal contact.

See Also the Following Articles

Family Therapy ■ Gestalt Therapy ■ Logotherapy

Further Reading

Ascher, L. M. (1989). *Therapeutic paradox.* New York: Guilford Press.

Frankl, V. E. (1975). Paradoxical intention and dereflection. *Psychotherapy: Theory, Research and Practice, 12,* 226–237.

Frankl, V. E. (1985). Logos, paradox, and the search for meaning. In M. J. Mahoney & A. Freeman (Eds.), *Cognition and psychotherapy* (pp. 259–277). New York: Plenum.

Haley, J. (1973). *Uncommon therapy: The psychiatric techniques of Milton H. Erickson, M.D.* New York: Norton.

Seltzer, L. F. (1986). *Paradoxical strategies in psychotherapy: A comprehensive overview and guidebook.* New York: John Wiley and Sons.

Watzlawick, P., Weakland, J., & Fisch, R. (1974). *Change: Principles of problem formulation and problem resolution.* New York: Norton.

Weeks, G. R., & L'Abate, L. A. (1982). *Paradoxical psychotherapy: Theory and practice with individuals, couples, and families.* New York: Brunner/Mazel.

Wegner, D. M. (1994). Ironic processes of mental control. *Psychological Review, 101,* 34–52.

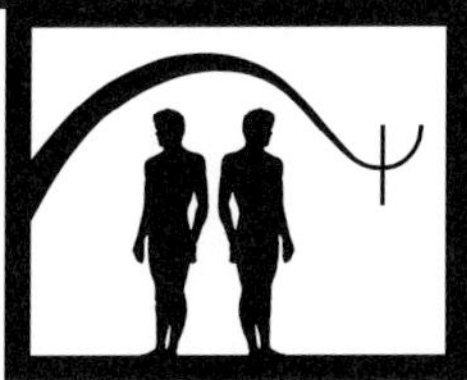

Parent–Child Interaction Therapy

Brendan A. Rich, Jane G. Querido, and Sheila M. Eyberg
University of Florida

GLOSSARY

clinically significant The extent to which the effect of an intervention makes an important difference to the individual or has practical or applied value.

negative reinforcement The removal of a negative stimulus (e.g., child whining) contingent on the occurrence of a behavior (e.g., parent yelling), which causes the behavior to occur more often.

prevalence rate Percentage of cases in the general population at one time.

Parent–child interaction therapy (PCIT) is a psychosocial treatment for preschoolers with conduct problems and their parents. In this article we describe the assessment procedures that guide the course of treatment and the treatment procedures in each major phase of treatment: (1) the child-directed interaction (CDI) phase in which parents learn play therapy skills, and (2) the parent-directed interaction (PDI) phase in which parents learn discipline skills. We address the significance of conduct problem behavior for children and families and present the theoretical foundation of PCIT, which draws from both attachment theory and social learning theory in teaching parents to interact with their child in new ways to change the child's behavior. Finally, we review the PCIT outcome studies and the directions for future research.

I. DESCRIPTION OF TREATMENT

A. Assessment in PCIT

Parent–child interaction therapy is an assessment-based treatment in which progression through treatment is guided at every point by the data. To begin treatment, the PCIT therapist must have a thorough understanding of the child's problem behaviors and the context in which they occur. This information is obtained by an assessment approach that involves multiple methods and informants, including parent interviews, parent and teacher ratings scales, and behavioral observations in the clinic and school or day care setting.

The initial clinical interview with the parent is designed to establish rapport and obtain information about the child's family that will impact treatment planning, including the parents' attitudes and beliefs about child rearing and their goals and expectations for treatment. Family factors known to present barriers to treatment, such as transportation problems for low-income families, are discussed with the family as well, so that they can be resolved immediately. Following the clinical interview, a structured diagnostic interview is conducted to determine whether the child meets criteria for oppositional defiant disorder. Children whose behavior problems are less severe may not require a treatment as intensive as PCIT. The diagnostic interview is also important for the identification of comorbid disorders that must be considered in tailoring PCIT to the specific needs of the child and family.

The Eyberg Child Behavior Inventory (ECBI) is a 36-item parent rating scale of disruptive child behavior used initially as a baseline measure and regularly throughout PCIT to assess the child's progress. Richard Abidin's parent self-report scales, the Parenting Stress Index—Short Form and the Parenting Alliance Measure, are given as baseline measures at the initial assessment session as well, to enable assessment of the effects of treatment on the parents' functioning.

The Dyadic-Parent Child Interaction Coding System-II, developed by Sheila Eyberg and colleagues, is used to assess parent–child interactions during three brief, structured play situations in which the degree of control required by the parent is varied. These initial observations provide baseline data for comparison throughout treatment, and specific situations are coded at the beginning of the treatment coaching sessions to monitor change in the parents' skills, to provide direction for the coaching, and to determine when the parents are ready to move to the next phase of treatment.

For children who present behavior problems at school or day care as well as at home, their teachers are asked to complete the Sutter-Eyberg Student Behavior Inventory—Revised, a measure of oppositional and inattentive behavior in the classroom. In addition, classroom observations are often conducted to assess disruptive behavior using the Revised Edition of the School Observation Coding System (REDSOCS). These measures are repeated at the end of treatment to assess the degree of generalization of treatment effects to the school.

B. The Format of PCIT

Treatment sessions begin as soon as the initial assessment is completed. PCIT is typically conducted in 1-hour weekly sessions and is usually completed within 9 to 16 weeks. The first phase of treatment, CDI, is focused on developing the parents' use of prosocial skills, and the second phase of treatment, PDI, emphasizes the parents' use of consistent disciplinary techniques. The principles and skills of each interaction are first presented to the parents alone during a single didactic session using modeling and role-play, and the subsequent sessions in each phase involve direct coaching of the parents to use the skills with their child. During these coaching sessions, the parents take turns being coached by the therapist as they interact with their child while the other parent observes the coaching.

1. Child-Directed Interaction

In CDI, parents learn to follow their child's lead in play by avoiding commands, questions, and criticism, and using the nondirective "PRIDE" skills: *P*raising the child, *R*eflecting the child's statements, *I*mitating the child's play, *D*escribing the child's behavior, and being *E*nthusiastic during the play. The parents learn to manage the child's behavior by directing the PRIDE skills to the child's appropriate play and ignoring the child's inappropriate behavior. Parents are asked to practice CDI skills at home for 5 minutes each day. Handouts summarizing the CDI skills are given to parents for their review (see Table I), and additional handouts on topics of relevance to individual families, such as social support or modeling appropriate behavior, are provided to parents during the course of CDI as needed.

Each of the CDI coaching sessions begins with a 5-minute observation of the interaction, coded by the therapist, which indicates the primary focus of the session. During coaching, the therapist prompts and reinforces the parents' use of the PRIDE skills and points out their positive effects on the child's behavior. The therapist uses this time to encourage and shape reciprocal interactions and responsive parenting. The CDI phase of treatment continues until the parents meet criteria for skill mastery: 10 behavioral descriptions, 10 reflective statements, 10 labeled praises, and no more than 3 questions, commands, or criticisms within the 5-minute interval. The criteria also include ignoring the child's inappropriate behavior.

2. Parent-Directed Interaction

During PDI, parents continue to use their CDI skills, but they also learn to direct their child's behavior using effective commands and specific consequences for compliance and noncompliance. Parents first teach the child to mind using "running commands," which are commands to perform a specific behavior immediately. Parents are taught the eight rules of effective commands (see Table II) and the precise steps that must be followed after a running command is given to the child (see Fig. 1). Parents are taught to give a labeled praise if the child obeys or to initiate the time-out procedure if the child disobeys.

During the PDI didactic session, the entire time-out procedure is role-played with each parent, and the parents are asked to review handouts summarizing PDI techniques prior to the next session. Parents are

TABLE I
CDI Skills Handout

Child		
Rules	*Reason*	*Examples*
Praise your child's appropriate behavior	• Causes your child's good behavior to increase • Lets your child know what you like • Increases your child's self-esteem	• Good job of putting the toys away! • I like the way you're playing so gently with the toys.
Reflect appropriate talk	• Shows your child that you are listening • Demonstrates that you accept and understand your child • Improves your child's speech	• Child: The doggy has a black nose. Parent: The dog's nose is black.
Imitate appropriate play	• Shows your child that you approve of the activity • Shows that you are involved • Teaches your child how to play with others and take turns	• Child (drawing circles on a piece of paper) Parent: I'm going to draw circles on my paper just like you.
Describe appropriate behavior	• Shows your child that you are interested • Teaches your child concepts • Models speech for your child • Holds your child's attention on the task	• You are putting together Mr. Potato Head. • You put the girl inside the fire truck.
Be Enthusiastic	• Lets your child know that you are enjoying the time you are spending together • Increases the warmth of the play	• Parent: You are REALLY being gentle with the toys.
Avoid Commands	• Takes the lead away from your child • Can cause unpleasantness	*Indirect commands:* • Could you tell me what animal this is? *Direct commands:* • Please sit down next to me.
Avoid Questions	• Leads the conversation • Many questions are commands and require an answer • May seem like you are not listening to your child or that you disagree	• We're building a tall tower, aren't we? • What sound does the cow make? • What are you building? • You're putting the girl in the red car?
Avoid Criticism	• Often increases the criticized behavior • May lower your child's self-esteem • Creates an unpleasant interaction	• That wasn't nice. • I don't like it when you make that face. • Do not play like that. • That animal doesn't go there.
Ignore negative behavior (unless it is dangerous or destructive)	• Helps your child to notice the difference between your responses to good and bad behavior • *Consistent* ignoring decreases many behaviors	• Child: (sasses parent and picks up toy) Parent: (ignores sass; praises picking up)
Stop the play time for aggressive and destructive behavior	• Teaches your child that good behavior is required during special play time • Shows your child that you are beginning to set limits	• Child: (hits parent) Parent: (CDI STOPS.) Special play time is stopping because you hit me.

TABLE II
Eight Rules for Effective Commands

Rule	*Reason*	*Examples*
1. Commands should be *direct* rather than indirect	• Leaves no question that child is being told to do something • Does not imply a choice or suggest parent might do the task for child. • Is not confusing for young children	• Please hand me the block. • Put the train in the box. *instead of* • Will you hand me the block? • Let's put the train in the box.
2. Commands should be *positively stated*	• Avoids criticism of child's behavior • Provides a clear statement of what child should do	• Come sit beside me. *instead of* • Don't run around the room!
3. Commands should be given *one at a time*	• Helps child remember the command • Helps parent determine if child completed entire command	• Put your shoes in the closet. *instead of* • Put your shoes in the closet, take a bath, and brush your teeth.
4. Commands should be *specific* rather than vague	• Permits child to know exactly what is to be done	• Put this lego in the box. *instead of* • Clean up your room.
5. Commands should be *age-appropriate*	• Makes it possible for child to understand the command	• Draw a square. *instead of* • Draw a hexagon.
6. Commands should be given *politely and respectfully*	• Increases likelihood child will listen better • Teaches child to obey polite and respectful commands • Avoids child learning to obey only if yelled at	Child: (Banging block on table) • Parent: Please hand me the block. *instead of* • Parent: (Said loudly) Hand me that block this instant!
7. Commands should be explained *before* they are given or *after* they are obeyed	• Avoids encouraging child to ask "why" after a command as a delay tactic • Avoids giving child attention for not obeying	• Parent: Go wash your hands. Child: Why? • Parent: (Ignores, or uses time-out warning if child disobeys). Child: (Obeys) • Parent: Now your hands look so clean! It is so good to be all clean when you go to school!
8. Commands should be used *only when necessary*	• Decreases the child's frustration (and the amount of time spent in the time-out	Child: (Running around) • Parent: Please sit in this chair. (Good time chair)to use this command) *instead of* • Parent: Please hand me my glass from the counter. (Not a good time to use this command)

instructed to spend the following week faithfully practicing their CDI skills at home, so that the child's first "time-outs from CDI" will be especially salient. Parents are coached through their first PDI with the child in the clinic so that the therapist will be available to provide the parents with emotional support during the initiation of the time-out procedure.

As the family progresses in PDI, the child's rate of compliance increases rapidly. Parents' homework assignments gradually expand their use of running com-

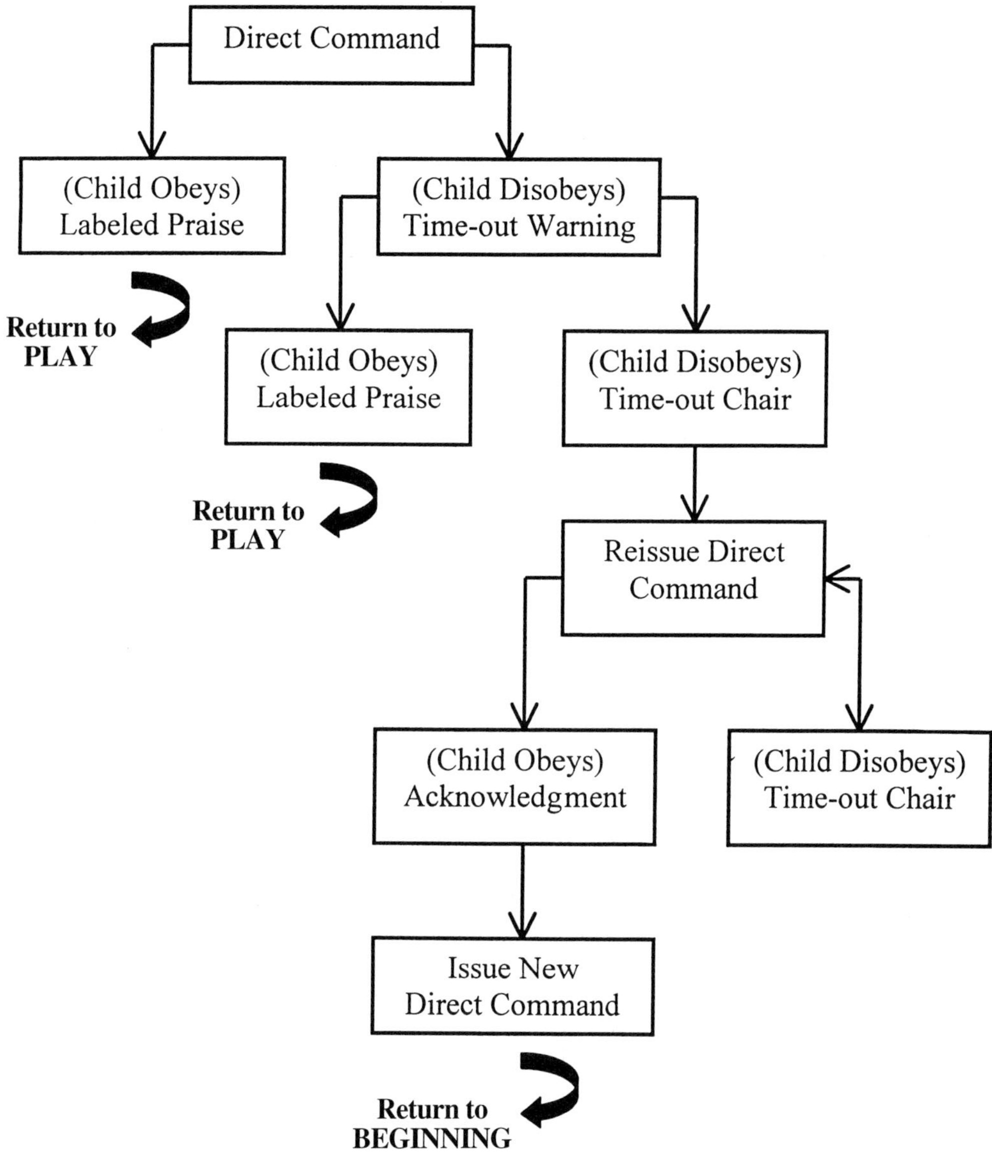

FIGURE 1 Parent-directed interaction diagram. (Copyright Sheila Eyberg, 2000).

mands to address specific problems that were identified during the assessment. For example, to encourage the child's use of words to indicate wants, the parent might give a command directing the child to say the name of the object the child is pointing to, and then follow the child's compliance with an enthusiastic labeled praise that explains the reason that the behavior is important, such as, "Nice job of using your words! Now that I know you want me to hand you the hat, I can give it to you really fast without guessing."

3. House Rules

As they progress in PDI, parents frequently want help with their child's aggressive behavior that is not decreased by parental ignoring and is not easily corrected with running commands. After a child's compliance to running commands is under control, parents may be introduced to the house rules procedure, which is a "standing command" variation of PDI. In teaching this procedure, parents are instructed first to label the target behavior problem for the child for 3 days to ensure that the child is aware of the label and the specific behavior it refers to, before a house rule to decrease that behavior is put into effect. For example, each time the child hits another person, the parent would say "You are hitting. Starting on Sunday, each time you hit, you will go to time-out." Once a house rule is in effect, the parent must use the time-out procedure when the targeted behavior occurs and must praise the child for behaviors incompatible with the target behavior, for example, "Good job of keeping your hands to yourself when she messed up your track." Parents keep a record of each house rule and the daily frequency of rule violations so that the effectiveness of the technique can be evaluated by the therapist. A new house rule may be added when the child shows improvement in an earlier target behavior, although a child should have no more than two active house rules at a time.

4. *Public Behavior*

Toward the end of PDI, another problem that may remain for some children is disruptive behavior in public places. To apply the PCIT principles to this situation, parents are advised to describe to the child their expectations for the child's behavior prior to entrance into the public area. Parents are then prompted to think of ways to give positive attention to the child's appropriate public behavior and ways to implement a time-out procedure for unacceptable behavior that cannot be ignored. The parent is given the opportunity to practice the new strategy with coaching as the therapist accompanies the family to public areas, such as a waiting room or parking lot.

Mastery of the PDI skills is demonstrated during clinic observations when 75% of the parents' commands are effective commands that allow the child time to obey, and when the parent follows through correctly at least 75% of the time after the child responds to a command, either with praise after compliance or initiation of time-out after noncompliance. The final PCIT session includes specific discussion of ways to maintain treatment gains and methods to deal with setbacks or new problems that arise in the future.

5. *Follow-Up*

Follow-up strategies are important to ensure the maintenance of parenting skills and the child's improved behavior. Maintenance techniques range from letters from the therapist reminding the family of the importance of daily practice sessions, to booster sessions in the clinic. One promising model of maintenance treatment currently under empirical study is an aftercare model in which the therapist continues contact with the parent with short, monthly telephone calls to monitor maintenance and determine the level of intervention indicated, if any. Three levels of intervention are used during the maintenance period, with Level 1 consisting of supportive services. A Level 2 intervention includes the components of Level 1 in addition to the implementation of a problem-solving approach for an identified problem. A Level 3 intervention is a clinic session and is indicated for significant problems or crisis situations. The components of a Level 3 intervention include support, problem solving, clinic observations of parent–child interactions followed by coaching, and the development of a plan for problem resolution. The goal of the maintenance model is to monitor treatment gains and intervene immediately at the first sign of new or recurrent problems so as to prevent relapse.

II. THEORETICAL BASES

A. Conduct Problem Behavior in Preschoolers

In young children, the prevalence of clinically significant conduct problems is thought to be rising. Recent studies have found as many as 23% of preschool children in the general population score in the clinically significant range on parent-rating scales of externalizing behavior problems. Not surprisingly, conduct problems are the most common reason for referral to child mental health services.

Although once dismissed as a transient phase of children's development, we now know that, without treatment, conduct problem behavior that begins in early childhood tends to persist and worsen with time. Evidence indicates that early parent–child interactions have a powerful influence on the development of conduct problems, particularly in children with difficult temperaments, and parenting practices continue to play an important role in the maintenance of conduct problem behavior throughout the child's development. Fortunately, evidence has also shown that parent training interventions with young conduct-disordered children can reverse their behavior and may produce lasting change.

Parent training programs for young children with conduct problems have historically taken either a relationship enhancement approach, as exemplified by Bernard Guerney in 1964, or a behavioral approach, as exemplified by Robert Wahler in 1965. In relationship enhancement therapies, parents are trained to use nondirective play therapy techniques to strengthen the parent–child bond, foster greater independence and self-acceptance on the part of the child, and increase parental acceptance of the child. In contrast, behavior therapies train parents in the application of learning principles to alter specific child behavior problems. In 1969, Constance Hanf developed a behavioral model of therapy that focused on coaching parents *in vivo* as they played with their child. Her treatment consisted of two stages, in which parents were first taught to change their child's behavior by using differential social attention, which involves ignoring inappropriate behavior and attending to positive behavior. In the second stage, parents were trained to change their child's behavior by giving direct commands, praising compliance, and punishing noncompliance with time-out.

Parent–child interaction therapy is a parent–child treatment for young children with behavior problems that places a dual emphasis on relationship enhancement and behavioral parent management training. The goal of PCIT is to create a nurturing, secure relationship by teaching parents to increase their child's prosocial behaviors while decreasing their child's inappropriate behaviors. Like the Hanf model, PCIT includes two primary phases in which parents are coached in the treatment skills as they play with their child. Goals of the first phase, CDI, are to strengthen the parent–child relationship, increase positive parenting, and increase child prosocial behavior. Goals of the second phase, PDI, are to decrease child noncompliance and defiance by improving parents' ability to set limits and be fair and consistent in disciplining their child. PCIT is most distinct from the Hanf model in its emphasis on teaching parents to use traditional play therapy techniques and the skills of reciprocal interaction in the first phase, and, in the second phase, on teaching parents to use problem-solving skills to apply general discipline paradigms to problem behavior, with an overarching objective to improve the quality of parent–child interactions.

B. Theoretical Underpinnings of PCIT

PCIT draws on both attachment and social learning theories. Children's optimal emotional, behavioral, and social development is enhanced by a secure, stable attachment and healthy interaction patterns with their parents. Attachment theory asserts that attentive and sensitive parenting during infancy leads children to develop a cognitive-affective model that their parents will be responsive to their needs. Children whose parents are cold, distant, and unresponsive to their child's needs are likely to develop a maladaptive attachment with their parents and peers, display increased aggression, and have poor self-esteem, coping skills, and social competence. The CDI emphasizes responsive parenting to establish or strengthen a secure attachment relationship as the foundation for establishing effective child management skills.

Gerald Patterson's coercion theory also provides a transactional account of early disruptive behavior in which children's conduct problems are inadvertently established or maintained by negative reinforcement in the parent–child interaction. Dysfunctional interactions must be interrupted by a change in parent behavior involving clear limit-setting that is consistently enforced early in the child's life. PDI incorporates these social learning principles by teaching parents a highly structured algorithm of positive and negative consequences to follow once they have issued a command or set a rule in place.

III. EMPIRICAL STUDIES

Parent–child interaction therapy outcome research has demonstrated significant findings in the treatment of conduct-disordered behavior of preschool children, including improvements in children's behavior at the end of treatment on parent and teacher rating scales and direct observation measures and significant changes on parents' self-report measures of psychopathology, personal distress, and parenting locus of control. Important changes in the interactional styles of fathers and mothers in play situations with the child, such as increased reflective listening, physical proximity, and decreased criticism have also been demonstrated at treatment completion. Treatment effects have been found to generalize to the school setting and to untreated siblings. Comparison studies have found PCIT superior to wait-list control groups and other treatments including parent group training.

Several studies have addressed the issue of maintenance of behavioral improvements following completion of PCIT by examining the short- and long-term recurrence of conduct problems for study participants in later childhood. In a study conducted by Toni Eisenstadt and her colleagues in 1993, short-term maintenance of treatment effects for 14 families was found on parent ratings of behavior problems, activity level, and maternal stress, and observational measures of parenting skills and child compliance. Two years later, 13 of these families were located for follow-up, and 9 (69%) of these families had maintained treatment gains on measures of behavior problems, activity level, and parenting stress at the same level as found at the end of treatment. Most of the children (7 of 13 or 54%) also remained free of diagnoses of disruptive behavior disorders. Recently, maintenance of treatment gains in child behavior and parenting confidence at 4 to 6 years after treatment have been found.

Daniel Edwards and colleagues examined differences in long-term outcomes between 23 PCIT dropouts and 23 PCIT completers. Ten to 30 months after their pretreatment assessment, mothers of children who dropped out of PCIT reported significantly more symptoms of the disruptive behavior disorders and higher levels of parenting stress than did those who completed treatment. The follow-up scores for dropout families showed no differences from their scores before treatment started, whereas follow-up scores for the families who completed treatment showed no differences from their scores at the end of treatment. These data suggest that PCIT can alter the developmental path of disruptive behavior for those young children and families who complete treatment, and they also highlight the problem of attrition.

Addressing attrition must become a research priority. The rate of attrition from PCIT has ranged from 0 to 32% in recent studies, which compares favorably to the average 40% to 60% attrition rate typically found in child clinic samples. Neither the poorest families nor the children with the most severe problems drop out more than other families, but maternal distress has been identified as a significant predictor of dropout from PCIT. Such findings indicate the necessity of addressing broader contextual issues in treatment to prevent attrition in the high-stress families of conduct-disordered children. In particular, attention to the parents' personal concerns will need even greater emphasis in PCIT.

Further attention to treatment maintenance is a second research priority. Although long-term maintenance of PCIT effects has been documented, the effects of treatment do not last for every family. Given the persistent and recurrent nature of early-onset conduct disorder, it may be unrealistic to expect that the current models of short-term treatment, which end immediately on initial resolution of the presenting problems, will lead to lasting changes in child and family behavior as the child develops and the family faces new challenges. In addition to testing promising models of maintenance treatment, it will be important to examine both the course and the predictors of long-term maintenance to identify the factors related to long-term behavior change, which will help in designing more effective interventions for all families.

IV. SUMMARY

Parent–child interaction therapy is a treatment for preschool-age children with conduct problems and their families. This treatment is theoretically based, assessment driven, and empirically supported. During PCIT sessions, parents play with their child while the therapist coaches them to use specific skills to change their child's behavior. In the first phase of treatment parents learn the CDI skills, designed to strengthen the parent–child attachment relationship and to increase positive parenting and the child's prosocial behavior. In the second phase, parents learn the PDI skills, designed to decrease child noncompliance and aggression by improving parents' ability to set limits and be fair and consistent in disciplining. Treatment ends when parents demonstrate mastery of these relationship enhancement and child management skills with the child and report that the child's behavior problems are within normal limits on standardized measures. Studies have clearly demonstrated the effectiveness of PCIT in decreasing disruptive behavior and increasing prosocial behavior of the child and improving the psychological functioning of the parents. The early long-term follow-up studies suggest that the changes seen at the end of treatment tend to last for most children and families, although further study of both maintenance and attrition is imperative.

See Also the Following Articles

Animal-Assisted Therapy ■ Child and Adolescent Psychotherapy: Psychoanalytic Principles ■ Communication Skills Training ■ Family Therapy ■ Home-Based Reinforcement ■ Primary-Care Behavioral Pediatrics ■ Therapeutic Storytelling with Children and Adolescents ■ Transitional Objects and Transitional Phenomena

Further Reading

Brestan, E., & Eyberg, S. M. (1998). Effective psychosocial treatments for conduct-disordered children and adolescents: 29 years, 82 studies, and 5272 kids. *Journal of Clinical Child Psychology, 27,* 179–188.

Eisenstadt, T. H., Eyberg. S., McNeil, C. B., Newcomb, K., & Funderburk, B. W. (1993). Parent-child interaction therapy with behavior problem children: Relative effectiveness of two stages and overall treatment outcome. *Journal of Clinical Child Psychology, 22,* 42–51.

Eyberg, S. M., & Boggs, S. R. (1998). Parent-child interaction therapy for oppositional preschoolers. In C. E. Schaefer & J. M. Briesmeister (Eds.), *Handbook of parent training: Parents as co-therapists for children's behavior problems* (2nd ed., pp. 61–97). New York: Wiley.

Eyberg, S. M., Edwards, D., Boggs, S. R., & Foote, R. (1998). Maintaining the treatment effects of parent training: The role of booster sessions and other maintenance strategies. *Clinical Psychology: Science and Practice, 5,* 544–554.

Foote, R., Eyberg, S. M., & Schuhmann, E. (1998). Parent-child interaction approaches to the treatment of child conduct problems. In T. Ollendick & R. Prinz (Eds.), *Advances in clinical child psychology.* New York: Plenum.

Funderburk, B. W., Eyberg, S. M., Newcomb, K., McNeil, C., Hembree-Kigin, T., & Capage, L. (1998). Parent-child interaction therapy with behavior problem children: Maintenance of treatment effects in the school setting. *Child and Family Behavior Therapy, 20,* 17–38.

Hembree-Kigin, T., & McNeil, C. (1995). *Parent-child interaction therapy.* New York: Plenum.

McMahon, R. J., & Estes, A. M. (1997). Conduct problems. In E. J. Mash & L. G. Terdal (Eds.), *Assessment of childhood disorders* (3rd ed.). New York: Guilford.

Querido, J. G., Bearss, K., & Eyberg, S. M. (in press). Theory, research, and practice of parent-child interaction therapy. In T. Patterson & F. Kaslow (Eds.), *Comprehensive handbook of psychotherapy, volume two: Cognitive/behavioral/functional approaches.* New York: Wiley.

Schuhmann, E. M., Foote, R. C., Eyberg, S. M., Boggs, S. R., & Algina, J. (1998). Efficacy of parent-child interaction therapy: Interim report of a randomized trial with short-term maintenance. *Journal of Clinical Child Psychology, 27,* 34–45.

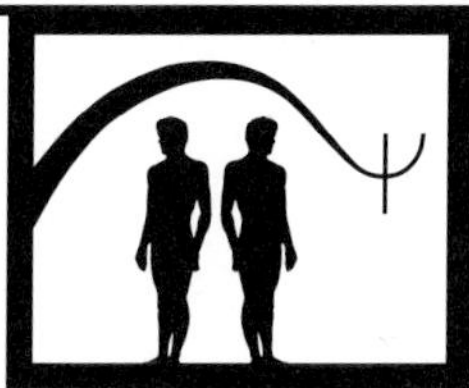

Patient Variables: Anaclitic and Introjective Dimensions

Sidney J. Blatt
Yale University

GLOSSARY

anaclitic A developmentally-oriented perspective on traits, behaviors, capacities, psychological structures, and psychopathological configurations that emphasizes relatedness, interpersonal relations, and attachments across the spectrum of maturity. The term is derived from the idea of "leaning upon."

introjective A developmentally-oriented perspective on traits, behaviors, capacities, psychological structures, and psychopathological configurations that emphasizes the establishment and maintenance of a sense of self. It literally means, "to take in."

Psychotherapy research usually assumes an homogeneity among patients and treatments. A number of research methodologists and psychotherapy investigators have questioned these assumptions and have noted the need to differentiate among patients and to examine systematically the role of the patient in the treatment process. As observed by the distinguished research methodologist, Lee Cronbach almost a half century ago, differences in the effects of various forms of therapeutic intervention may be a function of the congruence of certain characteristics of the patient with particular aspects of the treatment process. Rather than assuming that all patients respond to treatment in the same way, it may be more productive to distinguish among patients and to examine interactions between types of treatment and types of patients expecting some patients to respond more effectively to one form of treatment whereas other patients might respond more effective to another form of treatment. Jerome Frank, a major figure in initiating systematic psychotherapy research, noted in 1979 that research consistently suggests that "major determinants of therapeutic success appear to lie in aspects of the patients' personality and style of life." He saw as crucial the development of better criteria for the assignment of different types of patients to different therapies. He suggested that patients who conceptualize their subjective worlds in greater complexity might do better in unstructured situations whereas less conceptually complex patients may respond better to a more structured therapy. Mardi Horowitz and colleagues, in a study of brief therapy for bereavement in 1984, found that patients with developmentally more advanced levels of self-concept had better outcome in insight-oriented treatment, whereas patients with developmentally lower self-concept responded better to supportive techniques.

In an analysis of data from the National Institute on Mental Health (NIMH) sponsored Treatment of Depression Collaborative Research Program (TDCRP), Stuart

Sotsky and colleagues in 1991 identified several pretreatment characteristics of patients that were predictive of treatment outcome. Higher social functioning predicted a generally favorable outcome (completion of treatment and reduction of severity of depression at termination), particularly in responsiveness to interpersonal therapy (IPT). Higher cognitive functioning also appeared to predict good outcome, (i.e., reduction of severity of depression), especially to cognitive-behavior therapy (CBT). Patients with both impaired social and work functioning responded best to medication (imipramine) plus clinical management (i.e., reduction of depression severity and completion of treatment). These findings led the authors to suggest that "each psychotherapy relies on specific and different learning techniques to alleviate depression, and thus each may depend on an adequate capacity in the corresponding sphere of patient function to produce recovery with the use of that approach." Patients with relatively good social functioning are better able to take advantage of interpersonal strategies in IPT to recover from depression, whereas patients with relatively less cognitive impairment are better able to utilize cognitive-behavioral techniques to reduce depression. In a 1994 review of attempts to predict therapeutic outcome from a host of patient personality variables (e.g., rigidity, ability to feel deeply, ego strength, coping capacities, extroversion, and neuroticism), assessed via both objective and projective procedures, Sol Garfield concluded that "although a number of investigations have reported some positive findings, most of the relationships secured between personality variables and outcomes have been of limited strength."

The study of the interactions of patient characteristics with process and outcome variables in psychotherapy research was initially proposed by Lee Cronbach in 1952 in his demonstration that differential efficacy of various teaching procedures was a consequence of the congruence of particular educational procedures and teacher's style with characteristics of the individual student. As Cronbach noted, these findings not only have implications for educational psychology, but they have important implications for psychotherapy research in their suggestion that the investigation of patient-treatment (PT) and patient-outcome (PO) interactions may provide a more productive methodology for psychotherapy research. The investigation of the interaction between patient characteristics with aspects of the treatment process might facilitate the investigation of the efficacy of various types of treatment, as well as the exploration of possible differences in treatment outcome and process. Different types of treatment may not only be differentially effective with different individuals, but different individuals may experience different, but equally desirable, outcomes with the same therapeutic intervention. The identification of patients' characteristics that interact with particular therapeutic modalities and different outcomes could provide fuller understanding of important aspects of the therapeutic process.

The view that different types of patients might have differential responses to different types of therapy has been discussed since Cronbach's initial observations, more recently emphasized in a 1991 special issue of the *Journal of Consulting and Clinical Psychology* devoted to this topic. Donald Kiesler noted in 1966 that among the most salient obstacles to the development of methodologically sophisticated psychotherapy research are the assumptions of "patient and therapist uniformity." Patient uniformity is based on the assumption that "patients at the start of treatment are more alike than they are different." Kiesler stressed the need to abandon these uniformity myths in favor of "designs that can incorporate relevant patient variables and crucial therapist dimensions so that one can assess which therapist behaviors are more effective with which type of patients." Later in 1991, Larry Beutler called for more specific operational definitions of therapy and of patient characteristics if we are to develop effective predictive models. However, he stressed that the inclusion of PT and PO interactions in psychotherapy research requires conceptual models to identify the personality variables that might mediate the responses to different types of treatment and result in different types of therapeutic outcome.

The primary difficulty in developing this line of research is the identification of certain qualities, out of the infinite array of possible personal characteristics of patients, that might be relevant to the treatment process. Research not guided by theoretically derived or empirically supported principles could lead investigators into a "hall of mirrors" because of the complexity of the potential interactions. Cronbach noted in 1975, "One can avoid entering (this) hall of mirrors by exploring the interactions between theoretically meaningful ... variables" that are grounded in conceptual models. The choice of patient qualities needs to be theory driven and include dimensions relevant to the processes that are assumed to underlie psychological change. One possible model for introducing patient variables into psychotherapy research is the theory of personality development and psychopathology that articulates two primary dimensions in personality development—interpersonal relatedness and self-definition—and notes their differential role in different forms of psychopathology as well as their possible impact on the treatment process.

Sidney Blatt and colleagues beginning in 1974 proposed a theoretically derived and empirically supported model of personality development and psychopathology that has the potential to facilitate the introduction of patient variables into psychotherapy research. Blatt and colleagues conceptualized personality development as involving two fundamental developmental lines: (a) a relatedness or anaclitic line that involves the development of the capacity to establish increasingly mature and mutually satisfying interpersonal relationships, and (b) a self-definitional or introjective line that involves the development of a consolidated, realistic, essentially positive, differentiated, and integrated self-identity. These two developmental lines normally evolve throughout the life cycle in a reciprocal or dialectic transaction. An increasingly differentiated, integrated, and mature sense of self is contingent on establishing satisfying interpersonal relationships, and, conversely, the continued development of increasingly mature and satisfying interpersonal relationships is contingent on the development of a more mature self-concept and identity. In normal personality development, these two developmental processes evolve in an interactive, reciprocally balanced, mutually facilitating fashion throughout life.

These formulations are consistent with a wide range of personality theories ranging from fundamental psychoanalytic conceptualizations to basic empirical investigations of personality development. Sigmund Freud, for example, observed in *Civilization and Its Discontents,* that

> the development of the individual seems ... to be a product of the interaction between two urges, the urge toward happiness, which we usually call "egoistic," and the urge toward union with others in the community, which we call "altruistic." ... The man who is predominantly erotic will give the first preference to his emotional relationship to other people; the narcissistic man, who inclines to be self-sufficient, will seek his main satisfactions in his internal mental processes.

Freud also distinguished between object and ego libido and between libidinal instincts in the service of attachment and aggressive instincts necessary for autonomy, mastery, and self-definition. Hans Loewald, a distinguished psychoanalytic theorist, noted that the exploration of

> these various modes of separation and union ... [identify a] polarity inherent in individual existence of individuation and "primary narcissistic union"—a polarity that Freud attempted to conceptualize by various approaches but that he recognized and insisted upon from beginning to end by his dualistic conception of instincts, of human nature, and of life itself.

John Bowlby from an ethological viewpoint considered striving for attachment and separation as the emotional substrate for personality development. Michael Balint, from an object-relations perspective, also discussed these two fundamental dimensions in personality development—a clinging or connectedness (an ocnophilic tendency) as opposed to self-sufficiency (a philobatic tendency). Shor and Sanville, based on Balint's formulations, discussed psychological development as involving a fundamental oscillation between "necessary connectedness" and "inevitable separations" or between "intimacy and autonomy." Personality development involves "a dialectical spiral or helix which interweaves these two dimensions of development." A wide range of more general personality theorists including David Bakan, David McClelland, and Jerry Wiggins have also discussed relatedness and self-definition as two primary dimensions of personality development.

Various forms of psychopathology can be conceptualized as an overemphasis and exaggeration of one of these developmental lines and the defensive avoidance of the other. This overemphasis defines two distinctly different configurations of psychopathology, each containing several types of disordered behavior that range from relatively severe to relatively mild forms of psychopathology. Based on developmental and clinical considerations, anaclitic psychopathologies are those disorders in which patients are primarily preoccupied with issues of relatedness, ranging from symbiotic and dependent attachments to more mature relationships, and utilize primarily avoidant defenses (e.g., withdrawal, denial, repression) to cope with psychological conflict and stress.

Anaclitic disorders involve a primary preoccupation with interpersonal relations and issues of trust, caring, intimacy, and sexuality, ranging developmentally from more to less disturbed, and include non-paranoid schizophrenia, borderline personality disorder, infantile (or dependent) character disorder, anaclitic depression, and hysterical disorders. These patients utilize primarily avoidant defenses like denial and repression. In contrast, introjective psychopathology includes disorders in which the patients are primarily concerned with establishing and maintaining a viable sense of self ranging from a basic sense of separateness, through concerns about autonomy and control, to more complex and internalized issues of self-worth. These patients utilize primarily counteractive defenses (projection, rationalization, intellectualization, doing and undoing, reaction formation, overcompensation) to cope with conflict and stress. Introjective patients are more ideational and concerned with establishing, protecting, and maintaining a viable self-concept than they are about the quality of their interpersonal relations and achieving feelings of trust, warmth, and affection. Issues of anger and aggression, directed toward the self or others, are usually central to their difficulties. Introjective disorders, ranging developmentally from more to less severely disturbed, include paranoid schizophrenia, the schizotypic or overideational borderline, paranoia, obsessive–compulsive personality disorders, introjective (guilt-ridden) depression, and phallic narcissism.

The distinction between these two broad configurations of psychopathology can be made reliably from clinical case records. In contrast to the atheoretical diagnostic systems established in the diagnostic and statistical manuals of mental disorders developed by the American Psychiatric Association based primarily on differences in manifest symptoms, the diagnostic differentiation between anaclitic and introjective pathologies is based on dynamic considerations, including differences in primary instinctual focus (libidinal vs. aggressive), types of defensive organization (avoidant vs. counteractive), and predominant character style (e.g., emphasis on an object vs. self-orientation, and on affects vs. cognition).

The theoretical model of personality development and psychopathology based on the polarity of relatedness and self-definition provides a theoretically grounded, empirically supported, conceptual framework for introducing personality variables into psychotherapy research. Differences in the nature of therapeutic outcome and in the treatment process between anaclitic and introjective patients were examined in three different research programs: (a) in the study of therapeutic change in the long-term, intensive, psychodynamically oriented inpatient treatment of patients who are seriously disturbed and treatment resistant (the Riggs–Yale Project), (b) in the comparison of the therapeutic efficacy of psychoanalysis and long-term supportive-expressive outpatient psychotherapy (the Menninger Psychotherapy Research Project), and (c) in the comparison of four different, brief (16-week), outpatient interventions for major depression (the NIMH-sponsored TDCRP).

Sidney Blatt and colleagues demonstrated that the distinction between anaclitic and introjective patients facilitated the identification of important differences in the processes of clinical change in long-term intensive treatment with both inpatients and outpatients. The results of these two studies indicate that anaclitic and introjective patients have different needs, respond differentially to different types of therapeutic interventions, and demonstrate different treatment outcomes. Analyses of the data in these two studies based on more conventional diagnostic differentiations (e.g., psychosis, severe borderline, and neurotic psychopathology) were not as effective in identifying differences in change over the course of treatment. This conclusion is consistent with earlier findings that patient characteristics based on psychodynamic indices, as compared to symptomatic and descriptive distinctions, seem to have greater utility in predicting aspects of the therapeutic process and outcome.

I. THE AUSTEN RIGGS-YALE STUDY

Therapeutic change was studied in young adult inpatients who were seriously disturbed and treatment resistant in long term (at least 1 year), intensive, psychodynamically oriented treatment, including at least four times weekly individual psychoanalytic psychotherapy, in an open therapeutic facility. The differentiation of anaclitic and introjective patients was based on a review of admitting clinical case reports prepared during the first 6 weeks of hospitalization. Two judges made this differentiation from the case records at a high level of reliability. Systematic differences were found in the response of anaclitic and introjective patients on a number of measures of therapeutic change reliably derived from clinical case records and independent psychological test protocols that had been obtained at the outset of treatment and again after, on average, 15 months of inpatient treatment and, on average, 10 months prior to discharge from the clinical facility. Patients generally demonstrated significant improvement across these multiple independent assessments. Introjective patients, however, had greater overall improvement than did anaclitic patients on many of the measures. Independent of the degree of therapeutic gain, anaclitic and introjective patients expressed their therapeutic change (progression and regression) in different ways. Introjective patients expressed therapeutic change primarily through changes in their clinical symptoms, as reliably rated from clinical case reports and in their cognitive functioning, as independently assessed on psychological tests—in thought disorder on the Rorschach and in intelligence as assessed on the Wechsler Adult Intelligence Test. In contrast, anaclitic patients expressed change primarily in the quality of their interpersonal relationships, as reliably rated from clinical case reports, and in their representation of the human form on the Rorschach. Thus, anaclitic and introjective patients changed primarily in the dimensions of their basic concerns and preoccupations. Anaclitic patients changed primarily on measures of interpersonal relatedness; change in introjective patients was found primarily in measures of cognitive functioning and of clinical symptoms.

II. THE MENNINGER PSYCHOTHERAPY RESEARCH PROJECT (MPRP)

The Menninger Psychotherapy Research Project compared the therapeutic response of outpatients in 5-times weekly psychoanalysis with patients in long-term, psychodynamically oriented, twice-weekly, supportive-expressive psychotherapy. Extensive prior analyses of the clinical evaluations and psychological test assessments, conducted both before and after treatment, have repeatedly failed to find any significant differences in the therapeutic response of patients to these two types of therapeutic intervention. Significant differences between psychotherapy and psychoanalysis, however, were found when patient variables were introduced into the data analyses. Anaclitic and introjective patients were reliably differentiated by two judges who reviewed the pretreatment case reports. Independent evaluation of psychological test data gathered at the beginning and the end of treatment indicated that anaclitic patients had significantly ($p < .05$) greater improvement in psychotherapy than they did in psychoanalysis. Introjective patients, in contrast, had significantly ($p < .05$) greater improvement in psychoanalysis than they did in psychotherapy. Not only were these differences between the two types of treatment significant within each type of patient, but the patient-by-treatment interaction was a significant ($p < .001$) cross-over interaction. Thus, the relative therapeutic efficacy of psychoanalysis versus psychotherapy was contingent, to a significant degree, on the nature of the patient's pathology and pretreatment character structure. It seems consistent that the dependent, interpersonally oriented, anaclitic patients were more responsive to a therapeutic approach that provided more direct interaction with the therapist. It also seems consistent that the more ideational introjective patients, preoccupied with separation, autonomy, and independence, would be more responsive in psychoanalysis.

The findings of both these studies—the comparison of outpatients in two different forms of treatment and the therapeutic response of inpatients who are seriously disturbed and treatment resistant in long-term, intensive treatment—clearly indicate that aspects of patients' personality interact with dimensions of the therapeutic process to determine the nature of therapeutic change and the differential response to different therapeutic modalities. Patients come to treatment with different types of problems, different character styles, and different needs, and respond in different ways to different types of therapeutic intervention.

III. THE TREATMENT OF DEPRESSION COLLABORATIVE RESEARCH PROGRAM (TDCRP)

The availability of the empirical data from the large-scale, multicenter, treatment program for depression, the TDCRP, sponsored by The National Institute of Mental Health (NIMH), provided opportunity to explore the role of patient dimensions in the brief outpatient treatment of depression. The NIMH TDCRP was a comprehensive, well designed, carefully conducted, collaborative, randomized clinical trial that evaluated several forms of brief (16-week) outpatient treatment for depression. Two hundred thirty-nine patients were randomly assigned to one of four treatment conditions: cognitive-behavior therapy (CBT), interpersonal therapy (IPT), imipramine plus clinical management (IMI-CM) as a standard reference, and pill placebo plus clinical management (PLA-CM)[1] as a double-blind control condition. It seemed particularly appropriate to explore patient differences in the TDCRP with regard to the fundamental polarity of relatedness and self-definition, given the considerable evidence by Aaron Beck in 1983 and Sidney Blatt in 1974 that indicated the reliability and validity of the distinction between anaclitic and introjective forms of psychopathology, especially in the study of depression.

Patients were nonbipolar, nonpsychotic, seriously depressed outpatients who met RDC criteria for major depressive disorder and had a score of 14 or greater on a modified, 20-item, Hamilton Rating Scale for Depression (HRSD). Among patients who began treatment, 70% were female, 38% were definitely endogenous by RDC criterion, and 64% had had one or more prior episodes of major depression. The average age was 35.

Patients were systematically assessed at intake, at 4-week intervals until termination at 16 weeks, and again at three follow-up evaluations conducted 6, 12, and 18 months after termination. Assessments included an interview and a self-report measure of depression HRSD

[1] Clinical management (CM) was a 20-min nonspecific supportive interaction.

and Beck Depression Inventory [BDI], respectively), an interview and a self-report measure of general clinical functioning (Global Assessment Scale [GAS] and Hopkins Symptom Checklist [HSCL-90], respectively), and an interview assessment of social adjustment, the Social Adjustment Scale (SAS). In addition, patients, therapists, and independent clinical evaluators (CEs) rated various aspects of therapeutic progress during treatment, at termination, and at the three follow-up assessments (therapists did not participate in the follow-up assessments). Prior analyses of the TDCRP data indicated some differences in therapeutic outcome at termination among these brief treatments for depression; IMI-CM and IPT, but not CBT, were more effective than PLA-CM, but only with patients who were more severely depressed. Though at midtreatment, IMI-CM resulted in more rapid reduction of symptoms than CBT and IPT, no significant differences in the extent of symptom reduction were found among the three active treatment conditions in the TDCRP (CBT, IPT, and IMI-CM) at termination. In addition, no significant differences in the intensity of symptoms were found among all four treatment condition at the three follow-up assessments conducted at 6, 12, and 18 months. However, Blatt and colleagues found significant differences between the two psychotherapy conditions and the medication condition at the follow-up evaluations in the degree to which patients thought treatment had a constructive impact on their development of adaptive capacities to deal with interpersonal relationships and their experiences and symptoms of depression.

The development of these adaptive capacities early in the follow-up period, at the 6-month follow-up assessment, significantly moderated the degree to which subsequent stressful life events resulted in increases in depressive symptoms at the final follow-up assessment conducted 18 months after the termination of treatment. Thus, despite frequent claim of the efficacy of the medication condition in the TDCRP, analyses of data from all three follow-up assessments, including the last assessment conducted 18 months after termination, indicate that patients in the two psychotherapy conditions, CBT and IPT, reported greater satisfaction with their treatment and that their treatment had significantly greater positive effect on their life adjustment in a number of important areas—in their ability to deal with interpersonal relationships and their experiences and symptoms of depression than did patients in the medication condition. The development of these adaptive capacities decreased patients' vulnerability to subsequent stressful life events. These findings raise questions about the relative value of reduction in symptoms versus reduction of vulnerability as measures of therapeutic progress.

A. Impact of Patient Variables on Therapeutic Outcome

To introduce patient variables into analyses of data from the TDCRP, an experienced judge reviewed the intake clinical evaluations to see if he could differentiate anaclitic and introjective patients but found that these clinical case reports contained primarily descriptions of patients' neurovegative symptoms and lacked sufficient detail about aspects of the patients' lives to allow the judge to discriminate reliably between anaclitic and introjective patients. Fortunately the Dysfunctional Attitudes Scale (DAS) had been included in the TDCRP protocol, primarily to assess the effects of treatment on dysfunctional cognitions. A factor analysis conducted on the pretreatment DAS in the TDCRP data set, consistent with several prior studies, indicated that the DAS is composed of two primary factors—need for approval (NFA) and perfectionism (PFT) or self-criticism. Prior research indicated that NFA factor on the DAS assesses primarily the relatedness or anaclitic dimension whereas the PFT factor in the DAS assesses primarily the self-definitional or introjective dimension. Thus, the pretreatment DAS provided the basis for introducing differences among patients on the dimensions of relatedness and self-definition into analyses of data from the TDCRP.

Pretreatment PFT significantly (*ps* = .032 to .004) predicted negative outcome, assessed by all five primary measures of clinical change in the TDCRP (HSRS, BDI, GAS, SCL-90, and SAS across all four treatment groups. Factor analysis of the residualized gain scores of these five outcome measures at termination revealed that these measures all load substantially ($p > .79$) on a common factor with an eigenvalue of 3.78, accounting for 75.6% of the variance, indicating that this factor is a consistent measure of therapeutic change. Pretreatment PFT had a highly significant ($p <.001$) negative relationship to this composite residualized gain score at termination. NFA, in contrast, had a marginal, but consistently positive, relationship to treatment outcome as assessed by each of these five outcome measures and by the composite outcome measure ($p =.11$).

Pretreatment PFT also had a significant negative relationship to outcome ratings made by therapists, independent CEs, and the patients at termination. This negative impact of perfectionism on the therapeutic process persists even as late as the last follow-up assessment, 18 months after termination. Pretreatment

PFT correlated significantly with follow-up ratings by CEs of poorer clinical condition and a need for further treatment, and with ratings by patients of dissatisfaction with treatment. Perfectionistic patients gave poorer ratings of their current condition, said that they experienced less change in treatment, and said that treatment had less impact on their general life adjustment and their coping skills (i.e., dealing with relationships and their ability to recognize and deal with their symptoms of depression).

It is important to note that not only did patients with elevated pretreatment PFT feel subjectively less satisfied with treatment and report less impact of treatment on the ability to develop adaptive capacities, but ratings by the therapists (at termination) and CEs indicated a significant negative relationship between patients pretreatment PFT scores and ratings of the degree to which they thought the patients improved at termination and at the 18-month follow-up, independent of the type of treatment the patient had received. Thus, introjective personality traits significantly interfered with patients' capacity to benefit from short-term treatment, whether the treatment was pharmacotherapy (IMI-CM), psychotherapy (CBT or IPT), or placebo. These findings of impaired response of introjective (perfectionistic) patients in short-term treatment stand in contrast to the findings of more positive responses of introjective patients in the long-term, intensive treatment of inpatients who are seriously disturbed at the Austen Riggs Center and in the long-term, intensive treatment of outpatients evaluated in The Menninger Psychotherapy Research Project.

B. Impact of Patient Variables on the Therapeutic Process

The extensive data gathered as part of the NIMH TDCRP also provided Blatt and colleagues the opportunity to examine some of the dynamics of brief treatment and to identify when and how introjective personality characteristics interfere with the therapeutic process.

Therapeutic gain in the TDCRP was assessed every 4 weeks until termination, and thus it was possible to evaluate when in the treatment process pretreatment PFT began to disrupt therapeutic outcome. PFT significantly disrupted therapeutic progress primarily in the last one half of the treatment process. Until midtreatment at the 8th week, no significant differences were found in therapeutic gain between patients at different levels of PFT. Beginning at midtreatment, however, only patients in the lower one third of the distribution of PFT continued to make significant progress. When two thirds of the patients, those with higher pretreatment levels of perfectionism, approach the end of treatment, they seem to experience a sense of personal failure, dissatisfaction, and disillusionment with treatment. Even further, perfectionistic (introjective) individuals are very concerned about maintaining control and preserving their autonomy. Thus, another factor that may disrupt the therapeutic progress in the last one half of the treatment process of the more perfectionistic (introjective) patients in the TDCRP may be the unilateral, external imposition of an arbitrary, abrupt termination date.

Not only were we able to identify when introjective personality qualities began to disrupt therapeutic progress, but we were also able to discover some of the mechanisms though which this disruption occurs. Janice Krupnick and colleagues in 1996 had used a modified form of the Vanderbilt Therapeutic Alliance Scale (VTAS) to assess the contributions of patient and therapist in establishing an effective therapeutic alliance in the TDCRP. Judges rated videotapes of the 3rd, 9th, and 15th treatment sessions. They found that the VTAS comprised two factors: (a) a patient factor that assessed the extent to which the patient was open and honest with the therapist; agreed with the therapist about tasks, goals, and responsibilities; and was actively engaged in the therapeutic work; and (b) a therapist factor that assessed the extent to which the therapist committed self and skills to helping the patient and the degree to which the therapist acknowledged the validity of the patient's thoughts and feelings. The contribution of patients to the therapeutic alliance, but not that of the therapist, significantly predicated treatment outcome. Therapeutic outcome across treatment groups was predicted by the degree to which the patient became increasingly involved in the treatment process.

Using these ratings of the therapeutic alliance made by Krupnick and colleagues, David Zuroff and colleagues recently explored the impact of the pretreatment levels of PFT on the development of the therapeutic alliance and found that PFT significantly impedes the capacity of patients to develop a therapeutic alliance, particularly in the latter one half of treatment. Thus, not only were we able to identify when in the treatment process perfectionism disrupts therapeutic progress, but we also discovered how introjective personality traits impede patients' capacity to gain from the brief treatment of depression. Patients who make therapeutic progress usually become increasingly involved in a constructive collaborative relationship with their therapist, but this increased involvement in treatment is moderated by the patient's pretreatment level of perfectionism, independent of the treatment they were receiving. Increases in therapeutic alliance were significantly smaller or absent in patients at higher levels of perfectionism, particularly in the latter one half of the treatment process.

Perfectionistic individuals generally have limited capacities for developing open, collaborative relationships, and therefore it may take a more extended period of time for them to establish an effective therapeutic alliance. The effects of pretreatment PFT on therapeutic outcome is not only moderated by the quality of the therapeutic alliance, but, as Golar Sharar and colleagues demonstrated, it is also moderated by the extent to which patients are able to establish and maintain external social support during treatment and the follow-up period. Thus, the disruptive effects of pretreatment PFT on the treatment process is primarily the consequence of the disruptive effects of perfectionism on interpersonal relatedness both in the treatment process and in interpersonal relationships more generally.

Blatt and colleagues in 1996 also tried to identify aspects of the treatment process that could facilitate treatment outcome with these patients who are more difficult and highly perfectionistic. The TDCRP research team, using the Barrett–Lennard Relationship Inventory (B–L RI), asked patients, at the end of the second treatment session, to rate the degree to which they thought their therapist was empathic and caring. The B–L RI includes subscales to assess patient's perception of the therapist's emphatic understanding, level of positive regard, and congruence—qualities of the therapist that Carl Rogers believed were the necessary and sufficient conditions for therapeutic change. Prior studies demonstrated that the B–L RI was significantly related to treatment outcome at termination.

Overall, the degree to which patients in the TDCRP perceived their therapist as empathic and caring at the end of the second treatment session had a significant ($p < .05$) positive relationship to therapeutic outcome. However, this facilitating therapeutic effect of the patients' early view of the therapist as empathic and caring was very much contingent on the patients' level of perfectionism. An initial positive view of therapist had only marginal effects on treatment outcome at low and high levels of PFT ($ps < .10$ and .15, respectively). Patients who are highly perfectionistic did relatively poorly in treatment whereas patients low in perfectionism had relatively better outcome, independent of how they perceived the therapist early in treatment. However, at the middle level of PFT, the patient's early view of the therapist had a highly significant ($p < .001$) impact on treatment outcome. At the middle level of perfectionism, an early view of the therapist as empathic and caring significantly reduced the disruptive effects of perfectionism on treatment outcome, whereas a negative view of therapist significantly compounded these disruptive effects. Thus at the middle level, the effect of perfectionism on treatment outcome is significantly contingent on the degree to which the patient, very early in the treatment process, perceived the therapist as empathic and caring.

In sum, analyses of brief treatment of depression in the TDCRP indicate that therapeutic outcome is significantly influenced by pretreatment characteristics of the patient—by pretreatment level of perfectionism or self-criticism—independent of the type of treatment provided. This negative effect of pretreatment PFT on outcome occurs primarily in the second one half of the treatment process, as patients approach termination. This impact of pretreatment PFT on outcome occurs in large part through interference with patients' capacity to continue to be involved in interpersonal relationships both in the therapeutic alliance, particularly as termination approaches, as well as in interpersonal relations external to the treatment process. This negative impact of perfectionism on treatment outcome is significantly reduced, but only at middle levels of perfectionism, if the patient initially perceives the therapist as empathic and caring.

IV. SUMMARY

A fundamental polarity of relatedness and self-definition, central to many of Freud's theoretical formulations, as well as to those of many other psychoanalytic and non-psychoanalytic investigators, provides a basis for articulating a model of personality development: A model that involves a complex, mutually facilitating, dialectic transaction between the development of interpersonal relationships and of self-definition throughout the life cycle. This polarity also provides a basis for identifying two major types of depression: an anaclitic or dependent and introjective or self-critical depression. This polarity also provides a way for understanding a wide range of psychological disturbance, from schizophrenia to the neuroses, as emerging from disruptions in the dialectic development of the two fundamental developmental lines of relatedness and self-definition. This differentiation of two primary configurations of psychopathology—anaclitic and introjective—is based, not on differences in manifest symptoms, but on fundamental dimensions of personality organization: differences in primary instinctual focus (sexuality vs.

aggression), type of defensive organization (avoidant vs. counterphobic), and personality style (e.g., emphasis on relationships vs. a self-orientation and an emphasis on feelings and emotions versus cognition). This conceptual model of two major configurations of psychopathology developed by Blatt and colleagues facilitates an appreciation of the continuities between personality development and normal variations in personality or character style, as well as among various forms of psychopathology.

This conceptual model of personality development and psychopathology facilitated the introduction of personality dimensions into the study of therapeutic outcome and process in both short- and long-term treatment. These analyses demonstrated that anaclitic and introjective patients come to treatment with different capacities, needs, and problems, are differentially responsive to different types of treatment, and change in different, but equally, desirable ways. These theoretical formulations about a fundamental polarity of relatedness and self-definition provided a fuller understanding of personality development and the nature of psychopathology and facilitated a fuller exploration of important aspects of the therapeutic process and the nature of therapeutic change.

The introduction of patient variables into research on therapy outcome and process enables investigators to begin to identify factors that impede or facilitate therapeutic change. Even further, the inclusion of patient characteristics in research designs enables investigators to examine more systematically aspects of the therapeutic process and to identify when and how in the treatment process particular characteristics of the patients facilitate or impede therapeutic progress as well as identify particular aspects of the therapeutic process that can facilitate therapeutic change with patients who are treatment resistant.

See Also the Following Articles

Behavioral Assessment ■ Integrative Approaches to Psychotherapy ■ Neuropsychological Assessment ■ Outcome Measures ■ Projective Testing in Psychotherapeutics ■ Research in Psychotherapy ■ Therapeutic Factors

Further Reading

Bakan, D. (1966). *The duality of human existence: An essay on psychology and religion.* Chicago: Rand McNally.

Beutler, L. E. (1991). Have all won and must all have prizes? Revisiting Luborsky et al.'s verdict. *Journal of Consulting and Clinical Psychology, 59,* 226–232.

Blatt, S. J. (1974). Levels of object representation in anaclitic and introjective depression. *Psychoanalytic Study of the Child, 29,* 107–157.

Blatt, S. J. (1992). The differential effect of psychotherapy and psychoanalysis on anaclitic and introjective patients: The Menninger Psychotherapy Research Project revisited. *Journal of the American Psychoanalytic Association, 40,* 691–724.

Blatt, S. J. (1995). Representational structures in psychopathology. In D. Cicchetti & S. Toth (Eds.), *Rochester Symposium on developmental psychopathology: Vol. 6. emotion, cognition, and representation* (pp. 1–33). Rochester, NY: University of Rochester Press.

Blatt, S. J., & Felsen, I. (1993). "Different kinds of folks may need different kinds of strokes": The effect of patients' characteristics on therapeutic process and outcome. *Psychotherapy Research 3,* 245–259.

Blatt, S. J., & Ford, R. (1994). *Therapeutic change: An object relations perspective.* New York: Plenum.

Blatt, S. J., & Zuroff, D. C. (1992). Interpersonal relatedness and self-definition: Two prototypes for depression. *Clinical Psychology Review, 12,* 527–562.

Cronbach, L. J. (1953). Correlation between persons as a research tool. In O. H. Mowrer (Ed.), *Psychotherapy: Theory and research* (pp. 376–389). New York: Ronald.

Kiesler, D. J. (1966). Some myths of psychotherapy research and the search for a paradigm. *Psychological Bulletin, 65,* 110–136.

Sotsky, S. M., Glass, D. R., Shea, M. T., Pilkonis, P. A., Collins, J. F., Elkin, I., Watkins, J. T., Imber, S. D., Leber, W. R., Moyer J., & Oliveri, M. E. (1991). Patient predictors of response to psychotherapy and pharmacotherapy: Findings in the NIMH Treatment of Depression Collaborative Research Program. *American Journal of Psychiatry, 148,* 997–1008.

Zuroff, D. C., Blatt, S. J., Sotsky, S. M., Krupnick, J. L., Martin, D. J., Sanislow, C. A., & Simmens, S. (2000). Relation of therapeutic alliance and perfectionism to outcome in brief outpatient treatment of depression. *Journal of Consulting and Clinical Psychology, 68,* 114–124.

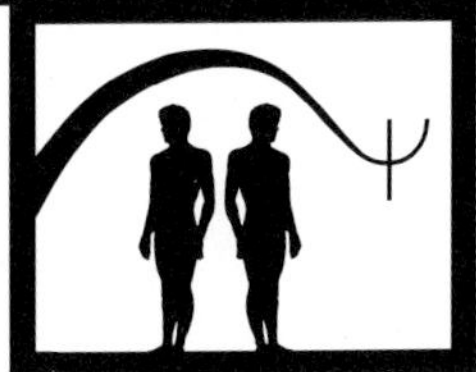

Positive Punishment

Alan Poling, Kristal E. Ehrhardt, and Ruth A. Ervin
Western Michigan University

GLOSSARY

aversive A nontechnical term often used to refer to punishment and negative reinforcement procedures.

conditioned punisher An event that acquires its capacity to serve as a punisher through learning.

negative punishers Punishers that involve removing something from an individual's environment.

negative punishment A procedure (or process) in which responding is weakened by its consequences, which involve removing something from an individual's environment.

negative reinforcement A procedure (or process) in which behavior is strengthened as a function of its consequences, which involve terminating a stimulus that is present or postponing (or preventing) the delivery of an otherwise forthcoming stimulus.

positive practice overcorrection A procedure that reduces the frequency of undesired behavior by having an individual emit appropriate relevant behaviors repeatedly each time the troublesome behavior occurs.

positive punishers Punishers that involve adding something to an individual's environment.

positive punishment A procedure (or process) in which responding is weakened by its consequences, which involve adding something to the individual's environment.

Premack principle A lower-probability behavior may be reinforced by allowing an individual to engage in a higher-probability behavior after the lower-probability behavior occurs. Conversely, a higher-probability behavior may be punished by requiring an individual to engage in a lower-probability behavior after the higher-probability behavior occurs.

punishers Consequences that weaken behavior.

punishment A procedure (or process) in which responding is weakened by its consequences, which are termed punishers.

respondent conditioning A procedure in which a previously neutral stimulus comes to control behavior by virtue of reliably preceding a stimulus that controls behavior at the onset of and throughout stimulus–stimulus pairings.

restitutional overcorrection A procedure that reduces the frequency of undesired behavior by requiring a person to repair the damage done by that behavior and to make the relevant parts of the world better than before the misdeed occurred.

simple correction A procedure that reduces the frequency of undesired behavior by having an individual emit appropriate relevant behaviors a single time after the troublesome behavior occurs.

stimulus An environmental event.

unconditioned punisher An event that does not require learning to serve as a punisher.

Many people consider punishment to be any attempt at disciplining a person by harming that individual, either physically or psychologically, when misbehavior occurs. When it is defined in this way, whether punishment increases, decreases, or has no effect on the future likelihood of occurrence of the misbehavior is irrelevant. Thus, spanking a child for cursing would be considered as punishment, regardless of whether the child curses more, less, or equally often after being spanked. When punishment is construed in this way, the behavioral function of the procedure is unclear and what stands out is that punishment is intended to hurt the person exposed to it. Not surprisingly, people who view punishment in this way typically object to its therapeutic use, although they may support it as retribution for heinous misdeeds.

To increase clarity and to avoid the negative connotations associated with "punishment" as the term is used in ordinary language, many behavioral psychologists define punishment not in terms of the intent of the person who implements it, but instead in terms of the nature of the operation and its effects on behavior. Specifically, punishment occurs when behavior is weakened by its consequences, which are termed *punishers*. The nature of those consequences, the intent of the person who administers them, and whether they harm the individual exposed to punishment are irrelevant to this definition, which we prefer. What is relevant is that the consequences of a particular behavior make it less likely that such behavior will occur in the future.

I. DESCRIPTION OF TREATMENT

It is convention to distinguish between positive and negative punishment. Positive punishment occurs when a response adds something to an individual's environment and is therefore weakened. If, for example, a parent says "don't poke your brother" when an older sibling jabs a toddler, and the subsequent rate of jabbing decreases as a result of this consequence, then the procedure is positive punishment. Negative punishment, in contrast, occurs when a response takes something away from an individual's environment and is therefore weakened. If, for example, the older sibling loses access to TV after poking the toddler, and the subsequent rate of jabbing decreases as a result of this consequence, then the procedure is negative punishment. In almost all cases, as in these examples, the response-weakening effects of punishment involve a decrease in the rate of responding. Other changes in behavior, however (e.g., an increase in response latency), can also be indicative of the response-weakening effects of punishment.

Positive punishment procedures can be divided into two general categories, those that involve presenting an external stimulus to a client and those that entail requiring the client to engage in nonpreferred (i.e., low-probability) behaviors. It is usual practice to refer to events that serve as positive punishers as "aversive" stimuli and to consider punishment as an "aversive" intervention. Unfortunately, these same terms also are often applied to negative reinforcers and negative reinforcement procedures, respectively, which is a source of confusion. Negative reinforcers are events that, when removed as a consequence of a particular kind of behavior, strengthen that behavior (e.g., pressing the "off" button on an alarm clock is strengthened by removal of the sound). Reinforcers always strengthen behavior, punishers always weaken it, and events that serve as negative reinforcers do not always serve as positive punishers. In addition, in everyday language "aversive" means "unpleasant" or "noxious," but the subjective effects of punishment are not a part of its technical definition. Punishment is defined functionally, in terms of how it affects behavior (i.e., it weakens it), not in terms of how it makes people feel. For these reasons, little is gained by labeling punishment as "aversive," although the practice is very common.

Positive punishment by presenting an external stimulus to a client when misbehavior occurs requires two steps. First, an effective positive punisher must be isolated and, second, conditions must be arranged so that this stimulus consistently and immediately follows the behavior that is to be reduced.

Positive punishers can be unconditioned (unlearned, or primary) or conditioned (learned, or secondary). Unconditioned punishers, which include events that provide extreme stimulation of any sensory system (e.g., loud sounds, bright lights, extreme cold or heat, strong pressure on the skin), suppress behavior automatically. That is, their delivery following a behavior reduces the likelihood that such behavior will recur in similar settings regardless of the history of the person in question. Events that serve as unconditioned positive punishers are similar across people. Moderate to intense electrical stimulation (shock) applied to the skin is a good example of such a punisher.

Unlike unconditioned punishers, conditioned positive punishers acquire their capacity to reduce responding through learning. This can occur through respondent conditioning when an established punisher reliably and shortly follows a neutral stimulus. For example, if a tone of moderate intensity that is not initially punishing occurs just before a person is shocked on a number of occasions, the tone eventually will acquire a punishing function. This function will be maintained so long as the tone is at least occasionally paired with the shock.

Conditioned punishers also can be established through verbal mediation. Consider, for instance, a music teacher who is giving voice lessons to a highly motivated student who is practicing singing on-key. The teacher says, "When you go too high, I'll raise my forefinger." By virtue of a unique learning history, the student is motivated not to sing at a pitch beyond that targeted by the teacher, that is, to "not go too high," and doing so is punishing. So is any indication that this is occurring, like the teacher's raised forefinger. Barring the teacher's explanation, the raised finger would not punish (i.e., reduce the future likelihood of) singing off-key in this student. In addition, unless their histories were similar to that of the student in our example, the teacher's raised finger would not serve as a positive punisher for the behavior of other people.

Once an effective unconditioned or conditioned punisher that is practical and ethically acceptable is isolated or established—which is an essential first step that can be difficult to accomplish—effective reduction of the targeted behavior is most likely to occur if:

1. The punisher immediately follows each occurrence of the behavior that is to be reduced.
2. The punisher is introduced at its optimum intensity initially, rather than being gradually increased in intensity over time.
3. The conditions of punishment are explained accurately to the client, if she or he has the verbal skill to understand them.
4. The reinforcer that maintains the troublesome behavior is made available for an alternative, desirable response.

As explained in later sections, positive punishment through the delivery of an external stimulus is not a common therapeutic procedure. More common, although still controversial, is requiring an individual to engage in a low-probability behavior when a high-probability, but troublesome, behavior occurs. This form of punishment is based on the Premack principle, which was devised by David Premack in the 1950s. It states that *(a)* the opportunity to engage in a higher-probability behavior will reinforcer a lower-probability behavior, and *(b)* the requirement of engaging in a lower-probability behavior will punish a higher-probability behavior.

Premack measured the probability of different incompatible behaviors by allowing an individual unconstrained opportunity to engage in them and measuring the amount of time spent in each activity. For example, a middle-school student on the playground during a 30-min recess would be given the opportunity to play soccer or softball, two independent activities that cannot occur together. If the student spent 24 min playing softball and 6 min playing soccer, then playing softball is the higher-probability, or preferred, activity. The Premack principle suggests that one could increase the amount of time the child played soccer by requiring this behavior to occur before the opportunity to play softball was provided. Conversely, the amount of time spent playing softball could be reduced if the child was required to play soccer for a considerable period after playing softball for a short time. In this case, however, neither behavior is necessarily undesirable and, unless they loved soccer and loved softball, there would be no reason for parents or teachers to punish playing softball in this manner. In other cases, however, the higher-probability behavior is clearly undesirable and the lower-probability behavior desirable (or innocuous), and the Premack principle of punishment can be used to good advantage. This is the case with overcorrection, a procedure that Richard Foxx and Nate Azrin developed in the early 1970s to reduce aggressive and other disruptive behaviors exhibited by clients with mental retardation living in an institutional setting.

In essence, overcorrection requires a client to engage in a low-probability (nonpreferred) behavior each time a higher-probability, but troublesome, behavior occurs. Two versions of overcorrection are distinguished, depending on the nature of the nonpreferred behavior that the client is required to perform. In positive practice overcorrection, the client is required to emit appropriate relevant behaviors repeatedly each time the troublesome behavior occurs. For example, a child who kicks a chained dog passed on the way to school might be required to walk the block on which the dog lives 10 times without approaching (or kicking) it.

A procedure similar to positive practice overcorrection is simple correction, in which the individual is required to emit appropriate relevant behaviors once after the undesired behavior occurs. For instance, the hypothetical child who kicks a chained dog would be required to walk past the dog once without approaching it.

In restitutional overcorrection, or restitution, each time the problem behavior occurs the client is required to repair the damage done by that behavior and to make the relevant parts of the world better than before the misdeed occurred. If, for instance, a child spits on the kitchen floor, she or he would be required to not only clean up the spittle, but also to mop and dry the entire kitchen floor. An advantage of restitution is that it has an educational, as well as a punishing, function.

Although they are not typically construed as overcorrection, a number of other interventions make use of the Premack principle to reduce inappropriate responding. One such procedure is contingent exercise, where a client who rarely exercises is required to do so when an undesired response occurs. Another is guided compliance, where a client who misbehaves while performing a task is physically guided through the task until it is completed. If, for instance, a child who is asked to turn off and put away a tape player begins to whine and argue (the undesired behavior), the parents may physically guide the child in performing the requested activity. Here, as in all cases involving punishment by requiring clients to engage in nonpreferred activities, when physical guidance is provided the stimulation resulting from such guidance may be punishing.

In some cases, it is difficult or impossible to get an individual to engage in nonpreferred activities, and attempts at doing so can create a host of problems. Among them are inconsistent application of the intervention and physical harm to the client, the therapist, or other people. In general, punishment based on the Premack principle is best used with compliant and easily managed individuals. One would not, for instance, attempt to physically guide a large, strong, and angry client in performing a task she or he abhorred.

II. THEORETICAL BASES

As discussed in the entry for operant conditioning, operant conditioning has been likened to natural selection in that both involve processes of variation, selection, and retention. Punishment "selects out" operants that produce certain consequences. Studies by neuroscientists may reveal the physiological mechanisms through which this occurs and, if so, contribute to a comprehensive theory of punishment. No such theory is currently available, which perhaps has contributed to widespread misunderstanding of what punishment entails.

Psychologists have been concerned with punishment from the discipline's early days. Although Edward Thorndike made no mention of what we now call punishment in the earliest versions of his well-known law of effect, by 1905 when his book *The Elements of Psychology* appeared, he recognized that the consequences of behavior could have bidirectional effects. That is, they could make it either more or less likely that such behavior would recur. Thorndike wrote:

> Any act which in a given situation produces satisfaction becomes associated with that situation, so that when the situation recurs the act is more likely than before to recur. [This is reinforcement.] Conversely, any act which in a given situation produces discomfort becomes disassociated from that situation, so that when the situation recurs the act is less likely than before to recur. [This is punishment.]

Later in life, Thorndike came to believe that punishment was not effective in reducing behavior. This belief was fostered by the results of studies conducted with college students learning to match English words with Spanish synonyms. Thorndike found that saying "Right" after correct matches facilitated learning, therefore, reinforcement was effective. But saying "Wrong" after incorrect matches had no effect on subsequent performance, therefore, punishment was ineffective. Although Thorndike's results are subject to alternative explanations, his view of punishment as ineffective was popularized in the lay press with respect to child-rearing practices.

B. F. Skinner greatly extended Thorndike's research and theorizing regarding the effects of consequences on behavior. Skinner acknowledged punishment as a principle of behavior, but throughout his life he argued that the effects of punishment are short lived and that, in general, punishment should not be used therapeutically or in the culture at large. Skinner's position regarding the short-lived effects of punishment were supported by his research findings with rats, and by the findings of his student, William Estes. In one study, Estes initially rewarded (reinforced) rats' lever presses with food. After the response was occurring reliably, food was no longer available, and each lever press produced an intense electric shock delivered to the rat's feet. This procedure reduced responding to near zero levels. If, however, a substantial period of time passed without the rats being tested, they would resume lever pressing. Thus, punishment did not eliminate behavior but only suppressed it so long as the punishment procedure was in effect.

Results such as these, as well as philosophical considerations, caused Skinner to have strong negative opinions regarding positive punishment. For example, the chapter in his 1953 book *Science and Human Behavior* that deals with punishment is titled "A questionable technique." He argues therein that *(a)* punishment does not produce lasting effects, *(b)* punishment often is used abusively, *(c)* punishment often engenders strong and negative emotional responding, *(d)* punishment engenders escape from and avoidance of stimuli associated with the experience, and *(e)* viable alternatives to punishment are available. He acknowledged, however, that relatively little research had been conducted on the effects of punishment and suggested that further work in the area was necessary.

Laboratory research concerning punishment by the delivery of aversive stimuli increased dramatically during the 1960s, but interest in the area soon waned. The studies that were conducted revealed a great deal about the variables that influence the degree of response suppression produced by positive punishment and also provided evidence that punishment could eliminate, or substantially reduce, behavior over long periods. In fact, after summarizing the research literature, Nate Azrin and William Holz concluded in 1966 that:

> As a reductive procedure, punishment appears to be at least as effective as most other procedures for eliminating responses. ... If we have not overlooked the effects of [important] variables, there is every reason to believe that our punishment procedure will be completely effective in eliminating the undesired response. The emotional state or enduring behavioral disruption of the punished subject are not necessarily undesirable outcomes of punishment, nor are the severity of the response reduction or the behavioral generalization of the punishing effects undesirable.

They suggest that disruption of social interactions, caused by the tendency of the individual exposed to punishment to avoid or react aggressively toward the person who inflicts punishment, is the major disadvantage of using punishment. Although Azrin and Holz' influential chapter is by no means a glowing endorsement for therapeutic applications of positive punishment, the studies reviewed therein make it clear that punishment can be effective in reducing behavior. These laboratory studies, which dealt with the application of external stimuli as punishers, provided an empirical basis for therapeutic applications of positive punishment during the 1960s and 1970s.

Although many theoreticians construe punishment as a process that is similar to reinforcement, but with opposite effects on behavior, there is an alternate view. From this perspective, the response reduction produced by punishment is due to passive avoidance responding. That is, organisms learn that emitting certain responses produce undesired (i.e., punishing) consequences and, because of this, they withhold such responses even though variables are present that would otherwise cause those responses to occur. Behavioral psychologists do not agree as to whether or not experimental data provide solid support for either the passive avoidance or direct response reduction theory of punishment. Although the issue is of theoretical significance, it does not appear to have important implications for clinical applications of positive punishment.

Most basic laboratory research in the area of positive punishment has involved delivery of aversive stimuli, and most theorizing has concerned the effects of such stimuli. There have, however, been some extensions of Premack's work concerning punishment by requiring the performance of low-probability (nonpreferred) activities. It is now generally accepted that forcing an individual to engage in a higher-probability behavior can punish a lower-probability behavior, so long as the individual is forced to engage in the higher-probability behavior for a longer period than would occur normally. Although this finding is interesting, it is of little clinical significance.

III. APPLICATIONS AND EXCLUSIONS

Restrictions on the use of positive punishment depend on the specific procedure under consideration. In general, ethical and legal considerations severely limit the use of positive punishment as a primary intervention in therapeutic settings. There is, however, debate about whether positive punishment should ever be used with protected populations (e.g., children, people with mental retardation).

No legitimate therapist recommends positive punishment as a first-line intervention, and advocates of "nonaversive" interventions contend that the procedure should never be used. Advocates of the right to effective treatment also acknowledge that positive punishment is a restrictive (harmful) intervention. They contend, however, that it may be appropriate to use the procedure to deal with serious behavioral problems that have not responded favorably to other, less restrictive, interventions. If fact, some argue that it is unethical to withhold a potentially valuable, although momentarily unpleasant, intervention if doing so maintains the client in a dangerous or uncomfortable state.

As a rule, the use of unusual unconditioned punishers (e.g., electric shock, aromatic ammonia) is more strongly restricted than are procedures that deliver common conditioned punishers (e.g., verbal reprimands) or that require clients to perform generally accepted, but (for them) low-probability behaviors. For instance, in 1990 the American Association on Mental Retardation condemned "aversive procedures which cause physical damage, pain, or illness" and procedures "which are dehumanizing—social degradaion, verbal abuse and excessive reactions." Common forms of conditioned punishment, as described in the example of the music teacher's raised finger, are common in many human interactions, including therapeutic interchanges in which clients and therapists talk to one another. Such interchanges are not, however, based primarily on punishment or generally considered as punishment procedures.

If punishment is to be used systematically as a part of therapy, it is important that appropriate safeguards be put in place to protect both clients and staff. In general, a clear decision-making process regarding the use of punishment should be in place. This process should recognize that punishment is a restrictive (harmful) intervention and adhere to the doctrine of the least restrictive alternative intervention. This doctrine states that other, less restrictive, interventions must be evaluated and found ineffective before punishment is considered.

Clear guidelines must be established regarding the exact nature of the punishment procedure, including who is to implement it and the specific standards of accountability. Input from clients and client's advocates, as well as behavior-change experts, should play a crucial role in determining the details of punishment, including who is to administer it and how its effects are to be monitored. Unambiguous rules regarding the behavioral data that will support continuation, modification, and termination of punishment must be established by a vigilant, expert, and caring treatment team before punishment is implemented, and these rules must be followed unless the good of the client dictates otherwise in the opinion of the team. Whenever possible, positive punishment should be avoided entirely.

IV. EMPIRICAL STUDIES

Most of the published studies of therapeutic applications of positive punishment involve attempts to reduce harmful behaviors in people with mental retardation and other developmental disabilities. A well-known example of research in this area concerns Ivaar Lovaas's successful use of electric shocks during the 1960s to reduce pernicious self-injury in children with autism. Other researchers replicated his findings concerning the effectiveness of electric shock punishment in reducing self-injury and also demonstrated that the procedure could be used to reduce other harmful behaviors to acceptable levels.

Several unconditioned primary punishers have been evaluated in published studies, including water mist sprayed in the face, ice cubes placed against the jaw, lemon juice squirted in the mouth, and aromatic ammonia held close enough to the client to be smelled. These stimuli have proven to be effective in reducing self-injury and other troublesome behaviors when presented immediately after such behavior occurred. In short, published studies provide clear evidence that punishment via the delivery of aversive stimulation can provide rapid, strong, and enduring suppression of target behaviors.

Even people who argue strongly against the use of punishment via the delivery of aversive stimuli generally acknowledge the procedure's efficacy. They point out, however, that the procedure can produce several harmful side effects, including aggression, undesirable emotional responses (e.g., crying), establishment of the person who delivers the punisher as a conditioned punisher, and general suppression of behavior. Although such effects certainly can occur, reviews of the research literature suggest that punishment is at least as likely to produce positive side effects, such as increases in social behavior, improved affect, and reductions in the problem behavior outside the treatment setting. Nonetheless, negative side effects remain a real concern.

So, too, is the possibility that caregivers may use punishment excessively and inappropriately in treating people with developmental disabilities, and that children who see punishment being used are likely to use punishment themselves. Such effects are documented in the literature, although they do not inevitably occur. Finally, because punishment is generally recognized as restrictive and is considered by many people as intrinsically dehumanizing, efficacy alone does not justify its use. When nonaversive alternatives are available, they are preferable. Although it is clear that such procedures have been used to manage a wide range of problem behaviors in protected populations, there is ongoing debate as to whether effective nonaversive alternatives to punishment via the delivery of an aversive stimulus are always available.

Positive punishment by requiring an individual to engage in nonpreferred activities has been evaluated in a substantial number of studies, most concerned specifically with overcorrection. In brief, such procedures, used alone or in combination with other strategies, have been effective in reducing a substantial range of behaviors emitted by a wide variety of persons in diverse settings. Among the behaviors that have been successfully controlled are self-injury, aggression, stereotypy, disruption, in-class masturbation, oral reading errors, oral spelling errors, writing errors, and failure to make eye contact. Although positive side effects, including decreased crying and increased smiling and social interactions have been observed in some studies, negative side effects also have been reported. These include aggression, avoidance of the setting in which the procedure is applied, screaming, and stereotypical responding. As noted previously, difficulties can arise in getting a client to perform low-probability behaviors. Moreover, selecting appropriate low-probability behaviors can be difficult in some settings.

Positive punishment by requiring individuals to engage in nonpreferred activities has engendered some controversy but appears to be generally accepted so long as the required behaviors are appropriate and the measures taken to get clients to perform them are humane. Positive punishment by the delivery of aversive stimuli, in contrast, is highly controversial and is best viewed as a treatment of last resort. Nonetheless, various forms of positive punishment are ubiquitous in everyday life and in therapy. They may teach people what not to do and be of value for that reason. But they do not establish appropriate behaviors, and they are unpleasant, and for these reasons many thoughtful people minimize their use.

V. CASE ILLUSTRATION

A study published by Thomas Sajway, Julian Libet, and Stuart Agras in 1974 provides a straightforward example of positive punishment through the delivery of an aversive stimulus. They treated a severely malnourished and dehydrated 6-month-old girl who regurgitated each time she was fed. As they described it, after being given food (e.g., milk in a bottle), she "would open her mouth, elevate and fold her tongue, and vigorously thrust her tongue backward and forward," which caused her to throw up the food she had just ingested. There was no sign of duress during these activities, and physicians could isolate no cause for their occurrence.

To reduce regurgitation, Sajway, Libet, and Agras squirted unsweetened lemon juice into the girl's mouth immediately after the tongue movements occurred. This procedure rapidly reduced regurgitation and, after 12 days of exposure to it, the vigorous tongue movements and regurgitation had totally disappeared. As a result, the girl's weight increased dramatically—by 50% in 2 months—and she became healthy. No untoward effects were observed, and it is no exaggeration to say that exposure to the mild punishment procedure saved the girl's life.

A study published by Richard Foxx and Nate Azrin in 1972 clearly illustrates punishment by requiring a person to emit nonpreferred behaviors. The client in this study was a 50-year-old woman with mental retardation who lived in an institution. Prior to treatment, for over 30 years she regularly (more than 10 times per day) upset furniture and engaged in other destructive acts on her ward. To reduce these destructive and high-probability behaviors, Foxx and Azrin used a restitutional overcorrection procedure in which the woman was required to correct immediately any damage caused by her actions and, in addition, to emit other behaviors that improved the quality of the ward. For instance, if she upset a bed, she was required to set it upright and make up the covers, and also to fluff the pillows on all of the other beds in the ward. (These were low-probability activities for the woman.)

Overcorrection rapidly reduced destructive acts. Within 1 week, fewer than four acts occurred per day. After 11 weeks of overcorrection, the behavior was totally eliminated. No adverse effects of the procedure were noted. Here, a behavioral problem that had existed for over 3 decades was solved by requiring the client to make amends for the damage caused by her inappropriate actions.

VI. SUMMARY

Positive punishment refers to a procedure in which a particular kind of behavior is weakened (decreased in rate) because a stimulus is presented, or the individual is required to engage in nonpreferred activities, as a consequence of that behavior. Positive punishment is effective in reducing a wide range of behaviors, but ethical and practical objections broadly restrict its therapeutic use.

See Also the Following Articles

Aversion Relief ■ Conditioned Reinforcement ■ Extinction ■ Functional Analysis of Behavior ■ Negative Practice ■ Negative Punishment ■ Negative Reinforcement ■ Operant Conditioning ■ Overcorrection ■ Positive Reinforcement ■ Self-Punishment

Further Reading

Axelrod, S., & Apsche, J. (1983). *The effects of punishment on human behavior.* New York: Academic Press.

Dinsmoor, J. A. (1998). Punishment. In W. O'Donohue (Ed.), *Learning and behavior therapy* (pp. 188–204). Boston: Allyn and Bacon.

Guess, D., Helmstetter, E., Turnbull, H. R., III, & Knowlton, S. (1986). *Use of aversive procedures with persons who are disabled: An historical review and critical analysis.* Seattle, WA: Association for Persons with Severe Handicaps.

Matson, J. L., & DiLorenzo, T. M. (1984). *Punishment and its alternatives: A new perspective for behavior modification.* New York: Springer.

Matson, J. L., & Taras, M. E. (1989). A 20 year review of punishment and alternative methods to treat problem behaviors in developmentally disabled persons. *Research in Developmental Disabilities, 10,* 85–104.

Miltenberger, R., & Fuqua, R. W. (1981). Overcorrection: Review and critical analysis. *The Behavior Analyst, 4,* 123–141.

Repp, A. C., & Singh, N. (1990). *Perspectives on the use of nonaversive and aversive interventionsn for persons with developmental disabilities.* Sycamore, IL: Sycamore Publishing Company.

Sidman, M. (1989). *Coercion and its fallout.* Boston: Authors Cooperative.

Singer, G. H. S., Gert, B., & Koegel, R. L. (1999). A moral framework for analyzing the controversy over aversive behavioral interventions for people with severe mental retardation. *Journal of Positive Behavior Interventions, 1,* 88–100.

Van Houten, R., Axelrod, S., Bailey, J. S., Favell, J. E., Foxx, R. M., Iwata, B., & Lovaas, O. I. (1988). The right to effective behavioral treatment. *Journal of Applied Behavior Analysis, 21,* 381–384.

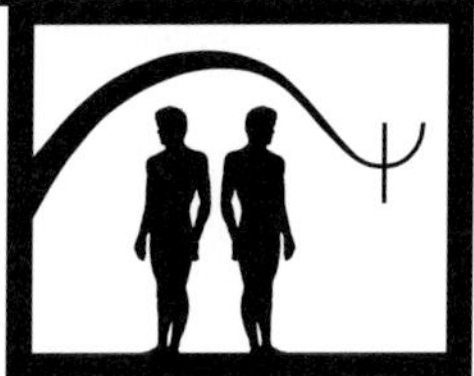

Positive Reinforcement

Alan Poling and Edward J. Daly III
Western Michigan University

GLOSSARY

chaining Reinforcing discrete responses in sequence so that all the behaviors occur as a single cohesive unit.

conditioned reinforcers Stimuli that acquire reinforcing properties through learning.

differential reinforcement of incompatible behavior A procedure in which a desired behavior that is incompatible with an undesired behavior is reinforced. The procedure is used to decrease undesired behavior and simultaneously increase desired behavior.

differential reinforcement of other behavior A procedure in which a reinforcer is delivered when a prespecified period passes without occurrence of an undesired response. The procedure is used to decrease undesired behavior.

primary positive reinforcers Stimuli that have reinforcing capacity in the absence of a special learning history.

prompt A verbal or physical antecedent that indicates to an individual how to respond in order to obtain reinforcement.

shaping Reinforcing successively closer approximations to a terminal, desired response.

Desirable as well as undesirable human behaviors often are operant responses, that is, they primarily are controlled by their consequences. Consequences are events (stimuli) that follow and are produced by a particular behavior. When the consequences of behavior make it more likely that such behavior will occur in a similar future context, or otherwise strengthen the behavior, the consequences are termed reinforcers and the process whereby responding is strengthened is termed reinforcement. Negative reinforcers strengthen behavior when responding removes them from the individual's environment, or prevents their occurrence. Positive reinforcers, in contrast, strengthen behavior when responding leads to their presentation.

Positive reinforcers can be learned (called conditioned or secondary) or unlearned (called unconditioned or primary). Stimuli that serve as primary positive reinforcers typically are of direct biological significance (e.g., food, water). Stimuli that serve as conditioned reinforcers do so because they precede the delivery of other reinforcers, or because of verbal mediation. Because people differ in their learning histories, the stimuli that serve as conditioned reinforcers differ substantially across people.

In a general sense, positive reinforcement comprises all procedures in which operant behavior is strengthened through the response-produced presentation of an object or event. Procedures based on positive reinforcement are useful in treating many kinds of behavioral problems in a wide range of client populations.

Moreover, understanding the role of reinforcement in the genesis and maintenance of inappropriate behavior is critical for understanding human psychopathology and for treating it effectively.

I. DESCRIPTION OF TREATMENT

Troublesome human behaviors generally can be categorized into those that involve the presence of inappropriate responses and those that involve the absence of appropriate responses. Because reinforcement by definition increases, or otherwise strengthens, responding, procedures based on positive reinforcement have an obvious role in treating individuals who fail to emit desired behaviors. To deal with such problems, a clinician typically begins by defining the desired behavior and selecting a measurement system that allows the behavior to be accurately quantified. Goals for performance of the desired behavior also are established at this point.

Next, a determination is made as to whether the absence of desired behavior involves a skill deficit or a performance deficit. In the former case, the client has not learned to perform the response. In the latter case, the client knows how to perform the response, but fails to do so. Often, the reason is that the desired behavior is not consistently reinforced in the client's everyday environment.

In many cases, planned reinforcement is used to treat performance deficiencies. For instance, an adult with mental retardation living in a group home may not regularly dress herself, even though she knows how to perform the task and does so on occasion. Making something valuable to the woman—perhaps tokens that can be exchanged for favored objects and activities—available only if she dresses herself appropriately each morning would in all likelihood lead to consistent self-dressing.

Treating a skill deficit typically begins with a task analysis, which involves breaking a complex behavior into its component parts. Dressing one's self, for example, begins with recognizing and laying out appropriate clothes and ends with fastening the final accouterment in place. Between the beginning and end of this chain of responses are many specific actions that depend on exactly what the person will be wearing. Several different procedures, all involving positive reinforcement, might be used in teaching a person to perform a new behavior, like dressing herself. Among them are shaping, modeling, prompting, chaining, and providing verbal instruction.

In shaping, successively closer approximations to the desired response are reinforced until the target (desired) behavior emerges. To teach a person to pull up a zipper, for instance, one might ask the person to do so then observe their performance. If they grasped the tab and pulled the zipper halfway up, praise (a positive reinforcer) would be provided. On the next trial, however, praise would be withheld until the zipper was pulled more than halfway up. This process would be repeated until the zipper was fully closed. At that point, another response in the self-dressing sequence would be taught.

In prompting, physical or verbal guidance in performing a desired response is provided. If the woman in our example were verbal, the therapist might say, "Keep pulling hard," as the zipper was raised. The therapist might also place a hand over the client's hand and help her to pull the zipper. In modeling, someone performs the target (desired) response while being observed by the individual who is to learn that behavior. Our therapist might operate a zipper one or more times before asking the client to do so.

In chaining, discrete responses are reinforced in sequence to form complex behaviors that eventually occur as a single cohesive unit. The completion of one response provides a cue (i.e., a discriminative stimulus) for performing the next response in the sequence and, eventually, reinforcement is provided only when the chain of responses is complete. By the time the client has learned to dress herself, she might earn praise only at the end of a long and integrated sequence of responses.

Verbal instructions can serve as prompts but also can specify relations among stimuli (events and objects) and responses, thereby changing the function of those stimuli and responses. The therapist might, for instance, tell the client "Your green top and your black slacks really go well together—I love how you look in them." This statement might establish the top and slacks combination as a positive reinforcer, which the client values and will work to get to wear. Absent the therapist's statement, or given another kind of statement, such as "Your green top and your black slacks look crappy together—I hate how you look in them," wearing the top and slacks together would not serve as a positive reinforcer.

In many cases, a behavior that is appropriate in one context is not appropriate in another. Therefore, once new behavior is established under conditions where it is appropriate, steps often must be taken to ensure that it does not generalize to other, inappropriate, contexts. This can be accomplished through differential reinforcement, which entails reinforcing behavior in contexts where the behavior is appropriate, and failing to reinforce that behavior in other contexts. Teaching multiplication tables to a child labeled with a learning disability in mathematics provides a good example of differential reinforcement at work. The child's saying "ten" is correct, and positively reinforced with praise ("that's right, good") when the child is reacting to "5 × 2 = ____." But that response is incorrect and is followed by corrective feedback that is not reinforcing ("no, that's wrong") when the child is reacting to "3 × 2 = ____." In this fashion, "5 × 2 = ____" is established as a discriminative stimulus for the verbal response "10." Differential reinforcement is used to establish stimulus control such that a particular response appears in the presence of appropriate stimuli, but not in their absence. In verbal humans, descriptions of appropriate stimulus control can sometimes be used as a substitute for actual differential reinforcement.

Positive reinforcement always strengthens the behavior that is reinforced, therefore, it may seem odd that procedures based on positive reinforcement can be used successfully to weaken undesirable behaviors. Two procedures that are frequently used in this way are called differential reinforcement of incompatible behavior (DRI) and differential reinforcement of other behavior (DRO) schedules. The DRI schedule makes use of the fact that some behaviors cannot occur simultaneously, therefore, increasing the rate of occurrence of one of these behaviors by reinforcing it also reduces the rate of occurrence of the other behavior. A client with a phobia cannot, for instance, simultaneously walk toward and avoid a feared object. So, by reinforcing approach responses, one can reduce avoidance responses.

The DRO schedule provides a reinforcer dependent on the passage of a specified period of time during which the behavior to be reduced does not appear; each time the behavior does occur, the interval is reset. If, for example, a DRO 5-min schedule is arranged to reduce self-stimulatory hand flapping by a person with autism, some positive reinforcer (perhaps a point on a counter that later could be exchanged for access to preferred music) would be delivered each time five consecutive minutes passed without a hand flap. This procedure should reduce the frequency of hand flaps relative to the preintervention level. But how can this be a reinforcement effect? The answer is that the unit of behavior that is strengthened is an interval of 5 min or longer without a hand flap. These units increase under the DRO and, as a result, incidents of hand flapping are reduced.

II. THEORETICAL BASES

A great deal is known about positive reinforcement. As discussed in the entry for operant conditioning, B. F. Skinner compared the selection of behavior by its consequences to natural selection and emphasized that both entail processes of variation, selection, and retention. Studies by neuroscientists may reveal the physiological mechanisms through which these processes allow behavior to be strengthened by its consequences. Attempts have also been made to explain at other levels of analysis why certain stimuli are positively reinforcing under certain circumstances. None of these attempts is universally accepted.

Be that as it may, over the past 50 years thousands of studies have documented the importance of positive reinforcement in controlling behavior in nonhumans in laboratory settings, and in humans in laboratory settings, in everyday life, and in clinical applications. Positive reinforcement directly or indirectly plays a crucial role in the production of an incredible variety of human behaviors, both healthy and pathological. The variables that influence positive reinforcement have been studied extensively and clinical applications of positive reinforcement are for the most part based on the resultant knowledge. Put simply, there is unequivocal theoretical support for the clinical application of procedures based on positive reinforcement.

III. APPLICATIONS AND EXCLUSIONS

As noted in the previous section, positive reinforcement can be used in a variety of ways to increase desired behaviors and to arrange for those behaviors to occur only in appropriate contexts. Arranged in other ways, positive reinforcement can be used to reduce or eliminate undesired behavior. Given this breadth of application, positive reinforcement is potentially useful in dealing with the behavioral problems of all clinical populations. Issues of client diversity do not limit the general use of positive reinforcement, which is widely accepted, but particular cultures and individuals may object to specific procedures based on positive reinforcement. Moreover, cultures may vary with respect to the behaviors that they deem acceptable and unacceptable, and in the objects and events that serve as positive reinforcers.

Some individuals object to contrived reinforcement procedures, that is, those that do not occur naturally, as a form of bribery. Bribery is rewarding an individual so that she or he will behave in a corrupt way that benefits the person who delivers the reward. Therapeutic applications of positive reinforcement are intended to benefit the person whose behavior is reinforced, and the behavior that is reinforced is appropriate responding, not unethical conduct. Positive reinforcement is not equivalent to bribery.

But, even if positive reinforcement is not bribery, certain critics claim that the purpose of using it is to control people's behavior, which to the critics is objectionable. It is true that the sole intent of therapists who use positive reinforcement, or, for that matter, any other psychological or psychiatric intervention, is to improve and in that sense "control" the client's behavior. But the control effected is such that the client's behavior, and as a result the quality of his or her life, improves. Moreover, the targeted changes in behavior characteristically are selected in consultation with the client, if she or he has the capacity to participate meaningfully in such decisions. If positive reinforcement is unacceptable because it controls clients, so are all therapeutic strategies.

Related to the foregoing concern is a third criticism of positive reinforcement, which is an ethical objection to rewarding people for doing "what they should do anyway." For example, Steve Higgins and his colleagues recently have had good success in treating cocaine abusers by paying them to produce drug-free urine samples. Although the procedure is relatively cheap as well as effective, some detractors claim that it is wrong to pay people not to engage in illegal behavior. People who raise this concern typically believe that individuals have the freedom to behave as they choose, and that those who behave inappropriately are ethically flawed and should be punished, not rewarded, for their shortcomings. Although this conception of human behavior has precedent in Western philosophy, theology, and jurisprudence, people who emphasize that much of human behavior is learned see it as little more than "blaming the victim."

A fourth criticism of positive reinforcement, one made popular by Edward Deci, is that the use of extrinsic reinforcers reduces an individual's "intrinsic motivation" to emit appropriate behavior. Such an effect has been demonstrated in a small number of studies in which children performed a task with no systematic reinforcement, then were reinforced for performing the task, and finally were retested with no systematic reinforcement. They worked less hard in the third condition than in the first, which is taken as evidence that extrinsic rewards (or reinforcers) reduced intrinsic motivation. In fact, the "intrinsic" motivation was acquired in large part as a result of prior reinforcement—people learn to do what they are asked to do because, historically, doing so was reinforced. In addition, the overwhelming majority of studies provide no evidence that positive reinforcement reduces people's intrinsic interest in tasks.

If the criticisms of positive reinforcement discussed earlier have little merit, why were they accorded so much space? Only because behavior-change interventions based on positive reinforcement should be used even more widely than they are. Paul Chance makes this point very nicely in an anecdote related in his 1998 book, *First Course in Behavior Analysis:*

> Once, when I was at a PTA meeting, the parents and teachers were discussing the problem of what to do about student misbehavior, which was getting worse and worse each year. The discussion focused on the kinds of punishment to provide for various offenses. They had compiled a list of student offenses and the consequences each offense should have. I made an innocent observation. "No one," I offered, "has said anything about what happens when a student behaves well. What about providing some *positive* consequences for *good* conduct?"
>
> Some parents strongly opposed the idea. "Nobody gave *me* anything for behaving myself when I was in school," said one. But the fact that schools haven't been very good about reinforcing desirable behavior does not mean that they should not do so now. Their schools never used to use computers, but that hasn't kept us from putting them in the schools.

IV. EMPIRICAL STUDIES

A very large clinical literature has documented the efficacy of positive reinforcement, alone and in combination with other strategies, in treating behavior disorders. Because of the size of this literature, and because positive reinforcement plays a role in such a wide range of interventions, it is impossible to provide a simple and meaningful summary of the efficacy of "positive reinforcement procedures." It is, however, the case that procedures based primarily on positive reinforcement have been shown to be effective with a wide range of settings, target behaviors, and client populations.

A good understanding of the principles of operant conditioning is required to design effective positive reinforcement procedures. Although they are rarely reported in the literature, failed attempts at using positive reinforcement are common in the everyday world of education and clinical practice. These attempts fail when the events selected as positive reinforcers do not, in fact, have this function, and when the intervention team cannot control the delivery of events that do serve as reinforcers. They also fail when reinforcement is too delayed or too inconsistent, and when the rules that a person follows regarding the consequences of his or her behavior reduce sensitivity to these consequences. Occasionally, positive reinforcement procedures fail because of their "side effects," that is, the negative emotional responding, aggression, escape, and avoidance that poorly designed procedures can engender. Although people characteristically enjoy positive reinforcement, such adverse reactions can occur when response requirements are substantial and reinforcers are few.

V. CASE ILLUSTRATION

Positive reinforcement is an equal opportunity employer. In other words, it is responsible for maintaining both appropriate and inappropriate behaviors. When the natural environment fails to provide sources of reinforcement for appropriate behaviors, inappropriate behaviors may emerge through the same mechanisms that govern adaptive behaviors. That is, the same behavioral processes that support appropriate behaviors may engender inappropriate behavior. This is the case in the following example that, although fictitious, is representative of many studies demonstrating the reinforcing properties of social attention in the classroom.

Imagine a second-grade classroom where children are busily filling out their math worksheets. The teacher is going around the room, checking on the children's work and assisting them as they need help. All of a sudden, there is an outburst. One of the children yells, "Give that back to me!" The teacher looks up and quickly becomes exasperated. Once again, Tommy is bothering another child. This time, he took Sarah's pencil. Tommy looks in the direction of the teacher. The teacher says, "Tommy, you give that back to Sarah right away! Get back to work!" A sly grin crosses Tommy's face. He complies, however, giving the pencil to Sarah and turning toward his paper. Tommy then looks at his blank paper. The numbers are almost as foreign to him as the crosses and dashes next to the numbers. He couldn't write the correct answer even if he wanted to.

After about 2 min, Tommy gets out of his seat. The teacher is on him this time. He is barely one step away from his desk when the teacher yells, "Get back in your seat! You know that you are not allowed out of your seat without my permission." Tommy begins to argue. He says, "My pencil is broken and I need to go to the bathroom," whereupon many of the other students snicker audibly. The teacher responds by reciting the rules for Tommy. She then comes over to his desk to make comments about his incomplete school work. In some cases, a scenario like this can last all day long. It is no wonder that teachers reach their frustration limits sometimes. An understanding of the variables controlling Tommy's behavior, however, may help Tommy to get his work done and reduce his class disruptions. It also will probably make the teacher's life easier if she is able to come up with an intervention that weakens or counteracts the primary controlling variable, social attention.

In this case, Tommy's inappropriate behavior is strengthened by teacher attention, which functions as a positive reinforcer. Unfortunately, virtually all of the attention given to Tommy is dependent on inappropriate behavior. In the scenario described earlier, there was not a single instance where social attention followed appropriate behavior. Every instance of inappropriate behavior, in contrast, produced attention. Therefore, we can conclude that Tommy's disruptive behavior is maintained by positive reinforcement in the form of teacher attention, and perhaps peer attention. One common, erroneous assumption is that positive reinforcement is "positive" in an evaluative sense. It is not.

In the case example, if the teacher is reflective or refers to a consultant who is knowledgeable about principles of behavior, she might be able to distribute her attention differently to promote more productive classroom behaviors. For example, she might praise Tommy for attempts to solve problems while ignoring (i.e., arranging extinction for) his inappropriate behaviors. In the process, she will probably discover that Tommy can't do the problems without assistance. Therefore, some additional instruction may be necessary. If she is consistent and if Tommy receives social attention for appropriate behaviors (e.g., numbers written on the page, holding his pencil appropriately) frequently enough to compete with the reinforcing effects of peers' attention for inappropriate behavior, the teacher may witness an increase in appropriate behavior and a decrease in inappropriate behavior.

It will be important for the teacher to keep in mind that Tommy's problem behaviors were strengthened over time and that they may be resistant to extinction for a period. In fact, they may increase briefly if the teacher stops providing social attention for inappropriate behavior. This fact alone is often the reason why adults stop an intervention quickly and conclude, "I tried that but it didn't work."

VI. SUMMARY

Positive reinforcement comprises all procedures in which behavior is strengthened through the response-produced presentation of an object or event. Such procedures can be used to increase desired behavior and to cause it to occur only in appropriate circumstances.

They also can be used to decrease undesired behavior. Thousands of studies document their efficacy with a wide range of clients and target behaviors in many different settings. Although they are not panaceas, positive reinforcement procedures are widely and effectively used by applied behavior analysts and other clinicians.

See Also the Following Articles

Chaining ■ Classical Conditioning ■ Extinction ■ Negative Punishment ■ Negative Reinforcement ■ Operant Conditioning ■ Positive Punishment

Further Reading

Carton, J. S. (1996). The differential effects of tangible rewards and praise on intrinsic motivation: A comparison of cognitive evaluation theory and operant theory. *The Behavior Analyst, 19,* 237–255.

Catania, A. C. (1998). *Learning* (4th ed.). Upper Saddle River, NJ: Prentice Hall.

Eisenberger, R., & Cameron, J. (1996). Detrimental effects of reward: Reality or myth? *American Psychologist, 51,* 1153–1166.

Sulzer-Azaroff, B., & Mayer, G. R. (1991). *Behavior analysis for lasting change.* Fort Worth, TX: Holt, Rinehart, & Winston.

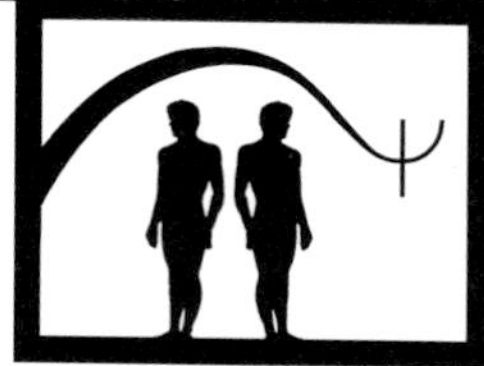

Posttraumatic Stress Disorder

Ann E. Norwood and Robert J. Ursano
Uniformed Services University of the Health Sciences

GLOSSARY

cognitive-behavioral therapies A wide range of programs including anxiety management, exposure treatments, cognitive restructuring, and combinations of these.

cognitive processing therapy A treatment designed especially for female sexual assault victims and uses features of exposure therapy and cognitive therapy.

diagnostic and statistical manual A manual of psychiatric diagnoses and statistics that has been published in multiple editions by the American Psychiatric Press, Inc.

eye-movement desensitization/reprocessing therapy A treatment in which trauma survivors are asked to recall disturbing elements of the trauma while the therapist invokes saccadic eye movements.

exposure therapy A form of therapy that consists of exposure to anxiety-provoking stimuli.

impact of events scale A scale that assesses PTSD symptoms.

stress inoculation training A treatment in which patients learn to manage anxiety that is conditioned at the time of the trauma and then generalized to many situations.

I. INTRODUCTION

The diagnosis of posttraumatic stress disorder (PTSD) was introduced into the *Diagnostic and Statistical Manual (DSM)* as an anxiety disorder in 1980. In the current *DSM* (fourth edition), there are six major diagnostic criteria for PTSD. First, the person must be exposed to a traumatic event in which they experienced or witnessed an event that involved the threat of death or serious injury, and the individual must have experienced significant fear, helplessness, or horror in response to the event. The major symptom criteria are persistent reexperiencing of the event, persistent emotional numbing and avoidance of stimuli associated with the trauma, and persistent arousal symptoms. The duration of the symptoms must be 1 month or more and must cause significant distress or impairment.

Traumatic events occur more often than one might expect. For example, it has been estimated that 7% of the U.S. population is exposed to a major trauma on an annual basis. Lifetime trauma exposure rates in populations are often 50 to 80%. Those who have been exposed to a traumatic event are at risk for developing PTSD and other major psychiatric disorders. Epidemiological studies have found that one-third of women who were sexually assaulted experienced PTSD at some point in their lifetime. Similar rates were found for lifetime PTSD in Vietnam veterans.

A variety of treatments have been used for PTSD. Recent neuroimaging, neurophysiological, and neuroendocrine studies have suggested that PTSD creates biological alterations. These findings have prompted clinicians to investigate the usefulness of pharmacological interventions. However, psychotherapy remains the primary treatment of most PTSD, particularly acute PTSD. This chapter focuses on psychotherapeutic interventions for PTSD. Work on group psychotherapy and debriefing are less systematic and are not reviewed.

II. PSYCHODYNAMIC THERAPIES

A. Description of Treatment

In their 2000 review, Harold S. Kudler, Arthur S. Blank Jr., and Janice L. Krupnick summarized the theoretical basis and research findings of the use of psychodynamic psychotherapy in the treatment of PTSD. They note that brief psychodynamic therapy, as developed by James Mann, can be particularly useful in work with trauma survivors to explore issues of separation and loss. Mardi Horowitz developed a brief psychodynamic psychotherapy specifically for the treatment of trauma survivors. It is a transference-based, 12-session model that focuses on the ways in which the trauma survivor's preexisting personality style and psychological defenses interact with the traumatic experience to affect relationships especially in the context of the therapeutic relationship. Later, Charles Marmar and Michael Freeman developed a brief treatment based on Horowitz's ideas to manage narcissistic regression in the face of trauma. Also building on Horowitz's work, Daniel Brom, Rolf Kleber, and Peter Defares developed a manual on brief psychodynamic psychotherapy for PTSD. Horowitz recently revised his manual on brief psychodynamic therapies for stress response syndromes. His technique is a multimodal brief approach. In this model, systematic case formulations guide decisions on when to use behavioral techniques, cognitive techniques, and/or supportive and expressive dynamic techniques.

In supportive psychotherapy, which is built on the principles of psychodynamic psychotherapy, the therapist's knowledge of defensive structures and transference informs his or her work with PTSD. The defenses against intrusive withdrawal and arousal are strengthened through education, identification of successful defense operations, and attention to interpersonal withdrawal.

Interpersonal therapy is a time-limited, manualized treatment, which incorporates supportive elements into a psychodynamic approach. Rather than focusing on the transference, the therapist explores the patient's relationship with other people as the avenue to identify distress and interpersonal withdrawal. Work is underway to use interpersonal therapy as a group treatment for women with PTSD following sexual or physical assault/abuse.

B. Theoretical Bases

Josef Breuer and Sigmund Freud, in their 1895 *Studies in Hysteria,* proposed that psychological trauma can create psychiatric illness. They hypothesized that if the traumatic memory could be found and removed, the patient would be cured. Later, Freud speculated that hysterical patients defended against their traumatic memories by maintaining them outside of conscious awareness (repression). Physical and psychological symptoms represented a compromise that partially expressed the memory and also expressed the ego's defense against the memory and the feelings accompanying it. Influenced by World War I, Freud attributed psychological trauma to a breakdown in a psychic stimulus barrier in *Beyond the Pleasure Principle.* Trauma survivors' intrusive and avoidant symptoms (essential features of PTSD) were viewed as biphasic attempts to cope with the trauma. Freud hypothesized that survivors repeated the memories in the hope of mastering them (repetition compulsion). Both world wars compelled many therapists to further develop theoretical models and treatments. Abreactive techniques using sodium amytal and hypnosis were paired with support and psychoeducation to treat combat fatigue. Henry Krystal and Robert Jay Lifton documented that overwhelming life events could result in a kind of "death in life." Krystal developed an information-processing model of trauma that postulated that overwhelming events can disable the psyche's ability to use anxiety as a signal for the mobilization of defense. Once this system is disrupted, anxiety and other affects fail to serve psychic needs. Affect may become muted, overwhelming, or inappropriate. The ego, without its normal signal processing, is virtually defenseless. One possible outcome described was alexithymia (a profound disconnection between words and feelings).

More recent approaches focus on psychodynamic psychotherapy's attempt to understand and work through the meaning of symptoms. Reminders represent meaningful fears. Psychodynamic therapy also focuses on the experience of guilt, shame, and interpersonal avoidance. These feelings usually carry associated memories of early life experiences that have become attached to the recent events. Even events after the traumatic event, such as a diagnosis of cancer, can enter the meaning network and become a primary source of sustaining the PTSD symptoms. Attention to the meaning network and its anxiety, defense and transference patterns can aid in dissecting the symptoms from their sources. Attention to the complex countertransference responses of the therapist when treating trauma victims is a major theoretical perspective adopted by all psychotherapies of PTSD.

C. Empirical Studies

Empirical studies of psychodynamic psychotherapy of PTSD are few. During 1993–1995, Mardi Horowitz and his colleagues published work that examined the hypothesis that trauma survivors experienced heightened intrusive and avoidant symptoms related to traumatic memories and themes. The brief psychodynamic psychotherapy that was provided was manualized. They found that when a topic linked to the traumatic event was discussed, it was accompanied by intrusion and avoidance, warding off behaviors, stifling of facial emotional expression, emotionality, and fragmentation of important ideas.

In 1997, Susan Roth and Ronald Batson evaluated a year-long psychodynamic treatment of six adult female survivors of childhood incest with PTSD. There was significant clinical improvement in their diagnoses, trauma themes, and PTSD symptoms.

In 1989, Daniel Brom, Rolf Kelber, and Peter Defares compared the efficacy of trauma desensitization, hypnotherapy, and a brief psychodynamic therapy (based on Horowitz's model) in reducing PTSD symptoms of intrusion and avoidance in 112 survivors of associated traumas and wait-list controls. One limitation of the study was that not all subjects met *DSM-III* criteria for PTSD. They found a reduction in symptoms on the Impact of Events Scale (IES) using desensitization that was higher than the improvement in the other treatments, but was not statistically significant.

D. Clinical Studies

In 1988, Jacob Lindy reported on 37 Vietnam combat veterans, who were treated for PTSD that met *DSM-III* diagnostic criteria. The participants' psychological function and combat experience were assessed. These combat veterans were compared to a volunteer sample of Vietnam veterans who were recruited from clinical and nonclinical sources (n = 200). There was no placebo comparison group, and assignment was not randomized. Treatment was manualized and consisted of opening, working through, and termination phases. Twenty-three of the participants completed the treatment. Significant changes were noted on the Psychiatric Evaluation Form (based on clinical ratings made by independent clinicians, on global ratings made by both patients and therapists), and on the Symptom Checklist-90, the Impact of Events scale, and the Cincinnati Stress Response Schedule).

In 1993, Daniel S. Weiss and Charles Marmar described a 12-session, manualized psychodynamic treatment for adult survivors of single traumatic events. Systematic outcome measures were not used. They reported on results in work with over 200 patients.

E. Summary

Psychodynamic psychotherapy remains a major part of the psychotherapy of PTSD, particularly complex chronic PTSD in which meanings of the trauma have been generalized to the individual's past and present. The unique focus of pschodynamic psychotherapy on the complex countertransference experience with PTSD patients has been widely adopted across all psychotherapies. Psychodynamically informed supportive psychotherapy is perhaps the most widely used form of treatment in severe chronic PTSD with multiple comorbid disorders and in which psychopharmacologic agents are important symptom-reducing factors.

III. COGNITIVE-BEHAVIORAL THERAPIES

Cognitive-behavioral therapies (CBT) have been used widely in the treatment of PTSD and are the most rigorously studied to date. CBT encompasses a wide range of programs, including anxiety management, exposure treatments, cognitive restructuring, and combinations of these. Edna Foa has been instrumental in the use of CBT for PTSD and strengthening research methodologies of psychotherapeutic treatment of PTSD.

A. Exposure Therapy

1. Prolonged Imaginal and in Vivo Exposure Therapy

a. Description of Treatment Exposure therapy consists of exposure to anxiety-provoking stimuli. The core feature of all these methods is that the person is confronted by the frightening stimuli until his or her anxiety dissipates. There are a number of different techniques, which vary in terms of whether the stimulus is real or imaginal; whether the length of the exposure is short or long, and how much anxiety the subject experiences during the exposure (e.g., high for flooding, moderate to low for desensitization). Generally, a hierarchy of anxiety-causing stimuli is developed. Two types of exposures are employed, imaginal and *in vivo*. Imaginal exposure generally consists of the patient talking about the trauma as if it is happening in the present. In contrast, *in vivo* exposure entails the patient confronting situations that are objectively safe, but have been avoided due to fear generalized from the original trauma. For example, if a person were robbed on the subway and continued to avoid it, the goal of exposure would be for the person to ultimately return to the subway. Flooding begins with exposure to the strongest anxiety-provoking item, whereas other systematic desensitization begins with items of low intensity. Exposure therapy is often used in combination with other components such as relaxation training.

b. Theoretical Basis Exposure therapy is based on learning theory. It has been used very successfully in the treatment of phobias. Because PTSD shares features of phobic disorders, it was hypothesized that exposure therapy would be of benefit for PTSD. Elements of PTSD are believed to be conditioned. Using the classical conditioning paradigm, the trauma (unconditional stimulus) is paired with a neutral stimulus, for example darkness. The previously neutral stimulus, darkness, now becomes a conditioned stimulus associated with a conditioned fear response. Operant conditioning maintains the fear as the traumatized individual used avoidance (e.g., not going out after dark) to diminish anxiety and fear. The avoidant behavior, itself, perpetuates the fear and anxiety. By forcing the traumatized individual to face the conditioned stimulus (threat), the patient learns that the conditioned stimulus no longer needs to be avoided.

c. Empirical Studies There have been 12 studies on the use of imaginal and *in vivo* exposure therapy for PTSD, 8 of which meet the most stringent criteria for methodology. Four well-controlled studies and two uncontrolled studies of the use of exposure therapy with Vietnam veterans have been conducted. All found positive results. There have been two well-controlled studies examining the effects of exposure therapy with female rape victims, which also found improvement in symptomatology. In addition, four studies have examined exposure therapy's efficacy for a variety of other traumas.

d. Summary Studies of exposure therapy have demonstrated the strong data supporting efficacy of exposure treatments for PTSD. Imaginal exposure has generally become a part of all psychotherapies as the therapist frequently brings the patient back to the traumatic event to talk, recall, reconstruct, and reexperience in a safe controlled manner the events and their subsequent consequences. It has been important to recognize that a traumatic event is rarely a single moment in time. Therefore, identifying the traumatic event as it extended over time means exposure can be more complex than it may first appear.

2. Eye-Movement Desensitization/ Reprocessing (EMDR)

EMDR, developed by Francine Shapiro in 1995, incorporates elements of imaginal exposure therapy. In this treatment, trauma survivors are asked to recall disturbing elements of the trauma while the therapist moves a finger back and forth in front of the patient's eyes. The resultant saccadic eye movements in conjunction with the disturbing images are hypothesized to result in neural reprocessing of the trauma and symptom resolution. There has been substantial controversy surrounding this treatment, focusing primarily on the theoretical basis regarding the role of eye movements. Research findings have been mixed on its efficacy but have suggested that improvement is more likely due to the exposure therapy elements rather than the eye movements.

3. Systematic Desensitization

a. Description of Treatment Systematic desensitization is a form of exposure therapy developed by Joseph Wolpe in 1958. Based on reciprocal inhibition, it posits that an individual cannot be relaxed and anxious simultaneously. A hierarchy of the patient's fears is developed. In the first part of the therapy, the patient is taught relaxation training. Once proficiency in relaxation is attained, the patient is gradually exposed to the trauma-related items that frighten him or her, starting with the least feared situation object or memory. The patient is instructed to note the onset of anxiety symptoms, and the treatment is paused while the patient initiates relaxation techniques. When the patient has regained a sense of comfort, the exposure resumes. This cycle continues until the patient can tolerate all the stimuli on the fear hierarchy without anxiety.

b. Empirical Studies While there have been six studies of systematic desensitization for the treatment of traumatic stress reactions, however, only the 1989 study by Daniel Brom, Rolf Kleber, and Peter Defares (described earlier) was well controlled.

c. Summary Although several studies have found that systematic desensitization was effective in reducing trauma-related symptom, the studies suffer methodological problems. Most researchers have moved away from systematic desensitization, preferring exposure therapy. These two approaches have much in common and emphasize the importance of understanding and working with the actual events of the trauma and the cognitive and emotional responses.

B. Cognitive Therapy

1. Description of Treatment

Cognitive therapy was developed in 1976 by Aaron Beck for the treatment of depression and was later applied to the treatment of anxiety. Beck theorized that it is the individual's appraisal or interpretation of an event, rather than the event itself that determines mood states. "Automatic thoughts" are dysfunctional thoughts that interpret events with a negative bias that, in turn, contribute to negative feelings such as anxiety, depression, anger, and shame. In cognitive therapy, patients are taught to identify these automatic thoughts, challenge those that are unhelpful or inaccurate, and replace them with more accurate or beneficial thoughts. For patients with PTSD, it has been postulated that patients see the world as a dangerous place and view themselves as incompetent to navigate it. In order to be successful, treatments for PTSD are believed to need to change these distorted cognitions. Treatment programs are particularly focused on patients' self-concepts and appraisal of safety. A specific form of cognitive therapy, cognitive processing therapy, for sexual assault victims with PTSD has been suggested. This model focuses on correcting dysfunctional cognitions thought to be common in rape victims related to self-esteem, safety, trust, power, and intimacy.

2. Empirical Studies

One well-controlled study found that cognitive therapy, exposure therapy, and the combination of the two were all equally effective but more effective than relaxation therapy for patients who had sustained various traumas. Another study comparing cognitive therapy and systematic desensitization with wait-list controls, found cognitive therapy and systematic desensitization to be equally effective and superior to the wait-list controls. A third study found cognitive therapy to be as effective as exposure therapy in producing improvement relative to pretreatment for survivors of a variety of traumas.

3. Summary

Two controlled studies have demonstrated that cognitive therapy is effective in reducing trauma-related symptoms. Cognitive therapy focuses on the effects of the traumatic event as it spreads through time and across personality dimensions. In general, the cognitive therapies and the psychodynamic therapies often overlap on their goal to alter appraisals although their techniques differ.

C. Cognitive Processing Therapy

1. Description of Treatment

Cognitive process therapy (CPT) has components of exposure therapy and cognitive therapy. Patricia Resick and Monica Schnicke developed CPT specifically for rape-related PTSD. The exposure element consists of developing and reading a detailed history of the rape. This narrative is used to discover "stuck points," elements of the rape that challenge previously held beliefs or are especially difficult to accept. These "stuck points" are then addressed in the cognitive component. The cognitive component teaches patient skills in examining and challenging distorted cognitions, for example, self-blame, and attempts at "undoing" the event.

2. Empirical Studies

In 1992, Resick and Schnicke reported that cognitive processing therapy was effective in reducing PTSD and related symptoms in 19 female sexual assault survivors compared to a wait-list control group. This study was not randomized.

3. Summary

Cognitive processing therapy has only been used with women who have been sexually assaulted. Because it was designed specifically for this population, it requires modification for use in other settings.

D. Anxiety Management Therapies

In contrast to the other therapies described in this chapter, anxiety management therapies do not aim to change underlying beliefs or structures that maintain PTSD. Rather, their goal is to teach patients to manage their symptoms.

1. Stress Inoculation Training

a. Description/Theory In 1974, Donald Meichenbaum developed stress inoculation training (SIT) as an anxiety management treatment. SIT assists patients in learning to manage anxiety that is conditioned at the time of the trauma and then generalizes to many situations. Dean Kilpatrick, Lois Veronen, and Patricia

Resick modified the program to treat victims of sexual assault. Their program included training in muscle relaxation and breathing, education, guided self-dialogue, and thought stopping.

b. Empirical Studies All four studies of stress inoculation training have used women who have been sexually assaulted as subjects. Two studies had excellent methodology whereas two were less well controlled. As noted earlier in this chapter, Edna Foa has performed some of the most rigorous studies in the field. She and her colleagues have found that nine 90-min sessions of stress inoculation training were effective in reducing PTSD. SIT was also found to be as effective as peer counseling in a study by another group. A study comparing SIT with supportive therapy and assertiveness training, found them all to be equally effective.

c. Summary Although stress inoculation training has been shown to be efficacious in treating women who have been sexually assaulted, it is unclear whether this finding can be generalized to other trauma populations. In general, SIT is often seen as a combination of cognitive, behavioral, and relaxation elements.

2. Biofeedback and Relaxation Training

Biofeedback and relaxation therapy have also been used as techniques for managing anxiety for patients with PTSD. In biofeedback, patients learn to control their physiological responses. They learn to decrease muscle tension by watching their electromyographic (EMG) activity change on a monitor. Only one study has examined biofeedback in a controlled design, comparing it to eye-movement desensitization and reprocessing (EMDR) plus milieu and to relaxation therapy plus milieu. Biofeedback was not found to be effective. EMDR in conjunction with milieu therapy was more effective. Another group used a combination of biofeedback and relaxation training to treat six Vietnam veterans with PTSD. They reported symptom improvement on all measures. Biofeedback was also found to be helpful in reducing muscle tension, nightmares, and flashbacks in another group of Vietnam veterans.

IV. SUMMARY

The psychotherapeutic treatment of PTSD is increasingly studied with rigorous methodological designs. No studies have rigorously evaluated combined psychotherapeutic and medication treatments. Across the psychotherapies, there is a developing consensus on the need to attend to the specifics of the traumatic event. The interpersonal experience over time after the event, the meaning of the traumatic event, distortions of interpersonal and emotional perspection that derive from the experience of the trauma and for therapists to be alert to the countertransference issues in these often profoundly terrorized patients. The complex comorbidity often seen in PTSD also means that multiple therapeutic modalities are often needed in treatment.

See Also the Following Articles

Anxiety Disorders: Brief Intensive Group Cognitive Behavior Therapy ■ Biofeedback ■ Cognitive Behavior Therapy ■ Exposure ■ Eye Movement Desensitization and Reprocessing ■ Relaxation Training ■ Self-Control Desensitization ■ Trauma Management Therapy

Further Reading

Foa, E. B. (2000). Psychosocial treatment of posttraumatic stress disorder. *Journal of Clinical Psychiatry, 61*(5), 43–48.

Foa, E. B., Keane, T. M., & Friedman, M. J. (2000). *Effective treatments for PTSD.* New York: Guilford Press.

Fullerton, C. S., & Ursano, R. J. (Eds.). *Posttraumatic stress disorder: Acute and long-term responses to trauma and disaster.* Washington, DC: American Psychiatric Press.

Lindy, J. (1988). *Vietnam: A casebook.* New York: Brunner/Mazel.

Raphael, B. & Wilson, J. P. (2000). *Psychological Debriefing.* Cambridge, England: Cambridge University Press.

Saigh, P. A., & Bremner, J. D. (1999). *Posttraumatic stress disorder: A comprensive text.* Boston: Allyn and Bacon.

Sonnenberg, S. M., Blank, A. S., & Talbot, J. A. (1985). *The trauma of war.* Washington, DC: American Psychiatric Press.

Young, B., & Blake, D. (Eds.). (1999). *Group treatments for posttraumatic stress disorder.* New York: Brunner/Mazel.

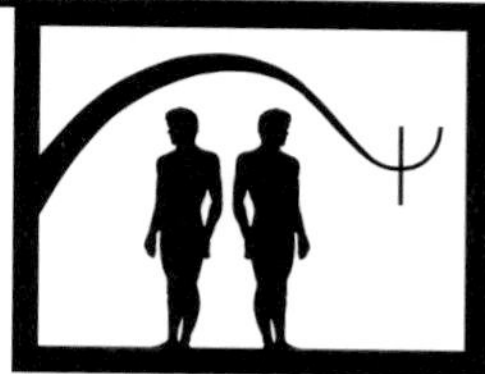

Primary Care Behavioral Pediatrics

Patrick C. Friman
University of Nevada, Reno

Nathan Blum
Children's Seashore House of Children's Hospital of Philadelphia

GLOSSARY

Berkson's bias The tendency in clinical research to study clinical populations with compound problems, especially hospitalized populations. The findings from the pertinent study are skewed because of the severity of the study groups.

encopresis Frequent fecal accidents occurring after the age of 5 and not due to an organic condition.

enuresis Frequent urinary accidents occurring after the age of 5 and not due to an organic condition.

incontinence Urinary or fecal incidents that occur in clothing or bedding.

primary care Branch of medicine devoted to prevention and early intervention.

temperament An aspect of a person's behavioral style that is more inherited than learned. Temperamental characteristics involve dispositions toward emotional reactions, mood shifts, and sensitivity to stimulation.

Tourette's syndrome An impulse control disorder involving the habitual emission of vocal sounds and motor movements referred to as tics. The tics sometimes involve obscene gestures or words.

trichotillomania Habitual hair pulling preceded by a mounting urge to pull and accompanied by detectable hair loss.

within series ABAB experimental design An experimental method applied to single subjects wherein the subject is intermittently exposed to treatment and no-treatment conditions. Differences in behavior observed during the varying conditions form the basis for conclusions about the effectiveness of treatment.

Behavioral pediatrics is the branch of pediatrics that addresses child behavior problems that populate the intersection between clinical child psychology, child psychiatry, and pediatric health care. Although problems of importance to behavioral pediatrics occur across all domains of medicine, the field upholds the longstanding tradition in pediatric medicine of emphasizing prevention over treatment or rehabilitation. In the words of Stanford Friedman, an early architect of the field of behavioral pediatrics, "curative and rehabilitative orientation (is) always second best to preventing the disease or defect in the first place...". This chapter focuses on the evaluation and treatment of child behavior problems that initially, and often only, present in primary care. We will refer to this as primary care behavioral pediatrics (PCBP). PCBP is an eclectic field but most practitioners are either primary care pediatricians who take a special interest in the management of behavior problems in their practices or pediatric psychologists whose practice includes close collaboration with their clients' primary care physicians.

I. DESCRIPTION OF PCBP TREATMENT

The term psychotherapy may not be appropriate for PCBP; it is grounded in a context of psychopathology or mental illness and is thus inconsistent with the preventive context of PCBP. Many definitions for psychotherapy exist but the most traditional and widely held involve primarily verbally based, processed-oriented treatment the goal of which is remediation of psychopathology or mental illness. In many cases the behavior problems seen in primary care are not indications of child psychopathology or mental illness. Rather they arise out of problematic interactions between children and their environment. For example, confident, experienced parents with abundant social support may not view their 8-week-old child's crying for 2 to 3 hours a day, which is less than one standard deviation above the expected mean for daily duration of crying for children this age, as a problem. However, less confident, experienced, and supported parents may interpret the same amount of crying in their similarly aged child not only as a serious problem but also as indictment of their parenting skills. These less experienced parents, however, might be unconcerned if the crying averaged only 1 to 2 hours a day (slightly less than the expected mean). Thus it would be inappropriate to assume that the crying, the average daily duration of which is above the mean but well within the range of normal, is an indication of psychological disturbance in the child or skill deficiencies in the parents. Providing health education about the extent to which behaviors such as extended crying are part of the normal variations in a child's life is an important part of PCBP practice and one we will discuss in greater detail later in the chapter.

Having emphasized that many behavior problems seen in PCBP are not reflective of psychopathology, it is also important to note that PCBP acknowledges the existence and importance of child psychopathology. The PCBP view, however, is that although the presence of psychopathology is always accompanied by behavior problems, the reverse is not necessarily true, especially for problems initially presenting in PCBP. Nonetheless, at least some of the problems presenting in PCBP are reflective of psychopathology and thus PCBP practitioners must be able to recognize when children have major disorders and be willing to refer those children to specialists. Moreover, a fundamental reason PCBP is viewed as preventive care is based on the belief that persistence of problematic interactions between children and their environment increases the likelihood that psychopathology will develop. The care provided for problems presenting in PCBP involves two intersected kinds of intervention, supportive counseling and prescriptive behavioral treatment.

A. Supportive Counseling

The primary goals of supportive counseling in PCBP are to provide emotional support and health education. To be effective, practitioners must be able to communicate care and compassion for parents of children exhibiting problem behaviors and an appreciation for the distress and disharmony those problems cause the family. Additionally, practitioners must have informative and persuasive answers for the parents' questions about the problems and a prime function those answers must serve is demystification. Parents want to know why their child is exhibiting the problematic behaviors and typically the answers they obtain on their own are overly pessimistic. Fortunately, many troubling aspects of childhood are actually normal and expected. For example, extended crying in the first 3 months, although stressful, is normal. Incontinence in children younger than 5, although unpleasant, is normal especially for boys. Limit testing, although exasperating, is common throughout early childhood. Separation anxiety spikes between 11 and 14 months, negativism is common in the second and third year, and thumb sucking is prevalent and harmless up to age 4. There are many other examples. The successful PCBP practitioner is knowledgeable about most or all of these and can communicate that knowledge in a respectful, accepting, and compassionate way.

In some cases supportive counseling is sufficient to address the presenting complaints. PCBP practitioners can reassure parents of a child presenting with behavior problems by informing them that the problems are not unusual at their child's age and are likely to resolve within specified age limits. For example, separation anxiety diminishes after 14 months in most children. However, if the problems persist (or emerge) beyond these age limits, substantially worsen, or begin to cause health concerns, supportive counseling is supplemented by prescriptive behavioral treatment recommendations.

B. Prescriptive Behavioral Treatment

When a child behavior problem presents in PCBP, practitioners place it in its appropriate developmental and prognostic context via supportive counseling (as indicated above). If the problem does not involve one of the major psychiatric conditions (e.g., major depression) at the boundary of PCBP, practitioners recommend a series of therapeutic steps to be followed at home (or school) to address the problem. The therapeutic advice typically emphasizes procedure over process and most procedures recommended are derived from the more pragmatic parts of the behavioral sciences, particularly those focused on learning and development. For example, according to Edward Christophersen, another major architect of the field, "Behavioral pediatrics is the application of the principles and procedures of the behavioral sciences to the prevention or resolution of problems encountered in the practice of pediatrics." Prescriptive behavioral treatments are the primary methods PCBP practitioners employ to remedy behavior problems. Treatments that work are valued for their own sake and their importance is not diminished because they are at odds with this or that theory. Efficiency, effectiveness, and acceptance are valued over and above theoretical consistency, precision, and scope. Furthermore, PCBP treatment, although predominantly verbal and thus consistent topographically with traditional child psychotherapy, differs from it in at least two important ways.

First and perhaps most fundamental, parents (or primary caregivers) rather than children are the direct recipients of treatment (i.e., supportive counseling and the recommendations that make up the prescriptive behavioral treatment regimens). Children are, of course, the ultimate recipients of PCBP treatment, regardless of its form and they are often present during its discussion and even participate in its preparation. But the most common vehicle for PCBP treatment is educational and prescriptive advice pertaining to the parent portion of parent–child interactions. Although the comparison is not perfect, it may be helpful to view PCBP treatment as a specialized form of parent training. The critical point, however, is that although child problems are the reason for PCBP treatment, parents are the proximal recipients of the therapeutic advice pertaining to those problems. Thus PCBP treatment is fundamentally different from traditional child psychotherapy wherein the child is the direct recipient of treatment.

Second, because of limitations on time and the emphasis on procedure in pediatric settings, PCBP treatments are often brief and protocol driven. In this respect they differ dramatically from the process-based, time-intensive interventions that characterize traditional child psychotherapy. PCBP treatment, however, is consonant with the increasing emphasis on empirically supported treatment and manualized practice in contemporary psychotherapy. The therapeutic armamentarium of the PCBP practitioners includes a variety of procedures each with abundant empirical support including (but not limited to) time out, contingency management, home-school notes, simple point systems, and various procedures for simple habits, chronic incontinence, bedtime struggles, and feeding problems.

C. More on the Practitioners

Because of the preventive emphasis in PCBP, clinical expertise in the treatment of major psychiatric problems of childhood is not a prerequisite for practitioners in the field. PCBP therapists, however, must have a strong appreciation for the variations commonly seen in normal child development, which then allows them to distinguish behavior problems that are best viewed as interactional from those that represent psychopathology. For example, hair play, twirling, and pulling in toddlers, although potentially problematic and certainly important enough to address in a PCBP visit, is not necessarily reflective of psychopathology or indicative of true trichotillomania. But compulsive hair pulling of long standing in a 12-year-old girl is a much more serious condition, one typically requiring more intensive care than that provided in PCBP. Thumb sucking in preschoolers is more likely a benign source of self-soothing than a malignant sign of oral fixation or regressive personality disorder. But chronic sucking in a school-aged child can be a serious problem and should, at a minimum, be regarded as a threat to optimal social development. Soiling in young children is much more likely to result from constipation than from psychic mechanisms such as resentment, regression, or anal fixation. Yet soiling in older children unaccompanied by constipation is likely to be the result of potentially serious psychogenic variables and unlikely to respond to a procedure-based PCBP treatment. There are many other examples.

Another important qualification for PCBP therapists is working knowledge of the biologic variables that are functionally related to child behavior problems. Many of the behavior problems managed in PCBP have important biologic dimensions (e.g., enuresis, encopresis, recurrent abdominal pain). To be effective, PCBP practitioners must at a minimum have a rudimentary understanding of variables such as bowel and bladder function, sleep physiology, and pain sensation.

Because the child problems that are appropriate for PCBP are diverse, the field is professionally eclectic. Thus primary care physicians (e.g., pediatricians, family practitioners) can specialize in behavioral pediatrics just as readily as pediatric, school, and clinical child psychologists or psychiatrists. And there are a growing number of specialized training programs for these various types of professionals. The limited emphasis on psychopathology and the eclectic makeup of the field make the PCBP orientation to child behavior problems a novel, perhaps even unusual, but nonetheless important candidate for an encyclopedia on psychotherapy.

Generally PCBP will favor those whose orientation to practice is guided by science more than art, whose claim to expertise is predicated on empiricism more than clinical or ex cathedra authority, and whose methods are typified more by procedure than process. Thus, there are similarities between therapists in PCBP and those in some branches of psychology (e.g., behavior therapy, applied behavior analysis, pediatric psychology) but not those in others (e.g., psychoanalysis, existentialist psychology, human potential psychology).

II. THEORETICAL BASES

Coverage of all the theoretical bases that underlie PCBP is beyond the scope of this chapter. Because of its inherent pragmatism and largely agnostic stance toward most psychological theories, virtually all of the principles of behavior, learning, and development that could be exploited for therapeutic benefit are potentially part of the theoretical base. Rather than providing shallow coverage of a large number of relevant principles, we will more fully cover four basic assumptions that are pertinent to supportive counseling and central to prescriptive behavioral treatment: (1) individual differences and temperament are real and important; (2) effective use of behavior change language is critical to effective management of behavior problems; (3) effective management of behavior problems requires more emphasis on what children do than on what they say; (4) child learning is governed largely by repetition leading to experiential contrast.

A. Individual Differences and Temperament

As emphasized above, the origin of behavioral problems presenting in PCBP usually involves an interaction between child characteristics and environmental variables. Although psychopathology is possible, it is infrequently present. A more accurate and less stigmatic perspective involves child behavior that is safely within the wide range of normal variation in development and/or behavioral style but that is outside of, or at odds with, environmental (e.g., parental) expectations. As stated by Stella Chess and Alexander Thomas, pioneering researchers in the area of individual variation, a good fit between an individual and the environment occurs.

> when the properties of the environment and its expectations and demands are in accord with an organism's own capacities, motivations, and style of behavior. When this consonance between organism and environment is present, optimal development in a progressive direction is possible. "Poorness of fit" involves discrepancies and dissonances between environmental opportunities and demands and the capacities and characteristics of the organism so that distorted development and maladaptive functioning occur.

In other words, misinterpretation of child skill level (i.e., under or over) and misunderstanding of normal individual differences cause discrepancies between what parents expect of a child and what the child can and does do. These discrepancies, in turn, result in problematic parent–child interactions and, pertinent to this chapter, many of the problems presenting in PCBP. For example, overinterpretation of children's cognitive abilities is widespread (and is discussed later in the section on effective use of behavior change language).

Variations in developmental processes can also contribute to the onset of child behavior problems. For example, variations in the development of sleep architecture can contribute to a range of potential bedtime problems such as infant night waking and sleep terrors in toddlers. Variations in child sensitivity to bladder distension, especially during sleep, can contribute to enuresis. Variations in appetite, especially the decreases that often accompany the natural reduction in growth rate during the second year of life, can lead to difficulties at mealtime. These, and many other examples not mentioned, underscore the theoretical assumption of PCBP that the process of development and its variation clearly influences the behavioral concerns likely to be seen in PCBP.

Elevated parental concern also contributes to child behavior problems and when variations in child behavioral style or temperament conflict with parental lifestyles, elevated concern is very likely. For example, a child with a low activity level may concern active athletic parents, but may not be a concern to less active parents. A toddler who is hungry or sleepy at irregular times may concern parents who are committed to a regimented schedule but may not concern parents in a less tightly scheduled family. The cluster of temperamental characteristics that is most likely to conflict with preferred lifestyles, especially for new parents, includes irregular biologic rhythms, frequent withdrawal from new stimuli, slow adaptation, frequent negative mood, and high intensity responding. This cluster is believed to occur in approximately 10 to 15% of children and its presence significantly increases the probability of parental concern and correspondingly, the probability of reportable behavior problems. But its presence in some children is of minimal concern to parents and correspondingly, the probability of behavior problems is substantially reduced.

The capacity to recognize and describe how variations in child behavioral style and temperament can conflict with parental expectations and lifestyles is a critical component of supportive counseling. Use of this capacity can help parents understand why some of their attempts at management (e.g., those recommended by family, friends, the media) have failed with their child. It can also provide relief for parents who have been on the receiving end of the widespread tendency to view child behavior problems as reflective of poor parenting and/or child psychopathology. The science of temperament helps explain why some obviously caring and talented parents sometimes have difficult children. These explanations and interpretations are necessary but sometimes insufficient for successful outcomes, however, and interventions that improve the interaction between child temperament, family environment, and parent teaching style are sometimes needed.

These interventions usually involve a combination of modifying the learning environment and teaching the child the behaviors necessary for meeting environmental requirements. For example, parents of an inattentive 4-year-old could be taught to use good eye contact and one-step instructions when teaching the child (a modification of the environment) while the child could be taught to follow the one-step instructions. A child who has tantrums when instructed to change activities (e.g., come to dinner) may have a temperamental difficulty of adapting to transitions. Teaching parents to provide warnings for incipient transitions may help their child cope with the changes and comply with the related commands. But the child would still need to be taught that a tantrum is not an acceptable response to an upsetting situation. There are many other examples that underscore the importance role theory and research on individual differences and temperament play in the practice of PCBP.

B. Effective Use of Behavior Change Language

From the earliest stages of human life, language is such a ubiquitous presence that subtle but powerful aspects of its unfolding development are widely missed or at least largely misunderstood. The result is a high likelihood of mismatches between parental assumptions about child knowledge and what the children actually understand. Fortunately, due to developmentally beneficial processes such as modeling, the mismatches are beneficial in many parent–child interactions. But when the interactions involve parental attempts to change child behavior (e.g., discipline), these mismatches can frustrate parental attempts to teach, thwart child efforts to learn, perpetuate established behavior problems, inaugurate new problems, and deteriorate parent–child relations. There are multiple behavior-relevant aspects of child language development and we will cover the two that emerge most frequently in PCBP, the capacity to conserve and instructional control.

1. Conservation

Although many child researchers have demonstrated the incremental nature of language development, perhaps the first, and if not, certainly the most authoritative, was Jean Piaget. Among his many discoveries was the relatively slow development of the child's ability to meaningfully understand abstractions and abstract relations. Piaget's studies and related theories in this regard are too multifaceted and systemized for a full discussion here, but his concept of conservation is sufficiently general to serve as vehicle for our purposes. Conservation is largely synonymous with abstraction; it involves the capacity to conserve a quality of an object or event and meaningfully apply to another object or event. The capacity to do so when objects or events closely resemble each other emerges early but when they do not, when the objects or events are formally or contextually dissimilar, the capacity to conserve emerges late (averaging between 5 and 7 years) and does not fully develop until the teen years.

Piaget (and other investigators) conducted numerous studies that demonstrated the young child's limited capacity to conserve. For example, when asked to hold a pound of lead and a pound of feathers and then asked which weighed more young children usually said the lead. When in the presence of two containers with identical volume capacities but different forms (e.g., one tall and thin the other short and fat) and asked which held more water young children usually said the tall one.

When shown two similar apples, one cut into fourths and one cut into eighths, and asked which they preferred, young children picked the one with eighths ("because there was more apple"). When shown five quarters in a bunch and five quarters in a row and asked which grouping had more quarters children usually said the row. There are many other examples. Those above generally pertain to children younger than 7 years of age. But there are also related tests that have been conducted with older children and they too underscore the difficulty children have in seeing sameness in the presence of manifest topographical or contextual difference.

One example involves the water level task. Typically the test includes four pictures of containers, holding an identical amount of water, arrayed in a row. There are usually several such rows and in each row the containers are positioned at different angles. The angles are different within rows and identical across rows. In each container a line depicts the level of water within. One row accurately depicts what happens to the water level when the angle of the container changes (i.e., the water level remains the same, parallel to the bottom of the container, regardless of the position of the container). In the other rows water levels are inaccurately depicted (e.g., they change with the angle of the container). Tests of the water level task have revealed that even early teens will sometimes fail to identify the row with the accurately depicted water levels. In conclusion, children—especially younger children—have difficulty seeing sameness in objects or events that have substantially different physical or contextual characteristics.

Conservation is important to PCBP because the effectiveness of behavior change language heavily depends on the child's capacity to discern similarity in differing behavioral episodes. No two episodes are completely alike and thus, to learn conduct-relevant relations between combinations of episodes, children must be able to conserve aspects that form the basis of the relevancy. For example, the inception of a disciplinary event often includes a parental attempt to forcefully assert similarities between a current and a previous behavioral episode (e.g., "Isn't that the same thing I warned you about yesterday?" "Didn't your father tell you not to do that last week?"). There are at least two conservation-based assumptions implicit in parental comments of this kind: (1) the child should have been able to see conduct-relevant sameness in the indicated behavioral episodes; and (2) the child can currently see the sameness because the parent has pointed it out verbally. But if conservation is weakly developed, which is true of most children younger than 7 years, there is a good chance both assumptions are incorrect. For example, if children have a difficult time seeing quantitative sameness between five quarters in a row and five quarters in a bunch, it seems safe to say they would have much more difficulty seeing conduct-relevant sameness between something they have just done and something they did hours or even days ago. Furthermore, the test situations with quarters are simple and uniform with the exception of the differing arrangement of the quarters. Behavioral episodes, however, are often very complex and differ in many ways including time frames, persons present, and physical locations.

Additionally, when conducting tests of conservation capacities in the laboratory, investigators exhibit calmness, acceptance, perhaps even gentleness. As much as possible, investigators attempt to expunge any hint of disappointment, judgment, or possible punishment. Most children respond in kind (e.g., by cooperating, trying their best). But in the prototypical disciplinary event, parents demonstratively exhibit disappointment, judgment, and sometimes anger and the possibility of punishment is always implicit and often very explicit. Many (probably most) children respond emotionally (e.g., by crying, yelling, denying). A large scientific literature shows that high levels of emotional arousal substantially diminish cognitive functioning. While in an intensely emotional interaction with their parents, children are probably functioning cognitively at a level much lower than their chronological age. Thus even children who exhibit a developed capacity to conserve in routine situations may be unable to do so in disciplinary situations.

2. Instructional Control

Many child behavior problems involve children failing to do what they are told to do by their parents and many of these failures occur because parental instructions are unclear and/or too complex. Similar to the discussion on conservation, mismatches between parent expectations and child understanding are the central problem. These mismatches are generally the result of parental overestimates of the clarity of their instructions and/or of their children's capacity to follow those instructions. Three decades of research on parent–child interactions and on parent training programs has shown strong correlations between vague instructions and delayed development of child instructional control. A representative (but not exhaustive) list of exemplar vague instructions includes those that are question-based (e.g., "Are you going to put that away?"), indirect (e.g.,

"You know you should really be getting ready for school"), veiled (e.g., "Somebody left the door open"), or multistep (e.g., "Go down stairs, pick up your clothes, sort out the dirty ones, put them in a basket, and bring them here"). It is important to note that instructional control is not necessarily achievable through a focus on clarity alone. Everyday exchanges between parents and children necessarily involve diminished clarity and it is ultimately necessary for children to learn to understand and follow instructions that are vague, offhand, imbedded in other grammatical structures (e.g., questions), or communicated through vocal inflection more than through word arrangement. To become proficient at following instructions in their everyday form, however, children must first have abundant practice at following instructions that are in a clear, simple, direct form. Without this preliminary practice, many children are slow to develop optimal instructional control skills and more likely to exhibit problem behavior as a result.

Two related findings from developmental psychology are among the more ironic and counterintuitive aspects of early child language and they are also directly relevant to the language of behavior change (especially for children between 2 and 4 years of age). The first is that children respond to instructions that involve action onset (i.e., "do" or "start" commands) more readily than to instructions that involve action offset (i.e., "don't" or "stop" commands). The ironic aspect is that parents are much more frequent users of "don't" or "stop" than of "do" or "start" instructions. The counterintuitive aspect is that telling a child to do something (i.e., other than what they are currently doing) can be a more effective way to halt the activity than actually telling them to stop.

The second finding is that young children often respond more to vocally intensified components within an instruction than to its semantic content. For example, when issuing an instruction such as "whatever you do, don't drop that cup" a parent may say the last three words much more intensively than the first four, resulting in a simple instruction, ostensible for the child, to drop the cup, inside of a more complex instruction, intended by the parent, to do the exact opposite. The ironic aspect is that attempts to ensure instructional compliance through selectively placed vocal intensity can result in noncompliance with the instructions issued. The counterintuitive aspect is that this noncompliance actually reflects instructional control, albeit with the instructions understood by the child and not the ones intended by the parent.

In conclusion, mismatches between parental assumptions (and expectancies) about child knowledge and actual child understanding are common, especially in early childhood. These mismatches, reflected in the language used by parents in their interactions with their children, set the occasion for problems especially when the interactions involve parental attempts to modify child behavior. A theoretical assumption of PCBP is that the mismatches play an important part in the inauguration and perpetuation of child behavior problems. A core goal in PCBP is to train parents to use language more effectively, especially when attempting to establish and enforce rules, implement discipline, and manage behavior problems. A major emphasis is placed on use of simple language, but care is taken to explain that use of complex language when the parental goal is not child behavior change is not problematic, that it can be beneficial. For example, modeling new and/or complex language can expedite children's ability to use and understand it. The purpose of behavior change interactions, however, is to teach children to exhibit appropriate behavior in everyday life (e.g., not to leave the house without asking) not to expand their command of complex language. To enhance effectiveness of behavior change language, especially in the early stages of child training, clear, simple, and direct should be the rule not the exception.

C. Emphasis on Doing

Another theoretical assumption of PCBP rests on a distinction between two types of knowing, knowing how to do and knowing how to say (or to specify verbally what is to be done). Although not the first to draw this distinction, the philosopher Gilbert Ryle most effectively brought it widespread attention with publication of his book, *The Concept of Mind* in 1949. The distinction has been drawn in many other ways since then (e.g., cognitive knowing versus behavioral knowing, knowing a rule versus behaving consistent with the rule, theory versus practice). The distinction is the basis for a theoretical assumption of PCBP that has three fundamental components: (1) knowing how to say does not entail knowing how to do; (2) adult attempts to change child behavior typically emphasize saying much more than doing; (3) the combination of 1 and 2 is an important source of child behavior problems.

For example, during toilet training it is routine to ask 2- and 3-year-old children if they have to go to the bathroom. Accurately answering the question can be difficult for such young children. First they must determine whether the question refers merely to a change in location (i.e., just going into the bathroom) or to an act of elimination. When (more accurately if) the children ascertain that the question involves elimination, an accurate answer requires that they examine their own bodily responses and determine whether their bowel is full and/or their bladder is distended and therefore that an act of elimination is imminent. If imminence is determined, the children then have to decide whether it is in their best interests to say so. Children in the early stages of toilet training are typically in Pampers or Pull-ups, both of which protect them from discomfort that would otherwise result from wetting or soiling themselves. In the absence of a toilet training program that reprograms the natural contingencies, most young children would typically rather eliminate in the Pampers or Pull-ups than stop what they are doing, go into the bathroom, take off their clothes, sit on the toilet, and attempt elimination there.

Thus the difficulty occasioned by the question "do you have to go to the bathroom?" is potentially problematic in at least five ways. First, the question places emphasis on an answer about toileting and not on a toileting action. In other words it calls for children to say, not to do. Second, the developmental limitations of 2- and 3-year-old children, coupled with the contingencies that typically prevail in interactions involving toileting, dramatically decrease the chances of an affirmative answer even when elimination is imminent. Third, nonaffirmative answers in such situations (e.g., child says "no" and has an accident shortly thereafter) set the occasion for punishment (or at least unpleasant parent–child interactions) because such answers make it seem as if the child has misbehaved (e.g., by being dishonest, stubborn, or stupid). Fourth, as a result of punishing exchanges during or following toileting episodes, toileting situations and behavior can acquire aversive properties. Fifth, young children will tend to avoid such situations and behavior in the future, resulting in delayed development of toileting skills.

A focus on doing instead of saying at the beginning of parent–child interactions involving toileting can obviate these problems and expedite training. For example, when timing (i.e., time elapsed since last act of elimination) or child responses (e.g., shifting weight from foot to foot) suggest elimination is imminent, rather than making an inquiry about toileting urge, parents should instead issue a toileting instruction requiring that their child make an attempt to eliminate in the toilet, guide them as they do so, and praise performance and any success achieved. This method removes the focus on saying and places it on forms of doing that are central to toileting. Additionally, by focusing on toileting instructions, this method contributes not just to development of toileting skills, but also to development of instruction control skills in general. Because it is easier for children to follow simple instructions (such as those that accompany successful toilet training programs) than to answer complex questions (such as those about toileting need), a focus on instructions (rather than inquiry) reduces the potential for contention between child and parent during the process.

From a slightly different perspective, the scientific literature on toileting supports the instruction-based approach by showing that children generally do not acquire the ability to succeed with an inquiry-based approach (i.e., respond accurately to questions about whether they have to go and independently conduct the act if they do) until late in their third or early in their fourth year. But the inquiry-based approach is widely used with much younger children resulting in many toileting problems that are ultimately brought to PCBP.

A focus on doing more than saying is also important for other reasons. For example, in many domains of children's lives their ability to say what they should do is learned before their ability to do it. That is, children can often readily say what they are supposed to do (or what they should have done) but lack the actual skill necessary for accomplishing the task. For example, they can easily say they should share their toys and yet not have the slightest inclination to do so because they lack the social and emotional skills that are essential for proficient sharing. Unfortunately, many adults assume that if children can say they should share it means they actually know how. For these adults, the children's subsequent failure to share is much more likely to be interpreted as evidence of a flawed character than of a skill deficit.

That a disparity between saying and doing exists and differential emphasis is more productively placed on doing is no surprise, at least where adults are concerned. Tell-tale examples are legion in everyday life. For example, all golfers know they should keep their head down during the golf swing but many (most) routinely lift their head up. Or more generally, lovers say they should look before they leap, readers say a book should not be judged by its cover, and fools say they should not rush in. Yet lovers often leap, readers frequently judge by the cover, and fools typically rush in all because their knowledge involves a facility for saying far more than it does a capacity for doing what has been said. Many proverbs, aphorisms, and epigrams make similar points and underscore the importance of doing over saying (e.g., "put your money where your mouth is"). The importance of doing over saying also suffuses the marketplace. As an example, the January

2001 issue of *Wired Magazine* included a symposium on marketing in the new millennium in which David Kelley, a prominent participant, said, "If you listen to the customers, they can't tell you anything. You have to *watch* the customer to really learn something. That's how you get at what they think and feel."

The surprise is actually how little this disparity is recognized where children with behavior problems are concerned and how minimally it is incorporated into attempts to modify those problems. As indicated above, children can often readily say what they should or should not do (e.g., not suck their thumb, pick on smaller children, take things without asking) but their ability to exhibit the requisite behaviors often lags far behind their ability to enunciate them. The related mistaken assumptions about what children know results in at least three sources of child behavior problems and corresponding difficulties. The first involves parental teaching efforts undermined by overemphasis on saying and underemphasis on doing, resulting in delayed child learning of behavioral skills (e.g., instructional control) critical to successful home and school life. The second involves the frequency of punitive discipline used with behavior problem children whose ability to say what they are supposed to do greatly exceeds their ability to do it. The third involves a widespread cultural tendency to interpret child behavior problems as a reflection of psychopathology rather than skills deficits. A fundamental assumption of PCBP is that the strength of these sources of problems and complications is substantially reduced when teaching focuses more on child doing than on child saying.

D. Repetition Followed by Experiential Contrast

The final theoretical assumption underlying PCBP that we will discuss involves how children derive meaning from the teeming multitude of events that compose their day-to-day life, how they learn to exhibit appropriate and inappropriate behavior, or more generally, how they learn. A century of research on learning with major contributions by eminent scientists such as John Watson, Edward Thorndike, B.F. Skinner, Albert Bandura, and Sydney Bijou shows that child learning largely results from the emergence of functional relations between what children do, what happened before they did it, and the change or contrast in experience generated by what they have done. The second theoretical assumption underlying PCBP we discussed dealt with antecedents or events occurring before children do things. Antecedents (e.g., instructions, rules) that compose a major portion of child teaching (e.g., by parents) were discussed, and the importance of salience, clarity, and simplicity as well as an emphasis on doing was stressed. The final theoretical assumption involves how children make adaptive (i.e., preferred by parents) connections between these types of antecedent events and what they subsequently do. Specifically, the assumption is that the connections result from repetition of behavior that follows the antecedent events and the changes or contrast in child experience that follows the behavior.

In very general terms, there are four classes or categories of experiential events that establish learning-based connections, two that make repetition of behavior more likely and two that make it less likely. The two classes that make behavior more likely are (1) contact with experientially pleasant or preferred events and (2) avoidance of, or escape from, experientially unpleasant or nonpreferred events. The two classes that make behavior less likely are (1) contact with experientially unpleasant or nonpreferred events and (2) disconnection from, or loss of contact with, pleasant or preferred events. An important corollary of the final assumption is that the number of repetitions necessary for children to make meaningful connections is governed by the amount of the experiential contrast that follows what they do. The more contrast, the fewer repetitions necessary for learning a meaningful relationship between a behavior, its antecedents, and its experiential consequences.

For example, flame or fire is a very salient (and attractive) antecedent event (e.g., the primary purpose of most fireplaces is for viewing fire, not for heating homes) but also very dangerous for children. Very young children who initially encounter fire are typically unaware of its dangers but are enthralled with its beauty and if unsupervised, they will often try to touch it. As a result a very important lesson (i.e., meaningful connection) is instantly learned. The learning results from the presence of fire (antecedent event), behavior that brings the child into contact with fire (touching), and the experiential (unpleasant, nonpreferred) consequences of that contact (being burned). These experiential consequences involve so much contrast (i.e., temperature of the body versus flame) that an instance of one-trial learning generating caution around fire occurs and it typically lasts a lifetime (i.e., the child will be unlikely to deliberately place his or her hand in open flame again). This is not to say that children who have been burned will not be burned again, but as the saying goes "once burned, twice shy." If the temperature of fire were lower, if it were much closer to skin temperature (e.g.,

102°F), many repetitions (and probably some supplemental aversive—disciplinary—consequences) would be necessary to establish a level of caution similar to that generated from flame.

The power of learning resulting from such extraordinary levels of experiential contrast is revealed by some parents who, after being unsuccessful in using other methods to teach their toddlers to avoid breakable household objects, achieve temporary success warning them that the objects are hot. A child with some experience of being burned and who has learned a connection between that experience and the antecedent event of hearing a parent say "hot" will often avoid, albeit temporarily, objects so described.

Critical to this discussion of learning is the logical necessity of incorporating the obverse of the primary point made above. That is, if behavior followed by high experiential contrast requires few repetitions to result in the learning of meaningful connections, responses followed by low experiential contrast will usually require many repetitions to result in a similar amount of learning. Numerous everyday examples corroborate this second point.

For example, many parents report high rate use of tactics such as nagging, reminding, warning, and threatening when attempting to teach their problem children appropriate behavior. Each of these tactics is a class of topographically similar antecedent events and in most teaching situations the events are repeated multiple times before a parent takes any further action, if indeed any action is taken at all. The reason for the repetition is that the children (who have been repetitiously nagged, reminded, warned, or threatened) have presumably not responded to the parent (i.e., they ignored their parent). Each instance of these parental tactics (e.g., each warning) sets the occasion for a learning trial in which the child actually learns to continue ignoring the parent. This unwanted and unfortunate result occurs for two reasons related to the theoretical assumption we are discussing here. First, the ignoring typically fails to generate the type (unpleasant) and the amount of experiential contrast necessary to reduce the likelihood of ignoring in the future. Second, the ignoring generates a consequential event of the type (avoidance of unpleasant or nonpreferred activity—i.e., whatever the parent wants the child to do or not do) that makes ignoring more likely to be repeated in the future.

Another type of learning trial that strengthens the learning of ignoring parents even further often accompanies the first type. In this second type of trial parents ignore or respond minimally when children actually do what they are told. That is, the tendency to ignore the parent, established by frequent parental warnings with no followup, is made even more likely when the child complies with the parent and still receives no followup. More generally, the learning of inappropriate behavior (e.g., ignoring as described above) is often accompanied by learning trials in which appropriate alternatives (e.g., compliance) are not followed by the type (pleasant, preferred) or the amount of experiential contrast necessary to increase the likelihood of the alternatives. In conclusion, many child behavior problems result from a confluence of learning trials where inappropriate behavior receives more of an experiential payoff for the child than its appropriate alternatives.

Making matters even worse is the devolution in parent teaching tactics that can result from these problematic teaching and learning processes. Many parents, frustrated by the extent to which their instructions and rules are ignored, resort to highly punitive consequences, especially yelling and sometimes even spanking. These consequences produce high levels of experiential contrast and thus readily instigate learning, but their potential benefits are outweighed by several potential risks. For example, children habituate to yelling and spanking quickly so more is gradually needed, an escalatory process that can lead to abusive child treatment. Additionally, frequent use of punishing tactics often creates so much distress for child, parent, and family that the quality of the family environment is usually diminished as a result. The effects of highly punitive tactics on child behavior are also reductive and so they are less likely to teach new skills than they are to increase avoidance and escape. Lastly, the tactics can cause unwanted side effects (e.g., fear, retaliation) that can worsen the parent–child relationship even further. For these reasons, the use of highly punitive consequences are neither recommended nor endorsed in PCBP.

1. The Experience of Nothing

For most disciplinary purposes, an alternative approach to discipline, derived from the fourth theoretical assumption of PCBP (i.e., repetition with contrast) as well other fundamental aspects of human life, is employed instead. Specifically, the approach involves the strategic use of the experience of nothing. Events in which very little stimulation occurs involve the type of experience (unpleasant, nonpreferred) that reduces the probability of behavior that produces it. Faced with the extended experience of nothing, children (and indeed most humans) prefer events that produce something, even if those events involve unpleasantness. Said slightly differently, most children ultimately prefer negative over nothing. Unfortunately, from a theoretical perspective nothing is hard to define and from an empirical perspective it can be difficult to document. But fortunately, from a procedural perspective experiences involving nothing, not much, or very little can be programmatically arranged, as we will discuss below.

a) Sensory Deprivation The importance of nothing as an experience is predicted on humans as sentient beings whose senses must be stimulated in order to maintain perceptual integrity and ultimately life itself. If one or more sensory modalities are cut off (e.g., through blindness or deafness) the acuity of those that remain increases substantially. It is as if a requisite amount of stimulation is necessary for humans to maintain perceptual health. An illuminating example of the power of the experience of nothing involves enclosure within sensory deprivation chambers. In the chambers persons lie in water the temperature of which is identical to that of the body. There is no light or sound and there is nothing to taste or smell. In other words, in sensory deprivation chambers the stimuli available for differential perception are held to a profound and potentially life-threatening minimum. In the short term, enclosure in the chambers has been associated with such experiences as exhilaration, relaxation, and awareness enhancement. In the long term, however, enclosure in the chambers has been associated with such experiences as hallucination, hyperventilation, and panic. Extended stays (e.g., more than an hour) are thought to be dangerous especially for novices. The point of this discussion is not to review sensory deprivation but rather to use a brief description of it to illuminate a correlate of the fourth theoretical assumption of PCBP. Specifically, programmed (i.e., planned contingent use of) consequences generating the experience of nothing powerfully reduce the likelihood of behaviors that produce those consequences.

We used the deprivation chamber example to reveal a very important dimension of the experience of nothing, the experiences where very little external stimulation occurs. Another equally important dimension is the experience of not being able to do anything about it (e.g., being powerless to provoke a reaction in a parent). In other words, situations in which there is nothing going on and nothing one can do about it are aversive for humans and particularly for children. One feature of the deprivation chamber that makes it tolerable is that the person within can readily terminate the experience and produce some external stimulation. Removing this feature, however, makes the experience highly aversive, one that few persons would willingly seek. There are many other examples that, although less exotic than the deprivation chamber, can be just as reflective of the influence the experience of nothing can have on learning and behavior, for example, parents on the telephone and the use of time out.

b) Parents on the Telephone The influence the experience of nothing can have on learning is often in evidence when young children are alone with a parent who takes an extended telephone call. Escalated child misbehavior and demonstrative child upset are two common results and both can puzzle parents. Viewed from the perspective of our discussion of nothing, however, there is little mystery here. The most treasured source of external stimulation for young children is usually the parent and during telephone calls the parent is mostly psychologically (and physically) unavailable; that is, they provide their child little or nothing. In the unlikely event that children behave appropriately during the call, for example, they sit on the couch and look at picture books, the likely consequence for them will be an extension of the call. When children are behaving appropriately there is no compelling reason for a parent to terminate an activity and attend to them. The unfortunate result for the children, however, is an extended experience of nothing, at least as far as the parent as a source of stimulation is concerned. In other words, appropriate child behavior occurring while a parent is on the telephone usually produces nothing for the child. Extended telephone calls in the presence of a young child, however, are not neutral from a learning perspective. They are learning trials in which appropriate behavior is followed by experiential consequences (i.e., nothing) that are of the type (unpleasant, nonpreferred) that make the behavior less likely to occur in the future.

Making matters worse is that inappropriate child behavior, especially of a highly escalated sort, can and often does terminate parental telephone calls. When this happens, parents are likely to express frustration or anger and possibly even impose some discipline. Despite this quite logical parental approach to the problem, child misbehavior during telephone calls often subsequently increases rather than decreases. Although counterintuitive, from a PCBP perspective this outcome is readily explained. Although the parental response to the child appears to involve unpleasant consequences, these consequences are something (experiential) and from the typical child's perspective as we have argued, something is better than nothing. Through misbehavior the child is, in effect, able to neutralize both of the dimensions of the experience of nothing that make it aversive. The first (nothing going on) is neutralized as soon as the parent interacts with the child because something begins to happen. The second (nothing the child can do about it) is neutralized by the instrumental quality of the misbehavior (i.e., it causes the parent to respond). More generally and from the perspective of the fourth theoretical assumption of PCBP, attempts to discipline child misbehavior that occurs in the context of nothing (as we have discussed it here) are more likely to increase than decrease the misbehavior. The reason is that when the disciplinary consequences occur, the context of nothing transforms them into the type (preferred) that make the behavior that generated them more likely in the future.

c) Time Out Another example of the role the experience of nothing can play in a child's life is a very common disciplinary procedure called time out. Time out, an abbreviation for Time Out From Positive Reinforcement, established in basic science experiments years ago, has become the most used method for disciplining children in this country, with the possible exception of verbal reprimands. A disclaimer, frequently heard in PCBP, is that time out has been tried and it did not work. The implicit assumption is that what was done in the name of time out closely resembles the procedure developed in the laboratory long ago. Unfortunately, close resemblance is the rare exception rather than the rule. In the laboratory, time out conditions involve what we have been referring to as the experience of nothing. Specifically the subject could not make contact with events that would be reinforcing, rewarding, stimulating, or interesting. In other words for laboratory subjects, a time out meant there was nothing going on, and for a specific period of time, there was nothing they could do about it. This laboratory experience, however, differs dramatically from the typical experience called time out in homes and schools across the country.

During the typical time out children are taken to a specific location, usually a chair, lectured briefly on the nature of their offense, and told they must sit quietly for a certain amount of time. A timer is often placed in the child's visual and/or auditory range so that the youngster can keep track of time passing. Verbal components such as warnings, rationales, and commands are frequently directed at the child. Children in time out are also often allowed to bring favored objects (e.g., teddy bear, book) with them. The location of the time out is often near rich sources of external stimulation such as the television or a picture window. So in terms of the first dimension of the experience of nothing, specifically nothing going on, most time outs often fail.

Also detrimental to the process is the ease with which children can do something about their situation, thereby neutralizing the intended effects of the time out experience. For example, simply calling out, crying out, or coming out of time out (without permission) are very successful means of fully engaging the attention of parents and thereby undermining the effects of time out. Other types of inappropriate behaviors (e.g., profanity, disrobing) also typically engage parental attention. The attention thus engaged is usually negative but, because it is delivered when the child is in time out, resulting in a temporary escape (the instant attention is delivered, time out functionally ends) it is more likely to increase rather than decrease the inappropriate behavior. In other words, negative attention is something and for children in time out, something is usually better than nothing.

Not surprisingly, helping parents to strategically apply the experience of nothing (e.g., time out, planned ignoring) as a disciplinary alternative to raising their hands or voices is an important part of PCBP. Much of this assistance involves helping them eliminate sources of social stimulation (e.g., warnings, criticisms, expressions of parental anger) that often occur while children are in time out. Perhaps even more important is assisting them to see that the experience of nothing is relative phenomenon. If little external stimulation is available for a child (e.g., they are bored because nothing is happening) time out, even when done well, produces little experiential contrast. Needed is an experience, resulting from an act of discipline, that is unpleasant or nonpreferred and that stands out starkly from what was happening before the discipline was imposed. Yelling or spanking can serve this purpose but we have already discussed the problems associated with their use. Time out is much more subtle but it can serve the purpose very well if three conditions are met: (1) sources of social stimulation are eliminated during the time out (as above); (2) the child's inappropriate attempts to terminate time out are ignored outright; and (3) the child's life was generally interesting and fun before time out was imposed. In other words, time out must be devoid of social interaction and must occur in a context called time in.

d) The Role of Time In As indicated, in order for time out to have desired effects, it must represent a change in the experience of the child and if nothing was going on before the time out occurred, and the child is then put in a situation with nothing going on, not much contrast and thus not much learning occurs. Actually, this principle applies to virtually any form of discipline. For example, if parents usually talk to their children with stern voices and then use a stern verbal reprimand for discipline, the reprimand produces little contrast and thus little possibility of learning. However, if parents usually talk to their children in soothing, affectionate, or emotionally positive ways and then use a stern verbal reprimand, the stark contrast between the typical parent–child interaction and the stern one increases the probability of children learning an important connection between what they have done and the parents' reaction to it. In honor of this principle, PCBP therapists are unlikely to recommend any form of discipline without first recommending ways for parents to increase the positive aspects of their child's daily life. Said slightly differently, PCBP practitioners routinely recommend procedures to increase time in, the functional opposite of time out, wherein multiple sources of preferred external stimulation (e.g., physical affection, parental participation in child activities,) are made available to children as well as a variety of minimally effortful methods accessing those sources.

In conclusion, a large part of PCBP involves provision of procedural advice generally based on developmental and behavioral science and specifically on the four theoretical assumptions we described above. That is, this advice almost always involves some combination of (1) consideration and explanation of child behaviorial style; (2) more effective use of behavior change language; (3) a focus on doing; and (4) the arrangement of teaching circumstances that result in the type and amount of experiential contrast necessary to produce children's learning of appropriate behavior.

III. APPLICATIONS AND EXCLUSIONS

Some children resist most, and most children resist some, key aspects of the socialization and education processes in this culture and a vast number and array of child behavior problems is the result. For example, nutritional and maturational health is predicated on food preferences that include the major food groups and yet some children, whose behavioral style may include slow adaptability and approach to new experience, resist parental attempts to introduce new tastes and textures into the daily diet. Adaptive child performance during the day is dependent on receipt of adequate sleep at night, yet children with slow adaptability or irregularity in sleep cycles may resist parental efforts to establish a reasonable bedtime. Most parents, preschools, and many day care programs require full toilet training during the third year of life, yet many children resist parental training efforts. Success in most life situations requires a reasonable amount of instructional control yet many children resist following important adult instructions. There are many other examples and they generally emerge in situations in which the requirement for adherence to family, school, or societal standards or requirements is not well matched with aspects of the child's behavioral style and/or learning history.

There are also a large number of child problems pertinent to PCBP that do not involve child resistance as much as they do child inability to emit, maintain, reduce, or cease important behavior. Although many of these problems are clinically unremarkable and resolve with time and routine parental efforts, some do not and require professional assistance for complete resolution. Furthermore, some of these problems resemble or, if unresolved, can lead to more serious conditions and thus they require some level of professional assessment prior to intervention. For example, simple tics and other child habits involving repetitive but nonadaptive behavior are common yet difficult for children to stop and highly resistant to routine parental efforts to help. In addition, tics may be an early sign of serious clinical conditions (e.g., Tourette's syndrome). Urinary and/or fecal incontinence is common, even in school-age children, yet without professional help incontinence can become a threat to physical and psychological health. School problems involving excesses or deficits of various behaviors critical to school performance (e.g., attention, activity) are common, stubborn, and absent effective intervention, can lead to serious problems later (e.g., school failure). There are many other examples and they generally emerge in situations requiring inhibition of potentially maladaptive behavior and increased exhibition of adaptive behavior.

The PCBP perspective on types of problems described above is that most are more productively viewed as a skill or performance deficit than as psychopathologies. Nonetheless, the problems are usually serious enough to warrant a professional opinion and sufficiently complex enough to require professional assistance for resolution. Psychopathology, however, is rarely the appropriate interpretive context for the assessment or the assistance warranted by these problems. As indicated, the problems emerge as a function of the friction between child style, preference, and/or skill level and the requirements inherent in socialization and education processes.

This "otherwise normal" perspective, unfortunately, is at odds with the vast majority of psychology and psychiatric literature on child behavior problems, which is focused almost entirely on detection of psychopathology with minimal regard for detection of child health. In fact, very few clinical assessment instruments are even designed to detect behavioral health. Behavior assessment instruments used in clinical research and practice on child behavior ask questions about symptoms or behavior problems and the typical intent is to determine whether a given child has significantly more than children of a similar age in the group used to norm the instrument. In other words, the de facto definition of child behavioral health within clinical child psychology and psychiatry is a composite of symptoms and problems that are below a threshold established for psychopathology, not a composite of healthful behaviors.

Perhaps the best way to view the PCBP approach to behavior problems is as early intervention. By providing parents and families with supportive counseling and prescriptive recommendations sufficient to improve interactions between children and their learning environment, PCBP aims to facilitate adaptive child development and behavior and thus prevent more severe problems in the future. For example, inadequate sleep leads to behavioral deterioration during the day and PCBP advice on how much sleep is needed and how to produce it can prevent these problems. Incontinence poses a number of risks to child health and development and PCBP advice on when and how to start toilet training can eliminate them. Resistance to adult instructions places children at risk for perpetuated conflict with adults. PCBP advice on instructional control can reduce child noncompliance with adult authority. The list of other examples is very long. They typically involve mild to moderate child behavior problems, most of which are responsive to changes in practices by parents (or teachers). Although some of the problems may meet diagnostic criteria for clinical conditions (e.g., enuresis, encopresis, simple phobias) the problems are usually in their early stages and are much more responsive to changes in teaching or training practices than problems that have been chronic for years. Thus even though PCBP provides treatment, the context of care is still characterized as preventive rather than curative or rehabilitative.

In conclusion, PCBP focuses on mild to moderate behavior problems exhibited by children who initially present in primary care. The context of care is one of prevention (preservation of health) much more than it is treatment (restoration of health) or rehabilitation (minimization of illness). Adopting this context, however, does not mean that PCBP denies the possibility of psychopathology or mental illness in children. Rather, the position taken is that children are deemed psychologically well until proven otherwise. Forms of such proof include resistance to PCBP treatment, an initial severe presentation, or incontrovertible assessment-based evidence; if any of these occur, cases are referred to appropriate specialists. PCBP, however, is an appropriate form of care for the vast array and number of child behavior problems presenting initially, and often only, in primary care settings.

IV. EMPIRICAL STUDIES

As emphasized, an important portion of PCBP involves educating parents about childhood and what to expect socially, emotionally, and behaviorally from their children. Thus virtually all child and developmental research is potentially relevant to PCBP. Three categories of this research are particularly relevant, however, the first two because they supply some justification for the well child focus of PCBP and the third because it reveals the size of the empirically supported armamentarium of the PCBP practitioner. The first category involves research on child temperament and individual differences, the second involves research assessing whether mild to moderate child behavior problems necessarily involve psychopathology, and the third involves research on PCBP appropriate treatments (pragmatic, procedure-based, outcome oriented, and time-limited) developed for various mild to moderate child behavior problems.

A. Temperament and Individual Differences

The expanding role of temperament or behavioral style in the professional approach to child behavioral problems is due in no small measure to the work of Stella Chess and Alexander Thomas and their colleagues working on the New York Longitudinal Study. This landmark research identified nine characteristics of temperament: activity level, rhythmicity (regularity of physiologic functions such as sleep, hunger, etc.), adaptability, intensity, mood, approach–withdrawal (to new stimuli), persistence, distractibility, and sensory threshold. There is, however, variation in the opinions of other researchers on the number and nature of the dimensions that compose variations in temperament, with more recent views favoring fewer dimensions.

These differences of opinion notwithstanding, there is consensus that dimensions of temperament do exist, play a significant role in behavioral expression, and are relatively stable over time.

Two other potent influences have contributed to the expanding role of temperament in the theoretical assumptions of PCBP. The first influence involves neonatal assessment of temperament, most notably with the instrument developed by T. Berry Brazelton. Related studies show that long before environmental influences could produce major changes in behavioral responses, substantial differences in behavioral expression exist in newborn children. The second influence involves assessment of temperament across early and later childhood, authoritatively (but not solely) documented in the papers and books authored by William Carey. The evolution of temperament from theory and basic science (e.g., Chess, Thomas) to routine assessment in a hospital setting (e.g., Brazelton) to routine assessment in a private pediatric practice setting (e.g., Carey) has contributed greatly to its current important role in PCBP practice.

B. Testing for Psychopathology

The second category of research is unfortunately small for reasons we have discussed briefly. For example, most of the research conducted on child behavior problems involves attempts to detect psychopathology and failure to do so usually means a failed experiment. As another example, children who do not exhibit psychopathology are much less likely to interest professionals (e.g., clinical child psychologists and psychiatrists) whose careers are focused on the study of it than children who do. Thus essentially healthy children are rarely the focus of clinical research.

There is, however, a small group of child studies whose group data were more reflective of clinical normality than psychopathology, despite presenting problems often interpreted as evidence of an underlying disorder. Examples include studies on children exhibiting problems such as enuresis, encopresis, chronic hair pulling, and thumb sucking. Note that these types of problems are very likely to present in primary care and thus are directly pertinent to this chapter. In these studies, the majority of children studied did not exhibit a sufficient number of clinical symptoms other than the target problem (e.g., enuresis) to justify a label of psychopathology. Rather, with the exception of the presenting problems, the groups appeared to be appropriately located within a spectrum of normality. There were extreme cases within the groups, but they were in a small minority.

Unfortunately for the empirical base of PCBP, however, the extreme case is much more likely to be the source of data for published papers than the routine case. This publication practice, sometimes referred to as selection bias (e.g., Berkson's bias), is typical not just of clinical psychology and psychiatry but also of clinical medicine. A long line of research shows that in any field of clinical science, extreme cases (multiple presenting problems) are more likely to be used for research and teaching than otherwise normal cases (one presenting problem). From the standpoint of professional education, this bias makes sense; the extreme case or the textbook case, as it were, provides a richer source of teaching material than the routine case. Yet the institutionalized practice of basing professional teaching mostly on extreme cases has its limitations. For example, the practice can result in the overinterpretation of routine cases, especially in clinical settings. Additionally, it probably diminishes incentives to study routine cases.

There are three important implications for PCBP to draw from the extant research on child behavior problems. First, a small but growing body of directly relevant research, as well as a long line of indirect study (e.g., on selection bias) supports our assumption that the initial evaluation and treatment of children with mild to moderate behavior problems is appropriate for PCBP. Second, it is incumbent upon PCBP practitioners to ably distinguish between routine and severe cases in order to make appropriate referrals. Third, the historical mainstream emphasis on the search for psychopathology in children with behavior problems and the resulting differential emphasis on extreme cases is a research opportunity for PCBP (e.g., research exploring the spectrum of normality in populations of children with bona fide psychological and behavioral problems is needed).

C. Evaluation of Treatments

The growing research on hair pulling in children is a good bridge from tests of psychopathology to research on treatment of behavioral problems presenting in PCBP. Reviews of the literature on chronic hair pulling or trichotillomania have shown that there is a spectrum of severity and that in many individuals, especially young children (i.e., younger than 10), hair pulling is a relatively simple habit (albeit with potentially serious consequences) similar in function and situational presentation to other simple habits such as thumb sucking. This point is not intended to downplay the seriousness of classic cases of trichotillomania where those afflicted experience frequent powerful urges to pull their own hair, psychological satisfaction when they do so, and cosmetically significant hair loss. Although effective therapy exists for such cases, its dependence on specialized knowledge and its inherent complexity places it well beyond the bounds of PCBP. Such cases are at the pathologic end of a spectrum of severity in which mild and moderate cases also exist. In fact, as research on trichotillomania evolves, mild and moderate cases may ultimately be classified in other ways, leaving only the more serious cases in the diagnostic category. Regardless, the children in the mild and moderate portions of the spectrum are indeed pulling their own hair and many present with serious hair loss. In support of the position we have taken, multiple published papers have described many cases of child hair pulling that resolved with treatments suitable for use in PCBP. Our case illustration (described below) will describe one of these cases. We used hair pulling for the case illustration because it, perhaps more than any other child problems appropriate for initial evaluation and treatment in PCBP, is believed by most clinicians to be reflective of psychopathology and in need of specialty care. Below we will briefly discuss some of these other problems with particular attention paid to the success of PCBP appropriate treatments that have been used with them.

1. Risky Infant Behavior

Crawling, cruising, and early walking infants explore their worlds with enthusiasm and tenacity. Although essential to healthy development, these explorations often lead to danger (e.g., electrical outlets, fireplaces, swallowable nonedible objects). Informed parents can minimize risks to their infants by "childproofing" their home, but no home is risk free. The parental task remaining after risks have been reduced involves actually teaching children to avoid the dangerous objects and situations that remain. Typical tactics include redirection, stop commands, warnings, threats, and even mild corporal punishment (e.g., slight slap on the hand). Despite use of these tactics, risky infant behavior often continues and sometimes even increases. From the theoretical perspectives of PCBP, this perpetuation of risky behavior is readily explained. Infants explore mostly when they are otherwise not engaged and most of their exploratory behavior produces little adult attention. When the behavior becomes risky, however, adult attention is quickly engaged, redirection and/or mild discipline is employed, and experiential contrast is produced for the infant. But because adult attention is such a powerful incentive for infants, and because the contrast it produces in these instances typically occurs in a context involving little or no social stimulation for infants, it can strengthen rather than weaken the infants' risky tendencies.

An important study, derived from this interpretation, was conducted with teenage mothers who had been reported for abusing their 1-year-old children. In the study, the mothers were taught to use language more effectively (e.g., eliminate threats, reasoning), focus on doing rather than on abstract personality traits (e.g., "you are so stubborn"), establish "time in" (e.g., by increasing physical affection, using more pleasing voice tones, more play times), and to use a brief time out (i.e., a few moments in a playpen) when their child engaged in risky behavior. Risky infant behavior dropped to near zero levels and mother–child interactions improved dramatically. Although some special training was necessary for these mothers, this approach is readily taught to older, more experienced mothers who bring their concerns to primary care.

2. Bedtime Problems

One of the most common presenting problems in PCBP involves resistance to bedtime (e.g., some combination of crying out, calling out, and coming out from the bedroom after bedtime). Several aspects of behavioral style may contribute to this difficulty. Children who are persistent and slow to adapt may resist and prolong the bedtime routine. Children with a low rhythmicity of relevant biologic processes may develop an erratic sleep schedule and not be tired at bedtime. Regardless of origin, bedtime resistance often generates experiential contrast of the type (e.g., contact with the parents) that perpetuates problem behavior.

Several PCBP appropriate treatments have been shown to be effective at curtailing resistance and establishing reasonable bedtimes. They achieve their success by modifying parental responses to achieve a more effective use of language, a focus on doing, an increased child experiential payoff for compliance, and a decreased experiential payoff for resistance. The bluntest form of PCBP treatment for bedtime problems involves ignoring the children altogether after they have gone to bed and extending appreciation for the night thus spent in the morning when they get up. This procedure is controversial because it can produce severe "bursts" of crying, especially in persistent children with slow adaptability to change and these bursts can be very difficult to manage even for confident, experienced parents. A more modulated version of this approach involves graduated ignoring (e.g., ignoring for 5 minutes the first night, 10 the second, and so on). An apparently equally effective (as indicated by comparative published research) less controversial technique involves establishing pleasant bedtime routines that occur when children comply with bedtime procedures and suspending the procedures when they do not.

A final technique was the subject of a recent scientific report and it is a classic demonstration of PCBP treatment as an early intervention. The technique is called the bedtime pass and it involves providing children with a pass, constructed by the parents, for use as an exchange for one trip out of the bedroom after bedtime. During the trip the children are allowed to make one request of their parents that can be satisfied readily with an action (e.g., request to use the bathroom, have a drink, obtain a hug). Once the action is satisfied, the children surrender the pass and return to bed. The recent report showed the program was highly effective with children who were routinely disruptive at and after bedtime. Additionally, the pass was deemed more acceptable than ignoring or the family bed by groups of pediatricians and parents.

3. Routine Oppositional Behavior in Younger Children (1 to 7 years)

Oppositional behavior in younger children is common. Instructional control is not an inherent trait; it is a learned skill and although children whose behavioral style is marked by easy adaptability, positive mood, and low intensity may learn it with minimal effort on the part of parents or teachers, other children learn it much more slowly. Relevant to the PCBP view, there is a very large literature, including numerous scientific papers and books that derive their message from those papers, on how to teach instructional control skills to younger children. The fundamental method emphasized in this literature involves the tactics we have discussed here. Specifically these include effective use of language, heightened focus on what the children do, increased time in, and imposition of experiential consequences that increase the likelihood of appropriate behavior and decrease the likelihood of inappropriate behavior. Detailed examples of this kind of child training are provided in a selection of books in our recommended reading section.

4. Routine Oppositional Behavior in Older Children (7 to 12 years)

As the social environment of children expands, the potential for direct parental control contracts. Said differently, as children's important social relationships increasingly develop outside their home and family, social influences that compete with parental influence mount and the possibilities for opposition to parental authority increase. As with younger children some of the opposition occurs in the home (e.g., chores undone) but increasingly with age some occurs outside the home (e.g., poor grades, school rules broken, curfew violations). Multiple studies have shown that effectively managing routine opposition in these older children involves the general tactics used with younger children (e.g., effective use of language). The critical difference involves the composition of the experiential consequences used to increase and decrease behaviors of concern. Whereas various forms of time out are usually sufficient for younger children, tactics such as contingent access to family and home resources (television, telephone, bike, etc.) and contingent permission to leave the home are needed, in addition to time out, for success with older children.

For example, an early (1972) study demonstrated that a simple home point system, where points earned or lost contingent upon appropriate and inappropriate behavior were used to "purchase" special privileges, dramatically improved the behavior problems of a group of misbehaving older children. Since then, many studies using similar tactics, although often in a less elaborate form (e.g., without a point system), have been used to successfully reduce opposition to parental authority in older children. Directly pertinent to this chapter is the fact that these methods can be prescribed readily in PCBP sessions.

5. Nocturnal Enuresis

Nocturnal enuresis involves nighttime urinary accidents that occur in children over the age of 5 who do not have a causal organic condition. The National Health Examination Survey estimated that as many as 25% of first-grade boys and 15% of first-grade girls were enuretic and not surprisingly, given its high prevalence, enuresis is one of the most frequent presenting problems in PCBP. Pertinent to this chapter is a voluminous body of scientific evidence showing the effectiveness of the urine alarm, a treatment for enuresis that is entirely consistent with the theoretical assumptions of PCBP and well suited to its practice. The alarm displaces the ineffective use of language (threats, reasoning, etc.) that often accompanies enuresis before it is seen professionally. Bedwetting children cannot be talked, threatened, or reasoned into continence. If they could, enuresis would be much more rare. The alarm is connected to a moisture-sensitive switching system and as little as one drop of urine completes the connection and turns it on. The alarm emits an unpleasant stimulus but the child can easily turn it off and thus continence-based learning occurs on two fronts. First, accidents produce the alarm (i.e., unpleasant experiential consequence) which reduces their likelihood. Second, turning off the alarm produces pleasant (or at least preferred) experiential consequences (escape from the alarm) that increase the likelihood of waking after or during the accidents. Initially the latency between the onset of urination and the alarm is large but it reduces over time until escape from the alarm segues into avoidance of it altogether (i.e., the latency ultimately decreases to the point where accidents do not occur and the alarm does not go off). This explanation of how the alarm works is accurate but highly simplified. The fundamental point is that the alarm can be used readily in PCBP and it works. The alarm has not just been shown to be effective; it has been shown to be more effective, in terms of continence achieved and relapse avoided, than any other treatment used for enuresis including all other behavioral approaches and a variety of medications.

6. Habit Disorders

Habitual repetitive behaviors are common in young children. For example, between 25% and 50% of children younger than 4 exhibit habitual thumb sucking. Smaller, but substantial, percentages of children exhibit other habitual behaviors such as head banging, body rocking, nose picking, fingernail biting, or hair pulling. These habits are typically benign in young children and the PCBP service offered is usually supportive counseling. But perpetuated (beyond specified age norms) or singularly intense practice of the habits places children at risk and in need of prescriptive behavioral pediatric treatment. A large collection of studies document the effectiveness of treatments, based on assumptions of PCBP (e.g., time in, simplified instruction, targeted consequences), for a broad range of problematic habits in young children (see case illustration below).

Effective treatment of habit problems in older children usually involves more complex approaches and more active participation of the child than treatment for young children. The most outstanding example of such treatment is habit reversal, a habit treatment package based on the assumptions underlying PCBP, suitable for use in PCBP, and more empirically supported for treatment of a broad range of habits (from tics to tantrums) than any other approach described in the literature. In its conventional form, habit reversal is a multicomponent procedure that includes relaxation training, self-monitoring, situations (where habits are likely to occur) review, awareness training, review of consequences (of the habit), social support, and competing response exercises. Although the number of components in habit reversal may make it seem impractical for some PCBP practitioners, especially those whose sessions are short (e.g., pediatricians), streamlined versions have been shown to be just as effective as the full package. For example, a recently published study showed that an abbreviated version of habit reversal, including only brief relaxation and competing response exercises, eliminated habitual mouth biting in a 16-year-old boy. The biting was a long time habit that occurred almost "unconsciously" especially when the boy was nervous or bored. Treatment was delivered in one session and results were produced almost immediately. This study (and many others like it) supplies the empirical basis for our conviction that habit reversal is a valuable part of the PCBP armamentarium.

7. Other Problems

The examples above represent only a small sample of empirically supported treatments for problems presenting in PCBP. Successes with similar treatments (i.e., PCBP appropriate) have been documented for many problems not mentioned, including difficulties with feeding, encopresis, recurrent abdominal pain, other "learned illnesses," early onset anxiety, simple phobias, other mild anxiety problems, attentional problems, and school problems. Collectively the breadth of the problems, and the extent of the evidence showing their successful treatment, supplies a major part of the empirical basis for the rapidly expanding view that PCBP is a highly appropriate and important approach to mild and moderate child behavior problems.

V. CASE ILLUSTRATION

A 3-year-old girl was seen for chronic hair pulling of 1 year's duration. The hair pulling had resulted in abnormal hair loss on the crown of her head (approximately a 13×8 cm patch). The hair pulling occurred mostly during sedentary activities or during the onset to sleep. She did not exhibit other significant behavior problems and was described by her parents as happy, compliant, and highly intelligent. The parents had tried several procedures to stop the hair pulling with no success. These included scolding, reasoning, hats, edible rewards for not pulling, and spanking.

The treatment for hair pulling involved three components: (1) increased nurturing (i.e., time in) was provided by asking each parent to increase physical touching by 50 touches per day and to play with their daughter at least 10 minutes per day, providing frequent praise and avoiding questions, commands, or criticisms. In addition, the usual bedtime routine was extended by 15 minutes. (2) The child was placed in time out for 3 minutes contingent on observed hair pulling. (3) Response prevention was used to help the child limit her hair pulling. The child agreed to select a pair of loose fitting cotton socks (hand socks) to be placed over her hands if she was observed pulling her hair while in time out. She also wore the hand socks to bed at night. Three days per week one parent observed the child for the presence or absence of hair pulling during 5 high-risk 1-hour time intervals. The percentage of intervals during which hair pulling occurred was recorded for each day.

A within-series withdrawal of treatment (ABAB) experimental design was used to assess the effects of treatment. This design involves periods of no treatment baseline (A) and periods of treatment (B). Experimental effects are determined based on differences between the A and B periods. For example, high levels of the target behavior during the baseline (A) periods contrasted with low levels during the treatment (B) periods are strong evidence that the treatment works (reduces the target behavior). During the initial baseline period in this case, hair pulling occurred in 76% percent of the observation intervals (see Figure 1). During the first treatment period, hair pulling reduced to 22% of intervals. During the second baseline period, hair pulling resumed at the original baseline levels and during the second treatment period it reduced to zero levels, where it stayed. The use of hand socks at bedtime was stopped after 2 months, but the parents continued the use of increased time in. Six months after the study, hair pulling was still at zero levels, and at a 2-year follow-up the child had a full head of hair, approximately 14 inches in length.

This case is a classic demonstration of PCBP, for at least three reasons. First, it involves a behavior problem, chronic hair pulling, that it is routinely viewed as evidence of psychopathology. The evaluation and treatment used here, however, negate this view. The pulling was not accompanied by other problem behavior, responded readily to direct treatment, and did not recur in another form during or after treatment. In other words, the pulling appeared to be a simple habit disorder presenting in an otherwise normal child and an appropriate context of care for such problems is PCBP. Second, the clinical approach involved both forms of PCBP, supportive counseling (e.g., the pulling was placed in its appropriate developmental and prognostic context) and prescriptive treatment. Third, the prescriptive treatment was based on the theoretical assumptions of PCBP. The parents' varbal interactions with their daughter regarding pulling were reduced to a highly simplified and quantitative minimum. The focus of their interactions was directed away from what their child thought, felt, and said about pulling and onto pulling itself (i.e., doing). For example, their repeated attempts to obtain an explanation for the pulling from their daughter or to reason with her about it were terminated. They imposed consequences (time out) for pulling that involved the type of experiential contrast (unpleasant, nonpreferred) that would reduce its likelihood in the future. Lastly, in order to increase the amount of contrast produced by time out, the parents employed various methods to increase the experientially pleasant aspects of their daughter's life (i.e., to increase time in).

VI. SUMMARY

There is a vast number and array of child behavior problems that, although not necessarily representative of true psychopathology, do pose psychological risks for the children who exhibit them and for their families. Almost all of these problems are initially seen in primary care settings and, absent a deterioration sufficiently serious to warrant specialty care, the majority are seen only in primary care. To remedy the problems early and obviate the risks they pose, we propose they be evaluated and treated within pediatric primary care itself via a special branch called primary care behavioral pediatrics. The principal types of therapies used in PCBP are supportive counseling and prescriptive behavioral treatment. Supportive counseling involves placing presenting problems in their appropriate developmental and prognostic context and prescriptive behavioral treatment involves the provision of procedure-based interventions for their remediation. PCBP is a multidisciplinary specialty but its practice is largely confined to psychologists and physicians. Limitations on time and in training, however, may reduce the physician's ability to deliver more complex procedures or to modify treatment in accord with unexpected responses. But because the physician is very likely the first professional to whom behavior problems are reported and because there often are medical considerations in the evaluation of behavior problems, the position of this chapter is that a partnership between physician and psychologist is optimal for practice. A representative sample of problems appropriate for PCBP includes risky infant behavior, oppositional behavior in younger and older children, bedtime problems, incontinence, and various habit disorders. It is important to stress that PCBP is not

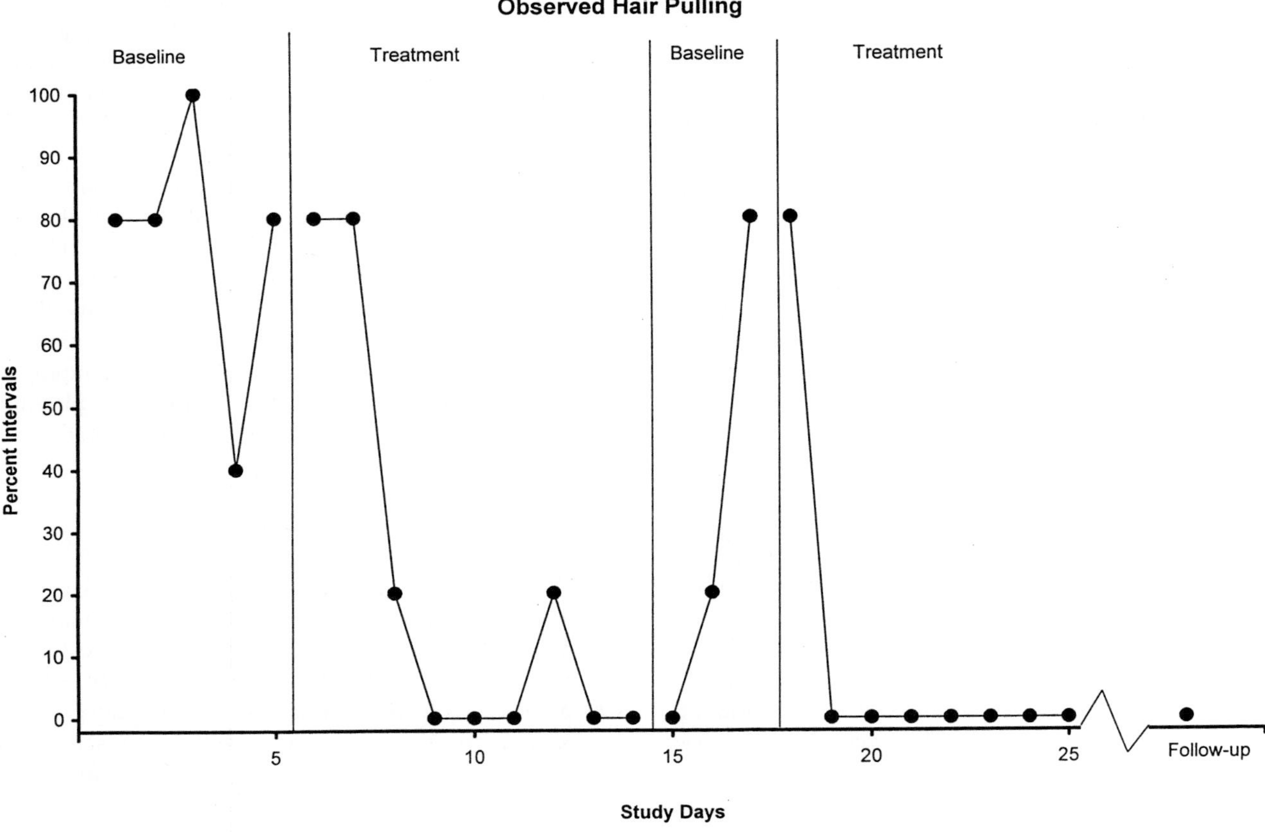

FIGURE 1 This figure shows the effects of treatment on hair pulling. The data points represent the percentage of intervals where hair pulling occurred. During baseline periods treatment was not administered. Reprinted with permission from *Pediatrics* **91**, 944. Copyright 1993, the American Academy of Pediatrics.

a universal approach for behavior problems in childhood. It is rather best viewed as the optimal domain for early intervention. Serious diagnostic conditions such as major depression, suicidal behavior, or delinquency represent boundary conditions for PCBP and should be referred for specialty care as soon as they are identified. Additionally, referral is recommended when presenting problems prove resistant to supportive counseling and prescriptive treatment. Behavioral pediatrics is thus proposed as a supplement to and not a substitute for existing care systems.

See Also the Following Articles

Behavioral Consultation and Therapy ■ Child and Adolescent Psychotherapy: Psychoanalytic Principles ■ Family Therapy ■ Home-Based Reinforcement ■ Nocturnal Enuresis ■ Parent–Child Interaction Therapy ■ Time-Out

Further Reading

Bijou, S. W. (1993). *Behavior analysis of child development.* Reno, NV: Context Press.

Blum, N., Williams, G., Friman, P. C., & Christophersen, E. R. (1995). Disciplining young children: The role of reason. *Pediatrics, 96,* 336.

Blum, N., & Friman, P. C. (2000). Behavioral pediatrics: The confluence of applied behavior analysis and pediatric medicine. In J. Carr & J. Austin (Eds.), *Handbook of applied behavior analysis.* Reno, NV: Context Press.

Brazelton, T. B. (1973). *Neonatal behavior assessment scale.* Philadelphia: Lippincott.

Carey, W. B., & McDevitt, S. C. (1995). *Coping with children's temperament: A guide for professionals.* New York: Basic Books

Christopersen, E. R. (1998). *Little people.* Shawnee Mission, KS: Overland Press.

Christophersen, E. R., Finney, J. W., & Friman, P. C. (Eds.) (1986). Prevention in primary care. *Pediatric Clinics of North America, 33.*

Forehand, R., & Long, R. (1996). *Parenting the strong willed child*. Chicago, IL: Contemporary Books.

Friedman, S. B. (1975). Foreword. *Pediatric Clinics of North America, 22,* 515–516.

Friman, P. C., & Jones, K. M. (1998). Elimination disorders in children. In S. Watson & F. Gresham (Eds.), *Handbook of child behavior therapy*. New York: Plenum.

Friman, P. C., & Rostain, A. (1990). Trichotillomania in children: A caveat for primary care. *New England Journal of Medicine, 322,* 471.

Levine, M. D., Carey, W. B., & Crocker, A. C. (1999). *Developmental–behavioral pediatrics*. Philadelphia: W. B. Saunders.

Webster-Stratton, C., & Herbert, M. (1994). *Troubled families, troubled children*. New York: John Wiley.

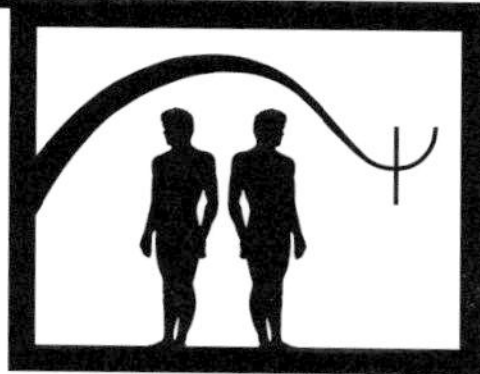

Progressive Relaxation

Rachel L. Grover and Douglas W. Nangle
University of Maine

GLOSSARY

autonomic nervous system The part of the nervous system that controls involuntary actions of the smooth muscles, heart, and glands. Consists of sympathetic and parasympathetic portions.

psychophysiological Pertaining to the branch of psychology that is concerned with the biological bases of psychological processes.

sympathetic nervous system The part of the autonomic nervous system that inhibits or opposes the effects of the parasympathetic nervous system, as in reducing digestive secretions, speeding up the heart, and contracting blood vessels.

systematic desensitization A behavior therapy technique that is used to reduce or eliminate anxiety. Deep muscle relaxation is paired with imagined scenes or actual anxiety-provoking situations that increase in intensity.

Progressive relaxation represents a group of therapeutic techniques that seek to reduce one of the physiological manifestations of anxiety by teaching a person to be aware of muscle tension and to release quickly that tension. One common system of progressive relaxation involves tensing and releasing various muscle groups until a deeply relaxed state can be accomplished through simply recalling the feeling of relaxed muscles. Progressive relaxation is used with a variety of populations to alleviate a range of complaints including anxiety, depression, and psychophysiological disorders.

I. DESCRIPTION OF TREATMENT

A. The Basic Procedure

Progressive relaxation training should take place in a quiet, dimly lit room with little chance of disruption. The client is seated in a chair that completely supports the body, thus enabling tension and relaxation of all required muscle groups. The client is encouraged to wear loose-fitting clothing to prevent the distraction of uncomfortable attire.

Progressive relaxation training involves teaching the client to tense and relax a series of 16 muscle groups: (a) dominant hand and forearm; (b) dominant biceps; (c) nondominant hand and forearm; (d) nondominant biceps; (e) forehead; (f) upper cheeks and nose; (g) lower cheeks and jaws; (h) neck and throat; (i) chest, shoulders, and upper back; (j) abdominal or stomach region; (k) dominant thigh; (l) dominant calf; (m) dominant foot; (n) nondominant thigh; (o) nondominant calf; and (p) nondominant foot. To begin, the client is encouraged to focus on the first muscle group and to tense the muscles in that group for a period of 5 to 7 sec. Then the client is instructed to relax the muscle group for 30 to 40 sec. During both tension and relaxation, the therapist helps focus the attention of the client on the muscular experience. Comments such as, "Notice what it is like to have tension/relaxation in these muscles" are useful. The tense–relax sequence then is repeated with the same muscle group, with an increase in relaxation time to 45 to 60 sec. The client is required to attain full muscle relaxation with each muscle group before progressing to the next group. The therapist asks the client to signal complete relaxation by raising a finger of the right hand before continuing to the next muscle group. If the client does not report total relaxation in the specified muscle group, the tense–relax procedure is repeated. To avoid muscle fatigue or pain, repetition should not exceed four or five times.

With the application of the tense–relax sequence to the chest, shoulders, and upper back, breathing cues are added to the instructions. The therapist begins including mild suggestions about breathing into the script (e.g., "Notice your slow and regular breathing"). In addition, the client now is instructed to take a deep breath and hold it during the tension phase and to release the breath during the relaxation phase of each subsequent muscle group.

Upon completion of the entire sequence, the therapist reviews the targeted muscle groups and encourages the client to continue to relax. Then, the client's overall level of relaxation is assessed. Once again, the therapist asks the client to signal when a state of complete relaxation throughout the body has been achieved. If the client does not signal complete relaxation, then the client is asked to signal tension in a muscle group as the therapist lists the possible groups. On the identification of tension, the tense–relax sequence is repeated. The assessment phase is continued until complete relaxation is obtained or until the therapist decides to terminate the training. Prior to concluding the training, the client is allowed to experience complete relaxation for a few moments. At this time, the therapist makes comments that aid the client in remaining focused on the feeling of relaxation. After a few minutes, the therapist may begin the termination process.

The therapist guides the client out of the relaxed state by asking the client to begin moving muscle groups. For example, the therapist may count backwards from 1 to 4, informing the client to move legs and feet at 4, arms and hands at 3, head and neck at 2, and to open the eyes at 1. The client is encouraged to continue feeling relaxed and calm. In addition, the client is prepared for the possibility that he or she may feel dizzy or disoriented on emergence from the state of deep relaxation.

Relaxation is a skill that cannot be perfected without practice. Therefore, the client should be encouraged to practice twice a day for 15 to 20 min. The therapist helps the client identify appropriate times and places to practice progressive relaxation. For best results, the client is asked to practice on a comfortable chair or bed when there is no time pressure and little chance of disruption.

B. Variations on the Basic Procedure

Once the client is able to completely relax the 16 muscle groups, the therapist condenses the progressive relaxation procedure to decrease the amount of time needed to reach a fully relaxed state. Frequently, the initial 16 muscle groups are decreased to 7 muscle groups including: (a) dominant arm; (b) nondominant arm; (c) facial muscles; (d) neck and throat; (e) chest, shoulders, upper back, and abdomen; (f) dominant thigh, calf, and foot; and (g) nondominant thigh, calf, and foot. The procedure can be further reduced to include 4 muscle groups in the tense–relax sequence: (a) arms, hands, and biceps; (b) face and neck; (c) chest, shoulders, back, and abdomen; and (d) thighs, calves, and feet. The client must master each variation both in session and during home practice before progressing to the next version.

Following competence in relaxation through the tense–relax sequence, the client is introduced to relaxation through recall, or muscle relaxation achieved through memory of the relaxed state, without the initial tension. The therapist encourages the client to think about a particular muscle group and then relax by remembering how to release those muscles. After focusing on the relaxed muscle for 35 to 45 sec, the therapist asks the client to signal if the muscle group in question is relaxed. Similar to the basic procedure, the client should achieve complete relaxation in a muscle group prior to proceeding to the next group. Also, the therapist may repeat a muscle group if needed. This new approach is incorporated into the home practice sessions.

When the client becomes proficient at relaxation through recall, the therapist transitions the client into relaxing the entire body by counting from 1 to 10. The therapist first introduces this technique when the client already is in a relaxed state. After relaxing each muscle group through recall, the therapist instructs the client to notice all the muscles in the body continuing to relax as the therapist counts to 10. Once the client has practiced this approach at home several times, the therapist works with the client toward reaching a relaxed state solely by counting from 1 to 10. Again, the client must practice this skill.

C. Applied Relaxation

The goal of progressive relaxation training is for the client to learn an effective way to reduce muscle tension in daily life. Therefore, the client needs to learn to transfer these skills from the twice-daily practice sessions to routine situations throughout the day. The process of using relaxation skills in specific stressful situations is called "applied relaxation." Applied relaxation training as described by psychologist Douglas Bernstein and colleagues, consists of four components. First, the client learns to monitor tension in the body and notice when the body begins to move away from a relaxed state. Second, the client becomes adept at implementing relaxation responses subsequent to the detection of tension. Next, frequent practice is recommended to improve the skill of the client at deploying relaxation strategies. Last, the client learns several different approaches for reclaiming a relaxed state to optimize the chance of success in a variety of anxiety-provoking situations.

II. THEORETICAL BASES

Several conceptual explanations have been theorized to account for the ability of progressive relaxation to reduce anxiety. Edmund Jacobson's work in the first half of the 20th century represented the first significant attempt to investigate this relationship. In his early studies, Jacobson observed that the subjective state of anxiety was accompanied by a contraction of muscle fibers. In subsequent investigations, he observed that thoughts of physical activity elicited corresponding electrical activity in the expected muscle group. Similarly, absence of thought was associated with negligible electrical activity in the musculature. Using the earlier information, Jacobson theorized that prolonged stress resulted in chronic tension. This chronic tension caused excessive strain on the musculature and a sustained increase in activity in the central nervous system that contributed to a variety of pathological conditions. In Jacobson's view, deep relaxation of the muscles would decrease activity in the central nervous system thus preventing and ameliorating psychological and/or physical distress. In 1938, he developed the tense–release procedure he named progressive relaxation and used it to treat anxious people. By 1962, the therapy was an intensive experience involving 15 muscle groups and extending over 50 hour-long sessions of training.

Around 1950, the inclusion of an abbreviated form of progressive relaxation in a successful treatment for anxiety called systematic desensitization precipitated another wave of empirical scrutiny. Systematic desensitization is a treatment approach that entails imagined or actual contact with the feared stimuli in stages progressing from least stressful to most distressing. At each stage, an individual is encouraged to experience the stimuli until a reduction of anxiety occurs, thus lessening the learned fear. The subjective experience of anxiety is thought to have cognitive, behavioral, and physiological components. When a person experiences anxious arousal, increased activity in all of the components contributes to the amplification and length of the anxious state. Psychologist Joseph Wolpe theorized that muscle relaxation was physiologically incompatible with the experience of anxiety. Therefore, relaxation intervenes in this process by reducing physiological arousal. As such, the presentation of a feared stimulus coupled with a physiological state incompatible with fear could eventually eliminate the conditioned anxiety response.

Additional research has supported this theory. The physiologist Ernst Gellhorn developed the most thorough explanation of the mechanisms by which progressive relaxation affects the autonomic nervous system. Gellhorn theorized that relaxed muscles correspond to a decrease in activity in the autonomic nervous system caused by the lack of feedback information from the skeletal muscles. The physiological aspects of anxiety are activated by the part of the brain that stimulates the sympathetic nervous system, or the reticular system. Gellhorn noticed that a large proportion of the nerve input into the reticular system came from fibers in the skeletal muscles. As such, progressive relaxation reduces autonomic arousal (e.g., decreased heart rate and blood pressure) by reducing input to the reticular system and therefore, the sympathetic nervous system. In addition, nerve fibers also connect the reticular system to the cortex: the area of the brain associated with the feeling of nervousness and increased vigilance. Thus, progressive relaxation may also dampen alertness and cognitive activity. Indeed, the research of psychologist F. J. McGuigan revealed that all thought is associated with muscular activity. Hence, reduction of muscular activity can result in a lessening of cognitive activity.

III. APPLICATIONS AND EXCLUSIONS

A. Applications

Progressive relaxation was developed to reduce tension in clients who have chronic anxiety problems; thus early applications were predominately limited to this population. However, in recent years the range has greatly broadened to include a variety of people who suffer from an extended scope of problems including insomnia, hypertension, tension headache, explosive anger, chronic pain, and depression. In addition, progressive relaxation occasionally is used to aid the therapeutic process. For example, relaxation training may enable a client to discuss a particularly distressing topic. On the other hand, research suggests that progressive relaxation works best when the central difficulty is tension. Progressive relaxation is appropriate for both adults and children, and there is a manual that includes suggested amendments in procedures for children with special needs.

In their 2001 manual, Bernstein and colleagues recommend a pretraining inventory to assess the appropriateness of a client for progressive relaxation training. First, any biological bases for the presenting problem should be ruled out. Second, the therapist should assess the possible risks of relaxation for that client. For example, a client may have an injury that is aggravated by repeated tensing and releasing of a muscle group. Next, if possible, the client should discontinue the use of any muscle-relaxing drugs as they may interfere with the client learning how to control tension and relaxation. Finally, the therapist should consider whether progressive relaxation training is likely to alleviate the client's complaint.

B. Exclusions

There are a few reasons why some clients may not benefit from training in progressive relaxation. However, adjusting some basic procedures can accommodate the limitations of most clients. For example, if a person has an injury that prevents tensing a muscle group, the therapist may instruct only to relax that muscle group thus forgoing the tension phase. Similarly, clients with breathing difficulties (e.g., chronic congestion due to smoking or allergies) may need to sit upright for the training to prevent coughing. Other exclusionary factors are more serious. For example, individuals who lack muscle control will, obviously, not benefit from this intervention. Second, a minority of individuals experience "relaxation-induced anxiety" that may prevent them from gaining any benefit from relaxation training. Relaxation-induced anxiety refers to a variety of symptoms including fear of losing control, increased tension, and increased indications of anxiety that appear to be triggered by relaxation. Third, relaxation approaches are ineffective when skill deficiencies rather than anxiety appear to be the problem. For example, highly test-anxious college students are helped more by instruction in test-taking skills than by relaxation methods. Finally, there are many disorders for which progressive relaxation has been found to be inappropriate (e.g., muscle pain disorder, excessive gastric acid output, tinnitus).

IV. EMPIRICAL STUDIES

Progressive relaxation has been applied to a large variety of physical and psychological complaints. This section reviews the research on those classes of disorders most frequently investigated in connection with relaxation methods. As the original progressive relaxation procedure was designed to counteract anxiety, the majority of the research falls within this topic area. In addition, a considerable amount of research has investigated progressive relaxation as a component in the treatment of depression. Finally, progressive relaxation also is used to help treat psychophysiological disorders such as headache, hypertension, insomnia, and chronic pain.

A. Anxiety Disorders

Progressive relaxation training is an element present in the treatment of almost all anxiety disorders including generalized anxiety disorder, panic disorder, specific phobias, and posttraumatic stress disorder. Progressive relaxation training is often used as an essential component in a more comprehensive treatment package targeting physical, behavioral, and cognitive aspects of anxiety. For example, although progressive relaxation reduces anxiety, the most successful treatment for generalized anxiety disorder is a multicomponent package that includes cognitive, behavioral, and physiological aspects. The empirical literature reveals that individuals with anxiety treated with a treatment package tend to report significantly less anxiety than people given a placebo, drug treatment, nondirective counseling, or no treatment. Similarly, in the treatment of panic disorder, progressive relaxation alleviates panic to a greater extent than no treatment. However, the therapies with the most empirical support are multicomponent composed of exposure to panic triggers, cognitive therapy, deep breathing, and progressive relaxation.

In the treatment of specific phobias, repeated exposure to the feared stimuli is essential. Contact with the feared object or situation is introduced in stages through systematic desensitization. At each stage, exposure is encouraged until a reduction of anxiety occurs, thus lessening the learned fear. Progressive relaxation has been used for decades as part of systematic desensitization to facilitate the fear reduction process. Indeed, in a few studies, the addition of a relaxation component to exposure has increased the effectiveness thereby demonstrating its validity as a necessary component of treatment.

Research on the treatment of posttraumatic stress disorder reveals that progressive relaxation alone is not a viable treatment. However, the treatment packages that have empirical support all include a relaxation module. In each therapy program, progressive relaxation is used to create a mood state that resists anxiety in a systematic desensitization, flooding, or stress inoculation procedure.

B. Depression

Applying progressive relaxation procedures to depression emerged from the observation that anxiety symptoms often occur along with depression. Moreover, depression can be exacerbated by stress. A few research studies have demonstrated the superior effectiveness of progressive relaxation alone to no treatment in adolescents and adults with mild to moderate depression and in women with postpartum depression. More frequently, research supports the inclusion of a relaxation component in a comprehensive treatment package for depression. One such treatment program has garnered an extensive amount of research endorsement. The Coping with Depression Course was designed by psychologist Peter Lewinsohn and colleagues to aid in the treatment of depressed adults and adolescents. In clinical trials, it has proven to significantly reduce depression scores and the rate of diagnoses in comparison to a wait-list control condition. Moreover, the empirical literature suggests that results are maintained over time. In addition to progressive relaxation training, the Coping with Depression Course is composed of several treatment components including cognitive therapy, social skills training, pleasant events scheduling, self-monitoring, and training in personal goal achievement in a group setting.

C. Behavioral Medicine

In recent years, progressive relaxation increasingly is used to alleviate the effects of stress-related and psychophysiological disorders such as headache, hypertension, insomnia, and chronic pain. Progressive relaxation training is an effective treatment for both tension and migraine headaches. Recent investigations demonstrated that in the treatment of tension headache, relaxation training is more effective at reducing the strength and frequency of headaches than headache monitoring, false biofeedback, medication placebo, and attention placebo. In addition, gains in treating tension headache through progressive relaxation tend to be long-term improvements. Progressive relaxation in combination with thermal biofeedback appears to be a successful treatment for migraines, proving more beneficial than headache monitoring and medication placebo. Component treatments that include progressive relaxation (or applied relaxation) and cognitive therapy also reduce and weaken migraine headaches more than headache monitoring, and at times, placebo conditions.

Early research on the effects of progressive relaxation on hypertension yielded promising results, leading research reviews at that time to conclude that relaxation training was effective in lowering blood pressure. Unfortunately, many of the positive results of these investigations have not been replicated. In fact, few studies continue to support the benefits of progressive relaxation over blood pressure monitoring and placebo. Currently, more attention is being paid to comprehensive treatment packages that include relaxation as a component along with stress management skills and healthy lifestyle behavior training. However, further research should be done to determine whether progressive relaxation is a useful component in the treatment of hypertension.

Insomnia is probably the most common behavioral medicine complaint that progressive relaxation has been applied to treat. Progressive relaxation is considered to be an effective treatment for insomnia. However, combination treatment packages that also include stimulus control and sleep restriction techniques tend to be more effective than relaxation training alone.

Similarly, multicomponent treatments for chronic pain have proven to be more effective than relaxation training alone. The more effective treatment packages for chronic pain are cognitive behavioral in orientation and composed of goal setting, increased activity and/or exercise, pain education, and medication management. These comprehensive treatments generate more favorable results than no-treatment control, standard physical rehabilitation, and attention placebo conditions. However, the overall effectiveness of progressive relaxation training on the treatment of chronic pain is unclear as the majority of research is based on lower back and joint pain and pain experienced as a result of rheumatoid arthritis.

V. CASE ILLUSTRATION

"Tom" was a 42-year-old male living alone subsequent to a recent divorce. Tom had no history of previous psychiatric treatment, although he did report a serious head trauma when he was a teenager. At the time of referral for depression, Tom was self-employed as a painter and also performed routine maintenance on several houses. Tom presented for treatment on the recommendation of his parents who were concerned about his lingering depression. In the initial interview, Tom stated that he was apprehensive about therapy and was willing to attend only because it relieved his parents' fears. Throughout the session Tom sat rigidly upright and gripped tightly the arms of the chair.

As Tom began to trust the therapist in subsequent assessment sessions, he confided that he had been depressed since his divorce 1 year ago. In addition, he had recently experienced suicidal thoughts in the form of visions of himself jumping off the roof of a house that he was painting. He reported that that he did not want to die, but was terrified that he would "lose control" and jump. He stated that this fear caused him a great deal of anxiety resulting in difficulty sleeping and an inability to concentrate on his work. These initial sessions were extremely difficult for Tom as he maintained his high level of muscle tension and stated that it was anxiety provoking to confide his fears to another person.

As a result of the assessment, the therapist concluded that Tom would benefit from cognitive-behavioral therapy for his depression. However, his high level of anxiety surrounding the therapeutic process was a significant barrier to this process. Therefore, the therapist introduced progressive relaxation training as a coping skill to be used during therapy and at his work. The therapist predicted that after mastering progressive relaxation, Tom would be able to discuss his concerns with less distress and be able to examine more readily his thoughts and behaviors.

Progressive relaxation training followed Bernstein and colleagues' 2001 manual for this purpose. The first four sessions focused on tensing and relaxing 16 major muscle groups. Tom was able to signal deep relaxation during the second training session. The therapist asked Tom to practice the training on his own at least twice a day. Tom reported practicing three times the first week, but increased his practice sessions in the following weeks as he became more familiar with the procedure. In the next two sessions, the therapist concentrated on tensing and relaxing 7 major muscle groups. Tom continued to report deep relaxation during the training sessions. He also appeared visibly more relaxed. He stopped gripping the arms of his chair during session and presented a more relaxed posture. Tom reported that he was less anxious at work and his suicidal thoughts had decreased. In the next few sessions, the therapist continued the tense-and-release training with four muscle groups. Finally, Tom was able to progress to relaxation with recall training and relaxation with counting training. Tom was instructed to continue to practice at least once daily during the continuation of therapy.

Following the progressive relaxation training, Tom obtained slightly lower scores on measures of depression and greatly reduced scores on measures of anxiety. More important, his fears of committing suicide disappeared. Tom was able to discuss his thoughts surrounding his divorce with less distress. He reported continuing the therapeutic process both for his parents and for himself.

VI. SUMMARY

Progressive relaxation refers to a closely related group of procedures designed to reduce muscle tension, one of the physiological symptoms of anxiety. The described technique involves repeated tensing and releasing of a series of muscle groups. The tense–relax process increases awareness of muscle tension and how to alleviate that tension. After a client achieves deep relaxation with the original procedure, the amount of muscle groups is systematically reduced. Once the client attains a state of deep relaxation using the tense–release system, the client then is introduced to a less intensive way to relax. For example, counting from 1 to 10 as the client relaxes the body is often used to encourage relaxation. In this way, the client learns to reach a relaxed state with less investment of time and energy. Learning the basic progressive relaxation skills enables the client to then utilize the skills in stressful situations in daily life. Progressive relaxation may be used with both adults and children and is easily adapted for individuals with special needs. However, relaxation training is not appropriate for people who cannot control their skeletal musculature. Progressive relaxation frequently is used to treat anxiety disorders, depression, and several psychophysiological complaints. Progressive relaxation is most effective when included in a multicomponent treatment package.

See Also the Following Articles

Applied Relaxation ■ Breathing Retraining ■ Panic Disorder and Agoraphobia ■ Relaxation Training ■ Stretch-Based Relaxation Training ■ Successive Approximations ■ Systematic Desensitization

Further Reading

Bernstein, D. A., Borkovec, T. D., & Hazlett-Stevens, H. (2001). *New directions in progressive relaxation training: A guidebook for helping professionals.* Westport, CT: Praeger.

Carlson, C. R., & Hoyle, R. H. (1993). Efficacy of abbreviated progressive muscle relaxation training: A quantitative review of behavioral medicine research. *Journal of Consulting and Clinical Psychology, 61*(6), 1059–1067.

Cautela, J. R., & Groden, J. (1978). *Relaxation: A comprehensive manual for adults, children, and children with special needs.* Champaign, IL: Research Press Company.

Goldfried, M. R., & Davison, G. C. (1994). *Clinical behavior therapy* New York: John Wiley & Sons.

Lehrer, P. M., & Woolfolk, R. L. (Eds.). (1993). *Principles and practice of stress management* (2nd ed.). New York: Guilford.

Roth, W. T. (Ed.). (1997). *Treating anxiety disorders.* San Francisco: Jossey-Bass.

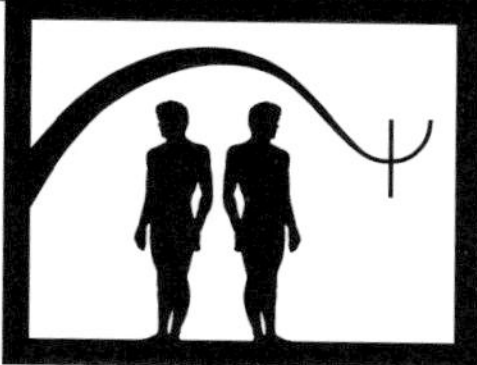

Projective Testing in Psychotherapeutics

J. Christopher Fowler

The Erik H. Erikson Institute for Education and Research

GLOSSARY

diagnostic evaluation report The vehicle for communicating interpretations of test data that illuminates the underlying personality structure, object-relations paradigms, sources of psychological distress, and the framework for understanding defense constellations, as well as providing treatment recommendations and consultation to the referring therapist.

early memories test Procedures to elicit early childhood memories work from the basic assumption that early childhood memories are retrospective narrative creations that reveal aspects of psychological functioning rather than objective truths about the person's life. Narratives are analyzed using a variety of content and structural scoring systems to assess object-relations themes, character styles, depression, and behavioral disorders.

personality assessment Utilizing various instruments, diagnosticians are able to synthesize an understanding of individual's cognitive style, emotional attitudes, and aptitudes, as well as primary defenses and conflicts.

projective techniques A broad array of assessment procedures utilizing ambiguous stimuli and opaque instructions to conceal the nature of the task and the personality structures being assessed. Ambiguity presses the individual to organize responses in terms of personal motivations, perceptions, attitudes, ideas, emotions, problem-solving strategies and core dynamic conflicts.

Rorschach inkblot method Hermann Rorschach's perceptual/projective test consisting of 10 standardized inkblots of varying color and form that are administered to the participant one at a time with the request to describe, "What the inkblot might be." From the free associations and the inquiry of the determinants making up a percept, the examiner applies one of several standardized scoring systems to develop hypotheses relevant to personality traits, perceptual and problem-solving styles, prototypic modes of interpersonal relating, degree of thought, mood, and impulse disturbance. Systems for analysis vary from a-theoretical empirical approaches to psychoanalytically derived systems.

thematic appreception test Conceived by Henry A. Murray as a narrative projective device, the TAT consists of 20 scenic pictorials from which participants are instructed to create narratives about the scenes and human representations. Through the participant's imaginative elaborations, the psychological examiner makes inferences about themes most important in the participant's life. From these themes, psychological datum such as the participant's needs and "press," prototypic relationship paradigms, object relations, and understanding of social causality can be ascertained.

word association methods A series of assessment methods utilizing stimulus words or phrases to elicit immediate associations. Thematic analysis and comparison of participant's responses to normative data allows for discerning complexes and defenses.

I. PROJECTIVE TECHNIQUES AND PSYCHOANALYSIS

The demand for assessment techniques that probe beyond the patient's conscious defenses and resistances could only have developed from clinical and theoretical systems that endeavored to comprehend the obscure layers of personality functioning, and to explore the interplay of conflicts and fantasies in the creation of symptoms. Inherent in the psychoanalytic model is the assumption that superficial layers of personality structure are readily available to consciousness, but to comprehend unconscious motivations, fantasies and complexes require the specialized techniques of free association, dream interpretation, and the analysis of the transference. Projective techniques are the logical application of psychoanalytic theory to assess underlying structures.

Assessment methods specifically designed to tap into hidden complexes and conflicts has a rich history involving luminaries and revolutionaries from the psychoanalytic movement. Carl Jung developed the first projective test with the Word Association Task to uncover hidden complexes and conflicts as an aspect of psychoanalytic investigations. Since Jung's test, numerous sentence completion tasks have sprung from the essential theory that irregularities in response style and repetitive patterns of themes reveal underlying conflicts that the patient would not readily reveal through traditional interview methods. Alfred Adler crafted a technique for analyzing early childhood recollections as a projective test that reveals the individual "lifestyle" and major life themes including self-schemas. Although somewhat outside the mainstream of psychoanalytic discourse, Adler's test is widely used by practitioners of the individual psychology movement. Martin Mayman, an analyst from the Menninger Foundation, drew on modern ego psychology and object-relations theory to develop a highly versatile assessment technique by inquiring into specific early childhood memories. Another class of projective test relies on complex pictures depicting people involved in various interactions to which the participant is pressed to create stories that are then analyzed for structure and content. Tests such as the Thematic Apperception Test rely on the participant's apperception of relationships to project their beliefs and emotional reactions in their stories.

Herman Rorschach, one of the first presidents of the Swiss Psychoanalytic Society, is best known for developing the now-famous inkblot method bearing his name. Rorschach believed his method did not uncover layers of unconscious processes. Rather, he thought of it as an experimental, atheoretical method for assessing personality styles based on the perceptual organization of patient's responses. In his 1921 monograph he made patently clear that the test could not be used to tap into the contents of the subconscious. Thus from its inception, the Rorschach Inkblot Method was considered a perceptual task based on objective scoring criteria of how participants organize the inkblots into images. In this way specific contents were less important than what portions and features of the blot were utilized in the development of the percept. It is now widely acknowledged that Rorschach underestimated the full application of his technique in its ability to reveal aspects of the individual's representational world of self and others. In the last four decades analysts and nonanalytic diagnosticians have broadened the scope of the method from essentially two angles. From an atheoretical stance of a perceptual task, diagnosticians and researchers have developed empirically validated structural variables by correlating them with behaviors and personality constructs. Working from psychoanalytic theory, David Rapaport, Roy Schafer, Steven Applebaum, Sidney Blatt, and Paul Lerner have not only articulated psychoanalytic test theory, they have brought their learning from projective testing to deepen and extend psychoanalysis as a science. Still other analysts have developed specialized psychoanalytic analog scales to assess intrapsychic phenomena such as primitive defenses, object representations, and interpersonal phenomena such as dependency.

Projective techniques encompass a number of methods for measuring personality constructs that makes an all-inclusive definition impossible. Nonetheless, they share some common features and purposes. First, their purpose is to gain insight into the individual personality as a system, rather than assessing one facet or a series of disconnected features. Most tests of this nature rely to some degree on ambiguous stimuli and opaque directions as catalysts for creating data. These tests pressure the examinee to draw on inner resources to respond to visual and verbal stimuli. This forces the examinee to utilize perception, apperception, associative processes, and memory to create responses to the examiner's questions: the more ambiguous the stimuli, the greater freedom to form idiosyncratic responses that reveal aspects of individual personality. A second feature of projective tests is the nature of data analysis—like the examinee's multitude of possible interpretations of the stimulus—the diagnostician interprets data from empirically derived scoring methods, to more "experiential" analysis that emanates from a well-organized theory of personality.

II. PROJECTIVE TECHNIQUES FOR DIAGNOSTICS AND TREATMENT PLANNING

Testing is generally undertaken to answer questions about puzzling diagnostic possibilities, to determine the presence and form of a personality disorders, and to provide consultation to therapists prior to, or during the course of psychotherapy. The standard method for answering these questions is to select a series of tests that have the greatest potential for answering the referral questions. A second consideration when compiling a battery of tests includes choosing measures that are differentially sensitive to unique manifestations of personality. For example, it is widely held that the TAT and Rorschach tap different levels of "implicit" personality functioning, and that findings from various tests, including self-report measures, provide the opportunity to observe the patient functioning under different circumstances. This data is then integrated into the formulation of the patient's character organization and the understanding of symptoms and defense configurations (Rapaport, Gill, and Schafer wrote the classic text on this topic).

A review of the diagnostic validity of projective tests in assessing symptoms, diagnoses, and prediction of outcomes would require volumes to complete. Rather than a specific review, the following is a brief sample of how projective testing is used in treatment planning and prediction in psychoanalytic treatments.

Early developments in theory-based psychological assessment can be traced to David Rapaport's efforts to interpret projective test responses using psychoanalytic theory of motivation, drives, and defensive structure. The fruits of such a major undertaking were best described by Martin Mayman:

> Rorschach inferences were transposed to a wholly new level of comprehension as Rapaport made a place for them in his psychoanalytic ego psychology and elevated psychological test findings from mundane, descriptive, pragmatically useful statements to a level of interpretation that achieved an incredible heuristic sweep.

Although Rapaport's approach was a considerable advance, a broadening of its scope was necessary to capture the experience and influence of the testing situation and its relation to transference paradigms as they are revealed in the testing situation. Roy Schafer, psychoanalyst and expert diagnostician, wrote the classic treatise on how the testing situation stimulates the expression of underlying dynamic configurations. For Schafer, the constraints of the patient role in being tested is an anxiety-arousing situation that stimulates and exacerbates defensive and transference reactions that can be scrutinized and integrated into the understanding of the patient. This approach brought the prediction of potentially disruptive and useful transference configurations into the scope of diagnostic testing.

Schafer and others were successful in shifting the focus from testing solely to determine analyzability to an approach that emphasizes the assessment of problems that interfere with the establishment of a therapeutic alliance to discover potential therapeutic levers, as well as predicting potential therapeutic stalemates and transference enactments that may not be readily discernible in the course of a standard diagnostic evaluation. The ability to employ new models for predicting transference enactments has become critical, as more patients were referred to treatment with severe character pathology and vulnerability to psychosis and suicide. Such patients create special challenges for therapists and hospital staff because premature terminations, turbulent transference–countertransference struggles and negative therapeutic reactions are more the rule than the exception. Predicting transference enactments are best done through a careful assessment of object relations prior to beginning psychotherapy because the capacity for interpersonal relations depends largely on an individual's internal array of object representations.

The strength of object relations theory when applied to psychological assessment is that it provides an understanding of the complex interactions among self and object representations, defenses, pathological formations, and ego strengths that make up the entire personality. The clinical utility of testing improved dramatically when diagnosticians shifted from more traditional focus on ego structures and impulse-defense configurations framed in abstract terms, to a middle language, grounded in a patient's phenomenology that create meaningful clinical generalizations about a patient. Diagnosticians who craft test reports in this middle language create a textured picture of a patient's character style, their modes of relating and vulnerabilities that alert the therapist to potential pitfalls that may emerge months later during an intensifying transference.

Test data from Rorschach, TAT, and Early Memories protocols are particularly well suited to these newer modes of data analysis. Psychoanalytic Rorschach scales have been crafted to examine features of self and object representations, generally along a developmental continuum from pathological to healthier and more mature modes of object representation. Two such scales are Sidney Blatt's Concept of the Object scale and Jeffery Urist's Mutuality of Autonomy scale. The former assesses the developmental level of object representations using a variety of projective tests including the Rorschach and the TAT. Utilizing structural variables, Blatt and his colleagues have studied the developmental progression of object representations along more cognitive lines by integrating the theories of Piaget and Werner into the system.

The Mutuality of Autonomy scale was developed for the Rorschach to assess the degree of differentiation of object representations, focusing primarily on the developmental progression of separation individuation from engulfing, fused relations, to highly differentiated self-other representations. Studies have demonstrated that the scale can be reliably scored, has a high degree of construct validity with behavioral ratings, and has been utilized in treatment outcome studies.

Drew Westen's Social Causality and Object Relations scale has been applied to TAT and Early Memories data, as well as interview and psychotherapy process data. Westen's scale assesses both cognitive and affective features of patient's understanding of interpersonal relations and the underlying structures of object representations and the affective quality of those representations. The scale successfully differentiates diagnostic groups and predicts behavioral outcomes such as early termination from treatment. A growing body research attests to its construct and convergent validity.

Early childhood memories have also been utilized to understand crucial aspects of personality functioning. Because of their reconstructive nature, early memories allow patients to express critical life themes in a camouflaged and unconscious way, while revealing their inner object relations, character structure, and prototypic transference enactments. Inner object-relation constellations intrude into the structure and content of early memories, just as they occur repetitively in important interpersonal relationships. This is precisely what makes early memories so revealing of the private inner world, allowing therapists to make informed decisions about therapeutic stance, and timing of interventions in order to facilitate a viable therapeutic alliance. A vast array of studies assessed early memories in treatment planning, determining character organization, and assessing potential transference paradigms.

III. EMPIRICAL EVIDENCE AND THE SCIENTIFIC STATUS OF PROJECTIVES

The fate of projective testing is continuously in question because heated disagreements over the scientific status of projective techniques, most notably the Rorschach Inkblot Method, are consistently engaged in scholarly journals. This article cannot address the scope of this debate but provides some evidence of the utility and empirical validity of the projective techniques, using the Rorschach as the prototype. A brief review is undertaken to examine the accuracy of Rorschach in assessing select disorders, in predicting treatment outcome, and in assessing change during and after intensive psychodynamic treatment.

Research has demonstrated the validity of some, but certainly not all Rorschach indexes in accurate diagnosis. When appropriately formulated, the Rorschach has demonstrated high degrees of validity in measuring specific personality constructs such as interpersonal dependency, ego strength, defense mechanisms, and quality of object relations. In terms of differential diagnosis, specific patterns of Rorschach responses have been correlated with independent diagnosis of schizophrenia; major mood disorders; and antisocial, narcissistic, and borderline personality disorders. Perhaps one of the most important uses of the test is in predicting dangerous behavior during treatment. The Rorschach when appropriately scored and formulated can predict with approximately 75% accuracy which patients will make a lethal suicide attempt within 60 days of the administration of the testing. The Rorschach has also demonstrated that scoring indexes can predict similar levels of accurate prediction of patients who will make a near lethal suicide attempt within 60 days of administration of the test.

Traditional applications of projective testing include their use in clinical settings to predict who will most likely benefit from certain forms of psychological treatment. Anecdotal evidence is far more abundant than scientifically sound studies that support the empirical validation of projective testing in predicting treatment outcome. This is in part due to the fact that most researchers in the field conduct exploratory studies rather than replicating others work. As a result research is not cumulative, making it difficult to summarize the general effectiveness of specific measures in predicting specific outcomes. One stunning exception is the myriad studies of Bruno Klopfer's Rorschach Prognostic

Rating scale (RPRS). In a sophisticated statistical and conceptual analysis, Meyer and Handler analyzed the results of 20 separate studies assessing the validity of the RPRS in predicting treatment outcome. This meta-analysis (involving 752 participants) revealed that the RPRS was highly predictive of subsequent therapy outcome. To examine its predictive power the authors compared the RPRS to other predictor-criterion pairs from various fields including medicine and education. They found the RPRS was a better predictor of psychotherapy outcome than the SAT and GRE scores are at predicting subsequent grade point average. The RPRS as a predictor of psychotherapy outcome was also superior to electrocardiogram stress tests in predicting subsequent cardiac disease. For an enlightening view of how psychological testing compares to medical diagnostic testing, readers will profit from Meyer and colleagues' latest work appearing in the *American Psychologist*.

Steven Applebaum produced two clinically based studies that directly compared inferences based on projective test data to inferences based on traditional interview data. In a small sample of 13 cases, Applebaum found test-based inferences were more accurate than inferences based on interview data. Psychological test-based inferences were most accurate in assessing ego strength, quality of interpersonal relationships, core conflicts, patterns of defense, and transference paradigms. In a second study, 26 additional cases were added to the original 13 to compare interview-based predictions to test-based ones. When psychiatrists and psychological testers disagreed on the predictions, most often testers made correct predictions about the patient's ego strengths, core conflicts, transference paradigms, defense configurations, and the degree of psychological mindedness. The results suggest that projective test data, in the hands of well-trained diagnosticians can be used for making predictions about treatment planning and outcome that is superior to that of clinicans who have clinical data from interviews.

One facet of assessment that has received relatively little attention is the application of projective tests in assessing changes in intrapsychic functioning as an aspect of psychotherapy outcome research. Given that psychoanalytic treatment endeavors to effect structural change, it is remarkable that few researchers have used sensitive measures such as the Rorschach to monitor change. Nonetheless, there are examples of how the Rorschach has been utilized in this manner. Irving Weiner and John Exner, for example, assessed 88 patients prior to starting exploratory dynamic therapy, then retested them on three occasions including at termination. A second group of 88 patients undergoing brief nondynamic psychotherapy were also assessed throughout the course of treatment and at termination. The researchers chose 27 Rorschach variables indicative of patient's ability to manage stress, perceive reality in conventional modes, modulate affective experience, adaptively utilize ideation, be self-reflected, and represent interpersonal relationships.

Results indicated that 24 of the 27 variables were significantly improved for patients in the long-term dynamic therapy, demonstrating progressive improvements at each testing through termination. Short-term patients also made significant improvement but to a lesser extent than patients in psychodynamic treatments. In a similar study Exner and a colleague replicated the first study with 70 patients, 35 in long-term treatment and 35 in brief therapy. The researchers added a fourth testing after termination. They found similar results with one major exception—improvements for patients in long-term treatments were more likely to be sustained, whereas short-term patients did not sustain improvements at follow-up.

In one of the most in-depth and extensive studies of intrapsychic change (involving 90 psychiatric inpatients with serious disturbances. Sidney Blatt and Richard Ford examined the nature of intrapsychic and behavioral change across all patients, while simultaneously assessing differential change in two distinct groups. At 1 year into treatment, the researchers found that the patients as a whole had made significant improvement in externally validated real-world behaviors such as social behavior and symptom expression (assessed from hospital case records). In terms of structural change measured by the Rorschach, they found statistically significant decreases in the degree of thought disorder, with the clearest improvements in the most serious forms of thought disorder frequently found among patients with psychotic disorders. Patients also demonstrated a greater capacity to engage adaptive fantasy and demonstrated a significant improvement in the quality of object representations, both in terms of decrease in their expectations of malevolent interactions and their ability to represent objects as separate and more autonomous.

Blatt and Ford then assessed the possibility that psychodynamic treatment might affect patterns of intrapsychic functioning in different ways depending on the patient's character structure. Blatt and his research group at Yale University had earlier distilled two essential developmental trajectories corresponding to two global character styles, the anaclitic and introjective.

The anaclitic character's actions are organized around defending against vulnerabilities to disruptions in need-gratifying interpersonal relationships. Anaclitic patients are highly dependent people who often experience somatic symptoms and seek solace and care from others including physicians and therapists. By contrast, the introjective character is focused primarily on issues of self-definition, autonomous identity, and self-esteem. Introjective characters often eschew dependent longings for fear they will disrupt efforts to secure autonomy and clarity of identity.

When patients were divided along anaclitic and introjective lines, interesting results emerged. For patients primarily concerned with maintaining need-gratifying relationships, changes were noted in moving from experiencing relationships as malevolent, controlling and fused, to more benign and differentiated. This structural change corresponded to the anaclitic patients' improved social competence and motivation for treatment. For patients with introjective character organizations, the greatest change occurred in decreased thought disorder on the Rorschach, with a corresponding improvement in clinician's assessment of symptoms—most notably, introjective patients demonstrated significant decreases in psychotic symptoms with corresponding improvement in affect modulation. Blatt and Ford's findings support decades of clinical case reports demonstrating that structural change occurs in specific arenas of functioning most related to the patient's psychopathology. An equally, if not more important finding is the fact that psychiatric patients with severe disturbances appear to benefit from intensive psychodynamic treatment. Finally, they demonstrate the way in which projective techniques can be sensitive to subtle changes in patients' intrapsychic processes and can be quantified to study treatment outcome for large groups of patients.

IV. SUMMARY

This article reported on the evidence for specific uses of projective tests in developing an accurate portrait of a patient's personality—their frailties and strengths. The diagnostic facet of projective testing can be integrated into treatment recommendations for specific patients to help the therapist develop a working model of the patient's functioning and to help predict potential transference developments. The scientific status of projective testing was considered in light of recent comparisons between the Rorschach in predicting treatment outcome and the ability of medical diagnostic tests in predicting the development of disorders such as cardiac disease. Finally, the use of projective testing to monitor intrapsychic change illuminates the current and potential uses of projective testing in measuring treatment outcome.

See Also the Following Articles

Behavioral Assessment ■ Manualized Behavior Therapy ■ Neuropsychological Assessment ■ Object Relations Psychotherapy ■ Single Case Methods and Evaluation

Further Reading

Applebaum, S. A. (1977). *The anatomy of change: A Menninger Foundation report on testing the effects of psychotherapy.* New York: Plenum.

Blatt, S. J., & Ford, R. (1994). *Therapeutic change: An object relations perspective.* New York: Plenum.

Lerner, P. (1998). *Psychoanalytic perspectives on the Rorschach.* Hillsdale, NJ: The Analytic Press.

Mayman, M. (1968). Early memories and character structure. *Journal of Projective Techniques and Personality Assessment, 32,* 303–316.

Meyer, G. J., Finn, S. E., Eyde, L. D., Kay, G. G., Moreland, K., Dies, R. R., Eisman, E. J., Kubisyn, T. W., & Ried, G. M. (2001). Psychological testing and psychological assessment: A review of evidence and issues. *American Psychologist, 56*(2), 128–165.

Meyer, G. J., & Handler, L. (1997). The ability of the Rorschach to predict subsequent outcome: A meta-analysis of the Rorschach Prognostic Rating Scale. *Journal of Personality Assessment, 69,* 1–38.

Rorschach, H. (1921/1942). *Psychodiagnostics.* Bern: Hans Huber.

Rapaport, D., Gill, M. M., & Schafer, R. (1968). *Diagnostic psychological testing.* New York: International Universities Press.

Schafer, R. (1954). *Psychoanalytic interpretation in Rorschach testing: Theory and application.* New York: Grune and Stratton.

Weiner, I. B. (1999). Contemporary perspective on Rorschach assessment. *European Journal of Psychological Assessment, 15*(1), 78–86.

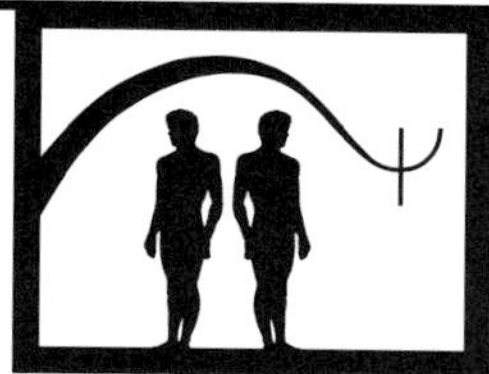

Psychoanalysis and Psychoanalytic Psychotherapy: Technique

Stephen M. Sonnenberg
Uniformed Services University of the Health Sciences, Baylor College of Medicine

Robert J. Ursano
Uniformed Services University of the Health Sciences

GLOSSARY

abstinence The refrain of the therapist/analyst from gratifying the patient's wishes.

adaptational perspective The perspective that addresses the patient's attempts to adjust and compromise with external reality.

clarification A technical intervention on the analyst's part asking the patient to consider the unconscious intentions of the patient's communications.

confrontation The technical intervention on the part of the analyst in which the analyst brings to the patient's awareness some aspects of feelings, thoughts, or context of which the patient has been unaware.

countertransference The experience of transference by analysts and therapists.

free association The technical instruction from the analyst for the patient to say anything that comes to mind, and to suspend the usual effort to think clearly and coherently and to pass judgement on the appropriateness of the idea.

freely hovering attention A mode of functioning and listening on the part of the analyst in which the analyst is sensitive to symbolic metaphorical communications, and listens in a creative, imaginative frame of mind, attempting to discern the underlying unconscious intentions of the patient's communication.

freely hovering role responsiveness The manner in which the analyst participates in the psychoanalysis, allowing himself or herself to experience the transference, as well as countertransference, forces at play in the relationship.

historical perspective The perspective of psychoanalytic thought that emphasizes the influence of past history on present behavior.

interpretation A technical intervention in which the analyst attempts to assist the patient to understand exactly how and why he thinks, feels, and behaves as he does.

neutrality The stance which the analyst/therapist takes in which he or she does not express personal preferences to the patient and does not ally himself or herself with important dimensions of the patient's conflict.

psychodynamic perspective The emphasis in psychoanalytic theory demonstrating conflict and compromise among various psychological structures to create new behaviors, symptoms, and psychological structures, such as wishes and fantasies.

structural perspective A psychoanalytic view that describes the components of the mind, emphasizing the specific functions and tasks of these components.

topographical perspective A psychoanalytic perspective that emphasizes there are two qualities of mental activity, conscious and unconscious.

transference The tendency to unwittingly construct and create, through an active but unconscious process, the pattern of imagined and real past relationships with an important person.

I. THE TALKING CURE

Psychoanalysis and psychoanalytic psychotherapy are often referred to as the talking cures. That term emphasizes that psychoanalysts help patients by talking with them and that a conversation is central to what heals the patient. However, although the term *talking cure* captures something very special about psychoanalysis, it is misleading. It fails to stress that at the core of what heals is the relationship between the analyst and the patient, and that their conversation is the way the aspects of that relationship are formed and expressed.

A. Basic Assumptions

An examination of the basic assumptions underlying psychoanalysis and psychoanalytic therapy will further clarify what has just been emphasized. In the past various groups of analysts have come together in more or less official schools, groupings that emphasize somewhat different theoretical perspectives. Today, there is an emphasis on harmonizing those groups, and finding the common ground in the basic assumptions they share. In a recent article, Donna Kline and Stephen Sonnenberg suggested that four basic assumptions were useful in describing contemporary psychoanalysis. These are (1) that the analyst is experienced by the patient as having characteristics of important people from the patient's past, (2) that the patient's actions in and outside the analysis repeat patterns from the patient's past, (3) that some mental activity of all people takes place outside of consciousness, and (4) that people have a wish to understand themselves, to know, and that what is known can lead to changes in the way they think, feel, and act.

It is very important that the analyst is experienced as having characteristics of people from the past. The technical term for this is *transference,* and because it occurs in the relationship between the patient and the analyst, that relationship becomes a living experiment in which the influence of the patient's past on the patient's present life can be explored.

Past patterns are repeated in the present that provide another component of the transference, again making possible an exploration of the effect of the past on the present.

The idea that some portion of mental activity takes place outside consciousness is also of vital importance in psychoanalysis. Certainly, it is that idea which was central when Freud invented psychoanalysis as a method of personal inquiry and healing: Freud reasoned that when an unconscious idea became conscious it could be examined, and if it was unreasonable, placed in a new perspective. For example, consider a person has a powerful unconscious wish to put a business competitor out of business and fails at his own business out of unconscious guilt over that unconscious wish. When the wish becomes conscious the individual in question can thoughtfully decide to abandon the idea/wish, or perhaps to follow through and develop a business plan that is acceptable and does not cause him second thoughts.

The desire to know is an assumption of psychoanalysis that has not always been sufficiently emphasized. If one pauses and gives serious thought to this matter, one must marvel at the human capacity to question and seek answers. Indeed, were it not for that capacity, one might realize there would be no field of psychoanalysis, no discipline that has at its purpose the illumination of the mysteries of what goes on in the human mind.

A corollary of this assumption is that the wish to know allows the patient and the analyst to come together in an alliance, sometimes called a working alliance, sometimes called a therapeutic alliance. It is certainly the case that a journey of deep self-inquiry will have many rough spots, many difficult times, and it is because the patient and the analyst are joined in a mutual commitment to knowing, to learning, that they can form a relationship in which they examine together often emotionally painful aspects of the patient's life. Put another way, it is the mutual wish to know that binds the patient and the analyst together in a relationship in which they both tolerate the frustration and sometimes painful challenge of the analytic journey.

II. ANALYSIS AS A DRAMA

Another useful metaphor in understanding the technique of psychoanalysis and psychoanalytic psychotherapy is that of a dramatic performance. In the treatment relationship the patient is asked to write a play about his life, and to act many of the roles in that play in his relationship with the analyst. For her part, the analyst is asked to give herself over to the playwright patient and psychologically assume various roles assigned by the patient in the course of their analytic relationship. This vivid process is described by psychoanalysts when they use the technical terms transference and countertransference.

A. The Transference

This term has already been introduced. The reason to discuss this term further in this section is to emphasize that it is the analyst's responsibility to teach the patient that the creation of the transference—the pattern of past relationships with an important figure—derives from the patient. Most often, the patient "creates" the transference out of an active, though unconscious, aspect of repeating a past experience. At times, this has been thought of as part of the wish to correct the past, but this is not a necessary part of the concept of transference. Rather, the pattern of interpersonal relationships laid down by early experience in our biopsychosocial world may give us few options of choice unless we become aware of our patterns of behavior. When the analyst helps the patient understand consciously this old pattern that is awakened (and is creating a drama driven by past experiences rather than present ones), the analyst helps the patient understand his contribution to the present conflict and for the life he lives.

Analysts are trained to both experience and observe the drama the patient constructs in words in the analytic consulting room. The analyst imagines herself in the world the patient creates, places herself in her imagination in the roles the patient describes for those with whom he interacts, and recognizes how in subtle ways similar patterns are created by the patient in the interactions with the analyst or therapist. The products of those reflections by the analyst are the various ideas the analyst conveys to the patient.

To illustrate this point, imagine a patient who feels helpless in all situations with authority figures. The patient will regard the analyst/therapist as an authority figure. The analyst will feel that role assigned to her, and that feeling will help the analyst understand the helplessness the patient feels.

B. The Countertransference

Psychoanalysis is neither an intellectual exercise nor a spectator sport. In the analytic relationship both the analyst and the patient experience the patient's life in an active, vivid way. In that spirit, psychoanalysts have stated that in their professional relationships with their patients they are participant observers, not simply outside observers. Therefore, analysts and therapists also experience transference—called countertransference—to the patient when the patient reminds the analyst of an important figure from the past. The analyst's awareness and attention to countertransference permits the analyst/therapist to have a fuller appreciation of the drama of the patient's life. The analyst does not act on the countertransference but rather uses her awareness of these feelings as further information to inform the understanding of the patient's world.

C. Abstinence and Neutrality: The Design of the Therapeutic Encounter

The analyst is restrained in interaction with the patient to words designed to help the patient learn about himself. In that spirit, the analyst strives to create an environment in which the patient feels safe to experience a part of the drama of his life and be able to observe it in this subtle form. This requires that the patient not be burdened with worry about the realities of the analyst's life, values, or ideas about living. The analyst maintains neutrality, does not express personal preferences to the patient, and provides limited information about his or her own life. A corollary of this is that the analyst maintains anonymity, thereby protecting the patient from knowledge of the analyst's personal style and values. The term abstinence refers to the fact that the analyst avoids gratifying the patient's wishes, whatever those might be—praise or punishment—direction or to be left alone. The analyst's task is to understand and to convey the patterns of interpersonal relating that emerge and reflect the past experience of the patient. This occurs in part because the analyst does not praise or punish or in general fulfill the unspoken wishes of the patient. When the patient's wishes remain unfulfilled, they are felt as obstacles by the patient and become available for examination. The concept of abstinence shares a common border with the concepts of neutrality and anonymity. As a group, these aspects of the analyst's behavior might usefully be seen as the way the analyst provides the context in which the patient can both experience and examine the interpersonal drama of his life and its past origins.

III. CORE TECHNICAL CONCEPTS

Four technical concepts of psychoanalysis and psychoanalytic psychotherapy are important to therapeutic process: free association, the metaphors in the patient's words, freely hovering attention as a mode of analytic listening, and freely hovering role responsiveness as a mode of establishing the countertransference during analytic listening.

A. Free Association

Psychoanalysts have observed that when people think and say what comes to mind their thoughts reveal a layering. On the topmost layer is rational thought, the kind of thinking that takes place when one performs an intellectual task or has a conversation about a particular topic. However, buried in that conscious rational verbal exchange and thinking are the hints of a parallel layer of thought that occurs simultaneously, outside conscious awareness. In this form of thinking, different rules apply. For example, many different things may be represented by a single symbol, a process sometimes described as condensation, sometimes described as symbolization. We see this same logic in other areas—such as a rebus in which a clock with wings represents "time flies," or when one recalls a vacation at the beach in childhood as a way to remember an entire year of one's life that may include many important but not yet recalled events.

Thus, when the psychoanalyst or psychodynamic psychotherapist listens to her patient, she first instructs the patient to say anything that comes to mind, to suspend the usual effort to think clearly and make sense. When the patient is able to do that, and it is not easy, the unconscious layer of thinking is more apparent, symbols are more apparent, and the analyst can hear somewhat more directly what goes on in the patient's mind outside usual awareness. In fact, this process of free association is always relative and only really becomes free as the patient resolves the conflicts that are the source of his or her pain.

B. The Focus on Metaphor

This core technical concept dovetails with free association. The psychoanalyst believes he or she can best help the patient if the analyst can equip the patient to examine his thoughts, recognize the clues to what is unconscious, examine the unconscious layer of mental activity, and determine how such thinking influences current behavior. Therefore, it is essential for the analyst to listen for the symbolic meaning in what the patient says.

For example, let us imagine that just as thoughts of dogs outside of conscious awareness may represent all four-legged animals, all similarly considered children who want love and praise may represent all adults who feel starved for love and praise. Let us also suppose that the patient in treatment is one such adult. When asked to free associate the patient may return repeatedly, in many forms, to the subject of children who need love and praise. Suppose also that the patient is a pediatrician who gives lectures to parents about the need of children for parental love and praise. Eventually, through noting when and in what context these associations occur, the patient's hints and verbal symbols about children and their need for parental love may be understood as the patient talking about his own need for love and praise when speaking of the children.

The analysis of dreams is a part of psychoanalysis and psychoanalytic psychotherapy. Dreams have been called the royal road to the unconscious, and certainly they often occupy an important place in a clinical psychoanalytic treatment. Dreams are used in the same way as free associations—a source of material to free associate to, as the patient and analyst/therapist listen for the unconscious concerns of the present and the forgotten links to the past. The analyst listens to the patient describe a dream in a search for symbols and for metaphor to educate the patient and facilitate an understanding of the meaning of the thoughts and the way of thinking, and an appreciation of all the mental activity which is outside conscious awareness.

C. Freely Hovering Attention as a Mode of Analytic Listening

As the analyst/therapist listens to the patient's free associations, he or she listens for the patient's unconscious mental activity. In this listening, the analyst is sensitive to the symbolic communications of the patient. This is not a process that is easy, nor ever automatic, no matter how well an analyst/therapist knows the patient. The analyst listens in a creative, imaginative frame of mind, in which layering of meaning and symbols become vivid experiences for the analyst. The analyst has as background the many previous topics that have been discussed by the patient and the context of these and of the present and past life of the patient.

For example, as the patient describes a needy child, the freely hovering analyst may note that a mental image of such a child has come to mind, and that image may change in the analyst's mind's eye into an imaginary mental image of the patient as a young child. The analyst/therapist continues to listen, now no longer freely hovering, but rather reasoning that perhaps the image is related to a subtle communication from the patient—how the patient phrased something or the empathy in the patient's associations. The analyst then wonders if he or she should ask the patient if he is talking about himself. If the patient responds in the affirmative, a piece of analytic information has been generated, and the patient has shared an experience of making the unconscious conscious.

D. Freely Hovering Role Responsiveness

Much that the analyst learns about the patient comes from being a participant observer in the analytic relationship. Imagine, then, that along with imagining the patient as a needy child, the analyst began to recognize the patient's subtle but demanding requests that the analyst praise him. That request by the patient and experience by the analyst could come in relatively hidden ways. For example, the pediatrician patient, despite having other alternatives, may ask his analyst to change the times of several hours because he must attend several national professional meetings, at which he has been asked to speak about the emotional needs of children. He may say to the analyst that he is available to meet at times he knows are not the usual working hours. For her part, the analyst may sense with great force the patient's request/demand for special treatment, as part of the recognition of what an outstanding pediatrician he is. The analyst practicing abstinence, neutrality, and anonymity, and using a freely hovering role responsiveness that has thus identified an unconscious meaning in this request, will be able to convey to the patient the particular meaning of the patient's associations and actions within the analytic relationship and wonder if the patient is alert to these feelings and wishes. With appropriate analytic inquiry on the part of the analyst, and a willingness to explore his desires on the patient's part, further insight will be gained by the patient of what he originally thought was only a "practical" request.

IV. CORE INTERVENTIONS

A critical part of an understanding of the technique of psychoanalysis and psychoanalytic psychotherapy includes how the therapist speaks to the patient. While the psychoanalyst listens to the wishes and feelings of the patient that are both conscious and out of awareness in order to have a deep understanding of the patient as another human being, the setting of that listening is specifically restrained. In addition, the ways of speaking to the patient are designed to effect change in specific ways. In sum, the analyst tries to speak in a way that enhances the patient's awareness of his own unconscious processes, and more generally of how his mind works, so that the patient can learn to practice effective introspection on his own. There are three technical ways the analyst speaks to the patient that are designed to enhance the capacity for insight: confrontation, clarification, and. interpretation.

A. Confrontation

At times in psychoanalysis, the analyst confronts the patient with information or observations. The term confrontation in this context does not mean a hostile exchange between analyst and patient, but bringing to the patient's awareness some aspect of feelings, thoughts, or context that the patient is not aware of. In keeping with the notion of the therapeutic alliance, the analyst attempts at all times to create a safe atmosphere in which the analysis will take place. This will be described in more detail later. Nevertheless, it is often the case that the analyst points out, in a kind way, that the expectations or ideas of the patient are quite different from what the patient realizes them to be.

For example, returning to our dedicated pediatrician, suppose he asked his analyst to see him on Saturdays, which she normally took off, and when she refused, said he was going to quit his analysis because she obviously did not care about him. In that instance, the analyst would appropriately point out to the patient that he was assuming that she could see him on Saturday and simply chose not to, and that on the basis of that unproven assumption was ready to stop a much needed treatment. This example, by the way, is common; there are many similar instances in which individuals desperately needing psychological help quit treatment without realizing that their actions are being guided by one of the problems for which they are seeking treatment. Thus, the analyst must be prepared to vigorously confront the patient, when necessary.

B. Clarification

There are other times when the analyst must ask the patient to clarify what he has said, or speak to the patient in a way that offers clarification from the analyst's viewpoint. Again, returning to our pediatrician, he might ask his analyst to give up her day off in a way so subtle that he unconsciously hopes she will not recognize that the request comes from him. Unconsciously, he desires her to feel spontaneously that she should offer to see him on Saturday. Consciously, he may be aware of none of this; not even that he has made an actual request of this kind. Here is a situation in which the patient requires clarification, rather than confrontation. The clarification may involve the analyst asking the patient to consider, in a thoughtful way, what he has said and to wonder if there may have been a subtle request, or a veiled threat if the wished-for offer was not spontaneously forthcoming from the analyst. Alternatively, the clarification may involve the analyst making such an observation to the patient.

C. Interpretation

Often interpretation is seen by analysts as the crown jewel of the methods available to help patients think more effectively about themselves. Interpretation involves telling patients in a convincing way that there is an unconscious process at work in their thinking and, in a complete interpretation, explaining exactly why and how that unconscious process works. In the example we are using, it might involve the analyst telling her patient that he requested sessions on her day off because he wanted to know that she loved and admired him, and that this was a strong desire of his for certain specific reasons that she would elaborate related to specific childhood experiences and needs which she would describe in detail. It is the addition of the developmental explanation of the feelings, wishes, and hopes that makes an interpretation a linking the past with the present in a convincing manner.

Interpretations are designed to help the patient understand exactly how and why he thinks, feels, and behaves as he does, but it is incorrect to think that they are more important than confrontations and clarifications. These three methods of communication are used throughout an analysis, and it is the judicious use of all three modes of communication that is an important skill of the clinical psychoanalyst.

V. PSYCHOANALYTIC PERSPECTIVES ON THE MIND

Psychoanalysis works by enhancing the patient's ability to examine the workings of his mind, especially workings that were previously unconscious. Put another way, psychoanalysis is a method of making the unconscious conscious or what is out of awareness available for the patient to consider and include in decisions and choices. However, there are several perspectives that psychoanalysts use in observing their patients, organizing their ideas about their patients, and which they try to convey to their patients in the belief that these perspectives will help them practice effective introspection during psychoanalysis and afterward on their own. These perspectives include the topographic, the structural, the historical, the psychodynamic, and the adaptational. These are, in effect, the smaller units into which the working of the mind can be divided. By understanding these, the patient has additional tools for introspection.

A. The Topographic Perspective

The topographic perspective emphasizes that there are two qualities of mental activity—conscious and unconscious. Much mental activity, increasingly supported by neurosciences of brain function, takes place outside conscious awareness. Forces pushing thoughts out of awareness appear to be always at work.

B. The Structural Perspective

The structural perspective describes the components of the mind, each of which has specific functions and performs certain tasks. Of course, these components do not really exist but rather are a way to group conceptually certain types of thinking and cognitive processes. For example, Freud described three components, or "structures" in the mind—the ego, the id, and the superego. Roughly, the first is where we do most of our thinking, the second where we do our wishing, and the third where our conscience and goals reside. Knowledge about these systems helps the clinician think more clearly about the patient. In addition, when understood in the specifics of one's life, it can help the patient think more clearly about himself.

Returning to our pediatrician, it is obvious that at the time he is asking his analyst to give up her Saturdays, there are desires (that we consider part of the id) that are very powerful, and ways of thinking (ego functions) that may allow him to implement his desire without it coming into full awareness. The knowledge that he has a mind that performs these different functions simultaneously can be helpful to this analytic patient.

C. The Historical Perspective

The historical perspective focuses on the aspects of mental function that show the influence of past history on present behavior and our attempts to resolve our conflicts and choices. This perspective, also, can be very helpful for the patient as one of the tools of introspection. It is essential that the analyst teach the patient to appreciate the ongoing nature of transference, and that transference takes place not only within the analysis, but in life outside the treatment setting. When the patient understands the ubiquitous nature of transference and the influence of the past and its important interpersonal relations, he has a perspective that will consistently enhance self-analysis.

D. The Psychodynamic Perspective

The psychodynamic perspective involves an appreciation of the conflicts we experience in our mental life and their path to compromise. From the psychoanalytic view, this means the way the different psychic agencies (structures) clash throughout mental life, and as a result, how much mental activity remains outside conscious awareness. For example, the dynamic perspective traces the evolution and alteration of a wish, a desire, or a hope from childhood and adulthood into being kept unconscious, molded by the ego into a compromise, and subjected to the judgment of the conscience. Returning for a moment to our pediatrician—the patient, thinking dynamically, recognizes his wish to be loved and his anger when love is not available. He recognizes his wish to threaten the person who does not bestow the love he wants, his compromise of lecturing on the need for love by others (young children), and that such lecturing brings him a loved feeling. In addition, he has come to realize that this process was previously outside awareness because such ignorance was more comfortable than knowing. With a new awareness of this complex set of feelings, thoughts, motives, and actions related to problems going back to childhood, the pediatrician may feel empowered to give up the wishes of childhood. The pediatrician recognizes that his previous frustration is replaced with a mature awareness that the disappointments of childhood no longer have the powerful impact they had when he was dependent on his parents for everything at the age of five.

E. The Adaptational Perspective

The adaptational perspective emphasizes how our feelings, thoughts, and behaviors are an adaptation, an adjustment and compromise with what was possible. This is important to the patient because it puts in context the patient's psychological strengths, his assets, and the reality of the world of the past and the present. Indeed, whatever compromises have been made throughout a person's development, part of the reason for them is that they have certain adaptational advantages. To avoid throwing out the baby with the bath water, it is crucial for the patient to have an enduring appreciation of how he came to be, what he was before psychoanalysis, and how he can and should retain the best of himself throughout the process. This includes an appreciation of the strengths of his personality structure, and the useful ways he has learned to use his thoughts and his feelings.

VI. HOW DO PSYCHOANALYSIS AND PSYCHOANALYTIC PSYCHOTHERAPY WORK?

Much has been written about the therapeutic action of these treatments. The goals of treatments include resolution of symptoms but, even more important, an enhanced maturity and ability to introspect and analyze one's mental conflicts on one's own after treatment. An enhanced maturity is indicated by more intimate, responsible, committed relationships. A more effective capacity to engage in self-analysis provides the patient with a tool for the future. Life is not static; human development involves ever new challenges. An effectively psychoanalyzed individual has developed the autonomous capacity to engage in productive self-reflection. What has occurred during a psychoanalysis, as a result of the techniques described, that promotes such personal maturation and self-reflection? These broad goals are reached through the patients obtaining:

1. A working understanding of his history, his psychodynamics, and his adaptational skills.
2. A mind now much more aware of itself than before. His unconscious mental processes are much more accessible to consciousness and, therefore, much more manageable.
3. A set of new and rearranged psychic structures, including an autonomous self-analytic, self-observing function, and a conscience that is both reasonable and appropriate.

VII. THE THERAPEUTIC ACTION OF PSYCHOANALYSIS AND PSYCHOANALYTIC PSYCHOTHERAPY

We have already established that analysis works because it is a relationship in which there is a process of examination, and that, during that process of examination, the patient changes in many ways. Analysts use the term working through to describe this. The process often takes several years. However, more recently, brief forms of psychodynamic psychotherapy have been introduced that are more focused, often to a single conflict-defense pattern, and rely much more on the patient's ability to carry on significant work after the treatment. For psychoanalysis, many analysts believe that at the start the patient needs to experience the examination as open ended. In this way, the patient is less able to use a special end point as a safe harbor, a place to which he can travel with the belief that once there he will be spared the difficult task of profound introspection. When the open ended treatment is not available, the therapist's and analyst's work must be even more alert to the patient's defensive choice of endings of the treatment or a protective definition of successful outcome.

The relationship with a psychoanalyst and a psychoanalytic therapist is unique in the modern world. Where else in adult life does someone listen to another person with such attention and concern? Such an environment provides the patient with what has been called a corrective emotional experience, an experience of being understood, accepted, held in a safe place, protected by someone with whom the patient can actually share his pain, his worries, his fears. This last activity is known as the analyst's containing function. Good parents of young children perform such a function. It is rarely available outside very close, loving relationships in adult life. Indeed, because most patients who seek analysis have trouble forming such close, loving relationships, the uniqueness to the patient of the analytic situation is evident.

Many analysts believe that the provision of such a safe and understanding environment provides the patient with such a new experience that the memories of the analyst's many functions and interactions can become the organizing psychological force behind the creation of a new psychic structure in the patient. As such, it can be an important, new idea in the patient's mind about what is possible in a human relationship. This new structure in turn permits the patient to develop a new structure of his self, a part of his mind in which his sense of himself is different than it was before. This new self is capable of the many psychological changes and behaviors described in this article because of psychoanalytic treatment. This self structure exists in a new and stable equilibrium, capable of loving itself and others, and working hard to do a good job in a wide range of life activities. In this new structure there are also new and old memories of others, memories that are now also stable, enduring, and either pleasing or relatively tolerable to the patient.

See Also the Following Articles

Confrontation ■ Free Association ■ Interpretation ■ Psychoanalytic Psychotherapy and Psychoanalysis, Overview ■ Research in Psychotherapy ■ Therapeutic Factors ■ Transference ■ Unconscious, The ■ Working Alliance

Further Reading

Kline, D. C., Sonnenberg, S. M. (In Press). Skepticism and science: An empirical construal of psychoanalytic experience. *Journal of Clinical Psychoanalysis.*

Malan, D. H. (1963). *A study of brief psychotherapy.* London: Tavistock Press.

Racker, H. (1968). *Transference and countertransference.* New York: International University Press.

Sandler, J., Dare, C., & Holder, A. (1973). *The patient and the analyst: The basis of the psychoanalytic process.* New York: International University Press.

Ursano, R. J., & Silberman, E. K. (1999). Psychoanalysis, psychoanalytic psychotherapy and supportive psychotherapy. In Hales, R. E., Yudofsky, S. C., & Talbott, J. A. (Eds.), *Textbook of Psychiatry* (pp. 1157–1184). Washington DC: American Psychiatric Press.

Ursano, R. J., Sonnenberg, S. M., & Lazar, S. G. (Eds.). (1998). *Concise guide to psychodynamic psychotherapy.* Washington, DC: American Psychiatric Press.

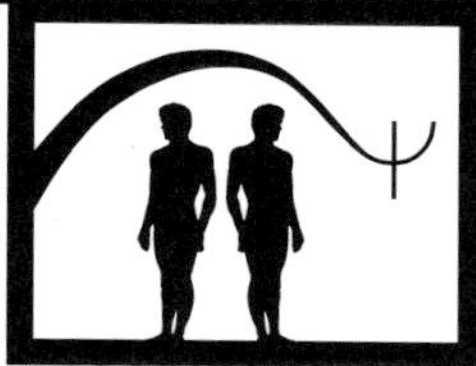

Psychoanalytic Psychotherapy and Psychoanalysis, Overview

Eric R. Marcus
Columbia University College of Physicians and Surgeons and Columbia University Psychoanalytic Center for Training and Research

GLOSSARY

analyze To make conscious and to describe the structure, relationships, meanings, significance, and origins of mental phenomena, especially emotional representations.

associations Experiences that come to mind, including memories and fantasies, that link emotionally to the topic under discussion. That topic may be a symptom or a pathological character trait.

cognitive A word for conscious thinking.

cognitive-behavioral therapy The use of conscious focus and will to overcome mental symptoms. The focus is on behavior and conscious thinking.

compromise formation A term used to refer to the result of conflicting forces. The compromise result may be a symptom or personality trait. A compromise formation may also be nonpathological. The difference is whether or not the compromise is adaptive to both the outer world and inner wishes and fears.

conflict The experience of opposed emotional forces causing anxiety and generating symptoms and pathological personality traits.

implicit memory Memory of aspects of experience inherent in, but not obviously part of, the content of events. Usually nonverbal and unconscious.

induction phase of psychoanalysis The first phase of psychoanalysis in which patients are engaging with the treatment process and emotional aspects of their own history start to emerge. The transference relationship to the analyst begins. The focus is on interpretation of resistances to the treatment process and to the transference.

mental representations The content and organization of mental experience. The term refers especially to self and object representations. Psychoanalysis is particularly interested in affect representations.

mental structure The relatively stable and lasting organizations of mental contents and functions.

middle phase of psychoanalytic treatment The phase of treatment when the patient's unconscious dynamic psychology unfolds in consciousness, the transference intensifies and focuses in a transference neurosis, and when interpretation of unconscious conflict and the working through of better compromises is occurring.

neurocognitive rehabilitation A method of teaching education techniques for learning to patients with neurological difficulties in learning.

neurotic A level of intensity of mental illness in which reality testing and emotional control are present.

parameters Noninterpretive techniques in psychoanalysis.

personality Characteristic attitudes and behavioral reaction patterns based on temperament and experience.

personality defenses Personality traits that are used to protect the conscious mind from painful mental experiences.

procedural memory The memory of processes that organize events. A type of implicit memory. Usually unconscious.

procedural rules The rules of organization and use of mental experience.

psychoanalysis A talking treatment method for eliciting and understanding the psychology of unconscious emotional experiences and representations. The method reveals the unconscious structures that organize emotional experience. The word also refers to a theory of human emotional development.

psychoanalytic psychotherapy A talking treatment method of less intensity than psychoanalysis. Usually conducted with the patient sitting up and facing the analyst, the treatment occurs one or two times a week. The goals are less ambitious. The objectives are more limited and focused. The treatment involves many different interventions, not just interpretation of conflict.

psychoanalytic treatment An intensive talking treatment method to understand the emotional conflicts in mental symptoms and personality. The patient lies on a couch with the analyst behind and is seen four or five times per week. The focus of treatment is especially on the emotional relationship with the analyst.

psychopharmacological treatment The use of medications to affect mental illness.

symbolization The representation of mental experience, particularly affect experience, that involve one image or element to refer to and express emotional meaning.

temperament Inborn reaction propensities composed of stimulus sensitivity, latency time, intensity of response, and dominant affect elicited.

termination phase The last phase of psychoanalysis. The transference neurosis resolves. Shifts in personality function and symptom improvement are consolidated. The psychoanalytic process itself is internalized.

transference The transfer of feelings about childhood relationships onto the experience of the relationship with the analyst.

unconscious Mental experiences, particularly emotional experiences, of which a person is not aware.

working through The process of applying insights from psychoanalysis to many different areas and to the working out of new compromise formations.

I. INTRODUCTION

Psychoanalysis is a theory and a method for understanding the development and functions of human psychology, especially the emotions. Psychoanalysis is a theory of human emotional development based on observations and treatment for emotional illness. Psychoanalysis and psychoanalytic therapy are talking treatments in which a person's psychology is explored in order to help the person master emotional conflicts. These conflicts are manifested in mental symptoms, in troubled relationships with others, in work, in love inhibitions and disruptions, in unhappiness, and in poor self-esteem. Through a detailed description of what troubles a person, and all the associations this brings to mind, the elaborate complexity of how the person's mind functions is brought to consciousness.

Psychoanalysis is based on the concept of unconscious mental representations that are built up from childhood. These mental representations of self and others include intense and conflicted emotions. The conflicted emotions involve wishes, associated fears, and attitudes that organize compromises among them. These representations are influenced both by temperament and experience. The representations are linked by association mainly of affect. They are mediated by and encompass the various groups of mental functions. They can be made conscious in an affect-stimulating relationship and changed if they can then be consciously observed and thereby better synthesized in more adaptive ways. The psychoanalyst achieves this goal by becoming the focus of and then analyzing the patient's projections of mental representations and attitudes.

Mental representations and attitudes include conflicted emotions. Emotional conflicts involve simultaneous wishes and fears. An example is envious hatred of, and longing feelings of love for, the same person, or the same type of relationship. The compromise might be avoiding love and having unhappy, longing feelings. If a compromise of distant love is rigid and fixed, the patient's love life will be lonely, sad, and unrequited. Psychoanalysis, tries to understand the conflict and its defensive avoidance so thoroughly that the patient can understand and achieve a new and better compromise that involves an intimate relationship.

The idea that we are not aware of all our feelings, of all the conflicts in our feelings, of the ways we defend against them, and the ways we compromise those feelings in our minds and in our everyday lives, or the rules that organize those compromises, was first thoroughly researched and systematized by Sigmund Freud. He discovered the rules of organization of emotional life in the late 19th century when the physical sciences were beginning to discover the rules of organization of physical matter. Freud's initial training was in physical science and neurology and he brought that intellectual approach to his study of human psychology and the unconscious.

II. GOALS AND OBJECTIVES OF PSYCHOANALYTIC TREATMENT

The goal of psychoanalysis is the relief of mental symptoms and life stalemates through understanding the contributing conflicted emotional forces involved. The objective is a shift in the compromises of those forces so that symptoms ease, psychological development renews, and life growth progresses. The specific objectives will depend on the particular categories of symptoms and behaviors in each case.

III. INDICATIONS AND CONTRAINDICATIONS

The indications for psychoanalysis are quite broad. Although classically limited to neurotic symptoms and personality disorders, the modern practitioner may attempt this method with a much broader spectrum of patients, either alone or in combination with other treatments.

The majority of patients in psychoanalysis have neurotic symptoms and neurotic personalty disorders. Psychoanalysis is particularly indicated for personality disorders because the illness affects almost all areas of interpersonal functioning and requires a model relationship to use as an example. The doctor–patient relationship in the psychoanalytic setting becomes that model.

Central to the treatment is the analysis of symptoms and of personality defenses. Symptoms are repetitive mental experiences the patient finds unpleasant. Personality defenses are attitudes the person experiences as part of themself, justified and valuable, which are used to protect the person, but at a price. Both symptoms and maladaptive personality traits are stable, psychological structures that encode conflicted feelings and responses from years of emotional feelings. These structures are associated with the memories they originated with and are partly in response to. They therefore encode the developmental history of the emotional life. Their structures involve the symbolization of emotional conflicts in symptoms and in attitudes.

Patients with neurotic symptoms and personality problems have their cognitive and emotional control functions intact. They are therefore able to understand and use a psychological treatment to gain conscious insight into the emotional forces at work in their problems. They have the capacity to apply this information to many different related areas. With insight, they can construct new compromises for the warring emotional forces so that the symptoms and personality traits that are the pathological compromises can change.

However, sicker patients are more and more being treated by this method in conjunction with medications, other treatments, and nonpsychoanalytic technique mixed with psychoanalytic technique. These parameters of treatment are aimed at strengthening cognitive and emotional control functions damaged by severe psychiatric illness. The sickest patients alter their view of reality to fit their conflicted emotional states. These patients cannot function well in psychoanalysis, and may even get worse, unless medications and other parameters of treatment are used. Such combinations can be highly successful.

The major contraindications for psychoanalytic treatment are, therefore, patients who have severe cognitive–integrative function disorders, patients who have extreme emotional control disorders, and patients whose reality testing is gone or severely limited. Of particular concern are those with emotional discontrol problems because they respond to intense emotion with disruptive actions or worsening emotional states. This is a problem in psychoanalysis because the technique is specifically geared to increase available affect for neurotic level patients, especially in the relationship with the therapist.

Relative contraindications are those patients who are not psychologically minded, or cannot use metaphor and meaning to generalize and apply to specific symptoms and concrete behavioral actions. Sometimes these functions can be rehabilitated or taught anew, making a psychological treatment possible.

IV. METHOD

The method of psychoanalysis has two components, the setting and the technique. The setting is an intensive psychotherapeutic setting where the patient is seen four or five times per week. The frequency of sessions is to achieve a persistence in focusing on pathological symptoms and actions and an intensity in the relationship to the analyst. This intensity is usually required for the conscious experience and analysis of unconscious emotional conflicts. The treatment lasts for a number of years, so that the deepest intensity and the deepest possible resolution of emotional conflict can be achieved.

The patient lies down on a couch with the analyst seated behind so that ordinary social interaction can recede and the patient's inner world of long-standing self and object relationships and attitudes can emerge. The frightening aggressive and loving fantasies that are organized in symptoms and personality attitudes can then be analyzed, and their earliest manifestations recovered in memory.

The method needs privacy and confidentiality. Because people are talking about their most intimate fears, wishes, and memories, the treatment cannot work unless the privacy of the analytic setting, and utmost confidentiality about any records of the treatment, is maintained. Breaches of this privacy and confidentiality barrier, whether casual or systematic, destroy the possibility of the treatment.

V. TECHNIQUE

The main technique of psychoanalysis is free association, in which the patient says whatever comes to mind about the symptoms and attitudes. Because associations are organized especially by affect-linked relationships, entering a free association pattern will reveal affect-organized self and object relationships. These patterns have a long developmental history beginning in early childhood. The free association method leads back to these early memories.

The free association method slowly discovers not only the content of thoughts, memories, and fantasies, and not only their historical antecedents in memory, but also their organizing procedural rules. Those procedural rules are crucial aspects of personality attitudes and form the basis of the experience of one's self and other people. The organizational rules of these emotional patterns may be stored in a special memory capacity that cognitive science calls procedural memory, a type of implicit memory. Psychoanalysis enters the procedural memory bank through the free association method.

By saying what comes to mind in free association, new historical information and/or new, previously unconscious, emotional attitudes to the life historical information become conscious. Crucial to this emerging story are the unconscious fantasies organizing attitudes and life history. Dreams and conscious fantasies are clues to this more unconscious material. More emotional and less factual dreams and fantasies show the surface of emotional conflicts, their historical associations, their present triggers, and their personality defenses more clearly. This allows for a more complete understanding of the life history, the emotional history, and their relationship. The influences on the development of the personality slowly become clear. Because of the intimacy of the setting, the intensity of the affect experiences, the pointing to resistances against associations and against the unfolding of affect experiences, the patient reexperiences the full force of affect associations, their memories, and their organizations.

The patient then has an emotional reaction to the listener. In this case, the listener is a psychoanalyst who can describe these reactions to the treatment and to the person of the analyst. These reactions are called transference reactions because they are transferred from formative relationship experiences in the past. When the analyst describes them in detail, the analyst is said to be analyzing the transference.

The transference is a crucial aspect of psychoanalytic technique because it gives the analyst a firsthand view of core emotional reactions in the patient. There is no other way to experience the specificity and the complexity of those emotional reactions because, being unconscious and composed of affect, the patient may not at first have descriptions in conscious language. The transference is the reason that the setting involves the supine position, frequent sessions, interpretation of resistance, and relative abstinence of the analyst. All of these techniques are to foster and catalyze an intense transference reaction that will reveal the deeper layers of personality.

The transference is different than the same old attitudes played out with other people in the patient's life for two reasons. The first reason is that the transference is usually clearer in its content and functions than interactions with people in the patient's present relationships because the associated conflicts become conscious. The second reason is that the conflicts are described in words. Language helps with new syntheses by reorganizing feelings into concepts. Logical sequence, cause and effect, and reality can now enter the new synthesis.

The technique of analyzing the transference allows for the slow emergence and better elaboration of the unconscious, and for understanding and integrating the new material that emerges. It is this emergence from the unconscious and from the past that allows more adaptive compromises in the present. This is what leads to more adaptive real-life relationships and to more emotional satisfaction. The unrealistic wishes, unrealistic fears, and resulting poorly adaptive compromises can now change. The more mature compromises form when patients are better able to see the unrealistic and impossible to satisfy nature of the previous conflicts and unhappy compromises. New compromises also form because the fears lessen and therefore more of the previously unacceptable wishes can find their expression in new reaction patterns and new attitudes that are both more generous and more realistic. This does involve giving up some of the intensity and unrealistic focus of these wishes but because it also involves giving up uncomfortable, unrealistic fears, new compromises can form that can achieve greater emotional and real-life satisfaction.

Interpretation is another crucial technique. Interpretation is the description by the analyst of what is unconscious, what the conflicts are, what the compromises are, and how they are linked to symptoms and attitudes. Interpretation describes the emotional link between the past and the present. Particularly important is the interpretation of transference, of resistance to transference, and of free association.

VI. INDUCTION PHASE

The treatment can be divided for discussion into three overlapping phases. The first is the induction phase, during which patients are becoming comfortable with the treatment process, and are telling their life history and present illness or unhappy state. Engagement with the treatment process and emotional aspects of their own history start to deepen. The real attributes of the analyst fade from view and patient's fears and wishes about other people begin to be focused on the analyst. In order for this phase to progress and be completed successfully, the analyst must pay attention to, and descriptively analyze, resistances to the analytic process and to treatment. Resistances use personality defenses and therefore are a leading edge of the personality neurosis of the patient. Because this personality neurosis is a primary focus of the psychoanalytic treatment, the resistances elicited by the induction phase form the crucial beginning to the treatment.

VII. MIDDLE PHASE

The middle phase of treatment is when the emotional history starts to progressively unfold. The transference intensifies, consolidates, and focuses intensely on the psychoanalyst. This focusing of the transference on the analyst, and the intense involvement the patient has with that transference, is called the transference neurosis. The transference neurosis provides crucial data about the subtleties of conflicts and compromises basic to the person. The transference neurosis allows the analyst as well as the patient to experience these attitudes, to thereby better understand their contents and their organizations, and to better reconstruct both their origins and present functions.

When the transference neurosis is established, the analyst and the patient are witness to the patient's full range of unique, emotional, personality reactions in a setting where they can be consciously experienced and their elements, conflicts, and troublesome compromise manifestations understood and analyzed.

A defense is an unconscious mechanism that protects the conscious mind from unconscious, conflicted emotional experience. Symptoms express defenses. Aspects of personality function are defensive. Conflicted emotional experience would be even more disruptive and painful than the defense in symptoms or personality. As defenses are analyzed and unraveled, as their functions become more known and more conscious, the underlying, conflicted emotional experiences they protect against emerge more clearly. Because this process is gradual, because each step of uncovering is preceded by a new and more satisfying organization of compromise, the patient can tolerate the uncovering of the deeper layers. A patient's tolerance is one of the factors requiring a long and intense treatment. The analysis of defense and of underlying conflicts allows for the better resolution of unhappy, symptom-generating, and maladaptive attitudes. The conscious mind, seeing the structure and functions more clearly in the course of analysis, and seeing their first origins in childhood, is better able to bring an adult perspective to bear, shifting mental problems in the direction of reality and emotional adaptation in the direction of new, more adaptive, and more satisfying compromises.

The application of insights about emotional conflict applied over and over again to different situations and manifestations, so that new compromises can be applied in all areas of mental life, is called the process of working through. The middle phase of psychoanalysis involves many intense periods of working through as each aspect of conflict is understood, and the insights gained are applied.

Analysis of the transference neurosis and personality defense, and the working through of conflict form together the major and defining aspects of the work of the middle phase. Both the analysis of the transference neurosis and the working through process require constant analysis of resistance defenses against the work. This analysis of resistance and defense is what opens up the character defenses in order to work them through to better compromises.

VIII. TERMINATION PHASE

The termination phase is the last phase and is also an intense period of the treatment. New data emerge making the life history and emotional history more complete, more understandable, and more useful. New compromises are applied to a range of life situations. Significant shifts in personality functioning and associated symptoms are consolidated. Conclusions to emotional stories and the transference neurosis are arrived at.

Crucial to this phase is the understanding of the full impact of the transference neurosis. In this phase, the analyst once again, as in the beginning, emerges more into the reality experience of the patient. The analyst is now seen more clearly as a person very separate from the projected attitudes and fantasies of the patient. This results in further conviction about the neurosis for the patient and further consolidation of the new, healthier compromises of personality conflict. During this phase, there is an internalizing of the psychoanalytic process itself, so that patients can continue understanding their mental life on their own. Patients are able to do some free association for themselves and to understand the central themes of their personality, dramatized in their fantasies and dreams. They can therefore figure out their new unhappy feelings and the reality triggers causing them, and plan to meet those reality challenges in ways that will be as satisfying as possible.

IX. CASE ILLUSTRATION

A 40-year-old man is in the perilous phase of fighting with his wife in a second marriage after a painful divorce ended his first. He is intensely unhappy and while he blames his second wife, as he did the first, it is he who is unhappy and it is he who cannot help but notice that the fight is the same one that ended his first marriage. He does not want the second one to end.

In consultation with a psychoanalyst, it is apparent in the first session that the same fight has gotten him into trouble at work and has retarded his career. The fight has something to do with who is in control. In analysis, this issue immediately affects his attitude to the analyst and he struggles over every issue, from time to money to the exact wording of interpretations by the analyst. Associations lead to a relationship with his mother in which there was a struggle over dominance. The relationship was filled with anger, recrimination, and humiliation. Years are spent untangling what seems to have been his mother, what seems to have been him, what seems to have been each one's reaction to the other, and how all this is played out now. He gradually comes to see that not every difference of opinion is a contemptuous judgment, not every variation is an attempt to humiliate, and not every suggestion is an attempt to control. He also comes to see that he is exactly like the mother he accuses. His personality gradually mellows, he becomes more flexible, and his career and marriage improve dramatically. Of added benefit is the great improvement in his relationship with his children, a benefit he had not expected because he never noticed it was also infected by his core issues. The transference to the analyst is quite stormy for the first few years and he berates and threatens the analyst with quitting treatment. Much careful confrontation, together with great tact and patience were required so that the analytic relationship could be useful to the patient.

X. TRAINING OF PRACTITIONERS

Becoming a psychoanalyst requires many years of training. The usual background for such a person is advanced training in one of the mental health fields and then psychonalytic training. In the United States, for many years physician psychiatrists dominated the field. In the past 20 years, Ph.D. psychologists have increasingly sought psychoanalytic training. More recently, clinical social workers and others have sought this training. Psychoanalytic training involves 4 to 5 years of classroom work, supervision of patients treated by the student, and a personal psychoanalysis. This intense course of study is necessary to learn the theory, practice the technique, and get enough self-analysis so that personality attitudes of the analyst do not interfere with the work. Another crucial advantage of personal psychoanalysis for the analyst is the ability to use emotional reactions to the patient as information about the patient, rather than only about the analyst. In this way, when one's own personality is well enough known, the analysts themselves can become, and can tolerate becoming, the vehicle of treatment. After many years of training and practice, psychoanalysts may undertake a formal certification process by the American Psychoanalytic Association if they are a graduate of the one of the institutes that comprise that association. On successful completion, the analyst may call himself or herself a certified psychoanalyst.

XI. PSYCHOANALYTIC PSYCHOTHERAPY

Psychoanalytic psychotherapy is a modified form of psychoanalysis. Its goals are similar in that it tries to achieve relief from mental suffering through a careful understanding of mental functions and contents. Although the goal is the same, the objectives, setting, and technique vary. The objectives are more focused and limited, the setting is once or twice a week with the patient sitting up, and the technique may be very much more active on the part of the therapist.

The indications are generally the same as for psychoanalysis but because the sitting position and active interventions of the therapist often prevent an intense emotional regression, this type of therapy may be better suited to sicker patients whose integrative mental functions cannot yet tolerate a full analysis. In addition, the method may be used when very specific, time-limited objectives are needed by the patient and no personality reconstruction is necessary for those objectives. Some examples of this situation are difficulty in mourning a lost one, panic attacks or social anxiety as isolated symptoms in an otherwise high-functioning person, difficulty adapting to a difficult spouse or boss, or help in understanding a troubled relationship with a child. This kind of therapy is often used in conjunction with medication. Examples are the treatment of depression, panic attacks, or social anxiety situations. The combination is a potent one. The duration of such treatments are weeks to months to a few years. In some situations, generally because of constraints of time or money on the patient's part, such therapy can stretch on for years with the goal of providing a modified psychoanalysis for the treatment of long-standing personality disorders.

The technique generally involves both interpretation of dynamic conflict and support of defenses and of self-esteem. The usual goal is to repair, not reconstruct. However, for those whom the technique is being used as a modified psychoanalysis, interpretation, reconstruction, uncovering, and the intensification of transference and its interpretation are important techniques just as they are in psychoanalysis.

The training of practitioners is difficult for the patient consumer to ascertain because there are few programs specifically teaching dynamic psychotherapy. Psychiatrists may learn dynamic psychotherapy in their residencies. Those who are psychoanalytically trained at psychoanalytic institutes after residency training at least are well grounded in the theory and technique of psychoanalysis, which is then applied to psychodynamic psychotherapy. Psychologists and social workers may get specific training in dynamic psychotherapy during the course of their degree programs. Some get further training in the few psychotherapy training programs that exist or go on for full psychoanalytic training themselves.

XII. COMBINATIONS WITH OTHER TREATMENTS

Psychodynamic psychotherapy and psychoanalysis are sometimes used with other treatments. The combination with medication for the treatment of depression is a very powerful combination because the psychopharmacological treatment treats the physical manifestations and the talking treatment treats the psychological manifestations. This combination is powerful because depression usually involves both components. Each component may catalyze or trigger the other component. A single uncombined treatment may or may not affect the other arm of the illness. Treating them both at the same time achieves a more rapid and more complete relief for more people. Although there is as yet little research proof of this, it is the overwhelming majority opinion among clinicians at this time.

Another combination that is growing in use is couples treatment combined with psychoanalysis or psychodynamic psychotherapy. The marital therapist can observe behavior that might otherwise go unreported in the individual treatments. Similarly, patients can gain insight into aspects of their own conflict that are counterproductive in their relationships. This may help in the more rapid uncovering of psychological conflict and in the more complete working through of its resolutions.

Another combination that is sometimes used is the combination with cognitive–behavioral therapy, which is highly focused on target symptoms such as phobias, panic, social anxiety, and obsessive–compulsive disorder. The combination with psychodynamic psychotherapy and psychoanalysis is especially helpful in two situations. The first is when a rapid resolution of symptoms is mandatory for the comfort of the patient and the progress of the psychodynamic treatment. The other is when the psychodynamic treatment has been going on for a long time without resolution of symptoms because the patient needs hand-on help in the working through and application process.

Another combination growing in importance is concomitant neurocognitive rehabilitation in patients who have severe learning disabilities, especially when those learning disabilities make it hard for them to integrate and apply a psychologically based treatment. Neurocognitive rehabilitation also helps the patient with academic work and with employment problems. Information from the neurocognitive psychologist to the psychoanalyst or psychotherapist can help the therapist understand better what the cognitive problems with the patient are so that the talking treatment can be better targeted, better framed, and more understandable.

XIII. RESEARCH

Research about psychoanalysis has a long history. Outcome studies of efficacy include Wallerstiene's small but intimately detailed study of 42 patients in psychoanalysis, Weber and Bachack's much larger study of outcome at the Columbia University Center for Psychoanalytic Training and Research, the Menninger psychotherapy research project for many years under the directorship of Otto Kernberg, and the largest study to date done by Joan Earle and colleagues at the New York Psychoanalytic Institute. These many studies tend to demonstrate certain conclusions. The first is that the longer and more intense the treatment, the better the result tends to be. The next is that even if patients fail to develop a full psychoanalytic process, and are instead in treatments with major psychotherapy parameters, the outcome in approximately 80% is excellent. What is left to be proved is whether the psychoanalytic process itself, rigidly defined if that is possible, is crucial to the beneficial outcome. My own reading of the data is that psychoanalytic psychotherapy aspects are crucial and the strict psychoanalytic process may or may not be crucial. One would expect this to vary not only because of the difficulty in standardizing psychoanalytic process but also because patients' needs vary according to illness.

Psychodynamic psychotherapy research has been advanced in a major way by Barbara Milrod and Fred Busch, who succeeded in manualizing a psychodynamic method of treating panic disorder and in showing the success of this method. Peter Fonagy and others who are psychoanalytic child researchers have succeeded in showing the excellent outcome of psychoanalytic treatments of children.

In conclusion, research over many years supports the general efficacy of psychoanalysis and psychoanalytic psychotherapy. The current challenges in research are to demonstrate the efficacy of the process, of various applications to different illnesses, of the efficacy of combination treatments, and of the relative efficacy against other treatments.

XIV. SUMMARY

A method is said to be psychoanalytic if it has certain crucial elements of treatment. The elements are the analysis of resistance and defense in the making conscious of unconscious conflicts and their compromises, the use of transference as a vehicle to understanding, some effort to reconstruct past patterns as they influence present functioning, and frequent sessions so that an intensity of treatment is achieved that can reveal these patterns. The goal is the progressive unfolding of personality psychology.

See Also the Following Articles

Cognitive Behavior Therapy ■ History of Psychotherapy ■ Psychoanalysis and Psychoanalytic Psychotherapy: Technique ■ Research in Psychotherapy ■ Therapeutic Factors

Further Reading

Balint, M., Ornstein, P. H., & Balint, E. (1972). *Focal psychotherapy.* Philadelphia: J.B. Lippincott.

Brenner, C. (1982). *The mind in conflict.* New York: International Universities Press.

Freud, S. (1932). New introductory lectures on psychoanalysis, Standard edition, (Vol. 22). London: Hogarth Press.

Rothstein, A. (1983). *The structural hypothesis and evolutionary prospective.* New York: International Universities Press.

Shapiro, D. (1989). *Psychotherapy of neurotic character.* New York: Basic Books.

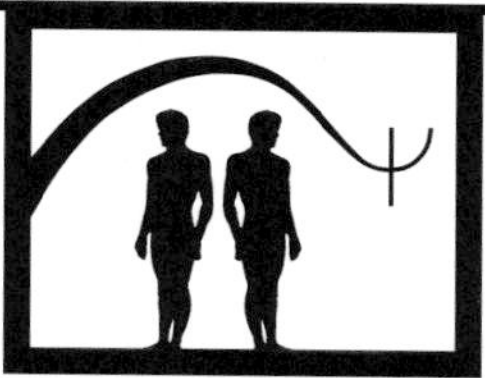

Psychodynamic Couples Therapy

Francine Cournos
Columbia University

GLOSSARY

countertransference The way the patient interacts with the therapist which induces feelings in the therapist towards the patient.

intrapsychic defenses Mental strategies developed to contain, and in some instances keep from consciousness, unacceptable wishes and impulses.

object relationships The internalized concepts of self and other that carry with it expectations, sources, type of gratification, and considerations of value.

temperament The biologically-oriented predisposition of a child towards particular ways of behaving, perceiving, and processing information and interactions.

transference The ubiquitous component of all human relations which in psychotherapy refers to how the patients experience the therapist.

Psychodynamic couples treatment involves interventions that incorporate concepts of mental functioning based on psychoanalytic theories. It is an approach that explores how any given couple acts, thinks, and feels, but also the meaning each partner attaches to these experiences. Such exploration is undertaken with the aims of reducing conflict and enhancing intimacy. In this approach, the therapist balances views of what is universally true about intimate relationships with respect for the uniqueness of every partnership between two people.

I. THEORETICAL MODEL

Psychodynamic couples therapists believe that adult behaviors and perceptions in intimate relationships are patterned on the interactions, and the associated feelings and fantasies, of important childhood connections with others, usually most powerfully with parents and siblings. Even under the most favorable circumstances, human development inevitably contains conflict and ambivalence as children struggle with such opposing needs and feelings as closeness and separation, love and hatred, and guilt over forbidden sexual or aggressive wishes. The mental strategies that develop to contain unacceptable wishes and impulses are called intrapsychic defenses, and their many variations and complexities are discussed in psychoanalytic literature. Some defenses are more adaptive than others. Those that allow people to recognize their feelings and take constructive action, for example, work better than those that involve the denial of feelings or self-destructive behaviors. Each person develops a unique repertoire of compromises between the expression of potentially dangerous (psychologically or otherwise) wishes or impulses and the efforts to contain them with intrapsychic defenses.

Because intrapsychic defenses develop in childhood, they contain irrational conclusions based on childhood reasoning. For example, young children imagine causal associations between unrelated events that occur at the same time. If a 4-year-old girl gets angry at her mother for bringing home a baby brother and then the baby gets seriously ill, the little girl might conclude that her angry feelings and wishes harmed the baby. Because seeing such a bad wish come true is frightening and guilt-provoking, the little girl may then develop intrapsychic defenses to contain her anger, which in turn may cause her to behave in a more inhibited manner. This resolution may persist as the little girl matures without her giving any conscious thought to its origins.

Intrapsychic defenses are well established by adulthood. They operate automatically and mostly unconsciously, but these defenses, and the impulses and wishes they protect against, can in part be indirectly observed through repetitive patterns of behavior and feelings in relationships. Exploration through psychodynamic couples therapy examines these patterns and the associated beliefs and fantasies that the patient uses to explain his or her interpersonal world. So, for example, the woman described earlier might return to the experience of her brother's illness if she seeks to understand in therapy why, when her husband's criticisms make her angry, she silently withdraws (her defense) rather than assert her opposing viewpoints (her aggressive wish).

Psychodynamic exploration also clarifies positive and negative internalized concepts of the self and of others, which are referred to as object relationships. For example, a boy who feels loved and cared for by his mother may have internal images of himself as handsome and appealing, and of his mother as protective and nurturing. By contrast, a little boy who feels his mother takes minimal interest in him and his well-being may have images of himself as unlovable and unworthy, and of his mother as remote and uncaring.

Although this example suggests that these images are created by a simple process, this is not at all the case. Children and parents bring to their interactions unique ways of behaving and experiencing the world, and there is also the matter of the fit between them. A father who is athletic and adventurous may perceive his highly active and mischievous son as great fun, whereas this same little boy could be perceived as a problem child to a quiet and studious father whose primary mode of expressing himself is through conversation. Children create images of themselves that incorporate how they believe they are seen in eyes of people who are important to them. This is affected by the child's temperament as well. So, for example, an easygoing child may both elicit more positive responses and reach more optimistic conclusions than a child with an irritable temperament. Subjective truths are as important as objective facts, and they help explain how two siblings can emerge from the same family with very different perceptions of childhood.

Children depend on their adult caretakers for nurturance, but because they are relatively helpless, they also fear being harmed by them. Young children cope with this contradiction by keeping the good and bad images of their caretakers separate. An example is their fascination with fairy tales that depict the good and bad images of mothers as fairies and witches. These contradictory images are integrated as the child grows and develops greater autonomy and more mature cognitive and emotional capacities. Integration allows for a more realistic view of others so that a range of negative feelings can be tolerated while still maintaining a predominantly positive image of an important person. Children can best accomplish this integration when they feel safe and loved.

Adults enter relationships using these mental structures constructed in childhood. We bring to our search for intimate partners our deepest hopes and fears and our preconceived ideas about how relationships work. We then think and act in ways that encourage a repetition of these expectations or perhaps seem to be an antidote to them. The attraction of one person to another is in large measure based on finding a fit for childhood constructs. When this fit results in the repetition of patterns that lead to excessive conflict, disappointment, or detachment, it can produce the suffering that is often the presenting complaint of a couple seeking treatment.

One of the central ways the psychodynamic therapist learns about the internal constructs a patient uses to guide relationships is by focusing on transference and countertransference. In individual therapy, transference refers to how the patient experiences the therapist. It is partly a response to the real qualities of the therapist and partly the unprovoked projection of expectations onto the therapist that are based on the internal constructs discussed earlier. For example, a man may anticipate that his therapist is going to be incompetent and judgmental because he perceived his father in that way. He may then doubt the therapist's opinions or perceive them as criticism. The degree of tact, respect, and reassurance the therapist manifests will to some extent enhance or discourage the patient's tendency to perceive the therapist in this manner.

The way the patient interacts with the therapist induces feelings in the latter known as countertransference, which are partly a response to the real qualities and interpersonal behaviors of the patient and partly a manifestation of the therapist's emotional reactions based on internal constructs from his own past. Psychodynamic therapists are trained to examine their countertransference feelings in such a way that they can use them constructively to help patients. For example, rather than respond to a patient's disdain by being offended or arguing to the contrary, the therapist seeks to understand what he can learn about how the patient approaches relationships. By examining the patient's transference feelings and the therapist's countertransference feelings, the therapist gains critical information about a patient's wishes, intrapsychic defenses, and object relationships. The therapist can then use this information to help the patient reconsider childhood assumptions and develop more adaptive adult strategies.

Most psychodynamically trained therapists learned their skills conducting individual therapy, which is by far the most commonly practiced form of psychodynamic treatment. However, with a shift in perspective, these same psychodynamic principles can be applied to couples interventions.

Transference is not a phenomenon unique to the process of therapy. Rather it is a ubiquitous component of human relationships. Each member of the couple is enacting models of the self and others that only partly correspond to the partner's reality. Thus, in effect, each member of the couple both projects expectations onto the partner (transference) and responds to the partner's projected expectations (countertransference). Negative transference and countertransference feelings can interact with one another in a vicious circle, each setting off the other in a spiral that can cause considerable pain and despair. A man who experienced his mother as inept and now reacts to his wife in the same way can easily elicit the wife's preexisting insecurities about her own abilities. The wife might respond by avoiding tasks in the marriage that could provoke her husband's criticism, which in turn confirms the husband's belief in his wife's ineptitude. Recognizing and exploring these cycles creates possibilities for profound change by allowing the couple to form more realistic and empathic views of one another, by separating the present relationship from past experience, and by creating clearer boundaries between what each person thinks and feels.

Psychodynamic couples therapy moves along much more rapidly than individual psychodynamic treatment. This is primarily because individual therapy brings together two strangers—the patient and the therapist—who develop a relationship over time. When a husband tells his individual therapist about a fight with his wife, the therapist hears only half the story. He does not know how the wife actually behaved, or how she perceived her husband's actions. In fact the individual therapist can best understand the whole story of how the patient relates to others from the experience of how the patient relates to him. Here the therapist is the partner in the relationship, and he knows how he felt and behaved in the interaction. He is learning firsthand about the patient's approach to others by observing and responding to the patient's transference and the therapist's countertransference. This takes time and unfolds with the development of the patient–therapist relationship.

By contrast, in couples therapy the couple brings an already existing intense relationship into the therapeutic process. By directly observing, for example, the hundreds of verbal and nonverbal exchanges that occur in only a few minutes of a couple's typical argument, the therapist begins to see how the wishes, disappointments, inhibitions, and preconceived ideas each member of the couple brings to the relationship play out between them.

The presence of three people in the session also greatly increases the complexity of what the therapist must attend to, including the interactions of the members of the couple with each other and the interaction of each of them with the therapist. This requires the therapist's intense and constant concentration because even a momentary lapse can result in a loss of crucial information. There is also a greater need to control what happens in the room lest the couple simply repeat destructive interactions or pull the therapist into their conflicts without achieving any therapeutic goals. This requires the therapist to make rapid decisions about interventions using less information than that upon which individual therapy interventions are usually based. Some dynamic therapists feel ill at ease with these requirements, whereas others find couples therapy lively and engaging, a remarkable opportunity to have a profound effect on the well-being of others in a relatively brief period of time.

Although Sigmund Freud laid the groundwork for the psychodynamic approach, many subsequent psychoanalytic clinicians and theorists have contributed substantial modifications to the original theories. Others have made an attempt to integrate these theories with new discoveries about the biology of the brain and the development of the mind. The skilled therapist uses a range of interventions within an overall framework based on psychodynamic principles and tailored to the particular couple's needs. So, for example, the therapist might employ behavioral interventions to improve a couple's skills in the areas of communication and negotiation, or he might refer a member of the couple who weeps throughout the session for an assessment of whether she would benefit from antidepressant medication. There is no single technique that provides an answer to every issue that arises. Skilled couples therapists know when to augment their primary approach with other strategies that are either more effective or more efficient but that do not undermine the framework of the overall treatment.

The psychodynamic therapist is interested both in what is universal and what is unique about people. She understands that just as no two people are the same, so it is that no two couples are the same. It follows that there are no simple formulas, instructions, or remedies for how couples should live their lives. Although the therapist uses her own emotional responses as a tool for understanding a couple's experiences, she has deep respect for the fact that her perspective is also unique to her own past and she avoids imposing her personal solutions on the couple. The psychodynamic therapist respects the couple's autonomy. With the exception of life-endangering situations, the therapist understands that only the couple can reach conclusions about the viability of their relationship, and that they are the ones who must live with the consequences of a decision to stay together or separate. The psychodynamic therapist also believes that all theories are only approximations of the truth, and that the couple's truth is more important than the therapist's theories. She is humbled by the knowledge that beneath every layer of truth is yet another layer. Each member of a couple selects what to reveal, and, however great a couple's willingness to be open, some truths will remain unconscious and therefore unavailable. An awareness of the enormous complexity of people and the irrational forces that influence them contributes to the depth and flexibility of the psychodynamic approach.

Because in most states anyone can hang up a shingle claiming to be a couples therapist, even with no training at all, complaints about the simple-mindedness and lack of success of couples treatment are commonplace, and such experience often leads to a jaundiced view of all couples treatment. Moreover, books and workshops abound that offer to teach couples how to have a more fulfilling relationship. Although these offerings may present meaningful opportunities for self-improvement, they are to be distinguished from psychodynamic couples therapy, which avoids one-size-fits-all solutions and involves a highly individualized assessment and treatment plan.

II. PRESENTING COMPLAINT

Sometimes a couple will present following an event that crystallizes a long-standing pattern of difficulties. Among the most dramatic of these precipitants are the revelation of an affair or an uncharacteristic act of physical violence. Couples may present because one member has given the other an ultimatum—for example, to marry or break up, to have a baby or divorce. Prenuptial agreements are sometimes experienced as ultimatums as well. Meeting with divorce lawyers prior to marriage may be economically sound, but it is a painful way to begin a marriage. Disappointment in the partner based on the perception of being emotionally and sometimes physically abandoned at a critical time of need, such as during job loss, infertility treatment, or an episode of serious illness may be the presenting complaint. Chronic feelings of anger are prominent in almost all these situations, and a reduction of sexual interest is common.

III. ASSESSMENT

Assessment begins with an evaluation of the presenting complaint. In obtaining this information, the therapist needs to convey the following complex set of concepts: that no two members of a couple see a story in the same way; that the therapist is more interested in subjective truth than objective fact; that the therapist listens for the purpose of understanding and not assigning blame; that the difference between the two stories that emerge will be useful to the therapeutic process; and that each member of the couple has the final say about his or her feelings or intentions. The therapist is in effect making an important intervention by creating an environment in which it is relatively safe to look at areas of disagreement and in the process clarify how each member of the couple may be projecting feelings or motivations onto the partner that create inaccurate perceptions of who the partner is. In the process, members of the couple can learn to separate past perceptions (e.g., "My father never took an interest in what I had to say.") and present reality (e.g., "I present my opinions in such an angry way that my partner finds it difficult to listen sympathetically.").

Elucidation of the presenting complaint leads naturally to inquiring about other areas essential for the therapist's understanding. These include the story of the relationship; the factors that attracted them; the history of their difficulties; their sexual functioning; the birth or adoption of children; the presence of any serious physical or mental illness in either of the partners or a child; and prior experience with individual or couples therapy. The couple's relationship then needs to be put into the context of each partner's family dynamics and, unless the couple is uncomfortable with discussing it, an understanding of previous important couples relationships. Religious and cultural factors also need to be taken into account For example, the marriage of a Japanese-born businessman to a musician of Irish extraction raised in the Midwest presents enormous complexity with regard to the differences in assumptions, patterns of communication, and expectations each brings to the relationship.

The assessment allows the therapist to begin to answer the following questions: Why is the couple presenting now? What has drawn them together or kept them apart? What is each member of the couple seeking from therapy? To what extent are their goals compatible? How does this relationship repeat patterns each partner learned in childhood? How does the couple function at their best and at their worst? To what extent is their anger and disappointment with one another balanced by a reserve of good feelings? What skills does each partner possess in communicating, negotiating, and empathizing with the other?

Maladaptive patterns of behavior are often passed from one generation to another. For example, a man who becomes verbally abusive or physically violent with his wife will often have experienced similar abuse as a child, and in turn risks raising a new generation of children who engage in such behavior. This man's maladaptive patterns are accompanied by painful internal constructs of a victimized, revenge-seeking self in relationship to undeserving and untrustworthy others. The roles of victim and perpetrator are intertwined.

One essential area of assessment that is often overlooked in couples treatment is the presence of major untreated psychiatric illness, most often depression, manic-depressive illness, anxiety disorders, and addictive disorders (e.g., alcohol, drugs, gambling). Each can place enormous stress on a relationship. For example, the irritability and pessimism of depression, the aggressive behavior seen in mania, the need for constant reassurance induced by anxiety disorders, and the loss of impulse control associated with addiction are each associated with interpersonal difficulties that can have a severe negative impact on how the couple functions. Personality disorders may also be present, and the therapist needs to assess what aspects can be addressed in the couples treatment and what difficulties are best handled by referral for individual therapy.

Consider a young woman who marries a middle-aged divorced man with two preadolescent sons from a previous marriage. Things go relatively smoothly until she gets pregnant, gives birth to a healthy baby girl, but then develops a severe episode of postpartum depression. She becomes withdrawn and irritable and expresses increasing annoyance with her stepsons. They feel rejected and displaced by the new baby, and become progressively more angry and defiant. This in turn reminds the new mom of her unhappy childhood experiences following her own parents' divorce and the subsequent emotionally distant relationship she developed with her father's new wife. She is frightened at finding herself in the position of becoming the evil stepmother. Although there are many psychodynamic issues for the couples therapist to explore, it is essential to consider the contribution that this woman's untreated depression is making to the deteriorating family situation and her inability to repair it.

The therapist also needs to appreciate what she is not likely to hear about in couples sessions: secrets that one partner wishes to keep from the other (e.g., an extramarital affair); hidden agendas (e.g., a plan to hide financial assets in the event of a divorce); full disclosure of each partner's feelings toward the other; and the type of intimate self-revelation that is the focus of individual psychodynamic treatment. Meeting with each member of the couple alone has the advantage of providing some additional information, and the potential disadvantage of burdening the therapist with secrets that the couple may not be prepared to confront. Whether or not the therapist elects to meet with each partner separately, she remains humbly aware that there are deep unconscious forces at work, that these will remain in place throughout the therapy, and that there is much that the therapist and even the members of the couple cannot understand.

Obtaining information from a couple stirs up strong feelings that need to be addressed, and thus the assessment process is also the beginning of the treatment.

IV. TREATMENT PLAN

Many couples enter therapy reluctantly, believing this admission of failure to solve problems on their own is the first step to separation or divorce. Not uncommonly, one partner has pressured the other to come to the initial session. A couple in angry conflict may fear that this form of passion is the only force that binds them. Often each partner puts the responsibility for problems on the other, and there is an almost universal desire to effect a change in one's partner rather than in oneself. Other common themes at the beginning of treatment include the wish to be understood without having to put feelings or requests into words, and the belief that one's own inner despair could be quelled by a more responsive partner.

The initial phase of couples treatment is the creation of a safe therapeutic environment in which discussion of painful issues does not cause further harm. This involves setting limits to destructive behaviors such as name-calling, shouting, interrupting, and other forms of angry interaction that serve no useful purpose. In their place, the therapist helps the couple use such strategies as identifying specific issues (e.g., "So you feel rejected when he comes home late every night."); adhering to the topic rather than engaging in global warfare (e.g., "Let's stay focused on the arguments you're having about the kids' bedtime rather than all the past failures to discipline them."); achieving useful goals (e.g., "Do you think that calling him a whining wimp will get you what you want?"); not invoking absent third parties (e.g., "Since your mother isn't here to concur that your wife is neglectful, let's focus on your own opinions."); and distinguishing past grievances from future hopes (e.g., "You're both bitter about the past, but perhaps there's enough good feeling between you to work on handling things differently from here on.").

The presence of physical violence is in a category of its own because it is unsafe to conduct couples treatment in this situation without setting very clear limits to what is acceptable behavior. The therapist's failure to do so can result in an escalation of violence. Consider the case of a lawyer who enters therapy after neighbors called the police in response to his wife's cries for help during a physical altercation. The husband accedes to his wife's demand to see a couples therapist because he is fearful that further police action could result in his being disbarred, but he believes his actions were amply justified by his wife's provocations. Both members of the couple act as if the husband has two different personalities: the good and caring one, and the out-of-control one. The therapist must indicate his belief that there is no provocation that justifies violence, that the threat of disbarment reflects a societal judgment that physically abusing a spouse is unacceptable under any circumstance, and that the husband has a single personality whose good and caring side must take responsibility for his angry and destructive side. It is essential as well to work with the wife on removing herself and her children from the situation (e.g., keeping clothes in the car, having a place to go to) when she observes the warning signs of impending violence. Exploring the feelings and barriers that might prevent her from taking such protective measures must be part of this process.

All sophisticated couples therapists use strategies for creating a safe environment regardless of theoretical orientation. When the psychodynamic couples therapist employs them, she maintains awareness of the powerful but unidentified intrapsychic forces each member of the couple brings to the joint creation of their repetitive pattern of painful and seemingly self-defeating behaviors. She knows that in childhood when each member of the couple developed the strategies they now use, these approaches were a way of coping with distressing feelings and creating some sense of safety. She has respect for the role of these strategies in maintaining each partner's emotional well-being, and is careful not to make matters worse.

The therapist's approach is then guided by her understanding of how much is at stake in making any changes. This is true whether she makes behavioral suggestions (e.g., "Let's work on how you'll carve out a time of the day to talk to one another without interruptions."); or addresses the underlying psychological problems (e.g., "I guess when your father died and left you alone to deal with your alcoholic mother, it felt like you should just learn to manage on your own and not have to depend on anyone.").

The goals of couples therapy depend on the motivation, capacities, and focus of the couple. They include such diverse possibilities as reducing conflict; improving communication; enhancing empathy and support; promoting trust; creating more effective teamwork; enhancing the depth of relatedness in such areas as self-revelation and sexual intimacy; using humor and pleasurable activities more effectively; improving relationships with extended family; and initiating appropriate treatment for coexisting psychiatric disorders. Because fewer conventional structures are in place and because discrimination exists, gay and lesbian couples, and sometimes interracial couples, may need to make a more conscious effort to integrate themselves into one another's families and work lives.

Although it raises cost and reimbursement issues, longer couples sessions are often more effective than shorter ones because they allow for greater closure of the topic under discussion. This reduces the likelihood that the couple will leave the office with feelings that they cannot successfully manage between sessions. The amount of time a couple needs to work on a particular goal can vary enormously from a few sessions to a lengthy treatment. Also, couples may be ready to focus on different issues at different times, and it is best to be open to the possibility of couples returning following an initial course of therapy. Decisions about how much collaboration to have with individual therapists, if present, and distinguishing between goals best met in couples therapy rather than individual therapy, are also important components of the treatment plan.

V. EMPIRICAL STUDIES

There is a substantial number of studies examining the outcome of a variety of models of marital therapy. However, most do not meet the current research standards for demonstrating the effectiveness of a treatment (e.g., random assignment, a control group comparison, use of questionnaires that have been shown to be reliable and valid, detailed protocols for administering and observing the intervention), and few of the studies test the outcomes of psychodynamic couples therapy. On the positive side, the direction of the findings taken as a whole suggests that marital therapy is effective and is more likely than individual therapy to solve marital problems.

VI. CONCLUSIONS

Psychodynamic couples therapy uses in-depth models of psychological functioning both within and between people to enhance intimacy and reduce conflict and suffering. This treatment works best when it takes advantage of the entire array of interventions known to improve couples functioning. This includes the diagnosis and treatment of psychiatric disorders present in either member of the couple and the use of cognitive and behavioral strategies as necessary to improve communication and interpersonal skills. The skilled psychodynamic couples therapist does not offer simple formulas, but rather assists each couple in finding solutions that are responsive to their unique needs and hopes.

See Also the Following Articles

Behavioral Marital Therapy ■ Couples Therapy: Insight Oriented ■ Family Therapy ■ Psychodynamic Group Psychotherapy ■ Spouse-Aided Therapy ■ Supportive-Expressive Dynamic Psychotherapy

Further Reading

Gabbard, G. O. (2000). *Psychodynamic psychiatry* (3rd ed.). Washington, DC: American Psychiatric Press.

Glick, I. D., Clarken, J. F., & Kessler, D. R. (Eds.). (1987). *Marital and family therapy* (3rd ed.). New York: Grune & Stratton.

Jacobson, N. S., & Gurman, A. S. (Eds.). (1986). *Handbook of marital therapy.* New York: Guilford Press.

Schaddock, D. (2000). *Contexts and connections.* New York: Basic Books.

Scharff, D. E., & Scharff, J. S. (1987). *Object relations family therapy.* Northvale, NJ: Jason Aronson.

Siegel, J. (1992). *Repairing intimacy.* Northvale, NJ: Jason Aronson.

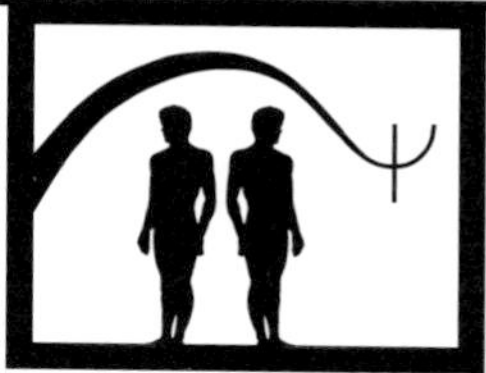

Psychodynamic Group Psychotherapy

Walter N. Stone
University of Cincinnati College of Medicine

GLOSSARY

countertransference Broadly defined, the emotional and behavioral response of the therapist stimulated by the therapeutic encounter.

group cohesion (cohesiveness) A property of the group in which the members are committed to the aims and work of the group, and from the satisfaction of being a member. Moreover, the properties of the group influence the members, creating a reciprocal experience in which individuals influence the group and the group influences the individual. The influences may be "positive" or "negative." This is akin to "the therapeutic alliance" in dyadic therapy.

identification An unconscious process in which the participant (patient) takes on parts or aspects of another. By taking on aspects of another, the individual changes by altering perceptions, behaviors, or affects.

norms Unwritten "rules," either conscious or unconscious, which evolve during the therapeutic process that regulate members' "behaviors." The behaviors may be either what is expected or what is sanctioned.

partial hospital A treatment setting that patients attend for portions of a day, evening, or night. Partial hospitals represent an alternative to full hospitalization.

personality disorder A constellation of inflexible and maladaptive personality traits that result in significant functional impairment or subjective distress.

posttraumatic stress disorder (PTSD) A set of symptoms that develop after a person sees, is involved in, or hears of an "extreme traumatic stressor." The symptoms must last more than 1 month. People reexperience the event in dreams or daily events. They attempt to avoid any stimulus that will reawaken the event. They may respond with numbness or hyperarousal.

psychosis The term is not precise, but is taken to mean grossly impaired in reality testing. It may be considered synonymous with major impairment of social and personal functioning.

repetition compulsion A person's tendency to repeat intrapsychic conflicts that have resulted from past traumatic experiences.

resistance Patients' difficulties in effectively collaborating in their therapy (They are late, forget to pay bills, miss sessions, unable to verbally participate). The source of these phenomena are thought to be unconscious.

transference A set of expectations, beliefs, or emotional responses displaced from prior experiences (often parents) to individuals in the present (often a therapist).

I. DESCRIPTION OF TREATMENT

Psychodynamic group psychotherapy is a treatment modality in which a specified number of individuals, who have been appropriately interviewed and prepared for the treatment, gather together at a regular day and time for treatment of their psychological problems. The groups may be of predetermined or indeterminate duration. They may have a fixed membership or be open to additional individuals, as space permits. Members, through examination of their in-group behaviors, learn about unconscious processes arising from prior experiences that distort present relationships with peers, authority, or with their relationship to the whole group (transferences). They become familiar with resistances and defenses against the emergence of unconscious processes, through manifestations in their relationships, slips (of the tongue), dreams, and fantasies as they emerge in the group process. Examination of the in-group process and dynamics are a primary, but not exclusive, focus of attention in members gaining insight into both conscious and unconscious aspects of themselves as they strive to understand and change their psychological problems.

A. Planning a Psychodynamic Psychotherapy Group

An essential element in the conduct of psychodynamic group psychotherapy is careful planning. Clinicians must determine the potential for finding sufficient individuals (6 to 10) who would benefit from and are willing to enter group treatment. They need to carefully plan for the space and time commitment involved in conducting this therapeutic modality, and they need to properly prepare members for participating in the group. A private practice setting differs from one in a clinic in which administrative and systems issues require particular attention.

The group format should be specified. One option is an ongoing, open-ended group, in which, as individuals leave, they are replaced. Another option is a time-limited group, which is usually defined as a predetermined number of sessions Generally, time-limited groups are closed for new admissions once they begin.

In composing treatment groups, consideration of ethnicity, age, gender, education, diagnosis, or degree of patients' psychological (functional) impairment should be taken into account. Groups may be heterogeneous as to these elements, but too great a disparity across these various dimensions would likely interfere with effective group treatment. Although each individual is unique, a degree of commonality along one or more of these dimensions is important in order to provide for linkages and identification(s) among members

Time-limited groups are often composed for a specific commonality (eating disorders, bereavement, reactions to a medical illness, victims of a disaster, including post-traumatic stress disorder) with the expectation that the commonality will enable the members to more readily identify with one another and facilitate sharing.

B. Therapeutic Factors

The therapeutic elements in group treatment arise from interactions among the members and with the leader. In addition, the image individuals develop of the group contributes to treatment outcome. The working theory posits that individuals will repeat their dysfunctional ways of experiencing and interacting (repetition compulsion) in the group setting, thereby providing a window into the person's conscious and unconscious emotional and cognitive processes. Individuals will experience the leader or other members as they have important individuals in their past (transference).

Insight into a person's unconscious emotional life as exemplified through their transferences has been the traditional cornerstone of the therapeutic action of dynamic group treatment. However, insight alone has never been sufficient explanation for a positive treatment effect. The value of the therapeutic relationship has always been appreciated as important, but only recently has it been differentiated from "nonspecific" or supportive categories. Cognitive elements, such as sharing of information or learning about an illness, have also been seen as useful.

Irvin Yalom, in 1975, working primarily in a framework of interpersonal relationships, listed 12 "therapeutic factors" that he believed were central to the mutative action of group psychotherapy. A cornerstone of this perspective was the potential for mutative impact from others' feedback as problematic transactions emerged in the course of the interaction. Yalom also emphasized group cohesion as a necessary, but insufficient, group element in effecting change. Group cohesion broadly defined as the commitment of the members to the aims and the work of the group, is a property of the entire group. Interpersonal influence (feedback) was most effective when a group was cohesive.

In 1997, Roy MacKenzie regrouped and modified Yalom's factors into four categories. The factors included in Yalom's formulation are indicated in bold:

1. *Supportive:* a sense of belonging to the group, which includes acceptance, **altruism**, **hope**, and **universality** (we are all human). **Group cohesion** is subsumed in this category.
2. *Self-revelation:* self-disclosure and **catharsis.** This included cognitive and affective dimensions.
3. *Learning:* **education**, guidance, **modeling**, and **vicarious learning** (observing how others interact and seeing similar aspects in one's self).
4. *Psychological work:* **interpersonal learning** and insight.

Psychological work is conceptualized as individuals' examine and learn about wishes, fears, hopes, and motivations that emerge in the manner they interact with others. Such work optimally takes place when the person feels supported, understood, and has revealed significant emotional aspects of her- or himself.

C. Recruiting and Preparing Members

Prior to recruiting members, clinicians need to attend to the composition and to an appropriate framework for the group. To form a group with the potential for achieving cohesion and a working atmosphere, the membership should not be too diverse along the dimensions of age, culture, socioeconomic background, or psychological awareness. Members should have a similar degree of psychological awareness as expressed in recognition of their inner emotional motivations or in their contributions to dysfunctional relationships. An individual might be excluded from a particular group, for example, on the basis of profession (a university professor with blue-collar workers), or age (a 65-year-old person with individuals in their twenties). Some exclusionary criteria based on traditional stereotypes are not valid if other aspects of the individual are basis for commonality (persons of color, if they have a similar occupation or common interests with others). However, using the theory of group process and dynamics described in the succeeding sections, modified psychodynamic groups can be formed with persons with persistent mentally illness or those with personality disorders who have significant deficits or absence of self-reflective capacities.

Fees for the sessions should be predetermined. Availability of appropriate space where members can sit in a circle with an unobstructed view of one another is necessary. In private practice settings adequate space may only be available in a waiting room, and under such circumstances, the clinician needs to assure privacy. Generally, groups are held in the evening after working hours. In the planning, clinicians must be aware of the extra time that is involved for administrative tasks (i.e., record keeping, patient contacts, or completing insurance forms). In clinics, arranging for a group requires collaboration with various levels of the administrative structure to assure collaboration with the clinician's needs in conducting a group in contrast to conducting dyadic treatment.

Any individual suitable for dynamically oriented psychotherapy is a prospective candidate for group treatment. However, most persons seeking psychotherapy request individual treatment. Thus, clinicians find it necessary to recruit and conduct careful preparatory interviews to determine an individual's motivation and psychological capacities to participate in group therapy. Clinicians also provide information regarding the treatment format.

Members may be recruited from the therapist's own practice. This has an advantage of both parties knowing each other and having worked together. Often therapists have insufficient prospects to begin or maintain an adequate group census. Other practitioners, or the clinician's usual referral sources, should be informed of the planning for a group to obtain additional candidates. In clinic settings, collaboration with persons in charge of admissions (intake), conferences reviewing patients' treatment, or in managing transfer from one clinician to another (often in the context of a therapist departing the clinic) provide additional referrals. Educational presentations serve to inform others of this treatment modality, as do flyers announcing the formation of a group. This latter method, however, seldom produces many referrals, but functions to remind others of the presence of a group that is seeking members.

Criteria for selecting individuals who would benefit from group treatment are linked to the therapist's goals for the group. Three basic criteria are: (1) an individual's motivation to work on his or her problems, (2) an ability to trust and share inner feelings, and (3) a capacity to examine one's inner states of mind and bodily responses.

General exclusionary criteria include persons (1) who show great reluctance or do not wish to join, (2) have mental retardation, (3) in a relational crises (i.e., divorce, death, loss of job), (4) in acute emotional reaction (i.e., a major depression or a psychosis), or (5) certain persons with certain personality characteristics (i.e., antisocial tendencies, limited frustration tolerance, or inability to maintain confidentiality). An additional consideration is individuals' life circumstances that prevent them from regular attendance (i.e., businesspersons, entertainers, or professional athletes who travel). None of these criteria are absolutes. Persons in crises may become good candidates when they recover. Insufficient data exist to define who should be excluded, because the attributes of the therapist and the characteristics of the specific group membership may be such that a particular individual may benefit from a particular group.

Candidates should be individually interviewed to determine their suitability for group treatment. The tasks of preparatory interviews as outlined by J. Scott Rutan and Walter Stone, include:

1. Obtaining a history and gaining a preliminary understanding of the person's problem(s).
2. Forming a relationship with the patient.
3. Setting treatment goals.
4. Providing information about the group.
5. Exploring initial anxieties about joining the group.
6. Gaining acceptance of the group agreement.

Interviews are not solely focused on determining a clinical diagnosis. They are conducted to learn, also, about an individual's prior role functioning in groups. Participation in the family, school, work, church, and recreational activities are almost universal group experiences. Therapists should inquire if individuals assumed leader or follower roles? Do they keep to task or have conflict with authority? Are they active or passive? Do they speak up or are they listeners? Can they keep secrets? The history and examination of role behavior alerts clinicians and patients to aspects of future group behaviors. Such an interview focus helps patients more clearly specify treatment goals. Furthermore, clinicians' interest in trying to understand the nature of their patients' problems in the various settings increases the likelihood of individuals negotiating the initial anxiety of entering and successfully remaining in the group.

Patients' treatment goals should be as specific as possible. These are usually formulated in interpersonal terms such as, "I need to understand why I become so angry at x," or "I seem to always get into relationships in which I am taken advantage of"; or "I cannot maintain a loving relationship with a man (woman)."

Information should be provided about the group. Usually this includes where the group meets, the time and duration of the sessions, gender composition, and if it will be an open or closed group. For ongoing groups, goals may be stated, "The group will provide members an opportunity to examine relationships both inside and outside the meetings." An additional explanation might include that a person's relational problem will emerge in the interactions among members and with the leader, and in this respect the group will be a microcosm of one's extra-group world. Learning about oneself in the group can be used in one's daily life.

Prospective members are informed that the group will be composed of persons who have no known prior relationships with each other. This leads into exploration of patients' initial anxieties about entering a group and further discussion of their ways of managing those feelings. Preparation serves to help patients work with their feelings and also provides an additional indication of the therapist's interest in the patient, further strengthening their alliance.

The group agreement (contract) is a central element in the preparation process and serves as a structure for the treatment. The elements include agreement to

1. Be present each week on time and remain throughout the entire meeting.
2. Work actively on the problems that brought you to the group, remain in the group until those problems are resolved, and provide sufficient time to say goodbye.
3. Put feelings into words, not actions.
4. Use the relationships in the group therapeutically, not socially.
5. Be responsible for your fee.
6. Protect the names and identities of your fellow members (confidentiality).

Each element can never be entirely fulfilled. Yet the agreement provides a structure and an indication of what behaviors are useful in the pursuit of treatment. The agreement alludes to patient safety, both physical and emotional. Proscribed actions include physical behavior and verbal attacks that are also considered actions. The ambiguous instruction to use groups therapeutically, not socially, leads to a discussion of extra-group contacts among members. They are asked to discuss in the group all salient contacts between them that take place outside of the meeting, as a means of learning more about themselves.

Fee arrangements should be explicit. The author distributes statements in the group at the initial meeting of each month for payment by the end of the month. If problems arise about payments, they should be discussed openly in the group. (This proves to be a very difficult assignment because money is not readily discussed in the American culture.) Groups cannot function without confidentiality, and it must be emphasized to the members. Members are not prohibited from speaking with others about the meeting, but they are instructed to do so in a fashion that no one can be identified. Members are reminded that confidentiality cannot be guaranteed, and each person is responsible to protect the information that is shared.

Failures to abide by the agreement provide opportunities to examine the reason and meaning of the particular behavior. It is easy to ignore members' slight tardiness or their delinquency in paying fees. Therapists need to overcome their own resistance to addressing such "violations" and help members to do the same.

The group agreement is incomplete without also informing members of the therapist's obligations. Therapists need to tell members about how they will use information gathered outside of the sessions, and how they will participate in the meetings. The former includes information from diagnostic or regularly scheduled (individual, family) therapeutic sessions, phone calls, chance meetings, or contact with other therapists. Moreover, patients should be told what information will be provided to insurance companies or of its use by the therapist in her or his professional capacity (i.e. writings or lectures). Finally, the therapist explains that he or she will try to help members understand themselves in their interactions in the group and in their lives. The members set the agenda. The therapist will intervene when a comment might be helpful.

D. The Therapist's Role

The clinician has the major initial responsibility for creating a group atmosphere that can be therapeutically useful to the members. The clinician must maintain a balance between understanding individuals, subgroups, and the whole group and be able to utilize that understanding for members' benefit.

Leaders need to initially establish boundaries between the group and the outside world, among members, and between themselves and the members. The concept of boundaries includes the time, place, and duration of the meetings (when do the session begin and end; where and when do we meet). The agreement is the first step in this process, because it defines aspects of the relationships among the members, and members with the therapist and with the group. For example, an external boundary is represented by selecting or excluding participants or by the emphasis on confidentiality. An internal boundary is exemplified by the element in the agreement to put feelings into words and not into action.

Clinicians help members begin to relate to one another in the here and now of the group. Yvonne Agazarian, in 1997, emphasized this process by pointing out similarities among pairs or subgroups. Such linking reduces members' sense of alienation. The therapist may identify a common group theme, which generally includes an assumption that silent members are participating, although they are not speaking. Moreover, not everyone has to be in agreement, because some members may favor a certain notion and others may "fight it," but all are reacting to it.

Therapists also have a responsibility in monitoring and, if necessary, helping members' contain or express their emotions, whichever is salient. Expression of intense emotions is inevitable. When feelings threaten to disrupt, rather than advance, therapy, the clinician must step in to prevent injury to an individual or to the group. Judgment is necessary in this task, and no rules are possible other than the general principle that safety is paramount.

The therapist also monitors and, when appropriate, comments on the unfolding group process, with the goal of alerting members to particular behaviors or interactions (confrontations) or of understanding unconscious elements in the transactions (insight). Many narratives seem only to describe events outside the meeting. However, they may be (displaced) communications or metaphors for unexpressed relationships or emotions within the group. Explaining these two levels (internal or external to the group) may lead to patients' insight into aspects of themselves.

Traditional theory elevates "insight" to a privileged place in helping patients. Insight may refer to understanding in the here and now of the meeting, to relationships in one's daily life or in the past. Interpretations provide insight into the transferences with linkages between "behavior" or feelings in the group, examples from the patient's current life, and from the patient's past. Interpretations illustrate the repetitious quality of patients' responses and their propensity to transport the past into the present. In the group, multiple opportunities for transferences are available with others representing parents, siblings, teachers, or other emotionally significant persons in the patient's life. The treatment setting opens transferences to examination and to understanding (insight). With insight the person can change.

Advances in theory have focused on the function of the relationships and interactions as significant in helping patients change their experience of others—this is often labeled a "corrective emotional experience," which means that people in the present respond differently than those in the past who have injured or traumatized a particular individual. A significant element in the therapist's task is to monitor the group atmosphere and try to form a setting in which such experiences can take place. The "relational experience" in itself is understood as mutative. Therapists, through their predictability, dependability, and reliability, contribute to the mutative impact of the treatment.

The focus of the therapist's activities is conceptualized by J. Scott Rutan and Walter Stone as encompassing two dimensions: role and focus:

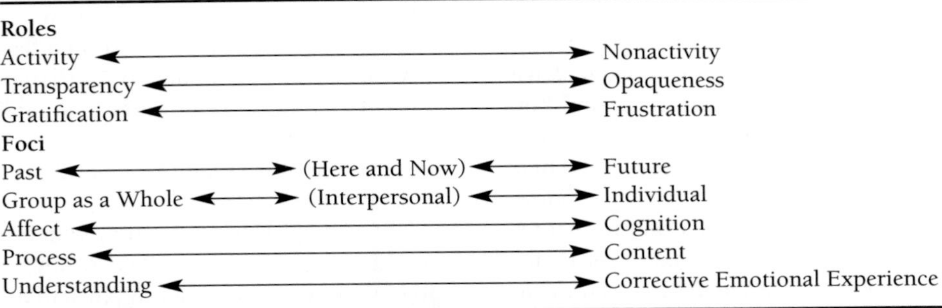

FIGURE 1 Roles and foci for the group therapist. Reproduced with permission from Rutan and Stone (2001). *Psychodynamic Group Psychotherapy,* 3rd ed. New York: Guilford Press.

1. Role

Role function addresses the leader's manner of engaging in the treatment. Each of the three dimensions is on a continuum. Clinicians may show considerable variation where they would be classified along theoretical or clinical places on a continuum. For instance, some clinicians might be active and gratifying during the initial meetings as a way of containing anxiety and creating a warm and accepting group atmosphere. Other clinicians might choose to remain inactive and opaque. They would view their position of nongratification of the "typical" leader role as creating anxiety that would help the members expose prior maladaptive relational patterns (transferences). It is unlikely that any therapist who rigidly adheres to one or another position on these continua would be therapeutically effective.

2. Focus

Leadership foci describe clinicians' stance regarding which aspects of the leadership will command their attention. No single dimension is the sole focus, nor is a single point along the continuum. For example, initially, individuals may not feel safe examining in-group feelings, and they resort to discussing events outside the meeting. The therapist may sense that such discussions promotes cohesion and identifications among members. At a later time, the therapists, hearing a similar discussion, may suggest that the discussion is a metaphor for transactions in the here and now of the group. Nevertheless, no matter which focus leaders choose, unanticipated responses are inevitable because many levels of individual and group experiences are simultaneously touched on. A comment to an individual about his or her behavior in the current transactions may reverberate to members' current life, their past, or imagined future.

E. The Group Process

Viewed from a perspective of a living organism, groups, somewhat akin to individuals, traverse developmental stages. These stages are not fixed or invariant but are subject to the capacities of the membership and the ability of the leader.

Like embarking on any enterprise, individuals enter a group needing to determine the nature of the task and of the emotional relations with peers and the therapist. The task in a psychodynamic group is to learn about and alter dysfunctional relationships and one's inner emotional responses. The therapist usually minimizes ordinary instructions in how to achieve these goals and leads by following—that is the clinician does not introduce topics or provide agendas but follows the members' lead and attempts to understand and convey understandings in a usable manner. This strategy of removing the "ordinary" expectable instructions creates a setting in which transferences, resistances, and unconscious processes are more available for examination.

The basic outline of group development was proposed by Warren Bennis and Herbert Shepard in 1956. An assumption of group developmental schema is that many of these processes are not conscious, yet they significantly affect an individual's emotions and behaviors. Knowledge of these processes serves to inform clinicians of influential elements that are outside of ordinary awareness.

1. The Formative Phase

On entering a group, members have two tasks—to determine how the group can be used to achieve their personal goals and to determine what is emotionally safe. With the leader providing only a bare outline of how to proceed, members naturally employ their usual strategies to obtain answers on how to proceed. Under the pressure evoked by meeting and having to reveal shameful or guilty aspects of themselves to unknown others, patients utilize previously learned strategies to manage the stressful situation. In the main, such strategies are unconsciously determined, having been arrived at during childhood, but are no longer adaptive. This process is termed *regression*. In this anxiety-laden context, members may cautiously reveal aspects of themselves while simultaneously assessing their emotional safety. Moreover, they invariably have an eye on the leader to determine if their behavior meets with approval, a reaction that suggests "childlike" dependency.

Members, through their interactions, unconsciously develop "rules" (norms) that will protect themselves from being emotionally injured. Norms serve as powerful restraints on the members, but simultaneously they function to protect members from overstimulation and intense discomfort. As these unconscious norms become established they partially replace the therapist, because they serve as rules. Under these circumstances the leader no longer has the same salience for dependency.

Members can benefit from this stage by studying how they respond to new situations. They can learn about their emotional adaptations (defenses) at an interpersonal and internal (unconscious) level, both in relation to authority and to peers. They may feel better because they have shared some of their problems (catharsis), discovered that they are not alone (universality), and they have been respectfully listened to. These represent relational elements inherent to group treatment.

2. The Reactive Phase

Similar to the manner in which children interpret rules rigidly, initial group norms often are experienced (unconsciously) as tyrannical, constricting, and impersonal. In response, clients begin to free themselves and assert their individuality. They may begin to argue or fight, and members' commitment to the group is tested. At times the group may feel on the verge of disintegration because of the tension. The process unfolds as if participants are saying, "I am an individual with my own feelings and responses, and I will not be controlled by the group." Thus the members' task is to find ways of remaining an individual in the group and simultaneously forgo a portion of their individuality. This is a difficult period because the process evokes powerful feelings, which may, for some, seem foreign and aversive. Members may threaten or actually drop out. During this phase, the therapist may lose confidence and may seriously question the value of the enterprise.

In most instances the group and the members survive, discovering that they can manage intense feelings they had not handled previously. They learn to recognize differences, and they learn about the use of their own and others "power."

3. The Mature Phase

This phase is characterized by clients being able to engage in deeply emotional interchanges and self-expression, with others recognizing the significance of what is being transacted and not interfering with the discourse. Members learn to explore their relationships, including their manner of handling conflict and affection within the group, and apply the new knowledge to their lives outside in a more mature and productive fashion. Not only do participants explore their interactions with others, they examine the personal meanings, as it may be contributing to both their life in the present and in the past. This is not a search for "absolute truth," but an attempt to examine patterns of behavior and feelings that have created ways of experiencing and interacting that continue from childhood into the present. The ongoing process allows members to experience their repetitious ways of handling relationships and to explore new ways of relating.

The therapist is no longer the only expert, as members learn that they can powerfully and effectively interact with others. This provides a sense of personal competence and efficacy, which is not present in dyadic therapy.

4. The Termination Phase

In ongoing groups clients enter and depart. Optimally, individuals do not leave abruptly. Rather, they provide sufficient time to say goodbye to others with whom they have formed meaningful relationships. Members usually have the opportunity to see others depart, and they familiarize themselves with a variety of responses to leaving. Their own departure, however, is much more personal. Often, under the stress, the departing person regresses to former behaviors. This provides an opportunity for "one more" chance to learn about oneself. No participant leaves entirely "cured." Group membership provides real relationships as well as transference experiences.

Termination is not easy, as members experience envy, resentment, sadness, and pleasure. Memories of other meaningful losses (separations or deaths) are stimulated. Some may try to convince the departing patient that he or she is not ready to leave, so that they will not have to face the departure. Others push to condense the termination period and diminish their associated affects.

Therapists are not immune to similar emotions. As they do with all phases of treatment, clinicians need to monitor their own emotional states (countertransferences [see later]) to help the group and the departing member experience, to the best of their ability, their departure.

F. Treatment Factors That Affect the Process

1. Cotherapy

Some groups are led by two therapists, which provides clinicians opportunities to share the therapeutic responsibility and to observe and learn from one another in direct action. Cotherapy is often used in training settings. The format requires that the clinicians spend time addressing the process and exploring their areas of agreement and difference.

For patients, the format provides two authority figures, often experienced as parents, with one being experienced as father and the other as mother. It creates an environment similar to a family, with members' associations to the positives and negatives of their family. They can observe how differences and inevitable conflict are managed by the therapists, which may serve as a corrective emotional experience to what was experienced in the family of origin.

Drawbacks to the model are the deemed inefficiency (two persons working where one may do) and the extra time involved in the clinicians addressing their relationship as the process unfolds. Assets of the model include its use in training, an opportunity to work directly with another colleague, and to hear differing perspectives about the conduct of treatment.

2. Combined Therapy

Some patients simultaneously participate in both individual and group treatment. Individual treatment may be either with the group therapist or another clinician. The advantages of such formats are that patients can address emergent problems in private, where there is more individual time for exploration than is available in the group. When the same clinician is therapist in both formats, patterns in the group can be linked to behaviors in the individual treatment, even if the patient does not observe them. Moreover, problems emerging in the dyadic treatment may be brought to the group for further elucidation. This is usually a responsibility of the patient, and not of the therapist.

Almost without exception, patients reveal in the group that they are participating in combined therapy. This information is examined like any other process element. Other members' common responses are of envy and wishes for special relationships. Opposite concerns suggest that the patient is more ill and requires extra treatment. Many clinicians endorse combined therapy as a very powerful treatment approach.

G. Certain Difficulties in the Treatment Process

1. Countertransference

In the modern therapeutic era, therapists' emotional responses in the treatment situation are examined as potential information about the therapeutic process. These responses may be in the form of the clinician's emotional states or behaviors that may be conscious or unconscious. Historically, countertransference was seen as an impediment to treatment due to the therapist's unconscious responses. Currently, therapists examine their emotional responses, fantasies, dreams, and interactions as sources of information about themselves and their patients. This expanded notion of countertransference separates clinicians' responses into those that can be useful in understanding either the individuals or the process from behaviors that may interfere with the treatment.

In group treatment therapists may respond to experiences from their past as stimulated by an individual, subgroups or the group-as-a-whole process. Mistakes and misunderstandings are inevitable. They may arise from a "reasonable" response to the emotions in the present or from the clinician's past. Interventions that are well intentioned may be heard, understood, or experienced by members in unintended or aversive fashion. Remaining alert to these possibilities enables the clinician to detect processes that may have been derailed.

2. Group Safety

For any treatment modality to function effectively, participants must have confidence in the safety of the situation. The agreement establishes a basic element—no physical contact. Patients who are unable to control themselves may not be able to continue in the group and may be asked to leave temporarily or permanently. In addition to physical actions, patients may threaten others verbally—an action that on a continuing basis is not compatible with group treatment.

3. Extra-Group Contacts

Members almost universally have contact with one another outside the treatment setting. This may naturally occur in the waiting room before the meeting or when leaving together at the end of a session. Ordinarily, this is not problematic. Not infrequently, though, patients will attempt to manage feelings emerging in the group by meeting with others. Sexual liaisons take place rarely. All salient contacts need to be openly discussed in the therapy, where patients can learn about themselves (see group agreement). Persistence of any emotionally laden extra-group contacts sets up destructive subgroups (i.e., there are secrets) and may be incompatible with an effectively functioning group.

4. Excessive Premature Terminations or Dropouts

Patients leave the group prior to completing treatment for a variety of reasons. Within the first 12 weeks, in almost every new group one or two members are likely to stop treatment, sometimes without notification. Reasons for dropping out may include fears that hearing others emotions may be harmful, or life changes interfere with regular attendance (these changes are sometimes are unconsciously "arranged" because of emotional responses).

To provide stability, replacements should be added to the group. If an excessive number of patients drop out, the viability of the group may be in doubt. Most groups do not function effectively with four or less members.

H. Other Populations

Groups described in this section are conducted with basic psychodynamic principles. Characteristically, patients have limitations in their ability to examine unconscious processes. This limitation does not obviate the unconscious processes that contribute to group dynamics. In these circumstances, treatment focuses more extensively on support, stabilization, and reintegration that in part arises from the supportive elements intrinsic to group dynamics. Examination of unconscious processes is limited, concordant with patients' limited capacities. Such groups represent the application of psychodynamics in an expanded range of setting and populations.

Psychodynamically informed groups have been shown to be useful in inpatient or in partial (day) hospitals. In these settings, patients may meet daily in dynamically oriented groups as an intrinsic element in a broader range of therapeutic activities. The increased meeting frequency serves as support and enables individuals to expose deeper layers of their personality. The results of this treatment have been encouraging for difficult patients who do not respond to more usual outpatient therapy.

Groups for victims of a common trauma or for individuals experiencing grief have been found to be effective in relieving individuals of the resultant acute and sometimes chronic symptoms. Such groups are generally time limited, and the dynamic theory often focuses on the termination issue, which may more specifically reexpose the experience of loss or death.

Psychodynamically informed groups benefit persons with chronic mental illness. Patients with diagnosis of schizophrenia, bipolar disorder, other persistent major illness, or severe personality disorders represent the greatest number of individuals in this category. These individuals are generally not seen as amenable to "insight," but they can benefit significantly from the slower developing, attenuated relationships. As described by Walter Stone in 1996, groups form in which some individuals attend regularly (core members) and others intermittently (peripheral members). Over time the group develops a workable degree of cohesion, and patients gradually develop trusting relationships. Members of these groups often do not thoroughly examine intragroup relationships and thus have limited potential for insight into their here-and-now transactions. Rather members achieve their benefits primarily through supportive, self-revelation and learning factors.

II. THEORETICAL BASES

Psychodynamic group psychotherapy arises from two theoretical bases: social psychology and psychoanalytic theory.

A. Social Psychology

Social psychology addresses the interaction between the social environment and the individual. Kurt Lewin, who developed field theory, conceives of a group not as a sum of its parts, instead groups form as a system that arises from interacting individuals. In turn, the system affects members' behavior and feelings. Groups have goals, roles, norms, boundaries, and develop cohesion, and evolve over time.

Psychodynamic groups have goals of improved individual functioning. Roles define the functions necessary to accomplish the task. The schema suggested by Roy MacKenzie posits four group roles: task, social, divergent, and cautionary. The task role, primarily cognitive, helps define what has to be done to accomplish goals. The social role attends to members' feelings. The divergent role challenges authority and questions normative views. The cautionary role hides feelings and thoughts. These roles are omnipresent and represent group, not solely individual, functions. Potentially any person could fill each role.

Norms are the conscious and unconscious rules of behavior that influence and regulate the members and the nature of the interactions (i.e., conscious: we should all be on time; unconscious: we will not express anger here). External boundaries define the time, place, and proper information to bring to the group (i.e., one is to tell about onself). Internal boundaries also define aspects of relationships among members (i.e., feelings are verbalized, not acted on or levels of communication: conscious/unconscious).

Over time, groups will "develop," as initially described by Warren Bennis and Herbert Shepard. As members resolve conflicts concerning authority and intimacy, roles become distributed and flexible; norms change, and exchanges are freer in the service of achieving goals of individual development and maturation. This is a sociopsychological process seen as somewhat akin to individual psychological development.

B. Psychoanalytic Theory

Sigmund Freud was the founder of psychoanalytic theory of the human personality. Basic theoretical tenets include individuals' behavior is influenced by unconscious processes, (which may be glimpsed through dreams and "mistakes," like slips of the tongue); individuals are in conflict with efforts to satisfy their instincts (aggressive or erotic), and their own or societal standards. Symptoms are a result of such conflicts. Individuals will transfer their childhood instinctual lives, often expressed as wishes and hopes, to persons in their current life (transference). They will be resistant to directly examining or acknowledging aspects of themselves (resistance) because of perceived danger associated with past childhood experiences or from their own internal prohibitions. They will repeatedly try to master these early conflicts (repetition compulsion) that will emerge in their present relationships. Psychoanalytic/dynamic theory attempts to help individuals understand the meaning of their behaviors or emotions, thereby freeing the person from unconscious forces.

Modifications of original Freudian theory have placed greater emphasis on wishes for relationships, rather than as gratifications of instincts. Moreover, more attention has been directed toward the role of culture in determining one's behavior.

Patients will exhibit repetitious patterns of behavior directed toward the therapist, peers, or to their image of the "group." The group then becomes a microcosm of their behavior in the external world, with allies, enemies, saviors, or as objects (others or the whole group) of affection or hate (transferences). Members learn about their unconscious motivations or wishes for relationships through their interactions (transferences) that emerge through their repetitious behaviors and emotional responses. This new knowledge will then be available for members to make changes as they are made conscious and examined in the group interactions.

III. EMPIRICAL STUDIES

Treatment efficacy of group psychotherapy has been explored for more than four decades. This has been a most problematic area of research because of the multiple elements contributing to treatment outcome. Nevertheless, meta-analytic reviews of group therapy have shown that group treatment is more effective than no treatment and has equivalent efficacy with individual therapy. These findings, however, need to be appreciated as generalizations, because most of the studies have been with cognitive behavioral treatments. Those with psychodynamic orientation have been limited by a lack of specificity along general demographic dimensions, including age, gender, diagnostic description of the patient populations, and duration of treatment.

Moreover, efficacy studies of group psychotherapy have emphasized individual patient outcome and underemphasize group outcome, that is some groups (therapist–client composition) appear to be more efficacious than others. Insufficient emphasis has been placed on assessing the contribution to outcome of leader behaviors, member-to-member interactions, or the group as a whole setting. In 1999, The National Advisory Mental Health Council's Clinical Treatment and Services research workgroup, concerned with fundamental flaws in present research designs, proposed much broader guidelines in hopes of learning more about the subtle factors of relationship and personality in the therapeutic venture.

Nevertheless, certain consistent findings have emerged that inform group therapy outcome. Patients are generally reluctant to enter into group treatment. Individuals assigned to group treatment are less likely to appear for their initial group meeting than persons assigned to individual treatment. Persons of lower social class and of color are more likely to drop out.

Groups that have a greater number of dropouts are less likely to have good outcomes than those with more stable membership. Individuals who successfully complete their group treatment are likely to credit their benefit to peer interactions, rather than their interactions with the therapist.

Studies of homogeneous populations have been few. Recently, however, reports of patients with borderline personality treated in partial hospital settings have shown improvement as reported by Canadian researchers, Anthony Joyce, Mary McCallum, and William Piper in 1999 and by the Norwegian research team including Theresa Wilberg, Sigmund Karterud, Oyrind Urmes, and colleagues in 1998. Individuals in these studies were treated with a variety group formats daily in a partial hospital for 16 to 18 weeks. The major emphasis was psychodynamically oriented group treatment. The Wilberg *et al.* study included a 30-month continued outpatient group treatment. Those participating in the continuing treatment had better outcomes than those who did not. The methodology did not include random assignment and therefore requires replication. These studies represent a focus on more homogenous populations with methodologies that include direct verification of therapists' behavior, thereby controlling for some of the variability.

Despite the overall limitations, research into the efficacy and the process variables that may contribute to the outcome of psychodynamic group psychotherapy remains promising.

IV. SUMMARY

Psychodynamic group psychotherapy is a treatment modality in which a small group of individuals (6–10) meet at a regularly scheduled time and place to address and seek to improve their emotional functioning. The theoretical bases for the treatment derive from social psychology and from psychoanalytic theory. Groups require careful preparation that includes setting goals for the group, recruiting, and preparing prospective members.

Therapists are responsible for creating a structure that facilitates open-ended discussion in which individuals can freely express themselves and examine the unfolding relationships among them, with the leader, and with the image of the group. In the therapeutic process members will, through repetition compulsion, recreate difficulties that brought them to therapy. Through the relationships and interpretations, participants will learn about their emotional responses and dysfunctional behaviors. The group provides a setting in which they may experiment with new behaviors before attempting them outside. Through the repeated opportunities to see, understand, and alter their behaviors and feelings, patients will mature and gain the capacity for greater intimacy and satisfying relationships and societal roles.

See Also the Following Articles

Anxiety Disorders: Brief Intensive Group Cognitive Behavior Therapy ■ Behavioral Group Therapy ■ Cognitive Behavior Group Therapy ■ Group Psychotherapy ■ Individual Psychotherapy ■ Posttraumatic Stress Disorder ■ Psychodynamic Couples Psychotherapy ■ Self-Help Groups

Further Reading

Fuhriman A., & Burlingame, G. M. (Eds.). (1994). *Handbook of group psychotherapy: An empirical and clinical synthesis.* New York: John Wiley & Sons.

Kaplan, H. I., & Sadock, B. J. (Eds.). (1993). *Comprehensive group psychotherapy* (3rd ed.). Baltimore: Williams and Wilkins.

Klein, R. H., Bernard, H. S., & Singer D. L. (Eds.). (1992). *Handbook of contemporary group psychotherapy: Contributions from object relations self psychology and social systems theories.* Madison, CT: International Universities Press.

MacKenzie, K. Roy. (1997). *Time-managed group psychotherapy: Effective clinical applications.* Washington DC: American Psychiatric Press.

Piper, W. E., McCallum, M., & Azim, H. F. A. (1992). *Adoption to loss through short-term group psychotherapy.* New York: Guilford Press.

Rutan, J. S., & Stone, W. N. (2001). *Psychodynamic group psychotherapy* (3rd ed.). New York: Guilford Press.

Stone, W. N. (1996). *Group psychotherapy for people with chronic mental illness.* New York: Guilford Press.

Yalom, I. D. (1995). *The theory and practice of group psychotherapy* (4th ed.). New York: Basic Books.

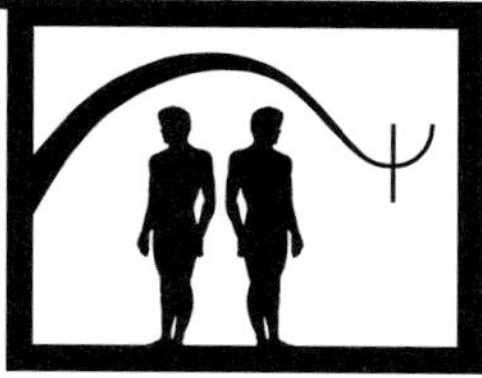

Psychogenic Voice Disorders: Treatment

E. Charles Healey
University of Nebraska, Lincoln

Marsha Sullivan
University of Nebraska Medical Center

GLOSSARY

aphonia Loss of voice.

breathiness Audible flow of air during phonation.

dysphonia Abnormal voice quality, heard as hoarseness, breathiness, or harshness.

conversion aphonia Voice loss in the absence of physical factors.

conversion dysphonia Voice disorder characterized by hoarseness, breathiness, or harshness that appears in the absence of physical factors.

harshness Phonation that has sudden onsets of phonation along with pitch and intensity abnormalities.

hoarseness Aperiodic vibration pattern of phonation, breathiness, pitch breaks, low pitch, and episodes of aphonia.

hyperfunctional Excessive function due to behavioral misuse or abuse.

laryngeal massage Therapeutic technique used to relax the musculature surrounding the larynx.

muscle tension dysphonia Voice disorder caused by excess muscle tension in the larynx.

mutational falsetto Voice disorder associated with a high-pitched phonation without structural abnormalities.

phonation Vibrations of the vocal folds creating voice.

puberphonia Voice of an adolescent.

psychogenic Referring to a voice that has psychological origins.

The human voice conveys a wide range of emotions, feelings, attitudes, and affections. It is a dynamic, complex mechanism that is central to verbal communication and is so individualized that for all practical purposes, no two voices are alike. A person's voice may be aesthetically displeasing or may convey a particular personality or emotional state. It is possible to hear a tremulous voice when a person faces fear or danger, an aphonic or dysphonic voice when someone endures extreme emotional stress, or an abnormal vocal pitch in which a man may sound like a woman or a woman like a child. Thus, the human voice has an extremely wide range of pitch, loudness, flexibility, and qualities, but the boundaries between normal and abnormal are not clearly defined. In 1990, Arnold Aronson defined a voice disorder as one that differs in terms of pitch, loudness, quality, or flexibility from the voices of other individuals of similar age, gender, and/or cultural group. However, there is no universal agreement of when either a normal or an abnormal voice exists.

There are a number of reasons why a person's voice might sound abnormal. Some voice problems can result from behavioral or hyperfunctional misuse of the vocal mechanism, abnormal medical and physical conditions, and psychological stress. Given the focus of this book, this article is limited to a discussion of the symptoms and treatments for three types of psychologically based voice disorders. These include *(a)* conversion reactions resulting in aphonia and dysphonia, *(b)* mutational falsetto or puberphonia, and *(c)* muscle tension dysphonia. These voice problems as commonly referred to as "psychogenic" voice problems because the disorder emerges from abnormal psychological factors in the presence of a physically normal voice.

I. DESCRIPTION OF TREATMENT

Before the treatment for these three psychogenic voice disorders is described, it is necessary to discuss some general features of patients with these types of voice disorders. In light of the strong connection between emotions and vocal behaviors, it is not surprising that emotional conflicts and stress change the way the voice sounds and functions. In 2000, Daniel Boone and Stephen McFarlane noted that increased emotionality or stress will cause significant perceptual changes in the voice because people will: *(a)* produce shorter and more shallow breathing patterns, and *(b)* increase the tension of the vocal folds and neck musculature, creating an elevation of the larynx in the neck. The vocal symptoms resulting from these physiological changes can range from compete aphonia to varying degrees of dysphonia characterized by hoarseness, breathiness, and abnormally high-pitched phonation.

Because emotions and vocal performance as so closely related, effective therapy for psychogenic voice disorders requires attention to the entire profile of the person rather than the simple remediation of the vocal symptoms. Therefore, most voice therapy involves a multidisciplinary team approach. Key team members include a speech-language pathologist, an otolaryngologist, a neurologist, and/or a psychologist. The speech-language pathologist and otolaryngologist are the primary members of the team and work collaboratively to rule out the presence of organic laryngeal disease, systemic illnesses, and any form of vocal fold movement disorder. A neurologist is called on to evaluate the voice disorder from a neurological perspective while a psychologist may provide important follow-up support to voice therapy when it is apparent that the voice problem is an expression of significant psychological difficulties.

One of the hallmark features of all psychogenic voice disorders is that the voice sounds abnormal yet the person doesn't have any form of organic laryngeal pathology or disease. In other words, the voice appears normal on visual inspection but is perceptually different from other normal voices. In most cases, the cause of the disorder can be traced to some form of life stress or to personality disorder. Interestingly, normal movement of the vocal folds usually occurs during a variety of vegetative laryngeal maneuvers such as quiet breathing, coughing, throat clearing, and laughing. Disordered vocal symptoms appear once the verbal communication is initiated.

The following is a description of voice therapy for conversion reactions, mutational falsetto, and muscle tension dysphonia.

A. Conversion Reactions: Aphonic and Dysphonic Voices

People who suddenly display hoarseness or lose the ability to phonate are thought to be suffering from a conversion reaction. These patients believe their voice problem is due to a physical or medically related disorder when, in fact, the problem is related to behavioral reposturing of their larynx due to unresolved interpersonal conflicts. They are unaware that they have translated an emotionally based communication problem into a physical voice problem. Typically, the voice symptoms are triggered by colds, flu, or a short period of laryngitis. Consequently, the person believes the vocal symptoms are a result of an upper respiratory infection rather than an unresolved emotional conflict that is related to communicating feelings toward others. The client's voice is characterized by aphonia, high-pitched squeaks, or varying degrees of hoarseness.

Treatment for this type of voice disorder involves the cooperation of the otolaryngologist and the speech-language pathologist. A patient needs to be reassured by both professionals that the larynx appears and functions normally. In 1995, Moya Andrews pointed out that it is important for the speech-language pathologist to build a positive relationship with the patient to help the patient discuss the main source of emotional conflict and stress. This should set the stage for having the patient accept the notion that the vocal condition is due to some type of emotional conflict. Once this issue is discussed, the speech-language pathologist explains to the patient how emotional stress and tension can interfere with the voluntary control of the voice. Next, the clinician should attempt to elicit a better-sounding voice pressing in, up, or down on the larynx while the patient sustains a vowel sound. Laryngeal massage, which involves using the fingers in a circular motion to reduce tension in the neck musculature around the larynx, is attempted also to help restore normal voicing. It is common to have the patient produce a significantly improved sounding voice during a cough, while clearing the throat, laughing, and shouting. If the voice improves dramatically during these involuntary forms of phonation, the problem is clearly a conversion reaction. A clinician can facilitate a normal sounding voice through the use of these vegetative vocal gestures. For example, the clinician can have the patient cough but then say a sustained vowel sound immediately after the cough. By extending the vocal sound of the cough into a sustained vowel gives the patient an auditory image of a normal sounding voice and also shows the patient that a normal sounding voice is possible. Therapy continues with having the patient recite the days of the week, counting, or simple oral reading. Gradually, the person should be asked to maintain the voice during a conversation with the clinician. If this occurs, then the patient can be encouraged to talk about the underlying emotional stress or conflicts that precipitated the aphonic or dysphonic voice. Follow-up therapy sessions might be needed to ensure that a normal sounding voice is maintained. In those cases in which the patient is unable to maintain voicing, referral to a psychologist or psychiatrist is recommended.

B. Mutational Falsetto (Puberphonia)

The second major type of psychogenic voice disorder is mutational falsetto, which is sometimes called puberphonia. This voice disorder is most commonly found in young adolescents, but it can also occur in adults. The main vocal symptom of this disorder is an abnormally high-pitched voice for either the male or female even though the voice has undergone its normal postpuberty changes. In other words, the patient has a mature larynx but for some psychosocial reason rejects the normal, lower-pitched voice. Typically, the mutational falsetto voice patient exhibits an elevated larynx, tightly stretched vocal folds creating a thin vibratory mass, and a shallow breathing pattern.

In 1995, Andrews pointed out that treatment of this disorder begins with medical confirmation that laryngeal maturation has occurred and that a laryngeal web or other structural deviations in the larynx have been ruled out. If there are no concerns about the physical condition of the larynx, the clinician can elicit a lower-pitched voice in the following ways. First, the clinician can use laryngeal massage to decrease extrinsic and intrinsic laryngeal muscle tension, adjust head position, and attempt to pull the larynx down to a lower neck position. Gradually, the fingers move down to the thyroid cartilage and thyroid notch where the larynx is gently moved into a lowered position. Some patients will resist the lowering of the larynx, but a clinician should be persistent and apply considerable force in pulling the larynx down to a more typical resting posture. Massage helps loosen tense musculature and stretches the laryngeal musculature, which contributes to a relaxed vocal mechanism. At the time the clinician is pulling the larynx down, the patient is instructed to cough, sustain a prolonged vowel sound, or repeatedly produce an abrupt onset of phonation. The patient also will produce a lower-pitched voice if a deeper breath is taken prior to phonation. In 1990, Aronson noted that the shift from a high- to a low-pitched voice will be sudden when the voice is produced forcefully and aggressively.

Once a lower-pitched voice is achieved, the clinician should have the patient habituate the lower pitch sound through repeated vowel productions using an abrupt or sudden onset of phonation. Eventually, the lower-pitched voice will become more consistent as the patient moves from vowel productions to words, and then phrases to spontaneous conversation. The speech-language pathologist will encourage the patient to use the lower-pitched voice because it is the most desirable and acceptable voice. Usually, only a few therapy sessions are sufficient to achieve a consistent, normal-sounding voice. At times, the patient rejects the lower-pitched voice because of the difficulty accepting the new vocal image. In those cases, it may be necessary to refer the patient for psychotherapy. Usually, patients return to therapy once they have accepted and become accustomed to the idea of the lower-pitch voice.

C. Muscle Tension Dysphonia

This type of voice disorder was first described by Murry Morrison, Hamish Nichol, and Linda Rammage in 1986. It is usually seen in young to middle-age adults who have difficulty coping with stress or use their voice in stressful situations. There is palpable muscle tension around the larynx, and during phonation, the suprahyoid musculature becomes tight. One of the main features of the disorder is that during indirect laryngoscopic exam, there is a visible space between the vocal folds in the posterior portion of the vocal folds during phonation. This posterior gap in the vocal folds contributes to the perception of a breathy voice and, to some degree, a harsh voice quality. Patients with muscle tension dysphonia usually complain that their voice is weak, lacks appropriate loudness, and tires easily.

Treatment for this type of pyschogenic voice disorder typically involves larygneal massage and a technique called "yawn-sigh." The yawn-sigh technique involves having a patient pretend to yawn, which creates an open vocal tract and helps the neck musculature to relax so that a lowered laryngeal position is obtained. When the patient exhales after the yawn, the patient is encouraged to create a gentle and brief phonation (i.e., a sigh) at the end of the yawn. Repeated practice of this technique may facilitate an improved voice quality. However, if this technique is ineffective in producing a better-sounding voice, a clinician will want to perform laryngeal massage and manual repositioning of the larynx, combined with simple vocalizations as done with conversion reactions and mutational falsetto patients. As stated earlier, the patient is asked to produce a sustained vowel sound while the laryngeal massage is taking place. A clearer voice quality and slightly lower pitch indicate that excessive muscle tension around the larynx is subsiding and/or the larynx is pulled down or the thyroid cartilage is gently squeezed. Once a better voice is achieved, the patient should practice using the voice in gradually more complex speech contexts. Patients can be taught how to massage their larynx and move it into a lowered position. In addition, the clinician explains the connection between emotional stress and its impact on increasing muscle tension levels in the neck as well as the direct effect muscle tension has on changing voice quality.

II. THEORETICAL BASES

In 2000, Boone and McFarlane stated that the most accurate theory that explains the mechanics of phonation is the myoelastic-aerodynamic theory of phonation developed in the late 1960s. The basic notions of this theory are that intrinsic vocal fold muscle contractions create elastic movements of the vocal folds, which interact with aerodynamic components. Specifically, airflow expelled from the lungs generates air pressure (aerodynamics) below the vocal folds as exhalation for speech begins. At the same time this aerodynamic process is initiated, there is simultaneous adduction of the vocal folds through contractions of the vocal fold adductor musculature. The vocal folds vibrate in response to the airflow passing between the vocal folds, separating the folds. The elasticity of the vocal fold mass brings the folds back toward the midline, and the vibratory process is repeated. The pitch of the voice and the flexibility of vocal fold movement are directly dependent on the mass, length, and internal tension of the vocal fold musculature.

In addition, the contribution of the epithelial covering and underlying lamina propria of the vocal folds (i.e., mucosa) cannot be ignored as an important component to vocal fold vibrations. Complex movements of the vocal fold cover create a mucosal wave that moves laterally across the superior surface of the each vocal fold at typical conversational pitch and loudness levels. Any type of voice disorder can be explained in terms of disruptions in any one or more components of the myoelastic-aerodynamic theory of voice production and alterations in mucosal wave activity. As stated earlier, changes in the internal position and tension levels of the larynx as well as changes in the airflow and air pressure characteristics of phonation can lead to abnormal voice qualities in psychogenic voice disorders.

III. EMPIRICAL STUDIES

Research confirming the effectiveness of the therapy approaches for psychogenic voice disorders are lacking. Perhaps the major reason for this is that most clinicians are able to achieve a normal or close-to-normal sounding voice within one or two therapy sessions. Moreover, clinicians may not have a sufficient number of these types of cases to warrant publication of the results of their clinical treatment. Our clinical results show that approximately 90% of the psychogenic patients we treat exit our clinics with normal-sounding voices. Relapse can occur but one or two treatment session(s) is usually sufficient to have the patient's voice return to normal.

The studies that are available indirectly address the effectiveness of the techniques used to treat psychogenic voice disorders. As discussed in the treatment section, laryngeal massage and repositioning of the larynx are used with all three psychogenic voice disorders described in this article. In 1993, Nelson Roy and Herbert Leeper showed that laryngeal massage was effective in improving the voices of 17 patients with voice problems that had no organic involvement.

In another study in 1998, Louis Luguna, Charles Healey, Debra Hope described the successful remediation of a patient with a voice disorder secondary to social phobia. At the outset of therapy, the patient was diagnosed with muscle tension dysphonia. The patient's voice was characterized by a combination of dysphonia, vocal tremors, and occasional spasmodic closure of the vocal folds. Treatment was successful in reducing the abnormal vocal symptoms and social phobia.

IV. SUMMARY

Psychogenic voice disorders represent a small portion of patients with voice disorders that a speech-language pathologist treats. However, the large majority of patients are capable of achieving a normal-sounding voice in a treatment session or two. This is possible because the voice disorder is not related to any organic involvement. Elevated levels of muscle tension in and around the larynx, a heightened posture of the larynx, and poor respiratory support for phonation can result in a voice problem ranging from complete aphonia to varying degrees of dysphonia. High-pitched, tense voices are always seen within the subgroup of the population with voice disorders. Treatment for psychogenic voice disorders involves convincing the patient that the problem is related to a functional misuse of the larynx. Through laryngeal massage and manual repositioning of the larynx while the patient produces simple vocalizations such as sustained vowels, coughing, or clearing the throat, a normal voice can quickly be established. Treatment for these types of voice disorders is effective when proper diagnosis and management are provided by a speech-language pathologist.

Further Reading

Andrews, M. L. (1995). *Manual of voice treatment: Pediatrics through geriatrics.* San Diego, CA: Singular Publishing Group.

Aronson, A. E. (1990). *Clinical voice disorders* (2nd ed.), New York: Thieme-stratton.

Boone, D. R., & McFarlane, S. C. (2000). *The voice and voice therapy* (6th ed.), Boston: Allyn and Bacon.

Laguna, L. B., Healey, E. C., & Hope, D. A. (1998). Successful interdisciplinary intervention with an initially treatment-resistant social phobia. *Behavior Modification, 22,* 358–371.

Morrison, M. D., Nichol, H., & Rammage, L. A. (1986). Diagnostic criteria in functional dysphonia. *Laryngoscope, 94,* 1–7.

Rosen, D., & Sataloff, R. (1997). *Psychology of voice.* San Diego, CA: Singular/Thomson Learning.

Roy, N., & Leeper, H. A. (1993). Effects of manual laryngeal musculoskeletal tension reduction technique as a treatment for functional voice disorders: Perceptual and acoustic measures. *Journal of Voice, 7,* 242–249.

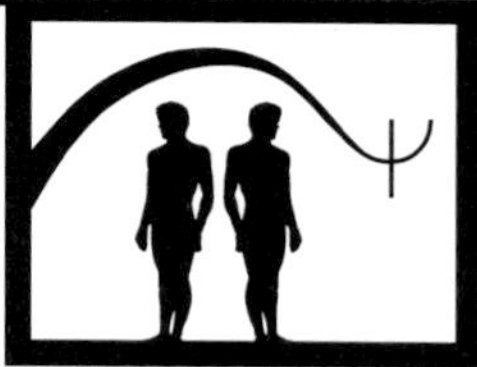

Psychopharmacology: Combined Treatment

Jerald Kay
Wright State University School of Medicine

GLOSSARY

combined treatment The simultaneous prescription of psychotherapy and pharmacotherapy in the treatment of a patient's mental illness.

integrative treatment The provision of pharmacotherapy and psychotherapy by the same clinician.

psychopharmacology The treatment of mental illness with classes of medications that include the following

1. *Anxiolytics*—compounds that possess antianxiety effects to relieve emotional tension.
2. *Antidepressants*—agents from a number of different classes used primarily to relieve depression although often useful in treating other symptoms.
   a. *Monoamine oxidase inhibitors*—medications that inhibit the degradation of monoamine oxidase in the brain thereby elevating levels of available biogenic amines.
   b. *Tricyclic antidepressants*—compounds that increase the availability of multiple neurotransmitters, (e.g., norepinephrine) in the brain.
   c. *Selective serotonin reuptake inhibitors*—medications that promote greater synaptic availability of the neurotransmitter serotonin.
3. *Hypnotics*—different classes of compounds (e.g., benzodiazepines) used to induce sleep.
4. *Mood stabilizers*—multiple types of medications that reduce or prevent mood lability and associated symptoms in affective disorders (e.g., bipolar disorder).
5. *Antipsychotics*—different classes of medications that target many types of malfunctioning neurotransmitter systems such as the dopamine system and relieve and prevent symptoms of psychoses.

sequential treatment The addition of psychotropic medication to psychotherapeutic treatment or psychotherapy to pharmacotherapy when a monotherapy is unsuccessful in alleviating symptoms of a patient's mental disorder.

split treatment The primary treatment of a patient by a psychotherapist in collaboration most often with a psychiatrist who is responsible for the management of medication.

I. DESCRIPTION OF TREATMENT

Throughout the last 10 years, managed behavioral health care has demanded an increasing accountability of mental health professionals to demonstrate both effectiveness and cost effectiveness in the treatments they provide. Because cost containment is the primary objective of managed care systems, the delivery of least expensive treatments has been paramount. This demand has resulted in a significant shift in the treatment models of patients or clients with mental illness toward therapies that are less costly and time intensive. However, the use of combined treatment, that is the employment of both psychotherapy and medication in the treatment of mental disorders, has been a preoccupation of modern psychiatry for more than 40 years and is becoming standard for many mental disorders and psychological problems. In the case of the physician mental health professional, managed care has, in general, preferred a model wherein psychotherapy is provided by a nonphysician mental health provider, and the physician, usually a psychiatrist, becomes responsible for the initiation and ongoing management of pharmacotherapy. For nonphysician mental health professionals, they have become increasingly obligated to adhere to guidelines that mandate a specific treatment for a specific disorder that frequently requires the use of medication. This type of treatment has been referred to most often as split or collaborative treatment. Managed care has undoubtedly refocused professional attention on collaborative care.

Although there is sparse data to support either the effectiveness or cost effectiveness of split treatment in naturalistic settings, nevertheless it has become a common practice. There are however a small number of studies that have suggested the possibility of reduced costs when medication and psychotherapy are provided by the psychiatrist under the auspices of a managed care arrangement.

The use of medication with psychotherapy is limited by neither the type of disorder nor the theoretical model of psychotherapy employed. Indeed in the case of interpersonal psychotherapy (IPT) medication issues where appropriate are routinely presented as a significant component in the treatment process from the start. Part of the appeal of this type of psychotherapy is the direct attempt to provide treatment in a situation that closely resembles the traditional nonpsychiatric doctor–patient relationship thereby reducing the stigma often associated with the need for mental health services. Similarly, the integration of psychotherapy and medication, when indicated, often characterizes cognitive-behavioral as well as psychoanalytically oriented psychotherapies.

II. THEORETICAL BASES

The prominence of a biologically based psychiatry within the last 40 years was in no small part facilitated by the substantial development of new compounds to treat mental disorders. Initially there was resistance to the introduction in psychotherapy of psychotropic medications. Some expressed concern that psychotropics irreparably altered the treatment relationship and dampened symptoms to such a degree that patients were no longer motivated to undergo psychotherapy. Others claimed that the introduction of medication encouraged a passive, dependent stance and perhaps the potential for magical thinking and symptom substitution. Still others claimed a lowering of the patient's self-esteem as a result of viewing himself or herself as being more ill and requiring some external agent to function. Some therapists feared that using medication raised unnecessary fears in patients that they were somehow less interesting to treat.

On the other hand, there may be benefits of employing medication within the psychotherapeutic relationship. These include:

- Patient self-esteem may be enhanced through symptom reduction.
- Greater safety and therefore increased expression of emotions by patients.
- Greater patient accessibility to psychotherapy through enhanced cognition, verbalization, and abreaction.
- Improvement in autonomous ego functions such as thought, attention, concentration, and memory permitting greater ego strength for verbal treatment.
- Reduction of stigma in help seeking through a positive placebo effect.
- Evocation of feelings and fantasies about receiving medication and the accompanying side effects that provide useful insights about the patient's personality and psychological state.
- Creation of an avenue to explore countertransference feelings around medication side effects or dose changes.
- Provision of a transitional connection between patient and therapist at times of unanticipated interruptions in treatment.
- Demonstration of patient conflicts about success when medication provides improvement.

Conversely, patient compliance or adherence to prescribed medication is a daunting problem for all physicians regardless of specialty. Some studies have found that nearly one-half of all patients prescribed a medication do not follow the prescription. Very often adding psychotherapy to a medication-based treatment program brings significant improvement in this problem because it establishes a format to explore noncompliance issues. In this respect, it is important to remember that effective treatment with pharmacological agents requires a solid therapeutic alliance as is the case when psychotherapy alone is provided. Helpful psychiatric treatment is based on correct diagnosis, however making a correct psychiatric diagnosis without a productive doctor–patient relationship does not assure that patients will take their medications.

Regardless of theoretical persuasion, therapists know that the prescription of medication has significance for each patient in psychotherapy. If the psychological meaning of taking medication can be understood, it can provide a useful resource for the psychotherapist. This is true for either a treatment plan in which a psychiatrist is both prescribing medication and providing psychotherapy or in those instances when a physician is directing the pharmacotherapy and a nonphysician mental health professional is responsible for the psychotherapeutic component.

Medications may have positive and negative meanings for patients. For some, the prescription of medication is a positive reflection that the professional or professionals are interested in and acknowledge the patient's emotional pain and discomfort. Other patients may feel that the introduction of medication into a psychotherapy can be a reflection of the therapist's disinterest or discomfort with the patient's plight. For most patients, medication is viewed as a trustworthy and effective intervention, yet for the suspicious patient medication may be experienced as toxic, hurtful, and an attempt on the part of the physician to control the patient. Similarly, although most patients view medications as relatively safe interventions, others attribute psychological significance to even the most benign side effects. Because for many psychotropics, improvement in symptoms does not occur for 2 to 3 weeks or longer, some patients view the gradual onset of action as a sign that the psychiatrist is inept and or uncaring and that the nonphysician collaborator is not to be trusted because of the questionable referral. For those who have difficulty following the medication regimen, the psychotherapist is obligated to explore the possible reasons. Is it a matter of the patient's denial, incompetency, lack of motivation, the presence of an recognized comorbid disorder, or might this nonadherence be a true reflection of a poor therapeutic alliance? Regardless of diagnosis, for some with a mental disorder, poor adherence may be a representation of an unstable, inconsistent, or chaotic lifestyle.

Despite the substantial scientific evidence demonstrating (alone and in combination) the efficacy of psychopharmacology and psychotherapy for many disorders, cognitive neuroscience does not offer a unified theory explicating the precise mechanisms about the interactions between the two types of treatment. Medications, by and large, are conceptualized in terms of their ability to enhance the capacity of the biological system to respond, experience, and integrate information. Psychotherapies address these issues as well, but fundamentally they are concerned with meaning. Different psychotherapies, of course, utilize different approaches at discovering and modifying the meaningfulness of certain events, feelings, conflicts, wishes, and fears. There is a growing knowledge, for example, about the neurobiology of psychotherapy that has described on the molecular and structural levels how learning and memory may bring about change in psychotherapy. Integrated neuroscience promises that someday what we call the mind will be explained from a biological point of view, at this point in time however, the clinician must juggle two conceptual approaches to understanding human behavior in illness and in health.

III. CLINICAL CHALLENGES IN USING PSYCHOTHERAPY AND PHARMACOTHERAPY

When a psychiatrist is providing both psychotherapy and pharmacotherapy there are some specific challenges to the delivery of effective combined treatment. These include:

- *The adoption of an overview to the patient that encompasses and integrates both biological and psychosocial domains.* This may require the clinician to adopt a more directive and educational manner of relating when discussing medication concerns, and perhaps, in the case of a psychoanalytically oriented psychotherapist, becoming more active than usual in this portion of the visit.
- *The establishment of a system for addressing medication issues with the patient.* The clinician may decide to raise medication issues at the start or very end of the session. In the former case, medication concerns are sure to be covered, and important and helpful material about the therapist–patient relationship may be introduced and explored throughout the entire visit. However, some therapists object to the physician setting the initial agenda for the meeting and favor permitting the patient to begin each session with whatever is most pressing. Others feel that by electing to discuss medication at the very end of a meetting, there is the possibility of premature closure of a significant discussion. Regardless of which approach is selected, it is vital to establish consis-

tency. Deviation from the traditional approach is often helpful in identifying potential countertransference events. For example, when a medication discussion is introduced by the clinician atypically in the middle of a session, it is often an indicator of some discomfort.

• *The development of a systematic format for addressing side effects, requests for changes in medication dose and type, and requests for discontinuation of pharmacotherapy.* In the first case, complaints about side effects may be an important manifestation of patient resistance to psychotherapy. If in the middle of a well-established insight-oriented psychotherapy, the psychiatrist considers raising the possibility of medication, this may be an indication of increasing frustration with the patient's lack of progress.

• *Acquiring a particular sensitivity to termination issues.* It is not uncommon for patients in some types of therapies to experience a recurrence of symptoms at the end stage of treatment. The clinician should not assume that such events require additional or reintroduction of medication. Invariably, this phenomenon is a reflection of the patient's conflicts about the end of the therapeutic relationship and requires appropriate exploration.

Professionals working in collaborative or split treatments face quite different challenges. These treatment relationships may consist of a nonphysician mental health professional and a psychiatrist, a primary care physician and a psychotherapist, and a psychoanalyst or psychiatrist and psychopharmacologist to name but a few formats. The practice of collaborative treatment is by no means rare and two-thirds of practicing psychiatrists have reported prescribing medication for patients in psychotherapy with other professionals. However, the greatest challenge in providing quality collaborative care is assuring adequate communication. This includes communication between the patient and each of the professionals but especially between the psychotherapist and physician.

The amount of time that is required to establish an effective relationship between two providers in a split treatment is by no means insubstantial. However failure to delineate many aspects of the collaborative relationship at the outset is undoubtedly the primary reason for poor patient outcome. First, cooperative treatment implies equal respect for the responsibilities and contributions of each provider. There is no place for ideological or professional tensions in the provision of effective split treatment. Second, the patient must be educated about the unique aspects of entering this type of treatment relationship. These include consent for the professionals to communicate frequently about the patient's progress, difficulties, and medication side effects. Confidentiality is defined differently in this type of treatment relationship, and patients must be aware that information from either professional will be discussed routinely and particularly at times of change or crisis in the treatment.

Informed consent in collaborative treatment should outline clearly the benefits and risks of each type of treatment component as well as explore the patient's expectations of the combined treatment. Organizational guidelines in the field of psychiatry suggest that there should be documentation of each party's responsibilities and that this information has been conveyed to the patient. This includes the need for periodic assessment of the treatment process. It is helpful to prepare a document that explains responsibility in times of emergencies, need for hospitalization, vacation coverage, and a method and frequency of collaboration that is not limited to times of crisis. In this regard, many professionals have begun to rely on electronic mail or fax to keep their collaborators up-to-date. Others prefer face-to-face meetings or telephone conversations.

Consistent communication between the treating professionals serves other purposes beyond legal concerns. Because transference is universal regardless of treatment modality, the introduction of a second professional may often provide some unique challenges. Depending on a patient's psychological problems, a three-person system may activate significant unresolved conflicts and unexpressed expectations about the treatment team. On the other hand, the propensity for splitting is high in some types of patients especially those with particular personality disorders. Idealization of the physician because he or she prescribes medication whereas the psychotherapist does not is common. Similarly, some patients experience a quick medication visit as being reflective of the disinterest of the physician, and the therapist is then held in much higher regard. Negative comments about either professional may serve as important indicators of the patient's problems and characterological style and require that their psychological importance be understood and explored with them within the treatment. Under no circumstances, except in cases of ethical misconduct or malpractice, should either professional collude with the patient to criticize another collaborator. Persistent negativity about one provider should be discussed within the collaborative relationship to decide how best to address this issue.

As noted previously, the suggestion to seek a pharmacological consultation invariably raises relevant patient concerns about the meaning of the current treatment relationship as well as the prognosis. How consideration for medication consultation is introduced has great influence on the patient's ability to follow through with the recommendation. The nonphysician professional should be clear for the reasons for referral. Is it a request for a second opinion about the patient's problems and suitability for psychotherapeutic treatment alone, a request for assistance in controlling disruptive symptoms, or even concern about the potential for an unmerited lawsuit.

IV. APPLICATIONS AND EXCLUSIONS

As will be reviewed shortly, the empirical evidence for employing combined treatment is growing. This is true across the spectrum of mental disorders from the most disabling to those disorders that are often associated with higher levels of functioning and coping. There appear to be no patient populations for which combined treatment is contraindicated although the usual culturally based reservations about psychotherapy or the taking of medication are always relevant. Beyond cultural considerations, the nonphysician professional must be aware that for some patients, medication is not an acceptable form of treatment and that a significant number of patients depending on their disorder will not respond to medication regardless of the type and duration of treatment.

There may be some clinical indications when combined treatment by a psychiatrist may be advantageous although there is no scientific evidence to support these assumptions. These might include those patients with highly complex medical conditions; cluster B personality disorders that have a history of significant self-harm and have experienced the need for frequent hospitalizations; and for those individuals with severe anorexia nervosa who require intensive medical care. Some, but not all, noncompliant patients with severe Axis I disorders such as schizophrenia and bipolar disorder may be candidates for this type of care as well.

V. EMPIRICAL STUDIES

A. Mood Disorders

With respect to combined treatment, unipolar nonpsychotic depression or major depression has been the most extensively studied disorder. Recent randomized controlled studies have provided the best evidence of the efficacy of psychotherapy and pharmacotherapy in the treatment of mood disorders. In a study of approximately 200 elderly patients with recurrent nonpsychotic major depression, interpersonal psychotherapy (IPT) in combination with a tricyclic antidepressant was found to be more effective than either medication or psychotherapy alone. More specifically, those receiving the combined treatment has a recurrence of 20% compared to 43% in those patients with medication alone, and 64% of those treated exclusively with psychotherapy. Those patients receiving only placebo in a typical medication clinic program had a recurrence rate of 90%.

The largest meta-analysis of approximately 600 subjects with nonpsychotic unipolar depression has established that combined psychotherapy and pharmacotherapy was more effective than psychotherapy alone. This study examined patients treated with either cognitive-behavior therapy (CBT) or IPT and compared them to those who were treated with IPT and medication. Combined treatment produced better outcome and also shorter time to recovery. However in patients with less severe depression, psychotherapy alone was equivalent to combined treatment.

A very recent study, the largest randomized controlled trial to date, demonstrated that medication and psychotherapy is clearly superior to either monotherapy. This study of nearly 700 patients found that psychotherapy and a newer antidepressant (nefazadone) provided greater relief than either treatment intervention by itself. This study used a manualized cognitive behavioral treatment called cognitive behavioral analysis system of psychotherapy (CBASP). Study participants receiving integrative treatment had an 85% response rate compared to 55% of those taking medication alone and 52% of participants being treated with psychotherapy alone.

European researchers were able to demonstrate the cost effectiveness of adding psychodynamic psychotherapy in outpatients with depression being treated pharmacologically. The addition of the psychotherapy resulted in fewer hospital days at the end of treatment as well as at 1-year follow-up. In addition to lower direct costs from hospitalization, combined treatment was also associated with less indirect costs for sick days.

As many as 40% of adolescents with chronic depression fail to respond to an initial trial with either a selective seratonin reputake inhibitor (SSRI) or psychotherapy. Some of these so called treatment-resistant teenagers may have comorbid disorders such as attention-deficit-hyperactivity disorder (ADHD), bipolar disorder, and/or substance abuse. However, in adolescents with only chronic depression, as many as 70% of these patients will respond when both medication and psychotherapy are provided.

In what order should medication or psychotherapy be added to either ongoing monotherapy is an important treatment issue. Sequential therapy refers to this clinical decision as to when to augment psychotherapy with medication or when to add psychotherapy to a pharmacotherapy. In the treatment of recurrent major depression it was found that in women who did not fully recover with IPT, the addition of an antidepressant was more effective than treating participants from the outset with combined treatment. Although this study was not a randomized controlled one, it did examine participants from a single patient population treated at one center. This treatment sequence may have particular appeal to women who are against taking medication during pregnancy or lactation.

The data from combined treatment in patients with dysthymia is inconclusive, but this is not the case in the treatment of bipolar disorder. Patients with bipolar and schizoaffective disorders are treated more effectively when they receive family therapy with medication as opposed to psychotherapy alone. Those in combined treatment had fewer relapses and hospitalizations, and researchers were able to demonstrate that family members viewed their affected relatives in a much more positive light.

B. Schizophrenia

There is a wealth of studies going back more than 20 years that has demonstrated the efficacy and effectiveness of treating schizophrenia with psychotherapy and medication. Contrary to some views, families and patients affected by this disorder value psychotherapy greatly. Early studies have demonstrated that patients living in families characterized as having high expressed emotion are more vulnerable to relapses. Such families are characterized by intense affect, frequent criticism, and intrusiveness which have been associated with noncompliance. One randomized controlled study of first-episode patients found only a 10% hospital readmission rate with participants who received both family therapy and medication. This figure compared to a 75% readmission rate in those patients who received no treatment. In addition to family therapy, individual psychotherapy has shown substantial promise. A recent 3-year randomized controlled trial of patients with schizophrenia who received medication and a type of individual treatment called personal therapy that addressed stress management, education about illness, and interpersonal relationship issues was found to be superior to medication and supportive measures. It also promoted enhanced social adjustment throughout the entire study period.

Patients in a British study whose illness did not respond to medication were helped with the addition of 9 months of CBT. Improvement persisted after the completion of formal therapy that was not the case for those patients receiving medication and a nonspecific befriending relationship. This study also noted that rational discussion of hallucinations and delusions when included as a formal component of the psychotherapy accounted for 50% less symptomatology. Another randomized controlled study of patients treated with 20 individual sessions of CBT showed significant improvement compared to groups who either received only medication or supportive psychotherapy plus medication.

Two other studies have demonstrated that CBT is helpful in the treatment of patients with schizophrenia. Treatment refractory patients started on an atypical antipsychotic medication and provided with CBT and social skills training showed greater improvement that a comparison group treated with supportive psychotherapy and medication. Another randomized controlled trial where CBT and medication were compared to medication plus routine care demonstrated nearly four times the improvement in the former group.

C. Anxiety Disorders

Compared to schizophrenia and affective disorders, there are considerably fewer studies of integrative and combined treatment in panic, generalized anxiety, and obsessive–compulsive disorders. In the case of panic disorder, a recent randomized controlled trial of approximately 300 patients receiving CBT and the tricyclic antidepressant imipramine demonstrated greater improvement at the end of the maintenance phase of treatment than those patients with panic disorder who were treated with either monotherapy. One report examined combined treatment of panic disorder with clomipramine and 15 sessions of brief psychodynamic psychotherapy. Patients who received both components showed greater improvement 9 months after the discontinuation of medication compared to those who were treated only with clomipramine. The efficacy of psychodynamic psychotherapy as a monotherapy in the treatment of panic disorder is currently under study, and preliminary reports are very promising.

In the 1980s there were numerous publications that supported the superiority of tricyclic antidepressants and behavioral therapy in combination for the treatment of panic disorder and agoraphobia with single interventions. However, there is considerable controversy regarding the advantage of using combined treatment compared to medication or psychotherapy alone in large part due to the high rate of relapse after medication is discontinued. The integrative treatment of social and specific phobias may be more helpful than is the case with panic disorder. It appears that the same may also be true for combined treatment of generalized anxiety disorder with CBT and medication. However the literature is very limited in this area. The clinician must remember that the vast majority of early studies in combined treatment of anxiety disorders employed older tricyclic antidepressants that often cause considerably more side effects than newer-generation medications. Therefore, studies using selective serotonin reuptake inhibitors may clarify the usefulness of these agents with psychotherapy.

Some practice guidelines support the use of medication and behavioral therapy in treating obsessive–compulsive disorder. Clinical consensus is that exposure and response prevention psychotherapy coupled with selective serotonin reuptake inhibitors is the treatment of choice. The superiority of behavioral therapy over medication alone is well established, but there are few substantive studies of combined treatments.

D. Substance Abuse

There are a number of reports that have noted the superiority of combined treatment with the opiate dependent. A randomized controlled trial assigned 84 opiate-dependent patients to either 4 months of counseling and supplemental drug counselling or counseling with supportive-expressive psychotherapy. At 6 months after treatment, those participants receiving the psychodynamic psychotherapy could be maintained on lower doses of methadone and also were less likely to test positive for cocaine. Another randomized controlled study of the same population found that those provided with psychiatric and vocational counseling services as well as family therapy were less likely to be hospitalized, experience job instability, and to be on welfare than patients who were assigned to medication or medication and counseling groups.

With regards to the treatment of alcoholism, two medications have been used traditionally and are FDA approved: disulfiram and naltrexone. The effectiveness of psychotherapy has been studied in a multisite effort called Project MATCH (Matching Alcoholism Treatment to Client Heterogeneity). This study of more than 1,700 patients, compared three forms of manualized treatment (CBT, motivational enhancement therapy, and 12-step facilitation) and found that all three treatments were effective in treating alcohol dependence with the last proving the most effective at 3-year follow-up.

E. Eating Disorders

At present there is only one randomized control trial addressing the treatment of women with bulimia nervosa. This study of 120 participants examined groups that were treated with CBT, supportive dynamic psychotherapy, and medication. Results indicated that CBT plus antidepressants was more effective than the psychotherapy by itself. Also patients given either CBT or supportive psychotherapy with medication experienced less depression and binge eating. The medication component of the study permitted the prescription of new-generation antidepressants if an older medication was unhelpful. This sequential treatment provided only modest improvement compared to the effectiveness of the CBT or supportive treatment.

F. Personality Disorders

There exists one randomized controlled trial of combined treatment for personality disorders, and therefore many clinicians follow consensus treatment guidelines. In this recent study of patients with borderline personality disorder treated with psychoanalytic psychotherapy and medication compared to patients receiving only standard care without psychotherapy, the former group showed decreased suicidal attempts, self-mutilating behavior, number and duration of hospital admissions, and the use of other psychiatric services. This group also demonstrated symptomatic improvement in anxiety, depression, and general symptom distress. There were also gains in interpersonal functioning and social adjustment.

The use of medications in the psychotherapeutic treatment of borderline personality disorder has been associated with a decreased treatment drop-out rate and fewer severely disruptive regressions. Some have cited a positive effect of medication in decreasing intense feelings of aloneness, a common characteristic of many patients with borderline personality disorder. Many clinicians use split treatment arrangements that augment the psychotherapy with medication for reducing target symptoms of aggression, impulsivity, affective lability, and behavioral dyscontrol.

From the review of the literature it is clear that many questions must be answered about the combined use of psychotherapy and pharmacotherapy. Which disorders are best treated with an integrative approach? What are the indications for sequential treatment, that is, when should treatment begin with psychotherapy and then be followed by the introduction of medication? For which patients and when in the treatment should psychotherapy be added to a pharmacological approach? Which psychotherapies are more advantageous for which disorders in a combined treatment? For which disorders is split treatment cost effective? Many mental health professionals work under significant fiscal pressure to be accountable to payors for the services they provide. Some of these constraints are not based on scientific support and require substantial investigation.

VI. CASE ILLUSTRATION

Ms. Jensen is a 27-year-old unmarried accountant who was referred by a recently relocated family physician to a social worker for assistance in managing the patient's depression and anxiety. According to her physician, the patient has not responded within the last 6 months to any of the various medications he has prescribed. She has a long-standing history of depressive episodes beginning as grade schooler and a well-established pattern of self-defeating behavior since her high school days. The patient has been difficult for the physician as she frequently calls for appointments because of a multiplicity of symptoms and complaints. He is unable to ascertain any significant illness in his patient, and all diagnostic tests have proven normal. Because the psychotherapist has not worked previously with the referring doctor, she recommends that they meet to discuss the patient before an evaluation for treatment is started. The doctor puts off the therapist saying he is pressed for time in his new practice and would prefer to send a summary of the patient's history. The social worker, not willing to disappoint a new referral source, agrees reluctantly to see Ms. Jensen.

The patient tells the therapist that her doctor seemed disinterested in her and stated that she was instructed to visit with a mental health professional for counseling. She describes her physician as very controlling and insisting that she take medication. The history indicated that the patient grew up in a household where both her mother and father were very demanding and rigid, always insisting that there was only one way to view life. This had major consequences for the patient particularly in her adolescence.

Ms. Jensen acknowledged that she had stopped taking the medications prescribed for her because of side effects despite the fact that her doctor had reassured her that they would pass after the first week of treatment. She felt he had been dishonest because some side effects, like her sexual dysfunction, did not improve. The patient was effusive in her praise for the psychotherapist who clearly was interested in her plight and gave her sufficient time to talk. This was not the case with her family doctor whom she experienced as somewhat rigid.

At the completion of the assessment, the social worker summarized her thoughts about the possible ways in which to proceed. She mentioned that the patient should discuss her side effects with her physician and that perhaps there might be another medication that would be less problematic for her. She instructed Ms. Jensen to return to her primary care doctor and share with him that psychotherapy would be helpful as well and that therapist was available to meet with this patient on a regular basis.

After trying to contact the referring physician without success, 4 days later the psychotherapist received a discouraging phone call from Ms. Jensen's doctor who felt he was undercut in his treatment decisions because the patient refused to take any of the medications he wished to prescribe and had nothing but glowing words about her interaction with the therapist. According to the physician, Ms. Jensen explained that she was instructed to tell him that psychotherapy was indicated and not medication treatment.

A. Discussion

This vignette illustrates the complications that can arise in a collaborative treatment when the expectations of both collaborators are never fully presented. First, even prior to the referral, the meaning of medication to this patient was never appreciated. She experienced her physician much like her parents who insisted they were correct at all times and that everything she did should conform to their wishes. In addition, there was a failure to explore side effects that resulted from the medication. This referral was made after the physician became frustrated with the patient and began to experience her as a difficult or problem patient. However, the psychotherapist should not have agreed to evaluate this patient because the necessary guidelines for the referral were never clear. Because the respective roles of the professionals were not delineated, the patient began even within the diagnostic sessions to polarize her treatment relationships with her physician and therapist. She also misconstrued what was recommended by the mental health professional, but this remained unclear because the physician had not returned the consultant's call in a timely manner. In short, this collaborative effort was doomed from the first.

It would have been helpful if the professionals had agreed to meet in person as this was their initial referral experience. At the very least, an in-depth phone conversation should have detailed the physician's concerns and expectations about the referral, and the social worker could also explain her requirements to evaluate and treat the referred patient. If treatment were indicated, the physician would be aware of the central need for communication and in what form and how frequently it should occur. There was no opportunity to discuss any of the groundwork either clinical or legal for this type of treatment relationship, and it was apparent from the outset that the physician did not respect or value the potential assistance from the mental health professional.

VII. SUMMARY

Integrated and combined treatment is the provision of both psychotherapy and pharmacotherapy to a patient. In the case of the former, therapy is most often administered by a psychiatrist. Combined, split, or collaborative treatment is administered jointly by a psychiatrist, other physician, or nurse practitioner with another mental health professional psychotherapist. Although collaborative or split treatment lacks scientific support for its effectiveness or cost effectiveness, it nevertheless is widely used. Mental health care financing has undoubtedly played a major role in the acceptance of split treatment. The psychiatrist who treats the patient with medication and psychotherapy must be hypervigilant to the meaning of medication for each patient and how it is reflected in the treatment relationship. Those clinicians working in collaborative treatment relationships must above all develop concise and consistent plans for professional communication about their patient's experiences if the treatment is to succeed.

Last, despite early efficacy initiatives, the clinician is in the best position to discover the benefits and challenges of treating clients or patients with multiple approaches. For the near future, the naturalistic setting is likely to provide the exciting findings and suggest new areas of inquiry. Mental health professionals will undoubtedly become more sophisticated in their ability to provide integrative and combined treatment.

See Also the Following Articles

Adjunctive/Conjoint Therapies ■ Eating Disorders ■ Integrative Approaches to Psychotherapy ■ Mood Disorders ■ Neurobiology ■ Schizophrenia and Other Psychotic Disorders ■ Sleep Disorders ■ Substance Dependence: Psychotherapy

Further Reading

Barlow, D. H., Gorman, J. M., Shear, M. K., & Woods, S. W. (2000). Cognitive-behavioral therapy, imipramine, or their combination for panic disorder: As randomized controlled trial. *Journal of the American Medical Association, 283,* 2529–2536.

Eells, T. D. (1999). Psychotherapy versus medication for unipolar depression. *Journal of Psychotherapy Practice and Research, 8,* 170–173.

Gabbard, G. O. (2000). Combined psychotherapy and pharmacotherapy. In B. J. Sadock, V. A. Sadock (Eds.), *Comprehensive textbook of psychiatry* (7th ed., pp. 2225–2234). Philadelphia: Lippincott, Williams and Wilkins.

Goldman, W., McCulloch, J., Cuffel, B., Zarin, D. A., Suarez, A., & Burns, B. J. (1998). Outpatient utilization patterns of integrated and split psychotherapy and pharmacotherapy for depression. *Psychiatric Services, 49,* 477–482.

Hogarty, G. E., Greenwald, D., Ulrich, R. F., Kornblith, S. J., Dibarry, A. L., Cooley, S., Carta, M., & Flesher, S. (1997). Three-year trials of personal therapy among schizophrenic patients living with or independent of family. I: Description of study and effects of relapse rates. *American Journal of Psychiatry, 154,* 1504–1513.

Kay, J. (2001). *Integrated treatment of psychiatric disorders.* Washington, D.C.: American Psychiatric Press.

Klerman, G. L., Weissman, M. M., Markowitz, J. C., Glick, I., Wilner, P. J., Mason, B., & Shear, M. K. (1994). Medication and psychotherapy. In A. E. Bergin, S. L. Garfield (eds.), *Handbook of psychotherapy and behavior change* (Vol 4, pp. 734–782). New York: John Wiley and Sons.

Riba, M. B., Balon, R. (1994). *Psychopharmacology and psychotherapy: A collaborative approach.* Washington, DC: American Psychiatric Press.

Thase, M. E., Greenhouse, J. B., Frank, E., Reynolds, C. F., Pilkonis, P. A., Hurley, K., Grochocinski, V., & Kupfer, D. J. (1997). Treatment of major depression with psychotherapy or psychotherapy-pharmacotherapy combinations. *Archives in General Psychiatry, 54,* 1009–1015.

Race and Human Diversity

Sandra Jenkins
Pacific University

GLOSSARY

culturation The process by which a peson learns, integrates and assumes the characteristics of a culture different from the person's original culture.

culture The sum total of human social organization, socialization, and learning.

ethnic group A group of people who share cultural norms and values and who identify with each other as a reference group different from other groups.

multiculturalism A branch of psychology that is based on the theoretical orientation that cultures are determining factors in the practice of psychology.

race A sociopolitical concept that describes a group of people who predominantly interbreed with one another and, therefore, share certain salient physical characteristics.

I. THE RISE OF MULTICULTURALISM

The field of psychology has evolved over time to include the dimension of race/cultural diversity as an area of professional competency. The American Psychological Association, the American Psychiatric Association, and the National Council of Schools of Professional Psychology have included guidelines for cultural competencies in their written policies for practice and training. It was not always so. A recent survey of the PscyhLit files showed a total of 19,418 references under the key term "cross-cultural." For the period between 1872 and 1950 there were 14 references cited, and most of these were rooted in anthropological origins. Then starting in the 1950s and 1960s the number of citations jumped to 863, and the numbers have continued to climb since then. This "burst" of interest coincides with the social reform movements during these periods, that is, the Civil Rights movement in the 1950s and 1960s and the women's and gay rights movements of the 1970s onwards. Clearly psychology as a field has responded to the forces of social change in the larger society.

There is no scientific evidence to support the existence of racial subgroups in the *homo sapiens sapiens* species. Physical anthropologists and geneticists have argued the point for over a century. Both definitions and typographies of racial groups have been difficult to establish. The reasons have to do with the distribution of genes in the human gene pool. No genes of significance are found in any human subgroup that are not found in all others. It seems certain that, after much scientific analysis, there are no human races, and yet the concept has had enormous social, economic, and political impact.

Since the beginning days of psychotherapy, problems have persisted when the client is an ethnic minority and

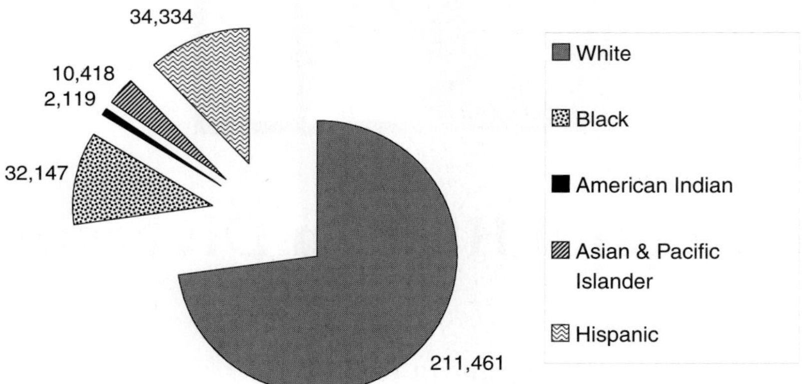

FIGURE 1 2000 population in thousands (U.S. Census Bureau).

the therapist is White. Eurocentric practitioners were prone to constructing improper judgments in diagnosis and treatment. For many years many minority clients were either misdiagnosed or treated with medications and hospitalizations in greater numbers than White clients with similar diagnoses. Many minority clients were denied psychotherapy because it was believed that they were either not verbally skilled or not intellectually capable of achieving insight into their psychological problems. Other studies have shown that minority clients do not present themselves for treatment as often, or drop out of treatment earlier than White clients. In many situations minority clients have been subjected to racial bigotry. Such bigotry is rarely intentional. Most therapists have been unaware of harboring racist attitudes and beliefs. Overall, the experiences of many ethnic minorities has been that psychotherapy has served as a means for furthering and promoting the "status quo" of the dominant White society. The prevailing dilemma is, despite the good intentions in the professional community, psychotherapy with ethnic minorities has frequently failed.

Efforts to solve the problem of ethnocentrist psychology practices have been organized under the general category of the "multiculturalism" movement in psychiatry and psychology. Other terms have been used previously. "Cross-cultural," "culture centered," "intercultural," "transcultural," and "culturally sensitive" have also been used as terms to define the struggle to expand the awareness and skills of practitioners working with clients from different cultural backgrounds.

The multicultural approach grows out of the debates in anthropology, which saw the concept of "races" give way to the concept of "cultures." From a "race" perspective it is clear that not all human groups are equal to each other and that some groups are subject to domination, extermination, and exploitation by other groups. When people are grouped in terms of "cultures," the possibility emerges for equality and relativism. That is, each group can be seen as equally valuable and equally deserving of respect and dignity as any other group. Proponents of multiculturalism have been acutely aware that the population "complexion" of the United States is rapidly changing. The changing demographics, with increasing numbers of non-White groups leads away from previous "assimilationists" thinking toward "cultural pluralism." (Figure 1 shows recent ethnic group figures for the 2000 census. Figures 2 and 3 are projections based on the 1990 census.)

The emphasis remains on ethnic minority clients, but the concept has also been extended to include many circumstances that place a person in a "minority position" in society. Clients who may be disadvantaged by their social position include persons from low socioeconomic backgrounds, women, gays and lesbians, disabled and elderly persons, certain religious groups, and immigrant/refugee clients. In other words, the multiculturalism movement potentially encompasses any clients who are not White, middle class, heterosexual, and mainstream in their social rank and values.

Multiculturalism addresses the failures of psychology to adequately treat diverse peoples, by positing that the cause of failure is the failure to fully realize existence of determining cultural factors. When client populations are viewed from a perspective of cultural/social determinism, a necessary set of questions arises. How does culture affect identity formation and pertinent social roles? What are the cultural factors that influence mental disorders? Are there culturally different norms for healthy or developmentally appropriate behavior? How does culture affect interpersonal behavior? Especially, how does culture influence the client–therapist relationship? How does

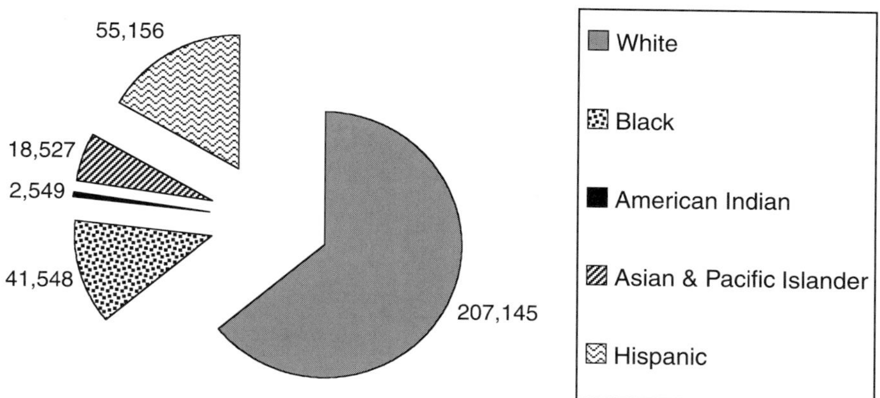

FIGURE 2 2020 projected population in thousands (U.S. Census Bureau).

culture affect help-seeking behavior? What are the implications for treatment and assessment?

Extending "culture" to include "diversity" means extending the concepts to include any significant social or environmental determinants that distinguish between dominant versus subordinate people. This means extending the same questions to incorporate variables, such as gender, age, socioeconomic status, and sexual orientation, and so on. How does a history of experiencing social oppression, discrimination, racism, sexism, and homophobia affect mental health and the development of healthy functioning? Again, what are the implications for assessment and treatment?

As the limits of ethnocentric practices became better understood, the multicultural thrust began to include development of cultural competence requirements for practitioners. In attempting to summarize various authors, a basic doctrine emerges throughout the literature. The multicultural position maintains that for therapists to be competent and successful:

1. Therapists must be knowledgeable about the history, beliefs, values, and norms of the client's reference group. They must also be knowledgeable about each group's status in relation to the dominant society.
2. The therapist must be mindful of the effects of social oppression and be willing to actively combat oppressive social forces.
3. To avoid pitfalls of bigotry and "cultural mismatches" the therapist must also be aware of their own cultural norms, beliefs, and values. They must be mindful of how their implicit cultural beliefs enter into and affect the therapy process.
4. The therapist must be aware of the ways in which their own worldview and the worldview of the client may be similar or different and accommodate the therapy to the client's worldview as much as possible.
5. The therapist must have the skills to respond appropriately to the client's verbal, non-verbal, affective, and cognitive cultural norms. This includes knowing and responding to culturally acceptable

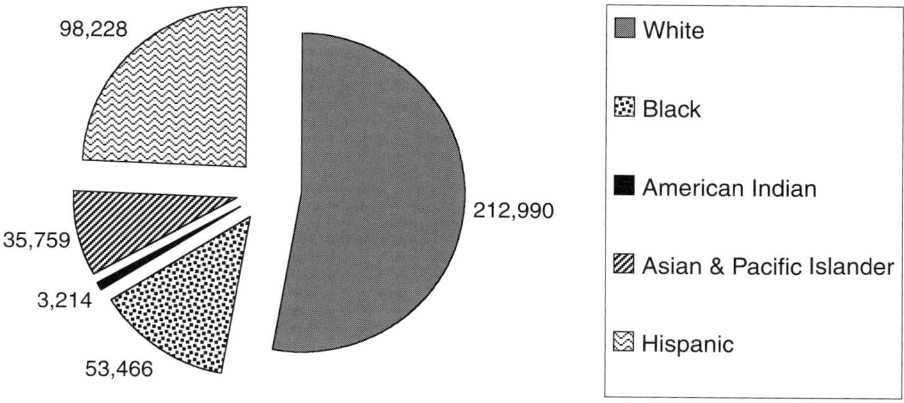

FIGURE 3 2050 projected population in thousands (U.S. Census Bureau).

norms for interacting with authority figures, non-family members, and strangers.

6. The therapist must possess knowledge of the cultural norms that govern asking for help and establishing a relationship.

7. The therapist must know the culturally prescribed expressions of different symptoms and must know how to accurately interpret and respond to the meaning of different affective and cognitive concepts.

8. The therapist must know the different cultural criteria for mental illness, as well as the criteria for healthy individual and social functioning.

9. Therapists must be knowledgeable of how cultural variables affect results of psychometric tests and measures. They must know which test instruments are suitable for use with which ethnic groups. They must be able to accurately interpret test results of various ethnic minorities.

10. Therapists must maintain an attitude of respect and valuing of each group, no matter how much that group differs from their own group. When therapists are able to maintain this attitude of "intercultural" valuing, both the therapist and the client can grow as human beings, developing from ethnocentric beings to a higher maturity of intercultural identities.

Based on a foundation of cultural relativism and pluralism, multiculturalists have attempted to establish new directions for psychology therapy practice, assessment, research, and training. To make psychotherapy culture sensitive, psychologists are encouraged to study the cultural norms of different groups, study specific personality traits relevant to each group, and explore developmental issues for each group. Culture-centered psychotherapies are also being developed. Assessment issues include test content, examiner bias, and culturally-competent test administration. A main focus of assessment is the degree of acculturation of the ethnic minority person being assessed. Identity development issues also play a strong part. The identity models that have been developed are generally consistent with one another. These models posit that ethnic minority identity develops along a series of cognitive stages. The stages begin with naive precontact with members of the dominant society and then some conflictual encounter leads to a rejection of the dominant society and an immersion into the ethnic group of reference. This stage eventually gives way to an autonomous/independence stage that eventually matures into a humanitarian/universal self. Research issues include problems with assessment, that is, reliability and validity studies of newly developed tests. Other important questions being studied are questions of operationalizing cultural competencies and evaluation of culture-sensitive therapies. Training issues concern development of training models and evaluation of effectiveness of training programs. There are two problems that persist in making these efforts difficult. One is the fact that there is more within-group than between-group variance, and another is that the process of acculturation is a fluid and changing, not static phenomenon.

II. MULTICULTURAL APPROACHES TO PSYCHOTHERAPY

A. Ethnographies

Ethnography has flourished in anthropology as a research method. Anthropological data are collected in the field when the anthropologist spends long periods living within the cultural community being studied. By using native informants to describe, translate, and clarify cultural beliefs, rituals, practices, values and norms, the anthropologist strives to understand unique and universal cultural realities. Two kinds of ethnographic data are used. Emic data are gathered directly from informants and are particular to the culture being studied. Etic data are the translation of emic data to universal cultural principles.

Various authors have presented ethnographic-based studies as one approach to culturally-sensitive psychotherapy. By adapting ethnographic descriptions of different ethnic groups, psychologists have utilized what might be called applied ethnography. The groups most represented in the literature are groups with the greatest increases in numbers in the U.S. population. Many applied ethnographic studies encompass African Americans, Asian Americans, Hispanic Americans and Native Americans. Other groups include immigrants from Eastern Europe and the Middle East.

When applied ethnographies are used for formulating treatment approaches three caveats are repeatedly emphasized:

1. Within-group variables are often larger than between-group variables.

2. The therapist must determine the extent to which cultural norms apply to the individual client.

3. Individual clients depict different social adaptations, identity formation stages, and acculturation issues.

1. Applied Ethnographies

a. African Americans. When working with African American clients the therapist must be knowledgeable about the impact of history. African Americans have had to struggle through slavery, in all of its brutal aspects, and racist attitudes toward Blacks continue in the larger society. Although there has been improvement, there are still crucial links between racism and poverty that affect large numbers of Blacks. Poverty rates are higher for Blacks than for Whites. Among lower-class Blacks, 70% of households are headed by single females. Black teens face an unemployment rate of 50%, and many are subjected to violence, including homicides. Black teen suicide rates are increasing.

African Americans often live in poor neighborhoods where substandard housing, crime, and violence are prevalent. Schools located in impoverished neighborhoods can be poor environments for learning. This combination of social problems leads to high levels of stress and higher incidence of both physical and mental illnesses associated with stress. Many lower-class Blacks, especially teenagers, feel that there is not much hope for a better future.

Since slavery, European physical characteristics have been preferred among many African Americans. Caucasian features such as light skin color, straight hair, thin lips, and light eye-color have been symbolic of higher status and greater attractiveness than African Americans with more African physical features. These preferences can cause social, economic, and interpersonal conflicts among African Americans. Although there were significant changes in these attitudes during the 1960s and the Black power movement, residual physical characteristics issues can cause additional stress and self-esteem problems.

Basic values present in Black culture include sharing responsibilities, respect for parents, pride in heritage, spirituality, and strong family ties. Many single women raise children with the help of extended family, boyfriends, and family friends. There is no empirical evidence that Black children raised in fatherless homes suffer from lower self-esteem than children raised in two-parent homes. Black churches have been a central source of community support since the days of slavery. In many Black families, whether headed by one parent or two, children often take on adult-level responsibilities at an earlier age than White children. African American men and women have traditionally shared domestic duties, with women working outside the home and men participating in child care and household tasks.

(1) Within-Group Differences. There are approximately 32,147 million African Americans in the United States. The majorities of Blacks are actually bicultural and have been able to adapt to living in a generally hostile dominant society. One third of Black Americans are middle class or higher. Most of these African Americans live in two-parent families and are pursuing lifestyles similar to European Americans. Yet, certain stressors are associated with the Black middle class. Job stress can come in the form of feeling that one has to compromise one's Black values to fit into work settings that are dominated by White values. Some middle-class Blacks must cope with racist attitudes at work, such as less chance for promotion or lower salaries than their White counterparts. There is some evidence that marital stress and alcohol abuse are often factors related to job stress. Middle-class Blacks do embrace White middle-class values to a larger extent than poor Blacks, but they are often victims of the stressors inherent in a bicultural lifestyle. Many middle-class Blacks live in predominantly White suburban neighborhoods and send their children to mostly White public and private schools. Yet, many of these African Americans seek out activities within the Black community to instill pride in heritage in their children.

(2) Treatment Approaches. Due to a history of racism many Blacks, especially Black families, are reluctant to seek outpatient mental health services. Despite such reluctance some studies show that people in Black communities do have knowledge of what is involved and expected in mental health centers and do believe that therapy can be helpful. Reluctance to seek services is usually based on the fear that White therapists will not understand the realities of African American racial oppression. Others have difficulties with transportation or child care arrangements. Many Blacks, especially those who have assumed adult responsibilities at an early age, are taught that they should take care of their own problems and are reluctant to ask for help.

Establishing trust is the most crucial aspect of forming a therapeutic alliance. There is no research support for matching Black clients with Black therapists as a therapeutic necessity. Trust is best established when the therapist behaves in a way that conveys honesty and sincerity and when differences in education and social status are not flaunted. It is important to provide straightforward answers to questions. The therapist should be easy to talk to but should avoid the pitfalls of "color blindness" and "paternalism" or feel that it is necessary to "buy into" a victim's stance. It is sometimes necessary to confront and challenge the client's thinking and beliefs if they are self-defeating or maladaptive.

In most therapy situations the Black client's attitudes and behavior in therapy are more likely to be determined by social class, personal experiences, and education status than by racial concerns. When a Black client behaves in a manner that is hostile, apprehensive or nonengaging it should not be assumed that the problem behaviors are racially motivated. To discover the basis of the problem it is necessary to distinguish between racial hostilities and fears versus the manner in which the therapy is being conducted.

Most authors agree that the White therapist must be open to initiating a conversation about racial differences within the beginning sessions. A frank, non-defensive discussion about the client's feelings and concerns, if there are any, suggests to the client that candid talk about racial matters is an acceptable part of the therapeutic process. Others suggest that it would be more prudent for the therapist to wait for the client to bring up the subject. In any case, the therapist must be prepared to discuss racial difficulties as openly as possible with Black clients.

It is also important for the therapist to pay attention to the possibility of practical problems. Black clients may need help with survival skills: finding employment, seeking further education, coping with crime and poor housing in their neighborhoods, and so on. The therapist may have to accommodate the therapy process to transportation and child care problems. It is best to be flexible and willing to negotiate scheduling, and fee arrangements that allow the client to attend sessions and pay for sessions in a way that works best with their job and family situations.

The client's family life should be explored and evaluated as part of the therapy process. It should be noted, however, that the Black family should not be evaluated in terms of healthy or desirable White family values. Healthy Black families have adapted to very different circumstances, and the healthy functioning of the Black family should be evaluated in terms of those norms. Family therapy work, including parenting training, can be constructive. It is also advisable to include the client's spiritual community.

Therapy should include exploration of the client's personal experiences with racism and the ways in which they have attempted to cope with it. Including extended family members and community and church resources can also augment therapy. There is evidence that African American clients, overall, respond best to a problem-focused, brief, cognitive-behavioral treatment approach. There is also evidence that African American clients respond favorably to a directive and educative approach to problem solving.

b. American Indians. The cultures of the American Indians were transformed dramatically with the arrival of Europeans. From 1492 until 1790 a series of disease epidemics greatly reduced their numbers. During the period from 1829 until 1890, a series of wars, White settlers claiming American Indian lands, and relocation of American Indians onto reservations were sources of further population devastation. It has been estimated that by the turn of the 20th century that the American Indian population had been reduced by over 90%.

The policy of the U.S. government has been to think of American Indians as a group to be "managed." Thus, the plight of American Indian cultural life has been governed by a series of treaties and laws, with the federal government. Until 1887 laws were designed to force American Indians onto reservations, prevent the practicing of their cultural traditions, and force a policy of assimilation into European culture. Thousands of American Indian children were routinely taken from their families and placed into boarding schools or adopted by White families. The subsequent loss of American Indian children from tribal communities is estimated at 25% to 55%. Traditional cultural practices, including religious ceremonies, were discouraged or forbidden. The policy of seizing American Indian lands continued into the 1920s, and the practice of placing American Indian children into boarding schools and other institutions continued until the 1970s.

American Indians were not granted U.S. citizenship until 1924, however, at this point racist policies gradually began to change. The 1934 Indian Reorganization Act terminated much of the federal controls over American Indian life, but many American Indians were relocated to urban centers where they were beset with expanding unemployment, welfare, and alcoholism. In 1955 the Indian Health Service was formed and established the Mental Health Services in 1969. In 1978 the Indian Child Welfare Act became the means to halt the seizing of children from American Indian families. The American Indian Religious Freedom Act of 1978 protected religious practices. With these recent legal freedoms has come a resurgence of interest in reclaiming cultural roots, with increasing numbers of American Indian peoples attending powwows and other cultural heritage events and ceremonies.

Depending on the political perspective, different terminology can be used when addressing this group of Americans. The term "Indian" began when European explorers thought they were in the Asian country of India and named the Caribbean tribes "Indians." Correcting this problem the term Native American became preferred. Native American, however, also has the problem of not distinguishing between native peoples and those Europeans whose ancestors settled in America before the 1700s. Generally, the term American Indian is used, despite its negative political connotations. In Alaska, the term Alaska Native is preferred. Really correct, is to address an American Indian person by his or her tribal or clan name, because personal identity usually acquires from the tribal affiliation, then extends to include the entire group of American Indian nations and finally extends to the larger U.S. citizenship.

In traditional American Indian society bonds within the tribal group and harmony with nature and others in the group are primary values. Giving and sharing with others is a major source of status in the group. One strives to maintain balance between the natural, human, and spiritual worlds. American Indian values predispose American Indians to have difficulty in situations that reward individualism, control over others, competition, verbal aggressiveness, and talking openly about personal problems with strangers. Prolonged eye contact can be interpreted as aggressive, but prolonged silence is tolerated. Shaking hands should be slight contact, not a firm grasp.

American Indians have the highest high school dropout rate of any ethnic group. Basic problems for many American Indian clients are problems with the loss of the family, isolation from the tribal group, poor education, depression, alcoholism, and underemployment.

(1) Within-Group Differences. Today there are approximately 2,119 million American Indians living within the United States. Estimates of the number of federally recognized "entities" range from 505 to 517; the number of state-recognized tribes is cited as between 304 to 365. There are approximately 200 to 250 tribal languages still being spoken. Yet, the definition of who is an American Indian is somewhat problematic. The U.S. Census Bureau figures are based on self-report, and the numbers of people reporting American Indian ancestry is increasing at a rapid rate. The Bureau of Indian Affairs and different tribal organizations have different systems based on percentages of blood ancestors; therefore, it is difficult to get a firm fix on the actual group numbers.

Vast differences exist within American Indian groups, including regional differences. It is important to remember that American Indian tribes populated the entire American continent. Tribal customs and languages varied considerably between in the eastern, southern, western plains, and northwestern regions of the country. Cultural worldviews vary from ethnocentrically isolated families who live mainly on reservations, to bicultural families who reside predominantly in urban areas, to acculturated families who may never have set foot on a reservation and have few connections to other American Indians in their daily lives.

Problems can occur with bicultural lifestyles. Many American Indians seeking work and education leave the reservations to live in urban areas. They may feel isolated from their families and cultures. Additional problems exist between generations as younger American Indians acculturate to European lifestyles and values. Younger generations may feel that they have little in common with older, more traditionally oriented parents and grandparents, thus causing further deterioration in family bonds.

(2) Treatment Approaches. It is a well-known fact that American Indians underutilize mental health services. This is true for three reasons. Many American Indians do not know about the existing services, there are few existing services and many distrust the reception and responses they will receive when they seek services. Several studies show that, on the whole, American Indians came to one therapy appointment and did not return for a second. Many American Indians fear that they will encounter a power difference that will amount to more forced assimilationism of European values. Many American Indians prefer to seek the services of traditional American Indian healers because, aside from the fact that they are probably effective, they are seen as the "keepers" of their cultural heritage.

When treating an American Indian client it is important for the therapist to understand the crucial necessity to spend sufficient time getting to know the client. It is important to establish a bond based on the degree of acculturation of the client. The therapist should take the lead to establish the structure and then proceed toward gathering personal history information. Questions about family relationships, education, employment, and where the client usually resides help to gauge the extent of acculturation. On the other hand, it is important to avoid prying too deeply at first, and avoid lengthy personal questions as well as lengthy questionnaires and agency forms. The therapist can encourage trust building by being willing to disclose information about themselves, as long as it is not too personal in nature. In American Indian culture words are considered important and lulls in conversation are not only acceptable, but also preferable to banter. The therapist should not expect the client to engage in emotional demonstrativeness, introspection, or self-examination. The therapist should take a directive but slow approach, allowing the client to pace the interview.

It is best to build a positive social support relationship. This can include family and friends who are available for participating in the therapy process. It is also advisable to inquire about use of traditional healers and to include those resources where appropriate.

The therapist should be willing to arrange flexible appointment times and be available for crisis interventions. American Indian clients might present a concrete problem at first to gauge the degree of social support and interpersonal bonding. When working with American Indians the therapist should be willing to bond with clients and their families. Connecting to clients outside the therapy structure is more important with this group than with any other.

Therapy approaches that appear to get the best results consist of social learning, behavioral, and family systems orientations. Teaching social skills, assertiveness skills, alcohol and drug education, suicide prevention, and parenting skills are effective and desirable treatment methods for American Indian clients. A homogeneous (only American Indians, separated by gender) group therapy can be especially helpful. The group should include pleasant and traditional activities. In a group approach elder American Indians can provide wisdom and guidance.

c. Asian Americans. Asian Americans are the fastest growing minority group and have the largest within-group variance. The Chinese began arriving in the 1840s to work on the railroads and gold mines. The Japanese began coming to the United States in the 1890s to work in the agrarian economies. Both groups soon encountered racist attitudes and were the victims of violent assaults, especially when work was scarce for White workers. The Federal Chinese Exclusion Act of 1882 banned immigration of Chinese. The Act was not repealed until WWII. In 1941, shortly after Pearl Harbor was bombed, Executive Order 9066 made Japanese Americans political prisoners. Japanese citizens were ordered into internment camps with no evidence of espionage or subversive activities. The Immigration Act of 1965 lifted restrictions on Asian immigration, and in 1988 The Civil Liberties Act offered reparations and apologies to Japanese Americans.

South East Asians have been arriving in large numbers since the mid-1970s. Many of the earlier 1970s immigrants were middle-class, educated Vietnamese, many of whom had worked for the U.S. government. Later South East Asian immigrants were poorer, and many were refugees escaping oppression after the fall of Saigon and the rise of the Cambodian Pol Pot regime. Many of these refugees have been victimized by pirates and subjected to brutal rapes, murders, and robberies. Many refugees have spent months and sometimes years, in refugee camps before arriving in the United States.

Ancient values based on Confucian and Buddhist thought are predominate moral and social codes in the cultures from Asia. Strong emphasis is placed on filial piety (respect, obedience, and loyalty for parents and other authority figures), emotional reserve, harmony with others, hard work, self-sacrifice, and endurance. Fathers are the respected heads of the family and mothers provide domestic nurturance. Fathers are to be obeyed by the children, including adult children, and mothers have a more supportive role. Interpersonal harmony is maintained by speaking indirectly around the point, rather than direct confrontation. Because expression of intense feelings in considered inappropriate, it has been theorized that Asian Americans tend to present with somatic symptoms, rather than emotional concerns.

Proper individual behavior and personal shortcomings are regulated by shame and guilt. Conformity to the group is valued and is also a way of avoiding being shamed or "losing face." Personal problems are kept in the family, because to reveal them to the community places people at risk for feeling shamed. There is strong parental pressure exerted on children to be successful. A poor work or achievement performance can result in intense feelings of shame and guilt.

(1) Within-Group Differences. There are approximately 10,418 million Asian Americans. The subgroups are numerous with large variations in history, culture, and languages. The largest subgroups are Chinese, Filipinos, Japanese, Koreans, Vietnamese, and Cambodians. There are also substantial numbers of Hmomg and Laotian citizens. Percentage wise more Asian Americans have college degrees than any other minority group. The median income is the highest of any group, including Whites. Yet, one half of Asian Americans are poor and undereducated. Urban ghettos, such as "Chinatowns" are often filled with poverty.

Some Japanese adults whose parents or grandparents were interned are often coping with the shame that the family experienced. Family members often refuse to talk about their internment experiences because of the shame and because talking about intense feelings is not culturally appropriate. Such suppression of feelings can lead to symptoms of anxiety and depression.

Many immigrants and refugees face problems with language barriers and with learning to fit in socially.

Pressure to acculturate is always in conflict with loyalty to family and cultural values. Recent immigrant children can face difficulties at school. They are sometimes subjected to racist attacks and ostracization. Children typically acculturate faster than adults, thus, Asian American children are often bicultural and speak native languages at home and speak English in school. This leads to intergenerational stress problems, which are difficult to deal with, especially when the children speak English and the parents do not. As children become acculturated they are often in conflict with values of strict obedience to authoritative parents. Problems with anxiety, loneliness, depression, and a sense of "not belonging" are common mental health concerns.

Many recent immigrants and refugees practice traditional healing methods of Chinese medicine, herbalists, and cope with evil spirits with coin rubbing. It has happened that Vietnamese parents were accused of child abuse when their son appeared at school with bruises on his torso. The school officials did not realize that well-meaning parents had rubbed his body with coins to heal his troubled spirit.

(2) Treatment Approaches. There is some evidence that Asian Americans underutilize mental health services. The problem appears to be fear of stigma and conflicting cultural values. When working with an Asian American client the degree of acculturation is a crucial consideration. If the families are recent immigrants or refugees, care should be taken to not offened and to behave in ways that are considered respectful and proper. Respect for authority is important in Asian culture, so the therapist should take an active, directive, teaching role. The therapists must show themselves to be credible and trustworthy. Many South East Asian clients expect concrete problem solving and advice giving. The therapist should be aware, however, that though they may offer advice it may not be followed. The therapist should not expect clients to talk about personal problems and personal feelings in an open fashion, especially in the beginning stages of therapy. Asian American clients often experience feelings of shame for having personal difficulties that require professional help and for bringing problems to a non-family member.

Language difficulties must be considered as well. Much literature has focused on the need for interpreters, but the results are mixed. Use of interpreters is generally discouraged unless they have been extensively trained in the proper role of an interpreter in a therapy context. It is not wise to use children or relatives as interpreters. A bilingual therapist is best, if one is available.

Major immigrant therapy issues include feeling socially isolated, struggling with gender and intergenerational adjustments in a new culture, and learning to adapt to new ways. Recent immigrants are often lonely and have lost loved ones or have lost social status by having to flee oppression. Japanese Americans may need encouragement to talk about the family internment history. South East Asian immigrants may need to talk about the traumas of refugee camps and victimizations by pirates.

Family therapy is advisable to deal with intergenerational problems if acculturated adolescents and traditional parents are not getting along. It is wise to show deference to the father, at least in the first session. It is never wise to insist that Asian adolescents, or adults, defy their parents openly. Acculturation takes time, and families can be helped to adjust if they are given hope for the future and a realistic sense of the amount of time it takes to adjust. Where possible, normalize problems to reduce feelings of shame.

d. Hispanic Americans. Hispanic Americans are growing rapidly in numbers. Due to high birth rates and a flow of immigrants, these Americans are the second largest minority group. The term Hispanic applies to all persons of Spanish-speaking descent. Other terms are in current usage including Latinos. Mexican American and Chicanos, are also common terms. Hispanic applies to a diverse group of peoples originally from Mexico, Puerto Rico, Cuba, and a number of Latin American countries, including Guatemala, El Salvador, the Dominican Republic, Honduras, and Nicaragua. The largest subgroups are Mexicans, many of whom have resided in parts of the southwest before the area became part of the United States in 1848, Puerto Ricans, who have been U.S. citizens since 1917, and Cubans many of whom have fled the Castro regime since the 1950s.

The history of Hispanics is filled with colonization and religious conversions. Many Mexican Americans have been victimized by racist policies, especially in the southwest. Many Hispanics are poor, with a median income below the national average. Migrant worker children drop out of high school at a rate of 50%, the second highest dropout rate.

Hispanics place great importance on the extended family and most live in two-parent families. Males are expected to value machismo, which has come to have many negative connotations, but has many positive ones as well, such being chivalrous, courageous, respectful, and protective. Men are heads of the household and are expected to be responsible providers. Women are taught to value marianismo, which means high moral virtue. Indeed, women are expected to set the moral standards for men. Boys are expected to be independent, but girls are often restricted by the close supervision of their families. Children assume adult responsibilities at an early age, for working and helping to raise younger children. The influence of the Catholic church is strong. It has been theorized that part of the church influence is that many Hispanics believe in the inevitability of fate and may display resignation during hard times or when faced with personal problems.

(1) Within-Group Differences. There are approximately 34,334 million Hispanic Americans in the United States today. Hispanic Americans live in diverse places. Most Mexican Americans live in the southwest, Puerto Rican Americans reside mainly in urban areas of the east and Cubans tend to reside in the south, especially Florida. Cuban Americans have the highest incomes, and Puerto Rican Americans the lowest. Rates of acculturation vary greatly. Some Hispanics are monolingual for English, some are monolingual for Spanish, and many are bilingual. Recent immigrants may have little knowledge of English. Intergenerational problems, including conflicts about gender roles, are family problems associated with acculturation. These problems appear less often if the family is middle class or not Catholic. Less acculturated Hispanic families also experience adjustment and educational problems with children in schools, especially where English is the dominant language.

After centuries of intermarriage with American Indians, Blacks, Europeans, and Asians, Hispanics show a wide variety or skin colors. Each skin shade has its own term and relative status. Since the Spanish colonizations, lighter-skinned children are preferred in some groups. Such preferences, however, are not a given.

(2) Treatment Approaches. Hispanics historically underutilize mental health services. The reasons appear to have to do with language barriers, seeking help inside the extended family and concerns about conflicting values. Many Hispanics first seek folk healers—the *curandera.* Many may use folk healers and professional healers simultaneously. Common mental health concerns include acculturation adjustments, alcoholism, drug use, and intergeneration family conflicts. Poverty is also a concern that should be considered.

The therapist should assess the degree of acculturation as a first step in the therapy process. The therapist should learn how to properly pronounce Spanish names and address people using their last names, at least in the first sessions. A therapist should also offer non-intimate self-disclosure to establish trust and to forming a working alliance. If the client offers a gift it is rude to not accept it.

Many Hispanic clients expect the therapist to offer suggestions that are practical and problem-solving oriented. Hispanics may think that therapy will be brief or perhaps only one session, so it is good to offer suggestions by the end of the first session. Problems with racism and identity formation should be explored and discussed. It is also advisable to address practical problems with jobs, food, clothing, and housing. The therapist should make flexible arrangements for session times, and be flexible if the client is late, misses appointments, or needs transportation.

Because of the importance of family ties, a family systems approach can be effective with Hispanic clients. Because of the emphasis on family cohesion and hierarchies, Structural family therapy is preferable to other approaches. It is important that the therapist show the family proper respect. Address the father first in the initial sessions.

Language problems must be dealt with. The literature is mixed concerning the use of interpreters. Some Hispanic clients resent the intrusion of a third party, whereas others feel that providing an interpreter is sign of caring about and respect for the cultural differences. A bilingual, bicultural therapist is preferable, if one is available.

Behavioral approaches tend to work best. Behavioral orientations have the cultural fit advantage of being goal oriented, action, rather than feeling oriented and here-now oriented, as well as brief. Social skills training and systematic desensitization are effective treatments for clients suffering from the stress and anxieties associated with making social adjustments. These are also methods associated with empowering clients and helping them to make changes in their adjustments to the new environment. Assertiveness training can be helpful for some clients, but with women clients the therapist should take care to not encourage role difficulties that make the client alienated from their families and cultures.

III. MULTICULTURAL ASSESSMENT

When assessing intelligence, achievement, and personality the psychologist is proceeding incompetently if certain culturally determined moderator variables are not taken into account. The major moderator variables that must be considered are acculturation, identity development, values, and attitudes toward the larger society. Misdiagnosis and misguided treatment failures are common problems when working cross-culturally. For example, two of the most widely used personality tests—the MMPI–2 and Rorschach—were standardized using a majority of European participants. Subsequently, the tests are used as etic measures, when in fact they are emic measures. That is, they are culturally specific in their underlying constructs and test designs but are being applied throughout the world in mental health settings as if they are measuring universals.

Cross-cultural application of culture-specific tests is prone to errors in predictive validity and reliability. It has also been demonstrated that ethnic minorities as a group show more pathology and have lower performance scores on all known psychometric and intelligence tests. Generally, when persons are unacculturated and have been poorly educated, especially combined with low social economic status (SES), then test scores show more pathology or lower intelligence.

The problem of test bias has yet to be solved. Instrument bias occurs when the test is designed in a way that the task is unfamiliar to the test participants. For example, some cultures do not have familiarity with pictorial tests, such as the Rorschach. It is then difficult to know whether the Rorschach scores are a result of the internal processes of the participants or their lack of knowledge about the test stimuli. Construct bias is a problem when the test does not have equivalent constructs in the other culture. It may be impossible to create a "culture-free" test, but it is also very difficult to construct a "culture-fair" test. For example, the MMPI–2, does not measure constructs like "face" or "harmony," both of which are immensely important social variables in Asian cultures. Moreover, it is not clear if concepts such as "depression," "guilt," "aggression," and "filial piety" are equivalent across cultures.

Language barriers are also a source of bias. Translations of the MMPI-2 may not provide cross-cultural accuracy, especially if the test is translated directly, (i.e., with one interpreter of the second version). The only method that appears to have language accuracy is back translation, where two interpreters are used. One interpreter translates from the first language into the second language, and then a back interpreter translates back into the first language. When the third translation matches the first, then accuracy of the second language version can be assumed.

Examiner bias is also a concern. If the examiner harbors a preference for Eurocentric, assimilationist thinking, then test administration and interpretation may be biased. Eurocentric norms can be applied to clients, and the given assumption is that any deviance for European norms is pathological. For instance, the examiner commits the error of functional bias if aggression is given a pathologic score for peoples for whom aggressive behavior is the norm in certain situations. Another example is to assume that the client is being negative, noncooperative or inept if they do not self-disclose in the assessment interview. Such behavior may be determined by the client's culture, values conflicts, the situation or the examiner's behavior, or all of these.

Multicultural research with the existing tests has been conducted for many years. Results are mixed. Research has also mainly focused on comparisons of African American tests scores and has not progressed very far with other ethnic minority groups. Research on the MMPI–2, for instance, has shown mixed results. Some authors report group differences comparing *T* scores of African Americans and White participants. Other authors, matching and controlling for social class and education background, found no significant differences between the two groups.

Accuracy in assessment outcomes can only be accomplished by first, assuming that cultural moderator variables are present, unless it is possible to rule them out. Second, the examiner has been carefully trained in recognizing the impact of culture on the testing and interview situation. Third, the tests themselves must be either altered to become culture sensitive or the norms of each group must be known or calculated. Fourth, and probably most important, the degree of acculturation of the client must be determined and the assessment process should be guided by this variable. Finally, test selection, administration, and interpretation should proceed only after all of these considerations have been met.

Few culture-specific intelligence and personality tests have been constructed, but existing tests are being researched for cultural accuracy, and new tests are under construction. Some researchers are working on developing truly etic, (i.e., universal measures, but these are not well developed yet). A number of culture-specific tests do exist to measure acculturation. Of the tests surveyed all were found to have adequate reliability and validity. Despite advantages of using these measures, they are currently used mainly for research purposes and have not become widely used for clinical work.

A number of scales exist to measure the attitudes, values, identity formation and degree of acculturation for different groups. Others measure acculturation and identity formation across groups. The number of existing scales is too numerous to offer a complete review here. Some scales that are gaining in recognition are measures specific to African Americans, and those have concentrated on developmental issues of identity and racial attitudes, rather than acculturation, because most African Americans are bicultural. The Racial Identity Attitude Scale (RIAS–B), the Black Identification Scale (BIS), and the Developmental Inventory of Black Consciousness (DIB-C) and the Black Personality Questionnaire (BPQ) are examples of measures currently available. Some measures of White identity have also been developed. The White Racial Identity Attitude Scale (WRIAS) and the White Racial Consciousness Development Scale (WRCDS) are currently in use.

Some measures are designed to measure degree of affiliation and the degree of acculturation with a specific group. Some examples include, the American Indian Self-Identification Scale, the Acculturation Rating Scale for Mexican Americans (ARSMA-II), the Measure of Acculturation for Mexican Americans, the Bicultural Involvement Questionnaire (for Cuban Americans), the Suinn-Lew Asian Self-Identity and Acculturation Scale (SL-ASIA), the Ko Mental Health Questionnaire (KMHQ), and the Chinese Personality Inventory (CPAI).

Other scales are designed for multiethnic use. These include, the Multigroup Ethnic Identity Measure (MEIM), the Bicultural Inventory (BI), the Acculturative Balance Scale (ASC), and the Scale of Effects of Ethnicity and Discrimination (SEED).

Some measures are being developed to assess the competencies of the mental health services and counselors. The Agency Cultural Competency Checklist, the Multicultural Environmental Inventory (MEI), and the Institutional Racism Scale (IRS) are available for agencies and degree programs. The Cross-Cultural Counseling Inventory–Revised (CCCI–R), the Multicultural Counseling Knowledge and Awareness Scale (MCKAS), and the Multicultural Awareness-Knowledge-and-Skills Survey (MAKSS) are measures of the cultural competency of the therapists.

It is still an important question, however, as to how to measure acculturation. Acculturation is not static, levels of acculturation change over time. Another problem is that there are such great variations within groups that the validity of any group measure can be questioned. There are also wide differences between different regions of the country, and between urban and rural residents. Persons may also be totally unacculturated (speaking little if any English and spending little, if any time in the larger society, bicultural (speaking both English and their native language or dialect and spending equal amounts of time in both cultures) or totally acculturated (speak only English and have little, if any contact with their native culture). How do these different levels, with many points in between, become accurately measured? Moreover, it is possible for an individual to have multiple identities, depending on the situation and the reference group. At present, until these problems are resolved, it is considered preferable to use available measures despite these difficulties.

IV. RESEARCH ISSUES

Research in multicultural assessment and practice has been moving along steadily, but much remains to be done. There are still at least five important problems to be addressed.

1. More information is needed on the epidemiology and prevalence of disorders in ethnic minority populations.
2. Further outcome data is needed to answer the questions as to whether or not alternative culture-sensitive therapies are actually more effective with minority clients.
3. Further research on usage patterns is needed to explain the mixed information existing in the literature.
4. More empirical studies are needed to evaluate ethnic-specific assessment instruments.
5. More work is needed on ethnic minority identity development and formation.

Not much is known on incidence and prevalence of various disorders. This is partly true because most studies have been carried out either in hospitals, where only limited diagnostic data is obtained, or in community mental health settings, with few minorities presenting for therapy. As has been pointed out, a lack of help seeking should not be equated with a lack of mental health problems. The research on usage is inconsistent. Many studies show that ethnic minorities tend to underutilize mental health services but other, more recent studies, show that some minority groups are utilizing services at a comparable rate to White clients.

Controlling for the different variables that affect mental disorders is not an easy task. In fact, it is very cumbersome. For instance, much has been written about the linkage between SES and mental illness. It is, therefore, important to have some consistency between studies as to how SES is determined. Should the criteria be the income of the head of the household, or occupation of the head of household or total extended family financial resources? Studies are being conducted using different criteria. How do these inconsistencies between studies affect the research results and conclusions? It is also difficult to get broad research participation in some minority communities, due to a historically based lack of trust between minority peoples and the larger society.

Most of the ethnic-specific instruments have been developed using college students. Analogue methods for test construction and clinical training have been shown to have drawbacks. Again, under these circumstances there can be confounds between power-level discrepancies, SES, gender, the acculturation of the participants and the constructs being measured. Test instruments need further norming within client settings and among the general populations of ethnic minorities. Questions of equivalence must be addressed. Are the tests measuring the same constructs? The cross-cultural equivalence problems with existing instruments are well known, but construction of truly etic measures will be a daunting task. Large sample sizes are needed, and these are hard to acquire. It will also be necessary to compare across more than two cultures, as well as controlling for the usual variables of age, education, SES, and so on. A particularly difficult problem concerns different meanings attributed to words in different cultures. More rigorous control for use of language, especially in personality tests, is required.

If alternative methods are more effective, the question then is which particular methods and with which ethnic groups? If alternative methods are not more effective then why not? Treatment satisfaction results are mixed. Most studies reviewed here report that minority clients prefer a directive approach. However, some studies dispute this, showing a preference for non-directive approaches. More research is needed on insight-oriented therapies, especially those that are conducted with culture-sensitive modifications. Given the present state of the research it cannot be assumed that insight therapies are not effective with ethnic minority clients. Nor, for that matter, can it be assumed that only directive/behavioral therapies are preferred. More is needed on effectiveness of ethnic and gender matching. Again, studies are mixed in the results obtained. Some studies show that minority women and men differ in their preferences on this dimension.

Bicultural identity development research work is barely beginning. As the demographics of the U.S. population change, more people are self-reporting biethnic or mixed ethnic identities. Minority and White identity development models need further clarification and research on the connection between identity formation and the therapy process. Definitions of ethnic identity must be widened to include persons who claim multiethnic or multicultural backgrounds.

Possible explanations for research results discrepancies include the following:

1. The variables being tested are not specific enough. In particular, the linkages between SES, gender, and treatment satisfaction have not been consistently controlled.
2. The acculturation levels of clients is another crucial variable that has not been adequately controlled for.
3. Many studies have been based on an entire ethnic subgroup, (i.e., Asian American or African American, or Hispanics, or even non-White vs. White clients, etc.). Studies such as these are not conducted with sufficient regard for the enormous within group differences.
4. Cultures are not separate or static. Whenever different ethnic groups encounter each other a series of mutual cultural exchanges and influences begin that forever alter the participants. This cultural exchange variable, while always present, is difficult to isolate.

V. TRAINING ISSUES

Many psychologists feel reluctant and ambivalent about treating poor and minority clients. The essential questions for training programs are "What happens when a therapist encounters a client who is different?" "Is the therapist able and willing to engage in conversations that are meaningful to the client?" This would include participating in appropriate discussions about group inequalities and the painful experiences of people who have been subjected to oppressive social conditions. Given our nation's history, the very subject of racial and social class relations is loaded with conflictual, painful, and anxiety-provoking content. These subjects have been treated as taboo topics, with little substantive conversation in the media or in school settings. Most psychologists are from White and/or middle-class backgrounds. They have had little, if any, experience living or working among poor or ethnic minority peoples. Their own degree of unfamiliarity can be felt as a barrier to forming meaningful therapy relationships. Furthermore, the topic of multicultural practice is loaded with complex concepts, complex skills and a long list of behaviors that a psychologist is expected to master. The prospect of becoming multiculturally competent can feel overwhelming.

Given the difficulties inherent in the subject matter, combined with the rapidly changing demographics in the country, it follows that graduate degree programs must step up their training efforts in multicultural practice. Up-to-date information on the curricula of degree program offerings in multicultural training is sketchy. What is apparent is that some programs offer specific courses, practica, and workshops, and so on, while other programs offer little, if anything, specifically designed to train graduates in this area. Some programs focus on specific cultural groups, that is, training in working with African Americans or working with American Indian clients, and so on. Others take a broad-based approach. In some programs multicultural training is a degree requirement, in others training is an elective.

The literature reviewed here is consistent on the viewpoint that effective training models should strive to integrate four major goals:

1. Increasing awareness of the student's own and other people's cultural norms.
2. Increasing specific cultural and clinical knowledge about different cultural groups.
3. Developing skills about how to interact effectively with peoples who are culturally different.
4. Consciousness raising about how cultural differences affect the therapy process and learning to become confortable with those differences.

Training should also be comprehensive enough to cover cognitive, behavioral, and affective learning.

Course work in a didactic format with lectures, discussions and term papers, and so on, is mainly viewed as a beginning platform to which other components are added. Specific knowledge about cultural groups, their histories, cultural norms, and so on, can be conveyed in this format. There are so many different groups, however, that programs should offer several subcourses that offer in-depth knowledge about different groups and the clinical issues associated with each. It is unlikely that a single comprehensive course can be designed to do justice to this entire topic.

Other goals intended to increase awareness and skills can only be achieved through combining multiple learning techniques. Increasing self-knowledge, including learning about one's own cultural norms and assumptions, is a crucial component. How to train students in this aspect is still being developed. The Pedersen Triad model is an example. In this model students role play working with a culturally different client while an "anticounselor" voices the negative thoughts of the client and the "procounselor" voices the positive thoughts of the client. This training technique is intended to bring to light the differences between the client and the counselor and to enhance the counselor's awareness of the impact of differences on the therapy process. Another model for increasing awareness is the Hines & Pedersen Cultural Grid, which offers comparisons of same versus different expectations, values, and behaviors. Another method is the use of "synthetic" cultures. Using IBM staff personnel from around the world, Hofstede identified four cultural dimensions: small versus large power distances, weak versus strong uncertainty avoidance, masculinity versus femininity, and collectivism versus individualism. From these dimensions synthetic cultures named Alpha (high power distance), Beta (strong uncertainty avoidance), Gama (high individualism), and Delta (high masculinity) were developed. The Leong and Kim Intercultural Sensitizer method presents students with a case story in which some culturally based misunderstanding occurs. After reading these short stories students choose from four possible explanations for the misunderstandings. Each possible choice is accompanied by a rationale for why each choice is correct or incorrect.

Using vignettes based on the Cultural Grid, synthetic cultures or Intercultural Sensitizer counselors can examine their assumptions, attitudes, and predispositions and how their cognitions affect the client case. Other methods for developing skills and awareness include role plays and real-life client–counselor sessions using videotapes and case studies. Students watch videotapes of cross-cultural interactions and then analyze the underlying cultural assumptions and their impact on the interactions.

To consolidate the learning process, it is important that training go beyond the classroom. A cultural immersion experience is suggested to complement academic and skills-building components. A number of immersion experiences are possible. In some cases the immersion experience is a placement in a community mental health center that serves ethnic minority clients. In other settings, especially where there are no suitable community placements, the immersion experience can be volunteer service work. Another approach is to use field trips to relevant ethnic communities, social programs, and agencies. Some schools have adopted a "buddies" system technique, in which students are paired with a foreign student and engage in social activities. After contact with peoples in the immersion experience it is advisable to provide debriefing sessions in which trainees can analyze their experiences.

It is important that graduate programs realize that multicultural training can be stressful. Training programs should be carefully planned to provide a format in which certain inevitable affective responses and reactions can be discussed and resolved. Students often feel anxious when asked to engage in open, honest discussions with or about people who are different. Many are anxious when in contact with people who are different. Students are often anxious about revealing any "hidden" or unintentional racism, sexism or homophobia, and so on. Students may experience feelings of guilt or shame. The training format should help students cope with these emotions. Students should learn to become comfortable with differences and the unavoidable interpersonal and intergroup conflicts that will arise. Trainees need a format that allows for the emergence of intergroup conflicts and that also allows for the resolution of conflicts. Trainees need to be trained in the appropriate, that is, therapeutic methods for establishing rapport with clients who may be identified with being social victims. Training needs to be conducted over a sufficient period of time, utilizing a stage model with increasing degrees of difficulty of course material, personal awareness, and interpersonal skills development as the training progresses.

As of yet, there is little information on the frequency of use of these models in training programs. There are few studies on the evaluation of training models. Little is known about the effectiveness of different models. For instance, there is little information on pre- and posttests to demonstrate effectiveness of graduate student training. More work is needed to examine the effectiveness of existing training models and to develop additional models. Degree-granting programs in psychology will eventually be pressured by the rapidly changing population demographics to provide sufficient training in working with ethnic minority and bicultural clients. For the first time the U.S. Census Bureau included a multiracial category in the 2000 census. 6,826,228 million (or 2.4 percent) respondents checked two or more races. The future arrives sooner than we think.

See Also the Following Articles

Addictions in Special Populations: Treatment ■ Cultural Issues ■ Economic and Policy Issues ■ Education: Curriculum for Psychotherapy ■ Modeling ■ Multicultural Therapy ■ Objective Assessment ■ Transcultural Psychotherapy

Further Reading

Arkin, N. (1999). Culturally sensitive student supervision: Difficulties and challenges. *The Clinical Supervisor, 18*(2),1–16.

Cartmill, M. (1999). The status of the race concept in physical anthropology. *American Anthropologist, 100,* 651–660.

Cuéllar, I., & Paniagua, F. A. (Eds.). (2000). *Handbook of multicultural mental health.* San Diego, CA: Academic.

Dana, Richard H. (2000). *Handbook of cross-cultural and multicultural personality assessment.* Mahwah, NJ:Lawrence Erlbaum Associates.

Gopaul-McNicol, S., & Brice-Baker, J. (1998). *Cross-cultural practice.* New York: John Wiley and Sons.

Jones, J. M. (1998). Ethnic minority psychology in the 20th century: Reflections and meditations on what has been and what is next. *Cultural Diversity and Mental Health, 4,* 203–211.

Klonoff, E. A., Landrine, H., & Ullman, J. B. (1999). Racial discrimination and psychiatric symptoms among blacks. *Cultural Diversity and Ethnic Minority Psychology, 5,* 329–339.

McKitrick, D. S., & Jenkins, S. Y. (2000). Considerations for ethnically diverse clients. In M. Hersen & M. Biaggio (Eds.), *Effective brief therapies: A clinician's guide* (pp. 411–431). San Diego, CA: Academic.

Morrison, L. L., & Downey, D. H. (2000). Racial differences in self-disclosure of suicidal ideation and reasons for living: Implications for training. *Cultural Diversity and Ethnic Minority Psychology, 6,* 374–386.

Pedersen, P. (Ed.). (1999). *Multiculturalism as a fourth force.* New York: Brunner/Mazel.

Pope-Davis, D. B., Lui, W. M., Nevitt, J., & Toporek, R. L. (2000). The development and initial validation of the multicultural environmental inventory: A preliminary investigation. *Cultural Diversity and Ethnic Minority Psychology, 6,* 57–64.

Ramirez, Manuel. (1999). *Multicultural psychotherapy: An approach to individual and cultural differences* (2nd ed.). Needham Heights, MA: Allyn and Bacon.

Strickland, B. R. (2000). Misassumptions, misadventures, and the misuse pf psychology. *American Psychologist, 55,* 331–338.

Sue, D., & Sue, D. (1999). *Counseling the culturally different: Theory and practice* (3rd ed.). New York: John Wiley and Sons.

Sue, S. (1999). Science, ethnicity, and bias: Where have we gone wrong? *American Psychologist, 54,* 1070–1077.

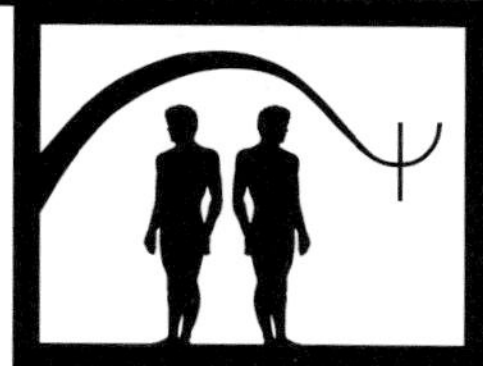

Rational Emotive Behavior Therapy

Albert Ellis

Albert Ellis Institute

GLOSSARY

desensitization The gradual overcoming of a symptom or behavior by the presence of a counter behavior or idea in the presence of the provoking stimulus, usually in a graduated degree of intensity.

exposure Behavioral technique that involves confrontation with the symptom provoking stimulus.

multimodal Refers to different modes of therapy that involve social, cognitive, emotional, behavioral, and biological dimensions of the individual's life. Also refers to different ways of doing therapy based on these different issues, such as family therapy, medications, psychotherapy, etc.

mustabatory An Ellis term referring to the set of ideas formed by the individual's sense of social necessity or the requirements of other important people. Frequently, these ideas have a rigid and premptory quality.

Rational emotive behavior therapy (REBT) was originated in January 1955 as a pioneering cognitive–experiential–behavioral system of psychotherapy. It is heavily cognitive and philosophical, and specifically uncovers clients' irrational or dysfunctional beliefs and actively and directively disputes them. But it also sees people's self-defeating cognitions, emotions, and behaviors as intrinsically and holistically connected, not disparate. It holds that they disturb themselves with disordered thoughts, feelings, and actions, all of which importantly interact with each other and with the difficulties they encounter in their environment. Therefore, with emotionally and behaviorally disturbed people, REBT employs a number of thinking, feel, and action techniques that are designed to help them change their self-defeating and socially sabotaging conduct to self-helping and socially effective ways.

REBT theorizes that virtually all humans consciously and unconsciously train themselves to be to some degree emotionally disturbed. Therefore, with the help of an effective therapist and/or with self-help materials, they can teach themselves to lead more satisfying lives—if they choose to do so and work hard at modifying their thinking, feeling, and behaving.

Albert Ellis, the originator of REBT, was trained in Rogerian person-centered therapy in graduate school in clinical psychology (1942–1947), found it too passive and abandoned it for psychoanalytic training and practice (1947–1953). But psychoanalysis, too, he found ineffective because it was too much insight-oriented and too little action-oriented. His clients often saw how they originally became disturbed—supposedly because of their family history. But when he stayed with typical psychoanalytic methods, he failed to specifically show them how to think and act differently and to thus make themselves more functional.

So Ellis went back to philosophy, which had been his hobby since the age of 16, and re-read the ancient philosophers (especially Epicurus, Epictetus, Marcus Aurelius, and Gautama Buddha) and some of the moderns (especially John Dewey, Bertrand Russell, and Paul Tillich) and found that they were largely constructivists rather than excavationists. They held that people do not merely get upset by adverse life conditions, but instead often choose to disturb themselves about these adversities. A number of philosophers also said that people could choose to unupset themselves about minor and major difficulties; if they made themselves anxious and depressed, they could reduce their dysfunctional feelings and behaviors by acquiring a core philosophy that was realistic, logical, and practical.

Following these philosophers, Ellis started to teach his clients that they had a choice of experiencing healthy negative emotions about the misfortunes they encountered—such as feelings of sorrow, disappointment, and frustration; or they could choose to experience unhealthy negative reactions—such as panic, depression, rage, and self-pity. By using rational philosophy with troubled clients, he saw that when they faced adversities with self-helping attitudes they made themselves feel better and functioned more productively. But when they faced similar adversities with irrational (self-defeating) philosophies they made themselves miserable and acted ineffectively. When he convinced them that they almost always had the choice of helping or hindering themselves, even when their desires and goals were seriously blocked, they often were able to make that choice.

I. THE ABCs OF RATIONAL EMOTIVE BEHAVIOR THERAPY

During the 1950s, Ellis put this constructivist theory into the now well-known ABCs of REBT. This theory states that almost all people try to remain alive and achieve basic Goals (G) of being reasonably content by themselves, with other people, productively working, and enjoying recreational pursuits. When their Goals are thwarted and they encounter Adversities (A) they are then able to construct Consequences (C)—mainly feelings and actions—that either help or hinder them satisfy these Goals. They largely (although not completely) do this by choosing to follow rational, useful Beliefs (B) or to follow irrational, dysfunctional Beliefs. Therefore, although the Adversities (A) they experience are important contributors to their emotional and behavioral Consequences (C), they do not directly or solely cause these Consequences. When at C, people feel and act dysfunctionally or self-defeatingly, their irrational Beliefs (B) and their experienced Adversities (A) bring on their disturbed reactions. So A does not by itself lead to C. A interacts with B to produce C; or $A \times B = C$. However, people tend to be aware that C follows A, but not that B is also included in the process. They therefore think that adverse A's automatically lead to disturbed C's—that their internal reactions are controlled by external events.

Ellis noted in his first paper on REBT at the Annual Convention of the American Psychological Association in Chicago in August 1956, that when people feel and act disturbedly (C), they have 12 common irrational or dysfunctional Beliefs (B) about the undesirable things that happen to them (A). When they change these to rational or functional Beliefs (in therapy or on their own) they become significantly less disturbed. Both these hypotheses have been supported by many empirically based studies, first by followers of REBT and then by other cognitive behavior therapists who largely follow and have tested the ABC theory of REBT. Hundreds of published studies have given much support to this theory.

After using REBT for a few years in the 1950s, Ellis came up with clinical evidence for Karen Horney's hypothesis about the "tyranny of the shoulds." He realized that the many irrational Beliefs with which people often disturb themselves can practically always be put under three major headings, all of which include absolutistic shoulds, oughts, and musts. With these three core dysfunctional ideas, people take their strong preferences for success, approval, power, freedom, and pleasure, and elevate them to dogmatic, absolutistic demands or commands.

The imperatives that frequently accompany dysfunctional feelings and behaviors seem to be (1) "I absolutely must perform well at important tasks and be approved by significant others—or else I am an inadequate person!" (2) "Other people absolutely must treat me kindly, considerately, and fairly—or else they are bad individuals!" (3) "Conditions under which I live absolutely must provide me with what I really want—or else my life is horrible, I can't stand it, and the world's a rotten place!"

These three common irrationalities lead to innumerable derivative irrational Beliefs and frequently are accompanied by disturbed emotional and behavioral Consequences. In fact, REBT hypothesizes that people would find it difficult to make themselves disturbed without taking one or more of their major preferences and transforming them into absolutistic demands. Individuals with severe personality disorders and psychosis also disturb themselves by turning their healthy preferences into unhealthy musturbating, but they often have other biochemical and neurological characteristics that help make them disturbed.

REBT also theorizes that the tendency to elevate healthy preferences to insistent demands, and thereby to think, feel, and act unrealistically and illogically, is innate in humans. People naturally and easily take some of their strong goals and desires and often view them as necessities. This self-defeating propensity is then exacerbated by familial and cultural upbringing, and is solidified by constant practice by those who victimize themselves with it. Therefore, especially with seriously disturbed people, psychotherapy and self-help procedures can, but often only with difficulty, change their dysfunctioning.

Many therapy techniques—such as meditation, relaxation, a close and trusting relationship with a therapist, and distraction with various absorbing activities—can be used to interrupt clients' musturbatory tendencies and help them feel better. But in order for them to get and stay better, REBT holds, they usually have to consciously realize that they are destructively escalating their healthy desires into self-sabotaging demands and then proceed to D—to actively and forcefully Dispute the irrational Beliefs that are involved in their disturbances. By vigorously and persistently Disputing these Beliefs—cognitively, emotively, and behaviorally—they can change their self-destructive shoulds and musts into flexible, realistic, and logical preferences. They thereby can make themselves significantly less disturbed.

II. RATIONAL EMOTIVE BEHAVIOR THERAPY TECHNIQUES

To help people specifically achieve and maintain a thoroughgoing antimusturbatory basic outlook, REBT teaches them to use a number of cognitive, emotive, and behavioral methods. It helps them gain many insights into their disturbances, but emphasizes three present-oriented ones:

Insight No. 1: People are innate constructivists and by nature, teaching, and, especially, self-training they contribute to their own psychological dysfunctioning. They create as well as acquire their emotional disabilities—as the ABC theory of REBT notes.

Insight No. 2: People usually, with the "help" and connivance of their family members, first make themselves disturbed when they are young and relatively foolish. But then they actively, although often unconsciously, work hard after their childhood and adolescence is over to habituate themselves to dysfunctional thinking, feeling, and acting. That is mainly why they stay disturbed today. They continue to construct dysfunctional Beliefs.

Insight No. 3: Because of their natural and acquired propensities to strongly choose major goals and values and to insist, as well as to prefer, that they must achieve them, and because they hold these self-defeating beliefs and feelings for many years, people firmly retain and often resist changing them. Therefore, there usually is no way for them to change but work and practice—yes, work; yes, practice—for a period of time. Heavy work and practice for short periods of time will help; so brief rational emotive behavior therapy can be useful. But for long-range gain, and for clients to get better rather than to feel better, they require considerable effort to make cognitive, emotive, and behavioral changes.

REBT clients are usually shown how to use these three insights in the first few sessions of psychotherapy. Thus if they are quite depressed (at point C) about, say, being rejected (at point A) for a very desirable job, they are shown that this rejection by itself did not lead to their depression (C). Instead they mainly upset themselves with their musturbatory Beliefs (B) about the Adversity (A). The therapist explores the hypothesis that they probably took their desire to get accepted and elevated it into a demand—for example, "I must not be rejected! This rejection makes me an inadequate person who will continually lose out on fine jobs!"

Second, clients are shown—using REBT Insight No. 2—that their remembering past Adversities (A), such as past rejections and failures, does not really make them depressed today (C). Again, it is largely their Beliefs (B) about these Adversities that now make them prone to depression.

Third, clients are shown that if they work hard and persistently at changing their dysfunctional Beliefs (B), their dire needs for success and approval, and return to mere preferences, they can now minimize their depressed feelings—and, better yet, keep warding them off and rarely falling back to them in the future. REBT enables them to make themselves less disturbed and less disturbable.

III. MULTIMODAL ASPECTS OF RATIONAL EMOTIVE BEHAVIOR THERAPY

To help clients change their basic self-defeating philosophies, feelings, and behaviors, REBT practitioners actively and directively teach and encourage them to use a good many cognitive, experiential, and behavioral techniques, which interact with and reinforce each other. It is one of the pioneering integrative therapies. Cognitive methods are particularly emphasized, and often include (1) Active disputing of clients' irrational beliefs by both the therapists and the client; (2) rational coping self-statements or effective philosophies of living; (3) modeling after people who coped well with Adversities similar to, or even worse than, those of the clients; (4) cost-benefit analyses to reveal how some pleasurable substances and behaviors (e.g., smoking and compulsive gambling) are self-sabotaging and that some onerous tasks (e.g., getting up early to go to work) are unpleasant in the short term but beneficial in the long run; (5) REBT cognitive homework forms to practice the uncovering and disputing of dysfunctional Beliefs; (6) psychoeducational materials, such as books and audio-visual cassettes, to promote self-helping behaviors; (7) positive visualizations to practice self-efficacious feelings and actions; (8) reframing of Adversities so that clients can realize that they are not catastrophic and see that they sometimes have advantages; (9) practice in resisting overgeneralized, black and white, either/or thinking; (10) practical and efficient problem-solving techniques.

REBT uses many emotive–experiential methods and materials to help clients vigorously, forcefully, and affectively Dispute their irrational demands and replace them with healthy preferences. Some of its main emotive–expressive techniques include the following: (1) Forceful and persistent disputing of clients' irrational Beliefs, done *in vivo* or on a tape recorder; (2) experiencing a close, trusting, and collaborative relationship with a therapist and/or therapy group; (3) steady work at achieving unconditional other-acceptance (UOA), the full acceptance of other people with their failings and misbehaviors; (4) using visualizations or live experiences to get in touch with intense unhealthy negative feelings—and to train oneself to feel, instead, healthy negative feelings; (5) role-playing difficult emotional situations and practicing how to handle them; (6) using REBT's shame-attacking exercises by doing "embarrassing" acts in public and working on not denigrating oneself when encountering disapproval; (7) engaging in experiential and encounter exercises that produce feelings of discomfort and learning how to deal with these feelings.

REBT uses many activity-oriented behavioral methods with clients, such as (1) Exposure or *in vivo* desensitization of dysfunctional phobias and compulsions; (2) taking deliberate risks of failing at important projects and refusing to upset oneself about failing; (3) staying in uncomfortable situations and with disturbed feelings until one has mastered them; (4) reinforcing oneself to encourage self-helping behaviors and penalizing oneself to discourage self-defeating behaviors; (5) stimulus control to discourage harmful addictions and compulsions; (6) relapse prevention to stop oneself from sliding back to harmful feelings and behaviors; (7) skill training to overcome inadequacies in assertion, communication, public speaking, sports, and other desired actions that one is inhibited about.

These are some of the cognitive, emotive, and behavioral techniques that are frequently employed in rational emotive behavior therapy. Many other possible methods are individually tailored and used with individual clients.

The main therapeutic procedure of REBT is to discover how clients think, feel, and act to block their own main desires and goals, and to figure out and experiment with ways of helping them get more of what they desire and less of what they abhor. As they make themselves less disturbed and dysfunctional, they are helped to actualize themselves more—that is, to provide themselves, idiosyncratically, with greater satisfactions. At the same time, clients are helped to stubbornly refuse to define their preferences as dire necessities and thereby tend to reinstitute their disturbances.

IV. REVIEW OF THE LITERATURE

When Ellis originated it in 1955, rational emotive therapy was unique. It was followed by somewhat similar forms of cognitive behavior therapy (CBT) in the 1960s and 1970s, particularly cognitive therapy of Aaron Beck, rational behavior therapy of Maxie Maultsby, Jr., cognitive behavior modification of Donald Meilchenbaum, and Multimodal Therapy of Arnold Lazarus. REBT was soon supported by about 300 published studies that showed its effectiveness with many different types of clients.

Many of these have been surveyed in comprehensive reviews by R. DiGiuseppe, N. J. Miller, and L. D. Trexler, by T. E. McGovern and M. S. Silverman, by D. Hajzler and M. E. Bernard, by L. C. Lyons and P. J. Woods, and by M. S. Silverman, M. McCarthy, and T. E. McGovern.

As a result of its many successful outcome studies, REBT has become one of the most practiced psychotherapies. It is widely used with children, adolescents, couples, families, people with sex problems, and in other forms of counseling and psychotherapy. In addition, it is often used in business and industry, in education, in sports, in assertion training, in stress management, in parenting, and in many other fields.

Finally, REBT has revolutionized the self-help industry and has been widely adapted in scores of best-selling books, workbooks, and audio-visual cassettes, such as Wayne Dyer's *Your Erroneous Zones,* Albert Ellis' *A Guide to Rational Living,* and David Burns' *Feeling Good.*

The Albert Ellis Institute in New York, and in its many American and foreign branches, trains therapists and counselors in REBT and certifies them in its practice. To date, it and its affiliates have certified well over 5000 therapists.

V. SUMMARY

Rational emotive behavior therapy (REBT) was originated in 1955 as the first of the major cognitive behavior therapies. It has been shown to have effective outcomes in hundreds of published studies and has become one of the most popular psychotherapies. It looks like it, as well as cognitive behavior therapy, will continue to thrive in the 21st century.

See Also the Following Articles

Beck Therapy Approach ■ Behavior Therapy: Historical Perspective and Overview ■ Cognitive Appraisal Therapy ■ Cognitive Behavior Therapy ■ History of Psychotherapy ■ Humanistic Psychotherapy ■ Multimodal Behavior Therapy

Further Reading

Bernard M., & Wolfe J. L. (2000). *The REBT resource book for practitioners.* New York: Albert Ellis Institute.

DiGiuseppe, R. A., Miller, N. J., & Trexler, L. D. (1979). A review of rational-emotive psychotherapy outcome studies. In A. Ellis & J. M. Whiteley (Eds.), *Theoretical and empirical foundations of rational-emotive therapy* (pp. 218–235). Monterey, CA: Brooks/Cole.

Ellis, A. (1994). *Reason and emotion in psychotherapy:* Revised and Updated. New York: Kensington Publishers.

Ellis, A. (1999). *How to make yourself happy and remarkably less disturbable.* Atascadero, CA: Impact Publishers.

Ellis, A. (2000). *How to control your anxiety before it controls you.* New York: Citadel Press.

Ellis, A., & Dryden, W. (1997) *The practice of rational emotive behavior therapy.* New York: Springer.

Ellis, A., Gordon J., Neenan, M., & Palmer, S. (1998). *Stress counseling.* New York: Springer.

Hajzler, D., & Bernard, M. E. (1991). A review of rational-emotive outcome studies. *School Psychology Qerly, 6*(1), 27–49.

Lyons, L. C., & Woods, P. J. (1991). The efficacy of rational-emotive therapy: A quantitative review of the outcome research. *Clinical Psychology Review, 11,* 357–369.

McGovern, T. E., & Silverman, M. S. (1984). A review of outcome studies of rational-emotive therapy from 1977–1982. *Journal of Rational-Emotive Therapy, 2*(1), 7–18.

Silverman, M. S., McCarthy, M., & McGovern, T. E. (1992). A review of outcome studies of rational-emotive therapy from 1982–1989. *Journal of Rational-Emotive and Cognitive Behavior Therapy, 10,* 111–186.

Walen, S., DiGiuseppe, R., & Dryden, W. (1992). *A practitioner's guide to rational-emotive therapy.* New York: Oxford.

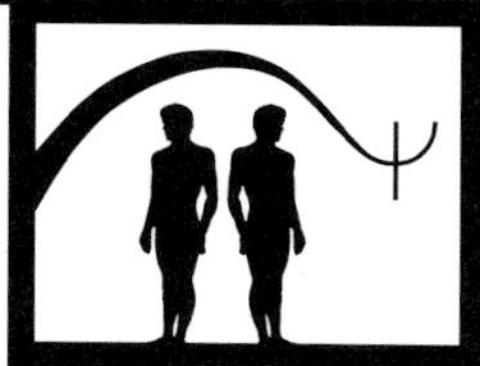

Reality Therapy

Robert E. Wubbolding
Center for Reality Therapy

GLOSSARY

choice theory The underlying principles of reality therapy that emphasize behavior as chosen for the purpose of satisfying inner genetic instructions or needs.

environment The therapeutic atmosphere or climate that serves as the basis for specific interventions.

WDEP The delivery system of reality therapy, signifying wants, direction and doing, self-evaluation, and planning.

Founded by William Glasser reality therapy has its roots in the work of Alfred Adler, who emphasized that human beings are social in nature and that behavior is goal centered. Glasser extended his early ideas to include genetic instructions or human needs as sources of human behavior. Accordingly, human beings originate their own behavior. It is not thrust on them by their families, their environment, or their early childhood conflicts. Rather, behavior is seen as chosen. In the early stages of its evolution, the formula for reality therapy was described as involving eight steps. Used widely in therapy, counseling, corrections, as well as in education, reality therapy attempted to avoid coercion and punishment and teach inner responsibility. Its current formulation as a delivery system, developed by Robert E. Wubbolding in his books *Using Reality Therapy* and *Reality Therapy for the 21st Century,* is summarized with the letters WDEP. Its use now extends to self-help, as well as management, supervision, and coaching employees.

Describing the root of human strife as flawed relationships, Glasser has provided a theoretical and conceptual blueprint for addressing human conflict. Wherever human relationships are improved, productivity increases in the workplace, families remain intact, students achieve, and organizations achieve their goals and function more humanely.

I. DESCRIPTION OF TREATMENT: ENVIRONMENT AND PROCEDURES

Figure 1 presents an outline of the delivery system for reality therapy. Establishing a safe atmosphere or environment provides the basis for the more specific interventions known as procedures. As in any therapy the therapist listens to clients' stories presented in their own words and seeks to become part of their inner discourse. In the language of choice theory the therapist becomes part of the clients' quality world (i.e., someone who is capable of providing needed help). The procedures are the specific tools for helping clients clarify and prioritize their wants, evaluate their actions and self-talk, and finally, make plans for effective change. The "Cycle of

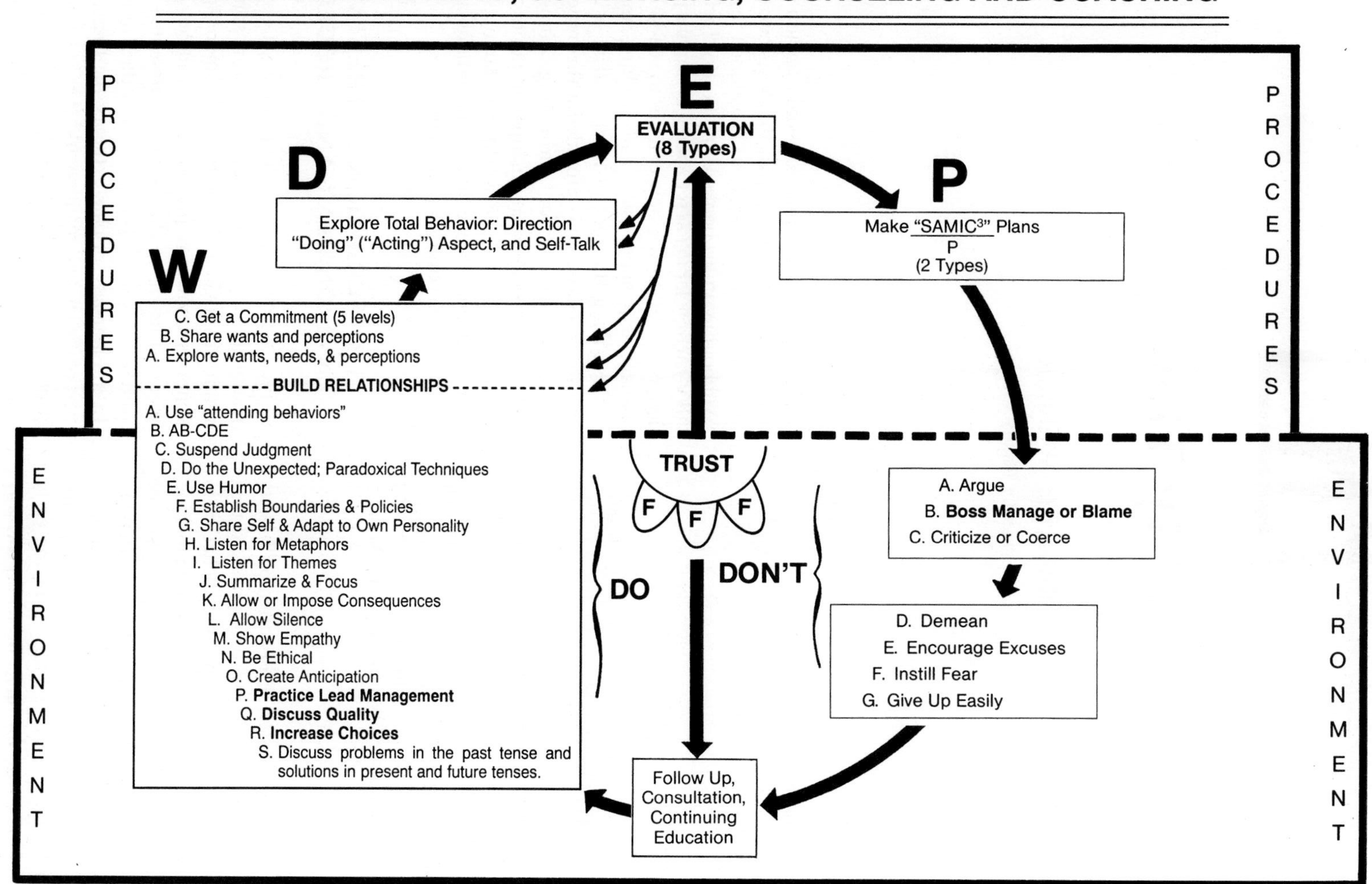

FIGURE 1 Outline of the delivery system for reality therapy. Adapted from the works of William Glasser. Copyright 1986 Robert E. Wubbolding. Reproduced with permission.

Summary Description of the Cycle of Managing, Supervising, Counseling and Coaching

Introduction:

The Cycle consists of two general concepts: Environment conducive to change and Procedures more explicitly designed to facilitate change. This chart is intended to be a brief summary. The ideas are designed to be used with employees, students, clients as well as in other human relationships.

Relationship between Environment & Procedures:

1. As indicated in the chart, the Environment is the foundation upon which the effective use of Procedures is based.
2. Though it is usually necessary to establish a safe, friendly Environment before change can occur, the "Cycle" can be entered at any point. Thus, the use of the cycle does not occur in lock step fashion.
3. Building a relationship implies establishing and maintaining a professional relationship. Methods for accomplishing this comprise some efforts on the part of the helper that are Environmental and others that are Procedural.

Environment:

DO: Build Relationship: a close relationship is built on TRUST through friendliness, firmness, and fairness.

A. Using Attending Behaviors: Eye contact, posture, effective listening skills.
B. AB = "Always Be..." Consistent, Courteous & Calm, Determined that there is hope for improvement, Enthusiastic (Think Positively).
C. Suspend Judgment: View behaviors from a low level of perception, i.e., acceptance is crucial.
D. Do the Unexpected: Use paradoxical techniques as appropriate; Reframing and Prescribing.
E. Use Humor: Help them fulfill need for fun within reasonable boundaries.
F. Establish boundaries: the relationship is professional.
G. Share Self: Self-disclosure within limits is helpful; adapt to own personal style.
H. Listen for Metaphors: Use their figures of speech and provide other ones.
I. Listen to Themes: Listen for behaviors that have helped, value judgements, etc.
J. Summarize & Focus: Tie together what they say and focus on them rather than on "Real World."
K. Allow or Impose Consequences: Within reason, they should be responsible for their own behavior.
L. Allow Silence: This allows them to think, as well as to take responsibility.
M. Show Empathy: Perceive as does the person being helped.
N. Be Ethical: Study Codes of Ethics and their applications, e.g., how to handle suicide threats or violent tendencies.
O. Create anticipation and communicate hope. People should be taught that something good will happen if they are willing to work.
P. Practice lead management, e.g., democracy in determining rules.
Q. Discuss quality.
R. Increase choices.
S. Discuss problems in the past tense, solutions in present and future tenses.

DON'T:

Argue, Boss Manage, or Blame, Criticize or Coerce, Demean, Encourage Excuses, Instill Fear, or Give up easily.

Rather, stress what they can control, accept them as they are, and keep the confidence that they can develop more effective behaviors. Also, continue to use "WDEP" system without giving up.

Follow Up, Consult, and Continue Education:

Determine a way for them to report back, talk to another professional person when necessary, and maintain ongoing program of professional growth.

Procedures:

Build Relationships:

A. Explore Wants, Needs & Perceptions: Discuss picture album or quality world, i.e., set goals, fulfilled & unfulfilled pictures, needs, viewpoints and "locus of control."
B. Share Wants & Perceptions: Tell what you want from them and how you view their situations, behaviors, wants, etc. This procedure is secondary to A above.
C. Get a Commitment: Help them solidify their desire to find more effective behaviors.

Explore Total Behavior:

Help them examine the Direction of their lives, as well as specifics of how they spend their time. Discuss ineffective & effective self talk.

Evaluation - The Cornerstone of Procedures:

Help them evaluate their behavioral direction, specific behaviors as well as wants, perceptions and commitments. Evaluate own behavior through follow-up, consultation and continued education.

Make Plans: Help them change direction of their lives.

Effective plans are Simple, Attainable, Measurable, Immediate, Consistent, Controlled by the planner, and Committed to. The helper is Persistent. Plans can be linear or paradoxical.

Note: The "Cycle" describes specific guidelines and skills. Effective implementation requires the artful integration of the guidelines and skills contained under Environment and Procedures in a spontaneous and natural manner geared to the personality of the helper. This requires training, practice and supervision. Also, the word "client" is used for anyone receiving help: student, employee, family member, etc.

FIGURE 1 (Continued).

Managing, Supervising, Counseling, and Coaching" is applicable to many relationships and is used in many settings where human relationships are paramount: teaching, therapy and counseling, consultation, management, and supervision. Moreover, reality therapy employs several strategies common to all counseling theories.

Also, although the environment is the foundation upon which the procedures are built, there is no absolute line of demarcation between them. Thus "Build Relationships" is both environmental and procedural. Nor is the "Cycle" a simplistic lock-step method to be entered unwaveringly at the same place with every patient. People using reality therapy in their human interactions, enter the "Cycle" at various points. Although a therapist generally establishes a friendly, warm relationship before employing procedures that lead to change, helping clients evaluate their own behavior and making plans often occurs early in the therapy process.

Finally, because reality therapy is used in corrections, in classrooms, and in many relationships besides therapy, specific helpful and hurtful and behaviors as well as attitudes are described under environment such as "don't criticize" and "don't encourage excuses."

A. Environment

The word "environment" implies an effort on the part of the therapist to establish an atmosphere in which the patient can feel safe, secure, and motivated. As shown in Figure 1, hindrances to establishing a trusting, helpful, safe environment include arguing, bossing, blaming, criticizing, demeaning, colluding with excuses, instilling fear, and giving up easily. In consulting with parents, educators, managers, and others, therapists often teach the ineffectiveness of such choices.

Opposite the ineffective environmental behaviors is a wide range of helpful, effective, and facilitative suggestions leading to a trusting atmosphere. These include attending behaviors, use of paradoxical techniques and metaphors, listening for themes related to procedures, skill in demonstrating accurate empathy, and helping clients find choices even amid their feelings of depression, perceptions of oppression, and lack of opportunities to fulfill their own needs.

B. Procedures: The WDEP System

The environment serves as a foundation for the effective use of procedures that lead to change. They are not a series of recipes used mechanically. Rather they are a network or a system defined by the acronym WDEP. Therefore, depending on the presenting and underlying problem, the therapist extracts from the system appropriate components for application.

W: Explore Wants, Needs, and Perceptions

Essential to the process of change, as well as facilitating the relationship, is a clear determination and definition of clients' wants or desires. They are asked to describe current pictures or to insert firmly in their "quality worlds," exactly what they want. Using the analogy of wants as pictures, it is evident that clients often have blurred wants. They are unclear about what they want, so when they are asked, "What do you want from your job, from your spouse, from your parents, from your children?" the answer is, "I don't know" or "I'm not sure." An adolescent often wants "my parents off my back" or "to be left alone" but is unable to provide a detailed and unambiguous description of this desire. Consequently, the reality therapist helps clients clarify and define wants, which is the process for the beginning of effective action on the part of clients.

Another part of the W is the exploration of clients' perception or viewpoint. The therapist asks the parent of a child, "How do you see your son or daughter?" In the case of a severely upset child, the parent might answer, "I see a lazy, rebellious, surly, uncooperative, and ungrateful child." Of course, such questioning is combined with an exploration of wants, for example, "What do you want from him or her?"

To the workaholic parent of a child, the therapist could say, "I see your 18 hour days not as a 'rendezvous with destiny' but as a collision course for you and your children." To the parent of the teenager, the counselor might say, "I see your son or daughter as a person who needs a compliment for even a minor success or change." In the practice of reality therapy, therapists take an active but nonauthoritarian role, and see themselves as a partners in the process of change.

D: Doing (Total Behavior)

Behavior is composed of four aspects: doing, thinking, feeling, and physiology. A popular misconception is that reality therapy neither deals with nor allows for a discussion of feelings and emotions. This erroneous perception is perhaps derived from the accurate statement that in reality therapy the action aspect of the behavioral system is emphasized (although not to the exclusion of the other components). Still, there are two important aspects to this procedure: exploration of overall behavioral direction and specific actions or choices.

The therapist encourages clients to be specific in the discussion of behaviors, such as exploring a specific segment of time: a day, a morning, an hour, an incident, or an event. Although it is important to examine the overall direction of total behavior, direction will change only with small measurable changes made one at a time. Thus, therapists help clients become a television camera describing specific rather than typical events.

E: Self-Evaluation

If the entire process of environment and procedures is a cycle, the procedures appear as an arch with its keystone self-evaluation. This component is a prerequisite for change in human behavior. No one chooses a more effective life direction or changes a specific behavior without making at least a minimal self-evaluation that the current course of action is not advantageous. Effective change rests on judgments related to total behavior, wants, perceptions, and other aspects of the client's life.

The term "Evaluation" has a meaning in reality therapy that is different from its meaning in other theories. In reality therapy, the procedure described here is not an assessment evaluation or "clinical diagnosis." Rather, it is a series of value judgments, decisions, and changes in thought made by the client. In the restructuring of thought, clients come to the conclusion that their life direction is not where they want to go, that a certain exact and specific current behavior is not useful or not helpful, that what they want is not attainable or helpful, that a perception is not effective, and that a future plan of action represents a more need-fulfilling behavior.

In the "Cycle" evaluation comprises an axis that closely connects procedures and environment. Reality therapists help clients evaluate their own choice systems (wants, behavior, perceptions) as well as devote considerable effort toward the evaluation of their own specific professional behaviors and generalized competencies.

P: Planning

If evaluation is the keystone of the procedures, planning is the superstructure or the goal. A plan of action is crucial to change. It can sometimes be complicated and sometimes simple. There must always be a plan. People who go through life without some sort of long-term plan, are like ships floundering without rudders. This procedure is the easiest to bring about if the therapist has prepared the way by the effective use of the more subtle procedures and environmental components already described. Nevertheless, if the plan is to be effective, it should be characterized by as many as possible of the following qualities summarized by the acronym SAMIC^3.

S = Simple: The plan is clear and not complicated.
A = Attainable: Realistically doable rather than grandiose and impossible.
M = Measurable. An effective plan is precise and exact.
I = Immediate. Implementation immediately after or even during the therapy session is desirable.
C = Controlled by the planner. A plan should not be contingent on the behavior of another person.
C = Committed to. The reality therapist elicits a firm commitment.
C = Consistent. The plan should be repeated.

The WDEP system should be seen as a unit, a system in which one component affects the others, and so, the subsystems W, D, E, and P are not isolated steps that must be followed one after another. Rather, it is more appropriate to extract from the system whatever component is most relevant at the moment. Through listening, practice, and supervision, a user of reality therapy can develop a sense of where to start and how to proceed through the "Cycle."

II. THEORETICAL BASES: CHOICE THEORY

The practice of reality therapy is based on choice theory. Previously lacking a theoretical framework for reality therapy, Glasser employed the relatively obscure principles of control system theory to explain its effectiveness, and extended the theory to provide a basis for clinical practice by presenting a detailed explanation of human needs, total behavior (actions, thinking, feelings), perceptions, and inner wants or "quality world," the phrase used to describe our specific wants and intense desires. Control system theory is based on the principle that living organisms originate their behavior from the inside. They seek to close a gap between what they have and what they perceive they need at a given moment. This discrepancy, called a "perceptual error," sets the behavioral system in motion so as to impact the external world. Human organisms act on their external worlds to satisfy needs and wants. They gain input from and generate output toward the external world. Because of the emphasis on inner control and especially because of the emphasis on behavior as a choice, the theory was renamed choice theory in 1996.

III. EMPIRICAL STUDIES

The question is often asked, "Does reality therapy work? Is it effective?" Robert Wubbolding has provided an extensive summary of research conducted on its efficacy. Investigators have found an increase in the self-esteem of clients and a greater realization of the meaning of "addict," a significant reduction in the rate of recidivism with juvenile offenders, and a complete resocialization of a large number of prison residents, all of whom received reality therapy treatment.

Much research has been conducted in schools measuring the effects of counselor and teacher training in reality therapy. Teaching students to self-evaluate their behavior and their work has resulted in a drop in teacher referrals for discipline and other problems.

A sampling of research in a variety of settings illustrates the wide use of this system. Participants in training workshops leading to certification represent psychology, social work, counseling, classroom teachers, administration, corrections, geriatrics, and other disciplines. Although there is ample research to demonstrate the viability of reality therapy as a therapeutic method, more is needed. Wubbolding recommends that close attention be given to the quality of training provided for therapists, teachers, and others who use the system so that the genuine use of reality therapy is measured. Also, more studies measuring outcome (i.e., change in behavior) are needed.

IV. SUMMARY

Reality therapy, formulated as WDEP, is a practical and jargon-free system based on choice theory. Its philosophical principles include the belief that people choose their behavior. It is not imposed from early childhood or by external stimuli. Therapists help clients define their wants, evaluate their behaviors as well as their wants, and make plans for future change.

See Also the Following Articles

Adlerian Psychotherapy ■ Control-Mastery Theory ■ Family Therapy

Further Reading

Glasser, W. (1965). *Reality therapy.* New York: HarperCollins.

Glasser, W. (1968). *Schools without failure.* New York: HarperCollins.

Glasser, W. (1998). *Choice theory.* New York: HarperCollins.

Glasser, W. (1999). *Reality therapy in action.* New York: HarperCollins.

Wubbolding, R. (1988). *Using reality therapy.* New York: HarperCollins.

Wubbolding, R. (1996). *Employee motivation.* Knoxville, TN: SPC Press.

Wubbolding, R. (2000). *Reality therapy for the 21st century.* Philadelphia, PA: Brunner/Routledge.

Wubbolding, R., & Brickell, J. (1999). *Counselling with reality therapy.* London: Winslow Press.

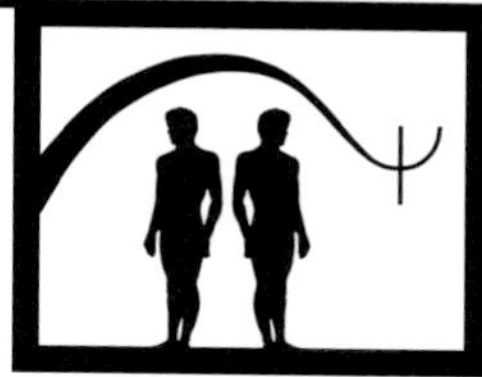

Reinforcer Sampling

Adrienne E. Fricker, Amy M. Combs-Lane,
Joanne L. Davis, and Ron Acierno
Medical University of South Carolina

GLOSSARY

behaviorism School of thought that stresses the importance of studying behavior objectively and dealing only with directly or potentially observable stimuli and responses.

reinforcer sampling rule Before using an event or stimulus as a reinforcer, sampling of the reinforcer is required in the situation in which it is to be used.

token economy Reinforcement system in which individuals earn symbolic reinforcers that can be exchanged for a tangible reward for performing adaptive behaviors, or lose symbolic reinforcers for performing maladaptive behaviors.

Reinforcer sampling is the procedure of noncontingently presenting a portion of a reinforcer prior to a response to (1) determine that a stimulus or event is, in fact, reinforcing, and (2) increase the motivation of the organism to engage in behavior to obtain the reinforcer. This article will present a review of the theoretical and empirical bases of reinforcer sampling, provide ways in which reinforcer sampling has been used in clinical populations, and provide other practical examples of its utility.

I. DESCRIPTION OF TREATMENT

Reinforcer sampling is a procedure to identify or increase the reinforcing value of a stimulus or event. In order to identify whether a potential reinforcer is desirable to the subject, the reinforcer is presented noncontingently (i.e., the subject receives or "samples" the reinforcer without doing anything for it). After the subject has sampled the reinforcer, the probability that the subject will work to gain access to the reinforcer in the future may change. A response or set of responses are then specified upon which the reinforcer is made contingent. It is hoped that since the subject has had a chance to experience the reinforcer, he or she will be more motivated to obtain it, and thus will be more likely to engage in the desired behavior.

Reinforcer sampling could be used in a situation in which a parent wishes to obtain a specific behavior from a child. For example, a mother may want her child to pick up his toys when he is finished playing with them. To alter his behavior using reinforcer sampling, this mother could noncontingently introduce a potential reinforcer, such as a new computer game, several random times in the home. Then, after it appeared that her son liked playing the game and looked forward to playing it, the mother could tell him that he would be able to play the computer game only after he picked up all of his toys, therefore making playing the computer game contingent upon picking up his toys. Importantly, prior experience, or sampling the computer game, would be necessary for this stimulus to have any relevance to the boy.

II. THEORETICAL BASES

Reinforcer sampling was described by Teodoro Ayllon and Nathan Azrin in their 1968 book on the token economy system of motivational and rehabilitational therapy. A token economy system requires individuals to earn tokens for adaptive behavior that can be exchanged for numerous reinforcers, such as meals, activities, and so on. The theory behind the token system is that individuals will engage in adaptive behaviors in order to gain access to available reinforcers. However, this will only be effective if the implementers of the token economy system accurately identify those stimuli or events (i.e., reinforcers) that may serve the function of increasing the probability of the occurrence of targeted responses (i.e., truly reinforcing stimuli). Ayllon and Azrin reported that many individuals in a token economy system would not engage in what was assumed to be a reinforcing activity. That is, the activity was not truly reinforcing to these individuals. Reinforcer sampling is a way of determining the reinforcing properties of a stimulus or event. Although the sampling of an event does not guarantee that it will be reinforcing, it will increase familiarity with the event. Thus, if the individual does not seek the reinforcer, one is assured that this is not simply due to unfamiliarity with it.

In their book, Ayllon and Azrin presented the Reinforcer Sampling Rule, which states that before using an event or stimulus as a reinforcer, sampling of the reinforcer is required in the situation in which it is to be used. This is important for several reasons. First, if an individual has not previously or recently come into contact with the potentially reinforcing event, then it may not be reinforcing to that individual. Second, a previously identified reinforcer may lessen or lose its reinforcing qualities in a new situation. In other words, while a stimulus may be familiar and somewhat reinforcing, it may not be worth the effort when subjects are required to engage in certain behaviors to obtain it.

The principle of stimulus generalization suggests that the probability of a response increases as a function of the degree of similarity of the stimuli to those previously present at the moment of reinforcement. Thus, to increase the odds that an individual will work for a reinforcer, the situation should closely approximate the original situation that existed when the individual initially obtained the reinforcer. Reinforcer sampling procedure allows the individual to be briefly presented with the reinforcer before the response, thereby reproducing all of the stimuli associated with the onset of the reinforcer. After the individual has sampled the reinforcer in the new situation, and thus has become familiar with the reinforcer in the new context, the remainder of the reinforcer could then be delivered after the individual has produced the desired response.

The sampling rule is often used in businesses. An example is the woman who hands out free food and drink samples at the grocery store hoping that shoppers will find the sample good (i.e., reinforcing) and buy the product (i.e., engage in the desired behavior).

III. EMPIRICAL STUDIES

In the 1960s, Ayllon and Azrin conducted a series of studies evaluating the use of reinforcer sampling with psychiatric inpatients. Each study evaluated the number of psychiatric inpatients that engaged in different activities, (e.g., a fair, a walk, watching a movie, a social evening, a music session, and religious services), without first being allowed to "sample" the event. The patients had to use one of their earned tokens to attend the event. In the second phase, patients were allowed to "sample" the event by being present at the fair grounds or watching the first few minutes of the religious service, and then were allowed to decide whether they wanted to use their token to attend the event for a longer duration. Ayllon and Azrin found that the patients were more likely to attend the event if they had been allowed to sample the event first. However, with a return to the regular procedure in which the patients were not allowed to sample the event before deciding whether they wanted to attend it, they were less likely to choose to use a token to participate. Ayllon and Azrin reported that this suggests that reinforcer sampling is an effective means of increasing utilization of a reinforcer, and that it can be used with a variety of different reinforcers. They also suggested that reinforcer sampling should be used for as long as the specific behavior is desired, as their results showed that patients decreased their utilization of the reinforcer event when the reinforcer sampling procedure was discontinued.

Reinforcer sampling does not appear to work solely by familiarizing individuals with reinforcers. That is, the experiments demonstrated an increased utilization of the reinforcer once sampling was available, even in patients who had previous experience with the event.

Since Ayllon and Azrin studied reinforcement sampling procedures in psychiatric inpatients, other studies have replicated their findings with other samples of psychiatric inpatients, as well as in different populations. Often, reinforcer sampling has been studied in the context of token economy systems used with severely mentally ill individuals or individuals with mental retardation. In these populations, reinforcer sampling is used to encourage individuals to work for reinforcers and activities that are available. For example, in token economy systems, individuals earn tokens by engaging in specific desirable behaviors and then are allowed to use the tokens to "purchase" meals, access to objects such as musical instruments, and activities such as social events or outdoor passes. In research conducted in the later 1960s through the 1970s, with an occasional study in the 1990s, researchers examined the effectiveness of reinforcer sampling in increasing mentally ill or developmentally delayed individuals' utilization of positive reinforcers (e.g., arts and crafts) provided in a long-term care setting. Similar to Ayllon and Azrin, researchers have predominantly found that allowing individuals to sample the reinforcer prior to using the reinforcer as a contingent event or stimulus has increased the chances that individuals will choose to engage in the reinforcing activity.

Researchers have also experimented with alternate forms of reinforcer sampling. For example, some have employed response exposure as a form of sampling. Response exposure involves allowing an individual to observe a desired response being chosen or enacted by another person followed by receipt of reinforcement.

IV. SUMMARY

Reinforcer sampling is a procedure that can enhance the relevance of a reinforcer. Reinforcer sampling involves presenting a potential reinforcer noncontingently to an individual prior to requiring a specific behavior so that the individual's motivation to obtain the reinforcer is increased. This procedure is useful when individuals are unfamiliar with the reinforcer, or are unfamiliar with the context in which the reinforcer will be used to obtain a desired behavior. Reinforcer sampling also helps to identify those events, objects, or activities that will be reinforcing to a specific individual or group of people. Reinforcer sampling has been used primarily with psychiatric inpatients and developmentally delayed populations. However, behavioral principles suggest that it could be useful with a variety of types of populations.

See Also the Following Articles

Behavioral Consultation and Therapy ■ Negative Reinforcement ■ Positive Reinforcement ■ Token Economy

Further Reading

Ayllon, T., & Azrin, N. (1968). *The token economy : A motivational system for therapy and rehabilitation* (pp. 88–103). New York: Appleton-Century-Crofts.

Ayllon, T., & Azrin, N. H. (1968). Reinforcer sampling: A technique for increasing the behavior of mental patients. *Journal of Applied Behavior Analysis, 1,* 13–20.

Kazdin, A. E. (1977). *The token economy: A review and evaluation* (pp. 157–158). New York: Plenum Press.

Spiegler, M. D., & Guevremont, D. C. (1993). *Contemporary behavior therapy* (2nd ed., pp. 105–137). Pacific Grove, CA: Brooks/Cole.

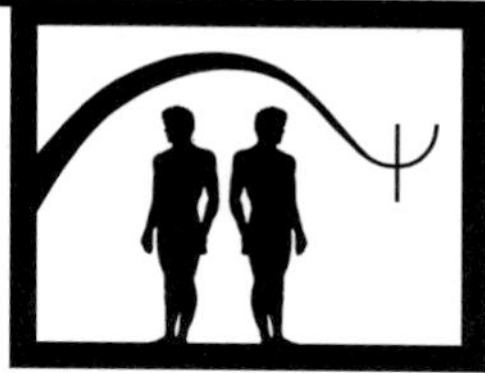

Relapse Prevention

Kirk A. Brunswig, Tamara M. Penix, and William O'Donohue
University of Nevada, Reno

GLOSSARY

abstinence violation effect (AVE) Occurs when a client lapses and irrationally concludes that the lapse is so severe that they may as well relapse (e.g., since I broke the rule and I had one shot of whiskey, I may as well finish the bottle); a form of perfectionist or "all or none" thinking.

high-risk situation A situation identified by client and therapist as one in which the client has a greater likelihood to experience a lapse or relapse. Part of a behavior chain that probabilistically could lead to a lapse or relapse.

idiographic A self-referenced, as opposed to norm-referenced, context (e.g., comparisons with the client's previous level of function would be idiographic, whereas comparisons with the client's peers would be nomothetic).

lapse An occurrence of an undesired behavior in the context of behavior cessation or reduction program (e.g., smoking a cigarette by the client in a smoking cessation program or visiting a bar by an alcoholic). A lapse is always less serious than a relapse.

problem of immediate gratification (PIG) The orientation to positive, usually smaller, short-term consequences with adverse, usually larger, long-term consequences, rather than to adverse or unwanted short-term consequences for a more beneficial long-term consequence.

relapse A violation of the contract or terms of the behavior cessation or reduction program. Sometimes defined as a return to pretreatment levels of the problem behavior.

seemingly irrelevant/unimportant decisions (SIDS/SUDS) Decisions early in a behavior chain that place the client in a high-risk situation (e.g., the pedophile deciding to get milk from the market near the day care center rather than the market near the commercial district).

I. OVERVIEW

When one thinks of psychotherapy, a picture comes into view of a more or less theoretically inspired set of techniques that are employed as a primary clinical intervention to treat a constellation of psychological symptoms. Unlike most of the psychotherapies that are described in this volume, relapse prevention (RP) did not evolve as a front-line treatment for a particular mental disorder. It was instead a calculated response to the longer-term treatment failures of other therapies. It was not conceived as an alternative to those interventions, but as a supplemental tool that would make a variety of treatments, particularly for addictive behaviors, more effective.

Another unique feature of RP is that it was not originally concerned with all of the phases of treatment; for example, it did not address the precontemplation, contemplation, preparation, and action stages of treatment. The original target of RP was the maintenance phase of treatment, when patients are no longer receiving a regular dose of the primary treatment and the positive effects brought about by regular treatment contact can begin to wane. RP was conceived as an answer to the problem of maintaining initial gains. Arguably the most difficult challenge for any patient is maintaining treatment gains over time without the structure and accountability of therapy, or the support of a therapist or group. RP provides some tools for maintaining treatment gains over time.

This article provides the history of RP and its evolution in the treatment of addictions and other impulse control problems. We describe some of the various forms of RP and its basic components. Relevant research is presented and we discuss the future potential of RP with the additions of motivational interviewing, stepped-care approaches to health, and harm reduction concepts.

II. THEORETICAL BASES

Relapse Prevention is a broad phrase that is used to describe a varied set of cognitive-behavioral techniques that are employed to maintain desirable addictive and impulsive behavioral changes. Alan Marlatt and Judith Gordon developed the approach over the course of several years and many discussions. Marlatt and his colleagues were working in the treatment of substance abuse and became increasingly concerned with follow-up data. Results indicated that although significant treatment gains could be produced in addictive behaviors such as drug, alcohol, and tobacco use, those gains also diminished significantly over time if no further intervention was implemented. In 1995 D. Richard Laws wrote of findings suggesting that within 1 year of ending treatment over 80% of patients would relapse (resume the undesired behavior) and two-third of these resumptions would occur in the first 3 months. Marlatt and his colleagues concluded that it was not the cessation treatments themselves that needed to be altered. These approaches initially appeared to facilitate abstinence for many patients. Instead, Marlatt reasoned that a supplemental treatment was needed that would focus on the maintenance of the gains that were acquired during the original treatment period.

The primary assumption of RP is that there it is problematic to expect that the effects of a treatment that is designed to moderate or eliminate an undesirable behavior will endure beyond the termination of that treatment. Further, there are reasons to presume a problem will reemerge, such as a return to the old environment that elicited and maintained the problem behavior; forgetting the skills, techniques, and information taught during therapy; and decreased motivation. Treatments typically involve an intense but limited period of time during which patients are brought into contact with new influences (some mental health workers, some patients like themselves), information, and contextual components that aid in creating changes in their behaviors. There is an accountability factor that is built into these techniques as well as a regular dose of treatment given reliably over a period of time. These accountability and dose elements are commonly removed after the client has reached his or her treatment goals (treatment is terminated) and the client must learn to implement the skills and knowledge he or she learned in a new context with little or no assistance. Generalizing the skills to varied situations poses a significant challenge and many treatment failures are the result.

Marlatt and his colleagues believed that treatment failures could be analyzed in order to discover internal and external variables that increased risk for relapse. They further reasoned that knowing items such as situational factors, mood states, and cognitions would identify individualized targets of change for clients, targets focused not on the acquisition of quitting behavior, but the maintenance of that behavior. Based loosely on Albert Bandura's 1977 social learning theory, the RP model proposes that at the cessation of a habit control treatment, a client feels self-efficacious with regard to the unwanted behavior and that this perception of self-efficacy stems from learned and practiced skills. Over time the client contacts internal and external risk factors such as seemingly irrelevant decisions (SIDS, sometimes seemingly unimportant decisions, or SUDS) and/or high-risk situations (HRS) that threaten the client's self-control, and consequently his or her perception of self-efficacy. According to the model, if the client has adaptive coping skills to adequately address the internal and external challenges to his or her control, the client will not relapse. However, if his or her skills are not sufficient to meet the challenge, a lapse or relapse may occur (this will be described in greater detail below). In response to a resumption of the change behavior at some level, the client has a reaction that either increases attempts to implement adaptive coping skills, or fails to cope effectively and engages in the undesirable behavior because it provides immediate gratification. Embedded in this model is Marlatt's supposition that the targets of intervention are cognitions and behaviors that are collectively referred to as coping skills. Marlatt and his colleagues' treatment therefore employs cognitive-behavioral techniques to improve the retention and accessibility of adaptive coping responses.

In the short period of time since its introduction, RP has evolved in numerous directions. It has been applied to new problem areas such as risky sexual behaviors, overeating, and sexual offending. It has additionally come into use as a full program of treatment and lifestyle change, instead of simply a supplemental intervention strategy. That is, RP is often a primary treatment program in addition to addressing the maintenance issue. Lastly, RP is emerging as a bona fide theory of compulsive habit patterns and the processes of relapse. It should be noted that RP is most widely used with behaviors deemed volitional in origin (e.g., behaviors of consumption); however, some practitioners have applied RP in problem behaviors where the volitional element is less clear (e.g., schizophrenia, depression).

Tony Ward and Stephen Hudson in 1996 argued that this conceptualization often fails to accurately capture the addictive processes for which it was used. For example, the theoretical link between high-risk situation and lapse, as well the link from lapse to relapse has not been sufficiently demonstrated. As Ward and Hudson suggest, RP has rightfully undergone increasing scrutiny in recent years. Additional researchers and scholars have critiqued and extended the RP theory that commenced with the ideas of Bandura, Marlatt, and Gordon. See the edited work by Laws, Hudson, and Ward (2000) *Remaking Relapse Prevention with Sex Offenders* for the latest developments in RP theory in general, and treatment applications for sexual offenders.

III. TREATMENT COMPONENTS

In 1995 Laws outlined the tenets of RP. He provides 12 principles that serve as the foundation of this approach. Briefly summarized, the components of RP are identification of a maladaptive behavior, a process of change defined by commitment and motivation, behavioral change and maintenance of behavior change, identification of lapses (a single instance of the maladaptive behavior) and relapses (a complete violation of the self-imposed abstinence rules), lifestyle balance between obligatory and self-selected behaviors, recognition of the ideographic aspects of the maladaptive behavior, and recognizing and planning behavioral responses for high-risk situations. In practice, RP addresses the issues of identifying high-risk situations, seemingly irrelevant decisions, and the problem of immediate gratification. Therapists using RP to treat sex offenders also include skills training components, such as social skills and coping skills.

In general, relapse prevention's foci are first, identification of high-risk situations, and second, employing appropriate self-control responses. High-risk situations are determined by an analysis of past offenses and by reports of situations in which the client feels or felt "tempted." These situations may be a bar or tavern for smokers and drinkers, playgrounds and shopping malls for sexual offenders, and casinos for gamblers. Appropriate responses are those behaviors that lead to avoidance of high-risk situations, or if in a high-risk situation, behaviors that foster nonoffending actions. For example, if an offender realizes he is having a fantasy about offending, he can employ a thought-stopping behavior, such as saying out loud "Stop!" or distracting himself such that the deviant fantasy is interrupted. Laws suggests that responding with an appropriate coping response to high-risk situations will lead to increased self-efficacy and a decreased probability of relapse. He also indicates that if appropriate coping responses are not utilized or not in the behavioral repertoire, there will be a decrease in self-efficacy, an increased likelihood of positive outcome expectancies (perception of positive experiences resulting from engaging in maladaptive behavior), a lapse, and an increased probability of future lapses.

A. High-Risk Situations

This component often involves the ideographic assessment of high-risk situations. The client and clinician work together to identify the situations in which the client has previously engaged in problematic behavior and those situations in which the client is likely to engage in problematic behavior. The client will be asked to generate a list of situations that are lowrisk, and to determine what aspects of those situations differentiate them from high-risk situations. The focus will be to train the client to recognize themes and commonalties in his or her high-risk situations so that the client can generalize the ability to assess level of risk in a novel situation. The therapist works with the client to ensure that the client is realistic in his or her assessment of the level of risk in a variety of hypothetical situations. For example, the therapist often creates a series of hypothetical situations, based on the client's self-report of risk factors, to assess the client's ability to determine the causes and severity of risk.

B. SIDs/SUDs

Seemingly irrelevant decisions (SIDs) (also seemingly unimportant decisions or SUDs) are those behaviors that might not lead directly to a high-risk situation, but are early in the path of decisions that place the client in a high-risk situation. For example, if the client reports that he is more likely to engage in the problematic behavior after drinking during lunch, a SID would be agreeing to attend a two-martini luncheon with a coworker. In addressing SIDs, the therapist works with the client to determine which decisions lead to high-risk situations. Coping skills are often taught in conjunction with therapeutic work on SIDs. Once the client can identify high-risk situations and SIDs, the client needs to learn effective coping strategies. For example, the therapist may direct the client to brainstorm strategies to resolve a high-risk situation without employing the problematic behavior. For example, the client may choose to walk away or the client may wish to change the situation so that the risk is lowered (e.g., for a smoker, moving a conversation to a room in which there are more nonsmokers, away from the break room or smoking area). The therapist must work with the client to ensure that client solutions and skills are adequate and appropriate. The therapist may also role-play situations with the client to allow the client a chance to practice skills in a hypothetical high-risk situation.

C. Problem of Immediate Gratification

The problem of immediate gratification (PIG) is the orientation of the client to smaller positive short-term consequences with larger adverse long-term consequences, rather than adverse or unwanted short-term consequences for a more beneficial long-term consequence. With smokers, the immediate relief from withdrawal symptoms provided by a cigarette is the proximal consequences, while emphysema, lung cancer, and death are more distal consequences. To address the PIG, the therapist typically employs psychoeducational approaches to teach the client how to create a decision matrix. This is usually a written exercise, in which the matrix contains the positive and negative outcome expectancies for engaging or not engaging in the problematic behavior, in both the immediate and short-term frame of reference. The therapist then confronts any unrealistic outcome expectancies until the client is able to generate more realistic outcomes. Following this, the therapist directs the client to analyze past situations in which the patient engaged in the problematic behavior, and to compare the immediate gratifications against the long-term consequences.

D. Abstinence Violation Effect

The abstinence violation effect (AVE) highlights the distinction between a lapse and relapse. Put simply, the AVE occurs when a client perceives no intermediary step between a lapse and a relapse. For example, overeaters may have an AVE when they express to themselves, "one slice of cheesecake is a lapse, so I may as well go all-out, and have the rest of the cheesecake." That is, since they have violated the rule of abstinence, they "may as well" get the most out of the lapse. Treatment in this component involves describing the AVE, and working with the client to learn alternative coping skills for when a lapse occurs, such that a relapse is prevented. The AVE occurs when a client is in a high-risk situation and views the potential lapse as so severe, that he or she may as well relapse. The client and therapist will practice identifying and coping with lapses. The treatment is not lapse prevention; lapses are to be expected, planned for, and taken as opportunities for the client to demonstrate learning. It is relapse prevention. Most often, relapse tends to be construed as a return to pretreatment levels of occurrence of the targeted behavior. Although there is some debate about the best definitions of lapse and relapse from theoretical and conceptual levels, these definitions should suffice.

E. Outcome Expectancies

An example of skills training is seen when addressing outcome expectancies. The client is asked to construct a decision matrix: on one dimension, the choice of offending versus not offending, on the second dimension, the positive and negative outcomes, and on the third dimension, the short- and long-term consequences. Often, the client will not generate accurate outcomes, and is instructed in more likely outcomes for their offending and nonoffending behaviors. Another component in some manifestations of RP is enhancing victim empathy. Clients are asked to do a variety of tasks, such as watching a videotape of victims telling of the effects of their victimization, imagining how the client and a loved one would feel if victimized, and writing a letter from the victim's point of view.

F. Cognitive Distortions

Therapists trained in CBT often find it necessary to address the client's cognitive distortions when dealing with clients who engage in problems of self-control. In 1989, as part of Laws's book on RP for sex offenders, Katurah Jenkins-Hall described the steps for changing cognitive distortions in sexual offenders as identification of the thoughts that lead to maladaptive behavior, analyzing the validity and utility of the thoughts, and an intervention designed to change the cognitive distortions into more adaptive cognitions. Jenkins-Hall details how cognitive therapy can be adapted to sexual offenders. Step one is providing alternative interpretations in that the "client is taught that his initial interpretation of a given situation may not be the most accurate. He is asked to generate a list of alternative explanations." Step two, utilitarian counters, asks the client to evaluate whether his thinking assisted or hindered the achievement of the desired outcome (e.g., did having a biased interpretation of the victim's behavior make it easier for you to justify your actions to yourself?). In step three, objective counters, the therapist helps the client analyze the logic behind certain types of thinking. Step four, disputing and challenging, is based in Ellis's rational emotive therapy. In this stage the client is asked to identify irrational types of thinking and beliefs, and these irrational statements and beliefs are challenged in therapy.

G. Social Skills

Another common problem in some self-control problems relates to deficits in social skills. Clients may be misperceiving both verbal and nonverbal behaviors by those in high-risk situations. An ideographic assessment can be used to learn which, if any, key social skill deficits are present. The clinician should address relative deficits in perception, interpretation, response generation, enactment, and evaluation. In conducting social skills training with these clients, clients and therapists typically discuss the abstract principles of the particular class of social skills. The therapist then models the specific set of social skills. The client and therapist then role-play a situation that emphasizes the specific social skills relevant for the client. For example, for a client working sexually inappropriate behavior in the workplace, the client and therapist may role-play joke-telling situations, socializing, or other critical situations common at the workplace. The therapist would then provide feedback for the client regarding the skills present and absent during the role-play.

H. Aftercare

As with any therapeutic intervention, therapists are obligated to design a plan for aftercare. With RP, one of the essential elements of the psychoeducational process is instructing the client about the role of misbehavior in the context of one's life. Although the goal of RP is the prevention of the occurrence of problematic behavior, the lifestyle must be addressed. The repairing of a damaged boat hull is an appropriate analogy. Patching the hole is well and good (reducing problematic behavior), but the pilot of the boat should also learn not to run the ship aground, through rapids, or into icebergs (lifestyle balance).

Often, the development of positive addictions is presented. Positive addictions are healthy behaviors and hobbies, such as reading and bowling, in which the client can engage without experiencing adverse consequences. Lastly, each element of the RP approach, e.g., high-risk situation, the PIG, the AVE, and cognitive distortions are reviewed in the larger context of RP. For example, in work with sexual harassers, the harasser is directed to review the role of cognitive distortions as a component involved in sexual harassment, and then relate to how cognitive distortions are involved in the RP model.

I. Planning for Lapses

To dissuade the client from buying into the AVE, a realistic aftercare plan should include a plan for addressing lapses, because they are likely to occur. To plan for lapses clients should know how they would handle situations in which they feel at risk for engaging in the problematic behavior. What is the client's support group? How will the therapist work with the client to devise strategies for seeking help, should the need arise after therapy? The therapist and client should also review plan to prevent a lapse from becoming a relapse. One way to do this is to practice these skills beforehand, for example, the client and therapist can role-play situations in which the client will need to ask a friend or loved one for help, call a therapist for an appointment, and tell a new friend about their history of problematic behavior and what the new friend can do to help the client when the client is in need.

There is gradual waning of the active role of therapy and the therapist in the client's life. However, practitioners employing RP typically inform their clients that the clients will struggle with this problem for life, and they will likely never be "cured." To enhance the gains made in therapy, and during RP aftercare for other primary interventions, RP sessions are often faded to biweekly, then later to monthly, then bimonthly, and sometimes continue annually for years.

J. Data on RP

In 1995 Gordon Nagayama Hall demonstrated the effectiveness of a community-based outpatient RP program for male sexual offenders, while Karl Hanson has spearheaded an effort to collect and organize data from an international pool of researchers on the effectiveness of RP programs with sex offenders. Most of these studies were limited by a lack of random assignment to conditions due to ethical and pragmatic difficulties. The effectiveness of RP with other problematic behaviors has been demonstrated as well, specifically with alcohol, tobacco, and overeating. Efforts to gather increasingly informative treatment outcome data are extensive and ongoing. In general, there is some evidence that RP can be an effective intervention to prevent the reoccurrence of many problematic behaviors. However, there exists a disconcerting lack of data on the theoretical foundations of RP, such as covert pathways to relapse and the role of motivation in treatment success. For example, there has not been a clear demonstration of the necessary and sufficient internal and external conditions that will predict instances of lapses and relapses. What the field does have is a bevy of clinical experience across a broad domain of client problems, all suggestive that RP is plausible as well as popular with both clients and therapists.

IV. FUTURE DIRECTIONS

A. Denial and Minimization—Motivational Interviewing

A common problem in working with clients who would likely benefit from RP is the evaluation and treatment of denial and minimization. In their 1993 work with sexual offenders, William O'Donohue and Elizabeth Letourneau developed an intervention that was designed to help the client to admit to the offense and be motivated to seek and participate in therapy. An adaptation of their techniques to the treatment of general self-control problems would include presenting the probable outcomes of receiving versus not receiving treatment (e.g., gainful employment versus lower wage or no employment) and likelihood and consequences of future instances of misbehavior (e.g., if treated, lower likelihood of re-offense, if untreated, higher likelihood of re-offense and more severe consequences).

In addition, therapists have successfully used intervention of motivational interviewing (MI). MI has been shown effective in a variety of other RP treatment evaluations (see the 1991 edited work by Miller and Rollnick, *Motivational Interviewing*.) MI involves presenting the client's data in a matter-of-fact manner in which problems are not discussed, but rather, a simple review of the facts is performed. This is thought to allow the client to make an informed choice about engaging treatment.

B. Stepped Care

Stepped care involves the gradual introduction of interventions of increasing cost and severity. The initial interventions are the least intensive, most costeffective, and have the lowest response cost to the client and have the greatest possibility of success. If this level of intervention fails, then more intense, high-cost interventions are introduced. As the level of intensity increases, fewer clients should require that level of intervention. As the active components of RP are better understood, the treatment dose and content may be tailored to the individualistic problem such that resources are used efficiently. In addition, as RP techniques are better documented and available to clients, the involvement of RP therapists may become limited or obsolete in some cases.

C. Harm Reduction

Laws describes the change in focus between RP and harm reduction (HR) as a difference based on expecting an absolute cessation of the problem behavior (RP) as opposed to a manageable and acceptable reduction (HR). In his work with sex offenders, Laws describes as recognizing that offenders may have the occasional fantasy or desire to act out sexually. By owning up to this reality, Laws indicates that client and therapist goals can be more realistic. Furthermore, lapses, when they occur in the HR model, can be seen as learning experiences rather than failures.

V. SUMMARY

Relapse prevention was not produced as a stand-alone treatment derived from theoretically based and empirically supported foundations. Instead, RP was created as a supplement to existing treatments to address as the treatment failures seen in other therapies for problematic behaviors often conceptualized as problems of self-control. Furthermore, RP was not an "intervention" per se, but rather a structured aftercare regimen to assist in the maintenance of treatment gains.

Over the course of time, RP was taken from the research laboratories at the University of Washington and field tested with problem drinkers, smokers, overeaters, and sex offenders, to name only a few. In its many manifestations, RP addresses high-risk situations, the avoidance of those situations, the management of those situations, and skills for recovery after encountering those situations. The data on RP, while sparse, suggest that RP is generally effective for a variety of self-control problems. The future of RP includes motivational interviewing, stepped care, and harm reduction, as well as further clarification of the theoretical underpinnings, mechanisms, and outcomes of relapse prevention.

See Also the Following Articles

Cost Effectiveness ■ Efficacy ■ Objective Assessment ■ Outcome Measures ■ Substance Dependence: Psychotherapy ■ Termination

Further Reading

Laws, D. R. (Ed.). (1989). *Relapse prevention with sex offenders.* New York: Guilford Press.

Laws, D. R. (1995). A theory of relapse prevention. In W. O'Donohue, & L. Krasner (Eds.), *Theories of behavior therapy: Exploring behavior change.* Washington, DC: American Psychological Association.

Laws, D. R., Hudson, S. M., & Ward, T. (Eds.) (2000). *Remaking relapse prevention with sex offenders:A sourcebook.* Thousand Oaks, CA: Sage.

Marlatt, G. A. (1998). *Harm reduction: Pragmatic strategies for managing high-risk behaviors.* New York: Guilford.

Marlatt, G.A., & Gordon, J.R. (Eds.). (1985). *Relapse prevention.* New York: Guilford Press.

Sandberg, G. G., & Marlatt, G. A. (1991). Relapse prevention. In D. A. Gravlo & R. I. Shader (Eds.), *Clinical manual of dependence.* Washington, DC: American Psychiatric Press.

Ward, T., & Hudson, S. (1996). Relapse prevention: A critical analysis. *Sexual Abuse: A Journal of Research and Treatment, 8,* 177–199.

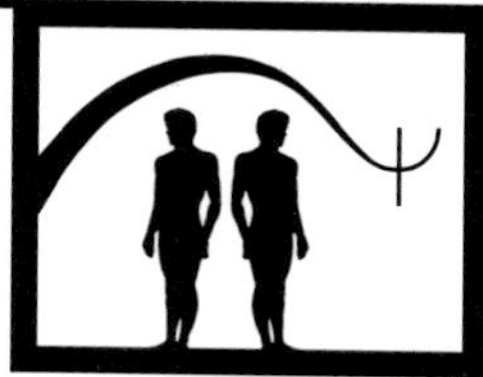

Relational Psychoanalysis

Spyros D. Orfanos
Stephen A. Mitchell Center for Relational Psychoanalysis

GLOSSARY

intersubjectivity A developmental achievement in which both individuals within a dyad recognize each other's subjectivity.

multiple selves The concept that people experience themselves not as unitary and unchanging but as consisting of multiple selves that may be compatible or incompatible with one another.

mutuality The idea that both patient and analyst participate in the analytic process, that they mutually regulate or influence each other, consciously and unconsciously.

projective identification A process by which the patient's disavowed feelings are projected onto the analyst who has become a container for the dissociated features of the patient's experience.

transference–countertransference matrix Transference and countertransference are interdependent, mutually determined experiences that are shaped by both patient and analyst.

I. DESCRIPTION

Relational psychoanalysis is an intensive form of psychotherapy that places human relations at the center of motivation, psychopathology, and treatment. It is an alternative to classical Freudian psychoanalysis (including its modifications in psychoanalytic ego psychology). It considers relations to others, not drives, as the basic building blocks of mental life. From the relational perspective, individual experiences and the internal structures of the mind are viewed as deriving from and are transformations of relationships with significant others.

The term "relational psychoanalysis" is a relatively new coinage. It refers to a theoretical and clinical sensibility that integrates a variety of psychoanalytic theories that have evolved following the promulgation of Freud's seminal ideas. Thus, it is a contemporary eclectic approach that has been in a process of growth and development in the United States for the last 20 years. This new perspective includes recent developments within, and cuts across, U.S. interpersonal psychoanalysis, the British school of object relations, self psychology, and currents within contemporary Freudian theory. It is concerned with the intrapsychic as well as the interpersonal, but the intrapsychic is seen as constituted by the internalization of interpersonal experiences. Although these internalized interpersonal experiences may be biologically mediated, relational psychoanalysis is primarily concerned with the psychological determinants of experience.

There is considerable variation in the practice of relational psychoanalysis, but all relational analysts share a sensibility in which the therapeutic relationship plays a superordinate role in the treatment. Thus, the analyst's subjectivity and personal involvement, including partially blinding entanglements, are given serious consideration. Gender, class, race, culture, and language are additional factors of great significance to relational analysts.

II. HISTORICAL DEVELOPMENT

The sea change that has been taking place in contemporary U.S. psychoanalysis in the last two decades is in sharp contrast to the popular view that modern-day psychoanalysis is a footnote to Freud. Psychoanalytic practice has evolved considerably since Freud's original creative contributions. Freud's body-based instinct (drive) model emphasizes intrapsychic conflict among id, ego, and superego as the child passes through the psychosexual stages of development. Interpretation, the main form of clinical intervention in Freudian analysis, is for the purpose of making unconscious content, such as sexual and aggressive impulses, conscious. In the Freudian model, relatedness is a derivative of the primary drives of sex and aggression.

The current paradigm shift away from the classical drive model to the relational model had its origins in the work of two psychoanalytic pioneers: the Europeans Sandor Ferenczi and Otto Rank. Both were students of Freud and in 1924 collaborated in exploring the primacy of experience in the here and now of the transference. After their collaboration, Ferenczi theorized about the mutuality of relationships in human development and clinical process. Rank went on to elaborate a theory of the birth of the self and the centrality of early relationships in the therapeutic interaction.

Working in the United States before World War II, Harry Stack Sullivan revised Freudian psychoanalytic ideas in his development of an interpersonal psychiatry. In an informal collaboration with Erich Fromm, Karen Horney, Freida Fromm-Reichman, and Clara Thompson, Sullivan came to disagree with the prevailing view of psychopathology as residing in the individual. He believed that human beings are inseparable from their interpersonal field and that focusing on the individual without considering past and present relationships is misdirected. Sullivan emphasized that human relatedness is a prerequisite of psychological well-being and a safeguard against anxiety. In treatment, he urged concentration on the here and now of the therapist–patient interaction. Subsequently, Thompson assembled the emerging concepts that constituted an interpersonal psychoanalysis and helped institutionalize them through the Washington School of Psychiatry and the William Alanson White Institute in New York City. Over time, two different clinical approaches emerged in the interpersonal tradition: Sullivan's emphasis on empathy and tact and Fromm's empahsis on frankness and confrontation. In stressing the role of actual and specific interpersonal relationships in personality development and psychopathology, interpersonal psychoanalysis came to be caricatured as social psychology by the mainstream and medical psychoanalytic power circles of the day. In recent years, however, interpersonal psychoanalysis has gained increased acceptance with the elegant writings of Edgar Levenson, who stressed that what was talked about between analyst and patient was also concurrently being enacted between the two.

Contemporary British object relations theories began to have a significant presence in the Unites States in the 1970s. The theoretical and clinical innovations of the British school stressed the importance of the pre-Oedipal stage and especially the early mother–infant relationship. Emphasis was placed on the conflictual nature of internalized relationships to others. Moreover, nonverbal phenomena, regressed states, and the actual relationship between analyst and patient were also highlighted. Melanie Klein's theorizing about greed, envy, aggression, and projective identification also played an influential role. As represented by Michael Balint, W. R. D. Fairbairn, D. W. Winnicott, and Harry Guntrip, the British school of object relations was a thorn for U.S. Freudian psychoanalysis in that the centrality of the Oedipus complex was downplayed.

A third psychoanalytic paradigm that contributed to relational approach is self psychology. In the late 1970s, Heinz Kohut reformulated Freud's ideas, first in terms of the concept of narcissism and then in terms of theory and practice. He emphasized the chronic traumatizing milieu of the patient's early human environment, not the intense sexual and aggressive pressures that Freud had defined as basic to human motivation. He viewed aggression and rage in treatment not as an expression of a fundamental force but as result of deep vulnerability. The self psychology school of psychoanalysis developed into a powerful presence and influenced the thinking and practice of many.

In their more contemporary cast, these three schools of psychoanalysis seemed to be moving along similar paths, toward a focus on self–other relations, an interest in feelings and experience rather than drives, and toward a less authoritarian stance on the part of the analyst. Furthermore, the clinical focus is often on the patient–analyst relationship and the way in which small, but subtle interactions and enactments dominate the clinical situation.

Other theoretical influences in the development of a relational approach were the works of Hans Loewald and John Bowlby. Hans Loewald, a prominent ego psychologist in the 1970s, redefined id, ego, and superego in terms of interpersonal experience giving drives a relational character. He argued against the Freudian idea that the human mind can be an independent unit of inquiry without taking into account the analyst's participation. John Bowlby's work on attachment theory in the 1960s and the subsequent rich research on attachment has also played an important role in recent relation theorizing. Bowlby and his followers have placed intimate attachments to others at the "hub" around which a person's life revolves throughout the life span.

In 1983, Jay R. Greenberg and Stephen A. Mitchell published their landmark treatise, *Object Relations and Psychoanalytic Theory,* in which they distinguished two distinct approaches to psychoanalytic theory: the drive-structure model and the relational-structure model. Despite its title, their book was not only about object relations theories. It compared various models including interpersonal theory and self psychology. In addition to making detailed comparisons, the authors argued that theoretical positions in psychoanalysis are inevitably embedded in social, political, and moral contexts. They used the term relational to bridge the traditions of interpersonal relations, as developed within interpersonal psychoanalysis, and object relations, as developed within contemporary British theorizing.

During the early 1980s, Merton Gill, a prominent leader in U.S. ego psychology, published a series of articles recognizing the contributions of the interpersonal theorists and their views. He contrasted the drive model with the more humanistic model in which relationships are given primary importance. He identified the depth of clinical process and the exploration of transference–countertransference issues as the defining characteristics of clinical psychoanalysis. Later in the decade, the English translation of *The Clinical Diary of Sandor Ferenczi* was published after having been suppressed for more than half a century. Consisting of Ferenczi's clinical experiments with mutual analysis, it demonstrated an objection to the hierarchical arrangement of the traditional analytic relationship between an analyst who dispenses interpretations and a patient who receives them.

Conceptually, two other broad developments occurred in the last two decades of the 20th century that facilitated the development of relational psychoanalysis. The first development was feminism. It launched a major critique on Freudian notions by deemphasizing the phallocentricity of its theories and practice. Sexuality was unlinked from both physical constitution and reproductive function, and homosexuality no longer pathologized. Using a feminist approach, Jessica Benjamin published *The Bonds of Love* in 1988. This work masterfully argued the importance for psychoanalytic theory to include both an intrapsychic and an intersubjective perspective. The second development was constructivism, in its moderate postmodern form. Basically, psychoanalytic theorists have used a constructivist approach to critique essentialism, positivism, and any pretext to objectivity. Constructivism is used to understand transference not as simply a distortion emanating from the patient as in Freudian psychology. Transference, according to Irwin Hoffman, is viewed as involving the analyst's subjectivity in a process of co-creation with the patient. In his 1998 book *Ritual and Spontaneity in the Psychoanalytic Process,* Hoffman brilliantly critiques theorists such as Sullivan, Kohut, and Winnicott charging that they are similar to Freud in that they suggest that analysts can keep their own subjective experience from "contaminating" their patients' transferences.

Organizationally, relational psychoanalysis was greatly bolstered by four developments. The Division of Psychoanalysis of the American Psychological Association operating outside the control of the traditional American Psychoanalytic Association acted as a forum for the relationally minded psychoanalyst and allowed for numerous creative and scholarly panel presentations at its annual conferences. This in turn gave relational psychoanalysis a national network and identity. The second organizational development took place in 1988 at the New York University Postdoctoral Program in Psychoanalysis and Psychotherapy where a "relational track" was established to go along with its Freudian, interpersonal, and independent tracks thus adding a prestigious university training legitimacy to relational psychoanalysis. Third, the establishment of the highly successful *Psychoanalytic Dialogues: A Journal of Relational Perspectives* in 1990 led to further consolidation of the identity of relational analysts. Finally, the formation of the International Association of Relational Psychoanalysis and Psychotherapy is well under way and will be inaugurated with a clinical conference in New York City in January 2002 titled *Relational Analysts at Work: Sense and Sensibility.*

III. THEORETICAL CONCEPTS

As articulated by Jay Greenberg and Stephen Mitchell, there are at least two different and incompatible views of human nature in psychoanalysis. Drive theory is derived from a philosophical tradition that sees a person as an essentially individual animal and human goals and desires as essentially personal and individual. In contrast, relational theory holds the philosophical position that a person is a social animal and that human satisfactions are realizable only within a social community. Consequently, the relational position is not interested in the single mind as a unit of study. It is interested in the relationship as a unit of study.

Although unconscious processes, the Oedipal complex, dreams, slips of the tongue, and free associations are of importance to relational theorists, they do not hold privileged positions. Wary of privileging any conceptual notion, relational theory nevertheless places the conscious and especially the unconscious relationship between patient and analyst at the heart of the therapeutic effort.

The relational matrix involves conflict, constructivism, and an overarching two-person perspective. Unconscious conflict is central to the drive model. In this model, the analyst strives to help the patient come to understand that sexuality and aggression are not as dangerous as they appear to be in the patient's fantasy-dominated child's mind. In the relational model, the traditional notion of conflict is maintained, but it is understood as containing conflicts over loyalties to parents, an idea attributable to W. R. D. Fairbairn's object relations theory. Thus, conflict is not located "in the person" but rather conflict may best be explained as both intrapersonal and interpersonal.

Constructivism in psychoanalysis holds that the observer plays a role in shaping, constructing, and organizing what is being observed. Psychoanalysis is a particular method for organizing what there is into unique patterns, but the patterns can be understood and organized in any number of ways. Thus, ambiguity and uncertainty are features of all human relatedness. This does not necessarily lead towards nihilism. On the contrary, it can propel theorists toward further elaboration and synthesis. For Irwin Hoffman, the paradigm shift in contemporary psychoanalysis is not necessarily from the drive model to the relational model, but from the positivist model to the constructivist model. Thus, the great divide is between dichotomous and dialectical thinking. What is meant by dialectic is a process in which each of two opposing concepts creates, informs, preserves, and negates the other, each standing in a dynamic relationship with the other. Among the pairs of phenomena Hoffman considers dialectically are doubt and certainty, possibilities and constraints, hierarchy and egalitarian relations; risk taking and responsibility; neurotic and existential anxiety; psychoanalysis as an instrument of healing and as cultural symptom; the analyst's intentions versus the patient's will; action and reflection; and analytic rituals and the analyst's spontaneity. Last, constructivism in psychoanalysis holds that analytic therapists do not have privileged access to their own motives, nor are they able to know exactly what is best for their patients. Hence, the patient's perception of the analyst's subjectivity is critical.

Stephen Mitchell has argued that the distinction between a monadic theory of mind (a one-person psychology) and an interactional relational theory of mind (a two-person psychology) is pivotal to understanding psychoanalytic concepts. In general, those theories greatly influenced by classical analysis have been referred to as one-person psychologies. They emphasize the individual experience of the patient and view the analyst as a blank screen onto which the patient projects wishes and fantasies. The two-person psychologies are influenced by the notion of the analyst as co-participant in the therapy. Emmanuel Ghent has described the history of psychoanalysis as constituted by dialectical shifts between one-person and two-person psychologies. Neil Altman has added to the dialogue by suggesting that we consider not a one-or two-person psychology but a three-person psychology. A good example of a three-person psychology would be thinking through the therapeutic relationship as it operates in a particular clinic or in conjunction with a specific insurance company.

Another important concept in relational psychoanalysis is that of intersubjectivity. Jessica Benjamin's work on intersubjectivity emphasizes mutual recognition as an intrinsic aspect of the development of the self. She argues that we need to maintain a tension in our theory between relating to others as objects and relating to others as separate subjects. The infant research of Daniel Stern on the development of a sense of self yields evidence for intersubjective relatedness, a relatedness that includes the recognition of subjective mental states in the other as well in oneself. By contrast, for Robert Stolorow and his colleagues, the term intersubjective is applied whenever two subjectivities constitute the field, even if one does not recognize the other as a separate subjectivity.

Recently, relational thinkers have been hypothesizing about how the mind is structured in an effort to redefine notions of the self. The self has usually been thought of as a continuous, unitary phenomenon. Philip Bromberg has described a state of multiple selves. This concept holds that people experience themselves not as unitary and unchanging but as consisting of multiple selves that may be compatible or incompatible with one another. For example, an adult self may be taking in a logical explanation about an interaction, while at the same time a child self simply feels vulnerable and angry. Multiple self-states are created not by unmet developmental needs, but by unintegrated, sometimes traumatic, early interactions with significant others. The therapeutic goal is to bring the different self-states into awareness and into a useful dialogue and not necessarily integration. For Jody Messler Davies multiple selves suggest a central role for the process of dissociation and consequently a very different vision of the unconscious. Unlike drive theory that utilizes the metaphor of an onion or an archaeological site for the unconscious, Davies prefers the metaphor of a kaleidoscope with which each glance through the pinhole of a moment in time provides a unique view and an infinite constellation of interconnectedness.

A fundamental principle in the relational model of psychoanalysis is that of mutuality. Mutuality is a process in which patient and analyst mutually regulate or mutually influence each other both consciously and unconsciously. What is regulated is subtle, but it can often involve feelings, thoughts, and actions. Heinrich Racker pointed out that analysis is not an interaction between a sick person and a healthy one, but rather an interaction between two personalities, each with healthy and pathological dynamics. Thus, the classical authority of the analyst has given way to a more democratic, respectful exploration of a joint reality. Mutuality means that the analyst and the patient are partners in the treatment, albeit unequal ones. This mutuality requires a certain type of emotional honesty from both participants. In the relational model, the analyst cannot function as a blank screen or a detached observer encouraging intense feelings in the patient and responding in a neutral manner. When mutuality in the clinical process is taken into account, dialectical tensions can arise. One such dialectical tension occurs between the patient's sense of the analyst as a person like himself or herself and the patient's sense of the analyst as a person with superior and magical power. Although the analyst engages in relative subordination of personal interests, the resolution of such tensions can be powerful emotional experiences for both participants.

IV. CLINICAL PROCESSES

The clinical attitude conveyed by a relational analyst depends very much on the particular analyst's personality, training, and the specific impact of a particular patient. She does not act as a judge of reality and nor does she presume that there is only one way to see something accurately. The patient's own sense of reality is greatly respected and encouraged. Compliant surrender to the analyst's presumed superior vision is not encouraged. The patient's observations and perceptions about the analyst are encouraged. Notwithstanding these attitudes, it is likely that there will develop repetitive reenactments of some of the most warping features of the patient's earlier experiences. These reenactments will likely involve the analyst and consequently also involve a range of feelings from attraction to conflict in relation to the analyst.

To a large extent, traditional analysis requires that the analyst interpret the true meaning of the patient's reactions to her. In contrast, when a patient feels discontent with her analyst, the relational approach requires both parties to examine how and why they are in conflict and to negotiate the conflict as best they can. This is a shift involving a move away from interpreting observer to active participant. The in-depth exploration will require that both parties track the way the patient's observations lead to conclusions about the analyst and how they might be reenactments in the here and now of earlier relationship difficulties.

Clinical psychoanalysts have tended to centralize the experiences of early childhood. The relational orientation acknowledges this importance as well, but it does not consider the uncovering of the past to be the major task of treatment. In the classical approach, the patient's problems are the result of repression; cure entails the release of impulses, fantasies, and memories from repression. The analyst interprets both the content of the repressed and also the ways the patient is defending against the content. The analyst helps the patient gain insight thereby releasing from repression unconscious conflicts and thus being cured. A number of relational approaches, particularly the British object relations school and the self psychology school, assume that from the moment of birth, the child's whole being has developed in the context of experiences with others. Normal development is thwarted due to inadequate parenting. What is curative in the analytic relationship is the analyst offering some form of basic parental responsiveness that was missed early on. The interpersonal approach regards the analyst's response to the patient as organized not along parent–child lines but rather along adult-to-adult lines requiring honest responses and engagement. Hence, relational analysts differ with respect to their use of efforts to reanimate stalled developmental processes or their use of frankness and authentic confrontations. For many espousing a more integrated relational approach, however, the belief is that the patient can be both child and adult. Both the realities and the fantasies of early childhood experiences are important to understand in detail, but the realities and fantasies of adulthood are also important to understand in detail.

In the most general sense, all psychoanalytic treatment paradigms value the analysis of transference. The relational paradigm, however, considers more than just the transference; it values the transference–countertransference matrix. Transference represents the emergence of feelings toward early childhood figures, displaced onto the person of the analysts. Historically, countertransference is the displacement of feelings from the analyst's past into the analytic situation. This was considered a seriously negative developmental in the analysis. The analyst was enjoined to rid herself of it through self-analysis or to return to her own psychoanalyst for help. Relational analysts have a different approach. They believe that countertransference is a normal state of affairs and that it can advance the analytic work. The transference–countertransference matrix is mutually determined and shaped by the conscious and unconscious beliefs, hopes, fears, and wishes of both patient and analyst.

The clinical approach of the relational model holds that the analytic situation is more that an arena for playing out the past; it is also where the patient is firmly engaged in the present. Thus, the patient is not simply displacing feelings from earlier relationships onto the analyst; he or she is likely to have observed a great deal about the analyst and to have constructed a plausible view of her. This view is, in part, based on the patient's own past and his typical way of organization experience. For example, an analyst can be experienced by a patient as critical of certain actions on the patient's part, and indeed that may be an opinion of the analyst. However, an indepth exploration of a patient's observations about the analyst can show that the criticism is different from the patient's mother and does not require allegiance from the patient for a personal connection to be maintained.

With the qualification that indeed psychoanalysts can suffer from the very same problems they are trying to assist patients with, relational ideas stress that countertransference can be (a) an ordinary, common responses to the sort of interpersonal positions and pressures a patient can set up; (b) an analyst–patient reenactment of a patient's past relationships; (c) a complex result of the patient's projective identification; and (d) something the patient is doing to strike responsive chords in the analyst.

Given that all analysts have a less than complete understanding of their own defenses, and that the patient may have picked up features of the countertransference that the analyst is not aware of, some analysts like Lewis Aron and Irwin Hoffman have argued for the usefulness of extended explorations of the patient's experience of and hypotheses about the analyst's experience. Such explorations give permission to patients who grew up feeling that their perceptions of their parents were forbidden and dangerous, and discounting their own observations albeit subtle and sometimes unformulated. Aron prefers to speak of the analyst's subjectivity instead of the analyst's countertransference. He believes that the term countertransference implies that the analyst's experience is reactive rather than subjective. The patient's perception of the analyst's subjectivity does not replace the historical analytic focus on the patient's experience, but it is seen as one component of the analysis.

To a large extent, relational analysts view self-disclosure as a form of intervention. It may involve the analyst revealing to the patient information, such as her thoughts or feelings about an interaction, something about the analyst's personal life, or the analyst's values and biases. Although the information may be useful, it is not disclosed as oracular. Other information besides the analyst's countertransference is necessary to confirm an idea about the patient's experience or to provide an interpretation. Nonetheless, many relational analysts believe that judiciously chosen self-disclosures can be helpful.

Finally, the two-person framework is interactive and makes more demands on the analyst to be attentive to the field—from disclosures that may momentarily focus attention on the analyst's mind, through analysis of interaction, to interpretation of the patient's intrapsychic activity. Clinical techniques are not to be objectified into a hard set of rules and regulations. Rather, psychoanalytic techniques are an interlocking set of clinical concepts that the analyst uses as a framework for analyzing the unique interactive matrix. The dialectical tension between the rules of restraint in the analytic relationship and the analyst's personal participation is a major controversy in contemporary psychoanalysis. The relational framework considers the joint critical reflection of such dialectical events crucial to the clinical process.

V. CONCLUSION

Relational psychoanalysis is a selective integration of various theoretical approaches. Its origins can be traced to contributions by various psychoanalysts and schools of psychoanalysis primarily interpersonal psychoanalysis, British object relations, and self psychology. In the last two decades it has evolved dramatically in the United States and is now the major challenge to the traditional Freudian school of psychoanalysis. Its current state of theoretical development and clinical innovations may make it a revolutionary challenge.

A major premise of relational analysis is that one's history of early relationships and present realities are critical. While classical Freudian theory holds that relatedness is a derivative of instinctual drives, relational theory considers relatedness to be at the center of human development and psychotherapy. In the clinical situation, relational analysts continuously track both the patient's subjectivity and their own. The relational matrix is understood to involve mutuality, conflict, and co-creation. Overall, the aim of relational psychoanalysis is to enrich the patient's experience, to expand the patient's degrees of personal freedom, and to examine the enormous complexities of the mind.

The success of the relational turn in psychoanalysis is consistent with a whole range of movements in other intellectual disciplines such as postmodernism. However, perhaps the major reason for its success is that it has proven to be a more useful approach to the problems in living that are presented in the consulting room of today. This utility in the day-to-day clinical work is based not on empirical research, which relational thinkers believe is only one of many narratives that can be useful, but on rigorous thinking, honest self-reflection and continuous cross-checking with clinical experience.

See Also the Following Articles

Acceptance and Commitment Therapy ■ Countertransference ■ History of Psychotherapy ■ Object-Relations Psychotherapy ■ Self Psychology ■ Sullivan's Interpersonal Psychotherapy ■ Transference

Further Reading

Altman, N. (1995). *The analyst in the inner city.* Hillsdale, NJ: The Analytic Press.

Aron, L. (1996). *A meeting of minds: Mutuality in psychoanalysis.* Hillsdale, NJ: The Analytic Press.

Benjamin, J. (1988). *The bonds of love: Psychoanalysis, feminism, and the problem of domination.* New York: Pantheon Books.

Bromberg, P. M. (1998). *Standing in the spaces: Essays on clinical process, trauma, and dissociation.* Hillsdale, NJ: The Analytic Press.

Davies, J. M., & Frawley, M. G. (1994). *Treating adult survivors of childhood sexual abuse: A psychoanalytic perspective.* New York: Basic Books.

Greenberg, J. R., & Mitchell. S. A. (1983). *Object relations in psychoanalytic theory.* Cambridge, MA: Harvard University Press.

Hoffman, I. Z. (1998). *Ritual and spontaneity in the psychoanalytic process: A dialectical-constructivist view.* Hillsdale, NJ: The Analytic Press.

Mitchell, S. A. (2000). *Relationality: From attachment to intersubjectivity.* Hillsdale, NJ: The Analytic Press.

Mitchell, S. A., & Aron, L. (Eds.). (1999). *Relational psychoanalysis: The emergence of a tradition.* Hillsdale, NJ: The Analytic Press.

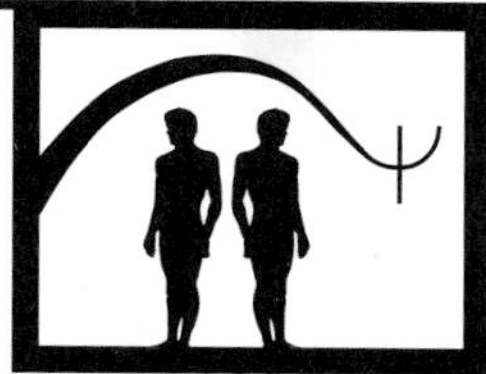

Relaxation Training

Daniel W. McNeil and Suzanne M. Lawrence
West Virginia University

GLOSSARY

autogenics Use of autosuggestions to evoke relaxation responses.

autosuggestion Process by which clients make self-statements, usually silently, that they then accept and believe.

biofeedback Integration of physiological assessment instrumentation (e.g., to record the temperature of the skin surface on one's finger) with audio or video stimuli (e.g., an outline of a human hand on a video monitor, with different colors indicating varying skin temperatures) to help a client learn to control physiological functions (e.g., skin temperature, muscle tension).

imagery Set of mental stimuli, existing cognitively, that can encompass all the senses (i.e., sights, sounds, tastes, smells, and tactile cues) that can be used to evoke a particular emotional or cognitive state (e.g., attention).

meditation Act of focused, quiet contemplation used to achieve a relaxed state.

patter Slow, rhythmic speech used by a therapist to maintain and enhance relaxation; repetition of statements often is involved.

relaxation Reducing or preventing levels of reactivity or arousal, in physiological, behavioral, or cognitive realms, which are so high as to constitute a problem.

I. DESCRIPTION OF TREATMENT

"Relaxation training" is a general term that refers to methods that are used to teach and learn specific techniques to help people moderate or control reactivity or arousal that is problematic to them. Often this term is associated solely with muscle relaxation, but given the commonalities among all relaxation-induction methods, we use it as an omnibus term. This label, then, includes various arousal control methods, such as muscle relaxation training, autogenics, biofeedback, meditation, imagery, and paced breathing. Hypnosis, often used to induce relaxation, has many similarities with these other methods, but is not reviewed in this article. The hyperarousal targeted by these techniques often is considered to be physiological (e.g., muscle tension), but can be cognitive (e.g., intrusive thoughts) or behavioral (e.g., fidgeting) as well. The widespread use and effectiveness of relaxation training have led some to call it "behavioral aspirin." The "training" component of relaxation training implies that it is a skill learned by someone, often a client or patient in a clinical setting, who ultimately can utilize it to induce relaxation on his or her own, in a variety of situations and settings. This procedure for producing relaxation then distinguishes it from other methods that are evoked by other persons (e.g., massage therapy) or substances (e.g., anxiety-reducing medications).

A. The Role of Relaxation Training in Behavior Therapy

Relaxation training often is used in behavior therapy as a means to reduce anxiety, tension, and stress. Research has shown it to be effective in a variety of disorders and conditions, primarily those related to anxiety, fear, and stress (e.g., specific phobias), but including those in the realm of behavioral medicine and dentistry, such as acute and chronic pain (e.g., tension headaches), hypertension, and coping with nausea related to chemotherapy. Training patients to relax typically involves providing a rationale, demonstrating exercises, and practicing relaxation in treatment sessions in clinics and hospitals. In addition, patients almost always are asked to practice ("homework") between therapy sessions. Often, forms or log books are used for patients to record details about their practice. Relaxation training can be relatively brief or long and more comprehensive. The former type has been referred to as "abbreviated" and the latter method as "deep," and has been associated with muscle relaxation.

Relaxation is a crucial ingredient in many empirically supported contemporary psychosocial treatments for various disorders, including such therapies as the Mastery of Your Anxiety and Panic program, which is a treatment for panic disorder. Relaxation training, in its various forms, is used most often as an adjunctive intervention, comprising one part of a comprehensive treatment program. Relaxation training also can be used to help facilitate communication during a therapy session with a client who may be too tense or anxious to communicate effectively with the therapist. Relaxation training (especially progressive muscle relaxation) often is used in conjunction with systematic desensitization, a procedure designed to lower fear or anxiety toward a specific stimulus (or stimuli) by pairing the feared stimulus or thoughts of the feared stimulus with relaxation.

B. Types of Relaxation Training

1. Progressive Relaxation Training

Progressive relaxation training (PRT) focuses on muscle relaxation; it is a widely used relaxation technique in behavior therapy, and has been the subject of considerable empirical research. Under the direction of the therapist, the client alternately tenses and then relaxes isolated muscle groups, until the entire body is completely relaxed. The rationale is that tensing the muscles before attempting to relax allows the client to become more aware of muscle tension, so as to be able to identify it when it occurs. The contrast between the tense and relaxed states also may help the client achieve a deeper state of relaxation than would be possible when begining from a resting state. By focusing on the feelings of tension and relaxation, the client can even learn to induce deep relaxation at a later time by using a recall procedure, allowing him or her to achieve a similar state of relaxation without actually creating muscle tension.

The exercises of progressive relaxation training follow a general sequence of individual muscle groups; each muscle group is relaxed as completely as possible before moving on to the next one. The most common contemporary methods include 16 muscle groups. As training progresses, the muscle tension exercises can be combined into 8 and then 4 groups. The specific order of muscle groups used varies according to the practitioner and his or her adherence to a particular sequence recommended in the literature, as well as to individual needs of the client. One possible sequence involves the following order:

1. Right (or dominant) hand and forearm
1. Right (or dominant) biceps
2. Left (or opposite) hand and forearm
3. Left (or opposite) biceps
4. Shoulders and upper back
5. Neck
6. Lower cheeks and jaws
7. Upper cheeks and nose
8. Forehead
9. Chest (breathing)
10. Abdominal region
11. Right (or dominant) thigh
12. Right (or dominant) calf
13. Right (or dominant) foot
14. Left (or opposite) thigh
15. Left (or opposite) calf
16. Left (or opposite) foot

The entire procedure is carefully controlled by the therapist; each exercise is precisely timed. Muscle tension is maintained for 5 to 7 seconds, during which the clinician may make such statements as "feel the tightness of the muscle; notice what the tension in the muscles feels like." The therapist will then instruct the client to relax, and make statements to direct the client's attention to the feelings of relaxation. This relaxation "patter" is used to capture the client's attention, to soothe and to encourage focusing of attention, and to promote quiescence. The relaxation part of the cycle continues for 30 to 40 seconds, after which the tension-release cycle is repeated. During early sessions of progressive relaxation training, the tension-release cycle typically is performed twice on each muscle group to ensure complete relaxation. In later sessions, after the client is familiar with the feelings of tension and relaxation, the procedure is often abbreviated, as already noted, to fewer steps by tensing combined muscle groups (i.e., both legs simultaneously instead of each leg individually).

Once clients are comfortable with the briefer procedure, a recall procedure may be taught that can be used in a wider variety of settings. This "cue-controlled relaxation" does not involve any actual tensing of the muscles, but rather the client recalls the feelings of relaxation using a cue word such as "relax." The cue word is paired with relaxation in treatment sessions and becomes associated with the feeling of deep relaxation through conditioning. Another use of PRT is in differential relaxation training, in which clients are taught to recognize the muscles that are necessary in which activities (e.g., while standing) so that one can ensure that muscles not involved in that activity have minimum tension.

Edmund Jacobsen pioneered PRT in the 1930s. In his research, he found that persons who deeply relaxed their skeletal muscles did not show a normal startle response. Expanding on these findings, he developed a technique in which alternately tensing and releasing individual muscle groups, and learning to attend to and discriminate between the feelings of tension and relaxation, could moderate tension and produce relaxation. In the 1940s and 1950s, progressive relaxation training came to the attention of Joseph Wolpe, who in his research with cats, had discovered that a conditioned fear response could be diminished and even eliminated if an incompatible response (such as relaxation) was induced at the time of fear. Wolpe shortened Jacobson's methods, to make it feasible to use them in clinical settings. He used PRT in conjuction with systematic desensitization, as a way of producing relaxation during the reconditioning of fears in clinical patients. In 1973, Douglas Bernstein and Thomas Borkovec also streamlined Jacobson's approach, and produced a step-by-step treatment PRT manual for therapists. Since that time, there has been a great deal of research on PRT, and numerous variants and extensions of it have been forwarded.

2. Behavioral Relaxation Training

In 1988 Roger Poppen published a book on behavioral relaxation training (BRT), a variant of PRT based on modeling and operant conditioning. Like progressive muscle relaxation training, it emphasizes overt motoric behavior, which is important because it facilitates direct observation of the behavior by both the client and the therapist. Behavioral relaxation training is unique from progressive muscle relaxation training in its emphasis on observable behavior, including posture. Clients are instructed to observe their overt postures, as well as to be aware of feelings of relaxation. BRT also is somewhat different from progressive relaxation in that it is composed of four discrete steps for each of 10 postures or activities, including the hands, breathing, and other components very similar to that of PRT.

1. *Labeling:* A one-word label (e.g., feet) is assigned to each behavior (or posture) to facilitate communication between client and therapist.
2. *Description and modeling:* The therapist explains and demonstrates the relaxed posture, and contrasts it with frequently occurring unrelaxed postures.
3. *Imitation:* The client displays each posture.
4. *Feedback:* The therapist praises accurate posture portrayal, or provides corrective cueing if the client's posture is incorrect. Gentle manual guidance may be used by the therapist if the client is unsuccessful in achieving correct relaxed postures after several attempts. Positive feedback is then given for the correct postures.

The client maintains each correct posture for 30 to 60 seconds while being aware of the relaxation feelings. There are specific postures or behaviors for the hands, feet, body, shoulders, head, mouth, throat, quiet breathing, and eyes.

As a method of behaviorally assessing relaxation, Poppen devised the Behavioral Relaxation Scale (BRS). There are 10 descriptions of postures and activities in the BRS that are considered to be characteristic of one who is completely relaxed. Relaxation is assessed during an observation session at the conclusion of the session, or before relaxation as a baseline measure. Although the BRS was designed for use with BRT, it can also be used to assess relaxation induced by other methods.

Poppen proposed a taxonomy for analyzing complex behavior that can be easily applied to relaxation. His conceptualization of behavior is that it occurs in four domains: motoric, verbal, visceral, and observational. Poppen claimed that most relaxation techniques emphasize only one or another of these modalities while ignoring the others. BRT is intended to address all four of these areas.

3. Applied Relaxation

Another variant, and an extension of PRT, is applied relaxation, which was described by Lars-Goran Öst in

1987. It is conceptualized as a coping technique that focuses on physiological reactions when a person encounters a phobic object or situation. The intent is for the relaxation skill to be applied rapidly when confronted with such an event, to foster coping. Applied relaxation is intended to counteract, and later to prevent, phobic-level physiological reactions. Training includes the recognition of anxiety signals early in the chain of reactions to phobic events. PRT is then taught, followed by a shortened version in which only the relaxation (or muscle release) component is included. Cue-controlled relaxation is then reviewed, followed by differential relaxation. A somewhat unique component of applied relaxation is its focus on rapid relaxation in the natural environment. Then, application training ensues, first in generally stressful but nonphobic situations, and later in actual exposure to phobic objects or situations.

4. Stretch Relaxation

Much like PRT, stretch relaxation also is based on achieving a quiescent state through decreased muscle tension. The major distinction is that stretch relaxation does not require the individual to tense and release muscle groups. Rather, the reduction in tension is achieved through the systematic stretching of individual muscle groups. This technique was developed by Charles Carlson and colleagues, in part because some patient populations find the tensing and releasing of muscles painful or distressing, or that it is inappropriate for them. For example, some pain patients find that tensing their muscles increases pain and does not readily allow subsequent relaxation. Patients with certain cardiovascular problems, such as patients in whom creating muscle tension could cause arrhythmias or elevated blood pressure, also may be inappropriate candidates for progressive muscle relaxation. Stretch relaxation training is often an effective alternative treatment for these patients.

The process involves a series of 14 muscle-stretching exercises. Prior to the actual stretching exercises, the individual is instructed to assume a quiet resting position and breathe slowly and deeply. After 3 to 4 minutes of physical resting and relaxed breathing, the client or patient begins the stretching exercises, starting with the lower right leg and progressing through the 14 muscle groups. Similar to PRT that involves muscle tensing, stretching is utilized for the separate muscle groups in the extremities, back, buttocks, stomach, chest, forehead, eyes, jaws, neck, and shoulders. Examples of stretching exercises are those for the upper leg, in which one knee is raised and placed over the other leg to sag, and those for the shoulders and upper arms, in which the fingers of the hands are interlocked and the arms are raised over the head.

Each stretch is held for 15 seconds, and is followed by 60 seconds of relaxation. Clients are instructed to focus their attention on the sensations of stretching and relaxation and to breathe using a slow, regular rhythm.

5. Autogenic Training

Autogenic training (AT) is a passive autosuggestion technique with the goal of self-produced relaxation with a minimal amount of training. AT is used extensively in Europe, Russia, and Japan, but is less popular in North America. Some of the conceptualizations and wording are not common in American culture. In contrast to progressive muscle and stretch relaxation, AT is passive rather than active. It consists of six mental exercises that are based on short autosuggestions, or "formulas." Sensory feelings and states are emphasized, including heaviness and warmth in the extremities, regulation of respiration and cardiac activity, abdominal warmth, and coolness of the forehead. The therapist uses a calm, relaxed voice and makes statements about these feelings and physical states, which the client then repeats internally. The exercises are learned in a specific sequence, and the client achieves each state before initiating the next exercise. The six exercises or "formulas" are:

1. *Heaviness formula:* This exercise is intended to affect the muscles and reduce muscular tension. The therapist might utter a statement such as: "My left leg is very heavy."
2. *Warmth formula:* Blood circulation and dilation of blood vessels is the focus of this formula. The clinician focusing on this area with clients might suggest: "My right arm is very warm."
3. *Heart regulation:* Encouraging awareness of heart activity is the primary consideration, after which regulation of heart activity is the goal, consistent with statements such as "My heart is beating calmly and strongly."
4. *Breathing regulation:* Regular respiration is the key issue for this formula. Voluntary changes in breathing pattern are considered undesirable because that can involve tensing muscles and movement. Passive phrases are used, such as "It breathes me."
5. *Regulation of the visceral organs:* Clients focus their attention on the solar plexus as the central nerve center for the internal organs. A typical statement may be "Warmth radiates over my abdomen."

6. *Regulation of the temperature of the head:* Using statements such as "My forehead is cool," clients imagine the feeling of a cool cloth on their forehead, with the result of localized movement of blood away from the surface of the skin (i.e., vasoconstriction) on the forehead, creating sensations of coolness.

Autogenic training developed along a similar timeline to progressive relaxation training. In 1932, a German physiologist named Johannes Schultz began developing AT as a passive form of controlling arousal. Early psychophysiological studies led him and his colleagues to assert that the state brought about by AT was unique, and different from conscious awareness, sleep, or hypnosis. Electroencephalograph (EEG) recordings during AT led to the conception of the autogenic state as similar to a "pre-sleep state." Schultz believed that the shift from consciousness to the autogenic state was a specific process that involved changes in both psychological and physiological functioning, and allowed the person to "step behind" or "dive under" the usual conscious waking state. Schultz and his colleague Wolfgang Luthe believed that the mental and physical relaxation brought about by their procedure could eventually lead to relief from many physiological and psychological problems.

6. Biofeedback

The term biofeedback refers to a variety of procedures that provide ongoing information about physiological activity to persons attempting to learn to modify their physiological levels and responses. In particular, electromyographic (EMG) biofeedback is often employed as a relaxation technique to help people to control their levels of muscle tension. Thermal biofeedback also is common, in which the temperature of the skin surface is monitored, usually on a finger or foot, as increased blood flow to the skin surface is associated with relaxation. The general aim of biofeedback is to teach clients to use the feedback to gain conscious control of biological responses (e.g., skin temperature, heart rate) that have been operating maladaptively and that were previously thought to be uncontrollable. Biofeedback is shown to be effective across a variety of conditions, most notably anxiety disorders, tension headache, insomnia, and hypertension. In many cases biofeedback does more than teach individuals how to regulate their biological functions; it can also help improve their sense of personal control and ability to cope with stressful situations by showing that it is in fact possible to control the physiological events that accompany everyday life.

There are three major stages in biofeedback training. In the first stage, the client becomes aware of the maladaptive response (e.g., muscle tension) and learns that certain thoughts and biological events can influence the given response. The patient can relax some with a conscious effort. In the second stage, the client gains better control over the maladaptive response and can consciously relax with greater ease. The third stage marks the point at which the client can readily transfer the control to daily life, and can relax with little or no conscious effort.

Biofeedback training requires the use of instrumentation of varying degrees of sophistication. The essential requirement is that clients be provided with either visual or auditory information regarding their bodily state, usually in "real time," as the person's physiology is responding. The form of the feedback varies, can be shown visually on a video monitor, and/or can be transmitted by auditory tones or clicks, with higher or lower frequencies indicating the physiological response is increasing or decreasing.

Interest in biofeedback as a therapeutic technique burgeoned in the 1960s as a result of the work of various investigators. Among them, Joe Kamiya developed a technique of controlling alpha (EEG) rhythm by use of a tone to indicate that the brain was producing alpha waves. Second, Neal Miller demonstrated that autonomic responses could be conditioned through operant procedures in animals. Also, Thomas Budzynski and his colleagues built an alpha EEG feedback device with the intent of teaching subjects to produce more pleasant, tranquil alpha brain wave activity. Thereafter, attention shifted away from alpha feedback and toward skin surface feedback, generally measured through electrodes placed on the forehead to record facial muscle activity. This progression in research was based on investigations that found that the frontalis muscle of the forehead was a reliable indicator of anxiety, tension, and arousal. Over the years since this early research, EMG biofeedback has been demonstrated to be effective in helping clients to learn to reduce tension in the muscles of the head and scalp, thereby producing long-lasting reductions in tension headaches, among other uses.

7. Meditation

One of the currently most popular methods of relaxation is meditation. Examples are transcendental meditation and mindfulness meditation. In many forms, meditation enjoys widespread use across many lands and cultures. Quite old forms of meditation are involved in yoga practice; Japanese Zen, Chinese Tao, Hindu, and

Buddhist meditation are other forms. Some forms of meditation are associated with religious and spiritual beliefs about lifestyle. Others have no connection with religion or spirituality, but focus specifically on feelings of peacefulness and concentration. Across types of meditation, there are some qualities that are common to most or all of them.

First, meditation requires a comfortable position, usually sitting or lying down. Second, like other relaxation techniques, it usually must take place in a quiet, peaceful setting where interruption is unlikely. Thirdly, individuals regulate their breathing to a slow steady pace. Fourth, mental or cognitive activity during meditation often is focused on a particular word or phrase (e.g., a "mantra"). Some types of meditation, however, require the individual to empty the mind, think of nothing, and meditate on that mental silence.

One meditation technique that deserves special attention is one developed by Herbert Benson in 1975 termed "the relaxation response." Benson based his technique on laboratory observations of practitioners of transcendental meditation. He found that during meditation, the oxygen consumption and blood lactate levels of his subjects dropped to levels similar to those seen in sleep or hibernation. He concluded that meditation led to a hypometabolic state, which he termed the "relaxation response." Benson went on to specify a method to meditate in which one can acheieve the desired response through four crucial elements:

1. *Quiet environment:* A quiet place is essential for meditation practice, so as to eliminate distracting noises. Also, in this and most other forms of relaxation, the client closes his or her eyes, to reduce distracting visual stimuli.
2. *Target object to dwell on:* The target can be a repeated word, phrase, sound, symbol, or image, or can involve focusing on a particular feeling.
3. *Passive attitude:* The individual should allow thoughts and feelings to drift in and out of awareness without concentrating on them. Ongoing self-evaluation of progress with meditation practice should be avoided. Maintaining a passive attitude was identified by Benson as the most crucial factor in eliciting the relaxation response.
4. *Comfortable position:* As with most forms of relaxation, it is usually necessary for the person to be in a sitting position that can be comfortably maintained for at least 20 minutes.

Although Benson's technique has not been subjected to the same amount of empirical research as other techniques such as PRT or biofeedback, it has enjoyed widespread popularity in the United States and elsewhere.

8. Guided Imagery

In the use of guided imagery, the therapist and client develop imagery scenes that produce feelings of calmness, tranquility, or pleasure for the client. It is critical that the therapist consult with the client as to the appropriateness of scenes, as a scene thought to be calming (e.g., sitting at a waterfall) may not be relaxing to a particular individual (e.g., one who is phobic of water). The scenes are embellished with as much sensory detail as possible, both to make the imagery seem more real and to completely involve or "absorb" the client in the experience. Common settings for guided imagery include the beach, a tranquil forest, or a mountaintop. Note the sensory detail in these scene instructions:

> Close your eyes, sit back, take a few deep breaths, and relax. While your eyes remain closed, sitting in the chair and feeling relaxed, think about yourself on a tropical island. Make this image as real as possible, as if you really are there. As you look up, there are a few wispy clouds scattered across the brilliant blue sky. The turquoise ocean tumbles toward the shore in gentle, foam-capped waves. Gulls fly overhead; you hear their distant squawks. You feel the bright, warm rays of sun over your entire body and the light breeze blowing over your skin. You taste the salt from the air, as the wind blows in from the water. Walking along the beach, you encounter pleasing flowery scents from the nearby groves of tropical trees.

Actual scenes can be much longer. After the scene has been developed, clients are instructed to practice using the scene. In practicing, clients often focus on the scene for approximately 30 seconds, trying to picture, feel, and otherwise sense as much detail as possible. Over time, they should be able to readily and reliably evoke the image, leading to relaxation. It is possible also for clients to use the imagery to inoculate themselves from stressful or fear-provoking situations, or to mediate those reactions once they have begun. Guided imagery is often used as a distraction from pain during medical and dental procedures, or to combat anxiety during a feared situation.

Guided imagery relies somewhat on the clients' abilities to vividly imagine scenes, so in clinical practice, it may be important for the therapist to assess the clients' abilities in this area. Imagery ability can be assessed informally by asking clients to recall a particular event they enjoyed. Allowing clients to relax, the therapist then asks for as many details as they can provide, after which clients rate the vividness of the image, for example, on a 1 to 10 scale. Another way to assess imagery ability is to use a rating scale in which the clients are instructed to imagine a variety of scenes and to rate the vividness of each. For clients whose skills are not well developed, imagery training can be employed to help them effectively utilize guided imagery.

9. Paced Breathing

Deep, regular breathing is a component of most relaxation training strategies. Many clients who experience problem levels of stress often have breathing-related complaints, and most of the symptoms associated with stress are those associated with hyperventilation. Variations in breathing patterns have an effect on cardiovascular functioning. Diaphragmatic breathing is a technique that teaches clients to breathe deeply using the diaphragm, expanding the abdomen rather than the chest. One of the most common ways of teaching diaphragmatic breathing is to have clients place their hand on the abdomen while breathing slowly. The client is instructed to breathe so that the hand on the abdomen raises up, minimizing any movement in the upper chest. Breathing in this manner allows the individual to inhale more air than normal shallow breathing. Deep breathing has been shown to release stress and tension, build energy and endurance, help with pain management, and to enhance mental concentration and physical performance. It can be taught as part of another relaxation technique or alone. Deep breathing usually is easily taught in one therapeutic session, and has the advantage that it can easily and unobtrusively be used by clients during the day whenever a stressful situation emerges.

C. Clinical Assessment and Treatment Issues

As with any treatment, assessment is a key issue in relaxation training. Identifying who can and cannot benefit from a given treatment is a critical consideration, although psychological science has not yet evolved to the point that it is known which treatments match to which clients. Those relaxation methods that focus on muscle tension or stretching may be particularly appropriate for clients who have high levels of tension and tension-related ailments, such as tension headache. Persons with highly reactive cognitive processes (e.g., worry, intrusive thoughts) may be well suited for those techniques that emphasize control over one's thinking. Relaxation skills can be taught in individual or group settings. There are numerous commercially available relaxation programs, including various media (e.g., audiotapes), for clients and therapists.

There are some considerations to be addressed in employing relaxation training. The first of these considerations is medical in nature. Before deciding on relaxation training, the clinician should ensure that medical problems have been properly evaluated, and that treatment has been provided or is ongoing. Many times, relaxation methods are a helpful adjunctive treatment for clients who have diseases (e.g., cardiovascular disease), and can be used in conjunction with medications. Another consideration is the possibility of contraindications to the use of relaxation training. Some clients (such as chronic pain patients, and those with temporomandibular joint [jaw] dysfunction) are advised not to tense certain muscle groups, so techniques that involve the tensing or stretching of muscles may not be the treatment of choice, although if only a few muscle groups are involved, the tension component can be skipped for them. Another issue to consider in using relaxation training is the source of the tension. If a person's tension is excessive or out of proportion to a situation, then relaxation training may be particularly appropriate. If, however, there is a life situation (e.g., marital disharmony) that is amenable to change that is leading to the problem tension, then addressing that problem directly (e.g., marital therapy) may be the treatment of choice. Another point to consider is that tension may be a conditioned response to some specific environmental stimuli. In this case, relaxation training alone may not be sufficient. Instead, systematic desensitization or *in vivo* exposure may be more appropriate. Finally, the preference of the client should be a prime consideration in choice of a relaxation strategy. As there presently are no hard and fast guidelines about which methods to use with which persons, client preferences may well be one of the most important factors currently in predicting treatment success.

Not everyone will benefit from relaxation training. Although it is rare, relaxation training sometimes can actually induce anxiety or even panic in some clients. There have been several explanations offered for such a reaction. One is that relaxation causes new and unusual sensations in the body, such as feelings of disorientation, or "floating." These unfamiliar feelings may provoke anxiety in some clients. Other patients may have a fear of losing control. It has been hypothesized that some people with chronic, pervasive anxiety may have learned to control their anxiety by never letting go or permitting themselves to relax. The feeling of loss of control associated with relaxation can cause excess anxiety in such individuals.

II. THEORETICAL BASES

By emphasizing "training," the conceptual underpinnings of relaxation training obviously include learning. It is assumed that individuals learn a new skill, enhance existing abilities, or learn to utilize existing adaptive responses. Some individuals may need relaxation training because of extreme life circumstances (e.g., undergoing chemotherapy). Others may have a unique psychophysiology, behavioral functioning, or cognitive processing that predisposes them to psychological problems that are amenable to relaxation training. The problem response may either be chronic (e.g., hyperactivity in the muscles due to job-related stress), acute (e.g., intense response to a phobia, such as public speaking phobia), or both. Regardless of the reason for the problematic physiological, cognitive, or behavioral response, training is utilized to develop, enhance, or prompt relaxation-related skills.

There are elements of classical conditioning, operant conditioning, and observational learning in relaxation training. The relaxed state is classically conditioned to various stimuli (e.g., sitting in a dimly lit room, closing one's eyes while sitting in a relaxed posture). Operant conditioning principles are employed, for example, when therapists use positive reinforcement for praising clients for proper use of relaxation procedures. When therapists model or demonstrate appropriate relaxation postures, for example, observational learning occurs. Moreover, in some forms of relaxation training (e.g., PRT), the individual is specifically taught to discriminate between tense and relaxed states. This training allows clients to discern more accurately tense and relaxed states, particularly in terms of muscle tension, which should allow then to prevent tension before it reaches problematic levels. In other types of relaxation training, the focus is on learning the relaxation response itself, and clients are encouraged to turn their attention away from impediments to relaxation (e.g., intrusive thoughts).

III. EMPIRICAL STUDIES

There is a wide body of literature that supports relaxation training as an effective therapy for a wide range of disorders. One problem with much of the existing data, however, is that most studies combine relaxation training with other forms of therapy; it rarely is used in isolation. Charles Carlson, who originated stretch relaxation, and a colleague, conducted a review in 1993 of 29 experiments with relaxation training. Their statistical analyses suggested that relaxation training is effective for a range of disorders, particularly including tension headache. Individual training was found to be superior to group sessions, and training audiotapes for home practice were determined to increase treatment effectiveness. Longer treatment duration in each session, and greater numbers of sessions, also were associated with more positive treatment outcome. In addition to this "meta-analysis" of the findings of a number of studies, recent individual experiments also provide strong support for the effectiveness of various forms of relaxation training.

One example is an investigation by F. Dudley McGlynn and colleagues in 1999; they examined the effects of PRT on levels of fear and arousal during *in vivo* exposure to phobic stimuli. There were 10 snake phobic individuals who were given six sessions of progressive relaxation training, while another 10 were not. All participants were then exposed six times to a 4-minute viewing of a caged snake on a conveyor; they were able to control how close the snake came to them. The distance between the subject and the snake was measured, a self-report measure of fear was obtained, and heart rate and sweat gland activity were recorded. Data analyses showed that the individuals trained in progressive relaxation had significantly lower fear ratings, and a smaller degree of heart rate change, throughout the course of snake exposure. These findings support the use of PRT prior to *in vivo* desensitization procedures.

As another example, a study of applied relaxation by Lars-Goran Öst and a colleague in 2000 compared it to cognitive therapy in the treatment of generalized anxiety disorder. There were 36 patients who met criteria for this anxiety disorder who were randomly selected to receive either one or the other of the treatments. At posttreatment assessment, both treatment groups showed clinically significant and lasting improvements in a variety of areas, including worry, cognitive and somatic anxiety, and depression.

IV. SUMMARY

Varying types of psychosocially based relaxation inductions have been used across known history. In the latter part of the 20th century, and into the 21st century, empirically tested forms of relaxation training have become widely available. There are many commonalities among the various forms of relaxation training, but each has its own unique characteristics. Some of the differences among these methods are based on societal perceptions, and the different labels that are used to describe them. Some of the similarities of these methods include the client being in an environment relatively free of distractions (e.g., a quiet, dimly lit room) so as to reduce distractions, reposing in a relaxed posture (usually sitting), focusing on a specific stimulus (such as the therapist's voice in PRT, or a "mantra" in meditation), and having guidance by a practitioner using a soothing voice and calm manner. Clinicians now have a wide array of relaxation methods to choose from, allowing more individualized treatment for clients with complaints including anxiety, hypertension, insomnia, pain (including tension headaches), and many others. As in any science, research will progress to reveal more information about relaxation and its beneficial effects and limitations, and techniques will continue to improve.

See Also the Following Articles

Anxiety Management Training ■ Applied Relaxation ■ Applied Tension ■ Biofeedback ■ Emotive Imagery ■ Progressive Relaxation ■ Stretch-Based Relaxation Training

Further Reading

Benson, H. B. (1975). *The relaxation response.* New York: William Morrow.

Bernstein, D. A., Borkovec, T. D., & Hazlett–Stevens, H. (2000). *New directions in progressive relaxation training: A guidebook for helping professionals.* Westport, CT: Praeger.

Carlson, C. R., & Hoyle, R. H. (1993). Efficacy of abbreviated progressive muscle relaxation training: A quantitative review of behavioral medicine research. *Journal of Consulting and Clinical Psychology, 61,* 1059–1067.

Cautela, J. R., & Groden, J. (1978). *Relaxation: A comprehensive manual for adults, children, and children with special needs.* Champaign, IL: Research Press.

Davis, M., Eshelman, E. R., & McKay, M. (1988). *The relaxation & stress reduction workbook* (3rd ed.). Oakland, CA: New Harbinger.

Jacobson, E. (1970). *Modern treatment of tense patients.* Springfield, IL: Charles C Thomas.

Lichstein, K. L. (1988). *Clinical relaxation strategies.* New York: Wiley.

Öst, L-G. (1987). Applied relaxation: Description of a coping technique and review of controlled studies. *Behaviour Research and Therapy, 25,* 397–409.

Poppen, R. (1988). *Behavioral relaxation training and assessment.* New York: Permagon.

Wolfgang, L. (1990). *Autogenic training: A clinical guide.* New York: Guilford.

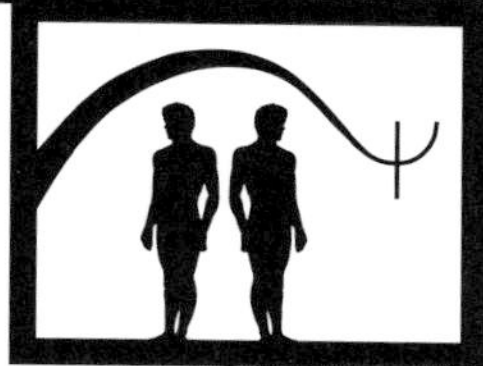

Research in Psychotherapy

Karla Moras
University of Pennsylvania

GLOSSARY

effect size A statistic that often is used in therapy research to indicate the magnitude of the difference in outcomes (or "effects") found in a research study between alternative treatments or between a treatment and an un- or minimally treated control group.

external validity A concept that refers to the inferences that can be accurately drawn from a research study's findings, specifically the confidence with which findings can be assumed to "generalize" or extend to situations, people, measures, times, and so on other than those particular to the study. A study's research design and methodology are major determinants of the external validity of its findings.

internal validity A concept that refers to the inferences that can be accurately drawn from a study's findings, specifically the confidence with which a causal relationship can be assumed to exist between a study's independent variables (e.g., forms of therapy) and dependent variables (e.g., outcomes or effects in a therapy study). The fit between a study's hypotheses, research design, and methodology is a major determinant of its internal validity.

managed care corporation A for-profit business that sells health care insurance contracts to employers and to individuals. Managed care corporations differ from traditional indemnity insurance companies in that the former directly oversee and control access to treatment by those who hold its contracts.

outcome research Studies that are designed primarily to test hypotheses and answer questions about the effects of psychotherapy and other treatments. "Outcome" is used as a synonym for "effects." For example, outcome studies can be designed to answer comparative treatment questions like, "Is cognitive-behavioral therapy associated with more improvement in depression than interpersonal psychotherapy?"

patient In the therapy research literature one of two words, "patient" or "client," usually is used to refer to a person who is the direct recipient of psychotherapeutic services. "Patient" typically is used in more medically dominated settings such as departments of psychiatry, "client" in more psychologically dominated settings such as university counseling clinics. Herein, the term patient is used.

psychoneurotic A global psychodiagnostic term that was in common use until about 1980. It connotes a wide range of problems that now (2002) are called anxiety disorders, unipolar depressions, and personality disorders in the American Psychiatric Association's diagnostic nomenclature (*Diagnostic and Statistical Manual of Mental Disorders*). "Psychoneurotic" typically did not refer to what are considered more severe disorders such as schizophrenia and bipolar disorder.

psychopathology research A field that is focused on (a) distinguishing normal and abnormal human psychological, emotional, and behavioral functioning; (b) identifying causes for abnormalities; and (c) developing methods to assess and taxonomies for varieties of abnormal functioning.

psychotherapy Psychotherapy is used in this article as a synonym for "psychological therapies." It refers to all forms of treatment in which the primary therapeutic agent is a person (e.g., in contrast to an instrument or machine) who relies exclusively on verbal/conceptual, psychoeducational, or behavioral methods, rather than on pharmacological or other somatic methods (such as electroconvulsive treatment or rapid transcranial magnetic stimulation), to ameliorate a broad array of behavioral and psychological problems, many of which fall under the contemporary medical terms, "mental illnesses" and "psychiatric disorders."

statistical significance A mathematically derived index of the probability that a research finding is valid versus due to chance.

I. INTRODUCTION

Psychotherapy research in the United States is a relatively young field, about 60 to 80 years old depending on the perspective taken. It encompasses a diverse array of activities, a uniting goal of which is to create a scientific foundation for the practice of psychotherapy. Alan Kazdin, a contemporary expert on psychotherapy research, described its aims this way: "To understand alternative forms of treatment, the mechanisms and processes through which these treatments operate, and the impact of treatment and moderating influences on maladaptive and adaptive functioning."

A broad mix of research strategies and methods are used to achieve the preceding aims. They span a continuum from relatively "uncontrolled" methods (e.g., systematic, naturalistic observation) to experimental procedures that are used to control (reduce the potential impact of) some variables so that the operation of others can be observed more clearly and precisely. Psychology and, in particular, clinical psychology often are said to be the parent disciplines of psychotherapy research in the United States. Other disciplines, notably psychiatry, also have made important contributions to it from the outset. The relatively short history of psychotherapy research includes marked shifts of focus ("turning points" herein), as well as scientific advancements ("milestones" herein). The field also has some long-standing, unanswered fundamental questions.

One goal of this article is to convey the dynamic nature of psychotherapy research—its responsiveness to social issues, government needs for information on which to base policy, developments in related fields—as well as to its own discoveries and other advances. A second goal is to provide an overview of some of the field's defining, substantive features as they have evolved to the present. The features described are primarily key research questions. A few, related research methods also are described. Detail on the conduct of psychotherapy research is not provided, nor are findings on different questions reviewed in depth. Relevant research methods (e.g., study design, measurement, statistical data analysis strategies) are extensive and are well described in many excellent sources, a few of which are listed in Further Reading. Similarly, sophisticated and comprehensive reviews of findings from the thousands of psychotherapy research studies that have accumulated over the years can be found in the five editions to date of *The Handbook of Psychotherapy and Behavior Change.*

A single article on an entire field of research requires many inclusion and exclusion decisions. This article is focused solely on the development of psychotherapy research in the United States. It also is limited to research on individual psychotherapy (not group or family therapy) for adults (not children or adolescents). The content pertains most directly to therapy research for problems other than addictions (e.g., to alcohol and drugs of abuse such as heroin) because substance abuse treatment research in the United States followed a partially separate developmental path. Within the preceding delimitations, a guiding principle was to highlight scientific milestones and turning points. Turning points herein are findings or events that changed the direction of at least a notable constituency of therapy researchers. Milestones are findings or other research-related developments that improved the possible scientific quality of research or its immediate value for informing clinical practice (the two are not distinct: "findings" from studies with poor scientific quality rarely if ever are properly regarded as having immediate implications for practice). Of course, the identification of milestones and turning points lies in the eyes of the beholder. To reduce the extent to which the topics discussed mainly reflect idiosyncratic biases of the author, several dedicated experts in psychotherapy research graciously reviewed the article (see Acknowledgments).

The preceding precaution could not eliminate another type of limitation. Doing psychotherapy research teaches well the general lesson that some "facts" are highly dependent on the perceiver. The author has been involved in therapy research for over 25 years in a variety of settings. Nevertheless, a participant–observer's perspective always is limited to just part of "the elephant" that is one's field. In addition, the perspectives herein on the primary forces that prompted turning points are likely to both overlap with and differ somewhat from descriptions by others who had different vantage points and who were influenced by different contingencies.

II. HISTORICAL OVERVIEW

Psychotherapy research is a branch of research on treatments for psychological, emotional, and behavioral problems, that is, for problems often referred to by the medically oriented term, "mental illnesses." The development of psychotherapy research has a strong historical link to clinical psychology. The link was solidified in 1949 at the Conference on Graduate Education in Clinical Psychology that was held in Boulder, Colorado. The "Boulder model," also known as the scientist–practitioner model of graduate-level training in clinical psychology, was established then. The essence of the Boulder model is that the doctoral degree (Ph.D.) in clinical psychology should be based on training both in research methods and in the clinical application of (i.e., direct use with people) psychotherapeutic interventions. To this day, Ph.D. clinical psychologists are expected to be able to conduct and evaluate research relevant to their field, as well as to provide psychotherapeutic services.

The psychotherapy studies done by clinical psychologists and other therapy researchers examine a broad range of questions. Some are designed mainly to answer more basic questions (e.g., "How do psychotherapies work?"), whereas others are designed to answer questions that have immediate implications for the practice of psychotherapy such as, "Which of the available forms of treatment has the best probable outcomes for depression in adults?" Both types of studies are said to have "applied" aims. Treatment-relevant research that primarily has applied aims is referred to as "clinical research." Psychotherapy research correctly is regarded as a branch of clinical, mental health research.

A. How Psychotherapy Research Relates to Other Mental Health Research

Psychotherapy research is distinguished from other types of clinical mental health research such as psychopharmacology (medication) research, which is strongly linked to the field of psychiatry and to the pharmaceutical industry. However, from the mid-1980s to the present an increasing number of outcome studies include psychotherapeutic interventions, pharmacological interventions, and their combination, thereby blurring the boundaries between psychotherapy and psychopharmacology research. Psychotherapy research also is distinguished from mental health services research. Traditional services research is intended to obtain data on the natural functioning of community-based, clinical care delivery systems. Typical data include how such systems are organized, their accessibility, fiscal features, and outcomes at a global level (e.g., recidivism). Services research usually utilizes large databases (e.g., several thousand service recipients and clinic "contacts" or visits) and provides information useful at a programmatic level. It is not designed to test and develop specific treatments. Psychotherapy research also can be differentiated from psychopathology research, although the two fields historically and presently overlap.

B. Psychotherapy Research versus Behavior Therapy Research

For many years (from about the 1950s through the 1970s), therapy researchers themselves drew a clear distinction between behavior therapy research and psychotherapy research. The distinction reflected what aptly has been described as an internecine struggle between those who endorsed forms of therapy that were grounded in theories and findings of subdisciplines of psychology known as learning and behavior ("behavioral" therapies), and those who favored therapies derived from Freudian psychodynamic theory or from humanistic principles (e.g., Rogerian client-centered therapy). The distinction was instantiated in the founding by psychologists of two scientific organizations at approximately the same time: the Association for the Advancement of Behavior Therapy (1966) and the Society for Psychotherapy Research (circa 1968). Both flourish to this day.

By the late 1970s, tangible signs of a rapprochement between the two camps emerged. One such sign was the "psychotherapy integration movement" that was spearheaded by psychologists such as Paul Wachtel and Marvin Goldfried. The period of rapprochement was spurred in part by outcome findings that indicated that behavior therapy-based and psychotherapy-based treatments both were associated with measurable benefits, often of comparable magnitude. Neither camp could claim unqualified victory. Indeed, contrary to the hopes and expectations of many, some studies in which a behavioral therapy was compared directly to a non-behavioral therapy (e.g., psychodynamic psychotherapy) failed to detect statistically significant outcome differences. A prototypic study like this was published in a 1975 book by Sloane, Staples, Cristol, and colleagues, *Psychotherapy vs. Behavior Therapy*.

At least partially due to mutually humbling outcome research findings, animosity between the camps substantially diminished, and some cross-fertilization even occurred. The two arms of therapy research also retained some distinctiveness, as reflected in one of the field's most influential recent milestones, a listing of empirically supported forms of therapy ("ESTs") for specific types of problems. The list was first published in 1995, based on the work of the American Psychological Association's Task Force on Promotion and Dissemination of Psychological Procedures. The Task Force was chaired by Dianne Chambless from 1993 to 1997. (Initially, the term "empirically validated therapies" was used for the list. It was changed to ESTs in part because the word "validated" could mistakenly connote that the process of validation for a therapy had been completed and no additional research on it was needed.) The list includes some therapies that are essentially behavioral (e.g., exposure and response prevention for obsessive–compulsive disorder), as well as some that are not such as interpersonal psychotherapy for depression (a type of psychotherapy that was developed by psychiatrist Gerald Klerman and colleagues, published in 1984).

The long-standing distinction in the literature between behavior therapy and psychotherapy, and between the corpus of research focused on each, marks a historically important epoch in the development of research on psychologically based interventions. Herein the term "psychotherapy research" includes research on all forms of psychologically based treatments.

C. "Coalescence" Phase of the Field of Psychotherapy Research

So, when did all this start? Several reviews of therapy research indicate that the earliest outcome studies of psychotherapies were published in the late 1920s, slightly over 80 years ago. A 1916 study was mentioned in a review by Allen Bergin, an unusually knowledgeable reviewer. The number of outcome studies published per year was very low at first—about two every 5 years between 1920–1930. The rate increased to about 10 every 5 years after that and during World War II. Starting in the early 1950s, the publication rate of psychotherapy outcome studies began to increase exponentially.

By 1958, the field of psychotherapy research definitely had emerged in the United States. In that year, the Division of Clinical Psychology of the American Psychological Association held the first national conference on psychotherapy research. The National Institute of Mental Health (NIMH) provided financial support for the conference. Broadly stated, its purpose was to evaluate the status of therapy research and to thereby provide information that also could stimulate further research. An important additional aim was to strengthen research collaboration and interdisciplinary relations between psychologists and psychiatrists. Psychiatrists were among the invited participants and also were asked to join the conference planning committee.

Several forces are likely to have contributed to the accelerating growth of psychotherapy research that was evident by the 1950s. The end of World War II played a role. For example, resources of many types became more available, and the kinds of acute problems that psychiatrists observed in soldiers led to greatly expanded interest in psychotherapy after the war. A closely related development was the U.S. Veterans Administration's promotion of the use of psychologists both to administer psychotherapy and to conduct research. Another factor was the methodologically groundbreaking and exemplary psychotherapy research program that was developed by Carl Rogers, his colleagues, and students at the University of Chicago beginning in 1949. The availability of funding from the NIMH, after it was established in 1949, was certainly growth promoting. The previously noted adoption in 1949 of the scientist–practitioner model for education in clinical psychology also contributed. Moreover, doubtless, what was reacted to by many as a gauntlet thrown down by Hans Eysenck in 1952 energized and focused psychotherapy outcome research initiatives.

In perhaps the most widely cited therapy research publication of the era, Eysenck presented data that he interpreted as evidence that existing outcome studies did not show that psychotherapy was associated with better improvement rates than occurred, over time, in untreated individuals who had comparable problems. The latter was termed "spontaneous remission." Eysenck used two previously published naturalistic data sets to estimate improvement rates that would occur in psychoneurotic problems over 2 years without the benefit of "systematic psychotherapy." One set of figures was from discharge records of neurotic patients from New York state hospitals; the other was from an insurance company's disability claims for psychoneuroses for a 5-year period. According to Eysenck's calculations, improvement rates found in psychotherapy outcome studies and improvement rates for the same types of problems in those who did not receive psychotherapy both were about 66%.

The validity of Eysenck's methods and conclusions were challenged by many therapy researchers over the years. The kinds of questions asked included "Was his assumption accurate that those in the naturalistic studies had not received any psychotherapy?"; "Were the improvement criteria used in the naturalistic studies comparable to those used in therapy outcome studies?"; "Was spontaneous remission an established finding," as Eysenck's argument suggested it was? It was not until 1977 that data were presented (by Mary Smith and Gene Glass) that finally put to rest Eysenck's conclusion that no evidence existed that psychotherapy was effective. More about this in Section III.

Before leaving the topic, a key fact is worth noting. The heated debate stimulated by Eysenck's 1952 paper (and by a later, similar paper of his published in 1960) was to some extent both fueled by and a manifiestation of, the aforementioned behavior therapy versus psychotherapy struggle. Eysenck, himself, became a leader in the behavior therapy movement.

Despite the field's burgeoning growth since the 1950s, as recently as 20 years ago (1980) psychotherapy research was quaintly described as a "cottage industry" by some observers. The term seems to have originated mainly from comparison of psychotherapy research to psychopharmacology research, a field whose primary and huge funding source is the pharmaceutical industry. Among other things, cottage industry status connoted that outcome studies of psychotherapy typically had relatively small sample sizes—20 or fewer individuals included in each treatment condition. In addition, many studies were un- or underfunded and conducted by individual investigators who did not closely coordinate their efforts with those of others working on the same or related questions. Thus, findings did not typically build on each other, thereby creating a cumulative and obviously progressing body of knowledge. Although the quality of studies could be excellent, their findings typically were not highly influential in terms of affecting either the practice of psychotherapy or public policy on mental health treatment. (Cottage industry or not, the field was an active one. According to Michael Lambert who reviewed the psychotherapy research literature in 1980, 4,000 studies of various types had been published by then.)

D. "Coming of Age" Phase: Therapy Research Enters the Mainstream of Clinical Mental Health Research

The milestones and turning points described in the next subsections, with one exception (the NIMH treatment development grant mechanism), were in some way controversial within the field of therapy research. Indeed, controversy probably is a marker for publicly observable events that have the potential to precipitate widespread change. The points of contention are not discussed here but readily can be found in the psychotherapy research literature.

1. Large-Sample, Multisite Studies, Randomized Clinical Trial Design

A clear turning point for the field of therapy research began to take shape in about the late 1970s. Larger-scale outcome studies of psychotherapies—250 or more individuals treated—began to be undertaken with the assistance of substantial funding from the NIMH. The shift was at least partially due to a leadership role taken by NIMH staff like Morris Parloff and Irene Elkin, both of whom were experienced psychotherapy researchers. Psychiatrist Gerald Klerman also facilitated the changes from his position at the helm of the Alcohol, Drug Abuse and Mental Health Administration, the federal government agency that oversaw the NIMH at the time.

One study, in particular, marked the defining shift for psychotherapy research from its so-called cottage industry status to a recognized, influential branch of clinical research. The study is known as the NIMH Treatment of Depression Collaborative Research Program (TDCRP). Irene Elkin of the NIMH played a key role in the study's oversight and conduct throughout its course. Work began on conceptualizing and designing the TDCRP in 1977. Its initial outcome findings were published in 1989, a mere 13 years ago. The TDCRP was the first time that a collaborative, multisite outcome study of psychotherapies (i.e., the same research design and procedures were implemented simultaneously at three, geographically distant research settings) was conducted using the randomized, controlled clinical trial research strategy. Until then, collaborative clinical trials were commonly used for pharmaceutical company-funded research on psychoactive medications but not for psychotherapy research.

2. Selection of Patient Samples by Psychiatric Diagnoses

The TDCRP also illustrates the impact of a development external to the field of psychotherapy research that became a momentous turning point for it shortly after 1980. In 1980, the American Psychiatric Association published the third edition of its diagnostic nomenclature of psychiatric disorders, the Diagnostic and Statistical Manual of Mental Disorders *(DSM–III)*. The *DSM–III* was a major revision of the Association's existing nomenclature. The overhaul was undertaken in part to remediate features of prior versions of the *DSM* that made it an inadequate diagnostic system to support clinical research—both psychopathology studies and outcome studies of psychopharmacological and other treatments. For example, the descriptions of diagnoses were not specific or detailed enough to enable diagnoses to be assigned reliably to the same patient by different, even expert, psychiatrists. Poor interrater reliability of diagnoses was a fatal handicap from a research perspective, and it created many problems from a practice perspective too.

The *DSM–III* had a major impact on psychotherapy research despite the fact that many mental health professionals from all disciplines and many psychotherapy researchers did not endorse it. Some even condemned it. They did not believe that the *DSM–III* was either a valid system for classifying psychopathology or a treatment-relevant nosology for selecting and planning most types of psychotherapeutic interventions. Despite rejection of the nomenclature by many therapy researchers, the *DSM–III* and its subsequent editions changed the direction of psychotherapy research. After the mid-1980s, psychotherapy outcome studies started to be focused on disorders as they were defined in the *DSM*, such as panic disorder and major depression. The TDCRP was a harbinger of this trend.

Developments at the NIMH in 1985 contributed to the impact on psychotherapy research of the *DSM–III* and its later editions. In 1985, the NIMH Division of Clinical Research was reorganized such that many of its subdivisions or "branches" were identified by disorders that appeared in the *DSM–III*. For example, the existing Psychosocial Treatments Research Branch was abolished and replaced by the Affective and Anxiety Disorders Research Branch. ("Psychosocial" was a term that was adopted at the NIMH by branch chief Morris Parloff in part to span the aforementioned rift in the field between behavior therapy and psychotherapy.) Prior to the NIMH reorganization, psychotherapy researchers often sought guidance from staff of the Psychosocial Treatments Research Branch on their grant applications. After the reorganization, many therapy researchers did not know which, if any, branch was the appropriate one to contact about their treatment study ideas and potential proposals. Moreover, it became evident rather quickly to researchers that the NIMH grant review committees were, in essence, requiring grant applications for psychotherapy outcome studies to be focused on a specific disorder. Study patients were to be selected primarily by diagnostic criteria, and disorders as defined in the *DSM* seemed most likely to be viewed as acceptable by review committees.

For the last 20 years and into the present, the largest and most influential psychotherapy outcome studies have been designed to test psychotherapies for specific *DSM* disorders—despite the continuing reservations of many therapy researchers, practicing mental health professionals, and psychopathology researchers about the validity of much of the nomenclature. One major result is that a cumulative body of treatment research findings has been achieved. At the same time, substantial and scientifically well-founded skepticism about aspects of the nomenclature continues among mental health researchers and practitioners from all disciplines, including psychiatry.

3. "Time-Limited" Courses of Therapy

The TDCRP illustrates yet another characteristic feature of therapy outcome research during its coming-of-age phase through the present. The length of therapies studied typically has been relatively short—12 to 24 sessions over 3 to 4 months. Particularly to psychotherapy research pioneers who espoused the psychodynamic orientation, examining therapies of less than 1 or more years duration was of uncertain relevance, at best, to the phenomenon of psychotherapy. Several forces converged by the late 1970s that resulted in the focus of psychotherapy outcome research, particularly federally funded studies, on time-limited treatments. Society's and insurance companies' concerns about the costs of long-term psychotherapy played a role, as did scientific considerations that made the conduct of interpretable studies of long-term psychotherapy problematic. Indeed, few outcome studies of long-term psychotherapy exist at this time. A study done of psychodynamically oriented therapy at the Menninger Foundation in Topeka, Kansas, from about 1954 to 1974 is a famous exception.

Findings from studies of time-limited treatments, particularly for depression, are renewing interest in conducting studies of longer-term therapy—up to 1 year. Disappointing percentages of individuals who reach a "recovery" criterion and evidence that a notable proportion of patients relapse after time-limited treatments support the interest. Indeed, 18-month follow-up findings from the TDCRP contributed to the currently nascent tendency to conduct outcome studies of longer-term courses of psychotherapy. A well-established trend is outcome studies of "maintenance" therapeutic interventions (e.g., monthly "booster" therapy sessions following time-limited, acute phase treatments) to determine if posttreatment relapse rates can be reduced. A contrasting direction, consistent with economic considerations and cost-cutting interests of managed care organizations, is the examination of very short treatments—three sessions for some types of anxiety problems. In addition, the potential of technological advances, such as handheld computers ("Palm Pilots"), to enhance psychotherapy is being explored, e.g., between-session use of Palm Pilots by patients with panic disorder to prompt behavior change and to reduce the amount of contact with a therapist that is required to get desired outcomes.

4. Treatment Development Grants

Efforts of NIMH staff, such as psychologist Barry Wolfe, led to another pivotal milestone in the history of psychotherapy research. In 1993, the NIMH made available a type of funding opportunity called a "treatment development grant." NIMH's action followed a similar initiative by the National Institute on Drug Abuse that was cultivated by Lisa Onken, then of its Clinical and Experimental Therapeutics Branch. The appearance of the treatment development grant was embraced by psychotherapy researchers as a crucial attempt to help offset a very long-standing handicap from which the field suffered, particularly in comparison to psychopharmacology research. Pharmaceutical companies are and have been a major source of non-federal funding for psychopharmacology outcome research, as well as for the development and initial testing of new medications for psychiatric problems. The field of psychotherapy research never had a counterpart to this mammoth corporate funding source for treatment development. The development of new forms of therapy, or modified versions of existing ones, was completely dependent on the unfunded initiative of individuals before treatment development grants became available. The preceding major impediment to the development of psychotherapies was long recognized by therapy researchers.

E. Unfolding Directions

Three more turning points for psychotherapy research surfaced in the 1990s, the ultimate impact of which on the field and on the practice of psychotherapy in the United States is yet to be known. Two of the three were spawned directly by the NIMH. It, in turn, was responding to a host of forces, prominently including economic concerns (continually increasing costs of all forms of health care) and public health policy issues (e.g., what direct recommendations for typical clinical care settings could be made from existing treatment research?). One turning point was a call for cost data to be included in mental health treatment studies. A second began as the "efficacy versus effectiveness debate" and culminated in the intentionally revolutionary endorsement by the NIMH of "the public health model" as a new paradigm for mental health treatment research. The third, not completely distinct from the other two in terms of causal forces, was the introduction to therapy research of a "patient-focused" research paradigm.

1. Cost-Effectiveness, Cost-Benefit, and Related Methodology

By the mid-1970s if not before, insurance companies and various U.S. social institutions voiced concerns about the cost of mental health treatment. By the early 1990s, rising health care costs were a major focus of the U.S. Congress. In addition, managed care treatment delivery systems, an intended antidote for rising costs, were actively seeking cost-effectiveness data on mental health treatments. Concurrently, the NIMH began making concerted efforts to get investigators to obtain cost data in treatment outcome studies. (The concept of costs is very broad and includes resources of many types that are used in the delivery of treatments such as office space, supplies, and transportation.) Various types of cost information were needed by federal and local health care policymakers and by managed care entrepreneurs—the comparative costs of alternative treatments, such as medication and psychotherapy for the same problem; the relative benefit obtained for resources consumed by different treatments (cost benefit); and savings in medical expenses, work days lost, and so on, that might be associated with mental health treatments (cost offset).

Highly sophisticated and complex methods for assessing costs associated with treatments existed though they rarely were used in psychotherapy outcome research at the time. The NIMH recommended that health care economists be added to outcome study grant applications to ensure that adequate cost data would be obtained. Now, in 2002, experts in cost analysis are on NIMH treatment grant review committees. The impact is not yet widely evident of cost data from outcome studies on practice patterns and on directions in psychotherapy research.

2. From Efficacy versus Effectiveness to the Public Health Research Paradigm

From a public health perspective, a core issue of what often is called "the efficacy versus effectiveness debate" is the generalizability to community-based, clinical practice settings of treatments examined in, and outcome findings from, randomized controlled studies. Sometimes the issue is characterized as the "transportability" of treatments from research into typical practice settings. From a scientific perspective, the debate's core issues are: (a) alternative experimental designs and methods that can be used for clinical treatment studies, and (b) the kinds of inferences (conclusions) for practice in non-research, community settings that most confidently can be drawn from them.

The seeds of the efficacy versus effectiveness debate were sown years before its rise to the forefront as a bonafide scientific debate in the mid-1990s. Its emergence then was a side effect of several forces, including: (a) dramatic shifts in health care delivery that occurred in the United States beginning about the mid-1980s, (b) the U.S. Congress's (failed) attempt in 1993 to reform national health care, and (c) escalating dissatisfaction of practitioners with the output of therapy research (e.g., manuals for therapists that describe how to implement specific types of psychotherapy).

In the mid-1980s, health care delivery patterns increasingly moved away from indemnity insurance coverage toward managed care. The managed care model gained momentum from the mid-1980s on as a way to contain and cut health care costs. Both managed care and the health care reform movement spotlighted the need for valid information about existing treatments to guide decisions of government policymakers and managed care entrepreneurs. Both groups were motivated to make decisions rapidly that would affect the treatments that millions of citizens could receive using insurance benefits. Gaps became widely evident between the types of information wanted by these and other stakeholders in mental health treatment (e.g., its "consumers" and clinical providers) and what was available from existing therapy and other mental health-related research. Recognition of the limitations fostered lively debates about how treatment research, particularly federally funded research that is mandated to meet broad public health needs, should be designed.

From a scientific standpoint, two concepts that are key to the efficacy versus effectiveness debate are internal and external validity. The concepts first were proffered in the early 1960s by Donald Campbell and Julian Stanley as part of a conceptual framework that linked different experimental designs and methods to the types of questions that could most validly (logically correctly) be answered with them. Internal validity relates to designs and methods that increase a study's logical strength for drawing causal conclusions about the relationship between its independent (e.g., form of psychotherapy) and dependent (e.g., outcome indices) variables. When a therapy outcome study has a design and methods that maximize internal validity (e.g., random assignment of patients to the treatment conditions that are being compared; inclusion of a "control" condition of some type to provide an estimate of the improvement that could occur, without treatment, over the same period of time that a study treatment is provided), confidence is maximized that its findings can be interpreted as evidence that the therapy or therapies examined caused the outcomes obtained. Studies that have high internal validity are referred to as "efficacy" studies in the parlance of the debate. The aforementioned TDCRP is a prototypic efficacy study.

External validity relates to study designs and methods that enhance the generalizability of study findings. Generalizability means the confidence with which a study's results can be assumed to extend to situations, people, measures, times, and so on, other than those particular to the study. For example, say a finding is that cognitive therapy plus progressive muscle relaxation for generalized anxiety disorder is associated with more reduction in anxiety than nondirective therapy plus relaxation. The external validity features of the study's design and methods determine the types of "real-world" clinical settings, therapists, patients, and treatments to which we can confidently generalize the expectation (i.e., infer) that the same cognitive therapy plus relaxation will be associated with more reduction in anxiety in generalized anxiety disorder than an alternative therapy will be. Studies with designs and methods that achieve high external validity are referred to as "effectiveness" studies in the efficacy versus effectiveness debate.

In a series of actions that became clearly evident to psychotherapy researchers by about 1998, the NIMH indicated it wanted to receive grant applications for studies that were designed to have external validity strengths in the sense of having direct implications for practice in typical care settings. In actuality, a much more dramatic and far-reaching change was in progress, a change that has the potential to affect therapy research at least as profoundly as the 1985 NIMH reorganization did.

Another major reorganization of the NIMH funding by programs occurred in 1997 under the leadership of a new director. Once again, as in 1985, psychotherapy researchers interested in federal funding needed to determine what new branch of the NIMH they should contact with their ideas, and so on. In addition, a Clinical Treatment and Services Research Workgroup was established and charged by the new NIMH Director Steven Hyman to advise on "strategies for increasing the relevance, speeding the development, and facilitating the utilization of research-based treatment and service interventions for mental illnesses into both routine clinical practice and policies guiding our local and national mental health service systems." In 1999, the Workgroup's report, *Bridging Science and Service,* became available. Moreover, in 1999, Dr. Hyman co-authored a publication with key NIMH treatment research administrators that said that NIMH was now dedicated to advancing "a public health model approach to clinical research." The model is intended to eventually fill the information gaps that various stakeholders need and want. It also is expected to meet the treatment dissemination and other goals, described earlier, that the Workgroup was charged to consider.

Obviously, yet another major turning point for therapy research is underway, spurred by the NIMH's recent transformation and new aims. As yet, the field's new directions, questions, and findings largely remain its unforeseen future.

3. Patient-Focused (versus Treatment-Focused) Research

In 1996, Kenneth Howard and colleagues presented a research strategy that was new to the field of therapy research. It was called "patient profiling." The strategy was an outgrowth of Howard's direct knowledge of contemporary trends in the provision of psychotherapy in managed care delivery systems and lifelong career doing therapy research in naturalistic settings. Patient profiling also was an outgrowth of the application of developments in data analysis techniques. Other therapy researchers concurrently pursued similar directions, using what now are sometimes classified as "patient-focused" research strategies. In general, patient-focused research answers questions like, "Is this patient's therapy working?" It is contrasted with conventional or "treatment-focused" therapy research that addresses questions like, "Does this type of therapy work?"

A main difference between patient-focused and treatment-focused studies (like the TDCRP) is that the aim of the newer strategy is to provide information that can be used to evaluate the progress of a specific patient's treatment by comparing his or her ongoing treatment response in real time to an expected response of clinically comparable individuals. The expected (or predicted) response is estimated from archival data on many treated patients, that is data of the type collected by managed care corporations.

The potential value and impact of patient-focused research on the main questions in therapy research is yet to be known. A hope is that it will, at minimum, provide one type of bridge across an ironic and chronic gap between therapy research and clinical practice. For example, the utility of patient-focused research currently is being examined for giving community-based therapists up-to-date information on how a patient is progressing compared to a predicted course so that therapists can consider modifying the treatment that they are providing.

F. Comment

The foregoing has been a thumbnail sketch of trends in and forces that have shaped psychotherapy research in its first 60 or so years. One aim was to illustrate that psychotherapy research is characterized so far by noteworthy shifts in focus and style. Many of the shifts described reflect the responsiveness of the field to external forces rather than to its own findings or findings in closely related fields such as psychology and other behavioral sciences. Therapy research has responded to research priorities established by the NIMH to meet public health and policy needs; developments in psychiatry; and insurance providers' demands for data on the efficacy, safety, and costs of psychotherapies to form and defend their mental health care reimbursement policies. Indeed, the applied (practice-relevant) potential of psychotherapy research can make it a quickly changing, exciting field both to work in and to observe. Unfortunately, many of the sources of excitement and the sense of urgency associated with studying practice-relevant questions also can challenge the maintenance of scientific integrity.

III. KEY QUESTIONS

Fundamental features of a scientific field are its focal aims, focal questions, theories, and primary research methods. In research, aims are instantiated in the form of specific questions and hypotheses. Several key questions that have been examined by psychotherapy researchers are reviewed in this section. The emergence of milestones and turning points along the way is noted.

A. What Can Be Learned about Personality Psychology from Psychotherapy?

During the late 1940s and 1950s when psychotherapy research was beginning to coalesce as a scientific field, an aim endorsed by many investigators was to use psychotherapy as a method to advance personality theory, a major subdiscipline of psychology. At least into the early 1960s, some psychologists were exploring the question of whether psychotherapy provided a "valid method for the science of psychology." In other words, psychotherapy as a vehicle for advancing basic academic, rather than applied, research questions was of considerable interest.

Psychotherapy had several features that suggested its promise as a sort of laboratory for systematically investigating human personality and behavior. Psychotherapy provided a relatively standard, simple-to-construct situation in which a person and his or her psychological processes could be observed closely. Moreover, to achieve therapeutic goals, the psychotherapy situation specifically was designed to enable people to reveal themselves in the most complete and honest way possible. This feature also afforded a unique opportunity to achieve scientific goals. It was hoped, for example, that both observations of people and information they revealed about themselves and their life histories might answer basic questions about personality, its developmental antecedents, and also provide data from which a valid taxonomy of personality traits (cross-situationally consistent patterns of perceiving and behaving) might be derived and tested. In turn, from the preceding types of knowledge, principles of personality change could be developed.

The foregoing early trend in psychotherapy research reflected, in part, Freud's legacy. Freud viewed psychoanalysis as both a treatment and a method to examine hypotheses about personality and its development. A similar perspective was prominently displayed at the first conference on psychotherapy research in 1958 that was mentioned in Section I. The authors of a summary of the conference, Morris Parloff and Eli Rubinstein, noted that many of the researchers present were relatively uninterested in outcome studies compared to research that was intended to advance understanding of personality.

B. What Is "the Problem" to Be Treated?

The early interest of psychotherapy researchers in personality psychology points to the intrinsic link between psychotherapy research and models of psychopathology. The development and identification of efficacious, efficient psychotherapeutic interventions are fundamentally contingent on conceptualizations of the problem(s) to be treated. Widely endorsed models of psychopathology have been elusive, although models have not been in short supply. None have generated widespread acceptance despite their lynchpin role for the development, refinement, and evaluation of psychotherapies. The lack of consensus has been an enduring handicap for psychotherapy research, as well as for other types of clinical mental health research.

Why has the development of consensually agreed-on models of psychopathology been unattainable to date? One reason is that many problems that seem to be legitimately regarded as mental health concerns are neither objectively observable nor measurable deviations from clearly definable and delimited "normal" functioning and states of mind. Even though behaviors of the type that often are the focus of mental health treatment can be observed, their deviation from "normalcy" frequently is a judgment call. (The preceding two statements do not apply to psychotic and manic symptoms of conditions like schizophrenia and bipolar disorder that are associated with obvious impairments in adaptive functioning. The two conditions exemplify a few that are consensually viewed as more "severe" by mental health professionals across disciplines.) In brief, the nature of the problems that can be the focus of psychotherapy (and of psychopharmacology by current practice patterns) often is much different than the physical anomalies and abnormal processes that typically are the focus of medical treatment.

Medicine characteristically has the relative luxury of being directed to physically observable and, thus, readily agreed-on deviations from equally observable, normal functioning of the human organism. Obvious examples are broken limbs, flesh wounds, and cancers. Many serious medical problems are not observable by the unaided eye, but technological aids such as microscopes, x-rays, and imaging equipment allow their presence to be observed and consensually assessed. Mental health complaints often are not similarly available to visual inspection or verification and, thus, to consensual agreement on the nature of (or even presence of) the problem to be treated. Moreover, attitudinal, emotional, and behavioral functioning that is regarded as in the normal range seems to be much more heterogeneous than physical functioning in the normal range. Thus, using indices of normality as a benchmark from which to create models of psychopathology is unlikely to be as helpful as it has been in medicine. The medical model is only partially applicable, at best, to dimensions of "mental" functioning.

Unfortunately, attempts so far to develop models of psychopathology that could provide strong foundations for psychotherapy research and for other mental health treatment research often have elicited, or have been notably influenced by, guild interests of the various mental health professions. Such factors compound the difficulty of an extremely difficult, yet crucial conceptual challenge for psychotherapy research and for mental health treatment, in general.

C. Does Psychotherapy Work?

Alternatively stated, the question is, "Is psychotherapy effective?" Its answer requires results from studies that are designed to determine if a type of psychotherapy is associated with greater or different change than no treatment, using a standard criterion to judge whether or not a difference exists.

1. A Compelling, Affirmative Answer

It was not until 1977 that data were presented that provided a widely influential and convincingly positive answer to the simplistic yet fundamental question, "Does psychotherapy work?" The answer came from the application of meta-analysis, a statistical technique, to data from nearly 400 (in 1977) and then 475 (in 1980) therapy outcome studies, many of which included a no- or minimal treatment control condition. The two meta-analyses (the first authored by Mary Smith and Gene Glass; the second by Smith, Glass, and Thomas Miller) were a major milestone for the field of psychotherapy research. The larger one showed that when findings were pooled from outcome studies in which treated individuals were compared in the same study with either (a) untreated or minimally treated individuals, or (b) groups who received placebo treatments or "undifferentiated counseling," the average person who received a form of psychotherapy was better off on the outcomes examined than 80% of those who needed therapy but were not treated. The advantage for psychotherapy was larger when the meta-analysis included only studies in which therapy groups were compared to no- or minimal treatment groups. Subsequent meta-analyses to date, often focused on the effects of psychotherapy for specific problems (like depression), have supported the conclusion that it is an effective treatment modality.

As noted previously, numerous and often painstaking prior attempts were made to effectively challenge Hans Eysenck's 1952 conclusion that no evidence existed from outcome studies that psychotherapy was associated with a higher rate of improvement than could be expected to occur, over time, without therapy. For some years, a major impediment to disproving Eysenck's conclusion was a lack of psychotherapy outcome studies that included a no- or minimal treatment condition whose outcomes were compared with those of the therapy of interest. The presence of such a condition provides an experimental way to estimate or "control for" change that might occur without treatment—with just the passage of time and normal life events. Randomized controlled psychotherapy outcome studies became increasingly prevalent over the years following 1952. Thus, a lack of controlled studies was not the only impediment to the appearance, before 1977, of a compelling counterargument to Eysenck's proposition.

Before Smith and Glass applied meta-analysis to controlled outcome studies of psychotherapy, others had summarized the results of such studies using a "box score" or tallying method. That is, the results of available studies were coded on whether or not the therapy of interest was associated with statistically significantly more improvement than was the no- or minimal therapy control condition. Conclusions based on the box score method were not as convincing as those of a meta-analysis. This was partially because the possibility of finding differences between therapy conditions in outcome studies is heavily influenced by a study's sample size. Larger studies have a greater probability of obtaining statistically significant differences between therapy and control conditions.

2. How Should the Question Be Formulated?

Even while many therapy researchers were trying to disprove Eysenck's conclusion that psychotherapy did not work, they already had concluded that the global question, "Does psychotherapy work?," was not a productive one to guide research. For example, in a 1966 paper that, itself, qualifies as a milestone for the field, Donald Kiesler argued for the need to study "which therapist behaviors are more effective with which type of patients." In a similar vein, in 1967 Gordon Paul framed the question for outcome research as: "*what* treatment, by *whom* is most effective for *this* individual with *that* specific problem, and under *which* set of circumstances" (original emphasis)? Others, such as Nevitt Sanford noted as early as 1953 that the global question, "Does psychotherapy work?," was inadequate from a scientific standpoint to guide the field and suggested alternatives—"which people, in what circumstances, responding to what psychotherapeutic stimuli . . . ." However, it was Paul's phrasing of the question that essentially became a mantra for psychotherapy research.

One of the most recent and major milestones in the history of psychotherapy research illustrates the field's answers so far to a partial version of the applied question that Paul formulated for it 30 years earlier. The milestone was the aforementioned 1995 (updated in 1998) American Psychological Association list of empirically supported psychotherapies for various types of problems, such as depression and panic attacks.

D. What Is "the Treatment"?

For years, many researchers' energy and attention was directed toward answering the question, "Does psychotherapy work?," before methods were developed that enabled them to know of what, exactly, "the therapy" consisted that was done in outcome studies. Particularly for research on non-behavioral therapies, the field essentially was in the position of saying "it works (or it doesn't), but we don't really know for sure what 'it' is." More interesting, many therapy researchers were not fully aware that they were in the foregoing position. Investigators often assumed that study therapists were conducting the type of therapy that they said they were (e.g., "psychodynamic"), and that all therapists who said that they used a particular form of therapy implemented it more similarly than not. Donald Kiesler brought "myths" like the foregoing ones to the field's attention in 1966 in his previously mentioned, classic critique of conceptual and methodological weaknesses of therapy research at the time. The increasing use of audiotaping technology in therapy research no doubt contributed to the uncovering of mythical "therapist uniformity assumptions" like those which Kiesler identified.

It was not until the mid-1980s that detailed descriptions of non-behavioral psychotherapies were put into written, manual form for therapists to learn from and follow in outcome studies. (Manuals began to be used in behavior therapy research about 20 years earlier, the mid-1960s.) The development of therapy manuals for all types of therapy was a crucial milestone for psychotherapy research. In effect, manuals were operational definitions of the main independent variable(s) of psychotherapy outcome studies. They also enhanced the scientific quality of research on psychotherapies in other ways.

Manuals made it more possible for all the therapies examined in a study to be implemented as they were intended to be. Manuals contributed to consistent, correct implementation in two primary ways. First, they facilitated systematic training of therapists in the conduct of a study's therapies. Second, they provided criteria that could be used to monitor each therapist's implementation of a therapy for accuracy (i.e., Is the therapist "adhering" to the manual?) throughout the entire course of each study therapy that he or she did. In addition, and very important from a scientific perspective, therapy manuals greatly facilitated attempts to replicate outcome findings in different settings, with therapists from different disciplines and experience levels, for example. Finally, from both the practice and public health perspectives, manuals aid widespread and efficient dissemination of therapies that are found to be efficacious in outcome studies.

In 1984, Lester Luborsky and Robert DeRubeis observed that "a small revolution in psychotherapy research style" had occurred with the use of manuals. What is particularly interesting is not that the revolution of manualization occurred, but that this fundamental methodological advance did not occur earlier. How could a clinically-relevant, scientific field conduct valid tests of its treatments without first clearly articulating and defining them? As already noted, manuals were used in behavior therapy research almost 20 years before they were widely used in research on other forms of therapy. The lag largely reflected different fundamental assumptions of those who endorsed psychodynamic and some humanistic therapies, compared to therapies based on principles of learning and behavior. For example, a common view among psychodynamically oriented researchers and practitioners was (and is) that the treatment could not be "manualized" because it essentially requires artful and ongoing responsiveness of the therapist to shifts in the patient. When the aforementioned emphasis on time-limited forms of therapy occurred, it began to seem more possible to advocates of non-behavioral therapies to extract the theoretically essential change-promoting principles and techniques from their therapies, and codify them into manuals for the conduct of time-limited versions of the therapies.

As alluded to earlier in this article, ironically, one of the most important scientific advances for psychotherapy research—*therapy manuals*—became one of its most ferociously criticized accomplishments by practitioners in the 1990s. The reaction is only one example of a well-chronicled, perpetual gulf between research and practice. Historically, a central problem was that practitioners ignored therapy research and described its findings as irrelevant to or otherwise unhelpful for their work. More recently, practitioners do not feel as free to ignore findings. External pressures exist (e.g., from managed care payers) to make their care conform with findings by being able to provide manualized treatments found to be efficacious in treatment studies. The gulf is, of course, especially fascinating given that therapy research was fostered largely by the scientist–practitioner (Boulder) model of training in clinical psychology.

E. What Does It Mean to Say a "Psychotherapy Works"?

Two of many basic, yet conceptually and methodologically difficult questions that therapy researchers encountered early on were: "What effects (outcomes) should be measured to evaluate the usefulness of a psychotherapy?," and "How can the effects of interest be measured reliably (with precision) and validly (correctly)?" As investigators formulated answers to the first question, and both used and contributed to developments in psychometric methods to answer the second one, their findings revealed considerable additional complexity. Some of the complexity will become evident in topics that are discussed next. Many, if not most, of the relevant issues continue to be debated: "How frequently should effects of interest be measured in a therapy outcome study?"; "What is the impact on the validity of outcome data of repeated measurement?"

1. The "Perspective" Problem

By the early 1970s, findings unequivocally indicated that the answer to the outcome question often depended on whom was asked. The patient's assessment typically differed from the therapist's perspective on the same effect (e.g., degree of improvement in self-esteem). For example, it was not unusual to find very low coefficients of correlation—0.10—between patients' and therapists' ratings of patients' status on the same outcome variable. (A correlation of 0.80 or larger typically is regarded as high. Squaring a correlation coefficient indicates how much overlap, or "shared variance" scores on two measures have—0.80 × 0.80 = 64%.) Moreover, both perspectives could differ from the judgment of a clinically experienced, independent assessor. (Independent assessors' ratings came to be included in outcome studies for several reasons such as to obtain a judgment from someone who was not invested in either the benefit experienced by individual patients or the study results). In the rare instances when family members or others who knew a patient well were asked to evaluate outcomes, this "significant other" perspective did not necessarily agree with any of the other three.

In 1977, Hans Strupp and Suzanne Hadley presented a conceptual "tripartite model" of mental health and therapy outcomes. The model helped to resolve the problem of ambiguous outcome findings posed by low agreement between perspectives. It identified three parties who have a vested interest in a person's mental health ("stakeholders" in current parlance): the individual, mental health professionals, and society. The model included the idea that no one perspective was inherently more valid than another, although each perspective differentially valued aspects of an individual's functioning and experience. For example, the individual can be expected to be most interested in subjective experiences of well-being and contentment. Society is likely to be most interested in the adaptive qualities of a person's behavior. Another research-relevant idea of the tripartite model was that multiple perspectives should be obtained on the primary outcomes measured in an outcome study. The standard continues to this day.

The perspective problem was only one of many discoveries along the way that indicated the complexity of the focal phenomenon of interest in psychotherapy research. It also illustrates the challenges that the phenomenon poses for obtaining simple answers from even the most sophisticated applications of scientific methods to the study of psychotherapy.

2. Statistical Significance versus Clinical Significance of Effects

In a series of papers from the mid-1980s to 1991, Neil Jacobson and colleagues provided a solution to a basic limitation of what were then state-of-art psychotherapy research methods. Their contribution was a major conceptual and methodological milestone for psychotherapy outcome research. At the time, statistical significance typically was the sole criterion used to determine if study results indicated that a therapy worked or worked better than an alternative treatment. For example, if the difference between a therapy group's and a minimal treatment control group's posttreatment scores on an outcome measure was statistically significant favoring the therapy group, the therapy was concluded to be efficacious (assuming, of course, that the study design and methods had adequate internal validity to test the question).

An important problem was that the criterion of statistical significance could be met even if treated individuals remained notably impaired on the outcomes of interest. For example, a therapy group's average posttreatment scores could indicate that, although statistically significant improvement had occurred in symptoms of depression, most people's outcome scores were still not in the normal (non-depressed) range on the outcome measure. Thus, statistical significance did not give a full picture of the potential usefulness or effectiveness of a therapy. Jacobson and colleagues' milestone contribution was a set of logical and statistical procedures that provide information on how close to normal or to individuals with non-impaired scores on outcome measures those who receive a therapy are.

3. A Note on Data Analytic Techniques

The development of clinical significance methodology for evaluating outcomes illustrates the central role that data analytic techniques and statistics play in the kinds of conclusions that are possible from therapy research. As noted previously, the topic is excluded from this article. However, many developments in data analysis have been stimulated by or appropriated for psychotherapy research and are properly regarded as milestones for the field because they have had a profound impact on the kinds of questions that can be asked and answered. For example, effect sizes—as described by Jacob Cohen in 1970 and as used in the aforementioned technique of meta-analysis—came to be preferred over statistical significance indices for comparing the outcomes of treatment and control conditions. An effect size is a statistic that can indicate the magnitude of differences between two alternative treatments or a treatment and a control condition. Random effects regression and hierarchical linear modeling are other examples of techniques that were not available to therapy research during its coalescence phase that subsequently extended how outcome and other questions can be examined and answered.

4. *Stability and Longevity of Effects*

Obtaining data from outcome studies on the question, "How long do the desired benefits of a psychotherapy last?," was recognized as important early in the development of psychotherapy research. For example, Victor Raimy's 1952 chapter in the *Annual Review of Psychology* noted both the importance and absence of posttreatment follow-up data on the outcomes of psychotherapies. By about the mid-1960s, the collection of follow-up data was regarded as a crucial component of therapy outcome studies.

The need to know how long a therapy's effects last to fully evaluate its utility is another fundamental question that has proven to be an intransigent one. Over time, as more and more alternative treatments for the same problem have become available (e.g., various forms of psychotherapy and various medications for depression), data on the stability of effects of treatments have become particularly important because they bear directly on the relative desirability of the alternatives. Yet, it seems accurate to say that as of 2001 it is impossible to derive conclusive, no caveats, answers to stability of effects questions using currently available research methods.

A major problem is the phenomenon of attrition (loss) of study subjects during follow-up periods. Posttreatment follow-up periods typically range from 3 months to 2 years. Some portion of treated individuals inevitably become unable to be located or unwilling to continue to provide data. The longer the follow-up period, the larger the attrition problem typically becomes. The lack of complete follow-up data from all individuals treated in a study raises the possibility that the data obtained are biased in some way, that is, do not reflect the follow-up outcomes of the entire original sample (also called the "intent-to-treat" sample). For example, perhaps those who experienced more positive outcomes are more likely to agree to provide follow-up data. One obvious solution is to offer study participants large financial incentives to provide follow-up data. However, such a procedure raises the ethical concern of coercion of participants and typically is frowned upon by human subjects research review committees.

All the limitations associated with collecting unequivocally interpretable stability of effects data notwithstanding, interesting evidence exists for a variety of problems. For example, a recently completed multisite comparative outcome study of cognitive-behavioral therapy, medication, and their combination for panic disorder by David Barlow and colleagues suggested that the treatments that included medication (medication alone or combined medication and therapy) were associated with less stable benefits after treatments were discontinued than were treatments that did not include medication (i.e., therapy alone or therapy plus pill placebo).

F. How Does Psychotherapy Work: Mechanisms of Action

The question of how psychotherapy works often is stated in the contemporary therapy research literature as a "mechanisms of action" question: "What are the primary mechanisms and processes by which psychotherapeutic treatments potentiate desired changes (outcomes)?" Using no jargon, William Stiles and David Shapiro stated the essential question this way in 1994: "How do the conversations between therapists and clients (psychotherapy process) reduce psychological suffering and promote productive, satisfying ways of living (psychotherapy outcome)?" Many therapy researchers have devoted substantial parts of their careers to this and related questions.

Mechanisms of action questions have been examined since at least the 1940s when Carl Rogers and associates began doing methodologically groundbreaking research on them. Such questions have been studied from widely divergent vantage points—a range that has been characterized as "elephant to amoeba." For example, at a macro level, studies are done to identify therapeutic processes that might operate in all forms of psychotherapy (i.e., "nonspecific" or "common" factors) and that, thus, characterize psychotherapy as a treatment modality. At a more intermediate level, mechanisms of action are tested that are posited by the theory of a specific type of psychotherapy ("specific" factors) such as Beckian cognitive therapy for depression. At a micro level, "therapeutic change events" are examined—patterned sequential shifts in a patient's focus of attention and affect states in a therapy session—that might constitute universal psychological change processes that can be prompted by specifiable therapist interventions.

The importance of mechanisms of action research cannot be overemphasized. Without knowing the causally dominant processes by which a form of psychotherapy can prompt desired changes, therapists cannot structure their interventions to achieve a therapy's potential effects as quickly and as completely as is possible. Therapists can identify very specific goals for a patient's progress and improvement. Yet, without knowing a therapy's active mechanisms, they cannot rationally guide their interventions in the most effective and efficient ways to help a patient attain identified goals. Without mechanisms of action knowledge, therapists' moment-to-moment choices between alternative interventions must be based mainly on their knowledge of the theory that underlies a form of therapy, more general theories of how therapeutic change can be facilitated, or on their reflexive sense of what to do (or not do) next. Even the most well developed theories are not detailed enough to guide all the momentary decisions that therapists must make. Moreover, theories remain just that until posited mechanisms of action are tested and supported by empirical findings.

1. Process and Process-Outcome Research

The importance of conducting research on mechanisms of action questions has been matched so far by the difficulty of answering them. Pursuing such questions required therapy researchers to develop new methods, a task on which great strides have been made. The relevant methods collectively are referred to as process research methods. The development and refinement of process methods was a key advance for the field of therapy research during the last 50 years. Several colleagues and students of Carl Rogers at the University of Wisconsin in the 1960s such as Donald Kiesler, Marjorie Klein, and Philippa Mathieu-Coughlan made major early contributions to the needed methodological infrastructure.

The traditional type of process methods are observational. The researcher(s) or trained raters are the observers. Observational process methods involve systematic examination of actual therapy session material (i.e., the "process" of therapy), such as videotapes and/or transcripts of therapy sessions. Process methods extend to the collection of other types of data on therapy sessions such as patient and therapist self-report questionnaires completed immediately after sessions. The term "systematic examination" is a deceptively simple one that masks much complexity when used to describe process research methods. For example, it refers to detailed procedures for selecting (sampling) therapy session material to examine in order to answer a particular research question. It also refers to the development of psychometrically sound instruments that are needed to observe and quantify therapy process variables of theoretical or pragmatic interest (e.g., the therapeutic alliance). Process outcome research is a subset of process research that specifically involves combining therapy process data and outcome data from the same patients with the aim of identifying the aspects of therapies that can be either helpful or harmful.

Donald Kiesler authored a classic, still relevant text on observational process research, *The Process of Psychotherapy: Empirical Foundations and Systems of Analysis.* The book was the first attempt to compile and systematically review process methods, methodological issues, and "systems" (instruments and related instructions for their use) that had been developed. Seventeen major therapy process research systems of the time are reviewed in detail. Only process methods used to study non-behavioral types of psychotherapy are included, an omission consistent with the aforementioned bifurcation of the field at the time into "behavior therapy" and "psychotherapy" research. In 1986, Leslie Greenberg and William Pinsof edited a similar volume that included many of the then, major process research systems. A succinct contemporary summary of process research methods and issues can be found in Clara Hill and Michael Lambert's chapter in the most recent edition (5th edition) of the *Handbook of Psychotherapy and Behavior Change.*

2. Process-Outcome Research: Problems with the Paradigm

David Orlinsky and colleagues described process-outcome research in their 1994 review of existing studies this way: "Process-outcome studies aim to identify the parts of what therapy is that, singly or in combination, bring about what therapy does." An enormous amount of effort has been devoted to investigations of this type. Even after using specific definitions to delimit process-outcome studies, Orlinsky recently estimated that about 850 were published between 1950–2001. However, the yield from them, in terms of identifying mechanisms of action, was judged to be disappointing by many therapy researchers as of the late 1980s. Newer studies have not modified the overall disappointment of researchers' and practitioners' wish to know precisely (a) what the active agents of change are, and (b) how they can be reliably initiated and supported by a psychotherapist's actions. Yet, useful knowledge has been obtained from process outcome research.

Cardinal advances to date include the identification of overly simplistic conceptualizations that drove much process outcome research, that is, hypotheses about how therapeutic interventions might causally potentiate desired outcomes. For example, advances include: (a) elucidation of limiting assumptions that underlie the correlational design, a traditional one in process outcome research; (b) enhanced recognition that a network of contributing variables must be taken into account in this type of research; and (c) proposals for alternative, more complex strategies that incorporate (a) and (b).

a. Limiting Assumptions: The Drug Metaphor. Several limiting assumptions were highlighted for the field in a 1989 paper by Stiles and Shapiro with the attention-getting title: "Abuse of the Drug Metaphor in Psychotherapy Process-Outcome Research." The authors' general thesis was that "slow progress" in identifying the mechanisms of action of therapies was due to the ubiquity of a research paradigm in which therapeutic techniques were tacitly assumed to act like medications. So, for example, study designs reflected the assumption that therapeutic "ingredients" were dispensed by a therapist to a passive patient. Many studies also reflected the assumption that the relationship between a therapy's potentially helpful interventions and desired outcomes was linear and ascending—more is better.

The linear dose–response assumption guided many, if not most, of the mechanisms of action studies through the 1980s. That is, theoretically posited or other possible agents of change, measured with process methods in therapy session material, were correlated with outcome scores obtained at the end of a therapy. Such correlational designs are based on the assumption that a linear function accurately describes the relationship between two variables. For example, severity of depression scores (outcome variable) might be correlated with the frequency of therapist interventions in sessions that were intended to help the patient identify and change ways of thinking and behaving that (theoretically) were creating and maintaining symptoms of depression.

Most therapy researchers were at least dimly aware of the limitations of correlational designs for examining mechanisms of action hypotheses and of the other conceptual simplicities that Stiles and Shapiro elucidated. Yet, the research strategy continued to be used (overused) for a variety of reasons. As Stiles and Shapiro noted, the correlational design is not inherently flawed for use in process outcome research. Rather, it is highly unlikely to reveal all of the ways in which therapeutic interventions might robustly potentiate desired changes.

The drug metaphor analysis of process outcome research fostered widespread awareness of the need to formulate and test alternative hypotheses about relationships between outcomes and theoretically posited and other possible mechanisms of action of psychotherapies. It helped to solidify, disseminate, and encourage the implementation of "new ways to conceptualize and measure how the therapist influences the patient's therapeutic progress," in George Silberschatz's words.

b. Network of Contributing Variables: Moderators and Mediators. Pioneers in psychotherapy research were very much on target when they endorsed Gordon Paul's aforementioned formulation of the overarching question for psychotherapy research, that is, "*what* treatment, by *whom,* is most effective for *this* individual ... and under *which* set of circumstances (original emphasis)?" Increasingly, therapy researchers have tried to identify "moderator" and "mediator" variables that might modify and determine the potential therapeutic outcomes of a psychotherapy. A paper by Reuben Baron and David Kenny that helped clarify therapy researchers' thinking on the issues appeared in 1986. In brief, moderators and mediators are "third variables" that can affect the relationship between independent variables (like a type of psychotherapy) and dependent variables (e.g., reduction in symptoms of depression). So, for example, a therapist technique that is specific to a form of therapy, as interpretation is to psychodynamic psychotherapy, is a therapy process variable that is hypothesized to be a primary mediator of the potential benefits of psychodynamic psychotherapy. Specifically, as defined by Baron and Kenny, a mediator is "the generative mechanism through which the focal independent variable is able to influence the dependent variable of interest." A moderator is "a qualitative (e.g., sex, race, class) or quantitative (e.g., level of reward) variable that affects the direction and/or strength of the relations between an independent or predictor variable and a dependent or criterion variable."

The impact of possible moderating and mediating variables on hypothetically important mechanisms of actions of therapies (which also are posited mediators of outcome) is increasingly being attended to in process outcome research.

G. How Does Psychotherapy Work?: Specific versus Non-Specific (Common) Mechanisms of Action

The specific versus non-specific question is an enduringly central one for psychotherapy process outcome research. The basic question is: "What is the contribution to therapy outcomes of the specific therapeutic techniques that characterize different forms of therapy, compared with other possibly therapeutic, but common (non-specific) features that characterize psychotherapy as a treatment modality?" The potential causal contribution of common factors to therapy outcomes was convincingly argued 40 years ago by Jerome Frank.

In a classic book, *Persuasion and Healing: A Comparative Study of Psychotherapy,* Frank tried to account for the fact that existing psychotherapy outcome studies typically failed to show that markedly different types of psychotherapy had different outcomes. He specifically noted three types of null or "no-difference" findings. One was that "about two thirds of neurotic patients and 40 percent of schizophrenic patients are improved immediately after treatment, regardless of the type of psychotherapy they have received." Second, comparable improvement rates were found even when patients had "not received any treatment that was deliberately therapeutic." Third, follow-up studies, although very few at the time, did not demonstrate differences in long-term outcomes of diverse treatments.

The lack of evidence for any clearly superior form of therapy was, itself, perplexing. It was completely inconsistent with the expectations of many therapy researchers and nonresearcher, practicing mental health professionals alike. Different forms of therapy, such as Rogerian client-centered therapy and Freudian-derived psychodynamic therapy, were based on very different theories of the psychological processes that needed to be potentiated to achieve desired benefits. In addition, each theoretical orientation endorsed very different specific therapist techniques—techniques that were believed to potentiate the theoretically posited and theoretically required, psychological processes. In other words, a fundamental assumption was that the specific techniques of a type of therapy made a causal contribution to the outcomes that were sought. In addition, proponents of each orientation assumed that its underlying theory was more valid than the theories of alternative forms of therapy. Failure to find any one therapy that was superior to others was a stunning challenge to the preceding widely held assumptions.

Given that the results of therapy outcome research did not support the specific factors hypothesis (at least, not when using research methods and statistical analyses that were accepted at the time), Frank posited an alternate hypothesis. He suggested that similar improvement rates were due to psychologically influential elements that were common to all types of psychotherapy. Moreover, he posited that the common factors were those that operate in all human healing relationships and rituals, including religious healing. For example, he identified the arousal, or rearousal, of hope (e.g., the expectation of help) as one common factor. Frank did not, however, completely dismiss the role of specific factors. He hypothesized that improvement rates in outcome studies reflected changes due to common factors in many patients plus change due to specific factors in some patients who did, indeed, respond to the particular form of therapy that they received. So, Frank's common factors hypothesis included the idea that specific techniques of different forms of therapy could be helpful to certain individuals although they were not needed by all those who could benefit from psychotherapy.

By 1971, Frank had further developed his common factors hypothesis and identified six "therapeutic factors" that are present in all forms of psychotherapy. For example, one was giving the patient a rationale or "therapeutic myth" that included both an explanation for the cause of the distress and a way to remedy it. Frank posited that his or her therapeutic action of such rationales, whatever their specific content or validity, includes strengthening a patient's confidence in the therapist. This, in turn, can reduce a patient's distress by reducing anxiety, as well as make the patient more open to the therapist's "influence" (e.g., suggestions for needed changes in attitudes and behaviors, and possible ways to achieve such changes).

Currently, 40 years after Frank's common factors treatise, research designed to identify the contributions to therapy outcomes of specific therapeutic techniques compared to common factors still is of central importance to the development of maximally effective and efficient psychotherapies. In general, it continues to be true that much less evidence than expected exists for the contribution to outcomes of specific techniques endorsed by different forms of therapy. Many researchers have attempted to explain why the null findings persist, given that process research has repeatedly demonstrated that purportedly different forms of therapy (e.g., cognitive therapy for depression and interpersonal therapy for depression) are associated with observably different and theoretically consistent, specific therapist interventions. For example, Alan Kazdin summarized and evaluated the situation this way for the 1994 *Handbook of Psychotherapy and Behavior Change:*

> Comparative studies often show that two different forms of psychotherapy are similar in the outcomes they produce. ... This finding raises important questions about whether common mechanisms underlie treatment. Yet methods of evaluation are critical to the conclusion. It is possible that the manner in which treatment is studied may lead to a no-differences finding. The vast majority of therapy studies, by virtue of

their design, may not be able to detect differences among alternative treatments even if differences exist.

It is of interest that a similar situation exists for medications commonly used to treat depression. Classes of medications that have demonstrably different effects at the level of brain neurochemistry, such as selective serotonin reuptake inhibitors and tricyclics, have not yet been found to be associated with notably different outcomes. (Side effect differences are documented, however.) The similar failure to find outcome differences in medication treatments that differ at another level of observation lends some credence to contentions that current, standard methods for evaluating therapy outcomes might not allow different effects of psychotherapies to be observed. It also could be that the current difficulty demonstrating outcome differences between therapies that are demonstrably different at the level of implementation (therapeutic techniques) is a repetition of the fact that it could not be convincingly demonstrated that psychotherapy was better than no psychotherapy until the effect size statistic was applied to the task.

H. Do Some Forms of Psychotherapy Work Better Than Others?

Questions about the comparative efficacy of different forms of therapy have been a central focus of therapy research. As already noted, to the continual amazement of advocates of various specific forms of therapy, an enduring finding when different forms of therapy are compared is that their effects are not demonstrably different.

Over the years, the creative language skills of many experts in psychotherapy research have been stimulated by the frequent failure to demonstrate differential efficacy of different forms of therapy. For example, in a widely-cited 1975 paper, Lester Luborsky and colleagues adopted the Dodo Bird's salubrious verdict from *Alice in Wonderland* that "all have won and all must have prizes" to describe the weight of the evidence. Almost 10 years later, in 1984, Morris Parloff similarly summarized the findings as "all psychotherapy works, and all psychotherapy works equally well." However, the title of Parloff's paper highlighted a less sanguine implication of the no difference results: "Psychotherapy Research and Its Incredible Credibility Crisis." Shortly thereafter in 1986, William Stiles and colleagues analyzed possible reasons for the "equivalence paradox," that is, the fact that comparative outcome studies repeatedly found no differences in outcomes, yet the therapeutic techniques used in the different treatment conditions had been demonstrated (via process research methods) to be different.

As of now, 2002, very detailed and comprehensive reviews of the comparative outcome study literature on different types of problems (e.g., anxiety disorders like obsessive–compulsive disorder and generalized anxiety disorder) and different patient groups (e.g., children, adolescents, and adults) suggest that it is not completely true that all therapies work and work equally well for every type of problem. For example, evidence exists that different specific forms of behavior therapy (such as exposure plus response prevention vs. progressive muscle relaxation) are differentially effective for obsessive–compulsive disorder. However, the general situation remains that less evidence for differential effects of specific forms of therapy exists than predicted by prevailing theories of psychotherapy and their posited mechanisms of action.

I. How Well Do Psychotherapies Work Compared to and Combined with Medications?

Increasingly, since about the early 1980s, psychotherapy researchers have collaborated with experts in psychopharmacology research to design and conduct comparative outcome studies of medications and psychotherapies. Comparative studies that include a combined medication plus psychotherapy condition also have become more frequent. A keen interest currently exists in comparative medication, psychotherapy, and combined medication and therapy outcome studies. The interest reflects the fact that medications have become more and more widely used in mental health treatment. Increased use can be traced to many forces including, of course, the aforementioned national emphasis on cost containment and cutting in mental health care.

In the early 1960s, Hans Strupp noted that chemical means were likely to be a challenge for psychotherapy. Indeed so. Within the past 3 years (since 1999), psychoactive medications (e.g., for depression) started to be advertised in television commercials in the United States. Viewers now are even encouraged to inform their doctors when new forms of existing drugs are available (e.g., an extended time release, once weekly, Prozac pill). As yet, no forms of psychotherapy are advertised in this way.

Conducting comparative psychotherapy and medication outcome studies heightened therapy researchers' awareness of some of the assumptions on which their standard research methods were based. For example, in therapy outcome studies the posttreatment outcome assessment traditionally is done after therapy sessions have been discontinued. The procedure is consistent with both internal and external validity aims because of a general assumption about how psychotherapeutic interventions work. Historically, diverse forms of therapies all were expected to continue only for a time, to foster desired changes during that time, and then end when the patient had learned or otherwise "internalized" the ameliorative psychological processes that the therapy was intended to potentiate. When therapy researchers started to collaborate with psychopharmacology researchers, they observed alternative procedures for measuring outcome. For example, in medication studies, the convention was to obtain outcome assessments while patients still were taking the study medication. Differences in research methods made therapy researchers more aware of alternative methods and indicated the need for careful selection of methods that would yield "fair" and clinically-relevant findings from comparative studies of psychotherapies and medications.

Focal questions examined in comparative medication and therapy studies include rate of reduction in symptom severity, percentage of treated patients who reach a recovery criterion, stability and longevity of recovery, length of continuing treatment needed to retain response, and cost-effectiveness. Additional questions are associated with testing combined medication plus therapy treatments such as, "In what sequence should each intervention be administered to obtain the best outcomes?" An example of such a sequence is: Provide medication alone first for 2 months, then add in psychotherapy for 3 months, then discontinue medication while therapy continues for 3 months.

Fascinating, yet now completely unknown mechanisms-of-action questions about how medications and psychotherapies can interact are likely to be key to our ability to ultimately devise the most effective and efficient combined treatments. For example, do a particular medication and a psychotherapy interact in an additive way to affect certain problems so that the benefits of combined treatment are equal to the sum of the separate effects of each component? Alternatively, is the interaction "permissive" meaning that the presence of one component is needed to enable the other component to have its potential benefits? Alternatively, is the nature of the interaction inhibitory so that the presence of one component reduces the potential effects of the other component?

It is difficult to provide concise, general summaries of the findings from comparative studies of psychotherapies and medications, and their combination. Results exist for a variety of problems that differ markedly in symptoms and functional impairment (e.g., various anxiety disorders, types of mood disorders, schizophrenia). The findings are not the same across disorders. It is of interest, though, that for at least some disorders (major depressive episode, panic disorder) the common expectation that combined treatment would be more effective than single modality treatment (either medication or psychotherapy alone) generally has not been supported yet. For example, as mentioned previously, some evidence exists that combined treatment of panic disorder is associated with poorer stability of response after treatment is discontinued than cognitive-behavior therapy alone is. For major depression, the evidence now indicates that combined treatment is not generally more effective than monomodality treatment of either type except, perhaps, for individuals with more severe or chronic (e.g., ≥ 2 years) symptoms of unipolar depression.

J. Can Psychotherapy Be Harmful?

The importance of conducting research to determine the frequency and nature of negative effects of psychotherapeutic interventions has been recognized by various therapy researchers over the years, such as Allen Bergin in the early 1960s, and Daniel Mays and Cyril Franks in the early 1980s. In the mid-1970s, Strupp and colleagues received a contract, initiated and funded by the NIMH to examine the topic. Their conclusions were published in a 1977 book, *Psychotherapy for Better or Worse: The Problem of Negative Effects.* In 1983, Edna Foa and Paul Emmelkamp edited a book focused on unsatisfactory outcomes, not negative effects per se, *Failures in Behavior Therapy.* The book illustrates the effort to improve the effectiveness of existing therapies by studying cases in which their effects are disappointing. The value of studying poor outcomes was noted in 1954 by Carl Rogers in a book that reported on the first 5 years of the therapy research program at the University of Chicago Counseling Center, *Psychotherapy and Personality Change:* "The field of psychotherapy cannot come of age until it understands its failures as well as it understands its successes."

Research on deterioration, negative effects, and failures associated with psychotherapeutic interventions has not been prolific, but many questions have been examined. For example, the possible contribution of therapist personality features to poor outcomes has been studied as has the interaction of treatment approach (e.g., supportive vs. more "confrontational") with patient characteristics.

A review of research on the important topic of negative effects is included in Michael Lambert and Allen Bergin's chapter in the 1994 *Handbook of Psychotherapy and Behavior Change.* The review does not include relevant findings and methods that now are emerging from patient-focused research strategies. Such information can be found in Lambert and Ogles' chapter, "The Efficacy and Effectiveness of Psychotherapy" in the fifth edition of the *Handbook of Psychotherpy and Behavior Change*.

IV. CONCLUDING COMMENTS

Much ground has been covered in this article. Even so, some milestones in psychotherapy research have not been discussed, such as research on the therapeutic alliance (a subject that is covered in a separate article in this volume). Important topics have been skipped (e.g., research on training in psychotherapy) or referred to only in passing (e.g., the gulf between therapy research findings and clinicians' satisfaction with their utility for practice). Moreover, the Key Questions section doubtless has left the impression that some crucial and basic discoveries are yet to be made. For example, much more remains to be learned than is known about the major causal agents of change in existing therapies, and the relevant moderating variables.

Bountiful evidence has been provided that conducting informative, reasonably conclusive research on psychotherapy is difficult. Sol Garfield, one of the field's major contributors and astute critics, is among those who observed that a core problem is that clinical research is very unlike controlled laboratory experiments. The central variables in therapy research (e.g., patients, therapists, extratherapy events, outcomes) have proven to be particularly intransigent both to evaluation and to the kind of experimental controls needed to obtain unambiguous findings. Given the challenges, many of which were revealed as researchers tried to answer the field's fundamental questions, Michael Lambert and Allen Bergin's appraisal of progress as of 1992, seems apt: "Psychotherapy research has been exemplary in facing nearly insurmountable methodological problems and finding ways of making the subjective more objective."

Given the difficulties of the endeavor, one might ask, "Why do psychotherapy research?" The field's first 60 to 80 years has revealed that the work can be painstaking and can yield results that, although very informative and important, are surprising and disappointing—sometimes especially to those who worked to find them. But what are the implications for clinical practice and for the patients who are served by it if therapy research is not pursued? Lee Sechrest, in an electronic mail message to the Society for the Study of Clinical Psychology in 2000, observed: "reliance on authority (teachers, supervisors, trainers) or on one's experience does not allow you to know whether you are right or wrong." In the same message, Sechrest credited C. P. Snow for saying: "Science cannot guarantee that you will be right forever, but it can guarantee that you won't be wrong forever." For those who are dedicated to the responsible and ethical provision of mental health treatments, Paul Meehl's observation in 1955 (*Ann. Rev. Psych.* 6) exemplifies a compelling justification for psychotherapy research:

> The history of the healing arts furnishes ample grounds for skepticism as to our nonsystematic "clinical" observations. Most of my older relatives had all their teeth extracted because it was 'known' in the 1920's that the clearing up of occult focal infections improved arthritis and other disorders ... Like all therapists, I personally experience an utter inability not to believe I effect results in individual cases; but as a psychologist I know it is foolish to take this conviction at face value.

Acknowledgments

Morris Parloff, Donald Kiesler, and Marvin Goldfried all key contributors to and observers of the development of psychotherapy research in its first 60 to 80 years, generously provided comments and perspectives on the content of this article. Lisa Onken and Barry Lebowitz, two experts on the field who view therapy research from leadership positions at the U.S. National Institutes of Health, also graciously provided comments. Winnie Eng, a student of therapy research, made helpful suggestions. Responsibility for errors, omissions, and interpretations of events remains the author's. Quote page 541: Copyright and used by permission of John Wiley & Sons, Inc.

See Also the Following Articles

Cost Effectiveness ■ Effectiveness of Psychotherapy ■ Efficacy ■ History of Psychotherapy ■ Outcome Measures

Further Reading

Beutler, L. E., & Crago, M. (Eds.). (1991). *Psychotherapy research: An international review of programmatic studies*. Washington, DC: American Psychological Association.

Chambless, D. L., & Ollendick, R. H. (2001). Empirically supported psychological interventions: Controversies and evidence. *Annual Review of Psychology, 52*, 685–716.

Freedheim, D. K. (1992). Psychotherapy research (Section III, Chapters 9–12). In D. K. Freedheim (Ed.), *History of psychotherapy: A century of change* (pp. 305–449). Washington DC: American Psychological Association.

Handbook of psychotherapy and behavior change. (1971–). (Editions 1–4, 5th ed., in press). New York: John Wiley and Sons.

Kazdin, A. E. (1994). Methodology, design, and evaluation in psychotherapy research. In A. E. Bergin & S. L. Garfield (Eds.), *Handbook of psychotherapy and behavior change* (4th ed., pp. 19–71). New York: John Wiley and Sons.

Kazdin, A. E. (Ed.). (1998). *Methodological issues & strategies in clinical research* (2nd ed.). Washington, DC: American Psychological Association.

Kraemer, H. C., & Telch, C. F. (1992). Selection and utilization of outcome measures in psychiatric clinical trials: Report on the 1988 MacArthur Foundation Network I Methodology Institute. *Neuropsychopharmacology, 7,* 85–94.

Orlinsky, D. E., & Russell, R. L. (1994). Tradition and change in psychotherapy research: Notes on the fourth generation. In R. L. Russell (Ed.), *Reassessing psychotherapy research* (pp. 185–214). New York: Guilford Press.

Persons, J. B. (1991). Psychotherapy outcome studies do not accurately represent current models of psychotherapy. *American Psychologist, 46,* 99–106.

Schooler, N. (Vol. Ed.). (1998). Research methods. In A. Bellack & M. Hersen (Series Eds.), *Comprehensive clinical psychology* (Vol. 3). London: Elsevier Science.

Wilson, T. (1996). Manual-based treatments: The clinical application of research findings. *Behaviour Research and Therapy, 34,* 295–314.

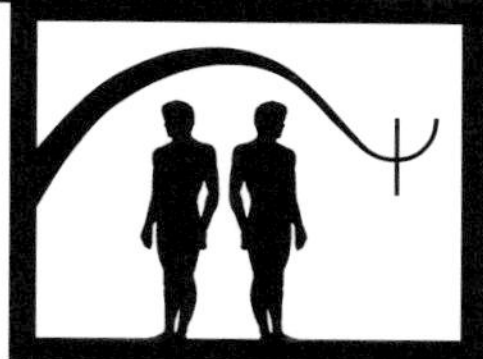

Resistance

Kay McDermott Long and William H. Sledge

Yale University School of Medicine

GLOSSARY

character A person's enduring patterns of thinking, feeling, and acting, as well as habitual ways of resolving inner conflict.

compromise formation The mind's attempt to resolve conflict between various aspects of a person's inner world and external reality by reorganizing the various aspects of the inner world so that competing interests are all given expression. For example, a fantasy may represent a compromise formation in that it expresses a wish, as well as defenses against the wish and ways a person imagines being punished for the wish.

defense A general term used to describe the mind's, usually unconscious, attempts to protect itself from felt dangers, such as loss of love or of the loved one, loss of physical integrity, or a harsh conscience and all the attendant uncomfortable feelings.

drive (instinctual drive) A strong endogenous motivational force, especially of a sexual or aggressive nature, that motivates behavior toward a particular end.

interpretation The analyst puts into words his or her understanding of what the patient has been expressing, perhaps even without knowing it, to add new knowledge about a patient's mental life.

object relations The particular, individual patterns of relating to others that are characteristic of a person.

repression The exclusion of painful ideas, impulses, and feelings from conscious awareness.

transference The largely unconscious process of shifting feelings, thoughts, and wishes originally experienced with significant figures in childhood onto current figures in one's life.

unconscious Mental content that one is not aware of at any given time, though one may get glimpses of it through dreams, slips of the tongue, and disconnected thoughts.

Resistance is a term used to describe the various ways patients in psychotherapy oppose the process of change. This article briefly traces the development of this concept in Freud's thinking and then presents contemporary psychoanalytic views of resistance. In addition, psychoanalytic views will be contrasted with a behavioral perspective. Finally, clinical examples illustrate how a psychoanalytically oriented psychotherapist might understand and treat resistance in a treatment situation.

I. DEFINITION

Perhaps the clearest and most direct definition of resistance was Freud's deceptively simple statement in 1900, in his landmark work, *The Interpretation of*

Dreams: "Whatever disturbs the progress of the work is a resistance." His discovery of the phenomenon, his attempts to understand it, and his work with it led him to some of his most important technical and theoretical discoveries in psychoanalysis. The concept of resistance still stands today as a cornerstone of psychoanalytic theory and practice; however, precise definition of the term remains elusive. In fact, any comprehensive definition of resistance includes almost all the key analytic concepts: drive, defense, compromise formation, character, and transference.

II. FREUD ON RESISTANCE

Early in his psychotherapeutic career Freud worked with Joseph Breuer treating women with hysterical symptoms. In their jointly published book, *Studies on Hysteria,* Freud describes his work with Fraulein "Elisabeth von R.," his first reported full-length analysis of hysteria and his first case report of resistance. By this time Freud had seen the limitations of using hypnosis and the power of suggestion to help his patients give up their hysterical symptoms, and he had already turned to encouraging his patients to talk freely as a method of cure. As Freud worked with Elisabeth, she would fall silent and refuse to speak. When Freud asked her what was on her mind she replied, "Nothing." Freud surmised that her not talking was a way of resisting treatment. Undiscouraged, Freud was able to make virtue out of a defect. He realized that resistance was not an obstacle to be overcome, but a way in and of itself to reach the repressed and overcome neurosis.

Freud learned through clinical experience how tenacious and persistent resistance could be even in patients truly interested in symptom relief and in the process of therapy. Anything could be used as a resistance to treatment: falling silent, forgetting, intellectual discussions about theory and treatment, coming late, seeing the therapist as the enemy. Equally suitable for resistance was coming on time, finding everything the therapist says helpful and brilliant, talking without hesitation.

At first blush, resisting treatment seems irrational. Why would someone who is suffering and coming for help in relieving that suffering resist efforts to get better? The attempt to answer this question led Freud to the discovery of key aspects of his theory and therapy. Freud posited that people fall ill due to the repression of painful memories or wishes, that is by pushing painful experiences out of conscious awareness. They get better by remembering those painful experiences. However, to readmit those warded-off mental contents into consciousness is inherently marked by conflict. It entails undoing or giving up the mental structures that have been created to achieve some form of adaptation, however costly and unsuccessful. The patient, understandably, resists recognition of painful experiences, and, in essence, mounts the same efforts that brought about the repression of the pain in the first place.

When Freud attempted to overcome this resistance through suggestion and authority, he was met with increased resistance. This led him to recognize the importance of interpreting the resistance rather than directly interpreting the warded-off aspects of the patient's experience. Resistance to treatment begins to seem more understandable in light of the patient's fear (perhaps even unconscious) that the "cure" may be worse than the "disease." Competing wishes are doing battle within the patient: the wish to leave well enough alone and the desire to ally with the therapist to be able to "remember" in the hopes of eventual relief of suffering. Ultimately the patient must ally with the therapist well enough to develop a partnership in exploration, and first and foremost exploration of his resistances.

In one of Freud's technical papers "Dynamics of Transference," he elaborates: "Resistance accompanies the treatment at every step; every single association, every act of the patient's must reckon with this resistance, represents a compromise between the forces aiming at cure and those opposing it." In fact, Freud defined psychoanalysis in terms of resistance. In a later work he wrote,

> It may thus be said that the theory of psychoanalysis is an attempt to account for two striking facts of observation which emerge whenever an attempt is made to trace the symptoms of a neurotic back to their sources in his past life: the facts of transference and resistance. Any line of investigation which recognizes these two facts and takes them up as the starting point of its work has a right to call itself psychoanalysis, even though it arrives at results other than my own.

Freud's first attempt to inventory resistances was in his previously cited book, *Studies on Hysteria.* Here he recognized that some resistances are manifest and some are hidden which led him to recognize the unconscious aspects of resistance and ultimately to see that his current model of the mind (topographic theory of conscious and preconscious) was not sufficient to account for the clinical phenomena he observed. Consequently he developed the structural theory of id, ego, and superego. Reflecting the further development of his ideas

Freud was still expanding his inventory of resistances 25 years later in "Inhibitions, Symptoms and Anxiety" in which he outlined three types of resistances: ego resistances—repression, transference resistance, and secondary gain from illness; superego resistances—unconscious guilt and need for punishment; id resistances—such as the repetition compulsion.

As Freud developed his theories of psychoanalytic technique he continued to emphasize the central role of interpreting resistance, along with the transference (i.e., relating to the therapist as if he or she were an important figure from the patient's past). In fact, he viewed transference itself as, in part, a resistance in that the patient was enacting a prior relationship rather than remembering and verbalizing it. Freud came to see that transference and resistance both impede and facilitate cure. The desire to remember is opposed by the desire to forget. According to Freud, analytic technique must first and foremost address itself to overcoming resistance.

III. CONTEMPORARY PSYCHOANALYTIC VIEWS

Psychoanalytic thinking, including the theory of resistance, has developed along several paths since Freud laid down his original ideas. Psychoanalytic thinkers since Freud have been trying to sort out his somewhat diverse legacy concerning resistance. At times Freud seemed to consider resistance as something to be overcome and at other times as psychical acts that could be understood. That same duality persists today in those who endorse techniques designed to overcome or bypass resistance and make the unconscious conscious, and those who would seek to recognize and clarify resistance at work and to try to analyze the perceived threat to the patient's functioning posed by trying to overcome the resistance. Adherents to the work of Melanie Klein in Great Britain (Kleinians) have been responsible for the development of the former view, while ego psychologists in North America (contemporary Freudians) have been developing the latter view. In addition, another school of thought has developed inspired originally by the works of Hans Kohut (self psychology, interpersonal or relational psychology) that has taken psychoanalytic theory and technique in quite a different direction. Although the ego psychological perspective has been the dominant view in North America, the influence of the Kleinians and the self psychologists is increasingly felt and is working its way into the mainstream of analytic thinking.

A. Ego Psychology

The central role of resistance in theory and technique has been best preserved in analysts schooled in an ego psychological approach (contemporary Freudians). Resistance, along with its successful interpretation by the analyst, is held as the essential unit of clinical psychoanalysis. A patient resists not just remembering but also resists understanding the nature of the felt dangers that caused the original repression. The patient is seen as struggling with internal conflicts not with the therapist. Resistance is a ubiquitous, recurring, ever-present aspect of the psychotherapeutic work. Successful therapy does not bring about removal of resistances but an understanding of them so that a new set of resistances can emerge and be explored. Successful psychoanalysis is the successful negotiation of one resistance after another. Problems occur when the patient becomes stuck in one particular resistance and cannot move on to other ones.

Contemporary Freudian efforts to develop Freud's ideas on resistance have focused on the defensive aspects of resistance. In this vein contemporary analytic thinkers view resistance as whatever gets in the way of a patient being able to recognize what comes to mind, as well as how and why it comes to mind. Paul Gray and his followers have led the field in contemporary efforts to develop Freud's ideas on resistance. Gray is particularly interested in the defensive aspects of resistance. He argues that traditionally analysts work to get past the resistance to get at what the patient is experiencing but not why the experience is so painful that the patient resists knowing it. Gray and his adherents argue for an approach that takes into account the importance of understanding why something is resisted as well as what it is that is being resisted. In Gray's view, it is not just that an experience is painful that it is avoided but that it threatens the patient with feeling overwhelmed and losing the capacity to function adequately.

B. The Kleinian School

In this school the emphasis has been on penetrating interpretations aimed at reaching the deepest levels of a person's unconscious experience. Trying to locate and articulate unconscious fantasies takes precedence over interpreting resistance. Resistances are seen in terms of object relationships rather than as impersonal mechanisms of the mind. That is to say they occur in the context of the relationship between the analyst and patient or between figures in the person's internal world.

C. Self Psychology, Interpersonal or Relational Psychology

In this framework resistances are not viewed as ways the patient is avoiding communicating or knowing something about the self, but as yet another way the patient has of communicating something important about the self to the analyst. What another analyst might see as resistance, a relational analyst would view as a communication from the patient to the analyst about something the patient wants the analyst to know and to hold in the analyst's mind because the patient cannot yet tolerate knowing it consciously. It is then the analyst's job to "contain" the communication and eventually to put this "unspeakable, unknowable" mental content into words.

In sum, a contemporary analyst might hear Freud's patient, Elisabeth's response of "Nothing" when asked what was on her mind as an attempt to keep painful experience out of mind and hence avoid feeling overwhelmed (ego psychology); as an unconscious repetition of an internal object relationship (Kleinian); or as an attempt to communicate something about herself to the analyst (self psychology/interpersonal psychology).

IV. BEHAVIORAL THERAPY PERSPECTIVES

Behavior therapy, of course, is a multifaceted approach about which generalizations should be made cautiously. So it would be misleading to state that there is a particular perspective or approach to the idea of resistance emanating from behavior therapists. Nevertheless, certain similarities and differences can be noted. For one, although behavior therapists and psychodynamic psychotherapists both believe that human behavior is more or less lawful and ultimately understandable, the laws that are in question are fundamentally different between the two approaches. Behavior therapy is based on the idea of the preeminence of the environment in controlling and shaping actions whereas the psychodynamic psychotherapist is concerned with the internal environment of the individual actor and the role of unconscious mental processes in governing behavior. Naturally then, when faced with the inevitable difficulty of the patient in complying with the prescribed treatment, adherents to the two approaches will see different (from one another) forces at work. Behavior therapists will look to the environment as the source of the problems while the psychoanalytically oriented therapist will see the key environment driving the patient as being located within the patient.

The definitions of resistance of the two perspectives are also different. For behavior therapists resistance is antitherapeutic behavior. For the psychodynamic psychotherapist resistance is the force working against making conscious unconscious processes in the context of the patient's effort to make changes in action, thinking, and feeling. In both perspectives, the patient acts in a way to keep the therapy from having a full effect. Behavior therapists tend to see resistance as something that has to be changed or eliminated. Psychoanalytic therapists see resistance as an essential element of the change process. For the behavior therapist, resistance is usually conceptualized as the therapist's failure to perceive accurately and fully the lawful rules by which the environment is influencing the behavior of the patient. The behaviorists think of resistance as just another part of the patients' world that has to be taken care of in the delivery of the therapy. For the behaviorist, it is not a central or core concept.

V. CLINICAL EXAMPLES

Though psychotherapists today may not be familiar with the history of Freud's thinking about resistance they are intimately familiar with the same clinical phenomena that led Freud to his theoretical and technical innovations. Day by day, hour by hour, psychotherapists confront powerful resistance on the part of even the most motivated patients.

Ms. A., usually very responsible in her time management, found herself over the course of a number of weeks arriving later and later for her psychotherapy appointment. At times she was as much as 15 or 20 min late and would berate herself for wasting valuable time. "How will I ever get better if I can't even get here on time to talk about my problems?" she asked. Her therapist suggested that perhaps she had mixed feelings about her therapy, wanting to be here to get better, but perhaps she was also aware of something that felt uncomfortable about being here. Several weeks later Ms. A. arrived only a few minutes late and saw the previous patient leaving her therapist's office. She felt a wave of jealous, competitive feelings come over her that she immediately wanted to disavow. Instead she decided, reluctantly, to talk to her therapist about her feelings of jealousy and dislike for the woman who saw him in the hour before her. As they talked about this the therapist suggested that these jealous feelings that clearly disturbed her might be playing a part in her recent pattern of coming late to her sessions. Immediately she saw that she had unwittingly avoided these feelings by coming so late she would never run into any "rivals" leaving her therapist's office. This understanding of her resistance led her to talk more about the role of jealous and competitive feelings in her life and also led her to resume coming to her therapy hour on time.

Mr. B. came to treatment feeling desperately unhappy about almost every aspect of his life. He had few friends, was not able to sustain romantic relationships, and felt stymied in trying to choose among various career paths open to him. Mr. B.'s therapist noticed that no matter what kind of comment she made to Mr. B., Mr. B. rejected it. For example, Mr. B. was talking about being in a social situation the previous evening and described becoming extremely anxious as he began to talk to a particular woman he found attractive. His therapist, thinking she was empathically reflecting what he had already said, responded that Mr. B. seems to become anxious around women he finds attractive. Mr. B. immediately responded, "Well, not exactly. I mean maybe but not always." After repeated efforts to try to talk with Mr. B. about his feelings and dilemmas the therapist realized that the work would go nowhere until the resistance was explored. The therapist pointed out to Mr. B. that every time she attempted to say something, even if it was something the patient has just described, the patient would reject it. The therapist interpreted that the patient seemed to be having trouble taking in anything from the therapist. Over time with the therapist's help the patient was able to observe this response over and over again in their conversations, and he began to be curious about it. He came to understand more about his attempts to shut out the therapist in this way and about the ways this related to his experiences with his intrusive mother as well as with others in his present life.

In these examples we can see that resistance is not just an obstacle to be overcome but the expression of essential aspects of the patient's characteristic ways of relating to themselves and others, the exploration of which can lead to significant therapeutic gains, as well as open doors to further areas of conflict and to transference manifestations.

VI. SUMMARY

All psychotherapists are faced with the many ways patients seek and resist help in the same endeavor. How that resistance is defined, understood, and worked with varies widely between schools of therapy, as well as within a particular school of thought. There is no single voice in psychoanalysis or in behavioral therapy, yet meaningful distinctions between the two schools of thought exist.

Practitioners of behavior therapy and psychoanalysis treat the clinical phenomenon of patients' opposition to the effects of the treatment in very different ways. Adherents of both perspectives recognize the clinical phenomenon and its salience for the effectiveness of the treatment. In the case of the psychoanalytic perspective, resistance is seen as an essential, indeed necessary element of the treatment process. It is inevitable, and there are technical, specific strategies and clinical rules and theoretical formulations designed to address this phenomenon. Of course, this conceptualization depends on the existence of an unconscious mental process that can both enhance as well as oppose conscious motivations and intentions at the same time.

Behavior therapy practitioners, on the other hand, tend to conceptualize the patient's inability to follow the treatment program as a lack or defect on the part of the therapist in not accurately understanding and formulating the contingencies in the patient's life. Behavior therapy provides no such motivational construct of patient-originated resistance to the treatment. Rather, behavior therapists locate the problem as existing in a faulty understanding of and/or application of treatment on the part of the therapist. Indeed, behavior therapists make room for the prospect that it would be impossible for all therapists at all times to understand all patients. The responsibility, however, for the treatment progress or lack thereof rests clearly on the shoulders of the therapist.

The different ways of conceptualizing the phenomenon of patient-originated opposition goes to the core of the differences between behavior therapy and psychoanalysis. Psychoanalysis postulates underlying and unwitting motivational complexes that can be in conflict with one another, and behavior therapy locates these conflicts entirely in the contingency environment of the patient.

See Also the Following Articles

Countertransference ■ Engagement ■ Interpretation ■ Object-Relations Psychotherapy ■ Termination ■ Transference ■ Unconscious, The ■ Working Alliance

Further Reading

Boesky, Dale. (1990). The psychoanalytic process and its components. *Psychoanalytic Quarterly, 59*, 550–584.

Busch, Fred. (1992). Recurring thoughts on unconscious ego resistances. *Journal of the American Psychoanalytic Association, 40*, 1089–1115.

Gray, Paul. (1987). On the technique of analysis of the superego-an introduction. *Psychoanalytic Quarterly, 56*, 130–154.

Kris, Anton. (1985). Resistance in convergent and in divergent conflicts. *Psychoanalytic Quarterly, 54,* 537–568.

Renik, Owen. (1995). The role of an analyst's expectations in clinical technique: Reflections on the concept of resistance. *Journal of the American Psychoanalytic Association, 43,* 83–94.

Schafer, Roy. (1973). The idea of resistance. *Journal of the American Psychoanalytic Association, 54,* 259–285.

Spezzano, Charles. (1995). "Classical" versus "contemporary" theory—the differences that matter clinically. *Contemporary Psychoanalysis, 31,* 20.

Wachtel, Paul. (Ed.). (1982). *Resistance psychodynamic and behavioral approaches.* New York: Plenum.

White, Robert. (1996). Psychoanalytic process and interactive phenomena. *Journal of the American Psychoanalytic Association, 44,* 699–722.

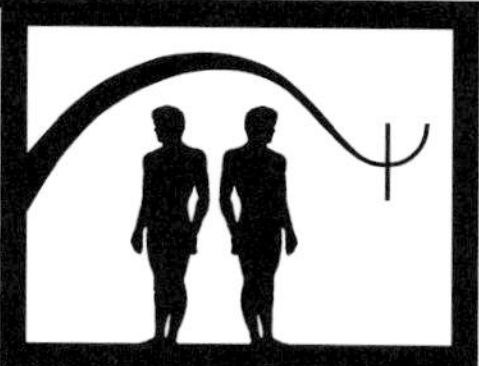

Response-Contingent Water Misting

J. Grayson Osborne
Utah State University

GLOSSARY

AB design A case study design in which the behavior of interest is first measured in the absence of treatment (during Condition A). Treatment is then applied (during Condition B). Changes of the behavior in Condition B cannot be attributed to the change from Condition A to Condition B.

ABAB withdrawal design A single subject research design in which A = baseline (no treatment) conditions; B = treatment conditions in which, after the occurrence of baseline (no treatment) treatment is presented for a number of sessions and then is withdrawn, and then is re-presented. The intent is to establish the effect of treatment.

aggression Behavior directed toward another individual that either produces or intends to produce physical or emotional damage.

alternating treatment design A research design in which several treatments are presented in succession in random order within sessions.

aromatic ammonia The use of ammonia as a punisher by holding it under an individual's nose contingent upon the emission of undesirable behavior (often pica).

BAB design Where B = treatment and A = no treatment; same as ABAB withdrawal design except that the study starts with the treatment condition immediately.

demand condition A diagnostic condition in which an individual is asked to perform a response the result of which is aggression by the individual against the asker with the intent that the aggression will make it less likely that the demanded response will be performed.

differential reinforcement of incompatible behavior (DRI) Reinforcement of a response (R_1) that is functionally incompatible with another response (R_2) with the intent of reducing in frequency that other response (R_2). The intent is that R_1 will occur frequently enough because it is being reinforced so there is limited opportunity for R_2 to occur.

differential reinforcement of other behavior (DRO) Reinforcement of the absence of a response (R_1) for a period of time with the intent of reducing it in frequency. At the end of the period of time whatever response (R_0) is occurring, as long as it is not the response that is supposed to be absent (R_1), is reinforced. As with DRI, the intent is that R_0 occurs frequently enough because it is being reinforced so there is limited opportunity for R_1 to occur.

facial screening A punishment technique in which the individual's face is briefly covered with a towel whenever an undesirable behavior occurs.

fading procedures Any of a number of procedures in which the known controlling stimuli of a discriminated response are gradually diminished in their apparentness such that their stimulus control passes to other stimuli that are more apparent in the current environment.

forced arm exercise Raising and lowering the arms of an individual in rapid succession as a punishment technique.

generalization of punishment The occurrence of the effects of punishment (i.e., the reduced frequency of the punished response) in an environment in which the response was not formally punished.

hand biting A self-injurious response in which the hand is inserted in the mouth and bitten, often with resulting tearing of the skin.

head banging/hitting Any response of an individual that brings the head into forceful contact with an object or body part.

lemon juice (therapy) Typically a squirt of lemon juice in the mouth contingent upon the emission of an undesirable behavior; often used with individuals who ingest nonedible substances in an attempt to punish such ingestion.

mental retardation Any endogenous or exogenous condition the result of which is an individual who has significant challenges in functioning independently in everyday life.

mouthing Putting an open mouth on objects or more typically on other body parts (e.g., skin) usually to the point where the other body part is damaged.

multiple baseline across settings The sequential treatment of a response in each of several settings; while being treated in one setting measurements of the frequency of the treated behavior occur in the other settings. If no change in frequency occurs in the other settings until and only if the behavior is treated in that setting, causal inferences about the treatment are typically thought to be strengthened.

pica The ingestion of inedible substances.

positive reinforcement Response-contingent presentation of a stimulus that has the effect of increasing the frequency (strength) of the response that it follows; both parts of this definition are necessary to the inference of positive reinforcement.

prepunishment baseline The frequency of occurrence of a response before punishment of the response.

programmed generalization The processes that produce the occurrence of a behavior therapeutic outcome in an environment in which it was not treated.

punisher A punishing stimulus, the presentation of which causes a decrease in the frequency of the response on which it is contingent.

punishment Either the presentation of a stimulus or the withdrawal of a stimulus, which has the effect of reducing the frequency of the response on which such presentation or withdrawal is contingent.

punishment procedure Either the response-contingent presentation or withdrawal of a stimulus, which has the effect of reducing the frequency of the response on which such presentation or withdrawal is contingent.

response Anything an organism (person) does or says that can be reliably observed and reported.

response-contingent faradic shock Electrical current delivered to an individual contingent upon the emission of a response, typically a self-injurious or aggressive response.

response-contingent water mist Water misting a person contingent upon that person's emission of a response, typically a self-injurious or self-stimulatory response.

restitutional overcorrection The overcorrection procedure in which the individual undergoing the procedure returns the environment to its former (presumably unspoiled) state, such as righting furniture that may have been thrown over during a tantrum. May also include a component in which the individual is required to improve on the unspoiled environment, such as polishing the furniture.

self-choke Any response of an individual that has the effect of cutting off the supply of oxygen to the brain.

self-injury Tissue damage caused by an individual's own behavior, such as head banging or head slapping.

self-injurious (behavior) responses Any response an organism emits that is either immediately tissue damaging or is tissue damaging in the long term.

self-stimulatory behavior (responses) Behavior that occurs in the absence of apparent, empirical reinforcement; typically assumed to be inherently reinforcing.

side effects Unprogrammed outcomes of behavioral procedures that may be positive or negative.

skin tearing Picking/pulling at loose pieces of skin.

stereotypic behaviors Peculiar responses that are emitted repetitively across long periods of time (e.g., mouthing), may be synonymous with self-stimulatory responses.

time-out (from positive reinforcement) Either the removal of a person from a reinforcing environment for a few minutes or the removal of the reinforcing environment from the person for the same few minutes contingent upon the emission of some undesirable response; a punishment technique.

water mist The spray from a water bottle.

water misting The act of spraying water mist at a person; typically a reaction to the occurrence of a self-injurious behavior by that person.

Response-contingent water misting has been used as a mild punisher to suppress self-injurious behavior (SIB) and/or self-stimulatory behavior in people with mental retardation. It is the subject of a little over a dozen clinical and research papers in the literature. Response-contingent water misting came to prominence as a function of the search by behavior analysts for mild punishers to use when reinforcement-based behavior reduction techniques had failed and stronger punishment techniques were inappropriate, as discussed by Bailey and colleagues in 1983. This article describes the use of the technique, its effectiveness, and drawbacks to its use. It also provides a chronological, annotated bibliography of the known literature.

I. EQUIPMENT

In its most prevalent use, water, at room temperature, is placed in a plastic spray bottle. Spray bottles used for the purpose of water misting are those commercially obtained for household use. They are manufactured in a variety of sizes that hold up to 1 liter of water. Spray is emitted from the nozzle of the spray bottle when a hand pump/trigger that is part of the nozzle and the cap to the bottle is squeezed. Each squeeze of the pump dispenses about 0.5 cc. The nozzle is usually adjustable to produce gradations from a thin stream of water (like that from a squirt gun) to a fine mist. The mist usually describes a diffuse arc of water greater than 90 degress and travels no more than about 46 cm. Thus, those operating the water mist must hold the spray bottle within 30 cm of the subject of the water misting.

II. OPERATIONAL DEFINITION

Room temperature water mist is sprayed in the recipient's face from a distance of 30 cm contingent upon the emission of a defined response. As is the case with all punishment procedures, unless the procedure is being used for research purposes, water misting does not occur absent concurrent positive reinforcement for behavior incompatible with the water-misted response.

III. FUNCTIONAL OUTCOME

The desired outcome is complete cessation of the water-misted response. Such an outcome is rare. Rather, the technique most often produces good, but partial, suppression of the response. Thirty to 90% suppression of the contingent response roughly encompasses the range of suppression in the literature. Suppression of the contingent response appears to be enhanced by the concurrent positive reinforcement of behavior incompatible with the contingent response. Response-contingent water mist does not appear to produce permanent suppression of the contingent response, as there is often recovery when the procedure is withdrawn, as discussed by Bailey et al., in 1983, Dorsey et al. in 1980, and Osborne et al. in 1992. Recovery is often incomplete; that is, the rate of the punished response does not return to the prepunished baseline. One implication of the recovery finding is that the procedure must be used chronically to maintain suppression of the responses on which it is contingent. However, fading procedures, in which the spray bottle is kept near to hand but where its presence cannot be discriminated by the subject, are effective in producing generalization of suppression beyond the occasions and environments of therapy, (according to research by Jenson et al. in 1985 and Rojahn et al. in 1987. In these procedures, the bottle has been made smaller so that it can be easily concealed.

IV. SUBJECTS

Subjects in the clinical and research literature have been primarily individuals with severe to profound mental retardation, often with additional challenges such as impaired vision and hearing and limited mobility. Most subjects described in the literature had been exposed to many other procedures to reduce the self-injurious or self-stimulatory responses that are frequently the focus of their behavioral programs, in the absence of good effect. These procedures are often the differential reinforcement of other behavior (DRO) or the differential reinforcement of incompatible behavior (DRI) in which the attempt is made to strengthen behavior that—when it occurs—precludes the occurrence of the self-injurious or self-stimulatory behavior. The literature is silent on how effectively these other procedures were applied. As these other procedures usually are mentioned as the reason to proceed with water misting, their ineffectiveness is assumed.

V. SIDE EFFECTS

No negative side effects have been reported. However, as with any punishment procedure there is always a chance of aggression against the therapist, according to Rojahn et al. in 1987. It may be notable that many of the subjects of this procedure appeared to be less than capable of aggression against a therapist because they were nonambulatory and confined to wheelchairs as discussed by Dorsey et al. in 1980, or they had visual impairments according to Dorsey et al. in 1980, Fehr & Beckwith in 1989 and Osborne et al. in 1992. Positive side effects appear to include enhanced effectiveness of concurrent positive reinforcement, as described by Fehr and Beckwith in 1989, and increased social interaction, as discussed by Singh et al. in 1986, which are common to other punishment procedures as well, according to Risley in 1968.

VI. OBSERVATIONS AND OPINIONS

Water misting was initially used for several reasons, as discussed by Dorsey et al. in 1980. First, it was easier to administer than other punishment procedures such as faradic shock or restitutional overcorrection. Second, the equipment (a spray bottle) was inexpensive and highly portable. Thus, it could be used in many different environments. Third, unlike other punishment procedures (e.g., response-contingent faradic shock), water misting appeared not to present any health risks to those on whom it was used. Fourth, because of its relative simplicity, it was easy to train staff in its use. Fifth, staff had fewer objections to using water mist than they did other punishment procedures. Sixth, given all of the foregoing, water misting—as punishment—could be considered relatively innocuous.

Notwithstanding these reasons, no evidence suggests that the technique has been used in the past decade. Since this time period is concurrent with the absence of virtually all other applied punishment research, it is concluded that the national crusade against the utilization of formally described punishment procedures is responsible. (I say formally here, because most therapists involved with institutionalized people understand that informal punishment procedures continue to be used by the staff of such institutions.)

Water misting is not a completely effective punishment procedure. If it were, it would produce complete cessation of responding, no negative side effects, no avoidance of the therapist, and generalization outside treatment sessions. Therefore, it is possible that the reason that it is no longer used is that it was not effective enough. However, absent complete suppression, there are no negative side effects of the procedure, there is no evidence of avoidance of the therapist, and there is some evidence of generalization outside treatment sessions. Therefore, response-contingent water misting is an effective—if not completely effective—punishment procedure. Utilization of the procedure has suffered the fate common to the formal application of all other punishment procedures.

In the beginning, water misting was used as an alternative to more effective punishment procedures, such as response-contingent faradic shock, according to Dorsey et al. in 1980. It was used also because it was thought that society would tolerate its use better than had been shown to be the case for faradic shock. Clearly, this was an incorrect supposition. No behavior analyst ever feels good about administering any form of punishment during therapy sessions, particularly to a subject who is not capable of escape. Water misting was no exception. Colleagues worried about changes in subjects' dignity and self-worth. Yet, such concerns were overridden by the felt need to help reduce what was, and is, perceived to be serious self-injury and its long-term effects. Response-contingent water misting seemed a good compromise.

A possibly serious restriction on the effectiveness of response-contingent water misting is the absence of application of this procedure to normal populations. The procedure would seem, on its face, to constitute a possible backup to ineffective verbal reprimands by parents of their young children. It could constitute a viable alternative to the more ungoverned use of corporal punishment. Absent any such information, however, it should be understood that generalization of the effectiveness of contingent water misting beyond the rather restricted populations on which it has been successfully used is unwise.

VII. CHRONOLOGICAL ANNOTATED LITERATURE REVIEW

1. Peterson, R. F., & Peterson, L. W. (1977). Hydropsychotherapy: Water as a punishing stimulus in the treatment of a problem parent-child relationship. In B. C. Etzel, J. M. LeBlanc, & D. M. Baer (Eds.), *New developments in behavioral research, theory, method, and application*. Hillsdale, NJ: Lawrence Erlbaum.

Study Design. Single subject, ABAB withdrawal design imbedded in contact/no-contact context; punishment only in contact context; during no contact, parent ignored child's head banging; followed by time-out phase.

Subject. 3.5-year-old male; with mental retardation.

Response. Head banging/hitting.

Treatment. 4-oz water splash delivered by parent from a water glass from a distance of 18 to 30 cm concurrently with a shouted, "No!"

Results. Good suppression by water splash over baseline in contact and no-contact periods; suppression not as good during no-contact context; but no-contact period provided evidence of generalization of punishment. Recovery during withdrawal phase, but phase stopped before recovery could further increase. Time-out was about as effective as water splash. Suppression maintained during follow-up, however, time-out was continued during this period.

Critique. Not really water misting. Study included because it appears to be a precursor to the water-misting procedure. Note difficulty of governing amount of water to be splashed and how much less water appears to be as effective when using water misting.

2. Murphrey, R. J., Ruprecht, M. J., Baggio, P., & Nunes, D. L. (1979). The use of mild punishment in combination with reinforcement of alternative behaviors to reduce the self-injurious behavior of a profoundly retarded individual. *AAESPH Review, 4*, 187–195.

Study Design. Single subject, BAB design.
Subject. Profoundly retarded male.
Response. Self-choke.
Treatment. Water squirt in the area of the mouth for self-chokes; positive reinforcement of other behaviors; treatment application in six different settings; utilization of seven different therapists.
Results. Good suppression of self-choking (near 90%); quick recovery during treatment cessation (A); considerable recovery by follow-up after 20 months.
*Critique.*Treatment begun in the absence of a recorded baseline. Good attempt at programmed generalization.

3. Dorsey, M. F., Iwata, B. A., Ong, P., & McSween, T. E. (1980). Treatment of self-injurious behavior using a water mist: Initial response suppression and generalization. *Journal of Applied Behavior Analysis, 13,* 343–353.

Experiment 1:
Study Design. ABAB within-subject, reversal designs.
Subjects. Seven nonambulatory persons with profound mental retardation, with additional auditory and visual impairments, 5 to 37 years old.
Responses. Mouthing; hand biting; skin tearing; head banging.
Treatments. Water mist contingent upon SIB.
Results. Substantial reductions in SIB frequencies during treatment conditions—but not to zero—followed by recovery (instantly in four of the seven cases) to prior levels during treatment absence (baselines).
Critique. No concurrent positive procedures. No generalization outside sessions.

Experiment 2:
Study Design. Single subject; case study with successive treatments, across two environments; i.e., AB1B2B3 where A = baseline; B1 = response contingent "No"; B2 = "No" + water mist + DRO 1 minute; B3 = "No" + DRO.
Subjects. 21-year-old female, nonambulatory, with profound mental retardation; 26-year-old female, nonambulatory, from Experiment 1.
Response. Hand biting.
Results. Little or no suppression during B1; good suppression in one environment each for each subject during B2, but not in the second environment; addition of DRO helped with suppression for one subject but not the other in the second environment; upon withdrawal of water mist (B3) there was continued suppression in both subjects in the previously successful environment and good suppression in the remaining environments for both subjects.
Critique. No measurements beyond treatment sessions. Authors anecdotally note no generalization in terms of long-term maintenance of suppression across the entire day.

4. Gross, A. M., Berler, E. S., & Drabman, R. S. (1982). Reduction of aggressive behavior in a retarded boy using a water squirt. *Journal of Behavior Therapy & Experimental Psychiatry, 13,* 95–98.
Study Design. Single subject; ABAB design with follow-up.
Subject. 4-year-old male with mental retardation.
Response. Biting; gouging (i.e., aggression).
Treatment. Baseline continued a hand slap and "No!" contingent on aggression that was already in place; treatment consisted of water misting—with mister set to the concentrated stream setting.
Results. Good suppression by water squirt over the hand slap procedure; some recovery during withdrawal of water squirt, but not back to original baseline; subsequent good suppression during second treatment application; zero frequencies at 6-month follow-up.
Critique. All day use of technique may have helped its success. Note that the study is only one of two (see work by Peterson and Peterson in 1977) that use water not in mist form.

5. Bailey, S. L., Pokrzywinski, J., & Bryant, L. E. (1983). Using water mist to reduce self-injurious and stereotypic behavior. *Applied Research in Mental Retardation, 4,* 229–241.
Study Design. Single subject; ABAB design with no treatment probes.
Subject. Ambulatory 7-year-old male with severe mental retardation with autism.
Response. Mouthing; hand biting.
Treatment. Water misting contingent upon finger/hand mouthing; all other contingency-based programs continued; including time-out for aggression during water misting.
Results. Excellent, but not complete, suppression during treatment periods; suppression also during no-treatment probes but not nearly as much as during treatment periods; recovery—but not complete recovery—during withdrawal phase; good suppression thereafter in no-treatment probe conditions.
Critique. Lengthy study, but no follow-up.

6. Friman, P. C., Cook, J. W., & Finney, J. W. (1984). Effects of punishment procedures on the self-stimulatory behavior of an autistic child. *Analysis and Intervention in Developmental Disabilities, 4,* 39–46.
Study Design. Single subject; ABACADAB where A = baseline; B = water mist; C = lemon juice; D = vinegar with follow-up.

Subject. 11-yr-old male with severe mental retardation and autism.

Response. Hand touching (hand clapping; hand jabbing; finger jabbing).

Treatment. Water mist to the face or lemon juice squirted in the mouth; or vinegar squirted in the mouth.

Results. Partial suppression during water mist followed by complete recovery during withdrawal; less suppression with lemon juice; about same suppression as water mist with vinegar; more suppression in second water mist phase; follow-up was continued use of water mist by staff and teacher with very good suppression.

Critique. Sessions were only 5 minutes. Baseline conditions and background in all treatment sessions consisted of structured play that involved therapists telling subject what to do explicitly—a demand condition that may have contributed to baseline frequencies.

7. Reilich, L. L., Spooner, F., & Rose, T. L. (1984). The effects of contingent water mist on the stereotypic responding of a severely handicapped adolescent. *Journal of Behavior Therapy & Experimental Psychiatry, 15,* 165–170.

Study Design. Single subject; multiple baseline across settings and teachers with follow-up.

Subject. 15-year-old female, deaf and blind.

Response. Stereotypic behavior (e.g., picking up coats, paper, etc., and covering her head with these items).

Treatment. Head coverings removed and water mist applied to subject's face immediately, while during baseline she was allowed to keep covered for 2 minutes before covering was removed.

Results. Good, but not complete, suppression on application of water misting in each environment only when water mist applied; good suppression in the presence of each teacher. Zero frequency at 17 months follow-up.

Critique. Not a very exciting response. There did not seem to be anything life threatening about it, nor did it have the qualities of stereotypic behavior (that is, on its face, did not seem highly self-stimulatory). Rather, response appeared to be attention getting. However, DRO had been tried and had failed.

8. Jenson, W. R., Rovner, L., Cameron, S., Peterson, B. P., & Keisler, J. (1985). Reduction of self-injurious behavior in an autistic girl using a multifaceted treatment program. *Journal of Behavior Therapy and Experimental Psychiatry, 16,* 77–80.

Study Design. Single subject; case study with generalization and follow-up.

Subject. 6-year-old-female, autistic, with moderate to severe mental retardation.

Response. Hand biting.

Treatment. Contingent water mist plus loud "No!" Size of spray bottle reduced across phases (fading). Parents also used program at home.

Results. Virtually complete suppression. Long-term follow-up showed almost complete suppression also.

Critique. Case study design. However, fading size of bottle and having parents do procedure at home, may have contributed substantially to long-term effectiveness.

9. Singh, N. N., Watson, J. E., & Winton, A. S., (1986). Treating self-injury: Water mist spray versus facial screening or forced arm exercise. *Journal of Applied Behavior Analysis, 19,* 403–410.

Experiment 1:

Study Design. Single subject; alternating treatments design with follow-up.

Subject. 17-year-old female, with profound mental retardation.

Response. Face slap.

Treatment. Alternation of contingent water mist with facial screening counterbalanced across the two daily sessions.

Results. Substantial reductions in frequencies of face slapping by both water misting and facial screening with slightly more reduction by the facial screening.

Critique. No generalization or measurement to other times of day.

Experiment 2:

Study Design. Same as Experiment 1.

Subject. 17-year-old female with profound retardation.

Response. Finger licking.

Treatment. Same as Experiment 1.

Results. Only about 25% reduction by water mist; much greater reduction by facial screening; socially positive interactions increased.

Critique. No generalization or measurement to other times of day.

Experiment 3:

Study Design. Same as Experiment 1.

Subject. 17-year-old female, with profound retardation.

Response. Ear rubbing.

Treatment. Water misting alternated with forced arm exercise.

Results. Water mist reduced ear rubbing by 80%; but forced arm exercise reduced it by 90%; socially positive interactions increased.

Critique. No generalization or measurements to other times of day. Forced arm exercise may have been more effective because subject was precluded from ear rubbing during the exercise.

10. Rojahn, J., McGonigle, J. J., Curcio, C., & Dixon, M. J. (1987). Suppression of pica by water mist and aromatic ammonia: A comparative analysis. *Behavior Modification, 11,* 65–74.

Study Design. Simultaneous (alternating) treatment design with fading.

Subject. 16-year-old female, autistic, with severe mental retardation, with mild cerebral palsy.

Response. Pica (tacks, staples, crayons, strings, woven material, paper, cigarette butts).

Treatment. Three daily sessions (7.5 minutes). Water mist, aromatic ammonia, and no treatment alternated across these sessions; location of bottle faded; generalized to other therapists.

Results. Virtually complete suppression of pica by water mist. Early ammonia administration produced increase in pica followed by decrease. Possible increase in collateral mild aggressive behavior. No increase in collateral SIBs.

Critique. No long-term follow-up. Absence of concurrent positive reinforcement program.

11. Fehr, A., & Beckwith, B. E. (1989). Water misting; Treating self-injurious behavior in a multiply handicapped, visually impaired child. *Journal of Visual Impairment and Blindness, 83,* 245–248.

Study Design. Single subject; case study; combined multiple baseline across settings and ABA design.

Subject. 10-year-old male; visually impaired; auditory agnosia; profound mental retardation.

Response. Head hit.

Treatments. Fine water mist spray to face contingent upon head hit, preceded with "No!" Food contingent on peg placement and toy play.

Results. Substantial reductions of head hitting in breakfast and lunch environments but not in class or residence hall until positive reinforcement for appropriate behavior was added in the latter two.

Critique. No follow-up. No measurement of response outside of treatment sessions and environments.

12. Paisey, T. J. H., & Whitney, R. B. (1989). A long-term case study of analysis, response suppression, and treatment maintenance involving life-threatening pica. *Behavior Residential Treatment, 4,* 191–211.

Study Design. Single subject.

Subject. 16-year-old male with profound mental retardation.

Response. Wandering; pica.

Treatment. Phase 1: Assessment. Pica observed in 4 settings—observers present; subject alone; baits on the floor but neck screen on (blocked vision of floor); neck screen on but baits on furniture, unlimited edibles, contingent mesh hood (did not permit ingestion); contingent water mist accompanied by loud "No!", contingent lemon juice. *Phase 2. Lemon juice punishment for pica and boundary training using water mist; Phase 3: Residential treatment package.* Lemon juice punishment for pica; water mist contingent upon crossing a taped line (wandering); DRI; DRO.

Results. Assessment. Pica greatest during alone context; pica lowest during lemon juice, mesh hood, and ad lib edibles, high during water mist contingency. Still mean frequencies of pica were reduced by half during water misting. *Program Development.* Excellent suppression of pica by lemon juice; good suppression of boundary crossing by water mist and warning. *Residential treatment package.* Lemon juice suppressed pica about 50%; with addition of water mist for boundary crossing there was additional suppression; upon withdrawal of lemon juice and water mist after 30 months there were some increases in pica but suppression was still about 50%.

Critique. Water mist shown not to be too effective with pica, but more effective with boundary crossing (wandering); Excellent study length, although disappointing to see that after so much time there was still an increase in pica after withdrawal of water misting and further increase in pica after withdrawal of lemon juice.

13. Peine, H. A., Liu, L., Blakelock, H., Jenson, W. R., & Osborne, J. G. (1991). The use of contingent water misting in the treatment of self-choking. *Journal of Behavior Therapy and Experimental Psychiatry, 22,* 225–231.

Study Design. Single subject, case study; AB design with treatment generalization and follow-up.

Subject. 25-year-old deaf, blind, male with profound mental retardation.

Response. Self-choke.

Treatments. Fine water mist spray to face contingent upon self-choke, paired with "No!" 20-second absence of self-choke produced face wipe, juice sip, and hug or pat on back.

Results. Approximately 2 responses/min in baseline to .03 to .12 responses/min during treatments—17- to 70-fold reduction. Zero responses during 8-month follow-up.

Critique. AB case study design; no disaggregation of water misting and the positive reinforcement procedure. Except for follow-up—an important exception—no measurement of response outside of treatment sessions and environment.

14. Osborne, J. G., Baggs, A. W., Darvish, R., Blakelock, H., Peine, H., & Jenson, W. R. (1992). Cyclical self-injurious behavior, contingent water mist treatment, and the possibility of rapid-cycling bipolar disor-

der. *Journal of Behavior Therapy and Experimental Psychiatry, 23,* 325–334.

Study Design. Single subject, case study; multiple probe design in which pre- and posttreatment baselines were taken before and after each treatment session.

Subject. 45-year-old female; visually impaired, with profound mental retardation.

Response. Head slap.

Treatments. Water mist spray to face contingent upon head slap, paired with "No hitting!" DRO 1 to 6 minutes for social and tangible reinforcers. Session end contingent upon a successful DRO interval.

Results. Subject cycled between high- and low-frequency periods of SIB lasting 4 to 14 weeks. Mean reduction from presession baseline during treatment was 71% for high-frequency periods; mean reduction from presession baseline during treatment baseline was 85%. No difference between presession baseline and treatment during low-frequency periods; reduction to zero in posttreatment baselines after treatment during low-frequency periods.

Critique. Use of pre- and posttreatment baselines shows recovery of SIB frequencies from posttreatment to next pretreatment baselines. DRO procedure not uncoupled from water mist procedure. No effect of water mist procedure on length of this subject's high- and low-frequency SIB periods.

See Also the Following Articles

Differential Reinforcement of Other Behavior ■ Fading ■ Negative Punishment ■ Overcorrection ■ Positive Punishment ■ Response Cost ■ Time-Out

Further Reading

Bailey, S. L., Pokrzywinski, J., & Bryant, L. E. (1983). Using water mist to reduce self-injurious and stereotypic behavior. *Applied Research in Mental Retardation, 4,* 229–241.

Dorsey, M. F., Iwata, B. A., Ong, P., & McSween, T. E. (1980). Treatment of self-injurious behavior using a water mist: Initial response suppression and generalization. *Journal of Applied Behavior Analysis, 13,* 343–353.

Fehr, A., & Beckwith, B. E. (1989). Water misting: Treating self-injurious behavior in a multiply handicapped, visually impaired child. *Journal of Visual Impairment & Blindness, 83,* 245–248.

Friman, P. C., Cook. J. W., & Finney, J. W. (1984). Effects of punishment procedures on the self-stimulatory behavior of an autistic child. *Analysis and Intervention in Developmental Disabilities, 4,* 39–46.

Gross, A. M., Berler, E. S., & Drabman, R. S. (1982). Reduction of aggressive behavior in a retarded boy using a water squirt. *Journal of Behavior Therapy and Experimental Psychiatry, 13,* 95–98.

Jenson, W. R., Rovner, L., Cameron, S., Petersen, B. P., & Kesler, J. (1985). Reduction of self-injurious behavior in an autistic girl using a multifaceted treatment program. *Journal of Behavior Therapy and Experimental Psychiatry, 16,* 77–80.

Osborne, J. G., Baggs, A. W., Darvish, R., Blakelock, H., Peine, H., & Jenson, W. R. (1993). Cyclical self-injurious behavior, contingent water mist treatment, and the possibility of rapid-cycling bipolar disorder. *Journal of Behavior Therapy and Experimental Psychiatry, 23,* 325–334.

Paisey, T. J. H., & Whitney, R. B. (1989). A long-term case study of analysis, response suppression, and treatment maintenance involving life-threatening pica. *Behavioral Residential Treatment, 4,* 191–211.

Peine, H. A., Liu, L., Blakelock, H., Jenson, W. R., & Osborne, J. G. (1991). The use of contingent water misting in the treatment of self-choking. *Journal of Behavior Therapy and Experimental Psychiatry, 22,* 225–231.

Peterson, R. F., & Peterson, L. W. (1977). Hydropsychotherapy: Water as a punishing stimulus in the treatment of a problem parent-child relationship. In B. C. Etzel, J. M. LeBlanc, & D. M. Baer (Eds.), *New developments in behavioral research, theory, method, and application* (pp. 247–256). Hillsdale, NJ: Erlbaum.

Reilich, L. L., Spooner, F., & Rose, T. L. (1984). The effects of contingent water mist on the stereotypic responding of a severely handicapped adolescent. *Journal of Behavior Therapy and Experimental Psychiatry, 15,* 165–170.

Risley, T. R. (1968). The effects and side effects of punishing the autistic behaviors of a deviant child. *Journal of Applied Behavior Analysis, 1,* 21–34.

Rojahn, J., McGonigle, J. J., Curcio, C., & Dixon, M. J. (1987). Suppression of pica by water mist and aromatic ammonia. *Behavior Modification, 11,* 65–74.

Singh, N. N., Watson, J. E., & Winton, A. S. W. (1986). Treating self-injury: Water mist spray versus facial screening or forced arm exercise. *Journal of Applied Behavior Analysis, 19,* 403–410.

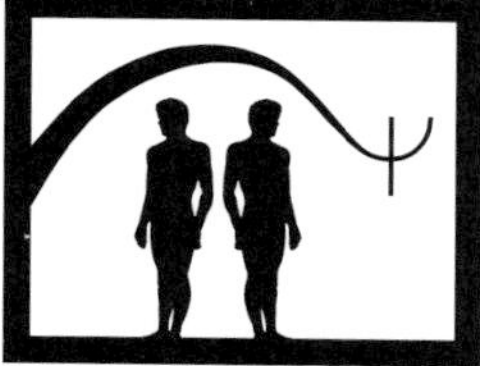

Response Cost

Saul Axelrod
Temple University

GLOSSARY

point-based response cost procedure Point removal in a point economy contingent on a targeted undesirable behavior.

response cost A punishment procedure in which a person loses a reinforcer or a portion of reinforcers following an undesirable behavior. A naturally occuring example of response cost is a traffic fine following an arrest for speeding.

I. DEFINITION

Response cost is the removal of a person's or group's reinforcer(s) as a consequence of an undesirable behavior. Although the entire reinforcer can be removed, more commonly, only a portion is removed. Response cost derives from the notion that the probability of the occurence of a behavior is related to its physical or monetary cost. That is, the greater the cost of performing a behavior, the less likely it is that the behavior will be performed. Some authors specify that the lost reinforcers must be conditioned, but they may also be primary, as in the loss of a portion of a person's edible reinforcers.

II. CONCEPTUAL SYSTEM

A response-cost procedure that results in a decrease in the future rate of a certain behavior is classified as Type II punishment. It differs from Type I punishment in that a reinforcer is removed rather than an unpleasant event (e.g., a loud verbal reprimand) being applied. Response cost differs from extinction, which involves termination of the delivery of ongoing reinforcers. It differs from time-out, which specifies a period of time in a less reinforcing environment following an inappropriate behavior. Response cost does not involve a temporal component, although a person can lose alotted minutes from a desired activity. Response cost is similar to time-out in that both procedures have an aversive component.

Hierarchies of restrictiveness of decelerative procedures usually place response cost as more restrictive than extinction and equal in restrictiveness to time-out procedures. The present author recommends that this classification be revised because response cost is quicker acting and associated with fewer undesirable side effects than extinction. Also it does not require physical intervention (e.g., removing people from ongoing activities), as do many time-out applications.

III. FORMS

The most common form of response cost is evident when a government fines its citizens for traffic violations, paying taxes late, or failure to obey health and safety regulations. A precondition for its application is that an individual have something to lose. Therefore, in order for a response-cost procedure to be applicable, a person must either have reinforcers to lose or must be provided with them.

Often, response-cost procedures are carried out in the context of token-reinforcement programs. Tokens in the form of points, stars, chips, check marks, smiley faces, and so on are removed contingent on display of inappropriate behaviors. The tokens are conditioned reinforcers that can be exchanged periodically for backup reinforcers. The amount of tokens an individual is penalized is crucial since it must be large enough to impact behavior, but not so large that a person quickly loses all of her or his reinforcers.

In one common form of response cost, people lose reinforcers from an existing pool. The pool of reinforcers can already exist in the person's possession or can be provided to the person by the program implementer. For example, a client could be fined $25 each time she missed an appointment at a weight-control clinic. Or a teacher could give a student 15 tokens each day and remove one each time he violated a classroom rule.

In a second form of response cost, a person could start the day with no reinforcers, but earn reinforcers for appropriate behavior and lose them for inappropriate behavior. The popular television quiz show, "Jeopardy," is conducted according to this format. People residing in group homes often experience programs of this type. Thus, the individuals may receive points for carrying out household chores and for prosocial behaviors and lose points for violations such as fighting and failing to do assigned work.

Variations of each of these approaches can also be applied. First, response cost can be carried out on a group-contingent basis. Thus, students can be given 10 extra minutes of free play, but lose 1 minute each time a classmate breaks a classroom rule as follows:

~~10~~,~~9~~,~~8~~,7,6,5,4,3,2,1,0

In this case there were a total of three violations; thus, each member of the class had 7 extra minutes of free time.

In a second variation, free reinforcers can be retained on an all-or-none basis. This modification, frequently mislabeled as differential reinforcement of low rate of response (DRL), could involve allowing a child to stay up an extra 15 minutes if she takes her brother's toys less than three times during the day. If she violates the rule three or more times, she loses the privilege of staying up 15 minutes late.

Finally, as was the case in the two previous examples, program implementers can program penalties from a bonus pool. That is, people can be offered a bonus for refraining from inappropriate behavior. Rule violations then result in the loss of the bonus, rather than what was already due the individual (e.g., the regular recess time). This variation can reduce ethical objections to the use of response cost.

IV. APPLICATIONS

The variety of settings, populations, and behaviors to which response cost has been successfully applied is immense. Settings include traditional homes, schools, clinics, group residences, work sites, correctional facilities, playgrounds, and athletic fields. Populations include children and adults, with and without handicaps. A partial list of behaviors comprises classroom disruptions, aggressiveness, sleep difficulties, excessive drinking, overeating, inattentiveness, speech disfluencies, psychotic speech, food scavenging, toileting accidents, failure to use seatbelts, occupational injuries, failure to keep appointments, failure to hand in assignments punctually, and hair and eyelash plucking. In a naturalistic environment, it has been shown to radically reduce directory assistance calls and could probably be employed to combat resource shortages involving fuel usage and water consumption.

V. ADVANTAGES

Response cost is one of the most effective interventions available. It commonly produces immediate, large, and enduring changes in behavior. It can be applied immediately, easily, and precisely following an undesirable behavior. The application typically does not interfere with the ongoing activity. Unlike time-out, response cost does not remove a violator from the setting in which the problem behavior occurred. Thus, a student who committed an infraction would not lose academic time. Unlike time-out and overcorrection, response cost does not involve physical interaction that could lead to injury. Compared to extinction, response cost works more quickly and produces greater decreases in behavior.

Unlike other punishment procedures, response cost is seldomly associated with adverse side effects. At times it results in desirable side effects. Thus, a reduction in disruptive behavior through response cost has sometimes resulted in appropriate social interactions. Also response cost rarely incurs public objections. It tends to fall within society's norms on how people should treat each other and is compatible with the principle that those who break a rule should pay proportionally.

VI. DISADVANTAGES

Although uncommon, adverse side effects of response cost have been noted. These include emotional responses and aggression following reinforcer removal and avoidance of the environment in which response cost occurs. Also response cost calls attention to the inappropriate behavior, possibly reinforcing its occurrence. All of these problems can be reduced or eliminated by combining response cost with positive reinforcement for appropriate behavior. Thus, a person will not avoid an environment that is mostly reinforcing, but employs occasional response cost. Also attention to appropriate behavior will lessen the likelihood that response cost will reinforce inappropriate behavior.

A significant problem that can occur is that a person could lose all of her or his reinforcers, thereby nullifying the response-cost procedure. In such cases a back-up system such as time-out might be necessary. Another problem is that, due to its effectiveness and ease of implementation, response cost can be overused. It might, for example, be effectively applied to minor infractions that do not justify a punishment procedure. Finally, given the numerical nature of many response-cost procedures, some mastery of quantification is often necessary. This may limit its usefulness with very young or severely cognitively limited individuals.

VII. CONSIDERATIONS IN USING RESPONSE COST

Given that response cost is a punishment procedure, it should only be used when more constructive approaches, such as positive reinforcement, are unreasonable or ineffective. Also the usual operations concerning any behavioral intervention should be employed. This includes defining the behavior(s) of concern, measuring its occurrence during baseline and intervention, specifying the rules of the operation, and revising the procedure when necessary.

In point-based response-cost procedures, point removal should be immediate, obvious, and follow all infractions. The point removal should be done in such a manner as to provide feedback to the offending individual, but should not involve comments that could reinforce inappropriate behavior (through attention) or trigger additional problems.

Significant issues with point-based response cost are setting the upper limit and determining how many points to remove on each occurrence. As indicated earlier, the procedure can be negated when all points are lost. Baseline measures can help set the upper limits for response cost. Thus, the upper limit for a person who displays 40 misbehaviors might be 20, whereas the upper limit for someone who displays 5 misbehaviors might be 3. Research has indicated that the removal of two points per infraction is more effective than removing one. Yet, removing two points might cause the upper limit to be exceeded more quickly than removing one point. In general, the effectiveness of response cost is so great that the upper limit is seldom reached.

Without exception response-cost procedures should be combined with positive reinforcement for appropriate behavior. This can take the form of bonuses or can simply consist of praise for appropriate behavior. The combination of response cost and positive reinforcement is more effective than either procedure used alone. The combination of procedures also allows for the possibility of gradually removing the response-cost procedure and maintaining improved performance with positive reinforcement procedures alone.

VIII. SUMMARY

Response cost is a punishment procedure in which a person loses a reinforcer or a portion of reinforcers following an undesirable behavior. It is powerful, easily implemented, and socially acceptable. It has been successfully used across a wide variety of behaviors, populations, and settings. For reasons of effectiveness and humaneness, it is best combined with positive reinforcement for appropriate behavior.

See Also the Following Articles

Differential Reinforcement of Other Behavior ■ Extinction ■ Good Behavior Game ■ Overcorrection ■ Positive Reinforcement ■ Punishment ■ Token Economy

Further Reading

Alberto, P. A., & Troutman, P. A. (1999). *Applied behavior analysis for teachers*. Columbus, OH: Merrill.

Heron, T. (1987). Response cost. In J. O., Cooper, T., Heron, & W. L., Heward, (Eds.), *Applied behavior analysis*. Columbus, OH: Merrill

Kazdin, A. E. (1972). Response cost: The removal of conditioned reinforcers for therapeutic change. *Behavior Therapy, 3*, 533–546.

McSweeny, A. J., (1978). Effects of response cost on the behavior of a million persons: Charging for directory assistance in Cincinnati. *Journal of Applied Behavior Analysis, 11*, 47–51.

Pazulinec, R., Meyerrose, M., & Sajwaj, T. (1983). Punishment via response cost. In S. Axelrod & J. Apsche (Eds.), *The effects of punishment on human behavior* (pp. 71–86). New York: Academic Press.

Reynolds, L. K., & Kelly, M. L. (1997). The efficacy of a response-cost based treatment package for managing aggressive behavior in preschoolers. *Behavior Modification, 21* 216–230.

Thibadeau, S. F. (1998). *How to use response cost*. Austin, TX:Pro-Ed.

Weiner, H. (1962). Some effects of response cost upon human operant behavior. *Journal of the Experimental Analysis of Behavior, 5*, 201–208.

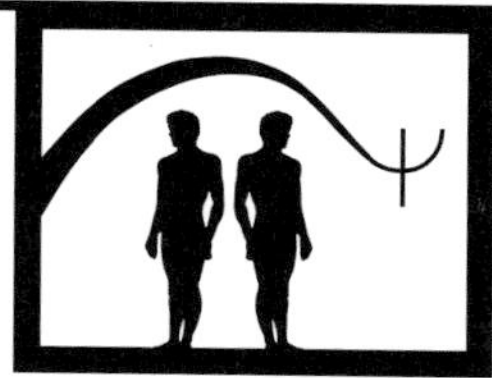

Restricted Environmental Stimulation Therapy

Jeanne M. Bulgin and Arreed F. Barabasz
Washington State University

W. Rand Walker
University of Idaho

GLOSSARY

chamber REST A type of REST that involves secluded bed rest in a small light-free and sound-attenuated room.

dry flotation REST A type of REST that involves a sound and light attenuated enclosed chamber designed so that the research participant is separated from the fluid, a solution of $MgSO_4$, by a velour-covered thin plastic polymer membrane.

restricted environmental therapy/treatment (REST) An experimental psychotherapeutic practice that, through the use of a solitary environment and a drastically reduced level of external sensory stimulation (i.e., light, sound, touch, and gravity) can produce beneficial effects on medical, psychological, and behavioral health outcomes, particularly when used in conjunction with other therapies.

wet flotation REST A type of REST that involves the use of a specially designed sound and light attenuated enclosed tank filled with a skin temperature aqueous solution of Epsom salts and water.

I. DESCRIPTION

Two decades ago, Peter Suedfeld coined the term restricted environmental therapy or technique (REST) as a less pejorative description of sensory deprivation. REST was born out of experimental methods designed to study the affects of environmental stimulus reduction on human beings. The earliest and most relevant preliminary research was published in the 1950s by Donald Hebb of McGill University who, with his students and collaborators, described the effects of "severe stimulus monotony" on his research participants to test his theory of centrally directed behavior. Hebb's experimental setup consisted of a completely light-free and sound-attenuated chamber in which the participant was isolated on a bed for a period of 2 to 3 days. Further sensory reduction was attempted by using variations of the basic setup such as having the participant wear translucent goggles and cardboard sleeves that fit over the hands and arms to limit visual and tactile stimuli and/or enclosing research participants in "iron lungs."

Shortly after publications involving chamber REST methods, John C. Lilly, a neuropsychologist at the National Institute of Mental Health, published findings from his sensory reduction research that focused on the effects of many natural or non-experimental experiences of isolation. These included details of autobiographical accounts from individuals who were isolated geographically or situationally. As a result of these findings, Lilly and his associate, Dr. Jay Shurley, pursued the origins of conscious activity within the brain and whether the brain required external stimuli to keep its conscious states active. To fully address this question, Lilly designed the flotation tank, which restricted environmental stimulation as much as was practical and feasible.

The experimental setup of flotation REST required that the research participant be submerged up to the neck in an enclosed tank of water. A diving helmet acted to block out outside visual stimulation and a breathing apparatus was used so that the participant could respire if the nose and mouth should drop below the level of the water. Although the helmet decreased visual stimuli, the breathing apparatus was anything but noise free. Over the years, Lilly continued his experiments with flotation, simplifying and improving the general design of the tank. Lilly found that one could float in a more relaxing supine position, rather than suspended feet downward in fresh water, if more buoyant salt water was used. This method allowed for the subsequent elimination of the breathing apparatus. Other refinements, such as water heaters, air pumps, and water filters for the reuse of the Epsom salts, were added and by the early 1970s, Lilly had developed the flotation tank in much the design that is used today.

Early studies addressing chamber and flotation REST tested participant endurance, often up to several days, and included setups that were ultimately stressful (being enclosed in iron lungs, cardboard sleeves and/or goggles, or having to rely on a noisy breathing apparatus for respiration as well as being almost completely submerged). It was no wonder that many of the findings from the initial reports were dramatic and negative. Such findings included aversive emotional reactions, disruptions of conscious states, negative hallucinations, interference with thinking and concentration, and sexual and aggressive fantasies. Later research suggested that these negative findings could be understood on the basis of a negative experimental set (aberration and endurance), of an excessive duration of isolation, and of demand characteristics. The most frequent and replicable results of REST are an openness to new information, increased suggestibility, increased awareness of internal cues, decreased arousal, and attentional shifts. These results not only contradict earlier studies, they actually hint at some potential benefits of REST. Research evidence indicates that REST consistently has beneficial effects on medical, psychological, and behavioral health outcomes, particularly when used in conjunction with other therapies.

Current use of REST involves three differing optimal methods and one method that can be used in clinical settings without substantial accommodations. The first, chamber REST, involves secluded bed rest for a variable amount of time, generally 24 hours or less, in a small, completely dark, and sound-attenuated room. Most of the data to date has been generated through the use of this technique. The second method, wet flotation REST, involves the use of a light-free, sound-attenuated flotation tank, resembling a large covered bathtub filled with a skin temperature solution of saturated Epsom salts and water. The research participant floats supinely in the tank for a time period that is generally 90 min or less. The third method is termed dry flotation REST. This method includes a rectangular chamber that is designed so that the research participant is separated from the fluid, a solution of $MgSO_4$, by a thin, plastic polymer membrane. Again, the float time is generally 90 min or less. In clinical settings it is possible to restrict the environment by using darkened goggles, earplugs, sound maskers, and a room with reasonable sound attenuation.

II. BIOLOGICAL AND PSYCHOPHYSIOLOGICAL EFFECTS

The research examining the biological and psychophysiological effects of chamber and flotation REST has been based on more than 1,000 incidents in which 90% of the individuals interviewed reported marked feelings of relaxation and a greater focus on internal processes because external stimuli is limited. A summary of specific findings regarding the relaxation response and cognitive processes are discussed in this section. Such findings include both subjective and objective measurements of various effects.

The relaxation response can be understood by studying several different biochemical and psychophysiological parameters. First, subjective measures of REST have been collected to study relaxation effects using various instruments including the Spielberger State Anxiety Scale, Zuckerman Multiple Affect Adjective Checklist, subjective units of disturbance scale (SUDS), and the profile of mood states (POMs). These instruments conclude that REST participants perceive significantly lower levels of subjective measures of stress and feelings of calmness, alertness, and deep relaxation.

Endogenous opiate activity has been studied, as it is frequently associated with increased pleasure responses and is related to a reduction of stress and pain, and increased relaxation. Results of these studies suggest that REST increased central nervous system availability of opioids across sessions. In addition, a state of relaxation can be defined as exhibiting low levels of the biochemical substrates involved in the stress response. The stress response is a fairly complicated reaction that involves hormone changes from the adrenal glands in particular. Basically, the hormones triggered by stress in this response include norepinephrine, epinephrine (commonly known as adrenaline), adrenocorticotropin (ACTH), cortisol, renin, and aldosterone. Each of these hormones play a role at various organ systems that results in the increase of heart rate, blood pressure, respiration, and muscle tension. Therefore, stress response parameters studied in REST research include blood pressure, muscle tension, and heart rate, as well as the adrenal axis hormones mentioned earlier.

Research studies that have examined heart rate, muscle tension, blood pressure, and various plasma and urinary adrenal hormones conclude that REST consistently produces significant decreases both within and across sessions of these measurements. Other hormones have been measured in conjunction with those mediating the stress response to provide an experimental control. These hormones have included testosterone and lutenizing hormone (LH) and have been found to remain consistent in a 1990 study by Charles R. Turner and Thomas H. Fine. Significant reductions in blood pressure was a finding that was established through case studies of hypertensive individuals, and later in controlled research studies that began in the early 1980s. Researchers that studied REST's effects on hypertensives included Fine and Turner, Jean L. Kristeller, Gary E. Schwartz, and Henry Black, and Suedfeld, Cuni Roy, and Bruce P. Landon, to name a few. This research concludes that a significant decrease in both systolic and diastolic blood pressure can occur in hypertensives. Furthermore cortisol and blood pressure have been shown to maintain these effects 9 months after cessation of repeated REST sessions in a follow-up study by Kristeller, Schwartz, and Black in 1982. Thus, the effects of REST are more than an immediate response that is reversible.

Cognitive effects of REST include a shift in cognitive processing strategies away from analytic, sequential, and verbal thinking toward non-analytic, holistic, and imaginal thought processes. A review of common reports by Helen Crawford in 1993 describes a decrease in external stimuli with redirection to internal stimuli or more narrowly focused external stimuli with possible shifts in attentional processing (changes in focused and sustained attention). The increases in internally generated stimuli, such as fantasies and thoughts, tend to be more vivid and involving. Since 1969, researchers have studied the effects of REST and increased suggestibility. Arreed F. Barabasz and Marianne Barabasz found that floatation REST enhances hypnotizability in participants who scored low on the Stanford Hypnotic Susceptibility Scale: Form C in 1989. Findings by A. Barabasz have also revealed that chamber and dry flotation REST dramatically influence hypnotizability whereas wet flotation REST elicits spontaneous hypnosis in participants that are highly hypnotizable.

A 1990 A. Barabasz study involving measurements of electrocortical (EEG) activity showed significantly increased theta (4–8 Hz) after flotation REST. Fine, Donna Mills, and Turner compared frontal monopolar EEG and frontal EMG readings of wet flotation versus dry flotation REST in 1993. The results showed that wet flotation REST had higher amplitude alpha frequency components. They concluded that wet flotation REST is qualitatively different in terms of central nervous system activity and may resemble the "twilight learning state." This state is induced through hypnosis and Stage 1 sleep. Differences between dry and wet flotation REST include humidity, temperature, and amount of tactile stimulation available to the participant. It is unknown which of these factors may contribute to differences in EEG readings.

III. APPLICATION EFFICACY

In 1982, Suedfeld and Kristeller suggested that, based on the implications of research and theory, REST should be "particularly appropriate" in two types of clinical situations: habit change and states of lower arousal and relaxation. Habit change, is based on the known cognitive effects of REST. The lack of distraction, increased hunger for stimuli, and increased openness to new information associated with the stimulus reduction experience, leads to a uniquely focused state of awareness. Lower arousal or relaxation effects of REST facilitate treatments addressing problems associated with chronic or acute stimulus overload such as dysfunction of information processing and stress-related disorders. Research findings have shown that chamber REST applications are particularly effective for the modification of habit disorders, whereas flotation REST sessions have been applied and have been found to be effective in the treatment of stress-related disorders, chronic pain, anxiety disorders, and sports performance enhancement. Notwithstanding the promising outcomes of REST as a treatment, as well as an augmentation strategy, the status of REST is predominantly an experimental procedure with many open questions regarding its utility and appropriateness in the clinical setting. Subsequently, REST research has been applied to a variety of problems, disorders, and opportunities for performance enhancement.

Smoking cessation studies combining REST with other traditional treatments have shown considerable promise as an augmentation strategy with multiple research sites demonstrating success rates of over 50% with follow-up periods ranging from 12 months to 5 years. In a few clinical studies, 1 to 2 years in duration, REST has been combined with weekly support groups. In those instances 75 to 80% with support group and tailored message have maintained abstinence for the length of the study.

Controlled studies have also demonstrated efficacy in decreasing the alcohol consumption of heavy drinkers. In 1987, Henry B. Adams, David G. Cooper, and John C. Scott studied the effects of REST on heavy social drinkers treated with 2.5 hours of REST with an antialcohol educational message during the treatment. The results of the study showed 55% reduction in alcohol consumption in the first 2 weeks after the treatment whereas control participants showed no significant reduction. A replication of this study showed similar results and alcohol reduction was maintained at 3- and 6-month follow-ups. A 1990 study by M. Barabasz, A. Barabasz, and Rebecca Dyer found that, for heavy drinkers, after exposure to one 12-hour or 24-hour chamber REST session, the average daily consumption of alcohol continued to drop over 6 months of follow-up. The 24-hour group's average consumption before REST was 42.7 ounces per day, immediately post-REST, it was 23.3 ounces per day, 16.0 ounces per day at 3 months, and 12.7 ounces at 6 months. Chamber REST was studied by David Baylah in 1997 as a relapse prevention technique with substance abusers enrolled in outpatient substance abuse treatment programs. At the end of 4 years of follow-up, 43% remained continuously sober and drug free, whereas none of the control group did after an 8-month follow-up.

Eating disorders have also been responsive to REST in a number of controlled studies. In a study that examined REST as a treatment for bulimia, the elimination of purging behaviors was a significant finding with a 50% success rate. In three studies using REST as a treatment for obesity, a slow continuous weight loss over a 6-month follow-up period after treatment was noted. In 1990, Dyer, A. Barabasz, and M. Barabasz utilized a true experimental design using a 24-hour REST treatment with a message (participants were asked to focus on the importance of diet and exercise and the role their particular problem foods had in their weight problems) and a REST treatment with problem foods (problem foods were brought into the chamber with the participants). Participant's total caloric consumption, problem food consumption, and body fat percentage were significantly lowered, and interviews revealed that REST appears to facilitate the resolution of conflicting attitudes and behaviors about food. Those individuals who had 25 to 30 or less pounds to lose benefited most from the study, whereas participants who had more weight to lose reported initial losses of 5 to 10 pounds and then reported that they were unable to maintain diet and exercise regimens. Non-REST participants did not show significant weight loss in the study.

Recreational, competitive, and intercollegiate sports including basketball, archery, tennis, gymnastics, rowing, darts, skiing, and rifle marksmanship have been the focus of flotation REST treatments to enhance performance. A performance enhancement study has also been done on commercial pilots, and REST treatments showed significant improvement on instrument flights tasks as opposed to control in a Lori G. Melchiori and A. Barabasz study. REST greatly enhances mental imagery, relaxation, and visualization of skills and has been shown to produce remarkable results in anecdotal and controlled performance studies. Studies in 1991 by Jeffery D. Wagaman, A. Barabasz, and M. Barabasz have been done on improving basketball performance. In these studies, improvements on shooting foul shots in a non-game session has been shown with REST, as well as improvements on objective performance skills and coaches' blind ratings as compared to a control group. Six sessions of flotation REST plus performance enhancement imagery of approximately 50 min over a 5-week period produced improved skill in passing, dribbling, shooting, and defense game and non-game measures when compared with an imagery-only control group.

An intercollegiate tennis study by Patrick McAleney in 1991 controlled for relaxation and guided imagery confounds noted in previous research on the enhancement of human performance using REST. Twenty participants took part in 50-min flotation REST treatments with visual imagery group or an imagery-only group. Participants were pre- and posttested on athletic performance and precompetitive anxiety measure. The analyses of performance scores revealed a significant performance enhancement effect for first service winners for the flotation REST plus visual imagery group in contrast to the group that received visual imagery only. No other performance analyses (key shot, points won or lost) were significant. The results of the analyses of anxiety scores were not significant. Another study by A. Barabasz, M. Barabasz, and James Bauman in 1993 looked at the enhancement of rifle marksmanship scores to determine the effects of dry flotation REST versus hypnotic relaxation, which is a confounding variable because flotation REST elicits spontaneous hypnosis in participants that are highly hypnotizable. Twelve participants who took part in a rifle marksmanship training course, and who were exposed to dry-flotation REST, showed significantly higher rifle marksmanship scores than 12 participants who were exposed to relaxation only. This suggests that REST's positive effects on marksmanship go beyond the induction of relaxation by hypnosis.

As mentioned previously, REST increases relaxation effects and pleasurable effects via endogenous opiate activity. Flotation REST has been studied as a treatment for chronic low back pain and chronic pain in rheumatoid arthritis, fibromyalgia, and premenstrual syndrome. Wet flotation REST was consistently associated with improved range of motion and grip strength and decreased pain both within and across sessions in all participants involved a Turner, Anna DeLeon, Cathy Gibson, and Fine 1993 rheumatoid arthritis study. Responses with dry flotation REST were less consistent and less vigorous. The moisture and heat associated with wet flotation REST are likely factors in the differences between the two types of REST treatments because rheumatoid arthritis is relieved by moist heat. A different study found that the pain associated with rheumatoid arthritis significantly decreased in participants treated by REST and autogenic training (a form of self-hypnosis). Studies on low back pain, fibromyalgia, and premenstrual syndrome also yielded significant relief of pain from REST treatments.

Stress and anxiety-related disorders are the focus of many flotation REST studies because of the role that REST plays in decreasing adrenal axis hormones associated with the stress response. Many foundational studies have been done that have illuminated REST's effects on lowering specific stress-related hormones. Other studies on anxiety-related disorders such as social anxiety, obsessive–compulsive disorder (OCD), trichotillomania (chronic hair pulling), psychophysiological insomnia, and induced stress have added to the growing body of research demonstrating that REST is effective at reducing physiological arousal related to stress and anxiety.

REST has also been used as an augmentation strategy for exposure treatments. In one case study involving a treatment refractory OCD patient, REST was used, along with an imaginal exposure treatment (using a loop tape), to treat severe contamination obsessions and compulsions. It was determined that the primary reason for the patient's unresponsiveness to traditional exposure treatments was his inability to focus on the stimulus. Subsequently, he would not meet the basic requirements of a sufficient time of exposure, as well as a lack of focused arousal. After an initial period of "REST only," the patient was exposed to the loop tape containing the fear-evoking material. This unconventional use of REST resulted in a substantial reduction of OCD symptoms.

IV. SUMMARY

REST has come a long way since its conception in the 1950s. Although it was initially used to test hypotheses about human endurance in monotonous, sensory-deprived environments and to test theories regarding brain processes, several side effects emerged from that early research that included an openness to new information, increased hypnotizability, increased focus on internal processes, and lower arousal. These cognitive and relaxation effects of REST were studied as they were seen as potential treatments for a wide variety of psychophysiological problems, addictive behaviors, and performance enhancement. In the past decade, REST has emerged as an effective therapeutic treatment with a low occurrence of negative side effects. The relaxation and pleasurable effects of REST have been used as a mechanism to decrease anxiety and pain in treatments of stress-and pain-related disorders. The cognitive effects of REST have been effective in modifying addictive behaviors and treating phobias and compulsive behaviors. Although there are many theoretical questions that remain to be answered as well as many possible applications that have yet to be studied, continued research builds its credibility and increases its visibility and practicality as a sound therapeutic treatment.

See Also the Following Articles

Applied Relaxation ■ Arousal Training ■ Neurobiology

Further Reading

Barabasz, A. F., & Barabasz, M. (1993). *Clinical and experimental restricted environmental stimulation: New developments and perspectives.* New York: Springer-Verlag.

Suedfeld, P., Ballard, E. J., & Murphy, M. (1983). Water immersion and flotation: From stress experiment to stress treatment. *Journal of Environmental Psychology, 3,* 147–155.

Suedfeld, P., & Kristeller, J. L. (1982). Stimulus reduction as a technique in health psychology. *Health Psychology, 1,* 337–357.

Suedfeld, P., Turner, J. W., & Fine T. H. (1990). *Restricted environmental stimulation Theoretical and empirical developments in flotation REST.* New York: Springer-Verlag.

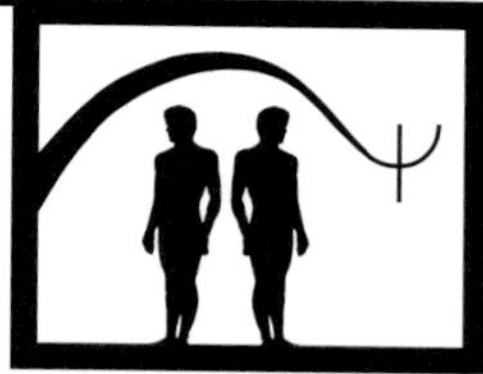

Retention Control Training

Kurt A. Freeman and Elizabeth T. Dexter

Pacific University

GLOSSARY

enuresis Involuntary discharge of urine after an age at which urine control should have been established.

micturition The passage of urine; urination.

Retention control training (RCT) is an intervention developed for the treatment of nocturnal enuresis. This article discusses the basic components of RCT, incorporating a brief description of the clinical phenomena for which it is used. Next, the theoretical and empirical basis for the development and use of this intervention is described. Finally, a review of the effectiveness of this intervention with nocturnal enuresis is provided.

I. COMPONENTS OF THE INTERVENTION

Enuresis is a condition that involves the involuntary passage of urine by a child after the age at which urinary control would be expected. According to the American Psychiatric Association's *Diagnostic and Statistical Manual, Fourth Edition, Text Revision (DSM-IV, TR)*, an individual must be at least 5 years of age, chronologically or developmentally, in order to be diagnosed as enuretic and experiencing repeated voiding of urine into bed or clothes, either intentionally or involuntary, at least two times per week for 3 consecutive months. If the enuretic behavior has not been present for the specified period of time, then clinically significant distress or impairment in social, academic, or other important areas of functioning must be present. Enuresis cannot be the result of a medical condition or the physiological effect of a substance, such as a diuretic. Furthermore, enuresis can be classified as either nocturnal (during sleeping hours), diurnal (during waking hours), or both. In addition to the subtypes of enuresis, it can also follow two different courses. Primary enuresis is characterized when the individual has never had a period of time with urinary continence, whereas enuresis is characterized as secondary when it begins after the individual has once established urinary continence.

Enuresis has a relatively high prevalence rate among young children and decreases as age increases. The literature reports there to be a 14 to 20% prevalence rate for 5-year-olds, 5% for 10-year-olds, 1 to 2% for 15-year-olds, and approximately 1% for 18-year-olds. In addition to differences across ages, the prevalence rate of enuresis also differs across gender. Males are twice as likely to be enuretic than females: 7% and 3%, respectively, at age 5; 3% and 2%, respectively, at age 10; and 1% and less than 1%, respectively, at age 18. Enuretic individuals may also experience a period of spontaneous remission without treatment. The likelihood of spontaneous remission is reported to be approximately 14% between the ages of 5 and 9, 16% between the ages of 10 and 14, and 16% between the ages of 15 and 19. Finally, a strong indicator of enuresis has been found to be family history. According to the *DSM-IV, TR,* 75% of children with enuresis have a first-degree biological relative who also experienced the disorder.

RCT is an intervention technique used for the treatment of nocturnal enuresis. As an intervention, RCT is relatively simplistic and typically involves the implementation of procedures during waking hours as a means of indirectly altering urine retention during sleeping hours. In general, RCT involves instructing the enuretic child to delay micturition from the time that he or she first senses the urge to urinate. In this manner, the child is learning to increase the amount of urine that can be held in the bladder prior to urination, thus establishing appropriate inhibitory responses. In addition to delaying urination, children are typically instructed to increase fluid consumption above normal levels. By doing so, they experience more frequent urges to urinate, providing more frequent opportunities for mastering retention control.

There are several variations in the basic procedures of RCT described in the current literature. First, procedures may differ regarding the method used to delay urination. One model instructs the child to delay micturition by programming successively longer periods of time. For example, the child is encouraged by parents to increase the delay between feeling the urge to urinate and doing so by 10 minutes across successive weeks. During the first week of intervention, the child is requested to delay urination for 10 minutes. The delay is then increased to 20 minutes and 30 minutes during the second and third weeks of treatment, respectively. In contrast, another variation of RCT entails the requested delay to be systematically increased over time by first instructing the child to go to the bathroom and urinate. The child is then provided with 500 ml of fluid and coached to delay urination as long as possible. Parents note the time at which the child requests to use the toilet, ask the child to delay urination for as long as possible, and then note when the child uses the restroom. From this information, postponement time can be calculated. This latency period serves as the baseline used during subsequent training trails so that the parents and therapists can monitor that the child is delaying urination 1 to 2 minutes longer with each consecutive attempt. Finally, RCT can involve a procedure that involves instructing the child simply to delay urination for as long as possible.

Second, the use of rewards for successful retention of fluids may also differ. Parents may be instructed not to provide any tangible reinforcement contingent upon successful delay of urination, to administer praise only, or to utilize procedures that involve the delivery of tangible rewards contingent upon increased fluid consumption and/or successful delay. Further, methods of reinforcement may also include instructing the child to change his or her own bed linens after voiding during sleep prior to returning to bed.

A third variation in RCT involves the child delaying urinations during the night. With this method the parents are instructed to give a large drink (i.e., 1 pint) to the child before bed and wake him or her every hour. At each awakening, the child is asked if he or she could delay urination for another hour. If so, the child returns to bed. If not, he or she is encouraged to delay urination for a few more minutes, is praised for doing so, and then is allowed to void. The child is then given another large drink and returned to bed; the amount of fluid loading may vary. Current research has only evaluated using this specific routine during the first night of treatment.

As mentioned earlier, methods of RCT may vary. To date, research has not systematically compared the various methods of administering RCT to determine which is most effective. Therefore, deciding which variation of the intervention to use depends on the structure of the child's environment (i.e., the willingness of the parents and the child) and the comfort level of the therapist with the different methods of the procedure.

II. BLADDER CAPACITY AND ITS ROLE IN NOCTURNAL ENURESIS

Various theories have been put forth to explain enuresis. Currently, enuresis is considered to be a functional disorder that is multiply determined, often with more than one causal mechanism operating with any given child. Physical causes accounting for the disorder include, but are not limited to, urinary tract dysfunctions and infections, nervous system dysfunctions, and bladder capacity deficits. Further, psychological and behavioral causes that have been shown to account for enuresis include toilet training practices and emotional disturbances.

Some research suggests that a proportion of children who experience nocturnal enuresis display small functional bladder capacities (i.e., the volume of urine at which contractions designed to evacuate the bladder occur). Thus, although the structure of the bladder is normal, its capacity to hold typical amounts of urine is underdeveloped. This smaller-than-expected functional bladder capacity may result in excessive urination diurnally in response to small amounts of urine in the bladder, resulting in fewer opportunities to learn micturition inhibitory responses. In fact, researchers have determined that a significant portion of enuretic children urinate more frequently than nonenuretic peers. At night, this may translate into an enuretic episode given the likelihood of decreased sensitivity to urination urges while asleep. RCT is based on the assumption that increasing functional bladder capacity will result in a decrease in enuretic episodes. In order to increase the bladder capacity, enuretic children are prompted to engage in certain behaviors during the day to train their bladders to hold increasing amounts of urine before voiding.

III. EFFECTIVENESS OF RETENTION CONTROL TRAINING

A significant amount of research has been conducted over the years in regards to the effectiveness of RCT and other behavioral treatments for nocturnal enuresis. Not surprisingly, RCT has been empirically demonstrated to increase functional bladder capacity. For example, in 1960 S. R. Muellner demonstrated that enuretic children produced greater urinary output following the use of RCT. Further, in 1975, Daniel Doleys and Karen Wells demonstrated that RCT resulted in normalized functional bladder capacity for a 42-month-old child. Regarding its effectiveness in treating nocturnal enuresis, RCT alone has been found to be effective in decreasing enuretic episodes in 50 to 75% of individuals. Further, it has been shown to be 30 to 50% effective in producing complete cessation of bedwetting episodes.

RCT reduces enuresis by normalizing bladder capacity and is thus more beneficial to those with a low functional bladder capacity. A child's bladder reaches full development around the age of 4 to 5. In a 1996 study, Tammie Ronen and Yair Abraham found that the rate of increase in bladder capacity is directly related to the age of the individual utilizing RCT. Specifically, they reported that the closer one is to the typical age of bladder maturity, the faster one can increase bladder capacity. Further, the rate of increase is slower for children much younger and much older than age 4 to 5. This is consistent with the results found in a 1990 study by Sandra Bonser, Jim Jupp, and Daphne Hewson. They implemented RCT with a 13-year-old female. Prior to implementing the treatment, the adolescent female was required to track her daily number of urinations and number of wet and dry nights for 5 weeks. This information continued to be monitored during the treatment and then for 1 week during each of the 2 months following termination of the intervention. In this study, RCT involved the adolescent holding her urine for successively longer periods of time. During the first week of treatment, she was instructed to hold her urine for 15 minutes after she first felt the urge to urinate. After 15 minutes, she was allowed to void. During the second week she was instructed to hold her urine for 20 minutes and then follow the same procedure as the previous week. In weeks 3 through 8, the adolescent was required to load her bladder with extra fluid as a means of increasing bladder capacity while continuing to hold her urine for 20 minutes. To accomplish this, she drank three large glasses of fluid in addition to her normal daily fluid intake throughout the day at breakfast, lunch, and after school. Finally, a reward system was in place based on the number of dry consecutive nights experienced. It took 8 weeks for her to decrease from seven wet nights per week to two wet nights per week and at 6-month follow-up she was experiencing only one wet night per week.

In 1970 H. D. Kimmel and Ellen Kimmel were among the first to systematically investigate the use of RCT in modern times. Three female children ages 4 and 10 participated. Baseline data revealed almost nightly bedwetting for all participants. RCT involved encouraging fluid intake (via reward contingent upon consumption) at any hour of the day and rewarding successively longer periods of retention of urine in the bladder, up to 30 minutes. Results showed that complete cessation of nocturnal enuretic episodes occurred for two of the participants within approximately 7 days of the initiation of RCT, and within 14 days for the third. Further, follow-up data indicated that none of the subjects had more than one enuretic episode during the year following treatment.

In 1972 A. Paschalis, H. D. Kimmel, and Ellen Kimmel conducted a more extensive investigation of RCT with 35 children who exhibited nocturnal enuresis. Treatment was essentially the same as that described by Kimmel and Kimmel in 1970 and was conducted for 20 days. Results showed that 40% of the participants met the criteria for success (i.e., seven consecutive nights without an accident) during the treatment period, and an additional participant achieved success through a continuation of the treatment beyond 20 days. Of those who were successful, no relapse was noted over a 90-day period.

As mentioned previously, reinforcement methods are at times used as a component of, or in addition to, RCT. In 1987, M. Carmen Luciano used an A-B-C single-subject design to test the effects of RCT plus reinforcement on nocturnal enuresis in two male participants, ages 11 and 12. After first obtaining baseline data, Luciano introduced RCT for 5 weeks in order to evaluate the effects of increasing bladder capacity on enuretic behaviors. RCT entailed the children drinking as much fluid as possible throughout the day and then holding their urine as long as possible for progressively longer periods of time until they reached 45 minutes. In addition, the children were told to practice stream interruption exercises (i.e., physically stopping and starting the voiding of their urine) three to five times each time they voided. The boys received points throughout the day for following directions as part of a reward system. The occurrence of bedwetting was recorded daily. Results showed that the use of RCT both increased bladder capacity and reduced the number of wet nights. However, because complete cessation of the enuretic episodes was not achieved, Luciano introduced differential contingency dry wet bed (DCDWB). DCDWB entailed an inspection of the child's bed each morning with a parent. If the bed was dry, a token reward system was implemented and the parent praised the child. If the bed was wet, the child was instructed to replace the dirty linens with clean ones and to wash his soiled nightclothes. From the point at which DCDWB was initiated, the nocturnal enuresis stopped within 5 to 6 weeks for both boys. At weeks 17 and 18, fading procedures were implemented by gradually decreasing the daily monitoring, exercises, and reward system. These findings are consistent with other studies demonstrating that providing tangible rewards plus fading as a treatment for nocturnal enuresis has a higher success rate (85%) and lower relapse rate (37%) than both dry bed training and the urine alarm.

In 1982, J. Bollard and T. Nettlebeck implemented a component analysis of dry bed training, a comprehensive treatment for enuresis consisting of the urine alarm, RCT, waking schedule, and positive practice/cleanliness training. This study included 177 enuretic individuals between the ages of 5 and 17. Each individual was randomly assigned to one of the eight groups. Group 1 was considered the standard condition, which entailed the use of the urine alarm during sleep. Group 2 involved the use of a waking the schedule in addition to the urine alarm. The waking schedule consisted of waking the individual every hour to void during the first night and one time 3 hours after falling asleep during the second night. Then after each dry night, waking would occur one-half hour earlier than the previous night, until the waking time was equal to 1 hour after sleep onset. Group 3 entailed the use of the urine alarm in addition to RCT. Here, RCT included the third variation of RCT at night that was discussed earlier (i.e., fluid loading before bed, hourly waking, prompting urine retention). The fourth group included the use of positive practice, cleanliness training, and the urine alarm. Positive practice entailed the child lying in bed with the lights off and counting to 50. When the child reached the set number, he or she was to go to the toilet and try to void. This process was repeated 50 times before falling asleep. Immediately following an enuretic accident, the child was reprimanded and sent to the toilet. The child then implemented cleanliness training, which involved changing one's nightclothes, removing and replacing the soiled bed linens, and drying and repositioning the detector pad of the urine alarm. Prior to returning to bed the child again had to carry out the positive practice exercises 20 times. There were also four additional groups that were composed of combinations of the first four groups. Group 5 included waking and RCT. Group 6 entailed waking, positive practice, and cleanliness training. Group 7 included RCT, positive practice, and cleanliness training. Finally, Group 8 was composed of the full dry bed training package. Bollard and Nettlebeck found that groups 6 and 8 had significantly fewer wet nights than each of the other groups. Further, they found no significant differences between the other groups. However, they did report that each of the four groups that included the waking schedule responded faster to the treatment than those without the waking schedule. In the RCT group specifically, 11 of the 12 participants met the criterion for becoming dry with an average of 24 wet nights during the 20-week treatment period.

As noted, studies have evaluated the combined effectiveness of RCT and other intervention methods as a means to stop enuresis. In 1986, Gary Geffken, Suzanne Bennett Johnson, and Dixon Walker compared the effects of the urine alarm alone against the urine alarm plus RCT with 50 5- to 13-year-old enuretic children. Baseline measures of wetting frequency were collected over a 2-week period of time; in addition, classification of either a small or large maximum functional bladder capacity was determined prior to randomly assigning participants to each of the groups. All participants were instructed to use the urine alarm. Half were also instructed to implement RCT based on Paschalis, Kimmel, and Kimmel's 1972 model of RCT. In this study, children in the RCT plus urine alarm group were instructed to hold their urine for progressively longer periods of time until they reached 45 minutes beyond the initial urge. Over the course of treatment, 10 participants dropped out. Of the 40 remaining participants, 92.5% ($n = 37$) achieved 14 consecutive dry nights, although 41% ($n = 16$) of the children relapsed. The fewest bedwetting accidents occurred in children with a large functional bladder capacity who were in the urine alarm only group and with the children who had a small functional bladder capacity and were in the urine alarm plus RCT group, suggesting a relationship between functional bladder capacity and method of treatment. This decrease in bedwetting may have also been a result of the increase in nighttime arising to use the toilet. This suggests that RCT was able to increase the sensitization to a full bladder but not actually increase functional bladder capacity as has been suggested throughout the literature.

Research on the effectiveness of RCT and other behavioral methods, such as dry bed training and the urine alarm, continue to provide information regarding the effective treatment of nocturnal enuresis. Further, treatment of nocturnal enuresis tends to produce a high dropout rate due to the demands placed on the parents to implement and follow through with the treatment. As discussed, different variations and combinations of RCT and other methods will result in different outcomes. It is important to choose a method that best suits the therapist and the family being treated.

IV. SUMMARY

RCT is an intervention model used to decrease the presence of nocturnal enuresis. Enuresis is the voluntary or involuntary voiding of urine in clothes or in bed after the age of 5. RCT encourages the holding of urine for extended periods of time after the first urge to urinate is detected. This functions as means of increasing the functional bladder capacity of an individual. Variations of RCT may also include fluid loading and reward systems as methods of reinforcement for increased fluid consumption, delayed urination, or both. On average, RCT is effective with 50 to 75% of individuals in reducing nocturnal enuresis, and with 30 to 50% of individuals in completely eliminating bedwetting. Based on the varying methods of implementation and the results of previous studies, specific intervention programs for treating enuresis should be tailored to the specific family and individual being treated.

See Also the Following Articles

Bell-and-Pad Conditioning ■ Child and Adolescent Psychotherapy ■ Modeling ■ Nocturnal Enuresis: Treatment ■ Primary-Care Behavioral Pediatrics

Further Reading

American Psychiatric Association. (2000). *Diagnostic and Statistical Manual, 4th Edition, Text Revision*. Washington, DC: author.

Friman, P. C., & Jones, K. M. (1998). Elimination disorders in children. In T. S. Watson & F. M. Gresham (Eds.), *Handbook of child behavior therapy* (pp. 239–260). New York: Plenum.

Friman, P. C., & Warzak, W. J. (1990). Nocturnal enuresis: A prevalent, persistent, yet curable parasomnia. *Pediatrician, 17*, 28–45.

Geffken, G., Bennett Johnson, S., & Walker, D. (1986). Behavioral interventions for childhood nocturnal enuresis: The differential effect of bladder capacity on treatment progress and outcome. *Health Psychology, 1986*, 261–272.

Lyman, R. D., Schierberl, J. P., & Roberts, M. C. (1988). Enuresis and encopresis: Psychological therapies. In J. L. Matson (Ed.), *Handbook of treatment approaches in childhood psychopathology* (pp. 397–428). New York: Plenum.

Ronen, T., & Abraham, Y. (1996). Retention control training in the treatment of younger versus older children. *Nursing Research, 45*, 78–82.

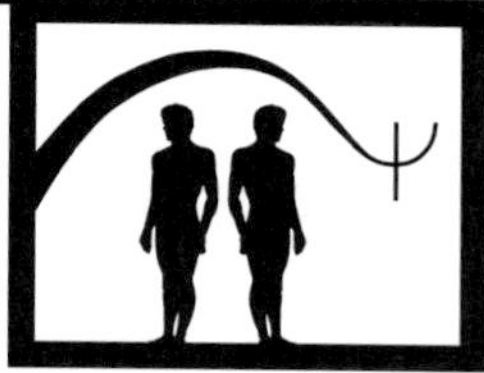

Role-Playing

Joanne L. Davis, Adrienne E. Fricker, Amy M. Combs-Lane, and Ron Acierno

Medical University of South Carolina

GLOSSARY

confederate An individual who pretends to be a participant in a research study, but is actually part of the research study.

modeling A procedure in which a particular behavior or behaviors is/are demonstrated for an individual to allow that individual to emulate the behaviors.

operant conditioning A theory of behavioral modification that states that behaviors are controlled by contingencies that occur following the behavior.

role reversal The client acts "as if" they are another individual involved in a problematic situation.

Role-play is a procedure in which scenarios are designed to elicit particular behaviors from an individual. The individual is asked to respond "as if" the situation were actually occurring. The individual may respond to another person or to a situation presented by video-or audiotape. This article presents a review of the uses of role-play in therapy, guidelines for use, advantages and disadvantages of this techniques, and information regarding empirical studies of the technique.

I. DESCRIPTION

Role-playing, also known as behavioral rehearsal, has a number of uses in behavior therapy, in terms of both behavioral assessment and treatment. Whether used as part of an assessment or intervention, role-playing requires the client to act "as if" they are in a real-life situation involving a problematic behavior. Role-play may enable clinicians to directly observe deficits (e.g., unassertiveness) or excesses (e.g., aggression) in an individual's behavioral repertoire. Role-play may also be used in treatment for a number of behavior-based problems including phobias, anxiety, social skills training, and interpersonal difficulties.

Role-play sessions can be audio- or videotaped in order for the behaviors to be rated by either the therapist, the client, or an objective judge. Frequently, behavior checklists are used to rate target behaviors the client is attempting to learn. Behaviors can be rated in terms of their effectiveness, frequency of occurrence, duration, or presence or absence. Clients can also provide ratings of self-perceived competence or level of arousal while performing the behaviors. Based on the ratings, a therapist provides feedback to the client. Feedback includes specific information regarding the individual's performance and suggestions for improvement and additional practice.

A. Assessment

Often, it is not possible for a therapist to observe directly a problem behavior in the natural setting in which it occurs. In these cases, it may be possible to re-create the situation in the therapists' office. Role-play frequently involves the therapist and client reenacting a problematic interpersonal situation. Outside models may also be used to better simulate the actual situation. For example, if the client is a male college student reporting difficulties asking women for dates, the therapist may want to recruit a young female assistant to assist in the role-play.

Role-play may also be beneficial if the client has a difficult time verbally expressing the nature of the problem. Enacting a similar situation with the client may provide the therapist with specific knowledge of the client's behavioral excesses and deficits that he or she is not able to verbalize. For instance, if the college student described above is not able to explain the nature of his difficulties interacting with women, conducting a role-play may clarify the specific nature of the problem.

B. Intervention

Role-play is often conducted within the therapy session to assist clients in learning and practicing new skills, decrease and extinguish undesirable behaviors, and increase and reinforce desirable behaviors. Through role-play exercises, the therapist is able to observe the client's behaviors directly and provide feedback regarding strengths and limitations, and to reinforce the target behavior. For example, a therapist engaging in social skills training may describe the procedure to the client, provide a rationale for its use, establish several scenarios that approximate the problematic situations, model the appropriate behavior with a confederate, then ask the client to respond to a confederate (live, audio, or video) "as if" the situation is occurring. Feedback is then provided to the client on her or his performance. Role-play is also frequently used is to assist parents in teaching new skills or modifying behavior of a child. Role-play may be first conducted in session with parents. The parents are then instructed to engage in role-play practices at home with their child. For example, role-play may be appropriate for teaching an aggressive child socially appropriate means of interacting with other children.

Role-play is also useful for helping a client attend to internal processes of which they are unaware. For instance, while enacting a scene in which the client is practicing assertive behavior, the therapist may call attention to thoughts, feelings, and stimuli to which the client typically does not attend. Once the client has identified the internal processes, role-play can be used to learn new ways of responding to the situation. For example, clients with social anxiety may not be aware of automatic, distorted cognitions (e.g., "Everyone in the audience thinks I'm stupid") that may be increasing their levels of anxiety.

Role-play is frequently used to introduce the concept of generalization of therapeutic techniques to other contexts. For example, if a client has been working on increasing his assertive behavior with his wife around money issues, the therapist may ask him to role-play confrontation with a friend or a problem at work. Further, a therapist may ask the client to take on various roles to gain other's perspectives on a problematic situation. This type of role-play is termed role reversal and is useful in challenging and modifying automatic thoughts concerning how a client is perceived by others.

Other forms of behavioral rehearsal that may be used as an adjunct to role-play are instruction, physical guidance, modeling, and imagery rehearsal. The decision to incorporate other techniques will depend on the desired skill or the behavior to be changed, the nature of the situation, and the current level of client functioning. For example, if the goal is acquisition of a new skill or if the client's behavioral repertoire is lacking, modeling appropriate behaviors may be required prior to initiating role-playing. Effective intervention with complex new skills may require breaking the skill down into smaller components and role-playing each component, gradually piecing together the total skill. An individual with a severe snake phobia may need to practice imaginal exposure or watch others interact with snakes before he or she is able to role-play exposure to a toy snake.

C. Guidelines for Use

The effectiveness of role-play techniques may be increased with the following strategies:

1. Make the scenarios as realistic and as close to the actual problematic situation as possible.
2. Start role-play with simple situations and graduate to more complex situations and behaviors.
3. Use a variety of different scenarios to help generalize skills to different contexts.
4. Specific role-plays should target the most salient problem behaviors for each client.
5. Monitor a client's progress over time. It may be helpful to provide a graphic depiction of the client's progress. For example, if the frequency of occurrence of target behaviors is the rating focus, the

therapist can plot changes in this frequency within and across sessions.

5. If role-plays are to be conducted across time as part of an ongoing assessment, care should be taken to standardize instructions and scenarios to ensure that it is the client's behavior that is being assessed, not changes in the scene, environment, or other individual(s) in the scene.

D. Advantages and Disadvantages

As with any procedure, there are numerous advantages and disadvantages to the use of role-play in assessment and as a therapeutic intervention.

1. Advantages

Role-play allows for the direct observation of clients' verbal and nonverbal behaviors. It can be used to corroborate self-reports of problem behaviors. Role-play assessments of target behaviors are easily conducted in the research laboratory or the therapist's office and are inexpensive. It provides a rich record of client responses that are difficult to assess using paper and pencil measures or interviews. Role-play scenarios are typically brief, so many can be conducted within one session.

Role-play can have many advantages in therapy. Clients frequently experience difficulties completing homework assignments at home. Role-playing within session may help decrease fears about the assignment and increase compliance. Role-play allows clients to achieve small successes, which in turn increase motivation for change. Further, role-play can be used as a steppingstone for performing more complex skills or conducting *in vivo* practice of target behaviors.

2. Disadvantages

There are also several disadvantages to consider. Scenarios need to be standardized in order to provide an accurate assessment of behavior change. Inconsistencies in the behavior of a confederate or the format of stimuli used may impact the behavior of the client and may inaccurately suggest improvement and make comparisons difficult. Perhaps the most salient limitation is the questionable criterion validity of role-play. The participants' or clients' behavior in session or in a research setting may not be an accurate representation of their behavior in a natural situation. Also, the therapist is not able to sample all possible scenarios, thus there is a potentially erroneous assumption of cross-situational consistency. Finally, the accuracy of the simulations themselves may not be completely acceptable in all scenarios.

II. THEORETICAL BASIS

In this discussion, role-play is presented as a behavioral technique and its utilization is based on the behavioral principle of focusing assessment and treatment on observable behaviors. It is not meant to provide an understanding of the etiology of a behavior; rather, problematic behaviors are identified and modified through practice in simulated situations regardless of etiology.

The theory of operant conditioning holds that the probability of the occurrence of specific behaviors is determined by the contingent consequences of those behaviors. The frequency of a behavior can be increased through positive (i.e., adding a desired stimulus) or negative (i.e., removing an aversive stimulus) reinforcement and decreased through positive or negative punishment. In cases in which the target behavior does not occur or is not yet a part of the client's behavioral repertoire, modeling (i.e., observational learning) may be used to introduce the behavior. Depending on the complexity of the target behavior, shaping (i.e., reinforcing approximations of the target behavior) may be incorporated in the role-play.

Once the skill is learned and the behavior performed, the therapist uses positive reinforcement to increase the occurrence of the behavior and to encourage the client to engage in the behavior outside of the therapy session. It is hoped that the modified behavior will positively impact the contingencies, further reinforcing the client's desire to engage in the behavior.

III. EMPIRICAL STUDIES

Research evaluating the validity of the use of role-play in either an assessment or as part of a therapeutic intervention is somewhat limited and dated. One of the primary difficulties involved in conducting such research is the lack of standardization of role-play stimuli used across studies. For the most part, research demonstrates that ratings of subjects' behavior responding to simulated situations correlates highly with evaluations of those who knew respondents well. Role-play (alone or as part of a treatment protocol) has been found to be effective for emotional and behavioral disorders including depression, social skills training, anxiety, phobias, aggression, and interpersonal problem solving. Role-play also has some support for prevention efforts. In 2000, Arthur Perlini and Christine Ward investigated the effectiveness of HIV prevention interventions and found that role-play was associated with increased knowledge about AIDS and HIV in comparison to video, lecture, or no intervention.

IV. SUMMARY

Role-play techniques have been widely used in behavioral assessment, as part of therapeutic interventions, and as a means of evaluating therapeutic interventions. Empirical support for role-play is fair; however, there are a number of factors that limit one's ability to evaluate techniques across studies. There are numerous advantages (e.g., brief and inexpensive) and disadvantages (e.g., questionable criterion validity) to consider when deciding whether or not to use role-play. However, it appears to be an appropriate technique for a variety of difficulties including anxiety and interpersonal interactions.

See Also the Following Articles

Behavioral Assessment ■ Behavioral Therapy Instructions ■ Behavior Rehearsal ■ Corrective Emotional Experience ■ Heterosocial Skills Training ■ Self-Statement Modification ■ Modeling ■ Working Alliance

Further Reading

Bellack, A. S., Hersen, M., & Kazdin, A. E. (1985). *International handbook of behavior modification and therapy.* New York: Plenum Press.

Cormier, W. H., & Cormier, L. S. (1991). *Interviewing strategies for helpers* (3rd ed.). Pacific Grove, CA: Brooks/Cole Publishing Company.

Schizophrenia and Other Psychotic Disorders

Richard L. Munich
The Menninger Clinic

GLOSSARY

psychosis A mental state characterized by loss of reality testing as in delusions and hallucinations, often accompanied with severe interferences with the capacity to meet the ordinary demands of life, maintaining social and personal boundaries, manage profound levels of anxiety, focus attention, and experience pleasure.

schizophrenia A disorder of cognition and behavior that lasts for at least 6 months and includes two or more of the following: delusions, hallucinations, disorganized speech (positive symptoms), grossly disorganized or catatonic behavior (disorganized symptoms), emotional flattening, poverty of thought, and speech and severe impairments in motivation (negative symptoms).

I. INTRODUCTION

Contemporary treatment of patients with schizophrenia is an amalgam of its biopsychosocial determinants, heterogeneous presentation, and phasic course. It includes psychopharmacological, psychoeducational, and rehabilitative interventions, and a continuum of care with a variety of ambulatory-based alternatives. Comprehensive treatment tailors these interventions to the phase of illness and is reinforced with a variety of flexible and supportive psychotherapies that emphasize medication compliance, problem-solving tasks, community reintegration and tenure, and in its most stable phase, conflict resolution and personal growth. This article describes the evolution and implementation of these psychotherapies as well as their interface with the various above-mentioned interventions.

II. HISTORY

Although Sigmund Freud was skeptical about the use of psychoanalytical therapy for patients with schizophrenia, many practitioners from early in the 20th century applied his methods for these patients. Because of their withdrawal from the external world and essential narcissism (e.g., autism), Freud felt that patients with psychotic disorders were unable to form a meaningful, stable, and workable transference, the basis of psychoanalytic treatment. This inability made it difficult to work through unconscious conflicts and their accompanying defenses as they appeared in relation to the therapist. Other psychoanalytic pioneers and followers of Freud, such as Paul Federn, Karl Abraham, and Carl Jung, felt otherwise and began a long tradition of utilizing insight-based techniques that developed side by side with psychodynamically oriented psychotherapy generally. To the earliest list was added the work of Victor Tausk, A. A. Brill, Wilhelm Reich, Gregory Zilboorg, Sandor Ferenczi, and Ernst Simmel. Simmel and Georg Groddeck introduced the psychodynamic approach into the mental hospital. It is noteworthy that all these early practitioners recommended modifications of the traditional analytic technique to be more directive, less focused on the transference, and employing more techniques than interpretation alone.

Use of these modified approaches reached its peak in the United States in the post–World War II decades of the 1940s and 1950s. Represented in the work of Harry Stack Sullivan, Frieda Fromm-Reichman, and Harold Searles, practitioners of the interpersonal school of psychiatry worked with patients as if schizophrenia were fundamentally a disorder of interpersonal relatedness. Along with British object relations theorists and practitioners such as Melanie Klein, Wilfred Bion, and Herbert Rosenfeld, these therapists believed that the illness was caused and could ultimately be cured, or at least significantly ameliorated, by interpersonal, psychotherapeutic, and interpretive techniques. Although much of the focus of treatment remained with an elucidation of the meaning of various symptoms and their relationship to the patient's past and current stressors, modifications in classical technique continued with patients being seen face to face, often less than daily, and with much more interaction between patient and therapist.

In the decades of the 1960s and 1970s clinicians like Lewis Hill, Milton Wexler, and Victor Rosen continued the psychodynamically oriented approach to patients with the idea that psychosis was just like neurosis only more so. Others, like Ruth and Ted Lidz, Steven Fleck, and Lyman Wynne, supported somewhat by the previous work of Searles, believed that schizophrenic pathology made it difficult to attain adequate separation from important figures in the patient's life. As opposed to the primacy of intrapsychic conflict, this more developmental or family point of view focused on the etiological role of dysfunctional events and faulty communication patterns within families. At the same time, this approach led to a more reality-based, adaptive thrust with straightforward language and problem-solving techniques. Unfortunately for those espousing this approach, the dysfunctional impact on families of living with a family member with schizophrenia was not adequately considered.

After reaching a peak in the two decades between 1950 and 1970, the clinical use of, reimbursement for, and educational input toward the psychodynamically informed psychotherapy for patients with schizophrenic, schizoaffective and psychotic depression steadily declined in the United States. The causes for this decline are well known and reflect a myriad of documented social, scientific, and economic realities. The development of the earliest antipsychotic medications dramatically reduced some of the most dramatic symptoms of psychosis. Research efforts were unable to confirm the effectiveness of psychotherapy, whereas others demonstrated a lack of its effectiveness. Questions about patient selection invalidated many of the remarkable and compelling anecdotal case reports of successful treatment. In addition, there was a dramatic proliferation of nonpsychological forms of treatment, and trends in the overall practice of psychotherapy itself shifted in ideology from psychodynamic to interpersonal to cognitive-behavioral modalities of therapy.

III. CONTEMPORARY APPROACHES

This nearly 30-year decline in the practice of dynamically informed psychotherapy for patients with psychotic disorders appears to be slowing down and even leveling off. There are several factors that account for this shift, not the least of which, paradoxically, is the revolution in and explosive growth of neuroscience over the last two decades. This growth directly affected psychotherapeutic work in two ways. First, there has been a clear-cut, experimentally verified recognition of the dynamic interplay between heredity and environment, between hard wiring and experience and between protein synthesis at the receptor site and input from the perceptual apparatus. Thus, a modern conception of severe mental disturbance suggests that the structure of a psychosis derives from the patient's genetic predisposition, prenatal environment, constitution and brain; whereas its content (the expression and experience of illness) issues from the patient's developmental environment, meaning system and mind. Because the interaction of psychosocial stressors and brain vulnerability leads to dysfunctional adaptation, optimal treatment addresses both sides of the interaction.

The second and more practical effect of the remarkable advances in *neuroscience* is the ability to design pharmacological agents to enhance effectiveness with the positive and disorganizing aspects of the illness and diminish some of those agents' most irritating side effects. Far from being perfect, the new so-called atypical antipsychotics also show promise for mitigating negative symptoms without the troubling extrapyramidal side effects of earlier neuroleptics. Much like the application of a brace to the paralyzed limb of a stroke victim, the antipsychotics appear to protect the receptor site on an affected neuron against continued overstimulation. Neither intervention cures the fundamental pathological condition, but in both cases their removal activates the symptoms: in the first case, hemiplegia; and in the second, decompensation and the exacerbation of psychotic symptoms.

The ability to manage positive, negative, and disorganized symptoms, the most debilitating aspects of schizophrenic illness, have made the patient more available for psychotherapy and brought the following crucial treatment issues into bolder relief: personality and character, treatment compliance and therapeutic alliance, and long-standing cognitive, social, and vocational deficits. With respect to personality and character, it was within the past decade that many believed that a diagnosis within Axis I of schizophrenia or schizoaffective illness precluded the personality or character diagnoses of Axis II. This was because regression to psychotic levels was presumed to have a fundamental and disorganizing effect on identity, personality, and coherence of the self-concept. Most people who work closely with these patients, however, believe the personality remains essentially intact and, depending on its configuration, can have both facilitating and inhibiting influences on the treatment, the treatment alliance, and the course of illness. The emergence of personhood in the previously withdrawn and disorganized patient makes the patient available to discuss the substantial problems of living that result from debilitating illness and form the centerpiece of an effective psychotherapeutic process. Other issues that may come to the foreground as a result of effective medication include depression, negative symptoms, and a profound demoralization and despair about the afflicted individual's deviance from the mainstream of friendship and social life.

The reduction of disorganizing symptoms also makes it possible to look more closely at the treatment alliance and some of its resistances, and secondarily, of course, the whole question of treatment compliance. Treatment alliance is critical for the success of any of the therapies proposed in this section and takes us immediately into the realm of object relations and interpersonal theories. Unlike Freud's conceptualization of the narcissistic neurosis, it is now more commonly believed the problem with the transference in these patients is not that there is not enough for a treatment alliance; rather, the issue appears over and over to be a very intense and highly unstable alliance and difficult to manage transference reaction. As mentioned there is by this time an enormous anecdotal literature on this subject, most of which precedes the modern pharmacological era. Clinicians continue to report on this kind of work with patients. In these highly evocative accounts, the vicissitudes of attachment and separation and transference and countertransference suggest much that can be reexplored and investigated with today's patient in an entirely new context and without the same level of anxiety about losing or doing damage to a patient. Psychodynamically oriented psychotherapy, however, with its emphasis on the regressive transference neurosis, may well be overstimulating for many of these patients especially in the early and more volatile phases of the illness. Thus, keeping in mind issues of separation and attachment while helping the patient reintegrate and cope—without focusing on them—becomes the task of the therapy.

Very often the psychotherapist of the patient with schizophrenia must perform auxiliary ego functions such as reality testing, assistance with impulse control, anticipation of consequences (judgment), and sharpening self-object differentiation. Therefore, the most widely practiced form of psychotherapy for patients with schizophrenia is supportive. The techniques include the establishment and maintenance of the therapeutic alliance, a steady focus on medication compliance and side effects, and paying attention to and helping reduce stress. These techniques are supported with clarification, education, and reassurance and are the heir to the psychodynamic tradition in which the relationship between therapist and patient is crucial and adaptive defenses are encouraged and reinforced. Finding the appropriate synthesis of the modifications from traditional psychotherapeutic technique, developing and maintaining a stable and durable therapeutic alliance, while keeping in touch with the dynamic unconscious, comprise the art of the therapeutic work with these patients. Furthermore, supportive psychotherapy is the basis of the majority of contemporary psychotherapies for the illness in virtually all its forms and phases. Figure 1 outlines the historical trends in the psychodynamically oriented psychotherapy of patients with schizophrenia.

Compliance with effective medication regimens is one of the most important issues in the ongoing treatment of patients with schizophrenia. The idea of learning in more detail about a patient's reluctance to continue a medication that is fostering the reintegration of his or her personality may be quite helpful. Is noncompliance the same or does it go beyond the same kind of denial of illness that one sees in any chronic illness, diabetes for example, in which issues of pride and autonomy play such a strong role in problems with compliance? Or is this denial significantly connected to the patient's low awareness of symptoms?

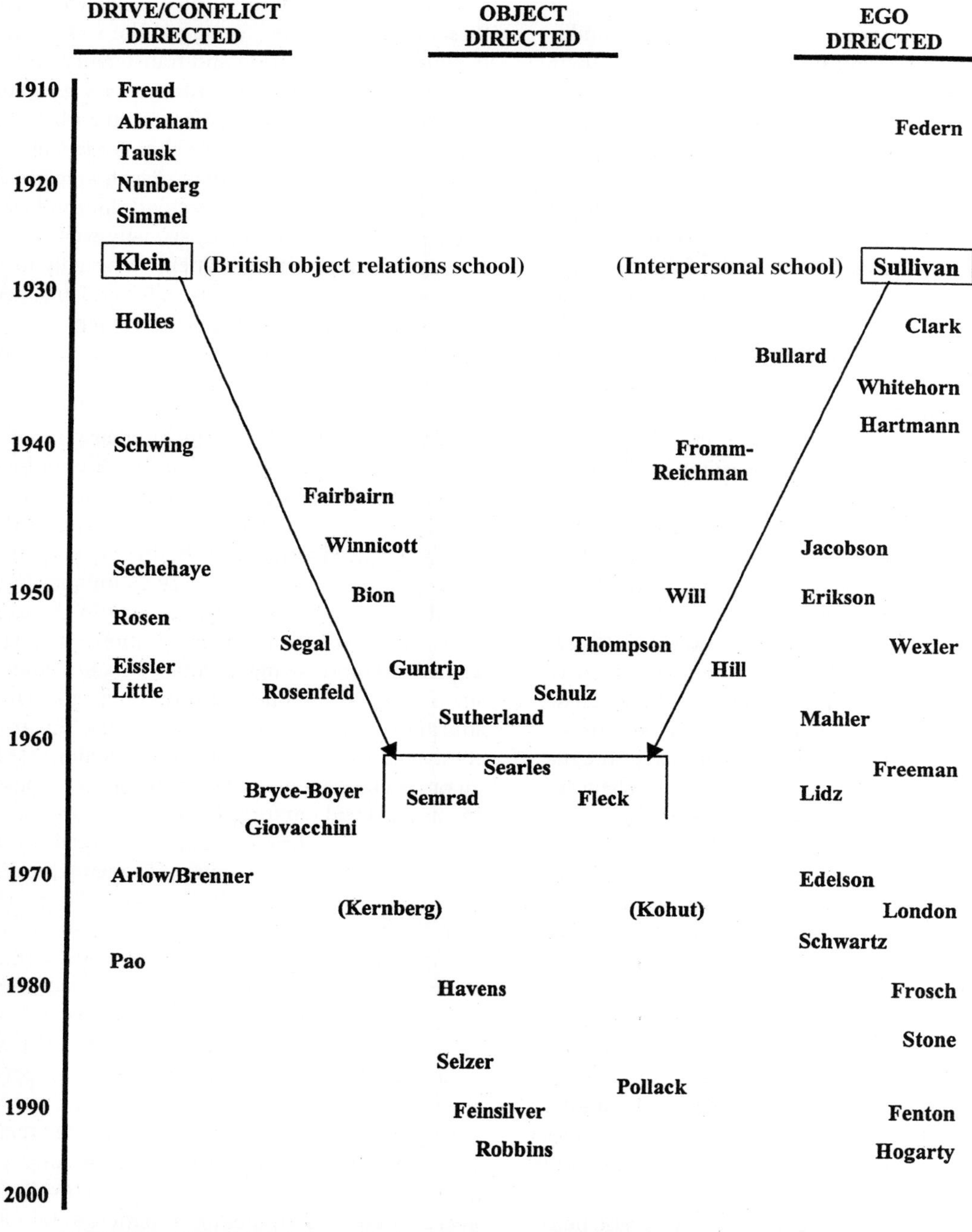

FIGURE 1 Major theoretical/clinical trends in psychotherapy of schizophrenia. Reproduced with permission from Spiegel (ed.). (1999). *Efficacy and Cost-Effectiveness of Psychotherapy.* Washington, DC: American Psychiatric Press.

Or is the reluctance to continue medication more like the patient with a bipolar disorder who stops their lithium or valproic acid because they miss the intense high associated with a manic state? Or is it a flight from inner deadness, a manipulative effort to obtain more from the treatment team, or a retreat from the despair associated with the many demands of external reality in the absence of requisite adaptive skills? Or finally, is it yet another manifestation of basic faults in internalized object relations alluded to when speaking of issues of attachment and separation earlier?

When a patient is not threatened so immediately and unpredictably by disorganizing symptoms, the psychotherapist is in a much better position to understand the dysfunctional interaction of these relevant and dynamic issues. It is noteworthy, however, that these issues may be sidestepped in many contemporary educative and rehabilitative approaches that take the position that noncompliance has more to do with a poor understanding of the illness, its symptoms, and the role of medications.

One of the most painful but important issues to emerge as a result of more effective psychotropic medication is the clear-cut cognitive, social, and vocational deficits that inhibit the functional adaptation of many of the patients with serious and persistent mental illness. In an increasingly technological age it may be preferable, in fact, to be considered mentally ill than it is to labeled a "drop-out." There are many patients who have emerged from several years of psychosis and withdrawal only to discover they are way behind their peers in the capacity to solve the problems of everyday life, to feel socially attuned, to enter the workforce, or otherwise construct a meaningful life. These represent another kind of deficit, a deficit that results from being more or less "out of it" and which adds a new dimension to the illness itself. Various forms of psychotherapy are especially helpful with the problems in living that are functional and emotional sequelae of severe mental illness.

IV. LINKING PSYCHOTHERAPY WITH PHASE OF ILLNESS

Growing from the work of John Strauss and his colleagues at Yale utilizing longitudinal patterns and an interactive-developmental model, Wayne Fenton and his colleagues at the Chestnut Lodge Hospital formulated a set of phases through which symptoms develop, progress and retreat. The phases include

1. A prodromal period signaled by a constellation of symptoms including sleep difficulty, perceptual abnormalities, and social isolation.
2. An acute or active phase with the characteristic signs of decompensation.
3. A subacute or convalescent phase characterized by a reduction in florid symptoms, some reorganization of function, especially reality testing, and postpsychotic depression.
4. Moratoriums or adaptive plateaus during which, somewhat like the latency period of psychosexual development, there is a consolidation of gains, a gradual restitution of personal identity and a strengthening of confidence and adaptive skills.
5. Change points, called "mountain climbing" by Strauss during which there may be upward shifts in functioning (moving from halfway house to community; beginning a job, etc) either self-motivated or initiated by others but that carry potential for improvement or relapse.
6. Stable plateaus which can be more or less enduring and range from remission to fixed deficits or persistent symptoms.

Instead of a monolithic therapeutic approach to patients with psychotic disorders, the contemporary clinician flexibly modifies his or her interventions and contact according to the phase of illness. In this approach, that sensitive clinicians have long understood, therapeutic contact may range from quite time limited, reality based, problem solving, and ego supportive along one end of the continuum to more exploratory, nondirective, interpretive, and insight oriented along the other end. More specifically, during the acute phase, at onset of the psychosis, exacerbation or relapse of illness, the focus is on acute symptom stabilization, and the therapist is encouraged to be supportive and directive. Because patients in the acute phase are often out of touch with reality and highly sensitive to social stimulation, group therapy is contraindicated at this time.

In the subacute and convalescent phase, the supportive and directive approach is continued with the additional task of assessing stressors and vulnerabilities, mobilizing social supports and constructing the treatment team. The subacute and convalescent phase corresponds in timing and intervention to the basic phase of so-called personal therapy outlined by Hogarty and his colleagues at Pittsburgh. If group modalities are used during this phase, they should also be supportive and interactive as opposed to uncovering and insight oriented. Group therapy can be helpful in this phase if the patient does not have prominent paranoid or negative symptoms, and it can be helpful with discharge planning and return to the community.

In the first moratorium or adaptive plateau, the therapist can begin focusing on the treatment alliance and helping the patient with problem solving. In this phase interventions are tempered with considerable reassurance, supporting defenses and strengths. This approach is consistent with the idea that this is a phase in which the patient is consolidating gains and restoring self-esteem. It is at this point that Hogarty's personal therapy would also introduce a step-by-step plan for the resumption of expected roles as well as the provision of social and avoidance techniques from social skills training. Group therapy during this phase is dependent on the patient's baseline level of functioning: for patients who can converse normally and function well between episodes, an interactive, non-insight-oriented approach is recommended; for those with chronic conditions and relatively good premorbid functioning, behaviorally oriented approaches should be used (see later).

When the patient moves to the next phase, begins to contemplate or becomes involved in changing status or venue, the therapy, now based on a reasonably solid treatment alliance, might begin to identify individual-specific prodromal and relapse factors because this is a very vulnerable time. This is also a phase when denial of illness may become prominent, so the therapist must pay attention to the patient's level of acceptance of illness. This phase roughly corresponds to Hogarty's intermediate phase. At this point his team provides internal coping strategies that include the identification of individual, cognitive and somatic indicators of distress, and the appropriate application of basic relaxation and cognitive reframing techniques.

After stable plateaus have been achieved and community reintegration and tenure sustained, the regular and by this point more traditional admixture of supportive and expressive psychotherapy can be employed. Here, interpretations continue to be quite modest, signs of regression are monitored very closely, and it is the patient who sets the pace of discovery. The later phases of recovery from the illness are usually those in which rehabilitative modalities are employed, inevitably highlighting the patient's premorbid difficulties, stressful familial patterns, and vulnerability to the social and technological demands of modern culture. This phase corresponds to Hogarty's advanced phase of personal therapy and includes encouragement for social and vocational initiatives in the community, progressive awareness of one's affect, together with its expression and perceived effect on the behavior of others. This latter phase also includes principles of criticism management and conflict resolution. Although it is a relatively recent addition to technique, personal therapy has modest research support.

Higher functioning patients may utilize an interactive group psychotherapy on an outpatient basis to learn more about their illness, to understand and utilize their medications more effectively, apply reality testing as positive symptoms threaten to emerge, and learn communication and problem-solving skills. Ambulatory patients with more severe disorders are best served with approaches derived from cognitive and problem-solving techniques, as well as skill training derived from more recent psychiatric rehabilitation methods. Many recommend co-therapists in groups for patients with schizophrenia, somewhat more personal disclosure as compared to that in groups for patients with character disorders, and a steady focus on the techniques of clarification, support, and the here and now of interpersonal interactions. There is virtually universal agreement that interpretive activity aimed at uncovering unconscious conflict is contraindicated in group work with this population.

In the resurgence of psychotherapy for patients with serious disorders, the psychodynamics are far more part of the understanding than they are of the technique. The psychotherapy is much more a part of the treatment than the principal element in or the guide of the treatment. The psychotherapy is more flexible, adjusting to the phase of illness and primarily supportive, focal and educative rather than explorative, general and insight oriented. It is more about coping, adapting, problem solving, and coming to terms with deficits rather than collaborating in a regressive enterprise to uncover and resolve conflict. Emerging from the ego psychological point of view, this version of supportive psychotherapy is more reality based and adaptive and closer to a developmental and educative rather than an interpersonal and interpretive focus. It might even be called rehabilitative psychotherapy. This point of view is closest to that held by Lidz and others, and it contrasts with a more interpersonal and interpretive point of view outlined by Harry Stack Sullivan and held by Otto Will, Elvin Semrad, and Michael Robbins (see Table 1).

V. COGNITIVE STRATEGIES

The last two decades have seen a rapid increase in an interest in schizophrenia from a neurocognitive perspective, beginning with a focus on attentional dysfunction and moving to the more recent focus on working memory and its various components. This interest has naturally led to innovative treatment approaches. Cognitive-behavioral therapies (CBT) for patients with schizophrenia and other psychoses represents a radical departure from traditional, and even from the flexible

TABLE I
Listening to the Patient with a Psychotic Disorder: Interpersonal and Developmental Psychodynamic Views

Issue	*Interpersonal*	*Developmental*
Advocacy	Sullivan, Will, Semrad, Selzer, Robbins	Lidz, Fleck, Wynne, MacFarland, Leff
Etiology	Interpersonal Primary versus secondary incapacity to cathect an object	Interfamilial Actual Dysfunctional events Faulty communication patterns
Symptom	Failure to connect with objects	Failure to separate from objects
Best theory	Closer to object relations	Closer to self-psychology
Treatment goal	Address deficits interfering with therapeutic alliance (self-other differentiation, faulty reality testing, observing ego).	Address pathogenic family transactions interfering with continuing development (marital schism, marital skew, double binds)
Individual psychotherapy	Conflict resolution Transference-countertransference Relate associations, restitutional phenomena to alliance	Problem solving Real, tangible life problems Discourage free association and exploration of restitutional phenomena
Milieu organized to:	Support psychotherapy; more confrontation	Support adaptive skills; less confrontation
Similarities	Both approaches look for and reinforce health functioning, tolerate regression, and minimize the use of somatic modalities.	

Reproduced with permission from Spiegel (ed.). (1999). *Efficacy and Cost-Effectiveness of Psychotherapy.* Washington, DC: American Psychiatric Press.

and personal psychotherapies of the last decade. CBT shifts the focus of intervention from the internal, dynamic, and supportive expressive to the external, symptom centered, and highly structured. Rather than a model of the mind based on psychoanalytic thought and various theories about the etiology of severe psychopathology, CBT addresses distortions in the cognitive sets or schemata that individuals develop to organize and understand their experience. These distortions may effect social-cognitive, perceptual, and inferential processes and lead to such diverse phenomena as hallucinations or delusional beliefs. Thus, rather than confronting or interpreting a delusion, the form and content of that false percept or belief, CBT's approach establishes a therapeutic alliance that increases the awareness and inconsistency of the belief. The goal is the replacement of the dysfunctional and maladaptive belief with one that is more evidence and reality based.

CBT for patients with schizophrenia and psychotic symptoms are based on the cognitive therapy developed in the 1960s and 1970s by Albert Ellis and Aaron Beck for patients with depression and anxiety. The emphasis placed on a nonthreatening and supportive therapeutic alliance, the effort to find aspects of the patient that are normal to help solve problems and a focus on adaptation and current problems harkens back to the developmental perspective on individual psychotherapy and have much in common with other contemporary psychotherapeutic treatments. The collaborative and accepting mode of the treatment focuses on the symptoms and problems that the patient wishes to address. A rational and common-sense approach is taken to the patient's attitudes, underlying assumptions, symptoms, and problems of daily living.

The major CBT approaches to these disorders include belief modification, focusing/reattribution, normalizing, cognitive therapy following acute psychosis, cognitive therapy for early psychosis, coping strategy enhancement and combinations of these. In belief modification, the patient is urged to view a delusion as only one possible alternative explanation of events. Without telling the patient that the belief is wrong, evidence for the belief may be challenged while inconsistencies are pointed out. Nonconfrontational verbal challenge and empirical testing help modify the degree of conviction patients may hold toward their beliefs.

Focusing/reattribution is the intervention most suited for patients with auditory hallucinations. Over a series of sessions the patient is asked to focus on specific aspects of the hallucinatory experience, from the characteristics of the voices, their content, and the patient's beliefs and thoughts about the voices. Following sessions, patients are given "homework" assignments to record these matters that are then used to discuss the timing and context of the hallucinations. The ultimate goal of this technique is to change the attribution of the voice from external to the patient to the patients themselves. Similarly, in the normalizing technique, the therapist attempts to help the patient describe the situation and stressors immediately preceding the onset of symptoms, as well as elucidate the cognitive distortions at the time of the onset. Normalizing also utilizes relaxation and anxiety management techniques, as well as the diary and notebook assignments as in the homework sessions described earlier. Much like the interpersonal school of psychoanalysis, every effort is made to emphasize the continuity of psychotic and normal experience and to reduce stigma and distress.

CBT interventions in acute psychosis and early psychosis combines many of the elements listed earlier but also include small group work in which patients are exposed to the irrationalities and inconsistencies of other group members, thus reducing some of the pressure on the individual patient. Efforts are also made to help patients integrate the experience, much like in the normalization technique, and families are encouraged to cooperate in helping reduce stress. These techniques also include illness education and focus on issues of motivation and stigma. Many of these techniques mirror the early phase of illness work in flexible and personal psychotherapies described earlier.

Coping strategy enhancement involves the reinforcement of those techniques already employed by patients to compensate for their illness. This method helps patients identify those environmental stressors that trigger dysfunctional cognitive, behavioral, and physiological reactions leading to psychotic symptoms. The process includes the careful and systematic identification and following of symptoms and their contexts, enhancement and development of ongoing strategies in response to the symptoms, and practicing new strategies in the sessions, and with homework assignments between sessions. Patients are taught to prioritize symptoms, whether or not to increase or decrease their activity, sensory input or social involvement in response to each symptom.

Because cognitive therapies have clear protocols, it is easier to design studies of effectiveness than with more dynamically oriented treatments. Since 1990 there have been well over a dozen variably controlled studies of the types of CBT mentioned earlier. The results are best for those patients with clear-cut symptoms and who acknowledge those symptoms as ones to be addressed. Within that group the most effective results are with those patients with delusional symptoms. Investigators in the field are calling for better controlled studies with better and more random patient selection with respect to severity and concurrent treatments.

VI. RELATED MODALITIES

The final developments that have modified the practice of psychotherapy for patients with psychotic disorders is the increased sophistication in other modalities of treatment beyond psychotherapy and psychopharmacology. These techniques include psychoeducation, psychiatric rehabilitation, case management and assertive community treatment. These techniques serve to reduce stressors, facilitate adaptation, improve thinking, and mobilize resources in ways that reinforce self-esteem and enlarge the conflict-free zone, freeing the psychotherapist to more collaboratively share a focus with the patient in a more expansive and interrelated manner. These modalities address areas that were rarely meant to be dealt with in traditional psychotherapies.

Psychoeducational approaches do not dwell on the past and do not employ confrontative nor particularly interpretive techniques; rather, they make an effort to increase the family's knowledge of the illness and facilitate a rapprochement between parent and afflicted child, thus decreasing the pressure on both. Gone are the efforts to separate patients and their families. By reducing the stressors associated with dysfunctional interactions, experimental evidence has indicated a reduction in relapse rates. Then, like the early advertisements about medication, the patient becomes more amenable to and more continually available for the previously described, phase-appropriate psychotherapeutic interventions.

It is clear that medication, dynamic, personal, psychoeducational, and cognitive-behavioral therapies do not solve all the problems confronting the patient with a psychotic disorder. This is the case because most problems in living, especially for someone recovering from psychosis, have many interrelated components. With respect to the matter of social adjustment, for example, it is worth noting just how much might be involved from the different neuropsychological spheres encompassing sending, receiving, and processing. Starting at the foundation, social adjustment requires molecular skills such as eye contact and what to say in an introductory conversation—sending information. Acquiring these skills requires a sufficient level of motivation. Another critical element at the foundation for social adjustment is the ability to perceive social cues, such as knowing when one might be welcome versus when one might be interrupting—receiving information. Acquiring social perception requires the capacity for self-object differentiation as well as the ability to recognize affects in the other. The final element in the foundation is problem solving. As mentioned, problem solving depends on intact cognitive processes, especially as has been more recently demonstrated, memory and visual-spatial mechanisms—processing information. Thus, effective treatment for social adjustment—a crucial factor in community reintegration and tenure—could involve cognitive remediation, social skills training, and psychotherapy—three separate treatment modalities, before coalescing into the molar skills necessary for social competence. And even then, these instrumental skills must be integrated with attachment needs. Insofar as some patients have the instrumental skills premorbidly, then a dynamically oriented psychotherapy that is helpful around issues of affiliation and attachment may be all that is needed. It is unusual, however, that this kind of intervention is sufficient for the modal patient with a psychotic disorder. Personal therapy as practiced by Hogarty and his colleagues appears to combine the elements most important for social adjustment. Their recently published study of 151 patients demonstrated a steady improvement in social adjustment for those patients living within a family. Their treatment had no effect on symptoms or anxiety and actually increased relapse rate in those patients living outside a family. Thus, like the recommendations of Fenton, they recommend that the later phases of their treatment await symptom and residential stability. Figure 2 outlines the many factors involved in social adjustment.

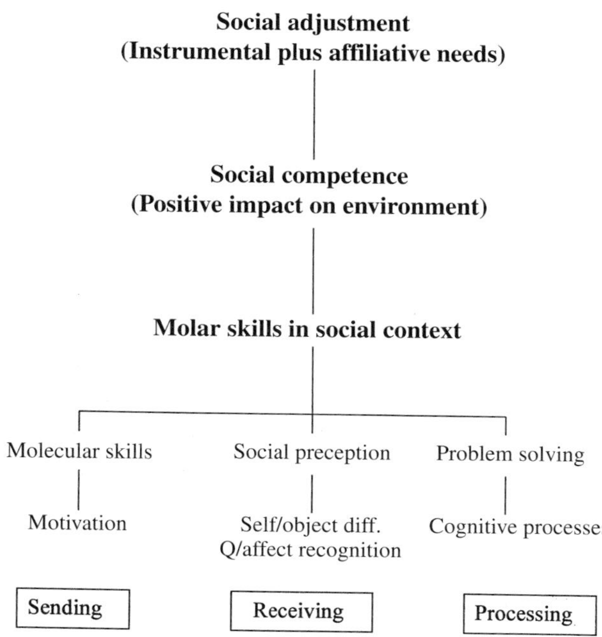

FIGURE 2 Elements of social adjustment.

There is an important note to be made about the new modalities in the context of psychotherapy. Incompatible as they may seem on the surface, there are aspects of the contemporary treatment of schizophrenia and other psychotic disorders that are heir to the psychodynamic tradition in the continuing treatment of the seriously and persistently mentally ill. In determining a patient's specific rehabilitation goals, ideal environment and readiness for these interventions, the patient's interest and motivation, meaning system, symbolic, and value-laden world are critical. These emerge from the biopsychosocial model of illness and a thorough understanding of the patient and provide the energy for and shape of the treatment plan.

Expecting too much from or being too quickly discouraged with the lack of progress of a recovering patient can replicate exacerbating features such as high levels of tension or demoralization. Therefore, issues of psychological safety and trust are paramount, leading to difficulty coming to a shared reality and experiencing helpful intentions from a caregiver. A familiarity with the principles of psychodynamic psychiatry, with its emphasis on unconscious mental life, its principle of multiple determinants of actions, thoughts, and feelings, areas of sensitivity and vulnerability, and the presence of the past in the present—especially as represented in self- and object relations and transference phenomena, can only enhance the sensitivity and effectiveness of the treatment professional. Finally, the effectiveness of other treatments makes it possible for more appropriate technical neutrality than has often been the case in the psychotherapy for patients with a psychotic disorder. This is not meant in the sense, of course, of being a neutral object; rather, it means freeing the psychotherapist to shape the psychotherapy to fit the patient, whether it be from the point of view of therapeutic activity as previously mentioned, or whether it concerns itself with the patient's drives, ego operations, object relational, interpersonal, or self-system paradigms.

See Also the Following Articles

Attention Training Procedures ■ Cognitive Behavior Therapy ■ Object Relations Psychotherapy ■ Psychopharmacology: Combined Treatment ■ Sullivan's Interpersonal Psychotherapy ■ Vocational Rehabilitation

Further Reading

Dickerson, F. B. (1999). Cognitive behavioral psychotherapy for schizophrenia: A review of recent empirical studies. *Schizophrenia Research 2000, 43,* (2–3): 71–90.

Fenton, W. S. (2001). Individual psychotherapies in schizophrenia. In Gabbard, G. O. (ed.), *Treatment of psychiatric disorders* (2nd ed., pp. 47–66). Washington, DC: American Psychiatric Press.

Fromm-Reichman, F. (1950). *Principles of intensive psychotherapy.* Chicago: University of Chicago Press.

Gunderson, J. G., Frank, A. F., Katz, H. M., Vannicelli, M. L., Frosch, J. P., & Knapp, P. H. (1984). Effects of psychotherapy in schizophrenia. II: Comparative outcome of two forms of treatment. *Schizophrenia Bulletin, 10,* 564–598.

Hogarty, G. E., Kornblith, S. J., Greenwald, D., DiBarry, A. L., Cooley, S., Ulrich, R. F., Carter, M., & Flesher, S. (1997). Three-year trials of personal therapy among schizophrenic patients living with or independent of family. I. Description of study and effects on relapse rates. *American Journal of Psychiatry, 154(11),* 1504–13.

Kates, J., & Rockland, I. H. (1994). Supportive psychotherapy of the schizophrneic patients. *American Journal of Psychotherapy. 48,* 4543–4561.

Munich, R. L. (1999). Contemporary practice of inpatient psychotherapy. In Spiegel, D. (Ed.), *Efficacy and cost-effectiveness of psychotherapy* (pp. 87–109). Washington, DC: American Psychiatric Press.

Perris, C., & McGorry, P. D. (Eds.). (1998). *Cognitive psychotherapy of psychotic and personality disorders: Handbook of theory and practice.* New York: John Wiley & Sons.

Stone, M. (1999). The history of the psychoanalytic treatment of schizophrenia. *Journal of the American Academy of Psychoanalysis,* 27(4), 583–601.

Sullivan, H. S. (1962). *Schizophrenia as a human process.* New York: Norton.

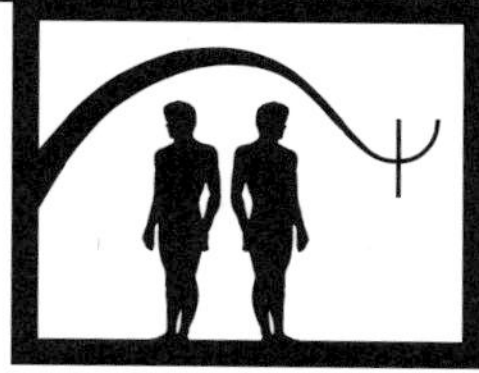

Self-Control Desensitization

E. Thomas Dowd
Kent State University

GLOSSARY

anticipatory anxiety Anticipating one's future anxiety when thinking about an anxiety-producing situation.

counterconditioning The replacement of one conditioned response to a stimulus by another.

hierarchy An arrangement of anxiety-producing scenes, from low anxiety arousal to high anxiety arousal.

in vivo desensitization Desensitization based on exposure to real-life anxiety-producing situations, generally by the practice of coping strategies.

proprioceptive responses Internal physiological responses, such as muscle tension, that occur in response to anxiety-producing situations.

reciprocal inhibition The inhibition of a learned anxiety response by pairing a new adaptive response with the original anxiety-producing situation.

self-control desensitization Desensitization based on a coping skills mediational format involving sensitivity to proprioceptive cues and cognitive relabeling.

systematic desensitization Reducing the connection between an anxiety-producing stimulus and anxiety by pairing an anxiety-incompatible response with the original stimulus.

I. DESCRIPTION OF TREATMENT

Self-control desensitization is a variant of systematic desensitization that gives more control of the procedure to clients than does the latter, which is therapist run. It is also based on a somewhat different theoretical model. In self-control desensitization, clients are given a rationale that is essentially coping skills oriented in nature. They are told that they have learned, on the basis of past experience, to react to certain situations by becoming anxious, tense, or nervous. They are then told they will learn new coping strategies to replace these negative reactions with more adaptable ones. They are taught the relaxation skills and other coping methods, such as breathing control and attention to internal sensations, and are then instructed to use them in a hierarchy of anxiety-producing situations to relax away tensions and provide covert rehearsal for situations they may face. The anxiety-producing scenes in the hierarchy are constructed jointly by the therapist and the client, and the client is asked to imagine them for 10 to 15 sec if there is no anxiety response. If there is such a response, the client is asked to terminate the scene and concentrate only on relaxation, relaxing away any tension. It is important that the use of these coping strategies be practiced repeatedly for the new coping skills to become well learned. This is especially important for scenes that arouse considerable anxiety.

The construction of the hierarchy originally followed the guidelines described by Wolpe in which it was considered necessary to construct separate hierarchies for each specific anxiety-producing situation. However, in accordance with a more mediational paradigm, clients were taught to cope with their internal proprioceptive responses rather than coping directly with the situations that caused the anxiety. Thus, early on the use of exact hierarchies was not considered to be as important in self-control desensitization. In fact, the therapist was urged to include items that reflected a series of different anxiety-producing situations.

In systematic desensitization, it was considered important that scenes in the hierarchy be terminated if anxiety was aroused. In self-control desensitization clients are encouraged to remain in the scene if anxiety increases and to cope with this anxiety by relaxation or other coping strategies. Clients are encouraged to practice these new skills in real-life *(in vivo)* situations. The *in vivo* practice of these coping strategies in actual anxiety-producing situations should lead to enhancement of these skills.

II. THEORETICAL BASES

Systematic desensitization, as originally developed by Joseph Wolpe, was theoretically based on reducing anxiety by causing a response antagonistic to this anxiety to occur in the presence of the anxiety-producing stimulus. Thus, if the presence of a snake (the anxiety-producing stimulus), which normally produces anxiety, was paired with relaxation (a response antagonistic to anxiety), then a reduction in anxiety should occur. Wolpe thought that in this fashion the bond between the fear-producing stimulus (the snake) and the anxiety response would be weakened or reciprocally inhibited. Wolpe thought that it was important that a hierarchy of fear-producing stimuli (ranging from looking at the snake to approaching the snake to touching the snake) be constructed so the individual was not overwhelmed by anxiety early in the process. The procedure was based on the counterconditioning model in which the original bond between stimulus and anxiety response was automatically reduced or eliminated by the introduction of an antagonistic response.

Self-control desensitization was originally developed by Marvin Goldfried in 1971 and was based on a somewhat different theoretical rationale. Rather than considering relaxation as "reciprocally inhibiting" the anxiety response, Goldfried proposed a mediational model that was a forerunner of cognitive-behavior therapy. This mediational model consists of two aspects: the active construction of the muscular relaxation response and a cognitive relabeling of the entire sequence between the fear-producing stimulus and the fear response. Theoretically, the client learns a method of actively coping with the anxiety rather than an automatic weakening of a psychological bond taking place. The client also learns to identify proprioceptive cues that are associated with muscular tension and to relax them away, essentially coping with these proprioceptive anxiety responses rather than the actual situations that elicit the anxiety. With considerable repetition, the client also learns to react to anticipatory anxiety with anticipatory relaxation, and eventually this process can become automatic in nature. However, both self-control desensitization and systematic desensitization are based on an important assumption of the counterconditioning model that the relaxation response must be stronger than the anxiety response for counterconditioning to occur.

Both systematic desensitization and self-control desensitization originally postulated that the construction and use of a hierarchy of anxiety-producing stimuli was important because a too-rapid introduction of an anxiety-producing stimulus might overwhelm the new relaxation response. If that occurred, it was thought that anxiety would reduce the relaxation rather than the reverse. However, research by Goldfried and Goldfried indicated that the use of a hierarchy of target-relevant behavior was not necessary for effective self-control desensitization. More recent research conducted on systematic desensitization itself has shown that a hierarchy may not be as necessary as originally thought. Implosive therapy (or "flooding"), in fact, is based on the opposite rationale—that it is more effective to begin at the top of the hierarchy rather than the bottom so that rapid extinction might take place. Thus, the construction of a hierarchy has been deemed less important as the theoretical explanatory model shifted from a counterconditioning to a coping skills model. Likewise, in line with the mediational model, it was not considered as important to terminate the anxiety-producing scene if anxiety increased; rather the client should implement the model by coping with the anxiety itself and relaxing it away. Only if the client is unable to tolerate the anxiety should the scene be terminated. The coping skills model assumes that skills are enhanced by practice and success under somewhat adverse conditions.

III. EMPIRICAL STUDIES

The majority of the empirical research on self-control desensitization was conducted in the 1970s and early 1980s, with some doctoral dissertations conducted in the late 1980s. Summary literature and case studies combining self-control desensitization with similar techniques, such as applied relaxation and Suinn's Anxiety Management Training, have appeared well into the 1990s. Especially noteworthy are the series of studies conducted by Jerry Deffenbacher and his colleagues on comparisons of self-control desensitization with Anxiety Management Training and self-control relaxation. Other studies have compared it to systematic desensitization, rational restructuring, and neurolinguistic programming. Its use has been investigated primarily with anxiety disorders but also with related problems such as phobias, vaginismus, and the management of psychotic patients and individuals with mental retardation.

The research has shown that, although self-control desensitization is effective when compared to control groups receiving no treatment, it is no more effective than a variety of alternative treatments. Furthermore, the use of a graduated targeted hierarchy does not appear to be necessary. What appears to be the mechanism of its effectiveness is the gradual installation of coping skills by practice, perhaps with the attendant nonspecific effects of hope, confidence, and optimism.

IV. SUMMARY

Self-control desensitization is a modification of systematic desensitization, as originally developed by Joseph Wolpe. It relies on a an active, mediational, coping skills model of change rather than a passive counterconditioning model. It utilizes coping skills such as relaxation as alternative responses to an anxiety response in the presence of anxiety-producing stimuli. A hierarchy of anxiety-producing situations is often used although research and clinical observation have shown that it is not as necessary as was once thought. Rather than terminate the scene as soon as anxiety is felt, clients are encouraged to remain in the situation and relax away the anxiety. *In vivo* practice in actual anxiety-producing situations is encouraged. It is similar in many ways to other self-control anxiety reduction techniques such as applied relaxation and Anxiety Management Training. Research has shown that self-control desensitization is effective for a variety of anxiety disorders but is not more effective than other cognitive or behavioral techniques.

See Also the Following Articles

Coverant Control ■ Eye Movement Desensitization and Reprocessing ■ Self-Control Therapy ■ Self-Statement Modification ■ Systematic Desensitization ■ Vicarious Conditioning ■ Vicarious Extinction

Further Reading

Barrios, B. A., & Shigetomi, C. C. (1979). Coping skills training for the management of anxiety: A critical review. *Behavior Therapy, 10*(49), 1–522.

Borkovec, T. D., & Whisman, M. A. (1996). Psychosocial treatment for generalized anxiety disorder. In M. R. Mavissakalian & R. F. Prien (Eds.), *Long-term treatments of anxiety disorders* (pp. 171–199). Washington DC: American Psychiatric Press.

Costello, E., & Borkovec, T. D. (1992). Generalized anxiety disorder. In A. Freeman & F. M. Dattilio (Eds.), *Comprehensive casebook of cognitive therapy* (pp. 53–60). New York: Plenum.

Goldfried, M. R. (1971). Systematic desensitization as training in self-control. *Journal of Consulting and Clinical Psychology, 37,* 228–234.

Goldfried, M. R., & Goldfried, A. P. (1977). Importance of hierarchy content in the self-control of anxiety. *Journal of Consulting and Clinical Psychology, 45,* 124–134.

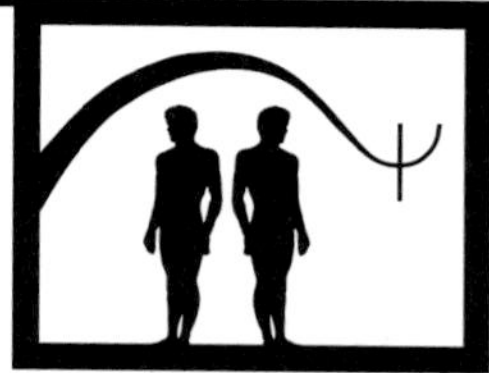

Self-Control Therapy

Lynn P. Rehm, Elisia V. Yanasak
University of Houston

GLOSSARY

self-management therapy A highly structured manualized, cognitive-behavioral therapy program for depression. Based on Frederick Kanfer's model of self-control, the treatment involves self-monitoring, self-evaluation, and self-control.

self-reward A strategy to increase probability of accomplishing difficult subgoal behaviors by setting up contingent rewards for their completion using a list of pleasurable activities for that purpose.

Self-control therapies involve teaching people skills and techniques for controlling their own behavior when striving to achieve long-term goals. It is usually assumed that people employ self-control implicitly in their efforts to change behavior, such as when starting a diet or exercise program. The self-control therapies attempt to teach these strategies in an explicit way. Many theories and therapies can be considered self-control theories. This article focuses on self-management therapy for depression developed by Lynn Rehm and his colleagues.

I. DESCRIPTION OF TREATMENT

Self-management therapy is a highly structured, manualized, cognitive-behavioral group therapy program for the treatment of depression. The program is currently presented in 14 weekly, one-and-a-half-hour sessions. Each session includes a didactic portion, a discussion period, in-session paper-and-pencil exercises, and weekly homework assignments that are reviewed at the beginning of the next session. It is an illustration of self-control therapies in that it is "transparent" to the participants. They are told that the depressive target of the intervention is identified, they are instructed in applying the intervention on their own, and they are told the theoretical rationale for the intervention. Participants are consciously applying psychological principles to change their own behavior.

Self-management therapy can be thought of in three ways. First, it is targeting specific components of depression and teaching the participants self-change techniques for modifying each target behavior. Second, it can be thought of as teaching principles of self-change in the context of depression. Third, it can be seen as teaching behaviors that are the opposite of depression, that is, positive self-esteem and self-control behaviors. People with positive self-esteem are people who accurately view their world, have a realistic sense of their abilities, set reasonable standards and goals, and are able to control their behavior with feedback to themselves.

The first session of the self-management therapy program serves to introduce the participants to one another and to the program. The nature of depression is described and related to the symptoms presented by the participants. A brief overall description and rationale for the program is presented by the therapist. Homework for this first session involves keeping track of daily mood by rating average mood for each day on a scale of 0 to 10, where 0 is the worst most depressed day ever and 10 is the happiest day ever. The purpose of the assignment is to focus on daily variations in mood and to get participants used to the mood scale.

In the second session homework is reviewed with emphasis on participants' observations on their mood variability during the week and any correlates of their mood that they might have observed (e.g., felt better on days when they got out of the house). The didactic presentation in this session conveys a central idea in the program. The program is premised on the idea that mood in influenced by behavior and cognition, that is, activities that people engage in daily and the "self-statements" they make to themselves about what they do. Although the relationship may go both ways, the program is premised on the idea that depressed participants can change their daily mood and, thus, their depression by changing activities and self-statements. In various ways the rest of the program involves strategies for increasing positive activities and positive self-statements. The homework assignment is to continue monitoring mood and, in addition, to list positive activities and self-statements. This self-monitoring assignment is continued throughout the program with a variation in focus with each new topic.

In session three, the relationship between mood and events is demonstrated to participants by graphing their week's homework. For each day of the week the mood rating is graphed with a connected line. Then the total number of activities and self-statements for each day is graphed on the same form. Parallel lines illustrate the relationship between mood and activity. The homework assignment is to continue the self-monitoring logs daily.

The topic covered in the next session is the idea that any event has both positive and negative immediate and delayed consequences. When they are depressed, people tend to focus on immediate consequences. Activities can be positive either because they are immediately pleasurable or because they produce some delayed, or long-term positive outcome. Eating ice cream is immediately pleasurable whereas mowing the lawn may be a positive activity because the end product of a nice-looking lawn is pleasing. The homework assignment is to list each day at least one positive activity that is positive because it has a delayed positive effect. Each time such an activity is listed, a positive self-statement is to be listed noting the positive long-term effect.

Having covered the effects of activities, the next few sessions focus on their causes. Depressed persons are seen as making external, unstable, and specific attributions for positive events. "That was nice, but it wasn't my doing. It was just luck and may never happen again." Exercises in the session teach the participants to realistically take credit for positive activities. The exercise includes having participants take positive events from their self-monitoring logs and examine their causes. The homework assignment is to include in each day's self-monitoring log, one positive self-statement recognizing credit for taking responsibility for a positive activity.

In a parallel session, the idea is presented that depressed people tend to blame themselves for negative events. For a negative event, depressed persons tend to make internal, stable, and global attributions. In effect they are saying "It was my fault. I always fail in this way and I fail in everything else of this type." Again an exercise takes participants through a series of examples teaching them not to take excessive blame for negative effects, but instead, to see the that some of the reasons for negative events are external, unstable, and specific. The homework assignment is to write a self-statement daily that diminishes blame from oneself for negative events.

Goal setting is the focus of the next sessions. Depressed persons tend to be disconnected from long-term goals, and they often set goals poorly. Drawing from the behavioral literature on goal setting, good goals should be positively stated, concretely defined, in the person's control, and attainable. Participants are asked to choose any goal of intermediate range that they can work on in the next few weeks. With a goal-setting form they are guided through an exercise to define their goal and to establish a list of component subgoals necessary to reach the main goal. The homework assignment is to include the accomplishment of subgoals on the daily self-monitoring log list of positive activities. The intent of the homework is for participants to acknowledge to themselves progress toward the distal goal.

Following the goal-setting topic, the idea of self-reward as a means of motivating oneself to pursue the goal is introduced. Essentially one can increase the probability of accomplishing difficult subgoal behaviors by setting up contingent rewards for their completion. Participants construct a list of pleasurable activities that they could use to reward themselves when they accomplish difficult subgoal behaviors. For example, when completing shopping for the materials necessary for a goal of completing some home repairs, the participant might self-reward with a stop at a favorite donut shop.

The homework here is to list the subgoal activities accomplished on the self-monitoring log and also to record contingent reward activities.

The final topics of the program deal with the way in which depressed people talk to themselves. Depressed persons typically talk to themselves in ways that are punishing and diminishing of motivation. For example, "Why should I try to do this? I'll never succeed. I always make a fool out of myself by failing at things like this." The idea presented is that talking to oneself in realistically more positive ways can increase rather than decrease motivation. Self-talk can be a self-administered reward or punishment. In one exercise, participants are asked to make a list of comfortable statements that acknowledge a positive accomplishment. As one person might say to a friend "You did a great job with that task," the person might list for him-or herself "I did a great job with that task." The corresponding homework assignment is consciously to practice contingent self-rewarding statements daily and to record them in the self-monitoring log as positive self-statements.

A final session allows for continued practice of the lessons taught in the program and review of the ideas involved. The therapist is given some latitude in deciding when to go on to a new topic during the weeks of the program. The extra sessions may be spent earlier to go over a topic that the therapist feels needs further effort.

II. THEORETICAL BASES

The self-management therapy program is based on an integrative model of depression that takes elements identified by other models and subsumes them in a larger coherent framework. In doing so, the model adds a focus on depression as a problem in disconnection from long-term goals. Frederick Kanfer's model of self-control provided the basis for Rehm's self-control model of depression. According to Kanfer, when an individual initiates an attempt to achieve a new long-term goal (e.g., quitting smoking, losing weight, getting "in shape"), that person regulates his or her own behavior via a three-phase feedback loop, including self-monitoring, self-evaluation, and self-reinforcement. Self-monitoring involves observing one's own behavior, including antecedents and consequences. Self-evaluation involves comparing one's behavior to an internal criterion or standard. On the basis of this comparison one feels good or bad about progressing toward the goal. Rehm added another consideration in thinking about self-evaluation. To self-evaluate and feel good or bad about a behavior, an internal attribution is necessary. The person does not experience self-control if the control is actually external (e.g., spent the day in a nonsmoking environment).

The third phase of Kanfer's model is self-reinforcement. Kanfer argues that people influence their own behavior in the same way they may influence another person, by rewards and punishments. Metaphorically, if people are successful in their self-control attempts they "pat themselves on the back," and if they do poorly they "kick themselves." The reactions function as rewards and punishments to maintain the self-controlled behavior in the face of external stimuli and reinforcers operating against the behavior change (e.g., smoking urges, the effort of exercising). Self-reinforcement can be overt (rewarding oneself with a movie) or covert (feeling good about an accomplishment).

Rehm's model of depression uses Kanfer's self-control model as a framework. Rehm views depression as a failure of self-control to supplement external controls. When people are depressed they are hypothesized to show six deficits in self-control behavior. First, depressed people tend to self-monitor negative events to the relative exclusion of positive events. They are vigilant for things to go wrong. A similar idea is described by Aaron Beck as selective abstraction and a negative view of the world. Second, depressed people tend to self-monitor the immediate as opposed to the delayed consequences of behavior. Although they may ruminate about long-term goals they tend to be self-indulgent and respond to immediate consequences (watch TV rather than complete the housework).

Third, in terms of self-evaluation, depressed persons tend to set stringent self-evaluative standards for themselves. They view their own behavior as never good enough and tend to make all-or-none judgments that their behavior was either perfect or a complete failure. Perfectionism has been cited by various authors as a component of depression. Fourth, depressed people make negative attributions for their behaviors. Martin Seligman has elaborated this point in an extended attributional analysis of the behavior of depressed people.

The fifth and sixth deficits in the depression model are lack of contingent positive self-reinforcement and excessive self-punishment. Peter Lewinsohn's behavioral model of depression posits a loss or lack of response contingent positive reinforcement as the source of depression. This model assumes that self-administered rewards and punishments supplement external sources. A person with good self-control skills can successfully manage to get through a time of lack of external reinforcement with self-reinforcement and other self-control skills.

As can be seen, the elements of the model are dependent on earlier elements. The person who focuses on negative events and immediate consequences does not take credit for positive events, sees efforts as not meeting standards, fails to self-reinforce, and excessively self-punishes will be disconnected from long-term goals and suffer depression when the environment does not reinforce behavior benignly. The model forms the basis for the therapy program. Each deficit is focused on in sequence with a didactic presentation of the idea, an exercise to help participants understand the idea, and a homework assignment to try out more effective self-control behavior.

III. EMPIRICAL STUDIES

Self-control therapy was first examined in a series of six studies conducted by Rehm and his colleagues. The first two studies conducted were traditional outcome studies, in which self-management therapy was compared to a control group. In 1977, C. Fuchs and Rehm randomly assigned depressed female community volunteers to 6 weeks of self-control therapy, nonspecific group therapy, or a wait-list control condition. Self-control therapy was found to be the most effective treatment for alleviating symptoms of depression. In a second study in 1979 Rehm, Fuchs, D. Roth, S. Kornblith, and J. Romano assigned depressed women from the community to 6 weeks of self-control therapy or a behavioral assertion skills training program. Self-control therapy was found to be more effective than the assertion skills training program with regard to improving self-control and reducing symptoms of depression, whereas the assertion skills training program more effectively improved assertiveness. One year follow-up data on participants in these two studies, reported by Romano and Rehm in 1979, indicated that treatment gains were maintained over time. However, differences between the self-management and other active treatment conditions were no longer significant. Individuals in the self-management condition did report fewer additional depressive episodes and less severe recurrences of depression.

Next, to examine the various components of self-management therapy, two dismantling studies were conducted. The first study, conducted in 1981 by Rehm, Kornblith, M. O'Hara, D. Lamparski, Romano, and J. Volkin, examined five conditions, including: (1) self-monitoring plus self-reinforcement; (2) self-monitoring plus self-evaluation; (3) self-monitoring alone; (4) the complete therapy package; and (5) a wait-list control condition. All four treatment groups outperformed the wait-list control condition with regard to self-reported and clinician measures of depression, with no consistent differences found between the active treatment groups. In a similar study, Kornblith, Rehm, O'Hara, and Lamparski compared four groups, including: (1) self-monitoring and self-evaluation alone; (2) self-management training without homework assignments; (3) the complete self-management therapy program; and (4) interpersonally oriented group psychotherapy, serving as the control condition. All four groups were successful in alleviating symptoms of depression, with no significant differences found among the groups.

Next, specific behavioral and cognitive targets of self-management therapy were examined. The self-control manual was revised, and programs were developed that focused primarily on cognitive targets (i.e., focusing on self-statements), behavioral targets (i.e., focusing on increasing activities), or both (i.e., the "combined" version). In 1985, Rehm, Lamparski, Romano, and O'Hara compared the three versions of treatment with a wait-list control group. All three treatment groups improved more than control subjects with regard to symptoms of depression, with no differences found between the treatment groups. In 1987, Rehm, N. Kaslow, and A. Rabin again compared the three versions of self-management against each other, using a larger number of participants. Again no differences were found between the three groups, with each group showing significant improvement in self-reported and clinician measures of depression over time. They also improved equally in behavior and cognition.

Self-management therapy has been evaluated by a number of other researchers in various contexts. B. M. Fleming and D. W. Thornton, in 1980, assigned depressed volunteers to self-management therapy, cognitive therapy, or a nondirective therapy control condition. At posttest and follow-up all three groups showed significant improvement, with the self-management group showing the greatest improvement on a number of measures. In 1980, D. P. Tressler and R. D. Tucker conducted a disassembly study in which depressed female volunteers were treated with either the self-monitoring and self-evaluation components alone, or the self-monitoring and self-reinforcement components alone. The self-monitoring and self-reinforcement combination was found to be superior at posttest and at a 12-week follow-up. In 1982, D. Roth, R. Bielski, M. Jones, W. Parker, and G. Osborn compared self-management therapy alone, to the combination of self-management therapy and a tricyclic antidepressant; although there was a faster response in the combined condition, no significant differences were found between the two groups at posttest and a 3-month follow-up in self-reported symptoms of depression. S. Rude in a 1986 paper assigned depressed women to both cognitive self-control treatment (a modified version of Rehm's therapy) plus assertion skills training (administered in random order), or to a wait-list control group. Participants who received the combination of self-control and assertiveness training experienced significantly larger reductions in depressive symptoms than the control group. However at the midtreatment point, when each participant had only received one form of therapy, no significant differences were found between the three groups. R. Thomas, R. Petry, and J. Goldman in a 1987 paper assigned depressed female volunteer participants to 6 weeks of self-control therapy or cognitive therapy. Both forms of therapy were effective in alleviating depression, with results remaining at a 6-week follow-up. In 1995, J. H. C. van den Hout, A. Arntz, and F. H. J. Kunkels compared 12 weeks of self-control therapy plus standard treatment, to standard treatment alone, for depressed patients in a psychiatric day-treatment center. The addition of self-control therapy was significantly more effective than standard treatment alone with regard to improving self-control, self-esteem, and depression. Although gains were maintained at a 13-week follow-up, significant differences were no longer found between the two groups.

Self-management therapy has also been applied to diverse populations. In 1982, P. Rogers, R. Kerns, Rehm, E. D. Hendler, and L. Harkness found self-management therapy to be more effective than nonspecific individual psychotherapy in reducing depression in renal dialysis patients. S. Bailey in a 1996 study examined the effect of self-management therapy compared to a wait-list control condition as a treatment for abused women. Treated participants experienced significantly greater improvement than control subjects in symptoms of depression, self-control, and dysfunctional attitudes.

Self-management therapy has also been modified for use with depressed children and adolescents. In 1986, W. Reynolds and K. I. Coats assigned moderately depressed high school students to self-management therapy, relaxation training, or a wait-list control condition. Both therapy groups, compared to the control group, experienced significant reductions in depression and anxiety, as well as improvements in academic self-image. K. Stark, Reynolds, and Kaslow (1987) assigned children, ages 9 to 12, to either behavioral problem solving, self-control therapy (a child version), or a wait-list control condition. At posttest and 8-week follow-up, both treatment groups showed significant improvements in self-reported and clinician-rated depression, whereas the wait-list control group showed little change. In 1996, Rehm and R. Sharp reported the results from a study in which self-management therapy was provided to fourth- and fifth-grade students; although little improvement was seen in depression across participants, those children who were classified as "depressed" at pretest significantly improved with regard to symptoms of depression, social skills, and attributional style.

Self-management therapy has also been applied to older adults (age 60 or older). P. Rokke, J. Tomhave, and Z. Jocic in a 1999 paper assigned depressed older adults to one of two forms of self-management therapy (one with a cognitive focus and one with a behavioral focus), or to a wait-list control condition. Both self-management groups, compared with the control group, experienced significant reductions in depressive symptoms (with gains maintained at a 3-month and 1-year follow-up), as well as improvements in depression-related cognitions, learned resourcefulness, self-control, and self-reinforcement. No differences were found between the two versions of self-management therapy. In a similar study published in 2000 Rokke, Tomhave, and Jocic randomly assigned depressed older adults to 10 weeks of self-management therapy, an educational support group, or to a wait-list control condition. No differences were found between the two treatment groups, each of which was more effective than the control group in alleviating depression and improving self-reinforcement, learned resourcefulness, and self-control knowledge. In addition, reductions in depression levels were maintained at the 1-year follow-up.

IV. SUMMARY

In sum, Rehm's self-management therapy program is a structured, manualized, cognitive-behavioral group therapy program, designed for the treatment of depression. The therapy is designed to address deficits in the three phases of the self-control feedback loop, including self-monitoring, self-evaluation, and self-reinforcement. A number of empirical evaluations have validated the efficacy of self-management therapy as an effective treatment for depression.

See Also the Following Articles

Grief Therapy ■ Self-Control Desensitization ■ Self-Help Groups ■ Self-Help Treatment for Insomnia ■ Self Psychology ■ Trauma Management Therapy

Further Reading

Rehm, L. P. (1977). A self-control model of depression. *Behavior Therapy, 8,* 787–804.

Rehm, L. P. (1995). Psychotherapies for depression. In K. S. Dobson & K. D. Craig (Eds.), *Anxiety and depression in adults and children* (pp. 183–208). Thousand Oaks, CA: Sage.

Rehm, L. P., Mehta, P., & Dodrill, C. (2001). Depression. In M. Hersen & V. B. Van Hasselt (Eds.), *Advanced abnormal psychology* (2nd ed., pp. 307–324). New York: Kluwer Academic/Plenum.

Rehm, L. P., & Sharp, R. N. (1996). Strategies in the treatment of childhood depression. In M. Reinecke, F. M. Dattilio, & A. Freeman (Eds.), *Comprehensive casebook on cognitive-behavior therapy with adolescents* (pp. 103–123). New York: Guilford Press.

Rokke, P. D., & Rehm, L. P. (2001). Self-management therapies. In K. S. Dobson (Ed.), *Handbook of cognitive behavior therapies* (2nd ed., pp. 173–210). New York: Guilford Press.

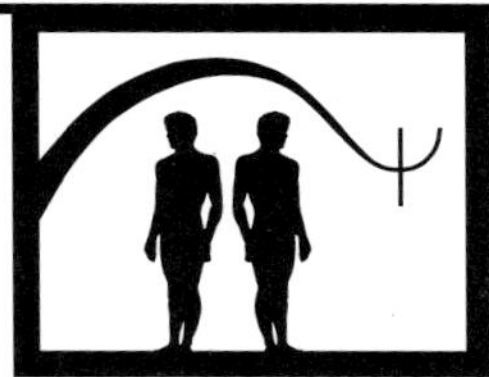

Self-Help Groups

Gary M. Burlingame and D. Rob Davies

Brigham Young University

GLOSSARY

helper-therapy principle Introduced by Riessman in 1965 to convey the notion that in the act of helping others, the member is empowered, both to help others and simultaneously to help him- or herself.

professional-centrism The tendency of professionals to view self-help groups with higher levels of professional involvement as being more helpful than non-professional self-help groups. This leads them to be more likely to refer to and support groups with higher levels of professional involvement.

self-help clearinghouses Organizations dedicated to cataloging and referring interested parties to the self-help groups in a particular district or region.

self-help groups Voluntary associations of persons who share common concerns or problems and who try to support and help each other at little or no cost.

self-help organizations Refers to a more complex and broader level of organization (regional, national, or international associations) that foster the development and management of local self-help groups.

I. OVERVIEW AND HISTORY

Despite rather humble beginnings, self-help groups have become a pervasive phenomenon in the United States. Although their history can be traced as far back as the guilds in the Middle Ages and likely before, the origination of modern self-help organizations is most typically associated with the start of Alcoholics Anonymous (AA) in June of 1935. AA is the largest and oldest self-help organization in the United States. It started as the brainchild of two recovering alcoholics, Robert Holbrook Smith and stockbroker William Wilson. AA is the prototype for modern self-help groups in the United States and Canada and, in fact, has become one of the most commonly utilized groups among those seeking treatment for alcohol problems. There are now estimated to be more than 55,000 AA groups in the United States, and Canada.

Other well known self-help groups include Recovery, Inc., the National Alliance for the Mentally Ill (NAMI), Narcotics Anonymous, and Schizophrenics Anonymous as well as lesser known groups for epileptics, families of suicide victims, a variety of neurological diseases, eating disorders, a multitude of serious emotional crises (retirement, widowhood, loss of a child, various illnesses, handicaps, unemployment, divorce), almost all chronic diseases, minorities, marginalized peoples, and parenting to name but a few of the groups available. This list is by no means exhaustive because estimates suggest that there are over 400 distinct types of self-help groups in the United States alone.

Self-help clearinghouses have sprung up due in part to the wide variety and the sheer number of self-help groups in any one geographical area. These clearinghouses are dedicated to cataloging and referring interested parties to the self-help groups in a particular district or region. For example, Gerald Goodman reports that in 1993 the California Self-Help Center clearinghouse alone, with 4,600 groups in its database, referred about 120 people a day to self-help groups.

Self-help groups have grown at an astounding rate. At present, it is estimated that the number of people being treated in self-help groups exceeds those in professionally-led individual and group therapy combined. It is surmised that roughly 25 million Americans have attended one of 500,000 self-help groups at some point in their lives. Telephone surveys of random individuals indicate that almost 7% of people admit to being actively engaged in a self-help group at any one time.

Despite the ubiquitous nature of self-help groups, there is less clarity on what is meant by the term. Mental health professionals have struggled for years to define these groups. Part of the difficulty lies in the fact that the concept itself is somewhat fluid. For instance, each one of the estimated 500,000 self-help groups add their own unique contributions to the definition. Despite this challenge most researchers have settled on four basic definitional tenants:

1. Members have common concerns or problems that they are dealing with.
2. Members of the group have control over the structure and format of the group.
3. Help that is received is given primarily through other members in the group.
4. There is little or no cost for the members of the group.

Although this definition has utility as an anchor point, it is important to keep in mind that individual self-help groups will vary on each one of these dimensions. For example AA groups and other "Anonymous" groups are built on a structured 12-step approach in which local chapters are facilitated by a larger national organization. Thus, although local members have some control over the structure and format of the group, much of what happens in group is a result of the structure set by the national program.

Other self-help groups are entirely controlled by local members without any affiliation with local or national organizations. In fact, given the earlier definition, a group of three or four single mothers who get together a couple of times a month for lunch to talk about their struggles could be classified as a self-help group. Of course, these self-help groups will never be classified by clearinghouses, receive publicity, and are closed to other outsiders; nonetheless they fall under the rubric of self-help groups.

Given the aforementioned definitional variability, is there a typical self-help group? The answer depends on whether one includes AA and the approximately 150 other 12-step groups as the model group. A persuasive argument for such is offered by Kathryn Davison and colleagues who found that out of 12,596 self-help groups identified in four major cities for 20 different diseases or disorders, 10,966 (87%) were AA groups. Given the pervasive nature of AA groups, a brief overview is warranted.

AA meetings are divided into four types.

1. Open Meetings: Any interested person may attend.
2. Closed meetings: Only people who are alcoholic or who have a desire to stop drinking may attend.
3. Discussion meetings: Typically the chairperson suggests a topic for the group.
4. Speaker meetings: The speaker presents his or her life before entering the group and gains made since then.

AA and other "Anonymous" groups follow a 12-step program. The first 3 of the 12 steps deal with the admission of defeat or powerlessness over addiction. Steps 4 through 9 consider healing the ruin of the past, and the last 3 steps deal with maintaining peace and serenity. There is an unmistakable emphasis on religious or spiritual influences in 12-step groups, which has led to their marginalization in some contexts. Nevertheless, 12-step programs have flourished and are considered by many professionals today to be an integral part of treatment for addictions.

The majority of all self-help groups (about two-thirds) formally introduce existing group members to new members and have new members introduce themselves. Some (about one third) ask new members to share personal experiences related to the group's stated purpose. With few exceptions new members are welcomed and accommodated. In recent comprehensive surveys, as many as 40% of self-help groups were oriented toward the treatment of physical illness. Attendance at these group meetings varied considerably, with some being very large (50 people in attendance) and others involving only 2 to 5 individuals (average attendance is in the range of 13 to 21 people). Most self-help groups recruit new members by word of mouth, but a significant number also use newspaper or magazine advertisements or solicit professionals for referrals.

Some authors have tried to differentiate self-help and mutual support groups (also referred to simply as support groups). The usual distinction is the level of professional involvement in leading, sponsoring, or otherwise controlling the nature of the group. Support groups are more frequently aligned with mental health professionals and are often led by a trained therapist. On the other hand, self-help groups are usually viewed as being relatively autonomous from professional involvement, and peer leadership is endorsed.

Critics of professional involvement voice their concern about the loss of the self-help group's ideology and effectiveness when a professional assumes the leadership role. This is based on an important therapeutic principle that self-help group members experience autonomy, control of the group, and a sense that they are the experts on their difficulty. Opponents to professional involvement postulate that when an authority steps in, the unique benefits of self-help groups are lost, and the members of the group may begin to engage in docile "patient behavior." This concern has led some writers in the field to characterize groups by the presence or absence of professional involvement with the former being classified as a treatment group (psychotherapy or psychoeducation).

The distinction between groups with and without professional involvement may have more ideological and historical value because modern self-help groups often incorporate professionals. More specifically, recent research indicates that most "self-help" groups have some professional involvement. In 1993, Morton Lieberman reported that over 60% of observed groups were professionally facilitated while simultaneously being characterized as self-help. Eight years earlier (1985), Jennifer Lotery randomly sampled 850 self-help groups in California and found that 14% "frequently" had professionals in the role of solo leader with another 35% using professionals as co-leaders. Thus nearly one half the groups experienced a professional as part- or full-time co-leader. More recently, Scott Wituk's work in 2000 found that in a sample of 253 randomly selected self-help groups only 27% were peer led with no professional involvement. Other recent random samples have also shown similar results, that is, a growing trend to include professionals in self-help groups.

Lotery's survey suggests that most self-help groups welcome professionals, especially as a referral source, speaker, teacher, student, or co-leader. Respondents also stated an interest in having professionals serve as solo leaders or coordinators/organizers. In general, most self-help organizations echo this sentiment. For instance, a recent study reports that groups with a combination of both peer and professional leadership had greater longevity and continued group membership than either professional or peer-led groups. Thus, peer-leadership versus professional leadership seems to fall on a continuum rather than the dichotomous variable that early researchers conceptualized.

Despite potential for collaboration and consultation, it is important to note that self-help groups and professionals often view the consulting role rather differently. Self-help group members can view professionals as wanting to control the group using their clinical experience and training. Thus, it is important for professionals to approach self-help groups with an attitude of mutual respect and partnership rather than as a source for expert solutions that may conflict with self-help group ideology. Several recent studies of mental health professionals' perceptions of self-help groups suggest that the majority view groups with higher levels of professional involvement as being more helpful, effective, good, strong, healthy, understandable, active, interesting, predictable, and safer than groups with less professional association. This phenomenon has been labeled by Mark Salzer as "professional centrism" and has been well documented. Professionals are more likely to refer to and support those groups with higher levels of professional involvement. Paradoxically, scant research exists to either support or refute professionals faith in self-help groups with more professional involvement.

II. HOW SELF-HELP GROUPS WORK

Members of self-help groups are empowered by not only being responsible for helping themselves, but also by being accountable for helping others. This is known in the self-help literature as the "helper-therapy principle." In helping his or her peers the member is enabled, both to assist others and at the same time to help him- or herself. The opportunity to help others with a similar problem is often a catalyst for personal change. Some research supports the help-therapy principle. Specifically the number of helping statements made by a member has been directly and significantly correlated with increasingly positive outcomes by Linda Roberts and her colleagues. Being in a position to help others with similar problems may be a unique experience for members of self-help groups, an opportunity not present in individual psychotherapy. In most self-help groups, even members who are experiencing serious challenges are given an opportunity to help others in the group.

A second source of therapeutic potential for self-help groups is the opportunity to observe strong role models of individuals who have overcome similar problems. According to Festinger's social comparison theory, people have a drive to evaluate their opinions and abilities by comparing themselves to others that they deem as similar. Self-help groups provide a unique opportunity to compare oneself with homologous others who have overcome analogous problems. Strong role models can exemplify success, reinforce group norms, provide empathy, and promote identification and motivation. In self-help groups, many successful members continue to attend to share their success and offer support to new or struggling members. This continued long-term involvement is possible because the groups are usually free from financial obligations. Moreover, research suggests that the longer a person participates in a self-help group the more likely they are to benefit from it.

III. EFFECTIVENESS

The scientific study of self-help groups has been slow and difficult at best. The traditional research paradigm for studying the effectiveness of psychotherapy groups involves randomly assigning participants to experimental and control conditions and then observing differences between the two groups. Application of this protocol to self-help groups is problematic because they are not under the researcher's control and participants cannot be randomly assigned to a no-treatment or wait-list control condition. More specifically, refusing or delaying fellowship to interested members is in direct opposition to the open philosophy of the self-help movement.

Critics have also argued that there is an inherent selection bias in studies that assess the outcome of self-help groups. Indeed, research has shown that individuals who do not expect to benefit from self-help groups drop out. This phenomenon led Leon Levy to argue those who remain in self-help groups will undoubtedly find the group to be effective thereby skewing the effectiveness results in the "positive" direction.

A final obstacle in the scientific study of self-help group effectiveness lies in the purported effects. In traditional group psychotherapy therapists focus on the removal of symptoms by treating the underlying causes for pathology (maladaptive relationships, distorted cognition, etc.). On the other hand, self-help groups focus on mutual support. In short, the expected outcomes for the self-help and traditional psychotherapy groups are different. More specifically, one measure of effectiveness for self-help groups may be the amount of support these groups give to each other and not the reduction of psychopathology. Members often highlight the salubrious effect of the group on their feelings of isolation and social seclusion rather than reduction in pathology reporting high levels of satisfaction. Although robust empirical data on the effectiveness of self-help groups is scarce, the current literature does support their effectiveness. Participation in self-help groups has been linked to improved subjective well-being, attenuated use of professional services, strengthened coping skills, shorter hospital stays, less denial of problems, less identification with the patient role, and reduced psychiatric symptomatology. Self-help groups also help individuals form a new identity, give them a sense of belonging and association, and assist in personal transformations through support, advocacy, and empowerment. Self-help groups are recommended by a majority of treatment programs for substance disorders. In fact, studies that evaluated AA as one element in a treatment program suggest that alcoholics who attend AA in addition to other treatment modalities do better than those who attend only AA or use professional treatment alone. In general 12-step groups have produced beneficial outcomes.

It is important to note that not all research has supported the effectiveness of self-help groups. In 1999, Sally Barlow and colleagues focused on self-help groups in the medical field. Seventeen studies that compared controls with active self-help treatment groups when examined as an aggregate found no evidence that members of medical self-help groups improve more than a non-treated control group. However, this does not mean that members of the self-help groups were not satisfied with their groups or that they did not receive benefits other than those objectively measured by the researchers.

IV. THE FUTURE

Self-help groups are not an endangered species. Gerald Goodman and Marion Jacobs predicted that self-help groups will become the nation's "treatment of choice" in the next 10 to 20 years. Given self-help groups' exponential growth in recent years, it is hard to imagine a mental health field without them. In fact, with the increasing scarcity and lack of availability of mental health services to the general public, self-help groups are virtually assured a position of prominence in the future. It is also likely that professional involvement in self-help groups will not only continue but intensify over time. Self-help groups are being recognized as a legitimate resource for clients and, as such, increasing numbers of professionals will vie to become involved with these groups.

Online groups are beginning to gain acceptance as a viable treatment alternative to the formal self-help group venue. They are likely to become increasingly common as more and more people gain access to this mode of communication. Advantages of online self-help groups include their availability (24-hours-a-day), breadth (worldwide), specificity (support for those with relatively rare conditions), and lower level of interpersonal risk (anonymity and indirect participation). Online self-help groups appear to be expanding despite the fact that almost no research exists to delineate whether participation is helpful or satisfying—a topic in need of future research.

V. SUMMARY

Self-help groups have grown exponentially since the inception of AA and are now a primary treatment method for many individuals. Although defining self-help groups has been problematic given the variety of groups available, they are typically composed of members with common concerns who have control over the structure and format of the group and who give mutual aid and support to each other for little or no cost. Of the over 400 documented types of self-help groups, most have some professional involvement, especially as a referral source, speaker, teacher, or consultant. Core therapeutic principles include giving members opportunities to help others, motivating them to emulate successful others in the group, and offering friendship and support. The study of how effective self-help groups are has been fraught with a number of problems that center around self-selection. Despite these problems, most research indicates that they are effective. In addition, most members of these groups report being highly satisfied with their group experience and rate the group as beneficial. It is likely that in the coming years self-help groups will become even more common.

See Also the Following Articles

Anxiety Disorders: Brief Intensive Group Behavior Therapy ■ Behavioral Group Therapy ■ Cognitive Behavior Group Therapy ■ Group Psychotherapy ■ Matching Patients to Alcoholism Treatment ■ Minimal Therapist Contact Treatments ■ Psychodynamic Group Psychotherapy

Further Reading

Barlow, S. H., Burlingame, G. M., Nebeker, R. S., & Anderson, E. (2000). Meta-analysis of medical self-help groups. *International Journal of Group Psychotherapy, 50*(1), 53–69.

Goodman, G., & Jacobs, M. K. (1994). The self-help, mutual-support group. In A. Fuhriman, & G. M. Burlingame (Eds.), *Handbook of group psychotherapy: An empirical and clinical synthesis* (pp. 489–526). New York: John Wiley & Sons.

Kurtz, L. F. (1997). *Self-help and support groups: A handbook for practitioners*. Thousand Oaks': CA Sage.

Wituk, S., Shepherd, M. D., Slavich, S., Warren, M. L., & Meissen, G. (2000). A topography of self-help groups: An empirical analysis. *Social Work 45*(2), 157–165.

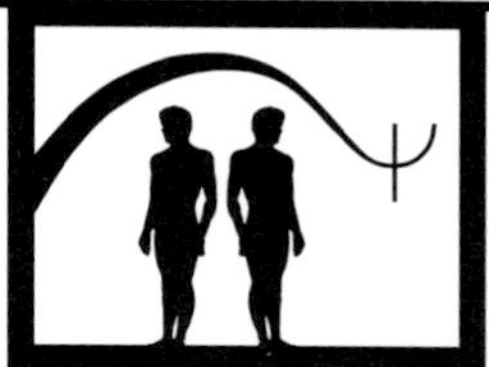

Self-Help Treatment for Insomnia

Annie Vallières, Marie-Christine Ouellet, and Charles M. Morin

Université Laval

GLOSSARY

chronic insomnia Insomnia persisting more than 1 month.

insomnia A condition involving difficulties falling asleep, staying asleep, early morning awakening, or nonrestorative sleep.

meta-analysis A quantitative method using a common metric (z score) to summarize the data from different studies.

primary insomnia Insomnia that is not associated with another medical, psychiatric, or sleep disorder.

self-help treatment Intervention based on printed information or audio/video material designed to improve a medical or psychological condition.

sleep efficiency A measure of sleep continuity obtained by dividing the total amount of time slept by the time spent in bed, multiplied by 100.

sleep hygiene Education about the impact of lifestyle and environmental factors on sleep.

sleep-onset latency Time required to fall asleep at bedtime.

sleep restriction therapy Behavioral procedure consisting of limiting time in bed to the actual time spent sleeping.

stimulus control therapy Behavioral procedures aimed at establishing a consistent sleep-wake rhythm and reassociating the bed and bedroom with sleep rather than with insomnia.

I. INTRODUCTION AND DEFINITION

Insomnia is a prevalent condition affecting about 10% of the adult population on a chronic basis. It involves either difficulties falling asleep, staying asleep, early morning awakenings, or nonrestorative sleep. Insomnia can occur as a unique disorder, as in primary insomnia, or may be secondary to an another medical (e.g., cancer) or psychological condition (e.g., depression or anxiety). Chronic sleep disturbances are often associated with negative daytime consequences such as fatigue and mood disturbance, thus significantly affecting one's quality of life. Despite its high prevalence and potential impact on social or occupational functioning, only a small portion of individuals with chronic primary insomnia actually receives any treatment. For those who do seek relief for their insomnia, the first interventions are usually self-initiated and generally involve medications bought over-the-counter, natural products, or the use of alcohol. When insomnia is brought to the attention of physicians, pharmacotherapy is the most widely used and often the only recommended treatment option, despite the controversy existing over the long-term use of hypnotic medications. In the past 20 years, there has been an increasing interest in psychological and behavioral factors contributing to insomnia. This had led to the development of diverse psychological therapies for insomnia, many of which have been shown to produce significant and durable effects. However, these interventions remain underutilized because they are not well known to health care practitioners and are less easily accessible, both physically and financially, than pharmacotherapy. A self-help treatment for insomnia is a valuable alternative to overcome some of these barriers by making treatment more accessible, at a low cost, to a larger number of individuals with insomnia. Self-help treatment refers to any intervention, either for a psychological or physical condition, that is implemented with the assistance of printed material (e.g., books, pamphlets), audio- or videotapes, or any other medium (e.g., Internet). It can be implemented with or without guidance from a health care professional. The objective of this article is to provide an overview of self-help treatments that have received empirical validation in the management of primary insomnia.

II. DESCRIPTION OF TREATMENTS

Self-help treatments for insomnia incorporate much of the same information and material provided in a face-to-face therapy. Interventions that have received adequate empirical support and that are usually included in self-help treatment programs include stimulus control, sleep restriction, cognitive therapy, sleep-hygiene education, and relaxation procedures. The main goals of these interventions are to induce sleep rapidly at bedtime, to sustain it with minimal interruptions throughout the night, to enhance sleep quality and duration, and to improve daytime functioning. To achieve these outcomes, treatments focus on psychological and behavioral factors presumed to perpetuate sleep difficulties. They seek to curtail maladaptive sleep habits, to regulate the sleep schedule, to correct faulty beliefs and attitudes about sleep, to reduce autonomic arousal, and to educate patients about good sleep hygiene. Another common goal of these therapies is to teach self-management skills for coping with residual sleep disturbances once treatment is completed. Some interventions, such as stimulus control instructions, or sleep restriction, are more amenable to a self-help format because they are primarily educational or instructional in nature. Others, like relaxation or cognitive therapy, are likely to require more direct guidance, possibly with the help of a therapist, if they are to be fully effective. Provided next is a brief description of several of the psychological interventions that can be applied in a self-help format.

A. Stimulus Control

Stimulus control therapy consists of a set of behavioral rules designed to bring the patient to reassociate the bed and bedroom with sleep rather than with arousal or the frustration caused by the inability to sleep. This is achieved by curtailing sleep-incompatible activities. A second objective is to establish a consistent sleep-wake rhythm by setting a regular arising time and by avoiding naps. Standard stimulus control instructions are:

- Go to bed only when sleepy.
- Use the bed and bedroom for sleep and sexual activity only; do not read, watch TV, or worry in bed.
- When unable to sleep within 15 to 20 min, leave the bed and go into another room; return to bed only when sleepy again (this step is repeated as often as necessary throughout the night).
- Arise at the same time every morning regardless of the amount of sleep obtained the night before
- Do not take naps during the day.

B. Sleep Restriction

Individuals with insomnia sometimes spend excessive amounts of time in bed in a misguided effort to obtain more sleep. In turn, this practice may cause more fragmented sleep and perpetuate insomnia. The standard sleep restriction procedure consists of curtailing time in bed to the actual sleep time. Once the usual sleep time and time spent in bed have been estimated with the help of a sleep diary kept for at least one week, an initial time window is defined in which the patient can sleep or attempt to sleep (i.e., total time allowed in bed). This window is set to correspond to the average total sleep time and is readjusted periodically (usually weekly), either decreased or increased, based on estimations of sleep efficiency that can be easily calculated from the sleep diary (ratio of total sleep time over time spent in bed x 100). As sleep efficiency improves, the sleep window is progressively extended until an optimal sleep duration is achieved. Although the task of setting and adjusting the sleep window is usually left to the therapist in face-to-face treatments, this procedure, if well explained in written material, can be easily implemented by the individual. Sleep restriction guidelines are fairly operational and easy to follow for adjusting the sleep window: for example, if a person has been able to maintain a sleep efficiency of at least 85% for 1 week, the time allowed in bed is increased by a small amount, usually 15 to 20 min. Conversely, if sleep efficiency is lower than 80%, the time allowed in bed is decreased by the same amount. Sleep restriction induces a mild state of sleep deprivation, which promotes a more rapid sleep onset, more efficient and consolidated sleep, as well as less internight variability. This procedure should however be used with caution with individuals who engage in hazardous activities (e.g., construction workers, truck drivers). In all circumstances, the time allowed in bed should never be less than 5 hrs to prevent excessive daytime sleepiness.

C. Relaxation Therapies

Patients with insomnia are often tense and anxious, both at night and during the day. Relaxation-based interventions are the most commonly used nondrug therapy for insomnia. A variety of techniques target different types of arousal. For example, progressive muscle relaxation, autogenic training, and biofeedback are used to reduce somatic arousal such as muscle tension. Cognitive or emotional arousal in the form of worries, intrusive thoughts, or a racing mind are addressed using attention-focusing methods such as imagery training (i.e., focusing on pleasant or neutral mental images) or meditation. Relaxation therapies may be less easily self-implemented than stimulus control or sleep restriction because they require the learning of specific relaxation techniques through appropriate training. Professional guidance or an audiotape is often necessary, particularly in the initial phase of treatment (e.g., the first 3 weeks), to optimize an adequate use of the techniques. Regardless of the training method selected, therapeutic gains usually require at least 2 to 3 weeks of relaxation training.

D. Cognitive Therapy

Poor sleepers tend to entertain faulty beliefs and attitudes about sleep, which feed into the vicious circle of insomnia, emotional distress, and more sleep disturbance. As such, insomnia often becomes a self-fulfilling prophecy. For instance, the belief that 8 hrs of sleep is an absolute necessity, or the perception that one is unable to function after a poor night's sleep is often enough to produce anxiety and exacerbate sleep disturbances. The objective of cognitive therapy is to alter these types of sleep-related cognitions by challenging them and replacing them with more adaptive substitutes. Several clinical procedures, modeled after those used in treating anxiety and depression, can be used for changing patients' misconceptions about sleep. Such techniques include attention shifting, reappraisal, reattribution training, and decatastrophizing. Cognitive therapy is also used to teach patients strategies to cope more adaptively with residual difficulties that recur occasionally even after treatment.

E. Sleep Hygiene

Sleep hygiene education fosters healthy habits through simple recommendations about diet, substance use, exercise, and environmental factors that promote or interfere with sleep. Standard sleep hygiene measures include the following:

- Avoid stimulants several hours before bedtime. Caffeine and nicotine, both central nervous system stimulants, can impede sleep onset and reduce sleep efficiency and quality.
- Do not drink alcohol too close to bedtime. Alcohol consumption prior to bedtime can lead to more fragmented sleep and early morning awakenings.
- Avoid heavy meals too close to bedtime, as they can interfere with sleep. A light snack may be sleep inducing.
- Regular exercise in the late afternoon or early evening can deepen sleep. Conversely, exercising too close to bedtime could have a stimulating effect and delay sleep onset.
- Keep the bedroom environment quiet, dark, and comfortable.

III. TREATMENT FORMATS AND PROCESS

Several formats have been used to implement self-help therapies for insomnia, including printed material (books or pamphlets), audiotapes, and videotapes. Some Internet sites are also under construction, a format that should make treatment more interactive. Most treatments available tend to combine different formats, for example by offering a self-help book in conjunction with an audio- or videotape.

The basic structure of a self-help intervention for insomnia is similar to a therapist-led treatment. The first step is to provide basic information about sleep and insomnia. A brief self-assessment method is introduced to ensure proper diagnosis. The daily use of a sleep diary throughout treatment is an essential feature of any self-help intervention for insomnia. Indications and contraindications of self-help treatment are also underlined. Patients should be informed to seek professional help when they are not sure whether they suffer from insomnia or from another condition (e.g., sleep apnea, depression). Once these preliminary steps have been completed, a conceptual model of insomnia is described, and the rationale behind the treatment is explained. This is particularly important because some treatment procedures, such as sleep restriction or stimulus control for instance, can appear paradoxical to individuals seeking relief for their insomnia, especially when they are sleep deprived. Consequently, it is important to inform the patient that mild sleep deprivation might occur in the initial phases of treatment, and to explain how this procedure will help them if they adhere to the treatment protocol. This understanding may influence the patient's willingness to invest time and efforts in carrying out the therapeutic recommendations.

Although therapist-led treatments often comprise 6 to 10 therapy sessions spread over a period of 10 to 12 weeks, there is no standard time frame when it comes to implementing a self-help treatment. Nonetheless, 4 to 6 weeks of strict adherence to treatment is usually necessary for sleep improvements to become noticeable. As treatment is often multifaceted, it is preferable to introduce each therapeutic component in a sequential fashion. Once basic information about sleep and insomnia and the rationale for treatment has been provided, sleep restriction and stimulus control procedures may be introduced. When these components are well integrated (about the 3rd week), treatment can move on to cognitive restructuring of dysfunctional beliefs and attitudes about sleep. Sleep hygiene education can be incorporated at any point in the treatment. If a relaxation-based component is added to the treatment, it should be introduced early on to allow sufficient time for training.

IV. EMPIRICAL STUDIES: EVIDENCE FOR EFFICACY

The efficacy of psychological treatments (mostly behavioral in nature) for chronic and primary insomnia has been well documented in the last 20 years. Two meta-analyses have shown that psychological treatments are effective in treating sleep-onset insomnia (problems falling asleep) as well as sleep-maintenance insomnia (problems staying asleep). Overall, it is estimated that about 70% to 80% of individuals with insomnia achieve some clinical benefits with behavioral interventions. Typically, treatment is likely to reduce the main target symptoms of sleep-onset latency and wake after sleep onset below or near the 30-min criterion initially used to define insomnia severity. Sleep duration is increased by a modest 30 to 45 min, but patient's satisfaction with sleep quality is significantly enhanced. Moreover, treatment gains are well sustained or even enhanced up to 24 months after completion of treatment.

There have been only five studies conducted on the topic of self-help treatment for insomnia. Table 1 presents a summary of these studies. The first investigation of self-help treatment for insomnia was conducted in 1979. It was designed to compare the efficacy of two self-administered treatment manuals for sleep-onset insomnia with a waiting-list control condition. One manual included relaxation and standard stimulus control instructions, whereas the other involved a different form of relaxation plus a countercontrol procedure in which participants were instructed to stay in bed when unable to sleep. Sleep-onset latency, number of awakenings, and worries about sleep were assessed with sleep diaries completed daily by the participants. Twenty-nine participants aged between 17 and 80 years old were enrolled in the study. The results showed a significant reduction of sleep-onset latency in both treatment conditions, although the standard stimulus control condition was superior (59% versus 32%). Participants receiving the manual with the standard relaxation and stimulus control procedures also reported higher ratings of sleep quality. Greater improvements were observed in younger individuals as compared to the elder participants. The authors suggest that the higher prevalence of medical conditions in the elderly might interfere with sleep and thereby moderate treatment efficacy.

The next study was performed 10 years later by David Morawetz in Australia. Three questions motivated his study: *(a)* Is self-help treatment more effective than no treatment? *(b)* Is self-help treatment as effective as a therapist-led treatment? and *(c)* What factors moderate the treatment response to self-help interventions? One-hundred-and-forty participants aged from 23 to 63 years took part in the study, including 63 who were taking sleep medication. Daily sleep diaries were again used to evaluate the comparative efficacy of three conditions: a self-help treatment, a therapist-led treatment, and a waiting-list control. The treatment material included basic information on sleep physiology and sleep disorders, a description of the standard stimulus control instructions, and relaxation training instructions. Whether they were in the self-administered or in the therapist-led treatment group, participants

TABLE 1
Summary of Empirical Studies on Self-Help Treatment for Insomnia

Authors	*Sample*	*Design*	*Self-help format*	*Treatment content*
Alperson & Biglan (1979)	*N* = 29 17–80 years old	Relaxation + stimulus control Relaxation + counter control Waiting-list	Printed manual	Relaxation + Stimulus control relaxation + in-bed activities
Morawetz (1989)	*N* = 141 23–60 years old	Self-help treatment Therapist-led treatment Waiting-list control	Audiotape/manual	Sleep information + relaxation + stimulus control
Oosterhuis & Klip (1993)	*N* = 325 15–86 years old	Single group, quasi-experimental design	Television and radio segments, booklet and audiotape	Sleep information + relaxation + stimulus control + sleep hygiene
Riedel et al. (1995)	*N* = 100 > 60 years old	Video treatment with or without therapist guidance; good sleepers controls	Videotape/pamphlet	Sleep information + sleep restriction
Mimeault & Morin (1999)	*N* = 54 18–54 years old	Self-help treatment Self-help treatment + phone consultation Waiting-list control	Treatment manual	Stimulus control, sleep restriction, sleep hygiene education, cognitive interventions

received the same therapeutic components. The results showed significant reductions of sleep-onset latency for the two treatment groups, both at posttreatment and at a 3-month follow-up assessment. No significant improvement was observed in the waiting-list condition. The authors noted only limited improvements among participants who received treatment but were concurrently using a sleep medication. These improvements were nonetheless greater for the group receiving therapist-led treatment than for the group receiving the self-administered intervention. These results suggest that self-help treatment is effective but also highlight the importance of therapist assistance in cases where complicating issues, such as medication use, are present.

In 1993, a Dutch public television channel scheduled a series of television and radio programs that were broadcast in the Netherlands to offer educational material about insomnia and its treatment. There were eight television (15 min each) and nine radio segments. In addition, participants received by mail a relaxation tape and a booklet summarizing the critical information covered during the television and radio programs. The written material incorporated basic information about sleep and sleep hygiene education, relaxation training, and stimulus control techniques. Psychologists Aart Oosterhuis and Ed Klip evaluated the impact of this program. Participants were recruited via a survey and completed a daily sleep diary and different sleep and mood questionnaires. This program reached an estimated 23,000 individuals. Of 400 participants who volunteered for the evaluation of this program, a total of 105 returned their assessment material. The results showed a significant decrease in sleep-onset latency and in the number of awakenings as well as a significant increase in total sleep time. In addition, 40% of the participants discontinued their medication during treatment. Although the results must be interpreted carefully because of the absence of control, this type of innovative program has the advantage of reaching a large number of individuals who may suffer from insomnia without ever consulting for it.

In a 1995 study, Brant Riedel, Kenneth Lichstein, and William Dwyer evaluated if therapist guidance, added to a self-help video program, influenced the efficacy of a self-help treatment for insomnia in older adults. Participants kept daily sleep diaries and completed a questionnaire evaluating knowledge about sleep. The video lasted about 15 min and contained information about sleep in the elderly, the benefits of restricting time in bed, and the possible hazards associated with the use of sleep medications. Subjects in the video-only condition and the video-plus-therapist guidance condition viewed the video twice with 2 weeks between viewing sessions. Participants in the therapist-guided condition received two additional group training sessions with a therapist. During these sessions, the therapist emphasized the importance of restricting time in bed. Participants were evaluated before and after each session, and 2 months after the end of the intervention. The results indicate that both self-help interventions were effective to improve several sleep variables, but also that the addition of therapist guidance enhanced treatment outcome.

Véronique Mimeault and Charles Morin conducted the most recent study of self-help treatment in 1999. This investigation examined the efficacy of cognitive-behavioral therapy with and without professional guidance. Fifty-four adults were enrolled in this study after being carefully screened with structured diagnostic interviews. Participants were excluded if there was evidence of another sleep disorder, severe depressive or anxiety symptoms, as well as if they were using an antidepressant medication or if they were concurrently involved in psychotherapy. Participants were randomly assigned to a condition involving a self-help treatment manual only (bibliotherapy), a self-help treatment manual plus weekly telephone consultation (15–20 min), or a waiting-list control group. Treatment outcome was evaluated with daily sleep diaries and different questionnaires. Treatment was implemented over a 6-week period. Participants in both treatment groups were mailed one booklet per week, with each booklet introducing a new treatment component, its rationale, and methods to foster its implementation. Treatment components included basic information about sleep and sleep hygiene, stimulus control, sleep restriction, cognitive therapy, methods for discontinuing sleep medications, and relapse prevention. The results showed that sleep efficiency and total sleep time improved significantly at the end of treatment for both self-help conditions, and that therapeutic gains were well maintained at the 3-month follow-up evaluation. The addition of a weekly telephone consultation enhanced outcome at posttreatment but not at follow-up.

Taken together, the results of these five studies support the efficacy of insomnia treatment implemented in a self-help format. This approach may therefore be considered as a useful and cost-effective alternative to therapist-led treatments. It is important to note, however, that several factors may moderate the efficacy of self-help treatment, including the individuals' age, the use of sleep medications, the presence of medical or psychological factors (e.g., generalized anxiety disorder, depression) and, naturally, the individuals' willingness to comply with behavioral procedures. Older adults are more likely to suffer from sleep disturbances complicated by medical factors and may require a more thorough evaluation before undertaking a self-help treatment for insomnia. Likewise, individuals who are chronic users of hypnotic medications are more likely to present comorbid anxiety or depressive disorders and may require therapist guidance, both for the initial evaluation and for treatment.

V. ADVANTAGES AND LIMITATIONS OF SELF-HELP APPROACHES

The main advantage of a self-help treatment format for insomnia is that it allows for a greater dissemination of treatment knowledge. The best example of this is with the Dutch television program, which was estimated to reach several thousands of individuals, many of which, might never have sought out treatment for their sleep difficulties. In this regard, it is possible that widespread dissemination of self-help interventions can actually prevent the development of more severe and chronic insomnia. Another advantage of self-help approaches is their low cost, rendering treatment more accessible to individuals who may never have consulted a professional for insomnia because of financial limitations.

Self-help interventions also have several drawbacks. First of all, there is always a danger of self-misdiagnosis. Insomnia can be easily confused with other sleep (e.g., apnea, periodic limb movement) or psychological disorders (e.g., generalized anxiety disorder, depression). In the presence of such disorders, insomnia should not be the initial target of treatment. Second, there is also a risk of inappropriate application of treatment techniques, particularly if the rationale is unknown or misunderstood. The third limitation concerns treatment failure, which can occur either because of misdiagnosis or inappropriate technique application, or because the problem is so severe that the individual is unable to sustain treatment long enough to make any improvement. Regardless of the cause of failure, it may lead to a worsening of the problem and may discourage patients to seek help from a health care professional. Another danger of self-help treatment is that there is no provision for monitoring patient's compliance and for ensuring adequate follow-up.

VI. SUMMARY

Insomnia is often undertreated and behavioral interventions remain underutilized, partly because they are more time-consuming and are not always known or accessible. Self-help behavioral therapies are a cost-effective alternative to drug therapy for the management of primary insomnia. This type of intervention offers several advantages such as lower costs and greater availability. Treatment information that can be conveyed in a self-help format includes basic facts about sleep and insomnia, standard stimulus control and sleep restriction instructions, relaxation methods, sleep hygiene education, and cognitive restructuring techniques. It cannot be overemphasized that compliance is a critical element for insomnia treatment to be effective, and this is particularly true for self-help approaches. Although guidance from a therapist is not always essential for a self-help method to be effective in improving sleep, it can be particularly useful to enhance motivation and willingness to adhere to the treatment protocol. Professional guidance is more likely to be needed when there is a complicating medical (e.g., chronic pain) or psychiatric condition (e.g., generalized anxiety disorder, depression) or when an individual is using a medication for sleep, because such factors can influence the course and effectiveness of the treatment. It may also be indicated to consult a professional prior to initiating a self-help treatment for insomnia to ensure a proper evaluation and diagnosis. Additional research is needed to determine what is the most adequate administration format (e.g., printed material, audio- or videotapes, Internet), who are the best candidates for this treatment modality, and what are the predictors of the response to self-help treatment for insomnia. More important, it remains to be evaluated whether widespread dissemination of information about healthy sleep habits (through simple self-help programs) could be useful in preventing the development of severe and persistent insomnia in the general population, thus significantly reducing health care costs.

See Also the Following Articles

Behavioral Treatment of Insomnia ■ Bibliotherapy ■ Relaxation Training ■ Self-Control Therapy ■ Self-Help Groups

Further Reading

Alperson, J., & Biglan, A. (1979). Self-administered treatment of sleep onset insomnia and the importance of age. *Behavior Therapy, 10,* 347–356.

Bootzin, R. R., Epstein, D., & Wood, J. M. (1991). Stimulus control instructions. In P. Hauri (Ed.), *Case studies in insomnia* (pp. 19–28). New York: Plenum.

Clum, G. A., & Gould, R. A. (1993). A meta-analysis of self-help treatment approaches. *Clinical Psychology Review, 13,* 169–186.

Mimeault, V., & Morin, C. M. (1999). Self-help treatment for insomnia: Bibliotherapy with and without professional guidance. *Journal of Consulting and Clinical Psychology, 67,* 511–519.

Morawetz, D. (1989). Behavioral self-help treatment for insomnia: A controlled evaluation. *Behavior Therapy, 20,* 365–379.

Morin, C. M. (1993). *Insomnia: Psychological assessment and management.* New York: Guilford Press.

Morin, C. M. (1996). *Relief from insomnia.* New York: Doubleday.

Oosterhuis, A., & Klip, E. (1993). Behavior therapy without therapists: Treating the complaint of insomnia. *International Journal of Health Sciences, 4,* 27–32.

Riedel, B. W., Lichstein, K. L., & Dwyer, W. O. (1995). Sleep compression and sleep education for older insomniacs: Self-help versus therapist guidance. *Psychology and Aging, 10,* 54–63.

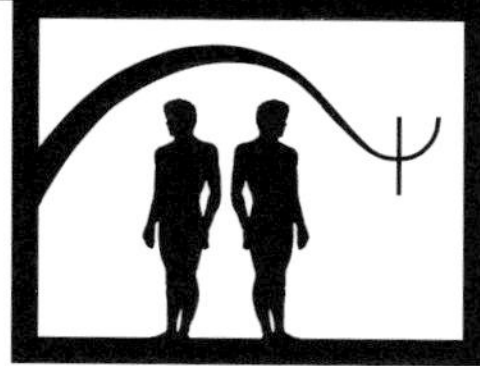

Self Psychology

Arnold Wilson and Nadezhda M.T. Robinson
Columbia University Center for Psychoanalytic Training and Research and St. Mary Hospital

GLOSSARY

empathy A cognitive tool, how a clinician comes to know the internal states of another. Called "vicarious introspection" in the case of the analyst at work, with the aim of understanding another's experience. Kohut describes empathic ambience as the positive attunement of analyst to analysand and empathic failures as the misattunement of analyst to analysand.

introspection A person's ability to use self-reflection to know his or her own internal states, including emotions, thoughts, fantasies, and values.

narcissism Used primarily in two ways—first, a way of conceiving of human development, characterized by the growth and stability of the self independent of its transactions with externally experienced others; second, a line of development (vs. a fixed stage or pathological state) characterized by the strivings to form and maintain a vital self. Kohut distinguished between healthy narcissism, a strong and vital self with ambition and ideals striving toward the realization of individual talents and skills, and pathological narcissism wherein self strivings are unsuccessful in maintaining a cohesive and stable self-representation.

self-object The manner by which another is experienced as if that person were an extension of the self and performs functions necessary for the smooth continuity of the functioning of oneself. A self-object relationship aids the experience of the self as cohesive, harmonious, firm in limits of time and space, connected to the past and present. Self-object relationships according to Kohut support mirroring, idealization, twinship, and alterego functions in the development and maintenance of a cohesive self.

transference When the patient responds to the analyst as if the analyst were some significant figure of the patient's past. Transference provides the self psychologist the means to accurately diagnose the patient's developmental level.

I. SELF PSYCHOLOGY DEFINED

Self psychology refers to the method, observations, and theory that grew from the novel clinical descriptions put forward by a pioneering psychoanalyst from Chicago, Heinz Kohut, primarily in the late 1960s and 1970s. However, the seeds for the development of self psychology were put in place by Kohut in a seminal 1959 paper titled "Introspection, Empathy, and Psychoanalysis." In this early paper, Kohut set the groundwork for what was to come by defining the faculties of introspection and empathy as crucial tools and determinants of the clinician in the analytic encounter. Much as an internist uses a stethoscope, an analyst uses introspection and empathy. Introspection was defined as a person's ability to use self-reflection to know his or her own internal states, including emotions, thoughts, fantasies, and values. By contrast, empathy was defined as "vicarious introspection," by which Kohut meant a person's ability to be cognizant of and accurately apprehend another's mental states, that necessarily involved accessing one's own internal cognitive skills, memories, and emotional states. In defining the arena of psychoanalysis as within the jurisdiction of that which is comprehended by empathy and introspection, Kohut moved psychoanalysis away from a preoccupation with forces, vectors, and structures, and toward subjective states and more explicitly phenomonological processes. It was the "self" rather than a more abstract metapsychological concern that dominated Kohut's thinking, and which was made accessible by introspection and empathy.

How self psychology and classical analysis fit together is a fascinating study of politics in psychoanalysis. In some ways, over the years, self psychology has taken its own path and departed from the mainstream of classical analysis in the United States. However, in other ways, certain key aspects of self psychology have more recently been integrated into the mainstream of classical analysis and has fueled and enriched the entire corpus of contemporary psychoanalytic theory. Thus, although there are many clinicians who think of themselves as "self psychologists," some of the principles of self psychology can now as well be found in the mainstream and are the source of many different and helpful ways of formulating clinical interaction.

II. HEINZ KOHUT

Heinz Kohut was an analyst who emigrated to Chicago from Vienna as a young man. As so many immigrant pioneers in the psychoanalytic movement did, he brought with him the enormous charm and intellectual prowess characteristic of old world scholarship. In a relatively short amount of time, and at a young age, he established himself as one of the leaders of the psychoanalytic world. Trained in analysis at the Chicago Institute, he rapidly rose up in the ranks and was soon to become the leading luminary in the Chicago milieu, the acknowledged leader and pacesetter within that institute. At first a conservative analyst, quite loyal to the tradition of Hartman and ego psychology, he was to break ranks and found the self psychology movement that he came to see was markedly at odds with classical psychoanalysis.

It was largely the description of narcissistic patients that led Kohut to develop his original and, at the time, controversial views. While practicing as a classical analyst, Kohut found that what he called a patients' "self-cohesion" was disrupted when the patient perceived the analyst to have committed an empathic failure. Kohut came to believe that many failures in analysis were not due to a narcissistic patients' predisposing pathology, but rather to the clinicians' failure to tune in to the analysand's underlying states. Believing that many failures in analysis were due to this factor, Kohut sought to expand the range of patients treatable by psychoanalysis. Although always a controversial topic, prior to Kohut many considered the narcissistic patient untreatable for a variety of reasons attributable to the patient, but rarely the clinician. Most telling, however, was the sense that such patients could not be reached by clinical interpretations, because they would contemptuously reject insight while at the same time displaying characteristics of extreme fragility and hypersensitivity. It was Kohut's inspiration to design a treatment that did not emphasize interpretation and insight, and in so doing, soon was to develop a whole new way of looking at people and the treatment situation. In moving away from interpretation as the primary mutative factor in psychoanalysis, Kohut spoke of "transmuting internalization" as a key concept, when the patient is enabled to take in those experiences that are empathically offered, and then convert them into psychic structure, thereby remediating early developmental failures that had been laying dormant for many years. The concept of transmuting internalization explains how patients change through the provision of empathic ministrations rather than through the acquisition of insight and understanding.

In 1968, Kohut published his first views on narcissistic disorders, which was to lead to his eventual postulate that narcissism was a line of development, rather than a stage, type of energy, or a personality disorder. At first, Kohut sought to meld his views with those of mainstream psychoanalysis. However, as his ideas developed, he perceived the need to carve out an independent niche for self psychology, which took the theoretical form of claiming that a self/narcissistic line of development follows an independent course from what he termed the "object-libidinal" line of development more typically described by classical analysis. Still, in 1971, when his first major book was published, titled *The Analysis of the Self*, it was framed in the patois of classical analysis. In this book, Kohut laid out the fundamentals of his views concerning the treatment of narcissistic patients, including transference and countertransference considerations. Most important, the analyst had to maintain an empathic immersion in the psychological field of the patient and tolerate the emptiness of their own emotional reaction to such individuals. What Kohut termed "empathy" was crucial, for departures from such empathic immersion lead to profound disruptions in the patient's personality, what Kohut called "fragmentation" of the self. The self became the focus of the analyst treating the narcissistic patient, which was phenomonologically closer to clinical experience than the reigning tripartite model of the classical analysts. The patient grew in the crucible of the analyst's empathic immersion, rather than through the analytic imparting of insight by way of interpretation. The actual experience of the clinical interaction became more important than the knowledge that could be deduced from the interaction.

The fragmented self was seen to result from early failures in what Kohut termed "self-object experiences," which were seen as failures in caregivers' empathic relationship to their children and which tended to get covered over by what Kohut termed the "compensatory structures" of development, that is, defense-like structures that covered over and protected the individuals' self-esteem from these early deficits. Although covered over by subsequent life span experiences, such early failures lurked in the personality of the child and could only be altered through an isomorphic reevocation of the early self-object experience, which Kohut termed a "self-object transference." In particular, he identified two kinds of self-object transference, an idealizing and a grandiose one. Loosely speaking, the idealizing transference can be equated with paternal object relations and the grandiose transference with maternal object relations. The idealized self-object transference referred to the normative need of a child to see the other in perfectionistic terms. The grandiose self-object transference referred to the normative need of a child to experience themselves as omnipotent as mirrored by a caregiver. Eagle has critically written about a develomental psychology based solely on these two types of reconstructed transferential configurations. Over the years, Kohut's vision of the child embedded in a world of self-objects has held up to research scrutiny far better than his description of these two types of transferences, which were reconstructed from the analytic situation of adults rather than actually observed in the behaviors of children and their caregivers.

Note again the emphasis on the concept of "self" in Kohut's thinking. The self is quite different than the ego of Freud. Kohut thought of the self and defined it as the center of initiative and action. The self develops through experiences of being independent, mirrored properly, and empathically understood until "self-cohesion" has formed. Self-cohesion is the term Kohut chose to describe the self of an emotionally strong, vigorous, expansive, and resilient person. The developing self is understood as potentially traumatized through subtle ways, such as a caregiver's rigidity, lack of empathy, or inability to affectively attune to a growing child. The child is seen as formed into a world of self-objects and is natively happy and prone to fit into such relationship patterns. The mind of the child is more akin to a tabula rosa than that described in classical analysis—children are born good and made bad, rather than inevitably suffering from the frustrations and limitations of intrapsychic conflicts as implied by an epigenetic psychobiological blueprint. This self psychology take on early development is in stark contrast to the classical view of trauma, which is understood more explicitly as an external assault on a psychic apparatus incapable of withstanding overstimulation, understimulation, and affective regulation.

The reception to his 1971 book was mixed. As Kohut inquired deeper and his clinical experience deepened, he felt the need to expand the scope of his investigations. As a consequence, Kohut began to describe what he called "the psychology of the self in the wider sense" that referred to a vision of self psychology as an approach to most patients, not just narcissistic ones (and which he contrasted with the "psychology of the self in the narrow sense"). Encouraged by many of his early followers in Chicago and elsewhere, such as Paul and Anna Ornstein, John Gedo (who was soon to break from this group), Arnold Goldberg, Michael Basch, Marian Tolpin, Joseph Lichtenberg, and Ernest Wolf, self psychology became a movement in its own right. In 1976, Kohut published a book titled *The Restoration of the Self* that became a virtual manifesto of this new movement. No longer seeking a rapprochement with classical analysis, a new vocabulary and new way of looking at virtually all clinical phenomena was born. It was also only a short amount of time before self psychology was to expand far beyond the frontiers of four to five times a week clinical psychoanalysis and become a treatment modality and method of investigation that addressed and incorporated psychotherapy, brief treatments, informed a tremendous amount of research, as well as a remarkable fecundity of applied psychoanalysis (art, history, politics, and literature). Reaching far beyond the borders of Chicago, self psychology became an international movement with chapters worldwide. It also was picked up by many nonmedical practitioners, who sensed a sympathetic and compatible view of people and treatment that they found lacking elsewhere.

As mentioned, in a subtle shift, self psychology overtly became a method of investigation into narcissism as a line of development rather than as a type of personality disorder. The narcissistic line of development was defined as the relationship of the self to the self, and the object-libidinal line as the relationship of the self to the other. Individuals were seen as growing up among and requiring self-object relationships of all sorts. The self was not seen as boundary by the skin. Self-objects were defined as environmental objects that fulfilled functions required by the self, and in fact were experienced as if they were a part of the self. Although outside the self, they were experienced as if they were inside. Thus, soothing and/or self-regulating self-objects were sought if an individual did not have internalized capacity for self-soothing or self-regulating; then, these functions were treated as if they were internal although they belonged to someone external. This framed a kind of attachment to others, and so individuals were seen as embedded in a social and interactive matrix far more than classical analysis had emphasized. The classical emphasis on infantile sexuality and aggression was markedly deemphasized, in favor of self cohesion and empathic immersion. Self-objects were also defined as incorporating not necessarily people but also ideas, ideals, and other factors such as goals and values.

In his 1976 book, Kohut also addressed many aspects of the treatment situation that were the pillars of the classical approach; for example, he reexamined the Oedipus Complex and claimed that its turbulence was a "breakdown product" resulting from developmental failures in empathic self-object relations rather than a universal period of conflict stemming from entry into the world of triadic object relations. In a series of sharp exchanges, Kohut and Otto Kernberg, a New York-based analyst with a more classical persuasion, engaged in a scintillating and intriguing series of exchanges concerning the treatment of patients with severe disturbances, particularly those termed borderline. At the time, it was unfortunate that many clinicians perceived a rubicon of sorts between classical analysis and self psychology and were drawn into taking sides. This probably delayed or prevented an integrative assessment of the significance of self psychology, as many felt they either had to reject or accept it in its entirety.

Kohut, after the 1976 book, was yet to publish a great many influential papers. One such paper that has captured the attention of a great many scholars of psychoanalytic history was titled "The Two Analyses of Mr. Z" which he said was his analysis and reanalysis of a particular patient; the first employing the techniques of classical analysis, and a second employing the techniques of self psychology. Needless to say, he reported that the second analysis was far more helpful and reached areas that the first analysis could not. Kohut reported that it was this analysis that truly opened his eyes to the depths and powers of self psychology. Although this cannot be confirmed, several independent sources hypothesize that Mr. Z. was Kohut himself. The two analyses referred to were actually the two analyses Kohut himself underwent.

III. TRANSFORMATION

Heinz Kohut died in 1981. His last book *How Does Analysis Cure* was published posthumously in 1984. With his death, self psychology underwent a profound transformation, as it became unclear whether it consisted of one theory or many. Clinicians such as Robert Stolorow and colleagues, Arnold Goldberg, Michael Basch, Howard Bacal, and others too numerous to name carried on the tradition. Many went their own way without the unifying force of Kohut's vision. As the group of adherents to self psychology grew, several individuals worked hard to clarify the specific principles of therapy native to self psychology. Although there was disagreement, the unifying thread seems to be that the main goal of treatment is to strengthen the sense of self and to facilitate growth. Treatment works to facilitate the latent potential for self-vitalizing experiences, largely through the positive and affirming experiences that take place in the transaction between the therapist and the patient. It did not necessarily require four or five visits per week nor a couch. As the principles of therapy expanded, so to did the theory of self psychology informing treatment. For example, Stolorow went on to elaborate on a worldview he termed "intersubjective." Goldberg sought something of a rapprochement with classical analysis, emphasizing that interpretation is and always has been the primary instrument of self psychology. Goldberg wrote persuasively of how empathy and introspection alone cannot define the field of psychoanalysis. Basch went on to describe psychoanalysis as "applied developmental psychology" and using a self psychology framework, brought in the method and findings of general psychology (perception, developmental psychology, brain-behavior correlations, etc.) to elaborate upon such issues as empathy, Freud's corpus of writings, and principles of psychotherapy.

Many of these authors took issue to some extent with some of the basic and fundamental tenets of Kohut's work. For example, Stolorow criticized Kohut's model of the bipolar self for having the potential for reification of self-experience, for mechanistic thinking, and for limiting the number of potential self-object transferences that can be found in the clinical situation. Basch also criticized the notion of the bipolar self and replaced it with his own version of a functional self-system, with a brain psychology integrating the affective and cognitive information processing activities governing the individual's adaptation to the environment. Bacal argues that self psychology is in reality an object-relations theory, and that the self-object transference is itself a particular type of object relationship; Kohut was explicit that he was not defining an object-relational psychology, which he pejoratively referred to as a "social psychology" that was outside of the arena of psychoanalysis.

As previously touched on, self psychology was informed by and spawned a significant amount of empirical research, particularly in developmental psychology. In many ways, the pioneering research of Daniel Stern in the early 1980s that pointed toward an interactive baby swept up in developmental currents was closer to Kohut's reconstruction of childhood then the child of classical analysis. Relationships rather than intrapsychic conflicts assumed a research priority. Other developmentalists, such as Louis Sander, Edward Tronick, and Beatrice Beebe, found the inspiration and a model in Kohut's description of childhood that fostered a great deal of creativity in their empirical research. Joseph Lichtenberg, himself not an infant researcher, was particularly active in conceptually seeking to integrate experimental and observational infant research with self psychology. Eventually, he was to go on to describe five motivational systems as the engine of action in self psychology, roughly equated with the drives in classical analysis. In several important publications, he described principles of treatments for the self psychological perspective that utilized his notion of these five motivational systems. Certainly one major advantage of these five motivational systems was their grounding in the developmental literature of the time, which in some people's view provided for a scientific grounding that could not be found in Freud's psychology of personality.

Self psychology was to develop its own diagnostic system (a kind of nomenclature) quite different from any other. A good example is depression. Many self psychologists spoke of "empty depression," a sort of experience of depletion or lack of vitality that characterize a sense of futility in connecting with others. Others were concerned with severely disturbed patients. They addressed how patients can develop the all-important capacity to sustain a stable self-object transference and defined this as the border between narcissistic and borderline states. Each has characteristic treatment implications in the self psychology diagnostic nomenclature. In borderline states, the transference was not stable, and "secondary compensatory structures" interfered too readily, so as to make such an individual not amenable to analysis (although, to be sure, psychotherapy could be embarked on with such individuals). Narcissistic states could thus best be diagnosed from an assessment of the transference, rather than from stable intrapsychic personality factors standing apart from the treatment situation. A very important step became the articulation of translation rules from the diagnostic nomenclature of self psychology to others in the psychodynamic arena thinking and practicing with a different theoretical frame of reference. In many ways, this is a work still in progress.

The study of dreams became a focus of self psychology as it expanded its network of influence. Some self psychologists expanded upon Kohut's notion of a "self-state dream." Whereas classical analysis looked for infantile wish fulfillments lurking within the patient's associations to the manifest content of a dream, self psychology looked for "self-states" in dreams that provided an indication of the patient's sense of connection, mood, and integration. Ernest Wolf, a colleague of Kohut's in Chicago, was one of the first to investigate the self psychology construal of dreams and the departure therein from the prevailing classical analytic theory dating back to Freud's revolutionary portrayal of the role and functions of dreams.

IV. SUMMARY

As is true for many branches of contemporary psychoanalysis, self psychology at present is in a state of flux. In the classical world, it is certainly clear that after an initial period of rejection, many of Kohut's ideas have found their way into the mainstream. For example, Kohut's observations concerning the fragility of the narcissistic person and the need not to interpret transference early on until the patient is able to make constructive use of it now seems to be the dominant view in classical theory. Many classical analysts, such as Evelyn Schwaber, have described how they proceed by always assuming that the patient's perceptions are primary, and that empathically the analyst must always understand the world as seen through the eyes of the patient. Such sensitivity to the subjective states of the patient is an example of the type of technical advancements attributable to Kohut's writings and influence. It is unclear, looking toward the future, whether self psychology will continue as a monolithic tradition, become a loose confederation of post-Kohutian psychologies, or proceed apace toward an integration with the very same points of view it rejected

40 years earlier to make its own way in the evolving psychoanalytic tradition.

See Also the Following Articles

Relational Psychoanalysis ■ Self-Control Desensitization ■ Self-Control Therapy ■ Self-Help Groups ■ Self-Statement Modification

Further Reading

Basch, M. (1977). Developmental psychology and explanatory theory in psychoanalysis. *The Annual of Psychoanalysis, 5,* 229–263.

Basch, M. (1983). Empathic understanding: A review of the concept and some theoretical considerations. *Journal of the American Psychoanalytic Association, 31,* 101–127.

Goldberg, A. (1989). *A fresh look at psychoanalysis: The view from self psychology.* Hillsdale, NJ: The Analytic Press.

Kohut H. (1971). *The analysis of the self.* New York: International Universities Press.

Kohut H. (1977). *The restoration of the self.* New York: International Universities Press.

Kohut H. (1984). *How does analysis cure?* Chicago: University of Chicago Press.

Lichtenberg, J. (1989). *Psychoanalysis and motivation.* Hillsdale, N.J.: The Analytic Press.

Wolf, E. (1989). *Treating the self.* New York: Guilford.

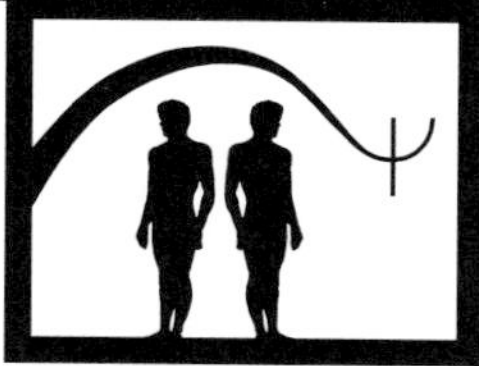

Self-Punishment

Rosiana L. Azman
University of Hawaii, Manoa

GLOSSARY

extinction The weakening of a behavior by withdrawing reinforcement.

learning theory Pertaining to learning through classical conditioning, operant conditioning, or modeling.

reinforcement The presentation of a positive stimulus or the removal of a negative stimulus to increase a desired behavior.

Self-punishment is a behavior in which a person is responsible for removing a positive stimulus or presenting an aversive stimulus to himself to decrease an undesired behavior. This article explains the concept of self-punishment, its behavioral underpinnings, and the limits to its effectiveness.

I. DESCRIPTION

To most people, punishment tends to be equated with a harsh consequence that is expected to teach a lesson, whether it is a part of childrearing, education, or civil law. A child may be grounded for missing curfew, a student kept in for recess because she failed to complete her homework assignment, or a criminal sentenced to jail for committing a felony. This definition, although adequate for everyday usage, is insufficient to describe the psychological connotations.

Behavioral psychologists, and others familiar with learning theory, appreciate punishment to be the presentation of a negative stimulus or the removal of a positive stimulus so that a particular undesired behavior will be decreased. The lay definition may include the aversive situation that comes with either the presentation of a negative stimulus or the removal of a positive one, but it is often irrelevant as to whether or not the behavior being punished will likely be deterred.

For persons to engage in self-punishment means that they are responsible for implementing the appropriate consequences without external support. For example, if a student tends to daydream while studying, a self-punishment tactic she could use to keep herself from going off-task would be to cancel her usual evening phone call with her best friend whenever she catches herself daydreaming (removal of a positive stimulus). The girl's decision not to call her friend must be self-generated for it to be self-punishment. Should her father revoke her phone privileges whenever she daydreams, it would be an external form of punishment. Similarly, every time a man deviates from his diet by eating fast food he could punish himself by having to drink an extra serving of wheat grass juice (presentation of an aversive stimulus) instead of having a fruit smoothie (removal of a positive stimulus). If his wife decides that he cannot eat dessert after dinner, it would be external punishment.

II. THEORETICAL BASIS: A BEHAVIORAL PERSPECTIVE

In behavioral psychology, three possible events other than punishment can follow a behavior: negative reinforcement, positive reinforcement, or extinction. Punishment should not be confused with negative reinforcement, which is the removal of an aversive stimulus to increase a desired behavior. Although homework is not designed to be an aversive stimulus, most students would insist otherwise because they have other tasks on which they would much rather spend their time. Therefore, a teacher could negatively reinforce students to participate in class discussions by canceling the homework assignment whenever the entire class actively participates. Another example of negative reinforcement would be the use of an umbrella during a rainstorm: the action of opening the umbrella removes the negative stimulus of becoming wet. Therefore, this reinforces the use of an umbrella when it rains.

Positive reinforcement also serves to increase a desired behavior, but it is achieved by presenting a positive stimulus after a desired response. The term reward is often equated with a positive reinforcement, although it is important to keep in mind that a reward in lay vernacular does not necessarily imply a positive reinforcement. For example, a person may receive a monetary reward for finding a lost pet. The money is meant as a gesture of gratitude, not as a means to induce a person to continue to find more lost pets. In the true psychological sense of the concept, a child who is rewarded with praise and congratulations from his parents for earning good grades at school is likely to continue to earn good grades so that he may continue to receive the positive parental reinforcement.

Extinction is often confused with punishment because it also involves the removal of a particular stimulus to weaken or decrease a behavior. However, extinction is the decrease of a behavior that had been previously learned. A rat could be trained not to press a lever if he no longer receives food pellets with every depression. The rat must have been originally trained to receive the pellets as positive reinforcers for this action to be interpreted as becoming extinguished. Had the action not been trained, it would more likely be interpreted as punishment when the pellets were not supplied.

Extinction is much more complicated in real-life situations than it is in the laboratory. The withdrawal of reinforcers tends to result in the immediate eruption of the undesired behavior. In addition, even if the original behavior has abated, other unexpected patterns of behavior may surface that prove equally problematic. For example, persons who are attempting to quit smoking may use nicotine gum to decrease the number of cigarettes smoked. Eventually, the use of the nicotine gum must also be eliminated, but it is quite possible that they will have uncontrollable nicotine cravings and smoke cigarettes because they no longer have the consolation of the gum.

Extinction is also difficult to implement in nonlaboratory settings because the stimuli that reinforce the undesired behavior are not always known, nor are they easily controlled. It is common for students to misbehave in class because of peer reaction. If a young boy sneaks a frog into the classroom, supportive students will applaud and others will most likely scream, but both reactions serve to reinforce the student for his deed by bringing attention to him. It would be possible although most likely difficult for a teacher to instruct students not to be supportive of such a disruptive act, but it would be even more difficult to tell others not to be afraid. Unless both forms of reinforcement are removed, the behavior cannot be extinguished.

The main problem with any form of punishment is that it does not teach a desired behavior. By definition, it only decreases an unwanted behavior; it does not increase the behavior that is wanted. If you are trying to teach your child to eat all his vegetables at dinner, scolding him when he hides his brussels sprouts in his napkin will not necessarily make him eat his brussels sprouts on a future occasion. Instead, he will find other means to avoid eating his vegetables. Similarly, punishing yourself whenever you eat junk food will not necessarily cause you to eat more healthily.

Punishment can be quite helpful when you are trying to decrease a particular behavior instantly. If you punish your child immediately after he has run into the street, it is likely that you have deterred that dangerous behavior from occurring again. It does not mean, however, that your child will angelically walk alongside you from that point forward. It simply means he will not run into the street again.

With all forms of reinforcement, and punishment, it is important for the ensuing action to be immediate, strong, and consistent. It is difficult to learn a new behavior or terminate an old behavior if the consequences are not easily discerned. It was quite common several decades ago for fathers to be the disciplinarian of the household. When children misbehaved early in the day, they would often have to wait several hours until their father came home before they were punished for their bad behavior making it difficult for them to associate their punishment with their earlier misbehavior. Instead, they would probably associate their punishment with their father coming home, and learn to fear the return of their father, instead of learning not to misbehave.

Delayed or inconsistent self-punishment would yield similar results. Suppose you are trying to teach yourself not to skip classes. You could tell yourself that every time you fail to attend a class, you would punish yourself by having to spend an extra hour in the library studying. This form of punishment is not likely to be successful because the punishment would not be immediate. For example, because it is such a beautiful day you decide to go to the beach instead of attending class. As you reach that decision, you tell yourself that you will go to the library that night for 3 hrs instead of two because of your truancy. Not only would your punishment be far removed from the misbehavior, but you have also unintentionally positively self-reinforced yourself for missing class by enjoying yourself at the beach. The positive stimulus immediately followed the decision to be truant; therefore, you are more likely to have trained yourself to skip class more often, the exact opposite of your original intentions.

III. EMPIRICAL STUDIES

There is limited evidence that self-punishment, used alone, is an effective method to change one's behavior. In fact, some research even suggests that more harm than good tends to come from self-punishment. In her doctoral dissertation, Sister Mary of St. Victoria Andreoli, R.G.S. found a strong positive correlation between self-punishment and later propensities to be aggressive toward others.

Many therapists have tried to use self-punishment to stop clients from smoking or from overeating. Clients are often instructed to pay a fine (removal of positive stimulus) whenever they engage in the unwanted behavior. Although this form of self-punishment avoids the ethical concerns associated with the presentation of a negative stimulus, M. J. Mahoney, N.G.M. Moura, and T. C. Wade found in 1973 that forcing someone to give up something of value was not an entirely effective means to deter a behavior.

In a study by M. J. Mahoney in 1971, a client was instructed to snap a large rubber band that was worn around his wrist to decrease the target behavior. This form of self-punishment did prove effective but not because of the presentation of mild pain (aversive stimulus). The punishment interrupted the misbehavior, which then alerted the client to regulate his actions.

W. H. Morse and R. T. Kelleher found that punishment should supplement programs that utilize reinforcement. The punishment can decrease the acute problematic behavior while the reinforcement supports the desired behavior. For example, if parents are trying to convince their teenage son to wear his seatbelt when he drives his car, they should revoke his driving privileges (removal of positive stimulus) whenever he is caught without his seatbelt. They should also extend his curfew (positive reinforcement) whenever he does remember to buckle up without inducement. This theory can be extended to apply to self-punishment. Using self-reinforcement in lieu of or in conjunction with self-punishment punishment would prove more effective. In his study, "Coping with temptations to smoke," Saul Shiffman found that people who used strategies other than self-punishing thoughts resisted the urge to smoke more than their self-punishing counterparts.

IV. SUMMARY

Punishment in any form is not a completely ineffective method to change one's behavior. However, given that it can only decrease a particular action, also engaging in a form of reinforcement would prove more logical and efficient. Although not many studies have been done directly on the concept of self-punishment, it is not unreasonable to extend findings from studies on punishment and apply them to self-punishment. People interested in self-modification will have better results using forms of self-reinforcement than they would if they engage solely in self-punishment.

See Also the Following Articles

Aversion Relief ■ Conditioned Reinforcement ■ Extinction ■ Negative Punishment ■ Negative Reinforcement ■ Positive Punishment ■ Positive Reinforcement ■ Self Control Therapy ■ Self Psychology

Further Reading

Bufford, R. K. (1981). *The human reflex: Behavioral psychology in biblical perspective*. San Francisco: Harper and Row.

Seligman, M. E. P. (1994). *What you can change and what you can't: The complete guide to self-improvement.* New York: Knopf.

Shapiro, E. S., & Cole, C. L. (1994). *Behavior change in the classroom: Self-management interventions.* New York: Guilford Press.

Shumaker, S. A., Schron, E. B., & Ockene, J. K. (Eds.). (1998). *The handbook of health behavior change.* New York: Springer.

Watson, D. L., & Tharp, R. G. (2001). *Self-directed behavior: Self-modification for personal adjustment* (8th ed.). Belmont, CA: Wadsworth.

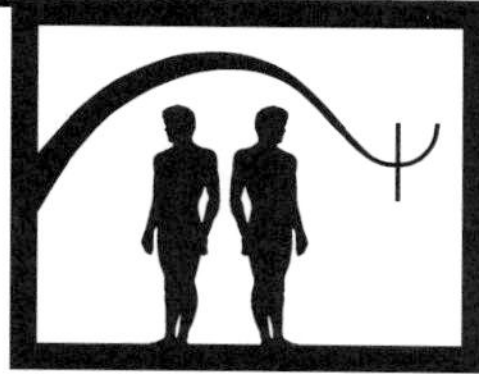

Self-Statement Modification

E. Thomas Dowd
Kent State University

GLOSSARY

cognitive contents The content of people's self-talk; what they think and the sentences they use. They are close to or just below the level of conscious awareness.

cognitive processes The cognitive distortions people use in interpreting sensory data, for example, overgeneralizing, personalization, and dichotomous thinking.

cognitive structures The network of tacit rules and assumptions people use in interpreting the world that are laid down at an early age. They consist of tacit cognitive contents organized around a theme. They are also called core cognitive schemas and consist of unrecognized assumptions about the self and the world, for example, "I'm unlovable."

covert behaviors (or coverants) Behavior (such as internal verbalization) that is observable only to the behaving and observing individual.

internal dialogue A series of automatic self-statements about a situation or behavior.

operant conditioning Consequential learning based on reinforecement, which increases subsequent behavior, or punishment, which decreases it.

self-instructional training (SIT) A training package that trains people how to assess what they are saying to themselves and then to modify what they say to themselves to overcome behavioral difficulties.

self-statement The self-verbalizations or self-talk in which people engage, either overtly (aloud) or silently (covertly).

I. DESCRIPTION OF TREATMENT

Self-statement modification is rarely attempted alone; rather it is generally presented as one component of a treatment package that includes other therapeutic ingredients such as modeling, role-playing, behavioral rehearsal, verbal reinforcement, problem-solving, or social skills training. There are two parts of self-statement modification, the assessment of maladaptive self-statements and the learning and production of new, more adaptive self-statements.

There are several methods for assessing self-statements, which were described (in another context) by Dowd in 1995. Interview-based methods include "think-aloud methods" (in which clients are instructed for a period of time to verbalize whatever comes to mind), "thought-listing" (in which clients list for a period of time whatever thoughts they might have had about a specific situation), "prompted recall" (in which clients view a video or audiotape of them in a problematic situation and indicate what their thoughts were at certain times), and "imagery assessment" (in which clients are asked about images they had during problematic situations). Questionnaire methods include such instruments as the Assertive Self-Statement Test (ASST), the Social Interaction Self-Statement Test (SISST), the Automatic Thoughts

Questionnaire (ATQ), the Dysfunctional Styles Questionnaire (ASQ), and the Irrational Beliefs Test (IBT). Some of these assess attitudes at least as much as self-statements but there is no clear demarcation between the two.

Once the maladaptive self-statements have been identified, clients are then taught to emit adaptive or coping self-statements in place of the maladaptive ones. Following the developmental theory of Luria and Vygotsky, Meichenbaum and Goodman in 1971 developed the prototype of the modification of self-statements:

> First, E *(experimenter, therapist)* performed a task talking aloud while S *(subject, client)* observed (E acted as a model); then S performed the same task while E instructed S aloud; then S was asked to perform the task again while instructing himself aloud; then S performed the task while whispering to himself (lip movements); and finally S performed the task covertly (without lip movements). (p. 117, italics added)

Thus, the therapist gradually takes clients from overt verbalization of the new self-statements to covert verbalization, recapitulating the development of private speech or self-statements in children.

Examples of maladaptive self-statements might be, "I'll never be able to do this task!", "I just don't have what it takes!", "I'm not as smart as other people." Examples of coping or adaptive self-statements might be, "I can develop a plan to handle this," "I can do it if I slow down and take it one step at a time," "Just relax and let the fear subside," or "It worked! I did it — not perfectly but pretty good!"

As with other therapeutic procedures, repetition is very important in self-statement modification. People do not easily or quickly change long-entrenched and automatic ways of responding, including self-statements. Often they are not even aware of their self-talk until after it has occurred and sometimes not even then, even with therapist prompting. Practice outside of therapy as well as during the sessions is important for sustained progress.

II. THEORETICAL BASES

Self-statements are a universal aspect of human cognitive function and their modification is an important part of cognitive behavior therapy procedures. Indeed they are found in all of the important Cognitive-behavior therapy (CBT) interventions, although often by different names. Self-statements are the statements that people say to themselves in a variety of situations and they can be either positive or negative. Sometimes they are within the area of conscious recollection although often they are not; that is, we sometimes recognize that we are making these statements while much of the time we do not.

Self-statements are similar in many ways to the automatic thoughts of Aaron T. Beck's cognitive therapy, to the irrational thoughts of Albert Ellis's rational-emotive-behavior therapy, to Marvin Goldfried's cognitive (or rational) restructuring, and to Daniel Araoz's negative self-hypnosis. What they all have in common is an assessment and modification of the covert self-talk that lies at and just below the level of conscious awareness. They are what Meichenbaum and Gilmore refer to as "cognitive contents," or the actual content of our cognitive processes. Perhaps because self-statement modification is functionally similar to or part of other CBT procedures, some writers have not clearly distinguished it from other CBT procedures, such as self-instructional training, cognitive restructuring, rational disputing, and imagery work. It has therefore appeared on occasion that the differences among them are insignificant. Nevertheless, there are distinctions. The automatic thoughts in Beck's cognitive therapy are more idiosyncratic in nature than the more standard irrational thoughts of Ellis. Cognitive restructuring is a more generic term for a set of techniques. Hypnosis and imagery work represent a class of more nonverbal techniques.

Perhaps the best theoretical development of self-statement modification can be found in the self-instructional training (SIT) of Donald Meichenbaum. Meichenbaum based his work on both behavioral and developmental theories, out of which he derived his own cognitive theory of change. His early work in cognitive behavior modification was based primarily on self-statement modification with impulsive children in order to reduce their level of impulsivity. Behaviorally, he considered self-statements to be examples of covert behaviors, subject to the same laws of learning and modification as other behaviors. Generally, the theoretical basis for these laws was operant conditioning. In this, he followed Lloyd Homme's notion of coverants (or covert operants/behaviors) as obeying the same laws as overt behaviors. Covert behavior was reinforced or punished according to the same principles as overt behavior. Developmentally, he referred to the work of the Soviet psychologists Alexander Luria and Lev Vygotsky, who viewed the internalization of self-statements as fundamental to the human development of self-control and regulation of behavior. Luria and Vygotsky argued that self-statements in young children are first overt in nature and mimic the overt talk of significant adults. Later, the child's self-statements become covertly subvocalized and then entirely automatic and nonconscious in nature. It is these automatic thoughts or self-statements that result in adult behavioral regulation. Children who do not internalize these self-statements have difficulty with self-regulation (most obviously in impulsivity) but internalization of maladaptive self-statements can result in later psychological problems.

Meichenbaum's cognitive theory of change has three phases. The first phase is self-observation, in which clients first become aware of their own behavior. They begin to monitor, with increasing accuracy, their own thoughts, feelings, physiological reactions, and interpersonal behavior. They gradually become aware that their self-statements (internal dialogue) are negative, repetitive, and unproductive and come to reconceptualize or redefine their problems, in part according to the theoretical orientation of the therapist. Thus, the client of a psychoanalyst may come to see his problems as stemming from his early relations with his father while the client of a behavior therapist may come to see her problems as arising from inadequate reinforcement for exploratory behavior as a child. In the process, both gain understanding (and therefore control and hope) of their feelings, behaviors, and thoughts. They begin the process of thinking differently about their problems.

The second phase is incompatible thoughts and observations. Here, as a result of the observations in Phase One, clients begin a translation process from the maladaptive internal dialogue to a more adaptive internal dialogue. They begin to reconceptualize their problems differently. The new internal dialogue affects their attention, their appraisals, their physiological responses, and even instigates new behavior. The increased attention in Phase One helps change the internal dialogue in Phase Two, which in turn guides new behavior.

The third phase is the development of new cognitions about change. In this phase, clients begin a new internal dialogue about the changes they have been undergoing and the new behaviors they have been producing. These changes provide evidence for a change in self-statements that make up the internal dialogue. If their interactions with other people change, they will then reflect on this in their changed internal dialogue. The modified internal dialogue is similar to what in other systems might be referred to as "insight." In other words, behavior change precedes insight, rather than following it, a point made in 1962 by Nicholas Hobbs.

The implication of this theory of change is that therapeutic interventions might profitably focus first on instigating behavior change and then fostering cognitive change as clients reflect on their behavioral change and its implications. But cognitive therapists in general have often focused first on changing cognitive contents (self-statements) or cognitive processes (cognitive distortions). Indeed, Jeffery Young, in his schema-focused therapy, focuses on cognitive structures, or the network of rules and assumptions that determine how we interpret the world.

III. EMPIRICAL STUDIES

There has been considerable research conducted on self-statement modification, even within relatively recent years. Two meta-analyses of the effects of self-statement modification were published by Dush, Hirt, and Schroeder, in 1983 and 1989, one on adults and the other on children. In the adult meta-analysis, the results for self-statement modification were impressive. Self-statement modification produced a greater effect size than alternative therapies when compared both to no-treatment controls and to placebo controls. However, the effect sizes were smaller when compared to placebo controls than to no-treatment controls. The efficacy of self-statement modification was found to be greater when combined with other cognitive-behavioral procedures. Similar results were obtained in the children's meta-analysis. Self-statement modification produced greater effect sizes than either no-treatment controls or placebo controls, although there was no significant difference between the two types of comparisons, indicating that placebo treatment with children may not be more effective than no treatment. Comparing the two meta-analyses, the effect of self-statement modification appeared to be less for children than for adults, especially when compared to no treatment.

A related meta-analysis examining the treatment of impulsivity in children by Baer and Nietzel found comparable results. The interventions were associated with improvements ranging from one-third to three-fourths of a standard deviation when compared to untreated controls. Self-statement modification in these studies was combined with other cognitive-behavioral interventions.

Other studies have found self-statement modification to be effective in preparing patients for various stressful medical procedures such as coping with office routines and illness management, particularly for children. It has also been found to be effective as part of a treatment program for anger management and in treating such problems as heterosexual effectiveness, assertive training, and dating-skills training. Because it has sometimes been evaluated in combination with other CBT techniques, it is not always clear what unique contribution it makes. However, it has been shown to be at least as, if not more, efficacious than alternative treatments.

IV. SUMMARY

Self-statements, positive and negative, appear to be a ubiquitous aspect of human cognitive and developmental functioning and are heavily implicated in self control. Self-statement modification is found in many of the cognitive-behavioral theories, including those of Aaron Beck, Albert Ellis, Marvin Goldfried, and Donald Meichenbaum, and is designed to replace negative self-statements with positive ones. However, it often goes by different names in different theories. Perhaps the fullest and most complete expression of the technique is found in Meichenbaum's self-instructional training. Self-statement modification consists of assessing the self-talk that clients use about a problematic situation and then training them to emit different, more adaptive, self-statements instead. Research has shown that it is a very effective and versatile technique, although it is often used in combination with other techniques.

See Also the Following Articles

Behavior Rehearsal ■ Coverant Control ■ Modeling ■ Objective Assessment ■ Role-Playing ■ Self-Control Desensitization ■ Self Psychology ■ Vicarious Extinction

Further Reading

Baer, R. A., & Nietzel, M. T. (1991). Cognitive and behavioral treatment of impulsivity in children: A meta-analytic review of the outcome literature. *Journal of Child Clinical Psychology, 20,* 400–412.

Dowd, E. T. (1995). Cognitive career assessment: Concepts and applications. *Journal of Career Assessment, 3,* 1–20.

Dush, D. M., Hirt, M. L., & Schroeder, H. (1983). Self-statement modification with adults: A meta-analysis. *Psychological Bulletin, 94,* 408–422.

Dush, D. M., Hirt, M. L., & Schroeder, H. E. (1989). Self-statement modification in the treatment of child behavior disorders: A meta-analysis. *Psychological Bulletin, 106,* 97–106.

Goldfried, M. R., & Davison, G. C. (1994). *Clinical behavior therapy* (2nd ed.). New York: Holt, Rinehart & Winston.

Kendall, P. C., & Hollon, S. D. (1979). *Cognitive-behavioral interventions: Theory, research, and procedures.* New York: Academic Press.

Kendall, P. C. & Hollon, S. D. (Eds.). (1981). *Assessment strategies for cognitive-behavioral interventions.* New York: Academic Press.

Meichenbaum, D. (1977). *Cognitive behavior modification.* New York: Plenum.

Meichenbaum, D., & Goodman, J. (1971). Training impulsive children to talk to themselves: A means of developing self-control. *Journal of Abnormal Psychology, 77,* 115–126.

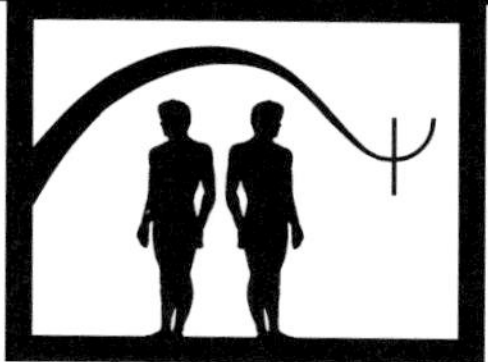

Setting Events

Mark R. Dixon
Southern Illinois University

GLOSSARY

consequence Any object or event that immediately follows the emission of a response.

discriminative stimulus A stimulus in the presence of which a response is reliably reinforced.

establishing operation A current environmental event, operation, or condition of the organism that alters the relative strength of the discriminative stimulus to control responding.

functional analysis An assessment technique whereby the experimenter directly manipulates potential controlling variables to directly assess their effects on the targeted behavior of interest.

punishment A contingent relationship between a behavior and a behavioral consequence, in which that consequence causes the behavior to decrease in frequency.

reinforcement A contingent relationship between a behavior and a behavioral consequence, in which that consequence causes the behavior to increase in frequency.

I. DESCRIPTION OF TREATMENT

A setting event is a distinct stimulus event or a specific level of a dynamic state of an organism that precedes and interacts with a particular stimulus and response function. Setting events may momentarily alter the relative control of a discriminative stimulus, resulting in a potentially different response than usually occasioned by that same discriminative stimulus. If a treatment was designed whereby a participant has been trained to emit a vocal response in the presence of a teacher's vocal prompt and subsequently reinforced with praise, the setting event of another person, say the participant's friend, may result in an altered probability of that same vocal response being emitted. In this case the setting event of the friend may result in a higher or lower probability of response emission by the participant. The relative change in response probability is a function of the participant's past history of reinforcement or punishment for similar responses in the context of that setting event. Assuming that the participant has been reliably reinforced for emitting a vocal response following a vocal prompt of the teacher, if now exposed to a similar situation where the friend is present he fails to emit the correct response. The occasioning ability of the teacher's prompt and the reinforcing function of the teacher's praise has been momentarily weakened in the presence of the participant's friend. Figure 1 provides a visual illustration of this example.

In order to establish new behaviors most effectively, one should be aware of the potential influence of setting events on a given treatment approach. Several variables will enhance the likelihood that the resulting treatment will be successful. First, attempts should be made to incorporate into treatment those setting

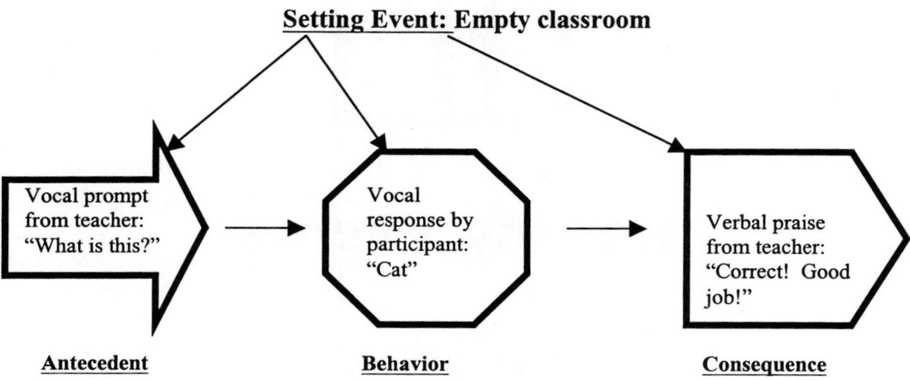

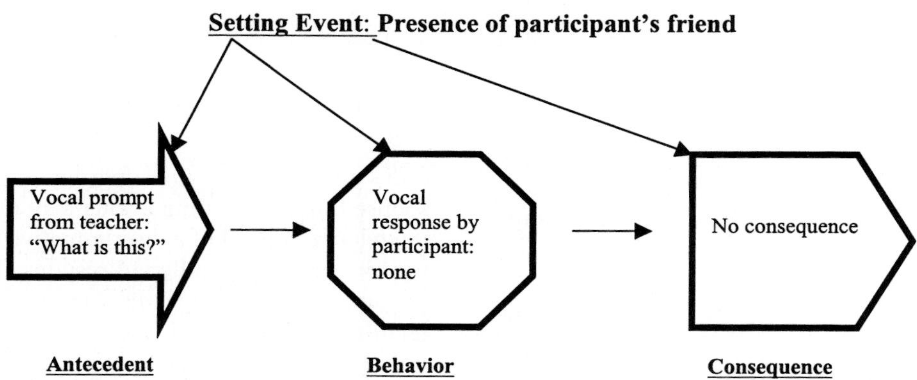

FIGURE 1 Conceptual illustration of the potential influence of a given setting event.

events that have been associated with increased emission of the desired response and eliminate those setting events that have been associated with decreased response emission. Proper identification of the relevant characteristics of the participant's environment that may be functioning as such setting events might be accomplished via an interview with relevant persons, direct observation, or a functional analysis. Second, it should not be assumed that a particular setting event will be directly observable or in temporal proximity to the stimulus–response function question. Setting events such as food deprivation, a fight with a spouse, and stomach pains may either be unobservable or currently absent from the immediate setting. In such cases, proper identification is still possible, yet may require additional exploration. Third, when the elimination of setting events that reduce the probability of treatment success are not possible, one should attempt to minimize their effect. This might be done by withholding the discriminative stimulus, which will now not occasion the appropriate response, providing additional discriminative stimuli for the appropriate response, or altering the magnitude, density, or salience of the reinforcement to be delivered contingent for the appropriate response. In the earlier example this might consist of the teacher not prompting the participant for a vocal response until his friend leaves the training environment, the teacher providing additional prompts such as "Show your friend how much you know" before presenting the original discriminative stimulus prompt, or the teacher providing a piece of candy coupled with praise as the consequence for a correct vocal response.

II. THEORETICAL BASIS

The concept of setting event was theoretically discussed as early as 1959 by J. R. Kantor, under the name "setting factors." He conceptualized the setting factor as a general circumstance surrounding the interaction between the stimulus and the response. According to Kantor, the setting may have an effect on the stimulus object, the reacting individual, or the interaction between the two. The role of the setting factor was to facilitate or hinder the occurrence of the particular stimulus–response function. Although the original name has changed in contemporary discourse from "factors" to "event," the theoretical role it plays on subsequent behavior has not.

The notion of setting event is often added to theoretical conceptualizations of the traditional three-term contingency of (1) discriminative stimulus, (2) response, and (3) consequence, to aid in accounting for the periodic variability in otherwise assumed predictable responding. Setting events differ from other conceptualizations of an additional influence on the three-term contingency in terms of their scope. Setting events can be present in the current environmental context such as the case with food deprivation prior to meal time, yet they can also be somewhat removed in time such as the case with engagement in strenuous exercise the day before coming to therapy, or getting a traffic ticket on the way to work. The former example of food deprivation might be theoretically equivalent to the notion of an establishing operation, although the latter examples would not. Yet all three might exert some change in control over responding. In general the conceptualization of a setting event is broad and not limited by space–time proximity to a current emission of a participant's behavior.

Additionally setting events may take the form of complete stimulus–response interactions that also affect other stimulus–response interactions that follow it. In other words, the setting event may be both an environmental event and the participant's response to that event. For example, assume a college student whose studying behavior in her room is typically followed the next day by exceptional test performance, is now interrupted from studying in her room throughout the night by her brother's playing of the drums downstairs. The no studying–being in her room interaction serves as a setting event for bad test performance the next day. Here it is the case that the previous night's stimulus–response interaction has a latter effect on observed behavior the next day.

Setting events influencing control over behavior can be identified in ways theoretically similar to those of discriminative stimuli and/or reinforcing consequences. One form of potential identification is through an interview or a rating scale. Caregivers or those known to the participant might be surveyed for potential awareness of the presence of a given setting event. These might include questions regarding the participant's daily sleep or eating patterns, medication changes, experience of recent traumatic life events, and the presence or absence of particular persons in a given setting. The interview or rating scale is a cost- and time-effective method for potential setting event identification. This method is also prone to potential problems. First, the skill of the interviewer must be such that appropriate questions are answered. Second, accuracy of responses is subject to the interviewee's ability to remember specific events. Third, the responses will provide correlated and anecdotal information at best. Current control by a specific setting event may or may not be identical to what has been post hoc reported.

Another form of identification is through observation. The clinician or the participant directly observes the behavior of interest and records current features of the present context that may be in part functioning as a setting event. In the case of the clinician, he or she might have a checklist or scorecard whereby a checkmark or tally is made when the observed behavior is emitted (or not emitted) by the participant in the presence of certain conditions. Self-monitoring might also be conducted whereby the participant attempts to observe and record data on their own behavior and its relation to potential setting events. Self-monitoring is useful when direct observation by another party is limited or not possible. One should keep in mind that accuracy is questionable with self-monitoring Without contingencies in place to ensure reliability of data collection, there may be incentives for the participant to inaccurately report the presence of a specific setting event. An example here might be a participant who just experienced a toileting accident and fails to record it on her daily tracking sheet of self-initiated activities outside of the house because she is embarrassed.

Like interviews and rating scales, the direct observation of setting events has potential problems. First, observers might not properly identify all relevant setting events. This is especially true when setting events are not in close temporal or spatial proximity to the behavior of interest or when they are covert events such as headaches, feelings of depression, or food deprivation. Second, direct observation is very time consuming to effectively train observers. Third, direct observation will only provide correlational data on the potential effects of a particular setting event. Causal inferences are not possible.

A last form of identification is through experimental manipulation. This technique is often termed functional analysis. A functional analysis assessment would require the clinician manipulate directly the presence or absence of a particular setting event and then assess subsequent performance. From experimental manipulation, causal inferences can be made about the relative contribution of an assumed setting event on a targeted behavior. For example, if it is assumed that the administration of a given drug to a participant is responsible for that participant's aggressive behavior at the workplace when prompted to complete tasks, the clinician might withhold drug administration on certain days to determine if drug-free days differ from drug-induced days' levels of aggressive behavior.

As with the previously mentioned methods, there also are potential problems in the functional assessment strategy for identification of setting events. Problems include the extensive time and cost for training of clinicians to identify and subsequently manipulate variables, as well as the increased ethical concerns regarding intensifying or postponing treatment for a problematic behavior. In summary, the clinician should use the assessment method for identifying potential setting events that is best suited for the individual circumstances, and be aware of and attempt to control for potential problems with its implementation.

Through the adoption of a theoretical perspective whereby setting events might influence stimulus–response relationships, and upon the utilization of appropriate identification techniques for such setting events, clinicians might eventually accomplish more effective treatments for the participants they serve.

III. EMPIRICAL STUDIES

The following empirical studies demonstrate that through proper identification and manipulation of a particular setting event(s), one can alter the strength of a stimulus–response relationship. Proper techniques should enhance treatment success.

For example, in 1993 Craig Kennedy and Tina Itkonen examined the effects of setting events on the problem behavior of students with severe disabilities. In a series of two studies they examined the relative frequency of problematic behavior occurrences in the presence and in the absence of hypothesized setting events. One of their studies involved a girl who exhibited both aggressive acts during daily transitions and frequent running away or inappropriate grabbing of objects in the presence of dogs, jewelry, or men. The authors assessed possible setting events for these classes of behaviors via a review of the girl's records, a structured interview, and direct observation of her behavior. Once it was deduced that the potential setting event influencing the occurrence of her inappropriate behaviors was "awakening late in the morning," a reversal design coupled with a setting event elimination strategy was introduced. The setting event intervention consisted of providing additional incentives for the girl to awake within a set period of time, along with requiring her to shut off her own alarm clock. Resulting frequencies of her problem behavior reduced dramatically upon the removal of the setting event. Similar results were obtained in the authors' second study that involved a girl whose problem behaviors were eliminated upon the removal of the setting event of being transported to school via the city streets. Here the intervention was simply to transport the girl to school via the highway.

A study conducted in 1997 by Mark O'Reilly demonstrated the correlation between the setting event of otitis media (a recurrent or persistent inflammation or infection of the middle ear) and episodic self-injury in a 26-month-old girl with developmental disabilities. In this study, the participant frequently engaged in back banging and ear poking. Upon completion of assessment interviews with the mother and doctor, it was deduced that her problem behavior occurred around 3 to 10 days a month and was thought to correlate with the presence of ear infections. To further investigate these correlations, a comparison across the naturally occurring conditions of ear infected and ear uninfected was conducted. This comparison yielded high rates of problem behavior during most conditions when the girl had an ear infection, and no rates of the problem behavior when her ears were infection-free. These results led the author to further explore the possibility that the setting event of otitis media might have been enhancing the sensory escape function from noise of the self-abusive behavior. Further functional assessment conditions showed this to be the case.

It is often the case that one particular setting event alters the probability of a given response, as in the above studies. Yet, it may also be possible that a combination of two or more setting events will have a collective effect on behavior. For example, in 1992, Lynette Chandler, Susan Fowler, and Roger Lubeck examined the effects of multiple setting events on the social behavior of preschool children with special needs. In their two studies, they attempted to identify the most optimal combination of setting events to produce the greatest number of social interactions of seven preschoolers. After implementing a series of systematic combinations, they concluded that the ideal combination of setting events to facilitate peer interactions was (1) the removal of the teacher from the activity location, (2) the inclusion of only a limited number of play materials, and (3) a pairing of the child with a socially skilled playmate.

IV. SUMMARY

Setting events are contextual stimuli that momentarily alter the strength of the relationship between a stimulus and a response. Appropriate identification of setting events can assist the clinician in explanation of potential variability in responding. They can also be useful for the development of more appropriate and effective training opportunities. Reinforcement is not a static process uninfluenced by anything other than a simple discriminative stimulus. Rather, the strength of the discriminative stimulus – response – reinforcement relationship is dynamic. That dynamic relationship is often a direct result of the impact of a given setting event on the current context.

See Also the Following Articles

Forward Chaining ■ Habit Reversal ■ Negative Reinforcement ■ Positive Reinforcement ■ Response Cost

Further Reading

Kantor, J. R., & Smith, N. (1975). *The science of psychology: An interbehavioral survey.* Chicago, IL: Principia Press.

Koegel, L. K., & Koegel, R. L. (Ed.). (1996). *Positive behavioral support: Including people with difficult behavior in the community.* Baltimore, MD: Paul H. Brookes.

O'Donohue, W., & Kichener, E. (Eds.). *Handbook of behaviorism.* New York: Academic Press.

Sulzer-Azaroff, B., & Mayer, G. R. (Eds.). (1991). *Behavior analysis for lasting change.* Orlando, FL: Holt, Rinehart, & Winston.

Wahler, R. G., & Fox, J. J. (1981). Setting events in applied behavior analysis: Toward a conceptual and methodological expansion. *Journal of Applied Behavior Analysis, 14,* 327–338.

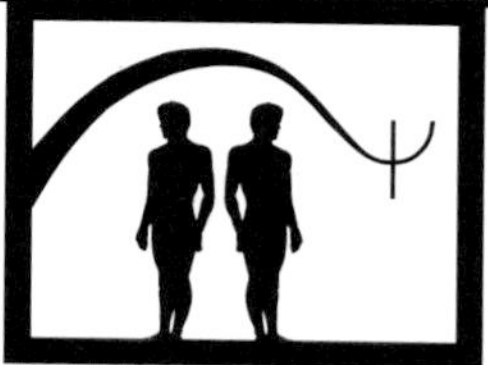

Sex Therapy

Heather J. Meggers and Joseph LoPiccolo
University of Missouri, Columbia

GLOSSARY

etiology All of the causes of a disease or abnormal condition.
organic Of, relating to, or arising in a bodily organ; affecting the structure of the organism.
psychogenic Originating in the mind or in mental or emotional conflict.

I. THE EVOLUTION OF SEX THERAPY: THEORETICAL UNDERPINNINGS

A. Early Views of Sexual Dysfunction

Although difficulties with sexual functioning have undoubtedly existed throughout time, early theories of the development and treatment of sexual dysfunctions first began to appear in the late 19th and early 20th centuries. In 1902, Richard von Krafft-Ebing published *Psychopathia Sexualis,* a book that addressed the existence of dysfunctions and deviations alike. Krafft-Ebing theorized that many sexual disorders resulted from the improper use of sexual energy, creating a state of moral degeneracy. For men, this loss was conceptualized as a waste of semen on nonreproductive activities such as childhood masturbation and excessively frequent sexual activity in adulthood. Mental health professionals at that time advocated preventive treatment through the use of restraining devices that inhibited children's masturbation, such as metal mittens, and through the maintenance of a bland diet in adulthood to avoid overstimulation of the senses.

Sigmund Freud presented a different view of sexual dysfunction in 1905 with the introduction of the Oedipal and Electra complexes. Sexual disorders were thought to be the result of failing to resolve these complexes and becoming fixated at an immature stage of psychosexual development. Treatment did not involve direct attention to sexual functioning, but instead revolved around indirect psychoanalytic approaches, such as insight attainment and transference techniques.

B. Behavioral Sex Therapy

Despite the failure of Freudian therapy in the successful treatment of sexual dysfunction, it was nearly 50 years before Freud's views were challenged by early behaviorists. These early behavioral psychologists posited that anxiety functioned to inhibit normal sexual arousal, resulting in dysfunction. Treatment consisted of techniques to reduce anxiety such as progressive relaxation and systematic desensitization.

In 1966 and 1970, William Masters and Virginia Johnson published their monumental works on the etiology and treatment of sexual dysfunctions. Masters and Johnson expanded on the theories of early behaviorists by stressing an informal social learning theory approach that emphasized the roles that negative messages about sexuality, lack of knowledge about sexuality, and traumatic first sexual experiences play in sexual functioning. In addition, they introduced the concept of sexual problems as self-maintaining cycles of dysfunctional sexual behaviors mediated by anxiety. They theorized that following a negative sexual experience, an individual might develop an anxious, self-evaluative spectator role that interferes with the normal sexual response cycle and results in the maintenance of sexual dysfunction. In addition to the anxiety reduction techniques utilized by early behaviorists, Masters and Johnson included the instruction of specific sexual stimulation techniques in their treatment protocol.

Later additions to the Masters and Johnson model for sex therapy have included elements of both cognitive and systemic theory. An emphasis was placed on a patient's thinking about sex, with various cognitive distortions becoming a major focus of treatment. Moreover, couple systemic considerations such as power struggles and difficulties with intimacy and trust have increasingly been included in both etiological considerations and treatment focus in a variety of sexual dysfunctions. In 1997, Joseph LoPiccolo termed this melding of theoretical approaches "post-modern sex therapy" and acknowledged that the procedures used by behavioral, cognitive-behavioral, and systemic therapists in treating sexual dysfunctions greatly overlap. As a result, the most comprehensive discussion of current treatment approaches to sexual dysfunctions must include an explanation of the theoretical underpinnings of postmodern sex therapy.

C. Post-modern Sex Therapy

Post-modern sex therapy is a therapeutic approach that uses behavioral, cognitive, and systemic methods to treat a variety of sexual disorders that affect both males and females. This approach is based on a theoretical foundation in which the etiology of sexual dysfunctions is considered to be multifaceted, with both psychological and physiological factors contributing to the onset of a particular disorder. As a result, both diagnosis and treatment of sexual dysfunctions must be considered in the context of a combination of behaviors, thoughts, and emotions.

Problems in sexual functioning are thought to have several potential causes that must be considered when designing the treatment approach. According to LoPiccolo, these include psychological factors, such as family of origin learning history, systemic relationship issues, cognitive distortions, and daily life stressors, as well as physiological or medical issues.

1. Family of Origin Learning History

Although Freudian theories of sexual dysfunction have largely been abandoned by modern mental health professionals, the idea that childhood can play a significant role in later sexual development has not. Most sex therapists today believe that childhood and adolescent experiences can play an important role in the development of both healthy and dysfunctional sexual relationships in adulthood. Issues in family of origin learning history often involve negative messages about sexual expression and a lack of sex education. In addition, many women and men who experience sexual dysfunctions have parents who have modeled unaffectionate and unhealthy sexual relationships.

The most common form of sex education for children who later develop sexual dysfunctions is the absence of sex education. Numerous adults who experience sexual difficulties report that they were not told about the positive aspects of sexuality by their families, and they often say that they did not receive any messages at all about sex. As noted by Susan Walen and Richard Perlmutter in 1988, the absence of communication about an issue does not indicate the absence of an underlying message, and often the topics that are never mentioned are the very topics that are seen as the most distasteful and inappropriate for discussion. By refusing to discuss sexuality, many parents set their children up for believing a multitude of myths about sex that they garner from peers, the media, and other unreliable outside sources of information. These can include misinformation about how one gets pregnant, the ways in which sexually transmitted diseases are transmitted, and the ways in which each partner must give and receive sexual pleasure.

Warren and Perlmutter outlined the "secrets of sex in families" that can contribute to the later development of difficulties in sexual functioning. One such secret is that sex is actually a pleasurable way to share feelings of love and affection with a partner, to express oneself as a healthy or happy person, or is a pleasurable form of recreation. Other deleterious family secrets include the secret that masturbation is a normal and healthy way to explore oneself and experience pleasure, the secret that children can have appropriate sexual feelings, the secret that adolescence is a normal time to experience sexual impulses and urges, and the secret that parents are sexual. In many of these families, the parents hide their affection and sexuality from their children behind closed doors, and children quickly learn that sex is an activity that needs to be hidden from others. Finally, the most serious sexual secrets that families keep are those associated with incest, rape, and paraphilias. Incest, in particular, is a family secret that very commonly leads to adulthood sexual dysfunction.

This lack of sex education not only leads to negative feelings about sexuality, but it also leads to sexual behavioral deficits in adulthood. Because they are discouraged from communicating with others about sexual issues and from sexual self-exploration, many children grow into adults who are ignorant of their partner's and their own anatomy, as well as the sexual response cycle. Common deficits in education that illustrate the problems associated with several sexual dysfunctions include uncertainty about the location of the clitoris, the belief that women must experience an orgasm through vaginal penetration only, the inability to recognize an orgasm when it does occur, the belief that men must ejaculate every time they have intercourse, the belief that men should be able to quickly regain erections after ejaculation, and the belief that orgasm through intercourse is the only acceptable end to sexual activity. These erroneous beliefs often lead to sexual behaviors that are detrimental to a functional sexual relationship, such as by neglecting to properly stimulate the clitoris to orgasm. In addition, cultural myths about sexuality and aging contribute to these cognitive and behavioral causes of sexual dysfunction. For instance, it is frequently thought that men should be able to attain and sustain an erection with little or no direct stimulation even as they get older.

While a lack of sex education is a common denominator in adults who have developed a sexual dysfunction, many children receive direct, harmful messages about the undesirability of sex. Negative messages about sexuality are communicated to children and adolescents in myriad ways. Strict prohibitions against childhood and adolescent masturbation, and parental negativism toward dating and premarital sexual activities are somewhat common methods of providing youth with messages about the shamefulness of sexual arousal and orgasm. In addition, traumatic first sexual experiences in childhood and adolescence have been found to be a common causative factor in the development of adult sexual dysfunctions. Finally, direct negative messages about sex and its consequences are often reported by individuals who suffer from a sexual disorder. Children might be told that sex is wrong, immoral, it hurts, or that it is dirty. Many females are informed that women do not enjoy sex, and if they do, then they are "sluts" or "whores."

Direct negative messages about sex have been linked to female orgasmic disorder by many clinicians and researchers. A "typical" history for these women has been described as involving strong parental prohibitions against nudity, masturbation, and sex play; no preparation for the onset of menstruation; a lack of sex education; and severe restrictions on adolescent dating. However, this same history is also common in women who do not later develop a sexual dysfunction. In 1986, Julia Heiman and colleagues reported that women who are both sexually functional and sexually dysfunctional experience similar culturally bound negative messages about female sexuality. It is still not clear what mediating variables may play a role in causing sexual dysfunction in some women, but not in others.

2. *Systemic Relationship Factors*

In the history of sex therapy, it has often been thought that sexual dysfunctions were extremely distressing to both the diagnosed individual and his or her partner. Marital dissatisfaction and sexual dysfunction were often considered to be separate problems, and assessment and treatment in one arena was compartmentalized such that marital therapy did not deal with sexual issues, and vice versa. More recently, however, it has been noted that sexual dysfunctions can play an important role in the couple's relationship. Indeed, sexual dysfunctions can sometimes be seen to develop in order to fulfill a role or convey a message within the relationship. As a result, post-modern sex therapy recognizes the important psychological needs that a sexual dysfunction can be meeting for an individual. In these situations, the dysfunction can be seen to introduce or maintain a level of homeostasis in the relationship structure. Understanding the psychological and relationship needs that sexual dysfunctions can help to fulfill is an important component of post-modern sex therapy. In 1997, LoPiccolo noted that inattention to the individual or couple dynamic needs that are being met by the sexual dysfunction commonly results in client sabotage and resistance toward therapeutic progress.

In 1988, LoPiccolo and Jerry Friedman formulated a list of several commonly occurring systemic issues that may be both causes and effects of sexual disorders. These issues include a lack of attraction to the partner, poor sexual skills of the partner, general dyadic unhappiness, fear of closeness or intimacy, a lack of basic trust, differences between the couple in the degree of personal space desired in the relationship, passive–aggressive solutions to a power imbalance, poor conflict resolution skills, and the inability to blend feelings of love and sexual desire. For example, some cases of low sexual desire disorder may reflect other relationship power disruptions. The diagnosed partner may use his or her lack of sexual desire to gain power in a relationship in which he or she feels very little control by becoming the sexual "gatekeeper." Alternately, the opposite could occur, where the nondiagnosed partner has a vested interest in the maintenance of the dysfunction because he or she gains some power in the relationship due to feelings of guilt in the diagnosed partner. In both instances, careful attention must be paid to the benefits that occur as a result of the dysfunction and treatment must address the underlying problems in the relationship.

3. Cognitive Distortions and Intrapsychic Factors

Cognitive contributions to the development and maintenance of sexual dysfunctions were first recognized by the early behaviorists who claimed that the major etiological factor associated with sexual dysfunction was anxiety. Masters and Johnson called this performance anxiety, a term referring to the excessive worrying about sexual performance that can in itself interfere with sexual arousal, resulting in sexual failure. Male erectile disorder is a sexual dysfunction that is often associated with performance anxiety, as men with this disorder tend to fear repeat occurrences of erectile failure, worry about it excessively, and spend much of their time during sexual encounters monitoring their arousal and strength of erection. As a result, they do fail to attain or sustain an erection, leading to even greater anxiety and the maintenance of a cycle of sexual dysfunction.

Many cognitive distortions play a role in the development and maintenance of sexual dysfunctions. Individuals who have problems with sexual functioning often engage in dichotomous thinking, in which they take an all-or-nothing attitude toward sexual functioning. A man who experiences premature ejaculation, for instance, may feel that if he cannot control his time to ejaculation, then he is a total sexual failure. This type of belief may even occur despite his bringing his partner to orgasm through other methods of sexual stimulation. Catastrophizing is also common, and can be seen when individuals make negative predictions about their future sexual functioning and their ability to overcome dysfunction. Imperatives, in which the client makes "should" and "must" statements about their sexual functioning, are characteristic of many people with dysfunctions. For example, a woman who has never experienced an orgasm during intercourse with her partner may tell herself "I should be able to have an orgasm just from having his penis in my vagina. I shouldn't have to stimulate my clitoris." Finally, people who experience problems in sexual functioning often engage in mind reading when it comes to the reactions of their partners, which can lead to even more anxiety. A woman who has vaginismus might make attributions about what her partner thinks about her as a person or a sexual being, such as, "He's thinking I'm frigid and undesirable."

According to LoPiccolo and Friedman, other intrapsychic and cognitive factors that are important contributors to a variety of sexual dysfunctions include a fear of loss of control over sexual urges, fears of having children, underlying depression, religious orthodoxy, gender identity conflicts, homosexual orientation or conflict, masked sexual deviation, aging concerns, sexual phobias or aversions, anhedonic or obsessive–compulsive personality, unresolved feelings about the death of a spouse, and attempting sex in a context or situation that is not comfortable for the client.

4. Daily Life Stressors and Operant Issues

A fourth psychological factor in the development and maintenance of sexual dysfunctions are the daily life stresses that an individual experiences and the operant value that the dysfunction may have for either partner. An operant value can be defined as a reinforcing consequence for a sexual dysfunction that comes from the external world, such as through the admiration of friends for sticking by a dysfunctional partner, or devoting extra time to work because of the impaired sexual and marital relationship and experiencing financial rewards as a result. Friends and family may admire a woman who devotes extra time to her children and their activities because she has distanced herself from her low-desire husband. As a result, she may have reservations about making real therapeutic gains on the low sexual desire.

5. Physiological or Medical Factors

Sexual dysfunctions are best understood as existing in a multidimensional realm, with both psychological and physiological factors playing differing roles in the development and maintenance of problems. Although some individuals may experience a disorder caused solely by physiological or psychological factors, most have a complex intermingling of etiologies that are unique to each individual. Many illnesses that affect the functioning of the neurological system, such as diabetes and multiple sclerosis, result in sexual disorders because they interfere with the very system that controls arousal and orgasm. Other illnesses and diseases that result in chronic pain or fatigue can also interfere with sexual arousal and enjoyment of a variety of sexual activities. Finally, many medications have side effects that interfere with functioning by inhibiting sexual responsiveness. These include a variety of psychotropics, particularly antidepressant and antianxiety medications, and drugs prescribed for various medical conditions, such as high blood pressure. Marijuana, alcohol, barbiturates, and other street drugs can also have a deleterious effect on sexual functioning.

These five categories not only serve a causative function in many instances of sexual dysfunction, but they can also work in a variety of combinations to maintain problems that are extremely disrupting to the lives of individuals with disorders. For instance, a man may experience his first erectile failure as a result of a medical problem, such as a reaction to an antidepressant. However, even when taken off of the antidepressant, he may continue to experience problems with attaining or sustaining an erection because he continues to make irrational and anxiety-provoking cognitive distortions. Similarly, a woman may originally experience anorgasmia due to the extremely negative messages she received about sex as a child and adolescent, but the problem may be maintained by her tremendously stressful life as a working mother who has little time to relax and resists adding a sexual role to the others for which she has already assumed responsibility. The combination of causative and maintaining factors that contribute to any individual case of sexual dysfunction must be thoroughly examined and treated within the context of fostering a healthy, mutually pleasurable sexual relationship for the dysfunctional couple.

II. BEHAVIORAL, COGNITIVE, AND SYSTEMIC TREATMENT FOR SEXUAL DYSFUNCTIONS

A. Treatment Overview

Post-modern sex therapy addresses the causal and maintaining factors of sexual dysfunction through a variety of behavioral, cognitive, and systemic treatment methods. In 1997, LoPiccolo outlined nine general principles of sex therapy through which couple change takes place. First, the sexual dysfunction is conceptualized as a disorder of the couple, with both partners bearing a mutual responsibility for treatment. It is important to take the blame out of sexual disorders and facilitate a team approach to treatment. Both partners should be engaged in the treatment process and willing to take on responsibility for the sexual dysfunction and its treatment. In cases where the nondysfunctional partner refuses to actively participate in therapy, the rates of treatment success can be seriously reduced.

Second, in many cases couples have limited knowledge of the basic anatomy and physiology of human sexual response. Consequently, it becomes necessary for the therapist to provide an informational and educational component to treatment. Clients often need to be educated about the process of sexual arousal in both males and females, as well as about human anatomy. For instance, many couples do not know where the clitoris is located, that vaginal lubrication is not automatic, or that men have a refractory period between the time they ejaculate and the time they can attain another erection. A sex therapist will assist their clients in learning about their bodies and the process of sexual arousal and orgasm.

The third principle of sex therapy is to foster an attitude change in clients who have negative attitudes toward the expression of their sexuality. As noted earlier, negative attitudes can come from a variety of sources, including the family of origin. The therapist must work to combat these negative attitudes and replace them with more positive, accepting attitudes toward sexuality.

A fourth mechanism of change in sex therapy is the elimination of performance anxiety. Many individuals who experience problems in sexual functioning possess negative self-fulfilling expectancies about their sexual abilities and how their sexual encounters will progress. There are many strategies used in sex therapy to help clients begin to enjoy the process of sex as opposed to focusing on sexual goals. Participants in therapy are taught that worrying about the outcome of sex guarantees that they will not attain their "goal," because it directly interferes with arousal. Instead, the emphasis is on enjoying the process of sex. This intervention is paradoxical: Often, as soon as clients are no longer worrying about maintaining an erection or attaining an orgasm, they are free to enjoy sex and experience normal sexual functioning.

A fifth goal of sex therapy is to increase communication skills in the couple. Dysfunctional couples often have many communication deficits that directly affect their ability to have satisfying sexual relationships. For instance, couples with sexual dysfunctions often have trouble communicating their likes and dislikes to one another for a number of reasons. Some couples are embarrassed about such communication, or they may not feel that it is part of their proscribed sexual role. Others may lack the knowledge of how to convey their preferences in an effective manner, resulting in their partners feeling criticized or humiliated by the communication that does take place. Another common difficulty concerns the initiation and refusal of sexual activity, with many couples developing indirect and ineffective ways of telling their partner when they do and do not want to engage in sexual activity. Sex therapy addresses these common problems by teaching couples effective communication strategies for conveying sexual preferences and responses in a clear, open, and supportive manner, and for initiating and refusing sexual activity in a clear, nonhurtful, and nonthreatening manner.

Changing destructive sex roles and lifestyles is the sixth mechanism of change in post-modern sex therapy. Many people have developed life habits that indirectly interfere with sexual functioning in a number of ways. Problems with extended family, children, and careers can all interfere with the sexual lives of adults. In addition, the sex roles that people acquire can interfere with sexual expression in a relationship. For instance, a common problem experienced by two-income households is the idea that the female partner is still responsible for the majority of housework and child care in addition to her career. This expectation leads many women to feel highly stressed and overworked, which in turn interferes with feelings of sexiness and sexual desire. A destructive sex role for men might include the expectation that they always initiate sexual relations, leading to pressure to be the pursuer and to feelings of uncertainty about their own sexual desirability. Sex therapy addresses these destructive lifestyles and sex roles by helping the client to initiate the life changes that will facilitate healthy sexual relationships.

Seventh, sex therapists must often help couples to change disruptive marital systems and enhance the marital relationship. Commonly, sexual dysfunctions are present in unhappy marital relationships. As such, it is unrealistic to believe that a couple can leave behind their disagreements about parenting, finances, or other issues while working solely on sexual issues. Often, therapists must address these issues in conjunction with sexual dysfunction in order to foster a more satisfactory sexual relationship. Current sex therapy frequently involves direct restructuring of the marital relationship.

Physical and medical interventions are sometimes needed to restore healthy sexual functioning. Many medical diseases can interfere with sexual functioning, including diabetes, heart disease, and neurological conditions such as spinal cord injury, multiple sclerosis, and pituitary/hypothalamic tumors. In addition, many prescribed medications can interfere with the arousal process. Antihypertensive medications and psychotropic medications such as antianxiety, antidepressant, and antipsychotic agents have been shown to interfere with arousal and orgasm for both men and women. Similarly, recreational drugs such as alcohol, marijuana, heroin, and cocaine can negatively impact sex drive, sexual arousal, and orgasm. Finally, hormone levels in the body can also have major effects on sexual functioning. Disruptions in the levels of testosterone, estrogen, and prolactin can suppress sex drive and negatively impact sexual functioning for men and women. As a result, team approaches to sex therapy are often warranted, with the therapist and a medical practitioner working together to improve sexual functioning.

Perhaps the most distinctive element of sex therapy is the behavioral component: changing sexual behavior and teaching effective sexual techniques. Stanley Althof outlined several goals of behavioral techniques in sex therapy in 1989. These goals include overcoming performance anxiety, altering the previously destructive sexual system, confronting resistances in each partner, alleviating the couples' anxiety about physical intimacy, dispelling myths and educating clients regarding sexual function and anatomy, counteracting negative concerns with body image, and heightening sensuality. For each sexual dysfunction, the therapist prescribes a series of specific sexual behaviors for the clients to perform in their own homes. Clients are confronted with the behavioral challenge of both changing their actual sexual behaviors and understanding the problems they have in implementing this change. In 1995, Walter Vandereycken outlined several common behavioral interventions that are used in sex therapy. Vandereycken divided these procedures into two categories: "nondemand" procedures aimed at decreasing sexual anxiety, and "excitement-awareness" procedures to increase sexual arousal. The nondemand interventions include deemphasizing sexual intercourse by placing a temporary ban on coitus, desensitization techniques, relaxation training, sensate focus, and graded noncoital contact and stimulation. Common excitement-awareness procedures include the development of sexual fantasies and imagery, role-play of an exaggerated orgasm, body awareness and self-exploration, directed masturbation, and guided stimulation by the partner. Although some of these behaviors may be similar for different disorders, the treatment for each sexual dysfunction includes unique behavioral prescriptions that will be described in detail later in this article.

It is important to note that these mechanisms of change are not a step-wise therapy, with each component being undertaken after the previous ones have been mastered. Instead, post-modern sex therapy is a conglomeration of these overriding principles, with the therapist using these techniques in conjunction with one another. Thus, throughout treatment, therapy is seen as a process for which both partners are mutually responsible, the therapist attempts to foster the development of more effective communication skills, and attention is paid to dyadic relationship satisfaction. All the while, specific behavioral modifications in sexual functioning are made.

B. General Strategies in Assessment and Treatment

Sex therapy usually begins with an evaluation and assessment of the particular sexual dysfunction and its impact on the marital relationship. This assessment has historically included taking an extensive sexual history of both partners, interviewed separately. Masters and Johnson advocated the use of a semistructured interview that typically lasted for several hours. However, as pointed out by LoPiccolo in 1995, the utility of this type of interview has not been empirically demonstrated and its application may not be the most efficient use of therapeutic time. Particularly in this time of insurance-placed restraints on the number of therapy sessions a given person is covered for, it is important for the therapist to be mindful of the benefits that a shortened sexual history assessment can provide for the therapeutic process.

Paper-and-pencil questionnaires are also commonly used to assess sexual history and current sexual functioning. The Sexual Arousal Inventory, developed by Peter Hoon, Emily Hoon, and John Wincze in 1976, and the Sexual Interaction Inventory, developed by LoPiccolo and Jeffrey Steger in 1974, are two questionnaires that can be particularly useful in the assessment and treatment outcome phases of sex therapy. These questionnaires can provide valuable information to the therapist by identifying arousal deficits and problem behaviors that can be the focus of treatment. They are also useful tools for identifying significant discrepancies in thoughts, feelings, and behaviors reported by the partners.

A physiological assessment by medical professionals is also indicated in the assessment of several sexual dysfunctions, including male erectile disorder and dyspareunia. Although vaginismus is not caused by organic factors, a medical assessment is still warranted to rule out the possibility that dyspareunia has not been incorrectly diagnosed as vaginismus. Premature ejaculation and female orgasmic disorder are not associated through empirical research with organic factors. Physiological assessments should include a pelvic examination by a specialist, such as a gynecologist or urologist, an assessment of current medications and their potential side effects, and tests for thyroid function, endocrine status, and glucose tolerance. In addition, vascular and neurological examinations are especially important in cases of male erectile disorder.

Following these initial assessment procedures, the therapist presents a comprehensive formulation of the etiology and maintenance of the dysfunction to the couple. Their sex histories, family-of-origin dynamics, cognitive styles, current relationship structure, external reinforcers, and any organic factors are used in this formulation, and the couple is informed about how these factors have interacted to create and maintain their sexual problems. This presentation is useful in initiating change procedures and sometimes has positive effects on the sexual problem itself.

After the completion of the assessment portion of therapy, some simple behavioral interventions are made that are common to all of the dysfunctions. First, the couple is asked to refrain from attempting sexual intercourse until it is prescribed by the therapist. Many sex therapists believe that this prohibition of coitus serves to alleviate performance anxiety, allowing the couple to rebuild their sexual relationship from the beginning. Next, the couple is typically asked to complete a series of sensate focus exercises. Sensate focus is a behavioral intervention that focuses the clients' attention on the sensuality of the body, without the pressure attendant upon sexual behaviors such as intercourse. These exercises include sensual touching of the clients' own bodies or their partners', and consist of caressing, hugging, kissing, and body massage. Participants in sex therapy are instructed to tune in to their sensual response to the touching. Sensate focus exercises serve to reduce anxiety in a number of ways, including providing a no-demand experience to the couple, eliminating the "spectator role," and increasing dyadic communication by giving feedback to the partner about what feels good. Breast and genital contact, intercourse, and orgasm are not allowed as part of these exercises. Vandereycken points out that the ban on intercourse and the inclusion of sensate focus exercises in the therapeutic process are of somewhat questionable value because they have never been systematically studied. However, their use is indirectly supported through their inclusion in several treatment protocols for different sexual disorders that have been empirically validated.

The next step in post-modern sex therapy is dependent on the exact nature of the couple's sexual dysfunction. Following is a description of each of the major sexual dysfunctions listed in the *DSM-IV*, along with the more specific treatment procedures used for each disorder.

C. Gender-Specific Sexual Dysfunctions

Several sexual disorders are unique to males, whereas some are experienced exclusively by females. These gender-specific disorders occur during both the arousal and orgasm stages of the human sexual response cycle. The male sexual dysfunctions include erectile dysfunction, premature ejaculation, and male orgasmic disorder. Disorders that commonly affect women are female arousal disorder, female orgasmic disorder, and vaginismus.

1. Male Sexual Dsyfunctions

a. Male Erectile Disorder Male erectile disorder is characterized by an inability to attain or maintain an erection, resulting in an incapacity to complete sexual activities such as intercourse. The etiology of male erectile disorder can be extremely complex, with a primarily psychogenic cause, a primarily organic cause, or most often, an interaction of the two. Neurological diseases such as multiple sclerosis and diabetes, a failure of blood flow to the penis, medication side effects, and surgical damage are all potentially physiological causes of erectile dysfunction. As stated before, a physical evaluation is extremely important in the assessment of this particular disorder. However, as LoPiccolo noted in 1995, the presence of some degree of organic impairment does not always negate the need for behavioral treatment. Men who suffer from mild organic impairment are often more vulnerable to psychological factors of erectile failure. As a result, treating the psychological difficulties can frequently enable a man to experience a fully functional erection even with the mild physiological impairment. Psychological treatment of erectile dysfunction in men with organic causes serves to help the client function at his optimum physiological capacity.

Psychogenic causes of male erectile disorder can include performance anxiety and the spectator role, as well as a lack of adequate physical stimulation of the penis. Commonly, men who experience difficulty attaining or maintaining an erection enter each sexual encounter with negative expectancies about their ability to "perform" and consequently, they constantly self-monitor their own level of arousal. These men become anxious observers rather than aroused participants. This sort of mindset prevents arousal, and as a result, the dysfunction is cyclically maintained. Problems with erection can also result from poor sexual techniques, such as inadequate stimulation of the penis. Especially as men age, direct stimulation of the penis for some period of time is necessary for the attainment of an erection. However, many couples expect erections to be automatic and effortless, and therefore do not give the penis adequate stimulation. Consequently, the predominant themes in the psychological treatment of erectile dysfunction are the reduction of performance anxiety and the increase of sexual stimulation.

After engaging in general sensate focus techniques, the couple is instructed to add genital contact to their sessions. They are taught the "tease technique" in which the couple is instructed to cease genital contact if the male should attain an erection. The couple can resume penile contact only after the erection is lost. This exercise teaches clients that erections occur naturally in response to stimulation, as long as the couple does not focus on performance. The male is paradoxically instructed throughout sensate focus that, "The purpose of this exercise is for you to learn to enjoy sensual pleasures, without focusing on sexual goals. Therefore, you should try to not get an erection." This demand to not get an erection frees the male to enjoy sensual situations without the accompanying anxieties that have worked against attaining an erection in the past.

After the couple experiences this process several times, they move on to intercourse. Intercourse is also attempted in several steps. First, the male partner lies on his back while the female partner kneels astride him and uses her fingers to push his flaccid penis into her vagina. This procedure, known as the "stuffing technique," frees him from having to have a rigid penis to accomplish entry. Sometimes called "quiet vagina," the woman remains still while his penis is inside of her. Gradually, the couple can add movement by the female gently moving her hips. Finally, the male is instructed to thrust and the couple resumes full sexual activity, with no further restrictions. Throughout this process, the couple is instructed to achieve the woman's orgasm through manual or oral sex, resulting in the reduction of pressure on the male to perform as well as partner compliance with treatment. In addition, Althof suggests that guided explicit fantasies can be used when the male is preoccupied with performance issues or when he is having difficulty becoming aroused.

This set of procedures seems to be effective in cases where there is no major organic impairment of erection. For men with more severe physiological problems underlying or complicating their erectile dysfunction, however, physical interventions may be warranted. One of several medical procedures may be useful for men who experience erectile failure as the result of a more severe organic impairment.

Penile injections of drugs that cause rigidity, such as prostaglandin E, phentolamine, and vasoactive intestinal polypeptide, can be an effective treatment for men with irreversible erectile dysfunction. These drugs are self-administered by the patient just before intercourse, and they work by dilating the penile arteries. Research indicates that most men who use penile injections experience erections as a result. In their discussion of organic treatment methods for male erectile disorder in 1989, Leonore Tiefer and Arnold Melman warn that this "quick fix" can often be tempting to men who have a more psychogenic basis for the disorder. However, they warn against using this method of treatment for these men, citing potential risks of scarring of the penis, and research results that indicate these types of men are often very dissatisfied with the treatment.

Another nonsurgical and noninvasive treatment method is the use of a vacuum constriction device. A hollow cylinder is placed over the penis, and a hand pump is used to pump the air out of the cylinder, leaving the penis in a partial vacuum. As a result, blood rushes into the penis. The cylinder is removed and a rubber constricting band is placed at the base of the penis to maintain the erection. This treatment method is most often used for men who have erectile dysfunction rooted in diabetes or neurological problems, and it does not have any known negative effects on the body. It can, however, be awkward and can interfere with the spontaneity of sex.

Artificial erections can also be manufactured in men with severe physical problems through the use of a penile prosthesis. This device consists of a semirigid pair of rods made of rubber and wire, and it is surgically implanted in the corpora. This device does not allow for growth of the penis in width or length during sexual activity. Instead, it can be bent up to an erect position when the man wants to have sex, and bent back down for normal wear. An alternative to this type of prosthesis is a hydraulic inflatable system that allows for tumescence. Inflatable hollow cylinders are surgically inserted into the penis, a reservoir of saline fluid is placed under the abdominal wall, and tubing connecting the cylinders to a pump is inserted in the scrotum. When he wishes to have sex, the man or his partner can squeeze the pump, forcing fluid from the reservoir to the penile cylinders, which expand and produce an erection. Tiefer and Melman caution that because of their invasiveness and annihilation of any capacity to produce an erection should they need to be removed at a later date, penile implants should be considered the last resort in the treatment of erectile disorder.

Finally, the recent proliferation of advertisements for Viagra speak to its popularity as a pharmacological treatment for erectile disorder. Viagra is an effective treatment, showing positive results in 70 to 80% of cases treated. The drug works by reducing venous outflow once blood has been pumped into the cavernous bodies, not by increasing arterial inflow. As such, men who use Viagra still need adequate sexual and emotional stimulation to achieve an erection. Some of the 20 to 30% of cases in which Viagra fails are not actually pharmacologic failures, but failures to provide adequate physical or emotional stimulation. Consequently, the use of Viagra is contraindicated in instances where couple systemic issues are the only etiological factor involved with erectile difficulties. In addition, Viagra is also contraindicated in instances where low desire is the cause of erectile failure, as the drug has not been shown to increase levels of desire.

b. Premature Ejaculation Premature ejaculation is defined as the persistent onset of orgasm and ejaculation with minimal stimulation, before or shortly after intromission occurs. An important determinant of premature ejaculation is that it causes marked distress in the male and/or his partner. Time criterion have had little use in the assessment of premature ejaculation, as differences in foreplay activity, age, and the use of distraction techniques can artificially increase or decrease the duration of intercourse. A more clinically useful conceptualization of premature ejaculation includes the couple's subjective opinions about the appropriateness of duration, and the pleasure and satisfaction that each partner gains from their sexual encounters. If both partners agree that their sexual encounters are negatively influenced by efforts to delay ejaculation, then premature ejaculation is considered a problem.

In 1970, Masters and Johnson reported that premature ejaculation can be treated with direct behavioral retraining procedures that are successful in nearly 100%

of cases. The standard treatment for premature ejaculation involves the "stop-start" or "pause" procedure, introduced by Semans in 1956. With this procedure, the penis is manually stimulated until the man is highly aroused and he feels that ejaculation is imminent. At this point, the couple stops stimulation until the arousal subsides, and they resume stimulation again when the male no longer feels that ejaculation is imminent. The "squeeze" technique can also be added to help the male delay ejaculation during manual stimulation. In this procedure, the female partner firmly squeezes the penis between her thumb and forefinger, at the place where the head of the penis joins the shaft. For some couples, this procedure can be an effective way to reduce arousal even further than that experienced with the stop-start technique. The stop-start and squeeze procedures are repeated many times so that the male can experience an immense amount of stimulation and arousal without the occurrence of ejaculation. Ultimately, the man should experience significantly more total time of stimulation than he has ever experienced before. These behavioral procedures lead to a higher threshold for ejaculation, with the male gradually gaining the capacity for participating in quite lengthy periods of penile stimulation without ejaculation.

After a few weeks of this training when the necessity of pausing diminishes, the focus of behavioral exercises shifts to include intercourse. The couple continues to practice a modified stop-start technique in which the penis is placed in the vagina without any thrusting movements. The most effective intercourse position during this period of treatment is the woman on top position. The "quiet vagina" exercise is utilized, and the male partner is encouraged to make no movement but to feel free to engage in erotic touching of his partner. If this stimulation produces high levels of arousal and a feeling of ejaculatory inevitability, the penis is withdrawn and the couple waits for arousal to drop off. When good tolerance for inactive containment of the penis is achieved, the training procedure is repeated during active thrusting exercises with a variety of sexual positions. After 2 to 3 months of practice, males who undergo treatment for premature ejaculation are generally able to enjoy significantly prolonged intercourse without the need to use pause and squeeze techniques.

In a 1989 publication of a treatment protocol for premature ejaculation, Barry McCarthy stressed the importance of the process of successive approximation in ejaculatory control exercises. The male is taught to become aware of his level of arousal and the point of ejaculatory control when he is still able to stop short of ejaculation. It is inevitable that the client will have at least one experience during treatment where he pushes the limits too far, and signals for his partner too late to stop the ejaculatory process. McCarthy emphasized that it is important for the therapist to confront the couple with this possibility early in therapy, and to encourage the couple to use it as a pleasurable learning experience about identifying ejaculatory inevitability rather than experience it as a failure in treatment. He also highlighted the importance of ensuring that the female partner's desires and preferences be given equal attention, with both manual and oral stimulation encouraged as a method to bring sexual satisfaction to the woman during the treatment period. The benefits of this are twofold. First, the female partner is more likely to remain invested in the treatment if the couple's sexual encounters are not always completely focused on the male partner's arousal. Second, the male can learn that women can be sexually satisfied in a number of ways that have little or nothing to do with the penis and intercourse, which in turn leads to the alleviation of performance anxieties. Finally, McCarthy suggested that cognitive restructuring procedures used in conjunction with behavioral interventions can have an important effect on the long-term success of therapy. Couples need to learn that sex is a collaborative process in which neither partner bears the responsibility for performing, in which both partners are integral to changing problematic sexual behaviors and maintaining those changes, and in which intimacy and sexuality are integrated to form a stronger sexual relationship for the couple.

c. Male Orgasmic Disorder Male orgasmic disorder is present when a man experiences a recurrent delay in, or absence of, orgasm following a normal phase of sexual excitement. Formerly known as inhibited ejaculation, male orgasmic disorder is a fairly rare sexual dysfunction, and the cause of the problem often remains unclear. Many psychological factors have been theorized as causes for male orgasmic disorder, such as an autosexual orientation and fear of intimacy with the partner, but there is little supporting empirical research. However, etiology has been established with several physiological factors, including multiple sclerosis, medication side effects, and damage to the hypothalamus.

Treatment of male orgasmic disorder is based on many of the standard strategies used with other sexual dysfunctions. Eliminating performance anxiety and ensuring adequate stimulation through paradoxical sensate focus exercises are the basis for treatment. The couple is instructed that during sex the penis is to be caressed manually and/or orally until the man is aroused, but that stimulation is to stop whenever he feels he might be close to orgasm. This procedure takes the focus of sex off of orgasm, and paradoxically, allows the man to fully enjoy the pleasurable sensations of stimulation. Additionally, in 1977 LoPiccolo reported that the use of electric vibrators, behavioral maneuvers called "orgasm triggers" (discussed in the section on female orgasmic disorder), and having the client role-play an exaggerated orgasm all seem to have some success with the treatment of male orgasmic disorder.

Physiological interventions are indicated when the primary cause is organic in nature. Drugs that increase the arousal of the sympathetic nervous system have been found to be helpful in some cases, as has increased stimulation of the scrotal, perineal, and anal areas. In particular, direct stimulation of the anus through the use of a vibrator has been found to be an extremely effective orgasm trigger in men who suffer neurological damage.

2. Female Sexual Dysfunctions

a. Female Sexual Arousal Disorder and Female Orgasmic Disorder A persistent inability to attain or maintain sexual excitement through the completion of sexual activity describes female sexual arousal disorder; female orgasmic disorder occurs when sexual excitement is normal, but orgasm does not occur. Both disorders can be successfully treated with many of the same behavioral techniques, including education, self-exploration, body awareness, and directed masturbation. These procedures are particularly effective for women who have never had an orgasm through any form of stimulation.

Directed masturbation, a treatment protocol for female arousal and orgasm disorders, has broad empirical support in individual, couple, and group modalities. This program of therapy is described in *Becoming Orgasmic,* a self-help book and accompanying film written by Heiman and LoPiccolo, and published in 1988. The directed masturbation protocol involves nine steps. In the first step, the inorgasmic woman is instructed to use various diagrams and reading materials to learn about her body, her genitals, and the female sexual response. She is also encouraged to work on her attitudes and cognitions surrounding the acceptability of female sexuality, and to examine her own sexual history to identify negative influences that have carried into her current functioning. Step 2 involves the woman exploring her body and genitals through both sight and touch. Next, in Step 3 the woman furthers her body exploration by locating erogenous zones, with a focus on the clitoris, breasts, and other genital regions.

The woman is directly instructed in techniques of masturbation in Step 4. She is encouraged to target the erotically sensitive areas that she has identified in previous sessions and increase the intensity and duration of stimulation. Step 5 is erotic masturbation, in which an attempt is made to make masturbation more erotic and sexual. The woman is encouraged to develop sexual fantasies, read erotic stories, or view sexually arousing pictures to increase her feelings of arousal.

The sixth step has three elements. If the woman has not yet reached orgasm, she will begin to use an electric vibrator to increase the intensity of stimulation. Women who experience their first orgasm through the use of a vibrator usually go on to have orgasms through other methods of stimulation, but the vibrator can be invaluable to the attainment of the first orgasm. Second, she will be instructed to act out or role-play an exaggerated orgasm. This procedure helps the woman overcome any fears about looking silly or losing control when she has a real orgasm. In the final element of the sixth step, "orgasm triggers," such as holding the breath, contracting the pelvic muscles, tensing the leg muscles, and thrusting the pelvis are used by the woman.

The final three steps of the directed masturbation protocol integrate the partner into treatment. In Step 7, the woman shows her partner how she likes to be touched and how she can have an orgasm. During this step, the partner also shares his or her own masturbation preferences with the woman so that she can feel less inhibited, and to ensure that the learning process is reciprocal. In the next step, her partner brings her to orgasm with manual, oral, or vibrator stimulation, using the woman's instruction and guidance to increase arousal and sexual satisfaction. Finally, in Step 9, the heterosexual couple resumes penile-vaginal intercourse in positions that permit one of them to continue clitoral stimulation.

During this final stage, it is essential to educate the couple that continued stimulation of the clitoris during intercourse is both normal and often necessary for many women to experience orgasm through this sexual behavior. Many women and their partners are wed to the myth that women should be able to experience orgasm through penile stimulation only. Educating them about the myth of vaginal versus clitoral orgasms is often necessary. In addition, it should be noted that the couple's goals can be vastly different—some couples are not as concerned with an ultimate goal of orgasm through coitus, and these individuals should be encouraged to see their treatment as successful if they learn to experience an orgasm through any method of stimulation that they find acceptable.

Not all women who seek treatment for arousal and orgasm disorders have difficulty becoming aroused or reaching orgasm in all situations. Such types of situational orgasmic dysfunction include only being able to reach orgasm in solitary masturbation, without a partner present, or through a circumscribed sexual activity, such as oral stimulation. It is important to note that sex therapists do not consider lack of orgasm during intercourse to be an indication for treatment, provided that the woman can have orgasm in some way with her partner, and that she enjoys intercourse. However, some women are distressed by their limited orgasmic experiences, and there are treatment techniques that can be utilized in these situations.

Treatment for situational lack of orgasm includes a gradual stimulus generalization approach developed by Antionette Zeiss, Raymond Rosen, and Robert Zeiss in 1977. This procedure helps the woman to expand the ways in which she reaches orgasm through a sequential series of changes in stimulation. For example, a woman who can masturbate to orgasm wants to experience orgasm during intercourse. The therapist will help her to identify a number of small, intermediate steps between the way she has orgasm now and the wished-for orgasm during intercourse with her partner. As a first step, the woman might be instructed to masturbate as usual, with the addition of having her finger passively inserted into her vagina from the beginning of stimulation. This procedure will enable her to learn to experience orgasm with something contained in the vagina. Other intermediate steps in this example might include thrusting the inserted finger, having the partner present while she masturbates, having the partner manually stimulate the clitoris with first her and then his finger inserted, passive containment of the penis in the vagina while the woman masturbates, and passive containment of the penis while the man manually stimulates the woman. Once the woman has been able to reach orgasm through each of these phases, the couple can attempt active intercourse with concurrent direct manual stimulation of the clitoris. By breaking down the differences between masturbation and intercourse into a series of very small and discrete changes, there is a much greater success in broadening the woman's range of orgasmic responsivity.

b. Vaginismus Vaginismus is characterized by the involuntary contraction of the muscles surrounding the outer third of the vagina. These contractions have a spasmodic quality, and they prevent the insertion of a penis or other objects into the vagina. Women who experience vaginismus are often capable of becoming sexually aroused and experiencing orgasms—it is the possibility of penetration that triggers the muscle contractions. However, they may also present with a variety of other disorders, including an aversion to sex, female arousal disorder, or female orgasmic disorder.

Relaxation training, Kegel exercises, and use of progressive dilators inserted in the vagina are the procedures used to treat vaginismus. The woman is taught deep muscle relaxation and diaphramatic breathing techniques in order to decrease her overall feelings of anxiety and to help her gain volitional control of her vaginal muscles. Voluntary control of the vaginal muscles is acquired through Kegel exercises, in which the woman practices contracting and relaxing the pubococcygeal muscle. Next, the woman is helped to overcome her fear of penetration by using a set of gradually larger dilators that she inserts into her vagina at home and at her own pace. Once the woman has been able to comfortably insert the largest dilator, she can begin to guide her partner as her or she slowly and gently inserts the dilators. It should be stressed to women in treatment for vaginismus that they go slowly and become comfortable with each step and each size dilator before moving on to the next. If a woman or her partner pushes treatment forward at too quick of a pace, the result is often increased anxiety about penetration and a rapid return to experiencing the spastic contractions. In addition, both partners should be educated about the need for effective stimulation of the woman's erogenous zones, so that the woman can learn to associate penetration with vaginal lubrication, pleasure, and arousal. The use of fantasies and erotic materials can also aid in this process.

After the woman and her partner have been able to successfully insert the graduated dilators, heterosexual couples can begin to attempt penile penetration. First, the partner lies passively on his back while the woman kneels above him and gradually inserts his erect penis into her vagina. Again, the couple is encouraged to go slowly, at the woman's pace. When the woman is able to contain her partner's penis in her vagina comfortably, she can begin to move. Once she is comfortable, the partner can begin to thrust and the couple can explore a variety of intercourse positions that are enjoyable to both of them.

D. Nongender-Specific Sexual Dysfunctions

1. *Dyspareunia*

The *DSM-IV* defines dyspareunia as persistent genital pain associated with sexual intercourse in either a male or a female. Although dyspareunia can occur in males or females, clinically, pain is much more frequently seen in female clients.

Most cases of dyspareunia involve an organic etiology, such as vaginitis, endometriosis, Peyronie's disease, unrepaired damage following childbirth in woman, and prostate conditions in men. However, this dysfunction must also have some element of psychogenic etiology in order to be diagnosed as a true case of dyspareunia. A complete medical examination is necessary to differentially diagnose dyspareunia from other, similar disorders such as vaginismus or simple medical conditions. In males, painful intercourse is almost always related to an underlying medical condition.

Because psychogenic dyspareunia is often attributed to a lack of arousal, the general sex therapy procedures and the specific techniques for enhancing female arousal and orgasm are commonly used. In addition, because dyspareunia is commonly linked with vaginismus and may in fact be an earlier stage of that disorder in some women, the treatment protocol for vaginismus is often used. Artificial genital lubricants and relaxation training can also be effective additions to therapy.

2. *Hypoactive Sexual Desire Disorder and Sexual Aversion Disorder*

Hypoactive sexual desire disorder, often called low sexual desire disorder, is characterized by the persistent absence of desire for sexual activity. A person with this disorder feels little or no interest in sex, but they do not have negative emotions associated with the sex itself. Sexual aversion, on the other hand, is defined as an aversion to and actual avoidance of sexual contact by a partner and is based on strong negative emotional reactions to sex that include fear, revulsion, and disgust. Differential diagnosis between these two disorders is imperative for good treatment results.

Low desire used to be thought to be more prevalent in women; however, more recent data suggest that it affects males and females at a relatively equal rate. According to a treatment guide authored by Cathryn Pridal and LoPiccolo in 2000, low desire is characterized by a very low level, or absence of, spontaneously occurring sexual interest. A distinction is made between receptive and proceptive sexual behaviors, with a lack of proceptive behavior most indicative of true low sexual desire. Just as differential diagnosis is important, so is an assessment of comorbid sexual disorders. Often, individuals with low desire also experience another dysfunction, such as lack of erection or orgasm. In these cases, it is difficult to determine if low desire is the cause or effect of other disorders. Careful assessment must be made to determine which disorder should be treated first. For instance, a woman suffering from posttraumatic stress disorder (PTSD) after a traumatic sexual history as a child should not be treated for low desire or sexual aversion until her abuse has been adequately dealt with.

In 1988, LoPiccolo and Friedman described a four-element sequential model for hypoactive desire and aversion that has been widely adopted. The first component of the treatment program, called affectual awareness, focuses on helping the client to become more familiar with his or her negative attitudes, beliefs, and cognitions about sex. Feelings of anxiety, fear, resentment, and vulnerability are uncovered as the client is encouraged to closely examine his or her attitudes about sex. Many clients begin therapy insisting that they do not have negative feelings about sex, but instead, are merely indifferent to it. Pridal and LoPiccolo recommended that therapists dispute this claim by using an "umbrella metaphor." In the umbrella metaphor, the therapist explains that all humans have an innate sexual drive. Their indifference to sex is an umbrella that blocks their awareness of the negative emotions that are working to block this innate sexual drive. During this stage, both partners are encouraged to make lists about the benefits of gaining a sexual drive, but also about the possible risks to each individual if sex drive increases, and the potential risks to the relationship. These lists help the low-drive partner gain some motivation for therapy, as well as point out any potential issues that would result in resistance to therapy. In addition, clients are encouraged to visualize sexual scenes and talk about sex in a more graphic way so that they can more accurately recognize negative emotions that they were not previously aware that they had. Finally, role-plays in which the low-drive partner pretends to have a sex drive and initiates sexual activity with his or her partner can be useful in helping the low-drive client track his or her emotional state during this process. In this way, individuals with low sexual drive can become more aware of their own negative attitudes and cognitions about sexuality.

The second phase of sex therapy for low sexual desire involves insight-oriented therapy. During the insight phase, clients are helped to understand the underlying causes for the negative emotions that they have identified. Family-of-origin experiences, religious teachings, depression, fear of having children, life stress, unresolved sexual trauma or abuse, masked sexual deviations, gender identity issues, and relationship problems are explored as possible initiating and maintaining causes of the low desire or aversion. In a sense, this and the previous step are preparatory. The more active treatment follows.

Stage 3 involves cognitive and systemic therapy. This phase of therapy serves to alter irrational beliefs that inhibit sexual desire and to identify and modify relationship problems that are suppressing sexual drive. First, clients are taught that irrational beliefs may be the main cause of their emotional reactions, and they are helped to identify self-statements that interfere with sexual desire. Therapist and client generate a list of coping statements that combat the client's irrational thoughts about sexuality and help him or her to cope with, rather than avoid, negative emotional reactions to sexual situations. Typical coping statements might be "If I allow myself to enjoy sex, it doesn't mean I am dirty or bad" and "When I was younger I learned to feel guilty about sex, but I'm grown up now, and I don't have to feel that way anymore." Second, relationship problems are addressed in the dyad. In couples in which one partner is low drive, a power imbalance in the relationship is often found. This disruption in power can be expressed with either the low- or normal-drive partner having a disproportionate amount of power in the relationship. Systemic therapy addresses this issue and works to make the couple feel more equal in both their sexual and nonsexual interactions.

The final element of treatment for low desire and aversion consists of behavioral interventions. These include sensate focus, skills training and other general sex therapy procedures, as well as some interventions that are more specific to these disorders. Frequently, couples in which one partner has low drive experience a drastic decline in nonsexual affectionate behavior. The normal-drive partner might misinterpret simple affectionate behavior such as a hug as an invitation to initiate sexual activity. Consequently, the low-drive partner learns to squelch all affectionate behaviors to guard against this type of misunderstanding. An important component to treatment, then, is to reintroduce these simple affectionate behaviors to the couple. The couple identifies a number of affectionate behaviors that they agree will not be used to initiate sexual activity. Next, treatment focus is turned to the ways in which sexual activity can be initiated. Once again, role-plays are used so that both partners can illustrate how they do and do not like to be approached for sex. Additionally, they can communicate with one another about acceptable, nonhurtful ways to refuse sexual activity. These types of assertion training and communication skills training exercises help couples learn how to negotiate their sexual relationship without being coercive or rejecting of their partner.

Pridal and LoPiccolo labeled this next set of behavioral procedures "drive induction." They posited that sometimes people do not become aware of their sexual drive until they expose themselves to external cues and stimuli that trigger it, and individuals with low drive have developed an extraordinary ability to avoid these sexually relevant cues. In therapy, then, low-drive clients are asked to begin attending to sexual cues. A number of interventions are used in drive induction. For instance, low-drive clients are asked to keep a "desire diary," in which they record all sexual stimuli, thoughts, and emotions. They are also instructed to watch films that have sexual content, read erotic books and magazines, read collections of sexual fantasies, note attractive people they see, and so forth. Finally, couples are also often asked to develop erotic fantasies, both alone and together. The low-drive partner is instructed to take several "fantasy breaks" during the day in which he or she spends some time fantasizing about the sexual scenes that have been developed.

III. APPLICATIONS AND EXCLUSIONS

Since Masters and Johnson published their groundbreaking work on sexual dysfunctions, most therapists have switched from treating these disorders individually to treating the couple. However, couples originally were accepted for therapy if they had very circumscribed problems in only the sexual area. Those clients with individual psychopathology and severe marital distress were systematically screened out, as were individuals with medically complicated histories. Today, there is a greater focus on treating all of these problems, as sex therapists have become more cognizant of the fact that the incidence of "pure" sexual dysfunction without concurrent marital problems is extremely rare. Sex therapists and marital therapists find it less important to try to distinguish between sexual and relationship problems, because it is often not possible to segregate these areas of distress in people's lives. Instead, couples can be helped to find ways of showing caring and love, to work on sex roles and role expectations within the relationship, to understand the effects that children have on the relationship, to deal with jealousy and outside interests, and to express their differing needs for intimacy, independence, companionship, and affection.

Similarly, there has also been a greater tendency in recent years to accept clients with major forms of psychopathology. Many nonsexual disorders have been associated with problems in sexual expression in the literature. For instance, low desire, erectile dysfunction, and problems reaching orgasm have all been associated with depression. Axis II disorders, such as antisocial personality and passive–aggressive personality disorders have also been found to severely complicate the treatment of sexual dysfunction. However, the presence of one of these disorders does not prevent successful sex therapy, provided that the therapist addresses the concurrent psychopathology.

Group therapy for both individuals and couples has also been found to be an effective modality for the treatment of sexual dysfunctions. Therapists often facilitate treatment groups for disorders such as female orgasmic disorder, premature ejaculation, and erectile dysfunction. Heiman and Grafton-Becker cited research in their work on female orgasmic disorder that indicates that group treatment, including assertiveness training, education, and directed masturbation procedures, can be nearly as effective as couples therapy. The group modality is particularly valuable for single individuals in that it provides an environment of mutual support and encouragement. The treatment of individuals without partners can be more difficult than couple-based treatment; however, assertiveness and social skills training, in addition to the procedures described above, can be helpful to single people with sexual disorders. Some procedures can be altered to handle the unique problems that arise when treating singles. For instance, in 1978, Bernie Zilbergeld described a treatment modification for premature ejaculation in which single men are taught skills in delaying ejaculation through masturbation and fantasy exercises. Similar modifications can be made for the treatment of other sexual disorders.

Several special populations present unique challenges to the traditional methods of treating sexual dysfunction. Sex therapy with gay men, lesbians, and bisexuals must be inclusive of sexual identity issues, the many variations of homosexuality itself, the fear of AIDS, and the internalization of heterosexism. In addition, some modification to techniques will most likely be warranted.

Treatment of clients who have experienced a sexual trauma such as rape or child sexual abuse can also be challenging. Judith Becker, in a chapter on this topic published in 1988, pointed out that some women who seek treatment for sexual dysfunction have had a history of sexual trauma. These women often present with symptoms of PTSD. Special attention must be paid to these symptoms, and the initial treatment goal should be to alleviate the impact of PTSD on sexual functioning. Finally, sex therapy with the chronically ill requires some adaptation. Cooperative work with a primary health provider, treating the client in an institutionalized setting, and adjustments in the behavioral interventions may be warranted. However, traditional treatment methods such as emphasizing education to help people understand their sexual functions and capabilities, deemphasizing genital sex as a necessary component to all sexual pleasure, and emphasizing the exploration of other forms of sexual expression beside sexual intercourse can contribute to the kind of program that is helpful for those who have to make adjustments in their sexual behavior because of a chronic medical condition.

IV. EMPIRICAL RESEARCH

This article has focused on the clinical techniques currently used to treat a variety of sexual dysfunctions. Unfortunately, much of this knowledge is based on clinical experience, rather than on empirical research. In 1980, LoPiccolo pointed out that much of the empirical literature in sex therapy is actually a series of demonstration projects that do not involve random assignment to experimental conditions, manipulation of independent variables, or assessment with objective, quantified dependent variables. Other methodological problems include the use of mixed-diagnosis samples, indirect outcome measures, and small sample sizes. Additionally, there have been very few studies attempting to identify which components of the total sex therapy package are active ingredients and which are "inert fillers."

William O'Donohue, Diane Swingen, and Cynthia Dopke published a comprehensive review of the empirical literature for female sexual dysfunctions in 1997. In 1999, they, along with Lisa Regev, published a similar article concerning male sexual dysfunctions. They cite methodological problems, a lack of long-term follow-up data, a lack of treatment manuals, and the disregard for several disorders in outcome research as major problems that have contributed to the lack of concrete information about the efficacy of sex therapy programs. Only approximately 20% of the published studies on male and female sexual dysfunctions met the inclusion criteria for the O'Donohue reviews: random assignment to treatment conditions, and at least one comparison or control group. For in-depth examinations of these studies, please refer to the O'Donohue and colleague reviews. For the purposes of this article, it is sufficient to note that strong arguments exist for further attention to research design and data analysis in the empirical study of sex therapy outcomes.

Despite the weaknesses in sex therapy outcome research, there is great reason to believe that the outlined treatments produce positive results in the majority of cases. As such, they have been validated in a very meaningful way. In 1995, the Task Force on the Promotion and Dissemination of Psychological Procedures included the directed masturbation program for female orgasmic disorder and behavioral treatment for male erectile disorder on their list of well-established treatments. However, further treatment outcome research is needed in order to firmly establish the efficacy of postmodern sex therapy procedures.

See Also the Following Articles

Arousal Training ■ Assisted Covert Sensitization ■ Aversion Relief ■ Couples Therapy: Insight Oriented ■ Oedipus Complex ■ Orgasmic Reconditioning ■ Women's Issues

Further Reading

Heiman, J., & LoPiccolo, J. (1988). *Becoming orgasmic: A personal and sexual growth program for women (revised and expanded edition).* Englewood Cliffs, NJ: Prentice-Hall.

Leiblum, S. R., & Rosen, R. C. (2000). *Principles and practice of sex therapy* (3rd ed.). New York: Guilford Press.

Masters, W. H., & Johnson, V. E. (1970). *Human sexual inadequacy.* Boston: Little, Brown.

O'Donohue, W., Dopke, C., & Swingen, D. (1997). Psychotherapy for female sexual dysfunction: A review. *Clinical Psychology Review, 17,* 537–566.

O'Donohue, W., Swingen, D., Dopke, C., & Regev, L. (1999). Psychotherapy for male sexual dysfunction: A review. *Clinical Psychology Review, 19,* 591–630.

Zilbergeld, B. (1999). *The new male sexuality* (Rev. Ed.). New York: Bantam Books.

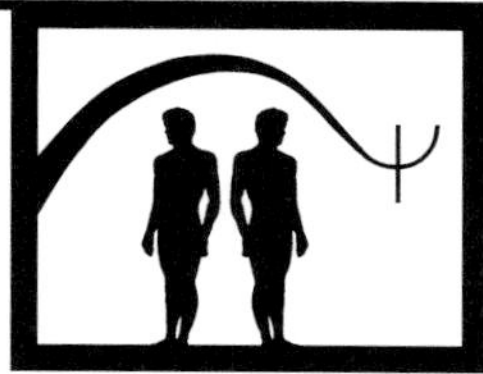

Short-Term Anxiety-Provoking Psychotherapy

John Tsamasiros

P. & A. Kyriakou Hospital, Athens, Greece

GLOSSARY

clarification The procedure aiming at the restructuring and differentiation of information brought by the patient to make certain points more easily understood.

compromise formation Connotes the product of the unconscious process in which the instinctual gratification (i.e., the discharge of sexual and aggressive instinctual impulses) and the demands of the opposing defensive forces are mutually satisfied through a compromise that partially expresses both tendencies allowing the repressed impulse to find expression in a substitute and disguised form (e.g., symptomatic phenomena).

confrontation The procedure that makes the phenomenon in question evident and explicit, aiming at the overcoming of the evasive and defensive tactics.

defense mechanisms The automatic, complex, and largely unconscious operations (e.g., repression, displacement, reaction formation, projection, etc.) used by the ego as a means of protection against internal (e.g., unacceptable wishes) or external (e.g., events, such as a loss, that elicit anxiety or painful affects) danger situations, aiming at the adaptive restoration of equilibrium.

dynamic Refers to the point of view according to which mental phenomena represent the outcome of a continuous conflict between opposing forces in general (i.e., the id, the ego, and the superego), and between the unconscious phenomena seeking discharge and a rigorous censorship (i.e., repression) aiming at their exclusion from conscious awareness in particular.

ego The agency of the psychical apparatus that mediates between the id, the superego, and the external reality, aiming at adaptation.

flight into health The phenomenon in which the resistant patient may exhibit a premature and temporary improvement of personal difficulties as a result of the unconscious wish to evade a further psychodynamic exploration of these conflicts.

focalization Refers to the active and collaborative attempt of the patient and the therapist to stay within the confines of the agreed-on focus and to work toward the attainment of specific therapeutic goals. Focalization is instrumental in the shortening of the treatment.

id The agency of the psychical apparatus that contains the instinctual drives.

interpretation The procedure of making the unconscious conscious.

object relations Refers to the distinctive organization of an individual's inner representational world, which stems from his or her interpersonal and developmental history and determines the mode of the individual's intrapsychic and interpersonal functioning. Furthermore, the term object relations, denotes the interplay between the external reality (i.e., interpersonal interactions with actual persons) and the patterns of inner mental representations (i.e., internalized object relations emerging from the interaction of the self with the external object). An inner mental representation is a mental image of the self or an object (self-representation or object representation), which constitute a complex enduring, cognitive structure within the ego, comprised of dynamic and effective elements. In psychoanalytic theory the term object refers to an actual person, or a thing, or an inner mental representation.

Oedipus complex Refers to the developmentally fundamental constellation of largely unconscious drives, defenses, thoughts, affects, and object relations relating to the child's wish to possess exclusively the parent of the opposite sex, which elicits feelings of rivalry, jealousy, and hostility toward the parent of the same sex and fears of severe retaliation (e.g., castration, loss of parental love) by the perceived rival parent.

Oedipal issues The derivatives of compromise formations (e.g., maladaptive coping strategies) and patterns of object relations (e.g., triangular interpersonal relationships) stemming from an unresolved Oedipus complex.

past–present link The process in which the therapist synthesizes the material brought by the patient in such a way as to help the patient understand the unconscious link between the past feelings for important people and the transference feelings for the therapist (therapist–parent or past-transference link), enabling the patient to utilize the insight to appraise personal behavior from a novel causative perspective, and to achieve a disconfirmation of the non-realistic inappropriate mode of viewing significant people in present life that entangles the patient in circular dysfunctional self-defeating patterns of relating and interacting.

psychodynamic The terms psychodynamic and dynamic are used interchangeably (See dynamic).

regression Denotes a return to an earlier, more developmentally primitive mode of mental functioning.

resistance Any kind of action, thought, or affect, which represents a manifestation of the patient's conscious or unconscious defensive functions and opposing forces, against treatment and the therapeutic progress in general, and the process of making the unconscious conscious in particular.

superego The agency of the psychical apparatus consisting of parental injunctions and inhibitions, as well as ideals and values.

therapeutic alliance The necessary condition for the progression of the psychodynamic work, consisting of an alliance between the patient's higher developmental ego processes and the therapist's facilitating analyzing ego, which alternately signifies the patient's capacity for empathic attunement and active involvement in a joint effort toward the overcoming of the patient's emotional conflicts, and further activates the patient's ability to work cooperatively and purposefully toward the accomplishment of the therapeutic goals.

transference A general, spontaneous, and universal phenomenon consisting of the process of unconscious displacement of feelings, impulses, defenses, thoughts, attitudes, expectations, and patterns of interaction derived from past interpersonal relations onto a person in the present. Transference is characterized by multiformity and ambivalence (i.e., co-existence of opposite feelings), and depending on its prevailing characteristics can be distinguished in positive (e.g., affectionate) and negative (e.g., hostile). The treatment situation fosters the development and expansion of transference, which is utilized explicitly, and helps in making feasible the resolution of conflict.

transference cure The phenomenon in which the patient may demonstrate an ephemeral symptomatic improvement in an unconscious effort to please the therapist as a result of a developing positive transference.

working through The repetitive process of assimilation and utilization of insight, aiming at the progressive elaboration and overcoming of the resistances that prevent the establishment of endurable adaptive structural, emotional, and behavioral changes.

Short-term anxiety-provoking psychotherapy (STAPP) is a radical, specialized, and research-based type of short-term dynamic psychotherapy (STDP) developed by professor of Psychiatry Peter Sifneos at the Harvard Medical School for the treatment of appropriately selected patients. This article presents the basic technical and theoretical principles of STAPP, as well as, a brief discussion on the research findings concerning treatment's effectiveness.

I. DESCRIPTION OF TREATMENT

STAPP is a kind of brief therapy based on psychoanalytic principles. The psychoanalytic principles include the analysis of transference, resistances, defense mechanisms, and unconscious processes, with the threefold aim of (a) investigating patient's psychodynamics, (b) facilitating the maturational process through the acquisition of insight (i.e., by making the unconscious conscious), and (c) working through the unconscious factors that hamper the accomplishment of the therapeutic goals.

Dr. Sifneos named his technique short-term anxiety-provoking psychotherapy (STAPP) to give emphasis to the basic technical component of his technique that consists of the constructive utilization of anxiety toward the obtainment of a higher level of psychical organization (i.e., increased capacity for anxiety, frustration and ambiguity tolerance, predominance of more adaptive ego defenses, better elaboration and reconciliation of inner conflict, improved affect regulation) and the attainment of more adaptive modes of coping. The STAPP therapist through the appropriate use of anxiety-provoking interventions (clarifications, confrontations, interpretations) is able to increase the emotional intensity during the session and to maintain patient's anxiety at an optimum level in which it can be utilized as a motivational force toward (a) the understanding of the nature of the nuclear emotional conflict (i.e., the specific emotional conflict—such as the Oedipal conflict—underlying the patient's psychological difficulties) and the recognition of the maladaptive defensive reactions used to deal with it, (b) the achievement of emotional reeducation, and (c) the acquisition of new learning and problem-solving techniques, in a brief period of time. The treatment can be successfully completed in 6 to 14, or at most 20 sessions.

The technique of STAPP consists of specific and intertwined components, which form four successive phases: (a) the patient–therapist encounter, (b) the early therapeutic phase, (c) the central therapeutic phase, and (d) the later therapeutic phase and the termination process.

A. The Patient–Therapist Encounter

The patient–therapist encounter includes two fundamental parameters: (a) the development of a facilitating therapeutic context, and (b) the psychiatric evaluation.

1. *The development of a facilitating therapeutic context*: In STAPP particular emphasis is placed on the development of a strong collaborative relationship between the patient and the therapist. The therapist is very active throughout the treatment. Through the judicious alternating of empathic, anxiety-provoking, supportive, and didactic interventions the therapist is able to establish rapport, to maximize the therapeutic alliance, and to utilize the positive transference to create a safe environment in which self-understanding, new learning, emotional reeducation, and change can take place. This involves the education of the patient about: (a) the importance of the establishment of a full, active, and joint cooperation for the specification, understanding and resolution of the patient's difficulties, (b) the requirements and the focal, goal-oriented, problem-solving, anxiety-provoking nature of the treatment and the ensuing resistances, and (c) the patient's psychodynamics concerning the therapeutic focus. The STAPP patient is considered capable of cooperating efficiently with the therapist focusing on the goal of resolving the emotional conflicts underlying the difficulties successfully over a short period of time, while the attainment of the mutually agreed therapeutic goals is viewed as a joint problem-solving venture.

2. *The psychiatric evaluation represents a global assessment of the patient's personality organization and psychopathology, which consists of five integral components:*

a. *The assessment of patient's presenting complaints*: The evaluator's primary task is to help the patient organize the presentation of chief complaints (i.e., by making the proper questions, and by emphasizing the importance of clarity, specificity, and immediacy for the successful outcome of their joint effort) and to assemble information concerning their onset, development, intensity, duration, sequence, timing, precipitating factors, as well as, other pertinent issues, to form a clear picture of the patient's problems. The presenting complaints of STAPP patients include interpersonal difficulties, specific, mild psychological symptoms, such as anxiety, depression, grief reaction, chronic procrastination, obsessive preoccupation, monosymptomatic phobia, as well as, physical symptoms of psychological origin (e.g., headaches).

b. *The systematic developmental history taking*: The evaluator through the judicious use of open-ended and forced-choice questions is able to obtain a clear and cohesive picture of the patient's emotional development on a longitudinal basis. The history taking follows a successive order from early childhood to the patient's current life. The evaluator investigates certain areas, such as the earliest memories, childhood relations with parents and other family members or key persons, the early family atmosphere and structure, the school history, interpersonal patterns and experiences during puberty, adolescent and early adulthood, the history of sexual development, and the medical history. The systematic history taking is crucial for (a) the identification of areas of conflict, maladaptive reactions, and repetitive difficulties, and (b) the understanding of the emotional problems in psychodynamic terms, which in turn, enables the evaluator to present to the patient a psychodynamic reformulation of his or her presenting complaints.

c. *The using of the appropriate selection criteria*: The evaluator uses five clear-cut criteria for the assessment of patient's ego strength, through which it can be established that the particular patient can be successfully treated in a short period of time. The STAPP candidate must have (a) the ability to circumscribe the presenting complaints (i.e., the patient, with the appropriate support and preparation by the therapist, must be able to make a compromise and to choose one out of a variety of problems for eventual resolution), (b) a history of at least one meaningful relationship (i.e., altruistic, give-and-take) during childhood, (c) the ability to interact flexibly with the evaluator (i.e., to be willing to consider the other person's view and be able to express positive or negative feelings openly and appropriately during the interview), (d) psychological sophistication (i.e., above-average intelligence and psychological mindedness), (e) a motivation for change, and not for only symptom relief. Motivation for change indicates the patient's willingness to work hard during the treatment assuming an active responsibility concerning the therapeutic task. According to Dr. Sifneos, the patient's motivation for change is probably the most important of all the selection criteria because it has a prognostic value concerning the therapeutic outcome. The evaluation of the patient's motivation for change is assessed on the basis of seven subcriteria: (a) a willingness to participate actively in the evaluation process, (b) honesty in self-reporting, (c) an ability to recognize that symptoms or difficulties are psychological in origin, (d) introspection and curiosity (i.e., self-inquisitiveness), (e) demonstration of openness to new ideas and ability to change, explore, and experiment, (f) realistic expectations of the results of psychotherapy, and (g) willingness to make a reasonable and tangible sacrifice (i.e., the patient is able to make a compromise concerning the appointment time or the fees of therapy) to achieve a successful outcome.

d. *The formulation of a specific focus for the psychotherapy*: The evaluator on the basis of the information offered by the patient constructs a dynamic formulation of the nuclear conflict underlying the emotional difficulties around which the treatment will revolve. The best therapeutic results can be achieved when the foci of the treatment relate to unresolved Oedipal conflicts, grief reactions, and certain difficulties relating to loss and separation issues. Concerning the unresolved Oedipal conflicts, which represent a common focus in STAPP, Dr. Sifneos proposed that there are three categories to be considered: in Category A the patient's attachment to the parent of the opposite sex is based only in the patient's fantasies of being the favorite child, while in reality there is no evidence of an actual encouragement by the parent; in Category B a more complex condition is presented that involves a reinforcement of the Oedipal attachment by the opposite-sex parent; and in Category C, which is the most difficult to resolve, Oedipal issues involve a complicated condition in which there is a combination of a strong reinforcement of the Oedipal attachment and an actual replacement of the parent of the same sex (i.e., as a result of divorce or death).

e. *The "therapeutic contract"*: The evaluator presents the therapeutic focus to the patient and expects an agreement about the resolution of the emotional conflicts underlying it. In addition the outcome criteria are formulated (these involve the specific therapeutic goals on which the success of the treatment will be evaluated). The mutual agreement concerning the therapeutic focus strengthens the patient's motivation to assume an active responsibility in expanding self-understanding and utilizing the insights to achieve the desirable emotional change. STAPP involves weekly, face-to-face, 45-min-long interviews, which take place at a mutually convenient specified time. The therapist informs the patient that the therapy will be brief but no specified number of sessions is set.

B. The Early Therapeutic Phase

In the early therapeutic phase, the patient's positive feelings for the therapist predominate. The most important technical principle involves the early utilization, and the vigorous and explicit analysis of patient's positive transference feelings. This procedure enables the therapist to establish the development of past–present links and to strengthen the therapeutic alliance.

C. The Central Therapeutic Phase

The central therapeutic phase represents the height of STAPP. The therapist uses repeated anxiety-provoking questions, confrontations, and clarifications in an effort to stay within the confines of the agreed on therapeutic focus, and to establish past–present links that constitute the fundamental technical aspect in STDP. A basic innovative unusual technical aspect of STAPP has to do with interpretations in the form of hypotheses prior to the analysis and clarification of resistances and defense mechanisms. The therapist utilizes the anxiety, which is elicited by the focal interpretive activity, to make explicit the emotional conflicts underlying the focus, as well as, to help to increase the patient's motivation for the acquisition of new more effective problem-solving strategies and for the resolution of old problems. Thus the patient is able to explicitly understand in which way his or her present mode of interpersonal relations is affected by the unconscious repetition of past interpersonal patterns. The patient's expanding awareness over hidden conflicts, fantasies, feelings, needs, and defensive operations, helps the patient to be able to exercise responsibility and control over them. Consequently the therapist by challenging the patient's neurotic entanglements and by providing empathic understanding and encouragement is able to support the patient's capacity to tolerate conflict and to explore new solutions to emotional conflicts. Through this procedure the therapist helps the patient to develop self-understanding and achieve emotional growth.

Even though it has been established through the careful evaluation process that a STAPP patient is sufficiently motivated to decisively achieve the therapeutic goals in a brief period of time, the emotional intensity of the anxiety-provoking focal interaction and the unpleasant realizations, may at times elicit strong resistance and evasive tactics. The therapist through careful note taking records certain verbatim statements of the patient, and at times of resistances is able to repeat the patient's exact words to present the facts which consolidate the patient's interpretations. Another technical tool, which is used for the resolution of the resistance-related impasse, is "recapitulation." This involves the presentation of a synopsis through which the therapist explicates how he or she arrived at the particular conclusion, based on the information that has been provided by the patient. Furthermore, the therapist by reviewing the recorded notes is able to make short-term predictions about the course and future development of treatment.

Patient's resistances and evasive tactics may include discussion of issues that are not relevant to the focus, or regression-like reactions (e.g., the patient may present him- or herself in a state of an apparently overwhelming anxiety) that actually represent a "pseudo-regression." It should be remembered that a STAPP patient has sufficient ego strength and anxiety tolerance. Under those circumstances the therapist's task is to explain to the patient the importance of focalization for the success of their specific agreed-on therapeutic goals and to reestablish the focus. The therapist through the active and systematic avoidance of early characterological issues (such as passivity, dependency, acting out, and manipulative tendencies), which may be used defensively, is able to prevent the emergence and the establishment of actual regressive modes of relatedness, and to accomplish the resolution of patient's nuclear conflicts within a short period of time.

As the therapeutic work is progressing the patient gradually internalizes the therapeutic processes. The demonstrated ability of the patient to utilize the assimilated knowledge to develop new attitudes and behavior patterns, as well as, to generate novel effective ways of dealing with past and present problems, is evidence of progress.

D. The Later Therapeutic Phase and the Termination Process

In the later therapeutic phase the therapist's task is to look out for tangible evidence of change, as well as, to make sure (e.g., through the exploration of specific examples brought by the patient) that the patient's improvement does not represent a fortuitous change, or a flight into health, or a transference cure that involve a superficial and transient symptomatic improvement without a clear-cut understanding of the psychodynamics concerning the emotional conflicts underlying the presenting difficulties. The acquisition of sufficient insight about the focal conflicts results in the establishment of tangible evidence of change and signals that the time has come for the termination process. Consequently the termination of the treatment takes place promptly when both patient and therapist agree that the basic therapeutic goals have been accomplished.

II. THEORETICAL BASES

STAPP is based on psychoanalytic theoretical premises consisting of six viewpoints: the topographical, the dynamic, the structural, the genetic, the economic, and the adaptive. A person's behavior or symptoms are interpreted as disguised representations of underlying unconscious processes (topographical viewpoint). The patient's difficulties or symptoms are viewed as an outcome of a conflict and a dynamic interaction in general, and a maladaptive compromise formation in particular (dynamic viewpoint), between: (a) the warded-off pleasure-seeking instinctual drives stemming from the id, (b) the restrictions by the reality-oriented ego that institutes defense mechanisms to maintain psychic equilibrium, (c) the prohibitions imposed by the superego (structural viewpoint). In addition, the patient's current conflict and maladaptive pattern of behavior are seen as parts of a continuum from infancy to adulthood (genetic or developmental viewpoint), consisting of two fundamental interrelated factors: (a) the nature of progressions, regressions, and fixations (economic viewpoint) in relation to the psychosexual development (oral, anal, Oedipal, latency, and genital stage), and (b) the quality of interpersonal relations and environmental influences and circumstances to which the individual adjust and to which he or she acts on (adaptive viewpoint).

Dr. Sifneos developed STAPP, while he was the director of the Psychiatry Clinic (from 1954 to 1968) at the Massachusetts General Hospital (a teaching hospital of Harvard Medical School). The prototype for STAPP was a 28-year-old male patient complaining of an acute onset of nervousness and phobias for all forms of transportation, who came to the clinic, requesting therapy to overcome his fears and be able to get married during the next 3 months. Dr. Sifneos decided to proceed with a therapeutic regimen that was successfully completed in eight sessions. A subsequent follow-up established that a lasting characterological dynamic change had taken place and patient's focal problems had been resolved. The successful results of this treatment encouraged Dr. Sifneos to look at the patient's character structure systematically and to develop criteria for selection of appropriate candidates to receive a similar psychotherapy. It was in this way that the evaluation process was developed, as well as, the anxiety-provoking technique. In sum the evaluation, techniques, and outcome, which were studied and improved over the years have made STAPP a systematic comprehensive and useful psychotherapeutic treatment.

III. EMPIRICAL STUDIES

STAPP represents the oldest type of brief therapy based on systematic research in the United States, and its effectiveness has been validated by several follow-up studies in United States and Europe. Between 1960 and 1987 Dr. Sifneos conducted extensive controlled research studies. These involved follow-up investigation of "experimental" patients who were immediately treated, and wait-list "control" patients who received treatment after a period of time. Impressive follow-up findings were presented, and studies in Europe showed similar and significant long-term follow-up results, as reported in 1985 by Dr. Ragnhild Husby in Norway.

An important educational and research tool in STAPP is the use of videotapes, which Dr. Sifneos called the "microscope of the psychiatrist." The videotape of the evaluation, the treatment, and the follow-up of patients who are willing to participate in research and to give an informed consent, makes the accomplishment of a detailed and systematic analysis of the therapeutic process and outcome, as well as, the accurate comparison of the pre- and the posttreatment condition feasible. The assessment of the efficacy of STAPP in follow-up studies is based on the evaluation of eight specific outcome criteria concerning patient's improvement in psychological or physical symptoms, interpersonal relations, self-understanding, the acquisition of new learning, the development of new effective problem-solving strategies, self-esteem, work or academic performance, and the development of useful new attitudes. According to follow-up outcome studies the STAPP patients after termination are able to efficiently utilize the new learning and problem-solving skills that they have assimilated during their treatment, through a process which Dr. Sifneos called "internalized dialogue," to solve new problems. This process, which facilitates continuous growth and maturation relates to the patient's ability to reconstruct the therapeutic dialogue with the therapist, to reproduce a therapeutic problem-solving effect for the resolution of new difficulties.

IV. SUMMARY

Short-term anxiety-provoking psychotherapy (STAPP) is an innovative, specialized, and systematically studied type of short-term dynamic psychotherapy (STDP), developed by Professor of Psychiatry Peter Sifneos at the Harvard Medical School. It is based on psychodynamic theoretical premises and constitutes the treatment of choice for the resolution of mild neurotic symptoms in appropriately selected patients. The basic technical principles include the establishment of a therapeutic focus, the use of anxiety-provoking interventions, the early utilization of positive transference feelings for the consolidation of a therapeutic alliance and the establishment of past–present links, the avoidance of characterological issues for the prevention of the development of regressive modes of relatedness, and the achievement of an early termination. STAPP is characterized by the establishment of clear-cut specific criteria for the selection of patients (i.e., circumscribed focus, history of a meaningful relationship, flexible interaction with the evaluator, psychological sophistication, and high motivation for change), and the evaluation of the therapeutic outcome (i.e., improvement in symptoms, in interpersonal relations, in self-understanding, in new learning and problem-solving strategies, in self-esteem, in work or academic performance, and in the development of new effective attitudes). The effectiveness of STAPP has been documented by extensive research studies in the United States and Europe.

Acknowledgments

The author gratefully thanks Dr. Peter Sifneos for reviewing the manuscript and offering his valuable comments and advice.

See Also the Following Articles

Brief Therapy ■ Confrontation ■ Interpretation ■ Object-Relations Psychotherapy ■ Oedipus Complex ■ Resistance ■ Supportive-Expressive Dynamic Psychotherapy ■ Working Alliance ■ Working Through

Further Reading

Brenner, C. (1973). *An elementary textbook of psychoanalysis.* New York: International Universities Press.

Glover, E. (1953). *The technique of psychoanalysis.* New York: International Universities Press.

Husby, R., et al. (1985). Short-term dynamic psychotherapy. *Psychotherapy and Psychosomatics, 43,* 1–32.

Langs, R. (Ed.). (1981). *Classics in psychoanalytic technique.* New York: Jason Aronson.

Sifneos, P. E. (1968). Learning to solve emotional problems: A controlled study of short-term anxiety-provoking psychotherapy. In R. Porter (Ed.), *The role of learning in psychotherapy* (pp. 87–96) Boston: Little, Brown.

Sifneos, P. E. (1972). *Short-term psychotherapy and emotional crisis.* Cambridge, MA: Harvard University Press.

Sifneos, P. E. (1984). The current status of individual short-term dynamic psychotherapy and its future: An overview. *American Journal of Psychotherapy, 38*(4), 472–483.

Sifneos, P. E. (1987). *Short-term dynamic psychotherapy. Evaluation and technique.* New York: Plenum Medical Book Company.

Sifneos, P. E. (1992). *Short-term anxiety-provoking psychotherapy. A treatment manual.* New York: Basic Books.

Sifneos, P. E., Apfel, R. J., Bassuk, E., Fishman, G., & Gill, A. (1980). Ongoing outcome research on short-term dynamic psychotherapy. *Psychotherapy and Psychosomatics, 33,* 233–241.

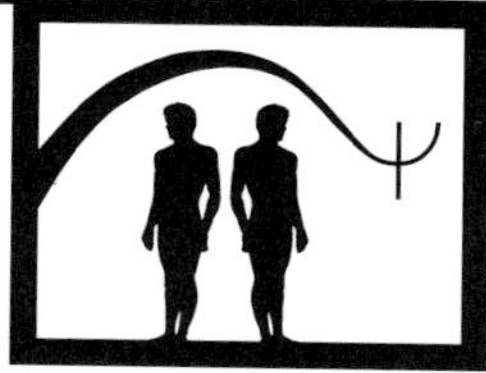

Single-Case Methods and Evaluation

Graham Turpin
University of Sheffield

GLOSSARY

external validity Concerns the extent to which experimenters can generalize their findings from one particular set of observations (e.g., individual clients, settings, therapists) to another.

idiographic The study of the individual. Common themes are identified by looking for similarities that emerge across individual profiles.

internal validity Concerns the extent to which observations of change can be interpreted as direct evidence that an intervention had a specific effect on the clinical outcome.

nomeothetic The study of groups of individuals. A common theme is extracted from the collective behavior of the group. This is usually based on the average of the group's responses.

Single-case methods can be defined with respect to psychotherapy, as a collection of techniques for evaluating the efficacy of a specific intervention(s) within a single clinical case or a series of cases. This article overviews the range of approaches and applications of these methods to psychotherapy research and practice. In particular, a set of principles underlying the implementation of the single case design within clinical practice is described.

I. APPROACHES AND METHODS

The fundamental questions within psychotherapy research about which treatments are the most effective or what works for whom are frequently mirrored in the mind of the clinician. Am I using the right approach with this client, are they really showing signs of improvement, should I be adopting a different approach? These questions and doubts are answered through the experience and judgments that clinicians make when reflecting on their practice either alone or when in supervision with other therapists. Nevertheless the search for evidence that therapy has been effective has always been part of the process of psychotherapy.

How can we reliably and objectively demonstrate clinical change within the individual? On a day-to-day basis, effectiveness of our interventions are demonstrated via our own perceptions of what seems to work; the satisfaction of the client that may be expressed verbally in terms of compliments or complaints; behaviorally by gifts, nonattendance, and the unplanned discontinuation of therapy; by comments from carers and relatives; or by peer evaluations during the process of "supervision" or clinical audit. However, do these sources of information really constitute evidence of effectiveness? Even if clinical change is observed, how confident are we that it was our own specific intervention, as opposed to a myriad of other influences ranging from the client's family through to other possible interventions of the multidisciplinary team, that brought about the real change? Single-case experimental designs have been developed in an attempt to provide proof of effectiveness within the individual. Accordingly, it can be argued that these techniques should provide therapists with an objective means of demonstrating the efficacy of their interventions. As such, they represent one approach to evidence-based practice that the psychotherapists might exploit to demonstrate their own effectiveness to a sometimes skeptical world.

Originally, evidence was presented in the form of what has become known as a "case study," which usually included an extensive account of the client including background history and problems, what happened within therapy frequently based on a session-by-session account, and also the therapist's attempts to understand and account for the process of therapy as described. Indeed, the case study became the major vehicle for documenting the nature of psychotherapy and communicating advances in the understanding of therapy to other practitioners. This approach is typified particularly within writings on psychoanalysis and the classical case studies published by Sigmund Freud.

Although case studies continue to be written, particularly during the course of training psychotherapists, today they are no longer considered as providing sufficient evidence that a particular therapy has been effective. Essentially they have been superceded by what are considered as more scientifically rigorous methods. Generally contemporary clinical research is based around the study of large samples of individuals who have been exposed to various different therapeutic approaches or regimes. So-called robust research methods have been developed relying on double blind procedures and randomized control trials to answer and further tease apart the questions of psychotherapy efficacy. Nevertheless there are circumstances when it is still appropriate to ask questions of effectiveness within a single client by a single therapist. This might arise in the course of developing an innovative therapeutic technique, treating a rare condition, or even as a means for therapists to satisfy themselves and others that their therapy has been effective. The purpose of this article is to describe methods that have been developed for systematically evaluating clinical evidence within the single client.

Single-case methods represent a wide range of approaches that have been used extensively across many different areas of study. The intensive study of the individual, as opposed to the usual nomeothetic approach of studying groups of individuals, can be readily identified across a range of different disciplines. The clinical case study is widely used within medicine and other clinical disciplines, but individually focused research strategies are also commonplace within educational research, experimental psychology, and sociology. Moreover, although it is common within psychology as a discipline to criticize single-case idiographic approaches on the grounds that they fail to generalize to groups of individuals, many basic laws of behavior within psychology have arisen by the careful and intensive study of just a few selected and usually well-trained individuals. With respect to psychotherapy, single-case methods can be defined as a collection of techniques for evaluating efficacy of a specific intervention(s) within a single clinical case or a series of cases.

The range of applications of single-case approaches is also reflected in a diversity of methods. Even the use of the term "case study" extends from anecdotal reports of therapy published in books through to the publication of brief clinical reports in journals, and formal presentations of case studies. The later are frequently used as assessments of assumed clinical competence within many forms of psychotherapy training. However, in 1981, Alan Kazdin in a now-classical journal article criticized the traditional clinical case study for being biased and unscientific. The subsequent demise of the clinical case study has given way to a range of more scientifically focused techniques, which are commonly described as "single-case experimental designs." These approaches commonly involve the comparison of data derived from a baseline period prior to when no intervention has been offered, with data obtained from an intervention period. The use of a follow-up assessment some months or years following the treatment is also frequently undertaken. These approaches are often termed AB designs, the letters referring, rather confusingly, to baseline (A) and intervention (B), respectively. Because they usually involve the collection of large amounts of data collected daily over time, they are also referred to as "time series" designs. The comparison between baseline and treatment is also frequently repeated either giving rise to "ABAB" designs or the use of several different measures concurrently that are termed "multiple baseline or phase designs." Occasionally, these designs will be repeated across a small series of individuals and this approach is called "a small *N* design."

In addition to the quantitative experimental approaches described earlier, the case study has also been developed to yield a range of qualitative methods that are commonly used within sociology. Indeed, observational case studies of particular services or institutions have resulted in dramatic insights and changes in attitudes. A classic example is Erving Goffman's ethnographic study of institutional life conducted in the 1950s and 1960s. Although qualitative approaches are not the main focus of this entry, their potential for understanding therapeutic processes are becoming increasingly recognized by psychotherapy researchers.

II. CLINICAL RESEARCH AND PRACTITIONER APPLICATIONS

Single-case experimental designs have a wide range of applications, which ought to prove useful to both researchers and practitioners. From a clinical research perspective, not every piece of clinical work will be treated as a potential piece of psychotherapy outcome research. Similarly, most practitioners will not be participating in psychotherapy outcome research. As a means of bridging this gap whereby practitioners become more involved in psychotherapy research, it could be argued that evaluating efficacy within a single clinical case is the bottom line as regards "evidence-based medicine." Indeed, it maybe that single-case methods are about to experience a renaissance as the requirements of demonstrating both the evidence base and clinical effectiveness for specific psychotherapy practices becomes more prevalent due to the influence of the "managed care" movement. David and Robin Morgan have recently made such an argument within an article in the *American Psychologist*.

A. Clinical Research Applications

There are several situations when therapists have a particular reason for evaluating their own work and communicating its outcome within the public domain. The most common reason for employing single-case designs is when the therapist is engaged in an innovative approach to therapy and wishes to disseminate through scientific publication the results of this new treatment approach. Single cases have provided the starting points for many commonly used therapeutic techniques that are widely employed today. For example, the cognitive treatment of panic disorder owes its origins to a series of single cases on the use of rebreathing and reattribution techniques published by David Clark and his colleagues some 20 years ago. Similarly, the cognitive therapy of psychotic symptoms was first published in 1994 by Paul Chadwick and Max Birchwood as a single-case series. Although these publications by themselves do not meet the full rigors of evidence-based medicine they have provided useful starting points for more systematic approaches to therapy. Indeed, in the case of both these examples, evidence from single-case studies has now been superseded by the findings from randomly controlled trials. Within psychotherapy outcome research, therefore, the single case plays a pivotal position as providing a starting point for the development of new therapies. It is also seen as a means by which regular practitioners may involve themselves in research because the demands of single-case methods tend to be less resource hungry than psychotherapy group evaluations.

Another reason for employing single cases includes the study of rare clinical conditions whereby the limited availability of clients precludes a group evaluation approach, especially in the first instance. Examples of this particular strategy include the evaluation of behavioral treatments of tic disorders and the in-depth investigation of neuropsychological patients with specific and unique head injuries. Single cases can also provide important illustrative material particularly about the practical implementation of new treatment approaches. Such accounts are frequently to be found in the appendices of published studies, which have relied on more traditional group evaluative approaches to outcome research. One particularly, important area for the use of such case material is when therapy is ineffective. Single-case approaches have much to offer the study of treatment-resistant cases. However, the degree to which unsuccessful cases are published and discussed tends to be limited by the implicit bias of scientific journals only to publish positive results. This form of bias may seriously distort the perceived efficacy of treatments, which have been evaluated using single-case approaches. It is usual, therefore, that only positive accounts of new treatment strategies are published at the expense of negative findings. A typical example of this involves the use of "ear plugs" to control auditory hallucinations in psychosis whereby singular and enthusiastically published positive results have tended to give way to later publications of case series that have been more skeptical and negative.

B. Practitioner Applications

The adoption of a single-case approach to clinical work may also have some benefits for clinical practice that are completely independent of research. For example, these approaches can be employed to demonstrate individual effectiveness of a particular approach to skeptical colleagues or managers. Within the context of cognitive behavioral work, using single-case approaches for data collection facilitates a collaborative relationship between therapist and client that can enhance both the client's motivation and "self efficacy." The approach enables client and therapist to sit down together to identify agreed treatment goals, decide on how individual outcomes should be assessed, and how the impact of therapy can be monitored. It is acknowledged, however, that such an open and goal-directed approach to treatment would not be consistent or appropriate for all forms of psychotherapy.

The demonstration of clinical change using objective measures can be particularly important when working indirectly with care staff. Many researchers have demonstrated that staff's subjective perception of clinical change is frequently biased and may not match more objective change measures, especially for chronic or irregular problems. It has been suggested that this might be due to "recency or memory effects," whereby care staffs' perceptions are determined by recent events that then makes it difficult for them to track accurately change over an extended period of time. The use a single-case approach allows a more objective assessment to take place. This can be particularly useful in motivating and informing staff that their efforts do yield positive effects particularly with individuals with challenging and chronic or even deteriorating problems who have previously been resistant to change.

Social work educators have argued that the use of evidence-based techniques such as single-case methods might also enhance the overall effectiveness of practitioners. They have suggested that training in single-case methods enhances clinical skills associated with assessment, formulation, and the implementation of therapy. If this were the case, the routine use of single-case approaches would not only provide the evidence of therapy efficacy but would also lead to enhanced effectiveness. To test these ideas effectiveness of various intervention programs have been compared when therapists have been differentially trained in and encouraged to use single-case approaches. Preliminary evidence from this research would suggest that training in these techniques does enhance therapy and that clients also may have a preference and greater satisfaction for working with a practitioner trained in single-case methods.

Finally, it is commonly believed that single-case methods can only be used by therapists working in either a behavioral or cognitive-behavioral framework. Although, it is undoubtedly the case that many examples of single-case work are published within behaviorally oriented journals, this doesn't have to be the case. Single cases have been studied using a wide variety of different therapeutic frameworks. What is required, however, are that certain goals of therapy can be established, that they are measurable in some way, and that there is a framework (e.g., formulation) that links the therapeutic model to intervention, together with some hypotheses relating to clinical change. The basic principles underlying single-case work will be further elaborated in the next section.

III. BASIC PRINCIPLES OF SINGLE-CASE DESIGN

Single-case experimental designs rely on several widely recognised and important principles, which have been widely discussed in classic texts such as David Barlow's and Michael Hersen's book published in 1984. These usually include: (a) repeated measurement, (b) stable baselines, (c) single and well-specified treatments, (d) reversibility, and (e) generalizability. To understand implementation of single-case designs, it is essential to appreciate the relevance of these principles. Moreover, it is these characteristics that distinguish the experimental single case from the ordinary case study. If a clinical study is unable to address these principles, it is likely that it will be classified as a case study.

Before expanding on the relevance of the earlier principles it is important to understand what a single-case design is attempting to accomplish. As emphasized by Alan Kazdin and others, the traditional case study is flawed because it relies on post hoc explanations that can be subject to different sources of bias and alternative interpretations. The purpose of single-case design is to identify these potential sources of bias, and control for their influence, and in so doing, to eliminate them as potential alternative explanations for the observed pattern of results that constitutes the case study.

What are the potential sources of confounding that might obscure the interpretation that a particular intervention has had a specific effect within a client on a particular outcome? For example, if during the course of therapy a client's relationship breaks down or a colleague alters the level of prescribed medication, to what extent is any clinical change a function of the therapy provided, the relationship difficulty experienced by the client, the change in medication or a combination of all three? Although some might argue that to attempt to disentangle these factors may be totally artificial, the single-case design attempts to place on the case study certain limits or boundaries that might distinguish or minimize the impact of these confounding variables.

A. Threats to the Validity of a Case Study

One of the foundations of experimental design in psychology is the identification of confounding variables that need to be controlled to rule out alternative accounts of a study designed to test particular hypotheses. These sources of confounding are frequently referred to as threats to internal and external validity. Internal validity concerns the extent to which the findings can be interpreted in support of the proposition that an intervention had a specific effect on the clinical outcome. A series of possible scenarios exist that if present would severely compromise the study and limit the validity of the conclusions drawn. These circumstances include the following:

- *History*: Here extraneous concurrent events (e.g., relationship break-up, change in medication) may happen alongside the clinical intervention studied. These events may either be known or unknown to the experimenter.
- *Maturation*: This refers to a change process, which may be endogenous to the client and independent of the applied experimental intervention or treatment. For example, neuropsychologists and physiotherapists frequently attempt early interventions aimed at facilitating recovery from brain injuries such as a stroke or a closed head injury. However, if left "untreated," most individuals with head injuries show a degree of spontaneous recovery in functioning following the injury. Any measurement of clinical change must, therefore, be interpreted against a moving baseline of endogenous change associated with recovery.
- *Testing (reactivity)*: The exposure of a client to the assessment process itself is not a neutral act, particularly when structured forms of assessment such as questionnaires or self-monitoring diaries are employed. The very task of inviting the client to self-assess requires a possible shift in self-awareness and focusing on possible new information. The nature of questionnaires might seek to clarify a client's understanding or attribution of events and by doing so, challenge their existing attributions and explanations. Thus, the very act of participation and assessment within a case study may bring about therapeutic change. Indeed, such changes are frequently observed during the baseline phase prior to the introduction of any formal intervention.
- *Instrumentation (reliability)*: Nearly every assessment tool, which a clinician will employ, will have associated with it some error of measurement, and it is, therefore, important that these incidental changes in measures across time are not misinterpreted as specific treatment effects.

Other sources of internal confounding include regression to the mean, multiple intervention problems, and instability.

Threats to external validity have also been identified as important sources of confounding that require experimental control. These concern the extent to which experimenters can generalize their findings from one particular set of observations to another. With respect to case studies, generalization refers to the degree to which a finding observed within a single individual can be extended to other individuals and in other settings. Essentially, two sources of bias that might limit generalizability may be identified:

- *Selected individuals/samples*: The degree to which individuals or samples are specifically identified will limit the generalizability of the findings. The more heterogeneous the sample from which individual cases are drawn, the more likely that the results will generalize across individuals. In the case of psychotherapy, the importance of generalizing across variables such as social class, education, gender, and ethnicity will be important for establishing the widespread applicability or otherwise of psychotherapeutic approaches throughout across service provision.
- *Biased interventions/settings*: The setting or the specific manner in which an intervention is delivered might affect the specific outcome within a particular individual. For case studies, the issue here is one of clinical replication. Are results obtained within specialized research clinics by presumably highly trained therapists, generalizable to practitioners attempting to replicate similar interventions within routine clinical practice?

These threats to validity need to be carefully considered by researchers wishing to employ single-case designs. Only by being aware of these threats, can the researcher consider and exclude common alternative explanations regarding the relationship between intervention and outcome. The use of a traditional case study exposes the researcher to a variety of interpretative biases that, at best, have to be accounted for when interpreting the results and, at worst, may be confounded with specific treatment effects leading to misleading conclusions. To compensate for these biases, "experimental" case study designs have been evolved that attempt to control for or minimize these threats to internal validity. For example, a common control for historical concurrent extraneous events is to repeat or replicate the treatment effect. If a specific treatment-outcome relationship can be observed, and this result is repeated a number of times on different occasions, it is unlikely that some other event unrelated to the intervention will have occurred successively to account for this particular repeating pattern of results. The more consistent the replication of the finding, the less likely it is that some other concurrent event has occurred alongside the specific intervention. Traditionally, group evaluation designs address historical threats to validity by examining replication of findings over a sample of different individuals. For single-case research, the replication is over different occasions within the same individual. Another example of designing against threats to validity concerns maturational effects. As discussed earlier, such endogenous changes may take the form of recovery functions. They may be distinguished experimentally from intervention effects, by observing within an individual the form of the recovery function under baseline conditions in the absence of an intervention, and comparing it following the introduction of the intervention. A specific treatment effect would predict a change in the gradient of any preexisting recovery function.

B. Design Principles

The following principles have been evolved for single-case designs to control for threats to validity and include repeated measurement, stable baselines, single well-specified treatments, reversibility, and generalizability. To understand the rationales underlying these principles, it needs to be acknowledged that their origins extend back to experimental studies of animal learning conducted largely in the middle of the previous century. Essentially, psychologists interested in animal learning conducted single-subject/animal experiments to investigate the effects of changes in various environmental contingencies on patterns of animal behavior. Hence, the knowledge base of animal learning derives very much from single-case experimental studies, together with replications, and has relied predominantly on the visual analysis of the graphical displays of results. This is in marked contrast to group nomeothetic approaches, used elsewhere within psychology, and the reliance on statistical testing.

It is these basic principles that have been extended to single-case experimental designs. An obvious reason for this extension was the application of learning theory in the form of applied behavioral analysis to a whole range of human problems, but particularly within the fields of learning disabilities and special education within the United States. This resulted in learning theory paradigms and methodologies being transferred into the clinical domain. It has to be emphasized, however, that the single-case approaches that these methods have inspired, are frequently used to evaluate interventions that are no longer associated with learning theory. In these circumstances, it is possible that rationales developed on the basis of learning theory may no longer apply. An example, which we will return to, is the use of either withdrawal or reversal techniques to demonstrate the specificity of an intervention. From a learning theory perspective, strong evidence of an environmental effect can be demonstrated if the contingencies can be manipulated to obtain withdrawal effects or reversals in the pattern of responding observed. Hence, a particular environmental event (e.g., social praise) could be shown to reinforce particular desirable behaviors (e.g., social interaction) in a young person with learning disabilities, if the behaviors increase when the praise is contingently offered but remains constant or decrease when the praise is withheld. Observation of a direct and repeated effect between the behaviors and the environmental effects provides evidence that the contingencies are reinforcing the behavior. However, this is based on certain learning theory assumptions concerning both the short-term and reversible nature of environmental contingencies. As we discuss later, these assumptions do not apply to the vast majority of interventions that are employed within psychotherapy. The evidence, therefore, that can be gathered from reversal or withdrawal designs is limited only to situations whereby the intervention will have short-term and reversible effects, and if these assumptions cannot be made, then the utility of reversal designs as a principle underlying single case methodology is markedly curtailed.

Bearing in mind the origins and possible limitations of the design principles underlying single case designs, each principle will now be briefly reviewed.

1. Repeated Measurement

Perhaps the most important distinguishing feature between a case study and a single-case experimental study is the number of observations or data points that have been obtained. A basic aim of an experimental study is to demonstrate within each individual intra-subject change using repeated measures. It is hypothesised that when comparing within an individual measures obtained prior to treatment with those during and following treatment, some therapeutic effect will be observed. The greater number of repeated measures obtained, and the greater the consistency of change across these measures, the more confidence that an effect has taken place. This is analogous to a group design comparing say therapeutic and placebo groups whereby the repeated measures are obtained across the different individuals constituting the groups, as opposed to the single case whereby the repeated measures are derived from a single individual but at many different points in time.

To achieve repeated observations, the measures used have to be easily replicable. This means that they can easily be repeatedly administered, reliable, and relatively free of error or bias. This may discount many traditional forms of psychotherapy outcome evaluation that use extensive psychometric questionnaires or interviews designed only to be used on a single or infrequent sessional basis. Instead, daily measures derived from structured self-report diaries or staff observational schedules are frequently employed. Hence, the case study that includes only a single psychometric measure of pre- and postintervention change should not be considered as a single-case design. However, inclusion of additional repeated daily diary measures would allow such an evaluation to be made. The question arises, therefore, as to what the minimum number of repeated measures has to be obtained? The strict minimum according to Barlow and Hersen is probably at least three baseline and three intervention observations per single measure.

2. Stable Baselines

The basic premise for using repeated measures is that clinical change will be self-evident following the introduction of some therapeutic intervention. The degree to which change is discernible depends both on the magnitude of the therapeutic impact and also on the nature of the preintervention baseline. The greatest confidence about therapeutic impact can only be made when a stable baseline has been obtained. If the baseline is unstable (i.e., it displays an existing trend or slope, cyclical variability or excessive variability or noise), the confidence of detecting therapeutic change is much reduced. It is frequently suggested that baselines should be collected until they demonstrate stability. However, this may not be practical within the psychotherapeutic situation and a frequent question posed is what is the minimum length of baseline acceptable? A review of the size of baselines used in 881 studies published in the *Journal of Applied Behavior Analysis* ranged between 3 and 10 observations. In practice, it is likely that baselines will be obtained perhaps within the second and third sessions as part of an overall assessment process. If derived from daily ratings, it is feasible to collect baseline data ranging from 7 to 20 or so observations across a period of a few weeks that ought to be more than sufficient, although this will depend ultimately on the type of analysis to be employed.

3. Treatments Are Well Specified and Documented

In order to assess the effects of an intervention, it is important that essentially only a single treatment is applied at any one time and that its nature can be specified. Many therapists have difficulties with this limitation because it forces them to assess and formulate the case and prescribe a particular therapeutic approach in advance. However, this does not mean that case reformulation and changes in therapy cannot occur; they need to be, if possible anticipated, and incorporated into the design. Another issue of contention is exactly how is "a single intervention" defined? Again this is the responsibility of the therapist and depends largely on why the case is being evaluated in the first place. Therapists frequently argue that they plan to use a combination of different treatment strategies or techniques. If the aim of the evaluation is to assess the overall impact of this package of strategies, then the package, if it can be defined, becomes synonymous with a "single treatment." Another problem frequently encountered is the presence of other therapeutic work such as medication or other inputs from a multidisciplinary team. Two possible approaches to this common problem are available: to negotiate keeping external therapeutic inputs constant (i.e., no planned changes in medication) or directly involving the other therapists in the design and attempting to evaluate the comparative effectiveness of these other approaches with respect to the psychotherapeutic intervention.

4. Designing against Threats to Validity: Replications, Reversibility, and Withdrawals

A myraid of single-case designs have evolved in an attempt by clinical researchers to rule out the various threats to internal validity that have been previously described. Usually these designs involve complex comparisons of different phases of intervention and baseline manipulated across behaviors, settings, and participants. The logic of many of these designs also originates from applied behavior analysis and the application of fundamental learning theory assumptions. As such it is debatable how relevant this complex myriad

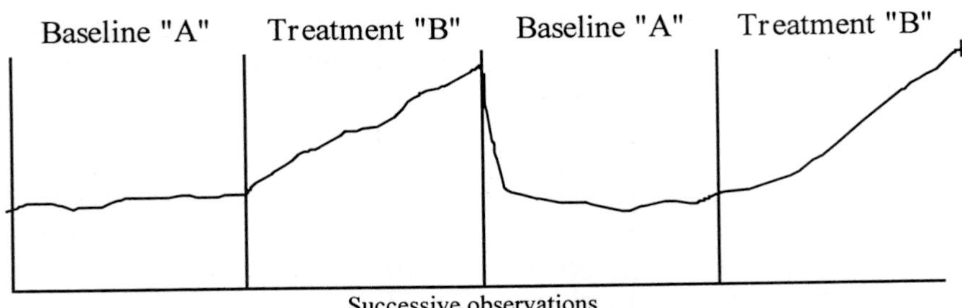

FIGURE 1 Withdrawal and reversal designs. The ideal single case design relies on intrasubject replication and is exemplified by the ABAB withdrawal design. The replication of a treatment effect (i.e., increasing slope) on both occasions that the treatment ("B") is introduced, and the return to baseline on the second baseline occasion ("A"), are seen as strong evidence that the original treatment effect is real and not spurious.

of designs is for psychotherapeutic applications? Accordingly we have avoided describing these different designs in any great detailed. Several of the cited references in Further Reading specify different designs, their rationales, and uses. Instead, we concentrate on the most influential design feature, which surrounds the questions of replication.

It is argued that greater confidence in the impact of treatment on intrasubject change can be demonstrated if the effects can be replicated within repeated measures, across different phases of a design, and that the effect of the intervention on the measures can be directly manipulated through either reversals or withdrawals. Replication is largely a means to protect against either historical or maturational threats to internal validity. Hence, if the results from the simplest AB design (baseline vs. treatment) can be replicated, then it less likely that some extraneous event can account for the original but replicated change from baseline to treatment. This is in essence the logic of ABAB design (see Figure 1), which is frequently advocated as a standard for experimental single cases. However, within the context of many psychological therapies such designs have important limitations. Essentially, their rationale depends on reversible treatment effects analogous to contingency manipulations employed within applied behavioral analysis. Fortunately, at least for the client, many interventions are considered as long lasting and hopefully resistant to reversal, relying on dynamic intrapersonal changes (e.g., cognitive therapy will promote schema changes). It is, therefore, neither theoretically likely nor ethically desirable that a positive treatment effect can be reversed. Hence, ABAB or ABA designs have their limitations because replication due to withdrawal of treatment and return to baseline may not actually be predicted due to the irreversible nature of the intervention employed.

Non-reversible treatments that are usually identified include psychoeducational approaches, skills-based therapies, schema-directed therapies, altered therapeutic environments, staff attitudes and training, and surgical or long-term pharmacological interventions. Nevertheless, introduction of a brief second baseline can be useful to assess and demonstrate the permanence or otherwise of therapeutic change. This can be practically incorporated into "therapeutic holidays," whereby clients are encouraged to assess progress by putting aside what has recently been learned or suspending temporarily homework exercises or self-coping techniques. Ethically this is defensible on the principle of demonstrating efficacy to the client of an intensive therapeutic regime. It is also likely, that a second baseline will also be introduced at the termination of treatment in the form of a follow-up to specifically assess the permanence and stability of change. If there has been deterioration in therapeutic improvement, this might argue for the introduction of "booster sessions": such a protocol would result in baseline and treatment phases not that indistinct from a classic ABAB design. A frequent rejoinder to those that criticize the ethics of single-case designs is that it might be considered a greater ethical problem to conduct psychotherapy in the absence of evaluation per se rather than to attempt evaluation through some manipulation of the therapy itself.

5. Evaluation and Interpretation

It is essential for a single-case design that the therapist has engaged in some critical and systematic evaluation of the data. There have been two competing approaches within single-case research: visual inspection and statistical analysis. Traditionally, single-case data have been analyzed visually using graphical presentation, sometimes presented alongside some simple descriptive statistics such as mean or medians. This tradition derives very much from applied behavior analysis and emphasizes the utility of complex designs that require phase changes and demonstrate intrasubject replication via reversals and withdrawals of treatment components relative to baseline. However, as the scope for replication based around the assumption of reversible treatments becomes less applicable, some authors have argued for a more systematic approach to evaluation using statistical methods. There has also been a concern that visual inspection might be biased toward "Type one statistical errors" where significant change is expected and inferred but not actually substantiated, and at the same time, biased away from "Type two statistical errors" whereby the inherent variability within single-case data prevents the easy detection of reliable change. Unfortunately, due to a unique statistical feature of single-subject data termed serial dependency, the assumptions underlying most of the commonly used statistical tests are violated and hence, this severely limits their application. Accordingly, application of statistical models of single-case data is a specialized area of evaluation and one that requires serious consideration by the single-case researcher.

Finally, even if change could be reliably inferred between treatment phases and baseline conditions, the meaning of these changes requires interpretation. Due to the design limitations of a single case and threats to both internal and external validity, it is essential that observed differences are not simply considered as treatment effects. The limitations of single-case designs are such that it is essential that the clinical researcher is able to identify and where possible rule out alternative interpretations or threats to validity. It is very unlikely that the rigor of the design will have already excluded these possibilities as maybe the case when employing double-blind, randomized control designs within group comparison studies of psychotherapy outcome.

6. *Generalizability*

A common misconception about single-case designs is that they involve only a single subject. To derive general explanations or laws of behavior change, effects should be generalizable. The converse of this is that these laws ought to account for known sources of variability, and this is often obscured in group designs. Although a single N=1 design has limited generalizability, a series of N=1 designs should identify sources of variability and lead to greater generalizability. Different types of generalizability include across individual clients or clients with similar attributes, across different therapists, and across different settings or situations. The issue of generalizability is resolved, therefore, through replication across different clients, therapists, and settings. Hence, N=1 studies lead on to N=1 series, small N designs with homogenous subjects and well-controlled conditions. Indeed recent exponents of single-case methods have also described meta-analysis procedures analogous to those used in group outcome studies with which to evaluate and summarize the results from a series of individual studies. Finally, it is also important to ensure that single-case research is not only generalizable but also clinically replicable within ordinary clinical settings.

IV. SUMMARY

We have attempted to review the general principles underlying single-case design and to suggest that they might play a role in helping to establish both the efficacy and effectiveness of psychotherapeutic interventions. Such a methodology might assist psychotherapists to address the combined agenda established by the influential "evidence-based medicine" and "managed care" movements and in doing so, encourage practicing clinicians to evaluate their clinical work and engage in clinical research. However, it should be recognized that much of the work published using single-case methods has derived from more experimentally based psychotherapies and that many of the fundamental principles underlying this approach might be antithetical to some psychotherapies, especially those that are more dynamically oriented. Notwithstanding these potential obstacles to the implementation of single-case approaches, I should like to invite the interested therapist to explore how these approaches might be integrated with their own therapeutic work. To achieve this, it will be important to identify clear clinical formulations, which link to therapeutic strategies. These strategies need to identify various therapeutic goals that can then be assessed as clinical outcomes and reliably and repeatedly measured. In addition, the clinician will also need to be disciplined so as to follow a predetermined therapeutic strategy but also to be sufficiently flexible so as to engage the client and be ready to reformulate and redirect the therapy, as the therapeutic process unfolds.

See Also the Following Articles

Efficacy ■ Outcome Measures ■ Research in Psychotherapy ■ Single-Session Therapy ■ Solution-Focused Brief Therapy ■ Termination

Further Reading

Barlow, D. H., & Hersen, M. (1984). *Single case experimental designs: Strategies for studying behavior change* (2nd ed.). New York: Pergamon.

Bloom, M., Fischer, J., & Orme, J. G. (1999). *Evaluating practice: Guidelines for the accountable professional* (3rd ed.). Boston: Allyn and Bacon.

Franklin, R. D., Allison, D. B. & Gorman, B. S. (1996). *Design and analysis of single case research.* Mahwah, NJ: Lawrence Erlbaum.

Hillard, R. B. (1993). Single case methodology in psychotherapy process and outcome research. *Journal of Consulting and Clinical Psychology, 61,* 373–380.

Kazdin, A. E. (1981). Drawing valid inferences from case studies. *Journal of Consulting and Clinical Psychology, 49,* 183–192.

Kratochwill, T. R., & Levin, J. R. (1992). *Single case research design and analysis: New directions for psychology and education.* Mahwah, NJ: Lawrence Erlbaum.

Long, C. G., & Hollin C. R. (1995). Single case design: A critique of methodology and analysis of recent trends. *Clinical Psychology and Psychotherapy, 2,* 177–191.

Morgan, D. L., & Morgan, R. K. (2001). Single-participant research design: Bringing science to managed care. *American Psychologist, 56,* 119–127.

Turpin, G. (2001). Single case methodology and psychotherapy evaluation: From research to practice. In C. Mace, S. Moorey, & B. Roberts (Eds.), *Evidence in psychological therapies: A critical guide for practitioners.* (pp. 91–113). East Sussex: Brunner-Routledge.

Yin, R. K. (1994). *Case study research: Design and methods.* Beverly Hills, CA: Sage.

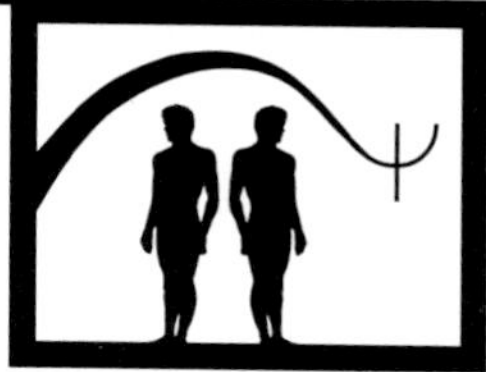

Single-Session Therapy

Brett N. Steenbarger
SUNY Upstate Medical University

GLOSSARY

brief therapy Psychotherapy, typically of short duration, in which efficiency in achieving change is an explicit aim. Sometimes referred to as time-effective or short-term therapy.

Ericksonian therapy Psychotherapy, typically brief, derived from the work of Milton Erickson. It seeks to maximize therapist influence through the strategic use of language, the accessing of altered states of mind via hypnosis, and the use of directed tasks.

single-session therapy A form of brief therapy in which there is a planned attempt to address the presenting concerns of clients within a single visit. Often makes use of techniques derived from Ericksonian, strategic, and solution-focused therapies.

solution-focused therapy Form of brief therapy that seeks to identify and/or construct exceptions to client problem patterns and reinforce these as solutions. Inspired by Ericksonian and strategic therapies.

strategic therapy Form of brief therapy that seeks to interrupt and alter self-reinforcing patterns in which attempted solutions to problems actually contribute to their maintenance. Inspired by Ericksonian therapy.

I. OVERVIEW

Single-session therapy is a general term that is used to describe any form of psychotherapy that seeks to address the presenting problems of clients within a single visit. It is hypothetically possible for any form of psychotherapy to be conducted in a single session and, indeed, Freud's case studies include cures that were achieved after one meeting. In practice, however, it is unusual to find either cognitive-behavioral or psychoanalytic brief therapists conducting single-session therapy. This is because the models of change underlying these approaches emphasize the value of repeated experience in building new patterns of thought, feeling, and behavior. The learning models associated with cognitive-behavioral modalities, for example, emphasize the acquisition of skills through deliberate rehearsal. Such practice generally requires more than one visit. (A notable exception would be massed practice in behavioral therapies, where desensitization might be undertaken in a single, extended session, as in the implosive therapy of Levis.) The relationship models underlying brief psychoanalytic therapies stress the importance of creating powerful emotional experiences for clients, which also are rarely undertaken in a highly abbreviated span.

Most single-session therapies draw on contextual models of change that emphasize the constructed nature of client presenting problems. Problems are seen as client construals, not necessarily as illnesses or problems that possess an independent existence. These construals are maintained by elements in the client's intrapersonal and interpersonal contexts and become reified over time. From this perspective, a long-standing problem is not necessarily any deeper than a recent one and might be amenable to short-term treatment. By shifting the contexts in which the client is operating and providing insights and experiences that dislodge problematic construals, therapists can catalyze significant change in a single meeting.

The majority of single-session therapies emphasize the role of the therapist in initiating change, rather than effecting a cure. Although problems can be dislodged and new construals introduced in a single visit, it is generally not possible for clients in single-session therapy to generalize these changes to a variety of life situations. As a result, single-session therapies are not seen as ideal treatment modalities for all people. Commonly cited contraindications for single-session therapy include the following.

- *Chronic, severe presenting problems*: The client with long-standing problems that significantly impair functioning often needs coordinated efforts at rehabilitation, rather than a brief episode of therapy. Although techniques derived from the brief and single-session literatures may be helpful for such individuals, they typically do not meet the full spectrum of client needs.
- *High need for support*: Clients who have poor support systems may want to rely on the therapist as a support and, indeed, may need that support to assist them in leaving an abusive relationship or changing an addictive pattern. A single-session treatment, by definition, cannot offer ongoing support to such individuals and could even prove detrimental to clients with issues related to attachment and separation.
- *Troubled interpersonal history*: Single-session therapies are effective to the degree that they utilize techniques that maximize the influence of the therapist. Clients who have experienced a history of abusive, neglectful, or highly troubled relationships often need an extended period of time before they can learn to trust a therapist. This severely limits the usefulness of single-session work.
- *Low readiness for change*: Clients who are ambivalent about making changes generally need to explore problem patterns and their consequences before developing the motivation to initiate and sustain efforts at change. This generally extends the duration of therapy beyond brief parameters, and certainly beyond the length of a single session.

Although these contraindications are significant, single-session therapies may be more useful for clients than is commonly acknowledged. Studies of utilization of therapy in outpatient settings suggest that approximately one third of all clients only attend a single session, often reporting that the brief intervention was sufficient for their needs. Appropriately utilizing highly abbreviated treatments for clients can preserve resources for others who most need them in capitated settings and clinics with staff limitations. Generally, clients who are the best candidates for single-session therapy display:

- *Adjustment problems, situational problems, and nonsevere disorders of recent origin*: Individuals who are not overwhelmed by their presenting problems are most likely to be able to take the results of a single visit and apply them to their lives.
- *High levels of motivation*: Because there will not be future sessions to carry the change process forward, clients who are to benefit from single-session work need to be able to sustain their own efforts at generalization.
- *Awareness of a focal problem*: Limiting therapy to a single session places therapist and client in an action mode from the start. If clients lack a focus for therapy, it is likely that more than one session will be needed to define and implement a therapeutic contract.

Although there are several different approaches to single session therapy, all share features that differentiate them from lengthier brief therapies. These include the following:

- *Beginning therapy before the first session*: A number of writers on single-session work emphasize that change begins at the time the first appointment is made. Often, the therapist will talk with the client at the time of first contact and suggest a task that can be accomplished prior to the first session. By encouraging pretherapeutic efforts at change, therapists can use their single session to focus on positive efforts already under way.
- *Addressing time at the outset of therapy*: Many approaches to brief therapy aim to be efficient but do not expressly address time during the first session. Single-session therapists generally preface treatment with an explanation that one visit is often enough for clients, even as they leave the door open for further meetings as needed.
- *Active attempts to utilize ideas and language introduced by the client*: Single-session therapists do not

have the luxury of stimulating and working through the resistances of clients. Rather, they attempt to build on frameworks already utilized by the client to elicit cooperation.

- *Rapid introduction of impactful interventions*: With a limited time available for catalyzing change, single-session therapists must move quickly from a problem-based mode to one in which new patterns are introduced. Often this is accomplished in ways that will maximize their impact, by employing vivid language, hypnotic suggestions, directed tasks, and novel reframings.

Just as brief therapy appears to represent an intensification of the common factors that account for the effectiveness of all therapies, single-session therapies are, in essence, a distillation of methods utilized in brief treatments. The quick establishment of rapport, rapid definition of a treatment focus, and active introduction of novelty in pursuit of change make single-session therapy a brief version of brief therapy.

II. THEORETICAL UNDERPINNINGS

Much of the writing on single-session therapy owes its inspiration to three strands of practice in the brief therapy literature:

1. *Ericksonian therapy*: A number of authors, including Jay Haley, Richard Bandler, John Grinder, and Stephen Lankton, have attempted to identify the elements of practice that distinguish the work of Milton Erickson. These elements include the creative use of language to influence clients, the introduction of hypnotic trance to shift clients' perception, and reliance on directed tasks to interrupt existing problem patterns. Many of these methods are attempts to bypass the normal, verbal, conscious awareness of individuals and introduce change experientially and emotionally. By affecting clients directly, Erickson found that the duration of therapy could be greatly reduced.

2. *Strategic therapy*: Therapists operating from a systems perspective, including Paul Watzlawick, John Weakland, and Richard Fisch, extended Erickson's pioneering work, creating short-term approaches to therapy that could be used for families and individuals. A central tenet of this strategic approach is that presenting problems are artifacts of self-reinforcing cycles, in which attempted solutions maintain the initial problems. For instance, a spouse hurt and angry over a perceived lack of attention may attack the partner, producing even further distance. By placing clients in contexts that could not support the self-maintaining cycles, strategic therapists provide powerful experiences that break the old patterns and allow for the introduction of new ones.

3. *Solution-focused therapy*: A new tradition was inspired by the work of Steve deShazer who conceptualized therapy as a search for solutions rather than an exploration and analysis of problems. This solution-focused approach, elaborated by such therapists as William O'Hanlon and Jane and Walter Peller, can be readily adapted to the single-session framework. By focusing on client goals and quickly initiating a search for imagined or experienced exceptions to client patterns, solution-focused therapists are able to quickly move treatment to an action phase, greatly abbreviating the change process.

Common to all three approaches is a postmodern epistemology, which emphasizes that reality is actively constructed, both in the cognitive processes of the individual and in social interaction. When something negative happens on multiple occasions, it becomes an object of attention and may be construed as a problem. Once so identified, the behaviors in question typically elicit further distress and efforts at coping. Many of these dampen distress in the short run, but exacerbate the initial concerns. By introducing novel approaches to the situation, through metaphor, story, or directed task, the therapist aids in the construction of a new reality. This opens the door to more flexible responding and the possibility of developing constructive behavioral patterns.

This postmodern conceptualization of problem formation and change provides much of the rationale of single-session therapies. Many alternate conceptions of therapy emphasize the existence of a problem that must be evaluated and subjected to various therapeutic interventions. The postmodern perspective stresses that the problem, in an important sense, does not exist other than in the eyes of the client; it is part of the client's mental map—not an enduring feature of the landscape. Even relatively small shifts in the map can produce new patterns of thinking, feeling, and acting that can assume a life of their own. This can be observed in the "pivot chords" described by Robert Rosenbaum, Michael Hoyt, and Moshe Talmon, who use ambiguity in client verbalizations to open the door to new ways of construing problematic situations.

An additional theoretical assumption that permeates single-session modalities is the notion that clients essentially possess all they need to overcome their problems.

Rather than view individuals as existing in a deficit state where they need treatment from professionals, single-session therapists emphasize their existing adaptive potentials. This is most clearly seen in solution-focused approaches, in which the emphasis of therapy is on exceptions to presenting problems and patterns. These exceptions may be imagined ("What would life be like if you did not have the problem?") or may be inferred from the client's own experience. By framing such exceptions as constructive actions that the client can initiate, the single-session approaches bypass much of the early phase of problem definition and analysis and quickly move to an action stage.

III. RESEARCH FINDINGS

Controlled outcome studies comparing single-session therapy to other forms of intervention have yet to be reported in the literature. Nonetheless, several strands of research represent initial attempts to build an empirical basis for these approaches. Moshe Talmon reports several studies that have found 30% of all clients attending therapy for a single session. Follow-up investigations with those clients found that approximately 80% were satisfied with the limited intervention and reported some or much improvement.

Studies at the Brief Family Therapy Center in Milwaukee have generally supported the effectiveness of solution-focused therapy and have found that pretreatment interventions result in noticed positive change in 60% or more of all clients. This is particularly true of Formula First Session Tasks, which ask clients to observe what is happening when things are going positively. Clients performing such tasks have been found to be more cooperative in therapy than clients not performing the tasks and have reported greater improvement by the second session. Other studies have found that the amount of change-related talk engaged in by therapists and clients is predictive of success.

Although these studies are encouraging, it will remain for controlled outcome studies comparing single-session interventions to other modalities to establish the long-term success of very brief work and the degree to which outcomes are attributable to specific interventions rather than general factors.

IV. SUMMARY

Single-session therapies are a collection of approaches that attempt to maximize change within a single visit. Most of these approaches owe their genesis to the pioneering work of Milton Erickson and the subsequent development of strategic and solution-focused therapies. Built largely on a postmodern epistemology, they emphasize the constructed nature of client concerns and the role of the therapist in identifying contexts and experiences that allow for alternate constructions. Such approaches are best suited for clients who are motivated to change focal patterns, especially those who are experiencing situational or adjustment concerns and are capable of establishing a rapid therapeutic alliance.

See Also the Following Articles

Brief Therapy ■ Cost Effectiveness ■ Individual Psychotherapy ■ Minimal Therapist Contact Treatments ■ Relapse Prevention ■ Solution-Focused Brief Therapy ■ Termination

Further Reading

Lankton, S. R., & Erickson, K. K. (1994). *The essence of a single-session success.* New York: Brunner/Mazel.

Miller, S. D., Hubble, M. A., & Duncan, B. L. (Eds.). (1996). *Handbook of solution focused brief therapy.* San Francisco: Jossey-Bass.

Rosenbaum, R., Hoyt, M. F., & Talmon, M. (1990). The challenge of single-session therapies: Creating pivotal moments. In R. A. Wells & V. J. Giannetti (Eds.), *Handbook of the brief psychotherapies* (pp. 165–192). New York: Plenum.

Talmon, M. (1990). *Single session therapy.* San Francisco: Jossey-Bass.

Watzlawick, P., Weakland, J., & Fisch, R. (1974). *Change: Principles of problem formation and problem resolution.* New York: W. W. Norton.

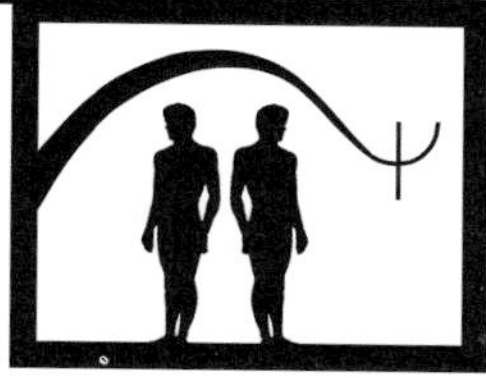

Solution-Focused Brief Therapy

Anne Bodmer Lutz
Cedarburg, Wisconsin

Insoo Kim Berg
Milwaukee, Wisconsin

GLOSSARY

coping questions Techniques that are designed to empower clients to manage their life more effectively by addressing their coping style.

miracle question Technical intervention in which the client is asked to think in an unlimited range of possibility and to identify changes that they want to see happen.

scaling questions Technical approach that encourages the client to prioritize and put into an ordinal relationship various issues, including efforts to problem solve, as well as problems.

SFBT (Solution Focused Brief Therapy) is an approach to delivering psychotherapy based on a variety of theoretical positions, such as Milton Ericson's ideas and Wittgenstein philosophy of language. SFBT focuses on solutions rather than problems.

Solution-focused brief therapy (SFBT) was developed through the work of Steve de Shazer, Insoo Kim Berg, and their colleagues at the Brief Family Therapy Center in Milwaukee, Wisconsin. It is a model that has been developed inductively based on 30 years of sessions with clients. It has been used successfully in a variety of settings including rehabilitation centers, psychiatric hospitals, residential treatment centers, child protection agencies, schools, and private practices. This treatment model is based on the hypnotherapeutic work of Milton H. Erickson, as discussed by Haley in 1967, and influenced by the 1974 work of John H. Weakland, Paul Watzlawick, and Richard Fisch of the Mental Research Institute.

I. BASIC POSTURE

As the name suggests, SFBT is defined by its emphasis on solutions rather than problems. Different from problem-based therapies in which a great deal of time is spent assessing problems, understanding in as much detail as possible what a client is doing wrong, or developing hypotheses about what is wrong with the client and family system, and the therapist prescribing solutions, SFBT focuses on finding solutions and gives minimal attention to defining or understanding presenting problems.

A description of the SFBT treatment model includes the following: therapist attitudes, socializing, goal negotiation, miracle question, exception questions, scaling questions, coping questions, and the consultation break and intervention message. In addition, three types of client–therapist relationships are described: visitor type, complainant-type, and customer-type.

Therapists' beliefs and attitudes influence how and what they listen to when talking with clients. SFBT emphasizes attitudes of client competence, and the importance of how language is used in conversation with clients. All therapists, regardless of their approach, come with certain attitudes and philosophies that affect how they do treatment. For example, all therapists are selective in their choice of what they ask about and what they ignore, depending on the underlying assumptions they hold about what is useful and helpful for their clients to talk about. Far from serving the "objective" purpose of "merely" gathering data, the questions therapists actually raise with clients influence and change clients' thinking about themselves. Solutions for clients are not scientific puzzles to be solved by practitioners, but rather changes in perception, patterns of interacting and living, and meanings that are constructed within the clients' frame of reference. The SFBT therapist assumes that clients are competent at conceptualizing an alternative more satisfying future and at figuring out which of their strengths and resources they can draw on to produce the changes they desire. The client is the expert of his or her problems and has legitimate goals and ways to facilitate change. For example, a client with an alcohol problem may want to improve his relationship with his wife and children and may not initially want to stop drinking. Accepting this initial goal as a reasonable first step makes it possible to further examine his desired state of life.

The therapist assumes a collaborative stance, with the client and therapist working together to bring about goals the client decides on. Berg and De Jong in 1996 described exploring and affirming clients' perceptions as clients describe them as a major share of what is done in SFBT. Even when clients are considering extreme actions—suicide or violence—they do so within a context of several associated perceptions. For example, to a client who thinks of hitting a child, an SFBT therapist might say, "What's happening in your life that tells you that hitting your child might be helpful in this situation? What else? Does it work? Suppose you were to do that, what would be different between you and your child? What would be different between you and your other children, the courts, your family?" As clients are respectfully asked about their perceptions, they usually are able to talk about less extreme possibilities. Berg and De Jong in 1996 described the therapist assuming a "not knowing" or curious stance in talking with clients. The therapist is always in the stance of learning the clients' perceptions and explanations, never knowing a priori the significance of the client's experiences and actions.

Finally, the therapist's job is to learn the language of the client. Rather than believing that language describes reality, it is believed that language also conveys information about what the therapist is interested in learning from the client. Being problem focused, clients often use language as if to describe their relationships and experiences, assuming, for example, that "being close" means the same for everyone. Often, although their language is very meaningful to them, it may be vague to a therapist. Clients use language to describe their relationships and experiences. Examples of techniques that begin to clear up the ambiguity are for the therapist to repeat key words used by a client, clarify what a client means by certain words, and use the actual words a client uses in the conversation. The therapist listens carefully for and explores each client's choice of words. This not only demonstrates respect for the client, it also begins a process in which, as therapists speak the client's language, clients begin to speak the solution-focused language of therapists.

II. SFBT PROCEDURES AND TECHNIQUES

All therapy, regardless of model, begins with a phase of socializing and orienting clients to what is to come. de Shazer and Berg describe initial questions directed at areas in which clients are successful or from which they draw satisfaction or esteem. Early on in the conversation, the SFBT listens for and highlights client strengths and successes. For example, beginning a conversation with clients by asking them what they are good at, what they enjoy, their job, hobbies, talents, past achievements, or ambitions for the future begins a dialogue between the therapist and client about identifying issues they both can agree are going well for the client. Client strengths, resources, and abilities are highlighted rather than their deficits and disabilities. This approach tends to look for what is right and how to use it. Asking clients early on what they are good at sets a different conversational path than "what problem brought you here today?" This communicates to the client that the therapist recognizes that even though the client has problems, he or she also has areas that are successful. Often these strengths, although unrelated to the presenting problem, bring early clues about how the client will solve their problems.

Co-constructing goals with clients is a very important feature of SFBT. Clients generally are much more aware of, for example, the problems and what they do not want in their lives than they are about what they want to be different. Many clients begin the discussion of goals as the absence of problems; however, SFBT conceptualizes goals as the presence of what the client wants. Berg and Miller describe goals as criteria that the client and therapist determine together that would tell them they have succeeded and can end therapy. They include the following: Goals must be important to the client and be viewed as personally beneficial; they must be small enough so they can be achieved; they must be concrete, specific, and behavioral and stated in positive, proactive language about what the client will do instead of what he or she will not do. Goals must also be perceived as involving hard work for the client. For example, instead of drinking, a client may make an arrangement for a designated driver before going out on the weekend, or get to work on time. This is in contrast to a vague goal of improving one's self-esteem or being happy.

III. THE MIRACLE QUESTION

Berg and De Jong describe how the miracle question gives clients permission to think about an unlimited range of possibilities, and identify changes they want to see happen. Because the question has a future focus, it begins to move the focus away from their current and past problems and toward a more satisfying life. The miracle question stated in the following way frequently draws a rich response from clients.

> Suppose (pause) after we talk today, you go home (pause) and sometime in the evening you go to bed (pause) and in the middle of the night (pause) while you are sleeping, a miracle happens and the problem that brought you here today is solved (pause), but because this happens while you are sleeping, you don't know that the miracle happened until you wake up in the morning. So when you wake up tomorrow morning, what will make you wonder, "something is different, maybe there was a miracle last night?"

Getting details of the miracle is important and the therapist's follow-up questions are crucial. Asking "what else will be different, what else?" is a helpful question to explore. The more opportunities a client has to rehearse a successful outcome verbally, the more chance the miracle has of beginning in small ways to become real for him or her. The miracle question can be an empowering experience for clients as they begin to imagine a painful life transformed to a more successful and fulfilling life. The gift of hope and a vision can be a truly healing experience for clients.

Exception finding questions are another tool used in SFBT. An exception to a problem occurs when the client engages in nonproblem behavior (e.g., does not drink, does not feel depressed, and does not fight with his wife). The therapist's job is to listen for and magnify a client's successes through repeated emphasis on those few, but important, exceptions. When repeated often and examined in detail, successes become more real to the client. The client can then begin to see their success and recognize that they actually have taken steps to improve their life. Thus the client can take responsibility and credit for the solution. An example would be exploring in detail those times when a client does not drink: What was she doing?—Who was she with?—Where was she?—What did other people notice during that time? Other questions to ask include inquiring about times when things have gone better between sessions, and helping clients describe times when some pieces of the miracle have already happened before therapy began. Getting as much detail about what was happening during these times (who, what, when, where, how) and including other important persons behaving differently during these times, provide further contextual information in these important moments.

Scaling questions are another useful technique used in SFBT. As deShazer states, "there is magic in numbers." An example of a scaling question is "on a scale from 0 to 10, with 0 representing the worst things could be for you and 10 the day after the miracle, where on the scale would you say you are now?" Frequently, clients will give a rating of "3." The therapist then helps them describe the differences between "0" and "3" and how other people might see those differences, and what it might take to "get all the way up to 3." Suppose a client answers "1." The therapist may respond "How are you able to keep going?" "What gives you the strength to continue?" When a client is asked to put problems, successes, hope, and level of self-esteem on a numerical scale, it gives the therapist useful information about a client's relationships, confidence in change, and self-esteem, and helps to determine an end point for therapy. An example is, "At what number on the scale will you be when things are going well enough that you no longer feel you need therapy?" It can also help the client describe contextual details of his or her experience. An example is, "Where would your mom/dad/best friend/spouse/boss/probation officer say you are on the scale?" Finally, scaling questions can also help clients create small goals for change. Asking a client what will be different when they go from a 3 to a 4 (not a 10), forces clients to think about taking small, more realistic steps toward change.

Coping questions can also be very useful in SFBT. Questions about how clients are managing their life can be very empowering to clients. Examples, include, "How are you able to keep going when your life feels like it's falling apart?" "How do you manage day to day?" Questioning clients about how they are coping with big problems shifts the conversation from hopelessness to hope and a sense of control. However small it may seem, the small things the client does to "barely cope" are the very things that the client must do more of "one day at a time" in order to create a basis on which to build more successes. "How come you life is not worse?" is used to "blame" the client for their success. Such "positive blame" assigns the responsibility for positive, helpful behaviors to the client.

Frequently, an SFBT session includes a team behind a one-way mirror and the therapist meets with them 10 to 15 minutes before the end of the session to develop a closing message to the client. Working alone (which is the most common practice) and taking a 5 to 10 minute break after 45 minutes of a session allows the therapist to review the session, take time to think about whether there are well-formed goals, and to decide on a feedback message for the client.

SFBT feedback messages include compliments, which are used with all cases and throughout the treatment process. All cultures use compliments as a means of cementing social relationships at all levels. Clients have personal qualities and past experiences that, if drawn on, can be of great help in solving their difficulties and creating more satisfying lives. Compliments can be direct or indirect. During the interview, for example, direct compliments can be developed from times when clients are resilient in the face of hardships, sober for even 1 week, able to hold down a job, care about their children, work hard, or are willing to come get help. Compliments are best when they are based on reality and incorporate the client's language. Indirect compliments are questions that imply that the client has done something positive. For example, "How have you managed to stay sober for one week?" "How have you managed to stay calm when things are so hectic?" This allows clients to speak aloud themselves about the details of their success. When clients are able to speak themselves, they appear more empowered in their ability to find solutions.

Suggestion for homework is frequently prescribed at the end of an SFBT interview. Deciding on what type of intervention to prescribe depends on what stage of relationship the client has with the therapist. SFBT describes three types of client–therapist relationships: visitor-type, complainant-type, and customer-type. Visitor-type relationships are those in which the client has not yet created a workable goal. Often these clients are mandated through probation officers, employers, or parents. Interventions with these clients focuses on giving frequent positive feedback on what the client is already doing that is helpful and working. Providing these clients with many compliments is often a very different message than what they have frequently heard, and may help make these clients more interested in treatment. Complainant-type relationships involve clients that have created some workable goals, but view their solutions lying outside of their control. In addition to using compliments, suggestions are made to shift the client's perception from someone who is a helpless victim to someone who can create solutions. Interventions encouraging clients to "observe and think" about what they will notice will be different when the miracle happens is an example. Because these clients are observers, but not yet "doers," this meets the client where he or she is. Customer-type relationships are those in which the client is willing to actively "do" something differently, to actually take steps to find solutions in his or her life. Clients are frequently asked to do more of what is working, pay attention to any part of the miracle that is happening, or imagine a miracle day.

IV. THEORETICAL FOUNDATION

The theoretical underpinnings of SFBT come from several sources including social constructionism, Wittgenstein's philosophy of language, and Milton Erickson's ideas on therapy. Social constructionism maintains that people develop their sense of what is real through conversation with and observation of others. Social constructionism holds that reality, as each individual perceives it, is by definition subjective and created through the process of social interaction and the use of language. SFBT asserts that problems occur in interactions between individuals and do not rest within any one individual. People define and create their sense of what is real through interaction and conversation with others, a form of negotiation carried out within the context of language. SFBT helps clients do something different by changing their interactive behaviors or the interpretations of behaviors. This approach makes no assumptions about the "true" nature of problems. SFBT has a strong orientation toward the present and future and further believes that everyone's future is negotiated and created. How clients are currently living their lives and their future goals are emphasized, thus orienting the client away from the past problem toward the future solution.

This model differs from the traditional "medical model" in a number of ways. Rather than assessing problems, signs, and symptoms, SFBT assesses for solutions, exceptions to problems, and strengths within an individual and his or her social context. It further focuses on past successes, coping strategies, and resources and collaboratively co-constructs a solution with the client.

Language is a resource that is vital to all therapists' practices and relationships with their clients. The importance of language in SFBT is crucial. Gail Miller and Steve de Shazer in 1998 wrote about how meanings of words are inseparable from the ways in which people use them within concrete social contexts. Problem-focused language emphasizes what is wrong with people's lives, and frequently portrays the sources of our problems as powerful forces that are largely beyond our control or understanding. In contrast, solution-focused language focuses on finding ways of managing one's problems. Solution-focused therapists ask, "Since we talk ourselves into problems and solutions anyway, why not emphasize solutions." This is not to deny the deprivations and injustices in clients' lives, but to help get through and beyond them. This model uses post-modern assumptions that problems and solutions are talked into being, and meaning is changeable based on our use of language.

V. FOLLOW-UP STUDIES

Having been inductively developed in clinical settings by de Shazer in 1985, Berg in 1994, Berg and Reuss in 1997, and Berg and Kelly, in 2000, rigorous research that shows its effectiveness is only beginning to emerge. There is a great deal of informal studies scattered throughout in a variety of settings. However, a rigorous study design using random selection of population, controlled, and experimental groups, and pre–post measures is just beginning to emerge. We recognize that such data are necessary. What has emerged so far seems to show promise in its effectiveness and cost in terms of human suffering and dollars.

In 2000, Gingerich and Eisengart performed a review of SFBT outcome research. This article critically reviewed a total of 15 studies. Additionally, it reviewed early follow-up studies documenting SFBT outcomes.

Early follow-up studies used follow-up surveys by asking clients at 6 to 18 months whether they had met their goal. In the first study, de Shazer in 1985 reported an 82% success rate on follow-up of 28 clients. The next year, de Shazer et al. reported a 72% success rate with a 25% sample of 1600 cases. Subsequent studies by De Jong and Hopwood in 1996 and Kiser in 1988 have reported similar results. Other follow-up studies of SFBT have similar, but somewhat smaller success rates and have used subjective outcome measures, such as those by Lee in 1997, Macdonald in 1997, Morrison, Olivos, Dominguez, and colleagues in 1993, and Schorr in 1997. Although these follow-up studies provide feedback on SFBT outcomes, their lack of experimental control does not permit causal inferences to be made about the effectiveness of SFBT.

Gingerich and Eisengart reviewed 15 controlled studies that implemented SFBT, employed some form of experimental control, assessed client behavior or functioning, and assessed end-of-treatment outcomes. These studies were further divided into well-controlled, moderately controlled, and poorly controlled studies based on the number of standards met for assessing empirical support for psychological treatments developed by the American Psychological Association.

The well-controlled studies included studies on depression in college students, parenting skills, rehabilitation of orthopedic patients, recidivism in a prison population, and antisocial adolescent offenders (the studies were those of Cockburn, Thomak, and Cockburn in 1997; Lindforss and Magnusson in 1997; Seagram in 1997; Zimmerman, Jacobsen, MacIntyre, and Watson in 1996; and Sundstrom in 1993). Four found SFBT to be significantly better than no treatment or standard institutional services. Because these studies did not compare SFBT with another psychotherapeutic intervention, they were not able to conclude that the observed outcomes were due specifically to the SFBT intervention as opposed to general attention effects. One study by Sundstrom in 1993 compared SFBT with a known treatment (IPT) and found SFBT produced equivalent outcomes (no significant differences were found). None of the five studies met all of the stringent criteria for efficacy studies and thus one cannot conclude that SFBT has been shown to be efficacious. They do, however, provide initial support for the efficacy of SFBT. The remaining 10 studies contain methodological limitations that preclude drawing firm conclusion, but their findings are consistent with the general conclusion of SFBT effectiveness.

Gingerich and colleagues identify several future areas of need in subjecting SFBT to empirical test. First is the specification and proceduralization of SFBT itself with the consistent use of detailed treatment manuals and treatment adherence measures. In addition, future efficacy studies will need to compare SFBT with other empirically validated interventions where therapist allegiance is equally balanced between treatments. Other considerations include specification of study sample, selection of the comparison group, adequate sample size, and using conventional diagnostic groupings.

Although the current studies fall short of what is needed to establish the efficacy of SFBT, they provide early support that SFBT is useful to clients, according to Gingerich et al. The wide variety of settings and populations studied suggests a broad range of applications, but this conclusion awaits more careful study.

See Also the Following Articles

Outcome Measures ■ Single Session Therapy ■ Working Alliance

Further Reading

Berg, I. K. (1994). *Family based services: A solution-focused approach.* New York: Norton.

Berg, I. K., & De Jong, P. (1996). Solution-building conversations: Co-constructing a sense of competence with clients. *Families in Society: The Journal of Contemporary Human Service, 77,* 376–391.

Cockburn, J. T., Thomas, F. N., & Cockburn, O. J. (1997). Solution focused therapy and psychosocial adjustment to orthopedic rehabilitation in a work hardening program. *Journal of Occupational Rehabilitation 7,* 97–106.

De Jong, P., & Berg, I. K. (1998). *Interviewing for solutions.* Pacific Grove, CA: Brooks/Cole.

De Jong, P. I., & Hopwood, L. E. (1996). Outcome research on treatment conducted at the Brief Family Therapy Center, 1992–1993. In S. D. Miller, M. A. Hubble, & B. L. Duncan (Eds.), *Handbook of solution-focused brief therapy* (pp. 272–298). San Francisco: Jossey-Bass.

Gingerich, W., (2000). Solution-focused brief therapy: A review of the outcome research. *Family Process, 39,* 477–498.

Lee, M. Y. (1997). A study of solution-focused brief family therapy: Outcomes and issues. *American Journal of Family Therapy, 25,* 3–17.

Lindforss, L., & Magnusson, D. (1997). Solution-focused therapy in Prison. *Contemporary Family Therapy, 19,* 89–103.

Macdonald, A. J. (1997). Brief therapy in adult psychiatry—further outcomes. *Journal of Family Therapy 19,* 213–222.

Miller, G., & de Shazer, S. (1998). Have you heard the latest rumor about...? Solution-focused therapy as a rumor. *Family Process, 37,* 363–377.

Seagram, B. C. (1997). *The efficacy of solution-focused therapy with young offenders.* Unpublished doctoral dissertation, York University, York, Ontario, Canada.

Uken, A., & Sebold, J. (1996). The Plumas Project: A solution-focused goal directed domestic violence diversion program. *Journal of Collaborative Therapies, IV,* No. 2, Summer.

Zimmerman, T. S., Jacobsen, R. B., MacIntyre, M., & Watson, C. (1996). Solution-focused parenting groups: An empirical study. *Journal of Systemic Therapies, 15,* 12–25.

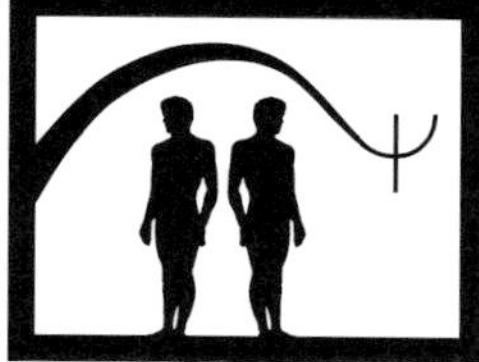

Somatoform Disorders

Ann Kerr Morrison
Wright State University

GLOSSARY

behavioral therapy Psychotherapy directed at changing observable and measurable behavior through a variety of techniques including monitoring, incremental change, shaping, and operant conditioning.

body dysmorphic disorder A preoccupation with an imagined defect in appearance.

cognitive therapy Psychotherapy directed at identifying and changing dysfunctional thoughts, perceptions, attitudes, and beliefs.

conversion disorder A symptom that mimics a neurologic problem (i.e., blindness, paralysis) that is not due to any neurologic problem, other medical condition, or substance but rather is thought to be due to psychological distress from a social stressor or psychological conflict.

factitious disorder Physical or psychological symptoms that are intentionally produced to assume the sick role.

hypnosis A mental state characterized by relaxation, concentration, and suggestibility in which perception and memory may be altered.

hypochondriasis A long-standing worry or fear of having serious illness in which one misinterprets physiologic sensations and minor symptoms.

iatrogenic Caused by a physician or his or her treatment.

narcotherapy An interviewing and psychotherapeutic technique involving sedative drugs, usually sodium amytal to induce relaxation.

pain disorder Pain complaints not completely attributed to a general medical condition. Purely psychological and combined medical and psychological types are described in DSM–IV–TR.

personality disorder A pervasive maladaptive pattern of relating to the environment and others that impairs function. Usually personality disorders arise in adolescence or the early adult years.

primary gain The decrease in anxiety or other unpleasant feeling attributed to the unconscious suppression of internal drives or conflicts.

psychoanalytic psychotherapy Psychotherapy derived from the theories of Freud that emphasizes the use of free associations, dream interpretation, and analysis of transference to bring to awareness repressed emotions and unconscious conflicts. Psychoanalytic psychotherapy focuses these techniques on the current conflicts and problems in the person's life rather than the very early life experiences and conflicts central to classical psychoanalysis.

psychodynamic psychotherapy Psychotherapy that incorporates a role for unconscious conflicts and motivations in human behavior but also recognizes the influence of life experience, current situational stressors, and biological predisposition in determining behavior. Techniques and issues emphasized are more varied than in either classical psychoanalysis or psychoanalytic psychotherapy.

secondary gain The support obtained from other people or systems due to a symptom or illness or the avoidance of an unpleasant, aversive situation due to a symptom or illness.

selective serotonin reuptake inhibitor (SSRI) Antidepressants that prevent the neuron from recycling serotonin released into the synaptic cleft, thereby increasing the amount of serotonin present at the synapse.

serotonin A neurotransmitter implicated in many mental disorders, especially major depression and obsessive–compulsive disorder.

social learning theory The theory that individual behavior is determined in large part by behaviors one has observed in others.

somatization The general process of presenting physical symptoms and concerns that are not explained by a general medical illness presumably as a manifestation of psychological distress or conflict or social stress.

somatization disorder A long-standing disorder involving multiple physical complaints and many organ systems usually developed at an early age and stable over time.

somatoform disorders The *Diagnostic Statistical Manual of Mental Disorders* category describing disorders that involve physical symptoms not attributable solely to general medical conditions or substances.

supportive therapy Psychotherapy directed at reinforcing a patient's defenses as a way of improving the ability to cope with psychological distress.

I. DESCRIPTION OF TREATMENT

Treatment of individuals with somatoform disorders represents a unique challenge for the psychotherapist in that the core deficit in these individuals is the inability to recognize the role of psychological and social conflicts and stressors in the development of their physical symptoms. These individuals are unlikely to present to psychotherapists for treatment initially and are often resistant to referral for psychiatric or psychological consultation. For many patients with somatoform disorder, the most important therapeutic relationship remains the primary care physician. The mental health consultant may assist this physician in maintaining a therapeutic stance with these often taxing and frustrating patients. For instance, the psychiatrist in this consultant role may assist the physician and patient by confirming the diagnoses and advising the referring physician about the general principles of management of somatoform disorders:

1. Maintain regular, consistent contact with a single physician.
2. Minimize invasive diagnostic procedures and aggressive treatments without objective evidence of physical disease.
3. Gradually, and in a nonconfrontative manner, work toward helping the patient recognize the connection between stressors in their lives and their physical symptoms.

The process of somatization is not limited to individuals with somatoform disorders. Other disorders, especially depression and anxiety disorders, frequently present with prominent somatic symptoms. In addition, individuals with somatoform disorders often suffer from other mental disorders such as depression, anxiety, and personality disorders. Treatment of these co-existing disorders may improve the individual's function even when the somatoform disorder persists.

The somatoform disorders, as described in *DSM–IV–TR* are a heterogeneous group of disorders that currently are lumped together due to the common characteristic of a physical complaint or complaints that are not completely explained by a general medical condition or a substance. Included in this category are somatization disorder, undifferentiated somatoform disorder (an abridged form of somatoform disorder), conversion disorder, pain disorder, hypochondriasis, body dysmorphic disorder, and somatoform disorder not otherwise specified (a residual category for presentations that do not fulfill criteria for the other somatoform disorders). Somatoform disorders vary greatly in the number and type of symptoms presented and systems affected, the duration of symptoms, the age of onset, the gender distribution, and the prognosis. In contrast to factitious disorder, the physical symptoms are not believed to be intentionally produced. Treatment approaches, for somatoform disorders, although unified by the general management principles already described also vary. Despite the fact that many of these disorders, especially somatization disorder (also known as hysteria, or Briquet's syndrome), conversion disorder (also named conversion reaction or hysterical conversion), and hypochondriasis have received much attention in the history of psychotherapeutic theories and treatments, there remains a dearth of well-controlled psychotherapeutic trials specific to each disorder. A general summary of treatment approaches for the principle types of somatoform disorder follows. Details of these treatments are discussed under the Empirical Studies section.

A. Somatization Disorder

Somatization disorder is characterized by the onset at an early age, usually late teens to early 20s but by definition by age 30 of multiple physical complaints. Females are afflicted over males by a ration of 10 or 20: 1. The disorder by definition has been present greater than 6 months. This disorder has in the past been known as Briquet's syndrome or hysteria. The complexity of the criteria has diminished over the years but still requires the presence of multiple symptoms involving several organ systems. The typical patient has had many surgeries at an early age, preceded by multiple workups for a variety of physical complaints. These individuals seldom seek psychiatric or psychological treatment because from their point of view, their problems are physical not mental in nature. In addition, to multiple surgeries and procedures, these patients may also suffer from iatrogenic side effects from a multitude of medications. Direction to the family physician to schedule regular, not as needed appointments, which include focused physical exams, to minimize testing and treatments and to gradually shift the focus of attention from physical complaints to stressors in the patient's life may help decrease health care utilization and avoid complications of procedures and treatments. Group therapy aimed at coping with the stress of a chronic medical condition has also been recommended. In a group setting, these individuals are said to be capable of recognizing and confronting this pattern of somatizing to an extent not possible in individual therapy. In addition, they may benefit from the support of others with similar conditions.

B. Conversion Disorder

Conversion disorder is characterized usually by only one symptom at a time, and this symptom, by definition, mimics neurologic disease. Historically, the type of symptoms has extended beyond those that mimic neurologic disease but neurologic-like symptoms (seizures, paralysis, numbness, deafness, or blindness) have always also been the most prominent. Commonly, the patient has both underlying diseases as well as conversion symptoms. Conversion disorder also is more common in women than in men and is found in both chronic (greater than 6 months) and acute (less than 6 months) forms. Due to the relatively high rate at which individuals either are later diagnosed with neurologic disease or have concurrent neurologic disease, the recommendation to minimize workups to exclude organic causes, generally made for somatoform disorders, is not applicable to conversion disorder. However once this workup is completed, the same principles of supportive, benign management prevails. Most authors advocate a nonconfrontative yet authoritative explanation that recovery is expected over a relatively brief period of time. An explanation that medical tests do not show signs of any serious progressive disease should be provided without confrontation or argument and without suggesting that the problems are "all in your head." These straightforward prescriptions for recovery allow most individuals to return to normal function. In cases in which suggestions and reassurance alone do not result in recovery, physical rehabilitation and other behavioral techniques such as relaxation and rest may be added. If the stressors presumed to be responsible for the conversion symptom in the first place cannot be ascertained from a standard history, then interviewing techniques such as narcotherapy or hypnosis may be used. The primary purpose of identifying the stressors is to be able to modify them through therapy. Narcotherapy and hypnosis may also be used to enhance the suggestion and expectation of recovery from the conversion symptom. Longer-term psychodynamic therapy is advocated by some for those individuals with chronic or recurrent conversion symptoms. Given that the stressor may well include marital or family issues therapy aimed at these areas may also be necessary.

C. Hypochondriasis

The essential feature of hypochondriasis is fear or worry that a symptom (often a minor physiologic sensation) represents a serious illness. This disorder is equally common in men and women. By definition, this preoccupation with disease must be present for longer than 6 months. The same general principles of conservative management with the primary care physician as principle clinician apply. Treatment of concurrent anxiety and depression is important. Cognitive therapies aimed at diminishing the focus and attention of these patients on physical sensations and reinterpreting these sensations as non-disease events has been used individually and in a group therapy format. Framing these therapies as techniques for dealing with physical distress, rather than a more direct psychological approach, may have positive results.

D. Body Dysmorphic Disorder

The essential feature of this disorder is a belief that a physical attribute is deformed or defective. These patients also do not seek mental health treatment but rather see dermatologists, plastic surgeons, and orthodontists. Psychotherapy using cognitive-behavioral techniques has seen the greatest use in recent years. Pharmacotherapy, particularly antidepressants which inhibit reuptake of serotonin into neurons, has also been shown to be effective.

E. Pain Disorder

Pain, even when the underlying cause is established, has long been known to be influenced by the psychological and social context in which it is experienced. Likewise, psychological techniques, as well as somatic treatments have long been known to modify the experience of pain. The overlap between pain disorder described as a somatoform disorder (those for which psychological factors are thought to play a major role in pain either alone or combined with a general medical condition) and pain due solely to a general medical condition is great. Pain disorder will not be dealt with extensively in this article, but the management principles of carefully coordinating care with one physician, minimizing potentially dangerous evaluations and treatments (especially addictive drugs and radical surgeries), focusing on improving function despite pain rather than curing all pain, and gradually helping the patient recognize the role of stressors in symptom exacerbation share much in common with management of the other somatoform disorders. Although pain management must be carefully coordinated by a primary physician, the multiple techniques employed often require a multidisciplinary team. Behavior therapy is the psychotherapy employed at least initially in most pain programs.

II. THEORETICAL BASES

As mentioned earlier, the disorders currently considered somatoform are quite varied. Historically, they have been united by an assumption that they represented the physical expression of an unrecognized underlying psychic conflict or a reaction to a social stressor. For somatoform disorders, the production of physical complaints is not believed to be under voluntary control as would be the case for a factitious disorder. More recent theories about the development of somatoform disorders have shifted to the role that social learning, amplification of bodily sensations, and even genetics may play. For somatization disorder, there appears to be a link between childhood trauma, especially physical abuse, illness as a child, growing up with an ill family member, and an increased likelihood of developing this disorder. Family studies of somatization disorder in females link it with sociopathy and alcoholism in male relatives. The great importance of establishing a therapeutic alliance, usually with a family doctor, which does not depend on ongoing physical complaints or illness behavior to be maintained ties together many of these etiologic theories. It is postulated that for many of these individuals, being ill themselves was the only way to either receive nurture and care or to avoid or counter mistreatment or abuse. Unfortunately, the frustration that these patients can engender in physicians and the invasive tests and procedures that they demand may easily lead to further abandonment or punishment-like experiences. Some neuropsychological studies indicate individuals with somatization disorder may have deficits in attention and memory as well as frontal lobe dysfunction and greater nondominant hemisphere dysfunction.

Conversion disorder contains in its definition an implication of the etiologic role of stress or conflict in the development of symptoms. These symptoms have been conjectured to have symbolic meaning, that is, being unable to hear due to a torrent of past verbal abuse or being unable to move one's arms after killing another in war or in an accident. However, studies have been unable to uphold this conjecture. Similarly, the belief that patients with conversion present with a "la belle indifference," showing little reaction or emotion to great impairment has not shown to be more characteristic of conversion symptoms versus impairment, due to an organic cause. The presence of secondary gain, whereby, the patient either derives some positive attention or care for the impairment or avoids some aversive responsibility or consequence, also was once believed to discriminate conversion symptoms from other medical conditions, but this does not appear to be true. Psychosocial factors that increase the likelihood of conversion symptoms include sexual abuse, exposure to medically ill relatives, lower social economic status, less education and a rural background, and having a neurological illness oneself. Theoretical outlook has shifted from one emphasizing unconscious conflicts, that is, aggression, sexuality, dependency, which are symbolically expressed to decrease anxiety and are complicated by a resistant indifference and secondary gain, to one that retains the idea that conflicts and stressors play a critical role in development of conversion symptoms but view these as more transparent to both the therapist and the patient. Treatment has shifted emphasis from longer uncovering insight-oriented psychodynamic psychotherapy to brief supportive therapy, which emphasizes suggestion, reassurance, and the prediction of recovery. This is sometimes coupled with behavioral and physical therapy approaches to address any issues of secondary gain, deconditioning, and other physical sequela and allow a face-saving mechanism for the patient to use in recovery. Psychodynamic therapy is still recommended by some for more chronic or relapsing cases of conversion symptoms.

Theories regarding the development of hypochondriasis include not only how it arises, but also whether it is a discreet disorder or simply a manifestation of other psychiatric illnesses such as anxiety or depression. With respect to anxiety disorders, analogies have been drawn between hypochondriasis and panic disorder, (both are sometimes involved in misinterpretation of normal physiologic sensations), hypochondriasis, and obsessive–compulsive disorder, (both incorporate the need to constantly check and be reassured that something bad hasn't happened with only temporary abatement of anxiety once reassured), and hypochondriasis and generalized anxiety disorder, (both are characterized by overreacting to and dwelling on common worries, often accompanied by physiologic symptoms of muscle tension, aches and pains, and hypervigilance). Somatic presentations of depression also show considerable overlap with hypochondriasis. Comorbidity is common, and treatment for concurrent conditions, for example with SSRI antidepressants may improve patients' overall function and in some cases ameliorate the hypochondriacal symptoms themselves. Psychodynamic theories have included a variety of beliefs including Freud's theories of object libido and later disturbed object relations, in which anger toward others is displaced as hostility toward the body. Other dynamic theories have described guilt, dependency needs, the need to suffer, as well as anger and hostility toward others as important in hypochondriasis. More recent psychological theories have focused on mechanisms of social learning and cognitive and perceptional distortions such as amplification, either alone or in combination. Hypochondriacal patients seem to misattribute normal physiologic sensations as evidence of underlying disease and believe to be free of serious illness one should be relatively free of any symptoms or distress. They are not, as they believe, more sensitive or accurate in detecting bodily sensations or symptoms, but rather they make errors of misattribution and overreporting. Because these patients then inaccurately identify themselves as ill, they then view themselves as entitled to assuming the sick role.

A direct or indirect experience with the sick role is thought by some to be an etiologic factor in development of hypochondriasis, however, data does not exist to confirm this theory. Cognitive-behavioral therapies have been developed to address the misperceptions and misattribution which hypochondriacal patients make. These therapies may be more successful and better accepted in the setting of a general medical clinic. As with somatization disorder, the initial focus of therapy may be on coping with physical distress rather than a more overtly psychological approach. The general management principles used for somatization disorder (for instance regular appointments with a single physician and minimizing testing procedures and treatments) are essential for hypochondriasis.

Body dysmorphic disorder has shared with hypochondriasis the debate whether it is a discreet disorder or arises from a spectrum of mood or anxiety disorders, especially obsessive–compulsive disorder. Recent successful treatment approaches with SSRI antidepressants and cognitive-behavioral therapies reinforce the belief that body dysmorphic disorder may be etiologically related to depression and/or obsessive–compulsive disorder. As with the other somatoform disorder, psychodynamic theories regarding the dysmorphic symptoms representing a displacement of a conflict on a body part had been made. Some have also commented on the role that societal preoccupation with appearance may play in the development of body dysmorphic disorder.

As noted earlier, the experience of pain has long been recognized to have a number of psychological, physical, and social determinates. Description of the specific theories of pain is beyond the scope of this article.

III. EMPIRICAL STUDIES

Because the somatoform disorders are quite different one from another, empirical studies typically focus on one specific syndrome, and the results from studies of one disorder should not be generalized across the entire category. With respect to general management principles of somatoform disorders, the most study has been done on somatization disorder. G. Richard Smith and coworkers in 1986 described the positive effects on decreasing health care utilization, without worsening health outcomes or changing patients' satisfaction with care, using psychiatric consultation followed by a letter to the referring primary care physician. The letter describes somatization disorder and recommends management with regularly scheduled appointments, physical exam at each visit, avoiding tests and procedures unless clearly indicated, and discourages physicians from telling patients "It's all in your head." This group published in 1995 a similar study on somatizing patients who did not meet full criteria for somatization disorder, showing similar positive results following a psychiatric consultation letter. The active ingredient here may be education of and support to the primary care physician. The importance of the therapeutic alliance between the primary care physician and the somatizing patient may need to be attended to in a way not formally done in most primary care settings. The primary care physician is coached to offer an analog of the "holding environment" more common psychotherapy settings. That is, to find a safe, predictable forum for the patient to present their distress albeit in the form of physical symptoms without fear of being rejected or abandoned by or overwhelming the physician, and without the sometimes unrecognized danger of being subjected to unnecessary tests and treatments.

When patients will accept overt psychological treatment, either individually or in a group setting, cognitive-behavioral therapies have been shown to improve the function of patients with somatization disorder as well as the other somatizing patients. As noted earlier, these patients may accept referral for these treatments when they are framed as "stress management." Disorders that have been shown to respond to cognitive-behavioral therapies include somatization disorder, hypochondriasis, body dysmorphic disorder, pain disorders, as well as a number of other illnesses in which somatic complaints figure prominently, including chronic fatigue, irritable bowel, chronic headaches, and non-cardiac chest pain.

Some studies of somatoform disorders, especially hypochondriasis, have attempted to answer whether or not these patients experience physiologic sensation differently or whether the error of somatization occurs secondarily in the area of interpretation, attribution, and reporting. Attempts are beginning to be made to discover whether these differences are learned or genetically determined. Explanatory therapy, an approach that emphasizes educating patients with accurate information about somatic sensations, including instruction regarding the amplification due to selective attention, providing reassurance and clarification and using repetition of this information was advocated by R. Kellner in the 1980s and was reintroduced in 2000 by G. A. Fava and colleagues for the treatment of hypochondriasis. They believe it is a simpler approach than cognitive-behavioral therapy and found it effective in a study of 20 patients.

Conversion disorders, sporadic and usually time-limited impairments, by nature have led to a relative lack of randomized control trials of therapeutic approaches. Anecdotal reports and clinical experience have led most to advocate suggestion and the expectation of recovery along with behavioral and physical therapy approach.

Supportive therapy to help patients identify and modify the psychological stressor postulated to be responsible for the conversion symptom may also be helpful. Sodium amytal interviews and hypnosis are also employed. However, well-controlled trials regarding these techniques for conversion disorder cannot be found. Further complicating studies is the broad range of conversion symptoms and the varying degree of functional impairment, for instance, hemi-paresis versus pseudoseizures. Taking into account the methodological weaknesses, there appears to be the most empiric support for suggestive and behavioral approaches. Amytal and hypnosis, although enjoying a long tradition of use for assessment and treatment of conversion disorder, suffer from the lack of control trials regarding efficacy. Some advocate there is enough suggestion of positive result utility that further studies are warranted. K. A. Phillips summarizing psychotherapeutic approaches for body dysmorphic disorder relates that cognitive-behavioral therapy including cognitive restructuring, exposure, and response prevention have been shown effective in body dysmorphic disorder. However, these studies have small numbers of participants, and as with other somatoform disorders more studies are needed.

In contrast to the few studies on body dysmorphic disorder, pain management has a relatively large literature. Pain disorders respond to cognitive-behavioral techniques, which include both cognitive restructuring and operant conditioning. Further review of the empiric studies of pain disorders is beyond the scope of this article.

IV. SUMMARY

The treatment of somatoform disorder involves both commonalties and differences. Those disorders that involve a chronic view of oneself as physically ill, somatization disorder and hypochondriasis, frequently present only to the primary care physician and the management principles of regularly scheduled rather than symptom dependent visits have already been summarized. Also critical is the avoidance of unnecessary diagnostic and therapeutic procedures and interventions. Those somatoform disorders in which a specific distortion of thinking can be identified, hypochondriasis and body dysmorphic disorder, are amenable to cognitive techniques aimed at this belief as well as behavioral therapy to change inappropriate behavioral responses such as reassurance seeking. Conversion disorder usually responds to suggestion, reassurance, and expectancy. Behavioral and physical therapy may enhance these general techniques. Pain disorder is best treated psychotherapeutically with cognitive-behavioral techniques. Although the somatoform disorders, especially somatization disorder, hypochondriasis, and conversion disorder provided some of the formative clinical material for psychiatry, especially psychodynamic psychotherapy, in practice psychodynamic therapy rarely finds itself at the forefront of treatment of somatoform disorders. In some cases of conversion disorder, particularly those for which the psychosocial stressor or conflict is not immediately apparent or which have a relapsing course, psychodynamic therapy continues to be utilized. In addition, skills in marital and family therapy are sometimes necessary particularly when somatoform disorders have resulted in patterns of secondary gain that involve couples or family systems.

See Also the Following Articles

Cancer Patients: Psychotherapy ■ Comorbidity ■ Medically Ill Patient: Psychotherapy ■ Pain Disorders

Further Reading

Avia, M. D. (1999). The development of illness beliefs. *Journal of Psychoanalysis and Research, 47*(3), 199–204.

Barsky, A. J. (1998). A comprehensive approach to the chronically somatizing patient. *Journal of Psychosomatic Research, 45*(4), 301–306.

Barsky, A. J., Stern, T. A. Greenber, D. B., & Cassen, N. H. (1997). Functional somatic symptoms and somatoform disorders. In N. H. Cassem, T. A. Stern, J. F. Rosenbaum, Jellinek (Eds), *Massachusetts General Hospital handbook of general hospital psychiatry* (pp. 305–336). Chicago: Mosby.

Epstein, R. M., Quill, T. E., & McWhinney, I. R. (1999). Somatization reconsidered incorporating the patient's experience of illness. *Archives of Internal Medicine, 159,* 215–222.

Folks, D. G., & Houck, C. A. (1993). Somatoform disorders, factitious disorders, and malingering. In A. Stoudemire, & B. S. Fogel, (Eds.), *Psychiatric Care of the Medical Patient* (pp. 267–287). New York: Oxford University Press.

Ford, C. V. (1983). *The somatizing disorders: Illness as a way of life.* New York: Elsevier Biomedical.

Martin, R. L., & Yutzy, S. H. (1997). Somatoform disorders. In A. Tasman, J. Kay, & J. A. Lieberman, (Eds.), Psychiatry (pp. 1119–1155). Philadelphia: W. B. Saunders.

Servan-Schreiber, D., Kolb, R., & Tabas, G. (1999). The somatizing patient. *Primary Care, 26*(2), 225–242.

Smith, G. R., Rost, K., & Kashner, T. M. (1995). A trial of the effect of a standardized psychiatric consultation in health outcomes and costs in somatizing patients. *Archives of General Psychiatry, 52,* 238–243.

Waurick, H. M. C., Clark, D. M., Cobb, A. M., & Salkouskis, P. M. (1996). A controlled trial of cognitive-behavioral treatment of hyponchondriasis. *British Journal of Psychiatry, 169,* 189–195.

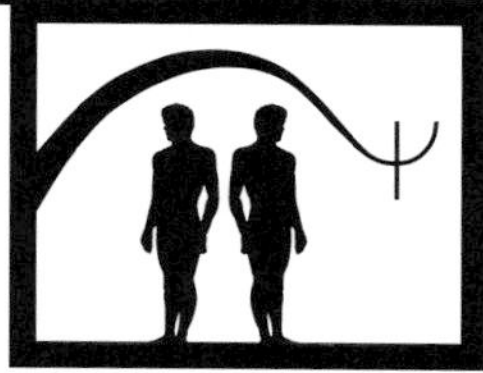

Sports Psychotherapy

Todd C. O'Hearn
Yale University

GLOSSARY

anorexia athletica Unofficial diagnostic term used to describe a syndrome found among athletes that closely resembles anorexia nervosa (AN), with the exception that an athlete's muscle mass maintains him or her above 85% of the minimum body weight.

creatine Performance-enhancing drug that increases energy transfer for muscle contraction.

deselection Forced suspension of play or retirement due to lack of physical competitiveness.

human growth hormone Performance-enhancing drug that stimulates skeletal and soft tissue growth.

neuropsychological assessment Systematic evaluation of learning and memory abilities commonly performed after an athlete sustains a head injury.

sports psychology Subspecialty of psychology that develops and applies psychological strategies to enhance and optimize athletic performance.

Yerkes-Dodson inverted U hypothesis Theory stating that optimal performance occurs at moderate levels of anxiety, while low and high levels of anxiety disrupt performance.

Sports psychotherapy is a subspecialty of psychotherapy that addresses the unique challenges and needs presented by athletes when they seek mental health services. Although sports psychotherapy has its roots in the sports psychology movement that has sought to enhance athletic performance, it extends beyond this practical goal. This article will present seven broad categories that illustrate the unique considerations of sports psychotherapy, including common psychological problems among athletes (drug use, eating disorders, and adverse reactions to injury) as well as the special developmental, social, and family factors that affect the athlete's mental health.

I. PERFORMANCE ENHANCEMENT AND THE ROLE OF THE SPORTS PSYCHOLOGIST

Performance enhancement refers to psychological interventions designed to increase an athlete's effectiveness and chances for success in competition. In a rapidly growing subspecialty, these interventions are designed and implemented by sports psychologists who provide consultation to college and professional athletic teams. In February 2001, a special issue of the American Psychological Association's journal *Professional Psychology: Research and Practice* discussed the roles and challenges of sports psychologists. For example, Frank Gardner noted that, particularly in professional sports, modern-day athletes are regarded as extremely valuable (even a kind of financial investment) and hence worthy of psychological support and protection that might optimize their performance. In the same special issue, Mark Andersen, Judy Van-Raalte, and Britton Brewer observed that sports psychologists often resemble coaches more than they do clinicians and have a correspondingly looser set of boundaries between themselves and their clients. For example, sports psychologists may accompany an athlete to a practice, a training meal, or a game.

Despite the fact that sports psychologists may not be regarded as mainstream clinicians, many of the techniques and interventions they employ are borrowed from psychotherapy treatments. In addition, the immediate goal of a performance enhancement intervention is often to reduce some negative feeling or cognitive state, although the more practical concern is competitive success. For example, performance enhancement interventions are often aimed at changing levels of competitive state anxiety, or the level of tension that an athlete feels at game time. Therapists may be guided by the "Yerkes-Dodson inverted U hypothesis," which states that optimal performance follows moderate levels of anxiety (while low and high levels of anxiety disrupt performance). To achieve this moderate level of anxiety, psychotherapists may use progressive muscle relaxation (PMR), deep diaphragmatic breathing (DDB), guided imagery, or hypnosis. PMR involves periodic tensing and relaxing of all muscle groups, typically beginning with the feet and working up toward the head. DDB involves breathing from the lower diaphragm rather than from the upper chest. Guided imagery involves the use of suggestions to create relaxing images (e.g., lying on the beach), while hypnosis also involves guidance and suggestion but in the context of a qualitatively different state of consciousness. Some therapists prefer PMR, DDB, and guided imagery because they are ultimately self-applied and the athlete can leave treatment with a tool to be used in better controlling his or her anxiety before and during competition.

In 1990, Richard Suinn presented a behavior therapy package called anxiety management training (AMT) designed to enhance athletic performance. In 6 to 8 sessions, athletes are taught self-control methods to manage their anxiety levels, including specific relaxation techniques and strategies to revise cognitive self-statements. AMT emphasizes between-session homework assignments that allow athletes to try the skills they have learned in real competitive contexts.

Sports performance may be indirectly enhanced via the psychotherapeutic exploration of an athlete's social support network. Social support has an established research base as a buffer against injury, stress, and the pressures of competition. Interpersonally oriented psychotherapy is one therapeutic modality that might be used by a sports psychologist to target relationship conflicts that can lead to social isolation. Through experiential role-plays and between-session practice exercise athletes can identify and change the problematic ways in which they interact with others. For example, role-plays may help an athlete get along better with teammates on and off the court, thereby improving the team's chances for success.

II. FAMILY THERAPY AND THE ATHLETE

Family therapy refers to the treatment of both individual and interpersonal problems within the context of a family system. In 1995 and 2000 expositions, Jon Hellstedt has described the "athletic family" as a family system that includes parents and their children who are involved in competitive sports. Although the athletic family is not necessarily destined to be problematic or dysfunctional in a clinical sense, it can be imbalanced if there is an overly intense and narrow focus on one member's sports activity. Family members, parents in particular, often project their own unfulfilled athletic (or financial and social) dreams onto their children, thereby becoming overinvolved and unduly pressuring.

Hellstedt has identified four common targets of psychotherapy with the athletic family: the level of cohesion, the nature of emotional boundaries, triangulation patterns, and developmental impasses in the family life cycle. Family cohesion, while it can provide a source of support and stability, may serve to hide tension and conflict. For example, the tightness of a family system may lead to undermining of a child's autonomy and decision-making; psychotherapy might explore this pattern, along with any unexpressed anger and resentment that accompany it. Boundaries refer to the space that separates the emotional and cognitive systems of different family members. These boundaries have been described as ranging from "enmeshed" (too little space between members) or "disengaged" (too much space between members). Psychotherapeutic intervention is typically directed at the two extremes, particularly the enmeshed boundaries often found among athletic families. Triangulation refers to avoidance of conflict between two people (e.g., parents) by focusing on a third person (e.g., athletic child). For example, parents may become overinvolved in their child's athletic activity as a way of avoiding their own marital discord. Hellstedt notes that a typical presentation in this regard includes a father who becomes overinvolved with his athletic son to the exclusion of his wife. Developmental impasses in the family life cycle refer to tasks and obstacles that arise as a family negotiates transitions. For example, most children leave home for the first time around age 17 or 18. However, young gymnasts often leave their families for extended periods of time for training, resulting in separation stress occurring sooner than is typical in the family life cycle.

Hellstedt summarizes the broad psychotherapy change goals in working with athletic families: identifying sources of stress, promoting healthy independence from the family, improving communication and problem-solving, negotiating developmental transitions, and developing the supportive capacity of the family while minimizing its role as a source of stress to the athlete.

Besides its relevance to specific athletic families, family therapy has been used as a model for understanding and intervening with sports systems and teams. Athletic teams, like family systems, often pursue goals of conflict resolution and facilitation of healthy cohesion. For example, in 1993 Toni Zimmerman and Howard Protinsky offered the following recommendations when using family therapy techniques in consultation to sports teams: meeting with both players and coaching staff, requiring attendance at consultation sessions, and utilizing family therapy models to monitor problematic patterns. Just as in families, athletic teams can experience damaging coalitions (e.g., coach singling out an athlete as his favorite) and significant communication problems.

III. LIFE SPAN DEVELOPMENT OF THE ATHLETE

Life span development refers to an age-appropriate context in which to better understand psychological issues and problems among athletes. For example, youth participation in sports can result in unique, and potentially negative, consequences. In a 1993 review, Robert Brustad explored how a child's psychological readiness for competition may impact on his or her emotional reactions to athletic activity. Psychotherapy with children who engage in sports competition too young (or perhaps too intensely) may involve discussion of the frustration, low self-esteem, and inappropriate achievement goals that have resulted from this involvement. When parents place undue pressure on children to perform the whole family can become involved in the problem, thereby necessitating a family therapy intervention to establish more realistic and healthy patterns of encouragement.

Undergraduates involved in intercollegiate sports are another group that have unique psychotherapeutic needs. Treatment must acknowledge their dual roles as both students and athletes. Stress management interventions are common among this group of athletes as they struggle to establish and balance multiple priorities. Particularly in Division I schools that serve as a training ground for professional sports, athletes may be exceedingly goal-oriented. This characteristic can be both an asset (e.g., compliance with psychotherapy homework assignments) and an obstacle (e.g., rigidity in the face of revising unrealistic or unhealthy goals) to treatment. Due to the college environment and related subcultural norms, student athletes often present with substance abuse problems, eating disorders, and adverse emotional reactions to sports injury (see later).

A third set of developmentally influenced issues arises in treatment with elite amateur and professional athletes who are retiring. In a 1993 review, Bruce Ogilvie and Jim Taylor discussed three factors that can precipitate career termination: (1) chronological age, (2) deselection (no longer physically competitive), and (3) injury. Although all three of these precipitants necessitate a process of acceptance in psychotherapy, they each bring additional unique considerations. For example, deselection often leads to marked erosion of self-esteem. Young, highly successful professional athletes who suffer career-ending injuries may need to clarify and revise their self-identity in long-term psychotherapy. Ogilvie and Taylor recommend proactive, preventive interventions for athletes who know they are facing retirement. These interventions might help athletes clarify values and goals beyond athletics, or perhaps encourage expression of feelings of frustration, doubt, and loss.

IV. DRUG USE AMONG ATHLETES

Drugs used by athletes include alcohol, recreational illicit drugs, and performance-enhancing drugs. Although there are no reliable data on the prevalence of substance abuse among athletes, alcohol, marijuana, and cocaine remain the most common recreational drugs of choice. Anabolic-androgenic steroids (AAS) are the most commonly used class of performance-enhancing drugs. AAS maximize gains in muscular strength and size, thereby conferring some competitive advantage to the athlete.

More recently athletes have begun to use human growth hormone and creatine to optimize performance.

An understanding of the reasons for drug use among athletes forms a starting point for many psychotherapeutic approaches to the problem. The question of why athletes abuse drugs has perplexed some members of the sports community who find it puzzling that individuals so committed to physical fitness would knowingly undermine this very commitment. In the case of performance-enhancing drugs, the motivations for use are relatively clear (e.g., the use of anabolic steroids for muscular power, the use of stimulants for cognitive focus and endurance), although these drugs can have unintended and negative psychological side effects. The reasons for athletes' use of other addictive recreational drugs are less clear. In 1991, Jim Taylor hypothesized that athletes at the professional and collegiate levels use recreational drugs because they have not developed effective interpersonal skills to cope with the pressures exerted by the media and fans. The peer pressure that originates in sports team subcultures can be especially potent, leading some athletes to use drugs to ensure acceptance. Finally, especially talented athletes may be less adversely affected by drug use, somehow still able to perform better than average when using, and thus more likely to deny that a problem exists.

Each of these potential reasons for drug use may lead to different psychotherapeutic interventions. For example, social skills training and anxiety management can be emphasized with athletes who are using recreational drugs as a coping strategy. Although the teaching of alternative coping strategies may help athletes who are using recreational drugs, long-term group-based rehabilitation may be necessary if serious addiction has resulted (see later). Psychoeducation may help athletes understand the short- and long-term risks of using performance-enhancing drugs (e.g., cardiovascular complications, liver damage, acne, mood swings, aggressive and antisocial behavior) and this alone may be sufficient in treating the problem, particularly where no addictive process has taken hold.

Confidentiality is a significant concern when athletes seek, or are required to receive, treatment for drug abuse. The potential stigmatizing effects of being labeled a drug abuser can be long lasting. Additionally, athletes may be very concerned about how initiation of treatment will limit their play, fearing that a sudden suspension will destroy the confidentiality of their treatment since teammates may not otherwise know a problem exists.

Long-term psychotherapy treatment programs for drug-abusing athletes, like those for members of the general population, usually include rehabilitation groups. For example, Alcoholics Anonymous and related 12-step programs may be especially effective if groups are composed of athletes with similar backgrounds. Often, athletes begin this kind of treatment at a residential inpatient (or at least day-treatment) facility where they can be fully immersed in the notion of sobriety and an alternative lifestyle. In the early 1980s, Gregory Collins was involved in one of the first organized programs for treating and preventing drug use among professional athletes. In a 2000 book chapter, Collins describes a self-help model used with the Cleveland Browns football team that included regular meetings of drug-involved players in a group called the "Inner Circle." This group placed a special emphasis on relapse prevention. Because the "Inner Circle" is composed of athletes at different stages of sobriety, members can discuss common pressures and triggers to use substances, provide and share effective support and coping mechanisms, and monitor each other's treatment progress.

Besides treatment of drug abuse, both college and professional sports teams have emphasized prevention. Although mandatory drug testing is one way of detecting a problem for early intervention, athletic staff would rather take action before a problem begins. For example, many teams have adopted programs to disseminate accurate information about drugs and to teach effective coping skills. Some prevention programs include required video and workshop orientations for new players where they are educated not just about drugs and their effects, but also about the availability of support and treatment services.

V. EATING DISORDERS AMONG ATHLETES

Sports that overvalue aesthetic appearance of the body (e.g., dance, gymnastics), low body fat (e.g., swimming, running), or maintenance of body weight (e.g., wrestling, horse-racing) may place athletes at a higher risk for developing eating disorders and related body image distortions. In 1994, Jorunn Sundgot-Borgen used the term "anorexia athletica" (diagnosed Eating Disorder, Not Otherwise Specified in *DSM-IV*) to describe a syndrome that closely resembles anorexia nervosa (AN), with the exception that these athletes do not meet AN diagnostic criteria because their muscle mass maintains them above 85% of the minimum body weight. As a clinical subpopulation, athletes are likely to respond to a distorted body image not just by restricting food intake but also by overexercising, which can in turn lead to further illness and injury (see later).

In a 1998 review, David Garner, Lionel Rosen, and Declan Barry emphasize the importance of confidentiality in working with athletes suffering from eating disorders, noting that they may be especially sensitive to how coaches and teammates will regard their problems. They specifically discourage the treating clinician from talking to other teammates about the athletes' eating problems. To avoid related marginalization, these authors recommend that athletic activity be suspended only if the athlete poses a physical health risk to themself.

Psychoeducation can be especially useful in psychotherapy with athletes suffering from eating disorders, specifically in motivating healthy dietary behavior change. For example, detailed discussion of the negative effects of restricted calorie intake on physiology and performance (e.g., reduced strength, impaired coordination, slower recovery from competition) can mobilize athletes at least to consider alternative strategies to enhance performance.

Recommended psychotherapeutic treatments for athletes with eating disorders include cognitive-behavior therapy (CBT) or interpersonal therapy for bulimia and CBT for binge-eating disorder. CBT attempts to bring eating habits under control through a system of monitoring and dietary change. Interpersonal therapy focuses on how the athlete's disrupted relationships with others (perhaps teammates) result in the impetus to engage in binge and purge cycles.

VI. REHABILITATION FROM ATHLETIC INJURY

Athletic injuries may result from relatively acute, discrete trauma, or from overtraining/overuse. Although it is rather obvious that athletic injury necessitates physical rehabilitation, only recently have psychotherapists become involved in the recovery process. Psychotherapy may facilitate both physical and emotional recovery. As an adjunct to physical rehabilitation, clinicians may help athletes set realistic goals for recovery, which is particularly important for "overuse injuries" and for those athletes who are characteristically overachieving or overexerting. Psychotherapists may also work to increase motivation about and adherence to rehabilitation regimens. For those athletes who have negative thoughts and attitudes about the prospects for recovery, cognitive-behavioral therapists may help an athlete identify cognitive distortions (e.g., an athlete who catastrophizes by assuming "this is the end of my career") and work to challenge and revise these thoughts. Psychotherapists may also indirectly affect commitment to rehabilitation and recovery rate by facilitating positive, healing imagery (e.g., "picture the tissue repairing itself"). In a 1991 study, Lydra Ieleva and Terry Orlick found that athletes using goal-setting, stress control, positive self-talk, and healing imagery recovered faster than those who did not receive these psychological interventions.

Emotional responses to athletic injury, particularly career-ending injury, often resemble reactions to loss. For example, athletes have been observed to move through Kubler-Ross's five grief stages: (1) denial and isolation, (2) anger, (3) bargaining, (4) depression, and (5) acceptance. A first step in psychotherapy is to normalize this grief process. Before acceptance can be forged, athletes may spend extended periods consumed by anger, depression, and even posttraumatic stress. These emotional problems may necessitate targeted psychotherapeutic interventions. For example, injured athletes may experience a precipitous drop in activities they enjoy or "pleasurable events," a common behavioral trigger for major depression. Therapy may identify alternative pleasurable activities and then use behavioral reinforcement contingencies to improve mood functioning. Alternatively, depression following injury may be understood within a cognitive context—sustaining an injury may provoke feelings of vulnerability and the belief that life is a series of uncontrollable events. Cognitive therapy would attempt to change these unnecessarily extreme and distorted beliefs.

Common defense mechanisms employed by athletes to avoid the unpleasant emotion associated with injury include reaction formation (displaying emotions that are the opposite of what is really felt) and intellectualization (discussing the injury in terms of thoughts and ideas without mention of emotion). Permissiveness to feel anger and sadness, and perhaps even induction of these emotions, is a primary objective of psychotherapy with athletes who are unable or unwilling to acknowledge their feelings.

The process of accepting a career-ending injury may require longer term psychotherapy to address erosion of self-esteem, particularly if an individual's valuation of himself or herself was primarily based on athletic success. This work may involve detailed discussion of what needs were fulfilled by athletic experiences and which alternative activities may now be substituted. Encouragement of seeking role models who have suffered career-ending injuries may help some athletes in psychotherapy, or even a support group of similar others if available.

Sports injury can be strategically exaggerated or even feigned by an athlete looking for secondary gain. For example, an athlete may wish to avoid some negative event (e.g., having parents watch him play) or acquire some positive benefit (e.g., insurance claim) by being injured. This kind of psychological motivation for injury may be addressed in psychotherapy by skills training that would emphasize (1) identifying more active and direct ways of making or denying requests from others, and (2) satisfying needs in a more forthright fashion.

VII. NEUROPSYCHOLOGICAL ASSESSMENT AND CONCUSSION

Neuropsychological assessment and concussion refers to the evaluation of cognitive functioning (e.g., learning and memory abilities) following a sports-related head injury. A developing body of research has suggested that multiple head injuries can have long-term negative psychological and physical health effects, with some players particularly susceptible to repeated head injury. In 1996, the National Hockey League (NHL) began an experimental pilot program to formally assess players who experienced head injuries. This program was intended to prevent a hasty return to play and thereby minimize the risk and consequences of multiple head injuries. The NHL extended this assessment program league-wide in 1997 while the National Football League also began to institute similar protocols.

In 1999, Michael Collins, Mark Lovell, and Douglas McKeag observed that there is some confusion as to when athletes should be examined because there is no universally accepted definition of concussion (e.g., some believe that loss of consciousness is central whereas others do not). Although evaluation of postconcussion effects may be conducted in a medical rather than psychotherapeutic context, sports clinicians are expected to be familiar with the testing and typical findings. For example, athletes with a history of concussion may experience slowness in processing speed (i.e., pace of response to verbal and visual stimuli) and decrements in executive functioning (i.e., ability to plan and execute decisions). When psychotherapists work with athletes who have suffered these kinds of effects from multiple head injuries, the content and pace of psychotherapy is usually adapted, as it is among other clients who present special cognitive considerations (e.g., young children, older adults).

See Also the Following Articles

Addictions in Special Populations ■ Cognitive Behavior Treatment ■ Collaborative Care ■ Eating Disorders ■ Family Therapy ■ Substance Dependence: Psychotherapy

Further Reading

Begel, D., & Burton, R. (Eds.). (2000). *Sport psychiatry: Theory and practice.* New York: W. W. Norton.

Collins, M. W., Lovell, M. R., & Mckeag, D. B. (1999). Current issues in managing sports- related concussion. *Journal of the American Medical Association, 282,* 2283–2285.

Gardner, F. L. (2001). Applied sport psychology in professional sports: The team psychologist. *Professional Psychology: Research and Practice, 32,* 34–39.

Garner, D. M., Rosen, L. W., & Barry, D. (1998). Eating disorders among athletes. *Sport Psychiatry, 7,* 839.

Russell, W. D. (1996). Utility of family therapy in the field of sport. *Family Therapy, 23,* 33–42.

Taylor, J., & Taylor, S. (1997). *Psychological approaches to sports injury rehabilitation.* Gaithersburg, MD: Aspen Publishers.

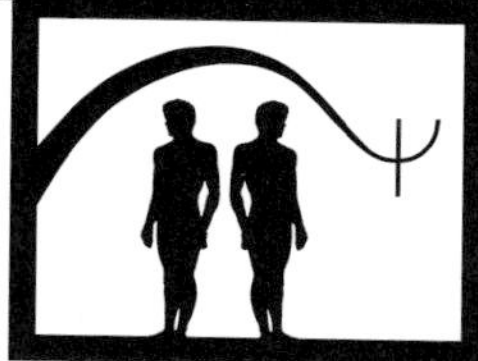

Spouse-Aided Therapy

Paul M. G. Emmelkamp and Ellen Vedel
University of Amsterdam

GLOSSARY

communication skills training A behavioral procedure designed to decrease stress in a couple by teaching attentive listening skills, effective ways to express positive and negative feelings, and how to request behavioral change in a nonhostile manner.

exposure Repeated confrontation with, or approach to, the object that is avoided.

interpersonal therapy Psychodynamically based treatment that aims to alter negative interpersonal situations that maintain depression. The focus is on one of the following domains: (1) loss, (2) role disputes, (3) role transitions, and (4) interpersonal deficits.

problem-solving training Teaching a set of sequential steps for solving problems that minimizes negative emotional undercurrents while maximizing the identification, evaluation, and implementation of the optimal solutions.

systems theory The basis premise of this theory is that the problem shown by the "identified patient" is a sign that something is wrong with the entire family. Problems of the patient are seen as only a symptom of more basic family problems. System-theoretically derived treatment deals with the relationship between the individual family members and the family system, rather than focusing on overt pathological symptoms.

I. DESCRIPTION OF TREATMENT

For present purposes spouse-aided therapy is defined as any psychological intervention in which the partner of the patient with a psychiatric disorder (e.g., anxiety disorder, depression, substance use disorders) is actively involved in the treatment, and the focus of the intervention is primarily on the psychiatric disorder. This means that marital therapy directed exclusively to the marital difficulties of the couple without due attention to the specific psychiatric disorder involved is not discussed here.

There are several advantages for spouse-aided therapy: (1) The spouse is informed about the psychiatric disorder and the kind of treatment delivered, (2) the spouse can give additional information about symptomatology of the patient and treatment progress, (3) the spouse can be emotionally supported, since living with a patient is often a heavy burden; and (4) the spouse can learn to deal more adequately with disorder-related situations, and, if necessary, general communication between partners can be improved.

A. Anxiety Disorders

In anxiety disorders, two different formats of spouse-aided therapy can be distinguished. In partner-assisted exposure the partner accompanies the patient to each treatment session. The couple receives a treatment rationale, in which the focus is on exposing the patient to phobic situations. The partner can assist in making a hierarchy, consisting of gradually more difficult exposure tasks. At each session the patient is given a number of exposure homework assignments. The role of the partner is to stimulate the patient to do these exercises, to help in confronting the phobic situations, to accompany the patient if necessary, and to reinforce the patient in mastering these exposure exercises successfully. The actual presence of the partner is gradually faded out during the exposure exercises. At the beginning of each new session, the patient's performance on the exposure tasks and the assistance of the partner are discussed with the couple and new homework assignments are given. More difficult tasks are given only if tasks lower in the hierarchy have been performed successfully. The pace at which the patient works through the hierarchy is determined by the couple. Thus, treatment focuses on the phobia. Relationship problems, if any, are not discussed.

Other spouse-aided approaches in anxiety disorders have focussed on interpersonal difficulties thought to maintain agoraphobic symptoms. These approaches include communication training and partner-assisted problem solving directed either at phobia-related conflicts or at general life stresses and problems.

B. Depression

Partner-assisted cognitive-behavior therapy for depression is based on Peter Lewinsohn and Aaron Beck's individual therapy of depression. It is assumed that depressed individuals do not engage in pleasant activities and hence do not get adequate reinforcement, resulting in mood disturbance. During spouse-aided therapy, partners join all sessions. Treatment focuses on the depression and on ways both partners can deal more adequately with depression-related situations rather than on relationship aspects per se. Therefore, spouses are involved in devising reinforcing activities, in stimulating patients to engage in rewarding activities, and participating in role-playing. Further, spouses are asked to attend to the dysfunctional thoughts of the patient and to discuss these with both patient and therapist. In addition, partners are actively involved in designing behavioral experiments to test (irrational) beliefs and are encouraged to take part in challenging the assumptions held by the patient.

In conjoint interpersonal therapy the partner is involved in addressing patient-related unresolved difficulties in one of the following domains: loss (e.g., of a child or parent), role disputes, role transitions, and interpersonal deficits. Moreover, five sessions of conjoint communication training are included.

In cases with co-occurring depression and marital discord, conjoint behavioral marital therapy may be applied. Here, the emphasis is not only on the mood disorder, but also on the communication between the partners. Generally, in the earlier phase of therapy problems associated with depression that could hinder a successful application of marital therapy are dealt with. Examples of such problems are complicated grief or a low activity level in the depressed patient. Later on the focus of the therapy is shifted to the training of communication skills in both spouses.

C. Substance Abuse

In general behavioral couple treatment for alcohol use disorders focuses on behavioral self-control and coping skills to facilitate and maintain abstinence, improving spouse coping with drinking-related situations, improving relationship functioning in general, and improving functioning within other social systems in which the couple is currently involved. The degree of emphasis on each of these four domains and the techniques used to target these domains varies across different treatment protocols. Two well-known protocols are the ones used in the Harvard Counseling for Alcoholics' Marriages (CALM) project by Timothy O'Farrell and the Alcohol Behavioral Couple Treatment (ABCT) protocol used by Barbara McCrady. The main differences between these two protocols are that O'Farrell's treatment is designed to be used in conjunction with or subsequent to a treatment focusing on cessation of drinking, whereas the treatment developed by McCrady is designed as a standalone treatment. Also, part of the CALM treatment is delivered in a group format whereas McCrady's treatment is delivered during individual couple sessions.

Some techniques often used are the sobriety or Antabuse contract to reduce conflict and distrust between the couple, identifying high-risk situations and teaching both partners alternative skills to cope with these situations, and improving communication between the partners by using role-play to reduce conflict, enhance marital satisfaction, and reduce the chance of relapse.

Behavioral couple treatment for substance use disorders other than alcohol are derived from these (and other) alcohol treatment protocols, focus on the same four domains, and use similar behavioral techniques. Another behavioral intervention in which the spouse is usually involved, but also other family members and other individuals from the patient's network, is Azrin's community reinforcement approach. Consistent with operant conditioning principles, this treatment is designed to remove drinking reinforcing behaviors by teaching family and friends to ignore drinking and reward nondrinking.

Originally designed for treating alcoholics, this treatment has been adapted by Stephen Higgens and colleagues for treating cocaine and other drug abusing patients.

II. THEORETICAL BASES

A. Anxiety Disorders

Systems-oriented clinicians hold that phobias and other anxiety symptoms have interpersonal meaning in relationships. For example, Jay Haley defined the martial relationships of agoraphobic patients as compulsory marriages, in which partners do not stay together out of love but are forced to stay together because of the symptoms. Further, the partners of patients with an anxiety disorder have been described by system-oriented clinicians as negativistic, hostile, compulsive, and anxious. It was assumed that improvement of the anxious patient would lead to an exacerbation of symptoms in the partner and/or to marital distress.

No convincing evidence has been provided that partners of patients with anxiety disorders are psychologically abnormal themselves. However, recent empirical studies comparing agoraphobic and obsessive–compulsive couples with healthy control couples suggest there might be some differences regarding marital satisfaction, adjustment, and interpersonal problem-solving skills. These differences, however, are usually rather small. Nevertheless, this view has given impetus to involving the partner of agoraphobic and obsessive–compulsive patients in the treatment.

B. Depression

Depressed persons are characterized by an aversive interpersonal style to which others respond with negativity and rejection. The interaction of depressed individuals with their partner has been characterized by a lower proportion of positive verbal behavior and a greater proportion of negative verbal and nonverbal behavior. A substantial number of depressed patients presenting for treatment also experience marital distress, whereas in approximately half of the couples who have marital problems at least one of the spouses is depressed. These data suggest that depression and marital distress are closely linked. Furthermore, marital distress is an important precursor of depressive symptoms. In addition, persons who, after being treated for depression, return to distressed marriages are more likely to experience relapse. When patients are asked about the sequence of depression and marital distress, most patients hold that marital distress preceded the depressive episode. Results of these studies suggest that it might be important to enroll the partner in the treatment of depressed patients.

C. Substance Abuse

From a behavioral or social learning perspective alcoholism is a biopsychosocial process, the course of which is determined by multiple factors. According to this model, alcoholism, as well as other addictive behaviors, are habitual, maladaptive methods for attempting to cope with the stresses of daily living. This maladaptive coping is triggered by internal and external cues and reinforced by positive rewards and/or negative punishment. Formerly spouse-aided interventions with substance use disorders were regarded most appropriate for only a subset of clients with severe marital or family problems. These clients were presumed to be in an "alcoholic relationship" with a specific pathological marital structure, in need of different treatment interventions. Research now points in the direction of also involving a significant other, across a broader spectrum of clients.

Within a behavioral framework drinking or drug taking is assumed to have a negative effect on communication between partners and marital satisfaction, and has also been linked to other marital issues such as domestic violence and sexual dysfunction. Research has differentiated families of alcoholics from healthier control families in that the former typically manifest poor communication, organization, problem-solving, conflict management, and affect regulation processes. However, comparing alcoholic couples with nonalcoholic but distressed couples revealed that the latter group was characterized by similar dysfunctional processes as the former. Alcoholic couples do differ from nonalcoholic couples in that they report more domestic violence. Even in nonalcoholic couples more drinking is associated with increased violence.

There is some evidence that specific behaviors of the spouse can function either as a cue or reinforcer in drinking or drug-taking behavior. Furthermore, marital stability has been found to be positively related to success of treatment. In studies of alcohol abusers recovering without treatment intervention, social support, especially from a spouse, was significantly related to successful changes in drinking behavior. Finally, there is some evidence that restoring marital satisfaction and reducing conflicts reduces the chance for relapse. Taken together, the results of these studies suggest a need to investigate the effectiveness of spouse-aided interventions in substance abuse.

III. EMPIRICAL STUDIES

A. Anxiety Disorders

In contrast to expectations derived from general systems theory, there is no evidence that exposure therapy with patients with agoraphobia or obsessive–compulsive disorder has adverse effects on the relationship or the partners' symptoms. The controlled studies in this area suggest that the relationship remains stable or improves slightly, and no exacerbation of symptoms in the partner of the patient has been reported. Thus, the empirical evidence does not support the systems conceptualization of anxiety disorders as being a symptom of more serious marital problems.

Studies investigating the effects of spouse-aided therapy in individuals with agoraphobia and obsessive–compulsive disorder have indicated partner-assisted exposure to be as effective as treatment by the patient alone. The results of the studies that have been conducted thus far indicate that it is not essential to include the spouse in the exposure treatment of patients with agoraphobia or obsessive-compulsive disorder.

The results of studies that evaluated the efficacy of interpersonal skills training interventions are rather mixed, so no general conclusions are allowed. Treatment focusing on general life stress rather than on relationship difficulties was found to be less effective than exposure by the patient alone. In contrast, studies that focussed on relationship issues in addition to exposure led to slightly better results, especially on follow-up. Notably, this was also the case in couples that were not maritally distressed. Given the finding that criticism of the spouse may be related to relapse at follow-up, this may require specific attention to communication training in couples with a critical partner.

B. Depression

In this paragraph only studies are reviewed in which at least one individual of a couple was clinically depressed. Marital distress hinders treatment of the depressive disorder and, given the link between relapse and being in a distressed relationship, increases the chance of relapse in the future. To date, three controlled studies have shown that conjoint behavioral marital therapy in depressed–maritally distressed couples may be a good alternative for individual cognitive-behavior therapy. Taking the results of these studies together, in depressed–maritally distressed couples behavioral marital therapy seems to have an exclusive effect on the marital relationship, which is not found in individual cognitive-behavior therapy, while it is as effective as cognitive therapy in reducing depressed mood. Not surprisingly, behavioral marital therapy was hardly effective in depressed patients who did not experience marital problems.

Thus far, only one controlled study has investigated the effects of partner-assisted cognitive-behavior therapy and only one the effects of conjoint interpersonal therapy in depressed individuals. The results of partner-assisted cognitive-behavior therapy were comparable with those of individual cognitive-behavior therapy. Both treatments led to statistically significant improvement on depressed mood, behavioral activity, and dysfunctional cognitions. However, none of the treatment formats affected relationship variables, which comes as no surprise because all couples were non–maritally distressed prior to treatment. Thus, partner-assisted cognitive-behavior therapy was as effective as individual cognitive-behavior therapy in depressed individuals. In addition, conjoint interpersonal psychotherapy was equally effective as individual interpersonal psychotherapy on measures of depressive symptomatology. There was some evidence that the conjoint version was slightly more effective than the individual therapy on relationship variables. Finally, there is some evidence that treatment focusing on the interaction of depressed couples is slightly more effective than antidepressants.

C. Substance Abuse

The results of spouse-aided treatment programs in substance use disorders are encouraging. Research suggests that spouse involvement in the treatment of alcohol and drug use disorders produces significant reductions in alcohol and/or drug use, and improves marital functioning. There are also indications that behavioral couple therapy reduces violence in violent alcoholic couples. It should be noted, however, that most research to date was conducted in academic centers and has focused on white, male, higher educated alcoholic subjects. Typically, subjects in these studies had few other axis I or axis II disorders and were in relatively steady relationships with non–substance-abusing partners. It remains to be shown whether these spouse-aided treatment protocols will be as effective when delivered to other populations in a community setting.

IV. SUMMARY

Spouse-aided therapy consists of psychological interventions in which the partner of the patient with a psychiatric disorder is actively involved in the treatment, which focuses primarily on the psychiatric disorder.

Spouse-aided exposure has shown to be effective in treating anxiety disorders (e.g., agoraphobia and obsessive–compulsive disorders). However, there is little evidence of it being more effective in reducing anxiety symptoms, compared to individual exposure treatment programs. There is some evidence that spouse-aided therapy focusing not only on the phobic disorder but also on communication is more effective than treatment of the patient alone. Specific attention to communication training may be required in anxious patients with an overcritical partner.

Evidence suggests that spouse-aided therapy that focuses not only on the mood disorder, but also on improving communication skills and problem-solving skills of both partners, should be the treatment of choice in maritally distressed patients with dysthymia or major depression. Finally, the results of spouse-aided treatment programs in substance use disorders are encouraging.

Although a number of studies have evaluated the effectiveness and efficacy of spouse-aided therapy in anxiety disorders, depression, and substance use disorders, no conclusions may be drawn from these findings regarding its efficacy in other disorders. There is some clinical evidence that spouse-aided therapy might also be used in chronic pain management and in schizophrenia, but controlled studies are needed before firm conclusions about the effectiveness of spouse-aided therapy in these disorders are warranted.

See Also the Following Articles

Aversion Relief ■ Behavioral Marital Therapy ■ Communication Skills Training ■ Couples Therapy: Insight Oriented ■ Family Therapy ■ Home-Based Reinforcement ■ Homework ■ Interpersonal Psychotherapy ■ Parent-Child Interaction Therapy ■ Psychodynamic Couples Therapy ■ Sex Therapy

Further Reading

Baucom, D. H., Shoham, V., Mueser, K. T., Daiuto, A. D., & Stickle, T. R. (1998). Empirically supported couple and family interventions for marital distress and adult mental health problems. *Journal of Consulting and Clinical Psychology, 66,* 53–88.

Beach, S. R. H., Fincham, F. D., & Katz, J. (1998). Marital therapy in the treatment of depression: Towards a third generation of therapy and research. *Clinical Psychology Review, 18,* 835–861.

Carr, A. (2000). Evidence-based practice in family therapy and systemic consultation: II. Adult focused interventions. *Journal of Family Therapy, 22,* 273–295.

Daiuto, A. D., Baucom, D. H., Epstein, N., & Dutton, S. S. (1998). The application of behavioral couples therapy to the assessment and treatment of agoraphobia: Implications of empirical research. *Clinical Psychology Review, 18,* 663–687.

Craske, M., & Zoellner, L. (1996). Anxiety disorders: The role of marital therapy. In N. Jacobson & A. Gurman (Eds.), *Clinical handbook of couples therapy* (pp. 394–410). New York: Guilford Press.

Emmelkamp, P. M. G., & Gerlsma, C. (1994). Marital functioning and the anxiety disorders. *Behavior Therapy, 25,* 407–429.

Epstein, E. E., & McCrady, B. S. (1998). Behavioral couples treatment of alcohol and drug use disorders: Current status and innovations. *Clinical Psychology Review, 18,* 689–711.

McCrady, B. S., Epstein, E. E., & Hirsch, L. S. (1999). Maintaining change after conjoint behavioral alcohol treatment for men: Outcome at 6 months. *Addiction, 94,* 1381–1396.

O'Farrell, T. J., & Cowles, K. S. (1995). Marital and family therapy. In R. K. Hester & W. R. Miller (Eds.), *Handbook of alcoholism treatment approaches.* Needham Heights, MA: Allyn & Bacon.

Prince, S., & Jacobson, N. (1995). A review and evaluation of marital and family therapies for affective disorders. *Journal of Marital & Family Therapy, 21,* 377–401.

Rotunda, J. R., & O'Farrell, T. J. (1997). Marital and family therapy of alcohol use disorders: Bridging the gap between research and practice. *Professional Psychology: Research and Practice, 28,* 246–252.

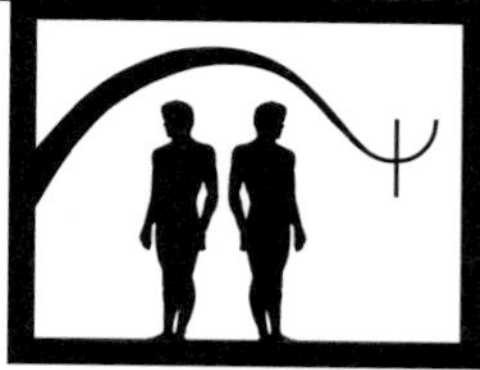

Stretch-Based Relaxation Training

Charles R. Carlson
University of Kentucky

GLOSSARY

masticatory muscle pain Chronic muscle pain disorder affecting the muscles used for chewing and moving the jaw.

musculoskeletal pain Pain involving structures of the musculoskeletal system that includes muscles, bones, joints, ligaments, and tendons.

PBS A three-step strategy for reducing muscle tension that focuses on positioning (P), breathing (B), and stretching (S).

self-monitoring Process of making regular assessments of personal behavior or activity for the purpose of understanding the frequency with which those behaviors or activities under study occur.

stretch-based progressive relaxation A progressive relaxation training approach that uses gentle muscle stretches to teach sensory awareness of muscle groups and to promote volitional relaxation.

Stretch-based relaxation training was developed as an alternative to more traditional progressive muscle relaxation procedures focusing on muscle tension exercises to teach relaxation skills. In contrast to the tense-release strategy of traditional progressive muscle relaxation, the stretch-based approach uses gentle stretches of major muscle groups to teach sensory awareness and volitional control of muscle activity. Results from randomized clinical trials have demonstrated the clinical efficacy of the stretch-based approach for addressing a range of problems that include face pain, neck pain, and general anxiety. This article presents the theoretical rationale, outcome data, and clinical applications of stretch-based relaxation training.

I. INTRODUCTION

Psychotherapists are faced with a broad array of options for conducting relaxation training. Generally, the goal of relaxation training is to reduce activation, both physical and mental, and promote self-efficacy for regulation of internal states. These skills of self-regulation can be used to enhance the management of personal and interpersonal challenges. Although there are a variety of relaxation training approaches, the use of progressive relaxation is often a method of choice.

Progressive relaxation was introduced just after the turn of the 20th century by Edmund Jacobson. As a physician, he became interested in the processes by which his patients controlled their own levels of physical and psychological activity. He believed that control over muscle tension and cognitions could be obtained through guided practice where an individual learned to manage her or his level of muscle tension and focus of attention. His primary strategy for teaching this control was conscious activation and relaxation of various muscle groups in a systematic manner. Originally, he conceptualized relaxation training as requiring 40 to 60 sessions of deliberate practice in tensing and relaxing various muscles. Often an entire hour-long session was devoted to only one muscle group. This rather laborious technique of relaxation training spurred an interest among other practitioners for developing shorter progressive relaxation training programs.

One of the most popular variants of Jacobson's original relaxation procedure was the abbreviated progressive relaxation (APR) approach developed by Bernstein and Borkovec. The original series of Jacobson's exercises was reduced to 16 major muscle groups in the initial APR training session. Like the Jacobsonian approach, the basic strategy for APR is to tense the muscle group for 15 to 20 seconds and then quickly release the muscle tension and let the muscle relax for an extended period. The sequence of muscles that are relaxed generally begins with the hands then progressively moves upward to the head and down to the feet. There is a substantial literature attesting to the effectiveness of APR for a wide variety of clinical problems, as is documented in Carlson and Hoyle in 1993 and Carlson and Bernstein in 1995. This literature includes information on anxiety disorders, depression, and medical conditions such as headache, insomnia, and hypertension.

There are conditions, however, where the use of muscle tensing strategies is not indicated. In cases where muscle tension increases pain, or there is a history of cardiac disease such as arrythmias, muscle tensing strategies should be avoided. Furthermore, the muscle contractions used in progressive relaxation training may increase muscle nerve sympathetic activity and not promote general relaxation. Finally, the rationale for use of muscle tension–based strategies that increase tension in order to reduce tension can often be difficult for clients to accept in the initial phase of treatment when pain, tension, or anxiety is intense. Because of these issues, an alternative to the use of muscle tensing exercises for progressive relaxation training is needed.

From a physiological perspective, if a muscle is contracted, a slow, gentle stretch of the muscle that does not overstretch or tear the muscle fibers will foster the relaxation of the muscle when the stretch is released. One common example of this principle is the familiar case of the "Charley horse" in which the muscle spasm of the lower back leg is most easily reduced by stretching that muscle gently (by moving the toes several inches toward the head and holding them in that position) for an extended period of time. Physical therapists and athletic trainers use muscle stretching on a regular basis to quiet contracted, overly active muscles. Muscle stretching results in reduced excitability of the motoneuron pool that can lead to reduced muscle activity, increased blood flow, and less pain. The value of muscle stretching is well-recognized in the empirical literature related to muscle function.

Jacobson's original intent in using muscle tensing exercises was primarily to teach the discrimination of muscle groups so that one's sensitivity to motor activation was enhanced. His ultimate goal for a client was to learn how to relax without the use of muscle tension exercises. The tense-release sequences were not a necessary part of the process of relaxing a muscle, but rather a learning tool to foster the acquisition of relaxation skills by teaching awareness of subtle sensations of muscle tension. Substituting a gentle stretch of a muscle for a contraction of that muscle is an alternative means by which sensory awareness can be improved while at the same time taking advantage of the natural relaxation effects associated with the release of a gentle muscle stretch.

Given this background, muscle stretches were developed for each of the 16 major muscle groups associated with the APR procedures of progressive relaxation. Although muscle stretches of these muscle groups cannot be performed by an individual without using some muscle tension (e.g., stretching the muscles of the lower back leg by gently drawing the toes of the feet toward the head), the focus of the procedures was on the muscle stretches themselves and the sensory experiences following the stretches. The sequence of the muscle stretches began with the lower legs and proceeded upward to the head region. Each of the muscles was stretched for 15 to 20 seconds and followed by relaxation for 60 seconds. An example of the instructions for a muscle stretch of the forehead (frontalis region) from Carlson and Collins follows:

> In order to stretch the muscles of the forehead, place the fingertips of both hands slightly above the eyebrows and gently push the fingers upward toward the hairline, stretching the muscles by applying light pressure. When you reach the hairline, hold the stretch by maintaining the upward pressure of your fingers on the skin.

The stretch-based progressive relaxation approach is presented in either a five-session format for individuals or a six-session group format. The protocol includes therapist scripts, home practice guidelines, audiotape for home practice, and videotape for therapist training. Diaphragmatic breathing entrainment is included in the presentation of the relaxation procedures to aid in relaxation, as well as to assist in the timing of the stretch-relaxation sequences. The goal of this program is to teach volitional skills of relaxation in as efficient manner as possible using a focus on muscle stretching procedures.

II. REVIEW OF CLINICAL TRIALS

Following completion of a successful clinical case study involving the use of the stretch-based relaxation approach to address a generalized anxiety, 24 individuals self-referred for moderate muscle tension and anxiety were assigned randomly to a stretch-based relaxation group, tension-based relaxation group, or a wait-list control group. After the treatments were delivered, participants in the stretch-based group reported significantly less muscle tension at four muscle sites (right trapezius, right brachioradialis, left tricep, and left tricep) and had significantly less electromyogram (EMG) activity in the right masseter region than did participants in the tension-based relaxation group. These preliminary data from this randomized clinical trial indicated that the stretch-based progressive muscle relaxation procedures were effective in reducing both subjective and objective indices of muscle tension in persons reporting moderate tension and anxiety.

Carlson and colleagues then applied the stretch-based approach to persons with masticatory muscle pain disorder. Masticatory muscle pain disorder is a disorder where there is no evidence of temporomandibular joint pathology, but the muscles of mastication (primarily masseter, temporalis, and pterygoids) are painful enough to cause impaired chewing function. A group of 34 persons with masticatory muscle pain were assigned randomly to either a stretch-based relaxation protocol or to a condition in which the participants were asked to rest in relaxed positions. Results revealed that persons with elevated muscle activity assigned to the stretch-based group had greater reductions in EMG activity at both left and right masseter sites than persons assigned to the rest control condition. There were, however, no differences in self-reports of muscle tension between the two groups. For persons with masticatory muscle pain disorders, the use of the stretch-based relaxation approach was an effective means for reducing ongoing muscle activity even though reductions in self-reports of muscle tension did not differ from persons given instructions to relax by assuming positions of rest.

Kay and Carlson in 1992 directly compared the stretch-based relaxation approach to the tense-release and rest control relaxation procedures in a group of 60 persons reporting chronic neck muscle tension. The effectiveness of the procedures was evaluated by having the participants use one of the relaxation strategies after being exposed to a standard laboratory stressor. Participants were randomly assigned to one of the experimental groups and it was found that those assigned to the stretch-based condition reported greater overall reductions in muscle tension and lower left trapezius muscle activity than those assigned to either of the other two groups. Additionally, the stretch-based group had an overall increase in peripheral skin temperature, whereas the other two groups did not. This latter finding suggests that sympathetic nervous system activity was reduced for the participants using the stretch-based relaxation procedures. Overall, these data indicated that the stretch-based relaxation approach provided an effective relaxation strategy for persons with chronic neck tension.

Sherman and colleagues in 1997 evaluated the influence of stretch-based relaxation procedures on the immune function of persons experiencing persistent facial pain. Twenty-one participants were assigned randomly to either a stretch-based relaxation condition or a rest-control condition. Participants in the stretch-based relaxation condition had greater salivary immunoglobulin A (IgA) secretion rates than those in the rest-control condition. These results indicated that stretch-based relaxation training may have benefits beyond reduction of muscle tension for persons with chronic pain conditions.

Finally, Wynn in 1995 and 1998 conducted a series of controlled trials of stretch-based relaxation training with persons at risk for developing hypertension. This first study involved 32 young adult males with a family history of hypertension. Participants randomly assigned to six sessions of stretch-based relaxation training displayed lower heart rate and blood pressure (systolic and diastolic) responses to a laboratory stressor than did a comparable group of persons randomly assigned to a control condition. Additionally, participants trained in stretch-based relaxation reported less anger and anxiety than the controls. These findings were followed-up in a second study of 48 Black American males at risk for developing hypertension. It was found that those randomly assigned to the stretch-based relaxation protocol demonstrated lower diastolic blood pressure reactivity to a laboratory stressor, as well as lower emotional reactivity than did persons randomly assigned to a group that underwent a health education program as a comparative control. Taken together, these two studies demonstrated the efficacy of the stretch-based relaxation protocol for reducing reactivity to laboratory stressors in persons at risk for the development of hypertension.

Overall, the data from a series of clinical trials support the use of stretch-based relaxation among persons with muscle tension and facial and neck pain, and those prone to excessive reactivity to environmental stressors. One of the shortcomings of the presently available data is that they are based on studies conducted within the clinical laboratory of the primary author of the stretch-based relaxation protocol. Other well-controlled clinical trials outside the author's laboratory are needed to provide independent confirmation of the effectiveness of the stretch-based relaxation approach. Based on the available data, however, there are strong preliminary data indicating the efficacy of the stretch-based progressive relaxation protocol.

III. TECHNIQUE

A. Initial Evaluation

Before beginning stretch-based relaxation training, the clinician should complete a thorough initial evaluation with the client to ensure that relaxation training is appropriate for that individual. The primary concern in this initial consultation is to determine the nature of the presenting complaints and to understand how the use of progressive relaxation training may be of benefit. There are also conditions for which stretch-based relaxation training may be contraindicated. These conditions would include a history of loss of contact with reality or an ongoing thought disorder whereby there would be significant difficulty with interpreting or understanding instructions. Medical conditions such as diabetes or seizure disorders may be contraindicated in some cases, or need to be closely monitored by medical personnel during the training program. Women who are pregnant should have the approval of their health providers before beginning a relaxation program. Any medical condition that requires ongoing medications (e.g., hypertension) also requires an approval of the health care provider responsible for prescribing the medication, because relaxation training may potentially alter how the body responds to current medication intake. Progressive relaxation training has the potential to alter the level of an individual's overall physiological activity, in addition to altering cognitive and emotional processes. Therefore, clients should be carefully screened for their participation in a progressive relaxation training program.

B. Presentation of Program

There are four elements to the initial presentation of the stretch-based relaxation program. The first element is to provide the client a historical overview of progressive relaxation training and the stretch-based approach. This overview would include a discussion of the natural use of muscle stretching and the value of systematic application of muscle stretching in the strech-based relaxation protocol. The second element to discuss with the client is the concept of learning the skill of muscle relaxation. The emphasis of the program is to develop specific and effective skills of quieting the body whenever the individual chooses to do so. The third element of the initial presentation involves the importance of regular practice of the skills introduced in the training sessions. Without systematic practice, the skills are difficult to perfect and to employ in ongoing daily routines. Finally, the central focus of the program is on learning relaxation skills that are under volitional control. The program is not about a therapist "relaxing" the individual, but rather it is about the individual learning how to relax themself with the skills that she or he has learned through regular practice.

C. Introduction to Basic Techniques

The basic series of 14 muscle stretches is introduced by first describing the importance of not invoking or increasing pain with any of the stretch-based relaxation activities. The client must be assured that the program is not centered on "enduring pain" in hopes of future gains. Then the client is told that each muscle stretch is done for 15 to 20 seconds and followed by a 60-second period of relaxation. The stretching of muscles is always done slowly and only to the point at which a slight muscle stretch is felt. Overstretching or "bouncing" of muscles is not appropriate.

After introducing the general approach to stretch-based relaxation, the client is shown each of the muscle stretches that includes both lower legs, both upper legs, the lower right/left back, stomach, chest, forehead, eyes, jaw, right/left neck, lower arms, and upper arms. The stretches are usually performed from a comfortable, reclined position in which the client's head is supported, eyes are closed (not necessary if closing the eyes creates discomfort), hands in curled and relaxed position, and legs are quiet with toes pointing away from one another at a 45 to 90 degree angle. Breathing slowly and regularly is also part of the relaxation program and will be important in later sessions of practice as a timing mechanism for each of the stretch-relaxation exercises.

Once the introduction of the exercises has been completed, the client is reminded of the importance of maintaining a relaxed and comfortable position throughout the period of training. Any tight clothing (e.g., belt) may want to be loosened for the training session, and if eyeglasses, contact lenses, heavy jewelry or watches are bothersome, they should be removed for the duration of the training session as well. When the client is ready to begin the relaxation training, the therapist can begin with the following instructions from Carlson and Collins in 1997:

> Before beginning the first exercise, take time to breathe in and out slowly and regularly (wait 2–3 minutes).
>
> We are ready to begin the exercises now. For each exercise I will first describe the exercise. Then, when I say the words, "ready, begin" I want you to begin the stretch.
>
> The first exercise involves stretching the muscles in the lower right leg. When I say "ready, begin" you are going to stretch the muscles in the lower right leg by pulling the toes of the right foot toward your head until you meet resistance in the muscles along the back of the right leg. Ready, begin the stretch by pulling the toes toward your head until you feel resistance. Hold the toes at that position while you feel the muscles stretching in the back of the right leg. Hold the stretch (wait 15 seconds) and now release the stretch and let the toes return to a resting position. Notice the difference in the muscle sensations in the back of the lower right leg as the muscles are now relaxing. Just let the muscles relax and become quiet (wait 30 seconds). You can help the muscles continue to relax by focusing your attention on the muscles in that lower leg and encouraging them to become less tense (wait 30 seconds).

Each of the remaining exercises follows a similar format and is done in a prescribed sequence. The sequence of the muscle stretches is designed so that if a muscle is activated to perform a stretch, it will then be stretched, in turn, to foster further relaxation of that muscle. The exercises are sequenced to move from the feet to the head region.

Following completion of the relaxation instructions, the client is encouraged to reactivate herself or himself with the following:

> At this time, I will begin counting backwards from 5 to 1. With each number you should gain more awareness. When I reach "1" you will be fully alert and ready to begin you next activity but you will still be feeling relaxed and comfortable. 5—begin to move your feet and legs. 4—move your arms and hands. 3—move your head and neck. 2—open your eyes. 1—you should now be alert with your eyes open; feeling relaxed and refreshed. Should you be lying down, you may want to roll to your side or stomach and then begin to lift yourself. That concludes your initial training session.

The relaxation exercise series should be practiced at least once a day for 5 out of the next 7 days. Generally, the training sessions are spaced at one week intervals. Audiotape instructions are available to assist in this home practice as it has been shown by Carlson and Holye in 1993 that audiotapes can improve the effectiveness of relaxation training. It is also helpful for the therapist to review with the client the importance of practice and addressing common beliefs such as "these exercises are so easy, I don't need to practice," "I can't relax, so why would these exercises work," or "When I relax, I am afraid that...". Finally, the client should be given some sort of self-monitoring forms to take home to record periodic levels of muscle tension on a daily basis and to record when relaxation practice sessions occurred. One effective self-monitoring strategy involves the use of 10 cm visual analogue scales (anchored at one end with "least tension" and at the other with "most possible tension") that the client can fill out periodically. These can be quickly and efficiently scored with a computer program. Another recently developed strategy is to use a hand-held computer that has been programmed to prompt for and to accept self-monitoring data.

The stretch-based relaxation protocol has four additional elements of training after the first session. The first additional element involves completing the entire series of stretches with a shortened set of instructions. The second element involves the use of music during the session and the use of breathing to self-pace the stretches. The third element includes muscle scanning, a procedure for taking "mental measurements" of muscle tension throughout the body, skills for reducing any areas of identified tension, and a shortened version of the muscle stretching protocol. The skills for reducing areas of identified muscle tension involve a stepped-process involving changes in posture, control of breathing, and isolated muscle stretches of those muscle areas identified as tense. The posture, breathing, and stretching (PBS) provides a systematic and progressive strategy for managing tension in the natural environment. The shortened version of the muscle stretching protocol begins from the stomach region so that the stretches of the legs and lower back are eliminated from the relaxation procedures. The fourth and final element of the relaxation program involves coping with thought intrusions, deepening levels of relaxation, and addressing life stressors that may be contributing to muscle tension. Each of these four elements is introduced in each of the subsequent sessions following the initial training session.

IV. REPRESENTATIVE CLINICAL APPLICATION

The use of stretch-based relaxation training in the clinical environment is generally part of a comprehensive and multicomponent approach to problem management. Within many clinical settings, stretch-based relaxation training can provide a foundation on which to build a comprehensive set of self-regulation skills. It is rare that progressive relaxation training is the sole focus of treatment.

This can be illustrated by the sample case of Ms. X. Ms. X was a 48-year-old female who presented with the chief complaint of excessive muscle tension, pain, and anxiety following an automobile accident. During the initial consultation, the client reported that she now had intense and persistent fears associated with being in and driving an automobile. The fears were so acute that she was very anxious and sweated profusely while in the car. Moreover, she was only able to drive very slowly and in certain geographic areas of her community. There were areas of her community that she fastidiously avoided for fear of being in another accident. Ms. X's clinical presentation was consistent with the diagnostic criteria for Specific Phobia of *(DSM-IV)*.

After the initial evaluation, Ms. X was presented with a formulation that described the events leading up to the development of her phobia, accounted for the subsequent elaboration of her phobia, and explained its continuation. Additionally, she was presented with a treatment plan that included a program of systematic desensitization. The first step in the treatment plan was to establish skills in control of muscle tension. Since she reported muscle pain in the region of her neck and shoulders, she was first asked to receive medical clearance for relaxation training. Following the receipt of medical clearance, the stretch-based program for progressive relaxation training was introduced.

Following the five sessions of the individual stretch-based relaxation training, Ms. X reported a decrease in overall tension and pain, but her fears of driving remained high. Therefore, the second phase of treatment that included constructing a desensitization hierarchy and performing systematic desensitization was initiated. The stretch-based relaxation skills, especially the PBS strategy for decreasing noticeable levels of tension, was used during the desensitization program. The treatment ultimately included an *in vivo* session in which the client demonstrated her driving skills while maintaining control over her level of anxiety and muscle tension.

V. SUMMARY

There are many successful approaches to progressive relaxation training as indicated by the substantial experimental clinical literature that is available (for example, see Carlson and Hoyle in 1993 and Carlson and Bernstein in 1995 for reviews). The stretch-based progressive relaxation protocol provides the clinician with an alternative to the traditional tense-release progressive relaxation programs. It is an approach based on fundamental physiological principles and experimental clinical data. Application of stretch-based relaxation can help a client develop a set of self-regulation skills to maintain volitional control of muscle tension. Particularly for persons with musculoskeletal pain disorders, the stretch-based relaxation protocol offers a viable alternative to the tense-release strategies for achieving effective relaxation skills.

See Also the Following Articles

Applied Relaxation ■ Applied Tension ■ Breathing Retraining ■ Pain Disorders ■ Progressive Relaxation ■ Relaxation Training

Further Reading

Carlson, C. R., & Bernstein, D. A. (1995). Relaxation skills: Abbreviated progressive relaxation. In W. O'Donohue & L. Krasner (Eds.), *Handbook of psychological skills training*. Needham, MA: Allyn & Bacon.

Carlson, C. R., & Collins, F. L. (1997). *A guided approach to stretch-based relaxation training, 2nd ed.*

Carlson, C. R., Collins, F. L., Nitz, A. J., Sturgis, E. S., & Rogers, J. L. (1990). Muscle stretching as an alternative relaxation training procedure. *Journal of Behavior Therapy and Experimental Psychiatry, 21*, 29–38.

Carlson, C. R., & Curran, S. L. (1994). Stretch–based relaxation training. *Patient Education and Counseling, 23*, 5–12.

Carlson, C. R., & Hoyle, R. L. (1993). Efficacy of abbreviated progressive muscle relaxation training: A quantitative review. *Journal of Consulting and Clinical Psychology, 61*, 1059–1067.

Carlson, C. R., Okeson, J. P., Falace, D. A., Nitz, A. J., & Anderson D. (1991). Stretch–based relaxation training and the reduction of EMG activity among masticatory muscle pain patients. *Journal of Craniomandibular Disorders: Facial and Oral Pain, 5,* 205–212.

Kay, J. A., & Carlson, C. R. (1992). The role of stretch–based relaxation in the treatment of chronic neck tension. *Behavior Therapy, 23,* 423–431.

McCubbin, J. A., Wilson, J. F., Bruehl, S., Ibarra, P., Carlson, C. R., Norton, J. A., & Colclough, G. W. (1996). Relaxation training and opioid inhibition of blood pressure response to stress. *Journal of Consulting and Clinical Psychology, 64,* 593–601.

Sherman, J. J., Carlson, C. R., McCubbin, J. A., & Wilson, J. F. (1997). Effects of stretch-based progressive relaxation training on the secretion of salivary Immunoglobulin A in orofacial pain patients. *Journal of Orofacial Pain, 11,* 115–124.

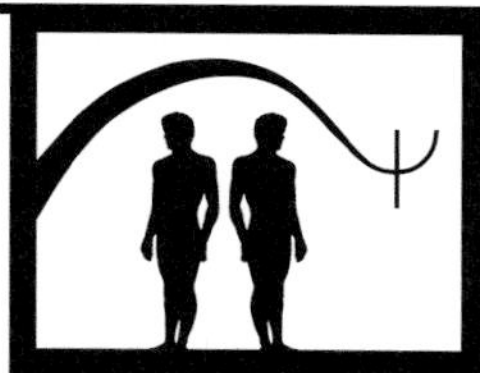

Structural Analysis of Social Behavior

Lorna Smith Benjamin

University of Utah

GLOSSARY

AG and DAG Attachment group and disaffiliative attachment group. Specific normal and pathological behaviors described by the SASB model.

case formulation A specific method of connecting the presenting problems to patterns learned in relation to early caregivers.

complementarity Natural interpersonal matches described by the SASB model.

copy process Links between current problem patterns and early attachments. The three main copy processes are (1) be like him or her; (2) act as if he or she is still there and in control; (3) treat yourself as did he or she.

core algorithm Focus each story on input, response, and impact on the self. Include the ABCs (affect, behavior, and cognition) and try to enhance the growth collaborator while minimizing the regressive loyalist.

five steps in IRT (1) Collaboration; (2) learn what your patterns are, where they are from, what they are for; (3) block maladaptive patterns; (4) enable the will to change; (5) learn new patterns.

growth collaborator (GC, or Green) is the part of the person that wants to be happier and more functional.

introjection SASB model descriptions of what happens when you treat yourself as you have been treated.

IPIR Important person and his or her internalized representation.

regressive loyalist (RL or Red) is that part of the person that is loyal to the old problem rules, norms, beliefs.

SASB Structural analysis of social behavior classifies interpersonal and intrapsychic interactions in terms of attentional focus and two dimensions: love/hate and enmeshment/differentiation. For example, maternal protectiveness consists of focus on other that is friendly and moderately powerful. Complex behaviors can be described by using more than one code. For example, demanding dependency is: <u>TRUST</u> plus **BLAME**.

similarity SASB model codes when you choose to be like him or her.

I. DESCRIPTION OF TREATMENT

Structural analysis of social behavior (SASB) is to the therapist as a telescope is to an astronomer. You can see some activity in the sky with the naked eye, but there is much more to see and understand if you have an instrument that effectively amplifies available information. In the interpersonal domain, the SASB lens can go beyond the familiar and help the clinician see the quintessence of interpersonal and intrapsychic patterns more clearly. The SASB model also can provide specific predictions about interactions. Of special interest in psychotherapy are the predictions about developmental antecedents and expectable consequences of identified patterns.

The SASB model and technology have been applied by researchers and clinicians to many aspects of psychotherapy, including interpersonal and intrapsychic assessment, therapy process, therapy outcome, and therapy relationship. The model is not limited to any one ideology. It has been successfully used by investigators exploring a variety of approaches such as client-centered, psychodynamic, psychoanalytic, interpersonal, and cognitive-behavioral therapies. Its usefulness extends beyond dyadic individual psychotherapy. There also are published SASB-based reports on individual, marital, family, and group therapy. The SASB system has been used to investigate related problems such as psychopathology, psychophysiology of interpersonal interactions, behavioral genetics, personality, therapist training, and more. For any approach that involves interpersonal or intrapsychic interaction, the SASB system offers precision in description of interactions, predictions, measurement methods (questionnaires for self-ratings, coding system for objective observer assessment), and software (to create well-validated cross-sectional and sequential parameters for use in clinical feedback or research hypothesis testing).

Although SASB technology is useful in a variety of contexts, this article focuses on Benjamin's recommendations for how to use the SASB model to define a specific individual's psychopathology and choose interventions in psychotherapy that consistently target the core of that individual's pathology. These recommendations have emerged from three decades of using the SASB model in research and practice. They are collected under the heading Interpersonal Reconstructive Therapy (IRT). IRT offers a tightly operationalized SASB-based method for assessing a patient's presenting problems, relating them to presumed underlying motivation, developing a treatment plan that explicitly and consistently addresses the organizing underlying motivators of the problem patterns, and then implementing and assessing the success of that treatment plan. Because SASB itself is generic, it is no surprise that IRT directs the clinician to draw from all schools of psychotherapy, using any available method of intervention. The guidelines require that the intervention conform to the case formulation, to the treatment plan, and to the IRT core algorithm. IRT is particularly appropriate for "nonresponders," people who have failed to improve in response to treatment as usual (medications and/or psychotherapy). Typically, these nonresponders carry the label personality disorder. IRT can facilitate profound change in some but certainly not all members of this population. It cannot, for example, help individuals who are unable or unwilling to control alcohol or substance use.

The IRT approach will be illustrated by a case example. Mary had an inpatient consultation with L. S. Benjamin following her second overdose attempt. During hospitalization and after discharge, Mary participated in psychotherapy with a graduate student learning IRT. Data presented here were gathered immediately after discharge and 4 months later, at the end of the school semester. Her history and presenting features, like those of many nonresponders, were severe and complex. She began this therapy with most scale scores on a symptom checklist at or beyond the 98th percentile for outpatients. Mary continued therapy with the same therapist through the next school year. She did quite well in that she made no further suicide attempts, needed no additional hospitalizations, discontinued medications, performed well in her new job, and improved in key social relationships. When the student therapist left on internship, Mary terminated earlier than necessary and said she did not need to use our offer of a referral to a new therapist. She failed to return any research forms at that time, but clearly had dropped a palpable distance from her original high level of symptomatology. But neither was she "cured."

Although IRT usually seeks to address the total picture, restricted aspects of Mary's presentation and the related history will be addressed here, because of space limitations. The selected focus is Mary's suicidality, very low self-esteem, and her apparent inability to look after her own interests.[1] These interpersonal and intrapsychic problems will be described in terms of the SASB model, shown in Figure 1.

The poles of the axes of the model, starting at the right-hand side and moving clockwise, are Love, Enmeshment, Hostility, and Differentiation. Points between poles consist of components of the nearest poles. Bold type indicates transitive focus on other; underlined type indicates intransitive focus on self. Italics depict introjected focus from other. For example, **IGNORE** describes behaviors relevant to focus on another person that is hostile and autonomy giving. <u>WALL-OFF</u> involves an intransitive focus on self reacting to another person with hostility and autonomy

[1] IRT theory prescribes that specific affects accompany specific interpersonal positions. Therefore, working with interpersonal patterns can help relieve symptoms. For a simple example, a person who fears rejection may be anxious. Transforming the fear as well as learning to handle actual rejection can reduce anxiety.

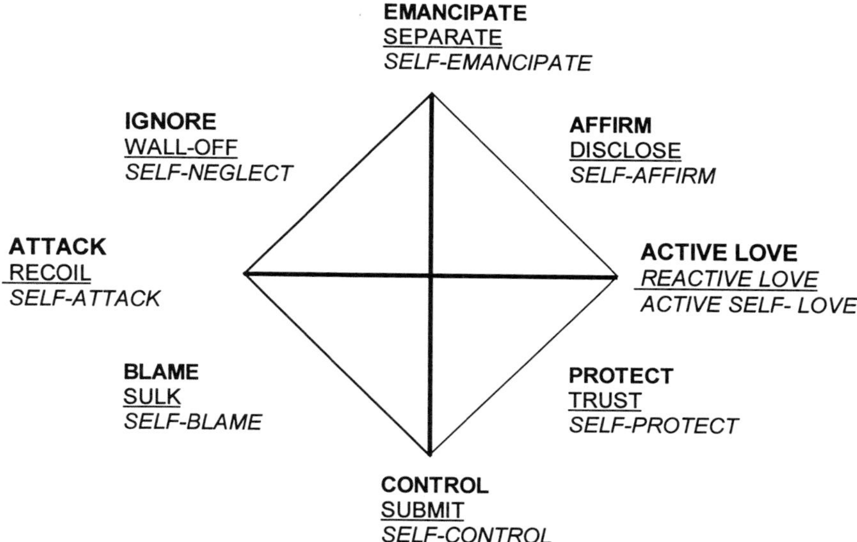

FIGURE 1 The simplified SASB cluster model. The poles of the axes, starting at the right-hand side and moving clockwise are Love, Enmeshment, Hostility, and Differentiation. Points between poles consist of components of the nearest poles (see text for further explanation). From Benjamin, L. S. (1996). *Interpersonal Diagnosis and Treatment of Personality Disorder*, 2nd ed. New York: Guilford Press.

taking. *SELF-NEGLECT* represents uncaring transitive focus on the self that is hostile and autonomy giving. Opposites are located at 180 degrees. For example, **PROTECT** is the opposite of **IGNORE.** Complements are show by adjacent **BOLD** and <u>UNDERLINED</u> pairs. For examples, <u>WALL-OFF</u> matches **IGNORE** and <u>TRUST</u> complements **PROTECT.**

Mary rated herself and important other persons on the SASB Intrex questionnaires. Selected results appear in Figure 2. The top part of Figure 2 shows the SASB-based description of Mary's self-concept (squares) compared to her view of the way in which she remembered her mother focusing on her when she was a child (diamonds).

A glance at the figure shows that Mary rated her mother high on items describing **BLAME, ATTACK,** and **IGNORE.** This picture is highly consistent with the content of the clinical narrative. Mary's mother was alcoholic and spent much of her time in bars. Mary, the oldest child, was responsible for running the household. If mother came home in the middle of the night and found a speck of dirt on a dish in the cupboard, Mary would be yanked out of bed and beaten and forced to wash every dish in the cupboard. The mother called Mary all kinds of names and assured her that no man would ever love her.

The data for Introject show how Mary internalized these messages. The two curves at the top of Figure 2 are similar. Mary's mother **BLAME**d her and she *BLAMED* her*SELF.* Her mother **ATTACK**ed her and she *ATTACK*ed her*SELF*. Mother **IGNORE**d her, and Mary *NEGLECT*ed her*SELF.* The current suicidal episode included all these elements. The suicidal attack was a conscious internalization of her husband's rejection and criticism ("Nobody wants to be married to me. I deserve to die") and after discharge from the hospital, she neglected herself markedly. For example, she moved out with essentially no overt protest and then she failed to engage a lawyer. Although she needed money and was a competent worker, she did not groom herself before her initial job interviews.

The lower part of Figure 2 compares Mary's self-concept at the beginning of the outpatient treatment (squares), and 4 months later (diamonds). The two curves are starting to separate, with the later assessment suggesting a shift in the direction of more friendly self-control. Her IRT therapy had initially focused precisely on these issues: the need to engage in more self-control and self-care. Her student therapist was competent and warm (**PROTECT**ive) and it is assumed that Mary internalized the structure and caring. The therapist's warm control offered the opposite of

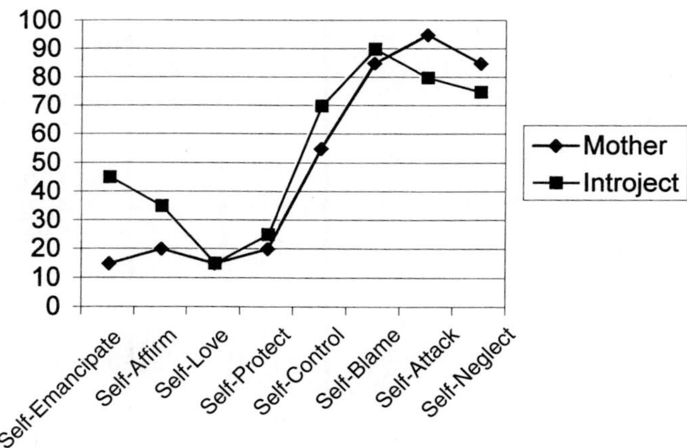

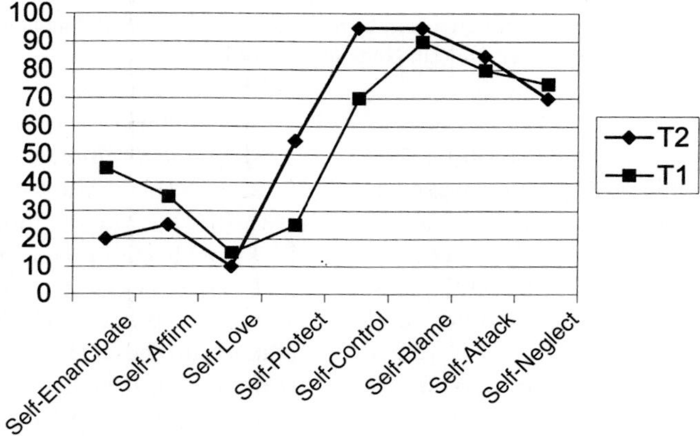

FIGURE 2 Mary's view of her mother is reflected in her introject (top). Her self-protectiveness and self-control began to improve early in IRT therapy (bottom).

Mary's mother's barhopping, coded, **IGNORE.** As she continued IRT, Mary internalized aspects of this corrective experience, and came closer to (but did not reach) the goal of letting go of the hope of rewriting childhood (discussed below). As time went by, the therapist offered less overt structure. Mary began to work on other skills, which included self-discovery, self-definition, and other "higher level" goals.

In general, the case formulation method in IRT requires that each presenting problem be linked to a key figure (usually a caregiver in childhood) by one of three copy processes. These are (1) be like him or her; (2) act as if he or she is there and in control; (3) treat yourself as did he or she. These processes of internalization are respectively called identification, recapitulation, and introjection. Usually copy processes are described directly by the SASB predictive principles. Copy process #1 applies the principle of similarity. Mary did not exhibit this process. Process #2 often reflects complementarity. Mary had recapitulated the violence in her relationship with her mother in her first marriage to a violent man. She retained the role of victim. Her second husband was not physically abusive, but he did specialize in neglect and rejection. She repeated the fate of being unwanted. Process #3 is introjection. As Figure 2 suggests, Mary introjected her mother's violence and degradation as well as the neglect. Copy processes can sometimes be seen in negative image, measured in terms of points 180 degrees apart on the SASB model. For example, Mary showed negative identification with her neglectful mother in that she had been very, perhaps too, protective of her own child.

This idea that patterns of disorder are replications of patterns learned long ago in relation to loved ones is startlingly simple. It is common for patients in IRT to say "I cant believe it, but it really is true: I am just like him!" Copying is universal, and, according to IRT, the difference between normality and pathology is simply in what is copied. Normal parents function from a baseline described by the SASB points **AFFIRM. ACTIVE LOVE,** and **PROTECT**, shown on the right-hand side of Figure 1. Normal children complement these behaviors with DISCLOSE, REACTIVE-LOVE, and TRUST. These baseline behaviors, described by SASB as friendly and moderately enmeshed and moderately differentiated, are called the attachment group (AG). Normal people internalize these benevolent ways of relating to themselves and others. Severely disturbed patients, like Mary, are more likely to have lived with baselines of **IGNORE, ATTACK,** and **BLAME**, called the disaffiliative attachment group (DAG) of behaviors. Like Mary, they internalize hatred of self and/or others.

The core issue in treatment planning in IRT therapy is to lock on to the motivation that is maintaining the copy processes that implement the problem patterns. Why are the copy processes sustained? For example, why does Mary continue her mother's norm of attacking herself? IRT's answer to the question is that it is for love. Every psychopathology is a gift of love. The "Gift of Love" hypothesis holds that behaving according to the "rules" of the internalized representation of the attachment figures, called important persons and their internalized representations (IPIRs), is an attempt to seek "psychic proximity." Doing things his or her way offers psychic security in the same way that the toddler is reassured by returning to the mother for a hug. This perspective is named the developmental learning and loving (DLL) theory of psychopathology. The fact that people will maintain patterns from childhood despite their enormous cost in adulthood is evidence of the stunning power of early figures in the development of the psyche.

It follows that if the problem patterns reflect early learning through copy process maintained by the gift of love, then the treatment plan must target that attachment. Somehow, the patient must give up the organizing wishes to rewrite history, or to wreak revenge (followed by reconciliation). The heart of reconstructive change will involve grieving what has been lost and what can never be. The patient must see and accept that childhood cannot be relived better and "righter." Letting go of those wishes is not easy. Tragically, the less secure and the more damaged the person, the more likely he or she is to cling to old fantasies of rescue or restitution. It takes good security and a solid psychological base to be able to let go of old patterns and move on to friendly independence.

IRT attempts to facilitate the development of new bases so that the patient can have the courage to let go and live differently and better. The therapy relationship is part, but not all, of the process of building a new base. Sometimes the parenting figure himself or herself can best serve this role.[2] The IRT therapist is quite active in helping the patient chose and maintain current relationships that are based in the normal (AG) range of behaviors. This is easier said than done, for there are powerful forces[3] that call the patient back to the familiar domain of DAG.

In the effort to transform the gift of love, every intervention in IRT is supposed to comply with three requirements: (1) It must conform to the case formulation, already discussed; (2) in addition, an intervention must implement one or more of five therapy steps; (3) finally, a good intervention implements the core algorithm.

The five therapy steps are (a) collaboration; (b) learning what your patterns are, where they are from, and what they are for; (c) blocking maladaptive patterns; (d) enabling the will to change; and (e) learning new patterns. Each of these five steps can be facilitated by any and all interventions known to the domain of psychotherapy. Therapy techniques are classified in two subgroups depending on whether they facilitate (a) experiencing or (b) self-management. In general, techniques from psychodynamic therapies encourage experiencing (e.g., discovery of ancient patterns and buried feelings through free association). Those from

---

[2] This requires that the parent is currently not defensive and, more important, that the therapist is not blaming. The assumption is that the pathology stems from the internalized representation, not the "reality."

[3] Complementarity with current figures is one such force for stasis. Most threatening, however, is the fact, that when people give up old patterns, they lose their identity. "I don't know who I am if I am not what I have been." This undefined state can be quite terrifying, and one resolution is to go back to the old ways.

behavioral therapies (e.g., learning and practicing skills in assertiveness) are more likely to invoke self-management techniques. Both domains of intervention are required in IRT: (1) The patient has to experience how it was and is to engage the will to change; (2) once he or she decides to change, learning better self-management can follow. According to IRT, the main difference between psychodynamic and behaviorally oriented therapies is in their relative emphases on (1) and (2).

When choosing an intervention, it often is helpful to think of the patient as, in effect, two people. The part that comes to therapy and hopes to change to function and feel better is called the growth collaborator (GC) or the "Green." The part of the person that wants to remain loyal to old ways is the regressive loyalist (RL), or the "Red." The conflict between the Green and the Red is everpresent and can be understood only after the case formulation is clear. In Mary's case, for example, the Red was often furious when someone showed signs of rejecting her; she was likely to react with self-destructive behavior. The Green, by contrast, would reflect carefully on why Mary was so panicked and angry about being left, and how her behaviors encouraged her husband to avoid her (step 2). For someone still in a problem relationship, these insights can help the patient contain the actions that alienate the spouse (step 3). Later, the patient can consider ways of relating to the spouse that might be more successful (step 5). Unfortunately, the Green cannot do much until the Red has had her say and the patient is truly sick of repeating the pattern. That decision to give up the ancient ways (step 4) is the most critical and most elusive part of therapy. It is facilitated if the therapist can minimize interventions that support the Red, and maximize those that encourage the Green. This can be altogether tricky. For example, after a fight with her husband, therapist efforts to encourage better patterns (help the Green) could easily be seen by Mary as blaming her (excite the Red). By using carefully chosen words informed by SASB codes of the therapy process and the case formulation, the therapist can make interventions that are perceived mostly as Green.

Finally, the core algorithm requires that the clinician extract from the therapy narrative a current episode that reflects the presenting problems. In Mary's case, for example, anything involving rejection, attack, or blame would be highly relevant. The clinician makes sure that each episode is fully explored in terms of (1) input, (2) response, and (3) Impact on self. A second feature of the core algorithm is to remember to attend to three domains, called the ABCs (affect, behavior, and cognition). The third feature of the core algorithm is that the clinician should try to enhance the Green and minimize the Red. For example, if Mary reports an episode of raging and crying when her date does not show up for lunch, it is appropriate to conduct a verbal walk through her morning up to the point where the rage erupted. This includes consideration of input (what set her off); response (rage and despair); and impact on self ("Nobody will ever love me"). The therapist encourages Mary to describe not only the situation and her behavior (B), but also her feelings (A) and her thoughts (C) about it. This could take most of a session. It would be excellent if the discussion also could contribute to her program of learning about how her repetition of patterns of rejection and abuse is related to the residuals of her attachment to her mother. (Her sexually abusive father also is an important part of Mary's story, but cannot be developed here.) After substantial repetition and lots of support, Mary eventually can "get the picture" emotionally and behaviorally as well as cognitively. That, of course, is the most difficult and challenging step for both patients and therapists. Various additional specific procedures to facilitate that realization and enhance the decision to let go are discussed in Benjamin. When the old wishes are given up, Mary and other IRT patients can give up the quest and the associated repetitions of the family scenario.

II. THEORETICAL BASES (CONCEPTUAL UNDERPINNING)

Bowlby argued that having reliable access to a supportive primary caregiver provides basic security required for independence. He emphasized that security is not the direct result of receiving food or the satisfaction of other needs. Harlow confirmed Bowlby's view of attachment by showing that baby monkeys gained more security and willingness to explore from having a huggable terry cloth laboratory mother that did not provide milk, than from a bare wire mother that did. Harlow suggested that contact comfort is a key component of attachment. Bowlby further proposed that children organize their behavior around internal working models derived from experience with their attachment persons. Copy process theory draws directly on Bowlby's concept of internal working models. Describing an individual's patterns in terms of the SASB model simply makes more explicit the nature of the internal models and their connection to the problem behaviors. Bowlby's work with attachment as a primary drive was revolutionary. Today's burgeoning literature continues to show that early attachment has a profound impact on mental and physical health.

IRT combines the fundamental principles from attachment theory with behavior theory. From behavior theory comes the idea that what works is likely to be repeated. Therapy must therefore identify and change the rewards. Attachment theory provides the definition of what "works." In other words, psychic proximity is the main "reward." IRT's focus on attachment demotes traditional "drivers" such as anger, rage, power, superiority, and the like. These human traits are very much a part of IRT, but they are not considered to be the primary targets of intervention. IRT centers instead on love for an important person and his or her internalized representation (IPIR). Once the loyalty to that internal representation is transformed,[4] the patient is free to learn and implement an entirely new and better way of living.

III. EMPIRICAL STUDIES

There have been many published studies of the methodological and clinical validity of the SASB model. There have been no formal published studies on the validity of IRT. However, IRT has repeatedly been successfully applied in a difficult-to-treat population, illustrated by Mary. The main measures have been in "testimonials" and in dramatic reductions in numbers of hospitalizations and suicide attempts. Scattered sets of before and after measures using Intrex questionnaires and symptom scales also are encouraging. However, with these severely disordered individuals, treatment may have to last for 2 or more years to achieve definitive and stable remission. The present hope is to conduct formal clinical trials at the University of Utah Neuropsychiatric Institute and possibly with colleagues at the University of Pittsburgh.[5]

IV. SUMMARY

IRT seeks to treat "nonresponders" by directly identifying and transforming the underlying motivations for the interpersonal and intrapsychic problems. The presenting problems are linked specifically to relationships with early caregivers in the form of three types of copy process: be like him or her; act as if he or she is still there and in control; treat yourself as did he or she. The motivation for copy process is to implement the rules or values of the persons being copied in order to provide testimony to their beliefs and to achieve reconciliation with them. The treatment implication of this "Gift of Love" hypothesis is that these now impossible wishes must be recognized, grieved, and given up. Then, personality reconstruction can begin. To reach that goal, IRT draws from any and every school of therapy as long as an intervention can achieve one of five therapy steps, use the core algorithm, and fit the case formulation. Assessment of patterns, copy links, therapy process, therapy content, and the effectiveness of therapy steps are greatly facilitated by clarity and explicitness provided by the SASB model and its associated technology.

[4] It is assumed that the neurologically based templates that have been implementing the problem patterns must be transformed by the new learning.

[5] Paul Pilkonis and Jennifer Skeem have teams of clinicians engaged in preliminary trials to gather pilot data preparatory to applying for grant support.

Acknowledgments

Thanks are expressed to Karla Moras, Linda Kidd, Tracey Smith, and the editors, who made helpful comments on an earlier version of this paper.

This chapter derives from and summarizes portions of Benjamin, *Interpersonal Reconstructive Therapy*, currently in press with Guilford Publications.

See Also the Following Articles

Configurational Analysis ■ Formulation ■ Sullivan's Interpersonal Psychotherapy

Further Reading

Benjamin, L. S. (1993). Every psychopathology is a gift of love. *Psychotherapy Research, 3,* 1–24.

Benjamin, L. S. (1996). An interpersonal theory of personality disorders. In J. F. Clarkin (Ed.), *Major theories of personality disorder* (pp. 141–220). New York: Guilford Press.

Benjamin, L. S. (1996). Introduction to the special section on Structural Analysis of Social Behavior (SASB). *Journal of Consulting and Clinical Psychology, 64,* 1203–1212.

Benjamin, L. S. (1996). *Interpersonal Diagnosis and Treatment of Personality Disorder.* Second edition. New York: Guilford Press.

Benjamin, L. S. (1998). Reconstructive Learning Therapy for Passive Aggressive Personality Disorder. *APA Psychotherapy Videotape Series II.* Washington, DC: American Psychological Association.

Benjamin, L. S. (2000). SASB Intrex users manual. Salt Lake City: University of Utah.

Benjamin, L. S. (2001). Known papers and books that use SASB technology. An electronic file that lists nearly two hundred SASB publications; available from Benjamin@Xmission.com.

Benjamin, L. S. (in press). *Interpersonal reconstructive therapy (IRT).* New York: Guilford Press.

Cassidy, J., & Shaver, P. R. (1999). *Handbook of Attachment.* New York: Guilford

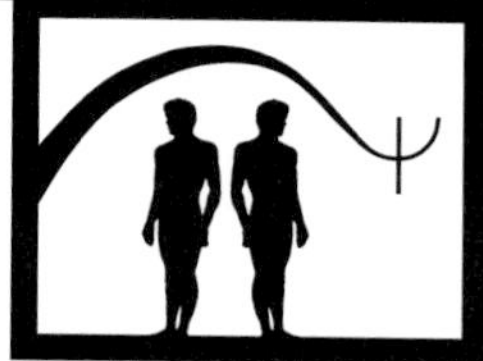

Structural Theory

Alan Sugarman

San Diego Psychoanalytic Society and Institute and University of California, San Diego

GLOSSARY

autonomous ego functions *Primary:* Inborn functions that follow a development timetable that unfold sequentially, so long as the environment does not interfere. Includes processes such as cognition, perception, and language. *Conflict free:* Refers to primary autonomous ego functions that arise without precondition of conflict. *Secondary autonomy:* Ego functions that arise out of conflict but become independent of such conflict.

compromise formations The balance of superego injunctions and id demands created by the ego and manifested in fantasies, symptoms, dreams, character traits, etc.

condensation A process whereby a sole idea represents several associative changes and is part of the functioning of the id.

displacement The process employed by the id in which an idea's emphasis, interest, or intensity is detached and passed onto other ideas.

drive derivatives The surface and conscious representation of id drives.

drives Psychic representation of instinctual and biological needs and urges.

ego The psychic structure posited by the structural theory developing out of the id, which functions as a synthesizing agency between the demands of the superego and the pressure for expression in the id. Functions include self preservation, perception, motility, learning, memory, cognition, language, reality testing, and the synthetic function.

ego psychology An offshoot of structural theory developed by Heinz Hartman and David Rapaport emphasizing the role of the ego in mental life.

id Identical to the earlier concept of the System Unconsious. The id is, in the structural theory, the reservoir for psychic representation of the two instinctual drives of libido and aggression.

infantile sexuality The idea that infants and children have sexual intentions, aims, and motivations.

intrapsychic conflicts Conflicts between intentions of the person, both conscious and unconsious, in conflict with the demands of external prohibitions.

libido The instinctual drive oriented towards merging, and is generally thought to be the basis of sexuality.

pleasure principle The economic concept of the organization of the mind under the structural theory that posits the motivating drive as the discharge of excitations, experiences, pleasure.

primary process A type of logic employed by the id in which the pleasure principle guides the direction of behavior. It is a timeless process that modifies distinctions in order to create representations and opportunities for pleasurable discharge.

reality principle The manner in which the ego carries out its work based on a perception and measurement of social reality demands.

resistance A defense aimed towards keeping the unconscious material activated by analysis or psychotherapy from reaching consciousness.

secondary process thinking The mode used by the ego that is based on logic, linear thinking, and time orientation.

structure A group of psychological functions or processes that are organized hierarchically and have a slow rate of change.

superego The psychological structure that represents the internalization of the parents' values and prohibitions and consequently those of the larger social cultural world.

topographical model An early model of psychoanalytic theory developed by Sigmund Freud which characterized mental phenomenon as being unconscious or conscious in postulated functions in a relationship to these qualities of mental life. This thinking included the ideas of systems unconscious, preconscious, and conscious.

I. LIMITATION OF THE TOPOGRAPHIC MODEL

Structural theory, sometimes referred to as the structural model or the tripartite model, refers to Freud's final and ultimate model of the mind that he first introduced with his book, *The Ego and the Id* in 1923, and elaborated in *Inhibitions, Symptoms, and Anxiety* in 1926. This shift in conceptualizing the workings of the mind away from the topographic model that had organized his thinking for over 20 years was prompted by Freud's realization that his topographic theory had too many theoretical inconsistencies to remain viable, and that it could not account adequately for a variety of clinical phenomena, most notably unconscious guilt. Freud came to see that understanding the workings of the mind, particularly the intrapsychic conflicts that give rise to most mental phenomena, needed to be based on something other than the relationship of mental contents and functions to consciousness. Thus, he changed his metaphors for understanding the mind away from the notion that mental contents moved from the depths to the surface. To accomplish this goal and to ensure that his new model more adequately explained the complexity of the psyche necessitated the relinquishing of his constructs of the systems Unconscious, Preconscious, and Conscious.

II. STRUCTURAL THEORY

These layers or stratas of the mind were replaced by what he first called agencies and later called structures—the id, the ego, and the superego. The term structure is an ambiguous one in psychoanalysis, although most analysts adhere to the definition of David Rapaport that the term refers to a group of psychological functions or processes that are organized hierarchically and have a slow rate of change. The id, ego, and superego are certainly not the only mental structures that comprise the mind. But they are thought to be its superordinate structures, leading Merton Gill to refer to them as macrostructures. It is assumed by most psychoanalysts that the mind is composed completely of these three superordinate structures, each of which can have substructures. The interrelationships within and between these three structures, particularly intrapsychic conflict, are what give rise to most mental phenomena and all psychologically mediated behavior.

Freud did not abandon all of the key concepts that he had developed during his topographic era of model building when he replaced it with the structural theory, however. His important concepts of infantile sexuality, libidinal and aggressive drives, unconscious mental functioning, and internal conflict remained as did more dubious concepts such as psychic energy. But these concepts were modified and integrated into structural theory with varying degrees of conceptual clarity and success. For example, the concepts of unconscious, preconscious, and consciousness were retained. But these concepts now became adjectives, used merely to describe whether any particular mental content or process was within the individual's conscious awareness or not. The terms no longer retained any structural or systemic implications. Despite this fundamental reconceptualization, it is not uncommon, even today, to hear psychoanalysts speak of the Unconscious as though it were a structure, to imply that unconscious mental phenomena are somehow deeper and more primitive than conscious mental phenomena, or to talk about the technical need to make the Unconscious conscious. Such analysts seem not to realize that such ways of thinking about analytic matters are outdated and at odds with how we have come to understand the workings of the mind.

III. THE ID

Nonetheless, conceptual overlap between the earlier topographic model and the later structural one remains important in understanding the intricacies as well as the necessity for utilizing structural theory in clinical situations. Perhaps the clearest overlap between the two models involves how Freud formulated the id. The id is virtually identical with the earlier concept of the system

Unconscious. Thus, it is the reservoir for psychic representations of the two instinctual drives, libido and aggression. As such its contents revolve around the basic, pleasure-seeking urges of mankind. It operates according to the pleasure principle and is organized according to the logic (or lack thereof) of the primary process. Freud retained his concept of psychic energy when he developed the structural model and he used differences in the nature of psychic energy to explain differences between structures of the mind. Psychic energy was thought to be mobile and its discharge rapid in the id, allowing for the clinical manifestations of primary process thinking—condensation and displacement. Drives were thought to be relatively unfused in this structure. Freud was drawn to the analogy of the id as a wild, untamed horse that had to be broken by the rider, the ego. Thus, he saw the ego as developing out of the id so that the individual could adapt to reality rather than run amok as the id's drives were given free rein. Freud viewed the contents of the id as dynamically unconscious; that is, they were defended against so as not to reach conscious awareness and cause unpleasure. He thought that they could only be known through their surface manifestations—what came to be called drive derivatives. More recent theorists such as Charles Brenner have questioned this dichotomy, arguing that the concept of drives is a purely theoretical and abstract one. To the degree that drive derivatives are the real clinical phenomena encountered, their availability to consciousness is a graded one. It is simply at odds with clinical experience to speak of completely unconscious drives.

IV. THE EGO

The ego is generally accepted as the most important structure of the mind in understanding the ability of humans to adapt and to survive in the world. In fact, it is so important that psychoanalytic thinkers such as Heinz Hartmann and David Rapaport developed an offshoot of structural theory, called ego psychology, between the late 1940s and the early 1960s. Their ideas are generally subsumed under the rubric, structural theory, today. But their wish to highlight the importance or even preeminence of the ego among the structures of the mind is worth noting. As will be described later, it has major implications for the clinical practice of psychoanalysis. Freud described the ego as developing out of the id because of the necessity to mediate between the drive wishes of the id and the demands and restrictions of external reality. As development proceeds, the ego comes to balance superego injunctions along with these other pressures. Thus, it is the source of compromise formations manifested in fantasies, symptoms, dreams, character traits, and so on. The ego accomplishes this complex task of mediating between the id, superego, and external reality according to the reality principle and through the use of secondary process thinking. The ego psychologists emphasized that the ego's structure was so complex and its mode of organization so substantially different than that of the id that it seemed more likely that both structures evolved out of an originally undifferentiated psychic matrix. This model of the mind developing through progressive differentiation is far more in keeping with modern concepts of developmental psychology than is Freud's metaphor of the rider ego.

Regardless of how one understands its origins, the ego remains understood as the "coherent organization of mental processes" that Freud described. Its most important clinical function is that of defense. That is, the ego monitors the conscious awareness and/or expression of id impulses and uses a wide array of defense mechanisms to keep them from arousing excessive unpleasure or causing danger to the individual. The ego does not just defend against the id, however. Defenses are just as readily deployed against the superego or against perceptions of external reality.

Defense is also not the only ego function. In *An Outline of Psychoanalysis* Freud discussed other ego functions including self-preservation, perception, motility, and learning. Later memory, cognition, language, reality testing, and the synthetic function of the ego were described by psychoanalysts including Anna Freud, Hartmann, Kris, and Loewenstein, Bellak, Arlow, and Brenner. All agree that it is impossible to develop a comprehensive list of ego functions because the mind is so complex. Nonetheless a particularly useful delineation of 12 ego functions that can be empirically measured has been developed by Leopold Bellak and his collaborators. These 12 functions include reality testing; judgment; sense of reality of the world and of the self; regulation of drives, affects, and impulses; object relations; thought processes; adaptive regression in the service of the ego; defensive functioning; stimulus barrier; autonomous functioning; synthetic-integrative functioning; and mastery–competence. This list is neither exhaustive nor theoretically consistent. But it does demonstrate the complexity of the ego and does offer a method of quantitative research.

Many of these functions also help to clarify another reason that the ego psychologists objected to Freud's idea that the ego developed out of the id. Freud's idea carried with it the notion that all ego functions arise out of intrapsychic conflict and are influenced by the id. Reality testing, for example, was thought to arise out of hallucinatory wish fulfillment conflicting with external reality. In contrast Heinz Hartmann argued that many ego functions are primarily autonomous. That is, they are inborn and follow a developmental time table that will unfold sequentially as long as the environment does not interfere. Processes such as cognition, perception, and language, for example, are conflict-free. Conflict was not necessary for their genesis or development. Other ego functions achieve what Hartmann called secondary autonomy. That is, certain functions or personality traits may originally develop out of conflict but over the course of development become functionally autonomous. Thus, conflict-related behaviors can become independent of their roots. This concept helps to explain the imperviousness of certain fantasies or character traits to interpretation, despite the therapist's ability to analyze and interpret all the various conflicts that gave rise to it.

V. THE SUPEREGO

The superego was the third structure of the mind in Freud's structural theory. In large part it is this structure and the clinical phenomena that it elucidates that caused Freud to develop his structural model in the first place. Prior to giving up the topographic model, Freud struggled to understand the phenomenon of unconscious guilt and its clinical manifestations, particularly the negative therapeutic reaction and issues pertaining to masochism. To explain these phenomena, he offered the concept of the superego as the internalization of the parents' values and prohibitions. He described it as developing out of the ego and becoming a full-fledged structure in its own right as part of the child's oedipal resolution. This latter point continues to be debated in the literature. Some contemporary structural theorists such as Paul Gray argue that the superego is just a specialized ego function and not a structure in its own right. In contrast some child psychoanalysts have noted the presence of a fully functioning superego far earlier than oedipal resolution and have argued that its function as a separate mental structure needs to be kept conceptually separate from the developmental level of the drives against which it is pitted. Despite these subtleties of theory, most psychoanalysts see the superego as crucial in understanding behavior. In essence it functions both as a conscience and as an internalized set of ideals, both of which are significant motivators of behavior.

VI. STRUCTURAL CONFLICT

These three structures of the mind—id, ego, and superego—function both on their own and interact in ways that determine every aspect of human behavior. But it is important to realize that calling structural theory a tripartite model is somewhat misleading. This is because external reality plays a far more prominent role in structural theory than it did in the earlier topographic model. Because the structural model stresses the importance of adaptation to an external environment, external reality is viewed as placing demands on the ego's mediating abilities just as much as the id and the superego. Thus, the compromise formations that the ego organizes to balance these sources of pressure must take into account reality's demands also.

The clinical implications of this model generally involve its role in intrapsychic conflict. Conflict between any of the structures can occur as can intrastructural conflicts wherein subprocesses or functions of each structure conflict with each other. Examples of the former include an ego defense arrayed against an id drive or a superego injunction deployed against an id drive or an ego function. An intrastructural conflict might involve competing ideals within the superego, for example. The fantasies, symptoms, behaviors, or character traits for which patients seek therapy are understood as compromise formations involving the ego's attempt to mediate the conflicts between these structures and external reality.

VII. TECHNICAL IMPLICATIONS

Only recently have psychoanalysts delineated a manner of working with patients that follows logically from this structural model. Fred Busch and Paul Gray are the two psychoanalysts most closely associated with a contemporary structural approach to technique. In essence, this way of working with patients emphasizes the need to expand the patient's autonomous ego functioning by teaching him or her to observe intrapsychic conflict as it becomes manifest in sessions. The patient is taught to closely observe his or her associations with a particular lookout for evidence of resistance. Resistance is monitored carefully with the analyst listening to and teaching the patient to listen for moments in the analytic process when resistance to the direct and unfettered expression of thoughts or feelings occurs. The patient learns to oscillate between being in analysis and observing the free associations that characterize the psychoanalytic process.

The goal of an analysis shifts from the topographic emphasis on making the unconscious conscious so that core unconscious fantasies can be changed to gaining mastery over them by thinking about them. Resistance analysis gains center stage in analytic technique guided by structural theory rather than being a means to an end with the end being making unconscious mental contents conscious. Self-analysis becomes a key criterion for termination, as patients master the analytic way of thinking and apply it to their own associations, particularly noticing unconscious defensive activity aimed at keeping thoughts out of awareness.

This approach to analytic technique is based on the realization that the way in which the ego handles its task of mediating the other structures and reality determines psychological health. Thus, the way in which a person thinks, and the amenability of that thinking to analytic interventions, are more important than the contents of that thinking. Oedipal, preoedipal, narcissistic, and so on refer to mental content. But structural theory, in contrast to earlier analytic models, focuses on mental structure. Analysts now try to help the patient to reestablish mental connections that have been disrupted by defense rather than to recover memories or fantasies. Structural theorists such as Busch or Gray take the ego's synthetic function seriously. Thus, insight becomes directed at understanding the workings of the patient's mind instead of at deep, hidden, mental content. New solutions to conflict emerge as a result of bringing the conflict between unconscious wishes and defenses or superego under the scrutiny of the autonomous ego.

Toward this end, vicissitudes of conflict are addressed by the analyst as they appear in sessions. Busch points out that the ego is regressed when in the midst of conflict so that thinking becomes preoperational and concrete. Thus, interventions by the analyst must be concrete and immediate in order to be grasped by the patient's regressed ego. Conflict, as it occurs in the associational processes, can be seen more readily by the patient than unconscious content, which is more abstract, and less immediately visible. Furthermore, interpretations of deep unconscious content as practiced under the topographic model risk analytic change occurring on the basis of identifying with the analyst's authority rather than on any expansion of the ego's ability to perceive and master conflict. Finally, the structural model postulates that the ego defends against unconscious id contents because they would stimulate excessive anxiety or guilt if they became conscious. To address these contents directly without first exploring and modifying the anxieties that motivate the defense will only increase the patient's anxiety and resistance.

Although such technical implications may seem obvious, they have only been elucidated over the past 15 years. Until then psychoanalysts practiced according to an implicitly topographic perspective despite their belief that they were operating from a structural orientation. This state of affairs was due primarily to Freud's writings on technique having been published during his topographic era of theorizing. He never returned to the theory of technique after formulating his structural model. Thus, too many psychoanalysts clung to outdated ways of working or of formulating their work because of their wish to remain true to Freudian technique. Even today it is not uncommon to hear analysts interpret unconscious anger, for example, before they have interpreted and understood the patient's reluctance to be aware of his or her anger. Furthermore, psychoanalysts of orientations other than Freudian have continued to misunderstand structural theory so that their critiques of so-called Freudian technique seem appropriate to technical concepts of the topographic era and not relevant to a truly structural approach to psychoanalytic practice. Modern day or contemporary structural theory offers a model and way of working with patients that is the most comprehensive and integrative of psychoanalytic approaches today. It is capable of integrating the clinical findings of self-psychology or object relations theory while retaining all of Freud's brilliant insights into the organization of the mind and the way in which this organization affects behavior.

See Also the Following Articles

Intrapsychic Conflict ■ Oedipus Complex ■ Structural Analysis of Social Behavior ■ Topographic Theory ■ Transference Neurosis ■ Unconscious, The

Further Reading

Bellak, L., Hurvich, M., & Gediman, H. K. (1973). *Ego functions in schizophrenics, neurotics, and normals*. New York: Wiley.

Boesky, D. (1995). *Structural theory*. In B. Moore & B. Fine (Eds.), *Psychoanalysis: The major concepts*. New Haven, CT: Yale University Press.

Busch, F. (1995). *The ego at the center of clinical technique*. Northvale, NJ: Aronson.

Gray, P. (1994). *The ego and analysis of defense*. Northvale, NJ: Aronson.

Moore, B., & Fine, B. (Eds.). (1990). *Psychoanalytic terms and concepts*. New Haven, CT: Yale University Press.

Sandler, J., Holder, A., Dane, C., & Dreher, A. V. (1997). Freud's *models of the mind*. Madison, CT: International Universities Press.

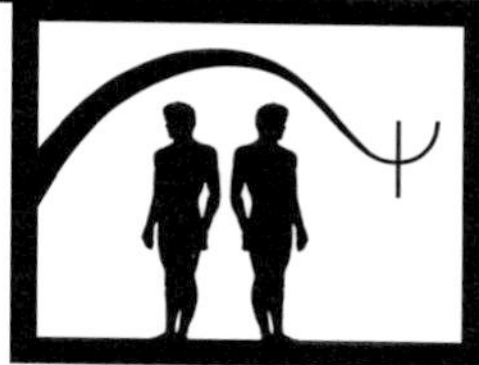

Substance Dependence: Psychotherapy

Kathlene Tracy, Bruce Rounsaville, and Kathleen Carroll

Yale University

GLOSSARY

community reinforcement approach Interventions based on learning theory that are designed to rearrange significant aspects of local communities, such as vocational, family, and social activities, to differentially support a non-substance-using lifestyle.

disease model approach Interventions that help the individual who abuses substances accept that they have an illness or disease and surrender by acknowledging that there is hope for sobriety through accepting the need for help from others and a higher power. A major goal is fostering active participation in self-help groups (e.g., AA, NA, CA).

methadone maintenance A pharmacological approach to the treatment of opioid dependence in which the individual who abuses opioids is maintained on an agonist, methadone, that has action similar to that of the abused drug but is considered to be less harmful.

substance abuse (*DSM–IV* criteria) A maladaptive pattern of substance use not due to dependence leading to significant impairment or distress that is characterized by one or more of the following occurring at any time in a 12-month period: recurrent substance use resulting in failure to fulfill major role obligations at home, work, or school; recurrent substance use in physically hazardous situations; recurrent substance-related legal problems; continued use despite having persistent or recurrent interpersonal or social problems exacerbated or caused by the effects of using.

substance dependence (*DSM–IV* criteria) A maladaptive pattern of substance use leading to significant impairment or distress that is characterized by three or more of the following occurring at any time in a 12-month period: tolerance; withdrawal; taking the substance in larger amounts or for longer periods than intended; expressing a desire to cut down on use or unsuccessful efforts to cut down or stop using; spending large amounts of time obtaining the substance, using, or recovering from the substance's effects; important social, occupational, or recreational activities have been given up or reduced because of the substance use; and continued use despite recurrent physical or psychological problems that is made worse or caused by the use.

therapeutic community An intervention that supports the individual's submission to group ideology of abstinence from substances. Every aspect of the individual's daily life is regimented often through confinement, structure, and daily work assignments.

Given the place of this article in a volume describing a variety of psychotherapeutic approaches, this article focuses on those aspects of individual and group therapy that are unique to the treatment of substance dependence. This article presents guidelines on therapy applicable to those both dependent on alcohol as well as those dependent on other drugs.

I. DESCRIPTION OF TREATMENT

Some form of psychotherapy or behavioral therapy is usually considered as a treatment option for virtually all patients seeking treatment for substance use disorders. Treatment seekers typically represent the more severe end of the spectrum of community members who meet criteria for current substance use disorders. Most of those who seek treatment do so only after numerous unsuccessful attempts to stop or reduce substance use on their own. The alternatives to psychotherapy are either pharmacological or structural limitations from access to drugs and alcohol such as in residential setting. Both these alternatives have limited effectiveness if not combined with psychotherapy or counseling. Removal from the substance-using setting is a useful and, sometimes, necessary part of substance treatment but is seldom sufficient, as is shown by the high relapse rates typically seen from residential detoxification programs or incarceration during the year following the patient's return to the community.

The major strategy that is now common to all currently practiced psychotherapies for individuals who abuse substances is to place primary emphasis on controlling or reducing substance use, while pursuing other goals only after substance use has been at least partly controlled. This means that either (a) the therapist employs techniques designed to help the patient stop substance use as a central part of the treatment, or (b) the therapy is practiced in the context of a comprehensive treatment program in which other aspects of the treatment curtail the patient's use of substances (e.g., methadone maintenance, disulfiram for alcoholics, residential treatment). Because people who abuse substances frequently react to increased anxiety or other dysphoric affects by resuming substance use, anxiety-arousing aspects of treatment are typically introduced only after a strong therapeutic alliance has been developed or within the context of other supportive structures (e.g., inpatient unit, strong social support network, methadone maintenance) that guard against relapse to substance use when the patient experiences heightened anxiety and dysphoria in the context of therapeutic exploration.

Psychotherapy to treat substance abuse can occur in a variety of settings. For example, individuals who are severely dependent remain unsuccessful at achieving abstinence may become inpatients or be admitted to a detoxification program. While in the detoxification program, the individual may receive brief directed psychotherapy that focuses mainly on controlling the impulse to use. In partial hospitalization or residential treatment programs, psychotherapy offered is typically longer in duration, and not only focuses on the impulse to use, but also includes a greater representation of managing and changing behavioral aspects that contribute to or maintain the person's substance use. In outpatient treatment settings, psychotherapeutic treatments often include all the components previously mentioned as well as an opportunity to engage in longer-term treatment that can address broader issues in the patient's life that may indirectly play a role in the individual's ability to remain abstinent.

Beyond setting differences, psychotherapy for substance use disorder may be delivered in a range of different modalities, such as group or individual. Major advantages to group substance treatment are: (a) cost savings, (b) given the social stigma attached to having lost control of substance use, having group members who acknowledge similar problems can provide comfort, (c) group members who have longer periods of abstinence can model that attempting to stop using is not a futile effort, (d) group members can act as social supports, and (e) the public nature of the group can provide powerful incentive to avoid relapse. Principal advantages to individual substance treatment are: (a) privacy for members whose careers or reputations may be damaged from more widespread knowledge of their substance use, (b) increased flexibility to address problems that are uniquely relevant to that patient, (c) easier resolution of logistics surrounding therapist caseloads where often there are not enough substance abuse clients to form a group or determent from individuals having to wait to engage in treatment until the group is formed, and (d) therapists may use the one-to-one relationship to explore relational elements not possible in group treatment.

II. THEORETICAL BASES

The history of individual psychotherapy for substance abusers has been one of importation of methods first developed to treat other conditions. Thus, when psychoanalytic and psychodynamic therapies were the predominant modality for treating most mental disorders, published descriptions of dynamics of substance abuse or of therapeutic strategies arose from using this established general modality to treat the special population of individuals who abuse substances. Likewise, with the development of behavioral techniques, client-centered therapies, and cognitive-behavioral treatments, earlier descriptions based on other types of patients were followed by discussions of the special modifications needed to treat substance abuse.

Although always present as a treatment option, individual psychotherapy has not been the predominant treatment modality for substance abusers since the 1960s, when inpatient 12-step informed milieu therapy, group treatments, methadone maintenance, and therapeutic community approaches came to be the fixtures of substance abuse treatment programs. In fact, these newer modalities derived their popularity from the limitations of dynamically informed ambulatory individual psychotherapy when it was used as the sole treatment for substance abusers. Many reported problems with dynamic treatment. Some of the difficulties reported for this form of treatment were premature termination, reaction to anxiety-arousing interpretations with resumption of substance use, erratic attendance at sessions, difficulties posed by attending sessions while intoxicated, and failure to pay fees because money was spent on drugs and alcohol.

Most schools of therapy, with widely varying rationales and strategies, have been adapted for potential use to treat substance abuse. Rather than focus on specific techniques associated with the different approaches, this article focuses on two topics that can guide substance abuse therapy within a variety of different schools: (a) specialized knowledge needed to apply psychotherapy to treat substance abuse, and (b) common goals and strategies that must be addressed by psychotherapists.

A. Areas of Specialized Knowledge to Treat Substance Abuse

1. Understanding the Effects of Using

The principal areas of knowledge to be mastered by the beginning therapist are the pharmacology, use patterns, consequences, and course of addiction for the major types of abused substances. For therapy to be effective, it is useful not only to obtain the academic knowledge about frequently abused substances, but also to become familiar with street knowledge about drugs (e.g., slang names, favored routes of administration, prices, availability) and the clinical presentation of individuals when they are intoxicated or experiencing withdrawal from the different abused substances. This knowledge has many important uses in the course of individual therapy with individuals who abuse substances.

First, it fosters a therapeutic alliance by allowing the therapist to convey an understanding of the addicted person's problems and the world in which he or she lives. This is an especially important issue when the therapist is of a different background from the patient who abuses substances. In engaging the patient, it is important to emphasize that the patient's primary presenting complaint is likely to be substance abuse, even if many other issues are also likely to be amenable to psychotherapeutic interventions. Hence, if the therapist is not comfortable and familiar with the nuances of problematic drug and alcohol use, it may be difficult to forge an initial working alliance. Moreover, by knowing the natural history of substance abuse and the course of drug and alcohol effects, the clinician can be guided in helping the patient anticipate problems that will arise in the course of initiating abstinence. For example, knowing the typical type and duration of withdrawal symptoms can help the individual recognize their transient nature and to develop a plan for successfully completing an ambulatory detoxification.

Second, knowledge of substance actions and withdrawal states is crucial for diagnosing comorbid psychopathology and for helping the person who is addicted to understand and manage dysphoric affects. Most abused substances such as opioids or cocaine are capable of producing constellations of symptoms that mimic psychiatric syndromes such as depression, mania, anxiety disorders, or paranoia. Many of these symptomatic states are completely substance induced and resolve spontaneously when substance abuse is stopped. It is frequently the therapist's job to determine whether or not presenting symptoms are part of an enduring, underlying psychiatric condition or a transient, substance-induced state. If the former, then simultaneous treatment of the psychiatric disorder is appropriate; if the latter, reassurance and encouragement to maintain abstinence are usually the better course. Over the last decade, co-occurrence of psychoactive substance use disorders with other psychiatric disorders have become much more widely recognized and are of common occurrence in most treatment facilities.

Third, learning about drug and alcohol effects is important for detecting when patients have relapsed or have come to sessions intoxicated. It is seldom useful to conduct psychotherapy sessions when the patient is intoxicated, and when this happens the session should be rescheduled for a time when the patient can participate while sober.

2. Understanding Treatment Philosophies

A second area of knowledge to be mastered by the psychotherapist is an overview of treatment philosophies and techniques for the other treatments and self-help groups that are available to patients who abuse substances. As noted earlier, the early experience of attempting individual psychotherapy as the sole treatment of the more severe types of substance abuse was marked by failure of an early dropout. Hence, for many individuals who abuse substances, individual psychotherapy is best conceived of as a component in a multifaceted program of treatment to help them overcome a chronic, relapsing condition.

Another major function of knowing about the major alternative treatment modalities for substance abusers is to be alert to the possibility that different treatments may provide contradictory recommendations that may confuse the patient or foster the patient's attempts to sabotage treatment. Unlike a practitioner whose treatment is likely to be sufficient, the individual psychotherapist does not have the option of simply instructing the patient to curtail other treatments or self-help groups while the treatment is taking place. Rather, it is vital that the therapist attempt to adjust his or her own work to bring the psychotherapy in line with the other treatments. It is also important to note that many treatments with high levels of empirical support are not the treatments most widely used clinically.

B. Common Goals and Strategies for Substance Abuse Psychotherapy

This section reviews issues presented by persons who abuse substances that should be addressed, if not emphasized, by any type of individual or group psychotherapy that is likely to be effective. As noted in reviewing the difficulties encountered by early psychodynamic practitioners, the central modification that is required of psychotherapists is always to be aware that the patient being treated is a substance abuser. Hence, even when attempting to explore other issues in depth, the therapist should devote at least a small part of every session to monitoring the patient's most recent successes and failures at controlling or curtailing substance use and being willing to interrupt other work to address slips and relapses when and if they occur.

Implicit in the need to remain focused on the patient's substance use is the requirement that psychotherapy with these patients entails a more active therapist stance than does treatment of patients with other psychiatric disorders such as depression or anxiety disorders. This is related to the fact that the principal symptom of substance abuse, compulsive use, is at least initially gratifying, and it is the long-term consequences of substance use that induce pain and the desire to stop. In contrast, the principal symptoms of depression or anxiety disorders are inherently painful and alien. Because of this key difference, substance abuse psychotherapy typically requires both empathy and structured limit setting, whereas the need for limit setting is less marked in psychotherapy with patients who are depressed or anxious.

Beyond these key elements, this section also elaborates on key tasks that are common to most approaches to psychotherapy for substance use: enhancing motivation to stop substance use, teaching coping skills, changing reinforcement contingencies, fostering management of painful affects, and improving interpersonal functioning. Although different schools of thought about therapeutic action and behavior change may vary in the degree to which emphasis is placed on these different tasks, some attention to these areas is likely to be involved in any successful treatment.

1. Enhancing Motivation to Stop Substance Use

Even at the time of treatment seeking, which usually occurs only after substance-related problems have become severe, patients usually can identify many ways in which they want or feel the need for drugs or alcohol and have difficulty developing a clear picture of what life without substances might be like. To be able to achieve and maintain abstinence or controlled use, individuals who abuse substances need a clear conception of their treatment goals. Several investigators have postulated stages in the development of ones' thinking about stopping use, beginning with precontemplation, moving through contemplation, and culminating with determination as the ideal cognitive set with which to get the most out of treatment.

Regardless of the treatment type, an early task for psychotherapists is to gauge the patient's level of motivation to stop substance use by exploring the treatment goals. In doing this, it is important to challenge overly quick or glib assertions that the patient's goal is to stop using substances altogether. One way to approach the patient's likely ambivalence about treatment goals is to attempt an exploration of the patient's perceived benefits from abused substances or perceived needs for them. To obtain a clear report of the patient's positive attitudes toward substance use, it may be necessary to elicit details of the patient's early involvement with drugs and alcohol. When the therapist has obtained a clear picture of the patient's perceived needs and desires for abused substances, it is important to counter these exploring advantages of a substance-free life.

As noted earlier although virtually all types of substance abuse psychotherapies address the issue of motivation and goal setting to some extent, motivational therapy or interviewing makes this the sole initial focus of treatment. Motivational approaches, which are usually quite brief, are based on principles of motivational psychology and are designed to produce rapid, internally motivated change by seeking to maximize patients' motivational resources and commitment to abstinence.

2. *Teaching Coping Skills*

One enduring challenge of treating substance abuse is to help the patient avoid relapse after achieving an initial period of abstinence. A general tactic for avoiding relapse is to identify sets of circumstances that increase an individual's likelihood of resuming substance use and to help the patient anticipate and practice strategies (e.g., refusal skills, recognizing and avoiding cues for craving) for coping with these high-risk situations. Examples of approaches that emphasize the development of coping skills include cognitive-behavioral approaches such as relapse prevention, in which systematic effort is made to identify high-risk situations and master alternative behaviors and coping skills intended to help the patient avoid substance use when these situations arise.

3. *Changing Reinforcement Contingencies*

As substance abuse worsens, it can take precedence over concerns about work, family, friends, possessions, and health. As compulsive substance use becomes a part of every day, previously valued relationships or activities may be given up so that the rewards available in daily life are narrowed progressively to those derived from substance use. When substance use is brought to a halt, its absence may leave the patient with the need to fill the time that had been spent using drugs or alcohol and to find rewards that can substitute for those derived from use.

An example of an approach that actively changes reinforcement contingencies is the approach developed by Steve Higgins and colleagues that incorporates positive incentives for abstinence into a community reinforcement approach (CRA). This strategy has four organizing features that are grounded in principles of behavioral pharmacology: (a) substance use and abstinence must be swiftly and accurately detected, (b) abstinence is positively reinforced, (c) substance use results in loss of reinforcement, and (d) emphasis on the development of competing reinforcers to substance use.

4. *Fostering Management of Painful Affects*

Dysphoric affects are the most commonly cited precipitant for relapse, and many psychodynamic clinicians have suggested that failure of affect regulation is a central dynamic underlying the development of compulsive substance use. To foster the development of mastery over dysphoric affects, most psychotherapies include techniques for eliciting strong affects within a protected therapeutic setting and then enhancing the patient's ability to identify, tolerate, and respond appropriately to them.

5. *Improving Interpersonal Functioning and Enhancing Social Supports*

A consistent finding in the literature on relapse to substance abuse is the protective influence of an adequate network of social supports. Gratifying friendships and intimate relationships provide a powerful source of rewards to replace those obtained by drug and alcohol use, and the threat of losing these relationships can furnish a strong incentive to maintain abstinence. Typical issues presented by individuals who abuse substances are: (a) loss of or damage to valued relationships occurring when using substances was the principal priority, (b) failure to have achieved satisfactory relationships even prior to having initiated substance abuse, and (c) inability to identify friends or intimates who are not, themselves, abusing substances. For some types of psychotherapy, working on relationship issues is the central focus of the work (e.g., interpersonal therapy, supportive-expressive treatment), whereas for others, this aspect is implied as a part of other therapeutic activities such as identifying risky and protective situations.

Again, although most approaches address these issues to some degree in the course of treatment, an approach that strongly emphasizes the development of social supports are traditional counseling approaches, 12-step facilitation, and other approaches that underline the importance of involvement in self-help groups. Self-help groups offer a fully developed social network of welcoming individuals who are understanding and, themselves, committed to leading a substance-free life. Moreover, in most urban and suburban settings, self-help meetings are held daily or several times weekly, and a sponsor system is available to provide the person in recovery with individual guidance and support on a 24-hour basis, if necessary. For psychotherapists working with substance abuse, encouraging the patient to become involved in a self-help group can provide a powerful source of social support that can protect the patient from relapse while the work of therapy progresses.

III. EMPIRICAL STUDIES

In general, the existing literature on behavioral treatment for substance dependence suggests the following:

1. To date, most studies suggest that psychotherapy is superior to control conditions as treatment for substance

abuse. This is consistent with the bulk of findings from psychotherapy efficacy research in areas other than substance use, which suggests that the effects of many psychotherapies are clinically and statistically significant and are superior to no treatment and placebo conditions.

2. No specific type of behavioral treatment has been shown consistently to be superior as a treatment for substance abuse or for other types of disorders as well. However, behavioral and cognitive-behavioral therapies may show particular promise.

3. The studies examining the differential impact of effectiveness of psychotherapy on those who abuse substances with and without coexistent psychopathology indicate with some consistency that those therapies shown to be generally effective were differentially more effective with patients who presented with high levels of general psychopathology or depression.

4. The effects of even comparatively brief psychotherapies appear to be durable among substance users as they are among other populations.

A. Specific Psychotherapy Approaches

In the following section we briefly describe some of the most promising behavioral therapies for substance use that have at least a minimal level of empirical support from randomized clinical trials. Although this is not exhaustive, many of these approaches are making their way into the field.

B. Contingency Management Approaches

Perhaps the most exciting findings pertaining to the effectiveness of behavioral treatments for cocaine dependence have been the recent reports by Higgins and colleagues discussed briefly earlier in the article. In this approach, urine specimens are required three times weekly to systematically detect all episodes of drug use. Abstinence, verified through drug-free urine screens, is reinforced through a voucher system in which patients receive points redeemable for items consistent with a drug-free lifestyle that are intended to help the patient develop alternate reinforcers to drug use (e.g., movie tickets, sporting goods). Patients never receive money directly. To encourage longer periods of consecutive abstinence, the value of the points earned by the patients increases with each successive clean urine specimen, and the value of the points is reset when the patient produces a drug-positive urine screen.

A series of well-controlled clinical trials demonstrated (a) high acceptance, retention, and rates of abstinence for patients receiving this approach relative to standard 12-step-oriented substance abuse counseling, (b) rates of abstinence do not decline substantially when less valuable incentives are substituted for the voucher system, (c) the value of the voucher system itself (as opposed to other program elements) in producing good outcomes by comparing the behavioral system with and without the vouchers, and (d) although the strong effects of this treatment decline somewhat after the contingencies are terminated, the voucher system has been demonstrated to have durable effects.

Moreover, the efficacy of a variety of contingency management procedures (i.e., including vouchers, direct payments, and free housing) has been replicated in other settings and samples, including cocaine-dependent individuals within methadone maintenance, homeless substance abusers, and freebase cocaine users. The use of contingency management procedures has also been effective in reducing substance use in individuals with schizophrenia and substance disorders in addition to individuals who may be homeless.

These findings are of great importance because contingency management procedures are potentially applicable to a wide range of target behaviors and problems including treatment retention and compliance with pharmacotherapy (i.e., including retroviral therapies for individuals with HIV). For example, in 1996, contingency management may be used effectively to reinforce desired treatment goals (e.g., looking for a job) in addition to abstinence.

However, despite the very compelling evidence of the effectiveness of these procedures in promoting retention in treatment and reducing cocaine use, these procedures are rarely implemented in clinical treatment programs. One major impediment to broader use is the expense associated with the voucher program; where average earnings for patients are about $600.

Recently developed low-cost contingency management (CM) procedures may be a promising approach to bring these effective approaches into general clinical practice. For example, Nancy Petry and colleagues have demonstrated that a variable ratio schedule of reinforcement that provides access to large reinforcers, but at low probabilities, is effective in retaining participants in treatment and reducing substance use. Rather than earning vouchers, participants earn the chance to draw from a bowl and win prizes of varying magnitudes. In a study of 42 alcohol-dependent veterans randomly assigned standard treatment or standard treatment plus CM, 84% of CM participants were retained in treatment throughout an 8-week period compared to 22% of standard treatment participants. By the end of the treatment period, 69% of those receiving CM had not experienced a lapse to alcohol use, but only 39% of those receiving standard treatment were abstinent. A controlled evaluation of this promising approach for the treatment of cocaine dependence is ongoing.

C. Cognitive Behavioral/Relapse Prevention Therapy

Another behavioral approach that has been shown to be effective is cognitive-behavioral treatment (CBT). This approach is based on social learning theories on the acquisition and maintenance of substance use disorders. Its goal is to foster abstinence through helping the patient master an individualized set of coping strategies as effective alternatives to substance use. Typical skills taught include: (a) fostering resolution to stop drug use through exploring positive and negative consequences of continued use, (b) functional analysis of substance use, that is, understanding substance use in relationship to its antecedents and consequences, (c) development of strategies for coping with craving, (d) identification of seemingly irrelevant decisions that could culminate in high-risk situations, (e) preparation for emergencies and coping with a relapse to substance use, and (f) identifying and confronting thoughts about substance use.

A number of randomized clinical trials over the last decade with several diverse cocaine-dependent populations have demonstrated: (a) compared with other commonly used psychotherapies for cocaine dependence, CBT appears to be particularly more effective with more severe cocaine users or those with comorbid disorders, (b) CBT is significantly more effective than less intensive approaches that have been evaluated as control conditions, and (c) CBT is as or more effective than manualized disease model approaches. Moreover, CBT appears to be a particularly durable approach, with patients continuing to reduce their cocaine use even after they leave treatment.

D. Motivational Approaches

For individuals with severe dependence who deny the seriousness of their involvement, a course of individual therapy in which the patient is guided to a clear recognition of the problem may be an essential first step toward more intensive approaches. Motivation enhancement treatment (MET) sets out to accomplish this in a brief therapy approach (i.e., 2–4 sessions). Included in these sessions are typically emphasis on personal responsibility for change with advice and change options, objective feedback of impairment, therapist empathy, and facilitation of patient self-efficacy.

MET has been used to treat a variety of substance disorders, including marijuana dependence. although marijuana is the most commonly used illicit substance, treatment of marijuana abuse and dependence is a comparatively understudied area to date, in part because comparatively few individuals present for treatment with a primary complaint of marijuana abuse or dependence. Currently, no effective pharmacotherapies for marijuana dependence exist, and only a few controlled trials of psychosocial approaches have been completed. In 2000, Robert Stephens and associates compared a delayed treatment control, a 2-session motivational approach, and the more intensive (14-session) relapse prevention approach and found better outcomes for the two active treatments compared with the delayed-treatment control group, but no significant differences between the brief and the more intensive treatment.

E. Family Therapy

Early intervention with individuals who abuse alcohol has historically been approached in some settings by addressing past crisis caused by the alcohol abuse into one dramatic confrontation by family and friends. This therapeutic approach is designed to combat denial by having family and individual close to the person present the negative effects of the individual's use in attempts to move the individual to agree to get treatment.

Moving beyond initial confrontation, others have included family in ongoing aspects of treatment. Edward Kaufman has identified three basic phases of family involvement in treatment: (a) developing a system for establishing and maintaining a drug-free state, (b) establishing a workable method of family therapy, and (c) dealing with the family's readjustment after the cessation of drug abuse. Where these three stages may vary is based on the substances abused, stage of the addiction, family reactivity, and gender of the individual.

M. Duncan Stanton and William Shadish in 1997 conducted a meta-analysis across 1,571 cases reviewing drug abuse outcome studies that included family couples therapy. Family therapy was seen as more beneficial than individual counseling, peer group therapy, and family psychoeducation. In addition, family therapy had higher retention rates than nonfamily therapies and was seen as a cost-effective adjunct to methadone maintenance.

F. Manualized Disease Model Approaches

Until very recently, treatment approaches based on disease models were widely practiced in the United States, but virtually no well-controlled randomized clinical trials had been done evaluating their efficacy alone or in comparison with other approaches. Thus, another important finding emerging from recent randomized clinical trials that has great significance for the clinical community, is the effectiveness of manualized disease model approaches. One such approach is 12-step facilitation (TSF). It is a manual-guided, individual approach that is intended to be similar to widely used approaches that emphasize principles associated with disease models of addiction and has been adapted for use with cocaine-dependent individuals. Although this treatment has no official relationship with Alcoholics Anonymous (AA) or Cocaine Anonymous (CA), its content is intended to be consistent with the 12 steps of AA, with primary emphasis given to Steps 1 through 5 and the concepts of acceptance (e.g., to help the patient accept that they have the illness, or disease, of addiction) and surrender (e.g., to help the patient acknowledge that there is hope for sobriety through accepting the need for help from others and a "higher power"). In addition to abstinence from all psychoactive substances, a major goal of the treatment is to foster active participation in self-help groups. Patients are actively encouraged to attend AA or CA meetings, become involved in traditional fellowship activities, and maintain journals of their self-help group attendance and participation.

Within Project MATCH, TSF was found to be comparable to CBT and motivational enhancement therapy in reducing alcohol use among 1,726 individuals with alcohol dependence; the findings from these studies offer compelling support for the efficacy of manual-guided disease model approaches. However, it is critical to recognize that the evidence supporting disease model approaches has emerged from well-conducted clinical trials in which therapists were selected based on their expertise in this approach and were trained and closely supervised to foster high levels of adherence and competence in delivering these treatments, and it remains to be seen whether these approaches will be as effective when applied under less-than-ideal conditions.

G. Combined Treatment Approaches

1. Combining Psychotherapies

At times it can be useful to combine different psychotherapies to treat patients who have ongoing specialized needs such as in the case of co-occurring disorders or if they are at a point in their treatment where they can benefit from combined approaches that address specific areas of concern. An example of the latter would be individuals in the initial stages of treatment receiving MET in conjunction with relapse prevention to address early treatment issues of decreased motivation to stop using that often occurs initially due to the uncertainty of how life would be without substances.

An example of the former would be combined treatments for posttraumatic stress disorder (PTSD) and substance dependence. Many women receiving substance treatment also meet the criteria for current PTSD. This may often cause the individual to experience a greater severity in the course of their illness than those who have only one of these. Other examples of combined treatments for patients who have co-occurring diagnoses include relapse prevention and exposure therapy for individuals who also have obsessive–compulsive disorder and relapse prevention and motivational long-term approaches for individuals who also have psychotic disorders.

2. Combining Psychotherapy with Pharmacotherapies

At times psychotherapy may be combined with pharmacotherapies to enhance adherence to the pharmacotherapy or synergistically enhance the effects of both treatments. Even when medications have been proven to be effective, dropout from treatment and compliance have still been a problem. Moreover, there has been no study that has demonstrated that the addition of psychotherapy did not help the medication effect.

The most powerful and commonly used pharmacologic approaches to substance abuse are maintenance on an agonist that has an action similar to that of the abused substance (e.g., methadone for opioid addicts, nicotine gum for cigarette smokers), use of an antagonist that blocks the effect of the abused substance (e.g., naltrexone for opioid addicts), the use of an aversive agent that provides a powerful negative reinforcement if the substance is used (e.g., disulfiram for alcoholics) and use of agents that reduce the desire to use the abused substance (e.g. naltrexone and acamprosate for alcoholics). Although all of these agents are widely used, they are seldom used without the provision of adjunctive psychotherapy, because, for example, naltrexone maintenance alone for opioid dependence is plagued by high rates of premature dropout and disulfiram use without adjunctive psychotherapy has not been shown to be superior to placebo.

Several studies have evaluated the use of contingency management to reduce the use of illicit drugs in addicts who are maintained on methadone. In these studies, a reinforcer (reward) is provided to patients who demonstrate specified target behaviors such as providing drug-free urine specimens, accomplishing specific treatment goals, or attending treatment sessions. For example, methadone take-home privileges contingent on reduced drug use is an approach that capitalizes on an inexpensive reinforcer that is potentially available in all methadone maintenance programs. Maxine Stitzer and George Bigelow, in 1978 and 1986, did extensive work in evaluating methadone take-home privileges as a reward for decreased illicit drug use. In a series of well-controlled trials, this group of researchers has demonstrated (a) the relative benefits of positive (e.g. rewarding desired behaviors such as abstinence) compared with negative (e.g., punishing undesired behaviors such as continued drug use through discharges or dose reductions) contingencies, (b) the attractiveness of take-home privileges over other incentives available within methadone maintenance clinics, and (c) the relative effectiveness of rewarding drug-free urine screens compared with other target behaviors. More recently in 1998, Andrew Saxon and colleagues further demonstrated that take-home doses of methadone serve as a reinforcer for abstinence among methadone maintenance program participants by showing fewer restrictions on their availability make them even more effective.

In 1996 and 1998, Kenneth Silverman and colleagues, evaluated a voucher-based CM system to address concurrent illicit drug use, typically cocaine, among methadone-maintained opioid addicts. In this approach, urine specimens are required three times weekly to systematically detect all episodes of drug use. Abstinence, verified through drug-free urine screens, is reinforced through a voucher system in which patients receive points redeemable for items consistent with a drug-free lifestyle that are intended to help the patient develop alternate reinforcers to drug use (e.g., movie tickets, sporting goods). In a very elegant series of studies, the investigators have demonstrated the efficacy of this approach in reducing illicit opioid and cocaine use and producing a number of treatment benefits among this very difficult population.

IV. SUMMARY

Psychosocial treatments should be considered as a treatment option for all patients seeking treatment for substance use disorders. The treatment itself can take place in a variety of settings including inpatient, residential, partial hospitalization, or outpatient treatment. In more controlled settings the frequency and duration of sessions increases.

Through our review of the literature, it becomes evident that individuals who abuse substances are a heterogeneous group reflecting much diversity. To address this diversity in treatment, it is useful to consider multidimensional outcomes. Consequently, no one form of treatment or psychotherapy is typically seen as universally effective across all substance disorders. However, one major strategy common to all currently practiced psychotherapies is to place primary emphasis on reducing substance use, while pursuing other goals only after substance use has been at least somewhat controlled.

The history of individual psychotherapy to treat substance abuse arose from using already established therapeutic strategies adapted for use to treat a special population of individuals who abuse substances. Most schools of therapy that have been adapted to address substance-related problems share common knowledge and common goals or strategies that must be addressed to provide successful treatment to substance-using populations.

The main areas of knowledge to mastered by the beginning therapist are pharmacology, use patterns, consequences, and the course of addiction for the major types of abused substances. It is important to go beyond textbook knowledge to street knowledge of frequently abused drugs as well as understand the clinical presentation of intoxicated individuals or withdrawal from different substances to fully understand the clinical picture and to aid alliance.

Common goals and strategies related to substance abuse psychotherapeutic treatment include enhancing motivation to stop using, teaching coping skills, changing reinforcement contingencies, fostering management of painful affects, and improving interpersonal functioning and social supports. The therapist needs to take a more active stance than in the treatment of other disorders such as depression of anxiety disorders due to the principal symptom, compulsive use, being initially gratifying until the long-term consequences of use induce pain and desire to stop.

Our review of rigorously conducted efficacy research on psychotherapies for substance abuse provides support for the use of a number of innovative approaches: individual substance counseling, and cognitive behavioral treatment for cocaine dependence; community reinforcement treatment with contingency management for cocaine dependence; and contingency management approaches combined with methadone maintenance in the treatment of opioid dependence as well as use with a wide range of other substance use disorders including alcohol dependence. Manualized disease model approaches have been as effective to other forms of psychotherapeutic substance abuse treatments. Substance psychotherapies have been combined with pharmacotherapies to enhance adherence to pharmacotherapies or synergistically enhance the effects of both treatments. Future studies are needed to evaluate the usefulness of combined psychotherapy approaches and further investigate less rigorously studied treatments.

See Also the Following Articles

Addictions in Special Populations: Treatment ■ Adjunctive/Conjoint Therapies ■ Comorbidity ■ Controlled Drinking ■ Gambling: Behavior and Cognitive Approaches ■ Matching Patients to Alcoholism Treatment ■ Psychopharmacology: Combined Treatment

Further Reading

Carroll, K. M. (1998). Treating drug dependence: Recent advances and old truths. In W. R. Miller & N. Heather (Eds.), *Treating addictive behaviors* (2nd ed., pp. 217–229). New York: Plenum.

DeRubeis, R. J., & Crits-Christoph, P. (1998). Empirically supported individual and group psychological treatments for adult mental disorders. *Journal of Consulting and Clinical Psychology, 66,* 37–52.

McLellan, A. T., Arndt, I. O., Metzger, D. S., Woody, G. E., & O'Brien, C. P. (1993). The effects of psychosocial services in substance abuse treatment. *Journal of the American Medical Association, 269,* 1953–1959.

McLellan, A. T., & McKay, J. R. (1998). The treatment of addiction: What can research offer practice? In S. Lamb, M. R. Greenlick, & D. McCarty (Eds.), *Bridging the gap between practice and research: Forging partnerships with community based drug and alcohol treatment* (pp. 147–185). Washington, DC: National Academy Press.

Stanton, M. D., & Shadish, W. R. (1997). Outcome, attrition, and family-couples treatment for drug abuse: A meta-analysis and review of the controlled, comparative studies. *Psychology Bulletin, 122,* 170–191.

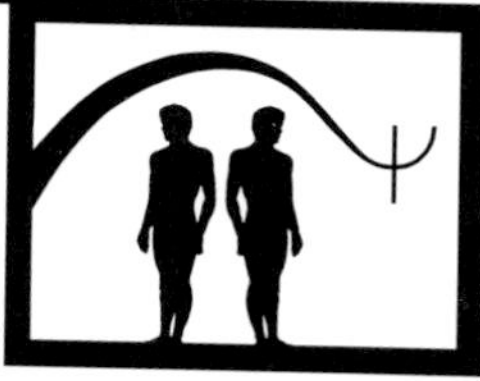

Successive Approximations

Patricia A. Wisocki
University of Massachusetts, Amherst

GLOSSARY

operant conditioning The process of increasing or decreasing the frequency of a behavior by altering the consequences that follow the performance of that behavior.

reinforcement Consequences that increase the likelihood that a behavior will increase.

systematic desensitization A therapeutic technique for anxiety reduction in which anxious clients are relaxed and exposed to an incremental, graded series of anxiety-provoking elements that approximate the ultimate event feared by the clients.

Successive approximations are responses that gradually increase in resemblance to the final behavior that is being shaped as part of a therapeutic program to develop new behavior. Shaping is the process of reinforcing responses that successively approximate the final desired behavior. Responses are reinforced that either resemble the final behavior or that include components of the final behavior. As new approximations are reached successfully and reinforced, the earlier ones in the sequence are allowed to extinguish.

I. DESCRIPTION OF USE

Before using successive approximations, a shaping program must be established. The shaping program consists of the following sequence: (1) a determination of the goal behavior and the criteria for successful performance; (2) a determination of the elements that resemble the goal behavior in gradually increasing steps (successive approximations) and a decision about the size of the intervals between steps; (3) a determination of the reinforcers to be given contingently as the incremental behavior is produced; (4) the application of the program. The goal behavior may be anything that the organism is physically capable of producing. It should be clearly specified in ways that may be unambiguously measured. In determining the elements that approximate the goal behavior, it is important to find a beginning point that has some resemblance to the final behavior. The beginning point may be as elementary as raising a hand, turning a head in a particular direction, or making a mark on paper. Progressive sequences of responses leading to the goal behavior and the intervals between the responses must also be determined. These are the successive approximations. The intervals between responses must be small enough so that the organism is able to succeed more often than not, for reinforcement is not given for failed responses. The interval must not be so small, however, that the organism becomes bored or inattentive. The organism may be reinforced at the same step for a short period of time in order to practice the response, but the demands for performance must be gradually increased sequentially so that the organism does not stop altogether at one step before reaching the goal.

II. THEORETICAL BASES

The procedure of response shaping by successive approximations was developed in the laboratories of Charles Ferster and B.F. Skinner in 1957, where pigeons were trained to peck at a response key. The birds were reinforced at first when their heads moved forward and ignored for all other behaviors. Once the forward movements occurred at a high rate, additional movements in the desired direction of the final goal of key pecking were reinforced. Reinforcements were withheld until the birds moved their heads in gradually increasing distances. Finally, the birds were reinforced for moving their heads in a position directly across from the response key. The pecking response could not fail to occur and the birds were reinforced only for pecking the key, the final desired behavior.

This technique is derived from the operant conditioning theoretical perspective, which holds that when rewarding consequences immediately follow the performance of a particular behavior, that behavior will increase in frequency. The principles of operant conditioning describe the relationship between behavior and environmental events, called antecedents and consequences, that influence behavior. This relationship is called a contingency. Antecedent events are those stimuli that occur before a behavior is exhibited, such as instructions, sounds, and gestures. Behaviors include actions made by an organism in response to the antecedent events. Consequences are those events that follow the performance of the behavior. For a consequence to affect behavior it must be contingent or dependent on the occurrence of that behavior.

In 1958 Joseph Wolpe reported on his work in the development of methods to reduce the laboratory-created experimental neurosis (anxiety) of cats. Wolpe gradually exposed the animals to a series of rooms that successively approximated the features of the room in which the anxiety had originally occurred. When the animals displayed a slight reduction in anxiety in the other rooms, Wolpe encouraged them to eat, reasoning that if the animals could engage in responses that competed with the anxiety response, the anxiety would be overcome. This systematically applied procedure was successful.

Using this information from the laboratory, Wolpe conceptualized the effects of the procedure from the viewpoint of classical conditioning in which environmental cues are said to elicit anxiety or fear responses. Anxiety may then be eliminated by conditioning an alternative response that is incompatible with it. For humans Wolpe used deep muscle relaxation as the competing response to anxiety. While relaxed, anxious clients were exposed to anxiety- producing stimuli, either in imagination or in real life. The stimuli were presented in gradually increasing intensity and resemblance to the original anxiety stimuli (i.e., successive approximations to the original event). As relaxation becomes associated with the anxiety events, the anxiety is reduced. Wolpe called this procedure "systematic desensitization."

III. EMPIRICAL STUDIES

Successive approximations is not a clinical technique per se, but a way of presenting material within a number of procedures. There has been no research on successive approximations independent of the clinical techniques in which it is embedded. The procedures of shaping and systematic desensitization have, however, been extensively reviewed and are presented elsewhere in this book.

IV. SUMMARY

Successive approximations are responses that gradually increase in resemblance to the final behavior that is being shaped as part of a therapeutic program. They are an element in the operant conditioning procedure of shaping and in the classical conditioning procedure of systematic desensitization.

See Also the Following Articles

Convert Reinforcer Sampling ■ Negative Reinforcement ■ Operant Conditioning ■ Positive Reinforcement ■ Progressive Relaxation ■ Reinforcer Sampling ■ Systematic Desensitization

Further Reading

Ferster, C., & Skinner, B. F. (1957). *Schedules of reinforcement.* New York: Appleton-Century-Crofts.

Kazdin, A. (1989). *Behavior modification in applied settings,* 4th ed. Pacific Grove, CA: Brooks/Cole.

Wolpe, J. (1958). *Psychotherapy by reciprocal inhibition.* Stanford, CA: Stanford University Press.

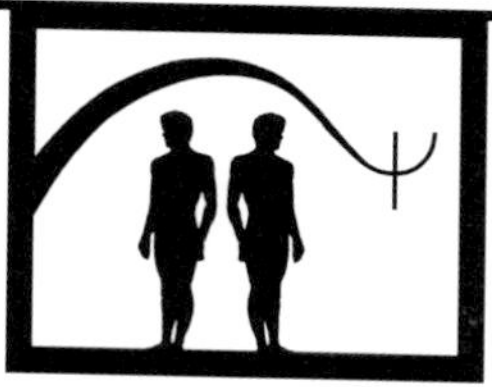

Sullivan's Interpersonal Psychotherapy

Maurice R. Green
New York University

GLOSSARY

counter-transference The personal reaction of the therapist to the patient including distortions that the therapeutic training helps him or her restrain.

field of awareness The content of the therapist's conscious attention to the interaction with the patient.

modifying the introject The therapist uses insight to modify by understanding the specific content he or she is experiencing directly from the patient.

object relations theory Within the traditional psychoanalytic framework W.R.D. Fairbairn introduced object relations to refer to the relations between the patient and a significant other person.

preverbalization Thoughts and feelings that give rise to specific language.

schizophrenia A term introduced by Bleuler to replace the term dementia praecox, referring to cognitive and emotional disturbances of a severe degree. Now a term designating a set of syndromes characterized by severe disturbances in thinking and reality perception.

security operations Verbal and nonverbal efforts of many kinds to prevent or ward off anxiety.

selective inattention Perceptions not attended to because they might arouse anxiety.

self-system The envelope of all the security operations.

transference The distortion of present experience by past experience as reflected in the patient toward the therapist.

I. INTRODUCTION

Harry Stack Sullivan's technique of psychotherapy was strongly influenced by his exquisite sensitivity to any sign of a patient's distress or discomfort in interaction with a therapist—himself or other. His theory of interpersonal psychiatry was the foundation for his practice of psychotherapy. He called his method of psychotherapy participant observation because the significant data included the psychiatrist's thoughts and feelings as well as those of the patient. Although Sullivan expressed an appreciation of Freud's work, it had little influence on his own thinking, which was firmly based on the philosophy of experience.

Sullivan was first and foremost an American psychiatrist, as Helen Swick Perry has brilliantly documented in her book *Psychiatrist of America*. However respectful and sensitive, he was firm, vigorous, and well-disciplined in his approach—contrary to the opinion of his critics who accused him of being too protective of his patients.

Sullivan had an extensive correspondence with Alfred Korzybski who, together with Kurt Lewin, organized their observations to a theoretical field in which many vectors of different force operated simultaneously with their counterparts in interpersonal transactions. Therefore, some part of a personality would enhance parts of another personality while other parts might diminish or suppress aspects of the other person. This could be elaborated with topological diagrams to clarify the ideas.

II. THEORETICAL BASES

Early in his career, Sullivan published a paper in his journal *Psychiatry* authored by Albert Dunham describing the important work of the American philosopher Charles S. Pierce and comparing it to the European philosophers on the nature of human responses. Pierce's three categories of experience, firstness, secondness, and thirdness, are logically parallel to Sullivan's prototoxic, parataxic, and syntaxic modes of experience.

The prototaxic mode of Sullivan is more or less equivalent to the Firstness of Pierce—that is, immediate, instant, forever, here and everywhere, with no differentiation before or after—"unione mystica." With differentiation and past, present, or future, here and there, we have the category of Secondness and the early part of the Parataxic mode, which includes myth, superstition, dreaming, and metaphor. Thirdness includes the logical, consensually validated, or scientific—which is the Syntaxic mode of Sullivan.

Sullivan introduced the term interpersonal for the first time in psychiatry in order to emphasize that the treatment, the work that was being done, was something that was done between two people, the patient and the psychiatrist, and not something that was being done to the patient by the psychiatrist. This was also emphasized in his term participant observation, which refers to the psychiatrist and the patient working together on the patient's difficulties in living in order to clarify them and to help the patient develop insight and better ways of coping more effectively.

The purpose of psychiatric treatment is to enhance the development of the syntaxic mode of experience, including the range of communication by word, gesture, and movement, between persons—interpersonal processes. In that way the problems of living that are contributing to the patient's distress and/or disablement can be clarified and addressed. Sullivan avoided the terms unconscious, preconscious, and conscious for their lack of precision and consistent meaning. He preferred to use the field of awareness, which ranged in content from unavailable to marginal to focal in its spectrum. This field spectrum can become wider or narrower with specific interactions, verbal or otherwise, blocked or opened up, as the interpersonal area changes, including the illusory or projected personification of "good me," and "bad me," "not me," as well as those of "good other," "bad other," and "non-other." In this context the psychiatrist or other mental health expert must manifest a precise sensitivity to nuances of speech and subtlety of movement. In this way the psychiatrist could avoid provoking anxiety that interfered with communication while eliciting information that was associated or accompanied by some anxiety. This has been described by others in the literature as coping with the mechanisms of defense. It is described later by Anna Freud in her well-known work *The Ego and Mechanisms of Defense*. Although Sullivan advocated various measures to minimize anxiety he vigorously opposed fraudulent reassurance or falsehood in any form. In his work with the severely mentally ill, he would sometimes use alcohol or mild sedation to help open up channels of communication.

III. THERAPEUTIC RANGE

Sullivan used the term parataxic for the phenomenon of transference and counter-transference—that is, generalizations from past experience that may not be appropriate to the present encounter, and may contribute to distressing interactions with others. As a participant observer, the therapist may reinforce some projections and diminish others. The content of this field of interaction was called the social geography or social landscape by Leston Havens. Sullivan insisted on obtaining detailed and precise descriptions of feelings and context—in one instance having a patient describe the New York subway system.

Sullivan also liked to set some distance by referring to a third party. He said that it is much easier for patients to tell the therapist what is important and unimportant, even about the therapist, if they talk about a third party. Sullivan objected to the patient lying on a couch with the therapist sitting behind the patient. Sullivan preferred to sit alongside the patient at an angle, which is the way I practiced analysis for 25 years, as did Clara Thompson, my training analyst. Sullivan referred to the content of transferences carried by the patient as false expectations, projections, and misconceptions.

For example, Sullivan said:

> If a patient says to me "You must think I'm terrible" and I don't feel that is just hysterical drama, but means something, I am apt to say, quite passively "about what?" as if I had not heard anything about such a

> notion. Quite frequently, just because my reaction seemed so astonished and annoyed, they tell me, and to that extent I have gotten somewhere.

Thereby he reduces the transference.

Sullivan was more interested in therapeutic change than he was in cognitive insight. This could be seen as deconditioning or in object-relations theory as modifying the introject. In some ways Sullivan's method is analogous to play therapy, with the transference projected onto the narrative or the world "out there."

In addition to correcting the transferences in a profoundly collaborative way, he used what can be called counterprojective statements. These statements talk about the important figure in the patient's life, which draws attention and projection to them. Sullivan may then join the patient in expressing appropriate feelings toward these persons such as desperation and rage. Sullivan was remarkably and dramatically effective with paranoid patients. The first step was establishing empathy with the paranoid person's rage and expressing it. At the same time Sullivan would avoid a direct face-to-face confrontation but would sit alongside the patient, joining the patient in a collaborative effort to look at the world from the patient's side. Third, he would cite some experiences of his own at distressing institutional behavior. However, this must be authoritative and not susceptible to being experienced by the patient as patronizing or false.

Sullivan examined and treated a variety of patients, but his central focus was always on schizophrenia and, to a lesser degree, obsessive–compulsive disorder. He saw conversion hysteria as a substitutive disorder wherein physical symptoms substituted for achievement in promoting an enfeebled self-esteem, and preventing anxiety, that is, the type of anxiety caused by a threat to one's sense of being a worthwhile human being.

Sullivan described the three most basic requirements for the effective psychotherapy of persons with schizophrenia. First, the therapist must review with the patient a survey of his or her conflicted growth and adaptation as skillfully as possible. Second, the therapist must provide some type of healthy "corrective" experiences in the patient's living of his or her life. Lastly, there is collaboration of the patient with an enlightened physician skilled in penetrating self-deceptions with the goal of improving the patient's self-esteem and social competence.

In assessing Sullivan's remarkable success at Sheppard Pratt Hospital it is important to note the linkage to the type of onset: Out of 100 patients who had slow insidious onset only two went on to a full recovery. Of 78 who had an acute onset, 48 showed marked improvement with most others experiencing a full recovery, according to (Sullivan in 1962.) In the Sheppard Pratt program Sullivan did very little psychotherapy directly with the patients but worked through a staff that he carefully selected, personally trained, and closely supervised.

Sullivan became interested in the criminal mind, the psychopath or sociopath, that had no empathy for fellow human beings, and no concern for anyone's welfare except their own. He expressed an opinion that they were not quite human, and that they should be studied by a method of studying animal behavior. However, he never developed this idea any further.

IV. TECHNIQUE

In his own psychotherapy practice Sullivan preferred to work indirectly with as much collaborative style as could be achieved. By sitting alongside or at an angle to the patient the two together could look at the "social geography" of the patient's life, examining the important relationships therein. In Sullivan's language this would "loosen or attenuate" the parataxes, or in object-relations theory modify the introjects. A corollary of this would be the counterprojective statements that would move the transference (parataxes, distortions) back to the original figures from the patient's past. In doing so Sullivan might not only refer to the significant figure (parent, sibling, etc.) and point it out, but also supply the appropriate feeling of hurt, anger, or rage in a corrective emotional experience.

Sullivan's verbal psychotherapeutic interventions could be described in four categories: interrogative, imperative, rhetorical, and declarative. Although the interrogative direct questions are obviously necessary, the imperative is only subtly apparent in the fundamental rule of free association—the verbal expression of empathy is rhetorical as it communicates the imaginative projection of one's own consciousness into the consciousness of another person. Declarative statements usually are made to clarify or interpret, but Sullivan used them also to direct attention elsewhere, away from the patient and therapist to the social field of other people. This is similar to doing play therapy with children. Thus these counterprojective statements move attention away from the patient; they point to the critical figures, and express appropriate feelings by the therapist toward those critical figures, setting an example for the patient. These counterprojective statements are especially useful in treating a paranoid patient or a psychotic transference. Again this is analogous to using play objects in treating children. Sullivan, in speaking of reconstructing the past, said, "What I would have seen if I had been there." The advantages gained are a clearer perspective on the past, differentiation of the structure (family, teacher, friend) internalized from the past, and best of all, freedom from the past.

In the beginning of this work, and in fact throughout the course of therapy or participant observation, the emphasis and direction were always on the concrete sharing of feelings and experiences in which the feelings and thoughts of the therapist were as important to share when appropriate as were the patient's. However, the therapist's only gratification from this experience was exercise of their competence and the pay that was received. He or she would not pursue friendship, gratitude, prestige, or anything else.

Sullivan never accepted general, vague, or speculative statements at face value. He would always try to pin down specifically and concretely what the patient was referring to, and that way the patient might become more aware of something that previously he or she had not paid attention to. Naturally, this required a very intense concentration on the part of the therapist, and a very disciplined approach to paying attention to what the patient meant by what was said. Therefore, theoretical hypotheses, structures, and jargon are completely avoided in accumulating very accurate and precise information. Therefore, Sullivan advocated questions that would be more productive than the interpretations. He also recommended attention to nonverbal communication of feelings such as a facial expression, tilting of the head, or a raising of the eyebrows that would communicate something to the patient that would be helpful in bringing out more useful data. In confronting delusional ideas that were communicated by the patient the therapist can show his or her puzzlement or questioning but should never flatly contradict or show a nonacceptance of this. The therapist should never pretend that he or she understands something when he or she does not. It is much better to say frankly that he or she does not understand and to ask for clarification or further explanation. In asking such questions the therapist might prefer indirect questions as they are less likely to be anxiety provoking, and they may yield more information than a direct question does. Indirect questions might also bring more attention to the interpersonal aspects of what was going on in the interaction between the two people referred to, rather than an attribute of somebody. Of course, at all times with either direct or indirect inquiry such questions for seeking more useful information and helping the patient should not in any way undermine the patient's self-esteem.

Sullivan was also very active as a therapist. He was opposed to the more traditional psychoanalytic position of passively listening to whatever the patient brings out. Instead, the therapist pursues data, striving for more details and more precise information until the issue is very clear and the patient understands it, and can go on to the next thing. Sullivan not only tended to avoid interpretations but he even objected to the word interpretation, which has an authoritarian aspect to it. Instead of using the word interpret he would employ words like comment, inquire, point out, indicate, and so on. There is a difference of viewpoint. He also recommended when pointing out particular aspects or data to a patient that the therapist should not try to do too much all at once but rather pace oneself properly so the patient has time to assimilate it, and express his or her own reaction to it. The therapist thus allows the interaction between the two of them to be productive, rather than to cut it short by overloading the patient with too much information at one time.

The thrust of the patient's work with the therapist is to become more aware of what goes on between himself or herself and other people, particularly the ones who are most significant in their life. To the extent that he or she can formulate this in words and share it with another person, namely the therapist, he or she is able to be in better health, and to be more effective in dealing with his or her problems in living. Therefore the work of therapy very often consists of paying attention to many small details that help the patient become more aware and to be able to use this awareness more effectively.

Sullivan believed very strongly that there was an innate movement toward health in the person and this thrust toward mental health would be more active as the barriers to it were removed in the collaboration between the therapist and the patient. Therefore, the therapist was never seen as curing the patient or making the illness go away; the therapist was seen as helping the patient be healthier and more competent in handling the emotional and personal problems of their life.

Sullivan uses the term anxiety in a way that is different from its general use in medicine and everyday life. He uses it as a category of all kinds of emotional anguish such as fearfulness, tenseness, guilt, inferiority feelings, shame, self-loathing, eerie feelings of personality change, and all other forms of emotional distress. Anxiety can vary in degree from a scarcely noticeable fear to incapacitating panic. There has to be some anxiety in order to know that you are getting somewhere, doing something useful; therefore, it is important for the therapist to (as it were) keep the finger on the pulse of anxiety to keep it manageable and constructive rather than interfering.

Sullivan was very skeptical about the value of direct reassurance. He saw that many schizoid and obsessional patients were able to respond to direct reassurance by having no response whatsoever and not allowing it to have any impact on them. Therefore indirect assurance was the only kind of assurance that would be effective. Sullivan was also very skeptical about the expression of admiration, gratitude, and affection from the patient. He did not believe that patients had enough feelings for themselves to be able to afford to appreciate him much. He believed patients may feel worthwhile only because this wonderful person is interested in them, but that is not very clinically useful and is not going to do them much good in their lives. It is much better that they discover how more effective and competent they are than they thought; and if that means disappointment in the therapist, that is beneficial. Being disappointed in themselves and feeling more inadequate is not of benefit, and indicates that their therapy is not going too well.

Sometimes the therapist can pick up anxiety that is blocking the patient by listening carefully to the pauses, missing data, and distortions in an account that the patient is giving them. The anxiety tends to block out an awareness of events, and things happening in the event, so by paying close attention, one may pick up on what is missing, and then find out what the anxiety was, and what it was all about. Rather than giving empty reassurance to the patient's anxiety, it is better for the therapist to specify the nature of the anxiety and the context in which it arose. For example, if the patient is feeling very angry with his parents it may make him feel guilty to point that out. It might be helpful for the person to be oriented to where he is emotionally because the anxiety interferes with the process. It may seem like stating the obvious, but when a person is in the midst of a breakup of a relationship, it may be useful to simply spell out the distress that the person is experiencing in the context of the breakup and how natural and normal it is to suffer such distress. Some people feel ashamed and embarrassed that they are a patient seeking help from a mental-health expert for their problems. This can be spelled out with the patient and put into its proper context. In doing such explorations with a patient, Sullivan was particular in adhering to objective data taking place in real time and a real place, and to not encourage the patient to go off into descriptions of fantasies. This is something he did not encourage and did not think was valuable. He believed it might even encourage unrealistic thinking; daydreaming might be present at times but it does not solve any problems.

Sullivan used the term security in a much broader sense to mean the opposite of anxiety: a sense of personal adequacy, or personal worth, personal value, or strong self-esteem and a complete lack of the negative feelings of worthlessness and other emotional distress. He saw the polar opposites of anxiety and security as being in a continual state of movement, trying to balance against each other like opposite ends of a see-saw. The ways of enhancing security and avoiding anxiety were called security operations by Sullivan and they could be either healthy or unhealthy. A healthy security operation increased a person's effectiveness and emotional health, and an unhealthy one could impair the interpersonal relationship. They are different from the Freudian notion of defense because the notions of defense occur in a hypothetical mind-structure and are not observable, whereas the security operations of Sullivan are behavioral.

Sullivan's whole system might be called a cognitive behavioral system. One of the unhealthy or sometimes healthy security operations is selective inattention. This occurs when individuals observe only a part of what is happening in their environment between them and authorities so that they pay attention to some things and avoid paying attention to others. This is analogous to Freud's concept of repression. Selective inattention is always an ongoing activity between two or more people whereas repression can be something between a person and himself in his mind. Sullivan was a fairly rigorous taskmaster in keeping the patient focused on the matter at hand, and not letting the patient go off into empty discussions of trivial subjects that were not particularly relevant to the basic problems for which help is being sought. Sullivan also discouraged pseudo-compliance wherein a patient becomes very eager to please and agrees with everything the therapist says without really confronting his or her issues. It is a way of dismissing the whole investigation with faint praise. Another way of avoiding confronting something that is painful or distressing is to get angry about something that is not to the point, and in the angry exchange the therapist may be put on the defensive unless he or she realizes what is happening.

The self-system is not exactly the same thing as the ego of psychoanalytic theories. The self-system that Sullivan refers to is what is characteristic of the individual and what defines that individual as a person that is known. Thereby the self-system protects patients against distress and enables them to live as comfortably as possible so that they can feel (that is, identify) who they are, and that they are worthwhile and recognized as such. The self-system is not something that exists as a thing in time and space. The self-system is simply a verbal convenience, a phrase to refer to an envelope of protective movements and ethics that the patient makes to avoid distress. The therapist must therefore use his or her skill to enable the patient to feel more worthwhile, and safer, and with more self-esteem while exploring relationships and experiences that might provoke embarrassment, shame, or other kinds of distress.

Sullivan paid great attention to this aspect of giving a kind of reassurance that was not sentimental, false, or difficult for the patient to assimilate. He would indirectly always provide a way for patients to see themselves with greater dignity and self-respect. Nonetheless, as Sullivan rigorously pursued the details of the patients' experiences with the important other persons in their life, it would provoke some distress. Sullivan was very careful to note this distress and to try to be helpful with it. Sometimes he would suggest a healthier, more constructive, way of dealing with a problem situation that the patient had never considered. When the patient is presented with the novel approach it must be something reasonable and practicable for the patient to follow.

Behavior and feeling patterns that recurrently characterize interpersonal relations—the functional interplay of persons and personifications, personal signs, personal abstractions, and personal attributions—make up the distinctively human sort of being. Sullivan characterized the manifestations in the interpersonal relations of activities as integrating, disjunctive, or isolative. He sometimes referred to the zones of interaction in which behavior takes place in interpersonal relationships, such as the oral zone, genital zone, anal zone, muscular activity zone, and so on. But he rarely referred to these zones.

In the course of treating very seriously ill persons Sullivan noticed that they sometimes manifested what he called a malevolent transformation. This occurs when the therapist or another person has shown a greater manifestation of tenderness and expression of a caring closeness to the patient than the patient is able to bear in his own experience of himself. Therefore the patient manifests a sense, or a feeling of hatred and hostility, and may even attack the person who is being tender and loving to him.

Sullivan did pay some attention to dreams but he never referred to it as dream interpretation. He would pick out salient features of the dream and then present them to the patient to ask the patient what the patient thought of it. For example, there was a dream of a Dutch windmill that the patient had in which everything was rack and ruin and when the patient finished reporting the dream Sullivan picked out two details, that the windmill was beautiful, active on the outside but utterly dead and decayed within, and the patient responded, "My God, my mother." Although this might be seen by others as interpretation it actually was presenting some details to the patient in such a way that the patient was able to use the dream, and use these details to get some insight into the relationship with his mother that he had not seen before. Sullivan not only showed a great respect for dreams and their content but he also showed much respect for the fantasies a patient might present. He objected strongly to the dismissal of these fantasies as mere wish-fulfilling fantasies. He insisted that they might actually provide some creative foresight and planning for the future.

The therapist needs to be aware of what he or she is communicating nonverbally to the patient as well as what the patient is communicating to him or her consciously or otherwise. Sullivan was against the idea of the therapist sitting behind the patient where he or she could not be seen, which reduces nonverbal communication to some extent, but of course it did not eliminate it. Sullivan was very much aware of the particular meanings that vary from one language or culture pattern to another. When therapists are not familiar with the language, or the cultural context of the patient, they may be misled by words or gestures from the patient. Because of Sullivan's experience with anthropology he was able to bring a much more sensitive cross-cultural awareness to his work.

In a case seminar with Dr. Kvarnes, an associate at Chestnut Lodge, Sullivan brought out the importance of looking at the apparent devotion and love of the patient's parents for him and seeing what there was in it that could be constructive for the patient. It could also be harmful in being overprotective. Sullivan was exquisitely sensitive not only to overprotective movements and gestures by significant people in the patient's life but also to overindulgence, which can be equally sabotaging of the patient's self-esteem.

A personified self is the whole fabric of how the patient presents himself and sees himself in relation to other people. He may mean that when important people around him are upset he retires and withdraws. If they upset him, also, that may mean that he cannot stand stress very well. However, he might mean that he has much inner emotional calm and secure self-respect that will enable him to cope with stress in a very effective manner.

Another area that is useful to explore is what the patient imagines about his future. It is good to encourage the patient to speculate about what he will be doing 3 years or 5 years or 10 years from now. However, if this arouses undue feelings of despair and hopelessness, one should not permit that to go on. In every case, in all categories of illness and types of patients, Sullivan was rigorously pursuing the precise and exact data of the patient's experience: What did occur, when did it occur, where did it occur, who was there, what did they say, what did they do, and so on. Sometimes the patient gets upset without the therapist knowing what the upset was triggered by, and what it is all about; one cannot let that pass. The therapist must investigate it and find out what has upset him, and what can be done about it.

Sullivan sometimes used what he called preverbalization when things were not going well with a patient; this is not the same thing as Freudian free association. Free association is usually employed as a method of therapy over a period of months or a year, whereas Sullivan used preverbalization as a tool for alleviating a block or a difficulty in communication. When there has been stagnation, he asked the patient to tell him everything that came to his mind about this particular aspect of his life. In the course of the interview in clarifying and straightening out misunderstandings, and the events and experiences of the patient's life, it was important for him to not only avoid any jargon himself but also to discourage the patient from using technical terms such as psychosis, complex, and so on. That way he could get down to the "nitty-gritty" and not be bogged down in terms of which neither person knew exactly the meaning.

Sullivan felt very strongly that the patient should get a summary of the important content of the interview or the course of treatment at some point. This could be done just before saying goodbye. The course of treatment could be summarized after each session. The therapist could give a summary of what was noteworthy in the session, and an anticipation of what will be looked for in the next meeting. In the course of such summaries the therapist may repeat the fact that he or she is a skilled person who has special training and knowledge; that the therapist is there to help clarify the problems that the patient has, and to help resolve them. This helps to keep the therapist/patient relationship on a professional level and reminds the patient of what he or she is about, and not to get lost in various distortions of what the therapist would like or fears or other anticipations that are not grounded.

Sometimes a patient who is grateful toward the therapist may experience a sexual urge to show his gratitude by submitting to a sexual experience, to giving the therapist sexual pleasure. In such cases the therapist needs to simply express an appreciation, and point to the fact that such an experience would be destructive to the therapeutic relationship. The professional nature of their relationship must be preserved so that work can go on, and the patient can get the most benefit from the relationship.

Sullivan was very familiar with the phenomenon of loneliness and stressed the important and powerful role it could play, referring to it as a driving force.

Sullivan had considerable experience of loneliness in his childhood and adolescence. He emphasized very strongly the importance of intimacy, and the devastating character of its lack from infancy throughout development to early adult life. He called loneliness or the need for intimacy one of the major integrating tendencies of life. He carefully separated it from other needs such as the need for satisfaction of lust.

Sullivan was very interested in the subtle and sometimes minute consequences of personal statements made to a patient. For instance, when a nurse told him some information about a patient, he was careful not to invade the patient's privacy by frankly communicating this to him. Instead he would do it indirectly so that the patient did not feel that people were spying on him. He did not want to undermine the patient's sense of confidence in the nurse's interest and her communication with him. He expected that their privacy would be fully respected. For example, the patient might confide something to the nurse that Sullivan felt was important to investigate and so Sullivan might say to the patient that he did not know how the nurse got this idea but he was glad that she was interested enough to speak to him about it. He would then ask the patient what he thought about it and what it was all about. In that way he got into it without violating the confidentiality of the nurse/patient relationship and at the same time he was able to explore this important information.

V. SUMMARY

In conclusion, it must be emphasized that Sullivan avoided jargon, theoretical systems, and language pertaining to such. He was very compassionate and at the same time very vigorous in collecting significant data from the patient that would be useful and helpful to the patient in living his or her life. Sullivan said that growth is still possible for the fortunate ones: If they are fortunate the growth goes on and on, they observe, formulate, and validate more and more; at the same time foresight continues to expand so that they can foresee their career line, not as it inevitably will be, but in terms of expectation and probability, perhaps with provisions for disappointment. Sullivan viewed a human as an enduring pattern of human relationships and also as a whole person, unique and alone. To him the structure of our human being and the core of our self-esteem is one with the continuity of specific kinds of relationships. The integrity of the self is one with the integrity of relating to others; reality of the self is one with the reality of the relationship, the "I am" of identity with the "you are" of identity—the enduring patterns of relatedness, with the whole person, alone in his uniqueness, related in his humanness.

See Also the Following Articles

Cognitive Behavior Therapy ■ Countertransference ■ History of Psychotherapy ■ Interpersonal Psychotherapy ■ Object Relations Psychotherapy ■ Rational Emotive Behavior Therapy ■ Schizophrenia and Other Psychotic Disorders ■ Transference

Further Reading

Chapman, A. H. (1978). *Treatment technique of Harry Stack Sullivan*. R. G. Kvarnes & G. H. Parloff (Eds.). New York: Brunner/Mazel.

Chryanowski, G. (1977). *Interpersonal approach to psychoanalysis. A contemporary view of Harry Stack Sullivan*. Halsted Press.

Dillingham, J. C. *A Harry Stack Sullivan Case Seminar: Treatment of a young male schizophrenic*. S. Jacobson, R. G. Kvarnes, & I. M. Ryckoff (Eds.). New York: W. W. Norton & Co.

Perry, H. Swick. (1982). *Psychiatrist of America*. Cambridge, MA: The Belknap Press of Harvard University Press.

Sullivan, H. S. (1962). *Schizophrenia as a human process*, H. S. Perry (Ed.). New York: W. W. Norton.

Sullivan, H. S. (1964). *The fusion of psychiatry and social science*. H. S. Perry (Ed.). New York: W. W. Norton.

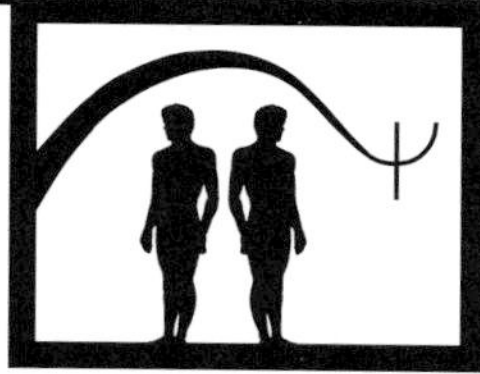

Supervision in Psychotherapy

Stephen B. Shanfield
University of Texas Health Science Center at San Antonio

GLOSSARY

evaluation Feedback in supervision allows the therapist to take distance from the therapy and is a form of ongoing evaluation.

parallel process The therapist re-creates the therapy in the supervision. This parallel process provides a guide to understanding the therapy.

supervision A relationship between a supervisor and a therapist to help the therapist more effectively engage in a purposeful relationship with a patient.

supervisor An individual experienced in psychotherapy and teaching.

therapist An individual engaging in helping patients with psychological problems.

Supervision is best viewed in the context of a relationship between supervisor and therapist. The supervisor, an experienced colleague and a teacher, helps the student therapist, a novice, to more effectively engage in a purposeful relationship with a patient. This is an apprenticeship to learn the craft of psychotherapy. A hermeneutic model provides an understanding of this process. The model holds that supervision is concerned with the meaning found in the supervisor–student interaction about patient-related issues. This is craft learning that as Alan R. Tom notes implies "an inexhaustible rule structure" because the "application of routinized skill sequences often fail to bring about desired results." The skilled therapist has the ability to analyze situations and has a broad range of therapy strategies that are then applied to a specific situation. In supervision, the student provides data about what occurred, and new knowledge is constructed in the supervisory interaction. Issues cluster around problems, which are analyzed by supervisor and student who then revise strategies for dealing with them. Over time there is an increasing understanding of problems, and the focus is on new concerns. The supervisory interaction provides new ways of framing problems and strategies to deal with them. The supervision process allows for the resident to take distance from psychotherapy and provides a method of ongoing evaluation of the psychotherapy.

I. CONDUCT OF SUPERVISION

A basic task of the supervisor is to provide a trusting relationship in which the student therapist can openly discuss work with the patient. An accepting and nonjudgmental attitude provides the context for the therapist to share unique concerns raised by the patient in an atmosphere of safety. Indeed, the alliance with the supervisor is at the center of supervision experience. So valued is this relationship that many former trainees view supervision as one of the most important elements of training. The supervisor allows the therapist's story about the therapeutic encounter to develop. Indeed, the identification and the tracking of the therapist's central and affectively charged concerns about the patient are essential elements of supervision. Different terms describe the therapist's concerns: blind spots, conflicts, difficulties, dilemmas, impasses, issues, lack of mastery, lead or main themes, problems, troubles, worries, and from the educational literature, messes.

A focus on the therapist's immediate experiences and an orientation to the specifics of the material are also essential to supervision. Indeed, therapist's concerns should be dealt with in the context of the material. Inquiry should be kept within the parameters described by therapist staying close to the understanding of the moment. For example, recommendations for interventions should be linked to issues presented by the therapist. Seemingly general questions should be reframed to focus on specific issues raised in the session. Similarly, each session is taken on its own understanding. Themes from previous sessions should be acknowledged in the changing context of current material. This is disciplined behavior on the part of the supervisor.

An accurate view of the patient using data provided by the therapist has the effect of affirming the therapist's observational and reporting skills. Even what is not discussed is perceived as an affirmation that the therapist's conduct with the patient is adequate.

Early, the novice therapist has to learn how to handle the data of the psychotherapeutic interaction and to maximize the production of new information. They learn over time how to discern problems and be able to share them with the supervisor. The task of the supervisor is to facilitate such discussion. In addition, a language of discourse develops between teacher and student about the patient interaction. The student's language and conceptual framework best guide this development.

Technical comments and jargon terms are used sparingly and in the context of the therapist's data. In addition, theoretical discussions are generally infrequent. This is in keeping with an early report by Joan Fleming and Theresa Benedict of the supervision of psychoanalytic candidates who called these discussions "surplus learning." Although scientific data and theory enhance reflection, such discussion should be also tied to the specifics of the material presented by the therapist.

The downside of not being in touch with the student therapist's concerns and not exploring underlying issues as well as interfering with the development of the therapists' story is to leave the novice therapist without direction or insight into the care of the patient. This leads to the therapist feeling discounted, devalued, and resentful.

Different methods of presentation of material from therapy sessions yield different information and are suitable for different tasks. Videotapes as well as audiotapes of actual sessions minimize distortion of what goes on in the therapy session. Videotapes have particular value early on in the supervisory experience. Discussion of videotaped data can alert the student therapist to the complexities of the interaction and are useful in group supervision. Audiotapes and detailed notes of the therapy (called process notes because they are filtered through the therapist) are more commonly used in supervision. In part, the use of each is a matter of personal preference. Audiotapes require a review of the tape by the therapist before the supervisory session. This allows the therapist to be an active participant. A downside of audiotapes as well as videotapes is that they are inefficient. For instance, observation of supervision using audiotapes reveals that considerable time is spent listening to the tape with minimal interaction between supervisor and therapist. Here, both supervisor and therapist are observed looking at the tape recorder as if it were the patient. Some supervisors base their discussion on the therapist's free-flowing summary of the session. Although this method addresses the therapist's understanding of the therapy it may be more suited to supervision of experienced therapists who have learned the complexities of therapeutic interaction. Notes drawn from an actual session force the therapist to capture the interaction and focus on problems raised in the interaction.

A. Focus of Comments: Parallel Process

The therapist recreates his or her view of the therapy in the supervision. In this sense, the therapist's data parallels what goes on in the therapy. An awareness of this parallel process provides a guide for the supervisor to help the therapist understand the therapy and is at the heart of supervision. The various levels of feedback implicitly use the parallel process strategy.

In terms of frequency, comments made by supervisors are directed at four levels:

1. Understanding the patient
2. Relationship of patient to therapist

3. Relationship of the therapist to patient
4. Relationship of therapist to supervisor in the context of understanding the patient

1. Understanding the Patient

The bulk of supervisory comments are directed to helping the therapist further understand the patient's actions, thoughts, and feelings. This is done through reframing the therapist's understanding of the patient. Questions about the meaning of a patient's comments should have continuity with the material and be asked in an open-ended manner. This leads the therapist to develop a broader understanding of the patient and the interaction.

Special attention is necessary for highly charged clinical dilemmas. These often involve the therapist's concerns about safety for themselves or for patients who are self-destructive, suicidal, angry, or violent. Guidance about dealing with these situations helps defuse the therapist's sense of helplessness. However, supervision based solely on management of difficult patients is better suited for supervision of more structured clinical experiences such as patients who are seen in an emergency center.

2. Relationship of Patient to Therapist

The most frequent relationship comments are directed to helping the therapist understand the patient's view of therapy or that relationship to the therapist.

3. Relationship of Therapist to Patient

Less frequent, although highly valued by therapists, are comments directed to deepening the therapist's understanding of concerns about his or her role in the interaction. The supervisor can reframe the interaction to help the therapist understand the role in the interaction. The highest praise is for the supervisor who uses a strategy of helping the therapist understand responses to the patient. This is a strategy for deepening the therapist's understanding that is particularly useful when the therapist feels immobilized. This level of discussion catches deeper levels of vulnerabilities and encourages the therapist to be more appropriately direct and active. Moreover, such concerns are highly personal. They can take many years to fully professionalize and can remain active for a considerable period of time after training.

Supervisors of developing professionals often acknowledge therapist's concerns about the impact of personal life experiences on the care of their patient. These concerns can involve poignant and emotionally intense experiences. Some are coincident with similar experiences in the patient's life. These include the impact on treatment of their own depression, transition to chief residency, impending marriage, divorce, pregnancy, and adoption of a child, or grief over the death of a loved one. Former therapists remain thankful for such discussions years after the supervisory experience and rate these supervisors as among the best of their training.

An adult developmental perspective is useful for understanding therapists' interest in discussing personal issues that affect their work. For therapists, the domain of work and caring for patients is at forefront of their lives. Usually, one other domain, perhaps two, are also operative in therapists' lives. The other domains include intimate relationships, family, religion, and community. Activity in these domains allows for the expression and gratification of deep values and needs. An important element in the professional developmental process involves integrating work with the other domains. This is a highly personal process that can involve considerable emotional conflict.

4. Relationship of Therapist to Supervisor

A discussion of the therapist–patient relationship in the context of the supervisory relationship can highlight issues in the therapy but has to be easily integrated with the therapist's data. This level of discussion is used infrequently but can be quite helpful in dealing with therapist's issues.

II. TERMINATION

Novice therapists worry about how well they are doing with their patients and how their patients will do after termination. Many worry that they have failed their patients and feel guilt over possible inappropriate termination plans. Some have unrealistic expectations of outcome and what can reasonably be accomplished. Discussion of expectations of outcome should be ongoing rather than just at termination. In addition, discussion of termination should focus both on clarification of the therapists' expectations of outcome as well as patient outcome.

III. EVALUATION

The feedback provided by the supervisor is a form of ongoing evaluation. This is called formative evaluation and is in contrast to the evaluation given at the end of a teaching period called summative evaluation. Here the supervisor summarizes what has occurred over the course of the supervision and provides recommendations for ongoing learning.

IV. CHARACTERISTICS OF THERAPISTS

The novice therapist's lack of experience in the conduct of psychotherapy can result in considerable emotional intensities. Indeed, the intensity of concerns about competence is easy to underestimate. Such concerns involve a sense of inadequacy to the task, feeling at a loss of how to conduct oneself with patients, and that others can do better. These underlying concerns can be acknowledged but do not need to be a major focus of discussion. Rather, the value of a sympathetic supervisor who acknowledges personal concerns provides a framework for helping the therapist achieve a sense of mastery. Indeed, development into a mature therapist takes years after training. With time, the student develops a personal style.

The ability among therapists to discuss and deal with problems varies considerably and guides the supervisor in the level of discussion. Indeed, supervisors adapt to the pace of the therapist's learning and adjust their discussion to the level of the therapist. Indeed, once a supervisory relationship is established, because of the variation in therapist abilities, it is difficult to discern the year of training by the level of sophistication of the presentation or the discussion. The range of therapist abilities mitigates against stage theories of learning supervision. Such theories posit stages of development as a psychotherapist based on year of training. These theories do not emphasize the personal development of the therapist.

V. LEARNING TO BE A SUPERVISOR

Discussing supervisory dilemmas with experienced colleagues is useful. This can be done in an ongoing group and is helpful for supervisors at all levels of experience. This discussion can aid the supervisor in understanding whether the problem is specific to the interaction, or a general problem that the therapist has with other supervisors. For instance the therapist may not be able to be open about discussing concerns about the patient. Such discussion can empower the supervisor to make appropriate interventions and also replicates the supervision process. Reading papers and texts on supervision is useful in orienting the supervisor to the conduct of supervision. However, they are often general and need to be applied to a specific situation.

Learning to be a supervisor is a matter of experience with a number of different therapists. Most supervisors initially model their behavior on their supervisory experiences during their training. They draw from these relationships until they develop a distinct supervisory style of their own. This also takes years to develop. Interestingly, supervisory behaviors become relatively stable even with different therapists.

VI. OUTCOME OF SUPERVISION

The intended outcome of the supervisory interaction is the transfer of new understanding to the patient encounter along with the transfer of patterns of interaction to other psychotherapeutic encounters.

See Also the Following Articles

Bioethics ■ Documentation ■ Economic and Policy Issues ■ Education: Curriculum for Psychotherapy ■ Informed Consent ■ Legal Dimensions of Psychiatry ■ Working Alliance

Further Reading

Fleming, Joan, & Benedek, Theresa. (1966). *Psychoanalytic supervision.* New York: Grune and Stratton.

Packer, M. J. (1985). Hermeneutic inquiry in the study of human conduct. *American Psychologist, 41,* 1081–1093.

Sergiovanni, Thomas J. (1985). Landscapes, mindscapes, and reflective practice in supervision. *Journal of Curriculum and Supervision, 1,* 5–17.

Shanfield, Stephen B., Matthews, Kenneth, & Hetherly, Vron. (1993). What do excellent psychotherapy supervisors do? *American Journal of Psychiatry, 150,* 1081–1084.

Shanfield, S. B., Hetherly, V., Matthews, K. L. (2001). Excellent supervision: The therapist's perspective. *Journal of Psychotherapy Practice and Research, 10*(1), 23–27.

Tom, Alan R. (1980). Teaching as a moral craft: A metaphor for teaching and teacher evaluation. *Curriculum Inquiry, 10,* 317–323.

Watkins, C. Edward (Ed.). (1997). *Handbook of supervision.* New York: John Wiley and Sons.

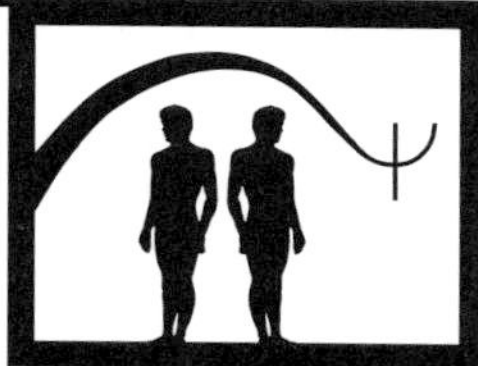

Supportive-Expressive Dynamic Psychotherapy

Lester Luborsky
University of Pennsylvania

GLOSSARY

alliance The concept of the therapeutic alliance, which refers to the positive bond that develops between patient and therapist.

blinding The use of controls on human judgments where the judges are restricted from access to information that could contaminate them.

cognitive-behavioral therapy A well-known form of psychotherapy that is built on the concepts of belief systems and consequent dysfunctional attitudes.

core conflictual relationship theme (CCRT) A method of formulating the essence of the relationship pattern between patient and other people, including the therapist. It is derived from the repetitions of the themes across the narratives in the sessions.

correlation A statistic in which the level of association of one item with another is computed.

dynamic A well-known theory of psychotherapy based on Sigmund Freud. It involves an assessment of both conscious and unconscious aspects of behavior and the concept of conflicts among the patient's wishes and other behaviors.

empirical As used here, it refers to the inclusion of a reliance on quantitative methods for data analysis.

empirically validated treatments Treatments that are designated as effective because of their relative performance in comparative treatment studies.

meta-analysis A collection of data across many studies that is summarized quantitatively.

researcher's allegiance The belief of a researcher in a treatment's efficacy—the bond between researcher and treatment.

I. DESCRIPTION OF TREATMENT

Supportive-expressive (SE) dynamic psychotherapy is now a standard form of psychotherapy. It was developed in the early 1940s at the Menninger Foundation and it has continued to be practiced there and in many other places around the world. In 1984, I published a book on supportive-expressive dynamic psychotherapy explaining the principles, procedures, and empirical supports for doing that psychotherapy.

The attractions to therapists for practicing this form of psychotherapy are multiply based: (1) it is a dynamic psychotherapy, (2) it is adaptable in terms of treatment length and applicability to patients with a wide range of severity and wide spectrum of diagnoses, and (3) it has the convenient capacity to be able to mix supportiveness and expressiveness so that the more severely sick patients are treated by greater supportiveness and lesser expressiveness and vice versa for less severely ill patients.

My books describe the two main formats of SE: time open-ended and time-limited psychotherapy. In 1998, Howard Book dealt with time-limited treatment and gave an unusual example: a verbatim complete case as treated by SE short-term psychotherapy. For most treatments the decision about the use of short-term versus open-ended treatment can be made even before the treatment starts, or sometimes in the early sessions. Most commonly, the time open-ended treatment is the preferred choice because with that the length of treatment tends to be a function of the patient's needs and wishes. When time-limited psychotherapy is the option chosen, it tends to be based on considerations of the limited time available, or considerations of the needs of a research protocol or of the preferred practice in a particular treatment setting.

A. How to Begin a Supportive-Expressive Psychotherapy

1. Treatment Arrangements

In the opening phase of psychotherapy, usually in the first session, treatment arrangements must explicitly be made. They include the frequency of sessions (usually one or two per week), the cost of each session, the method of payment, the handling of missed sessions, and a guide for the patient's style of speaking—the patient should speak about whatever is on the patient's mind, as well as the patient can.

2. Setting Goals

In the early phase of treatment, the setting of goals is essential. In the early sessions, and throughout the treatment, the patient should specify what it is that he or she wishes to change. That is a crucial first step because it can lead to achievement of the goals and to changes in the patient's goals. Both the patient and the therapist should be working toward the achievement of the same goals, and progress is gauged in terms of the achievement of these goals.

3. Development of the Therapeutic Alliance

The hope of both patient and therapist is that in the early sessions, and certainly as the treatment goes on, a relationship will be formed between patient and therapist of greater trust, rapport, and alliance. As examined by Safran, Muran, and Samstag in 1994 at times there is an oscillation between movement toward a rupture in the alliance that is usually followed by a movement toward reestablishing a positive relationship.

4. Focusing Interpretations around the Core Conflictual Relationship Theme

Starting early in the treatment, the therapist, and then the patient, will be able to understand and respond more effectively to the patient's problems. The therapist, by following the Core Conflictual Relationship Theme (CCRT) method described in 1998 in Luborsky and Crits-Christoph, will be able to formulate the central relationship problem. It is this pattern that will help the therapist to focus interpretive responses on aspects of the central relationship pattern and it is this focus that helps the therapist to shape the treatment into a focal treatment. The word "focal" means that the treatment is based on the gradually greater understanding of the main relationship pattern, which continues throughout the treatment and thereafter. There are likely to be major changes in understanding and behavior in the course of the treatment, but mostly there is a broadening, deepening, working through, and a mastering of the central theme.

B. Supportive Procedures and Principles

According to the dynamic theory of psychotherapy, a supportive relationship is vital.

1. Sigmund Freud in 1913 advised that the therapist's basic attitude should be as a sympathetic listener. Most comparative studies of psychotherapies actually have similar amounts of supportiveness, as shown in 1983 in Luborsky, Crits-Christoph, Alexander, Margolis, and Cohen. The most necessary supportive component, of course, is that the therapist is there to be helpful and to help the patient achieve the patient's goals and that the patient recognizes this.
2. In most psychotherapies a rapport with the patient is developed, which, in turn, develops into a therapeutic alliance. The alliance tends to improve when progress has been made and is recognized; in turn, the alternative sequence can also be that when progress has been made the alliance tends to improve, as shown by Tony Tang and colleagues in 2000.
3. A variety of measures of the alliance have been developed. These measures include two main types: self-report measures (for example, for self-ratings of the helping alliance), and the observer-judged alliance measures as developed by Luborsky in 1976 and 2000.
4. Paradoxically, the joint search for understanding can be classified under supportiveness as well as under expressiveness, for it can be both—the giving of interpretations can be experienced by the patient as supportive and the giving of interpretations also provides the patient with understanding.

C. Expressive Procedures and Principles

The other broad category of technique besides supportiveness is expressiveness. Expressiveness refers to the state of the patient that permits the patient to express his or her thoughts and feelings as fully as possible. The therapist then uses what is expressed by the patient to frame interpretations of the main relationship themes that are drawn from aspects of the CCRT as described by Luborsky, a theme that is reevaluated by the therapist in each session. The patients then use the therapist's responses, as well as their own knowledge of themselves to advance in mastery of their relationship conflicts. This sequence is essentially what is done in dynamic psychotherapies and in psychoanalysis.

The therapist tries to help patients to be free enough to share thoughts about themselves and their main problems in several ways:

1. Within each session, the therapist often responds to the patient by offering facets of the CCRT. The therapist should not try to encompass the entire CCRT in each of the few interpretations given, but instead, presents the separate components from time to time, so that the patient has a chance to build up a concept of the broader pattern of the relationship themes.
2. In the course of each treatment, there will be times in the sessions in which the patient's alliance moves toward a near-rupture, as noted earlier. These alliance shifts tend to occur when the patient experiences the relationship with the therapist in terms of a major negative pattern in the patient's CCRT.
3. Some expressions of the components of the CCRT can be thought of as a test of the relationship with the therapist. It has been shown in Weiss and Sampson and their research group in 1986 by examination of patients' responses that it is helpful for the treatment that the therapist pass the test.
4. The movements toward mastery are an important aim in psychotherapy. In the course of the sessions, most patients will succeed in achieving improved mastery of the relationship conflicts as shown by Brin Grenyer in 1996.

D. Ending Treatment

Both in time open-ended and in time-limited treatment, as the treatment ending approaches, the patient and therapist remind each other of when the termination will take place, so that they will be prepared. If a reference to termination does not happen spontaneously from the patient's side, the therapist will often bring it up.

Treatment endings tend to correspond to the achievement of the patient's goals; patients tend to complete treatment when they have achieved at least some of their goals, and even in a time-limited treatment some of the goals tend to be achieved.

A common event toward the end of treatment is the resurgence or reemergence of the initial symptoms. This event typically implies that the patient experiences the anticipation of not seeing the therapist at a time when the patient does not recognize that he or she has enough of a reliable internalized image of the therapist and the treatment. Usually, even a brief review by the therapist of the meaning of such recurrence of initial symptoms tends to bring back the patient's level of control.

II. THEORETICAL BASES

My 1984 book on the principles of psychotherapy explained and exemplified the principles for doing supportive-expressive psychotherapy. These principles were mostly based on Sigmund Freud's 1912 and 1913 writings on dynamic psychotherapy and on SE adaptations of Freud by Robert Knight in 1945 and other collaborators, including Karl Menninger.

III. APPLICATIONS AND EXCLUSIONS

One of the attractions of SE psychotherapy is its broad applications in terms of degrees of severity and varieties of diagnoses. Even the most severely ill patients can be treated through modifications of the method in terms of increased supportiveness and decreased expressiveness of SE psychotherapy, whereas the reverse is feasible for less severely ill patients.

IV. EMPIRICAL STUDIES

There are about 50 studies dealing with the uses and the effectiveness of supportive-expressive psychotherapy. Some representative studies are given in the Further Reading section of this article and in the books by Luborsky.

These are two typical examples of empirical studies: (1) Supportive-expressive psychotherapy for depression has been frequently studied, as reviewed in the 1984 book, the SE patients performed well. One of these studies is a comparison of patients diagnosed with major depression versus with chronic depression; there were no significant differences in outcomes in these two groups; (2) in the National Institute for Drug Abuse study of cocaine addiction four treatments were compared: supportive-expressive psychotherapy, cognitive-behavioral psychotherapy, drug counseling, and group psychotherapy. The results were that the supportive-expressive and cognitive-behavioral groups were not significantly different in their outcomes, but the most effective of the four in this study was the drug counseling.

It is also worth noting that the comparisons of one form of psychotherapy with another form of psychotherapy tend to show nonsignificant differences between them. This was true for supportive-expressive psychotherapy as well as for other psychotherapies. To cite some examples: In 1983, Woody, Luborsky, McLellan, and colleagues found nonsignificant differences between supportive-expressive psychotherapy and cognitive-behavioral psychotherapy for opiate addicts. In the psychotherapy for cocaine abuse, supportive-expressive and cognitive-behavioral therapies were not significantly different in their outcomes and also were not as effective as drug counseling, as reported by Crits-Christoph, Siqueland, and colleagues in 1999.

A meta-analysis summarizing the results of comparisons of different psychotherapies, such as Paul Crits-Christoph's in 1992, showed nonsignificant differences were most common. In 1993 analysis by Lester Luborsky and Louis Diguer showed a similar nonsignificant tendency.

In conclusion, there is not a lot of reliable consistent evidence for the special advantages of any one psychotherapy over another. In fact, the major positive evidence from comparative treatment studies is marred by a major limitation, that is, treatment comparisons are not done blindly by the researchers and perhaps cannot even be done blindly. The probable effect of this is that the differences in researcher's allegiance to forms of psychotherapy correlates very highly with the differences in outcomes of the treatments—the correlation is .85, according to a study by Luborsky, Diguer, and Seligman in 1999! Until such findings have appeared, the research field has been involved in a highly enthusiastic search for what are called "empirically validated treatments." The outcomes of these treatment comparisons have, in fact, even become part of advertisements as the "winners" of these comparisons. Unfortunately, the facts are that the field has to recognize the ambiguity of comparative treatment results, as just stated.

In summary, in practice it has become clear that the "empirically validated treatment comparisons" are ambiguous in their implications. The combination of the ambiguity introduced by the researcher's allegiance effect, as well as of the older problem of nonsignificant differences among the treatments compared, means that the field has a distance to go in terms of generating a trustworthy set of comparisons of one form of psychotherapy with another.

V. CASE ILLUSTRATIONS

Howard Book in 1998 offered a vivid, complete, and highly instructive book including a case illustration of a supportive-expressive psychotherapy in a generally well-functioning patient who developed a very positive alliance with her therapist.

Another example explains in greater detail the operation of the CCRT. Mr. EH, age 18, was a college student with problems of guilt, anxiety, sporadic pain in his penis, difficulty in dealing with a new girlfriend, and resentment of his parents. As a youngster he had never felt close to his father but had felt very close to his mother. He often felt he could not experience closeness from others. The seriousness of his conflicts were difficult to evaluate. They seemed either a worsening of normal adolescent development with intense guilt over sex or there was a thought disorder involved with his wishing to be an exaulted spiritual leader. The start of his treatment also showed that he had difficulties in being assertive and becoming separate from his family.

The relationship episodes in his session 3 contained six condensed examples. These six relationship episodes are followed here by a CCRT formulation in which the most frequent components are summarized: He wishes to be close, the other person rejects him, and he feels rejected, ashamed, and upset. What follows below are brief summaries of the six relationship episodes that he told during session 3 of his psychotherapy and the CCRT scoring of each one. This CCRT, as is usual, formed the basis for the interpretations given by the therapist:

CCRT Scoring	Precis of First Six Relationship Episodes
W: To get info about sex (W1): To get closeness RO1: Rejection RS1: Feel rejected RS2: Shame RS3: Upset	*Mother #1* This might have been a dream. Mother says it didn't happen. Up until we moved, when I had questions about sex, mother would explain to me. One day I asked and she said, "Sorry E. we can't talk about that anymore. You're getting to that age." Bothered me 'cause my young sister went into fits of laughter.
W: Get in bed with parents (W1): To get closeness RO1: Rejection RS1: (Rejected)	*Mother #2* Mother said this never happened: we, brother and I—before sister was born—when it was really cold, would sleep with parents. Parents took my brother in bed with them and they wouldn't take me.
W: To get rapport (W1): To get closeness RO1: Rejection RS1: Feel blank (empty)	*Therapist #3* T: What's happening now? P: I feel generally unresponsive. I'm getting a headache, tense, been thinking all week about relating all this stuff to what I was 10 years ago (sigh) and not getting any—I mean, nothing comes out ... like groups of guys who have embarrassing silences. It proves no perfect rapport exists. I feel blank.
W: To kiss mother RO1: M. criticizes him RO1: Rejection, kissing stopped RS1: Rejected, out in the cold	*Mother #4* Before I went to school I always used to kiss mother. I'm not sure it was a big thing, but it was a big thing when it stopped. She made a big thing about how I didn't want to kiss her anymore. I was suddenly out in the cold again.
(W1): Closeness to girlfriend RO: Doesn't like me RO1: Rejection, broke off RS2: Self-blame RS1: Rejected ("severed") RS3: Upset	*E (girlfriend) #5* I'm beginning to feel a lot of resentment to E (girlfriend). I went with her for a couple of years. It's just been severed. I'm fearful of seeing her and feeling something for her. She just doesn't give a dame Bothers me I used to be so screwed up about her.
(W1): To get a response RO1: Rejection RS: Resentment RS1: Rejected	*Mother #6* One thing that started my resentment against my parents. I told her about E (girlfriend) that everything was cut off. I said E's not writing and it upsets me. She said, "Well, I'm sure about you and you aren't sure about her." That really cut me up because she ... she ... a ... assumes between us is like between E and me.

N	*Total CCRT Formulation*
6 Wish 1	W1: To be close
6 Response from other 1	RO1: Rejection
6 Response from self 1	RS1: Feel rejected
2 Response from self 2	RS2: Shame
2 Response from self 3	RS3: Upset, anxious

VI. SUMMARY

Supportive-expressive psychotherapy is a common form of dynamic psychotherapy. Its main principles are basically derived from Sigmund Freud's as these were shaped by clinicians at the Menninger Foundation, starting around 1940. In each session the therapist allows the patients to express themselves in their own way and to choose their own goals. A main technique for helping the patient is provided by the therapist who formulates the patient's main conflictual pattern of relationships in terms of the Core Conflictual Relationship Theme. It is the patient's main pattern of relationships, especially those that are conflictual; this pattern of relationships is derived from narratives about relationships that the patient tells during each session. The treatment is called supportive-expressive because supportiveness and expressiveness are the two main techniques that the therapist uses. When the treatment conditions are more supportive, the therapist provides support when needed; when the help is more expressive, the therapist provides help with understanding by using what the patient expresses in interpretations. The length of the treatment is either time open-ended or time-limited. The treatment comes to a close when the main goals have been achieved and there has been sufficient occasion to work through the meanings of termination in order to optimize the retention of the gains.

See Also the Following Articles

Cognitive Behavior Therapy ■ Psychodynamic Couples Therapy ■ Psychodynamic Group Psychotherapy ■ Time-Limited Dynamic Psychotherapy

Further Reading

Book, H. E. (1998). *How to practice brief psychodynamic psychotherapy: The core conflictual relationship theme method.* Washington, DC: American Psychological Association.

Crits-Christoph, P. (1992). The efficacy of brief dynamic psychotherapy: A meta-analysis. *American Journal of Psychiatry, 149,* 151–158.

Crits-Christoph, P., Connolly, M., Azarian, R., Crits-Christoph, K., & Chappell, S. (1996). An open trial of supportive-expressive psychodynamic psychotherapy in the treatment of generalized anxiety disorder. *Psychotherapy, 33,* 418–430.

Crits-Christoph, P., Siqueland, L., Blaine, J., Frank, A., Luborsky, L., Onken, L. S., et al. (1999). Psychosocial treatments for cocaine dependence: Results of the National Institute on Drug Abuse Collaborative Cocaine Treatment Study. *Archives of General Psychiatry, 56,* 493–502.

Freud, S. (1912/1958a). The dynamics of the transference. In J. Strachey (Ed. and Trans.), *The standard edition of the complete psychological works of Sigmund Freud* (Vol. 12, pp. 99–108). London: Hogarth Press.

Freud, S. (1912/1958b). Recommendations to physicians practicing psycho-analysis. In J. Strachey (Ed. and Trans.), *The standard edition of the complete psychological works of Sigmund Freud* (Vol. 12, pp. 111–120). London: Hogarth Press.

Freud, S. (1913/1958). On beginning the treatment (Further recommendations on the technique of psycho-analysis). In J. Strachey (Ed. and Trans.), *The standard edition of the complete psychological works of Sigmund Freud* (Vol. 12, pp. 121–144). London: Hogarth Press.

Grenyer, B. F. S., & Luborsky, L., (1996). Dynamic change in psychotherapy: Mastery of interpersonal conflicts. *Journal of Consulting and Clinical Psychology, 64,* 411–416.

Knight, R. P. (1945). The relationship of psychoanalysis to psychiatry. *American Journal of Psychiatry, 6,* 777–782.

Luborsky, L. (1977). Measuring a pervasive psychic structure in psychotherapy: The core conflictual relationship theme. In N. Freedman & S. Grand (Eds.), *Communicative structures and psychic structures* (pp. 367–395). New York: Plenum Press.

Luborsky, L. (1984). *Principles of psychoanalytic psychotherapy: A manual for supportive-expressive (SE) treatment* (pp. 1–270). New York: Basic Books.

Luborsky, L. (in press). Psychoanalytic therapies. In A. F. Kazdin (Ed.), *Encyclopedia of Psychology.* Washington DC: American Psychological Association; Oxford University Press, USA.

Luborsky, L., & Crits-Christoph, P. (1998). *Understanding transference* (2nd ed.). Washington, DC: American Psychological Association.

Luborsky, L., Diguer, L., Luborsky, E., & Schmidt, K. A. (1999). The efficacy of dynamic and other psychotherapies: Is it true that "everyone has won and all must have prizes?"—An update. In D. Janowsky (Ed.), *Psychotherapy in the 1990s—Indications and outcomes* (pp. 3–22). Washington DC: American Psychiatric Press.

Luborsky, L., Diguer, L., Seligman, D. A., Rosenthal, R., Krause, E. D., Johnson, S., et al. (1999). The researcher's own therapy allegiances: A "wild card" in comparisons of treatment efficacy. *Clinical Psychology: Science and Practice, 6,* 95–132.

Luborsky, L., Rosenthal, R., Diguer, L., Andrusyna, T. P., Levine, J. T., Seligman, D. A., et al. (in press). The Dodo bird verdict is alive and well—Mostly! *Clinical Psychology: Science and Practice.*

Safran, J. D., Muran, J. C., & Samstag, L. W. (1994) Resolving therapeutic alliance ruptures: A task analysis investigation. In A. O. Horvath & L. S. Greenberg (Eds.), *The working alliance: Theory, research, and practice* (pp. 225–255). New York: John Wiley & Sons.

Weiss, J., Sampson, H., & the Mount Zion Psychotherapy Research Group. (1986). *The psychoanalytic process. Theory, clinical observations, and empirical research.* New York: Guilford.

Woody, G., Luborsky, L., McLellan, A. T., O'Brien, C., Beck, A. T., Blaine, J., et al. (1983). Psychotherapy for opiate addicts: Does it help? *Archives of General Psychiatry, 40,* 639–645.

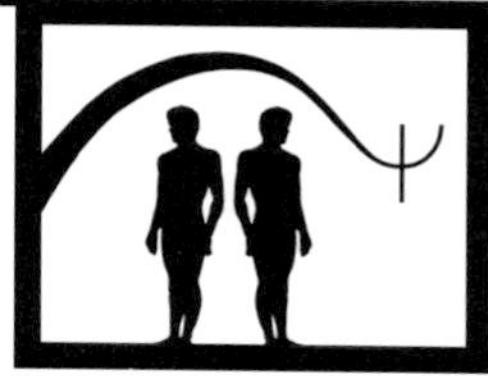

Symbolic Modeling

Michael A. Milan
Georgia State University

GLOSSARY

imitation The behavior of an observer that is similar to that of a model and that occurs subsequent to the observation of modeling.

model The individual or character who is observed and demonstrates the behavior that is to be imitated.

modeling (1) The act of demonstrating the behavior that is to be imitated and (2) the general term describing the treatment procedure.

observer The individual who observes and imitates the behavior of the model.

Symbolic modeling is one of two general forms of modeling: live and symbolic. In live modeling, the model is actually present and models behavior "live." In symbolic modeling, the model is not actually present but instead is pre-recorded, drawn, or described. Symbolically modeled behavior is typically presented on videotape or film; in animated or still cartoons; and in narratives read aloud by another, listened to on audiotape, or read silently to one's self from printed handouts, instruction manuals, and books. Silent reading, as well as imagining a model or one's self engaging in behavior, are considered covert forms of symbolic modeling.

I. DESCRIPTION

In its most basic form, symbolic modeling is a process in which one individual sees, hears, or reads a depiction of the behavior of a real or fictional individual or character and then engages in behavior that is similar to the behavior that was observed. Although the initial research on modeling focused on overt motoric behavior, more recent research has also explored the effects of modeling on covert affective and cognitive behaviors. The results of that research confirmed that modeling is indeed an important contributor to the acquisition and modification of both overt and covert behaviors, and that the manner in which modeling produces its effects is generally the same for both overt and covert behavior.

Although symbolic modeling alone can have powerful effects, it is often a part of multicomponent programs designed to teach social skills, such as assertiveness, anger management, and self-control. It is also often a component of programs designed to treat anxiety disorders, such a social phobias, agoraphobia, and animal phobias. Symbolic modeling can serve five general functions: It can teach a new behavior or skill that is demonstrated by a model; it can reduce anxiety by depicting a model engaging in a feared activity or making contact with a feared situation with no untoward consequences; it can encourage or disinhibit behavior by depicting positive consequences following modeled behavior; it can discourage or inhibit behavior by depicting negative consequences following behavior; and it can elicit or facilitate behavior by serving as a prompt to engage in the behavior at a particular time or place.

II. THEORETICAL BASIS

Since first recognized and studied by psychology, what is now typically referred to as modeling has been known by a variety of other terms, including observational learning, vicarious learning, identification, copying, matching-to-sample, and contagion. In their efforts to understand the modeling process, researchers have examined several theoretical issues raised by modeling and imitation, four of which will be discussed here. The first issue is whether the ability to imitate is innate or acquired. The general consensus among scientists in the field now is that the ability to imitate a broad range of behaviors modeled by a variety of both live and symbolic models is primarily an acquired skill.

The second issue involves the role of operant conditioning in modeling and imitation. Researchers have concluded that operant conditioning plays an important role in the acquisition and modification of overt, motoric behavior, as when a mother reinforces an infant when the infant produces a vocal sound similar to that the mother has made and as a result is more likely to imitate that and other vocalizations, or a child observes other children behaving aggressively and then does so as well.

The third issue involves the role of respondent conditioning. Again, researchers have concluded that respondent conditioning is primarily involved in the acquisition and modification of covert, emotional behavior, as when a child is terrified by a filmed depiction of a traumatic event happening in a dark room and as a result is fearful of dark rooms. Conversely, symbolic exposure to fear-producing stimuli can contribute to the deconditioning or extinction of anxiety responses in the treatment of anxiety disorders.

The fourth issue involves the adequacy of operant and respondent conditioning in the explanation of the full range of modeling and imitation phenomena. Cognitive theorists claim that conditioning theories ignore central processes. The cognitivists in general, and advocates of a social learning theory explanation in particular, postulate that a consideration of the action of a variety of intervening variables, such as anticipation, symbolic coding, and cognitive organization is necessary for an adequate understanding of the effects of modeling.

III. EMPIRICAL FINDINGS

Both live and symbolic modeling have long been accepted as an important contributor to the acquisition and modification of behavior. The major advantages of live modeling are that it typically allows more participatory learning and greater individualization of the content, pacing, and repetition of the modeled material to maximize its impact on the observer than does symbolic modeling. The major advantages of symbolic modeling are that it typically allows the modeling of behavior in situations that cannot be either practically or safely created live, it permits the widescale dissemination and cost-effective utilization of the modeling materials in a variety of settings, and it enables the assignment of homework or "self-study" modeling experiences as part of the course of treatment.

Several guidelines for the effective use of modeling have been identified. They address the characteristics of the observer, the characteristics of the model, and how modeling is conducted. The findings most relevant to the design of modeling programs will be noted here. The observer must have an adequate repertoire of imitation skills. If an assessment of the strengths and weaknesses of the observer indicates that the observer has not mastered the ability to imitate, imitative behavior must be taught.

The observer must attend to both the model and to the relevant aspects of the modeled behavior. Again, if assessment indicates that the observer does not have these skills, they must be taught; if the observer has these skills but does not use them, prompts must be provided and/or contingencies must be arranged to foster their utilization. Finally, the observer must imitate the modeled behavior. If the observer does not, impediments must be identified and eliminated and/or contingencies must be analyzed and altered to foster imitation.

To maximize the effects of modeling, the model should be similar to the observer and/or have high status or prestige for the observer. The modeled behavior should be expected to result in naturally occurring positive consequences for the model, such as the granting of a request, rather than arranged consequences, such as the award of a token. Modeling should portray a naturally occurring positive outcome for the model as a result of the modeled behavior. Models should be portrayed as coping successfully with the problems or tasks confronting them rather than achieving complete mastery and/or exhibiting flawless performance. To the degree possible, a variety of models using a number of variations of the skills being taught should be shown dealing with a range of problems or tasks in an array of settings appropriate to the observer.

The difficulty or complexity of the modeled behavior should be matched to the characteristics and abilities of the observer. More difficult or complex behavior should be broken down into components or approximations and taught in sequence. Self-instructions should be taught in order to assist observers to guide themselves through expected performances and deal with impediments to successful outcomes if they arise. Observers should be taught to evaluate their behavior, identify the strengths and weaknesses of their performances, and then self-reinforce for the strengths and determine how the weaknesses may be remediated. The modeled behavior should be actively practiced by the observer after it is modeled, and the practice should include feedback, reinforcement, and correction. Finally, arranged prompts and reinforcement that have been used to foster acquisition and performance of the modeled behavior should be faded out during the course of training to maximize the likelihood that the behavior will occur and maintained under natural conditions.

IV. SUMMARY

Symbolic modeling consists of a recording, depiction, description, or imaginal portrayal of behavior. The person demonstrating the behavior is termed the model; the actions of the model are termed modeling; the person observing the model is termed the observer; and the subsequent behavior of the observer that is similar to the modeled behavior is termed imitation. Explanations of symbolic modeling and imitation rely on operant conditioning, respondent conditioning, and cognitive social learning processes. Modeling has been shown to be effective in the teaching of overt behavior, such as social skills and anger management, and in the treatment of covert behaviors, such as fear and anxiety.

Successful modeling programs should include an assessment of the observers' strengths, weaknesses, and natural environment. The program should then be matched to observers' strengths, weaknesses, and the characteristics of their natural environment. Factors to be considered include the attributes of models, and the complexity and natural consequences of the modeled behavior. A variety of models, situations, and behaviors resulting in successful outcomes should be presented. Coping rather than mastery should be emphasized, and ample opportunities to practice and refine imitative performance should be provided. Prompts and reinforcement should be used as necessary to facilitate learning and performance and then faded out to foster success in the natural environment.

See Also the Following Articles

Behavior Rehearsal ■ Coverant Control ■ Heterosocial Skills Training ■ Modeling ■ Role-Playing ■ Self-Statement Modification

Further Reading

Bandura, A. (1969). *Principles of behavior modification*. New York: Holt, Rinehart and Winston.

Bandura, A. (1977). *Social learning theory*. Englewood Cliffs, NJ: Prentice-Hall.

Bandura, A. (1986). *Social foundations of thought and action: A social cognitive theory*. Englewood Cliffs, NJ: Prentice-Hall.

Martin, G., & Pear, J. (1999). *Behavior modification: What it is and how to do it*. Upper Saddle River, NJ: Prentice-Hall.

Mineka, S., & Hamida, S. B. (1998). Observational and nonconscious learning. In W. O'Donohue (Ed.), *Learning and behavior therapy* (pp. 412–439). Boston:Allyn & Bacon.

Mineka, S., & Zinbarg, R. (1996). Conditioning and ethological models of anxiety disorders. In D. Hope (Ed.), *Nebraska Symposium on Motivation, Vol. 43. Perspectives on anxiety, panic, and fear* (pp. 135–211). Lincoln: University of Nebraska Press.

Mitchell, Z. P., & Milan, M. A. (1983). Imitation of high-interest comic strip models' appropriate classroom behavior: Acquisition and generalization. *Child & Family Behavior Therapy, 5*, 15–30.

Spiegler, M. D., & Guevremont, D. C. (1998). *Contemporary behavior therapy*. Pacific Grove, CA: Brooks/Cole.

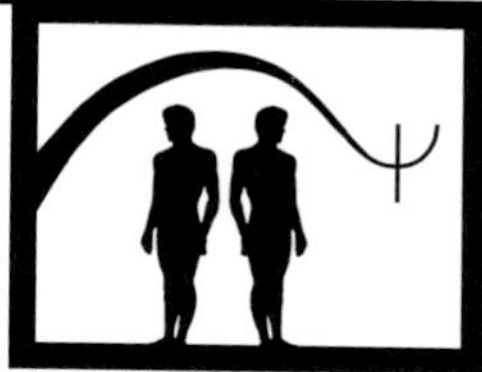

Systematic Desensitization

F. Dudley McGlynn
Auburn University

GLOSSARY

conditioned inhibition In the learning theory of Clark L. Hull the repetition of a learned response is accompanied by the buildup of a fatigue-like tendency to not respond called reactive inhibition. Stimuli present at the time of reactive inhibition become conditioned stimuli for inhibition or conditioned inhibitors.

counterconditioning An approach to learning associated with the theory of Edwin R. Guthrie; a relevant stimulus is maintained intact while a substitute response is practiced in its presence.

exposure technology Associated with Isaac Marks; refers to a therapeutic orientation according to which prolonged exposure to fear cues is the sole requirement for treatment success, and no interest is shown in how or why exposure produces beneficial outcomes.

extinction Associated with Ivan P. Pavlov's learning theory; denotes the repeated presentation of a conditioned stimulus in the absence of any unconditioned stimulus. Sometime refers to the response decrement that follows from repeated presentations of a conditioned stimulus alone.

habituation The decrement in a response due to repeated, predictable presentations of a stimulus. Sometimes habituation is said to be limited to unconditioned responses. Usually habituation refers to decrements in the neural substrate of behavior.

hierarchy As used in behavior therapy; a listing of verbal scenarios that describes situations in which a fearful person gradually confronts fearsome objects and/or events.

progressive relaxation training An approach to learning how to relax developed by Edmund Jacobson. Different groups of muscles are repeatedly tensed and relaxed in sequential order "up" or "down" the body while the different feedback from tense versus relaxed muscles is contemplated and deeper relaxation is suggested.

reciprocal inhibition The physiologist C. S. Sherrington's term that denotes the inhibition of neuronal activity by the activation of other, reciprocally inhibiting, neuronal activity. As used by Joseph Wolpe reciprocal inhibition refers to the inhibition of sympathetic activation by parasympathetic dominance.

spatiotemporal hierarchy A hierarchy for systematic desensitization in which increasing the fearsomeness of successive scenarios is accomplished by reducing the times and/or distances separating the patient from the frightening encounter.

SUD scaling The patient is taught to assign numbers from 0 (calm) to 100 (terrified) that reflect the level of fear or subjective units of discomfort (SUDs) associated with targeted activities or objects.

thematic hierarchy A hierarchy for systematic desensitization in which increasing the fearsomeness of successive scenarios is accomplished by increasing the clarity or poignancy of focal themes such as "being watched," "being criticized," "suffocating," "being confined."

Systematic desensitization is a venerable behavior therapy technique developed by Joseph Wolpe for the treatment of fear- and anxiety-related disorders. Systematic desensitization includes three basic procedural elements. The patient is taught to relax his or her voluntary musculature using a procedure known as progressive relaxation training. Concurrently the patient and therapist develop detailed descriptions of realistic encounters with the objects and/or events that provoke fear or anxiety, and arrange those descriptions in order of fearsomeness. Finally the patient is guided to visualize the scene descriptions in increasingly fearsome order while taking care to maintain a relaxed muscular state. In addition, treatment based on systematic desensitization often entails encouragement to rehearse the targeted encounters in real life after they have been visualized calmly. Systematic desensitization helped launch the behavior therapy movement and was the first psychological treatment that produced behavioral improvement reliably.

I. DESCRIPTION OF TREATMENT

A. Relaxation Training

As noted above one basic procedure in the use of systematic desensitization is training the patient to relax the voluntary musculature. Usually the training is done according to the "progressive relaxation" techniques that were developed by Edmund Jacobson during the 1930s. Ideally relaxation training is done using a procedural guide and detailed transcripts such as those in the manual provided by Douglas A. Bernstein and Thomas D. Borkovec in 1973 and in the book provided by Marvin R. Goldfried and Gerald C. Davison in 1976. Ordinarily the available transcripts for relaxation training provide the following: (1) a subdivision of the skeletal musculature into a number of muscle groups, usually 16; (2) a set of instructions that will produce tension in each of the muscle groups; and (3) another set of instructions that focus attention on the different sensations that arise from tense versus relaxed muscles. In the widely used manual of Bernstein and Borkovec there are transcripts also that subdivide the muscles into eight and four separate groups.

The 1976 book by Goldfried and Davison contains valuable information about how to set the stage for relaxation training, including information about such things as the purpose of relaxation training and how being deeply relaxed will feel. After the stage is set according to those or similar guidelines the therapist is ready to begin. The first step in relaxation proper is to demonstrate various exercises that will be used, exercises that create discernible tension in several groups of muscles. The second step is to encourage the patient to seek clarification about the exercises and, as needed, to repeat one or more of the demonstrations. In the third step the therapist reads the relaxation transcript with a few points in mind: (1) A training "trial" for a muscle group is a tension-relaxation cycle. After instructions for tensing a specific muscle group have been read, 10 seconds or so are allowed for maintaining the tension. At that time instructions for relaxing or "letting go" are read, after which another 20 seconds or so are allowed for relaxing and for attending to feedback differences from tense versus relaxed muscles. (2) Each muscle group is used for at least two consecutive trials. (3) The muscle tension should be easily discernible but not extreme. (4) The muscle groups will be relaxed in some progression (i.e., from the feet to the head-neck).

Some therapists provide patients with tape-recorded relaxation instructions and encourage them to practice relaxing at home. There is evidence that "live" relaxation is better than taped relaxation. Hence, taped relaxation is best viewed as an adjunctive procedure. If home practice of relaxation is important, then the patient should be instructed to record and submit regularly a diary of when, where, and how well he or she relaxed on each occasion.

B. Hierarchy Construction

Relaxation training usually takes from five to seven sessions. During this time the therapist and patient can construct what is known as a "desensitization hierarchy" provided that care is taken to construct the hierarchy when the patient is not relaxing. Behavioral assessment will have provided the information necessary to begin hierarchy construction. The information will include a complete and detailed listing of the various cue-stimuli for fear as well as a tentative arrangement of the fear stimuli according to groups. Each group of fears that has a common thread will ultimately be arranged into a single hierarchy or increasingly fearsome listing of targeted scenarios.

The most common types of desensitization hierarchies are spatiotemporal hierarchies and thematic hierarchies. In spatiotemporal hierarchies, increasing the fearsomeness of successive scenarios is accomplished by decreasing the times and/or distances that separate the patient from targeted encounters. For example, the times and distances separating a socially phobic student from a dreaded classroom speech can be reduced systematically from days, to hours, to minutes. In thematic hierarchies, increasing the fearsomeness of successive scenarios is accomplished by increasing the clarity or poignancy with which the scenario captures the fearsome theme. Given the same socially phobic student, for example, the successive scenarios in a public-speaking hierarchy could entail increasing scrutiny and/or increasing likelihood of failure. Choosing between spatiotemporal and thematic hierarchies is not always straightforward, nor is grouping disparate fears to form thematic hierarchies. The most common approach to the problem of grouping is to use traditional phobia categories. Wolpe, for example, arranged 14 "different" fears into four hierarchies: acrophobia, agoraphobia, claustrophobia, and fears related to illness.

The most common procedure for constructing desensitization hierarchies was developed by Wolpe and is called SUDs scaling. In this procedure, the patient is first taught to assign a numerical value of 0 subjective units of discomfort (SUDs) to reflect absolute calmness, and to assign a numerical value of 100 SUDs to reflect the most extreme fear imaginable. Each potentially useful scenario in a given hierarchy is then assigned a SUDs rating and the scenarios are ordered in terms of increasing fearsomeness. Then scenarios are dropped and new ones added until the first scenario (hierarchy item) is rated near 0 SUDs, and the zenithal scenario is rated near 100 SUDs. As is described later, each hierarchy of fearsome scenarios provides for systematic "exposure in imagination" to attenuated, then intermediate, than maximally fearsome forms of the cue stimuli for fear. Each successive scenario should be more fearsome than the last but the difference should not be over 10 SUDs at any point in the hierarchy and should be quite small toward the upper end of the hierarchy. The scenarios incorporated into the hierarchy should sample comprehensively the objects, events, situations, or themes that cue fear responses. Each scenario should be relatively complete and, where possible, relatively concrete. Initial hierarchies can be modified as desensitization proceeds and response to treatment can be monitored.

C. Systematic Desensitization

Systematic desensitization proper typically is performed in one of two ways. In the "orthodox" procedure the patient is first exposed to abbreviated relaxation training. (Abbreviated relaxation training is accomplished, after thorough training, by using fewer than 16 muscle groups, for example 8 or 4 groups as described by Bernstein and Borkovec.) Next the therapist instructs the patient to visualize for 10 to 15 seconds the least aversive hierarchy scenario and to signal by elevating an index finger if the visualization is accompanied by discomfort or fear. If the patient does not signal the presence of fear, then he or she is instructed to relax and, later, to visualize the scenario again. If the visualization occasions no fear on this second trial, then a 30 to 60 second period for relaxing follows and the next scenario on the hierarchy is presented for visualization. This process is repeated again and again as progressively more fearsome scenarios are visualized. Should the patient signal that fear is present, he or she is instructed to stop visualizing and relax. After time for relaxation the scenario is visualized again. If the fear signal recurs, then the therapist repeats the previously desensitized scenario and, after relaxation, repeats the troublesome scene. If the patient still signals the presence of fear, then the therapist and patient construct, on the spot, a new scenario that stands between the troublesome scenario and the last one that was successfully negotiated. Orthodox imaginal desensitization is complete when the most fearsome scenarios are visualized without fear signals.

Joseph Wolpe introduced the "improved" procedure for systematic desensitization in 1973. Here again treatment begins with abbreviated relaxation practice. Then the patient is instructed to visualize the appropriate scenario and to signal, by raising an index finger, when the imagery is clear. The therapist allows 10 to 15 seconds after a signal for the patient to continue visualizing fearsome material, then instructs the patient to drop the images and report orally a SUDs rating of the fear experienced during visualization. In this procedure visualization of each fearsome scenario is repeated until the patient reports 0 SUDs. "Improved" desensitization in imagination is complete when the patient visualizes the zenithal scenario(s) and reports that no fear was experienced.

Beyond the basic techniques discussed earlier there are a number of important considerations at the level of procedure. Discussions of specific procedures are available in Wolpe's various books and in the book by Goldfried and Davison. The following subset of those recommendations shows the flexibility of the approach.

1. The therapist should view any hierarchy as tentative and should be prepared to add, modify, or delete exact scenario descriptions as needed.

2. Multiple hierarchies should be dealt with simultaneously; no more than three or four scenarios in any given hierarchy should be dealt with during a given session.

3. Desensitization proper should last 20 to 30 minutes per session; sessions should occur at daily to weekly intervals.

4. Once a particularly troublesome scenario has been visualized calmly, it should be visualized repeatedly before the next one is attempted.

5. Throughout desensitization the patient should be reminded to include himself or herself as a participant in the scenarios. He or she is not merely visualizing fearsome situations, but is visualizing himself or herself behaving within the fearsome scenarios.

6. The patient should be encouraged to participate in the targeted real life scenarios after they have been imaginally desensitized; such participation should lag somewhat behind progress in imaginal desensitization.

II. THEORETICAL BASES

There are a dozen or so theories that explain how or why systematic desensitization brings about fear reduction. Many of them are only partial theories, nearly all are *post hoc* in nature. Theorizing about the causal efficacy of desensitization represents in microcosm many of the ills that have plagued general and clinical psychology for the past half century.

A. The Legacy of Learning Theory

The psychology of learning during the 1930s and 1940s incorporated several competing theoretical systems (e.g., the systems of Edwin R. Guthrie, Clark L. Hull, and Edward C. Tolman). There was not much disagreement about experimental data. The major facts of acquisition, extinction, generalization, discrimination, and the like were, for the most part, consensually endorsed. Nonetheless there was spirited argument at the seemingly basic levels of "what" was being learned, "what" was being unlearned, and so forth. Hull spoke of "habits." Tolman spoke of "expectancies." Guthrie spoke of S-R bonds.

Joseph Wolpe chose to articulate his explanation of desensitization effects using the language of Hull (see below). When he did so he invited rejoinders in the languages of Guthrie and Tolman. Once Joseph Wolpe's ideas gained some notoriety, these rejoinders did not take long to appear. Guthrie's language was used in the assertion that systematic desensitization embodies "counterconditioning." Tolman's language was used in the argument that desensitization works, in part, by engendering optimistic "expectancies."

B. The Psychotherapy Environment

The field of psychotherapy during the 1950s and 1960s also incorporated competing theoretical systems. Arnold Lazarus, for example, listed 36 psychotherapy systems in evidence as of 1967, adding that his list was incomplete. There was not much disagreement at the level of data in the psychotherapy field either. With the noteworthy exception of Carl Rogers and his followers, data did not play an important role in system development. From such a variegated and uncritical psychotherapy environment, it was inevitable that some would seize on opportunities to explain Joseph Wolpe's impressive results by recourse to their own preferred explanatory constructs. Thus, the beneficial effects of desensitization were said to depend on "the therapeutic alliance," on fortuitous psychodynamic accompaniments of desensitization treatment, and the like.

C. Empirical Problems

During the late 1960s and early 1970s scores of articles appeared that were intended to provide experimental answers to the theoretical questions made outstanding by the legacies of learning theory and the environment of psychotherapy. For one example, the outcomes of experiments on systematic desensitization with and without muscular relaxation were styled as evaluating "counterconditioning" versus "extinction" as explanatory vehicles. Unfortunately, the substantive yield from the many papers was confusing and contradictory; theorists remained free to "pick and choose" experimental support for the various explanations afforded by learning and psychotherapy theories.

D. Theories of Fear Reduction from Systematic Desensitization

By and large theories of the active mechanism(s) of systematic desensitization have not been theories at all. Rather, they have been uniformly *post hoc* (and often vacuous) claims that desensitization effects represent something else such as extinction, habituation, counterconditioning, deconditioning, and the like. Furthermore, these and similar concepts have been used uncritically, even interchangeably, as if the early behavior therapist acquired the lexicon of animal learning but little else.

1. Reciprocal Inhibition and Habituation

According to the reciprocal inhibition theory, systematic desensitization reduces anxiety by causing the cues for the anxiety to become cues for anxiety inhibition. Anxiety is composed of conditioned sympathetic responses. The occurrence of sympathetic responsivity during aversive imaging can be reciprocally inhibited by the parasympathetic underpinnings of concurrent muscular relaxation, provided that the imaging is graduated in fearsomeness. When reciprocal inhibition of the sympathetic response occurs during aversive imaging, the act of imaging acquires an anxiety-inhibiting function. This happens via a mechanism known as conditioned inhibition. Hence systematic desensitization reduces anxiety via conditioned inhibition based on reciprocal inhibition.

According to the habituation theory, systematic desensitization reduces anxiety due to habituation of sympathetic responses to clinically targeted stimuli. Sympathetic responsivity during aversive imaging is made to habituate over repeated imaging trials in much the same way that an orienting reflex habituates over the course of exposure to repeated novel stimuli. Theoretical accounts of habituation differ in minor ways and these differences appear in different renditions of how habituation is produced by systematic desensitization. Muscular relaxation plays a significant role by hastening or facilitating the rate of sympathetic response habituation.

2. Counterconditioning and Extinction

According to a theory based on counterconditioning, systematic desensitization reduces anxiety by causing the cues for anxiety-related behaviors to become cues for other behaviors. The display of emotional behaviors during conditioned aversive stimulation is prevented by rehearsing competing behaviors. (Relaxation is customary but any nonanxious behavior would suffice in principle.) In due course the conditioned aversive stimuli call forth the competing behaviors instead of the anxiety-related behaviors. Muscular relaxation plays a role by providing the substitute behaviors.

Throughout much of the early behavior therapy literature, clinically focal fears were regarded as conditioned emotional (Pavlovian) respondents. Accordingly, systematic desensitization was said to work by promoting respondent extinction. The role of muscular relaxation, in tandem with graduated exposures, was that of arranging for presentations of fear signals to be unreinforced.

3. A Variant of Exposure Technology

Beginning with Isaac Marks in the mid 1970s, most contemporary writers describe systematic desensitization as a variant of exposure technology. On the surface that characterization is not unreasonable because imaginal exposure is a prominent aspect of the procedure, and *in vivo* exposure is recommended adjunctively. However, characterizing systematic desensitization as a variety of exposure flies in the face of well-known history and does nothing to explain how systematic desensitization works.

4. Cognitive and Social Reinforcement Theories

Albert Bandura and Wallace Wilkins have both offered theories that explain the beneficial effects of systematic desensitization. Initially during the 1970s Albert Bandura developed his broadly applicable idea that "a sense of self-efficacy" is fundamental to success in psychological therapy. Relatively high self-efficacy influences successful outcomes by promoting persistent and vigorous self-change efforts. According to Albert Bandura systematic desensitization operates by increasing self-efficacy; the stronger self-efficacy promotes continued self-change efforts, and so forth.

In 1971 Wilkins offered a fairly elaborate theory explaining the beneficial effects of systematic desensitization. Among Wilkins' assertions are that systematic desensitization works because the therapist fosters an expectation of therapeutic success; because feedback during treatment affords information that the patient is improving; and because systematic desensitization teaches one how to control the onset and offset of fearsome imagery.

5. Other Theoretical Approaches

The notions that systematic desensitization effects arise from the therapeutic alliance and from fortuitous psychodynamic processes were alluded to earlier. Others have argued that systematic desensitization effects might rest on covert modeling of fearless behavior, or on social reinforcement of motoric approach responses, or on reinterpretations of the meanings of fearsome images. There is also the plausible notion, based on the contemporary work of Peter J. Lang, that systematic desensitization works by modifying the bioinformational import of fearsome imaging.

III. APPLICATIONS AND EXCLUSIONS

Over the past three decades creative clinicians have found numerous applications for relaxation-based fear treatments such as systematic desensitization and its variants. The most common applications have involved various specific phobias and social phobia. But applications to other anxiety-related disorders are not rare. Among the specific phobias with which systematic desensitization has been used are those related to death, injury, disaster, illness, water, storms, animals, birds, reptiles, airplanes, automobiles, injections, ambulances, sanitary napkins, and childbirth. Applications related to social phobia have included "social situations," heterosexual interactions, and authority figures. Among the other anxiety-related disorders treated heretofore with systematic desensitization are asthma, recurring nightmares, repetitive cleansing, chronic diarrhea, and urinary urgency.

For the past two decades clinicians have been opting for *in vivo* treatments that, in the aggregate, are called exposure technology. Hence, the first choice point in deciding to use systematic desensitization for any phobia or anxiety-related disorder is to establish that *in vivo* techniques are not feasible.

After a decision is made to consider using systematic desensitization there must be a relatively thorough assessment of the controlling stimuli for fear and the details of fearful responsivity. (Assessment of the sort used for diagnosis and for exposure treatment is rarely adequate.) Such specific assessment will afford answers to four important questions. (1) Can the cue-stimuli for fear be described in fairly concrete terms? (2) Does the patient show four or fewer different sets of fears? (3) Does the patient report clear imagery related to the fear cues? (4) Does the patient report or manifest fear, arousal, or discomfort while visualizing the relevant fear scenes? Affirmative answers to these questions prompt consideration of treatment via systematic desensitization.

Wolpe has written extensively on complications that arise from attempting systematic desensitization with inappropriate patients. Some patients simply cannot learn to relax. Others display what might be called a fear of relaxing or of "letting go." Still other patients do not seem to be able to conjure up the requisite imagery or to picture themselves as part of the targeted scenarios. Problems at these levels should prompt reconsideration of whether it is possible to use some sort of *in vivo* exposure procedure.

IV. EMPIRICAL STUDIES

Early reports about the successes of systematic desensitization did much to promote behavior therapy and the conditioning formulation of psychopathology on which behavior therapy was based. However, the tenor of those early reports was influenced by the Protestantism of that era; the subsequent four decades have witnessed some moderation of those early claims and no small amount of controversy.

A. Early Clinical Reports

The first reports of clinical success with systematic desensitization were reported by Joseph Wolpe via a series of papers published from 1952 to 1962. These papers were shadowed by a series of similar reports provided by Arnold Lazarus from 1957 to 1965. An extraordinarily thorough review of these and other early reports was prepared by Gordon L. Paul and published in 1969.

1. Joseph Wolpe

In his influential 1958 book, *Psychotherapy by Reciprocal Inhibition,* Joseph Wolpe reported that nearly 90% of 210 patients were either improved or much improved following treatment with his new methods. Gordon Paul pointed out later that some of those 210 patients were treated with methods other than systematic desensitization. He reanalyzed Wolpe's original reports, identified 85 patients who had been treated with systematic desensitization alone, and reported success in 78 (92%) of those 85 cases. He reported also that follow-up contacts with 21 patients after periods of 6 to 48 months yielded no report of relapse. In some cases the effects of systematic desensitization were gauged by direct observation and by reports from unbiased others. By and large, however, "success" was defined as self-reports of improved responses in the presence of previously anxiety-eliciting stimuli encountered in the natural environment.

2. Arnold Lazarus

In 1957 Arnold Lazarus and Stanley Rachman provided the first report of success when systematic desensitization was used by a therapist other than Joseph Wolpe. Through the first half of the 1960s Lazarus provided very careful case reports and summaries about a total of 220 patients with whom systematic desensitization had been used. The presenting problems were quite diverse; they included social anxieties, generalized anxiety, panic, and numerous phobias including agoraphobia. Of these 220 diverse cases Lazarus counted 190 as successes based on therapists' Likert-type ratings of patients' functioning in several adaptively significant arenas. He also acquired corroborative reports from referral sources in 70% of his cases.

3. Other Early Reports

The successes reported by Joseph Wolpe and Arnold Lazarus prompted numerous other reports about treating anxiety-related conditions with systematic desensitization. By 1969, Gordon L. Paul was able to locate 51 separate reports of individual cases or clinic series and several reports of systematic desensitization applied in groups. Successful outcomes were not universal in these reports, but there were relatively few failures.

B. The First "Controlled" Experiments

The earliest behavior therapists sought scientific support for the efficacy of their treatments. Thus when early experimental work done by Peter J. Lang and by Gordon L. Paul provided that support it received unprecedented attention.

1. Peter J. Lang

In 1963 and again in 1965 Peter J. Lang and his colleagues reported early experiments in which snake-fearful college students were exposed to standardized forms of systematic desensitization. In the aggregate the experiments achieved impressive control over sources of unwanted variance in the dependent-variable measures; they succeeded in supporting the argument that temporal pairing of muscular relaxation and graded imaging of snake-related scenarios was specifically responsible for observed reductions in avoidance and reported reductions in fear of snakes. They also provided 6-month follow-up data supporting the specific effect of systematic desensitization. Overall, 15 participants who nearly completed the standard course of systematic desensitization improved significantly by contrast with 10 participants who did not complete the standard course of desensitization, with 10 participants exposed to a procedural control for experimental demand/placebo influences, and with 11 participants who served as untreated controls.

2. Gordon L. Paul

In 1966 Gordon L. Paul reported an experiment that remains a methodological reference point three decades later, and that still affords the most convincing evidence available of the specific effectiveness of systematic desensitization. The participants were 96 college students most of whom would now be diagnosed as having generalized social phobia with particular problems in the domain of public speaking. After extensive assessment each of 74 participants was assigned to one of four experimental conditions that, taken together, served to compare the effects of systematic desensitization with those of insight-oriented psychotherapy under conditions that controlled for influence from experimenter (therapist) bias and from major extratherapeutic sources of variance. Fear during a standardized public speaking task was assessed by self-reports, by demonstrably reliable behavioral observation, and by pulse-rate and palmar sweat measures. The group treated with systematic desensitization improved significantly more than did any other group on fear measures in all three domains. Posttreatment differences were maintained as judged by self-reports acquired 2 years later from carefully selected respondents.

C. Analogue Experiments

The behavior therapy movement was up and running by 1970 complete with several new books, three new journals, and two new societies. In this context the early experiments reported by Peter J. Lang and his colleagues spawned scores of experiments in which pretreatment and posttreatment measures of fear of snakes among college students were used to evaluate the effects of systematic desensitization. Some of the experiments compared the effects of systematic desensitization with the effects of competing behavior-influence packages, notably implosive therapy and imaginal flooding. Most of the experiments compared the effects of systematic desensitization with those procedural variations that were germane for one reason or another. Many questions were asked. Is muscular relaxation training necessary for fear reduction with systematic desensitization? Must the imaging instructions proceed along a graded, increasingly fearsome hierarchy of scenarios? Must the participant be permitted to govern his or her own rate of progress along the scenario hierarchy?

Notwithstanding the effort and ingenuity that went into the so-called "snake desensitization studies" they afford very little by way of characterizing the clinical efficacy of systematic desensitization. This is true for at least two reasons. First, in the intellectual climate of the day the efficacy of systematic desensitization was virtually axiomatic; therefore most of the research was intended to answer other questions, such as questions about the "active ingredients" or causal mechanism(s) that explain the success of the approach. Second, the quality of systematic desensitization research with snake-fearful participants fell off sharply very soon after Lang's original reports; since 1972 the external validity of empirical generalizations based on orthodox "snake desensitization studies" has been very much in doubt.

D. Current Status

Throughout most of the decade of the 1960s systematic desensitization was clearly the treatment of choice for phobias and for other anxiety-related conditions. That popularity was based on the reports of clinical cases and series noted earlier and, in part, on the zeitgeist in which Joseph Wolpe's formulations appeared. Toward the end of the decade the work of Albert Bandura and his students began to receive attention also; phobia treatments such as graduated participant modeling began to compete with systematic desensitization. During the middle 1970s Isaac Marks began arguing persuasively that exposure to fear signals is the common element of the successful phobia treatments and that *in vivo* or real-life exposure is all that is needed for clinical success. Thus was born the approach known as "exposure technology."

One outcome of the competing efforts of Albert Bandura and Isaac Marks was an abrupt decline of interest in systematic desensitization. Thus when reports of experiments on the systematic desensitization of snake-fearful (and test-anxious and shy) college students disappeared suddenly from the mainstream literature in 1972 there was nothing about systematic desensitization to take their place. For the past 28 years the empirical literature has contained only episodic case reports about unusual or otherwise interesting applications of the procedure.

Because of the dearth of new data for a quarter century and the widely suspect external validity of "analogue" studies, there are essentially two ways to attempt answering questions about the efficacy of systematic desensitization. One can study and evaluate polemic papers, including papers based on meta-analytic studies, that include statements about clinical outcomes and/or one can retreat to information found in the early clinical series and experiments reported by people such as Joseph Wolpe, Arnold Lazarus, Peter J. Lang, and Gordon L. Paul. The polemics have occurred mainly between Joseph Wolpe and Isaac Marks who have championed the causes of systematic desensitization and exposure technology, respectively. The early clinical series and experiments were, as noted earlier, reviewed in painstaking detail, by Gordon L. Paul in 1969.

V. CASE ILLUSTRATION

The narrative that follows describes the treatment of a 45-year-old, married, white female (Helen) who had severe dental phobia. Behavioral interviewing revealed a clear history of aversive conditioning that involved both pain and ridicule during her extremely rare dental visits. The patient's goal in seeking treatment was to tolerate many sessions of restorative dental treatment. (She could more easily have been a candidate for dentures than for full-mouth restoration; she resisted dentures citing the implication of old age.)

A. Assessment

Early on Helen flatly refused to try direct exposure to dental care under any conditions. Systematic desensitization was then considered as a preparation for subsequent real-life exposure, provided that assessment data supported the use of systematic desensitization.

Initially a suitable dentist was contacted and together Helen and I visited the dentist's office in order to promote concrete imagery during the upcoming assessment. (The visit required a promise that no interaction with the dentist other than a "hello" would be expected.) Time was taken for Helen to get sufficient information for detailed mental pictures of the sights and sounds of that specific environment, and to tell that dentist about her fear.

A widely used structured interview produced diagnoses of claustrophobia and social phobia. (Usually fear of pain or of other oral discomfort plays a central role in dental fear and avoidance; the picture for Helen was surprising, especially given an apparent history of pain-related aversive conditioning.) Questionnaires, role-plays, and imaginal rehearsals were used to pinpoint the kinds of events that made Helen anxious and to describe her fear in three-channel terms. (For example, a questionnaire about the details of claustrophobia established that she was concerned with confinement but not with suffocation.) Helen was identified as a candidate for systematic desensitization in imagination based on the criteria in Joseph Wolpe's 1990 book. Importantly she reported clear imagery and considerable discomfort, including perceived heart-rate increase, during imaginal rehearsals of selected dental-visit scenarios. The kinds of events that made Helen anxious did, indeed, have more to do with confinement and with criticism than with pain.

B. Relaxation and Hierarchy Construction

An eight-session course of relaxation training was undertaken twice weekly using transcripts from the 1973 manual of Douglas A. Bernstein and Thomas D. Borkovec. During the last two sessions four muscle groups were used in order to set the stage for systematic desensitization. In general four repetitions of tension-relaxation cycles were used. Helen had no means of playing tape-recorded relaxation instructions. She was encouraged to relax at home when possible but no records were kept.

During several of the eight visits, at times when Helen was not relaxing, two initial hierarchies for systematic desensitization in imagination were prepared. The hierarchies were developed with an orthodox SUDs-scaling procedure based on scenarios initially provided by both of us. There was difficulty developing separate hierarchies for confinement and for devaluation/criticism that had the necessary gradations in SUDs. After considerable work we decided to begin with one hierarchy that contained scenarios related both to confinement and to devaluation/criticism. In addition we imbedded scenarios of both kinds in a spatiotemporal sequence that began 4 weeks before the first dental visit and that ended in the dental operatory. In the end the hierarchy included 21 scenarios that were at or near 5 SUDs apart from one another. Representative items include "Thinking about the dental visit one week away," "The assistant telephones to remind you two days before the appointment," "The dentist looks startled and asks you if you have ever brushed your teeth," "Reclining in the dental chair with tubes in your mouth so you cannot move."

C. Systematic Desensitization

Systematic desensitization occurred over 12 weekly visits. Each time it was preceded with 8 minutes of four muscle-group relaxation training. Then imaginal rehearsals of the hierarchical scenarios were begun. By and large the procedure involved "orthodox" systematic desensitization as described earlier. In general the actual desensitization trials lasted between 15 and 18 minutes. Each scenario was visualized calmly four times in succession before going to the next. No more than three scenarios were completed in any single session. Care was taken to end the trial on a successful item. On five occasions a scenario prompted repeated anxiety signals and a new, intervening scenario was used.

Beginning in the third week Helen was instructed to begin real-life practice of the spatiotemporal and behavioral aspects of the visualized scenarios. She was encouraged to not go too fast; to practice a week or so behind her progress along the imaginal gradient. As systematic desensitization progressed the dentist participated as an *in vivo* partner; various, long-duration *in vivo* exposure visits were added to the imagined scenarios.

VI. SUMMARY

Systematic desensitization is a venerable behavior therapy for fear and anxiety. Usually it entails remaining deeply relaxed while visualizing a series of increasingly fearsome scenes in which the patient confronts targeted events or situations. There are many theories about how systematic desensitization reduces fear; most "theories" are *post hoc* claims that systematic desensitization instantiates some other training regimen or process such as respondent extinction, habituation, counterconditioning, or self-efficacy augmentation. Joseph Wolpe's original theory of how systematic desensitization works appeals to learned inhibition of anxiety that is based on parasympathetic inhibition of sympathetic activation. Criteria have been developed to identify good candidates for systematic desensitization (e.g., there are four fears or fewer, there is evidence of a capacity for clear imagery, there is evidence of emotional discomfort while imaging frightening material). Scores of case studies and reports of clinical series attest to the efficacy of systematic desensitization. Several now classic experiments show the efficacy of systematic desensitization also. Much research on the outcomes of systematic desensitization was done in a way that renders it of little value. By and large research on the effects of systematic desensitization disappeared from the literature when exposure technology replaced systematic desensitization as the treatment of choice for phobic complaints. However, the earliest case studies and clinical series suffice to support the claim that systematic desensitization is effective and should be considered when *in vivo* exposure is not feasible or is initially refused. A case is described in which a 45-year-old female is treated for dental phobia that was based on claustrophobia and on social phobia.

See Also the Following Articles

Coverant Control ■ Emotive Imagery ■ Exposure ■ Eye Movement Desensitization and Reprocessing ■ Habit Reversal ■ Relaxation Training ■ Self-Control Desensitization ■ Successive Approximations

Further Reading

Bernstein, D. A., & Borkovec, T. D. (1973). *Progressive relaxation training.* Champaign, IL: Research Press.

Goldfried, M. R., & Davison, G. C. (1976). *Clinical behavior therapy.* New York: Holt, Rinehart & Winston.

McGlynn, F. D., Mealiea, W. L., & Landau, D. L. (1981). The current status of systematic desensitization. *Clinical Psychology Review, 1,* 149–179.

Paul, G. L. (1969). Outcome of systematic desensitization I: Background, procedures, and uncontrolled reports of individual treatment. In C. M. Franks (Ed.), *Behavior therapy: Appraisal and status* (pp. 63–104). New York: McGraw-Hill.

Paul, G. L. (1969). Outcome of systematic desensitization II: Controlled investigations of individual treatment, technique variations, and current status. In C. M. Franks (Ed.), *Behavior therapy: Appraisal and status* (pp. 105–159). New York: McGraw-Hill.

Thorpe, G. L., & Olson, S. L. (1997). *Behavior therapy: Concepts, procedures, and applications* (2nd ed.). Needham Heights, MA: Allyn & Bacon.

Wolpe, J. (1976). *Theme and variations: A behavior therapy casebook.* Elmsford, NY: Pergamon.

Wolpe, J. (1990). *The practice of behavior therapy* (4th ed.). Elmsford, NY: Pergamon.

Tele-Psychotherapy

Ann Oberkirch

Yale School of Medicine

GLOSSARY

bandwidth Data transfer speed for telecommunication data.

cable The widest pipes and the fastest but speed will vary. Pipelines are shared with neighbors, and are not dedicated lines like DSL. The maximum theoretical download speed is 27 gigabits per second. Upload speed may be 128 to 384 kbps.

chat rooms Virtual containers for instant e-mail correspondences from disparate locations.

DSL A digital subscriber line has no standard speed. Speeds vary from 256 kbps to 1.5 Mbps and thus are considerably faster than ISDN.

e-mail Electronic mail sent via the Internet.

fixed wireless Requires an antenna on the roof; download speed 1 to 2 mbps, and upload 256 kbps.

ISDN Integrated services digital network begins with a guaranteed 64 kbps, or two lines at 128 kbps, or four lines at 256 kbps or higher Data can be compressed as well to speed transmission.

POTS Plain old standard telephone has the slowest speed. Data are transmitted in analogue wave form. A computer modem converts outgoing digital data to analogue and on the other end incoming analogue data are converted back to digital. Download speed, which is variable at best is 50 kbps, and upload is 33 kbps.

satellite Speeds are on par with DSL and cable. Requires a rooftop dish.

videoconferencing Long distance meetings occurring with both picture and sound transmitted between two or more locations. Ideally transmission occurs in real time and there is perfect synchronization of voice and sound.

I. INTRODUCTION

Tele is a prefix from the Greek *tele* meaning at a distance, or far off. Thus, tele-psychotherapy is simply a term for psychotherapy conducted at a distance instead of taking place in the usual office setting with all participants physically present in one room. Tele-treatment is usually assumed to include new technology, either videoconferencing or e-words.

Videoconferencing technology has advanced sufficiently to deploy psychotherapeutic services that can span the globe, or even transmit to a space vehicle. At the present time, researchers funded by NASA are planning the psychological and medical care for a Mars probe planned for the end of this decade. Treatment will soon be supported from one end of our solar system to another. Truly, psychotherapy has been liberated from the office!

There is nothing new in psychotherapy occurring long distance. Letters have always been sent by surface mail from patient to therapist and vice versa, and should be considered a valid part of treatment. The telephone, as well, has routinely been used for brief consultation or full scheduled visits. Certainly, the initial call that plans the first visit and introduces the participants to each other is a form of tele-psychotherapy, although rarely recognized as such.

Telephone psychological support services have a long history, and provide much needed round-the-clock services sometimes with a more user-friendly interface than traditional medical settings. While suicide hot lines may be staffed by nonprofessionals, the ready access to a sympathetic voice has often sustained the troubled through difficult times.

Students who go off to be educated at a distant locale frequently remain in telephone relationships that are well established and proven salutary. Face-to-face visits are held at vacation times. Many adult patients who are attached to their therapists move, and choose to remain in a well-known trusted helpful partnership, rather than start over again with someone new. These patients should, and often do, have an occasional live office visit.

A colleague in psychoanalysis explained that at the beginning of the week she traveled to a city 3 hours away for an evening session, stayed overnight in a hotel, and had a visit the following morning, and then participated in two more telephone visits before the weekend. While this is unusual, it is not unheard of. Other patients traveling for work or pleasure, or simply too busy to commute to the therapist in the midst of a day of activities, will opt to keep a therapy appointment by phone, if the therapist is agreeable. This is more likely in the west than in the east. There are numerous surreptitious stories of telephone treatments. However, until now, the practice of telephone psychotherapy has always been utilized within treatments that began in a traditional office setting.

Today our new technology allows for treatments to begin outside an office container. What should we make of this psychotherapeutic brave new world? This article will introduce you to tele-psychotherapy: good or bad, safe or risky.

There is much reason for optimism: As new standards for telecare are written, and new regulatory law is encoded, good treatments will prevail, not wild teletherapies, and new, effective and improved tele-psychotherapies will be developed. We are at the point that quality care can be universal, if only we will share our resources.

II. TECHNOLOGY: VIDEO

Top-quality telephone or computer-driven videoconferencing has images that are similar to television or movies. The transmission of separate pictures is not detectible, and lip synchronization is perfect. Often there is little or no delay caused by distance, and communication flows easily. From the wide array of videoconferencing tools, equipment can be utilized with a guaranteed verisimilitude, the ideal, or for the most modest investment, inexpensive video that is unreliable, and/or so poorly reproduced that it is nearly useless. The quality of images relates to one factor: cost. The more money spent on equipment, software for computer applications, and transmission links, the better the result.

Videophones are now available that are simply telephones that can be plugged into a standard phone jack and produce excellent pictures. The image may appear on a lightweight portable phone screen that easily fits into an ample pocket or purse, or on a larger stationary telephone unit's screen, or displayed on a computer screen, or at the most lifelike projected on a television screen. These phones may have regular or plain old telephone system transmission links (POTS), or ISDN phones that utilize linkages two to four times as wide as POTS telephones. The best of them, often bought by the government to be used by the CIA, FBI, or military, cost well over a thousand dollars. The advantage of POTS videophones is ubiquity. The best videophones scramble information so privacy is almost guaranteed, hence their utility for the government.

Videoconferencing can also be conducted between computers with no telephones involved. When the widest pipe lines (known as broadband) are sending digital information, excellent images result. The cost of an individual long distance phone call is not incurred with every meeting, which is considerable when the videoconference lasts for a standard psychotherapeutic hour and crosses one or more oceans. The users pay a monthly fee for renting the broadband attachment (e.g., cable, ISDN, or DSL) to the local phone line. Such private stable computer linkages are often established between hospitals and satellite clinics. These networks may be set up by one of the large videoconferencing companies who sell their own connecting software or done more simply by downloading videoconferencing software off the web to go with a single PC.

Small clinics that cannot underwrite such expensive private networks can turn to the Internet for video transmission help. At least two companies will now permit downloading of videoconferencing software without charge into a PC/Windows based personal computer: CUSeeMe from White Pine and Microsoft's Netmeeting. With the addition of a 70 dollar videocamera on both ends, and an attachment to a high speed link like cable or DSL, without the addition of special software of equipment sold by the top videoconferencing companies, reliable intermediate quality images will result. For a military clinic in Hawaii with patients on a tiny island thousands of miles away, some video is far better than none, and improves care well above that done with mere sound.

Lower cost computer-driven video and low end videophones are, of course, available for pure POTS transmission, although diminishing expense is unfortunately correlated with decreasing quality. This would occasionally allow a therapist to receive video alongside audio, but the images are most likely to be delayed, and are prone to breaking up or fragmenting into component data, and transmission most often cannot be guaranteed, as crowded Internet lines prevent the flow of data at peak times. Thus, when a subject moves, the image conveyed breaks up into tiny parts or fragments. This is a disconcerting experience to view. The intermittent distorted weird displays are unsettling, and are not conducive to serious psychotherapeutic work.

How does videoconferencing compare to a real office visit? Is it nearly as useful? How much evaluative data are lost when a therapy patient is seen in only two dimensions? What happens when scent/olfaction is lost as a sensory cue? How much do we rely on intuition, whatever that is, as an evaluative measure and how much is it dependent on the actual sharing of physical space? How long will it take a generation of computer savvy people to process the mysteries of each other with a virtual contact? We have much to learn, but this should not hold us back.

III. TECHNOLOGY: E-WORDS

In the beginning, the portal of entry to the web was a computer. Access today can be instantaneous with a mere handheld wireless device that can fit in one small palm, even a child's. Alternatively a modestly priced electronic gadget designed only to link to the Internet equipped with a keyboard and large screen will do. The Internet's transmission of words, pictures, and other data is astonishing; the effluent is rapidly changing our civilization. Information of serious or dubious value is readily available for global consumption. The latest news can be read almost as it happens with the flick of a switch on a tiny unit. Nearly anyone can search the most knowledgeable medical databases from nearly anywhere. Sophisticated patients may know as much or more than their doctors about their illnesses as chat groups or bulletin boards run by victims of illnesses often provide the best information for dealing with disease. The Internet world has spun us topsy-turvy, replaced some pomposity with humility, and occasional ignorance with knowledge, and allowed a cave in a wilderness to headquarter a global terrorist war. The facile flow has brought all of us closer together, for good and for evil.

Groups, sometimes patients, can meet in real time in chat rooms that include participants from all over our planet. At the present time, these virtual settings allow only verbal messages, but in the near future, when broadband and POTS are near equally priced, and information that creates images races along, these virtual rooms will have multiple video-streams, one from each source. A dyad, or therapy pair, can now talk via instant messaging and share live real time e-conversation, usually typed and sometimes spoken.

E-mail is ubiquitous: The good news is the telephone has not deleted the written word, indeed letter-writing has returned in spite of television usurping hours spent on reading; the bad news is that much e-mail, whether spoken or typed, like much surface mail, is junk.

Amidst the deluge of e-correspondences, however, are useful interactions between therapists and patients. E-mail contact has a bad reputation because of the exploitation of cyberspace for felonious "activities". However, imagine the gain for a fragile person who can send a letter (albeit an e-letter) to a therapist at any time of night or day. In the loneliest hours when most are asleep, this may make the difference between life and death.

Properly used, the Internet will alter psychotherapy practice for the benefit of patients. Today, cyberspace is the "wild west," anything goes. Rest assured, this will not last.

IV. TELE-PSYCHOTHERAPY TODAY

A spare room in a centrally located community building can quickly be converted into a satellite psychotherapy clinic with the simple addition of a videoconferencing system, a scheduling administrator, and the requisite broadband link to a clinic with available psychotherapy staff. The earliest utilization of tele-psychotherapy has been the most natural: The technology has enabled the development of satellite clinics providing care in communities that cannot support full mental health clinics themselves.

The psychiatric and psychological sections of meetings for telemedical professionals have nearly always included clinical presentations from countries and states with large remote areas with low population density including Australia, Newfoundland, Norway, Alaska, Arizona, Michigan, and New Mexico, as well as other more exotic locales. These papers recount the benefit and efficacy of tele-treatments. The presentations are inspirational and usually have scenic photographs: one side of the videolink may be a well-known center of excellence, while the other is a few huts in the wilderness sometimes surrounded by reindeer and locked in by snow and ice. The patients, if depicted, are overwhelmingly grateful that care is available at long last for conditions that heretofore have gone neglected. The tele-psychotherapeutic visits are presumed to be almost as good as the real thing, and are justified as providing virtual care where real office care cannot exist.

A secondary proliferation of tele-psychotherapeutic services has been to prisons that are intentionally built far from population centers. A videoconferencing link allows for flexibility of delivery of services that could not be supported by importing mental health staff or exporting prisoner-patients with the requisite guard staff and a driver.

The United States Department of Health and Human Services Commission endorses long-distance treatment as the legitimate embrace of new technology by creating the first reimbursement codes for tele-psychotherapy, although in rural areas only. The preference for rural telemedicine and telepsychotherapy is echoed as well by the governmental agencies that fund telemedical programs: They are only willing to support programs in rural settings. Urban clinicians need not apply.

The military, of course, uses tele-treatments for troops and support staff who are stationed routinely in remote locations. The earliest implementation of the most sophisticated equipment would be allocated toward saving lives, hence tele-psychological services would be supported only when physical health needs are fully deployed. It is not yet widely accepted that providing adequate psychological support after the horror of battle and injury, if possible, speeds recovery from medical injuries.

Tele-treatments are slow in developing outside remote areas. There is little research on the potential exploitation of this new technology to improve delivery of care for patients who require the careful purview of a vigilant therapist with some exceptions. A project from Massachusetts General evaluates videoconferencing for OCD by Lee Baer and colleagues. A researcher from London, Paul McLaren, studies the use of videoconferencing in psychiatry in urban settings by inpatient units seeking specialty consultation at other hospitals.

Medical schools in and outside the United States show enormous zeal for developing consultation programs that bring in patients from distant locales. Many of these projects are developing to bring income into institutions facing funding cuts while they are simultaneously finding new and improved models of patient care. The comparative indifference to exploring the potential benefit of this new technology for local use seems shortsighted and overly cautious. In general, the prevailing opinion of tele-psychotherapy is that it is a second-rate alternative to in-the-flesh real care. Still, there is a surprising lack of creative effort for planning new techniques for conducting psychotherapy using this technology. Perhaps one explanation of this relative indifference is that grant money for pure clinical work is difficult to find. Much psychiatric research is drug company based, hence scientific research devoid of pharmaceuticals is more difficult to support. If this technology promises to bring relief of suffering to patients, and this opinion is popularized, scientific scrutiny is certain to ensue, although this seems not likely to occur soon. Today's adolescents have rich social lives in virtual settings sometimes all over the world, but the adult scientist generation is not yet ready to mine these virtual settings for clinical gain.

Psychotherapy in cyberspace or e-therapies are developing quickly. A web search will find a variety of dotcoms selling web treatments, and more added each day. The preponderance of e-psychotherapies are offered by nonmedical clinicians, and it is often difficult to evaluate the credentials of the practitioners. A minority of these web clinics include telephone conversations alongside e-mail chat. E-mail treatment is inexpensive but many clinicians believe it is of dubious value, hence you get what you pay for. How can words alone be beneficial to patients? If e-mail help is limited to informational help, rather than counseling or treatment, and goals are limited, and conceptually understood, it seems feasible that some useful parameters for e-service could be defined. If a life is saved by a well-timed persuasive e-comment, how would we discover this unknown benefit? The rapid condemnation of all e-services without exploring individually what each is doing seems hasty and gratuitously cautious.

Many psychotherapists exchange e-mail with patients. When this mail is sent within an active clinical exchange, the interaction is similar to a voice mail message, and is simply a new component of treatment. E-dialogue is another way for our patients to reach us, to confess secrets hard to admit face to face, to let us know more of aspects of a distraught inner self, and therefore provide more grist for the mill of an ongoing therapy.

V. IMPEDIMENTS, CONTROVERSIES, AND CAVEATS

Why hasn't tele-psychotherapy been embraced far and wide by practitioners with technical savvy when it seems such a logical extension of office treatment? The primary obstacle is probably money. As yet, there are no reimbursement codes for billing tele-psychotherapeutic videoconferencing visits unless your clinical work in done in rural areas. The managed care companies that underwrite much psychotherapy in the United States have not yet discerned that tele-psychotherapeutic visits are likely to save considerable funds when conducted in rural and urban settings. The studies demonstrating this have simply not been done yet.

There is also no reimbursement for e-mail correspondence, rural or otherwise. When clinicians permit e-mail correspondence, they either have to do this as a gift of time, or a billing arrangement must be agreed on with the individuals involved. When the patient's psychotherapy coverage is within a managed care program, the clinician is breaching the managed care contract by charging for e-mail treatment time. The concerned clinician is faced with an unpleasant dilemma when supplementing office visits for a fragile patient with an e-mail correspondence. If this exchange is done without fee, does this generosity have a tinge of self-sacrifice by the clinician? How would this effect the treatment over time? Alternatively, if a billing arrangement is set behind the back of managed care rules, what message does this give the patient about the therapist's ethics? There is no good solution given today's managed care contractual agreements for clinicians.

The solution might be to limit e-mail correspondence to self-pay patients. A policy of this sort would enhance the development of tiered mental health services with the best care given to the wealthiest patients who can afford to self-pay out of discretionary funds. This seems an unfortunate division of services for discerning who gets the most flexible treatment. Another solution might be to create public sector services for everyone offered by one government agency instead of our current complex system. We are a long way in the United States from a unitary mode.

In countries with government health care coverage for all citizens, it will probably prove easier to establish tele-psychotherapeutic practice. The complex challenges of finding liability coverage for clinicians for novel tele-treatments would be dealt with by a central authority, and reimbursement for telecare for all citizens could be efficiently planned. In the United States with its complex health care apparatus, each independent clinician will have to struggle to find tele-treatment liability coverage usually through a professional society. At the time of this writing there is scant malpractice liability coverage sold for tele-psychiatry by psychiatric insurers. The American Psychiatric Association is unfortunately not likely to make this available anytime soon even as an add-on to the usual malpractice package. Teletreatment programs operating out of medical schools and graduate psychology and social work departments that self-insure the malpractice of staff clinicians will have more flexibility.

The logical way to bill for e-mail time is by bytes of time or minutes. Just as lawyers charge for varying lengths of time, psychotherapists might do the same. But the reimbursement system in American medicine (and psychotherapy falls into this category) is by service code, roughly but not precisely based on time. How long will it take to convert the standard procedure code system to a more flexible scheme for tele-psychotherapeutic care that above all else should have flexibility for session lengths whatever the method of delivery? Since this constitutes a radical change in reimbursement structures, it is likely to be slow in coming. Another more novel appraoch for payment of e-mail correspondence might be a monthly set fee for e-mail privileges.

The regulatory barriers to tele-psychotherapy are enormous, and are likely to be more complicated in the future, not less. In the United States, licensures for psychotherapeutic practice is issued by state. Clinicians are credentialed to practice locally. Tele-psychotherapy would be confined to a geographic area when large clinics establish satellites, but how are clinicians to be licensed when the primary clinic is in one state and the satellite(s) in another? The medical-legal issues are compounded even more when the treatment is between two nations or several. The European Union is establishing guidelines for telemedical care that will enhance the flow of treatment within these countries. The World Health Organization has a larger global focus as it seeks to establish telemedical rules for all nations. It too is working on guidelines for telemedical practice. Ultimately, the nations of the world will have global pacts for telemedical and tele-psychotherapy treatments, protection of patient privacy regulations, conventions for flow of medical data, and even, one hopes, global pharmaceutical rules so patients who travel may easily get telemedical treatment and medications wherever they happen to be.

Today, whenever a therapist conducts tele-treatment with a patient in another country, or another state or province, the clinician is already operating in a legal gray area. Videoconferencing and telephone sessions held interstate or between national jurisdictions are not always clearly legally permissible, although they are also not quite against the law. For instance, does the clinician require a license to practice where the patient is located, however distant? Some would argue that an affirmative reply is correct, others not.

The G8 telemedical study group has members roughly comparable to the top eight global industrial powers. One of their strong recommendations is that when telemedical treatment is done, the license and governance in the location of the medical clinician should govern the transaction. Thus, clinicians will only require licenses, malpractice liability, and liability releases in one jurisdiction, not every location they are treating patients. It is not known, as sensible as this notion is, whether local governments will go along with such rules. How will chauvinism restrain itself from rearing its ugly head and launching protective turf battles? How will psychotherapy regional societies sit back and allow distant clinical intruders to compete for their available patient pool? Neither seems likely, although the alternative possibilities are dismal.

Who will be responsible for monitoring long distance treatments? Will this be done by the medical/psychotherapy societies in the clinician's jurisdiction or in the patient's? There is little agreement so far on what is considered adequate care utilizing videoconferencing, and even less of a consensus regarding e-word or text-based treatment. Standards of care must be determined, but given the paucity of scientific data on tele-psychotherapy, how will these be set? Interest in tele-treatment is not adequate yet for sufficient research to be funded to make these assessments. When agreement is finally reached, will it be possible to allow enough flexibility so creative clinicians can continue to generate new and exciting techniques and methods? Alas, in psychiatry, practice guidelines geared to protect patients and guarantee a high standard of care are being established that may eliminate deviation from a strict conservative norm. So in the short term patients are protected, at grave risk of an overall atrophy of creativity in the field.

The privacy issue has evoked much concern. When videoconferencing networks with a few private linkages are established, it is easy to create encryption of data and sufficient firewalls around the database server so the patients are as close to guaranteed privacy as is possible. But when the Internet is used for videoconferencing, or for e-mail, for modestly funded programs or treatments, how will privacy of data be promised if it flows between many servers that cannot be regulated by clinician or patients?

In the United States, extensive standards governing both privacy and security of health information are being developed and implemented under HIPAA (the Health Insurance Portability and Accountability Act of 1996). This law threatens high fines and even criminal penalties for unauthorized release of information. The security requirements will mandate some form of access control or encryption to protect electronic data traveling over a communications network. Other countries are enacting similar legislation. But how will every psychotherapist know these rules and follow them when the available unregulated Internet is so seductive?

The issue about which there is the most controversy is the entire matter of cyberspace psychotherapy or treatment by e-mail. Is it simply bad treatment and therefore negligent only designed to make a fast buck for its purveyors? Or are there circumstances when e-care might be appropriate or necessary? If so, what are these? Robert Hsiung, M.D., at the University of Chicago, is editing a book on e-therapy. He is well suited to do this as he runs a message board for patients with a million hits per month that he moniters himself, clearly not an easy task. Dr. Hsiung believes that e-care should not be carelessly relegated to tele-psychotherapeutic malpractice without a careful exploration of its salutary potential. But how will we decide what e-care is helpful and what is not in the face of the paucity of evidence-based clinical research to allow these determinations to be made based on scientific data?

Horror stories exist of Internet fraud: self-appointed therapists with no training setting up shop on the web. Who should regulate such practice? Should there be monitoring for consumer, or in this case, patient protection? Is this monitoring an invasion of privacy? Who will decide? No doubt, in time government commissions will develop to scrutinize web businesses, including all psychotherapeutic transactions, but if both parties have encryption and firewalls, this will not be an easy task.

One caveat: If you are going to utilize e-mail in your existing psychotherapeutic practice, make sure your patients know how often you read your letters. You do not want a new patient or anyone to send you an e-note full of suicidal ideation, homicidal yearnings, confessions of horrific crimes, or any other shared desperate feelings that you should have acted on but instead missed with dire consequences, because you had not had sufficient time to review your mail.

We have so much to discover and learn about tele-psychotherapy. The best of us is only an e-treatment toddler awkwardly staying up and finding the correct path.

VI. CLINICAL TALES AND THE ISSUE OF TELE-TRANSFERENCE

Patient confidentiality has been protected by eliminating or altering identifying data.

A. Case History 1

Thomas is a tall, elegant, middle-aged man with a large brood of interesting tow-headed children. He has had two brief courses of psychotherapy with me several years apart each involving e-technology. He came to his first visit with great reluctance, and arrived incredibly late to underscore that sentiment. He had always taken great pride in his competence and independence, and like many people, stigmatized psychiatric illness, and felt any need for treatment was an embarrassing weakness. His father had service-connected bipolar disease related to battle experiences during World War II; he viewed this man with both sympathy and pity. He sought help from me when he realized he was losing control of his most valuable commodity, time, and had given up any hope of remedying the situation himself.

His first treatment occurred when Internet access was considered quite precious and was sold by the minute, and was usually a privilege for the wealthy or a perk of academia. Thomas was neither. He described how he sat in his office at the end of a grueling day of back-to-back meetings, and signed on to the web to relax. Soon he found himself in chat rooms where he easily found women offering delightful e-company. Conversations would go on for hours, and were quite expensive. He found himself lying to his wife about his unusual long evening hours at the office. He was horrified by his dissembling, and the huge expense for his e-habit. He felt addicted to the web and its chat rooms, and his self-reproach for this loss of control was enormous. He believed he loved his wife and did not understand his incessant web flirtations.

In the past he had had several serious episodes of depression that he waited out; all of these had a seasonal component. His usual state was mildly ebullient: He needed little sleep, and his productivity was impressive. His only impulsive behavior in the past was with food; to his chagrin his weight went up and down. He exercised long hours to control his girth given his tendency to eat too much.

During several months of treatment, which involved an extraordinary number of cancellations, which he easily rationalized away as due to urgent situations at work, we discussed his marriage, its strengths and weaknesses. While it was apparent to me that Thomas was lonely in what appeared to be a faltering marriage, he had not allowed himself to acknowledge this. He saw his addiction to the web as analogous to overeating; and just as his weight would go up and down, so would his Internet time.

Thomas is a highly intelligent fellow. He enjoyed the opportunity to explore his past, his marriage, his parents' commitment to each other, and the nature of their relationship to him, and even our cautious study of his relationship with me. In time, he acknowledged how disappointed, sad, and bored he felt with his wife. His web friendships, which developed into romances, were thrilling.

One day he announced he was done with therapy, although he had just made a plan to meet one of his web girlfriends across the country during a business trip. He had never before considered infidelity and given his lapsed Catholicism, he would not abandon the sacrament of marriage without much soul-searching. Apparently he was not to do that with me as an accomplice.

Years later, Thomas contacted me again. He was now involved in a real love affair and was considering leaving his wife, and no, he had never met his cross country date when last we met. He was becoming increasingly depressed, and anxious about his confusing situation. His lover was pressuring him to end his marriage so she could leave her annoying husband, but he found himself reluctant to tear apart his children's family while they were still quite young. He enjoyed their company enormously and did not want to give up daily contact with them. Leaving his wife would be easier, though even this would be daunting.

At first his anxiety was nearly incapacitating and required the aggressive use of a tranquilizing SSRI antidepressant. When both his wife and his lovers' husband learned of the affair, not surprising given the frequent mid-day and evening assignations, he became deeply suicidal. Despite this, he refused to come in for office visits with the frequency his serious illness required, claiming work obligations. This explanation had already seemed a convenient cover for his avoidant behavior, which had not responded to interpretation.

I knew him well enough to understand his need to distance himself, even at a time when he felt extremely fragile, could not be altered. This very private man had to maintain his boundaries with me, no matter what the cost, including the risk of suicide. He was unwilling to plan telephone visits claiming an absence of privacy on all his phones; he was terribly worried that someone would listen in. (This treatment was before personal cell phones.)

So I turned to the web to supplement his visit schedule as the only alternative to having information from him about his level of potential lethality, and thus a site for titrating his medications frequently, and a place to nurture him with well-chosen words. I insisted he maintain an e-mail correspondence with me, daily when necessary at a frequency determined by me, so I could follow the depth of his suicidal ideation. His treatment consisted of a weekly visit and for a month near daily e-mail notes. During this time, he decided to end his affair and concentrate on improving his marriage. When his suicidal depression improved, we slowly weaned his e-mail nurturance.

He continued his treatment with decreasing frequency while he described the benefits of his newly discovered focus on his marriage. His wife was now experienced as his long lost best friend. The privacy each partner needed to sustain a long commitment did not allow for intimate lovemaking, and he adjusted to the lost thrill of his love affair versus the reliability of his marriage.

One day he cancelled a visit for what seemed like a spurious reason. A nonjudgmental inquiring e-mail went unanswered. Once again, his real and virtual treatments ended abruptly.

Thomas' second treatment could have been foreshortened when he became acutely suicidal but refused to allow me to determine the appropriate pace of our office meetings given his life-threatening illness. It was obvious that any attempt on my part to challenge or control him would have met with complete resistance, and the likely premature disruption of his treatment. My suggestion that we turn to a virtual conversation allowed for an ongoing discourse that could not be held elsewhere. Had we only had a weekly office visit with no supplementation, I would have never known if Thomas was safe. He could not be counted on to contact me if he became dangerously low. Plus I knew he could be overwhelmed by urges he could not control as he had been with spectacular binges of sweets. We both recognized that he might have become overwhelmed with suicidal impulses. The virtual conversations allowed for daily care, which he needed, without what for him would have been an overwhelming intensity of intimate real office dialogue. Thank goodness there was e-mail. It may have kept him alive.

B. Case History 2

Anna lives in Hong Kong with her husband and children. Her spouse has a lucrative and interesting job that pulled the family from a much appreciated community on the east coast. Anna's oldest daughter has just hit menarche, the youngest is still in diapers, and there are a few sons in between. Anna feels she should be content with the opportunity to live in a fabulous city especially with her recent affluence. Instead she is miserable. Her mother-in-law contacted me for help.

Anna, like many expatriates, is homesick and misses her family, her home, her language, and her culture. She speaks eloquently about her many travails, but she believes she should be happy. She is pensive about the origin of her gloom, offers biological and philosophical explanations, and also is deeply ashamed.

There are no English-speaking psychiatrists in her Asian city that she can find despite a circle of expatriate friends. She does not know the local language so cannot utilize local care. I agreed to have telephone consultations with her only if she had office visits with me regularly when she returns to the states on visits.

That was 6 months ago and since then she has sometimes been quite ill. One serious downswing reminded her of a postpartum illness when she stayed in bed for a month and had both infanticidal and suicidal thoughts. She often has high energy spells with racing thoughts and not infrequent fabulous shopping sprees at the many terrific stores.

I have arranged to have medication sent abroad to her but only products with a wide margin of safety. I have told her she needs more effective but riskier pharmaceuticals, but am waiting to prescribe mood stabilizers until we have videoconferencing visits. I hope this caution makes sense to her; I have explained that I need to see her if I am giving her a medicine that can be toxic. Voice alone will not give me adequate diagnostic cues.

We are planning a video link soon, so more aggressive care is imminent. In the meantime, she is feeling euthymic right now, though she doubts this will last long.

Anna's telephone psychiatric consultations will soon be enhanced with the addition of videoconferencing. She is likely to be my only transcontinental patient until telepsychiatric liability is available for long-distance care. Her telecare is untraditional but given her circumstances, it seemed the most reasonable alternative.

C. Case History 3

Maureen at 50 is finally happily married, though little else about her life is pleasurable. She sought my help about a year ago when her last psychiatrist moved away and she felt perilously close to a suicide. She did not want to do this to her beloved spouse, though she cared little for her own life.

She was often morbidly ill as a young woman and her arms are covered with innumerable scars from self-mutilation. She now will not wear clothing that shows her arms as she is so ashamed of these revealing white lines. So she hides beneath hand-woven fabrics in an interesting palette. Her overeating, always a problem, has recently gotten completely out of control. She has doubled her weight. An all too familiar feeling of deadness will not abate and she wonders, without any tears, if she will ever feel alive again, not that she cares much.

Recently a pain in her abdomen turned out to be the result of rare benign tumors in both kidneys. The largest was embolized, but her extreme discomfort continues and it seems likely that surgery will be necessary. During her weekly psychotherapy visits, she cracks black comedic jokes, and converses with my two French mastiffs, but says little to me.

Early on in her care, she accepted my invitation to send e-mails with reports of her food intake. We were not able to successfully curb her binge eating, though she described her struggles with control, and other critical emotional events. Recent notes are of visits with this specialist and that. She also in e-writing reveals her fears, her despair, and her anguish, all of which cannot be spoken. As her mood disorder does not respond to pharmaceuticals, we rely on therapy, real and virtual, to control her demons and one hopes, slowly heal her many wounds. She is witty and talented, and I am determined to enliven her—this will require ingenuity on both our parts, but luckily we have an abundance of patience. She has done so well in the past in overcoming her slicing impulses, there is room for optimism.

Maureen's e-mail correspondence is much like Thomas'. Her letters allow for self-revelation that is impossible to achieve face to face. She can accept warmth and kindness from me in writing that would seem disingenuous in my consulting room where she spends her time amusing me. Her e-treatments sometimes seems like the most useful treatment but I know she values our meetings as well. I like and respect her and recognize her talents that too often have been ignored. Our shared pleasant hours are salutary given the abuse in her childhood.

Many therapists will eventually use videoconferencing or e-mail in a similar fashion. Patients will insist on this flexibility, and therapists will comply. Teletreatments will be common, and will be understood to be nothing more or less than traditional care expanded by technology.

The relationship between patient and therapist will be equally available for scrutiny as an office treatment. Transference is a term that describes our predilection for misinterpreting relationships due to prior experiences usually in our childhoods. Thus an adult neglected in childhood will too easily find adult insult and injury. Tele-relationships will take longer to develop intensity but despite this attenuation, the full panoply of emotions will ensue. To be sure: tele-treatment will have transference aspects, despite the altered venue.

VII. TWO PRELIMINARY STUDIES

By early 1999, the web was suddenly abuzz with exciting activity. America Online was selling inexpensive global connectivity, and Amazon.com was selling books. How could this new technology be a potential source of benefit to my patients? The answer was not obvious.

After attending my first telemedicine conference in the fall of 1999, I decided to try out the technology in my practice to reduce the stress of separation at the time of my holidays, which seemed overwhelmingly distressing for some of my most fragile and dependent patients. These accounts are strictly anecdotal, there was never any plan to produce verifiable data. I was simply trying out what might be helpful in the most preliminary way. If my conclusions were positive, scientific studies might be warranted later.

A. Study 1: January 2000

The editor of a prominent telemedical journal suggested that low-cost videophones might suffice for long distance telepsychiatric treatment. Shortly before a trip to London for a conference sponsored by this colleague, I ordered six such videophones. Five were handed out to five fragile patients most likely to find the break in treatment troubling. The sixth phone went to England with me.

1. Results

2/5 Patients acted out by not appearing for their scheduled tele-visits.

3/5 had televisits with images appearing at a sluggish frame rate that had no semblance of reality. Voice and picture were poorly synchronized, not only did image lag way beyond sound, but the picture itself fragmented with movement creating a psychedylic effect.

1/5 A bipolar male used to long distance telephone treatment declared the video of no benefit.

1/5 A paranoid schizophrenic woman would not look at the camera, though her husband enjoyed the unique experience of a trans-Atlantic video-conversation

1/5 A bipolar woman was delighted with her video-talk with me and believed seeing me defused her anguish.

2. *Conclusion*

Low end videoconferencing is minimally better than telephone without video. Clinically useful videoconferencing should approximate real time with well synchronized movement and sound.

B. Study 2

I had announced a holiday to Nepal and invited patients to e-mail me if necessary during my lengthy absence. My practice would be covered by a local psychiatrist during this hiatus, but e-mail greetings were available during recuperative stays in Kathmandu between treks.

1. *Results*

Eighteen patients wrote, five more than once. No patient required a single visit with another psychiatrist during my holiday, or needed a day hospital or inpatient stay.

2. *Conclusion*

An e-mail during a long break in treatment may obviate the need for an office visit by another clinician. Such e-mails may alleviate suffering due to separation anxiety as well. Reimbursement for such e-mail correspondence might save on the overall cost of treatment.

VIII. TELE-PSYCHOTHERAPY TOMORROW

Today we are nearly at launch position for tele-psychotherapy (to use the space exploration metaphor again). Our current treatment model, except in rural areas, presumes patients will come to our offices for visits. In the not too distant future, the usual visit will be virtual. This will enable patients to access care from anyplace they happen to be that has appropriate telecommunication links.

In the case of a disaster, whether natural or manmade, health care relationships will be established almost immediately by bringing in videoconferencing and other telemedical equipment, if necessary, linked by remote satellite. When counseling is available immediately for victims, posttraumatic stress disorder will be prevented or diminished in at-risk populations.

Videoconferencing equipment will soon be on airplanes to calm nervous passengers, or support flight attendants handling challenging situations. Internet in real time will allow patients with phobias to find support as they fly. Such equipment will be on board ships, and even on space crafts!

Troops in combat will wear dog tags with lifetime medical histories; medics will carry small terminals to transmit this information to ships nearby, or to consultants across the ocean. Just as medically compromised patients will have access to improved immediate treatment, tele-psychotherapies will soon be supported for many emergencies.

Group therapies will be held with streaming video from disparate sites. Imagine the AA meeting with members from all seven continents.

If managed care has damaged the relationship between therapist and patient, tele-psychotherapy will promote healing of the wounds. Tele-treatment will restore the therapy relationship to the primacy it deserves, while the utmost of patient privacy will be guaranteed with encryption.

Someday we will have global conventions on licensing and global pacts on pharmaceutical distribution for people on the move.

Of utmost importance, should we develop and share our resources generously, is that rich and poor alike all over the globe could have access to the wisdom of our best clinicians. At last, worldwide excellent treatments are potentially an achievable goal, if only we make this our priority.

See Also the Following Articles

Cost Effectiveness ■ Economic and Policy Issues ■ Online or E-Therapy ■ Virtual Reality Therapy ■ Working Alliance

Further Reading

Baer, L., Cukor, P., Jenike, M. A., et al. (1995). Pilot studies for use of telemedicine for patients with obsessive-compulsive disorder. *American Journal of Psychiatry, 152,* 1383–1385.

Baer, L., Elford, D. R., & Cukor, P. (1997). Telepsychiatry at forty; what have we learned? *Harvard Review of Psychiatry, 5,* 7–17.

Hawker, F., Kavanagh, S., Yellowlees, P., et al. (1998). Telepsychiatry in South Australia. *Journal of Telemedicine and Telecare, 4,* 187–194.

Hill, J., Allman, L., & Ditzler, T. (2001). Utility of real-time video teleconferencing in conducting family mental health sessions: Two case reports. *Telemedicine Journal and e-Health, 7,* 55–59.

Kennedy, C., & Yellowlees, P. (2000). A community-based approach to the evaluation of health outcomes and costs for telepsychiatry in a rural population: Preliminary results. *Journal of Telemedicine and Telecare, 6* (suppl 1), 155–157.

McLaren, P. M., & Ball, C. J. (1997). Interpersonal communications and telemedicine: Hypotheses and methods. *Journal of Telemedicine and Telecare, 3,* 5–7.

McLaren, P. M., Blunden, J., Lipsedge, M. L., et al. (1996). Telepsychiatry in an inner-city community psychiatric service. *Journal of Telemedicine and Telecare, 2,* 57–59.

McLaren, P., Mohammedali, A., Riley, A., et al. (1999). Integrating interactive television-based psychiatric consultation into an urban community mental health service. *Telecare Journal of Telemedicine and Telecare, 5* (suppl 1), 100–102.

Simpson, J., Doze, S., Urness, D., et al. (2001). Evaluation of a routine telepsychiatry service. *Journal of Telemedicine and Telecare, 7,* 90–98.

Simpson, J., Doze, S., Urness, D., et al. (2001). Telepsychiatry as a routine service—the perspective of the patient. *Journal of Telemedicine and Telecare, 7,* 155–160.

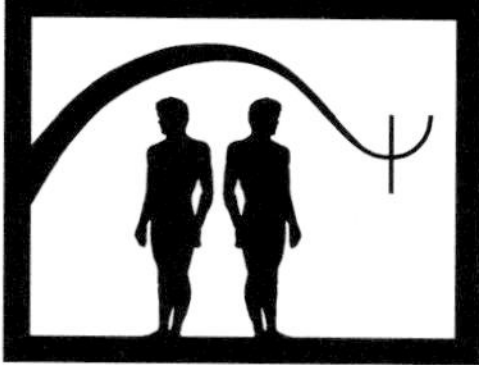

Termination

Georgiana Shick Tryon
City University of New York Graduate School and University Center

GLOSSARY

termination The end of psychotherapy.

All therapeutic relationships come to an end. This chapter discusses theoretical formulations and empirical findings concerning psychotherapy termination.

I. OVERVIEW

The ending of psychotherapy is commonly referred to as termination. The 1994 ethical standards of the American Psychological Association (APA) specify that therapists should terminate treatment with a client when the client does not require further therapy, or the client is not benefiting or is being harmed by continued service. Ideally, client and therapist make a mutual decision to discontinue therapy when the goals of treatment have been met.

In reality, however, the termination sometimes occurs because just one of the parties decides that it is time to end treatment. Client and therapist do not always agree on when termination should occur. Termination is sometimes forced on both client and therapist. Neither party may wish to terminate, but one of them may be moving to a new location or agency, insurance policies may limit therapy to fewer sessions than client and/or therapist view as sufficient, or agencies may have a rigid session limit.

The APA ethical standards require therapists to discuss termination with their clients and to provide "appropriate pretermination counseling." The nature of this pretermination counseling is not specified in the standards, but therapists are instructed to provide referrals for clients when appropriate. In 1994, Mathilda Canter and other colleagues who helped to construct the APA standards suggested that termination discussions should at least summarize the treatment and plan for the future. Oftentimes this future planning includes provision of referrals to other therapists and/or invitations to return to therapy in the future should the client encounter further difficulties.

II. THEORETICAL BASES

In 1993, Stephen Quintana summarized the major theoretical formulation of termination. He indicated that termination has been conceptualized from a psychoanalytic perspective as having two components—loss and development. The loss component was hypothesized to sometimes reach crisis proportions. It has received some attention with researchers such as Hans Strupp and Jeffrey Binder stating in 1984 that therapists must work to ensure that clients do not suffer a relapse of symptoms because of the loss of their relationships with their therapists. Therapists are also hypothesized to be affected by their loss of relationship with clients. In 1981, Rodney Goodyear argued that therapists who had not grieved past losses sufficiently were most likely to be disproportionately saddened by termination with clients. Quintana stated that some theorists even believed that anxiety surrounding termination has lead many researchers to avoid studying the process of termination altogether.

In 1933, Freud conceptualized that the loss triggered by psychotherapy termination facilitates the formation of an internal representation of the lost person (i.e., the therapist). The client compensates for the loss of the therapist by developing his or her own internal resources to replace what the therapist provided. Thus, termination is also viewed as a time of personal development. The client is viewed as maturing under the careful direction of the therapist much in the same manner that a child matures under parental guidance. When the client terminates therapy, he or she carries important internalized aspects of the relationship with the therapist that will facilitate the formation of new relationships with others.

Quintana updated this developmental conceptualization of termination to focus greater attention on the client's contribution to the therapeutic progress. He indicated that therapy is a process of continuing maturation of the client, and that termination is a time to call attention to the client's growth and the therapist's support of the client's progress. Quintana believed that termination is an opportunity to review the client's role in the therapeutic progress. In this way, the client clarifies what he or she did to facilitate change, and should problems arise after termination, the client may use these techniques to handle them. Finally, Quintana endorsed a conceptualization of termination as a sad time because of the loss of the relationship with the therapist that is tempered by the knowledge that the client has outgrown the relationship. Thus, termination represents a time to bid farewell to therapy and move on to new relationships. Quintana compared termination to graduation.

III. EMPIRICAL RESEARCH

Even though termination occurs in all therapy relationships very little research has been conducted on the termination process. Simon Budman and Alan Gurman suggested in 1988, that for many clients, therapy is an ongoing activity in their lives. They presented evidence that the majority of clients have had previous therapy, and 50 to 66% of clients who terminate will return to therapy within a year. This would tend to dampen the loss felt at termination, because therapy would not really be terminated in the sense that most clients return for further help in the future.

In 1985, Judith Marx and Charles Gelso asked 72 former clients at a university counseling center to indicate the most common behaviors and feelings surrounding their therapy terminations. Over 70% of the sample stated that they and their therapists summarized the therapy, assessed goal attainment, and planned for the future. Contrary to expectations, clients indicated significantly more positive than negative emotions surrounding termination. Clients also reported that more termination work was done when loss had been a theme of therapy, when the client had a closer relationship with the therapist, and when there had been more therapy sessions. The results supported a developmental view of termination rather than a conceptualization of termination as a crisis or loss.

In 1992, Stephen Quintana and William Holahan extended Marx and Gelso's research to therapists by asking 85 therapists what termination activities they engaged in and having them rate their clients' reactions to termination. Each therapist was asked to choose two recent short-term therapy cases—a case in which the therapy outcome was successful and a case where the therapy outcome was unsuccessful. Like Marx and Gelso, Quintana and Holahan found that clients' reactions (as rated by their therapists) to therapy termination were significantly more positive than negative. Not surprisingly, in unsuccessful cases, clients were significantly more likely to devalue therapy. The ranking of termination activities by therapists corresponded closely to client rankings of activities in the Marx and Gelso study. In successful cases, however, therapists were more likely to discuss the course of counseling, client affective reactions to termination, and the end of counseling than in unsuccessful cases. This research suggested that therapists did a more complete job of discussing termination issues with clients from successful therapy cases than from unsuccessful cases.

In 1993, Susan Boyer and Mary Ann Hoffman tested the hypothesis that therapists' reactions to termination would be affected by the impact of previous losses in their lives and their perceptions of clients' sensitivity to loss. They asked 165 licensed psychologists each to think of a client that they had seen for a minimum of 25 sessions. Therapists rated how sensitive they perceived these clients were to loss. Therapists also answered questions about their own grief reactions to past and present losses as well as questions about their perceptions and feelings surrounding termination with the client. They found that therapists' past grief reactions, present grief reactions, and perceived client loss predicted therapists' anxiety surrounding termination. Therapists' loss and perceived client loss, however, were unrelated to therapists' feelings of satisfaction with termination.

IV. SUMMARY

Termination is the capstone of psychotherapy. It should be a time when all that has gone before is discussed and solidified before the client leaves. Yet we know little about the process of termination. The results of the few studies of termination process suggest that for most clients and therapists psychotherapy termination is a relatively positive event rather than a traumatic loss. These findings support Qunitana's notion that termination serves a developmental function in which clients bid farewell to a relationship that they have outgrown. Loss appears to play a role in termination particularly when client and/or therapist have suffered past or present losses. In these cases, therapists are frequently more anxious about terminating, and loss is an important part of client–therapist termination discussions.

Study results show that most termination discussions cover what transpired during treatment, participants' feelings, and plans for the future. This seems to be particularly true when the outcome of therapy has been positive. When therapy has not been as successful, however, there is less discussion of the end of therapy, clients' reaction to termination, the course of therapy, and the client–therapist relationship. Thus, unsuccessful therapy is mirrored in a less thorough termination experience.

Much more research on the psychotherapy termination process is needed. Many variables need to be explored relative to termination. In particular, it is important to study client and counselor characteristics as they relate to the termination process.

See Also the Following Articles

Bioethics ■ Cost Effectiveness ■ Engagement ■ Informed Consent ■ Outcome Measures ■ Relapse Prevention ■ Resistance ■ Working Alliance

Further Reading

Gelso, C. J., & Woodhouse, S. S. (2002). The termination of psychotherapy: What research tells us about the process of ending therapy. In G. S. Tryon (Ed.), *Counseling based on process research: Applying what we know.* Boston: Allyn and Bacon.

Hill, C. E., & O'Brien, K. M. (1999). *Helping skills: Facilitating exploration, insight, and action.* Washington, DC: American Psychological Association.

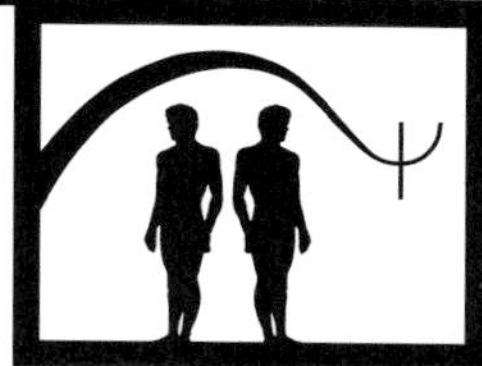

Therapeutic Factors

T. Byram Karasu

Albert Einstein College of Medicine/Montefiore Medical Center

GLOSSARY

analytic (or psychodynamic) therapy A primarily long-term, in-depth treatment concerned with conflictual intrapsychic forces, especially early libidinal urges and repressed childhood memories, which are uncovered and worked through via the interpretation by the analyst of the meaning of the patient's verbalizations.

behavior therapy (or behavior modification) Techniques of conditioning, shaping, and/or training—usually active, structured, time-limited, and directive—for the alteration of maladaptive symptoms and behaviors.

cognitive therapy A form of behavior therapy that addresses irrational beliefs and distortions of thinking, based on the fundamental idea that how a person perceives and structures the world determines personal feelings and behaviors.

existential approach (or analysis) A form of therapy that posits that a person's decisions, commitment, and responsibility for "choosing the future" give meaning to life, whereas choosing the past leads to boredom, meaninglessness, and despair.

interpersonal therapy A form of treatment that focuses on current life events—especially grief, developmental transitions, role disputes, and social deficits—based on the fundamental thesis that disorders are the result of unsatisfactory relationships and social maladaptation, the consequence of the individual's attempts to adapt to surroundings.

spiritual therapy A form of treatment based on six tenets of transcendence of soul and spirit—love of others, love of work, love of belonging, belief in the sacred, belief in unity, and belief in transformation.

I. INTRODUCTION

In an attempt to comprehend therapeutic factors in the total range of psychological treatments, one needs to differentiate the nonspecific elements that all psychotherapies are presumed to share, and the specific elements that may distinguish one school from the others. This article discusses the former under the headings of affective experiencing, cognitive mastery, and behavioral regulation, and the latter under the headings of analytical, behavioral, and experiential schools, each with its own variations. The therapeutic aspect of the therapist–patient relationship is discussed in its various forms: transferential and working alliances, and teacher–pupil and person-to-person relations. In clinical practice, these therapeutic factors are not categorical distinctions, but overlapping phenomena. An integration of past and present therapeutic factors is proposed.

II. NONSPECIFIC THERAPEUTIC FACTORS

The following features have been repeatedly cited as basic to all psychotherapies: an emotionally charged, confiding relationship; a therapeutic rationale (myth) that is accepted by patient and therapist; the provision of new information, which may be transmitted by precept, example, and/or self-discovery; the strengthening of the patient's expectation of help; the provision of success experiences; and the facilitation of the arousal of one's emotions. In their 1980 comprehensive analysis of the benefits of psychotherapy, Mary Lee Smith, Gene V. Glass, and Thomas I. Miller concluded that the weight of the evidence that now rests in the balance so greatly favors the general factors interpretation of therapeutic efficacy that it can no longer be ignored. Thus, above and beyond (or in addition to) the specific features of major modalities that technically differentiate them from one another, a number of universal conditions of therapeutic change have been hypothesized that unite all forms of treatment.

Aside from equivocal research findings from extensive comparison studies of outcome, other lines of support have been cited for a universality thesis. These include cross-cultural, historical, and religious examinations of the recurrent nature of healing agents, particularly the "placebogenic" roles of suggestibility, persuasion, trust, and hope, in changing or curing patients throughout the ages; the paucity of proof that special technical skill, type of training, theoretical orientation, or professional discipline is significantly related to therapeutic results; and, within the past decade, controlled studies of some commonly shared ingredients of successful outcome.

A. Affective Experiencing

Some form of strong emotional arousal was probably the primary tool in the psychotherapeutic cures of primitive man. Often seances were conducted in the presence of a select group of individuals (the psychotherapists of their day), and emotional excitement was induced through smoking, drinking, drugs, and rhythmic music. Such affectively charged situations facilitated patient regression and eased the confession of sins. This type of affective purging process was the prototype for the earliest known structured psychotherapeutic attempt to deal with man's problems.

The specific Freudian version of this was the now-classic "cathartic method," whereby abreaction occurred, with the emergence of repressed memories through the technique of free association. Behavior therapies have also had their affective counterparts in reproducing anxiety-evoking stimuli in imagination or *in vivo* (with or without the accompaniment of relaxation techniques for purposes of systematic desensitization). Flooding and implosion procedures, for example, re-create high-intensity exposure to feared objects or situations, with the expectation that patients will experience their anxiety as fully as possible and, exhausted with fear and relief, will no longer respond as they used to. Similarly, aversion therapy, by presenting an unpleasant and sometimes painful stimulus, at least temporarily disrupts emotional equilibrium as a precursor of change through reconditioning.

By far the most extensive resurgence of the therapeutic use of emotional arousal and release occurs in the "experiential" approaches. Reichian therapy, Lowenian bioenergetics, and Rolfian structural integration aim to express the affect trapped in the body posture not by analyzing defensive character armor as Wilhelm Reich originally did, but by physically manipulating the muscles that underlie it. Psychodrama enacts the expression of feelings through dramatic improvisations, while uninterrupted lengthy marathon sessions seek emotional access through the by-products of physical exhaustion. Comparably, primal scream and Morita use prolonged isolation and sensory deprivation to lower resistance and break down cognitive defenses—the former expressed in a sobbing, screaming, seizurelike episode to recapture the pain of the primal past, the latter by activating anxiety and distress as a preparatory step toward the creation of a state of spiritual readiness for rediscovering the beauty of life. A basic rationale for such diverse methods is that they aim to facilitate therapeutic change by producing excessive cortical excitation, emotional exhaustion, and states of reduced resistance or hypersuggestibility.

Emotional arousal is one of the major effective ingredients of successful psychotherapy. Following a strong abreaction, there occurs a period of exhaustion that produces heightened acceptance in which the patient appears bewildered, dependent, and eager to find a comforting solution from the therapist. Three experiments by Rudolf Hoehn-Saric in 1978 showed that heightened arousal made patients more receptive to suggestion and therefore more willing to change attitudes than they were under low-arousal conditions. Arousal combined with cognitive confusion yielded even better results than arousal in patients with undisturbed cognitive functions. Heightened arousal under conditions of cognitive disorganization helped to "unfreeze" attitudes necessary for change. Thus, affective experiencing—as a universal change agent in the psychotherapies—may be globally defined as arousing excitement and responsiveness to suggestion: unfreezing and expression of feelings.

The major roles and functions of affective experiencing thus are to set the emotional state for receptivity to change, to ease the cathartic release of repressed material, and to facilitate patient accessibility by reducing resistance and breaking down defenses. In short, the patient, through the dislodging of persistent chronic attitudes, is made more available for a new cognitive paradigm. However, Hoehn-Saric's results also reflect the finding (often observed clinically) that intense emotional arousal, however profound and necessary to set the stage for therapeutic change to occur, is difficult to sustain. Attitude changes that occurred were short-lived, and repeated interventions were required for such change to be established into a more stable new position. This observation parallels Sigmund Freud's earlier acknowledgment of the limitations of the cathartic method and his significant theoretical transition from release of repressed affects and traumatic memories to their systematic exploration and understanding, that is, from catharsis to insight as the ultimate aim of therapy. It is also consistent with the research conclusion that although heightened arousal under conditions of cognitive organization helps to unfreeze an attitude, it does not necessarily lead to a new solution unless it is followed by cognitive learning.

That is, perhaps the major role of affective experiencing is to emotionally prepare the patient for new cognitive input. Indeed, pure catharsis is considered most effective only in certain limited psychiatric conditions. Moreover, "peak experiences," which may offer attractive opportunities for rapid change, often do not carry over beyond the immediate encounter. In fact, when three therapy groups of differing duration were compared, the curative value of catharsis appeared to diminish in the longest-term group. Thus, some form of affective experiencing appears to be universally applicable, but perhaps largely as a preliminary stage of treatment. Ideally, this means that it should be succeeded by, or combined with, other therapeutic agents that have complementary roles and functions, to maximize or prolong its effectiveness.

B. Cognitive Mastery

All therapies, in some measure, provide the patient with cognitive mastery, whether they offer the classical, well-timed interpretations of Freudian psychoanalysis or, as in Albert Ellis's rational-emotive therapy, have the therapist "sing along" with the patient a litany of the patient's irrational false beliefs. Cognitive mastery thus refers to those aspects of treatment that use reason and meaning (conscious or unconscious) over affect as their primary therapeutic tools, and that attempt to achieve their effects through the acquisition and integration of new perceptions, thinking patterns, and/or self-awareness. A prototype of a cognitive change agent is the therapeutic application of insight, defined as the process by which the meaning, significance, pattern, or use of an experience becomes clear—or the understanding that results from this process.

Historically, primitive faith healing and the early stages of psychotherapy were very much alike in that neither initially attempted to provide insight. However, while faith healing continued only to maximize suggestion (essentially through affective experiences), Western psychotherapy became distinctive in departing from the primitive mode by moving into a second state—to correct problems by explaining them rationally. Going somewhat farther along this line, although the foundation of all therapies is the phenomenon of therapeutic suggestibility, primitive therapies are based almost entirely on irrational belief and dependency, whereas Western scientific therapies are more often founded on rational insight and independence.

Insight (through free association and interpretation) has been considered a *sine qua non* of the psychoanalytic process, yet all psychotherapies provide opportunities for change through cognitive channels—by means of explanation, clarification, new information, or even confrontation of irrational and self-defeating beliefs. Behavior therapies, once considered the antithesis of an insight-oriented approach, have increasingly incorporated cognitive learning techniques into their repertoire. Over time the behavioral model of treatment has radically changed from that of conditioning to social learning and information processing. The behavioral technique of thought stopping developed by David Wolpe, a cognitive variation of classical conditioning methods to extinguish anxiety, can be considered an early example of this change in approach. Albert Ellis's rational-emotive therapy, William Glasser's reality therapy, and Aaron Beck's cognitive therapy all share in direct attempts to correct stereotyped, biased, or self-defeating thinking patterns and dysfunctional attitudes and values, whereas others, like Victor Frankl's logotherapy and William Sahakian's philosophical therapy, are directed to the most profound cognitive reappraisals of life and its meaning. Even the most actively experiential therapies use cognitive techniques; for example, Gestalt "experiments" can be considered cognitively as a structured interpretation.

Thus, cognitive mastery as a universal therapeutic agent may be defined as acquiring and integrating new perceptions, thinking patterns, and/or self-awareness, whether this is effected through interpretations, explanations, practical information, or direct confrontation of faulty thoughts and images. In contrast to affective experiencing, it serves as a rational component of treatment—to inform, assess, and organize change and to establish or restore ego control. Despite their therapeutic utility in providing a new perspective, meaning, or way of thinking, cognitive approaches are not always sufficient as change agents. Put succinctly, not all change is attributable to insight and not all insight leads to change.

In the final analysis, the criteria for attaining lasting insight must be judged by its personal and social consequences. In short, new thinking (or insight) that has been achieved in therapy must be worked through and incorporated into one's actions and behavior in everyday life; it must be transferred from the structured and safe confines of the therapist's office and put into active practice in the real world outside treatment. Thus, cognitive mastery, like affective experiencing, needs to be complemented by other therapeutic change agents. More specifically, although an affective experience may prepare the patient for cognitive learning, the latter requires gradual assimilation and behavioral application of new input, if therapeutic effects are to endure.

C. Behavioral Regulation

Behavior modification approaches have directly sought behavioral change as an active goal, and learning to self-regulate or control one's habitual responses has become the thrust of their therapeutic efforts. Methodologically, this has meant the use of an extensive repertoire of reinforcement and training techniques based on research in experimental animal and human social learning laboratories—from classical conditioning to explicit rewards and punishments, to shaping and modeling methods in imagination and *in vivo*.

Nonetheless, as already implied, behavioral regulation as a major change agent is no longer limited to the classical confines of a conditioning model; nor is it restricted to the immediate territory of the behavior therapies. Even psychoanalysis, which has been considered relatively weak as a model for behavioral change, and whose therapists must ideologically refrain from direct suggestion or deliberate manipulation, is by no means exempt from the use of behavioral regulation, at least implicitly. All therapies, albeit in less systematic and sometimes unintentional ways, use methods of behavioral reinforcement, feedback, and modeling. Analytic interpretation influences behavior by labeling, defining a problem, providing permission, implying a course of action, facilitating foresight, and the like. Indeed, research has experimentally demonstrated that subtle cues can shape the responses of patients. Examination of actual excerpts of Carl Rogers's so-called nondirective therapy confirmed that even incidental nods or "hmms" by the therapist positively reinforced client responses. On a more inaccessible level, unconscious identification with the therapist is considered an essential aspect of shaping and modeling the patient's behavior. In the final analysis, all therapy may be a matter of emotional, cognitive, and behavioral learning.

III. SPECIFIC THERAPEUTIC FACTORS

Although universal features undoubtedly exist, this does not mean that we must *ipso facto* minimize differences in psychotherapy. There are comparative conceptual studies of various forms of psychotherapy that typically cite striking contrasts among them. More recently, experimental studies of different schools have lent some scientific support to the separatist stance. Exemplary of such findings are the systematic studies of analytically oriented psychotherapy versus behavior therapy, supporting the view that these are highly contrasting styles of treatment. Moreover, the treatment procedures created, developed, and chosen in one society or within the context of a particular belief system, may not be transposable to another. This is especially evident in attempts at cross-cultural psychotherapy.

The current state of the art attests to the lack of clarity and lack of resolution of the specificity versus nonspecificity controversy in explaining what is the quintessence of the therapeutic cure. This conflicting state of affairs is further compounded by comparative studies of various psychotherapies, which suggest that one's espoused theoretical orientation regarding the nature of the healing process may not always be synchronous with one's actual practices. In a comparison research study of Freudian, Kleinian, Jungian, and Gestaltist therapists, descriptive ratings of the different approaches in action did not differentiate the respective schools of thought, the investigators (and, no doubt, the proponents themselves) naturally expected.

A. Analytical Schools

For the analytic therapist the ultimate task, in its most parsimonious and famous form, is to make conscious the unconscious. The ongoing therapeutic charge is to facilitate the emergence and comprehension of unconscious content. That is, such a therapist seeks to undo the repressed material of the patient and to overcome the patient's natural resistances to this endeavor. The therapist attempts to accomplish this by means of a slow and scrupulous unraveling of the largely historical meanings of mental events and the characteristic ways in which they may serve to ward off the underlying conflicts through defensive camouflage. Understandably, the analytic goal is thereby a long-range one, perhaps even interminable. At best this concept of cure means opting for total personality reorganization in the final resolution of neurotic conflicts. The most crucial manifestation of this is the resolution of the Oedipal conflict, which is traditionally regarded as requisite for a healthy personality. This ultimate integration of personality would translate itself into final mastery of ego over id impulses or, as classically stated by Freud, "where id was, there ego shall be."

There are believed to be four successive stages in attaining therapeutic insight: (1) preparation, which is characterized by frustration, anxiety, a feeling of ineptness, and despair. It may be accompanied by much trial-and-error activity relevant to the solution of a certain problem and the falling into habitual patterns or ways of thinking, foreseeing no apparent solution to the problem; (2) incubation or renunciation, in which one desires to hide or escape from the problem and is resistant or unmotivated in therapeutic or insightful efforts; (3) inspiration or illumination, in which the whole problem becomes illuminated, and a solution or solutions suggest themselves (often there is a flood of vivid ideas and a sense of finality accompanied by a conviction in the truth of the insight); and (4) elaboration and evaluation, in which the validity of the insight is checked against external reality.

Furthermore, insight is most therapeutic when it meets all of the following specifications: (1) consistency, whereby the deductions based on the original insight are stable and logically sound, regardless of the truth or falsity of the particular content of the insight; (2) continuity, whereby insights must take place within some existing theoretical framework or stream of tradition in which the insight can be tested; (3) personal consequences, whereby the insight must be judged by the fruit it bears in terms of the ultimate use to which the insight is put; and (4) social consequences, whereby the acquisition of insight should allow the person to interact with others in a more honest and meaningful manner.

1. Variations on the Analytical Theme

The prototypic embodiment of the psychoanalytic or psychodynamic theme is, of course, classical psychoanalysis. The variations on the dynamic theme reflect overt and covert modifications of theoretical conceptualizations as well as methodological and technical applications in practice. These include attempts to partially or completely transcend the biological focus of Freud with more interpersonal, social, ethical, and cultural considerations (e.g., Alfred Adler, Karen Horney, Harry Stack Sullivan, Erich Fromm, Frieda Fromm-Reichmann, and Alfred Meyer); to extend or enhance the ego with earlier or more adaptive endowments (e.g., Federn and Melanie Klein); to enlarge man's temporality with a time focus on his primordial past (e.g., Jung), his present and/or his future (e.g., Adler, William Stekel, Otto Rank, and Rado); to expand treatment procedures by altering the range and goals of treatment (e.g., Otto Rank, Franz Alexander, Helena Deutsch, and Albert Karpman); to shift from ego to self psychology (e.g., Heinz Kohut), to narcissism as a character disorder (e.g., Otto Kernberg) to develop guidelines for short-term psychotherapy with anxiety-provoking techniques (e.g., Peter Sifneos), and even brief treatment of serious illness within the context of a single interview (e.g., David Malan); to revise the role of the therapist's personality and relationship to the patient by making the therapist a more direct, flexible, and/or active participant (e.g., Adler, Sullivan, Rank, Alexander, Stekel, Sandor Ferenczi, and Victor Rosen); to emphasize the developmental approach to diagnosis and treatment (e.g., T. Byram Karasu, James Masterson) at perhaps the opposing end of the analytic spectrum, to restore the psychophysical balance of man by focusing equally on the physical half of the psychophysical split (e.g., Sandor Rado and Jules Masserman) and/or substituting an approach to therapeutic cure from the somatic side by trading the traditional change mode of insight for a reversal back to the earlier catharsis by means of the bodily release of conflictual tensions (e.g., Wilhelm Reich).

The fundamental goals of the interpersonal approach relate to the need to maintain good interpersonal relations and social adaptability; they include reconstruction of present maladaptive relationships and, where possible, restoration of past losses. This means both coping with immediate stressful interactions and forming better or new relationships by developing problem-solving strategies and mastery in social skills. In 1984 Gerald Klerman and Myrna Weissman formulated a short-term, manualized form of interpersonal therapy (IPT), specifically applicable, but not limited to, depression.

In practice, a seasoned dynamic therapist is more broadly defined. This refers to the integration of drive, ego, object relations, and self approaches, and to the more global synthesis of conflict and deficit models.

This integrative model of psychotherapeutic practice acknowledges the joint impact on psychic structure formation of unresolved conflictual urges and wishes interfaced with early environmental deficiencies and traumas in the real-object world of the patient. In terms of treatment, it recognizes the pivotal roles of both erotic and narcissistic transferences in the therapist–patient relationship and in the respective stances and strategies of the listening and empathic presence.

B. Behavioral Schools

For the behaviorist, all problems are construed as pedagogical in nature, and therefore alterable only through direct teaching and learning of new behavioral associations, that is, stimulus–response connections. The patient must be taught new alternatives that have to be repeated and practiced within as well as outside the therapy situation. These alternative modes of functioning do not occur simply as a concomitant of cognitive or emotional understanding of one's problems—the patient needs to rehearse the new alternatives directly. Thus, in direct contrast to the psychodynamic schools, the behavioral approaches have tended to sustain the view that insight is not only unnecessary but can hinder the treatment of deviant behavior.

One implication of the behavioral view of the mode of therapeutic action is that change can presumably occur within a short period of time. In contrast to the dynamic therapists, behaviorists generally believe that all treatment of neurotic disorders is concerned with habits existing in the present, and their historical development is largely irrelevant. Moreover, some behaviorists have even suggested that it is possible to have a situation in which symptoms have been removed, with no knowledge at all their etiology.

Although all behaviorists may be viewed as seeking change through direct conditioning, shaping, or training, the classical conditioning paradigm sees all therapeutic learning or change (not just behavior therapy) as occurring within the reciprocal inhibition framework, incorporating the substitution of relaxation for anxiety in the reduction or elimination of symptoms. However, more critically, the difference between behavior therapy and other therapeutic modalities is that in the latter, counterconditioning of relaxation over anxiety occurs indirectly unsystematically, whereas in behavior therapy this process is overt, systematic, and under the direct control of the therapist.

In Jan Ehrenwald's 1966 words, the behavioral schools of psychotherapy actively relinquish "the methods of the couch" and replace them with "the methods of the classroom and the pulpit." Behavior therapists have at their disposal a large variety of conditioning, training, and other directive techniques. This repertoire may include any or all of the following: the more classical conditioning techniques of systematic desensitization combined with deep muscle relaxation, implosion, or assertiveness training; the operant techniques of positive or negative reinforcement, such as aversiveness training; shaping or modeling; and/or the direct transmission of advice, guidance, persuasion, and exhortation. The latter methods more typically reflect the means by which behavior modification has been extended recently to the teaching or conditioning of attitudes underlying specific behaviors, methods of philosophical indoctrination, or cognitive programming.

The behavioral counterpart of the psychodynamic procedure of working through is behavioral rehearsal within the confines of therapy, as well as assignments to be worked on outside of therapy; these are important parts of the total regimen. For example, the patient might be directly trained in certain social skills that may first be role-played or rehearsed within the course of therapy, and then explicitly instructed and tested out in outside, real-life situations, and reviewed in subsequent sessions.

1. Variations on the Behavioral Theme

Three broad types of behavior therapies or behavior modification are considered under the umbrella of the behavioral theme: one, based on the early classical Pavlovian paradigm, primarily uses systematic desensitization or extinction of anxiety techniques (e.g., reciprocal inhibition therapy); a second type, based on an operant paradigm, uses direct reinforcement by means of reward/punishment procedures (e.g., token economy); and a third type, based on a human social learning paradigm, is contingent on direct modeling or shaping procedures (e.g., modeling therapy). The last type extends to a variety of new systems of directive psychotherapy that expressly aim at attitudinal or philosophical restructuring, albeit using methods of the behaviorist's laboratory. Such so-called integrity therapies share the fundamental learning or problem-solving stance, yet are usually more actively advisory and/or exhortative in their therapeutic techniques (e.g., Albert Ellis's rational therapy. William Glasser's reality therapy, and William Sahakian's philosophic psychotherapy).

Another way of viewing the scope of these behavioral variations is through the evolution of their targets of change, from external to internal alterations in man's learnings. The earlier behavior therapeutic systems addressed overt behaviors and fears (e.g., Wolpe); the more recent systems are directed to more covert values and beliefs (e.g., Ellis). The most contemporary approaches even venture into the reaches of inaccessible and involuntary mental and physiological states and responses, such as heart rate, blood pressure, and brain waves (e.g., biofeedback).

Whereas in typical behavior modification, alterations in overt behavior are viewed as an end in themselves, with the cognitive approach they are considered a means to cognitive change. In 1979, Aaron Beck formulated a short-term, manualized form of cognitive-behavior therapy (CBT). The goals of this approach have been succinctly stated as: (1) to monitor negative, automatic thoughts (cognitions); (2) to recognize the connections between cognition, affect, and behavior; (3) to examine the evidence for and against the distorted automatic thoughts; (4) to substitute more reality oriented interpretations for these biased cognitions; and (5) to learn to identify and alter the dysfunctional beliefs that predispose the person to distort his or her experiences.

The major cognitive aims or processes of change have four successive components: recognition of faulty thinking through self-monitoring, modification of thinking patterns through systematic evaluation, empirical testing of the validity of automatic thoughts and silent assumptions, and self-mastery by means of homework and everyday practice on one's own. The initial phase of treatment, which aims at symptom reduction, emphasizes the recognition of self-destructive thoughts, whereas the subsequent phases, which aim at prophylaxis, concentrate on the modification of specific erroneous assumptions within and outside the treatment sessions. To isolate, control, and change illogical thinking—the cognitive concept of cure, treatment is organized to elicit and subject to rational examination the actual mental contents of conscious depressive ideation (current automatic thoughts, silent assumptions, attitudes, values, daydreams) and to trace their impact on dysphoric feelings and behaviors in current concrete situations. CBT has recently been applied to disorders other than depression. Its ultimate purpose is self-control and self-mastery—patients explicitly rehearse and train themselves to recognize and restructure their own faulty cognitions so that they can cope better in the future.

C. Experiential Schools

The experiential schools of psychotherapy trade intellectual cognition and insight for emotion and experience, forsaking the there and then of the distant past for the here and now of the immediate present. Experiencing is a process of feeling rather than knowing or verbalizing; occurs in the immediate present; is private and unobservable, but can be directly referred to by an individual as a felt datum in his own phenomenal field; acts as a guide to conceptualization; is implicitly meaningful, although it may not become explicitly so until later; and is a preconceptual organismic process. The many implicit meanings of a moment's experiencing are regarded not as already conceptual and then repressed; rather, they are considered in the awareness but as yet undifferentiated. Here therapeutic change occurs because of a process of experiencing in which implicit meanings are in awareness, and are intensely felt, directly referred to, and changed—without ever being put into words.

One variation of this thesis, especially applicable to Roger's client-centered therapy, reflects the underlying positive belief that every organism has an inborn tendency to develop its optimal capacities as long as it is placed in a optimal environment. The patient is offered an optimistic self-image and the understanding that the patient is basically good and full of potential. Therefore, the therapist does not need to challenge or shape the patient, only to offer a warm and understanding milieu that will enable the patient to unfold latent potentials.

Unlike transference, which is dependent on the revival of a former interpersonal relationship, experiential encounter works through the very fact of its novelty. Through encounter the therapist serves as a catalyst in whose presence the patient comes to realize his or her own latent and best abilities for shaping the self. In this behalf, there are schools of psychotherapy within the experiential theme that recoil at the idea of therapeutic technology. These schools, which are predominantly existential, renounce technique as part of their philosophy of understanding human existence. They feel that the chief block in the understanding of man in Western cultures has been an overemphasis on technique and a concomitant tendency to believe that understanding is a function of, or related to, technique. Rather, they feel that what distinguishes existential therapy is not what the therapist would specifically do, but rather, the context of the therapy. In other words, it is not so much what the therapist says or does, as what the therapist is. However, in this regard the existential schools of psychotherapy have been criticized for their vagueness about technical matters in the conduct of psychotherapy.

The experiential schools aspire to flexibility or innovation in their actual methods, as long as these methods are useful in the therapist's attempt to experience and share the being of the patient. Here the aim of all techniques would be to enter the phenomenological world of the patient. In direct contrast to the view of the analytic therapist, the experiential therapist does not concern himself or herself with the patient's past, the matter of diagnosis, the aspiration of insight, the issue of interpretation, or the subtle vicissitudes of transference and countertransference. Unlike the behavioral therapist, the experiential therapist expressly does not set goals for the patient and does not direct, confront, or otherwise impose his or her personality on the patient with directives in the form of behavioral instructions or problem-solving preferences.

Although they share the same basic faith in the therapeutic encounter and an emphasis on feelings, schools under the experiential umbrella are often antiverbal in approach. Such schools (e.g., Gestalt therapy) view overintellectualization as part of the patient's problem, that is, a manifestation of defense against experiencing or feeling, and discourage it as part of the therapeutic endeavor. These therapies attempt to accentuate activity over reflection, emphasize doing rather than saying, or, at the minimum, aim to combine action with introspection. The goal of experiencing oneself includes developing the patient's awareness of bodily sensations, postures, tensions, and movements, with an emphasis on somatic processes. Awareness of oneself as manifested in one's body can be a highly mobilizing influence. The main thrust of therapy is therefore to actively arouse, agitate, or excite the patient's experience of self, not simply to let it happen.

Among the techniques for expressing one's self-experience in such schools is the combination of direct confrontation with dramatization, that is, role-playing and the living out of a fantasy in the therapeutic situation. This means that under the direction (and often the creation) of the therapist, the patient is encouraged to play out parts of the self, including physical parts, by inventing dialogues between them. Performing fantasies and dreams is typical and considered preferable to their mere verbal expression, interpretation, and cognitive comprehension. In variations of the somatic stance, body and sensory awareness may be fostered through methods of direct release of physical tension, and even manipulations of the body to expel and/or intensify feeling.

In yet other attempts to unify mind, body, and more especially, spirit, the immediate experience of oneself by focusing on one's spiritual dimension is sought. This is most often accomplished through the primary technique of meditation. The ultimate state of profound rest serves to transcend the world of the individual ego, forming a higher reality or state of consciousness that the individual ego subserves. Major methods of will training and attention focused on a special word sound or mantra, for example, serve to create an egoless transcendent state.

1. Variations on the Experiential Theme

The therapeutic systems that have evolved under the experiential theme represent various approaches, each propelled by the immediate moment and geared toward the ultimate unity of man. These include the following: (1) a philosophic type, which reflects existential tenets as a basis for the conduct of psychotherapy and pivots on the here-and-now mutual dialogue, or encounter, while retaining essentially verbal techniques (e.g., Carl Roger's client-centered therapy and Victor Frankl's logotherapy; (2) a somatic type, which reflects a subscription of nonverbal methods and aspiration to an integration of self by means of focusing attention on subjective body stimuli and sensory responses (e.g., Fritz Perls' Gestalt therapy) and/or physical motor modes of intense abreaction and emotional flooding in which the emphasis is on the bodily arousal and release of feeling (e.g., Alexander Lowen's bioenergetic analysis and Janov's primal scream therapy); and, finally, (3) a spiritual type, which emphasizes the final affirmation of self as a transcendental or transpersonal experience, extending one's experience of self to higher cosmic levels of consciousness that ultimately aim to unify one with the universe. This is primarily accomplished by means of the renunciation of the individual ego. The establishment of an egoless state can occur by meditation (i.e., relaxation plus focused attention) in which one reaches a state of profound rest (e.g., Transcendental Mediation). Such a spiritual synthesis may be amplified by various techniques of self-discipline and will training, for example, practice of disidentification (e.g., Assagioli's psychosynthesis).

A most recent "variation on a theme" crosses the boundaries of the above three schools. Dialectical Behavior Therapy (DBT), originated by Marsha Linehan, Ph.D., in 1993, empirically supported multimodal psychotherapy, initially developed for chronically parasuicidal women diagnosed with borderline personality disorder (BPD). DBT blends standard cognitive-behavioral interventions with Eastern philosophy and meditation practices, as well as shares elements with psychodynamic, client-centered, Gestalt, paradoxical, and strategic approaches. DBT structures the treatment hierarchically in stages. It is based on Linehan's biosocial theory, whereby etiology of this dysfunction lies in the transaction between a biological emotional vulnerability and an invalidating environment.

IV. THE RELATIONSHIP AS THERAPEUTIC FACTOR

The patient's relationship to the therapist embodies one of the most powerful forces in the therapeutic enterprise. Psychotherapeutic changes always occur in the context of an interpersonal relationship and are to some extent inextricable from it. In the next section, these therapeutic relations are discussed under the three headings of transferential–therapeutic; teacher–pupil; and person–person. Again, they are far from being categorical distinctions. Rather, they simultaneously occur in different combinations and emphases.

A. Transferential Relations and Working Alliances

Deliberate, systematic attention to the vicissitudes of the special relationship between therapist and patient is crucial to the conduct of the psychoanalytic approach. It constitutes both the subject and the object of analysis. Historically, two stances—transferential versus nontransferential—have been described in portraying the psychodynamic psychotherapies: the primary stance with regard to the making of the transference relationship and, more recently, the secondary stance with regard to the making of a working or therapeutic alliance. Despite increasing acceptance of combining them in the therapeutic situation, these represent dual postures, even antithetical to each other, both in their essential purposes and in the actual requirements they make of the therapist.

The primary stance reflects Freud's original recommendations: (1) that the analyst be like a mirror to the patient, reflecting only what is reflected by the patient and not bringing personal feelings (attitudes, values, personal life) into play; and (2) that the analyst follow a posture of privation or rule of abstinence, that is, technical motives must unite with ethical ones in preventing the therapist from offering the patient the "love" that the patient will necessarily come to crave. These two basic requirements are traditionally made of the analyst, if the analyst must remain relatively removed and anonymous, a deliberately dispassionate observer and reflector of the patient's feelings. Such a therapeutic relationship is necessarily asymmetrical.

Conversely, the more recent concept of a working or therapeutic alliance reflects an alternatively nonregressive, rational relationship between patient and therapist. Although still in the service of analyzing transference and resistances, it means that the therapist aims at forming a real and mature alliance with the conscious adult ego of the patient and encourages him or her to be a scientific partner in the exploration of these difficulties. The real object need of the patient, deliberately frustrated by the transference relationship, is relatively satisfied by the therapeutic alliance. This therapeutic alliance has several variations and names, that is, working alliance, holding environment, corrective relationship, and empathic relationship. For example, self psychology introduced a new concept to psychology—the self, an experiential construction, the perceiver's own experience. Here the therapist provides an empathic atmosphere to foster development of a coherent self, and facilitates not so much insight as transmuting internalization, to crystallize the self. He or she is therapeutic through contemporary self-object functions for the self within an interpretive framework.

B. Teacher–Pupil Relations

The nature of the therapeutic relationship between therapist and patient in the behavioral therapies is an essentially educative, teacher–pupil relationship. It is a deliberately structured learning alliance in which, at its best, attention is drawn to the more current and presumably constructive aspects of the patient's personality in collaborating on the course of therapy. Here the behavior therapist has been depicted as a learning technician or social reinforcement machine. Although this rubric may apply to all therapies to greater or lesser degrees, usually the behavioral therapist openly regards him or herself as an instrument of direct behavioral influence or control, one who directly and systematically manipulates, shapes, and inserts individual values in the therapeutic encounter. In a comparable context, the therapist shapes personal behavior so as to be a social reinforcer for the patient. If the therapy does not proceed smoothly or effectively, the behavior therapist revises the behavioral plan or schedule to better fit the patient to treatment.

Behavior therapy deliberately does not dwell on the therapist–patient relationship; at most, it does so secondarily, only to the extent that this is seen to be important in securing the patient's cooperation with the therapist's treatment plan. The behavior therapist's use of warmth, acceptance, and any other relationship skills is common but relegated to the realm of secondary "relationship skills" that are not crucial therapeutic requirements for desired change to occur in the patient.

The term *collaborative empiricism* has been coined to characterize the major therapeutic relationship in cognitive therapy—CBT, a specific form of behavior therapy for treatment of depression—in which the therapist is continually active and deliberately interacting with the patient. The two participants have been further depicted as an investigative team; the content of each depressed thought is posed as a hypothesis to be tested by two scientists, who collect all the evidence to support or refute that hypothesis. Under the collaborative empiricism model, the major role of the therapist is primarily educative—to instruct and advise the patient in rational thinking and to provide active guidance during systematic reality testing, which is considered intrinsic to the cognitive approach. The therapist actively points out automatic thoughts, helps to identify cognitions from the patient's report of recent experiences, reviews patient records, assigns homework, and provides concrete feedback. Often part of this tutorial approach is a direct problem-solving, question-and-answer format, with which the therapist and patient can jointly explore the patient's cognitions.

Interpersonal therapy (IPT) shares elements with both the psychodynamic and cognitive approaches as it addresses four major foci or problem areas: interpersonal role disputes, especially between family members; difficult role transitions in coping with developmental landmarks or significant life events, such as getting married or divorced, having a child, changing careers or retiring from work; interpersonal deficits, including inadequate social skills; and abnormal grief reactions. It emphasizes the solving of interpersonal problems and entails supportive and behavioral strategies as well as both directive and nondirective exploratory methods—information, guidance, reassurance, clarification, communication skills education, behavioral modification, and environmental management. Didactic education techniques and environmental interventions are largely used in initial efforts to ameliorate overt symptoms, whereas support, exploration, behavioral modification, and social skills training are subsequently applied to specific interpersonal issues.

C. Person-to-Person Relations

Although methods may vary, the real here-and-now therapeutic dialogue or mutual encounter, between therapist and patient is the *sine qua non* of many of the experiential schools. It is an emotionally arousing human relationship in which each person tries to communicate honestly, both verbally and nonverbally. These approaches to psychotherapy ideologically aspire to an egalitarian treatment model. The human alliance is not of analyst to patient or teacher to student but of human being to human being. Here the therapist is still presumably an expert; but, if he or she is not first of all a human being, the expertness will not only be irrelevant, but even possibly harmful. Rogers stated that if the patient is viewed as an object, the patient will tend to become an object. Therefore, this type of therapist says in effect: "I enter the relationship not as a scientist, nor as a physician who can accurately diagnose and cure, but as a person, entering into an interpersonal relationship." Naturally, what one construes to fall within the domain of personal or real in a therapeutic relationship is open to interpretation. The state of the art of therapeutic factors suggests that new paradigms are necessary to combine and transcend diverse perspectives of schools. As there are transcending nonspecific elements, there are also transcending dimensions to all specific therapeutic relations and techniques.

The psychotherapeutic relationship possesses certain qualities of other relationships, such as between parent–child, teacher–student, and friend–friend, but it is also quite different from them. It is not natural, induced, or intended. It seems spontaneous but is not random, in fact, calculated. It has an intuitive quality but is learned, in fact, cultivated. It seems informal, but is quite serious. There is a system to this relationship—psychotherapy requires the systematic use of the human relationship. Based on the degree of consolidation of the patient's psychic apparatus, the therapist may modulate his or her activities to establish and maintain the relationship with the patient, no matter what technique used; and he or she may use any technique. Yet all techniques are implemented interpersonally, even prescribing of a medication.

The relationship is potentially a healthy medium in and of itself. The cumulative aspect of the interpersonal relationship was an inspiration for the emergence of the Sullivanian school. For analytically oriented therapists, their schools' contributions of four patient–therapist relationships (transferential, therapeutic alliance, object relations, self-object) are diagnostic and formative. The analytical therapist's first task is to establish a relationship, but the second task is to explore what that relationship reveals. For the nonanalytical practitioner, there are the patient's relational predispositions. The therapist does not need to use the relationship as a formative technique but must be aware that whatever technique used, these relationships will come to play.

V. AN INTEGRATION: THE PAST AND THE FUTURE

With shifting paradigms, every therapist must synchronize with the patient, not unlike meshed teeth of a cogwheel, and become a presence in the patient's psychic life. The technique evolves from such a presence. It has been said that the relationship is never sufficient. The technique alone is not feasible. The first task, the most fundamental technique, would be how to establish and maintain the therapeutic relationship. The second task is to apply any technique that is potentially useful and within the range of the therapist's competence and patient's receptivity.

Finally, we must not forget that there were "therapeutic factors" long before such a term was invented. Our professional ancestors used overarching teachings of their religions, the knowledge of their times, and their cultural myths in the service of the healing arts. Today, we can benefit from our professional ancestors by learning ways of the soul and the spirit, and by incorporating these into "spiritual psychotherapy," as recently described by T. Byram Karasu. Six tenets of transcendence incorporate the fundamental thesis that the way to soulfulness is through love—love of others, love of work, and love of belonging; and the way of spirituality is through believing—belief in the sacred (reverence for all life), belief in unity (i.e., oneness with nature and the universe), and belief in transformation (i.e., sense of the continuity and renewal of the life cycle)—the combination of which may turn out to be the superordinate therapeutic factors.

See Also the Following Articles

Behavior Therapy: Theoretical Bases ■ Cognitive Behavior Therapy ■ Existential Psychotherapy ■ Interpersonal Psychotherapy ■ Patient Variables: Anaclitic and Introjective Dimensions ■ Psychoanalysis and Psychoanalytic Psychotherapy: Technique ■ Working Alliance

Further Reading

Bugental, J. (1987). *The art of the psychotherapist.* London: Norton.

Friedman, A. (1988). *Anatomy of psychotherapy.* Hillsdale, NJ: The Analytic Press.

Karasu, T. B. (1992). *Wisdom in the practice of psychotherapy.* New York: Basic Books.

Karasu, T. B. (1996). *Deconstruction of psychotherapy.* Northvale, NJ: Jason Aronson.

Karasu. T. B. (1999). Spiritual psychotherapy. *American Journal of Psychotherapy, 53,* 143–162.

Karasu, T. B. (2001). *The psychotherapist as healer.* Northvale, NJ: Jason Aronson.

Pine, F. (1990). *Drive, ego, object and self.* New York: Basic Books.

Sheihk, A., & Sheihk, K. (1996). *Healing east & west: Ancient wisdom & modern psychology.* New York: John Wiley and Sons.

Weil, A. (1995). *Spontaneous healing.* New York: Fawcett Columbine.

White, M. (1993). *Therapeutic conversations.* New York: Norton.

Wilson, E. O. (1998). *Consilience: The unity of knowledge.* New York: Knopf.

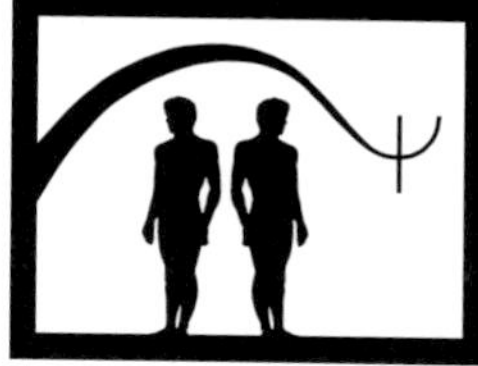

Therapeutic Storytelling with Children and Adolescents

Everett K. Spees
Devereux Cleo Wallace

GLOSSARY

arousal A heightened emotional or cognitive state in response to sensory input or internal neural stimuli.

attunement Alignment of the therapist and clients' emotional states so that each can experience the other's subjective world. This permits the sense of emotional communication and connection often described as "being together" and "feeling felt." The nonverbal signs of eye contact, body gestures, facial expressions, and tone of voice communicate the state of mind of each member of a dyad through the orbitofrontal cerebral cortex. Neurophysiological mechanisms use these stimuli to integrate several domains of the human experience, including emotional regulation, response flexibility, consciousness, social relationships, and the evaluation of meaning. Misattunements lead to emotional dysregulation, which require "interactive repair" through a sufficient number of beneficial interpersonal experiences for the child or adolescent to achieve or regain emotional regulation. Storytelling supports the "secure attachment" developmental state. This state tolerates arousal of excitement, interest, and enjoyment, and emotional resonance, which allows these pleasure effects to persist.

imagery The arousal of mental images through sensory neural stimuli.

resonance The mutual emotional alignment of the mental states of two individuals that persists within the mind of each individual after the direct interaction is no longer present. Secure developmental attachments allow children to tolerate the resonance of high-intensity emotional states without discomfort, while children with less secure attachments may experience affect blocking.

transitional phenomena Refers to a metaphorical dimension of living that does not belong to an external or internal reality, and a place that both connects and separates outer and inner. Donald Winnicott conceived of it as the area where cultural experience, creativity, playing, stories, and being occur. Contemporary developmental neurobiologists relate transitional phenomena to the complex neural interactions observed in attunement and resonance.

> ***The stories that people tell are the container that holds their world together and gives meaning to their lives.***
>
> *Andrew Ramer*

I. DESCRIPTION OF TREATMENT

Stories within a psychotherapeutic setting can facilitate positive interpersonal interaction between therapist and client, and can provide emotional enrichment and inner cognitive resourcefulness. Either therapist or client, in individual, family, or group therapy, may initiate the story. The setting can be a private office or an inpatient or outpatient institutional facility.

Both client and therapist often experience pleasure and camaraderie from following unwinding plots that stimulate mental images through curiosity, dilemma, suspense, delight, fear, and relief. Intimacy can occur because both therapist and client reveal much of themselves, their personal interests, values, attitudes, and playfulness. Clients may be able to speak of their issues more comfortably and indirectly in story or metaphor form than in explicit conversation. Developmental neurobiologists have suggested that metaphoric and story experiences help young people to organize emotions and integrate social experience through a process of "interpersonal neurobiology" of the developing mind.

Of particular value in therapy are young people's autogenic (spontaneous) stories, metaphors, and self-narratives, because these encode information about their developmental experiences, emotional maturity, and ability to achieve interpersonal synergy. The therapist who uses storytelling skillfully with these goals in mind can often build an alliance with young patients.

Early in the first encounter a well-chosen story may allay some of the child's natural anxiety, fear, and distrust, while energizing memory, emotion, and self-awareness. As psychotherapy progresses, stories can continue to serve treatment goals. Often the mutual exploration of an evolving spontaneous metaphor becomes the core of the helping enterprise.

One of the author's 7-year old clients enthusiastically referred to the stories in the therapy sessions as "word movies," thereby innocently naming the pleasant images he had experienced. At the start of each group session he would eagerly ask, "Will we have word movies today?"

Useful resources are increasingly available for the therapist interested in developing a storytelling approach, and customizing it to the specific client needs and clinical settings. Planning the therapist stories in advance, selecting an environment free of interruption, and orchestrating the necessary neurobiological dynamics that accompany effective storytelling, is necessary to optimize their therapeutic value. These necessary dynamic elements include attunement, resonance, imagery, modeling, transference, countertransference, social interaction, and interpretation, as shown in Table I.

TABLE I

Developmental, Neurobiological, and Dynamic Principles in Storytelling Sequence

Storytelling component	*Developmental/neurobiological correlate*
Private area	Allows focusing on group experience
Free of interruptions	Fosters attunement and resonance
Familiar staff members present	Provides comfort, safety, and trust
Drama, animation, stage props	Activates five senses, emotional arousal
Audience vocal participation	Activates interpersonal awareness
Vaguely mysterious storyteller persona	Excites curiosity, memories, images
Children gather around	Corporate experience is to be shared
Name recognition	Each child recognized, valued
Refocusing client's attention	Attunement gateway to rich experience
Storyteller's first story	Example of model structure to be realized
Children participate	Child plays role in enactment of model
Applause, discussion	Recognition, gratitude, challenging
Feedback from the children	Each child's peer input valued, used Opportunity for meaning making
Children volunteer their story	Permission to resonate and experiment New insights on personal self-narrative
"Storyteller hat," "storyteller seat"	Child earns status from staff and peers Social rewards for risk taking
Applause, discussion	Child's risk-taking is reinforced by peers Value of peer approval is learned
Staff attention to emotion and content	Can we decode child's emotional clues? What themes trigger arousal or anxiety?
Revealing autobiographical narratives	Child risks self-disclosure
"Oscar" calls	Narrative bridging object
Assessing the emotional experience	Transference, countertransference, synergy?

The mix of each of these elements varies with who is present at the storytelling session, who tells the stories, how interesting and well-told the stories are, how the group interacts socially, and many other factors. Because of the calls to memory and the unconscious, no two storytelling experiences are ever identical for an individual participant. Listening to children's after-story interpretations makes that phenomenon clear. Each child hears a unique story, and each storytelling is a unique never-to-be-repeated telling for the storyteller, because it is mysteriously nuanced by the presence and interaction of the listeners.

Knowledge of current literature and resources in storytelling presented in this article may facilitate selection, creation, and use of story techniques that can be shaped to specific client circumstances through the art of the therapist, and the use of client autogenic stories.

II. THEORETICAL BASIS

Storytelling and metaphors supplied by psychotherapists and clients are a universally recognized resource for developing rapport with children, and a technique that has a venerable reputation among psychotherapists since the early work of Helmut von Hug-Hellmuth, a Vienna psychiatrist, in 1913. He liked to make up disguised stories with young clients that might begin, "I used to know a little boy a lot like you who used to wet his bed, too, but he learned how to get over it." Over time the client would gradually begin to guess that he himself was the true protagonist, the "little boy" in the therapist's story.

Contemporary and later influential psychotherapists such as Sigmund Freud, Carl Jung, Anna Freud, Bruno Bettelheim, Milton Erickson, and Erik Erikson also advocated their own distinctive theories and treatment goals in the use of stories and metaphors, and commented on their relationship to play and dreams. David Gordon wrote in 1988, "Metaphors, in the form of fairytales, parables, and anecdotes, are consciously and unconsciously used by therapists in order to assist a client in making changes he wants to make."

Freud, through analysis of his own dreams, as well as those of his patients, gradually became aware of the resemblance of dreams to Greek tragedies and to mythology. Using the Sophocles *Tragedy of King Oedipus,* Freud made his interpretation of the Oedipus myth into one of the cornerstones of his scientific psychological system. He came to believe that the "Oedipus complex" was a critical key to the understanding of the history and evolution not only of social interaction, morality, and religion, but of normal and abnormal child development as well. As he put it, the Oedipus complex, with its unconscious guilt of imaginary patricide and incest, was "the kernel of neurosis." Carl Jung carried his teacher's ideas even further. He observed early in his psychoanalytic training that the powerful revelational emotional reactions and remembered experiences that occurred through the language of dreams, stories, metaphors, and childish play might relate to the presence of universal unconscious archetypes or archaic symbols that operated in the unconscious. Because of his theory that in the unconscious of modern man existed a vestige of the active mind of primitive man that was overtaken by later concessions to logic and written language, he later referred to archetypes as natural symbols or primordial images. The extensive findings of similar archetypal themes in his investigation of primitive cultures and myths from around the world, and in studies of medieval alchemy symbols, reinforced the validity of Jung's concept of archetype.

This wider cultural anthropological theme was further developed by Jung's friend Joseph Campbell, whose *The Hero with a Thousand Faces* in 1968 popularized Jung's concept of a universal subconscious archetype by showing the remarkable similarity of myths and legend themes from many unconnected cultures of the present and past. Not surprisingly Campbell's favorite lifelong venue was the New York Museum of Natural History.

Freud, Jung, and Campbell also called attention to important gender themes in human development. Myths and fairy stories frequently depict conflicts between maternal and paternal imperatives metaethically encoded in matriarchal and patriarchal social systems. These powerful archetypal images arouse both conscious and unconscious emotions. Homer's *Odyssey* provides us good examples in the protagonists Odysseus and Penelope. Penelope, the matriarch, embodies love, fidelity, care, and nurture and protection of children. She values ties to her (and Odysseus's) bloodline, ties to the earth (a live tree branch grows through the marital bed), universality, tolerance, acceptance of natural phenomena, longing for peace, and tender humanness. The woman's womb may produce many brothers and sisters to every human being, and all should have a chance to thrive. Meanwhile, Odysseus, the patriarch, embodies the archetype of adventurousness and risk-taking, obedience to divine authority, and a hierarchical order in society. In place of the feminine concept of equality of offspring and impartiality toward each, with Odysseus we encounter the concept of the favored son. Odysseus is as sexually promiscuous as his wife is chaste. He is crafty and ruthless in combat and takes the lives of many mothers' sons in order to win honor and fame for himself. He pillages cities, takes his enemies' treasure and his enemies' wives and children as slaves or concubines, and desecrates nature by killing bulls, cutting down trees, making bonfires, and raising elaborate buildings. Through recklessness and offense to the gods he loses all his comrades, ships, and plunder, and returns home alone to desolated families, leaving a trail of corpses behind. He arrives home just in time to slaughter all of Penelope's suitors, thereby keeping his honor and winning more fame. Having no womb to make children, the patriarchal archetype makes words, fame, commerce, theology, waste, and war.

In the Judeo-Christian Scriptures God is envisioned as a patriarch and patron, whose preexistence and authority mysteriously emanated from "the Word." The Gospel of St. John begins with the patriarchal vision, "In the beginning was the Word, and the Word was with God, and the Word was God." These gender themes preserved since the dawn of the human record continue to be relevant to the world we now inhabit, and are alluded to in a recent genre of gender psychology books that began with John Gray's *Men Are from Mars, Women Are from Venus.*

David Hicks, Headmaster at Darlington School, in Rome, Georgia, commented in a homily in 2001 on the persistence of metaethical archetypal themes, "Now, the influence of the world and the mind runs both ways. The world ultimately reflects the minds of those who inhabit it. At the same time, our minds mirror the world we inhabit" (and, we might add, the stories that reinforce these archetypes).

Using storytelling and metaphor allows the therapist access to a domain of childhood usually off limits to adults because storytelling can bypass both client anxiety and emotional resistances.

Richard Kopp in 1995 classified these resistances as both those known to the client (secrets actively avoided) and not known to the client (unconsciously avoided), both of which can be a barrier to learning the issues that prevent "living a free and full life." Because it specifically avoids confronting resistances, storytelling to and by children is usually more successful than direct questioning in assessing a child's attitudes, emotional intelligence, moral intelligence, assumptions, inner drives and conflicts, and the child's developing self-narrative. With children in groups, important information about the social interaction with peers and caregivers can also be assessed. Storytelling is also compatible and used with every major discipline of psychotherapy, and many psychotherapists use stories routinely.

III. APPLICATIONS AND EXCLUSIONS

The author conducts a regular weekly storytelling group for children ages 5 to 12 at a 300-bed child and adolescent psychiatric facility in Westminster, Colorado. One group of clients is inpatient, one is a day hospital group, and another a public school day-hospital group. Group size varies from 5 to 15. In addition, the author regularly uses selected storytelling along with autogenic autobiographical poems and fairy tales in a weekly adolescent values group with 10 to 20 clients ages 12 to 18. Because the ability to fathom abstract ideas and to activate the imagination is a necessary part of understanding metaphor and stories, young clients who suffer from, for example, developmental disability, obsessive–compulsive disorder, psychosis, or profound sedation from psychotropic drugs may not be able to benefit from storytelling. These children may have such a limited vocabulary or a concrete or unimaginative perception that the point of proverbs and metaphors may be a complete mystery to them. In fact, in every storytelling group the ability of children to attune, resonate, focus, engage, and interact varies, depending on many factors, including their developmental level, their degree of anxiety, their psychoactive medication, their underlying behavior disorder, and their ability to be playful.

For these reasons advance consultation with unit staff in planning a group helps the storyteller therapist understand each child's handicaps as well as to avoid distractions and logistical missteps. Children who are oppositional, acting out, or completely somnolent due to medication are best excluded from the storytelling activity group until their behavior permits their ability to participate and not distract others. On the other hand even some children who speak slowly or have speech impediments, are shy, or have other difficulties, should be allowed and encouraged to tell their stories if possible, and the therapist leader should help the other group members to be patient and respectful of the handicapped individual. This models the social values of tolerance and compassion. The presence of familiar unit staff members to calm or redirect children who are inattentive or who "act out" during a group is essential, since the storyteller is engaged and cannot take time out to deal with unexpected individual behavior. Fortunately the enthusiasm carried over by children and staff from week to week often makes the storytelling group familiar, popular, eagerly awaited, and fun. Because children are aesthetically discriminating, quality stories may help children overlook distractions. Both children and adolescents prize stories that are imaginative, dramatic, novel, subtle, intricate, and well told. Not infrequently children will request repetition of a story that they liked from the previous week.

IV. EMPIRICAL STUDIES

The quest for identifying the exact neurobiological pathway(s) by which storytelling and metaphor connects with development, consciousness, and unconscious goes back as far as Friederich Nietzsche, who coined the term "the third ear" in *Beyond Good and Evil* in 1886. Nietzsche proposed that with this imaginary extra ear we are able to hear and recognize the metaphorical language of our intuition.

J. L. Despert and H. W. Potter in 1936 reached the following conclusions from their clinical experience in therapeutic storytelling:

1. The story is a form of verbalized fantasy through which the child may reveal his or her inner drives and conflicts.
2. A recurring theme generally indicates the principal concern or conflict, which in turn may be corroborated with other clinical evidence (e.g., dream material).
3. Anxiety, guilt, wish fulfillment, and aggressiveness are the primary trends expressed.
4. The use of stories appears to be most valuable when the child determines the subject of the story.
5. The story can be used as both a therapeutic and an evaluation device. These observations are still valid.

Donald Winnicott wrote in 1971 of a "third area" of reality, as a dimension in which cultural experience is located between interior and exterior reality. He speculated that in this third area the young person experiences play, humor, metaphor, and stories as "transitional phenomena." Winnicott believed that the role of the child psychiatrist was to help the child who was unable to play attain the state of being able to play, and that "psychotherapy takes place in the overlap of two areas of playing, that of the patient, and that of the therapist."

Winnicott also described his experience with finding an unconscious meeting ground with children. He wrote of a "sacred moment" in the initial interaction of client and therapist when the child, aided by storytelling, believes that he or she is being understood in a common metaphorical language. He noted that the function of this sacred moment could either be to allow deep work during the first interview or serve as a "prelude to longer or more intensive psychotherapy."

Bettelheim, like Winnicott, was also highly aware of the "enchanted moment and place" phenomenon that stories could provide. He pointed out in 1975 an important subtlety of Grimms' and other traditional fairy tales: "The unrealistic nature of these tales ... is an important device, because it makes obvious that the fairy tale's concern is not useful information about the external world, but about processes taking place in an individual." Milton Erickson, who was himself a gifted and creative storyteller and metaphor artist, theorized in 1979 on the basis of extensive hypnotherapy experience that the location of the "third ear" of Nietzsche or "third area" of Winnicott was a specialized neuroanatomical site in the right cerebral hemisphere containing the primary process locus for processing not only metaphorical language but psychosomatic symptomatology as well. Erickson believed that this anatomical localization could account for the more rapid improvement in psychosomatic complaints when metaphorical and hypnotherapy rather than standard psychoanalytical approaches were employed.

Neurobiological research with infants by Daniel Siegel in 1999 and by Alan Schor in 2001 and the earlier work of Daniel Stern has identified primary processing in human preverbal and verbal stages of development that correlates with the appearance of symbolic and metaphoric thought, often described as nonlinear, nonsequential, metaphorical, and nonlogical. This neurofunctional distinction was made to contrast it to cognitive thought, which is said to be linear, sequential, nonmetaphorical, and logical S. Engle in 1999 theorized that this primary processing helps explain the objective basis by which self-composed stories may serve as the "most essential symbolic process" for reflecting on and describing experiences. Siegel, a developmental neurobiologist, described findings that the mind encodes internal and external experiences represented in different forms and creates a sense of continuity across time by linking past, present, and future perceptions is within the narrative process. The autobiographical self-narrative is a key evolving integrative process that influences the nature of interpersonal relationships, and is central to secure attachment relationships, and to how one constructs reality. These and other developmental findings about childhood and adolescence suggest ways to use neurobiologically advantageous strategies for storytelling with young clients suffering from mental or behavior issues.

In case there has been any doubt about the significant role of storytelling, Siegel stated that from the developmental neurobiological standpoint, "Storytelling becomes a proxy to the damaged or missing attachment relationships that are causing emotional despair and rebellion."

The hospital setting for a child away from family and among strangers and peers with behavioral problems may not seem so hospitable or safe. Consequently the therapeutic storyteller must make efforts to create a safe, comfortable, quiet environment so that each child can process as much sensory experience and emotion from the stories as possible, and feel free to contribute autogenic stories. The identification and timing of neurobiological factors, as well as psychodynamic concepts that can optimize the storytelling and autogenic narrative process, are summarized in Table I. The observation that adults outside the mental health setting also benefit from directed storytelling suggests that the effect is perennial and universal. Business leaders have recently written about the benefits of storytelling in the workplace to promote morale and teambuilding.

Theologians in recent years have reemphasized the narrative structure of the Scriptures and recommended narrative technique for homilies and teaching. More recently the U.S. Military Academies Academy Character and Leadership Divisions have adopted the practice of bringing in distinguished retired military officers to tell young cadet classes their personal stories of moral leadership struggles. For mentoring, small groups of cadets are given the opportunity to team with these elders.

The foregoing data support the author's belief that therapeutic storytelling facilitates the development of beneficial interpersonal relationships between client and therapist. Although each person experiencing a story has a unique psychic experience, stories activate important emotional and cognitive neural pathways that promote emotional enrichment and inner cognitive resourcefulness. Clarissa Pinkola Estes, the Jungian psychotherapist, poetic storyteller, and author of *Women Who Run With the Wolves,* once commented that we humans come not only from dust, but from stardust as well.

For children and adolescents whose brief life history has often been filled with grievous injustices such as parental neglect, physical and sexual abuse, violence, rejection, arrests, and pain, the redemptive personal attention, respect, ability to win peer approval, and the chance to develop a self-narrative through storytelling sessions may reopen an area of development and relationships that had been sealed. By approaching a side door rather than the main door, psychic resistance can often be bypassed so clients can willingly enter into a health-restoring personal psychotherapy program, the goal of which is to promote social and emotional maturation and healthy personal autonomy.

V. CASE ILLUSTRATIONS

Therapeutic storytelling preparation begins with finding and using or reworking story sources. Each therapist probably has at least a few and perhaps many favorite stories, and we encounter new stories daily in the various media. In general, little of the available children's story literature is immediately appropriate for psychotherapy storytelling. However, many of the following resources have been useful to the author in understanding, selecting, and working with a broad spectrum of storytelling options and psychotherapeutic approaches.

Jack Zipes' retranslation of classical folktales and his astute commentary on their archaic and modern cultural context, including feminist revisions, has enhanced their usefulness to psychotherapy. His books, such as *The Oxford Companion to Fairy Tales* in 2000, provide the therapist with a good background analysis of the genre. The Zipes references, taken in chronological order published from 1989 to 2000, make a thorough introduction to storytelling, as well as reviewing the state of academic "fairytale-ology." Bruno Bettelheim, who was intrigued by fairy tales and used them in therapy with adolescents, took off a year on sabbatical to write a book discussing his application of Freudian analysis to selected Grimms' (and other) fairy tales, and his 1975 publication *The Uses of Enchantment,* has been well received. Bettelheim's opinion was that fairy tales attract us because they permit our vicarious wish fulfillment in a seemingly perfect enchanted world. At the same time he said they help to affect sexual drives in a positive way, thus aiding resolution of oedipal tendencies and sibling rivalry.

Zipes, a nonpsychologist, disagreed with Bettelheim's analysis, writing that the appeal of the stories was more likely due to our desire to deal indirectly with repressed modern issues such as parental abuse, neglect, brutality, and our parental desire to abandon our children. Zipes wrote in 1995 that traditional fairy stories were originally written in raw detail for adults, and that the substitution of happy endings in order to dilute them for children was a travesty.

Ronald Murphy, a Jesuit priest and professor of German, pursued the religious themes in Grimm's fairy tales. Murphy journeyed to Germany for a detailed study of personal books, manuscripts, annotated personal Bibles, and other Grimm family items. In *The Owl, The Raven, and the Dove* in 2000, Murphy reconstructed from notations and background material in these original sources, the influences of Christian theology, oral culture, and German pagan mythology, choosing five selected fairy tales edited by Wilhelm Grimm.

William Bausch, another Catholic priest, published an extensive anthology of multicultural stories in several books (1996 to 1999), including *The Wizard of Oz*, with commentaries, which are potentially useful in psychotherapy, religious education, and homily composition. Recently other concerned educators have compiled story anthologies directed toward moral education of young people.

A recurrent dilemma in preparing traditional folktales or stories so that they are age appropriate and suitable for young mental health clients is how to maintain the charm and feel of the stories while making them more contemporary for young listeners. Ideally one should aim to preserve the authenticity, flavor, and meaning of the archaic story, as much as possible, although finding ways to deal with brutality, anti-Semitism, and sexual offenses may be a struggle.

John Stephens and Robyn McCallum in their 1998 *Retelling Stories, Framing Culture: Traditional Story and Metanarratives in Children's Literature*, showed how in traditional folktales and legends the encoded metaethics might impact the hearer on a deep moral or social level. They summarize the not-so-obvious cultural and ethnic baggage directed at the original audience, which they term the metanarrative in epics such as *The Arabian Nights*. In their opinion such ancient tales may transmit "implicit and usually invisible ideologies, systems, and assumptions that operate globally in a society to order knowledge and experience." Obviously the psychotherapist needs to consider these cultural and ethical overtones carefully for their positive or negative impact on today's clients.

Several resources have targeted specific children's behavioral health problems, such as kidney failure, bedwetting, and chronic illness, and the stresses from disruption of family life by divorce, useful for therapists who prefer modern stories. George Burns in his *101 Healing Stories: Using Metaphors in Therapy* in 2001 ranks high on the list of useful resources. Burns not only provides numerous engaging therapy stories, but he comprehensively discusses how to identify story resources from our own life experiences, from our patients, and from the secular world. He gives detailed, thought-provoking advice on how-to, and how-not-to develop and use stories with clients, and how to select and shape stories for specific client needs. Unlike other literary presentations, he comprehensively lists and discusses his interpretation of the psychodynamic themes in each of his healing stories from a psychoanalytic standpoint.

Lee Wallas in 1985 contributed 19 lively stories that she developed spontaneously in her Ericksonian hypnotherapy practice. She examines her personal experiences and insights about how she happened to hit upon these themes and develop the stories in the course of treating clients with various neuroses.

Richard Gardner in 1993 published his mutual storytelling techniques, *Storytelling in Psychotherapy with Children*, in which he relies upon autogenic (spontaneous undirected) stories told by the client, sometimes involving hypnotherapy. Gardner's therapeutic technique evolves from intense involvement with the client in therapy and, like Wallas, using reflections about the client's clinical problem as the kernel of a new story within the same metaphor and with the same characters used by the client. The therapist then tells the unique "new story" to the client in a way that suggests alternative methods for the client to deal with the problem issue(s). Gardner elaborates on further innovations including dramatized mutual storytelling, storytelling games, and bibliotherapy (the use of books in the therapeutic process).

Gardner's colleague, Jerrold Brandel in *Of Mice and Metaphors* in 2000, described his personal experience and his own modifications of Gardner's reciprocal storytelling technique. Brandel used the term "re-visioning" for his method of modifying struggling youngsters' own stories therapeutically and then "bouncing them back" to the client with the remedial editing and interpretation as part of a dynamic storytelling game. He might inquire of the client, for example, "How would you like this story to end?"

In 1997 Carlissa Pinkola Estes compiled a collection of deep and thought-provoking feminist fairy tales, *Women Who Run With The Wolves*, in both print and audiotape. She has used these in Jungian psychotherapy and hypnotherapy. Her tapes, published by the Sounds True Company in Boulder, Colorado, are a fascinating resource for grasping the immense possibilities of psychotherapeutic storytelling. Her audio performance of Hans Christian Anderson's *The Red Shoes* is an excellent example. She follows the story with a detailed and valuable interpretation of the Jungian insights of the fable. This author has found this story compelling in sessions with adolescent clients, who unerringly relate the theme of self-destructive obsession to their own life situation.

Ellen Wachtel in her 1994 *Treating Troubled Children and their Families*, wrote about helping parents compose and tell stories to their child at home as part of his or her therapeutic program, especially when there is poor clinical progress with conventional treatment methods. She reminds us of the immense pedagogical and spiritual value of parental life anecdotes that satisfy the child's developmental need to assimilate family tradition and parental role modeling as part of a healthy attachment and evolving self-story.

Personal storytelling tutorials, for example Nancy Shimmel's 1992 *Just Enough to Make A Story*, offer useful guidelines and some prime examples. Her title story highlights human persistence and thrift, and the underlying purpose of stories. It is about a tailor who buys a bolt of cloth to make himself an overcoat. When the overcoat begins to wear out he cuts it into a jacket, after further wear he pares it down into a vest, then a hat, and finally there is only enough to make a button. When the button is worn out there is "only enough left to make a story."

Zipes, in *Creative Storytelling: Building Community, Changing Lives* in 1995, offers novel ideas and model tales for telling, although he shares his skepticism about using stories for psychotherapeutic goals. Several authors, including Gionni Ronardi in *The Grammar of Fantasy* in 1973 have given memorable advice on inventing stories for telling.

Internet resources are considerable, and include "The Storytelling Ring," a popular site with a variety of public domain story resources (e.g., the interesting Southern mystery stories at www.themoonlitroad.com or www.storyteller.net). Friends, relatives, and community members, and especially senior citizens, often have poignant or funny anecdotes that can be creatively reworked.

Therapists may wish to seek out community storytelling groups in order to observe presentation techniques and content. Even more useful is the easily obtained opportunity to volunteer as a storyteller at a local library or elementary school. Another resource is the Storytelling Magazine and the live storytelling festival audiotapes of the National Storytelling Network.

A. Immediate Preparation

Ideally, the therapist should review the story list prior to the session. Preparation includes memorizing newly adapted stories, rehearsing, and developing an agenda on the evening before a group. When only one story is to be used the author selects it to fit a specific topic and proverb for that day. For example, if the group topic is coping with adversity, a story of the "Rapunzel" genre might fit.

B. Running the Group

A comfortable and private office is favorable for individual client stories during a treatment session. Storytelling with a group in a mental health center is more logistically demanding. One needs to find a space free of interruptions and arrange for familiar staff to be present.

Drama, animation, stage props, and audience participation enhance the choreography of this activity, while activating sensory and emotional pathways in the participants. Token costume items like a Turkish hat or cowboy jacket, according to the therapist's taste and intentions, can help the drama effect. The children gather around in chairs or sit on the floor with name cards in front of them so that the storyteller can identify and address each child by name. The first action of the group session is to refocus the children's attention by various techniques such as group singing, or asking the children to quietly listen to and identify various white noise sounds such as a downpour in a rainforest or a faraway train. These sounds can come from an inexpensive electronic generator operated by the storyteller. Alternatives might include juggling or harmonica playing by the storyteller.

Once attention is refocused, the storyteller begins, choosing first a story in which the children participate by repeating phrases, assuming roles, or making sounds to accompany the narrative. For example, in a story about a train trip designated children provide the sound effects of the "All aboard!," others the train wheels sound, and still others the train whistle at the appropriate times.

When the first story and applause are through, the storyteller asks for feedback from the children. What were their impressions and feelings during the story? What did the story mean to them? How did they feel when they were hearing it? Were they surprised or puzzled by some story element? Each child usually interprets the story somewhat differently. If a child is reluctant to share a personal interpretation, asking the child to briefly repeat the story aloud may be useful.

Next three children are recruited sequentially to tell an autogenic story. Offering the child a special "storyteller hat," and allowing the child to occupy a special "storyteller seat" can enhance the honor of this selection. Following each child's story there comes applause and feedback comments from the peers about each story. The staff and the therapist pay attention to the body language, facial expressions, emotion, and content of each child's story and the social interactions of others in the group. When clients tell revealing autogenic stories, their body language tends to become busier than usual. Sometimes a "poorly functioning" child surprises everyone with dramatic and sensitive stories, or with the ability to repeat someone else's story verbatim even though he appeared not to be paying attention.

Occasionally between stories the therapist's cellular phone "rings," because "Oscar" is phoning. The therapist explains that Oscar (the mythical caller and narrative continuity object) is a wizened old storyteller with a gruff voice. He "calls" to ask about the children's stories and describes where he is located geographically, and what his activities are. Recently Oscar reported that he was riding on a porpoise's back in the Bahamas.

The children are charmed but skeptical about Oscar. In every group meeting, and even in the cafeteria or while crossing the campus, the more experienced children ask the therapist whether Oscar will call in that day.

After three rounds of therapist and children's stories the author concludes the group by asking each child one-by-one to step up directly in front of him, hand the storyteller his or her name card, look the storyteller in the eye, and state which "word movies" he or she enjoyed. In that final moment of eye contact the therapist attempts to assess the magnitude, richness, and meaning of the emotional experience that child and the storyteller have shared during the hour, and to look for any signs of emotional upset.

VI. SUMMARY

Therapeutic stories generated by both therapist and client are valuable tools in individual and group therapy with children and adolescents. When used as part of any psychotherapeutic approaches they enhance the ability of the clients' developing minds to make beneficial alliances with staff and therapists, and to further develop their personal self-narrative. Developmental neurobiologists believe that storytelling acts as a substitute for unhealthy attachment relationships that are at the root of many behavioral disorders in children and adolescents. Taking advantage of the neurobiological and social mechanisms that occur during storytelling helps the therapist optimize the setting and choreography of storytelling.

In an era of cost-cutting pressure on behavioral health care providers, and an increasing reliance on psychoactive drugs, therapeutic storytelling as described in this article may be one of the truest forms of psychotherapy still being practiced. An important bonus to the use of stories is that they are a lively and enjoyable activity. Stories encourage children to share their experience and redevelop its meaning in an environment of human warmth, safety, trust, and curiosity.

Acknowledgment

This article could not have been completed without the impeccable assistance of Ms. Pam Roth, research librarian at Presbyterian/St. Luke's Medical Center in Denver, Colorado, and the help of my family.

See Also the Following Articles

Animal-Assisted Therapy ■ Art Therapy ■ Biblical Behavior Modification ■ Bibliotherapy ■ Child and Adolescent Psychotherapy: Psychoanalytic Principles ■ Dreams, Use in Psychotherapy ■ Emotive Imagery ■ Parent–Child Interaction Therapy ■ Primary-Care Behavioral Pediatrics ■ Transitional Objects and Transitional Phenomena

Further Reading

Anon. (1992). *A storytelling treasury.* Tales Told at The National Storytelling Festival. Five Audiotapes Recorded Live. Twentieth Anniversary Edition. Little Rock, AK: August House.

Bettelheim, B. (1975). *The uses of enchantment. The meaning and importance of fairy tales.* New York: Vintage Books.

Engel, S. (1999). *The stories children tell: Making sense of the narratives of childhood.* New York: W.H. Freeman.

Gardner, R. A. (1995). *Storytelling in psychotherapy with children.* Northvale NJ: Jason Aronson.

Kopp, R. (1995). *Metaphor therapy. using client-generated metaphors in psychotherapy.* New York: Bruner/Mazel.

Maguire, J. (1998). *The power of personal storytelling. Spinning tales to connect with others.* New York: Putnam.

Murphy, G. R. (2000). *The owl, the Raven, and the dove. The religious meaning of the Grimms' magic fairy tales.* New York: Oxford University Press.

Ronardi, G. (1973). *The grammar of fantasy. An introduction to the art of inventing stories.* New York: Teachers and Writers Collaborative.

Schimmel, N. (1992). *Just enough to make a Story: Inventing stories.* Berkeley, CA: Sisters Choice Press.

Siegel, D. (1999). *The developing mind. Toward a neurobiology of interpersonal experience.* New York: Guilford.

Spees, E. (2001). Stimulating emotional and moral intelligence: Innovative values groups for adolescents. *Annals of the American Psychotherapy Association, 4,* 14–17.

Stephens, J., & McCallum, R. (1998). *Retelling stories, framing culture. Traditional story and metanarratives in children's literature.* New York: Garland.

Wallas, L. (1985). *Stories for the third ear. Using hypnotic fables in psychotherapy.* New York: W.W. Norton.

Zipes, J. (Ed.). (2000). *The Oxford companion to fairy tales. The western fairy tale tradition from medieval to modern.* New York: Oxford University Press.

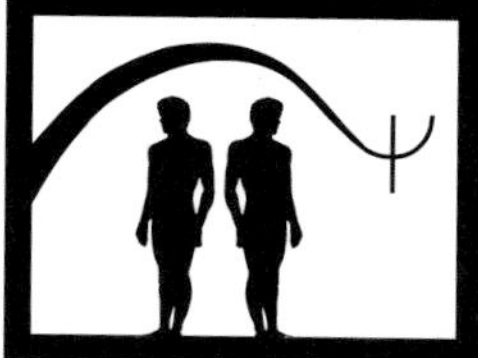

Thought Stopping

Melanie L. O'Neill and Maureen L. Whittal
University of British Columbia Hospital

GLOSSARY

counterconditioning A method to remove the original association between fear and the trigger for the fear and to replace it with a new trigger that is incompatible with fear.

covert sensitization A procedure in which an inappropriate response to a stimulus (e.g., a sexual response to children in an adult male) is broken by attempting to associate the stimulus with a new incompatible response (e.g., associating children with discomfort that may be produced by a puff of air in the eye).

escape conditioning A noxious stimulus is paired with anxiety/fear to terminate the fear and a more appropriate response is put in place (e.g., repeatedly pairing an intrusive thought with an electric shock. Over time the intrusive thought declines because of its association with the electric shock).

obsessive–compulsive disorder (OCD) An anxiety disorder that is characterized by the presence of obsessions and/or compulsions. Obsessions are defined as repetitive, unwanted, senseless thoughts, images, or impulses that may be repugnant or horrific. Compulsions are defined as overt behaviors or mental acts that are typically done in response to the obsession and function to decrease the anxiety. They are time consuming, excessive, and senseless. Persons are often aware that they are unnecessary but cannot stop themselves.

Thought stopping (TS) is a behavioral technique used to minimize the distress associated with unwanted intrusive thoughts. Clients are asked to sit with their eyes closed and verbalize a typical sequence of problematic thoughts. During this time the therapist suddenly shouts, "Stop!" The therapist then highlights that the thoughts did stop and proceeds to repeat the procedure several times until the client is able to subvocally disrupt the maladaptive thoughts.

I. OVERVIEW AND DESCRIPTION OF THOUGHT STOPPING

Joseph Wolpe describes TS as useful in the elimination of undesirable thoughts that are unrealistic, unproductive, and anxiety producing. Although used frequently by behavior therapists in the 1970s and early 1980s, TS has received relatively little rigorous empirical attention. Uncontrolled case studies and anecdotal reports of TS are generally favorable when used as both a stand-alone procedure or in conjunction with other cognitive and behavioral techniques. Our purpose is to summarize this work and draw conclusions about the usefulness of TS as a therapeutic technique.

Last, we will introduce a cognitive alternative to TS that has produced some initial success for clients with obsessive–compulsive disorder.

TS was introduced by James Alexander Bain and J. G. Taylor under the premise that thought control is important for positive mental health. Although TS is often viewed as an overly simplistic technique, it actually requires a thorough behavioral analysis. In 1977, Joseph Cautela and Patricia Wisocki suggest that the behavioral analysis should include a client's comprehensive list of disturbing and uncontrollable thoughts with particular importance placed on any overt or covert behaviors that have harmful societal implications (e.g., thoughts of seeking revenge).

Target thoughts are agreed on and the rationale for their elimination is discussed. Cautela recommends that clients be asked to close their eyes and raise their finger once deliberately thinking of the target thought(s). When the client raises a finger, the therapist loudly shouts "Stop!" that typically produces a startle response. The therapist explains that one is unable to think of two things at the same time (stop and the target thought[s]) and proceeds to teach the client the procedure for his or her own use by encouraging the the client to subvocally yell "Stop!" These rehearsals continue in-session for approximately 10 min or for 20 trials until the procedure is learned. Therapists emphasize that with the repeated and daily use of TS, the target thought(s) will gradually decrease in frequency until they disappear altogether. Subsequent sessions might allot 5 min for TS rehearsals including variations of the procedure (e.g., snapping a rubber band on the wrist instead of yelling "stop," substituting another word for "stop," visualizing a stop sign instead of yelling "stop").

II. THEORETICAL BASES

The theoretical underpinnings of TS are vague and sparse. Indeed, since the early 1970s, reservations concerning the adequacy of supporting theoretical arguments for TS have been expressed. Wolpe and Taylor did not discuss a conceptual basis for TS, however, Cautela and Wisocki suggested that the more likely interpretations include escape conditioning and counterconditioning.

Within the escape conditioning paradigm, TS functions to replace an inappropriate discomforting response with an appropriate alternative. In 1943, C. L. Hull contended that behaviors that reduce discomfort, such as anxiety, are associated with establishing a habit. Avoidance also strengthens a habit because it prevents clients from experiencing anxiety.

An anxiety-provoking thought is triggered by an internal or external cue. Counterconditioning is thought to function by replacing the old response with a new response in the face of the identical trigger. For example, once trained in progressive muscle relaxation, clients are instructed to think of the anxiety-provoking trigger while relaxed. The rationale behind this technique is that it is impossible to feel fear and relaxation at the same time. In 1958, Wolpe used a counterconditioning procedure and called it systematic desensitization. Cautela and Wisocki hypothesized that TS could be used to assist in the development of the new response.

III. EARLY EMPIRICAL STUDIES

Historically, TS was used in the treatment of obsessions, however, the technique has been used as an intervention for a variety of different disorders including smoking cessation, drug and alcohol dependence, psychosis, depression, panic, agoraphobia, generalized anxiety, and body dysmorphic disorder. Although numerous uncontrolled single case studies concluded that TS is a viable behavioral technique, there is little methodologically sound research with larger sample sizes to support the use of TS. After a thorough review of the literature in 1979, Georgiana Tryon concluded that the effectiveness of thought stopping had not been demonstrated. Another limitation preventing stronger conclusions about the efficacy of TS is the lack of a standard procedure when using TS. Many studies provide minimal detail regarding the procedure and use a variety of TS procedures in conjunction with various other techniques such as relaxation and self-monitoring.

TS is often used to treat obsessional difficulties. For example, in 1974 Raymond Rosen and Betty Schnapp reported that TS was helpful for a man who was ruminating about his wife's infidelities. In 1971, by instructing patients to snap a rubber band on their wrist in response to an obsessional thought, Michael J. Mahoney decreased the frequency of obsessive ruminations. In 1971, Toshiko Yamagami had success reducing color obsessions with four variations of TS. In 1982, Helen Likierman and Stanley Jack Rachman compared TS and habituation training for 12 individuals with obsessions and found little therapeutic benefit for both procedures. Of the six individuals in the TS group, four improved, one became worse, and, with one it was unclear.

TS has also been used in smoking cessation treatment. In 1974, Wisocki and Edward Rooney compared the effectiveness of TS, covert sensitization, and attention placebo in decreasing the number of cigarettes smoked. Initially, TS and covert sensitization significantly reduced smoking, however, this difference disappeared at 4-month follow-up. Another study conducted by Yves Lamontagne, Marc-Andre Gagnon, Gilles Trudel, and Jean-Marie Boisvert in 1978, compared four different treatments, including TS, group discussion, and wearing a badge, all with self-monitoring compared to self-monitoring alone. All treatments initially reduced the frequency of smoking; however, it was TS and self-monitoring that maintained a significant decrease at 6-month follow-up.

In another class of problems, Makram Samaan in 1975 reported that TS was successfully used to treat auditory and visual hallucinations in one client who did not experience a relapse 20 months after treatment. In 1979, John O'Brien applied TS to two cases of agoraphobia with no relapse at 1-year follow-up. However, the efficacy of TS is difficult to determine because the client received 1 year of treatment that included self-monitoring and some cognitive therapy. In 1978, John Teasdale and Valerie Rezin compared TS to placebo control for 18 individuals with symptoms of depression. TS had little effect in reducing the frequency of depressive thoughts or the intensity of depressed mood.

The previous paragraphs suggest that the efficacy of TS is based on single cases but its general usefulness is in question. Rachman and Padmal de Silva may have inadvertantly discovered one reason why TS is not helpful as a strategy. In a survey of people who lived in the general community, these researchers found that over 90% reported a multitude of intrusive thoughts, images, and impulses. The results of these and related studies suggest that experiencing unwanted intrusive thoughts is a completely natural, normal phenomenon. If so, the elimination of these thoughts through TS or other deliberate suppression attempts may be futile, at best, and harmful, at worst.

IV. THE IMPACT OF THOUGHT SUPPRESSION

Recent work in the area of thought suppression has confirmed that attempting to distract, ignore, or suppress thoughts may serve to increase their frequency. Dan Wegner's investigations on the effects of thought suppression have revolutionized the understanding of disorders characterized by persistent unwanted thoughts. In a series of two experiments, Wegner demonstrated that subjects who were asked to not think of a white bear during a 5-min time period actually thought of a white bear more frequently than another group of subjects who were told that it was okay to think of a white bear.

In a review of the literature in 1999, Christine Purdon indicated that thought suppression has now been identified as both a causal and/or maintaining factor in generalized anxiety disorder, specific phobia, posttraumatic stress disorder, obsessive–compulsive disorder (OCD), and depression. According to this line of research, purposely suppressing thoughts is associated with an unexpected and suprising increase in their frequency. For example, Paul Salkovskis and his colleagues in Great Britain have suggested that active and deliberate thought suppression in the form of neutralization is critical in the development of obsessions. Students who experienced frequent unwanted intrusive thoughts that they felt necessary to neutralize had their intrusive thoughts recorded and were asked to either neutralize the thought or distract themselves from it. Those students who neutralized the thought reported significantly more anxiety and a greater urge to neutralize when the thought was presented a second time.

V. A COGNITIVE ALTERNATIVE TO THOUGHT STOPPING

The work of Wegner, Salkovskis, and Purdon has demonstrated that thought suppression increases the frequency of the target thought(s). TS can be considered a form of thought suppression or control and will thus likely serve to increase the frequency of the thoughts. For example, if clients have a belief that they must be in control of their thoughts and emotions at all times, experiencing an unwanted thought (which we know from the work of Rachman and de Silva is a normal, natural phenomenon) will produce anxiety and the need to try to control the thought. Attempts at thought control often involve ignoring, distracting, or suppressing the thought. These strategies serve to increase attention to the thought process, likely making the thoughts more noticeable and seemingly more frequent. The apparent increase in the frequency of the unwanted thoughts likely serves to further heighten anxiety, attention to the thought process, and precipitate additional attempts at thought control. A vicious circle can quickly develop.

As part of recent developments in cognitive behavioral treatments for OCD, Maureen Whittal and Peter McLean have described a process coined "come and go." Clients are encouraged to experience the intrusive unwanted thought and not try to control it (i.e., do not try to ignore, suppress, distract or anything else that will serve to get rid of the thought). Rather, clients are instructed to let the thought leave naturally, typically when another thought logically takes its place. Clients are instructed to practice this "come-and-go" strategy and their usual style of thought control on alternate days and predict their anxiety and the frequency of intrusive unwanted thoughts on each of the days. Clients invariably predict that letting thoughts come and go will result in higher levels of anxiety and more frequent intrusive thoughts. They are often surprised that letting go of their efforts at thought control (i.e., letting thoughts come and go) lessens the anxiety and typically lowers the frequency of the target thought(s).

To date to the best of our knowledge, this "come-and-go" strategy has been tested only with clients with OCD. However, it is likely that it would also be helpful for other disorders that feature repetitive unwanted thoughts (e.g., eating disorders, impulse control disorders, and body dysmorphic disorder).

VI. SUMMARY

Thought stopping (TS) is a behavioral procedure used to minimize the distress and anxiety associated with unwanted intrusive thoughts. Clients are asked to sit with their eyes closed and verbalize a typical sequence of problematic thoughts. During this time the therapist suddenly shouts "Stop!" The therapist then highlights that the thoughts did stop and proceeds to repeat the procedure several times until the client is able to subvocally disrupt the maladaptive thoughts.

Although used frequently by behavior therapists in the 1970s, TS has received relatively little rigorous empirical attention. Uncontrolled cases studies and anecdotal reports of TS are generally favorable when used as both a stand-alone procedure or in conjunction with other cognitive and behavioral techniques. The few studies utilizing rigorous empirical methodology in their investigations of the efficacy of TS have been equivocal.

Recent empirical studies with thought suppression have demonstrated the paradoxical increase in thought frequency. TS can be considered a form of thought suppression or control and will, thus, likely serve to increase the frequency of the thoughts. With this in mind, Whittal and McLean developed a cognitive alternative to TS termed "come and go" that has shown success in treating individuals with OCD. The authors suggest that letting thoughts come and go will also be helpful with other problems that feature repetitive, unwanted thoughts (e.g., eating disorders, impulse control disorders, other anxiety disorders).

Acknowledgments

The authors wish to express their appreciation to S. Rachman, Ph.D. and Simon Rego, Psy. M. for providing comment on earlier versions of this manuscript.

See Also the Following Articles

Control-Mastery Theory ■ Coverant Control ■ Extinction ■ Orgasmic Reconditioning

Further Reading

Wegner, D. M. (1989). *White bears and other unwanted thoughts: Suppression obsessions and the psychology of mental control.* New York: Penguin.

Wegner, D. M. (1994). Ironic processes of mental control. *Psychological Review, 101,* 34–52.

Whittal, M. L., & McLean, P. D. (1999). CBT for OCD: The rationale, protocol, and challenges. *Cognitive and Behavioral Practice, 6,* 383–396.

Wolpe, J. (1958). *Psychotherapy by reciprocal inhibition.* Stanford, CA: Stanford University Press.

Wolpe, J., & Lazarus, A. A. (1966). *Behavior therapy techniques: A guide to the treatment of neuroses.* Toronto, Ont.: Pergamon Press.

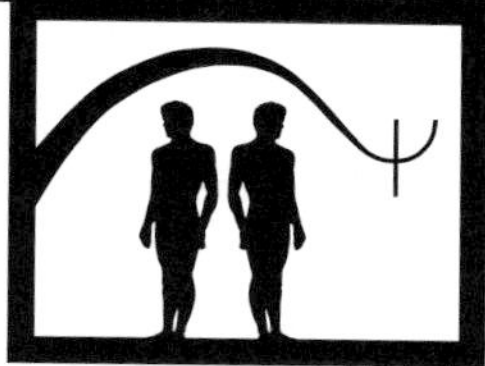

Time-Limited Dynamic Psychotherapy

Hanna Levenson
Levenson Institute for Training

Thomas E. Schacht
James H. Quillen College of Medicine

Hans H. Strupp
Vanderbilt University

GLOSSARY

attachment theory Pertains to how children become comfortable or anxious in relationship to their caregivers' behavioral and emotional responses; such attachment patterns are presumed to carry over into adult relationships.

behavioral A therapeutic approach that emphasizes that behaviors are learned (according to learning principles such as reinforcement and extinction) and therefore can be modified using these same principles.

case formulation The process of diagnosing problems for psychotherapeutic intervention. Case formulation differs from diagnosing psychopathological categories. Rather than producing a diagnostic label, case formulation seeks to create a minitheory linking current presenting problems with recurrent problem patterns and underlying core-ordering processes.

cognitive A therapeutic approach that emphasizes that how one interprets events in the world determines an individual's behavior and feelings; interventions therefore focus on changing the way one thinks and evaluates.

manualized treatment A psychotherapy with principles and techniques that have been specified in a written manual developed to specify the treatment variable in research contexts. Manualized treatments usually include associated psychometric instruments for measuring therapist's adherence to the precepts of the manual.

metacommunication Refers to communications in which the process of communication or the relationship between the communicators becomes the topic of conversation. In psychotherapy, metacommunication functions as a form of interpretive intervention focused on clarifying the ongoing interpersonal process between the patient and the therapist.

psychodynamic A therapeutic approach that emphasizes unconscious processes, the influence of early experiences, conflict, transference/countertransference, and resistance.

schema Stable, enduring, often unconscious, cognitive structures for screening, coding, evaluating, and organizing stimuli into patterns.

transference The tendency to reenact experiences and relationship patterns from past relationships in the therapeutic relationship.

working models A mental framework of what can be expected from others derived from both observation and inner schemas.

Time-limited dynamic psychotherapy (TLDP) is an interpersonal, time-sensitive approach for patients with chronic, pervasive, dysfunctional ways of relating to others. This article will present TLDP theory, assumptions, goals, formulation, intervention strategies, a clinical illustration, and empirical findings. The goal of TLDP is to help patients change their dysfunctional, interpersonal patterns by fostering new experiences and new understandings that emanate from the therapeutic relationships.

I. DESCRIPTION OF TREATMENT

A. Definition

Despite proponents dating to the 1920s, for decades the general response of the psychoanalytic establishment to short-term therapies was unreceptive. However, intense interest in brief dynamic therapy resurfaced in the 1970s and early 1980s, and by the 1990s brief intervention had become a treatment of choice for most patients. Confidence in the basic viability of brief therapy was buttressed by empirical research demonstrating that the majority of patients who benefit from psychotherapy do so within the first 6 months, and that success rates are not necessarily dependent on treatment duration.

Time-limited dynamic psychotherapy was developed with the intention of helping clinicians have more successful outcomes when treating patients with self-defeating interpersonal behaviors—the so-called difficult patient—seen in brief treatment. It was designed to target the specific subgroup of patients whose symptomatic problems (anxiety, depression, etc.) are embedded in underlying core patterns of recurrent dysfunctional interpersonal relationships and whose enactment of these dysfunctional patterns generalizes into the therapeutic relationship. When originally conceived, a liberal time limit of 25 to 30 hours was proposed. Currently the time frame is in the 15 to 20 session range, with the therapist maintaining a time-sensitive or focused approach rather than emphasizing a stipulated number of fixed sessions. The focus is not on symptom reduction per se, but rather on altering the way one relates to others and the self. More ambitious or perfectionistic goals, such as extensive personality reconstruction or plumbing the unconscious origins of experience, are generally inappropriate for TLDP.

Consistent with a general trend toward manualizing therapies for research purposes, the principles of TLDP were originally set forth in a manual published in 1984 under the title *Psychotherapy in a New Key*, authored by Hans Strupp and Jeffrey Binder with collaboration from Thomas Schacht. A subsequent volume produced a decade later by Hanna Levenson provides an updated perspective on TLDP. Levenson's approach places more emphasis on change through experiential learning, whereas the 1984 manual stresses insight through interpretation.

B. Assumptions Essential to TLDP Treatment

There are three core assumptions underlying the practice of TLDP.

1. Maladaptive interpersonal patterns acquired early in life underlie many presenting complaints of symptomatic distress and functional impairment.

Early experiences with parental figures inform the child as to what can be expected from others and what is necessary to maintain connectedness with them. These experiences from the building blocks in the mind of the child of what eventually become mental representations or working models of relationships in general.

2. Maladaptive interpersonal patterns acquired early in life persist and are maintained in current relationships, including reenactment in the therapeutic relationship.

Although one's dysfunctional style is learned early in life, according to the TLDP model, the individual's way of seeing the world must be supported in the person's present adult life for interpersonal difficulties to continue. For example, if one's parents were harsh and demanding, it would be understandable if such a child grew into a placating, deferential adult. Displaying such a subservient manner, such a person might inadvertently and unconsciously pull for others to respond in controlling ways—echoing the behavior of the parents.

This recursive focus is consistent with a systems-oriented approach, which holds that if you change one part of the system, other parts will shift as a result. In this manner, "pathology" does not exist solely within the individual, but rather resides in the totality of the interpersonal system that maintains the behavior. From a time-limited viewpoint, this emphasis on the present enables the therapy theoretically to be completed in a shorter amount of time, because the focus is on what is happening in the current interpersonal world of the individual rather than on an archeological dig into one's past.

The relationship that evolves between therapist and patient can be understood as a microcosm of the interpersonal world of the patient. The patient relates to the therapist in ways that are characteristic of interactions with significant others (i.e., transference), and hooks the therapist into responding in a complementary fashion (i.e., countertransference). Although this reenactment of interpersonal difficulties in the therapeutic relationship poses difficulties for the alliance, it is inevitable and also provides the opportunity to transform the therapeutic relationship into a specialized context for reflecting on and changing interpersonal patterns. In such a manner, the therapist has the opportunity to see the maladaptive interactions evolve in the therapeutic relationship and to discern dysfunctional patterns. Because such patterns are presumed to be sustained through present interactional sequences, the therapist can concentrate on what is happening in the session to alter the patient's experience and understanding.

As pointed out earlier, the therapist in attempting to relate to the patient is unwittingly enlisted into a reenactment of the patient's dysfunctional pattern; in other words, in addition to observing, the therapist becomes a participant in the interaction or a participant observer. The therapist is pushed and pulled by the patient's style and responds accordingly. The therapist's transactional reciprocity and complementarity are not viewed as a "mistake," but rather as a form of interpersonal empathy or role responsiveness. Eventually, the therapist must realize how he or she is replicating this interpersonal dynamic with the patient, and use this information to change the nature of the interaction in a healthier direction.

3. TLDP focuses on one chief problematic relationship pattern.

The emphasis in TLDP is on the patient's most troublesome and pervasive interactive pattern. Although other relationship patterns of less magnitude and inflexibility are important, in a time-limited format pragmatics dictate focusing on the most central interpersonal schema.

C. Goals

1. New Experience

The first and major goal is for the patient to have a series of new experiences through which he or she develops a different appreciation of self, of therapist, and of their interaction. These new experiences provide a foundation of experiential learning through which old patterns may be relinquished and new patterns established. The formulation of each particular case (see later) determines what specific types of new experiences will be most helpful in disconfirming the patient's interpersonal schemata and thereby undermining his or her maladaptive style. The concept of a corrective emotional experience described more than 50 years ago by Alexander and French is relevant. They suggested that with experiential learning individuals could change even without insight into the etiology of their problems. It is our current thinking that experiential learning broadens the range of patients who can benefit from a brief therapy format, leads to greater generalization to the outside world, and permits therapists to use a variety of techniques and strategies in addition to traditional inisght-promoting clarification and interpretation. For example, with the placating individual mentioned earlier, the goal might be for him to experience himself as more assertive and the therapist as less punitive within the give and take of the therapeutic hours.

2. New Understanding

The second goal of providing a new understanding focuses on helping patients identify and comprehend the nature, etiology, and ramifications of their dysfunctional patterns. To facilitate such an understanding, the TLDP therapist can point out repetitive patterns as they have manifested with past significant others, with present significant others, and with the therapist in the here-and-now of the sessions. Metacommunication occurs when the ongoing process of interpersonal transaction between the patient and therapist becomes the content of the therapeutic dialogue. Therapists disclosing their own reactions (i.e., interactive countertransference) to the patients' behaviors can be of benefit in this regard. In this way, patients can begin to recognize relationship patterns and discern their role in perpetuating the very dysfunctional interaction they wish to change.

D. Patient Suitability

TLDP may be helpful to anyone for whom adequate descriptions of their interpersonal transactions can lead to a dynamic focus. It is designed, however, for people who have lifelong interpersonal difficulties. Table I contains the five major selection criteria and four major exclusionary criteria for ascertaining a patient's suitability for TLDP.

E. Formulation

1. The Cyclical Maladaptive Pattern

In long-term treatments, therapists may rely on the patient's spontaneous organizing abilities to bring coherence, over time, to the tacit themes and patterns of their difficulties. However, a time-limited therapy requires a more systematic approach, a core theme or dynamic focus, which acts as a guiding beacon to direct and organize therapeutic activity. In TLDP this core theme is the repetitive dysfunctional interactive sequence that is both historically significant and also a source of current difficulty. This cyclical maladaptive pattern (CMP) provides a framework for deriving a dynamic, interpersonal focus for TLDP. It forms an organizational structure for the various components that contribute to the idiosyncratic vicious cycle of reciprocal interactions. By creating

TABLE I
Selection Criteria for Time-Limited Dynamic Psychotherapy

Inclusionary
1. Patient is sufficiently uncomfortable with his or her feelings and/or behavior to seek help via psychotherapy.
2. Patient is willing and able to come regularly for appointments and talk about his or her life.
3. Patient is willing to consider the possibility that his or her problems reflect difficulties in relating to others.
4. Patient is open to considering the possibly important role that his or her emotional life plays in interpersonal difficulties.
5. Patient evidences sufficient capacity for relating to others as separate individuals so that identifiable relationship predispositions can be enacted in the therapeutic relationship and then collaboratively examined.

Exclusionary
1. Patient is not able to attend to the process of a verbal give-and-take with the therapist (e.g., patient has delirium, dementia, psychosis, or diminished intellectual status).
2. Patient's problems can be treated more effectively by other means (e.g., patient has specific phobia or manic-depressive illness).
3. Patient cannot tolerate the active, interpretative, interactive therapy process, which often heightens anxiety (e.g., patient has impulse control problems, abuses alcohol and/or substances, or has a history of repeated suicide attempts).
4. Patient's problems are primarily due to environmental factors (e.g., social oppression, imprisonment, proverty).

Adapted from Strupp & Binder (1984) and MacKenzie (1988).

a narrative that incorporates the elements of the CMP, the clinician is guided in developing a treatment plan. A successful CMP should describe the nature and extent of the interpersonal problem, lead to a delineation of the goals, serve as a blueprint for interventions, enable the therapist to anticipate reenactments, and provide a way to assess if the therapy is on track.

2. *Constructing the CMP*

To derive a TLDP formulation, the therapist uses four categories to gather, organize, and probe for relevant information.

1. Acts of the self. These acts include the thoughts, feelings, motives, perceptions, and behaviors of the patient of an interpersonal nature. "I enjoy social gatherings because I am the life of the party!"
2. Expectations of others' reactions. This category pertains to how the patient imagines others will react to him or her in response to some interpersonal behavior (Act of the Self). "I expect that if I go to the party, everyone will want to talk with me."
3. Acts of others toward the self. This third grouping consists of the actual behaviors of other people as observed (or assumed) and interpreted by the patient. "When I went to the party, people were so concerned with making a big impression on the host, that no one spoke to me."
4. Acts of the self toward the self. In this section belong the patient's behaviors or attitudes toward oneself. "When I left the party, I told myself that it was their loss and felt better."

By linking information in these categories together, a narrative is formed from which emerges themes and redundancies in the patient's transactional interactions. This narrative forms the CMP describing the patient's predominant dysfunctional interactive pattern. The therapist then sets the goals for the treatment by considering what specific types of experiential interactions and new understandings would help weaken the strength, rigidity, and repetitiveness of the patient's CMP.

F. TLDP Strategies

Implementation of TLDP does not rely on a fixed set of techniques. Rather it depends on therapeutic strategies that are seen as embedded in a therapeutic relationship. The Vanderbilt Therapeutic Strategies Scale (VTSS) was designed to measure therapists' adherence to TLDP principles. The 10 items that contain TLDP specific strategies are included in Table II.

In general these therapeutic strategies emphasize clarification and understanding of actions and experiences in the here-and-now rather than excavation of the patient's past. Although a search for historical antecedents may help to clarify current events, archeological exploration of the patient's life history is subordinate to a thorough reconnaissance of present experiences, behaviors, and circumstances. In TLDP the patient and therapist collaboratively "make" the patient's life story, as contrasted with the traditional unilateral "taking" of a life history.

II. THEORETICAL BASE

Historically, TLDP is based in an object-relations, interpersonal framework with roots in attachment theory.

TABLE II
Vanderbilt Therapeutic Strategies Scale

TLDP Specific Strategies:

1. Therapist specifically addresses transactions in the patient–therapist relationship.
2. Therapist encourages the patient to explore feelings and thoughts about the therapist or the therapeutic relationship.
3. Therapist encourages the patient to discuss how the therapist might feel or think about the patient.
4. Therapist discusses own reactions to some aspect of the patient's behavior in relation to the therapist.
5. Therapist attempts to explore patterns that might constitute a cyclical maladaptive pattern in the patient's interpersonal relationships.
6. Therapist asks about the patient's introject (how the patient feels about and treats himself or herself).
7. Therapist links a recurrent pattern of behavior or interpersonal conflict to transactions between the patient and therapist.
8. Therapist addresses obstacles (e.g., silences, coming late, avoidance of meaningful topics) that might influence the therapeutic process.
9. Therapist provides the opportunity for the patient to have a new experience of oneself and/or the therapist relevant to the patient's particular cyclical maladaptive pattern.[a]
10. Therapist discusses an aspect of the time-limited nature of TLDP or termination.

Reproduced with permission from Butler, S. F., & Center for Psychotherapy Research Team. (1995). Manual for the Vanderbilt Therapeutic Strategies Scale. In Levenson, H. *Time-limited dynamic psychotherapy: A guide to clinical practice*. pp. 243–254. New York: Basic Books.

[a] Item written by H. Levenson.

According to object relations theory, people are innately motivated to maintain human relatedness. Basic tenets of interpersonal theory hold that, all else being equal, people learn to treat themselves in a manner that is complementary to how they are treated by others. Therefore, images of the self and others are considered to be products of social interactions. This relational view contrasts with that of classical psychoanalysis, which holds that drives for sex and aggression and their derivatives take preeminence. From a relational perspective, psychopathology results when recurrent dysfunctional interactions cause the individual to engage in patterns of maladaptive behavior and negative self-appraisal. Although recent applications of TLDP are grounded in psychodynamic theory, they also incorporate cognitive, behavioral, and systems approaches.

III. EMPIRICAL STUDIES

A series of studies done at Vanderbilt University in the 1970s found that therapists have difficulty being therapeutically effective when their patients are negative and hostile; in fact, the therapists themselves can often become hooked into responding with negativity, hostility, and disrespect. These findings led Hans Strupp and colleagues to develop TLDP.

Time-limited dynamic psychotherapy does not belong to the new research paradigm of the so-called empirically validated therapies (EVTs). Rather, TLDP was created to support a long tradition of basic research into the elementary processes distinguishing effective psychotherapy from interventions that are less effective or even harmful. Whereas the EVT concept furthers the idea that it is the technique of treatment that is most important, TLDP, in contrast, stems from a research tradition that underscores the importance of so-called common factors such as the personal qualities of the therapist, the interpersonal nature of the therapeutic relationship, and the quality of the therapeutic alliance. Thus, rather than producing an empirically validated "treatment" per se, TLDP research has sought to validate underlying generic therapeutic principles. TLDP was constructed to provide a fertile arena for investigating these principles, but it is by no means the only therapeutic environment in which similar research could be or has been conducted.

Although the primary emphasis of research has not been to demonstrate that TLDP is effective for particular disorders, many patients in studies involving TLDP have improved. Research on TLDP outcomes found that a majority of patients at a Veterans Administration outpatient clinic achieved positive interpersonal or symptomatic benefit, with almost three-quarters feeling that their problems had lessened by termination. Long-term follow-up of these patients revealed that patient gains were maintained and slightly bolstered, with 80% feeling helped. Other analyses indicated that patients were more likely to value their therapies the more they perceived that the sessions focused on TLDP-congruent strategies such as trying to understand their typical patterns of relating to people. A study examining relational change found that following TLDP, patients significantly shifted in their attachment styles (from insecure to secure) and significantly increased in their secure attachment themes. Other empirical studies have found that patients' images and treatment of themselves are a reflection of the way they were treated by their therapists, and that these internalizations are associated with better outcomes.

With regard to case formulation, empirical research suggests that the TLDP-CMP is a reliable and valid procedure. CMPs from patients who had completed TLDP were read by five clinicians unfamiliar with the cases. Based only on these CMPs, the clinicians' independent ratings showed high levels of interrater agreement with regard to the patients' interpersonal difficulties. Further analyses indicated that there was considerable overlap in problems the raters said should have been discussed with those that actually were discussed. Also the therapies were found to have better outcomes the more they stayed focused on CMP relevant topics. Another study found that themes derived from CMPs corresponded to themes obtained from another psychodynamic formulation method.

With regard to training in TLDP, research has demonstrated that although a programatic effort to train experienced therapists in TLDP was successful in increasing therapists' use of TLDP strategies, many of the therapists did not reach an acceptable level of TLDP mastery within the training period. Further inquiry into the data also revealed some unintended and potentially untoward training effects. For example, after training the therapists were more willing to be active and as a consequence made more "mistakes," inadvertently becoming less supportive and delivering more complex communications to patients.

In another training study, psychiatry residents and psychology interns changed their attitudes and values about brief therapy in a more positive direction as a result of a 6-month seminar and group supervision in TLDP. In a multisite investigation, similar attitudinal shifts have been found with experienced clinicians who attended 1-day TLDP workshops.

IV. CASE ILLUSTRATION

Ms. R. was a professional woman in her early forties, married for 15 years with three children. She sought psychotherapy for chronic symptoms of depression and anxiety that had been present for several years. Exploration of the interpersonal context of the presenting complaints indicated that Ms. R. frequently experienced others as emotionally distant or uncaring. She responded with complementary interpersonal distancing. For example, she felt that her husband had been unsupportive with child rearing and during a past time of physical illness but rather than expressing her concerns and wishes to him, she concealed her resentment and withdrew from sexual relations without explanation. Ms. R.'s description of her family of origin mirrored her current marital relationship. She did not feel close to her siblings. Her relationship with her father was notable for unrequited wishes for greater closeness and involvement. In a prior attempt at psychotherapy, Ms. R. found herself wishing for more time with the therapist, but could not bring herself to reveal this, ultimately choosing instead to discontinue therapy.

From the opening moments of the first interview, her TLDP therapist focused on Ms. R.'s current problems, especially as they were reflected in relationships with others and in concerns and expectations regarding the therapist. The beginning of the therapeutic relationship was a primary source of clues for a focal theme. Ms. R. expressed concern about the cost of treatment and added that she had not felt able to discuss this with her husband. She indicated that she was having second thoughts about therapy, and wondered if treatment would be a mistake. The therapist invited associations that eventually linked Ms. R.'s descriptions of uncomfortable affective states to accompanying interpersonal contexts. A search for similarities in patterns across contexts clarified how Ms. R.'s ambivalence about therapy stemmed from a fear that participation in treatment would disturb her marriage. In response to a comment from the therapist inviting associations to her apparent anger and resentment, Ms. R. reported a fear that her husband would perceive her seeking therapy as a rejection of him. She then wondered if therapy might also represent an indirect act of aggression toward him. Such early clarifications and interpretations allowed the therapist to assess Ms. R.'s capacity to participate in collaborative inquiry and probed her response to the work of therapy.

In emphasizing the interpersonal context of Ms. R.'s presenting complaints, the therapist set the stage for identification of a focal theme. In Ms. R.'s case, a theme was identified the essence of which was: "If I ask for what I want, I will be disappointed and will feel useless and worthless. If I don't want to be hurt or abandoned, I must always be polite and must do what others want. I must avoid standing up for myself and must never express anger toward men and must always subordinate my wishes to theirs. If something goes wrong in my relationships, it must be my fault and I am responsible for correcting the situation." Consistent with this theme, Ms. R. often perceived others as withholding what she wanted or needed, and as unresponsive to issues of relationship fairness that were important to her. Although the superficial expression of this theme takes the form of a subdued and unemotional exterior, there is a subtextual theme of covert hostility that finds indirect expression in complementary withholding, in withdrawal, or in subtle or passive forms of aggression.

The therapist used this theme as a heuristic to guide construction of organizing questions and comments designed to stimulate the patient's curiosity and foster collaborative effort. Even as Ms. R. was discussing her husband, other comments, behavior, and perceptions suggested that she often felt similarly toward the therapist. For example, she expected that the therapist would criticize her for her reluctance to tell her husband about seeking psychotherapy. Ms. R. expressed a fear that she would run out of things to say, and that the therapist would respond judgmentally and would refrain from helping her, leaving her cruelly tongue-tied. Similarly, when the therapist agreed to accept her into a time-limited 25-session treatment immediately following the initial interview, she did not experience this as a helpful gesture, but rather perceived the offer of help as a form of coercive pressure, as if the therapist had said: "You can be my patient, but only on my terms and my schedule, and you must choose now." The potential for such transference enactment was continuously in the background of the therapist's awareness.

As treatment progressed, Ms. R. and the therapist reencountered examples of the enactment of this focal theme in narratives about primary childhood relationships, other current family relationships, romantic relationships including her current marriage, and her relationship with the therapist. Within a few sessions, this dynamic focus was sufficiently salient that the therapist proposed to Ms. R. that working on the manifestations of this theme become a primary goal for their continuing sessions.

In future sessions, Ms. R.'s primary task was to verbalize whatever came to her mind. However, she often began her sessions with an awkward silence and an aloof stare that most likely reflected the vigilance associated with ingrained expectations that others will be displeased with her. At the beginning of therapy, as expected according to the principles of interpersonal complementarity, the therapist alternately felt bored, irritated, or subtly dismissive in response to Ms. R.'s criticality and withdrawn stance. For example, in the third session, the therapist, annoyed with the patient's indirect criticism of him, began to think about a highly successful intervention he had made with a previous patient. As he was in the midst of this self-congratulatory reverie, he lost track of what Ms. R. was saying. His emotional distance echoed the behavior of Ms. R.'s husband (and others in her life) and in fact was a reenactment of the very CMP that had become the focus of the therapeutic work.

Ms. R., hurt by her therapist's inattention, started to berate him and then trailed into a series of self-denigrating statements with sullen affect. The therapist, reflecting on this transactional process in the moment, realized that he had been countertransferentially responding to Ms. R.'s behavior and attitude. Rather than defensively denying his inattentiveness, the therapist admitted his lapse, and helped Ms. R. to express directly her disappointment and anger toward him. Together they explored the interactional sequence leading up to their mutual disconnect. The therapist did not punish Ms. R. or excuse his own dismissive behavior, but rather welcomed hearing her feelings, thereby providing her with a reparative interpersonal experience. As other such reenactments were therapeutically addressed, they became fewer and farther between.

For much of the therapy the therapist was able to support, clarify, elaborate, and link Ms. R.'s concerns to the core theme. Connections between Ms. R.'s current experience and the past helped to clarify Ms. R.'s perception of her circumstances, while also highlighting their anachronistic character and underscoring elements of distortion associated with transferential experience. Exploration of the past was important, but clearly subordinate to the therapist's endeavors to stay close to the patient's emotional experience. To this end, the therapist used simple evocative language and avoided complex constructions or abstract interpretations that were likely to move the patient away from her affective experience. Redundant encounters with the focal theme provided repeated opportunities for discussion and corrective emotional experience derived from the contrast between Ms. R.'s transference expectations and what actually occurred with the therapist. In this portion of the work, both the process and the content of the therapeutic dialogue had a healing impact. Indeed, the therapist's behavior often spoke more loudly than his words. A verbal profession of support for Ms. R.'s autonomy would have been of little value if the therapist's conduct simultaneously expressed criticism or infringed on that same autonomy.

Numerous examples of such corrective emotional experiences occurred as the therapy progressed. The therapeutic dyad encountered numerous variations on the focal theme, each a different facet of the theme's pervasive presence in Ms. R.'s life. Around the 20th session, Ms. R.'s concerns turned urgently to the impending termination date. She pressed the therapist for reassurance that therapy would not really have to stop at the agreed time. In response, the therapist maintained the same exploratory stance that had carried the relationship forward from the beginning. Thus, the therapist expressed curiosity about the patient's emotional experience and her wishes and fears associated with the anticipated end of the therapeutic relationship. The therapist did not attempt to reassure Ms. R. that everything would be OK or that the treatment had accomplished enough. Instead, he treated her responses to termination in the same manner as all other material that Ms. R. had brought to the therapy—as expressions of her central relationship issues.

As termination approached, Ms. R. initially pressed the therapist with rational arguments, protesting that while she had become much more aware of her automatic interpersonal predispositions, she needed much more therapeutic time to master alternative responses. When these arguments failed to elicit the desired amendment to the scheduled termination, Ms. R. then regressed temporarily, sarcastically stating that the therapist was putting her through hell and then withholding further disclosure by refusing to discuss her feelings. Despite Ms. R.'s provocative conduct, the therapist managed not to respond with complementary intensity or negative reaction, but instead maintained a gentle, receptive, and supportive curiosity. The therapist acknowledged Ms. R.'s experience of loss, empathized with her perception that she felt like a helpless child being summarily dismissed by an unfeeling parent, and clarified this fear of rejection and abandonment as a recapitulation of earlier traumas as expressed in the focal theme. The therapist also pointed out the realistic limitations of the therapy, emphasizing what Ms. R. had gained rather than what she imagined she may have foregone by terminating treatment at this time. In this way, the termination phase continued the primary work of the therapy, while also assisting the patient in a corrective emotional experience, namely experiencing the loss of the therapist via normal grief and mourning, rather than as a maladaptive resentment from perceived deprivation.

At their last session, Ms. R. indicated acceptance of the termination and reported that she felt "ready." She framed the termination positively via a metaphor of graduation, rather than negatively via analogy to divorce, abandonment, or ex-communication as would have been expected based on her focal theme. She verbalized comfort in the knowledge that further therapy was possible in the future if she encountered difficulties that she could not master on her own. She and the therapist parted with a sincere and warm good-bye.

V. SUMMARY

TLDP was developed to help therapists treat difficult patients within a brief therapy format. In TLDP, problems are defined in terms of a dynamic focus that formulates dysfunctional interpersonal patterns. The treatment process includes development and maintenance of a therapeutic alliance in the face of the patient's dysfunctional patterns and the therapist's own interpersonal proclivities. Therapeutic strategies include observing the inevitable reenactment of those patterns in the therapeutic relationship, metacommunicating about them, and providing opportunities for experiential learning.

See Also the Following Articles

Brief Therapy ■ Efficacy ■ Manualized Behavior Therapy ■ Minimal Therapist Contact Treatments ■ Outcome Measures ■ Single-Session Therapy ■ Solution-Focused Brief Therapy ■ Termination ■ Supportive-Expressive Dynamic Psychotherapy

Further Reading

Benjamin, L. S. (1993). *Interpersonal diagnosis and treatment of personality disorders*. New York: Guilford.

Henry, W. P., Schacht, T. E., & Strupp, H. H. (1986). Structural analysis of social behavior: Application to a study of interpersonal process in differential psychotherapeutic outcome. *Journal of Consulting and Clinical Psychology, 54,* 27–31.

Henry, W. P., Schacht, T. E., & Strupp, H. H. (1990). Patient and therapist introject, interpersonal process, and differential psychotherapy outcome. *Journal of Consulting and Clinical Psychology, 58,* 768–774.

Levenson, H. (1995). *Time-limited dynamic psychotherapy: A guide to clinical practice*. New York: Basic Books.

Levenson, H. (1998). Time-limited dynamic psychotherapy: Making every session count. Video and viewer's manual. San Francisco: Levenson Institute for Training.

Messer, S. B., & Warren, C. S. (1995). *Models of brief psychodynamic therapy: A comparative approach*. New York: Guilford.

Schacht, T. E., & Henry, W. P. (1994). Modeling recurrent patterns of interpersonal relationship with structural analysis of social behavior: The SASB-CMP. *Psychotherapy Research, 4,* 207–220.

Strupp, H. H., & Binder, J. L. (1984). *Psychotherapy in a new key: A guide to time-limited dynamic psychotherapy*. New York: Basic Books.

Wachtel, P. L. (1997). *Psychoanalysis, behavior theory, and the relational world*. Washington, DC: American Psychological Association.

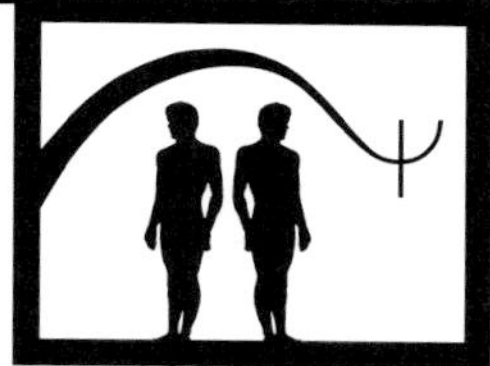

Timeout

Rebecca S. Griffin and Alan M. Gross
University of Mississippi

GLOSSARY

functional analysis Assessing a set of circumstances (e.g., through observation, interview, collection, and analysis of data) to identify and target variables that are influencing problematic behavior.

operational definition (of a behavior) A clear, specific description of a behavior so that it can be more easily targeted for change. For example, rather than targeting general "noncompliance," it is easier to target more specific "refusal to comply with direct instructions provided by an adult."

positive reinforcement (or reward) A situation or event, often pleasant in nature, which, when delivered contingent on the occurrence of a behavior, results in an increase in frequency of that behavior.

punishment An event following a behavior that thereby decreases the likelihood that the behavior will recur in the future.

Timeout is a punishment technique such that, following an act of negative behavior, a child spends a brief period of time in an environment less reinforcing than that in which the behavior originally occurred. This article will further define the concept of timeout, suggest typical methods for successful implementation of the timeout procedure, discuss the theoretical bases on which the technique relies, and identify several empirically supported variations of the technique.

I. DESCRIPTION OF TREATMENT

Timeout is a disciplinary technique that, when used correctly and consistently, can be quite effective in reducing maladaptive behavior patterns of children. Although several major principles of behavior modification may be involved with the use of timeout, the procedure is in its most basic form a punishment procedure, because it denies a child access to activities or situations that are sources of positive reinforcement. Thus, the term "timeout" suggests that a child is shifted from being in a reinforcing environment to being in an unpleasant or less reinforcing environment. It is important to note that timeout appears to be most effective when used in combination with other techniques, such as rewarding appropriate behaviors, and therefore encouraging greater frequency of positive behavior.

A. When to Use Timeout

The use of timeout can be effective for children from toddlerhood through adolescence, and in some cases even for adults, and can be used in many different settings. Schoolteachers often find the technique quite useful in handling classroom disruptions. The procedure is also valuable in working with individuals with developmental delays, inpatient residents in psychiatric settings, children who are aggressive toward siblings or peers, or in families with children who are defiant or noncompliant. Timeout can reduce behaviors such as tantrums, aggression, inattention, refusal to follow directions, inappropriate social comments or actions, or self-injurious behavior.

B. Functional Analysis

Before considering the use of timeout on a consistent basis, a functional analysis should be conducted to identify typical patterns of problematic behavior. A functional analysis can be conducted through the use of both formal and informal methods. Formal methods might include a distinct written operational definition of the target behavior, noting when and where the behavior does and does not occur (e.g., percentage of the time, duration of incidents, number of occurrences per time period). The graphing or charting of trends might be helpful both before and after starting the timeout strategy so that changes in patterns of behavior are easily evident. More informal methods of functional analysis might involve making notes on a calendar or simply being more attentive to potential triggers of behavioral outbursts. Jill Taylor and Michelle Miller provide several classroom case examples illustrating how a thorough functional analysis can lead to successful timeout implementation, or can help identify why the procedure is not producing desired results.

Whether formal or informal methods are used, the goal of the functional analysis is to determine typical antecedents and consequences of the child's actions. Determining the contingencies that could be reinforcing the undesired behavior can help the adult anticipate under what circumstances the behavior is likely to occur. In addition, this information can be used in setting realistic goals for timeout. It is important to set a clear goal (e.g., decrease the behavior by a certain amount) and to recognize and reward the child as positive changes happen and when goals are met.

C. Type of Timeout

Jennie Brantner and Michael Doherty defined three major categories of timeouts: isolation, exclusion, and nonexclusion. Isolation timeout is one in which a child is taken to a solitary, non-reinforcing area, separate in location from where the inappropriate behavior occurred. At home or at school, this might be a hallway or other specified room (where the adult can monitor the child, but without reinforcers present). Alternately, exclusion timeout means that the child is not actually removed from the room where the behavior occurred, but is also not allowed to participate in or view ongoing activities. An example of this would be having the child sit in a chair facing the wall. Russell Barkley suggests a modification of these ideas for use in public places, such that the child can be placed in a quiet corner facing the wall or can be taken to the car for a timeout.

The third category of timeout is nonexclusion, meaning that that the child is able to view ongoing activities but the child's participation is restricted for a period of time following undesired behavior. Brantner and Doherty identified three further variations of non-exclusion timeout. The first variation, titled contingent observation, requires the child to sit on the periphery of activities and watch what is occurring, which might include observing others continue to receive reinforcement. Another variation is removing reinforcing materials, or giving a "timeout" to the television, toys, games, or stereo being used by the child. This seems particularly effective for older children or adolescents. A third variation of non-exclusion time-out is simply ignoring the child, so that reinforcement is not being provided for a period of time. This could include turning away from the child or refusing to interact for a period of time.

To choose which type of timeout will be most effective, one must consider the disruptiveness of the behavior itself, the age, and developmental level of the child (i.e., a very young child may be far less receptive to an isolation timeout), whether or not the behavior occurred in a group setting, and any potential reinforcers in the setting where the behavior occurred (e.g., peer attention). Charles Wolfgang offers several examples of charts useful for record keeping if timeout is to be implemented in a school or group setting, and emphasizes the importance of implementing timeouts without allowing ridicule or social reinforcement from peers. Russell Barkley offers suggestions for training parents to use the technique, such as modeling the procedure for parents and dealing with frustration commonly experienced when implementing a new timeout program. Barkley also offers several adaptations in the procedure, such as incorporating a token economy system and taking additional measures to deal with a child's noncompliance with timeout.

D. Duration of Timeout

There has been considerable debate among researchers and behavior modification experts regarding the appropriate duration of timeout. The effectiveness of different lengths of time has been empirically tested and has produced varying results. Therefore, there is no absolute standard regarding how long a child should remain in a timeout. Some experts suggest a range of 1 to 5 min, whereas others suggest lengths of up to 20 min for older children. A typical rule of thumb is to require 1 min for each year of a child's age (e.g., a 5-year-old should receive a 5-min timeout). This rule seems logical, because a younger child will likely possess less patience than will an older child. However, this should not be an inflexible standard, because a child's developmental level should also be considered. For example, a 8-year-old who is developmentally delayed might receive beneficial effects from a timeout much shorter than 8 min in duration. For any child, use of a kitchen timer or buzzer can avert arguments or incessant questioning about when timeout has ended.

In determining appropriate timeout length, each child should be considered on an individual basis. The importance is to achieve the aversive and punishing nature of the timeout. That is, too short a timeout might not be perceived as aversive, whereas too long a timeout prevents opportunities to practice other behaviors. In either case, inappropriate duration of a timeout will ultimately be less effective in achieving the ultimate goal: reducing maladaptive behavior.

E. Providing Instructions

Before implementing timeout, the child must know ahead of time what the rules are and what consequences to expect when they are broken. R. Vance Hall and Marilyn C. Hall provide guidelines for explaining timeout to an individual. The adult must first explain to the child the specific target behaviors that will result in a timeout and convey that timeout will be enforced each and every time that behavior occurs. The length of timeout should be preestablished, and the child should know what indicates the end of a timeout. The adult should explain where the child is to spend timeout, and this designated area should be used consistently. If a "timeout chair" will be used, Russell Barkley suggests leaving the chair out for a few weeks to serve as a reminder of consequences. After explaining the entire procedure, younger children might benefit from practicing or role playing a pretend timeout, so they will know what to expect under real circumstances.

The child must also understand that certain behaviors can extend the duration of timeout. For example, screaming, arguing, leaving the timeout area, or other similar conduct should each extend the timeout (e.g., 1 minute for each infraction). The adult must enforce this rule, even if it initially leads to very long timeouts. Without enforcing this procedure, the child might manipulate his or her way out of the consequences and likely attempt that same tactic in later timeout sessions.

When a child's behavior actually warrants a timeout, the adult must deliver consequences in a calm, neutral manner. Russell Barkley suggests redirecting the behavior, waiting a 5 sec count, then warning the child that a timeout will occur if compliance with the request does not occur, waiting another 5-sec count, and if the child fails to respond appropriately, then direct the child to the timeout area. Many variations on this sequence can occur, depending on the child and the infraction. On the end of timeout, the child should be required to resolve the issue or behavior which necessitated timeout in the first place (e.g., if the timeout was for refusing to put away his toys, the child should put away his toys immediately following timeout). Otherwise, the child might begin using timeout as an escape from responsibilities. Consistent rewards, positive attention, and praise should be offered when the child demonstrates positive behavior following a timeout. In starting a new timeout program, the adult should initially expect resistance from the child, particularly if tantrums have been an effective ploy in the past. However, the adult must be willing to enforce timeouts in the same manner each time the behavior occurs. Without consistency, the technique will not be effective and will end up being more work for the adult than it is designed to be when used correctly.

F. When Timeout Does Not Work

If timeout seems ineffective, several factors could be the cause. Perhaps the target behavior is too vague, and the child is having difficulty understanding what behaviors are appropriate. On the other hand, perhaps the "timein" (time spent engaging in supposedly reinforcing activities) is not really rewarding. Thus, timeout might not seem so terrible an option. It could be that the child is using misbehavior and subsequent timeout as a way to gain attention or avoid being in particular environments. In addition, perhaps reinforcement is not being provided for positive displays of behavior. Adults who work to increase positive interactions with the child on a regular basis will be offering a more rewarding "timein," which builds a positive and supportive relationship and offers a little more leverage when disciplining the child.

Even if applied in a consistent and straightforward manner, some children react drastically to timeouts.

These reactions might include severe temper tantrums, physical aggression toward the adult, refusal to go to the timeout area, or leaving the timeout area before the required amount of time has been served. Adults must be prepared for these reactions so they can be dealt with accordingly. If a child is very young, he or she may be physically placed in the timeout area or restrained gently in the chair. If a child refuses to go to or repeatedly leaves the timeout area, extra time may be included or additional punishment (e.g., taking away other privileges) can be utilized.

II. THEORETICAL BASES

Timeout is based on the principle of punishment. Alan Bellack, Michel Hersen, and Alan Kazdin note that in his conceptualization of punishment, B. F. Skinner differentiated between two classes of punishment: one in which existing (often rewarding) stimuli are removed, and one in which new (often unpleasant) stimuli are introduced. A negative punishment (e.g., timeout) would fit into the first class, whereas a positive punishment (e.g., spanking) would fit into the second class. Barkley suggests that use of punishment should only be considered as an alternative after rewards or incentives fail to encourage positive behavior. He also notes that punishment usually fails to be effective when presented in a situation in which no regular positive interactions occur. Therefore, parents must accept some responsibility in finding ways to encourage positive behavior, as well as anticipating potential behavior problems. Simply reacting to negative behavior may encourage helplessness or guilt in a child, because few positive interactions are likely to occur on a consistent basis.

Karen Harris noted that the most important defining characteristic of an effective timeout is the discrepancy between "timein" and "timeout" environments. A timeout will not be perceived as a punishing event if the environment from which the child was removed was never rewarding to begin with. This idea also emphasizes the need for praise and positive social interactions between the adult and child, so that the child will value the "timein."

III. EMPIRICAL STUDIES

In considering length of timeout, Jennie Brantner and Michael Doherty reviewed timeout studies across different types of problem behaviors and in various settings. They were able to conclude that short intervals of timeouts (i.e., 5 min or less) can be quite effective with many populations and in many different settings. Successful use of the timeout technique has been documented with normal children in a family setting; with individuals in inpatient psychiatric settings; with defiant, assaultive, or delinquent adolescents; and in classroom settings at virtually all age and educational levels (to treat behaviors such as noncompliance with rules or inattentiveness). Timeout procedures can also be quite effective in working with autistic children and with children, who are mentally retarded particularly in dealing with aggressiveness or to shape new behaviors such as correct toileting habits. Timeout has been proven to be effective in dealing with a variety of undesirable behaviors, such as aggression, defiance, noncompliance with rules, temper tantrums, being argumentative, inappropriate social interactions, or engaging in self-injurious behavior. A timeout can also serve as a punisher during any type of training task, if the individual already understands and is capable of the desired response.

Robert Jones, Howard Sloane, and Mark Roberts targeted aggressive behavior, comparing the effectiveness of an immediate timeout versus a "don't" instructional command, which included "don't" directives, reinforcement for compliance, a warning for noncompliance, and finally a timeout for noncompliance with the warning. The immediate timeout proved more effective in reducing aggression, possibly because the "don't" procedure offered less immediate consequences and provided more social reinforcement and attention for misbehavior.

David Reitman and Ronald Drabman described an adjustment in implementing timeouts with children who typically become verbally noncompliant. The procedure is called "Read My Fingertips" and has the adult nonverbally adding additional minutes to the timeout, by touching each finger one by one, increasing the timeout one extra minute for each argumentative word spoken by the child. If the child understood the procedure ahead of time, the authors found the technique highly effective in reducing arguing that typically followed a directive to go to timeout.

R. M. Foxx and S. T. Shapiro implemented a nonexclusionary "timeout ribbon" procedure for use in a group setting with children with mental retardation. Following positive behavior, such children were given colored ribbons to wear and received edible reinforcers every few minutes for maintaining appropriate behavior. When misbehavior occurred, a timeout was issued, meaning that the child's ribbon was removed, and the child received no reinforcement for a brief period. The procedure was found to be useful in reducing undesirable behavior, it did not noticeably disrupt the group as a whole, and the teacher was usually able to continue the procedure alone without extra staff on hand to assist.

There are countless studies and reviews (e.g., Karen Harris; Bellack, Hersen & Kazdin; Brantner and Doherty) examining specific cases and providing continued support for the effectiveness of timeout, particularly when compared with other behavior modification procedures. Although timeout may not work for every individual, there is abundant data to suggest that its use can be quite beneficial in many cases and across many settings.

IV. SUMMARY

When implemented consistently and in combination with reinforcement for positive actions, timeout can be a beneficial method for decreasing negative behavior. As a punishment technique following misbehavior, timeout prevents an individual's access to a more rewarding environment for a brief period of time. There are various subcategories of timeout, which can be adjusted depending on an individual's age, developmental level, and setting in which timeout will be used. A functional analysis can help clarify target behaviors and goals for change, as well as encourage recognition and reward for positive change. Alternate methods of discipline should be in place if timeout fails to be successful. Although timeout may not be successful for every possible situation, there is much evidence to suggest its efficacy across numerous settings and populations.

See Also the Following Articles

Applied Behavior Analysis ■ Conditioned Reinforcement ■ Contingency Management ■ Functional Analysis of Behavior ■ Good Behavior Game ■ Negative Reinforcement ■ Positive Reinforcement ■ Primary-Care Behavioral Pediatrics ■ Response Cost ■ Token Economy

Further Reading

Barkley, R. A. (1997). *Defiant children: A clinician's manual for assessment and parent training* (2nd ed.). New York: Guilford Press.

Bellack, A. S., Hersen, M., & Kazdin, A. E. (Eds.). (1990). *International handbook of behavior modification and therapy* (2nd ed.). New York: Plenum.

Brantner, J. P., & Doherty, M. A. (1983). A review of timeout: A conceptual and methodological analysis. In S. Axelrod & J. Apsche (Eds.), *The effects of punishment on human behavior* (pp. 87–132). New York: Academic.

Foxx, R. M., & Shapiro, S. T. (1978). The timeout ribbon: A nonexclusionary timeout procedure. *Journal of Applied Behavior Analysis, 11,* 125–136.

Hall, R. V., & Hall, M. L. (1998). *How to use time out* (2nd ed.). Austin, TX: Pro-Ed.

Harris, K. R. (1985). Definition, parametric, and procedural considerations in timeout interventions and research. *Exceptional Children, 51*(4), 279–288.

Jones, R. N., Sloane, H. N., & Roberts, M. W. (1992). Limitations of "don't" instructional control. *Behavior Therapy, 23,* 131–140.

Reitman, D., & Drabman, R. S. (1996). Read my fingertips: A procedure for enhancing the effectiveness of time-out with argumentative children. *Child & Family Behavior Therapy, 18*(2), 35–40.

Taylor, J., & Miller, M. (1997). When timeout works some of the time: The importance of treatment integrity and functional assessment. *School Psychology Quarterly, 12*(1), 4–22.

Wolfgang, C. H. (1999). *Solving discipline problems: Methods and models for today's teachers* (4th ed.). Boston: Allyn and Bacon.

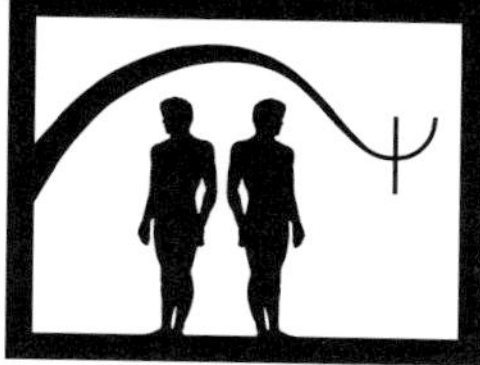

Token Economy

Paul Stuve and Julian A. Salinas

Fulton State Hospital and The University of Missouri School of Medicine

GLOSSARY

backup reinforcers Goods and privileges purchased with tokens that provide the token with its reward value.

change agent Person who administers reinforcers to a client contingent on the performance of a behavior or set of behaviors according to a prescribed plan.

extinction A reduction in the frequency of a behavior upon the cessation of its reinforcement.

generalized reinforcers Secondary reinforcers that are associated with a wide variety of reinforcing stimuli. Money is an example.

law of association by contiguity A fundamental law of learning that states that two events will come to be associated, or mean the same thing, if they are contiguous or occur together.

law of effect A fundamental law of learning that states that the frequency of a behavior is dependent on its resulting effects or consequences.

level system A supplementary system to a token economy program that involves different stages through which clients progress according to their mastery of specific behavioral competencies. Each stage, or level, is associated with more demanding reinforcement contingencies. The goal of such level systems is often to remove the use of tokens entirely.

negative punishment (response cost) The removal of a desirable event following a behavior that serves to reduce the frequency of that behavior.

negative reinforcement Increasing the frequency of a behavior by removing aversive stimuli as a consequence of that behavior.

positive punishment (aversion) The application of an aversive event following a behavior that serves to reduce the frequency of that behavior.

positive reinforcement Increasing the frequency of a behavior by applying desirable stimuli as a consequence of that behavior.

primary reinforcers Stimuli that have an "unlearned" reinforcing value. These are things that are critical to our survival, such as water, food, and sleep.

prompts Events that initiate a behavior, which is subsequently reinforced. These include a specific instruction of the expected behavior and its associated consequence.

punishment Arranging consequences of a behavior to decrease the frequency of that behavior.

reinforcement Arranging consequences of a behavior to increase the frequency of that behavior.

secondary reinforcers Stimuli that gain reinforcing value after being associated with primary reinforcers.

social reinforcers Social stimuli, such as attention, facial expressions, and verbalizations, that come to have a reinforcement value after being associated with other reinforcers.

stimulus sampling Procedure whereby clients are permitted to try a variety of reinforcers at no cost to generate interest and increase the likelihood that they will purchase the reinforcer with tokens once the sampling period is over.

time-out from reinforcement Removal of the client from all sources of reinforcement for a specified period of time to reduce the frequency of a particular behavior. Usually takes place in an isolated room or quiet area.

token Any symbolic material that can be exchanged for backup reinforcers. Tokens often consist of coins, poker chips, or cardboard squares.

I. DESCRIPTION

A token economy program (TEP) is a system whereby clients earn tokens in exchange for engaging in designated target behaviors. In some TEPs, clients will also lose tokens or be "fined" in response to engaging in inappropriate behaviors.

Just as we use money to buy the things we want, clients in a TEP exchange their tokens for a variety of desirable backup reinforcers, including food, beverages, magazines, toiletries, CDs, potted plants, toys, crayons, school supplies, and other desirable goods. Clients in residential settings may be given the opportunity to purchase a private bedroom, room furnishings, or home passes. Persons in TEPs in correctional settings often spend tokens to buy the privilege to wear their own, rather than institutional, clothes.

Backup reinforcers are available to the clients at specified times during the day, often through a well-stocked "token store" that functions like a small convenience store. In addition, other things purchased with tokens include time to watch TV or play a video game, trips to town for movies or other leisure events, and other desirable privileges. Because most people engage in such behaviors at a high rate when given the opportunity, these high-frequency behaviors are often used as reinforcers in TEPs. Improving the selection of backup reinforcers available, instituting time-limited sales, and holding auctions of highly desirable items all enhance token spending and associated client performance.

Tokens are disbursed by a change agent (e.g., psychiatric aide, educator, or parent) contingent on the performance of desired behaviors by the client. Change agents play active roles in TEPs, including informing the client of the contingencies for earning, spending, and/or losing tokens, and providing prompts as needed. In addition, as the goal of token economy programs is often for a behavior or set of behaviors to take place and be reinforced in the "natural" environment, token reinforcement and prompts are often withdrawn once consistent rates of the desired behaviors have been achieved. Change agents therefore deliver social reinforcers in addition to tokens to help maintain behavior when tokens are withdrawn. In addition, the transfer from a token economy back to a natural environment may include a transition from tokens to more abstract credit vouchers and eventually to money. This transition may be facilitated by a level system, whereby clients demonstrating the acquisition of certain competencies are "promoted" to a higher level that has more demanding contingencies associated with the client's improved functioning. The highest level of such a program could include elimination of tokens.

II. THEORETICAL BASES

B. F. Skinner's pioneering work in operant conditioning is generally credited with providing the theoretical foundation for the development of token economies. It is assumed that basic laws of learning account for the occurrence of behaviors, whether adaptive or maladaptive, and these same laws can be extended to change these behaviors through the thoughtful engineering of environmental events.

Two major laws synthesize theories of learning and have been validated by a body of basic and applied research. The law of effect states that the frequency of a behavior is dependent on the resulting consequences, or effects. Thus, behavior is strengthened or weakened by what follows it in the environment. In fact, a consistent finding has been that the more immediately a consequence follows a behavior, the greater effect it will have. Reinforcement always has the effect of increasing the likelihood or recurrence of behavior. In positive reinforcement this is done by adding a positive or desirable event (e.g., tokens) to the environment when a behavior occurs. In negative reinforcement, it is accomplished by removing an unpleasant or aversive event from the environment after a behavior occurs. A patient who utters threatening comments in a therapy group that she dislikes will have this behavior negatively reinforced if she is subsequently asked to leave the group (removal of an aversive event) and can be expected to make such statements with greater frequency to avoid that group.

Decreasing the frequency of a behavior is accomplished by removing reinforcement, or extinction. For example, some research shows that self-injurious behavior (e.g., head banging, hair pulling) in children with disabilities generally results in attention from caregivers (e.g., verbalizations of concern, physical intervention). Often, this attention positively reinforcers the self-injurious behavior. Brian Iwata and colleagues have repeatedly demonstrated that when such attention is withdrawn, a marked decrease in self-injury ensues.

Behavior can also be decreased by use of punishment. In positive punishment, this consists of applying an aversive event (e.g., spanking a child) following the target behavior, whereas in negative punishment the consequence involves removing a desirable event (e.g., removing a child's privileges). Punishment is most effective when used for brief periods and in combination with reinforcement for desirable behaviors. It is not recommended for use by itself.

The second law of learning is the law of association by contiguity. It states that two events will come to be associated if they are contiguous or occur together. Thus, things that are not reinforcing in and of themselves can become reinforcing by pairing them with things that are. By pairing tokens with a primary reinforcer such as food, the tokens become secondary reinforcers. Eventually, through association with a variety of primary and secondary reinforcers, tokens will become generalized reinforcers.

III. APPLICATIONS AND EXCLUSIONS

Because the operant conditioning principles on which TEPs are founded apply to all behavior, it is not surprising that TEPs have been developed to deal with a large variety of populations and target behaviors. They have been found to be effective in increasing exercise regimens in chronic pain patients; reducing cigarette smoking in psychiatric outpatients; improving outpatient therapy attendance and participation; reducing alcohol consumption and illicit drug usage in outpatient alcohol and substance abusers; increasing dietary compliance for individuals with diabetes or renal problems; promoting weight loss; improving word finding and decreasing misarticulations in aphasic patients; reducing temper tantrums, teasing, and other "acting out" by children in the home; eliminating thumb sucking; increasing self-care skills, social interaction, and exercise in geriatric patients; reducing stuttering; eliminating enuresis and encopresis; decreasing chronic nail biting; and improving marital satisfaction.

Token economy programs have also been applied to broader social issues, with successful implementations resulting in increased bus use at a major university, increased safety practices (and reduced injuries) at a pit mining operation, increased seat-beat use in youngsters, and increased litter control at a residential facility for individuals with mental retardation.

As should be apparent by now, participants for TEPs are not identified by focusing on psychological syndromes or diagnostic categories. Rather, the focus of the TEP is on the frequency and intensity of target behaviors. Thus, a TEP in a psychiatric hospital may focus on increasing grooming and hygiene, basic conversational skills, and vocational skills, and on decreasing assaultive and other maladaptive behaviors. It does not focus on treating "schizophrenia." Similarly, the social skills and academic skills of youth residing in correctional facilities may be addressed by a TEP. The TEP is not, however, used to treat "delinquency." In fact, although this article appears in the *Encyclopedia of Psychotherapy,* a TEP is not a "psychotherapy" or "treatment" per se. Rather, it is an extremely flexible organizational system used to deliver a wide range of plans for changing behavior. As Gordon Paul and Robert Lentz explained in 1977, the treatments delivered by two TEPs may be no more related to each other "than the action of heroin is related to that of penicillin, even though both are administered by injection."

IV. EMPIRICAL STUDIES

The bulk of the research on TEPs focuses on four populations: psychiatric patients, individuals with mental retardation, schoolchildren, and correctional populations. Although is certainly possible to apply diagnostic labels to these groups, it is important to reiterate that the focus of TEPs is on identifiable behaviors and not syndromes. Common targets across these populations include enhancing "motivation," increasing social and adaptive behaviors, and decreasing maladaptive and dangerous behaviors.

A. Psychiatric Patients

The first TEP for psychiatric inpatients with severe disabilities was implemented at Anna State Hospital in Illinois in the 1960s by Teodoro Ayllon and Nathan Azrin. Their research demonstrated that changes in the patients' off-ward job choices and increased performance of the non-preferred jobs resulted through use of token reinforcers. In another TEP at a VA hospital, John Atthowe and Leonard Krasner reported that previously catatonic, withdrawn, or isolated patients demonstrated a significant lessening of apathy indicated by requesting and receiving overnight passes with family, going to the canteen, and engaging in a variety of social interactions on the ward such as playing pool or card games (where betting was done with tokens).

Other target behaviors addressed by early TEPs with psychiatric patients included grooming and hygiene, bedroom care, attendance and participation in group activities, general cooperativeness with ward rules, and social functioning. Scores of publications show patient improvements in all of these areas, as compared to either their own pre-TEP behaviors, or to behaviors of patients on non-TEP wards.

In addition to these increases in appropriate and adaptive behaviors, psychiatric patients in TEPs have shown decreases in inappropriate and maladaptive behaviors as well. Some of these reductions occurred without being directly targeted, apparently as side effects of improvements in adaptive areas of functioning. Other TEPs have directly targeted such behaviors, generally by withholding reinforcement or using token fines. Results over the years show reductions in screaming, ritualistic behaviors, mannerisms, responsiveness to hallucinations, and the frequency of delusional talk. In addition, TEPs have shown dramatic decreases in threatening and assaultive behaviors, with corresponding reductions in use of seclusion and restraint with patients. Research shows that decreases in PRN or "as needed" medication usage as well as reductions in dosage of routine medications is common for TEP patients. In fact, some studies show that behavioral interventions such as the TEP are effective with psychiatric patients even in the absence of medications. Gordon L. Paul and colleagues reported that patients diagnosed with schizophrenia in a social learning program, which included a TEP, were able to be withdrawn from all psychiatric medications without a deterioration in functioning.

Finally, although discharge from inpatient settings and subsequent community tenure are affected by a number of political, financial, and social factors, TEP patients have nevertheless demonstrated decreased lengths of inpatient stay, increased rates of discharge, and decreased numbers of readmissions in comparison to non-TEP patients.

B. Individuals with Mental Retardation

Token economy programs for individuals with mental retardation (MR) have had similar results to those for psychiatric inpatients. Bathing, grooming, toileting, bed making, feeding, tooth brushing, and washing/combing hair have all been shown to increase for individuals with MR in TEPs. Improvements are also seen in vocational skills (punctuality and attendance, production rates, task quality) and academic skills (test preparation, study behaviors). Some TEPs even permit banking of tokens and will teach check-writing skills to their clients with MR to access tokens saved in this manner. Social behavior has also been affected, from behaviors such as making eye contact and asking questions to more complex skills like proper noun-verb agreement, correct grammar, appropriate use of articles or pronouns, and even speech volume and dysfluencies. For younger individuals, increases have been shown in cooperative and competitive play in comparison to solitary or parallel play.

Inappropriate behaviors of individuals with MR have been targeted as well. Research has demonstrated that aggression, rocking behaviors, and self-injury are responsive to treatment programs using token reinforcement, time-out from reinforcement, extinction, and token fines.

C. School Children

Schools have been a popular setting for TEPs, with participants including "normal" children as well as children with a variety of problems including learning disabilities, attention deficit hyperactivity disorder, and emotional disturbances. Participants have spanned the age range from elementary through high school and beyond.

A large TEP undertaking reported by Howard Rollins and colleagues in 1974 included more than 700 inner-city students in Grades 1 through 8. Students in the 16 TEP classrooms demonstrated increased attentiveness and superior improvements in IQ and academic achievement measures than students in the 14 non-TEP control classrooms. Other researchers have obtained similar results, including improved completion of homework and increased basic academic skills as measured by task completion, accuracy, and grades. These improvements are reported in "normal" children as well as those who demonstrate learning disabilities, hyperactivity, and emotional difficulties. In addition, TEPs have been successfully used to improve articulation in children with speech disorders and have even been successful in enhancing writing skills as measured by use of different adjectives, verbs, and story beginnings, and as rated by outside blind reviewers.

A comparison of multiple methods for controlling disruptive behaviors in the classroom was reported by K. Daniel O'Leary and colleagues, who examined the effects of rearranging the structure of the class periods, posting and reviewing of behavior rules, using praise and extinction, and finally adding a token economy. All methods were generally ineffective until the TEP component was added. Similarly, Marcia Broden and colleagues decreased disruptive behaviors as well as improved study behavior through use of a simple timer and a TEP. The timer went off at random intervals, at which time students who were quiet and in their seats received tokens. This and other research finds TEPs to be effective in reducing relatively minor disruptions (talking in class, being out of one's seat, interrupting, arguing), as well as more serious disruptive behaviors, such as threats and verbal or physical assaults.

As an alternative or supplement to individual contingencies, many classroom TEPs make use of group contingencies. In such an arrangement, it is the behavior of the entire group or class rather than the individual student that determines how much reinforcement each student receives. The "Good Behavior Game," developed by Harriet Barrish and colleagues, divides students into groups or teams, with each team earning or losing points depending on the behavior of the group's members. The team with the best score at the end of a specified time period receives reinforcement. Research using this game has successfully demonstrated its use to reduce disruptive behavior in the classroom. Variations on group contingencies in TEPs were examined by Ronald Drabman and colleagues. In different conditions, tokens were earned individually based on individual performance, or by the entire group based on the behavior of the best behaved child, the worse behaved child, or a randomly chosen child. Disruptive behavior decreased in all conditions, with no significant differences between them. Other research comparing individual versus group contingencies has reported similar results.

Although medications are often used to treat hyperactivity and disruptive behaviors in children, some researchers have found TEPs to be equally effective in controlling these behaviors. TEPs also have the added benefit of improving academic performance, a result not typically found with medication alone.

D. Correctional Populations

Token economy programs with youth engaging in criminal behaviors have also yielded favorable results, although these programs are generally conducted in institutional settings and not traditional classrooms. TEPs have resulted in improved self-care skills, conversational skills (including use of proper grammar), social functioning, classroom behaviors, academic skills, and vocational skills. Some programs, such as the Achievement Place program described by Elery Phillips and colleagues, involve using a client as a change agent to dispense tokens, levy fines, and assign jobs and other tasks. This innovative feature results in improved performance of target behaviors. In addition, decreases in aggressive and threatening behaviors have been reported, often through the adjunctive use of time-out from reinforcement and token fines.

Token economy programs in adult prisons have met with varying degrees of success. An effort in Missouri focused on the state's most problematic prisoners and involved a tiered token/point system. Prisoners initially earned tokens for lack of threatening or assaultive behaviors and for cooperating with the rules and could purchase privileges such as increased opportunities to shave and shower, exercise, and possess personal items. Improvement in behavior resulted in advancement through a level system and eventually a switch to points instead of tokens, with greater opportunities to access backup reinforcers such as visits to the commissary, outside phone call privileges, and paid "vacation" days from work. Plagued with legal problems throughout its existence, including charges of violating prisoners' rights, the program generally failed to meet its goals of returning its difficult prisoners to the general population and was closed after two years.

Less ambitious prison TEPs have been successful in improving compliance with basic prison routines (getting up on time, keeping cell neat, performing cellblock chores) and increasing academic skills in prisoners, including earning GEDs. Backup reinforcers in some innovative programs have included offering appointments with parole board officers, and even opportunities to go fishing or visit a women's prison.

E. Failures of TEPs

In spite of the success indicated here, research consistently shows that a small number of individuals fails to respond to TEPs. This may be due to individual differences in responsiveness to the contingencies arranged in a particular TEP. For example, providing cigarettes as a backup reinforcer to a non-smoking client is not likely to be very motivating. Similarly, offering reinforcers to a client who is unfamiliar with them may not generate much interest. Teodoro Ayllon and Nathan Azrin addressed this through the use of stimulus sampling. By permitting patients to "sample" new or unfamiliar backup reinforcers (e.g., attending a local fair or a concert) at no cost, they were able to increase interest in those reinforcers once token charges were reinstated.

Other TEP clients may not respond because they lack the skills necessary to perform the target behavior, or because they do not understand the relationship between the target behavior and the reinforcement. Devising individualized contingencies and personalized reinforcers can improve responsiveness in a TEP.

Finally, inadequate implementation of the TEP can attenuate client responsiveness. Some research shows that client change is related to the accuracy with which staff adhere to the planned contingencies. Inadequate training and/or oversight of the TEP can lead to poor results.

F. Generalization

Research indicates that gains made in TEPs do not always last after the token reinforcement has ended. Generalization of gains made in TEPs typically requires some advance planning and should not be expected to simply happen. Strategies for accomplishing this include a gradual rather than sudden cessation of token usage combined with a corresponding increase in naturally occurring reinforcers such as social praise. Other strategies include lengthening the delay between the behavior and the reinforcement, and providing reinforcement in a variety of settings so that the behavior is not limited to a narrow range of cues.

V. CASE ILLUSTRATION

Joe, 33, has spent most of his adult life in state psychiatric facilities. Periodically he gains discharge, only to be readmitted within a period of months. His current hospitalization has lasted over 3 years.

Joe typically spends his day in his bedroom. He rarely talks to anyone and only ventures out for coffee, cigarettes, and meals. He goes weeks without bathing, requiring strong staff encouragement or assistance on those occasions that he does bathe. Joe responds to auditory hallucinations and can frequently be heard talking and yelling at "Uncle Ed," his abusive and now-deceased uncle whom Joe believes is the source of his voices. At times, Joe assaults staff members and other patients in response to directives from "Uncle Ed."

On March 1, Joe is admitted to the hospital's TEP with identified goals of increasing socialization, improving self-care skills, decreasing responsiveness to hallucinations, and reducing/eliminating aggressive behaviors. Program staff orient Joe and explain the TEP to him, inducing a discussion of how to earn and spend tokens. Joe immediately begins a period of stimulus sampling, whereby all backup reinforcers are available to him free of charge so that he may be exposed to a wide variety of things that he may later wish to purchase with tokens. The free availability of backup reinforcers is gradually reduced over the next few days, and by March 5th Joe must have tokens to access his coffee and cigarettes. At first, Joe becomes angry when he does not receive a free cup of coffee and assaults a staff member. He receives a token fine for his behavior, which must be paid before he can purchase backup reinforcers for himself. Joe has similar incidents over the next few days but eventually realizes that assaulting others will not get him a cup of coffee, and by March 10th Joe is engaging in some simple behaviors to earn tokens. He starts attending a few scheduled treatment groups and begins to shower a couple of times a week. However, Joe doesn't use soap or shampoo while showering and only stands under the water for about 1 min. A decision is therefore made to individualize Joe's target behavior for showers. The next day, Joe earns a token for staying in the shower for 3 min. Eventually, he must use soap and then shampoo to earn his token. The change agents work closely with Joe to help him develop these skills. Slowly, over the course of about 2 weeks, Joe's showering skills advance to the point that he is taking full showers, with good use of soap and shampoo. His hygiene and grooming have improved immensely, and Joe smiles when staff compliment him on his appearance.

As Joe spends more time out of his room, he begins to notice other patients leaving the ward for vocational activities. He expresses an interest in this, but learns that he must be at Level 2 in the TEP to work, and he needs to participate in semistructured social activities to reach that level. Joe reluctantly begins showing up at a couple of the evening card games scheduled on the ward. When he discovers that he cannot earn tokens if he talks to his hallucinations, he angrily retreats to his room. Eventually, after this behavior costs him tokens in a number of activities, Joe begins to reduce the frequency of responding to hallucinations. By April 14th, Joe is promoted to Level 2 and starts attending work. Token payment for work activities is delayed at this Level, and patients are paid in a lump sum at the end of the week as the first step in gradually weaning them off the token economy.

While walking to and from work each day, Joe notices the Recreation Center on campus, as well as some of the gardens and nearby benches. His attendance and participation in other treatment groups starts to improve, as Joe tries to earn additional tokens to spend on grounds passes. An aggressive incident at work on May 10th results in a token fine and the loss of Level 2. Joe is frustrated and becomes sullen and withdrawn for a few days. Staff once again hear him speaking to "Uncle

Ed." However, after 3 days Joe shows up for the morning exercise group where he earns a token and receives a good bit of social praise from the staff. Joe focuses on regaining Level 2, and succeeds on May 22nd.

By late June, Joe rarely isolates himself in his bedroom. His aggressive behaviors are well under control, and he no longer talks to "Uncle Ed." Improvements in his group attendance and work performance result in a promotion to Level 3 on June 30th. Joe now receives a large weekly deposit of tokens into his "bank account," instead of receiving physical tokens at the time he performs each target behavior. He must learn to budget his token supply for an entire week, because no new token deposits will be received before the next week. Joe struggles with this for a few weeks, and often runs out of tokens after only 3 to 4 days, but with some teaching he learns to manage his funds for the entire week.

By late July, Joe is ready to make brief visits to local group homes in preparation for discharge. He continues to participate in treatment at the hospital during the day but starts engaging in evening and weekend leisure events at the group home where he wants to live. There are no tokens at the group home, and this is an additional step in helping Joe move from the token economy back to the community. When Joe is promoted to Level 4 on August 5th, he starts carrying money again and is taken off the token economy entirely. Staff continue to provide Joe with lots of social praise for engaging in positive and adaptive behaviors. By September 8th, Joe is ready for discharge.

VI. SUMMARY

Leonard Krasner once described TEPs as "the most advanced type of social engineering currently in use." Since their inception in the early 1960s, TEPs have been used to improve basic hygiene and grooming, social functioning, and vocational skills, and reduce agitation, assaultiveness, and other maladaptive behaviors. They have improved academic skills and have reduced classroom disruptions in schoolchildren. Individuals in correctional settings show improved social skills and rule compliance. Most participants respond favorably to TEPs, but poor implementation, including inadequate training or oversight, will reduce their effectiveness. In addition, people respond differently to reinforcement contingencies, and this will also affect the effectiveness of the TEP. Finally, planning for generalization can help ensure that client improvement continues after the token reinforcement has ended. Forty years after its inception, the token economy remains a powerful tool for changing an enormous array of behaviors with a wide range of populations in a variety of different settings.

See Also the Following Articles

Applied Behavior Analysis ■ Behavioral Contracting ■ Contingency Management ■ Good Behavior Game ■ Negative Punishment ■ Negative Reinforcement ■ Positive Punishment ■ Positive Reinforcement ■ Response Cost

Further Reading

Ayllon, T. (1999). How to use token economy and point systems. Austin, TX: Pro-Ed.

Kazdin, A. E. (1977). *The token economy.* New York: Plenum.

Kazdin, A. E. (1982). The token economy: A decade later. *Journal of Applied Behavior Analysis, 15,* 431–445.

Parker, H. C. (1996). *Behavior management at home: A token economy. program for children and teens.* Plantation, FL: Specialty Press.

Paul, G. L., Stuve, P., & Cross, J. V. (1997). Real-world inpatient programs: Shedding some light – A critique. *Journal of Applied and Preventive Psychology, 6,* 193–204.

Paul, G. L., & Lentz, R. J. (1977). *Psychosocial treatment of chronic mental patients* Cambridge, MA: Harvard University Press.

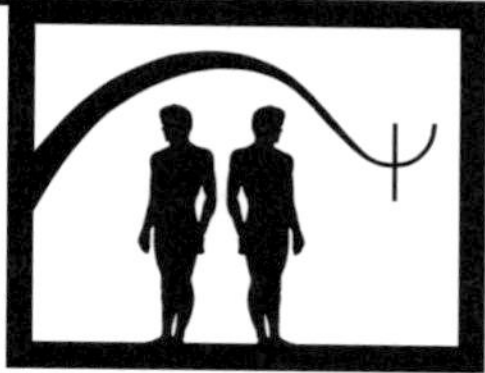

Token Economy: Guidelines for Operation

Teodoro Ayllon and Michael A. Milan
Georgia State University

GLOSSARY

backup reinforcer The positive reinforcers for which tokens are exchanged.

Premack principle The finding that the opportunity to engage in high-probability activities will serve as a reinforcer for engaging in lower probability activities.

radical behaviorism Based on the work of B. F. Skinner, it is the theoretical orientation that posits that behavioral principles provide an explanation and understanding of the full range of human behavior, thought, and emotion.

target behavior A desirable or undesirable behavior to be increased or decreased in the token economy program.

token The item earned or lost when desirable or undesirable target behavior occurs and which is exchanged for backup reinforcers.

I. HISTORICAL ANTECEDENTS OF THE TOKEN ECONOMY

Token economies have a long history. Perhaps the earliest description of what would now be considered a token economy was provided by Alexander Maconochie in the mid-1800s. While warden of the Norfolk Island, Australia prison, Maconochie concluded that the punitively oriented, torturous methods of inmate management common at that time did nothing to prepare offenders for a productive life in the community but instead increased the likelihood that they would return to their criminal ways when released. In an effort to bring humane management practices and meaningful rehabilitation programs to his prison, Maconochie developed a mark (token) system in which inmates earned marks for appropriate behavior and lost marks for inappropriate behavior. The inmates, in turn, used marks to purchase food, clothing, and privileges. Promotion through a levels system within the prison and even eventual release from prison were also determined by the number of marks accumulated.

It was not until the mid-20th century work of Ayllon and Azrin with severely disturbed psychiatric patients on one ward of a large state hospital and the work of Arthur Staats and his colleagues with children in a preschool setting that the token economy found acceptance and widescale use in modern psychology. Their work is a pioneering example of the extension of basic research conducted in the tradition of Skinner's radical behaviorism into applied settings.

II. OVERVIEW OF THE TOKEN ECONOMY

Stuve and Salinas provide a detailed description of the token economy in their contribution to this encyclopedia.

Our contribution therefore begins with only a brief overview of the token economy. We then offer a number of suggestions or guidelines for the operation of token economies that are based on both a consideration of published works in the area and our personal experience operating token economies in applied settings.

As Stuve and Salinas indicate, a token economy is a reinforcement-based motivational program that is used to encourage desirable, adaptive behaviors and to discourage undesirable, maladaptive behaviors. It differs from other reinforcement programs in that an artificial or contrived reinforcer (the token) is introduced to mediate the relationship and bridge the delay between behavior and more natural reinforcing consequences, such as extra recreational activities or special foods. Desirable behaviors are followed by the award of tokens, which are then exchanged for the natural reinforcers. Similarly, undesirable behavior is followed by the loss of tokens, which reduces or prevents access to the natural reinforcers. Token economies are typically employed with groups of individuals, such as all students in a classroom, all persons with developmental disabilities in a sheltered workshop, all psychiatric patients in a hospital ward, all delinquents in a group home, or all prisoners in a cell block. However, token reinforcement programs can also be used with individual children, adolescents, or adults. When this is done the program is usually referred to as a token or point system rather than as a token economy.

III. ESTABLISHING AND OPERATING A TOKEN ECONOMY

Token economies should be predominantly, if not exclusively, positive rather than punitive. That is, the target behaviors that lead to token award should far outnumber those that lead to token loss, and the participants should earn access to far more backup reinforcers than they are denied. Similarly, tokens should be awarded when earned by engaging in desirable target behaviors rather than given at the start of a day, for example, and taken away as punishment when desirable target behaviors are not exhibited. By emphasizing positive consequences for desirable behavior and for behavior that is incompatible with undesirable behavior, the token economy fosters cooperation and a sense of community among clients and staff while preventing the alienation and resistance that often is seen in punitively oriented programs. By so doing, the token economy fosters a positive attitude about the token economy, active participation in the token economy, and constructive relationships with those who carry it out on a day-to-day basis. Punitively oriented token economies tend to do just the opposite and explain much of the alienation and resistance commonly seen in such programs.

The major components of the token economy are the target behaviors, the tokens, and the backup reinforcers. In addition, the token economy includes the schedules relating target behaviors to the award or loss of tokens and the exchange of tokens for the acquisition of backup reinforcers. The token economy also includes provisions for the training and monitoring of staff, the use of behaviorally based methods for the development of the target behaviors to be reinforced, and procedures to ensure that behavior change is maintained as the client leaves the token economy. Finally, all aspects of the operation of the token economy and the progress of clients are monitored on a regular basis.

A. Target Behaviors

The token economy exists to increase and maintain desirable behaviors and to decrease and eliminate undesirable behaviors. In general, targeted desirable behaviors are those that contribute to or result in successful community adjustment and the living of a satisfying and productive life. Targeted undesirable behaviors are those that interfere with or prevent those outcomes. Quite often, the positive character of the token economy may be enhanced by targeting the desirable incompatible opposite behavior of an undesirable behavior for token award, rather than targeting the undesirable behavior for token loss.

The target behaviors should be in accord with the mission and goals those settings have established for themselves and their clients. A program for persons incompetent to stand trial that targets the signs and symptoms of mental illness, for example, is inadequate unless it also targets or even emphasizes the skills necessary to competently stand trial. Some behaviors may be targeted for all clients in the token economy. The target behaviors should also be based on an assessment of the strengths or abilities and the problems or deficiencies of the individual clients. As a result, clients may have several target behaviors in common, as well as several target behaviors that are unique to themselves or a small number of other clients.

The target behaviors or, in some instances, the products of the target behaviors should be described in unambiguous terms that make them observable and countable by a second party. This serves several important functions that advance the treatment effort. First, the clients know exactly what is expected of them and act in a manner that will earn tokens or avoid their loss. The staff also know exactly what is expected of the clients and can accurately award or deduct tokens accordingly. In addition, the objective definition of target behaviors reduces conflict between clients and staff about the occurrence or nonoccurrence of target behaviors that typically occurs when more subjective criteria are employed. Similarly, the clear specification of target behaviors fosters consistency in the manner in which different staff, often on different shifts, work with clients. Finally, the more objectively defined the target behaviors, the less likely it is that clients will be effective in manipulating staff by arguing, for example, that a staff member is discriminating against them by treating them more harshly than other staff members.

B. Tokens

Tokens should be awarded as quickly as possible, if not immediately, following a desirable target behavior and taken away as quickly as possible, if not immediately, following an undesirable target behavior. The tokens themselves should be tangible, durable, portable, counterfeit-proof, and personalized in a manner that allows their accumulation by participants. In a very real sense, a country's financial economy is a token economy, and the characteristics of these tokens are a good model for the tokens in any token economy. In general, the nickels, dimes, and quarters of the United States' economy are tangible, durable, and portable. These coins can be accumulated in considerable numbers, and are virtually counterfeit-proof. They can also be easily carried by staff and can be awarded to clients immediately following a desirable behavior. Perhaps the greatest problem the currency in the United States' economic system poses is that it is not personalized and as a result individuals can and do acquire these tokens through theft and other means without engaging in appropriate and desirable target behaviors.

Rather than use "real" money, of course, token economies typically employ other items as tokens. What is used as a token in a token economy is limited only by the ingenuity of the staff of the program. One example is the poker chip or similar item, perhaps personalized with a number or letter to discourage illegitimate acquisition through theft or coercion. Another example is the daily punch card on which staff punch holes in circles as clients earn tokens and cross off punched-out circles as clients spend tokens. At the end of the day the cards are collected by staff who determine the number of unexpended tokens, punch that number into the next day's cards, and distribute the individualized cards at the start of the next day. Still another example is a checkbook banking system in which clients are told to add tokens to their account as they earn tokens and write checks as they spend tokens. At the end of the day staff balance each account and inform the clients of their balance at the start of the next day.

The tokens in the three representative examples range from concrete or tangible to abstract or intangible. Where along that continuum the token should fall is dependent on the characteristics of the client population. Young preschool children should be provided more concrete or tangible tokens, whereas older adult offenders would most probably function well with more abstract or intangible tokens. When making that decision, one should keep in mind that one cannot err in the direction of using tokens that are too concrete or tangible.

C. Backup Reinforcers

The backup reinforcers are the natural reinforcers that give value to the tokens. The token economy should not deprive any clients of anything to which they are entitled by the Constitution or by statute. The backup reinforcers therefore are additions to these legally mandated minimums. They may involve access to additional amounts or enhancements of entitlements, such as additional exercise time or special foods, as well as anything to which the client is not legally entitled. In general, backup reinforcers fall in several categories. These consist of edibles or consumables, such as special food or drink; activities, such as extra recreational or computer game time; material objects, such as special athletic shoes or posters; and independence, such as reduced supervision or movement through progressively less restrictive levels in a structured levels program. Each can be considered a to-be-earned privilege.

A number of strategies may be used to identify backup reinforcers. The most straightforward consists of asking the clients what they would like and would work for. Another is based on the Premack principle and involves observing clients during free or unstructured time to identify the things they are most likely to do. These may then be used as backup reinforcers for the typically lower probability target behaviors. Finally, the staff can be asked what they believe will serve as backup reinforcers for their clients. It is important to note, however, that the information gathered through these strategies results only in the identification of potential backup reinforcers. The reinforcing properties of the potential backup reinforcers must be tested to determine whether they are true backup reinforcers. This is done by assessing whether clients will engage in target behavior to earn tokens and then exchange the tokens for the potential backup reinforcers.

What is reinforcing to one client may or may not be available to another client. The token economy must therefore offer a variety of backup reinforcers to ensure that there are sufficient reinforcers for all participants. Although some backup reinforcers may motivate most or all clients, additional backup reinforcers that function as such for only a few or, perhaps, only one client should also be made available to ensure that the unique interests of all clients are addressed. The backup reinforcers should be available to clients on a regular basis. Some should be available several times a day, others several times a week, and perhaps still others several times a month or only on a monthly basis. The schedule of availability of backup reinforcers is dictated, in part, by the characteristics of the clients, and a token economy cannot err in the direction of making backup reinforcers too frequently available to clients. Finally, the backup reinforcers must be available only through the token economy. The availability of "bootleg" backup reinforcers, that is, backup reinforcers that may be obtained through other means, will dilute or negate the reinforcing properties of backup reinforcers and should be prevented.

D. Additional Considerations

The token economy should be fair or balanced. That is, the backup reinforcers should be commensurate with the target behaviors. This is accomplished, in part, by ensuring there is a rich and variable array of backup reinforcers available to the clients, and by ensuring that the number of tokens earned is in accord with the nature of the to-be-rewarded target behaviors and the number of tokens expended are in accord with the nature of the to-be-purchased backup reinforcers. These ratios should be adjusted as participation in the token economy dictates. Clients should be included in the decision-making process to both better ensure fairness is maintained and to offer them the therapeutic benefit such involvement brings to the treatment setting. The token economy should also be as simple or straightforward as possible so that the relationship between target behaviors, point award or loss, and backup reinforcers is clear to all clients. Conditions, exceptions, and qualifications that obscure the direct relationship between target behavior, tokens, and backup reinforcers will work to dilute the effects of the token economy.

Although the token economy itself may provide experiences that foster a structure and an appreciation of the quid pro quo relationship between privileges and responsibilities that prepare individuals for life in the community, its greater power lies in its ability to motivate clients to participate in therapeutic and rehabilitative programs and activities. These should be identified while developing the target behaviors of each client's individualized treatment program. Staff require training to carry out the token economy and its treatment programs, or to support the staff that do. The general skills necessary to carry out a token economy include, among others, how to shape behavior, the use of prompting to increase desirable behavior and redirection to decrease undesirable behavior, how to use social reinforcement when awarding tokens and backup reinforcers, and the use of behavioral momentum, differential reinforcement, and chaining to further encourage appropriate behavior or discourage inappropriate behavior. Training in specific therapeutic skills is necessary to carry out the treatment programs called for by the characteristics and special needs of the client population. These should be in accord with the profession's movement toward the identification and adoption of empirically based treatments.

A monitoring system is an important part of the token economy. Not only should clients' progress be monitored and assessed on a regular basis, but the performance of the staff in carrying out the token economy should also be monitored and assessed on a regular basis. When the monitoring of clients indicates that their progress is not as is expected, changes in both the clients' individualized treatment plan and the design or implementation of the token economy should be considered and implemented as called for. When the monitoring of staff indicates that their performance is not as is called for, retraining and more intensive supervision should be considered and implemented as called for. More important, however, staff should participate in a positive organizational behavior management program to sustain high levels of work performance and morale.

Special procedures should be implemented to phase out the token economy when clients are eligible to move to another treatment setting or into the community. The general strategy to be followed is to give clients progressively more responsibility for the management of their own behavior. This may be done by moving clients through a structured levels program or by moving from the token economy to self-management in the absence of levels. One might begin, for example, by relaxing a requirement that staff evaluate clients' performance and award tokens as clients assume more responsibility for evaluating their performance of their target behaviors and awarding or deducting their tokens accordingly. Similarly, the next phase might involve the clients assuming responsibility for exchanging tokens for backup reinforcers. Finally, the tokens might be eliminated and clients assume full responsibility for continuing to engage in their target behaviors and, in exchange, have full but reasonable access to backup reinforcers. Staff should continue to monitor clients throughout this process to ensure that performance is sustained. Transitional programs should ensure that improvements are maintained as clients leave the token economy setting. These programs range from training those who will work with the clients in the additional behavioral skills employed by the token economy staff to training them to continue token economy procedures, if such prosthetic arrangements are deemed necessary.

IV. EFFECTIVENESS OF THE TOKEN ECONOMY

Maconochie's anecdotal reports indicate that the recidivism rate for inmates released from his program on Norfolk Island was markedly lower than that for other prisons in the British colonies. More recent empirical research provides general confirmation of the effectiveness of properly designed and implemented token economies. Perhaps the most influential of the empirical studies is Paul and Lentz's thorough-going experimental comparison of milieu therapy and social learning therapy with a severely disturbed psychiatric population in a large state hospital. They defined the milieu approach as consisting of increased social interaction and group activities, expectancies and group pressure directed toward normal functioning, more informal patient status, goal-directed communication, freedom of movement, and treatment of patients as responsible people rather than custodial cases. The social learning approach was described as the systematic extension of principles and techniques derived from basic research on learning to clinical problems, specification of specific behaviors for change, emphasis on response-contingent consequences, and the use of token economy programs.

In general, Paul and Lentz found the token economy to be superior to the milieu program in terms of both in-hospital improvement and then postrelease adjustment during a year and a half follow-up period. It was also found to be the more cost effective of the two approaches. The milieu approach, in turn, was found to be superior to routine hospital care for both the in-hospital and postrelease indices of program effectiveness. Findings such as these ensured that the token economy would become an important component of many treatment programs for persons with mental illness as well as in educational settings, training schools, and prisons.

V. SUMMARY

The token economy employs a conditioned reinforcer to mediate between clients' behavior and its more natural positive reinforcement. It is an effective motivational system to encourage desirable behavior and discourage undesirable behavior. It is also effective in ensuring clients' participation in individually prescribed treatment programs. Although simple in concept, it requires sophistication in implementation as well as staff training and continued monitoring to ensure its effectiveness.

See Also the Following Articles

Behavioral Contracting ■ Contingency Management ■ Good Behavior Game ■ Job Club Method

Further Reading

Ayllon, T., & Azrin, N. (1968). *The token economy.* New York: Appleton-Century-Crofts.

Ayllon, T., Milan, M. A., Roberts, M. D., & McKee, J. M. (1979). *Correctional rehabilitation and management: A psychological approach.* New York: John Wiley & Sons.

Chambless, D. L., Baker, M. J., Baucom, D. H., Beutler, L. E., Calhoun, K. S., Critis-Christoph, P., et al. (1998). Update on empirically validated therapies, II. *The Clinical Psychologist, 51,* 3–16.

Machonocie, A. (1847/1973). *Norfolk Island.* Hobart, Australia: Sullivan's Cove.

Paul, G. L., & Lentz, R. J. (1977). *Psychosocial treatment of chronic mental patients.* Cambridge, MA: Harvard University Press.

Paul, G. L., Stuve, P., & Menditto, A. (1997). Social-learning program (with token economy) for adult psychiatric patients. *The Clinical Psychologist, 50,* 14–17.

Premack, D. (1959). Toward empirical behavior laws: I. Positive reinforcement. *Psychological Review, 66,* 219–233.

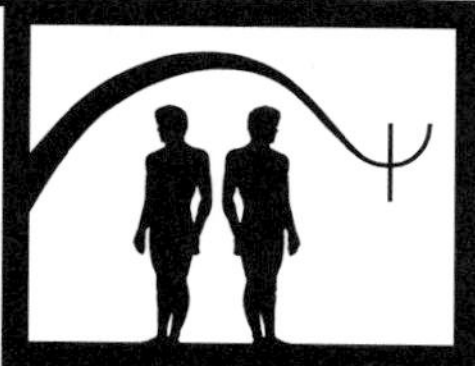

Topographic Theory

Alan Sugarman and Keith Kanner

San Diego Psychoanalytic Society and Institute and University of California, San Diego

GLOSSARY

defense The methods used by the ego to master and control id impulses or superego injunctions.

drives Another term for Freud's instincts. Two drives were postulated by Freud—sexual and aggressive. These were the major factors motivating the operation of the mind in his topographic model. They continue to be considered important but not the only motivating factors by modern psychoanalysts.

libidinal wishes Wishes infused with affectionate or sexual urges thought to be ubiquitous in human functioning.

libido The hypothetical psychic energy attached to the sexual instincts.

narcissism Love for the self. Modern-day psychoanalysts use the term primarily to refer to issues of self-esteem. Narcissistic defenses refer to defenses designed to protect or enhance self-esteem, for example.

object relations Refers to relationships to other people. In psychoanalysis, it is the internal representations of self and others that are important in motivating and mediating interpersonal interactions. A developmental distinction is often made between dyadic and triadic object relations. The former refer to relationships modeled on preoedipal experiences where the major goals of the child revolve around need satisfaction by the mother. Triadic relations are seen as more mature, implying oedipal engagement and the increasing mental complexity implicit in being aware of needs and wishes toward one parent vis-á-vis the other parent.

psychic determinism The tenet that all mental acts have meanings and causes. Psychoanalysis assumes that such causes have to do with mental phenomena that preceded the act in question.

resistance The manifestation of defense within the treatment process whereby the patient opposes the analyst's interventions.

transference The process by which the patient displaces onto the therapist or analyst feelings, impulses, attitudes, or defenses derived from important interactions in the past.

Topographic theory refers to Freud's second phase in developing his psychoanalytic model. It lasted from 1897 until he introduced his structural model in 1923. This phase was marked by rapid, significant evolution in psychoanalytic theory and technique. Many key concepts from it continued to inform psychoanalytic theory and practice including drives, unconscious mental functioning, defenses, unconscious conflict, object relations, and narcissism. Dream analysis, the importance of transference and resistance, and the importance of insight in bringing about psychoanalytic cure stem from Freud's interest in delineating the topography of the mind.

I. SEXUAL TRAUMAS

The most decisive clinical finding that led Freud to abandon his previous affect-trauma model and to develop his topographic one was his finding that the sexual traumas remembered by his hysterical patients thought to cause their symptoms had often not happened. He came to this startling conclusion when he realized that every patient blamed her problems on perverse actions of her father. The likelihood of such pervasive sexual abuse seemed too great to accept as Freud gained more experience with his new talking cure. Furthermore, he himself developed similar memories in his self-analysis. Yet he knew definitively that such actions had not truly happened. These realizations left Freud with the problem of how to account for the existence of such false memories as seemingly a part of the human condition. Puzzling over this problem, he realized that such memories were actually fantasies, fantasies from which he deduced the existence of sexual drives. The concept of defense was brought in to explain the patient's distortion of fantasies into memories. Thus was born the notion of intrapsychic conflict.

II. TOPOGRAPHIC THEORY

But Freud went far beyond the concepts of unconscious libidinal fantasies conflicting with defenses as he tried to understand a host of normal and pathological human characteristics during this stage of his thinking. In order to explain dreams, jokes, slips of the tongue, various types of psychopathology, and aspects of clinical technique he found it necessary to map out the terrain or topography of the mind. His topographic theory differentiated areas of the mind and mental characteristics according to their relationship to consciousness. A spatial metaphor of proceeding from the depths to the surface of the mind was used. Three regions or systems in the mind were delineated: (1) the system Unconscious; (2) the system Preconscious; and (3) the system Conscious. The mental contents of the system Unconscious, instinctual drives and wishes, were thought to be continually pushing to be discharged into the system Conscious. But the unpleasant affects anticipated were they allowed to emerge into consciousness gave rise to defenses that attempted to maintain them in the system Unconscious or to distort their expression so that only partial and disguised discharge was allowed into the system Conscious. This model of mental functioning, thought to give rise to the neurotic symptoms that Freud treated in his patients, led to the technical dictum of that era—make the unconscious conscious. Thus, Freud advocated that analysts impart insight of their patients' unconscious mental contents, and that this insight would lead to symptom relief.

The spatial metaphor that Freud relied on during this stage of his thinking was most clearly delineated in the seventh chapter of the *Interpretation of Dreams*, which he published in 1900. The model of the mind as composed of three systems or regions that he constructed was based on the concept of the reflex arc. This model held that mental contents had to proceed from the system Unconscious through the system Preconscious before becoming accessible to conscious awareness in the system Conscious. Each of these systems or regions of the mind had distinct characteristics, all of which combined to make mental functioning highly complex. Boundaries were thought to exist between each system, although the rigidity of the boundaries varied. When the mind was in a state of equilibrium or harmony, the boundaries between the regions were thought to be vague, but the dividing lines became quite defined during episodes of conflict.

III. SYSTEM UNCONSCIOUS

The system Unconscious was the most important system in this model. Indeed, the idea of unconscious mental functioning remains central to psychoanalytic understanding of normal and abnormal behavior to this day despite the concept of the system Unconscious having been eliminated. The idea that all behavior and psychological functioning have unconscious determinants remains central to psychoanalysis. Joseph Sandler and his colleagues have pointed out that this hypothesis assumes that the greatest portion of the mind operates outside conscious awareness. It follows from the assumption that most psychological adaptation occurs unconsciously. The principle of psychic determinism, so important in psychoanalytic theory, applies to unconscious mental functions and contents as well as conscious ones.

Perhaps the most noteworthy aspect of the system Unconscious are the contents that Freud thought it contained—the instinctual drives. The overall structure of the mind during this stage in his thinking was thought to occur so that instinctual drives from the system Unconscious could be controlled and expressed in a way that took into account both external reality and the need to allow drive gratification, albeit in disguised and attenuated forms. These contents of the system Unconscious were emphasized to play a dominant role in the individual's development and ultimate psychological functioning. Freud described the concept of instinctual drives as "a concept on the frontier between the mental and the somatic" in his 1915 paper, *Instincts and Their Vicissitudes*. He seemed to see the concept as a mental representation of somatic stimuli. Initially he emphasized only libidinal drives although aggression in the form of the death instinct was eventually added to psychoanalytic theory later in his life. But the aggressive drive has never been formulated as clearly as the libidinal one despite the indisputable importance of aggressive impulses in mental functioning.

Four components of the libidinal drive were described by Freud. The first was the pressure of the drive, by which he meant the degree to which it pressed for discharge. Freud was struck by the peremptory quality of libidinal urges; they seemed to exert a degree of pressure to act far more compelling than most other human urges. The aim of the instinctual drive was satisfaction. Satisfaction could only be obtained at the source of the instinct. The source referred to the part of the body from which the instinct was thought to derive. Oral impulses, for example, derived from the oral cavity and so could only be satisfied at that source. Finally the object of the drive is that person or object through which satisfaction is obtained. These objects can be part of one's own body. The wide range of perversity known to the human condition demonstrates how variable this component of instinctual drives can be.

The system Unconscious was postulated by Freud to be characterized by a number of unique processes. Perhaps the most important was what he called the primary process in contradistinction to the secondary process, which he saw as characterizing the systems Preconscious and Conscious. Underlying this concept of the primary process was Freud's economic model wherein he believed that a special form of energy, psychic energy, contributed to all mental functioning. Freud believed that the energy in the system Unconscious was freely mobile so that instinctual energy could shift between separate ideas, parts of ideas, memories, and so on, without consideration of logic or time. Thus, ideas could be combined or shifted in ways that the conscious mind would be unable to understand or accept. As a result unconscious thinking is often characterized by displacement or condensation. The former allows one idea to stand for another in the system Unconscious whereas the latter involved a fusing of two ideas that might not be logically compatible. These two primary process mechanisms—displacement and condensation—are what made dream analysis so complicated and interesting a task for Freud. In order to make the unconscious conscious, the analyst needed to decipher the unconscious mental contents that were disguised by these two primary process mechanisms.

Other unique characteristics of the system Unconscious were also described by Freud. Thus, he described its timeless nature. Temporal considerations were thought to be irrelevant in this system. Furthermore, it operated on the basis of the pleasure principle with no regard for reality constraints or logic. No distinction between memories of real or imagined experiences occurred in the system Unconscious. Furthermore, contradiction did not exist nor did negation. In this way opposites could be experienced as identical in the system Unconscious. Finally words (symbols) and that which they symbolized were experienced as identical in this system according to Freud.

IV. SYSTEM PRECONSCIOUS

The second deepest system or region of the mind according to Freud was the system Preconscious. It was defined as lying between the systems Unconscious and Conscious with its major task being to protect the system Conscious from being inundated by the instinctual drives of the system Unconscious. Freud's topographic model hypothesized that the system Preconscious developed gradually from the influence of both unconscious instinctual wishes and external reality. Over the course of childhood it was thought to become increasingly differentiated from the systems Unconscious and Conscious. Helping in this differentiation was the development of defenses that Freud first called censorship and later repression in this stage of his model development. Thus, the system Preconscious formed a censorship at its boundary with the system Unconscious in order to prevent the instinctual wishes from gaining direct access to the system Conscious. It is important to note that this defensive or censoring function of the system Preconscious was thought to operate unconsciously. But this type of unconscious was descriptive in nature, in contrast to the dynamically unconscious contents of the system Unconscious. That is, functions and contents in the system Preconscious were said to be capable of becoming conscious were attention directed at them. In contrast, the contents and functions of the system Unconscious are actively maintained as unconscious by the energic force (counter cathexis) that the preconscious censorship directs against them. This distinction between descriptively and dynamically unconscious content and functions remains relevant today.

Unlike the system Unconscious's operation according to the pleasure principle, the system Preconscious was postulated to adhere to the reality principle. Thus, the unconscious wishes that it allowed to pass through into the system Conscious were closely examined and modified to ensure that they would facilitate the individual's self-preservative needs and could be integrated with the individual's moral–ethical ideals. Secondary process thinking characterized the system Preconscious in order to ensure these adaptational needs also. Causality, logic, and temporality characterize the secondary process wherein language becomes the most important vehicle for harnessing the instinctual drives. The psychic energy assumed to characterize secondary process thinking was described as bound energy by Freud. Sandler and his colleagues have emphasized the multiple and complex functions the system Preconscious was thought to include: (1) unconscious scanning of thoughts and feeling states; (2) censoring of instinctual wishes and their derivatives; (3) formation of organized memory systems; (4) reality testing; (5) binding of psychic energy; (6) control of access to consciousness and motility; (7) affect modulation and development; (8) defensive functioning; (9) fantasy production; and (10) symptom formation.

V. SYSTEM CONSCIOUS

Freud described the system Conscious as being on the mind's surface. Unlike the two deeper regions, its contents were all conscious. Nonetheless the limitations of attention prevented all contents from being the focus of conscious attention at any one time. This system received input from both the system Preconscious and from stimuli of the external world. Thus, its contents were described as sliding back easily into the system Preconscious when conscious attention was completely removed from them. Accordingly, conscious contents are more fleeting than contents of the other systems. Self-preservation requires that the individual always be open to new perceptual experiences. Thus, attention cathexis was thought to be an important part of this system. It was described as based on psychic energy that had been neutralized of sexual or aggressive qualities. Otherwise the system Conscious was similar to the system Preconscious in its underlying structure. The reality principle dominated as did secondary process functioning.

VI. IMPORTANCE OF TOPOGRAPHIC MODEL

The topographic model remains important theoretically because all of Freud's papers on clinical technique were written during this stage in his thinking. Thus, it has continued to exert a prominent influence on psychoanalytic technique despite having been replaced with the structural model in 1923. Paying attention to transference and resistance, studying dreams as the royal road to the unconscious, and interpreting the unconscious content inherent in transference and resistance manifestations came to characterize the psychoanalytic process during this era. As mentioned above, the major curative factor was thought to involve making the unconscious conscious. These technical prescriptions are likely to still sound accurate to many today despite being based on an outdated theoretical model. In fact, Paul Gray has lamented what he calls a developmental lag in the psychoanalytic theory of technique wherein analysts have been slow to realize that the technical implications of the structural model call for a very different technique than that described earlier. Working in a typographic manner leads analysts to interpret unconscious mental content without analyzing the defenses that keep such content unconscious. This approach ignores the need to understand the motives for the defense. Failure to do so renders the patient vulnerable to maintaining these defenses. Also, interpretations that ignore defense can increase the patient's anxiety and, hence, resistance. Gray and his adherents have delineated the different technical implications of the structural model. Nonetheless, many contemporary analysts practice in a topographically informed manner without realizing that they are doing so or that such ways of working are outdated. Thus, it remains important to understand the topographic model as it may be some time before it becomes no longer used.

Furthermore, aspects of the topographic model remain important, even to those analysts whose theoretical understanding has been updated. Certainly the distinction between unconscious and conscious phenomena remains clinically relevant, as does the concept of psychic conflict. Unconscious, preconscious, and conscious are now used as adjectives describing mental processes and not as nouns depicting regions of the mind. The topographic concepts of instinctual drives also remain relevant. These concepts have been revised in an attempt to make them more scientifically viable. Furthermore, psychoanalysts have expanded the number of motivational factors that impel human behavior beyond sexual and aggressive impulses. Nonetheless, sexual and aggressive wishes remain quite important clinically and need to be addressed and analyzed in psychoanalytic treatment.

A major contribution of the topographic model not discussed earlier, but one that is quite important on the modern-day psychoanalytic scene, is that of object relations. The idea that individuals build up a subjective world of mental representations of self and important others, and that this representational world is a crucial component of the psyche is explicit in almost every variant of psychoanalytic theory adhered to today. Recognition of this fact has led analysts to a new acceptance of the inevitability of countertransference enactments. Such enactments are now thought to provide useful understanding about the patient rather than indicating psychopathology in the analyst or therapist. Object relations models have led to new ideas about what is curative in psychoanalytic treatment and to new technical prescriptions including the judicious use of self-disclosure on the part of the treater.

Many fail to recognize that Freud's key papers, *On Narcissism* and *Mourning and Melancholia,* written at the height of his topographic thinking, contain the seeds of all subsequent object relations models. Both these papers involve his explicit delineation of the importance of object relations in understanding psychopathology and in deriving treatment strategies. In those papers he laid out the importance of developing representational boundaries between self and other as well as the role of internalization in giving rise to important emotional states. Thus, the topographic model continues to exert a modern influence.

Joseph Sandler, one of the most prominent psychoanalytic thinkers of the last four decades, has argued for a more direct viability of the topographic model, albeit in a modified form. He believed that the transition from the topographic to the structural model left gaps and inconsistencies in conceptual understanding and in clinical technique; he believed that these could be overcome by a modification of the topographic model—what he called the three box model. He used this three box model to highlight the necessity for conceptualizing a second censor between the second and the third box or system of the mind. This censor gives the second box or system depth, acknowledging the clinical reality that unconscious ego activities have a range of closeness to consciousness. Even more important, this second system or box is oriented to the present, not to the past. It creates current unconscious fantasies and thoughts as ways of maintaining psychic equilibrium and helping to defend against the infantile, peremptory, and potentially disruptive fantasies of the first box as they push toward actualization.

The second censorship occurring between the second and third systems attempts to avoid shame, embarrassment, and humiliation. In essence it is a narcissistic defense. The contents of the third box are surface or conscious expressions of second system thoughts, impulses, wishes, and fantasies. Sandler believed that the technical importance of this model is to distinguish between the past Unconscious of the first box and the present Unconscious of the second. It is the present Unconscious content that lies behind the second censorship and is closest to consciousness. Sandler believed that his model would help analysts to avoid the topographic era strategy of interpreting deep or past unconscious content before having dealt with less deep, present unconscious content. He advocated that the analyst listen for current unconscious content that was being censored. Thus, his modification of the topographic model is an attempt to deal with the same sort of technical problems as that of contemporary structural theorists such as Paul Gray or Fred Busch. Their approaches are currently gaining greater acceptance than Sandler's three box model. Nonetheless, his efforts do highlight the continued attraction of topographic theory to many contemporary psychoanalytic practitioners.

See Also the Following Articles

Intrapsychic Conflict ■ Object Relations Psychotherapy ■ Oedipus Complex ■ Structural Theory ■ Transference ■ Neurosis ■ Unconsious, The

Further Reading

Dowling, S. (Ed.). (1991). *Conflict and compromise.* Madison, CT: International Universities Press.

Gill, M. M. (1963). *Topography and systems in psychoanalytic theory.* New York: International Universities Press.

Moore, B., & Fine, B. (1990). *Psychoanalytic terms and concepts.* New Haven, CT: Yale University Press.

Ritvo, S., & Solnit, A. (1995). Instinct theory. In B. Moore & B. Fine (Eds.), *Psychoanalysis—The major concepts* (pp. 327–333). New Haven, CT: Yale University Press.

Sandler, J., Holder, A., Dare, C., & Dreher, A. (1997). *Freud's models of the mind, an introduction.* Madison, CT: International Universities Press.

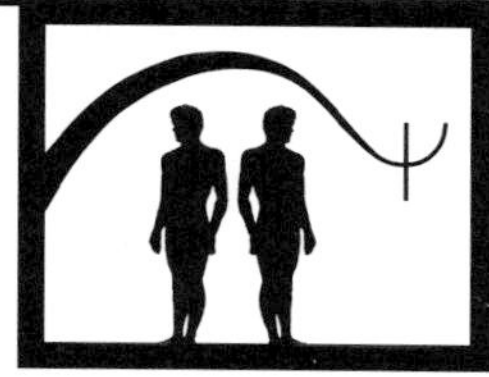

Transcultural Psychotherapy

Thomas E. Heise

Medical University of Hannover

GLOSSARY

culture-bound-syndrome (CBS) Term coined by P.-M. Yap (1967/1974) as pertaining to only locally spread diseases in opposition to current psychiatric diagnoses. Today they are seen as strongly culturally influenced diseases, finding their explanatory roots in folk medical beliefs. Examples include koro/suoyang, paleng, amok, latah, susto, brainfag, and ogba nje.

emic Culture-specific understanding; research by an insider; emphasized by the new cross-cultural psychiatry, comparing cultural aspects (e.g., A. Kleinman, B.J. Good, R. Littlewood, M. Lipsedge).

ethnopsychoanalysis Term, first used by G. Devereux in 1972, for a kind of work initiated by G. Róheim in 1932 and continued separately by P. Parin, G. Parin-Matthèy, and F. Morgenthaler in 1963. According to Devereux psychological and sociocultural explanations must be used separately. Modern interpretations of his ideas are controversial.

ethnopsychiatry Study of psychiatric diseases in other cultures. The term was first used by Devereux around 1950. He saw one of its tasks as being to create a culturally neutral psychotherapy.

etic Useful for global generalizations; a culture transcending view, as opposed to emic; research by an outsider.

immigrants first generation—5 phases Initially (1) the preparation for and (2) the act of migration. Communication barriers because of language problems are predominant. Overcoming many psychological problems by excessive effort, that is, (3) overcompensation occurs. However, this can have a negative impact, and (4) decompensation, occurs, especially on retirement. (5) Adaptation takes more than one generation.

immigrants second generation Mostly well-spoken new language, frequently hiding the problem of different meanings and losing their parents' language. Torn between traditional values of the family and place of origin and modern values of the new surrounding.

immigrants third and later generations On the surface mostly well adapted if belonging to a more educated social class, but—often unconsciously—still influenced by the family's cultural heritage. If belonging to a lower social class, they still might have difficulties in learning the new language sufficiently, while also not learning their original language well enough.

interpreters Should be neutral persons, not family members, trained in being translators without commentaries or cotherapeutic interventions.

qigong A therapeutic combination of movement, breathing, and hovering awareness as one example of therapeutic methods in traditional Chinese medicine (in addition to herbs, acupuncture, etc.). Many traditional medicines are used in diagnosis and treatment by their respective immigrants, often without mentioning it. Their traditional explanations of their disease might play an important role in Western psychotherapy.

shaman A traditional healer, found in most traditional cultures. He uses altered states of consciousness (ASC) if he is a real initiated healer.

transcultural psychotherapy (a) Using traditional methods from other cultures in Western psychotherapy. (b) Concerning all the sociocultural problems involved in the psychotherapeutic treatment of immigrants or refugees, deriving from the encounter of the two (or more) respective cultures. Often an interpreter is necessary.

I. INTRODUCTION

Mental health services rely not only on the physical body but also on the psyche, brain, mind, and soul. The body itself with its different physical afflictions, diagnoses, and treatments is viewed quite differently depending on the cultural context, according to Payer in 1996. Mental problems and sociocultural factors are so closely interrelated that they cannot be viewed separately, as discussed by Westen in 1996. With an ever-growing worldwide multiculturalism, it is imperative to integrate the results of international research. This concerns all theories of psychoanalytic, behavioral, humanistic, and other psychodynamic counseling and psychotherapy. To improve our understanding of transcultural psychotherapy I will introduce historical perspectives. Some of the main factors to be considered are aspects of migration and transcultural contexts. Short case studies, each emphasizing a particular facet, will illustrate this point.

II. THE HISTORICAL PERSPECTIVE

The foundation of transcultural psychotherapy is based on Middle European psychiatry. Known and unknown variations of familiar "mental illnesses" were discovered in distant and "exotic" countries. The scientific founders were Van Brero, who worked in the 1890s, and Emil Kraepelin in 1904. Their comparative psychiatric works dealt with mental disorders in Indonesia. Bronislaw Malinowski's work in 1924 on *Mother-Dominated Family and Oedipus Complex* represented a milestone in which he refuted Sigmund Freud's hypothesis on the general validity of the Oedipus complex by recording his observations on the Trobriand tribe in the Pacific. He was able to show that the complexes arising within the family core were a consequence of the social structure of the tribe or people. Nevertheless, he recognized the significance of Freud's attribution to the influence of the early childhood years. In 1957 Erik H. Erikson followed with his studies on *Childhood and Society,* a comparison between the North American Indian Yurok and Sioux tribes. Margaret Mead did her research with a scientific and objective point of view and described the customs and traditions of different races. In 1959 Mead introduced *Gender and Temperament in Primitive Societies* and was primarily interested in how children were raised within these societies. She was known as a representative of "Culture-Gestalt-Psychology," and her results are considered controversial.

Paul Parin, Golda Parin-Matthey, and Fritz Morgenthaler investigated African cultures according to psychoanalytical criteria. In the 1950s Georges Devereux coined the expression "ethnopsychiatry," and in 1972 he published the book *Ethnopsychoanalysis.* According to his ethnological studies, stress is traumatic when, within the respective culture, defense mechanisms are absent. He understood culture as a system of defense mechanisms. In 1982 he stated that shamans were mentally disturbed. The fact that in 1996, Asian shamans and African medicine men were invited to speak at the first World Congress of the "World Council for Psychotherapy," in Vienna, shows that today this situation is seen quite differently. Devereux's aim in 1970 was "the introduction of teaching and practice of cultural neutral psychotherapy," as described in 1982. This kind of psychotherapy should not be based on the attributes of any particular culture, but should be "comparable to affective neutral psychoanalytical therapy." Since this originated only in Devereux's culture, it is actually a contradiction in itself.

Jeanne Favret-Saada, a psychoanalyst and ethnologist like Devereux, introduced epochal standards to her field of research by participating in conversations and witchcraft ceremonials with the natives. These "natives" were not even "exotics" but a rural group of people from the western part of France. Favret-Saada allowed herself to become personally involved, and in doing so, pioneered a new scientific approach. Thus, in 1977, she added a third method of research. In 1966, R. Pike derived the already familiar "etic" approach, from linguistics, to be applied to ethnology. This meant gaining more culture-general information from scientific studies, in contrary to the rather culture-specific "emic" approach, which enabled a better understanding of the cultural aspects from the natives' point of view. Favret-Saada, as an insider among these "natives," was able to put herself into the position of examining the culture from both points of view, changing dialectically from inside to outside. These aspects were also considered by psychiatrists such as Christian Scharfetter, who, in 1987, published the book

Ethnopsychotherapy. His ideas were based on his own experiences with the Theravada-Buddhism method of meditation, and many discussions concerning altered states of consciousness (ASC). Thomas Heise used a similar method. He studied traditional Chinese medicine (TCM) for more than 2 years in China, and, in 1996, published the book *China's Medicine in Germany,* which also covered a broader view of "psychiatric-psychotherapeutic" aspects of TCM. Another book by Heise, published in 1999, dealt with *qigong* in the People's Republic of China, its historical development, theory, and practice. Michael Harner in 1972, 1973, and 1980 and Roger Walsh in 1990 also based their scientific books about shamanism and healing on their own experiences and participation. Similarly, Stanislaw Grof, in his works since the 1970s, investigated many traditional therapies in order to find common roots. He made the workings of the various subconscious layers and ASC more intelligible and understandable.

Eric Wittkower, Wolfgang Jilek, and Louisa Jilek-Aall influenced transcultural psychiatry in many ways. Wittkower in 1978 described its aim as the "identification of quantitative and qualitative differences when comparing mental illnesses in the various cultures, the investigation to determine these differences and the application of this knowledge for the treatment and prevention of mental illnesses." In 1980 he was concerned with the cultural and transcultural aspects of psychotherapy. On the one hand he placed emphasis on the introduction of foreign cultural methods to the West, such as yoga and Buddhist meditation, and on the other hand, on the use of Western psychotherapy outside the Western culture complex.

Based on his experiences in Taiwan in 1980, Arthur Kleinmann did research on the way in which cultural symbols and meaning influence the perception and expression of symptoms and therapeutic mechanisms. In 1985, he emphasized the theme in *Culture and Depression.* Wolfgang Pfeiffer concentrated on the analysis of dialogue and migration problems as well as on the contact between various medical systems. Having lived in Indonesia, he dealt in particular with those of Asia. His first work, *Transcultural Psychiatry,* published in 1971 and revised in 1994, is a phenomenological collection of culturally influenced expressions, corresponding to the various psychiatric groups of diagnoses. Erich Wulff, who worked in South Vietnam for 7 years, studied the methods of comparative psychiatry, and emphasized the social requirements for these methods, and thus their historical significance and subjectivity. Karl Peltzer, who spent many years researching in different parts of Africa, supported these ideas and coined the expression "postanalytical ethnopsychological research." In 1994 he published *Psychology and Health in African Cultures: Examples of Ethnopsychotherapeutic Practice.*

On the whole we can see in the historical development of transcultural understanding a start with a rather Eurocentric and limited approach. Scientists looked for the well known in foreign countries. The second step showed a deeper involvement into different cultures, but no change of scientific ideology, which only began with the third step. Here the dialectical switch between subjective involvement during field research and more objective scientific evaluation gave rise to new ideas. These are not limited to pure psychoanalytical or behavioral thinking and are more sincerely tolerant and humanistic, grounded on interdisciplinary cultural studies.

III. MIGRATION

Another pragmatically important topic concerns immigrants. They arrive for different reasons in historically varying waves, and experience specific stages of more or less successful adaptations to their problems. In Germany, for example, early research on the mentally related illnesses of foreign workers *(Gastarbeiter)* at the end of the 1970s was abandoned and thereafter temporarily forgotten. Other countries with a colonial or immigrant history were confronted with this problem to a greater degree. In the past two decades, in England and the United States, this has led to a growing literature on counseling. These perspectives on counseling apply to therapy as well. In past years the geriatric ailments of the "foreign workers" in Germany, the second and third generation of immigrants, and the increasing inflow of new immigrants and political refugees produced an escalation of problems in mental health and psychotherapy. It was found that for refugees suffering from posttraumatic stress disorder (PTSD) it is of utmost importance to assess the preflight personality, the circumstances that caused the flight, its conditions, and coping abilities. Around 20 years ago, *Counseling Across Cultures* was published by Paul. B. Pederson and colleagues. It deals not only with the specific ethnic groups in North America, but also with international students and refugees, gender conflicts, ethics, and cultural empathy. In 1989, Patricia D'Ardenne and Aruna Mahtani published the book *Transcultural Counselling in Action,* which demonstrated practical aspects of the transcultural therapist–patient relationship. That same year, Colleen Ward issued the volume *Altered States of Consciousness and Mental Health: A Cross-Cultural Perspective. Handbook of Multicultural Counseling* by Joseph G. Ponterotto and co-workers discusses theoretical and practical statements. A book series on multicultural counseling covers themes such as *Preventing Prejudice* by Ponterotto, *Improving Intercultural Interaction* by Richard Brislin and Tomoko Yoshida, *Assessing and Treating Culturally Diverse Clients* by Freddy Paniagua, *Overcoming Unintentional Racism in Counseling and Therapy* by Charles Ridley, and *Multicultural Counseling with Teenage Fathers* by Mark Kiselica. Colin Lago and Joyce Thompson compiled the book *Race, Culture and Counseling* and Suman Fernando published *Mental Health in a Multi-Ethnic Society.* The latter two books deal particularly with the problems of biological and cultural racism and the different, often multiprofessional management of inpatient and outpatient institutions for the care of mentally disturbed foreign citizens.

One prominent French author, Tobie Nathan, published such works as *The Madness of Others: An Essay on Clinical Transcultural Psychiatry* in 1986, and *The Influence That Cures* in 1994. Initially, he held the opinion that the ethnopsychoanalytical background was of prime importance. Later, however, he changed his mind and stated that patients could also be healed using the therapeutic means of their respective cultures. In 1998, Marie Rose Moro, who worked especially with immigrant children emphasizing the aspect of family therapy, published a book on these topics. In the Netherlands, in 1996, Joop De Jong developed, among other things, a handbook on transcultural psychiatry and psychotherapy. A number of German books show, by their titles alone, that there are numerous problems in the search for better solutions: Heribert Kentenich, Peter Reeg, and Karl-Heinz Wehkamp, 1990, *Between Two Cultures: Why Does a Foreigner Become Ill?;* Horacio Riquelme, 1992, *Other Realities—Other Approaches;* Eckhardt Koch, Metin Özek, and Wolfgang M. Pfeiffer, 1995, *Psychology and Pathology of Immigration: German-Turkish Perspectives;* Peter Möhring and Roland Apsel, 1995, *Intercultural Psychoanalytical Therapy;* Jürgen Collatz, Ramazan Salman, Eckhardt Koch, and Wielant Machleidt, 1997, *The Medical Report with Special Emphasis on Transcultural Issues: Quality Safeguarding of Social-Legal and Social-Medical Reports for Working Immigrants in Germany;* Thomas Heise, 1998, *Transcultural Psychotherapy: Helping to Treat Foreign Citizens;* and Heise, 2000, *The Situation of Transcultural Counseling, Psychotherapy and Psychiatry in Germany.*

Traumatization can occur as a result of ethnic, religious, sexual, or economic pursuit, if the preflight personality cannot cope. These differences must be taken into account when determining therapy, which varies for immigrants in the various generations. Each subjective reality is based on the individual's identity, perceptions, and experiences. Neglecting its relation to culture, diagnosis may be inadequate, the patient does not feel accepted personally, and therapy is likely to fail. For evaluating the five phases of migration (see Glossary) important issues include reflecting on the cultural influence of one's own behavior; being able to investigate another person's cultural background, if necessary with interpreters; reflecting on one's own prejudices and the cultural and historical relativity of values; understanding each other sufficiently; and being able to find acceptable solutions in a multicultural teamwork. According to Sluzki in 1996, the therapist must help the migrant to prepare to accept times of feeling lonely, to encourage him or her to learn the new language and new customs as quickly as possible, to get as much new information as necessary, and in order not to lose continuity, to remain in contact with compatriots and enhance the personal environment with pictures from the past or other symbols.

IV. TRANSCULTURAL CONTEXTS

There are many cultural barriers to communication and we are only aware of some of them. Less evident are attitudes toward one another; nonverbal behavior; customs and traditions of greeting and meeting; personal theories of communication; political differences; fear, perception, and expectations of one another; systems of belief and ethics; view of personal and institutional power; notions of acceptable and unacceptable behavior; patterns of interpersonal relationships; ways of learning, working, and living; and views of illness and disease as well as of therapy regarding meaning for oneself and others. In 1980 Geert Hofstede determined some main criteria in 40 different nations and distinguished between small and large "power distance" (the acceptance of the distribution of power in society), weak and strong "uncertainty avoidance," collectivist and individualist, and feminine and masculine dimensions.

In approaching different philosophical assumptions, as Lago and Thompson showed in 1996, general views of the world will be compared.

The Western system emphasizes a material ontology, appropriating a high value to the acquisition of objects. External knowledge derived from counting and measuring is assumed to be the basis of all knowledge. The logic of this conceptual system is dichotomous (either–or), like the basis of computer technology and other technological processes that are repeatable and reproducible. In consequence, identity and self-worth tend to be based on external criteria, such as status symbols.

In the Asian conceptual system, the ontology of a cosmic unity, as taught in Buddhism, Taoism, Shintoism, and Hinduism, is of the highest value, emphasizing the cohesiveness of the group and traditionally the interplay with nature. Thus the Asian logic does not separate the body, mind, or spirit. Harmony is necessary to make the internal and external cosmos, in their interrelatedness, a balanced model of unity. In consequence identity and self-worth are based on being and an internal and external reality.

The African system emphasizes both a spiritual and a material ontology, valuing above all the interpersonal relationship between women and men. Self-knowledge is assumed to be the basis of all knowledge. One acquires knowledge through symbolic imagery and rhythm. The logic is based on co-unity, and through this process, everything in time and space is interrelated through human and spiritual networks. In consequence identity and self-worth are intrinsic.

For the sake of brevity, these views of the world indicating such tendencies may seem somewhat simplistic. Transcultural psychotherapy should try to be aware of these different processes, cosmologies, and values and their consequences.

V. APPLIED TRANSCULTURAL PSYCHOTHERAPY

According to findings by Fernando in 1996, ethnic minorities are more often diagnosed as schizophrenic, compulsorily detained under the Mental Health Act, given high doses of medication, and not referred to psychotherapy. A research survey conducted on behalf of the Royal College of Psychiatrists in 1991 and reported by Lago and Collins in 1996, showed that 85% of the 2000 respondents believed that depression was caused by life events and that psychotherapy, not antidepressants, was the most appropriate form of assistance. A study by Bebbington and colleagues of 297 randomly selected women demonstrated a significant excess of marked life events in acute cases of psychiatric disorders (50%) compared to chronic cases (16.7%) and noncases (27.9%). The effect of chronic social difficulties was even more pronounced (33.3%) than, and independent of, the effects of life events. Here psychotherapy would be helpful.

We should keep in mind that we must not be intimidated by this subject, since a good education in psychotherapy equips one with all the tools necessary and can be effectively applied here. One must simply be more eager, more neutral and tolerant, more open minded and more empathetic, and display these attitudes in various ways. Patients want our help and will give us every possible assistance, if asked for, in understanding them in their cultural background. Let us use their cultural expertise by asking "What does this mean to you?" If they do not speak our language fluently, a neutral interpreter is needed and not an emotionally involved family member. If after the translating job we ask the interpreter separately for some commentaries, most of them will recognize our interest and be glad to help us. In order to broaden this point of view I will provide additional important aspects followed by short case histories, in full reported by Heise in 1998.

The term transcultural psychotherapy contains two aspects that are expressed in the prefix "trans." The monocultural aspect of illness should be trans-cended with regard to the diagnosis and also to the manifestation of the illness itself as a dis-ease. This kind of mental illness may arise in certain individuals as a result of the encounter of two different cultures. This fact must be taken into account in an empathetic and unprejudiced manner. A neutral attitude toward affect and culture and feigned objectivity as shown in the classic psychoanalysis with its rules of abstinence is not adequate.

In medical reports and testimonies the pathogenetic and therapeutic differences between political refugees with either acute depressive decompensation or posttraumatic stress disorders are of great importance. The task of the physician, as sometimes opposed to that of official authorities, may be challenging in the case of foreigners.

Case History 1: Pathogenetic and Therapeutic Differences between Two Kurdish Refugees with Acute Depressive Decompensation

A young Kurdish patient, accompanied by his father and older brother, was brought for examination. He suffered persistent abdominal pain and had already undergone unsuccessful surgery. The dependence on his family, who after 3 years were still awaiting political asylum, due to predominantly economic reasons, resulted in a conflict with his wish to return to his relatives in Turkey. No inpatient treatment was required for this case. The doctor treating the patient sent a letter recommending that the boy return to Turkey. The second case concerned a Kurdish female from Iraq, an accepted political refugee. Her husband, who as a physician had treated Kurdish rebels, was therefore killed by the Iraq authorities. She, due to administrative and domestic problems, had attempted to kill herself along with her little son. This case required inpatient treatment with client-centered therapy with the help of an interpreter.

The patient received support regarding her social problems, and finally gained enough self-confidence to cope alone with her difficulties. The medical role had to be determined regarding contact between the patient and the authorities for foreign citizens.

Some patients feel bewildered because of the foreign land and people, and have even more problems discussing their difficulties and emotions. Here, the use of guided affective imagery therapy according to Hanscarl Leuner, art therapy, Gestalt-therapy, or bodily oriented methods are helpful to understand, for example, depressive disorders followed by psychosomatic complaints. In addition it helps to introduce the "talking cure."

Case History 2: Guided Affective Imagery Therapy as the Turning Point in the Psychotherapy of a Russian Female with Chronic Reactive Depression

A Russian immigrant came for psychiatric help with acute suicidal thoughts and admitted to suffering from headaches and depression for 2 years. With the help of an interpreter, she was able to build up a sufficient basis of trust during client-centered psychotherapy, according to Carl Rogers, to give an account of her rape incident. She was raped by an unknown person after her arrival in Germany and had not yet summoned the courage to inform her husband of this event. As she had great difficulty in coming to terms with negative feelings or even to speak of them, the guided affective imagery therapy was invoked twice to help her express her feelings and thoughts. Only two themes (flower and mountain) were necessary to give her access to her split feelings. Of particular interest were the specific transference relation, the recalling of the situation, the confrontation with her feelings, the catharsis, and the reaction toward the symbolic image. Talking about the two images helped her to visualize her partnership conflict. After painting them she tried to speak about solutions, first in therapy and later with him.

This procedure proved effective and the patient was then able to relate the whole story to her husband. Finally, she succeeded in improving her newly found verbal abilities so that she was able to carry out a constructive discussion with her husband concerning their relationship, and also to take part with him in partner discussions. She was seen in the outpatient clinic for 8 more months. In these partner discussions her resistance to "talk" started again. The therapist introduced breathing and relaxation exercises that the patient could manage with increasing ease. Three months later, she indicated she was ready to take up the discussions once more.

The topic "guilt" brought back the accusation of her husband that she was also guilty as she had not offered enough resistance to her rapist. It then became evident that for the Jewish family of the husband, the topic "guilt" with reference to "why didn't they kill us like the others?", played a major role in association with the persecution of the Jews in Russia.

Before this admission to the psychiatric department, the patient had already experienced three occasions when she had tried to talk about these same problems with Russian-speaking therapists without success. During the first phase of her illness, she was treated by a neurologist in Moscow in order to find the organic reasons for her symptoms. The diagnosis offered was a psycho-vegetative complaint with labile personality traits, while symptoms increased again on the way to Germany. She later consulted a Russian guest doctor (not a psychotherapist or a psychiatrist) and here misunderstandings arose in the communication between him and the doctor treating her for her psychiatric symptoms, most likely due to incorrect translation. Finally, she was treated as an outpatient by a Russian psychiatrist practicing in Germany who, on the one hand, showed a preference to administering medication and, on the other, forgot about the mutual influences of the involved cultures, and never spoke to her without her husband. Therefore, in this part of the therapy, the "trans" cultural element was disregarded. To avoid any similar retraumatizations, transcultural sensibility training should be introduced to medical and, in particular, psychotherapeutic and psychiatric education.

Problems of translation, interpreters, a mono- or bicultural approach, and a change in the therapeutic procedures (verbal – nonverbal) were discussed. This shows that language, ethnicity, and culture are not identical. All conscious or unconscious processes, interactions, and experiences are culture related, family related, and individual related. These can be clarified to make therapy successful.

The diversity of so-called schizophrenic manifestations is transculturally even more obvious. Therefore, diagnosis and therapy must take into account both the individual and the cultural diversity. Other cultures might even present a more adequate way to cope with psychotic experiences. In the delusion of being possessed the understanding of the patient's bio-socio-psycho-spiritual world view is paramount. This, in addition to the application of client-centered psychotherapy according to Carl

Rogers and the inspiration by transpersonal psychology, may prove more helpful in transcultural psychotherapy. An understanding of the cultural "differences" of the patient helps to build up the patient's self-esteem.

Case History 3: A Korean Patient's Delusion of Being Possessed

A Korean priest of a Christian sect was responsible for inflicting a patient of the same nationality with short-term exogenous psychosis by means of a syncretistic atmosphere and deprivation of sleep. This led to an attempted suicide. Mutual trust between patient and doctor was developed by therapeutic intervention according to Roger's client-centered therapy. Further anamnestic details were obtained, particularly in connection with the dead grandmother who was a *mudang* or shaman priestess. Knowledge of the patient's cultural background explained her reaction of feeling possessed by a bad spirit, and we, by showing a neutral respect for this particular culture, including the involved shamanism, presented the patient with a favorable prognosis for successful therapy. The conclusions resulted in a transcultural–transpersonal portrayal for diagnosis and treatment; it became obvious that there were syncretistic factors, but no real shamanistic transformation act or traditional healing process involved.

The second "trans" aspect concerns, on the one hand, the intracultural cooperation between the indigenous medical system of the immigrant and the Western medical system. On the other hand, it deals with intercultural cooperation. This may be in the form of influence or inclusion of aspects and methods from traditional medical systems together with our Western medical system. Some patients have better access to psychotherapeutic measures from other cultures. The use of foreign and archaic instruments in music therapy or therapeutic means from traditional Chinese medicine or Indian ayurvedic or Arab unani-tibb medicine may prove effective.

Case History 4: Treatment of Hallucinatory Psychosis with Complementary *qigong* Exercises

Taiji quan (T'ai Chi Ch'uan) "shadow boxing" and *qigong* (Ch'i Kung) meditative "breathing exercises" are therapeutic methods based on traditional Chinese medicine (TCM), like herbal medicine or acupuncture. There are several forms of exercises, some of which are becoming more popular in the Western sphere. At first glance only the movements bear a vague resemblance to our established forms of gymnastic exercises, but the exercises based on TCM are, in fact, far more advanced. By means of a balanced form of movement according to the *yinyang* concept, the meridians are harmonized and the activated subtle energy *qi* also contributes to balancing the associated functional organic system. According to TCM theory, certain emotions and mental conditions are associated with specific organs, and with the help of these exercises, a psychotherapeutic effect is obtained. It was shown in a recent study by Heise in 2002, that *qigong* reduces in psychosis significantly state anxiety after each session and trait anxiety on the long term (STAI) and depression and psychoticism (SCL-90-R), increases relaxation and ability for enjoyment, helps exhaustion and achievement, and diminishes cenesthesia (case histories).

The 40-year-old patient complained of hearing voices for 4 years. The physical problems in his arms and legs and his headaches had persisted for 3 years and were induced by voices with their lips on his body. He initially tried to block out the voices by "drowning" them with beer, then gave up drinking, and since one year, had only consumed limited amounts of alcohol. The patient could for the first time be convinced of the advantage of persistent high-potency neuroleptics while undergoing day clinic therapy. Organic causes were ruled out and analgesic medication reduced. During the group therapies he demonstrated an aggressive inhibition with withdrawal tendencies on confrontation with conflicts. In addition, he took part in 5 of the above mentioned *qigong* therapy group sessions, and then a further 11 sessions on an outpatient basis following discharge. During day clinic therapy, the patient appeared to be considerably more relaxed, more lively, and more socially active with increasing clarity of mind, and experienced reduced physical pain and fewer headaches with weaker and less aggressive auditory hallucinations. It was noted on *qigong* therapy that even at the beginning he was able to rapidly develop the special "*qi*-feeling." On discharge from the day clinic he reported that immediately after the *qigong*, the voices disappeared for an hour and the headaches became less frequent. He felt an inner calm. Up to the 6th session he admitted to changes in his condition with regard to the voices and the "headaches," showing a slight improvement. The physical pains disappeared completely. He executed these exercises independently twice a week, and continued to do them when followed-up for research purposes 1 month and then 4 months later, as he found they helped to combat the more aggressive voices, which now appeared about two times each week. He then received his third kind of a typical neuroleptics, and although he was unable to differentiate between these medications, he was aware that they had a certain beneficial effect on his condition, but less so than the *qigong* exercises, which he would practice whenever needed.

In order to deal with ethnocentric feeling and thinking, new solutions are required for the basic points of transcultural psychotherapy. These are not yet statistically validated, but need further investigation in this rather new field of research. Special issues are the question of value and purpose ("honor") regarding self-responsibility and self-realization in different cultures together with its role in psychotherapy. For example, a supervisor of the same foreign culture in an analytically oriented self-experience group for social and medical professionals may help to combat hostility toward foreigners. He reduces defense mechanisms, because he has overcome these troubles himself.

Weekend seminars to discuss crisis intervention with youngsters of the same culture, using the group analytical method, may be effective in reducing violence. Thus underaged refugees may have the opportunity, during this session, to discuss, in an appropriate manner with their peers, their traumatic experiences of leaving their parents and their native culture. Different psychotherapeutic forms such as hypnotherapeutic and cognitive-behavioral therapeutic techniques may be effective, as well as ritual techniques and eye movement desensitization and reprocessing (EMDR) developed by Francine Shapiro and published in 1997, as discussed by Foa and colleagues in 2000 and Sack and co-workers in 2001.

For therapists treating in a foreign country, in their mother tongue, with deep psychological, systemic, and behavioral therapeutic elements, transference–countertransference and the risk of regression are important factors. Sociocultural circumstances influence drinking habits and drug consumption strongly and should not be disregarded in any therapy, according to Lala and Straussner in 2001.

Systemic individual and family therapy (mono- and bicultural) is resource- and solution-oriented by means of esteemed and engaged neutrality combined with respectful curiosity, as discussed by Krause in 1998. In addition to the routine service of psychotherapeutic-sensitive trained interpreters, the patient is also an expert in his culture. This induces a paradigmatic change.

Positive psychotherapy developed by Nossrat Peseschkian in the 1970s is derived from the narrative elements of Middle Eastern fables. This kind of therapy judges bodily feelings, senses, achievements, social contacts, and fantasy regarding future decisions. A comparison of giving life meaning in Eastern and in Western cultures is often added in this transcultural approach, similar to other humanistic psychotherapies.

All of these therapeutic methods concentrate on the way each individual interacts with his or her environment. The respective cultural background is responsible for influencing and molding the senses of perception and sensitivity of each human being. Culture is a term incorporating the material cultural relics and daily customs, everything that language makes "producible," "approachable," and "conceivable." This includes specific conditionable senses of perception (particularly apparent in the Yogis and Masters of the hard *qigong*) and metaphysical experiences, speakable and unspeakable expectations, and constructed models. All of these are attitudes that are more or less "culture-bound," without calling them a "culture-bound-syndrome." However varied the climate and the people they originate from may be, common denominators may remain with regard to the same generation, gender, spirituality, (un-) employment, wish for a better life of one's children, and so on.

All of these points need to be considered within the complete context of therapy—consciously or unconsciously. Certainly it would be more beneficial if this were to happen consciously and thus not uncontrolled. The rationalized, verbalized, and cognitive element has prevailed in the culture of the Western world over the past 2000 years; this is understandable when one reflects on its historical development. However, domination of this kind of thinking must not be accepted to such an overwhelming extent. Therapeutically, it is significant to attempt to discover the other elements in oneself, which one has either never or rarely recognized before, or which have not had the chance to develop properly. A feeling of amazement or astonishment must be produced, which leads to a realigning of the thoughts by thinking twice. This change of "sense(s)" cannot only be achieved by verbal tactics but also by other therapeutic techniques. This change of the senses may give another sense and meaning to living. This initiates a healing process that materializes into the human system and its culturally influenced relationships toward fellow humans and the cosmos, as a whole, in an intrapersonal, interpersonal, and transpersonal way. The therapist is the catalyst of this process, acting as a mediator to promote the self-curing efficacies of the patient.

It is interesting to note what effect this has on therapists, regarding their personal and professional development in relation to their feeling toward their own native culture, when one is constantly identifying with the patients and their foreign cultures, having to distance themselves in the next moment to assume the role of the catalyst once more.

VI. SUMMARY AND OUTLOOK

Many countries are faced with an increase in multiculturally based problems for which not only political but also specific psychotherapeutic solutions must be sought. On the basis of a bio-socio-psycho-spiritual view of humanity, there are two main tasks for "transcultural psychiatry and psychotherapy."

1. Adequate care that is suitably based on the individual and cultural background of mentally disturbed immigrants, along with their family and other close relations, is of prime importance. This should include a necessary and learnable sensitization of the therapist to cultural diversity, complemented by the use of professional interpreters when necessary.
2. With disregard for Americo- and Eurocentrism and school disputes, the vast area of transculturally comparative therapy research is concerned with offering the best forms of therapy to suit the requirements of the patients. Clarification for the culturally diverse self-understanding of mental illnesses in patients from other countries will ensue as a matter of course.

The experiences of many psychotherapeutic measures of other traditions are becoming of increasing interest in the Western world. For thousands of years these methods have demonstrated their value. These may not only be felt bodily but may be also related in language that uses subtle energetic–functional terms (not to be misinterpreted as purely symbolic). Consequently, methods taken from other cultures that influence the psyche are playing a more significant role in an increasingly globalized and multicultural society.

The future of psychotherapy will most likely be submitted to culturally reciprocal influences, which will not only affect the diagnostic criteria and the general attitude of life but also expectations regarding psychotherapy. Discussions in China have shown that Western forms of psychotherapy are gradually becoming better known and accepted; however, many Chinese emphatically believe that the use of Western methods in conjunction with their own methods and thinking will bring about some changes in Western psychotherapeutic procedures in China. In 1993, Louis Yang-ching Cheng, Fanny Cheung, and Char-Nie Chen described these mutual influences regarding practice in Hong Kong and for Chinese people in general. Sylvester Ntomchukwu Madu, Peter Baguma, and Alfred Pritz reported in 1996 the same relating to Africa. We must recognize that one culture can offer its therapeutic methods to other cultures, as discussed by Xudong in 2001 and Peseschkian in 2001. But it is up to each individual culture to decide what to accept, what to alter, and what to refuse.

See Also the Following Articles

Bioethics ■ Cultural Issues ■ Multicultural Therapy ■ Race and Human Diversity

Further Reading

Bebbington, P., Hamdi, E., & R. Ghubash (1998). The Dubai Community Psychiatric Survey, IV. *Social Psychiatry and Psychiatric Epidemiology, 33,* 501–509.

Devereux, G. (1982). *Normal und anormal. Aufsätze zur allgemeinen Ethnopsychiatrie.* Frankfurt: Suhrkamp.

Fernando, S. (Ed.). (1996). *Mental health in a multi-ethnic society* (2nd ed.). London: Routledge.

Foa, E. B., Keane, T. M., & Friedman, M. (2000). *Effective treatments for PTSD.* New York: Guilford.

Heise, T. (Ed.). (1998). Transkulturelle Psychotherapie. Berlin: VWB-Verlag.

Hiscox, A. R., & Calisch, A. C. (Eds). (1998). *Tapestry of cultural issues in art therapy.* London: Jessica Kingsley.

Jacobs, M. (Ed.). (1996). *Jitendra, lost connections. In search of a therapist.* Buckingham and Philadelphia: Open University Press.

Kareem, J., & Littlewood, R. (Eds). (1992). *Intercultural therapy: Themes, interpretation and practice.* Oxford: Blackwell Scientific.

Krause, I.-B. (1998). *Therapy across culture.* London: Sage.

Lago C., & Thompson, J. (1996). Race, culture and counselling. Buckingham and Philadelphia: Open University Press.

Lala, S., & Straussner, A. (Eds.). (2001). *Ethnocultural factors in substance abuse treatment.* New York: Guilford.

Parin, P., Morgenthaler, F., & Parin-Matthey, G. (1963). *Die Weißen denken zuviel.* Zürich: Atlantis.

Payer, L., & White, K. L. (1996). *Medicine and culture: Varieties of treatment in the United States, England, West Germany, and France.* New York: Owlet.

Pedersen, P. B., Draguns, J. G., Lonner, W. J., & Trimble, J. E. (Eds). (1996). *Counseling across cultures* (4th ed.). London: Sage.

Rowan, J. (1998). *The transpersonal. Psychotherapy and counselling* (2nd ed.). London: Routledge.

Sack, M., Lempa, W., & Lamprecht, F. (2001). Metaanalyse der Studien zur EMDR-Behandlung von Patienten mit posttraumatischen Belastungsstörungen. *Psychotherapic, Psychosomatik, Medizinische Psychologie, 51,* 350–355.

Sluzki, C. E. (2001). Psychologische Phasen der Migration und ihre Auswirkungen. In T. Hegemann, & R. Salman (Eds.), *Transkulturelle Psychiatrie* (pp. 101–115). Bonn: Psychiatrie-Verlag.

Smith, P. B., & Bond, M. H. (1998). *Social psychology across cultures* (2nd ed.). Hertfordshire: Prentice Hall Europe.

Ward, C. (Ed.). (1989). *Altered states of consciousness and mental health: A cross-cultural perspective.* Newbury Park, CA: Sage.

Westen, D. (1996). *Psychology: Mind, brain and culture.* New York: Wiley.

Wittkower, E. D. (1978). Probleme, Aufgaben und Ergebnisse der transkulturellen Psychiatrie. In E. Wulff (Ed.), *Ethnopsychiatrie.* Wiesbaden: Akadem. Verlagsges.

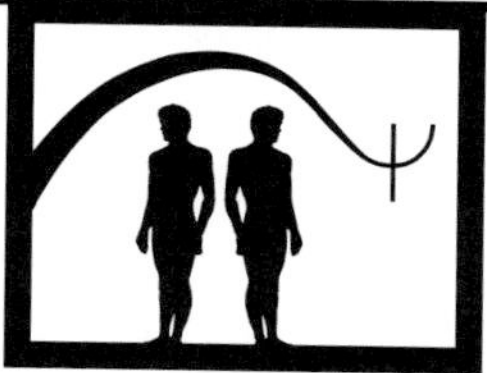

Transference

Eric R. Marcus

Columbia University College of Physicians and Surgeons and Columbia University Psychoanalytic Center for Training and Research

GLOSSARY

personality Characteristic attitudes and behavioral reaction patterns based on temperament and experience.

resistance Unconscious defenses to psychoanalytic treatment or to the transference. Resistance is a term for defenses that are used against the treatment process or against the transference.

transference The transfer of feelings about childhood relationships onto the experience of the relationship with the analyst.

transference resistance Unconscious blocks to experiencing the development of the transference; defenses against the transference.

I. INTRODUCTION

Transference refers to feelings the patient has for the analyst. The term transference was first used by Freud to refer to the neurotic feelings that were displaced or transferred from formative relationships in the patient's childhood. Transference is of crucial importance to psychoanalytic treatment because transference reactions help bring into consciousness the content and organization of the patient's unconscious self and object representations, and can dramatically demonstrate the effect of constituent conflicts, defenses, and compromises. Transference is the patient's experience in the present that comes closest to those formative relationships from the past.

As psychoanalysis widened its purview beyond mental symptoms to include the analysis of personalty, the definition of transference was broadened to include all feelings the patient had for the psychoanalyst. This broadened definition included emotional reactions in the here and now that are basic to personality function.

II. HISTORY

The term transference was first used by Sigmund Freud, who discovered the phenomena in the course of his earliest treatments. He at first felt these transference reactions prevented easy and thorough reports of the emotional associations to symptoms connected to the patient's history. Seen perhaps most clearly in fears about a judgmental attitude in the analyst, Freud thought such transference anxieties could block the treatment by inhibiting a full report of symptoms and associations. Therefore Freud at first felt that transferences were resistances to the treatment and were to be confronted by the psychoanalyst and consciously overridden by the patient. Later, Freud realized that these transference resistances were unconscious and were characteristic of the patient's personality defenses and adaptations. They displayed important aspects of the patient's symptoms. Freud further realized that the transference resistances often encoded and expressed the same themes as the patient's illness.

III. FUNCTION

Freud therefore began to focus on the transference and discovered that as the transference was allowed to intensify, the pathological attitudes and conflicts central to personality defenses rose to conscious intensity. This emotional intensity gave an experience of emotional validity to the treatment that was invaluable. Patients could see the emotional truth in their conflicts and compromise formations. Freud saw there was often little else that encoded so directly, so consistently, and so intensely these basic personality conflicts and compromise adaptations. When these compromise formations are part of personality attitude, the transference and personality disorder coincide. Analysis therefore more and more focused on transference, which became a hallmark of psychoanalytic treatment.

IV. TYPES

The emotional content of transference material may vary. The dominant theme of the content of the emotional transference is then used as a label to catagorize different types of transference reactions.

The maternal transference involves the emotional experience of the analyst as a mothering figure. Conflicts about dependancy needs and frustration, usually mobilizing intense conflicts between aggression and tender care, comprise the typical conflicts of this type of transference. Often associated with the personality features of the primary mothering figure, together with the child's reaction to the maternal personality, the two combine to form the projections onto the analyst, and the reactions to these projections, that form the maternal transference.

There is a similar transference possible to issues of authority and competition, often with fears of punishment. This type of material may be associated with the patient's early experiences of the father's personality. They condense together with the patient's personality reactions and the inevitable conflicts of growth and development. Together these form the projections onto the analyst, and the reactions to those projections, that are classically labeled the paternal transference.

Of course, sibling transferences (typically of competition and aggression), grandparent transferences (typically of tender care and an absence of competition), as well as transferences from other important figures during the patient's formative years are not only possible but probable.

Transferences may also be categorized according to the dominant emotional reaction. Erotic transferences involve sexual content irrespective of the formative figure involved. Aggressive transferences involve the emotional experience of anger. Idealizing transferences involve the projection of perfection. Denigrating transferences are the projection of feelings of devaluation.

Combinations of transferences are more the rule than the exception. The particular combinations are not just mixtures but highly specific condensations that reveal basic emotional compromise formations achieved in an attempt at emotional adaptation to constituent conflicts.

Because of these strong basic emotions and their combinations, containing the transference reaction both to the treatment setting and to the capacity of the patient to experience and describe rather than enact, the analyst must take great care in both the nurturing and containing of these reactions. The method of nurturing involves interpretation of resistances to the transference and the method of containing involves interpretation of the effects of the transference intensities. This is basic to psychoanalytic technique.

One of the most intense, most difficult to manage, and potentially destructive forms of transference and transference neurosis is the negative therapeutic reaction. In this form of transference, intense negative feelings are focused either on the analyst, the patient, or both as a result of the psychoanalytic treatment. Paradoxically, the reaction happens when things seem to be going well in the treatment. The negative therapeutic reaction is a reaction to accurate interpretation by the analyst, which then triggers an intense aggressive and guilt response. The danger is that the treatment may break off before the opportunity to thoroughly analyze the triggering factors, the constituents, and the destructive compromises inherent in the negative therapeutic reaction. The destructive nature of this reaction is often operating unconsciously at a lesser intensity throughout the patient's life and experience of themselves. It is one reason for life stalemate, life failure, chronic unhappiness, and self-destructive behavior.

V. TRANSFERENCE NEUROSIS

The focus on transference manifestations led Freud to the discovery of the transference neurosis. In the transference neurosis, the entire range of the patient's personality and neurosis is displayed in the psychoanalytic treatment relationship, and focused on the analyst and the treatment. This intense emotional involvement of the patient with the analyst and with the analytic treatment can reveal in great detail the emotional conflict elements and their psychopathological compromises. The analysis of the transference neurosis may take up the better part of the middle phase of psychoanalytic treatment.

Crucial to the use of the transference neurosis is the ability to catalyze its engagement, to manage its intensity, to analyze and interpret its meaning, to progressively unfold its developmental layers, and to show its relevance to the patient's symptoms and personality dysfunctions. It is for this reason especially that psychoanalytic training is long, arduous, and involves personal analysis for the practitioner.

Becuase transference is such a direct and felt experience, psychoanalytic technique attempts to bring it to an optimal level of intensity. This is why patients in analysis are seen many times per week and use the couch. Frequent sessions allow the intensity to build. Use of the couch helps because normal social interaction may dilute transference emotional reactions with reality representations or with reality experiences. Placing the patient out of sight of the analyst and reducing social interaction can increase the intensity, and therefore the consciousness of the transference.

Transference occurs as a part of all relationships but is not necessarily as consistently intense, nor verbalized, nor are its antecedents studied in an attempt to change. The transference neurosis can emerge in psychoanalytic treatment because the analyst is skilled at managing intensity. The analytic setting provides a safe setting because of the dependability, confidentiality, and lack of any agenda in the analyst other than the care of the patient.

VI. PHASES OF TRANSFERENCE

The different phases of psychoanalytic treatment can be defined in relationship to the transference. In the first phase, the transference is beginning to be catalyzed and engaged through the analysis of resistances to the transference. In the middle phase the transference neurosis forms, intensifies, progresses, and is analyzed. During the middle phase a deeper understanding of the transference and its origin occurs. During this phase, the insights from the analysis of the transference neurosis are applied to the patient's problems and pathological personality adaptations and these applications are worked through. The termination phase of analysis is the phase of resolution of the transference neurosis. During this phase, because of gains made in the analysis that resulted in psychological change, the neurotic transference reaches a kind of emotional conclusion. It then becomes less intense and disengages from the reality person of the analyst.

VII. USE IN PSYCHOTHERAPY

Transference is also triggered and used in psychodynamic psychotherapy. Although the focus may not be consistently on this level of the work with the patient, emotional reactions in and to treatment are used by the therapist to understand patients' reactions to people and problems that are the focus of treatment. The transference is thus a textbook of the patient's personality reactions to be read carefully by the analyst and analyzed thoroughly in psychoanalysis. Although not necessarily analyzed so thoroughly with the patient in psychodynamic psychotherapy, the transference is as crucial to the treating psychotherapist as it is to the psychoanalyst. The problem may be that because the psychotherapy is less intense, the exact nature of the transference is unclear. However, even in less intense or briefer treatments, the transference may be strong enough to reveal itself at least partially. Even this is useful to the treating analyst, who applies the information to understanding the patient's problems even if the transference is not usually the primary focus of psychodynamic psychotherapy.

VIII. APPLICATIONS OF TRANSFERENCE

Transference is important in all medical treatment. Emotional reactions may help or impede any form of helping relationship. In medical treatments, the most common cause of noncompliance to medication is an emotional problem in the doctor–patient relationship. In psychopharmacology treatments, patients may resist their medication because of emotional relationships they have either with the treating doctor or with the medication itself. The sophisticated psychopharmacologist understands these transference reactions and interprets especially the patient's attitudes toward medication.

Psychopharmacologists psychologically sophisticated in this way achieve better compliance with medication regimens and therefore better outcomes. Likewise, the sophisticated cognitive-behavioral therapist is attuned to even nascent transference reactions to the treatment or to themselves. This is especially so where either the reactions are negative resistances to the treatment or where the reactions are so idealizing that they imply the power of change is in the therapist rather than in the patient. Cognitive-behavioral therapists are adept at either sidestepping such transferences or including the attitudes as targets for their treatment. Their treatment aims at giving patients more conscious control over aspects of these attitudes that interfere with their treatment and support their symptoms.

The role of transference in all medical care is so powerful because illness tends to trigger emotional regression in patients, as does the setting of care in which trust and hope are to be vested in someone else, a dependency situation most like early childhood. Because of its application to medical care, to teaching, to social services, and even to institutions, the concept of transference is perhaps Freud's widest contribution.

IX. SUMMARY

All schools of psychoanalysis make use of transference. Ego psychology uses it to understand mental structure, its constituent conflicts, and compromises. Object relation theorists use it to understand the contents and functions of object relations. Self psychologists use it to understand the state of empathic attunement. Transference is basic to psychoanalysis.

See Also the Following Articles

Countertransference ■ Free Association ■ Intrapsychic Conflict ■ Resistance ■ Transference ■ Neurosis ■ Unconscious, The

Further Reading

Freud, S. (1915). *Observations on transference love.* (Standard ed. vol. 12.) London: Hogarth Press.

Sandler, J., Dare, C., & Holder, A. (1992). The patient and the analyst (2nd ed.). Madison, CT: International Universities Press.

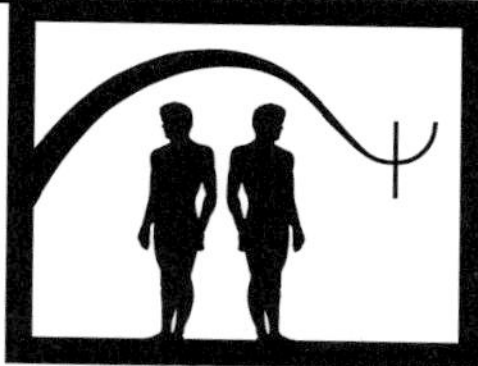

Transference Neurosis

Alan Sugarman and Claudia Law-Greenberg
San Diego Psychoanalytic Society and Institute and University of California, San Diego

GLOSSARY

compromise formation Any mental phenomenon that is the product of internal conflict and expresses all components of the conflict.

conflict Opposition between mental forces. These forces can be instinctual or Freud's structures of the mind (id, ego, superego).

countertransference The analyst's feelings toward the patient. Some restrict the term to the analyst's emotional responses to the patient's transference.

defense The methods used by the ego to master and control id impulses or superego injunctions.

ego The hypothetical construct defined in Freud's structural model to enable the mind to organize its various components and to adapt to the external world.

libido The hypothetical psychic energy attached to the sexual instincts.

psychic energy Freud believed there was a quantifiable mental energy, similar to physical energy, that fueled the activity of the mind. Two major types of psychic energy were postulated-sexual energy (libido) and aggressive energy.

repression The particular defense mechanism of the ego by which a conflictual mental content or process is rendered unconscious.

resistance The manifestation of defense within the treatment process whereby the patient opposes the analyst's interventions.

structural model Freud's final model of the mind introduced in 1923 in *The Ego and the Id*. The mind was conceived of having three structures (the id, ego, and superego). Interaction between these three structures is thought to account for all mentally mediated behavior.

topographic Freud's earlier model of the mind in which its systems were defined in terms of their accessibility to consciousness. Despite the topographic model having to be discarded because of its theoretical inconsistencies and clinical failings the term *topographic* remains useful for describing mental contents and functions in regard to their degree of consciousness.

transference The process by which the patient displaces onto the therapist or analyst feelings, impulses, attitudes, or defense derived from important interactions in the past.

The phenomenon of transference neurosis is arguably the most important (and perhaps most controversial) concept in the psychoanalytic theory of technique. For almost 50 years its presence or absence has been used to determine whether a psychoanalytic treatment process is, in effect, true psychoanalysis or whether it is psychoanalytic psychotherapy. Merton Gill, in 1954, was one of the earliest psychoanalysts to differentiate psychoanalysis from psychotherapy based on whether or not the patient had developed a regressive transference neurosis in the treatment that could be resolved by interpretation. Leo

Stone, another prominent analyst of that era, concurred with Gill. But by the time of Gill's death, Gill, himself, as well as others had repudiated both his definition of transference neurosis and its centrality to the analytic process.

I. FREUD'S CONCEPT OF TRANSFERENCE

Understanding this reversal and arriving at an adequate modern-day understanding of both the concept and its role require that one study its origins in Freud's thinking. As with most of Freud's other technical concepts, the term transference neurosis predates the introduction of his structural model. Hence the concept was never reformulated or adequately integrated into Freud's new manner of thinking, leading to inconsistences and ambiguities that continued to affect how the concept is used today. Freud first introduced the concept of transference in *Studies in Hysteria* when he discussed the "false connection" between feelings arising outside the treatment situation and those directed toward the therapist. That is, he recognized that feelings and thoughts originally experienced in regard to significant figures in the patient's life, usually from childhood, were displaced onto the analyst. Soon transference was viewed as a displacement of libidinal ties into the treatment situation.

In his *Introductory Lectures,* Freud introduced the concept of transference neurosis as a diagnostic category that included both hysterical and obsessional neuroses. Such transference neuroses were thought to be the most amenable to a successful psychoanalytic treatment because patients suffering from them were able to form a relationship with the analyst and to be influenced by their transference to the treater. Patients suffering from transference neuroses were differentiated from those suffering from narcissistic neuroses (paranoids, melancholics, and schizophrenics). Freud thought that the latter group had no capacity for a transference relationship with the therapist and, therefore, was incapable of being helped by psychoanalytic treatment.

Earlier in his thinking Freud had first understood transference as a resistance to the remembering of the past. At that stage in the evolution of his theory and technique, such resistance was quite important given that psychoanalytic cure was thought to occur when the patient was made aware of previously unconscious mental contents, usually sexual fantasies from the past. By 1912, however, Freud raised the analysis of transference to the forefront of analytic technique. He described the transference neurosis as the replacement of the patient's clinical neurosis with an artificial neurosis "through which the patient could then be cured through the therapeutic work" in his 1914 paper, *Remembering, Repeating, and Working Through.*

The transference neurosis was described as the creation of an intermediate region between illness and real life. This newly created condition was said to contain all of the conflicts or elements of the clinical neurosis, making them amenable to therapeutic intervention. In essence, Freud came to understand the transference neurosis as a phenomenon in which the libido shifted from the original object(s) and associated internal conflicts into the transference where it became concentrated on the analyst. The original conflicts were then experienced with emotional immediacy in the relationship with the analyst. The analyst could then analyze these conflicts in a context of intense affectivity that allowed their historical or unconscious roots to become evident. Fresh repression was avoided, and the freed up psychic energy then became available to the patient's ego.

II. GREENSON'S CONCEPT OF TRANSFERENCE NEUROSIS

This understanding of the transference neurosis held sway in American psychoanalysis into the early 1970s. It was given the greatest legitimacy by Ralph Greenson, arguably the greatest clinical analyst of his era, in his tome, *The Technique and Practice of Psychoanalysis.* Greenson made it clear that he viewed the development of a transference neurosis to be a central dimension of the psychoanalytic process. He described its phenomenology as involving an increase in the intensity and duration of the patient's preoccupation with the analyst and the analytic process. This intensified interest in the analyst is usually experienced by the patient as a mixture of love and hate as well as defenses against these emotional reactions triggered by anxiety and guilt. Reactions to the analyst were described as varying. They could be intense, explosive, subtle, or chronic; such constellations of affects become omnipresent once the transference neurosis takes hold. As the patient's preoccupation intensifies, his or her symptoms and instinctual demands revolve around the analyst while simultaneously remobilizing all the old neurotic conflicts. The transference neurosis, therefore, was described by Greenson as a repetition of the patient's past neurosis.

Greenson argued that the classical psychoanalytic attitude toward the transference neurosis must be to foster its development. The analyst has to safeguard the analysis to allow the best opportunity for a transference neurosis to develop. According to Greenson, contaminations or intrusions into the analytic space, such as the analyst's personal characteristics or values, can inhibit or limit the development of the transference neurosis. Thus, they must be avoided. He took pains to warn that the analyst's countertransference could impede the development of a transference neurosis. For example, undue warmth was thought to risk inhibiting the patient's hostile transference whereas incomplete transference interpretations could produce a treatment stalemate.

III. LEGITIMACY CONTROVERSY

By 1987, however, the phenomenon of transference neurosis was being called into question on a variety of grounds. An entire issue of the journal *Psychoanalytic Inquiry* was devoted to the question of its legitimacy—hence the title of that issue, "Transference Neurosis, Evolution or Obsolescence." Arnold Cooper was perhaps the harshest critic of the concept among the contributors to that volume. He argued that using the occurrence of a transference neurosis to differentiate psychoanalysis from other therapies left psychoanalysis in a difficult position because of the lack of precision in both the definition and the phenomenological recognition of the transference neurosis. Highlighting the term's conceptual ambiguity, he pointed out that those analysts who argued that the transference neurosis involved a heightened emotional experience of the analyst were at odds with Freud who had emphasized that the transference neurosis should be manifested more in memory than in enactment in the analytic situation. Cooper also quoted the writings of the early British analyst, Edward Glover, who had emphasized that transference neuroses developed only with regard to certain types of patients, generally those suffering from phobic, conversion, or obsessional symptoms. Thus, Glover did not see the occurrence of a transference neurosis as a differentiating factor for a psychoanalytic process.

Cooper also criticized the notion that the transference neurosis recapitulates the infantile neurosis. He pointed out the vagueness in defining the concept of the infantile neurosis. Some use the term to refer to the hypothetical childhood neurosis that presumably predated the adult one; others use the term to indicate oedipally based conflicts, while still others define it as concrete, observable, childhood, neurotic symptoms. To the extent that this concept is used in vague or inconsistent ways, it becomes impossible to describe the transference neurosis as a reactivation of it in any coherent fashion.

The connection between the concept of the transference neurosis and the infantile neurosis has also led to debate about the degree to which the transference neurosis is a regressive phenomenon. By the mid 1970s, some analysts, most notably Jacob Arlow, had argued that it was a fallacy to consider the analytic process and the activation of a transference neurosis as regressive. Rather than promoting regression, Arlow argued that the analytic situation created a context in which regressive aspects of the patient's mind could emerge in a clearly observable fashion. Merton Gill extended this view while pointing out that the transference neurosis did not involve the revival of the infantile neurosis. He challenged the entire thesis that an earlier developmental state could literally be reactivated. Rather, he believed that earlier developmental experiences that exert an active influence on present-day behavior did so because they remained active in the patient's personality. As such, he argued that such active influences would be manifested in patients' transferences to the analyst.

Such a position leads into another area of unclarity about the definition of transference neurosis. Traditionally, the concept of transference neurosis has been distinguished from the concept of transference. As mentioned earlier, the former concept has been used to distinguish a psychoanalytic process from a merely psychotherapeutic one in which many transferences develop. The latter are more fluctuating, less organized, and less intense than the sort of full-fledged transference neurosis described by Greenson. However by 1984, Gill was taking issue with this distinction. Thus, he argued that the reason for the more intense transference neurosis was not the difference in the type of treatment process involved. He believed, rather, that it was the analyst's failure to interpret earlier manifestations of transference in the treatment process that led to transferences intensifying to the point where they could not be ignored by the analyst. Thus, this sort of transference neurosis was thought by him to be a sign of poor technique, not of psychoanalytic process. For Gill there was no important clinical distinction between transference and transference neurosis. Instead he argued for early and consistent interpretation of the transference wherever it might be ferreted out in the patient's associations. Gill's technical strategy for transference interpretation has remained a minority view in psychoanalysis although his disinclination to distinguish transference from transference neurosis continues to be embraced by a number of psychoanalysts.

Charles Brenner is another prominent psychoanalyst who criticized the concept of transference neurosis. He argued, similarly to Gill, that there was nothing to be gained theoretically or clinically by distinguishing transference neurosis from transference. Brenner argued that the term *transference* was sufficient, and that transference manifestations were compromise formations that needed to be analyzed in the same manner as any other compromise formation.

Despite these debates about the nature of the transference neurosis and its role in psychoanalytic technique, the concept continues to be valued by most theorists of analytic technique. Both editors of the *Psychoanalytic Inquiry* issue devoted to the topic concluded that transference neurosis remains a useful clinical concept and one that distinguishes psychoanalysis from psychotherapy. Nathaniel London was probably the most eloquent on the subject. He argued that the distinction between transference and transference neurosis is complex and significant, that the emergence of a transference neurosis does distinguish a psychoanalytic from a psychotherapeutic process, and that those analyses in which a full-fledged transference neurosis fails to emerge are more limited in their clinical results.

These conclusions leave psychoanalysts with the problem of defining the transference neurosis and accounting for successful clinical analyses in which one has not been manifested. A modern view is that the latter problem rests on the former. That is, many contemporary analysts believe that the apparent lack of a transference neurosis reflects a problematic definition rather than an actual failure to develop one. Too many psychoanalysts continue to think of a transference neurosis in the way that Freud did when he developed the concept. That is, it is defined as a displacement of childhood libidinal and aggressive wishes or fantasies from the parents onto the analyst in a particularly organized and emotionally intense fashion. But this definition arose from the topographic era of Freud's thinking when unconscious impulses were viewed as the explanation of most psychopathology and personality traits. The advent of the structural model in 1923 offered a more complex way of understanding transference (and, hence, transference neurosis). Freud, himself, never integrated his concepts of transference or transference neurosis with his structural model. Thus, many analysts continued to think of these concepts in a topographic manner without realizing it.

IV. STRUCTURAL BASIS

Anna Freud, in her 1936 volume, *The Ego and the Mechanisms of Defense,* offered a structurally based understanding of transference. She discussed three types of transference. It is her transference of defense that is most appropriate to a modern-day understanding. This type of transference involves the patient's projecting or externalizing significant aspects of his or her defensive structure into the analytic situation, particularly the relationship with the analyst. Thus, patients who are reported not to develop a full-fledged transference neurosis generally are found, with closer scrutiny, to be using a variation of transference of defense. Rather than displacing unconscious drive impulses onto the analyst, they externalize their defensive structure into the analytic situation and relationship with the analyst. In these instances, the defensive structure generally involves prominent defenses against feeling or becoming aware of strong emotions toward others. The apparent absence of a transference neurosis is, in actuality, an intense one whereby the analyst is treated with the same emotional detachment and/or fearfulness that characterize the patient's relationships with most important objects in his or her world, including internal representations of the parents. Thus, analysis of the transference neurosis with such patients involves the consistent confrontation, exploration, and interpretation of their distancing defenses and the reasons for them. Such work is generally quite productive but requires significant activity on the part of the analyst. Nonetheless, working in this fashion generally demonstrates the fallacy of assuming the absence of a transference neurosis and deepens the analytic work in the same way that analyzing the more obvious forms of transference neuroses do.

Those analysts who practice in this manner tend to agree that it is this work—the analysis of the transference neurosis—and all its complexity that allows for the important conflicts that cause the patient's symptoms or personality problems to be experienced and mastered by the patient in an emotionally vivid fashion. The intensity of feeling and firsthand quality of such work allows for conflict mastery far more than other nontransferential elements of the analytic process. Although not scientifically demonstrated, such work does not happen in psychotherapy because the reduced frequency of sessions prevents the emergence of the sort of transference neurosis just described, although certainly transference manifestations do occur and can be worked with in a fashion that is therapeutically useful.

V. SUMMARY

In summary, the concept of transference neurosis continues to be a valuable one in psychoanalysis. It distinguishes psychoanalysis from other forms of psychotherapy, even psychoanalytic psychotherapy. Analysis of the transference neurosis remains a crucial aspect of the analytic process, one that many continue to view as the most important in promoting mastery of conflict. Thinking in terms of the transference neurosis serves as a useful guideline for the practicing analyst. After a certain point in analysis, most analysts begin to look for the emergence of one and to attempt to understand when one is not apparent. Utilizing a contemporary structural approach to analysis allows psychoanalysts in the latter situation to more carefully observe and listen to the patient's material for evidence of the defensive aspects against deeper feelings toward the analyst, defenses that the analyst brings to the patient's awareness to analyze the reasons that the patient feels it necessary to keep the analyst at such emotional distance.

See Also the Following Articles

Countertransference ■ Intrapsychic Conflict ■ Oedipus Complex ■ Resistance ■ Structural Theory ■ Topographic Theory ■ Transference ■ Unconscious, The

Further Reading

London, N. L. (1987). Prologue. *Psychoanalytic Inquiry, 7,* 457–463.

London, N. L. (1987). Discussion. In defense of the transference neurosis concept: A process and interactional definition. *Psychoanalytic Inquiry, 7,* 587–598.

Moore, B. E., & Fine, B. D. (1990). *Psychoanalytic terms and concepts.* New Haven, CT: Yale University Press.

Stone, L. (1995). Transference. In B. E. Moore & B. D. Fine (Eds.), *Psychoanalysis. The major conflicts.* New Haven, CT: Yale University Press.

Wallerstein, R. S. (1995). *The talking cures.* New Haven, CT: Yale University Press.

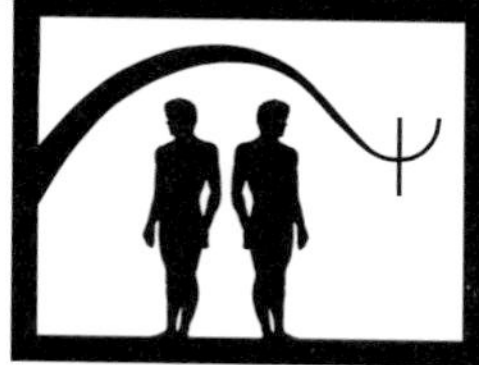

Transitional Objects and Transitional Phenomena

Arnold Wilson and Nadezhda M.T. Robinson

Columbia University Center for Psychoanalytic Training and Research and St. Mary Hospital

GLOSSARY

illusion A belief or experience that is based on unconscious material and is experienced as real.

objective External reality, that which is outside the individual and separate from the individual.

subjective Unconscious material such as drives, impulses, wishes, and fears that is particular to the individual and cannot be objectively defined.

transitional object An object, typically a soft toy, chosen by an infant or child. Irreplaceable, the object is imbued with the child's feelings for and experience of his or her primary caretaker. The child uses the transitional object to aid the transition from primary dependence to independence.

transitional phenomena Individual experiences characterized by the interplay of unconscious material and objective reality in forming a novel emotional experience or state.

It is not unusual for parents or caretakers to intuitively allow children the use of some kind of object, oftentimes soft and furry, less frequently hard and with rough edges, that becomes a special kind of beloved possession of the child. Blankets, teddies, things that easily mold to the flesh, that keep a telltale smell, that survive the transition from toddlerhood into latency, ideally serve such a purpose. It is little short of miraculous how adults recognize the life-sustaining urgency of the need for the child to cling to these possessions. Such objects are often named "momma" or some such appellation that implies an understanding that the object is a stand-in for the mother, providing similar soothing and comforting, and herein lies a key paradox of childhood—the child's ability to separate from the mother begins in holding firmly to her, or at least a rendition of her. Thus, the necessary separation from primary caretaker takes place with the assistance of some symbolic object (the transitional object) that provides the continuity of closeness to the primary caretaker.

I. D. W. WINNICOTT

This paradox—that separation can come to exist only in the context of a symbolic continuity—is the sort of recognition D. W. Winnicott set about to explore in his career. A British pediatrician turned psychoanalyst, Winnicott saw thousands of infants and mothers in London during the World War II years, while developing a remarkable oeuvre that remains influential to this day. Never a systematic thinker, his uncoordinated insights into mother–child relations, the inner life of infants and children, the relations between aggression, security, and creativity—remain the stuff to which many contemporary investigators turn for inspiration and guidance. In this article, the reader will recognize a certain allusive and poetic use of language. This is more Winnicott's than our style, for in order to grasp and communicate what Winnicott was trying to convey, one must remain true to his style of discourse.

II. TRANSITIONAL OBJECTS

In 1951, Winnicott published his classic paper "Transitional Objects and Transitional Phenomena," which investigated the relationship between symbol formation, maternal caregiving, and the development of creativity and, in fact, the mind itself. To Winnicott, the main function of a transitional object is to "start each human being off with what will always be important for them: a neutral area of experience which will not be challenged."

Winnicott provides sufficient material for a thorough understanding of transitional objects and transitional phenomena in his first paper on the topic. He presented these concepts with rich examples from infant observation and analytic work with adults. The topic appears in later articles but is only minimally refined or elaborated there. In the 1951 paper, Winnicott defines transitional objects and transitional phenomena, describes the key concepts, and identifies areas of further exploration, which have been taken up by theorists such as Paulina Kernberg, Arnold Modell, and Peter Giovacchini.

III. WINNICOTT AS THEORETICIAN

It is helpful here to say a bit about Winnicott the theoretician. Strictly speaking, Winnicott was less of a theoretician than he was a pragmatic yet intuitively driven observer. A member of the so-called middle school, his theoretical roots are both Freudian as well as Kleinian, especially in his uncanny understanding of the role of aggression in early mental life. His writings have contributed many fundamental concepts to the body of psychoanalytic thought (for example the good-enough mother, primary maternal preoccupation, the capacity for concern, and hate in the countertransference) which are not so much particular to a comprehensive theory as they are critical to what we might call the experience of being. Fogel explicates this in an article titled "Winnicott's Antitheory" wherein he explains that Winnicott was traditionally analytic in his theoretical beliefs but obviously singular and unique in terms of his distinctive application and elucidation of the concepts that stand alongside traditional theory. Transitional phenomena and objects are good examples of this. Truly grasping what Winnicott meant is crucial in order to undertake clinical work with children or psychoanalytic work with adults yet this knowledge does not necessarily alter in any way one's theoretical foundation. Thus, it is a challenge to fully describe Winnicott's concepts of transitional objects and transitional phenomena. On the one hand, understanding what he was trying to convey makes available an intellectual and, Winnicott would hope, experiential knowledge of self and other that deepens our contact with others. On the other hand, one will not find any particular alteration to one's structural understanding of the individual or technical view of the practice of psychotherapy on the basis of the knowledge.

IV. TRANSITIONAL OBJECTS

A transitional object is an object that is chosen, or, to be more explicit, Winnicott says "created," by the infant and that stands for the breast or object (bottle, caregiver's face) of the first relationship. It is developmentally appropriate, indeed a positive indicator of a healthy maternal–child bond, typically develops first between 6 and 9 months, and lasts often into the preschool years. It is the child's first possession and original "not-me" object. By this, Winnicott means that the child is sufficiently developed to have a growing sense of object permanence and constancy (see Piaget for discussion of object permanence.) Thus, the child is able to conceive of the transitional object's separateness from himself. Object use begins with an infant's use of fist-in-mouth, then thumb, then some mixture of fingers and thumb, and finally the infant moves to the use of an object. There is a gradual progression toward the use of objects that are part of neither the mother nor the infant but represent the shared experiences of both.

Certain features mark the relationship between the transitional object and infant. Perhaps most remarkable is the infant's assumption of possession of the object and the environmental cooperation with that. Caregivers hesitate to wash well-loved transitional objects and households are collectively turned inside out when a transitional object goes missing. The transitional object is "affectionately cuddled" and "excitedly loved and mutilated." The transitional object possesses a reality and vitality of its own. It is cocreated by the infant's objective perception of the object and his or her subjective projections of relating (in this case, loving and being loved) onto the object.

Winnicott talks of the "fate" of the transitional object in further defining it as well as further illustrating the depth and a particularly unique feature of his theory. Winnicott proposes a "third area" of "existing" or human life, which is where transitional phenomena grow and live. For the purposes of this article, they shall be called the first and second areas, as Winnicott did not name them. The first area is the fundamental reality of individual experience. It is the inner life, intrapsychic world, or "personal psychic world" in Winnicott's words. Here we find the genesis of dreams, hallucinations, and the creative process. The first area of existence is our store of preferences, idiosyncrasies, and "neuroses." The second area is the external world of the individual composed of our relations with others, standards of conscience, and the various roles we fulfill (husband, wife, worker, friend, parent, sibling). Winnicott calls this the "expanding universe which man contracts out of."

Transitional phenomena illustrate the joining of the first and second areas of consciousness, which Winnicott calls the "cultural life of the individual." This third area is the meeting of the objective–subjective, personal–political, internal–external realms of individual experience. Using the example of the teddy bear as transitional object, we see that the teddy is an external object (second area) real to the infant and his extended external reality (parents, siblings, etc.). Yet, the teddy also represents the material of the infant's inner life (first area) to the extent that the teddy is a cuddling, nurturing, soothing, nonretaliatory object of his or her aggression, and a constant reliable feature of his or her existence. The infant has made the teddy with the imbuing of these unconscious features while also, for the first time, using an object outside himself to serve as a receptacle for internalized experiences. It is useful to note here Winnicott's famous phrase that "there is no such thing as a baby." Winnicott's view of infant and mother are as a union, the "nursing couple" and, according to the infant's perceptions, the mother does not exist without him or her; indeed, mother exists because of him or her. With the development of transitional objects, and by implication, the ability to live in the third area, the infant is demonstrating his or her ability to perceive the external world as separate while simultaneously giving away his or her reliance on the unconscious/first area. The use of transitional objects demonstrates the emergence of the baby as separate from his or her primary caretaker.

The transitional object sits in the middle of the continuum between the subjective and objective. It is slowly moved more and more toward the objective as the child grasps reality, develops reality testing, and is confronted with the inevitable frustrations of external reality. Thus, the fate of the transitional object is to "fade away" but never leave. The object loses its importance in the maintenance of and elaboration of unconscious material; other mechanisms such as play, language, and interpersonal interactions serve this function. But, Winnicott argues, we see the vestiges of transitional objects and the vibrancy of transitional phenomena in the human activities of art and the appreciation of creativity and religion.

Winnicott is especially concerned with the ability to symbolize that the use of transitional objects implies. Symbolization implies a broader human activity, interesting to Winnicott, which is the use of illusion. The transitional object simultaneously serves the infant's unconscious life of merger and union and external life of independence and self-reliance.

Here we arrive at another particular element of Winnicott's thought and the aspect of the theory of transitional phenomena that continues to be the focus of theorists and practitioners today.

> From birth and thereafter the human being is concerned with the problem of the relationship between what is objectively perceived and what is subjectively conceived of.... The intermediate area to which I am referring is the area that is allowed to the infant between primary creativity and objective perception based on reality testing. The transitional phenomena represent the early stages of the use of illusion, without which there is no meaning for the human being in the idea of relationship with an object that is perceived by others as external to that being.

V. ILLUSION

Winnicott's exploration of the use of illusion was not without precedent at the time. Freud in 1920 had described his grandson's ability to symbolize his own reality and existence through play when briefly separated from his mother. Muensterberger describes two theorists whose work predates Winnicott's and is clearly in the same vein. Geza Roheim described the activity of filling one's mind with thoughts of the people and relationships we are separated from as the "theory of an intermediate object as stabilization between a trend that oscillates between clinging and going exploring." The reference here to the "intermediate object" is very similar to Winnicott's term the "intermediate area" and in fact, Roheim is clearly describing a transitional object (i.e., teddy bear) that helps the infant feel grounded enough to explore. Roheim later writes of the transitional phase "located somewhere halfway between the pure pleasure principle and the reality principle." Again, this description is very similar to Winnicott's description of the 1st, 2nd, and transitional areas of human experience. Here, Roheim is referring, in part, to an earlier work by Hermann, called seminal by Muensterberger, which is titled "To Cling—to go in Search." Hermann's view, very similar to Winnicott's, is that the infant requires a link between his or her inner experience and emerging external experience. When the link is concretized, it is a transitional object. The link may also be imaginal (the memory of a connection with a significant other) in which case, the memory lives and is sustained in the transitional area.

VI. THE FUTURE

Winnicott's concepts also provided the framework for generations of future papers. The most important aspect of his paper, in terms of the advancement of the field, is the explication of the transitional phenomena. Green states "It is easy to see that Winnicott has in fact described not so much an object as a space lending itself to the creation of objects." Indeed, after his death his wife Clare described how Winnicott considered this one of his most important achievements and it is evident that transitional phenomena, this area of the experiential field is the groundwork for much of his more important work including primary maternal preoccupation, playing in reality, and the facilitating environment. Describing transitional phenomena is a bit like describing a fog—we can only present the outline of it against the land and sky, note its thinner aspects, and watch its movement and effect. The transitional phenomenon is in fact an experience and one further complicated by its straddling of the objective and subjective experiences of the experiencer.

Winnicott described transitional phenomena as "an intermediate are of experience" and further stated "I am therefore studying the substance of illusion." This is a most remarkable statement for Winnicott to have made. The use of illusion is at the heart of the transitional phenomena. Here, Winnicott draws our attention to the activity of the early infant in perceiving the breast (or substitute) as created by and for him or her by virtue of the good-enough mother's repeated presentation of the breast at the moment the baby requires it—and early on, before the baby "knows" he or she requires. "The mother's adaption to the infant's needs, when good enough, gives the infant the *illusion* that there is an external reality that corresponds to the infant's own capacity to create." Our appreciation of and reliance on illusion is therefore with us from our earliest days. "From birth therefore the human being is concerned with the problem of the relationship between what is objectively perceived and what is subjectively conceived of." Gradually, reality seeps into the infant's sense of omnipotent control of the environment (still perceived as aspects of himself or herself) and the infant is confronted with the reality of the objective world. The good-enough mother allows the gradual impingement of reality, understanding the infant's need to be disappointed and thereby develop reparative capacities. The place where the objective and subjective meet, where our experience is created by the interaction between our subjective material and objective reality remains and is exercised in our appreciation of the arts, practice of religion, and ability to symbolize our daily experience lives. Winnicott called it the "neutral area of experience which will not be challenged." We do not argue with a person who cries during a soulful passage of a cello concerto or who believes in the sacrament of the Eucharist, nor do we argue with the poet who draws meaning from the curve of an arm. Only when an individual requires us to endorse the "objectivity of his subjective phenomena" do we "discern or diagnose madness." It is when a delusional patient asks us to believe a plot involving the FBI and CIA is the true source of his or her pervasive sense of danger, importance, and isolation that we see the bullying imposition of subjective experience in the intermediate/transitional realm of experiencing.

The nature of illusion and the transitional phenomena are important to current theorists for two general reasons. First, theorists who use clinical data to expand theory have advanced the importance of illusion; second, clinicians use theory to understand clinical material. While current theorists are typically psychoanalytic theorists, because Winnicott's theory is best applied to any two individuals conducting a relationship it is widely applicable. Clinically, researchers like Paulina Kernberg use the concept of transitional objects to identify her patients' abilities and frustrations of mediating internal impulses and fantasies while managing an overwhelming and confusing experience of the external world. Kernberg's most ill patients develop no transitional object use or maintain a transitional object that is cruel, rejecting, and a poor receptacle for feelings of love, hope, and forgiveness. Kernberg uses the theory of transitional objects to further clarify her patients' functioning. Peter Giovachinni in 1987 explicates the use of transitional objects and of transitional phenomena in adult borderline states from a broad clinical, phenomenological perspective. He expands the theory of the transitional object in his consideration of the borderline patient's inability to regulate affect states and adaptively use projection, thereby making impossible the use of a transitional object. Arnold Modell in 1962 detailed the idea that the adult borderline patient lives in an inner world devoid of transitional phenomena, starkly reality bound, with all the attendant harshness and abrasions of the unmitigated reality of life. In all applications, the theory of transitional objects and transitional phenomena is useful in understanding the intra- and interpersonal functioning of an individual.

Theoretically, Green tells us that Winnicott's place is in guiding any analytic work that does not strictly adhere to the tenets of classical analysis. Green states "It seems to me that the only acceptable variations of classical analysis are those whose aim is to facilitate the creation of optimal condition for symbolization." Symbolization is a transitional phenomenon. It is Winnicott's explicit assumption that reality acceptance is a never-ending task and that the intermediate area of experience, illusion, or transitional phenomena (all different names for the same, unchallenged experience) provide relief from the ongoing tension of relating internal and external reality. This experience is what many good therapists attempt to create and sustain for their patients. More precisely, therapists and patients work to cocreate this experience. The intermediate realm of experience is activated in what Winnicott termed "the holding environment," is present in unconditional positive regard, and whatever the orientation, facilitates the therapist's ability to understand his or her patient in a meaningful and intimate, beyond-language way.

Winnicott left a legacy of literature that remains vital, challenging, and inspiring. Moreover, he left detailed insights about what it means to be human, to love, to mourn, to long for, and to hope. His concept of the transitional object is one of his better known contributions. Perhaps teddy bears and blankies appeal to all of us, regardless of age. It would be a underestimation of Winnicott's contribution to characterize his thoughts on transitional phenomena as primarily about soft cuddly toys. He described a realm of experience, never before or since captured with such elegance, wherein we have the capacity to be moved by art, find solace in religion, and use illusion in various ways to adapt and meaningfully mediate one's constant grappling with reality.

In this article, the theory of transitional objects and phenomena was presented. Additional considerations of more current applications of the theory were also presented. It is the authors' hope that the reader has been both awed and bemused by Winnicott.

See Also the Following Articles

Animal-Assisted Therapy ■ Child and Adolescent Psychotherapy: Psychoanalytic Principles ■ Dreams, Use in Psychotherapy ■ Parent–Child Interaction Therapy ■ Primary-Care Behavioral Pediatrics ■ Therapeutic Storytelling with Children and Adolescents

Further Reading

Bak, R. C. (1974). Distortions of the concept of fetishism. *Psychoanalytic Study of the Child, 29,* 191–214.

Busch, F. (1974). Dimensions of the first transitional object. *Psychoanalytic Study of the Child, 29,* 215–229.

Busch, F., Nagera, H., McKnight, J., & Pezzarossi, G. (1973). Primary transitional objects. *Journal of the American Academy of Child Psychiatry, 12,* 193–214.

Coppolillo, H. P. (1967). Maturational aspects of the transitional phenomenon. *International Journal of Psycho-Analysis, 48,* 237–246.

Coppolillo, H. P. (1976). The transitional phenomena revisited. *Journal of the American Academy of Child Psychiatry, 15,* 36–48.

Escalona, S. K. (1953). Emotional development in the first year of life. In M. J. E. Senn (Ed.), *Problems of infancy and childhood* (pp. 11–12). New York: Josiah Macy Jr. Foundation.

Fogel, G. (1992). Winnicott's antitheory and Winnicott's art. *The Psychoanalytic Study of the Child, 47,* 205–222.

Gaddini, R., & Gaddini, E. (1970). Transitional objects and the process of individuation. *Journal of the American Academy of Child Psychiatry, 9,* 347–365.

Galenson, E., & Roiphe, H. (1971). The impact of early sexual discovery on mood, defensive organization, and symbolization. *Psychoanalytic Study of the Child, 19,* 448–469.

Green, A. (1978). Potential space in psychoanalysis: The object in the setting. In S. A. Grolnick & L. Barkin (Eds.), *Between Reality and Fantasy* (pp. 167–191). New York: Jason Aronson.

Hong, K. M. (1978). The transitional phenomena: A theoretical integration. *The Psychoanalytic Study of the Child, 33,* 47–78.

Jacobson, E. (1964). *The self and the object world.* New York: International Universities Press.

Kahne, M. J. (1967). On the persistence of transitional phenomena into adult life. *International Journal of Psychoanalysis, 48,* 247–258.

Kernberg, P. (1988). Children with borderline personality organization. In C. J. Kestenbaum & D. T. Williams (Eds.), *Handbook of clinical assessment of children and adolescents. Vols. I & II.* (pp. 604–662). New York: New York University Press.

Kernberg, P. (1989). Childhood psychosis: A psychoanalytic perspective. In S. Greenspan & G. Pollock (Eds.), *The course of life. Vol. III. Middle and late childhood* (pp. 115–134). Madison, CT: International Universities Press.

Modell, A. H. (1963). Primitive object relationship and the predisposition to schizophrenia. *International Journal of Psycho-Analysis, 44,* 282–292.

Muensterberger, W. (1962). The creative process: Its relation to object loss and fetishism. In *The Psychoanalytic Study of Society* (Vol. 2). New York: International Universities Press.

Stevenson, O. (1954). The first treasured possession. *The Psychoanalytic Study of the Child, 9,* 199–217.

Tolpin, M. (1971). On the beginnings of a cohesive self. *The Psychoanalytic Study of the Child, 26,* 316–352.

Winnicott, D. W. (1953). Transitional objects and transitional phenomena. *International Journal of Psycho-Analysis, 34,* 89–97.

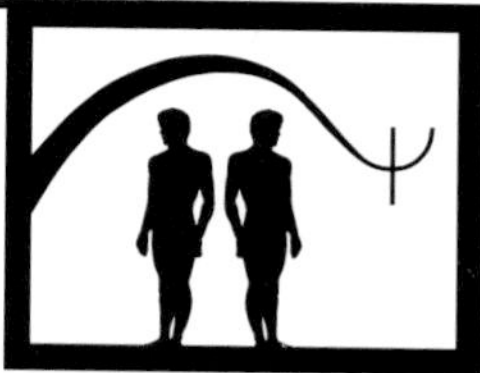

Trauma Management Therapy

B. Christopher Frueh
Medical University of South Carolina

Samuel M. Turner and Deborah C. Beidel
University of Maryland at College Park

GLOSSARY

exposure therapy A well-established behavioral treatment for anxiety disorders, it involves exposing individuals to feared thoughts, images, or other stimuli repeatedly and for prolonged periods in the absence of any actual threat until anxiety is reduced via habituation.

habituation A progressive decrease in the vigor of autonomic responses or behavior that may occur with repeated presentations of the eliciting stimulus.

posttraumatic stress disorder An anxiety disorder that may follow traumatic experiences (e.g., combat, physical and sexual assault), which is characterized by symptoms of re-experiencing the trauma (e.g., nightmares, "flashbacks"), emotional numbing and avoidance, and arousal (e.g., insomnia, hypervigilance, anger).

Trauma Management Therapy is a multicomponent behavioral treatment program for chronic combat-related posttraumatic stress disorder (PTSD). It is a comprehensive treatment designed to address all aspects of the clinical syndrome seen in veterans, via a combination of patient education, exposure therapy, social skills training, and relevant homework assignments.

I. DESCRIPTION OF TREATMENT

Trauma Management Therapy (TMT) is a multicomponent behavioral treatment program for chronic PTSD in veterans. It is a comprehensive treatment designed specifically to target various aspects of the clinical syndrome associated with chronic PTSD, particularly reducing emotional and physiological reactivity to traumatic cues, reducing intrusive symptoms and avoidance behavior, improving interpersonal skills and emotion modulation (e.g., anger control), and increasing the range of enjoyable social activities. The program is designed to incorporate exposure therapy, the PTSD psychosocial treatment approach with the most empirical support, with a social skills training component designed specifically for veterans with PTSD. It is a comprehensive treatment designed to address all aspects of the primary clinical syndrome seen in veterans, via a combination of patient education, exposure therapy, social skills training, and relevant homework assignments. It is important to note that this treatment is not merely a combination of exposure and traditional social skills training procedures. Rather, it includes strategies designed to remedy specific difficulties seen in veterans with chronic PTSD, and the particular sequencing and timing of the individual components are thought to contribute to its overall effectiveness. The major components of TMT are described next.

A. Education

All patients are provided with a general overview of chronic PTSD, including common patterns of expression, issues of diagnosis, comorbidity of other anxiety and Axis I disorders, etiological pathways, and a review of current treatment strategies. This phase is important for ensuring that veterans not only develop a realistic understanding about treatment prognoses, but also an overall positive expectancy regarding the efficacy of behavioral treatment. Finally, this phase is used to educate veterans about the treatment they will be receiving and what will be expected from them regarding their participation in TMT.

B. Exposure Therapy

Individually administered intensive exposure therapy is included as the first active component of TMT, because it has been shown to effectively address the unique features of each patient's fear structure, allowing for a reduction in general anxiety, physiological reactivity, and intrusive symptoms. Patients are exposed imaginally to feared or anxiety-producing stimuli in a prolonged fashion until there is a decrease in fear and anxiety (i.e., until habituation is obtained) within session. Repeated contact with the feared stimulus hastens the habituation process and, with sufficient pairings, the stimulus loses its ability to elicit the fear response. Typically, most veterans with PTSD escape or avoid feared stimuli, which functions to increase the intensity of the fear response. The goal of exposure therapy is to provide prolonged contact with the feared stimuli of sufficient duration that within session habituation occurs. Repeated pairing across a number of days also is important and hastens the habituation process. Fourteen sessions of exposure therapy are administered early in the sequence so that veterans may experience relatively quick relief from acute symptoms of PTSD, enabling them to then concentrate on developing emotional control and improving their social functioning. All sessions are terminated following a 50% reduction in within session reactivity to the traumatic cues, with reactivity monitored physiologically (i.e., heart rate) and/or by patient ratings of subjective distress. Based on our experience with PTSD, and data on behavioral treatment of other anxiety disorders, exposure sessions usually average about 90 min in duration.

C. Programmed Practice

The programmed practice component of TMT is implemented in the final seven individual exposure sessions and is a form of exposure that does not require therapist accompaniment (i.e., it is "homework"), but requires careful planning on the part of the therapist and patient together. Examples of suitable exercises focusing on traumatic combat fears include self-directed imaginal sessions at home, which may serve as an initial step toward *in vivo* activities, such as watching movies (e.g., *Platoon* or *Hamburger Hill*), visiting war memorials or museums, speaking with other veterans or loved ones about war experiences, and visiting airfields or helicopter pads. Experiences should also be devised that require the veteran to engage in other feared activities, the avoidance of which may interfere with quality of life. Examples of suitable activities include social events, shopping, attending movies, eating in a restaurant, etc.

D. Social and Emotional Rehabilitation (SER)

A highly structured group (3–5 people) social skills training component (SER) was developed to target PTSD features that are not improved by exposure therapy only. In other words, interpersonal difficulties, commonly associated with chronic PTSD, such as social anxiety, social withdrawal, excessive anger and hostility, explosive episodes, marital and family conflict are targeted via a number of specific interventions. SER includes instruction, modeling, behavioral rehearsal, feedback, and reinforcement. Following each SER session, veterans are given homework assignments to allow further practice and consolidation of newly acquired skills. A series of symptom-specific strategies were sequenced to build on one another in a cumulative fashion and are designed to serve multiple functions. One purpose is to teach veterans the requisite skill foundation for effective and rewarding social interactions. Patients with PTSD vary widely with respect to basic social skill, but most have room for improvement. In addition to general social skill, the program is divided into four components that target specific areas of dysfunction.

1. Social Environment Awareness

Social environment awareness involves teaching the nuances of when, where, and why to initiate and terminate interpersonal interactions. Veterans are taught the verbal and nonverbal mechanics of successful social encounters, including identification of appropriate conversation topics, attentional and listening skills, and effective topic transitions.

2. *Interpersonal Skills Enhancement*

Interpersonal skills enhancement is devoted to teaching how to establish and maintain friendships, appropriate telephone skills, and assertive communication. This component is designed to help patients learn those skills that are necessary to engage in new and diverse social activities to increase their social repertoires and the likelihood that social interactions will become intrinsically rewarding.

3. *Anger Management*

Anger Management involves teaching veterans how to better manage anger and other intense emotions. It is designed to reduce temper outbursts and the problematic expression of anger. This component is designed to give patients a range of strategies for expressing their anger, problem solving, improving their emotional modulation, communicating assertively with others, so that verbal and physical violence do not continue to disrupt their relationships with others.

4. *Veteran's Issues Management*

Veteran's Issues Management teaches how to improve communication regarding combat trauma and military issues with nonveterans, to increase the understanding of significant others. In addition, veterans are also taught to identify and challenge negative and dichotomous thinking patterns, which limit their quality of life by reducing their involvement with others.

TABLE 1
TMT Session Overview

Week	*Session*	*Format*	*Treatment component*
1	1	Individual	Education
1	2–3	Individual	Exposure
2	4–6	Individual	Exposure
3	7–9	Individual	Exposure + Prog. Practice
4	10–12	Individual	Exposure + Prog. Practice
5	13–15	Individual	Exposure + Prog. Practice
6	16–17	Group	SER: Social Environment Awareness
7	18–19	Group	SER: Interpersonal Skills
8	20	Group	SER: Interpersonal Skills
9	21	Group	SER: Interpersonal Skills
10	22	Group	SER: Interpersonal Skills
11	23	Group	SER: Anger Management
12	24	Group	SER: Anger Management
13	25	Group	SER: Anger Management
14	26	Group	SER: Anger Management
15	27	Group	SER: Veterans' Issues Management
16	28	Group	SER: Veterans' Issues Management
17	29	Group	SER: Veterans' Issues Management

E. Treatment Implementation

TMT consists of 29 treatment sessions ideally administered over a period of about 17 weeks. Sessions initially occur three times a week through the Exposure phase, then twice a week at the start of SER, and then once a week for the final 10 weeks of the program (see Table 1).

II. THEORETICAL BASES

A. The Clinical Syndrome

In 1980 the American Psychiatric Association's *Diagnostic and Statistical Manual (DSM)* formally defined and recognized the cluster of acute symptoms often seen in victims of traumatic events (e.g., combat, sexual and physical assault), naming this condition posttraumatic stress disorder (PTSD). It is defined by six basic criteria: (1) the historical antecedent of a traumatic event that involves both actual or threatened death or serious injury, and an intense response of fear, helplessness, or horror; (2) persistently reexperiencing the traumatic event through intrusive memories, dissociative flashbacks, recurrent distressing dreams, and/or psychological or physiological reactivity on exposure to associated cues; (3) the avoidance of stimuli associated with the event, or a numbing of general responsiveness, including efforts to avoid thoughts and feelings related to the trauma, efforts to avoid activities or situations that arouse recollections of the trauma, loss of interest in significant activities, social detachment, and/or reduced affect; (4) the existence of persistent symptoms of increased arousal such as hypervigilance, sleep disturbance, irritability or outbursts of anger, impaired concentration, and/or exaggerated startle response; (5) duration of the disturbance for at least 1 month; and (6) the pervasive effects of the disturbance causing clinically significant distress or impairment in social, occupational, or other important areas of functioning.

Posttraumatic Stress Disorder is frequently chronic, and many combat veterans still suffer severe symptoms from wars fought 30 (Vietnam) or 50 (WWII) years ago. Epidemiological estimates of PTSD put the current prevalence at as high as 15% and lifetime prevalence as high as 31% for veterans exposed to war zone trauma. Given that over 3 million American soldiers served in the Vietnam war alone, and many more have served in other foreign conflicts, the potential number of veterans currently with PTSD is well above the half-million mark.

Complicating the syndrome is the fact that PTSD is typically accompanied by multiple co-occurring mental disorders, including substance abuse (73–84%), major depression (26–68%), psychotic symptoms (15–40%), and panic attacks (21–34%), among others. Furthermore, chronic PTSD is also associated with a diverse set of symptoms associated with social maladjustment, poor quality of life, sleep disturbance, medical illnesses, and general symptom severity. This includes social avoidance, memory disruption, guilt, anger, social phobia, suicide attempts, and other debilitating behavioral features, such as unemployment, impulsive or violent behavior, and family discord. In fact, it is notable that a majority (69%) of veterans seeking treatment for PTSD within VA specialty clinics seek disability payments for the debilitating occupational impairment they experience. It recently has been documented that the costs associated with PTSD are extremely high and make PTSD one of the costliest mental disorders to society.

Although PTSD symptoms currently are grouped into three primary clusters, symptoms of reexperiencing (nightmares, intrusive memories, "flashbacks") and associated physiological reactivity, are what best distinguish PTSD from other affective or anxiety disorders. Supporting the prominence of autonomic symptoms are data from studies examining physiological responding in people with PTSD. Most notable is the finding of heightened reactivity. In these studies, combat veterans with PTSD have significantly larger blood pressure and heart rate responses during fear-relevant cue exposure than do combat veterans without PTSD.

B. Rationale for Exposure Therapy

Exposure therapy is a well-established behavioral treatment for a wide range of anxiety disorders (e.g., phobias, obsessive–compulsive disorder), which involves exposing individuals to feared thoughts, images, or other stimuli repeatedly and for prolonged periods of time. The rationale for this treatment is based on two-factor theory. As applied to the condition of PTSD, first, stimuli (e.g., combat images or sounds) that were once paired with actual danger and horror in combat now elicit a similar autonomic response (e.g., increased heart rate) and fear. Second, as a result of this fear response, those with PTSD tend to avoid or escape from such stimuli as much as possible. Thus, habituation to the stimuli never occurs, and the maladaptive condition is maintained. Exposure therapy involves exposing individuals to feared stimuli (e.g., combat images or sounds) repeatedly and for prolonged periods in the absence of any actual threat until habituation allows for a progressive decrease in the vigor of autonomic responses (e.g., heart rate). Therefore, anxiety and fear are reduced via habituation. In the case of individuals with PTSD, such exposure is usually accomplished, at least initially, via imaginal procedures, and is often then complimented later by *in vivo,* or "live," exposure experiences.

III. EMPIRICAL STUDIES

A. Treatment of PTSD

There are surprisingly few data available regarding treatment outcome for veterans or civilians with PTSD. To date only a relatively small number of randomized clinical trials of pharmacological and psychotherapeutic treatments have been published. Although a range of psychotherapeutic strategies for chronic PTSD have been suggested, cognitive-behavioral treatments, usually emphasizing various methods of exposure therapy, have been the most carefully studied and show the most promise.

1. Exposure Therapy for PTSD

Among civilians with PTSD, exposure has been found to be efficacious in a number of randomized, controlled trials. Exposure therapy has been found to be superior to stress inoculation training, progressive relaxation, supportive counseling, and wait-list control groups; and it is equally effective as cognitive therapy.

Among veteran samples, intensive exposure has proven partially efficacious for chronic PTSD, although the data are not as strong as for civilians. In an early trial, exposure therapy was compared to a wait-list control group using Vietnam veterans ($N = 24$). At post-treatment, the exposure group scored significantly lower than the control group on some clinical measures and received lower therapist ratings of startle responses, memory disturbance, depression, anxiety, irritability, and legal problems. These improvements were maintained at 6-month follow-up. Significant differences were not found for emotional numbing, sleep disturbance, or any measure of social adjustment. In another study, veterans who received both "imaginal flooding" and "standard" treatment were compared to a group of yoked patients who received "standard" treatment only ($N = 14$). The exposure group showed superior outcome on patient ratings of sleep, nightmares, and intrusive thoughts, but no differences were found for heart rate, and only minimal differences were found for measures of trait anxiety, depression, and violent tendencies. Again, the treatment appears to have been only partially efficacious. Another study included the use of physiological recordings (e.g., heart rate) and self-report inventories to assess outcome in inpatient veterans treated with exposure or individual counseling. Participants receiving exposure showed modestly superior improvement across most psychological and behavioral rating measures, but no significant differences were found between the groups on physiological parameters. Further, regardless of treatment condition, those participants who showed decreased physiological responding were improved on psychological inventories at 3-month follow-up. This suggests that reductions in physiological responding was a critical element of efficacious therapy and might be a predictor of long-term treatment success. Finally, results from two uncontrolled studies support the partial efficacy of exposure for treating PTSD symptoms in veterans.

Data from these studies indicate that exposure therapy helps reduce the hallmark features of chronic PTSD and much of the general anxiety that accompanies it. In fact, according to the consensus statement on PTSD by the International Consensus Group on Depression and Anxiety exposure therapy is the psychotherapy of choice for the disorder. However, exposure does not have a significant effect on the "negative" symptoms of PTSD (e.g., avoidance, social withdrawal, interpersonal difficulties, occupational maladjustment, emotional numbing), nor on certain aspects of emotion management (e.g., anger control). This is because exposure is narrowly focused on anxiety and fear reduction and hence does not address other features of the disorder. Specifically, exposure does not address basic skill deficits, impaired social functioning, unemployment, or anger control problems. In essence, exposure therapy does not address the many problems often associated with any chronic mental disorder. Thus, many scientists have suggested that a behavioral treatment program, targeting specific areas of dysfunction via different behavioral strategies is necessary to address the complex symptoms associated with this condition—hence, the development of Trauma Management Therapy.

2. Trauma Management Therapy

The efficacy of TMT was examined in an open trial with 15 male Vietnam combat veterans with PTSD. The veterans participating in this study had a mean severity rating of 6.09 on the 7-point rating scale of the Clinical Global Impressions scale, indicating that the sample was severely ill. Demographics were as follows: six were African American (40%) and nine were Caucasian (60%). The mean age of the sample was 47.9 ($SD = 2.1$; range = 44 to 52 years), mean education level was 12.7 ($SD = 1.2$), 8 (53%) were married, 6 (40%) were employed full-time, 5 (33%) had a prior history of arrests, 7 (47%) had a prior history of psychiatric hospitalization, 7 (47%) received some level of VA disability payments for PTSD prior to treatment, and 11 (73%) currently were seeking disability payments or increases in existing disability payments. Acute psychiatric diagnoses other than PTSD included major depression, panic disorder, social phobia, and obsessive–compulsive disorder. Personality disorder diagnoses included borderline, avoidant, and schizoid. Overall, 15 (100%) were diagnosed with a co-occurring acute psychiatric disorder, and 11 (73%) with a co-occurring personality disorder. The combination of the multiple psychiatric disorders and extreme severity ratings indicate this was a severely ill sample.

Eleven patients were included in the analyses because 4 of the 15 (27%) dropped out during the course of treatment. One veteran discontinued after a few sessions of exposure treatment without giving a reason. The remaining three dropped out after successfully completing the exposure phase and all reported benefiting from the treatment; two of these veterans dropped out because their employment took them to another city, and the other cited transportation problems for not being able to participate in the SER phase.

To summarize the results, significant pre- to posttreatment improvement on most of the outcome variables was noted (see Table 2), suggesting that TMT is a promising treatment for the chronic and multifaceted symptoms associated with combat-related PTSD. Over the course of 4 months significant improvements were made on most critical features of PTSD. Symptom reductions occurred across problematic features of sleep disturbance, nightmares, flashbacks, social withdrawal, heart rate reactivity; significant improvements were

TABLE 2
Pre- and Posttreatment Data for Outcome Variables ($N = 11$)

	Pre-	*Post-*	*t*	*p*
Clinician ratings				
Hamilton Anxiety	33.91 (9.38)	23.26 (4.20)	4.88	.0003***
Clinical Global Impression	6.09 (.70)	4.00 (.78)	6.10	.0001***
Clinician PTSD scale	82.46 (19.23)	65.55 (8.51)	2.77	.0099**
Patient symptom ratings				
Sleep (hours/wk)	30.55 (8.64)	36.09 (8.85)	4.45	.0006***
Nightmares (freq./wk)	9.73 (5.12)	5.55 (3.14)	4.44	.0007***
Flashbacks (freq./wk)	9.00 (5.53)	6.27 (4.65)	2.95	.0073**
Social activities (freq./wk)	.55 (.69)	2.55 (.93)	8.56	.0001***
Physiological reactivity				
Heart rate	89.73 (9.81)	77.00 (8.65)	5.34	.0002***
Self-report inventories				
Social Phobia Difference	94.67 (21.62)	85.00 (20.28)	1.97	.0423*
Beck Depression	28.91 (9.66)	28.64 (8.70)	.14	.4441
Spielberger Anger Scale	34.82 (13.64)	35.82 (10.38)	.40	.3480

* $p < .05$; ** $p < .01$; *** $p < .001$.

noted on clinician ratings of general anxiety, PTSD symptoms, and overall level of functioning.

Because TMT significantly improved patients' social functioning across a number of dimensions, the outcome generally appears to be superior to findings reported for combat veterans in treatment studies using exposure therapy only or other nonexposure treatments. Furthermore, the patients' overall ratings of their treatment indicate that they considered it a credible and positive therapeutic experience, and all but one said that they would encourage other veterans with PTSD to participate in TMT. Although significant improvement was found on many measures, the clinical syndrome was not remediated entirely, which is usually the case even for most "successful" treatments of anxiety disorders and most other severe psychiatric conditions. Nevertheless, overall the new treatment strategy appears to have resulted in broad improvement across the wide symptom spectrum of PTSD in a sample of veterans typical of those in most VA settings.

For purposes of examining component efficacy, assessments were administered after completion of exposure therapy at midtreatment (Session 15), but prior to the commencement of SER. These data indicate that veterans responded with significant improvement after completion of the exposure therapy phase, but only on certain symptoms (e.g., nightmares, flashbacks, physiological reactivity, sleep, and general anxiety). Significant improvement in the frequency of social activities occurred only after the implementation of social skills training, suggesting that this deficiency improved only after specific intervention with the SER component. This validates the need for a broad-based intervention to address the entire PTSD syndrome. Research is pending to extend these results for TMT in randomized, controlled efficacy research.

IV. SUMMARY

Posttraumatic stress disorder (PTSD) is a severe and chronic anxiety disorder that may follow traumatic experiences (e.g., combat, physical and sexual assault). The clinical syndrome is characterized by symptoms of reexperiencing the trauma (e.g., nightmares, "flashbacks"), emotional numbing and avoidance, and arousal (e.g., insomnia, hypervigilance, anger), as well as severe impairment of social functioning. Research shows that intensive exposure therapy helps reduce the hallmark features of chronic PTSD (e.g., symptoms of intrusion, physiological reactivity) and much of the general anxiety that accompanies it and is considered to be the psychosocial treatment of choice. However, exposure therapy does not have a significant effect on the "negative" symptoms of PTSD (e.g., avoidance, social withdrawal, interpersonal difficulties), nor on certain aspects of emotion management (e.g., anger control). Although exposure may reduce maladaptive arousal and fear, it does not address basic skill deficits, impaired relationships, or anger control problems. Trauma Management Therapy

(TMT) is a multicomponent behavioral treatment program for chronic combat-related PTSD designed to address all aspects of the clinical syndrome in veterans. It utilizes a combination of patient education, exposure therapy, social skills training, and relevant homework assignments. Preliminary evidence from an open trial shows that overall TMT appears to result in broad improvement across the wide symptom spectrum of PTSD, including social functioning, in veterans treated within the VA. Research is pending to extend these results for TMT in randomized, controlled efficacy research.

See Also the Following Articles

Exposure *in Vivo* Therapy ■ Grief Therapy ■ Post-Traumatic Stress Disorder ■ Self-Control Therapy

Further Reading

Ballenger, J. C., Davidson, J. R., Lecrubier, Y., Nutt, D. J., Foa, E. B., Kessler, R. C., McFarlane, A. C., & Shalev, A. Y. (2000). Consensus statement on posttraumatic stress disorder from the International Consensus Group on Depression and Anxiety. *Journal of Clinical Psychiatry, 61* (suppl. 5), 60–66.

Davidson, J. R. T. (2000). Pharmacotherapy of posttraumatic stress disorder: Treatment options, long-term follow-up, and predictors of outcome. *Journal of Clinical Psychiatry, 61* (suppl. 5), 52–56.

Frueh, B. C., Turner, S. M., & Beidel, D. C. (1995). Exposure therapy for combat-related PTSD: A critical review. *Clinical Psychology Review, 15,* 799–817.

Frueh, B. C., Turner, S. M., Beidel, D. C., Mirabella, R. F., & Jones, W. J. (1996). Trauma Management Therapy: A preliminary evaluation of a multicomponent behavioral treatment for chronic combat-related PTSD. *Behavior Research and Therapy, 34,* 533–534.

Foa, E. B., Keane, T. M., & Friedman, M. J. (2000). *Effective treatments for PTSD.* New York: Guilford Press

Keane, T. M., Fairbank, J. A., Caddell, J. M., & Zimering, R. T. (1989). Implosive (flooding) therapy reduces symptoms of PTSD in Vietnam combat veterans. *Behavior Therapy, 20,* 245–260.

Kessler, R. C. (2000). Posttraumatic stress disorder: The burden to the individual and to society. *Journal of Clinical Psychiatry, 61* (suppl. 5), 4–12.

Kulka, R. A., Schlenger, W. E., Fairbank, J. A., Hough, R. L., Jordan, B. K., Marmar, C. R., & Weiss, D. S. (1990). *Trauma and the Vietnam war generation: Report of findings from the National Vietnam Veterans Readjustment Study.* New York: Brunner/Mazel.

Turner, S. M., Beidel, D. C., Cooley, M. R., Woody, S. R., & Messer, S. C. (1994). A multicomponent behavioral treatment for social phobia: Social Effectiveness Therapy. *Behaviour Research Therapy, 32,* 381–390.

Unconscious, The

Alan Sugarman
San Diego Psychoanalytic Society and Institute and University of California, San Diego

Caroline DePottel
San Diego Psychoanalytic Society and Institute

GLOSSARY

cathexis Freud used this term to refer to changes in direction or quantity of psychic energy. Generally it means interest, attention, or emotional investment.

hermeneutic school This approach to psychoanalysis argues that the psychoanalytic process and theory should be understood as a humanities discipline, not a natural science. Thus, it disregards concepts such as causality to focus on the coherence theory of truth. Criteria such as internal consistency, coherence, comprehensiveness, and therapeutic efficacy are more important than empirical proof.

instinctual drives Freud's two drives, sexual and aggressive, were considered to be the major factors motivating the mind. They continue to be considered important but not the only motivating factors by modern psychoanalysts.

I. INTRODUCTION

The notion that most mental processes occur outside of consciousness and that these unconscious contents and functions exert tremendous influence on virtually all psychologically mediated behavior is perhaps the most central and long-standing of Sigmund Freud's many contributions. Although his definition and understanding of the role of unconscious phenomena have been revised and expanded, every practicing therapist who uses a psychoanalytic or psychodynamic orientation is always considering the role of unconscious psychodynamics in the symptoms and personality traits their patients want to change. Technical strategies for utilizing and working with these unconscious phenomena have evolved, but the basic idea that these phenomena are important and must receive therapeutic scrutiny has stood the test of time.

II. CONCEPT OF THE UNCONSCIOUS

The concept of the Unconscious was described in various sections of *The Interpretation of Dreams,* most notably Chapter 7, by Freud in 1900 as he delineated his topographic model wherein the regions of the mind were defined by their closeness to consciousness. But it was not until 1915 in his paper, "The Unconscious," that Freud elaborated on what he called the system Unconscious in detail. He began that paper by reviewing the justification for the inference of such a system. Thus, he pointed out what psychologists of most theoretical persuasions have come to acknowledge—that is, it is simply untenable to assume that everything that occurs in mental life can occur in the conscious mind. Even recent cognitive and information processing models acknowledge that the conscious mind can only be aware of a fraction of the contents and processes occurring in mental life. One has only to reflect on daily phenomena such as arriving at one's destination while driving without remembering any details of stopping for traffic lights, making turns, and so on, to be struck by the evidence supporting the occurrence of unconscious mental processes.

Freud also argued that it was conceptually necessary to postulate the existence of an unconscious mind to explain the many gaps in the contents of consciousness (e.g., slips of the tongue, dreams). Such gaps were simply unintelligible using only the information provided by the conscious mind. In fact, many of the books and papers of Freud's topographic stage of thinking (1897–1923) were devoted to demonstrating the unconscious logic of these consciously illogical phenomena. Dreams, slips of the tongue, jokes, and neurotic symptoms were all studied and shown to be comprehensible once one grasped the role of the system Unconscious in their genesis and subsequent maintenance. In fact, Freud was able to argue for the legitimacy of assuming that others also had unconscious minds as he was able to make sense of their previously unintelligible behavior by illuminating its unconscious meanings.

The basic thesis of the topographic model was that the mind was organized into three systems or regions, the systems Unconscious, Preconscious, and Conscious, organized to prevent the contents of the system Unconscious from breaking into and overwhelming the system Conscious so that the individual could continue to attempt to adapt to the constraints of reality while allowing enough discharge of the contents of the Unconscious to avoid excessive frustration, unpleasure, or symptomatology. In essence, the mind's major function was one of maintaining some sort of homeostatic equilibrium between the contents of the Unconscious and the need to behave in the external world in a manner that enhanced the individual's self-preservation.

III. THE DRIVES

What made this task difficult was the nature of the contents of the system Unconscious. Most of its contents were understood by Freud to be instinctual drives—generally libidinal ones. Freud had been driven by clinical necessity to postulate the presence of unconscious sexual drives in 1897 when he realized that the sexual abuse reported by his patients generally involved fantasies and not the actual reality that he had assumed during his previous affect-trauma stage of thinking. These sexual fantasies were theorized to derive from libidinal instincts in the system Unconscious, instincts that had a powerful, peremptory quality, always pushing the individual to discharge his or her accumulated sexual tension in the real world.

But to blindly run amok, seeking gratification of the multiplicity of sexual urges available to humanity, would place the individual at great risk for not surviving. The same could be said for the aggressive instinctual urges that Freud described later in his life. Thus, the mind needed to function so as to keep these libidinal and aggressive contents repressed, that is, in the system Unconscious. Thus, Freud hypothesized the existence of a censor at the boundary between the systems Unconscious and Preconscious. Freud always believed that some form of special energy, what he called psychic energy, provided the means by which the system worked. Each system had its own psychic energy to serve its functions. Explaining how censorship worked in his 1915 paper, he said, "there is a withdrawal of the preconscious cathexis, retention of the unconscious cathexis, or replacement of the preconscious cathexis by an unconscious one." Another form of energic cathexis, what Freud called an anticathexis, was also used to buttress repression. In this way the mind could keep the potentially most self-destructive or unpleasurable instinctual impulses from moving into the system Preconscious, from where they could make their way into the system Conscious. Some discharge of instincts had to be allowed to prevent excessive internal tension from occurring. Discharge generally occurred through the system Preconscious disguising the contents of the Unconscious and depleting them of some intensity before allowing their derivatives to proceed into the system Conscious.

IV. THE ROLE OF PSYCHIC ENERGY

Freud also described the system Unconscious as being organized and functioning in very different ways than the other two systems. In large part these differences were due to the primary process that characterized the system Unconscious. Primary process referred to the earliest, developmentally most immature form of mental activity according to Freud. In many ways it corresponds to what cognitive psychologists call preoperational thinking. Such thinking seeks immediate and complete discharge of drive impulses by attaching psychic energy *(cathexis)* to the visual memory traces of the object that gratified the drive in the past. Primary process mentation was characterized by the occurrence of both displacement and condensation. Displacement refers to immature thinking whereby one idea within a drive-connected associative network comes to symbolize another idea. Pars pro toto thinking is one example of displacement. For example, the color blond may come to symbolize the person toward whom the drive-wish was directed who had blond hair. Likewise, situations wherein the whole represents a part is another example of displacement. Condensation was the other primary process mechanism described by Freud. In condensation one mental content (idea, memory trace, etc.) can represent several others. For example, the occurrence of a church in someone's dreams might represent at the same time both wishes toward a particular figure who had been religious as well as memories of one's religious training. To account for the fluidity by which primary process thinking operated, Freud introduced the idea that the system Unconscious was characterized by mobile psychic energy that easily shifted from one mental content to another toward the goal of wish fulfillment.

V. CHARACTERISTICS OF THE UNCONSCIOUS

The system Unconscious was also said to operate according to the pleasure principle. Freud described the instinctual wishes that made up the contents of the system Unconscious as peremptory. They were so compelling that he believed they sought pleasurable discharge and the parallel reduction of unpleasurable tension at all costs. Drive stimulation was thought to arouse unpleasurable tension in what Freud called the psychic apparatus, and to push toward consciousness and motility so that satisfaction of the drive-wish could be achieved. As the wish proceeded through the other systems of the mind, its pressure for direct and immediate discharge often aroused conflict, leading the censorship between the systems Unconscious and Preconscious to transform it. If disguised sufficiently, such drive derivatives would pass into the system Conscious and provide instinctual gratification. Otherwise, they would be repressed and maintained in the system Unconscious by the censor. Thus, the contents of the system Unconscious included both the infantile sexual and aggressive drive wishes as well as their repressed derivatives that had originally been allowed into consciousness, but had subsequently aroused enough conflict that they were re-repressed.

As the individual developed, virtually all primitive sexual and aggressive wishes were said to be repressed and capable of conscious expression only after being disguised thoroughly by the system Preconscious. Repression of a drive derivative could occur at any time that it aroused unpleasure, generally in the form of anxiety, in an individual. In this way the system Unconscious was thought by Freud to be constantly changing as new repressions occurred. Strong repressions of drive wishes early on were said to serve as fixation points encouraging later repressions to regress to the fixation point.

The system Unconscious was also described by Freud as having other characteristics that differentiated it from the systems Preconscious and Conscious First it was timeless. Mental content and processes in this system were not affected by the passage of time or the concept of time. This characteristic was necessary to explain the clinical finding that childhood instinctual derivatives continued to play such vivid roles in the psyches of adult patients. Implicit in the concept of the pleasure principle was the notion that reality was disregarded in the Unconscious. This contributed to another special characteristic—the equating of psychic reality with external reality. That is, in the system Unconscious, memories of actual occurrences were treated as no different than imagined experiences. Thus, no reality–fantasy boundary existed. Contradiction was also said not to exist in the system Unconscious. Mutually incompatible ideas could be maintained simultaneously and without conflict because of this. Negation also did not exist in the system Unconscious. Finally words were treated as things in the system Unconscious so that the symbol of a concrete thing was treated as though it were the thing it symbolized.

It is impossible to overstate the importance of the system Unconscious during Freud's topographic era of model building. Treatment was guided by the dictum that the analyst needed to make the Unconscious conscious. Helping the patient to become aware of the unconscious drive wishes that were being repressed was believed to bring about cure, in part, by releasing the psychic energy that had been dammed up, and by alleviating the unpleasant sensation of drive frustration as well by insight. Dreams were described as the royal road to the Unconscious and psychoanalysts were taught to devote particular time and energy to unraveling the disguised unconscious wishes being expressed in the dream. The primary process mechanisms described earlier were of particular importance as knowledge of them became necessary in deciphering the symbolism of the dream.

VI. CONCEPTUAL PROBLEMS

Despite the many technical and theoretical contributions of this era, clinical findings and theoretical inconsistencies led Freud ultimately to replace the topographic model with the structural one and to give up the concept of the system Unconscious. As he gained greater appreciation for the complexity of defensive functioning, particularly the fact that it, too, operated unconsciously, he realized that organizing the mind in terms of its accessibility to consciousness was no longer clinically useful. In essence, he realized that his patients' symptoms and character traits were caused by conflicts between unconscious wishes and unconscious defenses. That is, the conflicting elements were both unconscious. At this point, consciousness or the lack of it ceased to serve a differentiating function. Furthermore, he became increasingly aware of the need to deal clinically with the phenomenon of unconscious guilt. Yet there was no easy way to explain this concept in terms of topography. He needed the construct of a superego, which he described when he replaced the topographic theory with his structural one in *The Ego and the Id* in 1923. From that point, to speak of the Unconscious as a noun became theoretically anachronistic. Today it should be used only as an adjective, describing mental contents or processes that are not conscious. Some analysts fail to grasp this point, however, and still talk of an Unconscious. Unfortunately adhering to an outdated concept often leads to outdated formulations about the process of psychoanalysis or psychotherapy and how it cures.

Nonetheless, unconsciousness remains an important concept. The contents of the system Unconscious—instinctual wishes—are now thought to reside in the id, a mental structure that retains most of the structural characteristics of the system Unconscious, in particular the pleasure principle and the mechanisms of the primary process. But psychoanalytic treatment no longer is geared toward making these contents conscious as a curative approach. The discovery of unconscious defensive functioning as well as unconscious superego prohibitions has led to a therapeutic strategy whereby psychoanalysts make their patients aware of the occurrence of mental conflict as it occurs in their thoughts during treatment sessions. The patient's attention is drawn to the evidence of such conflict and whichever aspect of it is most easily accessible to the patient at any particular time. This work leads to the exploration of unconscious defenses and their motives at one time, the analysis of unconscious superego injunctions or ideals at another time, and the elaboration of unconscious wishes at still another. But the point of the strategy is to expand the ego's awareness of such conflict, its elements, and the motives that cause it so that conscious ego mastery can occur. Drive satisfaction or tension reduction are no longer relevant to analytic cure, although the focus on unconscious features of mental functioning continue to remain important.

VII. THREE BOX MODEL

Joseph Sandler has also introduced what he calls the Three Box Model in which he tries to retain a place for the system Unconscious. In essence, he divides it into a Past Unconscious and a Present Unconscious in an attempt to argue the importance of interpreting the Present Unconscious content over ones from the Past Unconscious. Although most current-day analysts would support this technical dictum to interpret present before past, his theoretical modification has failed to receive widespread support. Other theoretical models, particularly the contemporary structural theories of Paul Gray and Fred Busch, offer similar technical emphases while not falling into the difficulties that describing the Unconscious as a system entail.

VIII. UNCONSCIOUS FANTASY

Another clinical arena in which the phenomenon of unconscious functioning remains salient today is the concept of unconscious fantasy. Freud first introduced the concept in *Formulations on the Two Principles of Mental Functioning* in 1911. He talked of an aspect of thinking that was split off and kept free of reality constraints. Fantasizing or daydreaming continued to operate according to the pleasure principle. Symptoms, dreams, moods, and character traits were all traced to derivatives of unconscious fantasies. Anna Freud, using the structural model, applied the concept of unconscious fantasy to explain defenses such as identification with the aggressor and denial in fantasy. Repressed masturbatory fantasies were shown to disrupt certain ego functions and to distort important object relations.

But it is Jacob Arlow who has brought this concept to current-day prominence while demonstrating its clinical utility. He pointed out that decisive conflicts during an individual's life become organized into a number of stable unconscious fantasies that provide constant stimulation to an individual's mind. In this sense they form a schema through which subjective experiences are perceived, interpreted, and reacted to. Such fantasies are organized hierarchically and group around drive wishes, allowing for different versions of the fantasy. Arlow described such fantasies as developing early in life, but only with the resolution of the Oedipus complex. These fantasies provide what hermaneutically oriented psychoanalysts have called narratives, giving a plot to the individual's life that organizes his or her multiplicity of experiences into a few consistent and cohesive themes. Needless to say, they are important in maintaining ego identity.

Unconscious fantasies are usually the basis for neurotic symptoms and character traits. Generally the development of these clinical phenomena can be traced to an event that is reminiscent of a persistent unconscious fantasy built around a corresponding traumatic event. But equally as often unconscious fantasies lead to selective perception and responding. It is important to realize that unconscious fantasies involve the contribution of the ego and superego, and not just instinctual wishes from the id. Arlow has shown how fetishism can involve an unconscious fantasy that women have penises, which can fend off castration anxiety. Such a fantasy serves a defensive function.

Arlow has gone on to explain the technical importance of the concept of unconscious fantasy. He explained that the analyst needs to infer the presence of an unconscious fantasy from the patient's associations and to show the patient how its derivatives affect the patient's actions and mental life. An example described by Arlow was a patient who could only perform sexually if he fantasized spanking a woman. Analysis of this fantasy led the patient to realize his need to be in charge and not to see the female genital that made him anxious. Such realization allowed him to be more assertive with his wife and subsequently to have a successful sexual experience with her. Arlow has also said that the analyst's ability to empathize with and to understand the patient requires the ability to allow an unconscious fantasy to be evoked in the analyst that is similar to that of the patient's. Thus, the concept of unconscious fantasy remains another example of the continued importance of the concept of unconscious mental functioning in clinical practice.

It is impossible and technically unwise to ignore unconscious mental functioning when doing psychodynamic psychotherapy or psychoanalysis. Unconscious resistances are both inevitable and problematic if they are not analyzed. They lie at the core of patients described today as treatment resistant. Likewise, becoming aware of unconscious intrapsychic conflict is crucial in expanding the patient's consciousness and mastery of his or her own mind. Thus, unconscious phenomena remain as important as ever in psychodynamically oriented treatment as long as therapists are careful not to think of an Unconscious with the technical implications carried by that outdated concept.

See Also the Following Articles

Intrapsychic Conflict ■ Oedipus Complex ■ Structural Theory ■ Topographic Theory ■ Transference Neurosis

Further Reading

Arlow, J. A. (1995). Unconscious fantasy. In B. E. Moore & B. D. Fine (Eds.), *Psychoanalysis: The major concepts* (pp. 155–162). New Haven, CT: Yale University Press.

Arlow, J. A., & Brenner, C. (1964). *Psychoanalytic concepts and the structural theory.* New York: International Universities Press.

Brakel, L. W., Kleinsarge, A., Snodgrass, M., & Shervin, H. (2000). The primary process and the unconscious experimental evidence supporting two psycho analytic presuppositions. *International Journal of Psycho-Analysis, 81,* 553–569.

Moore, B. E., & Fine, B. D. (1990). *Psychoanalytic terms and concepts.* New Haven, CT: Yale University Press.

Sandler, J., Holder, A., Dare, C., & Dreher, A. V. (1997). *Freud's models of the mind.* Madison, CT: International Universities Press.

Vicarious Conditioning

E. Thomas Dowd
Kent State University

GLOSSARY

classical conditioning Conditioning that is based on the association of one stimulus with another.

continuous reinforcement schedule A schedule in which reinforcements are given after every response.

coping model A model who initially performs the target behavior imperfectly or hesitantly but becomes better with repetition.

intermittent reinforcement schedule A schedule in which reinforcements are given fewer than once every response, according to a predetermined order. The schedules are fixed interval, variable interval, fixed ratio, and variable ratio.

mastery model A model who performs a target behavior perfectly and without hesitancy from the beginning.

model Someone who performs a target behavior and is reinforced or punished for it under observation.

operant conditioning Conditioning that is based on the reinforcing or punishing consequence of a behavior.

target behavior The behavior to be reinforced (increased in probability) or punished (decreased in probability).

vicarious conditioning Conditioning that occurs by an observer by watching a model perform the target behavior and being reinforced or punished for performing it. Also known as vicarious learning or vicarious reinforcement.

I. DESCRIPTION OF TREATMENT

In vicarious operant conditioning, the observer is exposed to a model who is reinforced or punished for performing a certain behavior. It is important that the model actually be observed being reinforced or punished for performing the behavior, not simply observed performing it, or vicarious conditioning will not occur. Usually it is important that the observer be repeatedly exposed to the model because conditioning may not occur after a single exposure. In addition, conditioning may not occur because the observer did not see the important features of the modeled behavior or may have no memory of it. It is helpful if the modeled behavior is symbolically represented by images or words or is mentally rehearsed. The observer, of course, must have the means to carry out the target modeled behavior.

In vicarious classical conditioning, the observer is exposed to a model who behaves fearfully when confronted with a feared object (such as a snake) or who has negative consequences occur when exposed to an object (such as being scared by a large animal or in association with that animal). As a result of making these observations, the observer may likewise learn to fear these objects or situations.

Whereas vicarious operant conditioning may require several trials and multiple models to become firmly established, vicarious classical conditioning may occur in a very few or even single trials or exposures. It is likely that the majority of human anxiety responses are learned in this manner because most people have not had personal experiences with many of the events or people they fear.

II. THEORETICAL BASES

Vicarious conditioning is theoretically based on the modeling paradigm as developed by Albert Bandura. In modeling, individuals may show increases or decreases in various target behaviors by observing a model being reinforced (to increase target behavior) or punished (to decrease target behavior). It is not necessary that the observing individual be directly reinforced or punished for behavior change to occur. This process has been called vicarious learning, vicarious conditioning, or in some instances, vicarious reinforcement.

Vicarious conditioning is the analogous process to *in vivo* or directly experienced conditioning. According to the operant conditioning paradigm, the observing individual watches a model being reinforced for performing a certain behavior and the probability of the observer subsequently exhibiting that behavior increases as well. Observation of rewarding consequences occurring to a model for exhibiting a certain behavior, such as aggressiveness, may increase the probability of the observer performing that behavior in the future. By contrast, observation of a model being punished for exhibiting aggressive behavior may decrease the likelihood of, or inhibit the observer from performing, a similar aggressive act.

In vicarious classical conditioning, an observer watches a model becoming afraid of certain activities or animals as a result of seeing these stimuli paired with fear-producing situations. For example, the observer may see a model being bitten by a large furry dog, and subsequently fears large furry dogs without having been personally bitten. Indeed, the conditioning may generalize to a fear of large furry objects in general or to animals other than dogs.

Vicarious conditioning has been thought to be a major contributor to fear and anxiety disorders in people because people are commonly afraid of, or anxious about, situations or events that they have never experienced directly. It is also thought to account for a higher level of aggression in individuals who have not themselves been exposed to aggressive responses. Vicarious conditioning can develop through familial influences, subcultural influences, or symbolic modeling by the mass media because, for example, the latter provide ample models for violence and aggression.

Bandura has described several mechanisms or functions by which vicarious conditioning may occur. There is the informative function, in which the model's actions and response consequences provide information to observers about the probable consequences to them if they engage in similar actions. There is the motivational function, in which seeing others reinforced (or punished) can act as a motivator for the observer to perform similar actions. There is the valuation function, in which observers may come to value certain things if they see a model being reinforced for similar things. There is the influenceability function, in which observers may be influenced more by models' actions that respond positively to reinforcing consequences than by those who resist such consequences. In other words, observers tend to be more influenced by modeled responsiveness than by modeled resistance. Finally, there is the emotional learning function, in which an observer's emotional reactions are aroused by the model's emotional reactions while undergoing the rewarding or punishing consequences. This last function is essentially a form of classical conditioning in which an observer's fear responses may be enhanced or reduced by the model's fear responses or lack of them.

Observing the model gradually and perhaps hesitantly approach the feared situation or be reinforced for initially imperfect responses may be especially useful. Bandura found that a coping model, who performed the behavior gradually, imperfectly, or hesitantly was a more effective model than a mastery model, who performed the behavior perfectly, quickly, or without hesitation. People may respond better to a coping model because of perceived similarity to themselves. A coping model appears to be more like them whereas a mastery model may make them feel too inadequate and therefore not be imitated. Of course, it is important that the observers see the model as similar to themselves so that they may reasonably assume that the rewarding or punishing consequences would likely happen to them as well. For example, rewarded aggression occurring to a soldier model may not result in an increase in aggression in a civilian observer. The model and observer are not similar enough. Likewise, similarity of model and observer in such attributes as gender, age, and race may enhance the modeled vicarious conditioning effect whereas dissimilarities may reduce it. The use of multiple models may also enhance vicarious conditioning.

It should be noted that the standard laws of conditioning also apply to vicarious conditioning. For example it has been shown that conditioning that has been established on an intermittent reinforcement schedule is acquired more quickly and established more firmly than that which has been established on a continuous reinforcement schedule. Whereas vicarious extinction may require many repeated trials, vicarious conditioning can often be accomplished in a few trials. In the case of highly intense or emotionally involving experiences, one-trial conditioning may occur.

III. EMPIRICAL STUDIES

There has been considerable research on the effectiveness of vicarious conditioning. Not only has it been found to be quite effective, it can be superior to direct reinforcement. This phenomenon is especially true if the tasks to be reinforced are more conceptual than manual. Vicarious conditioning is certainly more pervasive than direct conditioning, and likely accounts for the majority of human learning. In fact, a large number of behaviors exhibited in everyday life are probably conditioned vicariously by observing models being reinforced for performing these actions. The amount of vicarious classical conditioning has been found to be related positively to arousal level generated by psychological stress. It has been shown that the need for approval can increase the conditioning effect of vicarious reinforcement. Vicarious and instructional conditioning have been found to be major sources of childhood fears, more so than with adolescents, although they have often been combined with direct conditioning. Childhood fears have in fact been reduced or eliminated by this procedure. Vicarious conditioning has been found to be effective in eliminating maladaptive response patterns and increasing and maintaining new adaptive behaviors in children with mental retardation. It has been successfully implemented to train these children in more prosocial behaviors. It was found that children who were shown films in which a model showed either a fear response or a positive emotional response showed a lower rate of responding to the fear stimulus and a higher rate of responding to the positive stimulus. These effects were easily overridden by instructional and reinforcement conditions, however, and proved to be temporary. Only minimal cues from a model may be required for vicarious conditioning to occur as was demonstrated by one study that found that information about the model's heart rate was sufficient for it to occur. Thus, vicarious conditioning may account for a large part of human learning and be relatively easy to implement.

IV. SUMMARY

Vicarious conditioning is theoretically based on Albert Bandura's conditioning through modeling paradigm. It is analogous to direct trial conditioning, the difference being that it occurs when an observer learns by seeing a model performing a target behavior that is reinforced or punished. It is important that the observer actually see the model being reinforced for performing the behavior, not simply observed performing the behavior. Social behaviors, such as aggression and violence, are likely learned by this process. Vicarious conditioning can also occur through the classical conditioning paradigm whereby an observer sees a model learn to be afraid by being exposed to a noxious stimulus paired with an activity or event. Most human fears have likely been acquired by the latter process. Vicarious conditioning has been shown through research to be at least as effective as direct conditioning and possibly more so. It is a highly effective method for learning under a wide variety of situations and can be flexibly adapted to many conditions. Vicarious conditioning may be especially useful in learning conceptual material as opposed to manual skills. Mastery models may be less useful than coping models. Especially with vicarious classically conditioned fear, relatively few trials may be needed for conditioning to occur.

See Also the Following Articles

Classical Conditioning ■ Operant Conditioning ■ Response Cost ■ Self-Control Desensitization ■ Vicarious Extinction

Further Reading

Bandura, A. (1977). *Social learning theory.* Englewood Cliffs, NJ: Prentice Hall.

Minetka, S., & Tomarken, A. J. (1989). The role of cognitive biases in the origin and maintenance of fear and anxiety disorders. In T. Archer & L. G. Nilsson (Eds.), *Aversion, avoidance, and anxiety: Perspectives on aversively motivated behavior.* Hillsdale, NJ: Erlbaum.

Ollendick, T. H., & King, N. J. (1991). Origins of childhood fears: An evaluation of Rachman's theory of fear acquisition. *Behaviour Research & Therapy, 29,* 117–123.

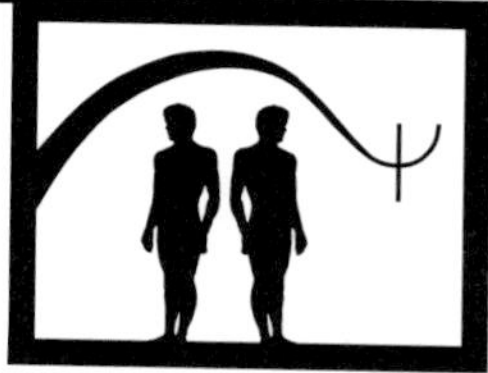

Vicarious Extinction

E. Thomas Dowd
Kent State University

GLOSSARY

classical conditioning Learning that is based on the association of one stimulus with another.

coping model A model who initially performs the target behavior imperfectly or hesitantly but becomes better with repetition.

extinction A change in behavior that occurs when it is no longer reinforced or punished.

intermittent reinforcement schedule A schedule in which reinforcements are delivered fewer than once for every response, according to a predetermined order. The schedules are fixed interval, variable interval, fixed ratio, and variable ratio.

mastery model An expert model who performs the target behavior perfectly and without hesitancy from the beginning.

model Someone who performs a target behavior and is reinforced or punished for it.

operant conditioning Learning that is based on the reinforcing or punishing consequence of a behavior.

thin reinforcement schedule A schedule in which few reinforcements are delivered for each response, for example, one reinforcement for every 50 responses.

vicarious extinction Extinction that occurs by watching a model perform a behavior that is no longer reinforced or punished.

vicarious learning Learning that occurs by an observer by watching a model perform the target behavior and being reinforced or punished for performing that behavior.

I. DESCRIPTION OF TREATMENT

In vicarious operant extinction, the observer is first exposed to a model who is reinforced or punished for performing a certain behavior. It is important that the model actually be observed being reinforced or punished for performing the behavior, not simply observed performing it, or vicarious learning will likely not occur. Then, the reinforcer or punisher is removed so that the observer simply sees the model performing the behavior. As a result, the observer is less likely to exhibit the behavior (if previously reinforced) or to suppress it (if previously punished).

In vicarious classical extinction, such as is commonly used to extinguish conditioned fearful avoidance behavior, the observer is first exposed to a model who behaves fearfully when confronted with an object, such as a snake, or who has negative consequences occur when exposed to an object, such as being knocked down by a large dog. As a result of seeing the model, the observer learns to fear the objects as well. Then the model is observed approaching the object (e.g., the snake) without fear or approaching the object (e.g., the dog) without adverse consequences. As a result, the observer is likely to feel less fear and to engage in less avoidance behavior in the future.

It is important that this extinction process be repeated a number of times, sometimes a large number of times, so that the previous learning will in fact extinguish. Overlearned or traumatic learning experiences may require many extinction trials. It may also be helpful for the model to exhibit gradual approach behavior to a feared object rather than approaching it too quickly. Finally, it may be helpful to use coping models for individuals who are fearful and avoidant themselves whereas mastery models may be more useful if precise skill development is desired in the relative absence of fear.

II. THEORETICAL BASES

Vicarious extinction is theoretically based on the modeling paradigm as developed by Albert Bandura. In modeling, individuals may show increases or decreases in various target behaviors by observing a model being reinforced (to increase target behavior) or punished (to decrease target behavior). It is not necessary that the individual be directly reinforced for behavior change to occur. This process has also been known as vicarious learning.

Vicarious extinction is the analogous process to *in vivo* or directly experienced extinction. According to the operant conditioning paradigm, the observing individual, after having vicariously learned a particular behavior by watching a model being reinforced for performing that behavior, now watches the model no longer being reinforced for exhibiting that behavior. Thus, the observer's target behavior likewise diminishes over time for lack of reinforcement.

In vicarious classical conditioning, an individual may have vicariously learned from a model to fear and therefore avoid certain activities or animals (such as avoiding members of the opposite sex or avoiding dogs) by watching a model learning to fear them (perhaps by being consistently rejected or by being knocked over by the dog). In vicarious extinction, the observer no longer sees the model performing fear-producing behaviors with adverse consequences (being rejected or knocked over); in fact the observer may see the model approach the dog without problems occurring. Thus, the fear that has become associated with either stimulus is gradually extinguished as the observer learns that the activities are safe.

Observing the model gradually and perhaps hesitantly approach the feared situation without problems occurring may be especially useful. Bandura found that a coping model, who performed the behavior gradually or imperfectly, was a more effective model than a mastery model, who performed the behavior perfectly or quickly. People may respond better to a coping model because of perceived similarity. It looks more like them whereas a mastery model may make them appear too inadequate and therefore not to be imitated.

It should be noted that the standard laws of learning also apply to vicarious learning. Therefore, the standard laws of extinction also apply to vicarious extinction. For example, it has been shown that learning that has been established on an intermittent reinforcement schedule is much more resistant to extinction than behavior acquired on a continuous schedule of reinforcement. Thus, vicarious learning that has been established on an intermittent reinforcement schedule would likewise be more resistant to vicarious extinction than that established on a continuous schedule. Likewise, a very thin vicarious reinforcement schedule would produce greater resistance to vicarious extinction than one involving a large number of reinforcers per response.

It is difficult to explain how fearful avoidance responses can be extinguished without ever being initially elicited. Bandura explains this by a dual-process theory of avoidance behavior. A conditioned aversive stimulus evokes emotional arousal that controls to some extent instrumental responding, and therefore if the arousal capacity of a fear-producing stimulus is extinguished, both the motivation and the avoidance stimulus are eliminated.

III. EMPIRICAL STUDIES

In the 1960s, there was substantial research conducted on vicarious extinction of fear and avoidance behavior, much of it conducted in Albert Bandura's laboratory. Vicarious classical extinction was found to be quite useful in extinguishing fear of certain animals in young children. Bandura and his colleagues also found that multiple models were more effective than single models in eliminating animal phobias in children, at least from posttest to follow-up. They also found that live modeling with participation (seeing an actual model perform the behavior with guided practice by the observer in performing the same behavior) was more effective than symbolic modeling (watching a film of the model performing the behavior) or systematic desensitization. Modeling appeared to account for about 60% of the behavior change and 80% of the attitude change. Guided participation accounted for the rest of the variance. Relaxation did not appear to increase the effectiveness of symbolic modeling alone in reducing fear arousal.

Other research, including some doctoral dissertations dating from the 1970s, has been conducted on vicarious classical extinction designed to reduce fear arousal and avoidance behavior and has found it to be effective in reducing sex anxiety in women, reducing frigidity, reducing fear of dogs through films (symbolic modeling), and reducing fear of snakes. Multiple models were again found to be more effective than single models. One study comparing systematic desensitization and vicarious symbolic extinction found greater improvement for systematic desensitization. Another study comparing symbolic desensitization, symbolic modeling, and live modeling combined with guided participation (contact desensitization) found the latter to be the most effective.

IV. SUMMARY

Vicarious extinction is theoretically based on Albert Bandura's learning through modeling paradigm. It is an analogous process to *in vivo* extinction, the difference being that the former occurs when an observer sees a model performing a behavior that is no longer reinforced, rather than not being reinforced (extinguished) directly. It was shown through research conducted in the 1960s and early 1970s to be an effective technique for extinguishing fear and avoidance behavior. It is more flexible and adaptable than *in vivo* extinction because the observer does not have to experience the extinction directly. However, live modeling combined with guided participation, which is essentially a combination of vicarious and *in vivo* extinction, was found to be more effective than other forms of vicarious extinction alone.

See Also the Following Articles

Classical Conditioning ■ Operant Conditioning ■ Self-Control Desensitization ■ Vicarious Conditioning

Further Reading

Bandura, A. (1969). *Principles of behavior modification*. New York: Holt, Rinehart & Winston.

Bandura, A., & Menlove, F. L. (1968). Factors determining vicarious extinction of avoidance behavior through symbolic modeling. *Journal of Personality and Social Psychology, 8,* 99–108.

Spigler, M. D., & Guevremont, D. C. (1993). *Contemporary behavior therapy*. Pacific Grove, CA: Brooks/Cole.

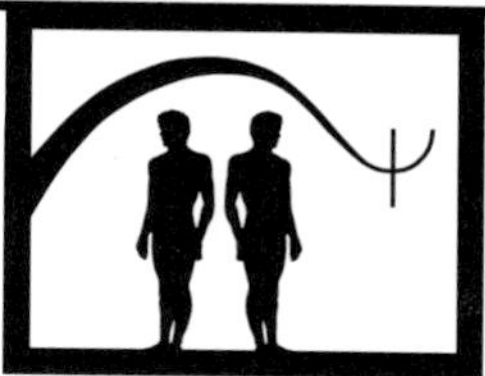

Virtual Reality Therapy

Max M. North and Sarah M. North
Kennesaw State University

GLOSSARY

virtual reality A technology that enables users to enter computer-generated worlds and interface with them through sight, sound, and touch.

Virtual reality therapy (VRT) is a new modality of therapy that enables clients to confront what troubles them and deal with irrational behavior using virtual reality technology. VRT is changing deeply held concepts about how human beings can overcome psychological disorders.

I. DESCRIPTION OF VIRTUAL REALITY THERAPY

VRT brings clients face-to-face with their deepest fears in a nonthreatening environment. That is the key. Entering a computer-generated world, clients know the situation is harmless, yet the re-creation of fearful scenes is lifelike, enabling them to deal with their fears in a realistic setting, confronting them through sight, sound, and touch.

VRT is similar to behavior therapy in its focus on exposing clients to fear-provoking stimuli. It differs from traditional behavior therapy modalities in that VRT computer graphics and various display and input technologies create real-life situations in the laboratory. These produce a sense of presence, so that the client feels immersed in the frightening scene. VRT can overcome some of the difficulties inherent in traditional treatment of psychological disorders. In traditional therapy, the therapist often has to imagine what is going on in the mind of the client. In VRT, the therapist can see how a phobic client reacts to fearful situations and is able to provide on-the-spot guidance. VRT generates stimuli of much greater magnitude than standard *in vivo* techniques can produce. It offers the added advantage of greater variety, efficiency, and economy in creating situations that might be either difficult or impossible with traditional techniques.

The centerpiece of VRT technology is a stereoscopic head-mounted video display with a head-tracking unit, along with a device that produces auditory and tactile stimuli (Figure 1). The effect can be startling, especially when the client is exposed to lifelike situations that have always produced fear. A set of VRT scenes is created before the therapy sessions begin. In the first laboratory session, which lasts approximately 20 minutes, the VRT client gets familiar with the virtual reality equipment. During this session, the client is asked to eliminate any virtual reality scenes that do not necessarily cause

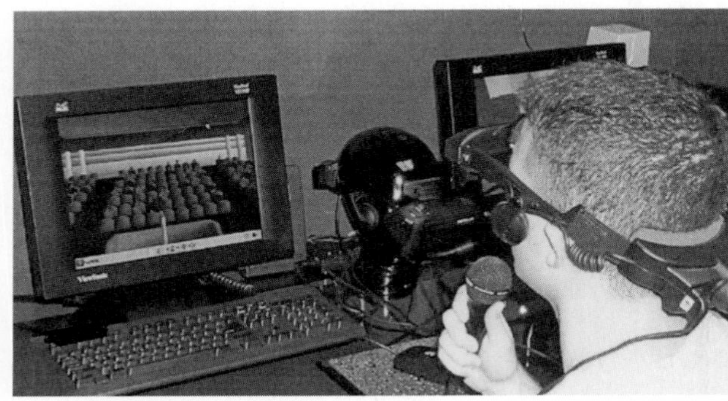

FIGURE 1 A typical virtual reality system with head-mounted display and head-tracking unit for use in VRT treatment.

anxiety. The client is asked to rank the remaining scenes from least to the most threatening. For the next eight weekly sessions, which last 15 to 20 minutes each, VRT is conducted in a standard format, tailored to individual needs.

The VRT session begins with the least fearful scene. Discomfort is measured every few minutes with the Subjective Units of Disturbance (SUD) scale. Clients rate their discomfort on a scale of 0 to 10. They progress systematically through each level of discomfort, and then are exposed to the next most threatening scene. Clients control their progress through the hierarchy of scenes. However, if the SUD score is 2 or less, the therapist may urge them to move up to the next level or next scene. Each new weekly session begins where the previous session ended. In addition to client-controlled subjective measurements, such as SUD, objective measurements of discomfort are also used. For instance, a heart-monitoring device, such as EEG/EMG, can be employed to monitor physical reactions.

II. THEORETICAL BASE OF VIRTUAL REALITY THERAPY

The principal aim of VRT is to help reduce or eliminate anxiety and fear. Phobias are nearly always linked to people's reactions to specific situations. VRT focuses on re-creating those situations in a controlled environment. When people encounter these disturbing situations under nonthreatening conditions they find ways to deal with them. In VRT, they learn new responses to old disturbing situations, thus gaining more control over psychological disturbances and their symptoms.

III. EMPIRICAL STUDIES

In testing military navigation software in a virtual reality setting in 1992, Dr. Max North and Dr. Sarah North discovered that it made some of the participants very fearful. They concluded that this technology could not only trigger phobias but could be used to combat these and other psychological disorders. Since then, they have successfully conducted numerous studies of VRT applied to specific phobias, such as fear of flying, heights, being inside a dark barn, crossing a river in an enclosed bridge, and being in the presence of various animals. Fear of public speaking; obsessive–compulsive behavior, and other psychological disorders were also found to be responsive to VRT treatment. These research activities have established a paradigm that is increasingly attracting scientists from the computer science, psychology, and medical fields.

As clients looking into the VRT head-mounted video display turn their heads, the scene changes appropriately. Visual, auditory, and tactile stimuli create a virtual world, with which the client can enter and interact. This controlled environment allows the client to reexperience events that have caused any psychological imbalance, and, most significantly, it takes place in the presence of the therapist. VRT, like current imaginal and *in vivo* modalities, generates stimuli that are unusually effective in therapy. Moreover, virtual reality generated stimuli are of greater magnitude than standard traditional techniques. VRT allows successful treatment of disorders that have often been difficult or impossible to treat with traditional techniques. A classic example is treatment of the fear of flying phobia. A virtual scene makes clients feel they are actually flying over cities. As VRT treatment progresses, these clients gradually become desensitized.

A substantial number of research activities have confirmed the success of VRT in treating psychological disorders. Table I shows a sampling of these innovative applications.

Mental and physical health risks associated with VRT can be greatly minimized by taking precautionary measures, as pointed out by Stanney in 1995. Clients at risk for psychological harm are primarily those who suffer from panic attacks, those with serious medical problems such as heart disease or epilepsy, and those who are (or have recently been) taking drugs with major physiological or psychological effects. A professional screening process will help identify these risks. Questions regarding physical and mental disabilities must be a standard part of the admissions process, and persons with these

TABLE 1
A Brief Report of Prior VRT Applications

Disorder to combat	*Experiment conducted*	*Researchers*
Fear of flying	Several case studies involving fear of flying were successfully conducted. After clients were exposed to virtual aerial views, they were given real world tests. A virtual helicopter and virtual commercial airplanes were used to fly the clients over realistic terrain. Afterwards, when clients flew long distances in real airplanes, they reported significant reduction in anxiety levels.	North et al., 1994 North et al., 1995 North et al., 1996 North et al., 1997a Hodges et al., 1996 Wiederhold et al., 1998
Fear of heights	Virtual scenes that were created for two major controlled studies and several case studies included belconies of various heights, an elevator, a canyon, bridges, and a series of balloons. The result: Clients comfortably accomplished real-life situations involving heights.	Rothbaum et al., 1995 North et al., 1996
Agoraphobia (fear of being in certain places or situations)	A major controlledstudy centered on helping clients who suffer from being in places from which escape might might have been either embarrassing to them or impossible. Several virtual scenes were created for this study. The scenes included a dark barn, a cat in the dark barn, a covered bridge over a river, empty room, and a few more related virtual scenes based on the request of the clients. In general, a subjective measurement showed that a majority of the clients' subjective measurements indicated their anxiety level was reduced and they became more comfortable in comparable real-life situations.	North et al., 1995, 1996
Autism	The challenge here was to create scenes of altered reality, of the kind clients were experiencing. Traditional treatments had often been ineffective for these clients. The virtual scenes closely tracked the distortion of environment that clients had personally perceived. This enabled them to gain new insight and to better understand the real situation.	Strickland, 1996
Body experience (eating disorders)	In this study, clients were exposed to a virtual environment that let them experience a modified body image. A partial reduction in negative feelings of body dissatisfaction was reported.	Riva, 1997a, 1997b
Fear of public speaking	Several case studies were conducted using a virtual auditorium with no audience initially. As treatmentprogressed, more audience and varieties of sound effects were introduced. Clients' symptoms reduced significantly, and they gained greater confidence in real-world speaking experiences after the therapy.	North et al., 1997b
Fear of closed spaces (claustrophobia)	Clients in several case studies were confronted with closed spaces in a virtual house. The spaces could be resized to suit the clients' progress, allowing them to gradually cope with their fear of closed spaces and significantly reduce their anxiety level.	Botella et al., 1998 Booth et al., 1992
Fear of driving	Volunteers tested the effectiveness of virtual reality technology in automobile driving situations. They were They were exposed to scenes that ordinary drivers might find themselves in, such as a series of stops, turns, heavy traffic, nearby buildings, and various hazards. Phobic participants significantly and consistently reported more anxiety than the nonphobic clients.	Schare et al., 1999
Posttraumatic stress disorder	In a case study, a Vietnam veteran was immersed in virtual jungle scenes, encountering thick foliage and armed combat, including machine guns and other weapons. The client reported significant decrease in symptoms as treatment progressed.	Hodges et al., 1999

(continues)

TABLE I
(Continued)

Disorder to combat	Experiment conducted	Researchers
Obsessive–compulsive disorder	Another case study involved a young client who had trouble remembering to take supplies she needed for school each day. She was encouraged to prepare a virtual schoolbag with all the articles she would need on a particular day. After treatment she reported more confidence in remembering what to take to school each day.	North et al., 2000
Attention deficit disorder	A virtual classroom scene was created to help a client stay focused on studying. She was exposed to an increasing number of classroom distractions, as well as activities that could be seen outside the window. VRT was shown to be more effective than previous traditional treatments had been.	Rizzo, 2000

characteristics must be excluded from VRT experiences. Additionally, some otherwise healthy people experience symptoms ranging from headaches to epileptic seizures when exposed to certain visual stimuli. Clients must be closely observed by therapists at all times. Both the client and the therapist must agree beforehand to terminate quickly the virtual reality session if there is any evidence of significant physical or psychological distress. As a routine precaution, the therapist should ask clients to sit in a chair rather than stand during the VRT procedure. It is also recommended that the therapist use a modified head-mounted display so clients can partially see their physical body, choose the head-mounted display with a narrower field of view, and, most important, keep the sessions brief (between 15 and 20 minutes). This configuration reduces the degree of immersion while increasing the physical and psychological safety of the clients. There is a need for more research in this area. In the meantime, it is strongly recommended that researchers take appropriate steps to minimize client risks.

Therapists must keep in mind that symptoms of anxiety while under VRT are distinctly different from simulation sickness. Anxiety symptoms evoked under VRT are the same as real world experiences, including shortness of breath, heart palpitations (irregular or rapid heartbeat), trembling or shaking, choking, numbness, sweating, dizziness or loss of balance, feeling of detachment, being out of touch with self, hot flashes or chills, loss of control, abdominal distress, and nausea.

See Also the Following Articles

Cinema and Psychotherapy ■ Emotive Imagery ■ Online or E-Therapy ■ Post-Traumatic Stress Disorder

Further Reading

Booth, R., & Rachman, S. (1992). The reduction of claustrophobia. *Behavior Research and Therapy, 30,* 207–221.

Botella, C., Baños, R. M., Perpiñá, C., Villa, H, Alcañiz, M., & Rey, A. (1998). Virtual reality treatment of claustrophobia: A case report. *Behavior Research and Therapy.*

Hodges, L. F., Rothbaum, B. O., Alarcon, R., Ready, D., Shahar, F., Graap, K., et al. (1999). Virtual Vietnam: A virtual environment for the treatment of Vietnam war veterans with post-traumatic stress disorder. *CyberPsychology & Behavior, 2.*

Hodges, L. A., Rothbaum, B. O., Watson, B. A., Kessler G. D., & Opdyke, D. (1996). Virtually conquering fear of flying. *IEEE Computer Graphics & Applications, 16,* 42–49.

North, M. M., & North, S. M. (2000). Virtual reality combats obsessive-compulsive disorders (OCD). Medicine Meets Virtual Reality 2000 Conference.

North, M. M., & North, S. M. (1994). Virtual environments and psychological disorders. *Electronic Journal of Virtual Culture, 2,* 37–42(ep.).

North, M. M., North, S. M., & Coble, J. R. (1995). Effectiveness of virtual environment desensitization in the treatment of agoraphobia. *International Journal of Virtual Reality, 1,* 25–34.

North, M. M., North, S. M., & Coble, J. R. (1996). *Virtual reality therapy, an innovative paradigm.* CO: IPI Press.

North, M. M., North, S. M., & Coble, J. R. (1997a). Virtual environment psychotherapy: A case study of fear of flying disorder. *PRESENCE, Teleoperators and Virtual Environments, 6.*

North, M. M., North, S. M., & Coble, J. R. (1997). Virtual Reality Therapy Combating Fear of Public Speaking. Medicine Meets Virtual Reality.

Riva, G. (1997). The virtual environment for body image modification (VEBIM): Development and preliminary evaluation. *PRESENCE, Teleoperators and Virtual Environments, 6.*

Riva, G. (1997). *Virtual reality in neuro-psycho-physiology.* IOS Press.

Rothbaum, B., Hodges, L., Kooper, R., Opdykes, D., Williford, J., & North, M. (1995). Effectiveness of computer-generated (virtual reality) graded exposure in the treatment of acrophobia. *American Journal of Psychiatry, 152,* 626–628.

Schare, M. L., Scardapane, J. R., Berger, A. L., Rose, N., & Berger, S. (1999). A virtual reality based anxiety induction procedure with driving phobic patients. Presented at Association for Advancement of Behavior Therapy, November 1999, Toronto.

Stanney, K. (1995). Realizing the full potential of virtual reality: Human factors issues that could stand in the way. *IEEE Proceedings of Virtual Reality Annual International Symposium, '95.* Research Triangle Park, North Carolina, pp. 28–34.

Strickland, D. (1996). A virtual reality application with autistic children. *PRESENCE, Teleoperators and Virtual Environments, 5,* 319–329.

Wiederhold, B. K., Gevirtz, R., & Wiederhold, M. D. (1998). Fear of flying: A case report using virtual reality therapy with physiological monitoring, *CyberPsychology & Behavior, 2.*

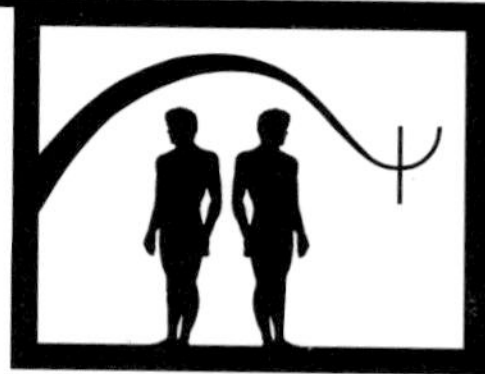

Vocational Rehabilitation

Ruth Crowther

University of Manchester

GLOSSARY

akathisia A state of motor restlessness ranging from a feeling of inner disquiet to an inability to sit or lie quietly.

clubhouse A building run by clients and staff along egalitarian lines, where clients meet for social activity, mutual support and graded work experience.

expressed emotion Refers to a family environment characterized by hostility, criticism, or emotional overinvolvement.

individual placement and support model A type of supported employment approach.

prevocational training A form of vocational rehabilitation that advocates a period of preparation before placing clients into open paid employment.

rehabilitation Restoration of an optimal state of health and functioning by medical, psychological, social, and peer group support.

supported employment A form of vocational rehabilitation that emphasizes placing clients directly into open paid employment without any extended period of preparation.

transitional employment A form of vocational rehabilitation that involves the placement of clients in a series of paid but temporary jobs owned by a Clubhouse with the aim of helping them develop the skills and confidence required to cope with competitive employment.

vocational rehabilitation A range of interventions that aim to improve the quality of life and functional capacity of people who are subject to social exclusion by virtue of their disabilities, by providing them with the skills and attributes necessary for them to return to open paid employment.

The aim of vocational rehabilitation is to improve the quality of life and functional capacity of people who are subject to social exclusion by virtue of their disabilities. The main outcome is to reintegrate individuals back into open paid employment integrated into a community's economy. This article will present a psychosocial approach to this form of rehabilitation including the significance of work for people with mental health problems, the types of approaches offered, as well as the impact vocational rehabilitation has on psychopathology, self-esteem, and social relationships.

I. EMPLOYMENT AND MENTAL HEALTH

Work is central to human existence. It enables an individual to possess a valued social position and identity that has a significant influence on self-concept and relationships with others. As an important aspect of life in today's society, work has a substantial effect on our fundamental aspects of personality and is a major contributing factor to our levels of self-esteem. In addition, work provides an opportunity for increasing social contact and improving skills while also providing income and financial security. Conversely, unemployment can produce high levels of stress, anxiety, and depression; low levels of self-worth; and decrease opportunities for self-development, autonomy, and social contact. The shift from being employed to unemployed is significantly associated with not only an increased risk of depression, alcohol dependence, anxiety states, and psychosomatic reactions, but also stigma, aimlessness, and poverty, which combine to trigger or amplify mental health problems. It appears that unemployment is associated with the conditions that substantially interfere with recovery from major psychopathology. This cycle of psychopathology, unemployment, and further distress, leading to further psychopathology, leading to further difficulty in adaptation and rehabilitation, is the vicious circle that spirals downwards in the lives of those with severe mental illness.

Unemployment is a major problem for all people regardless of their mental health status. However, for those people predisposed to mental health problems it makes sense that the effects of long-term unemployment could have a massive impact on their capacity to lead a happy fulfilled life. People who suffer from severe mental illness experience high levels of unemployment with rates estimated at 75 to 85%. Not only do these rates reflect the disability caused by severe mental illness, but also the discrimination experienced by this client group and the low priority given to employment by psychiatric services. Despite these high rates, surveys have consistently shown that psychiatric patients are strongly dissatisfied about not working and express a desire for competitive integrated employment.

II. THE ROLE OF VOCATIONAL REHABILITATION

Improving the course and management of severe mental illness involves not only the management of symptoms but also the social reintegration (or integration) of the psychiatric patient. Despite the recent advances in psychopharmacology for people with severe mental illness, medication is still unable to address the social impairment and skills deficits experienced by these groups that are a major contributing factor to high vulnerability for relapse. A comprehensive care package, therefore, would not only involve medication treatment and a psychotherapy approach, but also interventions that provide patients with the social and occupational skills necessary for them to function at their optimum capacity in the community. The provision of these skills requires a comprehensive infrastructure of community services, in particular housing and employment, and a means for ensuring continuity of care.

In response to this increasing awareness of skills deficit for psychiatric patients, vocational rehabilitation has assumed increasing importance in the treatment package for rehabilitating people with severe mental illness. In the mid-19th century, the moral treatment of insanity regarded work as an effective therapeutic task that distracted patients from their psychotic preoccupations. This school of thought has evolved over the last half century, which has been witness to the development of a range of approaches to vocational rehabilitation for psychiatric patients.

The emphasis within vocational rehabilitation programs is, in the first instance, to provide patients with a structured day, and provide skills training that will ultimately enable them to secure open paid employment at a level that they will be able to manage. It is important to note that all psychiatric patients will require differing levels of input and the rehabilitation they receive must be highly individualized to their needs and capacity to work. For some patients this may take as little as a few months, in others as many as a few years. The type of rehabilitation a patient receives is dependent on the level of their "work-readiness," and is usually provided in the form of one of the two ideologies described later.

III. TYPES OF VOCATIONAL REHABILITATION

Prevocational training (PVT) and supported employment (SE) are the two main ideologies that have developed to help people with severe mental illness return to work.

Prevocational training otherwise known as the "trained and placed model," assumes that people require a period of preparation before entering into competitive employment—that is, a job paid at the market rate, and for which anyone can apply. This includes sheltered workshops, transitional employment, work crews, skills training, and other preparatory activities.

Supported employment, otherwise known as the "placed and trained model," places people directly into competitive employment without an extended period of preparation, and provides time unlimited, on-the-job support from trained job coaches or specialists. Much work has been done in this area that has led to the development of a carefully specified variant of supported employment known as the individual placement and support (IPS) model. The IPS model is distinguished by six key principles. According to Becker in 1994, these are (1) the goal is competitive employment in work settings integrated into a community's economy, (2) clients are expected to obtain jobs directly, rather than after a lengthy period of preemployment training, (3) rehabilitation is an integral component of treatment of mental health rather than a separate service, (4) services are based on client's preferences and choices, (5) assessment is continuous and based on real work experiences, and (6) follow-up support is continued indefinitely.

In addition to these approaches, cross-fertilization between the two ideologies has led to the development of a number of hybrid models (or stepwise-eclectic models), that offer either a combination of, or all of, the services offered by both PVT and SE.

Although much research has been done on the effectiveness of prevocational models in terms of returning people to the workplace, up until the past 10 years limited evaluations have been done on supported employment programs. However, the past decade has been witness to a growth in supported employment programs and along with it has come a number of reviews of their effectiveness. These reviews have shown that SE appears to be more effective than PVT in terms of helping people with SMI obtain competitive employment.

An underlying assumption that has been related to work since the early asylum system is that "work is therapy." Work of the right type has been assumed to benefit patients in other nonvocational domains such as better controlling of psychiatric symptoms, increased levels of self-esteem and self-worth, and improved capacity for social relationships, all of which contribute to an overall improved quality of life. The relationship between vocational rehabilitation and each of these domains is outlined later.

IV. VOCATIONAL REHABILITATION AND PSYCHOPATHOLOGY

The pioneers of the early asylum movement hypothesized a direct relationship between employment and symptom alleviation. In modern times, however, the conceptual models within which psychiatry operates have not tended to include constructive activity as anything more than a mediating factor, intervening between sociodemographic or psychopharmacological variables and outcome in terms of symptom relief. With the treatment of severe mental illness increasingly moving into the community, this attitude is beginning to change and the measurement of symptoms is often included among outcome measures as an indication of social adaptation and community living skills. Increasingly, these measures are being incorporated into evaluations of vocational rehabilitation services by measuring outcomes in terms of improvements to a person's psychopathology in addition to whether or not they have obtained employment.

Given that long-term mental health problems are commonly linked with chronic unemployment, it is not surprising that an improvement in socioeconomic status in the psychiatric patient improves psychopathology and prognosis. There are two likely explanations for this. First, the direct financial benefits of moving from an impoverished lifestyle will produce both mental and physical health gains, and second, the problem of chronic patienthood relates to social marginalization. The emphasis on employment or work, in "normalization" or "social valorization" rehabilitation theory, reflects a strategy to reverse this marginalization.

An additional latent clinical benefit of some work schemes is that they provide structured opportunities for supervision and treatment compliance. Support is often provided in the workplace for those who need it and in addition to an awareness of whether a person has taken medication or not, often an individual will not want to jeopardize their job by failing to take their medication and increasing the likelihood of relapse. A negative aspect of medication is that for many people the sedation effects and akathisia caused by medication make work tasks difficult. Therefore, until the medication regimen is stable, work would not be considered a feasible option.

Not only does employment appear to have a positive effect on psychopathology, but symptom alleviation could also be seen as a consequence of improvement in other facets of an individual's life, which again, are influenced by vocational rehabilitation. This type of rehabilitation is thought to have a significant impact on the level of self-esteem, which in turn can promote improvements in mental state.

V. VOCATIONAL REHABILITATION AND SELF-ESTEEM

Self-esteem is the evaluation people make and maintain about themselves and has been defined as evaluation of one's own worth, value, or importance. It is essential to our ability to function in a healthy way. Without the foundation of a solid sense of self-worth, we are unable to take the risks and make the decisions necessary to lead a fulfilling, productive life. A low self-esteem has a negative effect on our relationships, careers, family bonds, and, most important, our internal sense of well-being. A high self-esteem, on the other hand, brings the high level of confidence, problem-solving abilities, and assertiveness needed to achieve what Maslow referred to as "self-actualization"—a continuous desire to fulfil potentials, to be all that you can be. Obviously this refers to everyone regardless of their mental health status; however, for psychiatric patients, this is a state that is particularly difficult to achieve. People who have positive self-esteem have healthier, stronger relationships with those with negative self-esteem. A strong sense of self-worth actually creates a type of self-fulfilling prophecy. The more people like themselves, the more they begin to act in likable ways, the more they believe they are able to achieve something, the more likely it is that they will.

The concept of self-esteem has been widely used as an outcome variable in studies of rehabilitation. This is based on the assumption that a higher level of functioning is coexistent with a higher level of self-esteem and feeling of self-worth. The sources of self-esteem are regarded as personality related and as a function of intrapersonal evaluation, individual roles, role accumulation, or early childhood experience. Self-esteem has two essential elements, social status and affirmative experience. Social status refers to an individual's position in society relative to others, and is most often measured in terms of household income, educational attainment, and occupation. As employment is a major source of social status, it may, therefore, be argued that employment in a respected occupation is a means of restoring the self-esteem of people with mental health problems that cannot be obtained in any other way. Affirmative experiences are experiences in which individuals receive positive reinforcement from others about their abilities and behavior. Affirmative experiences can usually be obtained through a variety of social encounters; however, people with mental health problems may have limited opportunities for social interaction. Hence, work in a nonstigmatized setting may enhance the self-esteem of people with mental health problems.

Goodman and colleagues in 1994 found that in psychiatric patients, low levels of self-esteem were found to be associated with higher levels of psychiatric disturbance and higher levels of external locus of control among African-American women. The potential of employment to influence self-esteem is shown by the Rosenfield model. Rosenfield's 1992 study of a Clubhouse took "mastery" as a pivotal concept, defined as "a personal resource that can moderate or help in coping with the effects of stress. ... A low sense of mastery affects subjective quality of life because it results in feelings of hopelessness and passivity." Rosenfield points out that many psychotherapists have suggested increasing a sense of mastery as the first task in psychotherapy for people with chronic mental health problems. Leading on from this she set out to explore associations among vocational rehabilitation, mastery, and quality of life. She concluded that economic resources and empowerment increased a sense of mastery and hence a better quality of life. Controlling for perceptions of mastery, she also found that having a greater time structure as imposed by work, increased people's quality of life.

Studies comparing people with mental health problems who were either in competitive employment or unemployed, found that those in competitive employment had significantly higher self-esteem than those unemployed. In addition, studies have also shown that patients working in sheltered workshops had a high level of self-esteem associated with the opinion that their job held a "valued social position."

Given the obvious importance self-esteem has on both people's capacity to lead a fulfilling life, and the type of employment they consider themselves suitable for, and able to do, rehabilitation in conjunction with psychotherapeutic interventions need to implement techniques that focus specifically on increasing levels of self-esteem.

VI. VOCATIONAL REHABILITATION AND SOCIAL RELATIONSHIPS

Our levels of self-esteem also have a significant impact on our ability to maintain social relationships. This can be seen as a self-perpetuating circumstance in that a low level of self-esteem severely disables a person's ability to interact and build social relationships. Conversely, interaction and social relationships can help build a person's feeling of self-esteem and self-worth and make them feel wanted. Social support or interaction can be seen as part of our basic need for belongingness and love and is defined as the degree to which a person's basic social needs are gratified through interaction with others.

Psychiatric patients commonly suffer deterioration of social relationships, particularly in the case of schizophrenia. Evidence for the importance of social support in schizophrenia is growing with research showing that psychiatric service users have smaller social circles than people without mental health problems. In addition, patients with schizophrenia also perceive themselves to have fewer people offering instrumental support, and fewer social companions than those suffering with depression.

Although an understimulating social environment has been shown to be associated with clinical poverty syndrome, or institutionalization, conversely, an overstimulating one can precipitate psychotic episodes. Given that patients with schizophrenia tend to react adversely to overstimulation it is unsurprising that they withdraw from social interaction and are reluctant to enter a work environment. The emphasis here is on both the level of stimulation and the level of communication required to operate within the workplace. Obviously both of these factors need to be at a level that is suitable for each individual, while acknowledging that thresholds will be different for each person.

It is important to note here that the quality of the relationships within work is of importance. Relationships are bidirectional in that they can be seen as reciprocal or dependent. Although psychiatric patients may consider themselves dependent on a relationship in terms of receiving support, they must possess a sufficient level of social skills to maintain that relationship. Therefore, diminished social interaction may be due to the breakdown of social skills, which then places the person at a disadvantage in terms of disabling his or her capacity for beneficial social interaction.

People with mental health problems who are entering a work environment are exposing themselves to an entirely new source of social supports. These supports can be seen as "natural" (e.g., from colleagues) or "constructed" (e.g., from supervisors or job coaches). These relationships can be then further built on in order to provide both emotional and instrumental support, in some cases becoming friendships that extend beyond the workplace. The Clubhouse movement advocates this ethos in its work intervention known as transitional employment. For psychiatric patients, constructed networks derived from therapeutic settings may serve as a substitute for poor social networks outside work.

Another important aspect of employment that may facilitate improvement is removal of psychiatric patients from the home environment where their social contacts may have a high level of expressed emotion (EE). Research in EE has clearly demonstrated that medication and removal from relatives who have high EE can protect the psychiatric patient from relapse. It therefore follows that a structured work environment to where the patient can "escape" on a regular, structured basis may serve as a protective factor. It is of obvious importance that the work setting does not replicate high levels of EE. This can be prevented by education of supervisory staff and colleagues about the concept and manifestations of EE.

VII. INTEGRATION OF VOCATIONAL REHABILITATION EFFORTS IN PSYCHOTHERAPY

Given the psychosocial aspects of vocational rehabilitation, there is a common link between this type of intervention and that of psychotherapy. Both interventions share the goal of increasing the functional capacity of the individual. The difference is that within psychotherapy, the improvement of psychopathology, self-esteem, and the capacity for social relationships are specific aims, whereas in vocational rehabilitation, they can be seen as by-products of improving an individual's capacity to work.

In terms of provision of these interventions it would be desirable to offer them within a framework where all aspects of the patient's care are provided collaboratively and communication between the services is common. Both interventions require the input of specialized individuals and it is unlikely that an individual or particular caregiver will be expert in both enough to integrate them into his or her practice. Therefore, it is often the case that both interventions will be carried out by separately trained practitioners who may not share the same views of the nature of psychopathology. They may have differing subtle and not so subtle goals and ideas about what is practical for an individual to achieve, and consequently the opportunity for conflict between the two may arise. Consequently if they are not organized out of the same agency providing care and leadership in treatment planning, they must commit themselves to a regular form of communication in which they share their ideas and assessments of individuals. Regular discussions need to take place concerning what the individual wants to achieve and whether it is feasible, what difficulties may be encountered, and perhaps most important any difficulties that may arise in their relationship with one another as they collaborate in the care of the individual. It is important to acknowledge here the existence of one such mechanism that aims to achieve treatment integration. This mechanism is known as case management, which involves a team of professionals with a limited number of cases for each intervention, thus reducing the workload and enabling more time and commitment for patients' care. The emphasis within the team is on collaborative working, with regular meetings for discussion about patients.

Only by collaborative working between all services involved in a person's care will we be able to bring the management and rehabilitation of psychiatric patients together in an organized cohesive manner. This will enable us to ultimately provide a seamless service working closely together with the common goal of improving the overall functioning and capacity of the psychiatric patient, thus facilitating (re)integration back into the community.

Acknowledgments

The author would like to acknowledge the funding support from the National Health Service Research and Development North West.

See Also the Following Articles

Job Club Method ■ Schizophrenia and Other Disorders

Further Reading

Becker, D. R., & Drake, R. E. (1994). Individual placement and support: A community mental health center approach to vocational rehabilitation. *Community Mental Health Journal, 30,* 193–206.

Bell, M. D., Lysaker, P. H., & Milstein, R. M. (1996). Clinical benefits of paid work activity in schizophrenia. *Schizophrenia Bulletin, 22,* 51–67.

Bond, G. R., Drake, R. E., Becker, D. R., & Mueser, K. T. (1999). Effectiveness of psychiatric rehabilitation approaches for employment of people with severe mental illness. *Journal of Disability Policy Studies, 10,* 18–52.

Crowther, R. E., Marshall, M., Bond, G. R., & Huxley, P. (2001). Helping people with severe mental illness to obtain work: A systematic review. *British Medical Journal,* January 2001, 204–208.

Lehman, A. F. (1995). Vocational rehabilitation in schizophrenia. *Schizophrenia Bulletin, 21,* 645–656.

Rosenfield, S., & Neese-Todd, S. (1993). Elements of psychosocial Clubhouse program associated with a satisfying quality of life. *Hospital and Community Psychiatry, 44,* 76–79.

Torrey, W. C., Mueser, K. T., McHugo, G. H., & Drake, R. E. (2000). Self-esteem as an outcome measure in studies of vocational rehabilitation for adults with severe mental illness. *Psychiatric Services, 51,* 229–233.

Women's Issues

Malkah T. Notman and Carol C. Nadelson

Harvard Medical School

GLOSSARY

gender identity The perception of oneself as being either male or female, and the acquisition of social roles culturally appropriate for that person that are gender linked.

gender role A cultural construct referring to the expectations, attitudes, and behaviors that are considered to be appropriate for a particular gender in a particular culture.

sexual orientation The sexual preference of a person based on gender, i.e. homosexual, heterosexual, bisexual.

I. INTRODUCTION

Gender is an important variable in psychotherapy. Gender can influence a patient's choice of therapist, the "fit" between therapist and patient, and the sequence and content of the clinical material presented. It also affects the diagnosis, length of treatment, and sometimes outcome. Gender differences in experiences affect the perception and interpretation of patient material. Biologic aspects of gender must be considered from a perspective that reflects emerging data that unify brain and mind, biological, and psychosocial factors.

Evidence of gender differences in the nervous system beginning in fetal life suggests that, from birth, boys and girls may not perceive and experience the world in the same way. Gender differences in neural maturity and organization influence behavior and reactions in infants that can also affect caretakers' response, further reinforcing differences. These differences in reactions can alter the growth and development of neuronal pathways. Experience modifies the structure and function of neurons and neuronal networks, and can modify gene expression. Brain structure, metabolism, and function are also affected by psychotherapy. These findings reinforce our understanding of the plasticity of the brain and how it is affected by behavior and experience. The implications of these data underscore that the distinction between biological and psychosocial is both artificial and misleading.

In this article we focus on the relationship between gender and psychotherapy, considering psychosocial and biological variables. We will examine biological influences, developmental and life experiences, gender differences in personality styles, and the effects of stereotypes and values.

II. VALUES AND TREATMENT

Personal and social values affect standards of normality and influence the perception, diagnosis, and treatment of mental disorders and emotional problems. Although there have been changes in concepts of normality, mental illness, and the range of behaviors and attitudes that are thought to characterize each gender, evidence suggests that there continue to be differences in what is considered normal for men and women, even by therapists. Broverman and colleagues in their classic 1970s study found that when male and female psychotherapists were asked to describe a mentally healthy person, psychological health was more closely associated with descriptions of "healthy, mature, socially competent" men than with concepts of maturity or mental health of women. Although a 1990 report by Kaplan and co-workers noted that attitudes toward gender roles have changed to some extent, and that male and female psychiatrists' beliefs regarding gender-appropriate behavior had become more similar and less stereotyped, ratings derived from the Bem scale indicated that female and male psychiatrists were still more likely to choose stereotypical traits to define mental health.

Although concepts of normal masculine and feminine behavior and attitudes have shifted, these changes are not necessarily integrated into a cohesive view of normality for either men or women. Attitudinal changes may be consciously adopted by those treating a patient, but unconscious views about what is "normal" may be unchanged and can affect therapy.

Values are communicated to patients in both overt and subtle ways in the process of evaluation and referral as well as during treatment. In psychotherapy, therapists communicate values by their selection of material to respond to, by the timing of their interpretations, and by their affective reaction to the content of what is said by the patient. This subtle communication conveys the therapist's judgment. For example, the therapist may emphasize or ignore the patient's references to menstruation, to taking drugs, or to engaging in risky sexual behavior and women patients may be more reluctant to discuss these with male therapists. By responding, the therapist expresses a judgment of what is important and to whom, and consequently may misinterpret the importance of these issues for the patient.

Gender also affects treatment priorities and approaches. It has been suggested, for example, that concern about some more characteristically male behaviors, such as violence related to alcohol abuse, may lead to the development of treatment methods that are more suitable for men. These methods may also be used for women, although there is evidence that they are less effective for them. Likewise, more attention may be paid to treating the adolescent schizophrenic or substance-abusing man, because of the threat of violence, than to treating the seriously handicapped but less threatening women with posttraumatic stress disorder (PTSD) or depression.

III. GENDER INFLUENCES AND DIFFERENCES IN EARLY DEVELOPMENT

Early influences and endowments, both biological and psychosocial, are important in the shaping of personality. In childhood, the presence or absence of continued stable care, styles of child rearing, the responsiveness and nurturance of people in the environment, physical health and illness, loss, and trauma, as well as biological endowment, are all determinants of the ultimate configuration of personality.

Complex integrative functioning, such as conceptualization and learning of language and social skills, derives from both biological and psychosocial influences. These may differ between males and females. The effects of particular cultural practices, including gender differences in child rearing, and ideas about gender-appropriate roles are also manifested very early in life and affect development. Parental behavior affects male and female roles and is a powerful developmental force.

Ideas about the determinants of gender identity have changed from the early views that the major determinants of gender development were anatomical, to a view that development and gender concerns represent a complex interplay of anatomy, genetic endowment, and environment including developmental experiences and cultural context. These include the structure of the family, the presence and roles of other siblings, the mother's other pregnancies, and many aspects of the child's relationship with extended family and others.

There seems to be a connection between early trauma and the development of personality disorders, especially borderline personality disorder, which is more commonly diagnosed in women than in men. There is evidence that developmental disruptions occur when an individual is traumatized early in life.

Gender role is a cultural construct referring to the expectations, attitudes, and behaviors that are considered to be appropriate for each gender in a particular culture. There are enormous differences in the roles and expectations of men and women in different societies. Some societies dictate more rigid and fixed roles than others. Not all value the same traits or see certain traits as gender specific in the same ways. For example, physical strength is often considered a male characteristic, but despite their smaller size and lesser physical strength women in some cultures are assigned the heavy work. The role most consistently assumed by women across cultures is early child rearing.

During early development, in all cultures, the mother remains the primary caregiver of young children. The earliest attachment is more likely to be made with her. She becomes the primary identification figure in early childhood, for both boys and girls. Therefore, for girls, the first identification is with the parent of the same sex. For boys, the first identification is with the parent of the opposite sex. As girls grow up, this same-sex identification does not have to change in order for feminine gender identity to consolidate. Thus, girls learn about being women in identifying with their mothers. Boys, on the other hand, must shift their primary identification away from their mothers in order to develop a male gender identification. Thus, they move away from their early attachment.

For girls, the continuity of attachment to their mothers, and the fear of loss of love by manifesting aggression that is disapproved of, may make it more difficult to establish autonomy and independence. Aggression, competitiveness, and anger may be difficult to manage because these affects can threaten loss of relationships. It can be difficult for women to express themselves freely, especially when they experience anger and aggression, and, at the same time to preserve relationships. This may be seen later in life in a woman's conflict about aggression, manifested in her difficulty in being appropriately assertive and in her inhibited risk-taking or autonomous behavior. Cultural values such as independence, initiative, and competitiveness have been considered positive characteristics for males, but not for females.

Because of the primacy of relational ties, women also may be more vulnerable to loss throughout their lives. One of the syndromes that has been seen as related to the conflict about autonomy and independence and the sense of vulnerability to loss is agoraphobia, which is more commonly diagnosed in women than in men. Although this syndrome has multiple determinants, it may represent anxiety about moving out into the world and feeling alone. Depression is also more frequently diagnosed in women than in men. The reasons for this are complex and unclear, but multidetermined, including conflicts about aggression and mastery, social depreciation of feminine roles, identification with depressed mothers, early loss, and biological factors.

In contrast, disturbances involving violent, aggressive behavior, and problems with impulsiveness are more often diagnosed in men. Conflicts around intimacy and socialization toward aggression and action are consistent with this picture in men. These findings raise questions about the factors affecting the process of diagnosis itself, particularly with Axis II disorders. Because these disorders more generally reflect clusters of observed personality characteristics rather than specific symptoms, incidence figures may reflect biases and sex-role stereotypes.

At times, women may also fail to act in their own best interests because of their desire to preserve relationships, even if these are abusive. This can result in behavior that may continue to put them at risk for victimization. The threat of loss then, may motivate behavior that can be interpreted as masochistic. For women, the conflict experienced about aggression can result in turning aggression inward, with excessive self-criticism and diminished self-esteem. Culturally supported passivity with consequent feelings of helplessness can be risk factors for depression. Problems in the development of self-esteem, for girls, appear to be intensified in adolescence. Gilligan found that there are gender differences in self-concept and identity in adolescence. Males generally define themselves in terms of individual achievement and work, and females more often in relational terms. Gender differences in depression, except in bipolar illness, appear to have their onset in puberty, a time when girls begin to assume adult feminine identities and roles.

IV. BODY IMAGE AND REPRODUCTION

With the beginning of puberty, girls and boys experience their reproductive identities in different ways. For girls, menarche signals a capacity for pregnancy. This change also brings a potential vulnerability for girls that is not in boys' experience. It is both a positive experience and a source of risk and anxiety. Girls develop new organs, breasts, transforming their bodies. This has no parallel in boys. For a girl, menarche is an organizer of sexual identity. It is also an undeniable physical experience, and it can be a source of pleasure and conflict about growing up and about femininity. Adolescent girls in Western cultures are bombarded with media images of women who are loved because of their physical appearance. Self-esteem and self-confidence rest heavily on physical attributes and body image especially during adolescence, for both sexes.

Conflicts around self-image and body image become more prominent during adolescence and can be expressed differently for boys and girls. Discomfort with body image and fear and ambivalence about mastery, independence, separation from family, and adulthood including sexuality, are difficult issues that are thought to contribute to the dramatic incidence of eating disorders in adolescent girls. They may literally attempt to starve themselves back into childhood and diminish female body characteristics (e.g., curves and breasts).

V. THE ROLE OF REPRODUCTIVE LIFE EXPERIENCES

Women's life cycles are closely connected to their reproductive potential. The acknowledgment of a woman's reproductive capacity is an important component of her sense of identity and femininity, regardless of whether or not she actually bears children. The knowledge that there is a finite time period for reproduction also influences her concept of time. She must make different decisions about career and family than men do. This difference can affect her emotional state, her decision to seek therapy, and the issues that will be raised in the course of therapy. With delays in the time of childbearing for contemporary women, many come to treatment as they approach 40 or in their early 40s to deal with issues around childbearing. They have not confronted their biological clocks and must deal with the issues of reproduction before it is too late.

Reproductive events, decisions, and choices may have different significance for men and women, thus affecting the process of therapy. Because reproductive issues are more likely to be addressed for female patients, male patients may find that their reproductively related concerns are not dealt with. Therapists often share the patient's reluctance to explore these issues. This avoidance may result from the conscious or unconscious conviction that exploration of a man's infertility or sexual dysfunction would be too great a threat to his view of his "masculinity."

Pregnancy as a life event marks a transition to motherhood and raises many issues for a woman, including her relationship and identification with her mother. Although pregnancy is usually experienced positively it also increases a woman's vulnerability to specific psychiatric disorders, particularly postpartum depression.

Infertility is also a different experience for men and women, and there are different issues to consider in treatment. Historically, and in some cultures today, women have been seen as the sole responsible partner when there is infertility. A woman's pregnancy has been viewed as a confirmation of a man's masculinity and potency. Infertility can be a threatening and distressing problem for both men and woman, but in different ways, depending on how important it is to each partner and what the etiology is. Social norms have supported men's resistance to be involved in infertility workups and treatment.

Menopause is a unique marker of the life cycle for women. Stereotyped expectations about women's life cycle and the attribution of midlife symptoms to menopause have resulted in the confusion of the experiences of this time of life, including concerns about the physical and emotional aspects of aging, family changes, shifts in goals, and retirement, with the effects of the physiological event of cessation of menses. Menopause has been linked with depression and loss, but there is no evidence supporting that this is an inevitable connection. Those women who become depressed in midlife are generally those who have had depressions at other times in their lives. The peak incidence of depression in women, in fact, is in early adulthood. Responses to menopause are also strongly influenced by cultural expectations, and in many cultures, women regard the cessation of menses and childbearing with relief and sometimes with greater enjoyment of sexuality.

VI. GENDER AND CHOICE OF THERAPIST

Patients give many reasons for their choice of a therapist. These reasons have often been based on stereotyped views such as "men tend to perpetuate patriarchal values," or "women are more nurturant."

The search for a role model is often a determinant of the choice of a therapist. Women frequently feel that a woman therapist will be more responsive to their wishes for achievement, success, and self-actualization or that because she has faced similar conflicts she could empathize with them more easily. Although this idea may facilitate the development of an alliance, it does not by itself resolve the patient's difficulties.

Women may also request to see a woman because they seek permission to succeed in certain goals, particularly those involving career. Permission, explicit or implicit, can result in improvement and can enable the patient to compete and succeed, even if the issues are not taken up specifically and explicitly. Identification with a therapist is also important. Although the reasons for the choice may be based on stereotypes, without regard for the characteristics of the specific therapist, the patient's feeling of greater comfort or empathy can facilitate the initial development of a positive therapeutic alliance.

A patient's gender-based choice can also derive from idealized fantasies about the characteristics and capacities of the clinician and what he or she can do for the patient. For example, if the clinician is a prominent person in the community, expectation based on this status can affect the therapeutic relationship. If the patient makes a choice because of particular political views, sexual orientation, or the cultural heritage of the therapist, treatment may begin with positive feelings, only to have these reversed if, in the course of treatment, the patient is disappointed. The recognition that the therapist is not omnipotent repeats past life experience. If there is a negative outcome it may be blamed on the therapist's gender. If the therapist is a woman who is not the fantasized omnipotent mother who can transform the patient, devalued ideas about women can be confirmed.

Choosing a therapist of a particular gender with the expectation that this will resolve the patient's problems can also be a resistance to therapy. A woman may want to see a woman for treatment because she feels unlovable and unattractive to men and can, in this way, avoid the experience of confronting her feelings or initially because she wants support, and later devalues the therapist or find herself in an angry competitive interaction, which can be a repetition of her relationship with her mother. She may be unaware of the origins of her feelings or the reasons for her choice of a therapist. Although there are conscious reasons for choices, unconscious factors or needs such as fear, anger, or a search for mothering may be important and should be considered in the initial encounter with a patient. For a woman, the choice to be treated by a woman can also represent a wish to restore the relationship with her mother or to have a better mother. A desire to see a male therapist can be based on the desire to avoid this maternal kind of relationship or the anxiety that these feelings arouse, or may reflect anxiety about the intense attachment that may be evoked by a woman.

Many support the view that women should be treated by women in order to avoid being misunderstood or treated from a male-oriented perspective. This oversimplifies the effects of gender and minimizes the necessary working through of ambivalence and conflict in the therapeutic relationship.

Concerns about sexualization and sexual relationships in treatment have become important factors in requests based on gender. For those patients who have actually been abused in previous treatment, trust can be severely damaged. It may be particularly difficult for such patients to see anyone who serves as a reminder of that previous experience. Women therapists are often asked to see women patients who have had sexual involvements with male therapists. Although it does occur, women are less likely to become sexually involved with their patients, either male or female, than are men.

Sexual orientation has also become a consideration for many gay individuals who request therapy with gay therapists. They feel that a gay therapist will better understand and empathize with them and will be less likely to judge their sexual object choice as pathological. Although there has been controversy about the appropriateness of disclosure of the therapist's sexual orientation, some therapists believe that this disclosure can be beneficial in therapy.

Stereotypes and expectations about women affect male patients as well. A man may seek treatment from a woman therapist in order to avoid a competitive or authoritarian relationship with a man, to avoid homosexual feelings, or because he has had poor relationships with women in the past and wants to work these out with a woman. His expectations may be that a woman will provide the cure for his problems with intimacy.

VII. THE THERAPEUTIC PROCESS

Understanding the concept of transference can clarify aspects of the therapeutic relationship that may otherwise be difficult to comprehend. The attitudes and feelings brought to a relationship from past experiences with important figures such as parents are components of future interpersonal interactions. The need to please or to gain love by acquiescence or seductive behavior can be brought into the therapist–patient relationship as if it were a response of the patient to the therapist as a real person in the present. The therapist can be seen as rejecting, authoritarian, giving, preferring other patients, and so on.

The classical conceptualization of transference assumed that both maternal and paternal transference could be developed toward both male and female therapists. Thus, the therapist's gender was not a particularly salient consideration. Freud came to believe that transference responses to a male analyst differed from those to a female analyst. Subsequently, however, Horney emphasized the importance of the competitive transference with the same-sex analyst, and Greenacre stated that strong gender preferences should be respected, but also carefully analyzed because prior wishes, expectations, and fantasies could affect not only the choice but also the course of the psychoanalytic process.

Gender can affect the initial relationship and the early evolving transference, as well as the sequence in which therapeutic issues emerge, and the pace at which therapy progresses. For example, working with a woman therapist can evoke maternal transference material earlier in therapy. Transference expectations may cause some patients to fail to reveal details of sexual abuse or other sexual experiences to a male or female therapist depending on the patient's view of how the therapist might hear or react to this information. This lack of disclosure may also be related to the patient's stereotypical ideas as well as the particular characteristics of both patient and therapist.

Assessment of the kinds of transference engendered may be complicated by the countertransference of the person doing the assessing. Although an erotic transference may occur in a man's transference to a woman therapist, it is more common for women patients to develop an erotic transference to either male or female therapists. This can create problems, particularly for the inexperienced therapist. The idea that a real romantic or sexual relationship can be therapeutic to a patient can be difficult to reject if the patient passionately pursues this or demands it, particularly if she is suicidal and it may be rationalized as life-saving. Sexual relationships with patients are ethical violations, boundary violations, and leave the therapist open to legal action as well as therapeutic failures. When these become an issue in therapy, a consultation and supervision is very important.

Transference can take many forms, including cross-gender manifestations. It is possible for a woman patient to develop a paternal transference to a woman therapist. It may be difficult for the therapist to imagine himself or herself as the cross-gender person or for a man to imagine himself as a mother or a woman as a father.

Current views of transference emphasize that the therapist or analyst plays a role in the creation of the transference, even if this is not consciously recognized. Thus, recognition of the effect of the gender of both participants is important.

Change or reassignment of a therapist on the basis of gender has been widely discussed and is often recommended. Some have suggested that a change of therapist might mobilize a stalemated situation. Transfers on the basis of the therapist's gender have also been made when there is a therapeutic impasse or failure.

Unless there has been a sexual interaction, however, it is rare that gender itself is the significant variable in the majority of cases that are not successful. A transfer based on gender may be a way of avoiding responsibility for failure or dealing with the embarrassment of a negative outcome. Person suggested that women therapists are often referred particularly difficult patients after these patients have failed a first therapeutic effort. Because gender affects trust and compliance in psychotherapy, change in the therapist based on gender might be helpful in some situations.

VIII. GENDER CHOICE IN COUPLES AND FAMILY THERAPY

As with all forms of therapy, gender is a consideration in the choice of a therapist for couples or families. In general, as with individual therapy, issues related to gender choice should be clarified and addressed. A couple with marital difficulties may request a female therapist because it is the wife who has made the call and it is her preference, perhaps because she feels intimidated by men or because she fears that she could be left out of the male dyad if the therapist were male. On the other hand, a husband may choose a woman or comply with his wife's choice of a female therapist because he is more comfortable and less threatened by women, because he does not take the therapy seriously, or because he has negative feelings about women. The choice of a male therapist for some couples may re-create, in the transference, a paternal or authoritarian relationship or even the fantasy of possible sexual abuse. This can be a special problem if abuse has actually occurred.

During the course of therapy, attention must be paid to bias regardless of whether the therapist is male or female. Transference issues in couples and family therapy are multiple and more complex because more people are directly involved in the therapy. For example, each partner and the couple as a unit will have different transference reactions to the therapist and to each other. If there are additional family members involved they too will add to the transference complexity.

Changes in family patterns have presented an increasing array of challenging issues for therapy. For example, the stress and demands of dual-career or commuting families, especially those with two achievement-oriented partners, can create enormous tension. This may be a greater source of conflict if the wife is earning more money, or if there is a job offer to either partner in another city. Because the husband's work has traditionally been the motivating factor in a relocation, a wife's job offer can create tensions, especially involving competition. A wife who achieves success later in life can be on a different timetable than her husband, who may wish to retire earlier.

Feminist critiques of family therapy express concern about the structural–hierarchical dominant role of males in the family, mother blaming, assumptions about sharing power and responsibility embedded in systemic concepts, and assumptions about therapist neutrality. Family therapy has also been criticized for biased treatment of men, for example, for reinforcing the socialized limitations of male roles.

IX. GROUP THERAPY

As with couples and family therapy, there are gender issues in group therapy. When group therapy is sought or recommended, the gender of the group therapist is not frequently considered, although the gender composition of the group is often thought to be important. There are data suggesting that group behavior between group members and with the leader is affected by gender.

Women often seek women's groups because in groups of men or even in mixed groups they feel powerless, intimidated, and uncomfortable about speaking up. One need only look at classrooms, professional meetings, and business groups to recognize that women speak less often than men, and when they do speak, their comments are more often ignored or attributed to men. Women report the same experiences, regardless of professional status or income. They may feel supported and less anxious in same-sex groups, although mixed groups may be helpful in confronting these issues.

Most often single-sex groups have been used for support and consciousness-raising. Both male and female self-help groups often form around a specific focus (e.g., substance abuse, divorce, family violence) and use problem-solving approaches.

Therapy groups with both male and female leaders permit men and women to deal with transference issues, both as peers and as leaders. It is important, however, that the leaders' relationship with each other, just as with male and female therapists in family therapy, be a facilitating rather than inhibitory factor. Mistrust, competition, and anger that are not addressed in either leader or group members can be unproductive and inhibitory to group process.

X. SEXUAL ABUSE

When there is a history of early trauma, especially sexual abuse, which is more common in women, the impact of the trauma and the betrayal by parental figures or those in authority can result in psychopathology that can emerge later. It can be understood as an etiological factor in the increased likelihood that survivors of childhood abuse will be victimized as adults. Studies also report profoundly self-destructive behaviors emerging after victimization. Somatic symptoms can also develop later. The aftermath of abuse, particularly after repeated abuse, is often a residual sense of helplessness and loss of autonomy. This may intensify conflicts about dependency and stimulate self-criticism, shame, and guilt in many areas of life. Difficulty handling anger and aggression, and persistent feelings of vulnerability are also common repercussions.

For those who have been abused, the ability to form a trusting therapeutic alliance may be difficult. This is an example of a situation in which patients may not seek or continue therapy if they are not comfortable with the therapist, and in this way gender may be a variable.

Some of the responses and behaviors of those who have been victimized evoke profound countertransference reactions in those treating them. It may be difficult to work with battered and abused women, who often evoke frustration and anger because of their tendency to displace anger, their passivity and failure to follow through on suggestions, and the frequency with which they return to the abusive situation. Some therapists overidentify with these patients and may also project their own feelings, fantasies, or experiences onto their patients. These may include judgment about the appropriateness of the patient's response. Rescue fantasies may occur in both male and female therapists when they treat abuse victims and can lead to therapeutic problems such as boundary violations. The therapist may attempt to become the loving, nonabusive parent that he or she thinks the patient should have had instead of the real, abusive parent. These countertransference problems can compromise the therapeutic relationship.

XI. ALCOHOL AND SUBSTANCE ABUSE

There is less known about the epidemiology and treatment of alcoholism and substance abuse in women than in men. Pharmacological treatments have often paid little attention to the different presentations, physiology, and needs of men and women. For example, women's smaller body size, higher body fat content, and lower alcohol dehydrogenase levels contribute to higher blood alcohol concentrations in women with the same alcohol intake, and to the greater effect of smaller amounts of alcohol in women. Likewise, there are psychological and sociocultural factors affecting the behavior of those with alcohol and substance abuse. Currently, treatment approaches are similar for men and women, and do not account for gender differences. For example, treatment programs attempt to dissociate abusers from their alcohol- or drug-using peers, placing women drug and alcohol abusers at a disadvantage because they are more likely to live with partners who are also abusers and who discourage or prevent them from seeking help with threats or actual physical and/or sexual abuse.

Women respond better to relational involvement in treatment programs. They are more likely to attend and participate in women's groups. Because women's substance abuse often is less visible than it is for men, their abuse is often not recognized by family and friends so they are not encouraged to seek treatment.

XII. CONCLUSION

It is apparent that gender is an important treatment variable and that attention to the particular needs and experiences of women, together with better understanding of the complex interaction of gender and other variables, will shed light on the therapeutic process and contribute to greater therapeutic effectiveness. We have seen that gender can influence the patient's choice of therapist, the "fit" between therapist and patient, the sequence and content of the clinical material presented, the diagnosis, length of treatment, and the outcome of the treatment. Stereotyped views, expectations, and unconscious transference and countertransference fantasies about gender differences and what they will mean in the therapeutic process often persist and are influential, regardless of whether they have demonstrable validity. As more attention has been paid to the real attributes of the therapist, age, race, culture, gender, life experiences, and other variables have been understood to play an important role in the therapeutic process.

See Also the Following Articles

Couples Therapy ■ Cultural Issues ■ Eating Disorders ■ Family Therapy ■ Feminist Psychotherapy ■ Multicultural Therapy ■ Race and Human Diversity ■ Transcultural Psychotherapy ■ Sex Therapy

Further Reading

Adler, D. A., Drake, R. E., & Teague, G. B. (1990). Clinicians' practices in personality assessment: Does gender influence the use of DSM-IIIAxis II? *Comprehensive Psychiatry, 31*, 125–133.

Chodorow, N. (1978). *The reproduction of mothering: Psychoanalysis and the sociology of gender*. Berkeley, CA: University of California Press.

Clarkin, J. F., & Kernberg, O. F. (1993). Development factors in borderline personality disorder and borderline personality organization. In J. Paris (Ed.), *Borderline personality disorder: Etiology and treatment* (pp. 161–184). Washington, DC: American Psychiatric Press.

Comtois, K. A., & Ries, R. K. (1995). Sex differences in dually diagnosed severely mentally ill clients in dual diagnosis outpatients treatment. *American Journal on Addictions, 4*, 245–253.

Gabbard, G. O., & Wilkinson, S. M. (2000). *Management of countertransference with borderline patients*. Washington, DC: American Psychiatric Press.

Gilligan, C., Rogers, A. G., & Tolman, D. L. (1991). *Women, girls and psychotherapy: Reframing resistance*. New York: Harrington Park Press.

Greenacre, P. (1959). Certain technical problems in the transference relationship. *Journal of the American Pschoanalytical Association, 7*, 484–502.

Gunderson, J. G., & Sabo, A. N. (1993). The phenomenological and conceptual interface between borderline personality disorder and PTS. *American Journal of Psychiatry, 150*, 19–27.

Johnson, J. G., Cohen, P., Brown, J., Smailes, E. M., & Berstein, D. P. (1999). Childhood maltreatment increases risk for personality disorders during early adulthood. *Archives of General Psychiatry, 56*, 600–606.

Kandel, E. R. (1999). Biology and the future of psychoanalysis: A new intellectual framework for psychiatry revisited. *American Journal of Psychiatry, 156*, 505–524.

Kauffman, E., Dore, M. M., & Nelson-Zlupko, L. (1995). The role of women's therapy groups in the treatment of chemical dependence. *American Journal of Orthopsychiatry, 65*, 355–363.

Merkatz, R. B., Temple, R., Sobel, S., Feiden, K., Kessler, D. A., and the Working Group on Women in Clinical Trials. (1993). Women in clinical trials of new drugs. *New England Journal of Medicine, 329*, 292–296.

Notman, M. T., Klein, R., Jordan, J. V., et al. (1991). Women's unique developmental issues across the life cycle. In A. Tasman, S. M. Goldfinger (Eds.), *American Psychiatric Press Review of Psychiatry* (Vol. 10, pp. 556–577). Washington, DC: American Psychiatric Press.

Schwartz, J. M., Stoessel, P. W., Baxter, L. R., Martin, K. M., & Phelps, M. E. (1996). Systematic changes in cerebral glucose metabolic rate after successful behavior modification treatment of obsessive-compulsive disorder. *Archives of General Psychiatry 53*, 109–113.

Weissman, M. M. (1991). Gender differences in the rates of mental disorder. In *Assessing future research needs: Mental and addictive disorder in woman*. Washington, DC: Institute of Medicine.

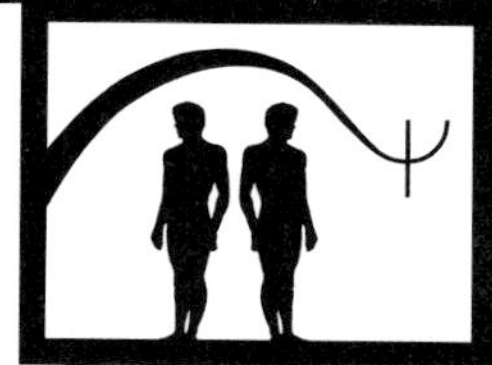

Working Alliance

Georgiana Shick Tryon

City University of New York Graduate School and University Center

GLOSSARY

common factors Procedures and processes that occur in all types of therapies regardless of the theoretical orientation of the therapist.

effect size The statistical degree to which differences or relationships between groups exist.

meta-analysis A statistical analysis that combines the results of several empirical studies.

working alliance Client–therapist bond and agreement on the goals of therapy and tasks to be undertaken to achieve them.

Working Alliance Inventory (WAI) A scale that enables assessment of the common alliance factors of client–therapist bond and agreement on goals and tasks of therapy. Ratings may be done by clients, therapists, and outside observers.

The working alliance is a collaborative relationship between client and therapist that is common to all types of therapies and enables therapeutic success. This article presents an overview of the theoretical foundations of the alliance and a review of research on the quality of the alliance and its relationship to therapeutic outcome.

I. OVERVIEW OF THE WORKING ALLIANCE

For years, researchers conducted numerous studies to determine whether or not various psychotherapies were effective in relieving clients' problems, and if they were, which types of therapy were most effective. Large-scale reviews of these studies in 1994 by Michael Lambert and Allen Bergin, in 1986 by William Shapiro and colleagues, in 1980 by Mary Smith and colleagues, and in 1997 by Bruce Wampold and colleagues established that psychotherapy worked and that there was little difference in the effectiveness of different forms of psychotherapy. Since different types of therapy are virtually equally effective, some researchers have focused on the characteristics that all therapies have in common that contribute to client improvement. These characteristics are known as common factors, because they are procedures or processes that occur in all types of therapy regardless of the theoretical orientation of the therapist.

The working alliance refers to the collaborative relationship between therapist and client where the two establish a bond and agree on the goals of therapy and tasks to be undertaken to achieve them. It is a common factor that impacts outcome across a variety of therapies. Some theorists and researchers even believe that the working alliance is more important to outcome than the type of therapy that the therapist uses. In 1988, in an article on the integration of all forms of therapy, Barry Wolfe and Marvin Goldfried called the working alliance the "quintessential integrative variable."

II. THEORETICAL BASES OF THE WORKING ALLIANCE

The concept of working alliance originated in psychoanalytic psychotherapy that is designed to make unconscious conflicts and feelings conscious. The analytic patient relates to the analyst in a distorted manner that mirrors these unconscious conflicts. In 1912, however, Sigmund Freud also posited a positive relationship between the analyst and patient that was based in the reality of their work together. This relationship later became known as the working alliance.

To humanistic therapists who believe that people are capable of helping themselves if they are provided with a facilitating relationship, the working alliance is both necessary and sufficient for client improvement. According to Carl Rogers in 1957, the therapist was responsible for creating this facilitating relationship by demonstrating empathy, genuineness, congruence, and unconditional positive regard toward the client. Within this accepting environment, the client was then able to achieve self-acceptance and self-actualization. This relationship would then generalize to other relationships outside of therapy. Thus, for Rogers, the working relationship was directly responsible for client improvement.

Behavioral and cognitive-behavioral therapy, which are based on learning principles, did not originally address the client–therapist relationship. In 1977, however, the Association for Advancement of Behavior Therapy (AABT) published ethical principles for behavior therapists. These principles emphasized client agreement with the goals and methods of treatments that are important components of the working alliance. Thus, most behaviorists and cognitive behaviorists stress the importance of the working alliance.

The working alliance is just one term for the collaborative relationship between client and therapist. Different theorists highlight different aspects of the alliance, and as a result, it is sometimes referred to as the helping alliance or therapeutic alliance. In 1979, Bordin put all the elements of the working alliance together into one conceptualization that applied to all types of theories and therapies. He defined working alliance as a bond between client and therapist and an agreement on the goals of therapy and the tasks necessary to achieve those goals.

III. EMPIRICAL STUDIES

Interest in the working alliance as a common factor in all types of therapies has spawned considerable research. This research is primarily, but not exclusively, concentrated in three areas: assessment of the alliance, the relationship of the alliance to outcome, and changes in the alliance across time.

A. Alliance Assessment

Because different researchers emphasize different aspects of the working alliance, they have developed scales to measure the alliance that reflect their theoretical interests. For instance, in the 1980s, Lester Luborsky and his colleagues at the University of Pennsylvania developed what are now known as the Penn Scales to assess client, therapist, and observer perspectives of the helping alliance. Also in the 1980s, Charles Marmar and Elsa Marziali and their colleagues developed the Therapeutic Alliance Rating Scale (TARS), and in 1989, Marmar and colleagues revised the TARS and named the new scale the California Psychotherapy Alliance Scales (CALPAS). In 1983, D. E. Hartley and Hans Strupp developed the Vanderbilt Therapeutic Alliance Scale (VTAS), and in 1989, Stephen Saunders and his colleagues developed the Therapeutic Bond Scales (TBS).

Each of these scales was based on the different theoretical conceptualizations of the working alliance, but most also incorporated Bordin's integrative formulations. One scale, however, was developed to specifically assess Bordin's conceptualizations. It is the Working Alliance Inventory (WAI) and was created in 1986 by Adam Horvath and Leslie Greenberg. It allows an overall alliance score and its three scales separately assess the therapeutic bond, agreement on goals, and agreement on tasks—the three dimensions of the working alliance identified by Bordin. The original WAI is 36 items long, with 12 items in each scale. In 1990, Terence Tracey and Anna Kokotovic developed a short form of the WAI that has 12 items.

Because they were designed to assess the same thing, the various working alliance instruments have been found by researchers, such as Victoria Tichenor and Clara Hill in 1989, to be highly positively correlated. In 2000 in a statistical analysis that combined the results of 79 empirical studies, using meta-analytic strategies. Daniel Martin and his colleagues found that each of these scales is associated with good reliability. With the exception of the TARS, each of the scales also related positively and significantly to therapy outcome. Thus, researchers investigating the working alliance could use any of these scales, with the exception of the TARS, in their inquiries with confidence. Martin and colleagues suggest, however, that the WAI is an appropriate choice for most investigations because of its applicability to all theoretical perspectives.

B. Relationship of Working Alliance to Therapeutic Outcome

The numerous studies relating the working alliance to various types of outcome (i.e., ratings of patient improvement, type of termination) are summarized by two meta-analyses. The first was a meta-analysis of 24 studies done in 1991 by Adam Horvath and Dianne Symonds. They found that the working alliance was moderately positively related to therapy outcome. The effect size, or the statistical degree to which working alliance and therapy outcome were related, was .26. Their findings applied regardless of the length of the treatment, the number of clients in each sample, and whether or not the study was published.

The recent meta-analysis in 2000 by Daniel Martin, John Garske, and Katherine Davis also found a moderate positive relationship between working alliance ratings and treatment outcomes. The effect size was .22. This meta-analysis corrected for some factors that might reduce effect size in the studies reviewed, but it did not correct for other factors (such as test reliability and validity). As a result, the effect size is an underestimate. This means that the impact of the working alliance is greater than the meta-analysis reported.

This relationship between alliance and outcome was obtained regardless of who did the alliance ratings (therapist, client, or observer), who rated the outcome (therapist, client, or observer), what outcome measure was used, the time in therapy that the alliance was assessed (earlier or later in treatment), the publication status of the research (21 studies of the 79 studies in the analysis were unpublished, 58 were published), or the type of therapy provided. Thus, Martin and colleagues' meta-analysis provided support for the inference that the working alliance is a common factor associated with outcome for all types of therapies.

C. Changes in the Working Alliance across Time

In their 1985 article on the relationship in psychotherapy, Charles Gelso and Jean Carter emphasized the importance of establishing a positive working alliance early in treatment so that the alliance would sustain the relationships through the difficult periods in treatment. They believed that the alliance becomes disrupted in the middle phase of therapy when most intense work on behavior and attitude change is undertaken. The alliance was then assumed to recover to more positive levels later in therapy.

The 1991 meta-analysis by Horvath and Symonds provided some support for this perspective. They found a larger effect size between working alliance and outcome in studies where the assessment of the working alliance was done early in treatment session than for studies that assessed alliance in the middle phases of treatment.

The 2000 meta-analysis by Martin and colleagues did not support the formulation that successful treatment is associated with a better working alliance at the beginning and end than in the middle of treatment. The relationship between working alliance and outcome was not influenced by the time in treatment when the alliance was assessed, and, as stated earlier, the alliance–outcome relationship is also not influenced by type of therapy used. The findings of Martin and colleagues' meta-analysis support the perspective advanced by Carl Rogers that the working alliance is itself therapeutic. Thus, if a good working alliance is established, client, therapist, and external observers will perceive the client's problems as improved.

IV. SUMMARY

When clients come to therapy, they expect to find therapists with whom they can develop a close relationship. They expect that their therapists will want the same outcomes for them that they want for themselves, and they expect that therapists will suggest ways to attain these goals that they will find acceptable. These are the elements of the working alliance endorsed by most theorists and researchers—client and therapist bond and agreement on the tasks and goals of therapy. The strength of the working alliance may be assessed by giving clients and therapists any of several instruments, but the Working Alliance Inventory is recommended because it was specifically designed to assess client–therapist bond, agreement on tasks, and agreement on goals as well as the overall alliance.

Research results confirm that the working alliance is a common factor in all types of successful therapies. If the working alliance between client and therapist is positive, the outcome of therapy will be positive. If the alliance is negative, the client will not improve and may even leave therapy before it is finished. Moreover, it could be said that the working alliance is itself a therapy. If they are part of a good working alliance, clients will improve regardless of what type of therapy is being conducted or when in therapy the alliance is assessed. These research results indicate that specific training in the establishment of positive working alliances should be done in all graduate programs regardless of the theoretical emphasis of the program.

See Also the Following Articles

Bioethics ■ Confidentiality ■ Engagement ■ Informed Consent ■ Integrative Approaches to Psychotherapy ■ Rational Emotive Behavior Therapy ■ Resistance ■ Termination ■ Working Through

Further Reading

Constantino, M. J., Castonguay, L. J., & Schut, A. J. (2002). The Working Alliance: A Flagship for the "Scientist-Practitioner" Model in Psychotherapy. In G. S. Tryon (Ed.), *Counseling based on process research: Applying what we know.* Boston, MA: Allyn & Bacon.

Greenberg, L. S., & Pinsof, W. M. (Eds.). (1986). *The psychotherapy process: A research handbook.* New York: Guilford.

Martin, D. J., Garske, J. P., & Davis, M. K. (2000). Relation of the therapeutic alliance with outcome and other variables: A meta-analytic review. *Journal of Consulting and Clinical Psychology, 68,* 438–450.

Tracey, T. J. G. (2002). Stages of counseling and therapy: An examination of complementarity and the working alliance. In G. S. Tryon (Ed.), *Counseling based on process research: Applying what we know.* Boston, MA: Allyn & Bacon.

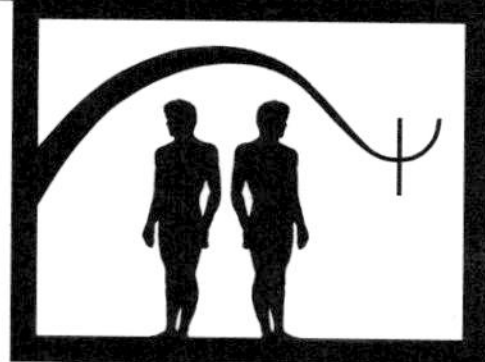

Working Through

Mark J. Sedler
State University of New York, Stony Brook

GLOSSARY

insight Understanding acquired in therapy that connects general themes with particular actions and emotions.

resistance Term that refers to a variety of intrapsychic forces that impede the progress of therapy.

working through A psychoanalytic concept that describes the effort by patient and therapist of overcoming resistance and effecting change.

I. DEFINITION

The psychotherapeutic concept of "working through" originated as a psychoanalytic construct that accounted for the failure of correct interpretive work to immediately result in symptom resolution and character change. It simultaneously invokes the fact that therapy takes time and that patience and persistence on the part of the therapist must be matched by active perseverance and effort on the part of the patient. If therapy is to produce genuine changes in patterns of thinking, feeling, and behavior then a process of transformation must take place, a process that achieves both self-understanding and that neutralizes the countervailing forces of inertia and defense. Although working through has at times seemed almost an afterthought for theorists, an epiphenomenon of the analytic work, others have viewed it as the quintessential activity that defines successful psychotherapy. Working through names the struggle to crystallize the insights gleaned from meticulous self-examination, to connect these insights not only to their putative origins, but to trace their consequences throughout one's subjective and interpersonal experience in an effort to establish a healthier, less fettered, character. This takes time and is often an elusive and arduous goal to reach. The tendency to reenact long-established patterns is not easily undone. In other words, therapy takes work and commitment if it is to result in something more profound than glib self-awareness, which is to say substantive change.

II. FREUD'S THEORY

Freud first makes reference to the notion of "working through" in his paper on technique "Remembering, Repeating, and Working Through" written in 1914. Troubled by the mounting recognition that often a patient's resistance persists in spite of the initial disclosures of a correct interpretation, Freud observed that the beginning analyst has

> merely forgotten that giving the resistance a name could not result in its immediate cessation. One must allow the patient time to become more conversant with

> this resistance with which he has now become acquainted, to work through it, to overcome it, by continuing in defiance of it, the analytic work according to the fundamental rule of analysis.

What the beginning analyst had forgotten was not always apparent even to Freud. In the early days of psychoanalysis, the work of therapy was admittedly "laborious and time-consuming for the physician" but the effort expended was directed toward bringing the pathogenic ideas to consciousness. The resistance of the patient was primarily a matter of repression; once the ideas were successfully retrieved and exposed to the light of conscious awareness symptom resolution followed in short order. Typically, this revelation was accompanied by an "abreaction" of affect associated with the offending idea. Where this failed, the affect was found to have been embedded in a series of affiliated memories and associations and only by a comprehensive "working over" of the pathogenic material could the symptoms be disposed of once and for all. This earlier term, "working over," was a prototype for the subsequent concept of working through and signified early on the fact that analytic progress is not always straightforward, even when it seems to be going well.

Clearly, resistance plays a key role in the analytic view of therapy and it is the antinomy of working through. In Freud's formulation working through engages the resistance once the patient has become acquainted with it. By its very nature resistance is an unconscious adversary that operates by subterfuge and stealth. It is protean in its manifestations and may appear as a failure to produce meaningful disclosures, as faulty remembering, by tenacious distortions and misconstructions, or through the distractions of a robust transference. This latter resistance was paradigmatic for Freud who was preoccupied with the dynamics of the transference throughout his papers on technique (1910–1919). Originally derived from techniques that employed suggestion, the psychoanalytic method first recognized in the transference a means of securing the cooperation of the patient and thus of facilitating the analytic work. Although there is no doubt that some degree of positive transference is indispensable to the progress of therapy, Freud learned from experience that transference is the "strongest weapon of the resistance." As a result of this discovery, the analysis of the transference proved to be a critical step in acquainting the patient with the fact of his resistance. Freud observed:

> Only when the resistance is at its height can the analyst, working in common with his patient, discover the repressed instinctual impulses which are feeding the resistance; and it is this kind of experience which convinces the patient of the existence and power of such impulses.

In this way the patient becomes aware of the resistances and their associated impulses. Becoming conversant with these manifestations constitutes the first phase of working through proper. This phase is time-consuming because recognizing resistances requires deep understanding and an appreciation for the common themes that run through what may appear on the surface to be totally unrelated attitudes and behaviors. It is this exercise that ultimately establishes insight.

Although the resistance exhibited in the transference may have been uppermost in Freud's thinking at the time he first wrote of working through, his subsequent deliberations on resistance called attention to the threat posed by the tendency to repeat. Freud had written variously of the "pertinacity of early impressions," of "psychical inertia," "fixation," and the "adhesiveness of the libido." All of these terms referred, in one way or another, to an obstinacy or lack of mobility on the part of the libido, its reluctance to give up its objects or to change its course. Writing of the general *modus operandi* of analytic treatment in the Introductory Lectures, Freud (1917) remarked:

> The more closely events in the treatment coincide with this ideal description, the greater will be the success. ... It finds its limits in the lack of mobility of the libido, which may refuse to leave its objects...

Freud traced this obstinacy on the part of neurotic fixations to the "resistance from the id" and its manifestation he termed the "compulsion to repeat." Even after the ego resistance has been identified and the pathogenic material rendered visible, the tendency to repeat remains. Thus, Freud observed in his *Inhibitions, Symptoms and Anxiety* in 1926:

> For we find that even after the ego has decided to relinquish its resistances, it still has difficulty in undoing the repressions; and we have called the period of strenuous effort which follows after its praiseworthy decision, the phase of "working-through." The dynamic factor which makes a working-through of this kind necessary and comprehensive is not far to seek. It must be that after the ego-resistance has been removed the power of the compulsion to repeat—the attraction exerted by the unconscious prototypes upon the repressed instinctual process—has still to be overcome. There is nothing to be said against describing this factor as the *resistance of the unconscious*.

In other words, what Freud discovered was that even after the patient has gained an awareness of his resistances and the pathogenic impulses underlying them, the perennial therapeutic imperative—"let go and move on"—is far easier said than accomplished. The resistance from the unconscious manifested by the repetition–compulsion remains to be dealt with. Overcoming this deeply mired complex of resistances represents an aspect of working through that differs from that involved in the acquisition of insight. Faced with the inherently conservative nature of the drive derivatives motivating neurotic life, the ego engaged in working through must wrest itself free from these bonds in order to foster meaningful change. The contest would appear not to be a matter of insight or of understanding, but of brute force. Knowing that one is, by nature, subject to the law of gravity does not help one to escape its influence. Only by overcoming this force can one move out of its orbit.

It is not surprising, then, that Freud in 1940 concluded the chapter on technique in his posthumously published *Outline of PsychoAnalysis* by remarking that:

> We shall not be disappointed, but, on the contrary, we shall find it entirely intelligible, if we reach the conclusion that the final outcome of the struggle we have engaged in depends on *quantitative relations*—on the quota of energy we are able to mobilize in the patient to our advantage as compared with the sum of energy of the powers working against us.

This conclusion suggests that working through is nothing less than a heroic process, one that calls for overcoming, defiance, and perseverance. Indeed, the decision to continue the analytic work over and against all such forces to the contrary Freud deemed "praiseworthy." And, not inconsequentially so, for Freud conceded from the outset that working through names that "part of the work which effects the greatest changes in the patient and which distinguishes analytic treatment from any kind of treatment by suggestion."

III. PERSPECTIVES ON WORKING THROUGH

Given the obvious importance of working through to the outcome of psychotherapy it remains a curiosity that Freud devoted so little actual discussion to the problem. One explanation may be that working through is as pervasive in actual practice as it is intangible and that Freud could only invoke it as the ineffable ingredient that distinguished analysis terminable from analysis interminable. Any attempt to define it further immediately devolves into a discussion of technique, or of metapsychology.

Of course, subsequent theorists have intermittently elaborated on the concept and have generated a series of sometimes divergent positions. Not surprisingly, these elaborations typically reflect the differing approaches to technique or theory espoused by their authors. Classically, Otto Fenichel in 1945 viewed working through from the analyst's point of view, that is, as a problem in technique.

> Systematic and consistent interpretive work, both within and without the framework of the transference, can be described as educating the patient to produce continually less distorted derivatives until his fundamental instinctual conflicts are recognizable. Of course, this is not a single operation resulting in a single act of abreaction; it is, rather, a chronic process of working through, which shows the patient again and again the same conflicts and his usual way of reacting to them but from new angles and in new connections.

Others such as W. Stewart in 1963 and M. Sedler in 1983 emphasized the patient's contribution to the process. P. Greenacre in 1956 conceived of working through as a "working out" of residual infantile traumas and memories that could not be adequately reconstructed or resolved solely by an analysis of current defenses. In 1991 L. Aron proposed the term "working toward" in an effort to "capture the sense of the work of both patient and analyst as co-participants in the analytic process. Patient and analyst not only work toward a new and corrective relationship, but work toward making the nuances of that relationship explicit..." Transcending such positions, Charles Brenner presented a view of working through that underscored its ubiquity in the analytic process. He argued simply that "working through is not a regrettable delay in the process of analytic cure. It *is* analysis. ... The analysis of psychic conflict in all of its aspects is what should properly be called working through."

Generally, there is agreement that working through is a concept made necessary in order to explain, "Why does psychoanalysis take so long?" Posing just this question, Charles Brenner in 1987 helped us perhaps to understand Freud's reticence on the subject by answering candidly, "we do not know." Brenner observed:

> that such analysis takes time, all analysts know. Why it takes as much time as it does is a question which remains

as yet unanswerable. However, we also know that when analytic work proceeds favorably—when working through is successful—it results in psychic changes which are of inestimable value to the patient and which no other form of psychotherapy can achieve.

III. SUMMARY

Many of the basic truths about character pathology, neurotic symptoms, and the possibilities for meaningful change discovered in the era of psychoanalysis have been obscured by the subsequent proliferation of derivative psychotherapies. Nevertheless, the promises and predictable results of "brief therapy" cannot negate the fundamental lessons about mental life learned from our experience of psychoanalysis. Serious conflicts rooted in the soil of constitutional factors and infantile residues are not easily brought to light, and are even less easily resolved. The method of psychoanalysis is a notoriously protracted one and its results are uncertain. For these reasons its popularity and its credibility have suffered. Nevertheless, the challenges defined by working through show why it must be so: Failures, uncertainty, struggle, and hope are facts of the human condition. Technical innovations in psychotherapy are not likely to fundamentally alter this reality. Insofar as the original meaning of "working through" has been assimilated by this psychotherapeutic pluralism, there may be a general understanding that successful therapy requires both time and hard work. At the same time, this assimilated meaning most likely designates the process only in its most generic sense, that is, as the struggle to replace one set of personal characteristics with another. In any context this is not an easy business.

See Also the Following Articles

Engagement ■ Outcome Measures ■ Relapse Prevention ■ Resistance ■ Termination

Further Reading

Brenner, C. (1987). Working through: 1914–1984. *Psychoanalytic Quarterly, LVI,* 88.

Cooper, A. (1989). Working through. *Contemporary Psychoanalysis, 25,* 34.

Freud, S. (1914). Remembering, repeating, and working through. *Standard Edition, 12,* 145, London; Hogarth, 1959.

Sedler, M. (1983). Freud's concept of working through. *Psychoanalytic Quarterly, LII,* 73.

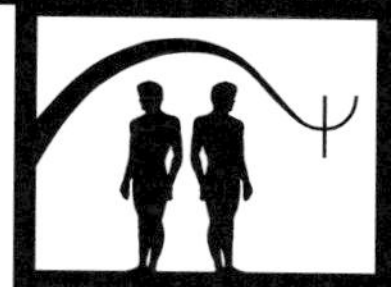

Contributors

Ron Acierno
Medical University of South Carolina
Charleston, South Carolina, USA
Behavioral Therapy Instructions
Reinforcer Sampling
Role Playing

Cynthia M. Anderson
West Virginia University
Morgantown, West Virginia, USA
Fading

Jennifer R. Antick
Pacific University
Forest Grove, Oregon, USA
Behavioral Case Formulation

L. Michael Ascher
Philadelphia College of Osteopathic Medicine
Philadelphia, Pennsylvania, USA
Paradoxical Intention

John Austin
Western Michigan University
Kalamazoo, Michigan, USA
Negative Punishment

Saul Axelrod
Temple University
Philadelphia, Pennsylvania, USA
Response Cost

Teodoro Ayllon
Georgia State University
Atlanta, Georgia, USA
Token Economy: Guidelines for Operation

Rosiana L. Azman
University of Hawaii at Manoa
Manoa, Hawaii, USA
Self-Punishment

Nathan H. Azrin
Nova Southeastern University
Fort Lauderdale, Florida, USA
Job Club Method

Arreed F. Barabasz
Washington State University
Spokane, Washington, USA
Restricted Environmental Stimulation Therapy

Dean E. Barley
Brigham Young University
Provo, Utah, USA
Outcome Measures

Judith S. Beck
Beck Institute for Cognitive Therapy and Research, University of Pennsylvania
Bala Cynwyd, Pennsylvania, USA
Beck Therapy Approach

Deborah C. Beidel
University of Maryland at College Park
College Park, Maryland, USA
Trauma Management Therapy

Donna S. Bender
New York State Psychiatric Institute/Columbia University
New York, New York, USA
Character Pathology

Lorna Smith Benjamin
University of Utah
Salt Lake City, Utah, USA
Structural Analysis of Social Behavior

Insoo Kim Berg
Milwaukee, Wisconsin, USA
Solution-Focused Brief Therapy

Larry E. Beutler
University of California, Santa Barbara
Santa Barbara, California, USA
Individual Psychotherapy

David Bienenfeld
Wright State University
Dayton, Ohio, USA
History of Psychotherapy

Gary R. Birchler
University of California, San Diego
San Diego, California, USA
Behavioral Marital Therapy

Sidney J. Blatt
Yale University
New Haven, Connecticut, USA
Patient Variables: Anaclitic and Introjective Dimensions

Nathan Blum
Children's Seashore House of Children's Hospital of Philadelphia
Philadelphia, Pennsylvania, USA
Primary Care Behavioral Pediatrics

Claude Boutin
Université Laval
Quebec, Canada
Gambling: Behavior and Cognitive Approaches

Jason W. Brown
New York University Medical Center
New York, New York, USA
Organic Brain Syndrome: Psychotherapeutic and Rehabilitative Approaches

Jodi H. Brown
The Institute of the Philadelphia Association for Psychoanalysis
Philadelphia, Pennsylvania, USA
Oedipus Complex

Kirk A. Brunswig
University of Nevada, Reno
Reno, Nevada, USA
Relapse Prevention

Jeanne M. Bulgin
Washington State University
Spokane, Washington, USA
Restricted Environmental Stimulation Therapy

Gary M. Burlingame
Brigham Young University
Provo, Utah, USA
Self-Help Groups

James N. Butcher
University of Minnesota
Minneapolis, Minnesota, USA
Objective Assessment

Karen T. Carey
California State University
Fresno, California, USA
Correspondence Training

Charles R. Carlson
University of Kentucky
Lexington, Kentucky, USA
Stretch-Based Relaxation Training

James E. Carr
Western Michigan University
Kalamazoo, Michigan, USA
Operant Conditioning

Kathleen Carroll
Yale University
New Haven, Connecticut, USA
Substance Dependence: Psychotherapy

Norman Andrew Clemens
Case Western Reserve University
Cleveland, Ohio, USA
Confidentiality
Documentation

Marcia Sue Cohen-Liebman
Philadelphia Children's Alliance, MCP Hahnemann University, and American Art Therapy Association
Cherry Hill, New Jersey, USA
Art Therapy

Amy M. Combs-Lane
Medical University of South Carolina
Charleston, South Carolina, USA
Behavioral Therapy Instructions
Reinforcer Sampling
Role Playing

Francine Cournos
Columbia University
New York, New York, USA
Psychodynamic Couples Therapy

Brian J. Cox
University of Manitoba
Winnipeg, Manitoba, Canada
Behavioral Group Therapy

Lisa W. Coyne
University of Mississippi
University, Mississippi, USA
Discrimination Training
Homework

Ruth Crowther
University of Manchester
Manchester, United Kingdom
Vocational Rehabilitation

Janet L. Cummings
The Nicholas & Dorothy Cummings Foundation
Scottsdale, Arizona, USA
Alternatives to Psychotherapy

Nicholas A. Cummings
University of Nevada, Reno and the Foundation for Behavioral Health
Reno, Nevada, USA
Collaborative Care
Economic and Policy Issues

Kirsten Dahl
Yale Child Study Center
New Haven, Connecticut, USA
Child and Adolescent Psychotherapy: Psychoanalytic Principles

Edward J. Daly III
Western Michigan University
Kalamazoo, Michigan, USA
Positive Reinforcement

D. Rob Davies
Brigham Young University
Provo, Utah, USA
Self-Help Groups

Joanne L. Davis
Medical University of South Carolina
Charleston, South Carolina, USA
Behavioral Therapy Instructions
Reinforcer Sampling
Role Playing

Jerry L. Deffenbacher
Colorado State University
Fort Collins, Colorado, USA
Anxiety Management Training

Caroline DePottel
San Diego Psychoanalytic Society and Institute
San Diego, California, USA
Unconscious, The

Elizabeth T. Dexter
Pacific University
Portland, Oregon, USA
Retention Control Training

Genevieve Dingle
University of Queensland
Brisbane, Queensland, Australia
Anxiety Disorders: Brief Intensive Group Cognitive Behavior Therapy

Mark R. Dixon
Southern Illinois University
Carbondale, Illinois, USA
Setting Events

Brad B. Doleys
Mt. View Hospital, Southeastern Psychiatric Institute
Montgomery, Alabama, USA
Bell-and-Pad Conditioning

Daniel M. Doleys
Pain and Rehabilitation Institute
Birmingham, Alabama, USA
Bell-and-Pad Conditioning

Brad Donohue
University of Nevada, Las Vegas
Las Vegas, Nevada, USA
Behavioral Contracting

E. Thomas Dowd
Kent State University
Kent, Ohio, USA
Coverant Control
Self-Control Desensitization
Self-Statement Modification
Vicarious Conditioning
Vicarious Extinction

T. Wayne Downey
Western New England Institute for Psychoanalysis and Yale University
New Haven, Connecticut, USA
Interpretation

Jack D. Edinger
Veterans Affairs and Duke University Medical Centers
Durham, North Carolina, USA
Behavioral Treatment of Insomnia

Martha E. Edwards
Alfred Adler Institute of San Francisco and Ackerman Institute for the Family
San Francisco, California, USA
Adlerian Psychotherapy

Tracy D. Eells
University of Louisville
Louisville, Kentucky, USA
Formulation

Kristal E. Ehrhardt
Western Michigan University
Kalamazoo, Michigan, USA
Extinction
Positive Punishment

Mark E. Ehrlich
University of Wisconsin, Madison
Madison, Wisconsin, USA
Behavioral Consultation and Therapy

Georg H. Eifert
University of Hawaii
Manoa, Hawaii, USA
Manualized Behavior Therapy

Albert Ellis
Albert Ellis Institute
New York, New York, USA
Rational Emotive Behavior Therapy

Karin Elsesser
University of Wuppertal
Wuppertal, Germany
Complaints Management Training

Paul M. G. Emmelkamp
University of Amsterdam
Amsterdam, The Netherlands
Aversion Relief
Exposure in Vivo Therapy
Spouse-Aided Therapy

Winnie Eng
Adult Anxiety Clinic of Temple University
Philadelphia, Pennsylvania, USA
Cognitive Behavior Therapy

Carolyn Zerbe Enns
Cornell College
Mount Vernon, Iowa, USA
Feminist Psychotherapy

Ruth A. Ervin
Western Michigan University
Kalamazoo, Michigan, USA
Positive Punishment

Sheila M. Eyberg
University of Florida
Gainesville, Florida, USA
Parent-Child Interaction Therapy

Aubrey H. Fine
California State Polytechnic University
Pomona, California, USA
Animal-Assisted Therapy

John P. Forsyth
University at Albany, State University of New York and the Center for Stress and Anxiety Disorders
Albany, New York, USA
Behavior Therapy: Historical Perspective and Overview

Edward F. Foulks
Tulane University School of Medicine
New Orleans, Louisiana, USA
Cultural Issues

J. Christopher Fowler
The Erik H. Erikson Institute for Education and Research
Stockbridge, Massachusetts, USA
Projective Testing in Psychotherapeutics

Kurt A. Freeman
Pacific University
Portland, Oregon, USA
Modeling
Retention Control Training

Adrienne E. Fricker
Medical University of South Carolina
Charleston, South Carolina, USA
Behavioral Therapy Instructions
Reinforcer Sampling
Role Playing

Deborah Fried
Yale University
New Haven, Connecticut, USA
Corrective Emotional Experience

Patrick C. Friman
University of Nevada, Reno
Reno, Nevada, USA
Primary Care Behavioral Pediatrics

B. Christopher Frueh
Medical University of South Carolina
Charleston, South Carolina, USA
Trauma Management Therapy

Eileen Gambrill
University of California at Berkeley
Berkeley, California, USA
Assertion Training
Bibliotherapy

Melissa K. Goates
Brigham Young University
Provo, Utah, USA
Efficacy

Eva K. Gold
Pacific University School of Professional Psychology
and Gestalt Therapy Training Center–Northwest
Vancouver, Washington, USA
Gestalt Therapy

Jerry Gold
Long Island University
Brooklyn, New York, USA
Integrative Approaches to Psychotherapy

Maurice R. Green
New York University
New York, New York, USA
Sullivan's Interpersonal Psychotherapy

Rebecca S. Griffin
University of Mississippi
University, Mississippi, USA
Timeout

William A. Griffin
Arizona State University
Tempe, Arizona, USA
Family Therapy

Alan M. Gross
University of Mississippi
University, Mississippi, USA
Discrimination Training
Timeout

Gerald Groden
The Groden Center, Inc. and Brown University
Providence, Rhode Island, USA
Covert Positive Reinforcement

June Groden
The Groden Center, Inc. and Brown University
Providence, Rhode Island, USA
Covert Positive Reinforcement

Rachel L. Grover
University of Maine
Orono, Maine, USA
Progressive Relaxation

Max Harris
Nova Southeastern University
Fort Lauderdale, Florida, USA
Dreams, Use in Psychotherapy

T. Mark Harwood
University of California, Santa Barbara
Santa Barbara, California, USA
Individual Psychotherapy

Leston L. Havens
Harvard University
Cambridge, Massachusetts, USA
Existential Psychotherapy

Susan M. Havercamp
University of North Carolina
Chapel Hill, North Carolina, USA
Differential Reinforcement of Other Behavior

Stephen N. Haynes
University of Hawaii at Manoa
Manoa, Hawaii, USA
Behavioral Assessment

E. Charles Healey
University of Nebraska, Lincoln
Lincoln, Nebraska, USA
Psychogenic Voice Disorders: Treatment

Richard G. Heimberg
Adult Anxiety Clinic of Temple University
Philadelphia, Pennsylvania, USA
Cognitive Behavior Therapy

Thomas E. Heise
Medical University of Hannover
Chemnitz, Germany
Transcultural Psychotherapy

Steven A. Hobbs
Georgia School of Professional Psychology
Atlanta, Georgia, USA
Overcorrection

Asle Hoffart
Research Institute, Modum Bad
and University of Oslo
Vikersund, Norway
Guided Mastery Therapy

Stefan G. Hofmann
Boston University
Boston, Massachusetts, USA
Panic Disorder and Agoraphobia

Debra A. Hope
University of Nebraska–Lincoln
Lincoln, Nebraska, USA
Heterosocial Skills Training

Mardi J. Horowitz
University of California, San Francisco
San Francisco, California, USA
Configurational Analysis

Sandra Jenkins
Pacific University
Forest Grove, Oregon, USA
Race and Human Diversity

R. Lanai Jennings
Western Michigan University
Kalamazoo, Michigan, USA
Extinction

Cynthia R. Johnson
University of Pittsburgh School of Medicine
Pittsburgh, Pennsylvania, USA
Functional Communication Training

Benjamin A. Jones
Georgia School of Professional Psychology
Atlanta, Georgia, USA
Overcorrection

Julie Stollger Jones
Georgia School of Professional Psychology
Atlanta, Georgia, USA
Overcorrection

Mairwen K. Jones
University of Sydney
Lidcombe, New South Wales, Australia
Danger Ideation Reduction Therapy

Nichole Jurbergs
Louisiana State University
Baton Rouge, Louisiana, USA
Communication Skills Training

J. H. Kamphuis
University of Amsterdam
Amsterdam, The Netherlands
Aversion Relief

Keith Kanner
San Diego Psychoanalytic Society and Institute and University of California, San Diego
San Diego, California, USA
Topographic Theory

T. Byram Karasu
Albert Einstein College of Medicine/Montefiore Medical Center
Bronx, New York, USA
Therapeutic Factors

Jerald Kay
Wright State University School of Medicine
Dayton, Ohio, USA
Neurobiology
Psychopharmacology: Combined Treatment

Alan E. Kazdin
Yale University
New Haven, Connecticut, USA
Applied Behavior Analysis

Christopher A. Kearney
University of Nevada, Las Vegas
Las Vegas, Nevada, USA
Contingency Management

William M. Klykylo
Wright State University School of Medicine
Dayton, Ohio, USA
Comorbidity

Robert J. Kohlenberg
University of Washington
Seattle, Washington, USA
Functional Analytic Psychotherapy

Joy R. Kohlmaier
Louisiana State University
Baton Rouge, Louisiana, USA
Behavioral Weight Control Therapies

S. Mark Kopta
University of Evansville
Evansville, Indiana, USA
Dosage Model

Thomas R. Kratochwill
University of Wisconsin, Madison
Madison, Wisconsin, USA
Behavioral Consultation and Therapy

Anton O. Kris
Boston Psychoanalytic Society and Institute and Harvard University
Cambridge, Massachusetts, USA
Free Association

Linda Laatsch
University of Illinois College of Medicine
Chicago, Illinois, USA
Neuropsychological Assessment

Stella Lachance
Université Laval
Quebec, Canada
Gambling: Behavior and Cognitive Approaches

Robert Ladouceur
Université Laval
Quebec, Canada
Gambling: Behavior and Cognitive Approaches

Michael J. Lambert
Brigham Young University
Provo, Utah, USA
Effectiveness of Psychotherapy
Efficacy
Outcome Measures

Robert C. Lane
Nova Southeastern University
Fort Lauderdale, Florida, USA
Dreams, Use in Psychotherapy

Sean Laraway
Western Michigan University
Kalamazoo, Michigan, USA
Negative Punishment

Claudia Law-Greenberg
San Diego Psychoanalytic Society and Institute and University of California, San Diego
San Diego, California, USA
Transference Neurosis

Suzanne M. Lawrence
West Virginia University
Morgantown, West Virginia, USA
Relaxation Training

Susan G. Lazar
Washington Psychoanalytic Institute
Washington, DC, USA
Cost Effectiveness

Arnold A. Lazarus
Rutgers University and Center for Multimodal Psychological Services
Princeton, New Jersey, USA
Behavior Rehearsal
Emotive Imagery
Multimodal Behavior Therapy

Linda A. LeBlanc
Western Michigan University
Kalamazoo, Michigan, USA
Negative Reinforcement
Operant Conditioning

Luc Lecavalier
University of North Carolina
Chapel Hill, North Carolina, USA
Differential Reinforcement of Other Behavior

Douglas S. Lehrer
Wright State University School of Medicine
Dayton, Ohio, USA
Neurobiology

Larry M. Leitner
Miami University
Miami, Florida, USA
Humanistic Psychotherapy

Hanna Levenson
Levenson Institute for Training
San Francisco, California, USA
Time-Limited Dynamic Psychotherapy

Donald J. Levis
Binghamton University
Binghamton, New York, USA
Implosive Therapy

Ronald Ley
University at Albany, State University of New York
Albany, New York, USA
Breathing Retraining

Paul B. Lieberman
Brown University
Providence, Rhode Island, USA
Existential Psychotherapy

Marsha M. Linehan
University of Washington
Seattle, Washington, USA
Dialectical Behavior Therapy

James W. Lomax
Baylor College of Medicine
Houston, Texas, USA
Education: Curriculum for Psychotherapy

Thomas W. Lombardo
University of Mississippi
University, Mississippi, USA
Homework

Kay McDermott Long
Yale University School of Medicine
New Haven, Connecticut, USA
Resistance

Joseph LoPiccolo
University of Missouri, Columbia
Columbia, Missouri, USA
Sex Therapy

Jenny L. Lowry
Loyola College in Maryland
Baltimore, Maryland, USA
Dosage Model

Lester Luborsky
University of Pennsylvania
Philadelphia, Pennsylvania, USA
Supportive-Expressive Dynamic Psychotherapy

James K. Luiselli
The May Institute Inc.
Norwood, Massachusetts, USA
Avoidance Training

Anne Bodmer Lutz
Cedarburg, Wisconsin, USA
Solution-Focused Brief Therapy

K. Roy MacKenzie
University of British Columbia
Vancouver, British Columbia, Canada
Group Psychotherapy

Steven Marans
Yale Child Study Center
New Haven, Connecticut, USA
Child and Adolescent Psychotherapy: Psychoanalytic Principles

Bethany A. Marcus
Virginia Commonwealth University and Central State Hospital
Richmond, Virginia, USA
Differential Attention

Eric R. Marcus
Columbia University College of Physicians and Surgeons and Columbia University Psychoanalytic Center for Training and Research
New York, New York, USA
Psychoanalytic Psychotherapy and Psychoanalysis, Overview
Transference

Johnny L. Matson
Louisiana State University
Baton Rouge, Louisiana, USA
Negative Practice

Margaret E. Mattson
National Institute on Alcohol Abuse and Alcoholism
Bethesda, Maryland, USA
Matching Patients to Alcoholism Treatment

Louise Maxfield
Lakehead University
Thunder Bay, Ontario, Canada
Eye Movement Desensitization and Reprocessing

Marita P. McCabe
Deakin University
Burwood, Victoria, Australia
Arousal Training

Nathaniel McConaghy
University of New South Wales
Paddington, New South Wales, Australia
Electrical Aversion
Orgasmic Reconditioning

F. Dudley McGlynn
Auburn University
Auburn, Alabama, USA
Systematic Desensitization

Dean McKay
Fordham University
Bronx, New York, USA
Behavior Therapy: Theoretical Bases

Daniel W. McNeil
West Virginia University
Morgantown, West Virginia, USA
Relaxation Training

Alice Medalia
Albert Einstein College of Medicine
Bronx, New York, USA
Attention Training Procedures

Heather J. Meggers
University of Missouri, Columbia
Columbia, Missouri, USA
Sex Therapy

W. W. Meissner
Boston Psychoanalytic Society and Institute and Boston College
Boston, Massachusetts, USA
Clarification
Confrontation

Ross G. Menzies
University of Sydney
Lidcombe, New South Wales, Australia
Danger Ideation Reduction Therapy

Mary A. Mich
The Marcus and Kennedy Krieger Institutes and the Johns Hopkins University School of Medicine
Atlanta, Georgia, USA
Nocturnal Enuresis: Treatment

Michael A. Milan
Georgia State University
Atlanta, Georgia, USA
Symbolic Modeling
Token Economy: Guidelines for Operation

Catherine Miller
Pacific University
Portland, Oregon, USA
Flooding
Informed Consent

Raymond G. Miltenberger
North Dakota State University
Fargo, North Dakota, USA
Competing Response Training
Forward Chaining
Habit Reversal

Doil D. Montgomery
Nova Southeastern University
Fort Lauderdale, Florida, USA
Biofeedback

Karla Moras
University of Pennsylvania
Philadelphia, Pennsylvania, USA
Research in Psychotherapy

Charles M. Morin
Université Laval
Quebec, Canada
Self-Help Treatment for Insomnia

Ann Kerr Morrison
Wright State University
Dayton, Ohio, USA
Somatoform Disorders

Richard L. Munich
The Menninger Clinic
Topeka, Kansas, USA
Schizophrenia and Other Psychotic Disorders

Amy R. Murrell
University of Mississippi
University, Mississippi, USA
Functional Analysis of Behavior

Carol C. Nadelson
Harvard Medical School
Cambridge, Massachusetts, USA
Women's Issues

Douglas W. Nangle
University of Maine
Orono, Maine, USA
Progressive Relaxation

Max M. North
Kennesaw State University
Kennesaw, Georgia, USA
Virtual Reality Therapy

Sarah M. North
Kennesaw State University
Kennesaw, Georgia, USA
Virtual Reality Therapy

Ann E. Norwood
Uniformed Services University of the Health Sciences
Bethesda, Maryland, USA
Posttraumatic Stress Disorder

Malkah T. Notman
Harvard Medical School
Cambridge, Massachusetts, USA
Women's Issues

Raymond W. Novaco
University of California, Irvine
Irvine, California, USA
Anger Control Therapy

Ann Oberkirch
Yale School of Medicine
New Haven, Connecticut, USA
Tele-Psychotherapy

William O'Donohue
University of Nevada, Reno
Reno, Nevada, USA
Relapse Prevention

Tian P. S. Oei
University of Queensland
Brisbane, Queensland, Australia
Anxiety Disorders: Brief Intensive Group Cognitive Behavior Therapy

Todd C. O'Hearn
Yale University
New Haven, Connecticut, USA
Sports Psychotherapy

Melanie L. O'Neill
University of British Columbia Hospital
Burnaby, British Columbia, Canada
Thought Stopping

Spyros D. Orfanos
Stephen A. Mitchell Center for Relational Psychoanalysis
New York, New York, USA
Relational Psychoanalysis

J. Grayson Osborne
Utah State University
Logan, Utah, USA
Response-Contingent Water Misting

Lars-Göran Öst
Stockholm University
Stockholm, Sweden
Applied Relaxation
Applied Tension

Robert Ostroff
Yale University School of Medicine
New Haven, Connecticut, USA
Adjunctive/Conjoint Therapies

Marie-Christine Ouellet
Université Laval
Quebec, Canada
Self-Help Treatment for Insomnia

Theodosia R. Paclawskyj
The Johns Hopkins University School of Medicine and The Kennedy Krieger Institute
Baltimore, Maryland, USA
Negative Practice

Tamara M. Penix
University of Nevada, Reno
Reno, Nevada, USA
Relapse Prevention

Zehra F. Peynircioğlu
American University
Washington, DC, USA
Covert Rehearsal

Cathleen C. Piazza
The Marcus and Kennedy Krieger Institutes and the Johns Hopkins University School of Medicine
Atlanta, Georgia, USA
Nocturnal Enuresis: Treatment

Joseph J. Plaud
Cambridge Center for Behavioral Studies, New School for the Learning Sciences, and Brown University
Concord, Massachusetts, USA
Assisted Covert Sensitization

Alan Poling
Western Michigan University
Kalamazoo, Michigan, USA
Extinction
Negative Punishment
Negative Reinforcement
Operant Conditioning
Positive Punishment
Positive Reinforcement

Jane G. Querido
University of Florida
Gainesville, Florida, USA
Parent-Child Interaction Therapy

Ruth Anne Rehfeldt
Southern Illinois University
Carbondale, Illinois, USA
Chaining
Omission Training

Lynn P. Rehm
University of Houston
Houston, Texas, USA
Self-Control Therapy

David Reitman
Louisiana State University
Baton Rouge, Louisiana, USA
Communication Skills Training

Sarah K. Reynolds
University of Washington
Seattle, Washington, USA
Dialectical Behavior Therapy

Brendan A. Rich
University of Florida
Gainesville, Florida, USA
Parent-Child Interaction Therapy

David C. S. Richard
Eastern Michigan University
Ypsilanti, Michigan, USA
Behavioral Assessment

Henry S. Roane
The Marcus and Kennedy Krieger Institutes and the Johns Hopkins University School of Medicine
Atlanta, Georgia, USA
Nocturnal Enuresis: Treatment

Rostyslaw W. Robak
Pace University
New York, New York, USA
Grief Therapy

Michael Robertson
Mayo-Wesley Centre for Mental Health
Taree, New South Wales, Australia
Interpersonal Psychotherapy
Mood Disorders

Nadezhda M. T. Robinson
Columbia University Center for Psychoanalytic Training and Research and St. Mary Hospital
New York, New York, USA
Self Psychology
Transitional Objects and Transitional Phenomena

Sheldon D. Rose
University of Wisconsin–Madison
Madison, Wisconsin, USA
Cognitive Behavior Group Therapy

Harold Rosenberg
Bowling Green State University
Bowling Green, Ohio, USA
Controlled Drinking

Johan Rosqvist
Pacific University
Forest Grove, Oregon, USA
Behavioral Case Formulation

Robak W. Rostyslaw
Pace University
Pleasantville, New York, USA
Grief Therapy

Deborah A. Roth
Center for the Treatment and Study of Anxiety, University of Pennsylvania
Philadelphia, Pennsylvania, USA
Cognitive Behavior Therapy

Bruce Rounsaville
Yale University
New Haven, Connecticut, USA
Substance Dependence: Psychotherapy

Anderson B. Rowan
Malcolm Grow Medical Center
Andrews Air Force Base, Maryland, USA
Minimal Therapist Contact Treatments

Jill Sabsevitz
University at Albany, State University of New York and the Center for Stress and Anxiety Disorders
Albany, New York, USA
Behavior Therapy: Historical Perspective and Overview

Julian A. Salinas
Fulton State Hospital and The University of Missouri School of Medicine
Fulton, Missouri, USA
Token Economy

Lori A. Sansone
Alliance Physicians, Kettering Medical Center
Kettering, Ohio, USA
Medically Ill Patient: Psychotherapy

Randy A. Sansone
Wright State University School of Medicine
Dayton, Ohio, USA
Medically Ill Patient: Psychotherapy

Gudrun Sartory
University of Wuppertal
Wuppertal, Germany
Complaints Management Training

Jeffrey Satinover
Yale University
New Haven, Connecticut, USA
Jungian Psychotherapy

Thomas E. Schacht
James H. Quillen College of Medicine
Johnson City, Tennessee, USA
Time-Limited Dynamic Psychotherapy

Douglas Schave
University of California, Los Angeles
Los Angeles, California, USA
Gifted Youth

Irving Schneider
Georgetown University Medical School
Washington, DC, USA
Cinema and Psychotherapy

Kirk J. Schneider
Saybrook Graduate School and Research Center
San Francisco, California, USA
Humanistic Psychotherapy

John Schowalter
Yale Child Study Center
New Haven, Connecticut, USA
Child and Adolescent Psychotherapy: Psychoanalytic Principles

Avraham Schweiger
Academic College of Tel Aviv
Tel Aviv, Israel
Organic Brain Syndrome: Psychotherapeutic and Rehabilitative Approaches

Mark J. Sedler
State University of New York, Stony Brook
Stony Brook, New York, USA
Working Through

Stephen B. Shanfield
University of Texas Health Science Center at San Antonio
San Antonio, Texas, USA
Supervision in Psychotherapy

Francine Shapiro
Mental Research Institute
Palo Alto, California, USA
Eye Movement Desensitization and Reprocessing

Ashvind N. Singh
Virginia Commonwealth University and Central State Hospital
Richmond, Virginia, USA
Differential Attention

Nirbhay N. Singh
Virginia Commonwealth University and Central State Hospital
Richmond, Virginia, USA
Differential Attention

Andrew E. Skodol
New York State Psychiatric Institute/Columbia University
New York, New York, USA
Character Pathology

William H. Sledge
Yale University School of Medicine
New Haven, Connecticut, USA
Cost Effectiveness
Countertransference
Resistance

Kellie E. Smith
Research Institute on Addictions
Buffalo, New York, USA
Addictions in Special Populations: Treatment

Susan Snycerski
Western Michigan University
Kalamazoo, Michigan, USA
Negative Punishment

Douglas K. Snyder
Texas A&M University
College Station, Texas, USA
Couples Therapy: Insight-Oriented

Douglas A. Songer
Wright State University
Dayton, Ohio, USA
Pain Disorders

Stephen M. Sonnenberg
Uniformed Services University of the Health Sciences, Baylor College of Medicine
Bethesda, Maryland, USA
Psychoanalysis and Psychoanalytic Psychotherapy: Technique

Everett K. Spees
Devereux Cleo Wallace
Westminster, Colorado, USA
Bioethics
Therapeutic Storytelling with Children and Adolescents

David Speigel
Stanford University School of Medicine
Stanford, California, USA
Cancer Patients: Psychotherapy

Paul R. Stasiewicz
Research Institute on Addictions
Buffalo, New York, USA
Addictions in Special Populations: Treatment

Brett N. Steenbarger
SUNY Upstate Medical University
Syracuse, New York, USA
Brief Therapy
Single-Session Therapy

Henry T. Stein
Alfred Adler Institute of San Francisco and Ackerman Institute for the Family
San Francisco, California, USA
Adlerian Psychotherapy

Walter N. Stone
University of Cincinnati College of Medicine
Cincinnati, Ohio, USA
Psychodynamic Group Psychotherapy

Julie M. Storey
Malcolm Grow Medical Center
Andrews Air Force Base, Maryland, USA
Minimal Therapist Contact Treatments

Eric Strachan
University of Nebraska–Lincoln
Lincoln, Nebraska, USA
Heterosocial Skills Training

Kirk Strosahl
Mountainview Consulting Group, Inc.
Moxee, Washington, USA
Acceptance and Commitment Therapy

Hans H. Strupp
Vanderbilt University
Nashville, Tennessee, USA
Time-Limited Dynamic Psychotherapy

Scott Stuart
University of Iowa and
Iowa Depression and Clinical Research Center
Iowa City, Iowa, USA
Interpersonal Psychotherapy
Mood Disorders

Paul Stuve
Fulton State Hospital and The University of Missouri
School of Medicine
Fulton, Missouri, USA
Token Economy

David Sue
Western Washington University
Bellingham, Washington, USA
Multicultural Therapy

Alan Sugarman
San Diego Psychoanalytic Society and Institute and
University of California, San Diego
San Diego, California, USA
Intrapsychic Conflict
Oedipus Complex
Structural Theory
Topographic Theory
Transference Neurosis
Unconscious, The

Richard M. Suinn
Colorado State University
Fort Collins, Colorado, USA
Anxiety Management Training

Marsha Sullivan
University of Nebraska Medical Center
Lincoln, Nebraska, USA
Psychogenic Voice Disorders: Treatment

Frank Summers
Northwestern University
Chicago, Illinois, USA
Object-Relations Psychotherapy

Caroline Sylvain
Université Laval
Quebec, Canada
Gambling: Behavior and Cognitive Approaches

Zebulon Taintor
New York University School of Medicine
New York, New York, USA
Online or E-Therapy

Marc J. Tassé
University of North Carolina
Chapel Hill, North Carolina, USA
Differential Reinforcement of Other Behavior

Steven Taylor
University of British Columbia
Vancouver, British Columbia, Canada
Behavioral Group Therapy
Classical Conditioning
Exposure

Ellen J. Teng
University of Wisconsin
Milwaukee, Wisconsin, USA
Backward Chaining

Daniel H. Tingstrom
The University of Southern Mississippi
Hattiesburg, Mississippi, USA
Good Behavior Game

Kathlene Tracy
Yale University
New Haven, Connecticut, USA
Substance Dependence: Psychotherapy

Georgiana Shick Tryon
City University of New York Graduate School and
University Center
New York, New York, USA
Engagement
Termination
Working Alliance

Warren W. Tryon
Fordham University
Bronx, New York, USA
Behavior Therapy: Theoretical Bases

Mavis Tsai
Seattle, Washington, USA
Functional Analytic Psychotherapy

John Tsamasiros
P. & A. Kyriakou Hospital
Athens, Greece
Short-Term Anxiety-Provoking Psychotherapy

Lynne E. Turner
Western Michigan University
Kalamazoo, Michigan, USA
Negative Reinforcement

Samuel M. Turner
University of Maryland at College Park
College Park, Maryland, USA
Trauma Management Therapy

Graham Turpin
University of Sheffield
Western Bank, Sheffield, United Kingdom
Single-Case Methods and Evaluation

Michael P. Twohig
University of Wisconsin–Milwaukee
Milwaukee, Wisconsin, USA
Home-Based Reinforcement

Robert J. Ursano
Uniformed Services University of the Health Sciences
Bethesda, Maryland, USA
Posttraumatic Stress Disorder
Psychoanalysis and Psychoanalytic Psychotherapy: Technique

Annie Vallières
Université Laval
Quebec, Canada
Self-Help Treatment for Insomnia

Wiljo J. P. J. van Hout
University of Groningen
Groningen, The Netherlands
Exposure In Vivo Therapy

Jennifer Vecchio
University of Nevada, Las Vegas
Las Vegas, Nevada, USA
Contingency Management

Ellen Vedel
University of Amsterdam
Amsterdam, The Netherlands
Spouse-Aided Therapy

David A. Vermeersch
Brigham Young University
Provo, Utah, USA
Effectiveness of Psychotherapy

W. Rand Walker
University of Idaho
Moscow, Idaho, USA
Language in Psychotherapy
Restricted Environmental Stimulation Therapy

Linda Wasserman
University of West Florida
Pensacola, Florida, USA
Biblical Behavior Modification

Joseph Weiss
San Francisco Psychotherapy Research Group, San Francisco Psychoanalytic Institute, and University of California
San Francisco, California, USA
Control-Mastery Theory

Lisa Solomon Weissman
University of Nevada, Las Vegas
Las Vegas, Nevada, USA
Behavioral Contracting

Richard L. Wessler
Cognitive Psychotherapy Services
New York, New York, USA
Cognitive Appraisal Therapy

Marney A. White
Louisiana State University
Baton Rouge, Louisiana, USA
Behavioral Weight Control Therapies

Maureen L. Whittal
University of British Columbia Hospital
Burnaby, British Columbia, Canada
Thought Stopping

Ben A. Williams
University of California, San Diego
San Diego, California, USA
Conditioned Reinforcement

Donald A. Williamson
Pennington Biomedical Research Center
Baton Rouge, Louisiana, USA
Behavioral Weight Control Therapies

Arnold Wilson
Columbia University Center for Psychoanalytic Training and Research and St. Mary Hospital
New York, New York, USA
Self Psychology
Transitional Objects and Transitional Phenomena

Kelly G. Wilson
University of Mississippi
University, Mississippi, USA
Functional Analysis of Behavior

Patricia A. Wisocki
University of Massachusetts, Amherst
Amherst, Massachusetts, USA
Covert Reinforcer Sampling
Successive Approximations

Paul T. P. Wong
Trinity Western University
Langley, British Columbia, Canada
Logotherapy

Douglas W. Woods
University of Wisconsin–Milwaukee
Milwaukee, Wisconsin, USA
Backward Chaining
Home-Based Reinforcement

Robert E. Wubbolding
Center for Reality Therapy
Cincinnati, Ohio, USA
Reality Therapy

Joel Yager
University of New Mexico School of Medicine
Albuquerque, New Mexico, USA
Eating Disorders

Elisia V. Yanasak
University of Houston
Houston, Texas, USA
Self-Control Therapy

Stephen G. Zahm
Pacific University School of Professional Psychology and Gestalt Therapy Training Center–Northwest
Vancouver, Washington, USA
Gestalt Therapy

Howard Zonana
Yale University and Connecticut Mental Health Center
New Haven, Connecticut, USA
Legal Dimensions of Psychotherapy

Michael J. Zvolensky
University of Vermont
Burlington, Vermont, USA
Manualized Behavior Therapy

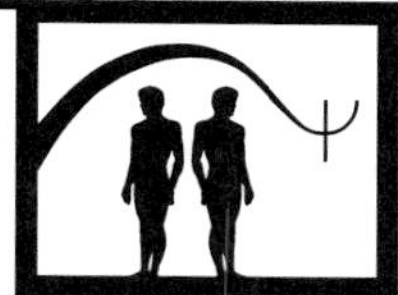

Index

Volume numbers are boldfaced, separated from the first page reference with a colon. Subsequent references to the same material are separated by commas.

A

B

C

D

E

G

I

J

K

L

M

N

O

Q

R

S

T

U

V

ISBN 0-12-343012-7

Date Due